BUTTERWOR
SECURITIES & FINANCIAL
HANDBOO
RECESSION SPECI
SUPPLEMEN

CW01502415

BUTTERWORTHS
SECURITIES & FINANCIAL SERVICES LAW
HANDBOOK
RECESSION SPECIAL 2009
SUPPLEMENT

Edited by

DEBORAH A SABALOT,
BA, DipLib, MLib, JD (Solicitor),
Professional Associate, Outer Temple Chambers

DR FELICITY MAHER
BA, LLB (University of Western Australia), BCL, MPhil, DPhil
(University of Oxford)
3 Verulam Buildings, Gray's Inn

Consultant Editor

SIR WILLIAM BLAIR
One of Her Majesty's Judges, Queen's Bench Division

LexisNexis
® Butterworths

Members of the LexisNexis Group worldwide

United Kingdom	LexisNexis, a Division of Reed Elsevier (UK) Ltd, Halsbury House, 35 Chancery Lane, London, WC2A 1EL, and London House, 20–22 East London Street, Edinburgh EH7 4BQ
Australia	LexisNexis Butterworths, Chatswood, New South Wales
Austria	LexisNexis Verlag ARD Orac GmbH & Co KG, Vienna
Benelux	LexisNexis Benelux, Amsterdam
Canada	LexisNexis Canada, Markham, Ontario
China	LexisNexis China, Beijing and Shanghai
France	LexisNexis SA, Paris
Germany	LexisNexis Deutschland GmbH, Munster
Hong Kong	LexisNexis Hong Kong, Hong Kong
India	LexisNexis India, New Delhi
Italy	Giuffrè Editore, Milan
Japan	LexisNexis Japan, Tokyo
Malaysia	Malayan Law Journal Sdn Bhd, Kuala Lumpur
New Zealand	LexisNexis NZ Ltd, Wellington
Poland	Wydawnictwo Prawnicze LexisNexis Sp, Warsaw
Singapore	LexisNexis Singapore, Singapore
South Africa	LexisNexis Butterworths, Durban
USA	LexisNexis, Dayton, Ohio

© Reed Elsevier (UK) Ltd 2009
Published by LexisNexis

This is a Butterworths title

A CIP Catalogue record for this book is available from the British Library.

ISBN: 978 1 4057 4721 9

Typeset by Columns Design Ltd, Reading, England
Printed in the UK by CPI William Clowes Beccles NR34 7TL

Visit LexisNexis at www.lexisnexis.co.uk

PREFACE

In his testimony to the Treasury Select Committee on the banking crisis, Mervyn King, Governor of the Bank of England said "We will never get rid of financial crises—a bank is inherently a dangerous institution that will generate crises from time to time—but what we ought to be really concerned about is that the impact of these crises and their frequency is not diminishing over time. We get used to the idea that aeroplane crashes are less frequent and that we make passenger transport more safe over time. In the financial sector it seems to be the other way round, and that is why we cannot, I think, just put the issue to one side and say practical people who understand the world know there is nothing you can do about it. That is a counsel of despair, and we cannot afford a counsel of despair given the damage that has been wreaked on the rest of the economy by the problems in the financial sector."

When the tenth edition of Butterworths Securities and Financial Services Law Handbook went to press in early 2009 we were able to include the text of the Banking Act 2009 but since that time a number of additional statutory instruments and other instruments made under the Act (including instruments made by the Bank of England under its powers under section 11(2) and 12(2) of the Banking Act 2009) have come into effect as Parliament and the regulators have moved to make the financial sector safer and to deal with the aftermath of the credit crunch and the failure of a number of UK financial institutions.

Due to the cross-over between material in the Butterworths Securities and Financial Services Law Handbook and Butterworths Banking Law Handbook it was decided to bring out a common supplement to cover the most recent orders and instruments affecting the special resolution regimes in relation to Bradford & Bingley plc, Heritable Bank plc, Kaupthing Singer & Friedlander and, most recently, the Dunfermline Building Society.

This Supplement provides an up-to-date and readily portable text of the Banking Act 2009 and its associated secondary legislation as well as relevant European legislative materials in force on 1 August 2009. However, later changes have been included wherever possible.

The Supplement is divided into six Parts, within which material is reproduced chronologically—

- Part I: Banking Act 2009

- Part II: Other Acts

- Part III: Statutory Instruments under the Banking Act 2009

- Part IV: Other Statutory Instruments

- Part V: EU materials

- Part VI: Other Materials

This Supplement follows the standard Butterworths Handbooks style, with amendments made by new legislation incorporated into the text of existing legislation. The notes which follow a provision detail the changes that have been made to the text and list any prospective amendments. In relation to the statutory material, the following points should be noted—

- Material in italics is prospectively repealed/revoked or substituted. The notes provide a detailed explanation of such prospective amendments.

- Material within square brackets is the subject of one or more insertions or substitutions of text. Again, the notes provide full details.

- Modifications of provisions are set out in full in the notes where relevant. In some cases, where modifications or extensions of scope have been made (for example, in relation to the Financial Services and Markets Act 2000 (Regulated Activities) Order 2001), this is noted as a cross-reference to the note at the beginning of that Part or section, etc.

- Where an Act or Statutory Instrument is amending only, it is not (generally) included in full, although the notes will provide a summary of the changes. The amendments made by such legislation are fully incorporated into the relevant provisions where they are within the scope of this work.

The main texts of Butterworths Securities and Financial Services Law Handbook and Butterworths Banking Law Handbook are regularly updated online.

Deborah A. Sabalot, Professional Associate, Outer Temple Chambers
Felicity Maher, 3 Verulam Buildings

August 2009

CONTENTS

PART V EU MATERIAL

PART VI OTHER MATERIALS

ALPHABETICAL LIST OF CONTENTS

PART I
BANKING ACT 2009

BANKING ACT 2009

(2009 c 1)

ARRANGEMENT OF SECTIONS

PART 1
SPECIAL RESOLUTION REGIME

Introduction

PART 2
BANK INSOLVENCY

Introduction

Bank insolvency order

PART 3
BANK ADMINISTRATION

Introduction

Process

Multiple transfers

(4)   Where a stabilisation power is exercised in respect of a bank, it does not cease to be a bank for the purposes of this Part if it later loses the permission referred to in subsection (1).

(5)   An order under subsection (2)(c)—
    (a)   shall be made by statutory instrument, and
    (b)   may not be made unless a draft has been laid before and approved by resolution of each House of Parliament.

(6)   Section 84 applies this Part to building societies with modifications.

(7)   Section 89 allows the application of this Part to credit unions.

[2]

NOTES

Commencement: 17 February 2009 (in so far as conferring or relating to any power to make subordinate legislation or codes of practice); 21 February 2009 (otherwise).

3 Interpretation: other expressions

In this Part—
    "the FSA" means the Financial Services Authority, and
    "financial assistance" has the meaning given by section 257.

[3]

NOTES

Commencement: 17 February 2009 (in so far as conferring or relating to any power to make subordinate legislation or codes of practice); 21 February 2009 (otherwise).

Objectives and code

4 Special resolution objectives

(1)   This section sets out the special resolution objectives.

(2)   The relevant authorities shall have regard to the special resolution objectives in using, or considering the use of—
    (a)   the stabilisation powers,
    (b)   the bank insolvency procedure, or
    (c)   the bank administration procedure.

(3)   For the purpose of this section the relevant authorities are—
    (a)   the Treasury,
    (b)   the FSA, and
    (c)   the Bank of England.

(4)   Objective 1 is to protect and enhance the stability of the financial systems of the United Kingdom.

(5)   Objective 2 is to protect and enhance public confidence in the stability of the banking systems of the United Kingdom.

(6)   Objective 3 is to protect depositors.

(7)   Objective 4 is to protect public funds.

(8)   Objective 5 is to avoid interfering with property rights in contravention of a Convention right (within the meaning of the Human Rights Act 1998).

(9)   In subsection (4), the reference to the stability of the financial systems of the United Kingdom includes, in particular, a reference to the continuity of banking services.

(10)   The order in which the objectives are listed in this section is not significant; they are to be balanced as appropriate in each case.

[4]

NOTES

Commencement: 17 February 2009 (in so far as conferring or relating to any power to make subordinate legislation or codes of practice); 21 February 2009 (otherwise).

5 Code of practice

(1)   The Treasury shall issue a code of practice about the use of—
    (a)   the stabilisation powers,
    (b)   the bank insolvency procedure, and
    (c)   the bank administration procedure.

(2)   The code may, in particular, provide guidance on—
    (a)   how the special resolution objectives are to be understood and achieved,
    (b)   the choice between different options,

PART I
BANKING ACT 2009

    (c)   the information to be provided in the course of a consultation under this Part,

    (d)   the giving of advice by one relevant authority to another about whether, when and how the stabilisation powers are to be used,

    (e)   how to determine whether Condition 2 in section 7 is met,

    (f)   how to determine whether the test for the use of stabilisation powers in section 8 is satisfied,

    (g)   sections 63 and 66, and

    (h)   compensation.

(3)   Sections 12 and 13 require the inclusion in the code of certain matters about bridge banks and temporary public ownership.

(4)   The relevant authorities shall have regard to the code.

(5)   For the purpose of this section the relevant authorities are—

    (a)   the Treasury,

    (b)   the FSA, and

    (c)   the Bank of England.

[5]

NOTES

Commencement: 17 February 2009 (in so far as conferring or relating to any power to make subordinate legislation or codes of practice); 21 February 2009 (otherwise).

Codes of Practice: see the Special Resolution Regime: Code of Practice at **[2000]**.

6 Code of practice: procedure

(1)   Before issuing the code of practice the Treasury must consult—

    (a)   the FSA,

    (b)   the Bank of England, and

    (c)   the scheme manager of the Financial Services Compensation Scheme (established under Part 15 of the Financial Services and Markets Act 2000).

(2)   As soon as is reasonably practicable after issuing the code of practice the Treasury shall lay a copy before Parliament.

(3)   The Treasury may revise and re-issue the code of practice.

(4)   Subsections (1) and (2) apply to re-issue as to the first issue.

[6]

NOTES

Commencement: 17 February 2009 (in so far as conferring or relating to any power to make subordinate legislation or codes of practice); 21 February 2009 (otherwise).

Codes of Practice: see the Special Resolution Regime: Code of Practice at **[2000]**.

Exercise of powers: general

7 General conditions

(1)   A stabilisation power may be exercised in respect of a bank only if the FSA is satisfied that the following conditions are met.

(2)   Condition 1 is that the bank is failing, or is likely to fail, to satisfy the threshold conditions (within the meaning of section 41(1) of the Financial Services and Markets Act 2000 (permission to carry on regulated activities)).

(3)   Condition 2 is that having regard to timing and other relevant circumstances it is not reasonably likely that (ignoring the stabilisation powers) action will be taken by or in respect of the bank that will enable the bank to satisfy the threshold conditions.

(4)   The FSA shall treat Conditions 1 and 2 as met if satisfied that they would be met but for financial assistance provided by—

    (a)   the Treasury, or

    (b)   the Bank of England (disregarding ordinary market assistance offered by the Bank on its usual terms).

(5)   Before determining whether or not Condition 2 is met the FSA must consult—

    (a)   the Bank of England, and

    (b)   the Treasury.

(6)   The special resolution objectives are not relevant to Conditions 1 and 2.

(7)   The conditions for applying for and making a bank insolvency order are set out in sections 96 and 97.

(8)   The conditions for applying for and making a bank administration order are set out in sections 143 and 144.

[7]

NOTES
Commencement: 17 February 2009 (in so far as conferring or relating to any power to make subordinate legislation or codes of practice); 21 February 2009 (otherwise).

8   Specific conditions: private sector purchaser and bridge bank

(1)   The Bank of England may exercise a stabilisation power in respect of a bank in accordance with section 11(2) or 12(2) only if satisfied that Condition A is met.

(2)   Condition A is that the exercise of the power is necessary, having regard to the public interest in—
    (a)   the stability of the financial systems of the United Kingdom,
    (b)   the maintenance of public confidence in the stability of the banking systems of the United Kingdom, or
    (c)   the protection of depositors.

(3)   Before determining whether Condition A is met, and if so how to react, the Bank of England must consult—
    (a)   the FSA, and
    (b)   the Treasury.

(4)   Where the Treasury notify the Bank of England that they have provided financial assistance in respect of a bank for the purpose of resolving or reducing a serious threat to the stability of the financial systems of the United Kingdom, the Bank may exercise a stabilisation power in respect of the bank in accordance with section 11(2) or 12(2) only if satisfied that Condition B is met (instead of Condition A).

(5)   Condition B is that—
    (a)   the Treasury have recommended the Bank of England to exercise the stabilisation power on the grounds that it is necessary to protect the public interest, and
    (b)   in the Bank's opinion, exercise of the stabilisation power is an appropriate way to provide that protection.

(6)   The conditions in this section are in addition to the conditions in section 7.

[8]

NOTES
Commencement: 17 February 2009 (in so far as conferring or relating to any power to make subordinate legislation or codes of practice); 21 February 2009 (otherwise).

9   Specific conditions: temporary public ownership

(1)   The Treasury may exercise a stabilisation power in respect of a bank in accordance with section 13(2) only if satisfied that one of the following conditions is met.

(2)   Condition A is that the exercise of the power is necessary to resolve or reduce a serious threat to the stability of the financial systems of the United Kingdom.

(3)   Condition B is that exercise of the power is necessary to protect the public interest, where the Treasury have provided financial assistance in respect of the bank for the purpose of resolving or reducing a serious threat to the stability of the financial systems of the United Kingdom.

(4)   Before determining whether a condition is met the Treasury must consult—
    (a)   the FSA, and
    (b)   the Bank of England.

(5)   The conditions in this section are in addition to the conditions in section 7.

[9]

NOTES
Commencement: 17 February 2009 (in so far as conferring or relating to any power to make subordinate legislation or codes of practice); 21 February 2009 (otherwise).

10   Banking Liaison Panel

(1)   The Treasury shall make arrangements for a panel to advise the Treasury about the effect of the special resolution regime on—
    (a)   banks,
    (b)   persons with whom banks do business, and
    (c)   the financial markets.

(2)   In particular, the panel may advise the Treasury about—

(a)   the exercise of powers to make statutory instruments under or by virtue of this Part, Part 2 or Part 3 (excluding the stabilisation powers, compensation scheme orders, resolution fund orders, third party compensation orders and orders under section 75(2)(b) and (c)),

(b)   the code of practice under section 5, and

(c)   anything else referred to the panel by the Treasury.

(3)   The Treasury shall ensure that the panel includes—

(a)   a member appointed by the Treasury,

(b)   a member appointed by the Bank of England,

(c)   a member appointed by the FSA,

(d)   a member appointed by the scheme manager of the Financial Services Compensation Scheme,

(e)   one or more persons who in the Treasury's opinion represent the interests of banks,

(f)   one or more persons who in the Treasury's opinion have expertise in law relating to the financial systems of the United Kingdom, and

(g)   one or more persons who in the Treasury's opinion have expertise in insolvency law and practice.

[10]

NOTES

Commencement: 17 February 2009 (in so far as conferring or relating to any power to make subordinate legislation or codes of practice); 21 February 2009 (otherwise).

The stabilisation options

11   Private sector purchaser

(1)   The first stabilisation option is to sell all or part of the business of the bank to a commercial purchaser.

(2)   For that purpose the Bank of England may make—

(a)   one or more share transfer instruments;

(b)   one or more property transfer instruments.

[11]

NOTES

Commencement: 17 February 2009 (in so far as conferring or relating to any power to make subordinate legislation or codes of practice); 21 February 2009 (otherwise).

12   Bridge bank

(1)   The second stabilisation option is to transfer all or part of the business of the bank to a company which is wholly owned by the Bank of England (a "bridge bank").

(2)   For that purpose the Bank of England may make one or more property transfer instruments.

(3)   The code of practice under section 5 must include provision about the management and control of bridge banks including, in particular, provision about—

(a)   setting objectives,

(b)   the content of the articles of association,

(c)   the content of reports under section 80(1),

(d)   different arrangements for management and control at different stages, and

(e)   eventual disposal.

(4)   Where property, rights or liabilities are first transferred by property transfer instrument to a bridge bank and later transferred (whether or not by the exercise of a power under this Part) to another company which is wholly owned by the Bank of England, that other company is an "onward bridge bank".

(5)   An onward bridge bank—

(a)   is a bridge bank for the purposes of—

(i)   subsection (3),

(ii)   section 77,

(iii)   section 79, and

(iv)   section 80(5), but

(b)   is not a bridge bank for the purposes of—

(i)   section 30(1),

(ii)   section 43(1), or

(iii)   section 80(1).

[12]

NOTES
Commencement: 17 February 2009 (in so far as conferring or relating to any power to make subordinate legislation or codes of practice); 21 February 2009 (otherwise).

13 Temporary public ownership

(1)   The third stabilisation option is to take the bank into temporary public ownership.

(2)   For that purpose the Treasury may make one or more share transfer orders in which the transferee is—
(a)   a nominee of the Treasury, or
(b)   a company wholly owned by the Treasury.

(3)   The code of practice under section 5 must include provision about the management of banks taken into temporary public ownership under this section.

[13]

NOTES
Commencement: 17 February 2009 (in so far as conferring or relating to any power to make subordinate legislation or codes of practice); 21 February 2009 (otherwise).

Transfer of securities

14 Interpretation: "securities"

(1)   In this Part "securities" includes anything falling within any of the following classes.

(2)   Class 1: shares and stock.

(3)   Class 2: debentures, including—
(a)   debenture stock,
(b)   loan stock,
(c)   bonds,
(d)   certificates of deposit, and
(e)   any other instrument creating or acknowledging a debt.

(4)   Class 3: warrants or other instruments that entitle the holder to acquire anything in Class 1 or 2.

(5)   Class 4: rights which—
(a)   are granted by a deposit-taker, and
(b)   form part of the deposit-taker's own funds for the purposes of section 1 of Chapter 2 of Title V of Directive 2006/48/EC (on the taking up and pursuit of the business of credit institutions).

[14]

NOTES
Commencement: 17 February 2009 (in so far as conferring or relating to any power to make subordinate legislation or codes of practice); 21 February 2009 (otherwise).

15 Share transfer instrument

(1)   A share transfer instrument is an instrument which—
(a)   provides for securities issued by a specified bank to be transferred;
(b)   makes other provision for the purposes of, or in connection with, the transfer of securities issued by a specified bank (whether or not the transfer has been or is to be effected by that instrument, by another share transfer instrument or otherwise).

(2)   A share transfer instrument may relate to—
(a)   specified securities, or
(b)   securities of a specified description.

[15]

NOTES
Commencement: 17 February 2009 (in so far as conferring or relating to any power to make subordinate legislation or codes of practice); 21 February 2009 (otherwise).

16 Share transfer order

(1)   A share transfer order is an order which—
(a)   provides for securities issued by a specified bank to be transferred;
(b)   makes other provision for the purposes of, or in connection with, the transfer of securities issued by a specified bank (whether or not the transfer has been or is to be effected by that order, by another share transfer order or otherwise).

(2)   A share transfer order may relate to—
  (a)   specified securities, or
  (b)   securities of a specified description.

[16]

NOTES
Commencement: 17 February 2009 (in so far as conferring or relating to any power to make subordinate legislation or codes of practice); 21 February 2009 (otherwise).

17   Effect

(1)   In this section "transfer" means a transfer provided for by a share transfer instrument or order.

(2)   A transfer takes effect by virtue of the instrument or order (and in accordance with its provisions as to timing or other ancillary matters).

(3)   A transfer takes effect despite any restriction arising by virtue of contract or legislation or in any other way.

(4)   In subsection (3) "restriction" includes—
  (a)   any restriction, inability or incapacity affecting what can and cannot be assigned or transferred (whether generally or by a particular person), and
  (b)   a requirement for consent (by any name).

(5)   A share transfer instrument or order may provide for a transfer to take effect free from any trust, liability or other encumbrance (and may include provision about their extinguishment).

(6)   A share transfer instrument or order may extinguish rights to acquire securities falling within Class 1 or 2 in section 14.

[17]

NOTES
Commencement: 17 February 2009 (in so far as conferring or relating to any power to make subordinate legislation or codes of practice); 21 February 2009 (otherwise).

18   Continuity

(1)   A share transfer instrument or order may provide for a transferee to be treated for any purpose connected with the transfer as the same person as the transferor.

(2)   A share transfer instrument or order may provide for agreements made or other things done by or in relation to a transferor to be treated as made or done by or in relation to the transferee.

(3)   A share transfer instrument or order may provide for anything (including legal proceedings) that relates to anything transferred and is in the process of being done by or in relation to the transferor immediately before the transfer date, to be continued by or in relation to the transferee.

(4)   A share transfer instrument or order may modify references (express or implied) in an instrument or document to a transferor.

(5)   A share transfer instrument or order may require or permit—
  (a)   a transferor to provide a transferee with information and assistance;
  (b)   a transferee to provide a transferor with information and assistance.

[18]

NOTES
Commencement: 17 February 2009 (in so far as conferring or relating to any power to make subordinate legislation or codes of practice); 21 February 2009 (otherwise).

19   Conversion and delisting

(1)   A share transfer instrument or order may provide for securities to be converted from one form or class to another.

(2)   A share transfer instrument or order may provide for the listing of securities, under section 74 of the Financial Services and Markets Act 2000, to be discontinued.

[19]

NOTES
Commencement: 17 February 2009 (in so far as conferring or relating to any power to make subordinate legislation or codes of practice); 21 February 2009 (otherwise).

20   Directors

(1)   A share transfer instrument may enable the Bank of England—
  (a)   to remove a director of a specified bank;

(b)   to vary the service contract of a director of a specified bank;

(c)   to terminate the service contract of a director of a specified bank;

(d)   to appoint a director of a specified bank.

(2)   A share transfer order may enable the Treasury—

(a)   to remove a director of a specified bank;

(b)   to vary the service contract of a director of a specified bank;

(c)   to terminate the service contract of a director of a specified bank;

(d)   to appoint a director of a specified bank.

(3)   Appointments under subsection (1)(d) are to be on terms and conditions agreed with the Bank of England.

(4)   Appointments under subsection (2)(d) are to be on terms and conditions agreed with the Treasury.

[20]

NOTES

Commencement: 17 February 2009 (in so far as conferring or relating to any power to make subordinate legislation or codes of practice); 21 February 2009 (otherwise).

21   Ancillary instruments: production, registration, &c

(1)   A share transfer instrument or order may permit or require the execution, issue or delivery of an instrument.

(2)   A share transfer instrument or order may provide for a transfer to have effect irrespective of—

(a)   whether an instrument has been produced, delivered, transferred or otherwise dealt with;

(b)   registration.

(3)   A share transfer instrument or order may provide for the effect of an instrument executed, issued or delivered in accordance with the instrument or order.

(4)   A share transfer instrument or order may modify or annul the effect of an instrument.

(5)   A share transfer instrument or order may—

(a)   entitle a transferee to be registered in respect of transferred securities;

(b)   require a person to effect registration.

[21]

NOTES

Commencement: 17 February 2009 (in so far as conferring or relating to any power to make subordinate legislation or codes of practice); 21 February 2009 (otherwise).

22   Termination rights, &c

(1)   In this section "default event provision" means a Type 1 or Type 2 default event provision as defined in subsections (2) and (3).

(2)   A Type 1 default event provision is a provision of a contract or other agreement that has the effect that if a specified event occurs or situation arises—

(a)   the agreement is terminated, modified or replaced,

(b)   rights or duties under the agreement are terminated, modified or replaced,

(c)   a right accrues to terminate, modify or replace the agreement,

(d)   a right accrues to terminate, modify or replace rights or duties under the agreement,

(e)   a sum becomes payable or ceases to be payable,

(f)   delivery of anything becomes due or ceases to be due,

(g)   a right to claim a payment or delivery accrues, changes or lapses,

(h)   any other right accrues, changes or lapses, or

(i)   an interest is created, changes or lapses.

(3)   A Type 2 default event provision is a provision of a contract or other agreement that has the effect that a provision of the contract or agreement—

(a)   takes effect only if a specified event occurs or does not occur,

(b)   takes effect only if a specified situation arises or does not arise,

(c)   has effect only for so long as a specified event does not occur,

(d)   has effect only while a specified situation lasts,

(e)   applies differently if a specified event occurs,

(f)   applies differently if a specified situation arises, or

(g)   applies differently while a specified situation lasts.

(4)   For the purposes of subsections (2) and (3) it is the effect of a provision that matters, not how it is described (nor, for example, whether it is presented in a positive or a negative form).

(5)   A share transfer instrument or order may provide for subsection (6) or (7) to apply (but need not apply either).

(6)   If this subsection applies, the share transfer instrument or order is to be disregarded in determining whether a default event provision applies.

(7)   If this subsection applies, the share transfer instrument or order is to be disregarded in determining whether a default event provision applies except in so far as the instrument or order provides otherwise.

(8)   In subsections (6) and (7) a reference to the share transfer instrument or order is a reference to—

(a)   the making of the instrument or order,

(b)   anything that is done by the instrument or order or is to be, or may be, done under or by virtue of the instrument or order, and

(c)   any action or decision taken or made under this or another enactment in so far as it resulted in, or was connected to, the making of the instrument or order.

(9)   Provision under subsection (5) may apply subsection (6) or (7)—

(a)   generally or only for specified purposes, cases or circumstances;

(b)   differently for different purposes, cases or circumstances.

(10)   A thing is not done by virtue of an instrument or order for the purposes of subsection (8)(b) merely by virtue of being done under a contract or other agreement rights or obligations under which have been transferred by the instrument or order.

[22]

NOTES

Commencement: 17 February 2009 (in so far as conferring or relating to any power to make subordinate legislation or codes of practice); 21 February 2009 (otherwise).

23   Incidental provision

(1)   A share transfer instrument or order may include incidental, consequential or transitional provision.

(2)   In relying on subsection (1) a share transfer instrument or order—

(a)   may make provision generally or only for specified purposes, cases or circumstances, and

(b)   may make different provision for different purposes, cases or circumstances.

[23]

NOTES

Commencement: 17 February 2009 (in so far as conferring or relating to any power to make subordinate legislation or codes of practice); 21 February 2009 (otherwise).

24   Procedure: instruments

(1)   As soon as is reasonably practicable after making a share transfer instrument in respect of a bank the Bank of England shall send a copy to—

(a)   the bank,

(b)   the Treasury,

(c)   the FSA, and

(d)   any other person specified in the code of practice under section 5.

(2)   As soon as is reasonably practicable after making a share transfer instrument the Bank of England shall publish a copy—

(a)   on the Bank's internet website, and

(b)   in two newspapers, chosen by the Bank of England to maximise the likelihood of the instrument coming to the attention of persons likely to be affected.

(3)   Where the Treasury receive a copy of a share transfer instrument under subsection (1) they shall lay a copy before Parliament.

[24]

NOTES

Commencement: 17 February 2009 (in so far as conferring or relating to any power to make subordinate legislation or codes of practice); 21 February 2009 (otherwise).

25   Procedure: orders

(1)   A share transfer order—

(a)   shall be made by statutory instrument, and

(b)   shall be subject to annulment in pursuance of a resolution of either House of Parliament.

(2) As soon as is reasonably practicable after making a share transfer order in respect of a bank the Treasury shall send a copy to—

  (a) the bank,
  (b) the Bank of England,
  (c) the FSA, and
  (d) any other person specified in the code of practice under section 5.

(3) As soon as is reasonably practicable after making a share transfer order the Treasury shall publish a copy—

  (a) on the Treasury's internet website, and
  (b) in two newspapers, chosen by the Treasury to maximise the likelihood of the instrument coming to the attention of persons likely to be affected.

[25]

NOTES

Commencement: 17 February 2009 (in so far as conferring or relating to any power to make subordinate legislation or codes of practice); 21 February 2009 (otherwise).

26 Supplemental instruments

(1) This section applies where the Bank of England has made a share transfer instrument in accordance with section 11(2) ("the original instrument").

(2) The Bank of England may make one or more supplemental share transfer instruments.

(3) A supplemental share transfer instrument is a share transfer instrument which—

  (a) provides for the transfer of securities which were issued by the bank before the original instrument and have not been transferred by the original instrument or another supplemental share transfer instrument;
  (a) makes provision of a kind that a share transfer instrument may make under section 15(1)(b) (whether or not in connection with a transfer under the original instrument).

(4) Sections 7 and 8 do not apply to a supplemental share transfer instrument (but it is to be treated in the same way as any other share transfer instrument for all other purposes, including for the purposes of the application of a power under this Part).

(5) Before making a supplemental share transfer instrument the Bank of England must consult—

  (a) the FSA, and
  (b) the Treasury.

(6) The possibility of making a supplemental share transfer instrument in reliance on subsection (2) is without prejudice to the possibility of making of a new instrument in accordance with section 11(2) (and not in reliance on subsection (2) above).

[26]

NOTES

Commencement: 17 February 2009 (in so far as conferring or relating to any power to make subordinate legislation or codes of practice); 21 February 2009 (otherwise).

27 Supplemental orders

(1) This section applies where the Treasury have made a share transfer order, in respect of securities issued by a bank, in accordance with section 13(2) ("the original order").

(2) The Treasury may make one or more supplemental share transfer orders.

(3) A supplemental share transfer order is a share transfer order which—

  (a) provides for the transfer of securities which were issued by the bank before the original order and have not been transferred by the original order or another supplemental share transfer order;
  (b) makes provision of a kind that a share transfer order may make under section 16(1)(b), whether in connection with a transfer under the original order or in connection with a transfer under that or another supplemental order.

(4) Sections 7 and 9 do not apply to a supplemental share transfer order (but it is to be treated in the same way as any other share transfer order for all other purposes, including for the purposes of the application of a power under this Part).

(5) Before making a supplemental share transfer order the Treasury must consult—

  (a) the FSA, and
  (b) the Bank of England.

(6) The possibility of making a supplemental share transfer order in reliance on subsection (2) is without prejudice to the possibility of making of a new order in accordance with section 13(2) (and not in reliance on subsection (2) above).

[27]

NOTES

Commencement: 17 February 2009 (in so far as conferring or relating to any power to make subordinate legislation or codes of practice); 21 February 2009 (otherwise).

28 Onward transfer

(1) This section applies where the Treasury have made a share transfer order, in respect of securities issued by a bank, in accordance with section 13(2) ("the original order").

(2) The Treasury may make one or more onward share transfer orders.

(3) An onward share transfer order is a share transfer order which—
  (a) provides for the transfer of—
    (i) securities which were issued by the bank before the original order and have been transferred by the original order or a supplemental share transfer order, or
    (ii) securities which were issued by the bank after the original order;
  (b) makes other provision for the purposes of, or in connection with, the transfer of securities issued by the bank (whether the transfer has been or is to be effected by that order, by another share transfer order or otherwise).

(4) An onward share transfer order may not transfer securities to the transferor under the original order.

(5) Sections 7 and 9 do not apply to an onward share transfer order (but it is to be treated in the same way as any other share transfer order for all other purposes, including for the purposes of the application of a power under this Part).

(6) Before making an onward share transfer order the Treasury must consult—
  (a) the FSA, and
  (b) the Bank of England.

(7) Section 27 applies where the Treasury have made an onward share transfer order.

[28]

NOTES

Commencement: 17 February 2009 (in so far as conferring or relating to any power to make subordinate legislation or codes of practice); 21 February 2009 (otherwise).

29 Reverse share transfer

(1) This section applies where the Treasury have made a share transfer order in accordance with section 13(2) ("the original order") providing for the transfer of securities issued by a bank to a person ("the original transferee").

(2) The Treasury may make one or more reverse share transfer orders in respect of securities issued by the bank and held by the original transferee (whether or not they were transferred by the original order).

(3) If the Treasury makes an onward share transfer order in respect of securities transferred by the original order, the Treasury may make one or more reverse share transfer orders in respect of securities—
  (a) issued by the bank, and
  (b) held by a transferee under the onward share transfer order of any of the following kinds—
    (i) a company wholly owned by the Bank of England,
    (ii) a company wholly owned by the Treasury, or
    (iii) a nominee of the Treasury.

(4) A reverse share transfer order is a share transfer order which—
  (a) provides for transfer to the transferor under the original order (where subsection (2) applies);
  (b) provides for transfer to the original transferee (where subsection (3) applies);
  (c) makes other provision for the purposes of, or in connection with, the transfer of securities which are, could be or could have been transferred under paragraph (a) or (b).

(5) Sections 7, 9 and 51 do not apply to a reverse share transfer order (but it is to be treated in the same way as any other share transfer order for all other purposes including for the purposes of the application of a power under this Part).

(6) Before making a reverse share transfer order the Treasury must consult—
  (a) the FSA, and

    (b)   the Bank of England.

    (7)   Section 27 applies where the Treasury have made a reverse share transfer order.

[29]

NOTES
    Commencement: 17 February 2009 (in so far as conferring or relating to any power to make subordinate legislation or codes of practice); 21 February 2009 (otherwise).

30   Bridge bank: share transfers

    (1)   This section applies where the Bank of England has made a property transfer instrument in respect of a bridge bank in accordance with section 12(2) ("the original instrument").

    (2)   The Bank of England may make one or more bridge bank share transfer instruments.

    (3)   A bridge bank share transfer instrument is a share transfer instrument which—
    (a)   provides for securities issued by the bridge bank to be transferred;
    (b)   makes other provision for the purposes of, or in connection with, the transfer of securities issued by the bridge bank (whether the transfer has been or is to be effected by that instrument, by another share transfer instrument or otherwise).

    (4)   Sections 7 and 8 do not apply to a bridge bank share transfer instrument (but it is to be treated in the same way as any other share transfer instrument for all other purposes, including for the purposes of the application of a power under this Part).

    (5)   Before making a bridge bank share transfer instrument the Bank of England must consult—
    (a)   the FSA, and
    (b)   the Treasury.

    (6)   Section 26 applies where the Bank of England has made a bridge bank share transfer instrument.

[30]

NOTES
    Commencement: 17 February 2009 (in so far as conferring or relating to any power to make subordinate legislation or codes of practice); 21 February 2009 (otherwise).

31   Bridge bank: reverse share transfer

    (1)   This section applies where the Bank of England has made a bridge bank share transfer instrument in accordance with section 30(2) ("the original instrument") providing for the transfer of securities to—
    (a)   a company wholly owned by the Bank of England,
    (b)   a company wholly owned by the Treasury, or
    (c)   a nominee of the Treasury.

    (2)   The Bank of England may make one or more bridge bank reverse share transfer instruments in respect of securities issued by the bridge bank and held by a person within subsection (1)(a) to (c).

    (3)   A bridge bank reverse share transfer instrument is a share transfer instrument which—
    (a)   provides for transfer to the transferor under the original instrument;
    (b)   makes other provision for the purposes of, or in connection with, the transfer of securities which are, could be or could have been transferred under paragraph (a).

    (4)   Sections 7, 8 and 51 do not apply to a bridge bank reverse share transfer instrument (but it is to be treated in the same way as any other share transfer instrument for all other purposes including for the purposes of the application of a power under this Part).

    (5)   Before making a bridge bank reverse share transfer instrument the Bank of England must consult—
    (a)   the FSA, and
    (b)   the Treasury.

    (6)   Section 26 applies where the Bank of England has made a bridge bank reverse share transfer instrument.

[31]

NOTES
    Commencement: 17 February 2009 (in so far as conferring or relating to any power to make subordinate legislation or codes of practice); 21 February 2009 (otherwise).

32   Interpretation: general

In this group of sections—
    "service contract" has the meaning given by section 227 of the Companies Act 2006, and

"transfer date" means the date or time on or at which a share transfer instrument or order (or the relevant part of it) takes effect.

[32]

NOTES
Commencement: 17 February 2009 (in so far as conferring or relating to any power to make subordinate legislation or codes of practice); 21 February 2009 (otherwise).

Transfer of property

33 Property transfer instrument

(1) A property transfer instrument is an instrument which—
   (a) provides for property, rights or liabilities of a specified bank to be transferred;
   (b) makes other provision for the purposes of, or in connection with, the transfer of property, rights or liabilities of a specified bank (whether the transfer has been or is to be effected by that instrument, by another property transfer instrument or otherwise).

(2) A property transfer instrument may relate to—
   (a) all property, rights and liabilities of the specified bank,
   (b) all its property, rights and liabilities subject to specified exceptions,
   (c) specified property, rights or liabilities, or
   (d) property, rights or liabilities of a specified description.

[33]

NOTES
Commencement: 17 February 2009 (in so far as conferring or relating to any power to make subordinate legislation or codes of practice); 21 February 2009 (otherwise).

34 Effect

(1) In this section "transfer" means a transfer provided for by a property transfer instrument.

(2) A transfer takes effect by virtue of the instrument (and in accordance with its provisions as to timing or other ancillary matters).

(3) A transfer takes effect despite any restriction arising by virtue of contract or legislation or in any other way.

(4) In subsection (3) "restriction" includes—
   (a) any restriction, inability or incapacity affecting what can and cannot be assigned or transferred (whether generally or by a particular person), and
   (b) a requirement for consent (by any name).

(5) A property transfer instrument may provide for a transfer to be conditional upon a specified event or situation—
   (a) occurring or arising, or
   (b) not occurring or arising.

(6) A property transfer instrument may include provision dealing with the consequences of breach of a condition imposed under subsection (5); and the consequences may include—
   (a) automatic vesting in the original transferor;
   (b) an obligation to effect a transfer back to the original transferor, with specified consequences for failure to comply (which may include provision conferring a discretion on a court or tribunal);
   (c) provision making a transfer or anything done in connection with a transfer void or voidable.

(7) Where a property transfer instrument makes provision in respect of property held on trust (however arising) it may also make provision about—
   (a) the terms on which the property is to be held after the instrument takes effect (which provision may remove or alter the terms of the trust), and
   (b) how any powers, provisions and liabilities in respect of the property are to be exercisable or have effect after the instrument takes effect.

[34]

NOTES
Commencement: 17 February 2009 (in so far as conferring or relating to any power to make subordinate legislation or codes of practice); 21 February 2009 (otherwise).

35 Transferable property

(1) A property transfer instrument may transfer any property, rights or liabilities including, in particular—

(a) property, rights and liabilities acquired or arising between the making of the instrument and the transfer date,

(b) rights and liabilities arising on or after the transfer date in respect of matters occurring before that date,

(c) property outside the United Kingdom,

(d) rights and liabilities under the law of a country or territory outside the United Kingdom, and

(e) rights and liabilities under an enactment (including legislation of the European Union).

(2) Section 32 applies for the interpretation of this section (with the necessary modification).

[35]

NOTES

Commencement: 17 February 2009 (in so far as conferring or relating to any power to make subordinate legislation or codes of practice); 21 February 2009 (otherwise).

36 Continuity

(1) A property transfer instrument may provide—

(a) for a transfer to be, or to be treated as, a succession;

(b) for a transferee to be treated for any purpose connected with the transfer as the same person as the transferor.

(2) A property transfer instrument may provide for agreements made or other things done by or in relation to a transferor to be treated as made or done by or in relation to the transferee.

(3) A property transfer instrument may provide for anything (including legal proceedings) that relates to anything transferred and is in the process of being done by or in relation to the transferor immediately before the transfer date, to be continued by or in relation to the transferee.

(4) A property transfer instrument which transfers or enables the transfer of a contract of employment may include provision about continuity of employment.

(5) A property transfer instrument may modify references (express or implied) in an instrument or document to a transferor.

(6) In so far as rights and liabilities in respect of anything transferred are enforceable after transfer, a property transfer instrument may provide for apportionment between transferor and transferee to a specified extent and in specified ways.

(7) A property transfer instrument may enable the transferor and transferee by agreement to modify a provision of the instrument; but a modification—

(a) must achieve a result that could have been achieved by the instrument, and

(b) may not transfer (or arrange for the transfer of) property, rights or liabilities.

(8) A property transfer instrument may require or permit—

(a) a transferor to provide a transferee with information and assistance;

(b) a transferee to provide a transferor with information and assistance.

(9) Section 32 applies for the interpretation of this section (with the necessary modification).

[36]

NOTES

Commencement: 17 February 2009 (in so far as conferring or relating to any power to make subordinate legislation or codes of practice); 21 February 2009 (otherwise).

37 Licences

(1) A licence in respect of anything transferred by property transfer instrument shall continue to have effect despite the transfer.

(2) A property transfer instrument may disapply subsection (1) to a specified extent.

(3) Where a licence imposes rights or obligations, a property transfer instrument may apportion responsibility for exercise or compliance between transferor and transferee.

(4) In this section "licence" includes permission and approval and any other permissive document in respect of anything transferred.

[37]

NOTES

Commencement: 17 February 2009 (in so far as conferring or relating to any power to make subordinate legislation or codes of practice); 21 February 2009 (otherwise).

38 Termination rights, &c

(1) In this section "default event provision" means a Type 1 or Type 2 default event provision as defined in subsections (2) and (3).

(2)   A Type 1 default event provision is a provision of a contract or other agreement that has the effect that if a specified event occurs or situation arises—

(a)   the agreement is terminated, modified or replaced,
(b)   rights or duties under the agreement are terminated, modified or replaced,
(c)   a right accrues to terminate, modify or replace the agreement,
(d)   a right accrues to terminate, modify or replace rights or duties under the agreement,
(e)   a sum becomes payable or ceases to be payable,
(f)   delivery of anything becomes due or ceases to be due,
(g)   a right to claim a payment or delivery accrues, changes or lapses,
(h)   any other right accrues, changes or lapses, or
(i)   an interest is created, changes or lapses.

(3)   A Type 2 default event provision is a provision of a contract or other agreement that has the effect that a provision of the contract or agreement—

(a)   takes effect only if a specified event occurs or does not occur,
(b)   takes effect only if a specified situation arises or does not arise,
(c)   has effect only for so long as a specified event does not occur,
(d)   has effect only while a specified situation lasts,
(e)   applies differently if a specified event occurs,
(f)   applies differently if a specified situation arises, or
(g)   applies differently while a specified situation lasts.

(4)   For the purposes of subsections (2) and (3) it is the effect of a provision that matters, not how it is described (nor, for example, whether it is presented in a positive or a negative form).

(5)   A property transfer instrument may provide for subsection (6) or (7) to apply (but need not apply either).

(6)   If this subsection applies, the property transfer instrument is to be disregarded in determining whether a default event provision applies.

(7)   If this subsection applies, the property transfer instrument is to be disregarded in determining whether a default event provision applies except in so far as the instrument provides otherwise.

(8)   In subsections (6) and (7) a reference to the property transfer instrument is a reference to—

(a)   the making of the instrument,
(b)   anything that is done by the instrument or is to be, or may be, done under or by virtue of the instrument, and
(c)   any action or decision taken or made under this or another enactment in so far as it resulted in, or was connected to, the making of the instrument.

(9)   Provision under subsection (5) may apply subsection (6) or (7)—

(a)   generally or only for specified purposes, cases or circumstances;
(b)   differently for different purposes, cases or circumstances.

(10)   A thing is not done by virtue of an instrument for the purposes of subsection (8)(b) merely by virtue of being done under a contract or other agreement rights or obligations under which have been transferred by the instrument.

[38]

NOTES

Commencement: 17 February 2009 (in so far as conferring or relating to any power to make subordinate legislation or codes of practice); 21 February 2009 (otherwise).

39   Foreign property

(1)   This section applies where a property transfer instrument transfers foreign property.

(2)   In subsection (1) "foreign property" means—

(a)   property outside the United Kingdom, and
(b)   rights and liabilities under foreign law.

(3)   The transferor and the transferee must each take any necessary steps to ensure that the transfer is effective as a matter of foreign law (if it is not wholly effective by virtue of the property transfer instrument).

(4)   Until the transfer is effective as a matter of foreign law, the transferor must—

(a)   hold the property or right for the benefit of the transferee (together with any additional property or right accruing by virtue of the original property or right), or
(b)   discharge the liability on behalf of the transferee.

(5)   The transferee must meet any expenses of the transferor in complying with this section.

(6)   An obligation imposed by this section is enforceable as if created by contract between the transferor and transferee.

(7) The transferor must comply with any directions of the Bank of England in respect of the obligations under subsections (3) and (4); and—

    (a)   a direction may disapply subsections (3) and (4) to a specified extent, and

    (b)   obligations imposed by direction are enforceable as if created by contract between the transferor and the Bank of England.

(8) In this section "foreign law" means the law of a country or territory outside the United Kingdom.

[39]

NOTES

Commencement: 17 February 2009 (in so far as conferring or relating to any power to make subordinate legislation or codes of practice); 21 February 2009 (otherwise).

40 Incidental provision

(1) A property transfer instrument may include incidental, consequential or transitional provision.

(2) In relying on subsection (1) an instrument—

    (a)   may make provision generally or only for specified purposes, cases or circumstances, and

    (b)   may make different provision for different purposes, cases or circumstances.

[40]

NOTES

Commencement: 17 February 2009 (in so far as conferring or relating to any power to make subordinate legislation or codes of practice); 21 February 2009 (otherwise).

41 Procedure

(1) As soon as is reasonably practicable after making a property transfer instrument in respect of a bank the Bank of England shall send a copy to—

    (a)   the bank,

    (b)   the Treasury,

    (c)   the FSA, and

    (d)   any other person specified in the code of practice under section 5.

(2) As soon as is reasonably practicable after making a property transfer instrument the Bank of England shall publish a copy—

    (a)   on the Bank's internet website, and

    (b)   in two newspapers, chosen by the Bank of England to maximise the likelihood of the instrument coming to the attention of persons likely to be affected.

(3) Where the Treasury receive a copy of a property transfer instrument under subsection (1) they shall lay a copy before Parliament.

[41]

NOTES

Commencement: 17 February 2009 (in so far as conferring or relating to any power to make subordinate legislation or codes of practice); 21 February 2009 (otherwise).

42 Supplemental instruments

(1) This section applies where the Bank of England has made a property transfer instrument in accordance with section 11(2) or 12(2) ("the original instrument").

(2) The Bank of England may make one or more supplemental property transfer instruments.

(3) A supplemental property transfer instrument is a property transfer instrument which—

    (a)   provides for property, rights or liabilities to be transferred from the transferor under the original instrument (whether accruing or arising before or after the original instrument);

    (b)   makes other provision of a kind that an original property transfer instrument may make under section 33(1)(b) (whether in connection with a transfer under the original instrument or in connection with a transfer under that or another supplemental instrument).

(4) Sections 7 and 8 do not apply to a supplemental property transfer instrument (but it is to be treated in the same way as any other property transfer instrument for all other purposes, including for the purposes of the application of a power under this Part).

(5) Before making a supplemental property transfer instrument the Bank of England must consult—

    (a)   the FSA, and

    (b)   the Treasury.

PART I
BANKING ACT 2009

(6)   The possibility of making a supplemental property transfer instrument in reliance on subsection (2) is without prejudice to the possibility of making of a new instrument in accordance with section 11(2) or 12(2) (and not in reliance on subsection (2) above).

[42]

NOTES
Commencement: 17 February 2009 (in so far as conferring or relating to any power to make subordinate legislation or codes of practice); 21 February 2009 (otherwise).

43   Onward transfer

(1)   This section applies where the Bank of England has made a property transfer instrument in respect of a bridge bank in accordance with section 12(2) ("the original instrument").

(2)   The Bank of England may make one or more onward property transfer instruments.

(3)   An onward property transfer instrument is a property transfer instrument which—
  (a)   provides for property, rights or liabilities of the bridge bank to be transferred (whether accruing or arising before or after the original instrument);
  (b)   makes other provision for the purposes of, or in connection with, the transfer of property, rights or liabilities of the bridge bank (whether the transfer has been or is to be effected by that instrument, by another property transfer instrument or otherwise).

(4)   An onward property transfer instrument may relate to property, rights or liabilities of the bridge bank whether or not they were transferred under the original instrument.

(5)   An onward property transfer instrument may not transfer property, rights or liabilities to the transferor under the original instrument.

(6)   Sections 7, 8 and 52 do not apply to an onward property transfer instrument (but for other purposes it is to be treated in the same way as any other property transfer instrument, including for the purposes of the application of a power under this Part).

(7)   Before making an onward property transfer instrument the Bank of England must consult—
  (a)   the FSA, and
  (b)   the Treasury.

(8)   Section 42 applies where the Bank of England has made an onward property transfer instrument.

[43]

NOTES
Commencement: 17 February 2009 (in so far as conferring or relating to any power to make subordinate legislation or codes of practice); 21 February 2009 (otherwise).

44   Reverse property transfer

(1)   This section applies where the Bank of England has made a property transfer instrument in accordance with section 12(2) ("the original instrument") providing for the transfer of property, rights or liabilities to a bridge bank.

(2)   The Bank of England may make one or more reverse property transfer instruments in respect of property, rights or liabilities of the bridge bank.

(3)   If the Bank of England makes an onward property transfer instrument under section 43 the Bank may make one or more reverse property transfer instruments in respect of property, rights or liabilities of a transferee of any of the following kinds under the onward property transfer instrument—
  (a)   a company wholly owned by the Bank of England,
  (b)   a company wholly owned by the Treasury, or
  (c)   a company wholly owned by a nominee of the Treasury.

(4)   A reverse property transfer instrument is a property transfer instrument which—
  (a)   provides for transfer to the transferor under the original instrument (where subsection (2) applies);
  (b)   provides for transfer to the bridge bank (where subsection (3) applies);
  (c)   makes other provision for the purposes of, or in connection with, the transfer of property, rights or liabilities that are, could be or could have been transferred under paragraph (a) or (b) (whether the transfer has been or is to be effected by that instrument or otherwise).

(5)   Sections 7, 8 and 52 do not apply to a reverse property transfer instrument (but it is to be treated in the same way as any other property transfer instrument for all other purposes including for the purposes of the application of a power under this Part).

(6)   Before making a reverse property transfer instrument the Bank of England must consult—
  (a)   the FSA, and
  (b)   the Treasury.

(7)   Section 42 applies where the Bank of England has made a reverse property transfer instrument.

[44]

NOTES
Commencement: 17 February 2009 (in so far as conferring or relating to any power to make subordinate legislation or codes of practice); 21 February 2009 (otherwise).

45   Temporary public ownership: property transfer

(1)   This section applies where the Treasury have made a share transfer order, in respect of securities issued by a bank, in accordance with section 13(2) ("the original order").

(2)   The Treasury may make one or more property transfer orders.

(3)   A property transfer order is an order which—
  (a)   provides for property, rights or liabilities of the bank to be transferred (whether accruing or arising before or after the original order);
  (b)   makes other provision for the purposes of, or in connection with, the transfer of property, rights or liabilities of the bank (whether the transfer has been or is to be effected by the order or otherwise).

(4)   Sections 7, 8 and 9 do not apply to a property transfer order.

(5)   A property transfer order is to be treated—
  (a)   in the same way as a share transfer order for the procedural purposes of section 25, but
  (b)   as a property transfer instrument for all other purposes (including for the purposes of the application of powers under this Part).

(6)   In the application of section 39 by virtue of subsection (5)(b) above, the power to give directions under section 39(7) vests in the Treasury (instead of the Bank of England).

(7)   Section 42 applies where the Treasury has made a property transfer order.

(8)   Before making a property transfer order the Treasury must consult—
  (a)   the FSA, and
  (b)   the Bank of England.

[45]

NOTES
Commencement: 17 February 2009 (in so far as conferring or relating to any power to make subordinate legislation or codes of practice); 21 February 2009 (otherwise).

46   Temporary public ownership: reverse property transfer

(1)   This section applies where the Treasury have made a property transfer order in accordance with section 45(2) ("the original order") providing for the transfer of property, rights or liabilities to a company wholly owned by—
  (a)   the Bank of England,
  (b)   the Treasury, or
  (c)   a nominee of the Treasury.

(2)   The Treasury may make one or more reverse property transfer orders in respect of property, rights or liabilities of the transferee under the original order.

(3)   A reverse property transfer order is a property transfer order which—
  (a)   provides for transfer to the transferor under the original order;
  (b)   makes other provision for the purposes of, or in connection with, the transfer of property, rights or liabilities which are, could be or could have been transferred.

(4)   Sections 7, 8 and 9 do not apply to a reverse property transfer order.

(5)   A reverse property transfer order is to be treated—
  (a)   in the same way as a share transfer order for the procedural purposes of section 25, but
  (b)   as a property transfer instrument for all other purposes (including for the purposes of the application of a power under this Part).

(6)   In the application of section 39 by virtue of subsection (5)(b) above, the power to give directions under section 39(7) vests in the Treasury (instead of the Bank of England).

(7)   Before making a reverse property transfer order the Treasury must consult—
  (a)   the FSA, and
  (b)   the Bank of England.

(8)   Section 42 applies where the Treasury have made a reverse property transfer order.

[46]

PART I
BANKING ACT 2009

NOTES
Commencement: 17 February 2009 (in so far as conferring or relating to any power to make subordinate legislation or codes of practice); 21 February 2009 (otherwise).

47 Restriction of partial transfers

(1)   In this Part "partial property transfer" means a property transfer instrument which provides for the transfer of some, but not all, of the property, rights and liabilities of a bank.

(2)   The Treasury may by order—

(a)   restrict the making of partial property transfers;

(b)   impose conditions on the making of partial property transfers;

(c)   require partial property transfers to include specified provision or provision to a specified effect;

(d)   provide for a partial property transfer to be void or voidable, or for other consequences (including automatic transfer of other property, rights or liabilities) to arise, if or in so far as the partial property transfer is made or purported to be made in contravention of a provision of the order (or of another order under this section).

(3)   Provision under subsection (2) may, in particular, refer to particular classes of deposit.

(4)   An order may apply to transfers generally or only to transfers—

(a)   of a specified kind, or

(b)   made or applying in specified circumstances.

(5)   An order—

(a)   shall be made by statutory instrument, and

(b)   may not be made unless a draft has been laid before and approved by resolution of each House of Parliament.

[47]

NOTES
Commencement: 17 February 2009 (in so far as conferring or relating to any power to make subordinate legislation or codes of practice); 21 February 2009 (otherwise).
Order: the Banking Act 2009 (Restriction of Partial Property Transfers) Order 2009, SI 2009/322 at [543].

48 Power to protect certain interests

(1)   In this section—

(a)   "security interests" means arrangements under which one person acquires, by way of security, an actual or contingent interest in the property of another,

(b)   "title transfer collateral arrangements" are arrangements under which Person 1 transfers assets to Person 2 on terms providing for Person 2 to transfer assets if specified obligations are discharged,

(c)   "set-off" arrangements are arrangements under which two or more debts, claims or obligations can be set off against each other,

(d)   "netting arrangements" are arrangements under which a number of claims or obligations can be converted into a net claim or obligation and include, in particular, "close-out" netting arrangements, under which actual or theoretical debts are calculated during the course of a contract for the purpose of enabling them to be set off against each other or to be converted into a net debt, and

(e)   "protected arrangements" means security interests, title transfer collateral arrangements, set-off arrangements and netting arrangements.

(2)   The Treasury may by order—

(a)   restrict the making of partial property transfers in cases that involve, or where they might affect, protected arrangements;

(b)   impose conditions on the making of partial property transfers in cases that involve, or where they might affect, protected arrangements;

(c)   require partial property transfers to include specified provision, or provision to a specified effect, in respect of or for purposes connected with protected arrangements;

(d)   provide for a partial property transfer to be void or voidable, or for other consequences (including automatic transfer of other property, rights or liabilities) to arise, if or in so far as the partial property transfer is made or purported to be made in contravention of a provision of the order (or of another order under this section).

(3)   An order may apply to protected arrangements generally or only to arrangements—

(a)   of a specified kind, or

(b)   made or applying in specified circumstances.

(4)   An order may include provision for determining which arrangements are to be, or not to be, treated as protected arrangements; in particular, an order may provide for arrangements to be

classified not according to their description by the parties but according to one or more indications of how they are treated, or are intended to be treated, in commercial practice.

(5)   In this section "arrangements" includes arrangements which—
- (a)   are formed wholly or partly by one or more contracts or trusts;
- (b)   arise under or are wholly or partly governed by the law of a country or territory outside the United Kingdom;
- (c)   wholly or partly arise automatically as a matter of law;
- (d)   involve any number of parties;
- (e)   operate partly by reference to other arrangements between other parties.

(6)   An order—
- (a)   shall be made by statutory instrument, and
- (b)   may not be made unless a draft has been laid before and approved by resolution of each House of Parliament.

[48]

NOTES

Commencement: 17 February 2009 (in so far as conferring or relating to any power to make subordinate legislation or codes of practice); 21 February 2009 (otherwise).

Order: the Banking Act 2009 (Restriction of Partial Property Transfers) Order 2009, SI 2009/322 at **[543]**.

Compensation

49 Orders

(1)   This Part provides three methods of protecting the financial interests of transferors and others in connection with share transfer instruments and orders and property transfer instruments.

(2)   A "compensation scheme order" is an order—
- (a)   establishing a scheme for determining whether transferors should be paid compensation, or providing for transferors to be paid compensation, and
- (b)   establishing a scheme for paying any compensation.

(3)   A "resolution fund order" is an order establishing a scheme under which transferors become entitled to the proceeds of the disposal of things transferred—
- (a)   in specified circumstances, and
- (b)   to a specified extent.

(4)   A "third party compensation order" is provision made in accordance with section 59 for compensation to be paid to persons other than transferors.

[49]

NOTES

Commencement: 17 February 2009 (in so far as conferring or relating to any power to make subordinate legislation or codes of practice); 21 February 2009 (otherwise).

Order: the Dunfermline Building Society Compensation Scheme, Resolution Fund and Third Party Compensation Order 2009, SI 2009/1800 at **[580]**.

50 Sale to private sector purchaser

(1)   This section applies if the Bank of England makes a share transfer instrument or a property transfer instrument in accordance with section 11(2).

(2)   The Treasury shall make a compensation scheme order.

(3)   An order made by virtue of subsection (2) may include a third party compensation order.

(4)   In the case of a partial property transfer, an order made by virtue of subsection (2) must include a third party compensation order.

[50]

NOTES

Commencement: 17 February 2009 (in so far as conferring or relating to any power to make subordinate legislation or codes of practice); 21 February 2009 (otherwise).

Order: the Dunfermline Building Society Compensation Scheme, Resolution Fund and Third Party Compensation Order 2009, SI 2009/1800 at **[580]**.

51 Transfer to temporary public ownership

(1)   This section applies if the Treasury make a share transfer order in accordance with section 13(2).

(2)   The Treasury shall make either—
- (a)   a compensation scheme order, or
- (b)   a resolution fund order.

(3)   A resolution fund order made by virtue of subsection (2)(b) may include—

    (a)   a compensation scheme order;

    (b)   a third party compensation order (which may, in particular, make provision, in respect of specified classes of creditor, for rights in addition to any rights they may have by virtue of the resolution fund order).

(4)   A compensation scheme order made by virtue of subsection (2) may include a third party compensation order.

[51]

NOTES

Commencement: 17 February 2009 (in so far as conferring or relating to any power to make subordinate legislation or codes of practice); 21 February 2009 (otherwise).

Note: For information regarding United Kingdom Financial Investments Ltd. see UKFI Business Plan 2009/10–2013/14 at http://www.ukfi.gov.uk/releases/UKFI%20Business%20Plan%2020090625.pdf and UKFI Shareholder Relationship Framework Document Revised Version 13 July 2009 at http://www.ukfi.gov.uk/releases/Framework%20Document%20July%20Revised%20Version.pdf.

52 Transfer to bridge bank

(1)   This section applies if the Bank of England makes a property transfer instrument in accordance with section 12(2).

(2)   The Treasury shall make a resolution fund order.

(3)   An order made by virtue of subsection (2) may include—

    (a)   a compensation scheme order;

    (b)   a third party compensation order (which may, in particular, make provision, in respect of specified classes of creditor, for rights in addition to any rights they may have by virtue of the resolution fund order).

(4)   In the case of a partial property transfer, the resolution fund order must include a third party compensation order.

[52]

NOTES

Commencement: 17 February 2009 (in so far as conferring or relating to any power to make subordinate legislation or codes of practice); 21 February 2009 (otherwise).

Order: the Dunfermline Building Society Compensation Scheme, Resolution Fund and Third Party Compensation Order 2009, SI 2009/1800 at **[580]**.

53 Onward and reverse transfers

(1)   This section applies where—

    (a)   the Treasury make an onward share transfer order under section 28,

    (b)   the Treasury makes a reverse share transfer order under section 29,

    (c)   the Bank of England makes a bridge bank share transfer instrument under section 30,

    (d)   the Bank of England makes a bridge bank reverse share transfer instrument under section 31,

    (e)   the Bank of England makes an onward property transfer instrument under section 43,

    (f)   the Bank of England makes a reverse property transfer instrument under section 44,

    (g)   the Treasury make a property transfer order under section 45, or

    (h)   the Treasury make a reverse property transfer order under section 46.

(2)   The Treasury may make—

    (a)   a compensation scheme order;

    (b)   a third party compensation order.

[53]

NOTES

Commencement: 17 February 2009 (in so far as conferring or relating to any power to make subordinate legislation or codes of practice); 21 February 2009 (otherwise).

54 Independent valuer

(1)   A compensation scheme order may provide for the amount of any compensation payable to be determined by a person appointed in accordance with the order (the "independent valuer"); and subsections (2) to (5) apply to an order which includes provision for an independent valuer.

(2)   An order must provide for the independent valuer to be appointed by a person appointed by the Treasury ("the appointing person").

(3)   An order may either—

    (a)   require the Treasury to make arrangements to identify a number of possible independent valuers, one of whom is to be selected by the appointing person, or

(b) require the appointing person to make arrangements to select the independent valuer, having regard to any criteria specified in the order.

(4) The independent valuer may be removed only—
  (a) on the grounds of incapacity or serious misconduct, and
  (b) by a person specified by the Treasury in accordance with the compensation scheme order.

(5) An order must include provision for resignation and replacement of the independent valuer (and subsections (2) and (3) apply to replacement as to the first appointment).

[54]

NOTES
Commencement: 17 February 2009 (in so far as conferring or relating to any power to make subordinate legislation or codes of practice); 21 February 2009 (otherwise).
Order: the Dunfermline Building Society Compensation Scheme, Resolution Fund and Third Party Compensation Order 2009, SI 2009/1800 at **[580]**.

55 Independent valuer: supplemental

(1) An independent valuer may do anything necessary or desirable for the purposes of or in connection with the performance of the functions of the office.

(2) The Treasury may by order confer specific functions on independent valuers; in particular, the order may—
  (a) enable an independent valuer to apply to a court or tribunal for an order requiring the provision of information or the giving of oral or written evidence;
  (b) enable or require independent valuers to publish, disclose or withhold information.

(3) Provision under subsection (2) may—
  (a) confer a discretion on independent valuers;
  (b) confer jurisdiction on a court or tribunal;
  (c) make provision about oaths, expenses and other procedural matters relating to the giving of evidence or the provision of information;
  (d) create a criminal offence;
  (e) make other provision about enforcement.

(4) An independent valuer may appoint staff.

(5) The Treasury may by order make provision about the procedure to be followed by independent valuers.

(6) The Treasury shall by order make provision for—
  (a) reconsideration of a decision of an independent valuer, and
  (b) appeal to a court or tribunal against a decision of an independent valuer.

(7) Independent valuers (and their staff) are neither servants nor agents of the Crown (and, in particular, are not civil servants).

(8) Records of an independent valuer are public records for the purposes of the Public Records Act 1958.

(9) An order under this section—
  (a) shall be made by statutory instrument, and
  (b) shall be subject to annulment in pursuance of a resolution of either House of Parliament.

[55]

NOTES
Commencement: 17 February 2009 (in so far as conferring or relating to any power to make subordinate legislation or codes of practice); 21 February 2009 (otherwise).
Order: the Dunfermline Building Society Independent Valuer Order 2009, SI 2009/1810 at **[599]**.

56 Independent valuer: money

(1) The Treasury may by order provide for the payment by the Treasury of remuneration and allowances to—
  (a) independent valuers,
  (b) staff of independent valuers,
  (c) appointing persons, and
  (d) monitors.

(2) An order—
  (a) must provide for the appointment by the Treasury of a person to monitor the operation of the arrangements for remuneration and allowances for independent valuers;
  (b) may require, or enable a compensation scheme order or third party compensation order to require, the monitor's approval before specified things may be done in the course of those arrangements;

(c) may include provision about records and accounts;

(d) may make provision about numbers of staff and the terms and conditions of their appointment (which may include provision requiring the approval of the Treasury or the monitor).

(3) In subsection (1) a reference to the payment of allowances to a person includes a reference to the payment to or in respect of the person of sums by way of or in respect of pension.

(4) Independent valuers (and their staff) are not liable for damages in respect of anything done in good faith for the purposes of or in connection with the functions of the office (subject to section 8 of the Human Rights Act 1998).

(5) An order under this section—

(a) shall be made by statutory instrument, and

(b) shall be subject to annulment in pursuance of a resolution of either House of Parliament.

[56]

NOTES

Commencement: 17 February 2009 (in so far as conferring or relating to any power to make subordinate legislation or codes of practice); 21 February 2009 (otherwise).

Order: the Dunfermline Building Society Independent Valuer Order 2009, SI 2009/1810 at **[599]**.

57 Valuation principles

(1) A compensation scheme order may specify principles ("valuation principles") to be applied in determining the amount of compensation.

(2) Valuation principles may, in particular, require an independent valuer—

(a) to apply, or not to apply, specified methods of valuation;

(b) to assess values or average values at specified dates or over specified periods;

(c) to take specified matters into account in a specified manner;

(d) not to take specified matters into account.

(3) In determining an amount of compensation (whether or not in accordance with valuation principles) an independent valuer must disregard actual or potential financial assistance provided by the Bank of England or the Treasury (disregarding ordinary market assistance offered by the Bank on its usual terms).

(4) Valuation principles may require or permit an independent valuer to make assumptions; such as, for example, that the bank—

(a) has had a permission under Part 4 of the Financial Services and Markets Act 2000 (regulated activities) varied or cancelled,

(b) is unable to continue as a going concern,

(c) is in administration, or

(d) is being wound up.

(5) There is nothing to prevent the application of the valuation principles in an order from resulting in no compensation being payable to a transferor.

[57]

NOTES

Commencement: 17 February 2009 (in so far as conferring or relating to any power to make subordinate legislation or codes of practice); 21 February 2009 (otherwise).

Order: the Dunfermline Building Society Compensation Scheme, Resolution Fund and Third Party Compensation Order 2009, SI 2009/1800 at **[580]**.

58 Resolution fund

(1) A resolution fund order must include provision for determining—

(a) who will be entitled to a share of the proceeds on disposal of things transferred,

(b) the way in which the proceeds will be calculated, and

(c) the way in which shares will be calculated.

(2) Provision under subsection (1)(b) may, in particular, provide for proceeds to be calculated net of—

(a) amounts required for the repayment of loans from public funds or for other payments in respect of public financial assistance;

(b) some or all of the administrative or other expenses incurred in connection with the provisions of this Part.

(3) A resolution fund order may include provision for—

(a) an independent valuer to make a determination under the order (in which case sections 54(2) to (5), 55 and 56 shall apply);

(b) valuation principles to be applied in making a determination (in which case section 57(2) shall apply).

(4)   A resolution fund order may confer a discretionary function on—
  (a)   a Minister of the Crown,
  (b)   the Treasury,
  (c)   the Bank of England, or
  (d)   any other specified person.

(5)   A resolution fund order may include provision for the determination of disputes about the application of its provisions (whether by conferring jurisdiction on a court or tribunal or otherwise).

(6)   A resolution fund order may require the Bank of England in managing a bridge bank to aim to maximise the proceeds available for distribution in accordance with the order; and an order which includes a requirement must—
  (a)   specify its extent, and
  (b)   include provision about how the Bank is to comply with it.

(7)   A resolution fund order may require the Treasury to ensure that a bank in temporary public ownership in accordance with section 13(2) is managed with the aim of maximising the proceeds available for distribution in accordance with the order; and an order which includes a requirement must—
  (a)   specify its extent, and
  (b)   include provision about how the Treasury is to comply with it.

(8)   A requirement under subsection (6) or (7) is to be complied with only in so far as is compatible with—
  (a)   pursuit of the special resolution objectives, and
  (b)   compliance with the code of practice under section 5.

[58]

NOTES

Commencement: 17 February 2009 (in so far as conferring or relating to any power to make subordinate legislation or codes of practice); 21 February 2009 (otherwise).

Order: the Dunfermline Building Society Compensation Scheme, Resolution Fund and Third Party Compensation Order 2009, SI 2009/1800 at **[580]**.

---

59   Third party compensation: discretionary provision

(1)   A power or duty in this Part to make a third party compensation order is a power or duty to make provision establishing a scheme for paying compensation to persons other than a transferor.

(2)   A third party compensation order may—
  (a)   form part of a compensation scheme order or resolution fund order, or
  (b)   be a separate order.

(3)   A third party compensation order may include provision for—
  (a)   an independent valuer (in which case sections 54 to 56 shall apply);
  (b)   valuation principles (in which case section 57(2) to (5) shall apply).

[59]

NOTES

Commencement: 17 February 2009 (in so far as conferring or relating to any power to make subordinate legislation or codes of practice); 21 February 2009 (otherwise).

See further: the Banking Act 2009 (Third Party Compensation Arrangements for Partial Property Transfers) Regulations 2009, SI 2009/319 at **[533]**, which specify provisions which must, or which may, be included in a third party compensation order made in accordance with this section in the case of a partial property transfer.

Order: the Dunfermline Building Society Compensation Scheme, Resolution Fund and Third Party Compensation Order 2009, SI 2009/1800 at **[580]**.

---

60   Third party compensation: mandatory provision

(1)   The Treasury may make regulations about third party compensation arrangements in the case of partial property transfers.

(2)   In making regulations the Treasury shall, in particular, have regard to the desirability of ensuring that if a residual bank enters insolvency after transfer, pre-transfer creditors do not receive less favourable treatment than they would have received had it entered insolvency immediately before transfer.

(3)   In subsection (2)—
  (a)   "residual bank" means a bank that is a transferor under a property transfer instrument,
  (b)   "pre-transfer creditor" means a person who—
    (i)   is a creditor of a residual bank immediately before a property transfer instrument takes effect, and
    (ii)   satisfies conditions specified by the regulations, and
  (c)   the reference to insolvency includes a reference to (i) liquidation, (ii) bank insolvency,

(iii) administration, (iv) bank administration, (v) receivership, (vi) a composition with creditors, and (vii) a scheme of arrangement.

(4) The regulations may—
  (a) require a compensation scheme order or a resolution fund order to include a third party compensation order;
  (b) require a third party compensation order to include provision of a specified kind or to specified effect;
  (c) make provision which is to be treated as forming part of a third party compensation order (whether (i) generally, (ii) only if applied, (iii) unless disapplied, or (iv) subject to express modification).

(5) Regulations may provide for whether compensation is to be paid, and if so what amount is to be paid, to be determined by reference to any factors or combination of factors; in particular, the regulations may provide for entitlement—
  (a) to depend in part upon the amounts which are or may be payable under a resolution fund order;
  (b) to be contingent upon the occurrence or non-occurrence of specified events;
  (c) to be determined wholly or partly by an independent valuer (within the meaning of sections 54 to 56) appointed in accordance with a compensation scheme order or resolution fund order.

(6) Regulations may make provision about payment including, in particular, provision for payments—
  (a) on account subject to terms and conditions;
  (b) by instalment.

(7) Regulations—
  (a) shall be made by statutory instrument, and
  (b) may not be made unless a draft has been laid before and approved by resolution of each House of Parliament.

[60]

NOTES
Commencement: 17 February 2009 (in so far as conferring or relating to any power to make subordinate legislation or codes of practice); 21 February 2009 (otherwise).
Regulations: the Banking Act 2009 (Third Party Compensation Arrangements for Partial Property Transfers) Regulations 2009, SI 2009/319 at **[533]**.

61 Sources of compensation

(1) This section applies to—
  (a) compensation scheme orders,
  (b) resolution fund orders,
  (c) third party compensation orders, and
  (d) regulations under section 60.

(2) An order or regulations may provide for compensation or other payments to be made by—
  (a) the Treasury,
  (b) the Financial Services Compensation Scheme, subject to section 214B of the Financial Services and Markets Act 2000 (contribution to costs of special resolution regime – inserted by section 171 below), or
  (c) any other specified person.

[61]

NOTES
Commencement: 17 February 2009 (in so far as conferring or relating to any power to make subordinate legislation or codes of practice); 21 February 2009 (otherwise).
Order: the Dunfermline Building Society Compensation Scheme, Resolution Fund and Third Party Compensation Order 2009, SI 2009/1800 at **[580]**.

62 Procedure

(1) This section applies to—
  (a) compensation scheme orders,
  (b) resolution fund orders, and
  (c) third party compensation orders.

(2) An order—
  (a) shall be made by statutory instrument, and
  (b) may not be made unless a draft has been laid before and approved by resolution of each House of Parliament.

[62]

PART I
BANKING ACT 2009

NOTES
Commencement: 17 February 2009 (in so far as conferring or relating to any power to make subordinate legislation or codes of practice); 21 February 2009 (otherwise).

Incidental functions

63   General continuity obligation: property transfers

(1)   In this section and section 64—

    (a)   "residual bank" means a bank all or part of whose business has been transferred in accordance with section 11(2)(b) or 12(2),

    (b)   "group company" means anything which is, or was immediately before the transfer, a group undertaking in relation to a residual bank,

    (c)   "group undertaking" has the meaning given by section 1161(5) of the Companies Act 2006 (interpretation),

    (d)   "the transferred business" means the part of the bank's business that has been transferred, and

    (e)   "transferee" means a commercial purchaser or bridge bank to whom all or part of the transferred business has been transferred.

(2)   The residual bank and each group company must provide such services and facilities as are required to enable a transferee to operate the transferred business, or part of it, effectively.

(3)   The duty under subsection (2) (the "continuity obligation") may be enforced as if created by contract between the residual bank or group company and the transferee.

(4)   The duty to provide services and facilities in pursuance of the continuity obligation is subject to a right to receive reasonable consideration.

(5)   The continuity obligation is not limited to the provision of services or facilities directly to a transferee.

(6)   The Bank of England may, with the consent of the Treasury, by notice to the residual bank or a group company state that in the Bank's opinion—

    (a)   specified activities are required to be undertaken in accordance with the continuity obligation;

    (b)   activities are required be undertaken in accordance with the continuity obligation on specified terms.

(7)   A notice under subsection (6) shall be determinative of the nature and extent of the continuity obligation as from the time when the notice is given.

[63]

NOTES
Commencement: 17 February 2009 (in so far as conferring or relating to any power to make subordinate legislation or codes of practice); 21 February 2009 (otherwise).

64   Special continuity obligations: property transfers

(1)   Expressions in this section have the same meaning as in section 63.

(2)   The Bank of England may—

    (a)   cancel a contract or other arrangement between the residual bank and a group company (whether or not rights or obligations under it have been transferred to a transferee);

    (b)   modify the terms of a contract or other arrangement between the residual bank and a group company (whether or not rights or obligations under it have been transferred to a transferee);

    (c)   add or substitute a transferee as a party to a contract or other arrangement between the residual bank and a group company;

    (d)   confer and impose rights and obligations on a group company and a transferee, which shall have effect as if created by contract between them;

    (e)   confer and impose rights and obligations on the residual bank and a transferee which shall have effect as if created by contract between them.

(3)   In modifying or setting terms under subsection (2) the Bank of England shall aim, so far as is reasonably practicable, to preserve or include—

    (a)   provision for reasonable consideration, and

    (b)   any other provision that would be expected in arrangements concluded between parties dealing at arm's length.

(4)   The power under subsection (2)—

    (a)   may be exercised only in so far as the Bank of England thinks it necessary to ensure the provision of such services and facilities as are required to enable the transferee to operate the transferred business, or part of it, effectively,

  (b) may be exercised only with the consent of the Treasury, and

  (c) must be exercised by way of provision in a property transfer instrument (or supplemental instrument).

[64]

NOTES

Commencement: 17 February 2009 (in so far as conferring or relating to any power to make subordinate legislation or codes of practice); 21 February 2009 (otherwise).

65 Continuity obligations: onward property transfers

 (1) In this section—

  (a) "onward transfer" means a transfer of property, rights or liabilities (whether or not under a power in this Part) from—

   (i) a person who is a transferee under a property transfer instrument under section 12(2) (an "original transferee"), or

   (ii) a bank, securities issued by which were earlier transferred by a share transfer order under section 13(2), and

  (b) the person to whom the onward transfer is made is referred to as an "onward transferee".

 (2) The continuity authority may—

  (a) provide for an obligation under section 63 to apply in respect of an onward transferee;

  (b) extend section 64 so as to permit action to be taken under section 64(2) for the purpose of enabling an onward transferee to operate transferred business, or part of it, effectively.

 (3) "The continuity authority" means—

  (a) the Bank of England, where subsection (1)(a)(i) applies, and

  (b) the Treasury, where subsection (1)(a)(ii) applies.

 (4) Subsection (2) may be relied on to impose obligations on—

  (a) an original transferee (where the original transfer was a property transfer),

  (b) a residual bank within the meaning of section 63 (where the original transfer was a property transfer),

  (c) the bank (where the original transfer was a share transfer),

  (d) anything which is or was a group undertaking (within the meaning of section 1161(5) of the Companies Act 2006) of anything within paragraphs (a) to (c), or

  (e) any combination.

 (5) Subsection (2) may be used to impose obligations—

  (a) in addition to obligations under or by virtue of section 63 or 64, or

  (b) replacing obligations under or by virtue of either of those sections to a specified extent.

 (6) A power under subsection (2) is exercisable by giving a notice to each person—

  (a) on whom a continuity obligation is to be imposed under the power, or

  (b) who is expected to benefit from a continuity obligation under the power.

 (7) Sections 63(3) to (7) and 64(3) and (4) apply to an obligation as applied under subsection (2)—

  (a) construing "transferred business" as the business transferred by means of the onward transfer, and

  (b) with any other necessary modification.

 (8) The Bank of England may act under or by virtue of subsection (2) only with the consent of the Treasury.

[65]

NOTES

Commencement: 17 February 2009 (in so far as conferring or relating to any power to make subordinate legislation or codes of practice); 21 February 2009 (otherwise).

66 General continuity obligation: share transfers

 (1) In this section and section 67—

  (a) "transferred bank" means a bank all or part of the ownership of which has been transferred in accordance with section 11(2)(a) or 13(2),

  (b) "former group company" means anything which was a group undertaking in relation to the transferred bank immediately before the transfer (whether or not it is also a group undertaking in relation to the transferred bank immediately after the transfer),

  (c) "group undertaking" has the meaning given by section 1161(5) of the Companies Act 2006 (interpretation), and

  (d) "the continuity authority" means—

   (i) the Bank of England, where ownership was transferred in accordance with section 11(2)(a), and

   (ii) the Treasury, where ownership was transferred in accordance with section 13(2).

(2)   Each former group company must provide such services and facilities as are required to enable the transferred bank to operate effectively.

(3)   The duty under subsection (2) (the "continuity obligation") may be enforced as if created by contract between the transferred bank and the former group company.

(4)   The duty to provide services and facilities in pursuance of the continuity obligation is subject to a right to receive reasonable consideration.

(5)   The continuity obligation is not limited to the provision of services or facilities directly to the transferred bank.

(6)   The continuity authority may by notice to a former group company state that in the authority's opinion—

(a)   specified activities are required to be undertaken in accordance with the continuity obligation;

(b)   activities are required be undertaken in accordance with the continuity obligation on specified terms.

(7)   A notice under subsection (6) shall be determinative of the nature and extent of the continuity obligation as from the time when the notice is given.

(8)   The Bank of England may act under or by virtue of subsection (6) only with the consent of the Treasury.

[66]

NOTES
Commencement: 17 February 2009 (in so far as conferring or relating to any power to make subordinate legislation or codes of practice); 21 February 2009 (otherwise).

67   Special continuity obligations: share transfers

(1)   Expressions in this section have the same meaning as in section 66.

(2)   The continuity authority may—

(a)   cancel a contract or other arrangement between the transferred bank and a former group company;

(b)   modify the terms of a contract or other arrangement between the transferred bank and a former group company;

(c)   confer and impose rights and obligations on a former group company and the transferred bank, which shall have effect as if created by contract between them.

(3)   In modifying or setting terms under subsection (2) the continuity authority shall aim, so far as is reasonably practicable, to preserve or include—

(a)   provision for reasonable consideration, and

(b)   any other provision that would be expected in arrangements concluded between parties dealing at arm's length.

(4)   The power under subsection (2)—

(a)   may be exercised only in so far as the continuity authority thinks it necessary to ensure the provision of such services and facilities as are required to enable the transferred bank to operate effectively,

(b)   may be exercised by the Bank of England only with the consent of the Treasury, and

(c)   must be exercised by way of provision in a share transfer instrument or order (or supplemental instrument or order).

[67]

NOTES
Commencement: 17 February 2009 (in so far as conferring or relating to any power to make subordinate legislation or codes of practice); 21 February 2009 (otherwise).

68   Continuity obligations: onward share transfers

(1)   In this section "onward transfer" means a transfer (whether or not under a power in this Part) of securities issued by a bank where—

(a)   securities issued by the bank were earlier transferred by share transfer order under section 13(2), or

(b)   the bank was the transferee under a property transfer instrument under section 12(2).

(2)   The continuity authority may—

(a)   provide for an obligation under section 66 to apply in respect of the bank after the onward transfer;

(b)   extend section 67 so as to permit action to be taken under section 67(2) to enable the bank to operate effectively after the onward transfer.

(3)   In this section "continuity authority" has the same meaning as in sections 66 and 67.

(4)   Subsection (2) may be relied on to impose obligations on—
    (a)   the bank,
    (b)   anything which is or was a group undertaking (within the meaning of section 1161(5) of the Companies Act 2006) of the bank,
    (c)   anything which is or was a group undertaking of the residual bank (in a case to which subsection (1)(b) applies), or
    (d)   any combination.

(5)   Subsection (2) may be used to impose obligations—
    (a)   in addition to obligations under or by virtue of section 66 or 67, or
    (b)   replacing obligations under or by virtue of either of those sections to a specified extent.

(6)   A power under subsection (2) is exercisable by giving a notice to each person—
    (a)   on whom a continuity obligation is to be imposed under the power, or
    (b)   who is expected to benefit from a continuity obligation under the power.

(7)   Sections 66(3) to (7) and 67(3) and (4) apply to an obligation as applied under subsection (2) with any necessary modification.

(8)   The Bank of England may act under or by virtue of subsection (2) only with the consent of the Treasury.

[68]

NOTES
Commencement: 17 February 2009 (in so far as conferring or relating to any power to make subordinate legislation or codes of practice); 21 February 2009 (otherwise).

69   Continuity obligations: consideration and terms

(1)   The Treasury may by order specify matters which are to be or not to be considered in determining—
    (a)   what amounts to reasonable consideration for the purpose of sections 63 to 68;
    (b)   what provisions to include in accordance with section 64(3)(b) or 67(3)(b).

(2)   An order—
    (a)   shall be made by statutory instrument, and
    (b)   shall be subject to annulment in pursuance of a resolution of either House of Parliament.

(3)   A continuity authority may give guarantees or indemnities in respect of consideration for services or facilities provided or to be provided in pursuance of a continuity obligation.

(4)   In this section "continuity authority"—
    (a)   in relation to sections 63 and 64, means the Bank of England, and
    (b)   in relation to sections 65 to 68, has the same meaning as in those sections.

[69]

NOTES
Commencement: 17 February 2009 (in so far as conferring or relating to any power to make subordinate legislation or codes of practice); 21 February 2009 (otherwise).

70   Continuity obligations: termination

(1)   The continuity authority may by notice terminate an obligation arising under section 63 or 66.

(2)   The power under subsection (1) is exercisable by giving a notice to each person—
    (a)   on whom the obligation is imposed, or
    (b)   who has benefited or might have expected to benefit from the obligation.

(3)   In this section "continuity authority"—
    (a)   in relation to section 63, means the Bank of England, and
    (b)   in relation to section 66, has the same meaning as in that section.

(4)   A reference in subsection (1) to obligations under a section includes a reference to obligations under that section as applied under section 65 or 68.

[70]

NOTES
Commencement: 17 February 2009 (in so far as conferring or relating to any power to make subordinate legislation or codes of practice); 21 February 2009 (otherwise).

71   Pensions

(1)   This section applies to—
    (a)   share transfer orders,
    (b)   share transfer instruments, and

(c)   property transfer instruments.

(2)   An order or instrument may make provision—
  (a)   about the consequences of a transfer for a pension scheme;
  (b)   about property, rights and liabilities of any pension scheme of the bank.

(3)   In particular, an order or instrument may—
  (a)   modify any rights and liabilities;
  (b)   apportion rights and liabilities;
  (c)   transfer property of, or accrued rights in, one pension scheme to another (with or without consent).

(4)   Provision by virtue of this section may (but need not) amend the terms of a pension scheme.

(5)   A share or property transfer instrument may make provision in reliance on this section only with the consent of the Treasury.

(6)   In this section—
  (a)   "pension scheme" includes any arrangement for the payment of pensions, allowances and gratuities, and
  (b)   a reference to a pension scheme of a bank is a reference to a scheme in respect of which the bank, or a group company of the bank, is or was an employer.

(7)   In subsection (6)(b) the reference to a group company of the bank is a reference to anything that is or was a group undertaking in relation to the bank within the meaning given by section 1161(5) of the Companies Act 2006.

[71]

NOTES

Commencement: 17 February 2009 (in so far as conferring or relating to any power to make subordinate legislation or codes of practice); 21 February 2009 (otherwise).

72   Enforcement

(1)   The Treasury may by regulations make provision for the enforcement of obligations imposed by or under—
  (a)   a share transfer order,
  (b)   a share transfer instrument, or
  (c)   a property transfer instrument.

(2)   Regulations—
  (a)   may confer jurisdiction on a court or tribunal;
  (b)   may not impose a penalty or create a criminal offence;
  (c)   may make provision which has effect in respect of an order or instrument only if applied by the order or instrument.

(3)   Regulations—
  (a)   shall be made by statutory instrument, and
  (b)   shall be subject to annulment in pursuance of a resolution of either House of Parliament.

[72]

NOTES

Commencement: 17 February 2009 (in so far as conferring or relating to any power to make subordinate legislation or codes of practice); 21 February 2009 (otherwise).

73   Disputes

(1)   This section applies to—
  (a)   share transfer orders,
  (b)   share transfer instruments, and
  (c)   property transfer instruments.

(2)   An order or instrument may include provision for disputes to be determined in a specified manner.

(3)   Provision by virtue of subsection (2) may, in particular—
  (a)   confer jurisdiction on a court or tribunal;
  (b)   confer discretion on a specified person.

[73]

NOTES

Commencement: 17 February 2009 (in so far as conferring or relating to any power to make subordinate legislation or codes of practice); 21 February 2009 (otherwise).

74 Tax

(1)   The Treasury may by regulations make provision about the fiscal consequences of the exercise of a stabilisation power.

(2)   Regulations may relate to—
   (a)   capital gains tax;
   (b)   corporation tax;
   (c)   income tax;
   (d)   inheritance tax;
   (e)   stamp duty;
   (f)   stamp duty land tax;
   (g)   stamp duty reserve tax.

(3)   Regulations may apply to—
   (a)   anything done in connection with an instrument or order;
   (b)   things transferred or otherwise affected by virtue of an instrument or order;
   (c)   a transferor or transferee under an instrument or order;
   (d)   persons otherwise affected by an instrument or order.

(4)   Regulations may—
   (a)   modify or disapply an enactment;
   (b)   provide for an action to have or not have specified consequences;
   (c)   provide for specified classes of property (including securities), rights or liabilities to be treated, or not treated, in a specified way;
   (d)   withdraw or restrict a relief;
   (e)   extend, restrict or otherwise modify a charge to tax;
   (f)   provide for matters to be determined by the Treasury in accordance with provision made by or in accordance with the regulations.

(5)   Regulations may make provision for the fiscal consequences of the exercise of a stabilisation power in respect of things done—
   (a)   during the period of three months before the date on which the stabilisation power is exercised, or
   (b)   on or after that date.

(6)   In relation to the exercise of a supplemental or onward instrument or order under section 26, 27, 28, 30, 42, 43 or 45, in subsection (5)(a) above "the stabilisation power" is a reference to the first stabilisation power in connection with which the supplemental or onward instrument or order is made.

(7)   The Treasury may by order amend subsection (2) so as to—
   (a)   add an entry, or
   (b)   remove an entry.

(8)   Regulations or an order under this section—
   (a)   shall be made by statutory instrument, and
   (b)   may not be made unless a draft has been laid before and approved by resolution of the House of Commons.

[74]

NOTES

Commencement: 17 February 2009 (in so far as conferring or relating to any power to make subordinate legislation or codes of practice); 21 February 2009 (otherwise).

---

75   Power to change law

(1)   The Treasury may by order amend the law for the purpose of enabling the powers under this Part to be used effectively, having regard to the special resolution objectives.

(2)   An order may be made—
   (a)   for the general purpose of the exercise of powers under this Part,
   (b)   to facilitate a particular proposed or possible use of a power, or
   (c)   in connection with a particular exercise of a power.

(3)   An order under subsection (2)(c) may make provision which has retrospective effect in so far as the Treasury consider it necessary or desirable for giving effect to the particular exercise of a power under this Act in connection with which the order is made (but in relying on this subsection the Treasury shall have regard to the fact that it is in the public interest to avoid retrospective legislation).

(4)   In subsection (1) "amend the law" means—
   (a)   disapply or modify the effect of a provision of an enactment (other than a provision made by or under this Act),
   (b)   disapply or modify the effect of a rule of law not set out in legislation, or

(c)   amend any provision of an instrument or order made in the exercise of a stabilisation power.

(5)   Provision under this section may relate to this Part as it applies—
(a)   to banks,
(b)   to building societies,
(c)   to credit unions (by virtue of section 89), or
(d)   to any combination.

(6)   Specific powers under this Part are without prejudice to the generality of this section.

(7)   An order—
(a)   shall be made by statutory instrument, and
(b)   may not be made unless a draft has been laid before and approved by resolution of each House of Parliament.

(8)   But if the Treasury think it necessary to make an order without complying with subsection (7)(b)—
(a)   the order may be made,
(b)   the order shall lapse unless approved by resolution of each House of Parliament during the period of 28 days (ignoring periods of dissolution, prorogation or adjournment of either House for more than 4 days) beginning with the day on which the order is made,
(c)   the lapse of an order under paragraph (b) does not invalidate anything done under or in reliance on the order before the lapse and at a time when neither House has declined to approve the order, and
(d)   the lapse of an order under paragraph (b) does not prevent the making of a new order (in new terms).

[75]

NOTES
Commencement: 17 February 2009 (in so far as conferring or relating to any power to make subordinate legislation or codes of practice); 21 February 2009 (otherwise).
Orders: the Amendments to Law (Resolution of Dunfermline Building Society) Order 2009, SI 2009/814 at **[565]**; the Amendments to Law (Resolution of Dunfermline Building Society) (No 2) Order 2009, SI 2009/1805 at **[598]**.

Treasury

76 International obligation notice: general

(1)   The Bank of England may not exercise a stabilisation power in respect of a bank if the Treasury notify the Bank that the exercise would be likely to contravene an international obligation of the United Kingdom.

(2)   A notice under subsection (1)—
(a)   must be in writing, and
(b)   may be withdrawn (generally, partially or conditionally).

(3)   If the Treasury give a notice under subsection (1) the Bank of England must consider other exercises of the stabilisation powers with a view to—
(a)   pursuing the special resolution objectives, and
(b)   avoiding the objections on which the Treasury's notice was based.

(4)   The Treasury may by notice to the Bank of England disapply subsection (3) in respect of a bank; and a notice may be revoked by further notice.

[76]

NOTES
Commencement: 17 February 2009 (in so far as conferring or relating to any power to make subordinate legislation or codes of practice); 21 February 2009 (otherwise).

77 International obligation notice: bridge bank

(1)   This section applies where the Bank of England has transferred all or part of a bank's business to a bridge bank.

(2)   The Bank of England must comply with any notice of the Treasury requiring the Bank, for the purpose of ensuring compliance by the United Kingdom with its international obligations—
(a)   to take specified action under this Part in respect of the bridge bank, or
(b)   not to take specified action under this Part in respect of the bridge bank.

(3)   A notice under subsection (1)—
(a)   must be in writing, and
(b)   may be withdrawn (generally, partially or conditionally).

(4)   A notice may include requirements about timing.

[77]

NOTES
Commencement: 17 February 2009 (in so far as conferring or relating to any power to make subordinate legislation or codes of practice); 21 February 2009 (otherwise).

78 Public funds: general

(1)   The Bank of England may not exercise a stabilisation power in respect of a bank without the Treasury's consent if the exercise would be likely to have implications for public funds.

(2)   In subsection (1)—
   (a)   "public funds" means the Consolidated Fund and any other account or source of money which cannot be drawn or spent other than by, or with the authority of, the Treasury, and
   (b)   action has implications for public funds if it would or might involve or lead to a need for the application of public funds.

(3)   The Treasury may by order specify considerations which are to be, or not to be, taken into account in determining whether action has implications for public funds for the purpose of subsection (1).

(4)   If the Treasury refuse consent under subsection (1), the Bank of England must consider other exercises of the stabilisation powers with a view to—
   (a)   pursuing the special resolution objectives, and
   (b)   avoiding the objections on which the Treasury's refusal was based.

(5)   The Treasury may by notice to the Bank of England disapply subsection (4) in respect of a bank; and a notice may be revoked by further notice.

(6)   An order under subsection (3)—
   (a)   shall be made by statutory instrument, and
   (b)   shall be subject to annulment in pursuance of a resolution of the House of Commons.

[78]

NOTES
Commencement: 17 February 2009 (in so far as conferring or relating to any power to make subordinate legislation or codes of practice); 21 February 2009 (otherwise).

79 Public funds: bridge bank

(1)   This section applies where the Bank of England has transferred all or part of a bank's business to a bridge bank.

(2)   The Bank of England may not take action in respect of the bridge bank without the Treasury's consent if the action would be likely to have implications for public funds.

(3)   Section 78(2) and (3) have effect for the purposes of this section.

[79]

NOTES
Commencement: 17 February 2009 (in so far as conferring or relating to any power to make subordinate legislation or codes of practice); 21 February 2009 (otherwise).

80 Bridge bank: report

(1)   Where the Bank of England transfers all or part of a bank's business to a bridge bank, the Bank must report to the Chancellor of the Exchequer about the activities of the bridge bank.

(2)   The first report must be made as soon as is reasonably practicable after the end of one year beginning with the date of the first transfer to the bridge bank.

(3)   A report must be made as soon as is reasonably practicable after the end of each subsequent year.

(4)   The Chancellor of the Exchequer must lay a copy of each report under subsection (2) or (3) before Parliament.

(5)   The Bank must comply with any request of the Treasury for a report dealing with specified matters in relation to a bridge bank.

(6)   A request under subsection (5) may include provision about—
   (a)   the content of the report;
   (b)   timing.

[80]

NOTES
Commencement: 17 February 2009 (in so far as conferring or relating to any power to make subordinate legislation or codes of practice); 21 February 2009 (otherwise).

81   Temporary public ownership: report

(1)   Where the Treasury make one or more share transfer orders under section 13(2) in respect of a bank, the Treasury must lay before Parliament a report about the activities of the bank.

(2)   The first report must be made as soon as is reasonably practicable after the end of one year beginning with the date of the first share transfer order.

(3)   A report must be made as soon as is reasonably practicable after the end of each subsequent year.

(4)   The obligation to produce reports continues to apply in respect of each year until the first during which no securities issued by the bank are owned by—
(a)   a company wholly owned by the Treasury, or
(b)   a nominee of the Treasury.

[81]

NOTES
Commencement: 17 February 2009 (in so far as conferring or relating to any power to make subordinate legislation or codes of practice); 21 February 2009 (otherwise).

Holding companies

82   Temporary public ownership

(1)   The Treasury may take a parent undertaking of a bank (the "holding company") into temporary public ownership, in accordance with section 13(2), if the following conditions are met.

(2)   Condition 1 is that the FSA are satisfied that the general conditions for the exercise of a stabilisation power set out in section 7 are met in respect of the bank.

(3)   Condition 2 is that the Treasury are satisfied that it is necessary to take action in respect of the holding company for the purpose specified in Condition A or B of section 9.

(4)   Condition 3 is that the holding company is an undertaking incorporated in, or formed under the law of any part of, the United Kingdom.

(5)   Before determining whether Condition 2 is met the Treasury must consult—
(a)   the FSA, and
(b)   the Bank of England.

(6)   Expressions used in this section have the same meaning as in the Companies Act 2006.

[82]

NOTES
Commencement: 17 February 2009 (in so far as conferring or relating to any power to make subordinate legislation or codes of practice); 21 February 2009 (otherwise).

83   Supplemental

(1)   In the following provisions references to banks include references to holding companies—
(a)   section 10(1),
(b)   section 13(3),
(c)   section 16(1), and
(d)   section 75(5)(a).

(2)   Where the Treasury take a bank's holding company into temporary public ownership in reliance on section 82—
(a)   section 20(2) applies to (i) directors of the holding company, (ii) directors of the bank, and (iii) directors of a bank in the same group,
(b)   section 25(2) applies as if references to a bank were references to a holding company,
(c)   sections 27 to 29 apply as if references to a bank were references to a holding company,
(d)   a share transfer may be made in respect of securities which were issued by the bank or by another bank which is or was in the same group; and a transfer—
(i)   shall be made by onward share transfer order under section 28 or by reverse share transfer order under section 29 (in addition to any that may be made under those sections as applied by paragraph (c) above),
(ii)   may be made under section 28 only in respect of securities held by (or for the benefit of) the holding company or a subsidiary undertaking of the holding company,
(iii) is not subject to section 28(4),
(iv)   may be made under section 29 only in respect of securities held by a person of a kind listed in section 29(3)(b), and
(v)   is not (otherwise) subject to section 29(3),
(e)   section 45 applies as if—

     (i)   the reference to a bank in subsection (1) were a reference to a holding company, and

     (ii)   a reference to the bank in subsection (3) were a reference to the holding company, the bank and any other bank which is or was in the same group,

(f)   sections 65 to 68 apply, with—

     (i)   references to the bank or the transferred bank taken as references to the bank, the holding company and any other bank which is or was in the same group, and

     (ii)   references to securities of the bank taken as including references to securities of the holding company (so that, in particular, sections 65(1)(a)(ii) and 68(1)(a) include references to the earlier transfer of securities issued by the holding company),

(g)   other provisions of this Act about share transfer orders apply with any necessary modifications,

(h)   section 214B of the Financial Services and Markets Act 2000 applies (contribution to costs of special resolution regime – inserted by section 171 below), and

(i)   the reference in section 214B(1)(b) to the bank, and later references in the section, are treated as including references to any other bank which is also a subsidiary undertaking of the holding company (but not to the holding company itself).

(3)   A reference in this Act or another enactment to a share transfer order in respect of securities issued by a bank includes (so far as the context permits) a reference to a share transfer order in respect of securities issued by a holding company.

(4)   In so far as sections 47 and 60 apply in relation to orders treated as property transfer instruments by virtue of section 45(5)(b) or 46(5)(b) (including those sections as applied by virtue of subsection (2) above) the reference in section 47(1) to the property of a bank includes a reference to the property of a holding company and of any other bank which is or was in the same group.

(5)   Expressions used in this section have the same meaning as in the Companies Act 2006.

(6)   A reference to two banks being in the same group is a reference to their being group undertakings in respect of each other.

                                                                     [83]

NOTES

Commencement: 17 February 2009 (in so far as conferring or relating to any power to make subordinate legislation or codes of practice); 21 February 2009 (otherwise).

Building societies, &c

84 Application of Part 1: general

This Part shall apply to building societies (within the meaning of section 119 of the Building Societies Act 1986) as it applies to banks, subject to the provisions of the Table.

Section	*Topic*	*Modification or note*
11	Private sector purchaser	A share transfer instrument may not be made.
13	Temporary public ownership	The procedure provided by section 85 has effect in place of share transfer orders.
14 to 32	Transfer of securities	The procedure provided by section 85 has effect in place of share transfer orders; and— (a) sections 28 and 30 do not apply, and (b) section 27 applies following an order under section 85 as following a share transfer order.
33	Property transfer instrument: nature	A property transfer instrument in respect of a building society may— (a) cancel shares in the building society; (b) confer rights and impose liabilities in place of cancelled shares (whether by way of actual or deemed shares in a transferee building society or by way of other rights and liabilities in relation to a transferee bank).

Section	Topic	Modification or note
33 and 36	Property transfer instrument: continuity	A property transfer instrument in respect of a bank which provides for transfer to a building society may confer rights and impose liabilities by way of actual or deemed shares in the building society.
34	Property transfer instrument: effect	A property transfer instrument may, in particular, have effect without causing sections 93 to 102D of the Building Societies Act 1986 (mergers and transfers) to apply.
42	Supplemental property transfer instrument	A supplemental property transfer instrument in respect of a building society may— (a) cancel shares in the building society; (b) confer rights and impose liabilities in place of cancelled shares (whether by way of actual or deemed shares in a transferee building society or by way of other rights and liabilities in relation to a transferee bank).
45	Temporary public ownership: property transfer	(a) Section 45 applies following an order under section 85 as following a share transfer order. (b) A property transfer order in respect of a building society may cancel shares in the building society.
49 to 62	Compensation	(a) A reference to a share transfer order includes a reference to an order under section 85. (b) A resolution fund order may not be made under section 51(2)(b). (c) If and in so far as an order under section 85 provides for the issue of new deferred shares, section 51(2) shall not apply.
63 to 75	Incidental functions	A reference to a share transfer order includes a reference to an order under section 85.

[84]

NOTES

Commencement: 17 February 2009 (in so far as conferring or relating to any power to make subordinate legislation or codes of practice); 21 February 2009 (otherwise).

85 Temporary public ownership

(1) For the purpose of exercising the third stabilisation option in respect of a building society the Treasury may make one or more orders for the purposes of—
 (a) arranging for deferred shares of a building society to be publicly owned,
 (b) cancelling private membership rights in the building society,
 (c) allowing the building society to continue in business while in public ownership, and
 (d) eventually either winding up or dissolving the building society.

(2) For the purpose specified in subsection (1)(a) an order may—
 (a) arrange for the transfer of existing deferred shares;
 (b) provide for new deferred shares.

(3) For the purpose of arranging for the transfer of existing deferred shares an order may—
 (a) provide for deferred shares to be transferred;
 (b) make other provision for the purposes of, or in connection with, the transfer of deferred shares (whether or not the transfer has been or is to be effected by the order, by another order under this section or otherwise);
 (c) relate to all or any specified class or description of deferred shares issued by the building society.

(4) For the purpose of providing for new deferred shares an order may—

    (a) issue or allow the Treasury to issue new deferred shares on behalf of the building society;

    (b) specify or allow the Treasury to specify the terms and effect of new deferred shares;

    (c) specify or allow the Treasury to specify the recipient of new deferred shares.

(5) For the purpose specified in subsection (1)(b) an order may—

    (a) cancel or permit the cancellation of shares (whether or not deferred) in the building society;

    (b) confer rights and impose liabilities, or allow them to be conferred and imposed, in place of cancelled shares;

    (c) prevent the issue or acquisition of shares in or other rights in respect of the building society otherwise than in accordance with the order.

(6) For the purpose specified in subsection (1)(c) an order may make any provision which the Treasury think desirable to facilitate the business of the building society after the making of provision in accordance with subsections (3) to (5).

(7) An order in respect of a building society may—

    (a) make provision expressly or impliedly disapplying or modifying the memorandum or rules of the building society;

    (b) disapply or modify an enactment about, or in its application to, building societies.

(8) The following sections apply to orders under this section as to share transfer orders: sections 17, 18, 20, 21, 22, 23, 25, 71, 72 and 73.

[85]

NOTES

Commencement: 17 February 2009 (in so far as conferring or relating to any power to make subordinate legislation or codes of practice); 21 February 2009 (otherwise).

86 Distribution of assets on dissolution or winding up

(1) The Treasury may by order make provision about the distribution of surplus assets of a building society which—

    (a) is the subject of a property transfer instrument or order, and

    (b) is later wound up or dissolved by consent.

(2) An order under section 85 may include provision about the distribution of surplus assets of the building society if it is later wound up or dissolved by consent.

(3) "Surplus" means remaining after the satisfaction of liabilities to creditors and shareholders.

(4) An order under or by virtue of this section—

    (a) may include any provision of a kind that may be made by order under section 90B of the Building Societies Act 1986 (power to alter priorities on dissolution or winding up),

    (b) may be made whether or not the power under that section has been exercised, and

    (c) shall be treated for all procedural purposes in the same way as an order under that section.

[86]

NOTES

Commencement: 17 February 2009 (in so far as conferring or relating to any power to make subordinate legislation or codes of practice); 21 February 2009 (otherwise).

87 Interpretation

(1) Expressions used in this group of sections and in the Building Societies Act 1986 have the same meaning in this group of sections as in that Act.

(2) An order under section 119(1) of that Act defining "deferred shares"—

    (a) may make special provision for the meaning of that expression in the application of this group of sections, and

    (b) shall otherwise apply to this group of sections as to that Act.

[87]

NOTES

Commencement: 17 February 2009 (in so far as conferring or relating to any power to make subordinate legislation or codes of practice); 21 February 2009 (otherwise).

88 Consequential provision

(1) The Treasury may by order make provision, in addition to the provisions of this group of sections, in consequence of the application of this Part to building societies.

(2)   An order may, in particular, amend or modify the effect of an enactment (including a fiscal enactment) passed before the commencement of this Part.

(3)   An order—

    (a)   shall be made by statutory instrument, and

    (b)   may not be made unless a draft has been laid before and approved by resolution of each House of Parliament.

[88]

NOTES

Commencement: 17 February 2009 (in so far as conferring or relating to any power to make subordinate legislation or codes of practice); 21 February 2009 (otherwise).

89   Credit unions

(1)   The Treasury may by order provide for the application of this Part to credit unions (within the meaning of section 31 of the Credit Unions Act 1979) subject to modifications set out in the order.

(2)   An order may disapply, modify or apply (with or without modifications) any enactment which relates, or in so far as it relates, to credit unions.

(3)   An order—

    (a)   shall be made by statutory instrument, and

    (b)   may not be made unless a draft has been laid before and approved by resolution of each House of Parliament.

(4)   Provision made under or by virtue of this Part may make special provision in relation to the application of this Part to credit unions.

(5)   In the application of this section to Northern Ireland the reference to section 31 of the Credit Unions Act 1979 is to be treated as a reference to Article 2 of the Credit Unions (Northern Ireland) Order 1985.

[89]

NOTES

Commencement: 17 February 2009 (in so far as conferring or relating to any power to make subordinate legislation or codes of practice); 21 February 2009 (otherwise).

PART 2
BANK INSOLVENCY

NOTES

Modification: this Part is applied with modifications in respect of building societies, by the Building Societies (Insolvency and Special Administration) Order 2009, SI 2009/805, art 3, Sch 1, Pts 1, 2 at **[557]**, **[561]**, **[562]**.

Introduction

90   Overview

(1)   This Part provides for a procedure to be known as bank insolvency.

(2)   The main features of bank insolvency are that—

    (a)   a bank enters the process by court order,

    (b)   the order appoints a bank liquidator,

    (c)   the bank liquidator aims to arrange for the bank's eligible depositors to have their accounts transferred or to receive their compensation from the FSCS,

    (d)   the bank liquidator then winds up the bank, and

    (e)   for those purposes, the bank liquidator has powers and duties of liquidators, as applied and modified by the provisions of this Part.

(3)   The Table describes the provisions of this Part.

Sections	*Topic*
Sections 90 to 93	Introduction
Sections 94 to 98	Bank insolvency order
Sections 99 to 105	Process of bank liquidation
Sections 106 to 112	Tenure of bank liquidator

Sections	Topic
Sections 113 to 116	Termination of process, &c
Sections 117 to 122	Other processes
Sections 123 to 135	Miscellaneous

[90]

NOTES

Commencement: 17 February 2009 (in so far as conferring or relating to any power to make subordinate legislation or codes of practice); 21 February 2009 (otherwise).

91 Interpretation: "bank"

(1) In this Part "bank" means a UK institution which has permission under Part 4 of the Financial Services and Markets Act 2000 to carry on the regulated activity of accepting deposits (within the meaning of section 22 of that Act, taken with Schedule 2 and any order under section 22).

(2) But "bank" does not include—
  (a) a building society within the meaning of section 119 of the Building Societies Act 1986,
  (b) a credit union within the meaning of section 31 of the Credit Unions Act 1979, or
  (c) any other class of institution excluded by an order made by the Treasury.

(3) In subsection (1) "UK institution" means an institution which is incorporated in, or formed under the law of any part of, the United Kingdom.

(4) An order under subsection (2)(c)—
  (a) shall be made by statutory instrument, and
  (b) may not be made unless a draft has been laid before and approved by resolution of each House of Parliament.

(5) Section 130 makes provision for the application of this Part to building societies.

(6) Section 131 makes provision for the application of this Part to credit unions.

[91]

NOTES

Commencement: 17 February 2009 (in so far as conferring or relating to any power to make subordinate legislation or codes of practice); 21 February 2009 (otherwise).

92 Interpretation: "the court"

In this Part "the court" means—
  (a) in England and Wales, the High Court,
  (b) in Scotland, the Court of Session, and
  (c) in Northern Ireland, the High Court.

[92]

NOTES

Commencement: 17 February 2009 (in so far as conferring or relating to any power to make subordinate legislation or codes of practice); 21 February 2009 (otherwise).

93 Interpretation: other expressions

(1) In this Part "the FSA" means the Financial Services Authority.

(2) In this Part a reference to "the FSCS" is a reference to—
  (a) the Financial Services Compensation Scheme (established under Part 15 of the Financial Services and Markets Act 2000), or
  (b) where appropriate, the scheme manager of that Scheme.

(3) In this Part "eligible depositors" means depositors who are eligible for compensation under the FSCS.

(4) For the purposes of a reference in this Part to inability to pay debts—
  (a) a bank that is in default on an obligation to pay a sum due and payable under an agreement, is to be treated as unable to pay its debts, and
  (b) section 123 of the Insolvency Act 1986 (inability to pay debts) also applies; and
for the purposes of paragraph (a) "agreement" means an agreement the making or performance of which constitutes or is part of a regulated activity carried on by the bank.

(5) Expressions used in this Part and in the Insolvency Act 1986 have the same meaning as in that Act.

(6) Expressions used in this Part and in the Companies Act 2006 have the same meaning as in that Act.

(7) A reference in this Part to action includes a reference to inaction.

(8) The expression "fair" is used in this Part as a shorter modern equivalent of the expression "just and equitable" (and is not therefore intended to exclude the application of any judicial or other practice relating to the construction and application of that expression).

[93]

NOTES

Commencement: 17 February 2009 (in so far as conferring or relating to any power to make subordinate legislation or codes of practice); 21 February 2009 (otherwise).

Bank insolvency order

94 The order

(1) A bank insolvency order is an order appointing a person as the bank liquidator of a bank.

(2) A person is eligible for appointment as a bank liquidator if qualified to act as an insolvency practitioner.

(3) An appointment may be made only if the person has consented to act.

(4) A bank insolvency order takes effect in accordance with section 98; and—
 (a) the process of a bank insolvency order having effect may be described as "bank insolvency" in relation to the bank, and
 (b) while the order has effect the bank may be described as being "in bank insolvency".

[94]

NOTES

Commencement: 17 February 2009 (in so far as conferring or relating to any power to make subordinate legislation or codes of practice); 21 February 2009 (otherwise).

95 Application

(1) An application for a bank insolvency order may be made to the court by—
 (a) the Bank of England,
 (b) the FSA, or
 (c) the Secretary of State.

(2) An application must nominate a person to be appointed as the bank liquidator.

(3) The bank must be given notice of an application, in accordance with rules under section 411 of the Insolvency Act 1986 (as applied by section 125 below).

[95]

NOTES

Commencement: 17 February 2009 (in so far as conferring or relating to any power to make subordinate legislation or codes of practice); 21 February 2009 (otherwise).

96 Grounds for applying

(1) In this section—
 (a) Ground A is that a bank is unable, or likely to become unable, to pay its debts,
 (b) Ground B is that the winding up of a bank would be in the public interest, and
 (c) Ground C is that the winding up of a bank would be fair.

(2) The Bank of England may apply for a bank insolvency order only if—
 (a) the FSA has informed the Bank of England that the FSA is satisfied that Conditions 1 and 2 in section 7 are met, and
 (b) the Bank of England is satisfied—
  (i) that the bank has eligible depositors, and
  (ii) that Ground A or C applies.

(3) The FSA may apply for a bank insolvency order only if—
 (a) the Bank of England consents, and
 (b) the FSA is satisfied—
  (i) that Conditions 1 and 2 in section 7 are met,
  (ii) that the bank has eligible depositors, and
  (iii) that Ground A or C applies.

(4) The Secretary of State may apply for a bank insolvency order only if satisfied—
 (a) that the bank has eligible depositors, and
 (b) that Ground B applies.

(5)   The sources of information on the basis of which the Secretary of State may be satisfied of the matters specified in subsection (4) include those listed in section 124A(1) of the Insolvency Act 1986 (petition for winding up on grounds of public interest).

[96]

NOTES

Commencement: 17 February 2009 (in so far as conferring or relating to any power to make subordinate legislation or codes of practice); 21 February 2009 (otherwise).

97   Grounds for making

(1)   The court may make a bank insolvency order on the application of the Bank of England or the FSA if satisfied—
  (a)   that the bank has eligible depositors, and
  (b)   that Ground A or C of section 96 applies.

(2)   The court may make a bank insolvency order on the application of the Secretary of State if satisfied—
  (a)   that the bank has eligible depositors, and
  (b)   that Grounds B and C of section 96 apply.

(3)   On an application for a bank insolvency order the court may—
  (a)   grant the application in accordance with subsection (1) or (2),
  (b)   adjourn the application (generally or to a specified date), or
  (c)   dismiss the application.

[97]

NOTES

Commencement: 17 February 2009 (in so far as conferring or relating to any power to make subordinate legislation or codes of practice); 21 February 2009 (otherwise).

98   Commencement

(1)   A bank insolvency order shall be treated as having taken effect in accordance with this section.

(2)   In the case where—
  (a)   notice has been given to the FSA under section 120 of an application for an administration order or a petition for a winding up order, and
  (b)   the FSA or the Bank of England applies for a bank insolvency order in the period of 2 weeks specified in Condition 3 in that section,
the bank insolvency order is treated as having taken effect when the application or petition was made or presented.

(3)   In any other case, the bank insolvency order is treated as having taken effect when the application for the order was made.

(4)   Unless the court directs otherwise on proof of fraud or mistake, proceedings taken in the bank insolvency, during the period for which it is treated as having had effect, are treated as having been taken validly.

[98]

NOTES

Commencement: 17 February 2009 (in so far as conferring or relating to any power to make subordinate legislation or codes of practice); 21 February 2009 (otherwise).

Process of bank liquidation

99   Objectives

(1)   A bank liquidator has two objectives.

(2)   Objective 1 is to work with the FSCS so as to ensure that as soon as is reasonably practicable each eligible depositor—
  (a)   has the relevant account transferred to another financial institution, or
  (b)   receives payment from (or on behalf of) the FSCS.

(3)   Objective 2 is to wind up the affairs of the bank so as to achieve the best result for the bank's creditors as a whole.

(4)   Objective 1 takes precedence over Objective 2 (but the bank liquidator is obliged to begin working towards both objectives immediately upon appointment).

[99]

NOTES
Commencement: 17 February 2009 (in so far as conferring or relating to any power to make subordinate legislation or codes of practice); 21 February 2009 (otherwise).

100   Liquidation committee

(1)   Following a bank insolvency order a liquidation committee must be established, for the purpose of ensuring that the bank liquidator properly exercises the functions under this Part.

(2)   The liquidation committee shall consist initially of 3 individuals, one nominated by each of—

     (a)   the Bank of England,
     (b)   the FSA, and
     (c)   the FSCS.

(3)   The bank liquidator must report to the liquidation committee about any matter—

     (a)   on request, or
     (b)   which the bank liquidator thinks is likely to be of interest to the liquidation committee.

(4)   In particular, the bank liquidator—

     (a)   must keep the liquidation committee informed of progress towards Objective 1 in section 99, and
     (b)   must notify the liquidation committee when in the bank liquidator's opinion Objective 1 in section 99 has been achieved entirely or so far as is reasonably practicable.

(5)   As soon as is reasonably practicable after receiving notice under subsection (4)(b) the liquidation committee must either—

     (a)   resolve that Objective 1 in section 99 has been achieved entirely or so far as is reasonably practicable (a "full payment resolution"), or
     (b)   apply to the court under section 168(5) of the Insolvency Act 1986 (as applied by section 103 below).

(6)   Where a liquidation committee passes a full payment resolution—

     (a)   the bank liquidator must summon a meeting of creditors,
     (b)   the meeting may elect 2 or 4 individuals as new members of the liquidation committee,
     (c)   those individuals replace the members nominated by the Bank of England and the FSA,
     (d)   the FSCS may resign from the liquidation committee (in which case 3 or 5 new members may be elected under paragraph (b)), and
     (e)   if no individuals are elected under paragraph (b), or the resulting committee would have fewer than 3 members or an even number of members, the liquidation committee ceases to exist at the end of the meeting.

(7)   Subject to provisions of this section, rules under section 411 of the Insolvency Act 1986 (as amended by section 125 below) may make provision about—

     (a)   the establishment of liquidation committees,
     (b)   the membership of liquidation committees,
     (c)   the functions of liquidation committees, and
     (d)   the proceedings of liquidation committees.

[100]

NOTES
Commencement: 17 February 2009 (in so far as conferring or relating to any power to make subordinate legislation or codes of practice); 21 February 2009 (otherwise).

101   Liquidation committee: supplemental

(1)   A meeting of the liquidation committee may be summoned—

     (a)   by any of the members, or
     (b)   by the bank liquidator.

(2)   While the liquidation committee consists of the initial members (or their nominated replacements) a meeting is quorate only if all the members are present.

(3)   A person aggrieved by any action of the liquidation committee before it has passed a full payment resolution may apply to the court, which may make any order (including an order for the repayment of money).

(4)   The court may (whether on an application under subsection (3), on the application of a bank liquidator or otherwise) make an order that the liquidation committee is to be treated as having passed a full payment resolution.

(5)   If a liquidation committee fails to comply with section 100(5) the bank liquidator must apply to the court—

     (a)   for an order under subsection (4) above, or

    (b)   for directions under or by virtue of section 168(3) or 169(2) of the Insolvency Act 1986 as applied by section 103 below.

(6)   A nominating body under section 100(2) may replace its nominee at any time.

(7)   After the removal of the nominated members under section 100(6)(c) the FSA and the Bank of England—

    (a)   may attend meetings of the liquidation committee,

    (b)   are entitled to copies of documents relating to the liquidation committee's business,

    (c)   may make representations to the liquidation committee, and

    (d)   may participate in legal proceedings relating to the bank insolvency.

(8)   Where a liquidation committee ceases to exist by virtue of section 100(6)(e)—

    (a)   it may be re-formed by a creditors' meeting summoned by the bank liquidator for the purpose, and

    (b)   the bank liquidator must summon a meeting for the purpose if requested to do so by one-tenth in value of the bank's creditors.

(9)   Where a liquidation committee ceases to exist by virtue of section 100(6)(e) and has not been re-formed under subsection (8) above or under section 141(2) or 142(2) of the Insolvency Act 1986 (as applied by section 103 below)—

    (a)   ignore a reference in this Part to the liquidation committee,

    (b)   for section 113(2) to (4) substitute requirements for the bank liquidator, before making a proposal—

        (i)   to produce a final report,

        (ii)   to send copies in accordance with section 113(2)(b),

        (iii)   to make it available in accordance with section 113(2)(c), and

        (iv)   to be satisfied as specified in section 113(4)(b),

    (c)   ignore Condition 2 in section 114, and

    (d)   for section 115(1) to (5) substitute a power for the bank liquidator to apply to the Secretary of State or Accountant of Court for release and requirements that before making an application the bank liquidator must—

        (i)   produce a final report,

        (ii)   send copies in accordance with section 115(2)(b),

        (iii)   make it available in accordance with section 115(2)(c), and

        (iv)   notify the court and the registrar of companies of the intention to vacate office and to apply for release.

[101]

NOTES

Commencement: 17 February 2009 (in so far as conferring or relating to any power to make subordinate legislation or codes of practice); 21 February 2009 (otherwise).

102 Objective 1: (a) or (b)?

(1)   As soon as is reasonably practicable, a liquidation committee must recommend the bank liquidator to pursue—

    (a)   Objective 1(a) in section 99,

    (b)   Objective 1(b) in section 99, or

    (c)   Objective 1(a) for one specified class of case and Objective 1(b) for another.

(2)   In making a recommendation the liquidation committee must consider—

    (a)   the desirability of achieving Objective 1 as quickly as possible, and

    (b)   Objective 2 in section 99.

(3)   If the liquidation committee thinks that the bank liquidator is failing to comply with their recommendation, they must apply to the court for directions under section 168(5) of the Insolvency Act 1986 (as applied by section 103 below).

(4)   Where the liquidation committee has not made a recommendation the bank liquidator may apply to the court under section 101(3); and the court may, in particular, make a direction in lieu of a recommendation if the liquidation committee fail to make one within a period set by the court.

[102]

NOTES

Commencement: 17 February 2009 (in so far as conferring or relating to any power to make subordinate legislation or codes of practice); 21 February 2009 (otherwise).

103 General powers, duties and effect

(1)   A bank liquidator may do anything necessary or expedient for the pursuit of the Objectives in section 99.

(2)   The following provisions of this section provide for—

(a)   general powers and duties of bank liquidators (by application of provisions about liquidators), and

(b)   the general process and effects of bank insolvency (by application of provisions about winding up).

(3)   The provisions set out in the Table apply in relation to bank insolvency as in relation to winding up, with—

(a)   the modifications set out in subsection (4),

(b)   any other modification specified in the Table, and

(c)   any other necessary modification.

(4)   The modifications are that—

(a)   a reference to the liquidator is a reference to the bank liquidator,

(b)   a reference to winding up is a reference to bank insolvency,

(c)   a reference to winding up by the court is a reference to the imposition of bank insolvency by order of the court,

(d)   a reference to being wound up under Part IV or V of the Insolvency Act 1986 is a reference to being made the subject of a bank insolvency order,

(e)   a reference to the commencement of winding up is a reference to the commencement of bank insolvency,

(f)   a reference to going into liquidation is a reference to entering bank insolvency,

(g)   a reference to a winding-up order is a reference to a bank insolvency order, and

(h)   a reference to a company is a reference to the bank.

(5)   Powers conferred by this Act, by the Insolvency Act 1986 (as applied) and the Companies Acts are in addition to, and not in restriction of, any existing powers of instituting proceedings against a contributory or debtor of a bank, or the estate of any contributory or debtor, for the recovery of any call or other sum.

(6)   A reference in an enactment or other document to anything done under a provision applied by this Part includes a reference to the provision as applied.

<table>
<tr><td colspan="3" align="center">**TABLE OF APPLIED PROVISIONS**</td></tr>
<tr><td>*Provision of Insolvency Act 1986*</td><td align="center">*Subject*</td><td align="center">*Modification or comment*</td></tr>
<tr><td>Section 127</td><td>Avoidance of property dispositions</td><td>Ignore section 127(2).</td></tr>
<tr><td>Section 128</td><td>Avoidance of attachment, &c</td><td></td></tr>
<tr><td>Section 130</td><td>Consequences of winding-up order</td><td>Ignore section 130(4).</td></tr>
<tr><td>Section 131</td><td>Company's statement of affairs</td><td>(a)   Treat references to the official receiver as references to the bank liquidator.

(b)   A creditor or contributory of the bank is entitled to receive a copy of a statement under section 131 on request to the bank liquidator.</td></tr>
<tr><td>Section 135</td><td>Provisional appointment</td><td>(a)   Treat the reference to the presentation of a winding-up petition as a reference to the making of an application for a bank insolvency order.

(b)   Subsection (2) applies in relation to England and Wales and Scotland (and subsection (3) does not apply).

(c)   Ignore the reference to the official receiver.

(d)   Only a person who is qualified to act as an insolvency practitioner and who consents to act may be appointed.

(e)   A provisional bank liquidator may not pay dividends to creditors.</td></tr>
</table>

PART I
BANKING ACT 2009

	TABLE OF APPLIED PROVISIONS	
Provision of Insolvency Act 1986	***Subject***	***Modification or comment***
		(f) The appointment of a provisional bank liquidator lapses on the appointment of a bank liquidator.
Section 141	Liquidation Committee (England and Wales)	The application of section 141 is subject to— (a) sections 100, 101 and 109 of this Act, (b) rules under section 411 (as applied by section 125 of this Act) which may, in particular, adapt section 141 to reflect (i) the fact that the bank liquidator is appointed by the court and (ii) the possibility of calling creditors' meetings under other provisions, and (c) the omission of references to the official receiver.
Section 142	Liquidation Committee (Scotland)	The application of section 142 is subject to— (a) sections 100, 101 and 109 of this Act, (b) rules under section 411 (as applied by section 125 of this Act) which may, in particular, adapt section 142 to reflect (i) the fact that the bank liquidator is appointed by the court and (ii) the possibility of calling creditors' meetings under other provisions, and (c) the omission of references to the official receiver.
Section 143	General functions of liquidator	(a) Section 143(1) is subject to Objective 1 in section 99 above. (b) Ignore section 143(2).
Section 144	Custody of property	
Section 145	Vesting of property	
Section 146	*Duty to summon final meeting*	*Section 146 is not applied—but section 115 below makes similar provision.*
Section 147	Power to stay or sist proceedings	An application may be made only by— (a) the bank liquidator, (b) the FSA, (c) the Bank of England, (d) the FSCS, or (e) a creditor or contributory (but only if the liquidation committee has passed a full payment resolution).
Section 148	List of contributories and application of assets	*By virtue of the Insolvency Rules the functions under this section are largely delegated to the liquidator—rules by virtue of section 125 may achieve a similar delegation to the bank liquidator.*
Section 149	Debts due from contributories	
Section 150	Power to make calls	

TABLE OF APPLIED PROVISIONS		
Provision of Insolvency Act 1986	*Subject*	*Modification or comment*
Section 152	Order on contributory: evidence	
Section 153	Exclusion of creditors	
Section 154	Adjustment of rights of contributories	
Section 155	Inspection of books by creditors	In making or considering whether to make an order under section 155 the court shall have regard to Objective 1 in section 99 above.
Section 156	Payment of expenses of winding up	
Section 157	Attendance at company meetings (Scotland)	
Section 158	Power to arrest absconding contributory	
Section 159	*Powers to be cumulative*	*Section 159 is not applied—but subsection (5) above makes similar provision.*
Section 160	Delegation of powers to liquidator (England and Wales)	
Section 161	Orders for calls on contributories (Scotland)	
Section 162	Appeals from orders (Scotland)	An appeal may be brought only if the liquidation committee has passed a full payment resolution.
Section 167 and Schedule 4	General powers of liquidator	(a) An application to the court may not be made under section 167(3) unless the liquidation committee has passed a full payment resolution (although a creditor or contributory may apply to the court with respect to any action (or inaction) of the liquidation committee, under section 101(3) above). (b) In exercising or considering whether to exercise a power under Schedule 4 the bank liquidator shall have regard to Objective 1 in section 99. (c) A reference to the liquidation committee is to the liquidation committee established by section 100. (d) The power in paragraph 4 of Schedule 4 includes the power to submit matters to arbitration. *Some additional general powers are conferred by section 104 below.*
Section 168	Supplementary powers of liquidator	(a) A direction or request under section 168(2) has no effect unless the liquidation committee has passed a full payment resolution. (b) Section 168(5) also applies in the case of the imposition of bank insolvency by order of the Court of Session.

TABLE OF APPLIED PROVISIONS

Provision of Insolvency Act 1986	Subject	Modification or comment
		(c) An application to the court may not be made under section 168(5) unless the liquidation committee has passed a full payment resolution (except as provided in section 100 or 102 above).
Section 169	Supplementary powers (Scotland)	(a) Ignore section 169(1). (b) Powers of the bank liquidator by virtue of section 169(2) are subject to Objective 1 in section 99 above.
Section 170	Liquidator's duty to make returns	The liquidation committee is added to the list of persons able to apply under section 170(2).
Section 172	Removal of liquidator	*Section 172 is not applied to a bank liquidator— but section 108 makes similar provision.* Section 172(1), (2) and (5) are applied to a provisional bank liquidator.
Section 174	*Release of liquidator*	*Section 174 is not applied—but section 115 makes similar provision.*
Section 175	Preferential debts	
Section 176	Preferential charge on goods restrained	
Section 176ZA	Expenses of winding up	
Section 176A	Share of assets for unsecured creditors	
Section 177	Appointment of special manager	
Section 178	Power to disclaim onerous property	
Section 179	Disclaimer of leaseholds	
Section 180	Land subject to rentcharge	
Section 181	Disclaimer: powers of court	
Section 182	Leaseholds	
Section 183	Effect of execution or attachment (England and Wales)	
Section 184	Execution of writs (England and Wales)	
Section 185	Effect of diligence (Scotland)	In the application of section 37(1) of the Bankruptcy (Scotland) Act 1985 the reference to an order of the court awarding winding up is a reference to the making of the bank insolvency order.
Section 186	Rescission of contracts by court	
Section 187	Transfer of assets to employees	
Section 188	Publicity	

TABLE OF APPLIED PROVISIONS		
Provision of Insolvency Act 1986	*Subject*	*Modification or comment*
Section 189	Interest on debts	
Section 190	Exemption from stamp duty	
Section 191	Company's books as evidence	
Section 192	Information about pending liquidations	
Section 193	Unclaimed dividends (Scotland)	
Section 194	Resolutions passed at adjourned meetings	
Section 195	Meetings to ascertain wishes of creditors or contributories	The power to have regard to the wishes of creditors and contributories is subject to Objective 1 in section 99.
Section 196	Judicial notice of court documents	
Section 197	Commission for receiving evidence	
Section 198	Court order for examination of persons (Scotland)	
Section 199	Costs of application for leave to proceed (Scotland)	
Section 200	Affidavits	
Section 206	Fraud in anticipation of winding up	
Section 207	Transactions in fraud of creditors	
Section 208	Misconduct in course of winding up	
Section 209	Falsification of company's books	
Section 210	Material omissions	
Section 211	False representations to creditors	
Section 212	Summary remedy against directors, &c	
Section 213	Fraudulent trading	
Section 214	Wrongful trading	
Section 215	Sections 213 & 214: procedure	
Section 216	Restriction on re-use of company names	
Section 217	Personal liability for debts	
Section 218	Prosecution of officers and members of company	(a) Ignore subsections (4) and (6).

PART 1
BANKING ACT 2009

	TABLE OF APPLIED PROVISIONS	
Provision of Insolvency Act 1986	*Subject*	*Modification or comment*
		(b) In subsection (3), treat the second reference to the official receiver as a reference to the Secretary of State. (c) In subsection (5) treat the reference to subsection (4) as a reference to subsection (3).
Section 219	Obligations under section 218	
Section 231	Appointment of 2 or more persons	
Section 232	Validity of acts	
Section 233	Utilities	
Section 234	Getting in company's property	
Section 235	Co-operation with liquidator	Ignore references to the official receiver
Section 236	Inquiry into company's dealings	Ignore references to the official receiver
Section 237	Section 236: enforcement by court	
Section 238	Transactions at undervalue (England and Wales)	Anything done by the bank in connection with the exercise of a stabilisation power under Part 1 of this Act is not a transaction at an undervalue for the purposes of section 238.
Section 239	Preferences (England and Wales)	Action taken by the bank in connection with the exercise of a stabilisation power under Part 1 of this Act does not amount to giving a preference for the purpose of section 239.
Section 240	Sections 238 & 239: relevant time	
Section 241	Orders under sections 238 & 239	Having notice of the relevant proceedings means having notice of— (a) an application by the Bank of England, the FSA or the Secretary of State for a bank insolvency order, or (b) notice under section 120 below.
Section 242	Gratuitous alienations (Scotland)	Anything done by the bank in connection with the exercise of a stabilisation power under Part 1 of this Act is not a gratuitous alienation for the purpose of section 242 or any other rule of law.
Section 243	Unfair preferences (Scotland)	Action taken by the bank in connection with the exercise of a stabilisation power under Part 1 of this Act does not amount to an unfair preference for the purpose of section 243 or any other rule of law.
Section 244	Extortionate credit transactions	
Section 245	Avoidance of floating charges	
Section 246	Unenforceability of liens	

TABLE OF APPLIED PROVISIONS		
Provision of Insolvency Act 1986	*Subject*	*Modification or comment*
Sections 386 & 387, and Schedule 6 (and Schedule 4 to the Pension Schemes Act 1993)	Preferential debts	
Section 389	Offence of acting without being qualified	Treat references to acting as an insolvency practitioner as references to acting as a bank liquidator.
Section 390	Persons not qualified to act	Treat references to acting as an insolvency practitioner as references to acting as a bank liquidator.
Section 391	Recognised professional bodies	An order under section 391 has effect in relation to any provision applied for the purposes of bank insolvency.
Sections 423–425	Transactions defrauding creditors	Anything done by the bank in connection with the exercise of a stabilisation power under Part 1 of this Act is not a transaction at an undervalue for the purposes of section 423.
Sections 430 to 432 and Schedule 10	Offences	
Section 433	Statements: admissibility	For section 433(1)(a) and (b) substitute a reference to a statement prepared for the purposes of a provision of this Part.

[103]

NOTES
    Commencement: 17 February 2009 (in so far as conferring or relating to any power to make subordinate legislation or codes of practice); 21 February 2009 (otherwise).

104   Additional general powers

(1)   A bank liquidator has the following powers.

(2)   Power to effect and maintain insurances in respect of the business and property of the bank.

(3)   Power to do all such things (including the carrying out of works) as may be necessary for the realisation of the property of the bank.

(4)   Power to make any payment which is necessary or incidental to the performance of the bank liquidator's functions.

[104]

NOTES
    Commencement: 17 February 2009 (in so far as conferring or relating to any power to make subordinate legislation or codes of practice); 21 February 2009 (otherwise).

105   Status of bank liquidator

A bank liquidator is an officer of the court.

[105]

NOTES
    Commencement: 17 February 2009 (in so far as conferring or relating to any power to make subordinate legislation or codes of practice); 21 February 2009 (otherwise).

Tenure of bank liquidator

106 Term of appointment

A bank liquidator appointed by bank insolvency order remains in office until vacating office—
- (a) by resigning under section 107,
- (b) on removal under section 108 or 109,
- (c) on disqualification under section 110,
- (d) on the appointment of a replacement in accordance with section 112,
- (e) in accordance with sections 113 to 115, or
- (f) on death.

[106]

NOTES

Commencement: 17 February 2009 (in so far as conferring or relating to any power to make subordinate legislation or codes of practice); 21 February 2009 (otherwise).

107 Resignation

(1) A bank liquidator may resign by notice to the court.

(2) Rules under section 411 of the Insolvency Act 1986 (as applied by section 125 below) may restrict a bank liquidator's power to resign.

(3) Resignation shall take effect in accordance with those rules (which shall include provision about release).

[107]

NOTES

Commencement: 17 February 2009 (in so far as conferring or relating to any power to make subordinate legislation or codes of practice); 21 February 2009 (otherwise).

108 Removal by court

(1) A bank liquidator may be removed by order of the court on the application of—
- (a) the liquidation committee,
- (b) the FSA, or
- (c) the Bank of England.

(2) Before making an application the FSA must consult the Bank of England.

(3) Before making an application the Bank of England must consult the FSA.

(4) A bank liquidator removed by order has release with effect from a time determined by—
- (a) the Secretary of State, or
- (b) in the case of a bank liquidator in Scotland, the Accountant of Court.

[108]

NOTES

Commencement: 17 February 2009 (in so far as conferring or relating to any power to make subordinate legislation or codes of practice); 21 February 2009 (otherwise).

109 Removal by creditors

(1) A bank liquidator may be removed by resolution of a meeting of creditors held pursuant to section 195 of the Insolvency Act 1986 (as applied by section 103 above) provided that the following conditions are met.

(2) Condition 1 is that the liquidation committee has passed a full payment resolution.

(3) Condition 2 is that the notice given to creditors of the meeting includes notice of intention to move a resolution removing the bank liquidator.

(4) Condition 3 is that the Bank of England and the FSA—
- (a) receive notice of the meeting, and
- (b) are given an opportunity to make representations to it.

(5) A bank liquidator who is removed under this section has release with effect—
- (a) from the time when the court is informed of the removal, or
- (b) if the meeting removing the bank liquidator resolves to disapply paragraph (a), from a time determined by—
  - (i) the Secretary of State, or
  - (ii) in the case of a bank liquidator in Scotland, the Accountant of Court.

[109]

PART I
BANKING ACT 2009

NOTES

Commencement: 17 February 2009 (in so far as conferring or relating to any power to make subordinate legislation or codes of practice); 21 February 2009 (otherwise).

110 Disqualification

(1) If a bank liquidator ceases to be qualified to act as an insolvency practitioner, the appointment lapses.

(2) A bank liquidator whose appointment lapses under subsection (1) has release with effect from a time determined by—

(a) the Secretary of State, or

(b) in the case of a bank liquidator in Scotland, the Accountant of Court.

[110]

NOTES

Commencement: 17 February 2009 (in so far as conferring or relating to any power to make subordinate legislation or codes of practice); 21 February 2009 (otherwise).

111 Release

A bank liquidator who is released is discharged from all liability in respect of acts or omissions in the bank insolvency and otherwise in relation to conduct as bank liquidator (but without prejudice to the effect of section 212 of the Insolvency Act 1986 as applied by section 103 above).

[111]

NOTES

Commencement: 17 February 2009 (in so far as conferring or relating to any power to make subordinate legislation or codes of practice); 21 February 2009 (otherwise).

112 Replacement

(1) Where a bank liquidator vacates office the Bank of England must as soon as is reasonably practicable appoint a replacement bank liquidator.

(2) But where a bank liquidator is removed by resolution of a meeting of creditors under section 109—

(a) a replacement may be appointed by resolution of the meeting, and

(b) failing that, subsection (1) above applies.

[112]

NOTES

Commencement: 17 February 2009 (in so far as conferring or relating to any power to make subordinate legislation or codes of practice); 21 February 2009 (otherwise).

Termination of process, &c

113 Company voluntary arrangement

(1) A bank liquidator may make a proposal in accordance with section 1 of the Insolvency Act 1986 (company voluntary arrangement).

(2) Before making a proposal the bank liquidator—

(a) shall present a final report on the bank liquidation to the liquidation committee,

(b) shall send a copy of the report to—

(i) the FSA,

(ii) the FSCS,

(iii) the Bank of England,

(iv) the Treasury, and

(v) the registrar of companies, and

(c) shall make the report available to members, creditors and contributories on request.

(3) A proposal may be made only with the consent of the liquidation committee.

(4) The liquidation committee may consent only if—

(a) it has passed a full payment resolution, and

(b) the bank liquidator is satisfied, as a result of arrangements made with the FSCS, that any depositor still eligible for compensation under the scheme will be dealt with in accordance with section 99(2)(a) or (b).

(5) The bank liquidator must be the nominee (see section 1(2) of the 1986 Act).

(6) Part 1 of the 1986 Act shall apply to a proposal made by a bank liquidator, with the following modifications.

(7)   In section 3 (summoning of meetings) subsection (2) (and not (1)) applies.

(8)   The action that may be taken by the court under section 5(3) (effect of approval) includes suspension of the bank insolvency order.

(9)   On the termination of a company voluntary arrangement the bank liquidator may apply to the court to lift the suspension of the bank insolvency order.

[113]

NOTES
Commencement: 17 February 2009 (in so far as conferring or relating to any power to make subordinate legislation or codes of practice); 21 February 2009 (otherwise).

114   Administration

(1)   A bank liquidator who thinks that administration would achieve a better result for the bank's creditors as a whole than bank insolvency may apply to the court for an administration order (under paragraph 38 of Schedule B1 to the Insolvency Act 1986).

(2)   An application may be made only if the following conditions are satisfied.

(3)   Condition 1 is that the liquidation committee has passed a full payment resolution.

(4)   Condition 2 is that the liquidation committee has resolved that moving to administration might enable the rescue of the bank as a going concern.

(5)   Condition 3 is that the bank liquidator is satisfied, as a result of arrangements made with the FSCS, that any depositors still eligible for compensation under the scheme will receive their payments or have their accounts transferred during administration.

[114]

NOTES
Commencement: 17 February 2009 (in so far as conferring or relating to any power to make subordinate legislation or codes of practice); 21 February 2009 (otherwise).

115   Dissolution

(1)   A bank liquidator who thinks that the winding up of the bank is for practical purposes complete shall summon a final meeting of the liquidation committee.

(2)   The bank liquidator—
    (a)   shall present a final report on the bank insolvency to the meeting,
    (b)   shall send a copy of the report to—
        (i)   the FSA,
        (ii)   the FSCS,
        (iii)   the Bank of England,
        (iv)   the Treasury, and
        (v)   the registrar of companies, and
    (c)   shall make the report available to members, creditors and contributories on request.

(3)   At the meeting the liquidation committee shall—
    (a)   consider the report, and
    (b)   decide whether to release the bank liquidator.

(4)   If the liquidation committee decides to release the bank liquidator, the bank liquidator—
    (a)   shall notify the court and the registrar of companies, and
    (b)   vacates office, and has release, when the court is notified.

(5)   If the liquidation committee decides not to release the bank liquidator, the bank liquidator may apply to the Secretary of State for release; if the application is granted, the bank liquidator—
    (a)   vacates office when the application is granted, and
    (b)   has release from a time determined by the Secretary of State.

(6)   In the case of a bank liquidator in Scotland, a reference in subsection (5) to the Secretary of State is a reference to the Accountant of Court.

(7)   On receipt of a notice under subsection (4)(a) the registrar of companies shall register it.

(8)   At the end of the period of 3 months beginning with the day of the registration of the notice, the bank is dissolved (subject to deferral under section 116).

[115]

NOTES
Commencement: 17 February 2009 (in so far as conferring or relating to any power to make subordinate legislation or codes of practice); 21 February 2009 (otherwise).

116 Dissolution: supplemental

(1)   The Secretary of State may by direction defer the date of dissolution under section 115, on the application of a person who appears to the Secretary of State to be interested.

(2)   An appeal to the court lies from any decision of the Secretary of State on an application for a direction under subsection (1).

(3)   Subsection (1) does not apply where the bank insolvency order was made by the court in Scotland; but the court may by direction defer the date of dissolution on an application by a person appearing to the court to have an interest.

(4)   A person who obtains deferral under subsection (1) or (3) shall, within 7 days after the giving of the deferral direction, deliver a copy of the direction to the registrar of companies for registration.

(5)   A person who without reasonable excuse fails to comply with subsection (4) is liable to a fine and, for continued contravention, to a daily default fine, in each case of the same amount as for a contravention of section 205(6) of the Insolvency Act 1986 (dissolution).

(6)   The bank liquidator may give the notice summoning the final meeting under section 115 above at the same time as giving notice of any final distribution of the bank's property; but, if summoned for an earlier date the meeting shall be adjourned (and, if necessary, further adjourned) until a date on which the bank liquidator is able to report to the meeting that the winding up of the bank is for practical purposes complete.

(7)   A bank liquidator must retain sufficient sums to cover the expenses of the final meeting under section 115 above.

[116]

NOTES
Commencement: 17 February 2009 (in so far as conferring or relating to any power to make subordinate legislation or codes of practice); 21 February 2009 (otherwise).

Other processes

117 Bank insolvency as alternative order

(1)   On a petition for a winding up order or an application for an administration order in respect of a bank the court may, instead, make a bank insolvency order.

(2)   A bank insolvency order may be made under subsection (1) only—
    (a)   on the application of the FSA made with the consent of the Bank of England, or
    (b)   on the application of the Bank of England.

[117]

NOTES
Commencement: 17 February 2009 (in so far as conferring or relating to any power to make subordinate legislation or codes of practice); 21 February 2009 (otherwise).

118 Voluntary winding-up

A resolution for voluntary winding up of a bank under section 84 of the Insolvency Act 1986 shall have no effect without the prior approval of the court.

[178I

NOTES
Commencement: 17 February 2009 (in so far as conferring or relating to any power to make subordinate legislation or codes of practice); 21 February 2009 (otherwise).

119 Exclusion of other procedures

(1)   The following paragraphs of Schedule B1 to the Insolvency Act 1986 (administration) apply to a bank insolvency order as to an administration order.

(2)   Those paragraphs are—
    (a)   paragraph 40 (dismissal of pending winding-up petition), and
    (b)   paragraph 42 (moratorium on insolvency proceedings).

(3)   For that purpose—
    (a)   a reference to an administration order is a reference to a bank insolvency order,
    (b)   a reference to a company being in administration is a reference to a bank being in bank insolvency, and
    (c)   a reference to an administrator is a reference to a bank liquidator.

[119]

NOTES
Commencement: 17 February 2009 (in so far as conferring or relating to any power to make subordinate legislation or codes of practice); 21 February 2009 (otherwise).

120 Notice to FSA of preliminary steps

(1)   An application for an administration order in respect of a bank may not be determined unless the conditions below are satisfied.

(2)   A petition for a winding up order in respect of a bank may not be determined unless the conditions below are satisfied.

(3)   A resolution for voluntary winding up of a bank may not be made unless the conditions below are satisfied.

(4)   An administrator of a bank may not be appointed unless the conditions below are satisfied.

(5)   Condition 1 is that the FSA has been notified—
    (a)   by the applicant for an administration order, that the application has been made,
    (b)   by the petitioner for a winding up order, that the petition has been presented,
    (c)   by the bank, that a resolution for voluntary winding up may be made, or
    (d)   by the person proposing to appoint an administrator, of the proposed appointment.

(6)   Condition 2 is that a copy of the notice complying with Condition 1 has been filed with the court (and made available for public inspection by the court).

(7)   Condition 3 is that—
    (a)   the period of 2 weeks, beginning with the day on which the notice is received, has ended, or
    (b)   both—
        (i)   the FSA has informed the person who gave the notice that it does not intend to apply for a bank insolvency order, and
        (ii)   the Bank of England has informed the person who gave the notice that it does not intend to apply for a bank insolvency order or to exercise a stabilisation power under Part 1.

(8)   Condition 4 is that no application for a bank insolvency order is pending.

(9)   Arranging for the giving of notice in order to satisfy Condition 1 can be a step with a view to minimising the potential loss to a bank's creditors for the purpose of section 214 of the Insolvency Act 1986 (wrongful trading).

(10)   Where the FSA receives notice under Condition 1—
    (a)   the FSA shall inform the Bank of England,
    (b)   the FSA shall inform the person who gave the notice, within the period in Condition 3(a), whether it intends to apply for a bank insolvency order, and
    (c)   if the Bank of England decides to apply for a bank insolvency order or to exercise a stabilisation power under Part 1, the Bank shall inform the person who gave the notice, within the period in Condition 3(a).

[120]

NOTES
Commencement: 17 February 2009 (in so far as conferring or relating to any power to make subordinate legislation or codes of practice); 21 February 2009 (otherwise).

121 Disqualification of directors

(1)   In this section "the Disqualification Act" means the Company Directors Disqualification Act 1986.

(2)   In the Disqualification Act—
    (a)   a reference to liquidation includes a reference to bank insolvency,
    (b)   a reference to winding up includes a reference to making or being subject to a bank insolvency order,
    (c)   a reference to becoming insolvent includes a reference to becoming subject to a bank insolvency order, and
    (d)   a reference to a liquidator includes a reference to a bank liquidator.

(3)   For the purposes of the application of section 7(3) of the Disqualification Act (disqualification order or undertaking) to a bank which is subject to a bank insolvency order, the responsible office-holder is the bank liquidator.

(4)   (*Inserts the Company Directors Disqualification Act 1986, s 21A at* **[347]**.)

[121]

NOTES
Commencement: 17 February 2009 (in so far as conferring or relating to any power to make subordinate legislation or codes of practice); 21 February 2009 (otherwise).

122 Application of insolvency law

(1)   The Secretary of State and the Treasury may by order made jointly—
(a)   provide for an enactment about insolvency to apply to bank insolvency (with or without specified modifications);
(b)   amend, or modify the application of, an enactment about insolvency in consequence of this Part.

(2)   An order under subsection (1)—
(a)   shall be made by statutory instrument, and
(b)   may not be made unless a draft has been laid before and approved by resolution of each House of Parliament.

[122]

NOTES
Commencement: 17 February 2009 (in so far as conferring or relating to any power to make subordinate legislation or codes of practice); 21 February 2009 (otherwise).

Miscellaneous

123 Role of FSCS

(1)   For the purpose of co-operating in the pursuit of Objective 1 in section 99 the FSCS—
(a)   may make or arrange for payments to or in respect of eligible depositors of the bank, and
(b)   may make money available to facilitate the transfer of accounts of eligible depositors of the bank.

(2)   The FSCS may include provision about expenditure under this section; and, in particular—
(a)   money may be raised through the imposition of a levy under Part 15 of the Financial Services and Markets Act in respect of expenditure or possible expenditure under this section, and
(b)   sums raised in connection with the scheme (whether or not under paragraph (a)) may be expended under this section.

(3)   (*Amends the Financial Services and Markets Act 2000, s 220 at* **[394].**)

(4)   The FSCS is entitled to participate in proceedings for or in respect of a bank insolvency order.

(5)   A bank liquidator must—
(a)   comply with a request of the FSCS for the provision of information, and
(b)   provide the FSCS with any other information which the bank liquidator thinks might be useful for the purpose of co-operating in the pursuit of Objective 1.

(6)   A bank liquidator may enter into an agreement under section 221A of the Financial Services and Markets Act 2000 (Compensation Scheme: delegation of functions) for the bank liquidator to exercise functions of the scheme manager for the purpose of facilitating the pursuit of Objective 1.

(7)   Where a bank insolvency order is made in respect of a bank, the fact that it later ceases to be an authorised person does not prevent the operation of the compensation scheme in respect of it; and for that purpose the bank is a relevant person within the meaning of section 213(9) of the Financial Services and Markets Act 2000 despite the lapse of authorisation.

[123]

NOTES
Commencement: 17 February 2009 (in so far as conferring or relating to any power to make subordinate legislation or codes of practice); 21 February 2009 (otherwise).

124 Transfer of accounts

(1)   This section applies where a bank liquidator arranges, in pursuit of Objective 1 in section 99, for the transfer of eligible depositors' accounts from the bank to another financial institution.

(2)   The arrangements may disapply, or provide that they shall have effect despite, any restriction arising by virtue of contract or legislation or in any other way.

(3)   In subsection (2) "restriction" includes—
(a)   any restriction, inability or incapacity affecting what can and cannot be assigned or transferred (whether generally or by a particular person), and

(b)   a requirement for consent (by any name).

(4)   In making the arrangements mentioned in subsection (1) the bank liquidator must ensure that eligible depositors will be able to remove money from transferred accounts as soon as is reasonably practicable after transfer.

[124]

NOTES

Commencement: 17 February 2009 (in so far as conferring or relating to any power to make subordinate legislation or codes of practice); 21 February 2009 (otherwise).

125, 126   (*S 125 amends the Insolvency Act 1986, ss 411, 413, Sch 8 at* **[299]**, **[300]**, **[315]***; s 126 amends s 414 of the 1986 Act at* **[301]***.*)

127   Insolvency Services Account

A bank liquidator who obtains money by realising assets in the course of the bank insolvency must pay it into the Insolvency Services Account (kept by the Secretary of State).

[125]

NOTES

Commencement: 17 February 2009 (in so far as conferring or relating to any power to make subordinate legislation or codes of practice); 21 February 2009 (otherwise).

128   (*Amends the Insolvency Act 1986, s 433 at* **[310]***.*)

129   Co-operation between courts

(1)   Provisions of or by virtue of this Part are "insolvency law" for the purposes of section 426 of the Insolvency Act 1986 (co-operation between courts).

(2)   (*Amends the Insolvency Act 1986, s 426 at* **[306]***.*)

[126]

NOTES

Commencement: 17 February 2009 (in so far as conferring or relating to any power to make subordinate legislation or codes of practice); 21 February 2009 (otherwise).

130   Building societies

(1)   The Treasury may by order provide for this Part to apply to building societies (within the meaning of section 119 of the Building Societies Act 1986) as it applies to banks, subject to modifications set out in the order.

(2)   An order may—
(a)   amend the Building Societies Act 1986 or any other enactment which relates, or in so far as it relates, to building societies;
(b)   amend an enactment amended by this Part;
(c)   replicate, with or without modifications, any provision of this Part;
(d)   apply a provision made under or by virtue of this Part, with or without modifications, to this Part as it applies to building societies.

(3)   An order—
(a)   shall be made by statutory instrument, and
(b)   may not be made unless a draft has been laid before and approved by resolution of each House of Parliament.

(4)   Provision made under or by virtue of this Part may make special provision in relation to the application of this Part to building societies.

[127]

NOTES

Commencement: 17 February 2009 (in so far as conferring or relating to any power to make subordinate legislation or codes of practice); 21 February 2009 (otherwise).

Note: On 21 July 2009 HM Treasury issued a consultation paper, Special resolution regime: the Building Societies (Insolvency and Special Administration) Order 2009 and related insolvency rules, and financial assistance to building societies to consult fully on the application of the Banking Act 2009 to building societies as the resolution procedures for building societies were not set out on the face of the Banking Act 2009 and time had not previously allowed for consultation before the new regime came into place. The closing date for this consultation paper is 30 October 2009. Following the consultation, HM Treasury will consider whether to bring forward proposals to amend the rules.

Order: the Building Societies (Insolvency and Special Administration) Order 2009, SI 2009/805 at **[556]**.

131 Credit unions

(1) The Treasury may by order provide for this Part to apply to credit unions (within the meaning of section 31 of the Credit Unions Act 1979) as it applies to banks, subject to modifications set out in the order.

(2) An order may—
   (a) amend the Credit Unions Act 1979, the Industrial and Providential Societies Act 1965 or any other enactment which relates, or in so far as it relates, to credit unions;
   (b) amend an enactment amended by this Part;
   (c) replicate, with or without modifications, any provision of this Part;
   (d) apply a provision made under or by virtue of this Part, with or without modifications, to this Part as it applies to credit unions.

(3) An order—
   (a) shall be made by statutory instrument, and
   (b) may not be made unless a draft has been laid before and approved by resolution of each House of Parliament.

(4) Provision made under or by virtue of this Part may make special provision in relation to the application of this Part to credit unions.

[128]

NOTES

Commencement: 17 February 2009 (in so far as conferring or relating to any power to make subordinate legislation or codes of practice); 21 February 2009 (otherwise).

132 Partnerships

(1) The Lord Chancellor may, by order made with the concurrence of the Secretary of State and the Lord Chief Justice, modify provisions of this Part in their application to partnerships.

(2) For procedural purposes an order under subsection (1) shall be treated in the same way as an order under section 420 of the Insolvency Act 1986 (partnerships).

(3) This section does not apply in relation to partnerships constituted under the law of Scotland.

[129]

NOTES

Commencement: 17 February 2009 (in so far as conferring or relating to any power to make subordinate legislation or codes of practice); 21 February 2009 (otherwise).

133 Scottish partnerships

(1) The Secretary of State may by order modify provisions of this Part in their application to partnerships constituted under the law of Scotland.

(2) An order—
   (a) shall be made by statutory instrument, and
   (b) shall be subject to annulment in pursuance of a resolution of either House of Parliament.

[130]

NOTES

Commencement: 17 February 2009 (in so far as conferring or relating to any power to make subordinate legislation or codes of practice); 21 February 2009 (otherwise).

134 Northern Ireland

In the application of this Part to Northern Ireland—
   (a) a reference to an enactment is to be treated as a reference to the equivalent enactment having effect in relation to Northern Ireland,
   (b) where this Part amends an enactment an equivalent amendment (incorporating any necessary modification) is made to the equivalent enactment having effect in relation to Northern Ireland,
   (c) references to the Secretary of State, except in section 122, are to be treated as references to the Department of Enterprise, Trade and Investment,
   (d) a reference to the Insolvency Services Account is to be treated as a reference to the Insolvency Account,
   (e) a reference to section 31 of the Credit Unions Act 1979 is to be treated as a reference to Article 2 of the Credit Unions (Northern Ireland) Order 1985,
   (f) the Judgments Enforcement (Northern Ireland) Order 1981 has effect in place of sections 183 and 184 of the Insolvency Act 1986 (applied by section 103 above), and
   (g) the reference in section 132 to the Lord Chief Justice is a reference to the Lord Chief Justice in Northern Ireland.

[131]

NOTES

Commencement: 17 February 2009 (in so far as conferring or relating to any power to make subordinate legislation or codes of practice); 21 February 2009 (otherwise).

135 Consequential provision

(1) The Treasury may by order make provision in consequence of this Part.

(2) An order may, in particular, amend or modify the effect of an enactment (including a fiscal enactment) passed before the commencement of this Part.

(3) An order—
    (a) shall be made by statutory instrument, and
    (b) may not be made unless a draft has been laid before and approved by resolution of each House of Parliament.

[132]

NOTES

Commencement: 17 February 2009 (in so far as conferring or relating to any power to make subordinate legislation or codes of practice); 21 February 2009 (otherwise).

Order: the Banking Act 2009 (Parts 2 and 3 Consequential Amendments) Order 2009, SI 2009/317 at [524].

PART 3
BANK ADMINISTRATION

NOTES

Application to Multiple Transfers: as to the application of this Part to multiple transfers, see the Banking Act 2009 (Bank Administration) (Modification for Application to Multiple Transfers) Regulations 2009, SI 2009/313 at [509].

Banks in Temporary Public Ownership: as to the application of this Part to banks in temporary public ownership, see the Banking Act 2009 (Bank Administration) (Modification for Application to Banks in Temporary Public Ownership) Regulations 2009, SI 2009/312 at [504].

Building Societies: this Part is applied with modifications in respect of building societies, by the Building Societies (Insolvency and Special Administration) Order 2009, SI 2009/805, art 3, Sch 1, Pts 1, 3 at [557], [561], [563].

Introduction

136 Overview

(1) This Part provides for a procedure to be known as bank administration.

(2) The main features of bank administration are that—
    (a) it is used where part of the business of a bank is sold to a commercial purchaser in accordance with section 11 or transferred to a bridge bank in accordance with section 12 (and it can also be used in certain cases of multiple transfers under Part 1),
    (b) the court appoints a bank administrator on the application of the Bank of England,
    (c) the bank administrator is able and required to ensure that the non-sold or non-transferred part of the bank ("the residual bank") provides services or facilities required to enable the commercial purchaser ("the private sector purchaser") or the transferee ("the bridge bank") to operate effectively, and
    (d) in other respects the process is the same as for normal administration under the Insolvency Act 1986, subject to specified modifications.

(3) The Table describes the provisions of this Part.

Sections	*Topic*
Sections 136 to 140	Introduction
Sections 141 to 148	Process
Sections 149 to 152	Multiple transfers
Sections 153 and 154	Termination
Sections 155 to 168	Miscellaneous

[133]

NOTES
Commencement: 17 February 2009 (in so far as conferring or relating to any power to make subordinate legislation or codes of practice); 21 February 2009 (otherwise).

137 Objectives

(1)   A bank administrator has two objectives—
    (a)   Objective 1: support for commercial purchaser or bridge bank (see section 138), and
    (b)   Objective 2: "normal" administration (see section 140).

(2)   Objective 1 takes priority over Objective 2 (but a bank administrator is obliged to begin working towards both objectives immediately upon appointment).

[134]

NOTES
Commencement: 17 February 2009 (in so far as conferring or relating to any power to make subordinate legislation or codes of practice); 21 February 2009 (otherwise).

138 Objective 1: supporting private sector purchaser or bridge bank

(1)   Objective 1 is to ensure the supply to the private sector purchaser or bridge bank of such services and facilities as are required to enable it, in the opinion of the Bank of England, to operate effectively.

(2)   For the purposes of Objective 1—
    (a)   the reference to services and facilities includes a reference to acting as transferor or transferee under a supplemental or reverse property transfer instrument, and
    (b)   the reference to "supply" includes a reference to supply by persons other than the residual bank.

(3)   In the case of bank administration following a private sector purchase the bank administrator must co-operate with any request of the Bank of England to enter into an agreement for the residual bank to provide services or facilities to the private sector purchaser; and—
    (a)   in pursuing Objective 1 the bank administrator must have regard to the terms of that or any other agreement entered into between the residual bank and the private sector purchaser,
    (b)   in particular, the bank administrator must avoid action that is likely to prejudice performance by the residual bank of its obligations in accordance with those terms,
    (c)   if in doubt about the effect of those terms the bank administrator may apply to the court for directions under paragraph 63 of Schedule B1 to the Insolvency Act 1986 (applied by section 145 below), and
    (d)   the private sector purchaser may refer to the court a dispute about any agreement with the residual bank, by applying for directions under paragraph 63 of Schedule B1.

(4)   In the case of bank administration following transfer to a bridge bank, the bank administrator must co-operate with any request of the Bank of England to enter into an agreement for the residual bank to provide services or facilities to the bridge bank; and—
    (a)   the bank administrator must avoid action that is likely to prejudice performance by the residual bank of its obligations in accordance with an agreement,
    (b)   the bank administrator must ensure that so far as is reasonably practicable an agreement entered into includes provision for consideration at market rate,
    (c)   paragraph (b) does not prevent the bank administrator from entering into an agreement on any terms that the bank administrator thinks necessary in pursuit of Objective 1, and
    (d)   this subsection does not apply after Objective 1 ceases.

(5)   Where a bank administrator requires the Bank of England's consent or approval to any action in accordance with this Part, the Bank may withhold consent or approval only on the grounds that the action might prejudice the achievement of Objective 1.

[135]

NOTES
Commencement: 17 February 2009 (in so far as conferring or relating to any power to make subordinate legislation or codes of practice); 21 February 2009 (otherwise).

139 Objective 1: duration

(1)   Objective 1 ceases if the Bank of England notifies the bank administrator that the residual bank is no longer required in connection with the private sector purchaser or bridge bank.

(2)   A bank administrator who thinks that Objective 1 is no longer required may apply to the court for directions under paragraph 63 of Schedule B1 to the Insolvency Act 1986 (applied by section 145 below); and the court may direct the Bank of England to consider whether to give notice under subsection (1) above.

(3)   If immediately upon the making of a bank administration order the Bank of England thinks that the residual bank is not required in connection with the private sector purchaser or bridge bank, the Bank of England may give a notice under subsection (1).

(4)   A notice under subsection (1) is referred to in this Part as an "Objective 1 Achievement Notice".

[136]

NOTES
Commencement: 17 February 2009 (in so far as conferring or relating to any power to make subordinate legislation or codes of practice); 21 February 2009 (otherwise).

140   Objective 2: "normal" administration

(1)   Objective 2 is to—
   (a)   rescue the residual bank as a going concern ("Objective 2(a)"), or
   (b)   achieve a better result for the residual bank's creditors as a whole than would be likely if the residual bank were wound up without first being in bank administration ("Objective 2(b)").

(2)   In pursuing Objective 2 a bank administrator must aim to achieve Objective 2(a) unless of the opinion either—
   (a)   that it is not reasonably practicable to achieve it, or
   (b)   that Objective 2(b) would achieve a better result for the residual bank's creditors as a whole.

(3)   In pursuing Objective 2(b) in bank administration following transfer to a bridge bank, the bank administrator may not realise any asset unless—
   (a)   the asset is on a list of realisable assets agreed between the bank administrator and the Bank of England, or
   (b)   the Bank of England has given an Objective 1 Achievement Notice.

[137]

NOTES
Commencement: 17 February 2009 (in so far as conferring or relating to any power to make subordinate legislation or codes of practice); 21 February 2009 (otherwise).

Process

141   Bank administration order

(1)   A bank administration order is an order appointing a person as the bank administrator of a bank.

(2)   A person is eligible for appointment as a bank administrator if qualified to act as an insolvency practitioner.

(3)   An appointment may be made only if the person has consented to act.

(4)   A bank administration order takes effect in accordance with its terms; and—
   (a)   the process of a bank administration order having effect may be described as "bank administration" in relation to the bank, and
   (b)   while the order has effect the bank may be described as being "in bank administration".

[138]

NOTES
Commencement: 17 February 2009 (in so far as conferring or relating to any power to make subordinate legislation or codes of practice); 21 February 2009 (otherwise).

142   Application

(1)   An application for a bank administration order may be made to the court by the Bank of England.

(2)   An application must nominate a person to be appointed as the bank administrator.

(3)   The bank must be given notice of an application, in accordance with rules under section 411 of the Insolvency Act 1986 (as applied by section 160 below).

[139]

NOTES
Commencement: 17 February 2009 (in so far as conferring or relating to any power to make subordinate legislation or codes of practice); 21 February 2009 (otherwise).

143   Grounds for applying

(1)   The Bank of England may apply for a bank administration order in respect of a bank if the following conditions are met.

(2)   Condition 1 is that the Bank of England has made or intends to make a property transfer instrument in respect of the bank in accordance with section 11(2) or 12(2).

(3)   Condition 2 is that the Bank of England is satisfied that the residual bank—
   (a)   is unable to pay its debts, or
   (b)   is likely to become unable to pay its debts as a result of the property transfer instrument which the Bank intends to make.

[140]

NOTES

Commencement: 17 February 2009 (in so far as conferring or relating to any power to make subordinate legislation or codes of practice); 21 February 2009 (otherwise).

144   Grounds for making

(1)   The court may make a bank administration order if satisfied that the conditions in section 143 were met.

(2)   On an application for a bank administration order the court may—
   (a)   grant the application,
   (b)   adjourn the application (generally or to a specified date), or
   (c)   dismiss the application.

[141]

NOTES

Commencement: 17 February 2009 (in so far as conferring or relating to any power to make subordinate legislation or codes of practice); 21 February 2009 (otherwise).

145   General powers, duties and effect

(1)   A bank administrator may do anything necessary or expedient for the pursuit of the Objectives in section 137.

(2)   The following provisions of this section provide for—
   (a)   general powers and duties of bank administrators (by application of provisions about administrators), and
   (b)   the general process and effects of bank administration (by application of provisions about administration).

(3)   The provisions set out in the Tables apply in relation to bank administration as in relation to administration, with—
   (a)   the modifications set out in subsection (4),
   (b)   any other modification specified in the Tables, and
   (c)   any other necessary modification.

(4)   The modifications are that—
   (a)   a reference to the administrator is a reference to the bank administrator,
   (b)   a reference to administration is a reference to bank administration,
   (c)   a reference to an administration order is a reference to a bank administration order,
   (d)   a reference to a company is a reference to the bank,
   (e)   a reference to the purpose of administration is a reference to the Objectives in section 137, and
   (f)   in relation to provisions of the Insolvency Act 1986 other than Schedule B1, the modifications in section 103 above apply (but converting references into references to bank administration or administrators rather than to bank insolvency or liquidators).

(5)   Powers conferred by this Act, by the Insolvency Act 1986 (as applied) and the Companies Acts are in addition to, and not in restriction of, any existing powers of instituting proceedings against a contributory or debtor of a bank, or the estate of any contributory or debtor, for the recovery of any call or other sum.

(6)   A reference in an enactment or other document to anything done under a provision applied by this Part includes a reference to the provision as applied.

PART I
BANKING ACT 2009

TABLE 1: APPLIED PROVISIONS: INSOLVENCY ACT 1986, SCHEDULE B1		
Provision of Sch B1	*Subject*	*Modification or comment*
Para 40(1)(a)	Dismissal of pending winding-up petition	
Para 41	Dismissal of administrative or other receiver	
Para 42	Moratorium on insolvency proceedings	Ignore sub-paras (4) and (5).
Para 43	Moratorium on other legal process	(a) In the case of bank administration following transfer to a bridge bank, unless the Bank of England has given an Objective 1 Achievement Notice consent of the bank administrator may not be given for the purposes of Para 43 without the approval of the Bank of England. (b) In the case of bank administration following transfer to a bridge bank, unless the Bank of England has given an Objective 1 Achievement Notice, in considering whether to give permission under sub-Para (6) to a winding-up the court must have regard to the Objectives in section 137. (c) In considering whether to give permission for the purposes of Para 43 the court must have regard to the Objectives in section 137.
Para 44(1)(a) and (5)	Interim moratorium	
Para 46	Announcement of appointment	Ignore sub-Para (6)(b) and (c).
Paras 47 & 48	Statement of affairs	
Para 49	Administrator's proposals	(a) Para 49 does not apply unless the Bank of England has given an Objective 1 Achievement Notice; for bank administrator's proposals before the Bank of England has given an Objective 1 Achievement Notice, see section 147. (b) Treat the reference in sub-Para (1) to the purpose of administration as a reference to Objective 2. (c) Before making proposals under sub-Para (1) in the case of bank administration following transfer to a bridge bank, the bank administrator must consult the Bank of England about the chances of a payment to the residual bank from a scheme established by resolution fund order under section 49(3). (d) Treat the reference in sub-Para (2)(b) to the Objective mentioned in Para 3(1)(a) or (b) as a reference to Objective 2(a).

TABLE 1: APPLIED PROVISIONS: INSOLVENCY ACT 1986, SCHEDULE B1		
Provision of Sch B1	*Subject*	*Modification or comment*
		(e) Ignore sub-Para (3)(b).
		(f) Treat references in sub-Para (5) to the company's entering administration as references to satisfaction of the condition in Para (a) above.
Paras 50–58	Creditors' meeting	(a) Treat references in Para 51(2) to the company's entering administration as references to the giving of an Objective 1 Achievement Notice.
		(b) The bank administrator may comply with a request under Para 56(1)(a) only if satisfied that it will not prejudice pursuit of Objective 1 in section 137.
		(c) A creditors' meeting may not establish a creditors' committee in reliance on Para 57 until the Bank of England has given an Objective 1 Achievement Notice.
		(d) Until that time the Bank of England shall have the functions of the creditors' committee.
Para 59	General powers	A bank administrator may not rely on Para 59 (or subsection (1) above) for the purpose of recovering property transferred by property transfer instrument.
Para 60 and Schedule 1	General powers	(a) The exercise of powers under Schedule 1 is subject to section 137(2).
		(b) In the case of bank administration following transfer to a bridge bank, until the Bank of England has given an Objective 1 Achievement Notice powers under the following paragraphs of Schedule 1 may be exercised only with the Bank of England's consent: 2, 3, 11, 14, 15, 16, 17, 18 and 21.
Para 61	Directors	
Para 62	Power to call meetings of creditors	
Para 63	Application to court for directions	(a) Before the Bank of England has given an Objective 1 Achievement Notice, the bank administrator may apply for directions if unsure whether a proposed action would prejudice the pursuit of Objective 1; and before making an application in reliance on this paragraph the bank administrator must give notice to the Bank of England, which shall be entitled to participate in the proceedings.
		(b) In making directions the court must have regard to the Objectives in section 137.

TABLE 1: APPLIED PROVISIONS: INSOLVENCY ACT 1986, SCHEDULE B1		
Provision of Sch B1	*Subject*	*Modification or comment*
Para 64	Management powers.	
Para 65	Distribution to creditors	(a) In the case of bank administration following transfer to a bridge bank, until the Bank of England has given an Objective 1 Achievement Notice a bank administrator may make a distribution only with the Bank of England's consent. (b) Ignore sub Para (3).
Para 66	Payments	
Para 67	Taking custody of property	
Para 68	Management	Before the approval of proposals under Para 53 a bank administrator shall manage the bank's affairs, business and property in accordance with principles agreed between the bank administrator and the Bank of England.
Para 69	Agency	
Para 70	Floating charges	The bank administrator may take action only if satisfied that it will not prejudice pursuit of Objective 1 in section 137.
Para 71	Fixed charges	The court may make an order only if satisfied that it will not prejudice pursuit of Objective 1 in section 137.
Para 72	Hire-purchase property	In the case of administration following transfer to a bridge bank, until the Bank of England has given an Objective 1 Achievement Notice an application may be made only with the Bank of England's consent.
Para 73	Protection for secured and preferential creditors	(a) Treat a reference to proposals as including a reference to the principles specified in the modification of Para 68 set out above. (b) Para 73(1)(a) does not apply until the Bank of England has given an Objective 1 Achievement Notice.
Para 74	Challenge to administrator's conduct	(a) The Bank of England may make an application to the court, on any grounds, including grounds of insufficient pursuit of Objective 1 in section 137 (in addition to applications that may anyway be made under Para 74). (b) Until the Bank of England has given an Objective 1 Achievement Notice, an order may be made on the application of a creditor only if the court is satisfied that it would not prejudice pursuit of Objective 1 in section 137.

TABLE 1: APPLIED PROVISIONS: INSOLVENCY ACT 1986, SCHEDULE B1		
Provision of Sch B1	*Subject*	*Modification or comment*
Para 75	Misfeasance	In addition to applications that may anyway be made under Para 75, an application may be made by the bank administrator or the Bank of England.
Para 80	Termination: successful rescue	*See section 153.*
Para 84	Termination: no more assets for distribution	*See section 154.*
Para 85	Discharge of administration order	
Para 86	Notice to Companies Registrar of end of administration	*See section 153.*
Para 87	Resignation	A bank administrator may resign only by notice in writing— (a) to the court, copied to the Bank of England, or (b) in the case of a bank administrator appointed by the creditors' committee under Para 90, to the creditors' committee.
Para 88	Removal	Until the Bank of England has given an Objective 1 Achievement Notice, an application for an order may be made only with the Bank of England's consent.
Para 89	Disqualification	The notice under sub-Para (2) must be given to the Bank of England.
Paras 90 & 91	Replacement	(a) Until an Objective 1 Notice has been given, the Bank of England, and nobody else, may make an application under Para 91(1). (b) After that, either the Bank of England or a creditors' committee may apply. (c) Ignore Para 91(1)(b) to (e) and (2).
Para 96	Substitution of floating charge-holder	Para 96 applies to a bank administrator, but— (a) only after an Objective 1 Achievement Notice has been given, and (b) ignoring references to priority of charges.
Para 98	Discharge	Discharge takes effect— (a) where the person ceases to be bank administrator before an Objective 1 Achievement Notice has been given, at a time determined by the Bank of England, and (b) otherwise, at a time determined by resolution of the creditors' committee (for which purpose ignore sub-Para (3)).
Para 99	Vacation of office: charges and liabilities	In the application of sub-Para (3), payments may be made only—

TABLE 1: APPLIED PROVISIONS: INSOLVENCY ACT 1986, SCHEDULE B1		
Provision of Sch B1	*Subject*	*Modification or comment*
		(a) in accordance with directions of the Bank of England, and
		(b) if the Bank is satisfied that they will not prejudice Objective 1 in section 137.
Paras 100–103	Joint administrators	Until an Objective 1 Achievement Notice has been given, an application under Para 103 may be made only by the Bank of England.
Para 104	Validity	
Para 106 (and section 430 and Schedule 10)	Fines	
Paras 107–109	Extension of time limits	(a) Until an Objective 1 Achievement Notice has been given, an application under Para 107 may be made only with the Bank of England's consent. (b) In considering an application under Para 107 the court must have regard to Objective 1 in section 137. (c) In Para 108(1) "consent" means consent of the Bank of England.
Para 110	*Amendment of provisions about time*	*An order under Para 110 may amend a provision of the Schedule as it applies by virtue of this section (whether or not in the same way as it amends the provision as it applies otherwise).*
Para 111	Interpretation	
Paras 112–116	Scotland	

TABLE 2: APPLIED PROVISIONS: OTHER PROVISIONS OF THE INSOLVENCY ACT 1986		
Section	*Subject*	*Modification or comment*
Section 135	Provisional appointment	(a) Treat the reference to the presentation of a winding-up petition as a reference to the making of an application for a bank administration order. (b) Subsection (2) applies in relation to England and Wales and Scotland (and subsection (3) does not apply). (c) Ignore the reference to the official receiver. (d) Only a person who is qualified to act as an insolvency practitioner and who consents to act may be appointed.

TABLE 2: APPLIED PROVISIONS: OTHER PROVISIONS OF THE INSOLVENCY ACT 1986		
Section	*Subject*	*Modification or comment*
		(e) The court may only confer on a provisional bank administrator functions in connection with the pursuance of Objective 1; and section 138(2)(a) does not apply before a bank administration order is made. (f) A provisional bank administrator may not pursue Objective 2. (g) The appointment of a provisional bank administrator lapses on the appointment of a bank administrator. (h) Section 172(1), (2) and (5) apply to a provisional bank administrator.
Section 168(4) (and Para 13 of Schedule 4)	Discretion in managing and distributing assets	In the case of bank administration following transfer to a bridge bank, until the Bank of England has given an Objective 1 Achievement Notice distribution may be made only— (a) with the Bank of England's consent, or (b) out of assets which have been designated as realisable by agreement between the bank administrator and the Bank of England.
Section 176A	Unsecured creditors	In the case of bank administration following transfer to a bridge bank, until the Bank of England has given an Objective 1 Achievement Notice distribution may be made in reliance on s. 176A only— (a) with the Bank of England's consent, or (b) out of assets which have been designated as realisable by agreement between the bank administrator and the Bank of England.
Section 178	Disclaimer of onerous property	In the case of bank administration following transfer to a bridge bank, until the Bank of England has given an Objective 1 Achievement Notice notice of disclaimer may be given only with the Bank of England's consent.
Section 179	Disclaimer of leaseholds	
Section 180	Land subject to rentcharge	
Section 181	Disclaimer: powers of court	
Section 182	Leaseholds	
Section 188	Publicity	
Section 213	Fraudulent trading	

	TABLE 2: APPLIED PROVISIONS: OTHER PROVISIONS OF THE INSOLVENCY ACT 1986	
Section	*Subject*	*Modification or comment*
Section 214	Wrongful trading	Ignore subsection (6).
Section 233	Utilities	
Section 234	Getting in company's property	
Section 235	Co-operation with liquidator	
Section 236	Inquiry into company's dealings	
Section 237	Section 236: enforcement by court	
Section 238	Transactions at undervalue (England and Wales)	
Section 239	Preferences (England and Wales)	
Section 240	Ss. 238 & 239: relevant time	
Section 241	Orders under ss. 238 & 239	(a) In considering making an order in reliance on section 241 the court must have regard to Objective 1 of section 137. (b) Ignore subsections (2A)(a) and (3) to (3C).
Section 242	Gratuitous alienations (Scotland)	
Section 243	Unfair preferences (Scotland)	In considering the grant of a decree under subsection (5) the court must have regard to Objective 1 of section 137.
Section 244	Extortionate credit transactions	
Section 245	Avoidance of floating charges	
Section 246	Unenforceability of liens	
Sections 386 & 387, and Schedule 6 (and Schedule 4 to the Pension Schemes Act 1993)	Preferential debts	
Section 389	Offence of acting without being qualified	Treat references to acting as an insolvency practitioner as references to acting as a bank administrator.
Section 390	Persons not qualified to act	Treat references to acting as an insolvency practitioner as references to acting as a bank administrator.
Section 391	Recognised professional bodies	An order under section 391 has effect in relation to any provision applied for the purposes of bank administration.
Sections 423–425	Transactions defrauding creditors	(a) In considering granting leave under section 424(1) the court must have regard to Objective 1 of section 137.

TABLE 2: APPLIED PROVISIONS: OTHER PROVISIONS OF THE INSOLVENCY ACT 1986		
Section	*Subject*	*Modification or comment*
		(b) In considering making an order in reliance on section 425 the court must have regard to Objective 1 of section 137.
Sections 430–432 & Schedule 10	Offences	
Section 433	Statements: admissibility	For section 433(1)(a) and (b) substitute a reference to a statement prepared for the purposes of a provision of this Part.

[142]

NOTES
Commencement: 17 February 2009 (in so far as conferring or relating to any power to make subordinate legislation or codes of practice); 21 February 2009 (otherwise).

146   Status of bank administrator

A bank administrator is an officer of the court.

[143]

NOTES
Commencement: 17 February 2009 (in so far as conferring or relating to any power to make subordinate legislation or codes of practice); 21 February 2009 (otherwise).

147   Administrator's proposals

(1)   This section applies before the giving of an Objective 1 Achievement Notice (at which point paragraph 49 of Schedule B1 to the Insolvency Act 1986 applies in accordance with section 145).

(2)   The bank administrator must as soon as is reasonably practicable after appointment make a statement setting out proposals for achieving the Objectives in section 137.

(3)   The statement must say whether the bank administrator proposes to pursue Objective 2(a) or 2(b) in section 140.

(4)   The statement must have been agreed with the Bank of England.

(5)   But a bank administrator who is unable to agree a statement with the Bank of England may apply to the court for directions under paragraph 63 of Schedule B1 to the Insolvency Act 1986 (as applied by section 145); and the court may make any order, including dispensing with the need for the Bank of England's agreement.

(6)   The bank administrator must send the statement to the FSA.

(7)   The bank administrator may revise the statement (and subsections (4) to (6) apply to a revised statement as to the original).

(8)   The statement shall be treated in the same way (subject to this section) as a statement under paragraph 49 of Schedule B1 to the Insolvency Act 1986.

[144]

NOTES
Commencement: 17 February 2009 (in so far as conferring or relating to any power to make subordinate legislation or codes of practice); 21 February 2009 (otherwise).

148   Sharing information

(1)   This section applies to bank administration following transfer to a bridge bank.

(2)   Within the period of 5 days beginning with the day on which the bank administrator is appointed, the Bank of England must give the bank administrator information about the financial positions of the residual bank and the bridge bank.

(3)   While the residual bank is in bank administration the bridge bank must give the bank administrator on request information about the financial position of the bridge bank that the bank administrator requires for the purposes of pursuing Objective 1 in section 137.

(4)   Until the Bank of England has given an Objective 1 Achievement Notice, the bank administrator must—

(a)   give the Bank of England information on request,

(b)   allow the Bank of England access to records on request,

(c)   give the bridge bank information on request,

(d)   allow the bridge bank access to records on request,

(e)   keep the Bank of England informed about, and allow the Bank to participate in, any discussions between the bank administrator and another person which relate to, or are likely to affect, pursuit of Objective 1 in section 137, and

(f)   keep the bridge bank informed about, and allow the bridge bank to participate in, any discussions between the bank administrator and another person which relate to, or are likely to affect, pursuit of Objective 1 in section 137.

(5)   The Treasury shall by regulations prescribe—

(a)   the classes of information that must be provided under subsections (2) to (4), and

(b)   the classes of record to which access must be allowed under subsection (4).

(6)   Regulations under subsection (5)—

(a)   shall be made by statutory instrument, and

(b)   shall be subject to annulment in pursuance of a resolution of either House of Parliament.

[145]

NOTES

Commencement: 17 February 2009 (in so far as conferring or relating to any power to make subordinate legislation or codes of practice); 21 February 2009 (otherwise).

Regulations: the Bank Administration (Sharing Information) Regulations 2009, SI 2009/314 at **[513]**.

Multiple transfers

149 General application of this Part

(1)   This section applies where more than one property transfer instrument is made in respect of a bank.

(2)   For that purpose "property transfer instrument" includes—

(a)   supplemental instruments under section 42,

(b)   onward property transfer instruments under section 43, and

(c)   property transfer orders under section 45.

(3)   This Part applies to the bank with any modifications specified by the Treasury in regulations.

(4)   The regulations—

(a)   shall be made by statutory instrument, and

(b)   may not be made unless a draft has been laid before and approved by resolution of each House of Parliament.

[146]

NOTES

Commencement: 17 February 2009 (in so far as conferring or relating to any power to make subordinate legislation or codes of practice); 21 February 2009 (otherwise).

Regulations: the Banking Act 2009 (Bank Administration) (Modification for Application to Multiple Transfers) Regulations 2009, SI 2009/313 at **[509]**.

150 Bridge bank to private purchaser

(1)   This section applies where the Bank of England gives a bank administrator—

(a)   an Objective 1 Achievement Notice in respect of a bridge bank, and

(b)   notice that Objective 1 is still required to be pursued in respect of a commercial purchaser who has acquired all or part of the business of the bridge bank.

(2)   An Objective 1 Achievement Notice accompanied by a notice under subsection (1)(b) is referred to in this Part as an Objective 1 Interim Achievement Notice.

(3)   Where an Objective 1 Interim Achievement Notice is given, Objective 1 continues to apply—

(a)   in accordance with section 138(3), and

(b)   with the commercial purchaser being treated as the "private sector purchaser".

(4)   An Objective 1 Interim Achievement Notice in respect of the bridge bank—

(a)   has effect as between the bank administrator and the bridge bank, but

(b)   has no other effect for the purposes of provisions of this Part which refer to the giving of an Objective 1 Achievement Notice.

(5)   When the Bank of England gives the bank administrator an Objective 1 Achievement Notice in respect of the commercial purchaser, section 139 and other provisions of this Part which refer to the giving of an Objective 1 Achievement Notice shall have effect.

[147]

PART I
BANKING ACT 2009

NOTES
Commencement: 17 February 2009 (in so far as conferring or relating to any power to make subordinate legislation or codes of practice); 21 February 2009 (otherwise).

151 Property transfer from bridge bank

(1)   This section applies where the Bank of England—
  (a)   transfers all or part of the business of a bank ("the original bank") to a bridge bank ("the original bridge bank") by making a property transfer instrument in accordance with section 12(2), and
  (b)   later makes or proposes to make an onward property transfer instrument under section 43(2) from the bridge bank to a transferee ("the onward transferee").

(2)   If the onward transferee is a company which is wholly owned by the Bank of England—
  (a)   the onward transferee is treated as a bridge bank for the purposes of this Part, and
  (b)   the original bridge bank is treated as a residual bank for the purposes of this Part.

(3)   In any other case, the Bank of England may determine that the original bridge bank is to be treated as a residual bank for the purposes of this Part.

(4)   Where the original bridge bank is put into bank administration in reliance on subsection (2)(b), Objective 1 shall apply in accordance with section 138(4) in relation to both—
  (a)   services provided by the original bank to the original bridge bank, and
  (b)   services provided by the original bridge bank to the onward transferee.

(5)   Where the original bridge bank is put into bank administration in reliance on a determination under subsection (3), Objective 1 shall apply in accordance with—
  (a)   section 138(3) in relation to services provided by the original bridge bank to the onward transferee, and
  (b)   section 138(4) in relation to services provided by the original bank to the original bridge bank.

(6)   But the Bank may determine—
  (a)   that subsection (5) does not apply, and
  (b)   that section 150 shall apply as if the Bank had given—
    (i)   an Objective 1 Interim Achievement Notice in respect of the original bridge bank, and
    (ii)   a notice under section 150(1)(b) in respect of the onward transferee.

[148]

NOTES
Commencement: 17 February 2009 (in so far as conferring or relating to any power to make subordinate legislation or codes of practice); 21 February 2009 (otherwise).

152 Property transfer from temporary public ownership

(1)   This section applies where the Treasury—
  (a)   make a share transfer order, in respect of securities issued by a bank (or a bank's holding company), in accordance with section 13(2), and
  (b)   later make a property transfer order from the bank (or from another bank which is or was in the same group as the bank) under section 45(2).

(2)   This Part applies to the transferor under the property transfer order as to the transferor under a property transfer instrument.

(3)   For that purpose this Part applies with any modifications specified by the Treasury in regulations; and the regulations—
  (a)   shall be made by statutory instrument, and
  (b)   may not be made unless a draft has been laid before and approved by resolution of each House of Parliament.

[149]

NOTES
Commencement: 17 February 2009 (in so far as conferring or relating to any power to make subordinate legislation or codes of practice); 21 February 2009 (otherwise).
Regulations: the Banking Act 2009 (Bank Administration) (Modification for Application to Banks in Temporary Public Ownership) Regulations 2009, SI 2009/312 at **[504]**.

Termination

153 Successful rescue

(1)   This section applies if—
  (a)   the Bank of England has given an Objective 1 Achievement Notice, and

(b)   the bank administrator has pursued Objective 2(a) in section 140 and believes that it has been achieved.

(2)   The bank administrator may give a notice under paragraph 80 of Schedule B1 to the Insolvency Act 1986 (notice bringing administrator's appointment to an end on achievement of objectives).

(3)   A bank administrator who gives a notice in accordance with subsection (2) must send a copy to the FSA.

(4)   Failure without reasonable excuse to comply with subsection (3) is an offence.

[150]

NOTES

Commencement: 17 February 2009 (in so far as conferring or relating to any power to make subordinate legislation or codes of practice); 21 February 2009 (otherwise).

154   Winding-up or voluntary arrangement

(1)   This section applies if—
  (a)   the Bank of England has given an Objective 1 Achievement Notice, and
  (b)   the bank administrator pursues Objective 2(b) in section 140.

(2)   The bank administrator may—
  (a)   give a notice under paragraph 84 of Schedule B1 to the Insolvency Act 1986 (no more assets for distribution), or
  (b)   make a proposal in accordance with section 1 of that Act (company voluntary arrangement).

(3)   Part 1 of that Act shall apply to a proposal made by a bank administrator, with the following modifications.

(4)   In section 3 (summoning of meetings) subsection (2) (and not (1)) applies.

(5)   The action that may be taken by the court under section 5(3) (effect of approval) includes suspension of the bank administration order.

(6)   On the termination of a company voluntary arrangement the bank administrator may apply to the court to lift the suspension of the bank administration order.

(7)   The bank administrator may not act under subsection (2) above unless satisfied that the bank has received any funds it is likely to receive from any scheme under a resolution fund order under section 52.

[151]

NOTES

Commencement: 17 February 2009 (in so far as conferring or relating to any power to make subordinate legislation or codes of practice); 21 February 2009 (otherwise).

Miscellaneous

155   Disqualification of directors

(1)   In this section "the Disqualification Act" means the Company Directors Disqualification Act 1986.

(2)   In the Disqualification Act—
  (a)   a reference to liquidation includes a reference to bank administration,
  (b)   a reference to winding up includes a reference to making or being subject to a bank administration order,
  (c)   a reference to becoming insolvent includes a reference to becoming subject to a bank administration order, and
  (d)   a reference to a liquidator includes a reference to a bank administrator.

(3)   For the purposes of the application of section 7(3) of the Disqualification Act (disqualification order or undertaking) to a bank which is subject to a bank administration order, the responsible office-holder is the bank administrator.

(4)   (*Inserts the Company Directors Disqualification Act 1986, s 21B at* **[348]**.)

[152]

NOTES

Commencement: 17 February 2009 (in so far as conferring or relating to any power to make subordinate legislation or codes of practice); 21 February 2009 (otherwise).

156   Application of other law

(1)   The Secretary of State and the Treasury may by order made jointly—

(a) provide for an enactment about insolvency or administration to apply to bank administration (with or without specified modifications);

(b) amend, or modify the application of, an enactment about insolvency or administration in consequence of this Part.

(2) An order under subsection (1)—

(a) shall be made by statutory instrument, and

(b) may not be made unless a draft has been laid before and approved by resolution of each House of Parliament.

[153]

NOTES
Commencement: 17 February 2009 (in so far as conferring or relating to any power to make subordinate legislation or codes of practice); 21 February 2009 (otherwise).

157 Other processes

(1) Before exercising an insolvency power in respect of a residual bank the FSA must give notice to the Bank of England, which may participate in any proceedings arising out of the exercise of the power.

(2) In subsection (1)—

(a) "residual bank" means a bank all or part of whose business has been transferred to a commercial purchaser in accordance with section 11 or to a bridge bank in accordance with section 12, and

(b) "insolvency power" means—

(i) section 359 of the Financial Services and Markets Act 2000 (application for administration order), and

(ii) section 367 of that Act (winding-up petition).

[154]

NOTES
Commencement: 17 February 2009 (in so far as conferring or relating to any power to make subordinate legislation or codes of practice); 21 February 2009 (otherwise).

158 Building societies

(1) The Treasury may by order provide for this Part to apply to building societies (within the meaning of section 119 of the Building Societies Act 1986) as it applies to banks, subject to modifications set out in the order.

(2) An order may—

(a) amend the Building Societies Act 1986 or any other enactment which relates, or in so far as it relates, to building societies;

(b) amend an enactment amended by this Part;

(c) replicate, with or without modifications, a provision of this Part;

(d) apply a provision made under or by virtue of this Part, with or without modifications, to this Part as it applies to building societies.

(3) An order—

(a) shall be made by statutory instrument, and

(b) may not be made unless a draft has been laid before and approved by resolution of each House of Parliament.

(4) Provision made under or by virtue of this Part may make special provision in relation to the application of this Part to building societies.

[155]

NOTES
Commencement: 17 February 2009 (in so far as conferring or relating to any power to make subordinate legislation or codes of practice); 21 February 2009 (otherwise).
Note: On 21 July 2009 HM Treasury issued a consultation paper, Special resolution regime: the Building Societies (Insolvency and Special Administration) Order 2009 and related insolvency rules, and financial assistance to building societies to consult fully on the application of the Banking Act 2009 to building societies as the resolution procedures for building societies were not set out on the face of the Banking Act 2009 and time had not previously allowed for consultation before the new regime came into place. The closing date for this consultation paper is 30 October 2009. Following the consultation, HM Treasury will consider whether to bring forward proposals to amend the rules.
Order: the Building Societies (Insolvency and Special Administration) Order 2009, SI 2009/805 at **[556]**.

159 Credit unions

(1)   The Treasury may by order provide for this Part to apply to credit unions (within the meaning of section 31 of the Credit Unions Act 1979) as it applies to banks, subject to modifications set out in the order.

(2)   An order may—
   (a)   amend the Credit Union Act 1979, the Industrial and Providential Societies Act 1965 or any other enactment which relates, or in so far as it relates, to credit unions;
   (b)   amend an enactment amended by this Part;
   (c)   replicate, with or without modifications, a provision of this Part;
   (d)   apply a provision made under or by virtue of this Part, with or without modifications, to this Part as it applies to credit unions.

(3)   An order—
   (a)   shall be made by statutory instrument, and
   (b)   may not be made unless a draft has been laid before and approved by resolution of each House of Parliament.

(4)   Provision made under or by virtue of this Part may make special provision in relation to the application of this Part to credit unions.

[156]

NOTES

Commencement: 17 February 2009 (in so far as conferring or relating to any power to make subordinate legislation or codes of practice); 21 February 2009 (otherwise).

Credit union: the Credit Unions Act 1979, s 31, provides that "credit union" means a society registered under the Industrial and Provident Societies Act 1965 by virtue of s 1 of the 1979 Act.

160–162   (*S 160 amends the Insolvency Act 1986, ss 411, 413 at* **[299]**, **[300]***; s 161 amends s 414 of the 1986 Act at* **[301]***; s 162 amends s 433 of the 1986 Act at* **[310]**.)

163 Partnerships

(1)   The Lord Chancellor may, by order made with the concurrence of the Secretary of State and the Lord Chief Justice, modify provisions of this Part in their application to partnerships.

(2)   For procedural purposes an order under subsection (1) shall be treated in the same way as an order under section 420 of the Insolvency Act 1986 (partnerships).

(3)   This section does not apply in relation to partnerships constituted under the law of Scotland.

[157]

NOTES

Commencement: 17 February 2009 (in so far as conferring or relating to any power to make subordinate legislation or codes of practice); 21 February 2009 (otherwise).

164 Scottish partnerships

(1)   The Secretary of State may by order modify provisions of this Part in their application to partnerships constituted under the law of Scotland.

(2)   An order—
   (a)   shall be made by statutory instrument, and
   (b)   shall be subject to annulment in pursuance of a resolution of either House of Parliament.

[158]

NOTES

Commencement: 17 February 2009 (in so far as conferring or relating to any power to make subordinate legislation or codes of practice); 21 February 2009 (otherwise).

165 Co-operation between courts

(1)   Provisions of or by virtue of this Part are "insolvency law" for the purposes of section 426 of the Insolvency Act 1986 (co-operation between courts).

(2)   (*Amends the Insolvency Act 1986, s 426 at* **[306]**.)

[159]

NOTES

Commencement: 17 February 2009 (in so far as conferring or relating to any power to make subordinate legislation or codes of practice); 21 February 2009 (otherwise).

166 Interpretation: general

(1)   In this Part "the court" means—

    (a)   in England and Wales, the High Court,

    (b)   in Scotland, the Court of Session, and

    (c)   in Northern Ireland, the High Court.

(2)   In this Part "the FSA" means the Financial Services Authority.

(3)   For the purposes of a reference in this Part to inability to pay debts—

    (a)   a bank that is in default on an obligation to pay a sum due and payable under an agreement, is to be treated as unable to pay its debts, and

    (b)   section 123 of the Insolvency Act 1986 (inability to pay debts) also applies; and

for the purposes of paragraph (a) "agreement" means an agreement the making or performance of which constitutes or is part of a regulated activity carried on by the bank.

(4)   Expressions used in this Part and in the Insolvency Act 1986 have the same meaning as in that Act.

(5)   Expressions used in this Part and in the Companies Act 2006 have the same meaning as in that Act.

(6)   A reference in this Part to action includes a reference to inaction.

[160]

NOTES

Commencement: 17 February 2009 (in so far as conferring or relating to any power to make subordinate legislation or codes of practice); 21 February 2009 (otherwise).

167   Northern Ireland

In the application of this Part to Northern Ireland—

    (a)   a reference to an enactment is to be treated as a reference to the equivalent enactment having effect in relation to Northern Ireland,

    (b)   where this Part amends an enactment an equivalent amendment (incorporating any necessary modification) is made to the equivalent enactment having effect in relation to Northern Ireland,

    (c)   the reference in section 159 to section 31 of the Credit Unions Act 1979 is to be treated as a reference to Article 2 of the Credit Unions (Northern Ireland) Order 1985, and

    (d)   in section 163—

        (i)   the reference to the Secretary of State is to be treated as a reference to the Department for Enterprise, Trade and Investment, and

        (ii)   the reference to the Lord Chief Justice is a reference to the Lord Chief Justice in Northern Ireland.

[161]

NOTES

Commencement: 17 February 2009 (in so far as conferring or relating to any power to make subordinate legislation or codes of practice); 21 February 2009 (otherwise).

168   Consequential provision

(1)   The Treasury may by order make provision in consequence of this Part.

(2)   An order may, in particular, amend or modify the effect of an enactment (including a fiscal enactment) passed before the commencement of this Part.

(3)   An order—

    (a)   shall be made by statutory instrument, and

    (b)   may not be made unless a draft has been laid before and approved by resolution of each House of Parliament.

[162]

NOTES

Commencement: 17 February 2009 (in so far as conferring or relating to any power to make subordinate legislation or codes of practice); 21 February 2009 (otherwise).

Order: the Banking Act 2009 (Parts 2 and 3 Consequential Amendments) Order 2009, SI 2009/317 at **[524]**.

PART 4
FINANCIAL SERVICES COMPENSATION SCHEME

169   Overview

This Part makes a number of amendments in connection with the Financial Services Compensation Scheme provided for by Part 15 of the Financial Services and Markets Act 2000.

[163]

PART 1
BANKING ACT 2009

NOTES
Commencement: 17 February 2009 (in so far as conferring or relating to any power to make subordinate legislation or codes of practice); 21 February 2009 (otherwise).

170–180   (*Ss 170–180 contain the following amendments to Part XV of the Financial Services and Markets Act 2000 (Part XV is at* **[383]** *et seq): s 170 inserts s 214A of the 2000 Act and amends ss 213, 218; s 171 inserts s 214B of the 2000 Act and amends s 223; s 172 inserts s 223A of the 2000 Act; s 173 inserts s 223B of the 2000 Act; s 174 inserts s 214(1A)–(1C) of the 2000 Act and amends s 417; s 175 amends s 215 of the 2000 Act; s 176 inserts s 218A of the 2000 Act and amends s 219; s 177 inserts s 223C of the 2000 Act; s 178 amends s 429 of the 2000 Act; s 179 inserts s 221A of the 2000 Act and amends s 222; s 180 inserts s 224A of the 2000 Act.*)

PART 5
INTER-BANK PAYMENT SYSTEMS
Introduction

181   Overview
This Part enables the Bank of England to oversee certain systems for payments between financial institutions.

[164]

NOTES
Commencement: 4 August 2009.

182   Interpretation: "inter-bank payment system"
(1)   In this Part "inter-bank payment system" means arrangements designed to facilitate or control the transfer of money between financial institutions who participate in the arrangements.

(2)   The fact that persons other than financial institutions can participate does not prevent arrangements from being an inter-bank payment system.

(3)   In subsection (1) "financial institutions" means—
  (a)   banks, and
  (b)   building societies.

(4)   In subsection (1) "money" includes credit.

(5)   A system is an inter-bank payment system for the purposes of this Part whether or not it operates wholly or partly in relation to persons or places outside the United Kingdom.

[165]

NOTES
Commencement: 4 August 2009.

183   Interpretation: other expressions
In this Part—
  (a)   a reference to the "operator" of an inter-bank payment system is a reference to any person with responsibility under the system for managing or operating it,
  (b)   a reference to the operation of a system includes a reference to its management,
  (c)   "the UK financial system" has the meaning given to "the financial system" by section 3(2) of the Financial Services and Markets Act 2000 (market confidence),
  (d)   a reference to the Bank of England's role as a monetary authority is to be construed in accordance with section 244(2)(c), and
  (e)   "the FSA" means the Financial Services Authority.

[166]

NOTES
Commencement: 4 August 2009.

Recognised systems

184   Recognition order
(1)   The Treasury may by order ("recognition order") specify an inter-bank payment system as a recognised system for the purposes of this Part.

(2)   A recognition order must specify in as much detail as is reasonably practicable the arrangements which constitute the inter-bank payment system.

(3)   The Treasury may not specify an inter-bank system operated solely by the Bank of England.
[167]

PART I
BANKING ACT 2009

NOTES
Commencement: 4 August 2009.

185   Recognition criteria

(1)   The Treasury may make a recognition order in respect of an inter-bank payment system only if satisfied that any deficiencies in the design of the system, or any disruption of its operation, would be likely—
(a)   to threaten the stability of, or confidence in, the UK financial system, or
(b)   to have serious consequences for business or other interests throughout the United Kingdom.

(2)   In considering whether to specify a system the Treasury must have regard to—
(a)   the number and value of the transactions that the system presently processes or is likely to process in the future,
(b)   the nature of the transactions that the system processes,
(c)   whether those transactions or their equivalent could be handled by other systems,
(d)   the relationship between the system and other systems, and
(e)   whether the system is used by the Bank of England in the course of its role as a monetary authority.
[168]

NOTES
Commencement: 4 August 2009.

186   Procedure

(1)   Before making a recognition order in respect of a payment system the Treasury must—
(a)   consult the Bank of England,
(b)   notify the operator of the system, and
(c)   consider any representations made.

(2)   The Treasury must also consult the FSA before making a recognition order in respect of a payment system the operator of which—
(a)   is, or has applied to become, a recognised investment exchange within the meaning of section 285 of the Financial Services and Markets Act 2000,
(b)   is, or has applied to become, a recognised clearing house within the meaning of that section, or
(c)   has, or has applied for, permission under Part 4 of that Act (regulated activities).

(3)   In considering whether to make a recognition order in respect of a payment system the Treasury may rely on information provided by the Bank of England or the FSA.
[169]

NOTES
Commencement: 4 August 2009.

187   De-recognition

(1)   The Treasury may revoke a recognition order.

(2)   The Treasury must revoke a recognition order if not satisfied that the criteria in section 185 are met in respect of the recognised inter-bank payment system.

(3)   Before revoking a recognition order the Treasury must—
(a)   consult the Bank of England,
(b)   notify the operator of the recognised inter-bank payment system, and
(c)   consider any representations made.

(4)   The Treasury must also consult the FSA before revoking a recognition order in respect of a payment system the operator of which—
(a)   is, or has applied to become, a recognised investment exchange within the meaning of section 285 of the Financial Services and Markets Act 2000,
(b)   is, or has applied to become, a recognised clearing house within the meaning of that section, or
(c)   has, or has applied for, permission under Part 4 of that Act (regulated activities).

(5)   The Treasury must consider any request by the operator of a recognised inter-bank payment system for the revocation of its recognition order.
[170]

NOTES
Commencement: 4 August 2009.

Regulation

188 Principles

(1)   The Bank of England may publish principles to which operators of recognised inter-bank payment systems are to have regard in operating the systems.

(2)   Before publishing principles the Bank must obtain the approval of the Treasury.

[171]

NOTES
Commencement: to be appointed.

189 Codes of practice

The Bank of England may publish codes of practice about the operation of recognised inter-bank payment systems.

[172]

NOTES
Commencement: to be appointed.

190 System rules

(1)   The Bank of England may require the operator of a recognised inter-bank payment system—

(a)   to establish rules for the operation of the system;
(b)   to change the rules in a specified way or so as to achieve a specified purpose;
(c)   to notify the Bank of any proposed change to the rules;
(d)   not to change the rules without the approval of the Bank.

(2)   A requirement under subsection (1)(c) or (d) may be general or specific.

[173]

NOTES
Commencement: to be appointed.

191 Directions

(1)   The Bank of England may give directions to the operator of a recognised inter-bank payment system.

(2)   A direction may—

(a)   require or prohibit the taking of specified action in the operation of the system;
(b)   set standards to be met in the operation of the system.

(3)   Before giving a direction the Bank must notify the Treasury.

(4)   The Treasury may by order confer immunity from liability in damages in respect of action or inaction in accordance with a direction.

(5)   An immunity does not extend to action or inaction—

(a)   in bad faith, or
(b)   in contravention of section 6(1) of the Human Rights Act 1998.

(6)   An order—

(a)   shall be made by statutory instrument, and
(b)   shall be subject to annulment in pursuance of a resolution of either House of Parliament.

[174]

NOTES
Commencement: to be appointed.

192 Role of FSA

(1)   In exercising powers under this Part the Bank of England shall have regard to any action that the FSA has taken or could take.

(2)   Before taking action under this Part in respect of a recognised inter-bank payment system the operator of which satisfies section 186(2), the Bank of England must consult the FSA.

(3)   If the FSA gives the Bank of England notice that the FSA is considering taking action in respect of the operator of a recognised inter-bank payment system who satisfies section 186(2), the Bank may not take action under this Part in respect of the operator unless—
  (a)   the FSA consents, or
  (b)   the notice is withdrawn.

[175]

NOTES
Commencement: to be appointed.

Enforcement

193   Inspection

(1)   The Bank of England may appoint one or more persons to inspect the operation of a recognised inter-bank payment system.

(2)   The operator of a recognised inter-bank payment system must—
  (a)   grant an inspector access, on request and at any reasonable time, to premises on or from which any part of the system is operated, and
  (b)   otherwise co-operate with an inspector.

[176]

NOTES
Commencement: to be appointed.

194   Inspection: warrant

(1)   A justice of the peace may on the application of an inspector issue a warrant entitling an inspector or a constable to enter premises if—
  (a)   any part of the management or operation of a recognised inter-bank payment system is conducted on the premises (whether by an operator of the system or by someone providing services used by an operator), and
  (b)   any of the following conditions is satisfied.

(2)   Condition 1 is that—
  (a)   a requirement under section 204 in connection with the payment system has not been complied with, and
  (b)   there is reason to believe that information relevant to the requirement is on the premises.

(3)   Condition 2 is that there is reason to suspect that if a requirement under section 204 were imposed in connection with the payment system in respect of information on the premises—
  (a)   the requirement would not be complied with, and
  (b)   the information would be destroyed or otherwise tampered with.

(4)   Condition 3 is that an inspector—
  (a)   gave reasonable notice of a wish to enter the premises, and
  (b)   was refused entry.

(5)   Condition 4 is that a person occupying or managing the premises has failed to co-operate with an inspector.

(6)   A warrant—
  (a)   permits an inspector or a constable to enter the premises,
  (b)   permits an inspector or a constable to search the premises and copy or take possession of information or documents, and
  (c)   permits a constable to use reasonable force.

(7)   Sections 15(5) to (8) and 16 of the Police and Criminal Evidence Act 1984 (warrants: procedure) apply to warrants under this section.

(8)   In the application of this section to Scotland—
  (a)   the reference to a justice of the peace includes a reference to a sheriff, and
  (b)   ignore subsection (7).

(9)   In the application of this section to Northern Ireland—
  (a)   the reference to a justice of the peace is a reference to a lay magistrate, and
  (b)   the reference to sections 15(5) to (8) and 16 of the Police and Criminal Evidence Act 1984 is a reference to the equivalent provisions of the Police and Criminal Evidence (Northern Ireland) Order 1989.

[177]

NOTES
Commencement: to be appointed.

PART I
BANKING ACT 2009

195 Independent report

(1)   The Bank of England may require the operator of a recognised inter-bank payment system to appoint an expert to report on the operation of the system.

(2)   The Bank may impose a requirement only if it thinks—
  (a)   the operator is not taking sufficient account of principles published by the Bank under section 188,
  (b)   the operator is failing to comply with a code of practice under section 189, or
  (c)   the report is likely for any other reason to assist the Bank in the performance of its functions under this Part.

(3)   The Bank may impose requirements about—
  (a)   the nature of the expert to be appointed;
  (b)   the content of the report;
  (c)   treatment of the report (including disclosure and publication);
  (d)   timing.

[178]

NOTES
Commencement: to be appointed.

196 Compliance failure

In this Part "compliance failure" means a failure by the operator of a recognised inter-bank payment system to—
  (a)   comply with a code of practice under section 189,
  (b)   comply with a requirement under section 190,
  (c)   comply with a direction under section 191, or
  (d)   ensure compliance with a requirement under section 195.

[179]

NOTES
Commencement: to be appointed.

197 Publication

(1)   The Bank of England may publish details of a compliance failure by the operator of a recognised inter-bank payment system.

(2)   The Bank may publish details of a sanction imposed under sections 198 to 200.

[180]

NOTES
Commencement: to be appointed.

198 Penalty

(1)   The Bank of England may require the operator of a recognised inter-bank payment system to pay a penalty in respect of a compliance failure.

(2)   A penalty—
  (a)   must be paid to the Bank of England, and
  (b)   may be enforced by the Bank as a debt.

(3)   The Bank must prepare a statement of the principles which it will apply in determining—
  (a)   whether to impose a penalty, and
  (b)   the amount of a penalty.

(4)   The Bank must—
  (a)   publish the statement on its internet website,
  (b)   send a copy to the Treasury,
  (c)   review the statement from time to time and revise it if necessary (and paragraphs (a) and (b) apply to a revision), and
  (d)   in applying the statement to a compliance failure, apply the version in force when the failure occurred.

[181]

NOTES
Commencement: to be appointed.

199 Closure

(1)   This section applies if the Bank of England thinks that a compliance failure—

(a)　　threatens the stability of, or confidence in, the UK financial system, or

(b)　　has serious consequences for business or other interests throughout the United Kingdom.

(2)　　The Bank may give the operator of the inter-bank payment system concerned an order to stop operating the system (a "closure order")—

(a)　　for a specified period,

(b)　　until further notice, or

(c)　　permanently.

(3)　　A closure order may apply to—

(a)　　all activities of the payment system, or

(b)　　specified activities.

(4)　　An operator who fails to comply with a closure order commits an offence.

(5)　　A person guilty of an offence is liable—

(a)　　on summary conviction, to a fine not exceeding the statutory maximum, or

(b)　　on conviction on indictment, to a fine.

[182]

NOTES

Commencement: to be appointed.

200　Management disqualification

(1)　　The Bank of England may by order prohibit a specified person from being an operator of a recognised inter-bank payment system—

(a)　　for a specified period,

(b)　　until further notice, or

(c)　　permanently.

(2)　　The Bank may by order prohibit a specified person from holding an office or position involving responsibility for taking decisions about the management of a recognised inter-bank payment system—

(a)　　for a specified period,

(b)　　until further notice, or

(c)　　permanently.

(3)　　A person who breaches a prohibition under subsection (1) or (2) commits an offence.

(4)　　A person guilty of an offence is liable—

(a)　　on summary conviction, to a fine not exceeding the statutory maximum, or

(b)　　on conviction on indictment, to a fine.

[183]

NOTES

Commencement: to be appointed.

201　Warning

(1)　　Before imposing a sanction on the operator of an inter-bank payment system or on another person the Bank of England must—

(a)　　give the operator or other person a notice (a "warning notice"),

(b)　　give the operator or other person at least 21 days to make representations,

(c)　　consider any representations made, and

(d)　　as soon as is reasonably practicable, give the operator or other person a notice stating whether or not the Bank intends to impose the sanction.

(2)　　In subsection (1) "imposing a sanction" means—

(a)　　publishing details under section 197(1),

(b)　　requiring the payment of a penalty under section 198,

(c)　　giving a closure order under section 199, or

(d)　　making an order under section 200.

(3)　　Despite subsection (1), if satisfied that it is necessary the Bank may without notice—

(a)　　give a closure order under section 199, or

(b)　　make an order under section 200.

[184]

NOTES

Commencement: to be appointed.

PART I
BANKING ACT 2009

202 Appeal

(1)   Where the Bank of England notifies a person under section 201(1)(d) that the Bank intends to impose a sanction, the person may appeal to the Financial Services and Markets Tribunal.

(2)   Where the Bank of England imposes a sanction on a person without notice in reliance on section 201(3), the person may appeal to the Financial Services and Markets Tribunal.

(3)   Part 9 of the Financial Services and Markets Act 2000 applies to appeals under this section; and for that purpose—

    (a)   a reference to the FSA is to be taken as a reference to the Bank of England,

    (b)   for section 133(9) of that Act substitute the proposition that a sanction may not be imposed while an appeal could be brought or is pending.

    (c)   Part 9 is to be read with any other necessary modifications.

[185]

NOTES

Commencement: to be appointed.

Miscellaneous

203 Fees

(1)   The Bank of England may require operators of recognised inter-bank payment systems to pay fees.

(2)   A requirement under subsection (1) must relate to a scale of fees approved by the Treasury by regulations.

(3)   Regulations under subsection (2)—

    (a)   shall be made by statutory instrument, and

    (b)   shall be subject to annulment in pursuance of a resolution of either House of Parliament.

(4)   A requirement under subsection (1) may be enforced by the Bank as a debt.

[186]

NOTES

Commencement: to be appointed.

204 Information

(1)   The Bank of England may by notice in writing require a person to provide information—

    (a)   which the Bank thinks will help the Treasury in determining whether to make a recognition order, or

    (b)   which the Bank otherwise requires in connection with its functions under this Part.

(2)   In particular, a notice may require the operator of a recognised inter-bank payment system to notify the Bank if events of a specified kind occur.

(3)   A notice may require information to be provided—

    (a)   in a specified form or manner;

    (b)   at a specified time;

    (c)   in respect of a specified period.

(4)   The Bank may disclose information obtained by virtue of this section to—

    (a)   the Treasury;

    (b)   the FSA;

    (c)   an authority in a country or territory outside the United Kingdom which exercises functions similar to those of the Treasury, the Bank of England or the FSA in relation to inter-bank payment systems;

    (d)   the European Central Bank;

    (e)   the Bank for International Settlements.

(5)   Subsection (4)—

    (a)   overrides a contractual or other requirement to keep information in confidence, and

    (b)   is without prejudice to any other power to disclose information.

(6)   The Treasury may by regulations permit the disclosure of information obtained by virtue of this section to a specified person.

(7)   The Bank may publish information obtained by virtue of this section.

(8)   The Treasury may make regulations about the manner and extent of publication under subsection (7).

(9)   Regulations under this section—

    (a)   shall be made by statutory instrument, and

    (b)   shall be subject to annulment in pursuance of a resolution of either House of Parliament.

(10) It is an offence—
  (a) to fail without reasonable excuse to comply with a requirement under this section;
  (b) knowingly or recklessly to give false information in pursuance of this section.

(11) A person guilty of an offence is liable—
  (a) on summary conviction, to a fine not exceeding the statutory maximum, or
  (b) on conviction on indictment, to a fine.

[187]

NOTES
Commencement: 4 August 2009 (sub-ss (1)(a), (2), (3), (4)(a), (b), (5), (6), (8)–(11)); to be appointed (otherwise).

205 Pretending to be recognised

(1) It is an offence for the operator of a non-recognised inter-bank payment system—
  (a) to assert that the system is recognised, or
  (b) to do anything which suggests that the system is recognised.

(2) A person guilty of an offence is liable—
  (a) on summary conviction, to a fine not exceeding the statutory maximum, or
  (b) on conviction on indictment, to a fine.

[188]

NOTES
Commencement: 4 August 2009.

206 Saving for informal oversight

(1) Nothing in this Part prevents the Bank of England from having dealings with the operators of payment systems to which this Part does not apply.

(2) Nothing in this Part prevents the Bank from having dealings, other than through the provisions of this Part, with the operators of payment systems to which this Part does apply.

[189]

NOTES
Commencement: to be appointed.

207–227 (*Part 6 (Banknotes: Scotland and Northern Ireland) outside the scope of this work.*)

PART 7
MISCELLANEOUS

Treasury support for banks

228 Consolidated Fund

(1) There shall be paid out of money provided by Parliament expenditure incurred—
  (a) by the Treasury for any purpose in connection with Parts 1 to 3 of this Act,
  (b) by the Treasury, or by the Secretary of State with the consent of the Treasury, in respect of, or in connection with giving, financial assistance to or in respect of a bank or other financial institution (other than in respect of loans made in accordance with section 229), or
  (c) by the Treasury in respect of financial assistance to the Bank of England.

(2) For the purpose of subsection (1)(b) expenditure is incurred in respect of financial assistance in respect of banks or other financial institutions if it is incurred in respect of an activity, transaction or arrangement, or class of activity, transaction or arrangement, which is expected to facilitate any part of the business of one or more banks or other financial institutions; and for that purpose it does not matter—
  (a) whether or not that is the sole or principal expected effect of the activity, transaction or arrangement, or
  (b) whether the sole or principal motive for the activity, transaction or arrangement is (i) its effect on banks or other financial institutions, (ii) its effect on the economy as a whole, (iii) its effect on a particular industry or sector of the economy, or (iv) its effect on actual or potential customers of banks or other financial institutions.

(3) In this section "financial assistance" has the meaning given by section 257 (and an order under that section may restrict or expand the effect of subsection (2)).

(4) This section has effect in relation to expenditure whether incurred—
  (a) before or after Royal Assent, and
  (b) in pursuance of obligations entered into before or after Royal Assent.

(5)   Expenditure which could be paid out of money provided by Parliament under subsection (1) shall be charged on and paid out of the Consolidated Fund if the Treasury are satisfied that the need for the expenditure is too urgent to permit arrangements to be made for the provision of money by Parliament.

(6)   Where money is paid in reliance on subsection (5) the Treasury shall as soon as is reasonably practicable lay a report before Parliament specifying the amount paid (but not the identity of the institution to or in respect of which it is paid).

(7)   If the Treasury think it necessary on public interest grounds, they may delay or dispense with a report under subsection (6).

[190]

NOTES
Commencement: 17 February 2009 (in so far as conferring or relating to any power to make subordinate legislation or codes of practice); 21 February 2009 (otherwise).

229   National Loans Fund

(1)   Where the Treasury propose to make a loan to or in respect of a bank or other financial institution, they may arrange for money to be paid out of the National Loans Fund.

(2)   The Treasury may make arrangements under subsection (1) only where they think it necessary to make the loan urgently in order to protect the stability of the financial systems of the United Kingdom.

(3)   The Treasury shall determine—
   (a)   the rate of interest on a loan, and
   (b)   other terms and conditions.

(4)   Sums received by the Treasury in respect of loans by virtue of this section shall be paid into the National Loans Fund.

(5)   Neither section 16 of the Banking (Special Provisions) Act 2008 (finance) nor any other enactment restricts the breadth of application of this section.

(6)   Where money is paid in reliance on subsection (1) the Treasury shall as soon as is reasonably practicable lay a report before Parliament specifying the amount paid (but not the identity of the institution to or in respect of which it is paid).

(7)   If the Treasury think it necessary on public interest grounds, they may delay or dispense with a report under subsection (6).

[191]

NOTES
Commencement: 17 February 2009 (in so far as conferring or relating to any power to make subordinate legislation or codes of practice); 21 February 2009 (otherwise).

230   "Financial institution"

(1)   The Treasury may by order provide that a specified institution, or an institution of a specified class, is or is not to be treated as a financial institution for the purposes of section 228 or 229.

(2)   An order—
   (a)   shall be made by statutory instrument, and
   (b)   shall be subject to annulment in pursuance of a resolution of either House of Parliament.

[192]

NOTES
Commencement: 17 February 2009 (in so far as conferring or relating to any power to make subordinate legislation or codes of practice); 21 February 2009 (otherwise).

231   Reports

(1)   The Treasury shall prepare reports about any arrangements entered into which involve or may require reliance on section 228(1).

(2)   A report must be prepared in respect of—
   (a)   the period beginning with 1st April 2009 and ending with 30th September 2009, and
   (b)   each successive period of 6 months;
but no report is required for a period in respect of which there is nothing to record.

(3)   The Treasury shall lay each report before the House of Commons as soon as is reasonably practicable.

(4)   A report must not—

(a)   specify individual arrangements, or
(b)   identify, or enable the identification of, individual beneficiaries.

(5)   The Treasury must aim to give as much information as possible in a report, subject to subsection (4) and other considerations of public interest.

[193]

NOTES

Commencement: 17 February 2009 (in so far as conferring or relating to any power to make subordinate legislation or codes of practice); 21 February 2009 (otherwise).

Investment banks

232   Definition

(1)   In this group of sections "investment bank" means an institution which satisfies the following conditions.

(2)   Condition 1 is that the institution has permission under Part 4 of the Financial Services and Markets Act 2000 to carry on the regulated activity of—
(a)   safeguarding and administering investments,
(b)   dealing in investments as principal, or
(c)   dealing in investments as agent.

(3)   Condition 2 is that the institution holds client assets.

(4)   In this group of sections "client assets" means assets which an institution has undertaken to hold for a client (whether or not on trust and whether or not the undertaking has been complied with).

(5)   Condition 3 is that the institution is incorporated in, or formed under the law of any part of, the United Kingdom.

(6)   The Treasury may by order—
(a)   provide that a specified class of institution, which has a permission under Part 4 of the Financial Services and Markets Act 2000 to carry on a regulated activity, is to be treated as an investment bank for the purpose of this group of sections;
(b)   provide that a specified class of institution is not to be treated as an investment bank for the purpose of this group of sections;
(c)   provide that assets of a specified kind, or held in specified circumstances, are to be or not to be treated as client assets for the purpose of this group of sections;
(d)   amend a provision of this section in consequence of provision under paragraph (a), (b) or (c).

[194]

NOTES

Commencement: 17 February 2009 (in so far as conferring or relating to any power to make subordinate legislation or codes of practice); 21 February 2009 (otherwise).

233   Insolvency regulations

(1)   The Treasury may by regulations ("investment bank insolvency regulations")—
(a)   modify the law of insolvency in its application to investment banks;
(b)   establish a new procedure for investment banks where—
      (i)   they are unable, or are likely to become unable, to pay their debts (within the meaning of section 93(4)), or
      (ii)   their winding up would be fair (within the meaning of section 93(8)).

(2)   Investment bank insolvency regulations may, in particular—
(a)   apply or replicate (with or without modifications) or make provision similar to provision made by or under the Insolvency Act 1986 or Part 2 or 3 of this Act;
(b)   establish a new procedure either (i) to operate for investment banks in place of liquidation or administration (under the Insolvency Act 1986), or (ii) to operate alongside liquidation or administration in respect of a particular part of the business or affairs of investment banks.

(3)   In making investment bank insolvency regulations the Treasury shall have regard to the desirability of—
(a)   identifying, protecting, and facilitating the return of, client assets,
(b)   protecting creditors' rights,
(c)   ensuring certainty for investment banks, creditors, clients, liquidators and administrators,
(d)   minimising the disruption of business and markets, and
(e)   maximising the efficiency and effectiveness of the financial services industry in the United Kingdom.

PART I
BANKING ACT 2009

(4)   A reference to returning client assets includes a reference to—
  (a)   transferring assets to another institution, and
  (b)   returning or transferring assets equivalent to those which an institution undertook to hold for clients.

[195]

NOTES

Commencement: 17 February 2009 (in so far as conferring or relating to any power to make subordinate legislation or codes of practice); 21 February 2009 (otherwise).

234 Regulations: details

(1)   Investment bank insolvency regulations may provide for a procedure to be instituted—
  (a)   by a court, or
  (b)   by the action of one or more specified classes of person.

(2)   Investment bank insolvency regulations may—
  (a)   confer functions on persons appointed in accordance with the regulations (which may, in particular, (i) be similar to the functions of a liquidator or administrator under the Insolvency Act 1986, or (ii) involve acting as a trustee of client assets), and
  (b)   specify objectives to be pursued by a person appointed in accordance with the regulations.

(3)   Investment bank insolvency regulations may make the application of a provision depend—
  (a)   on whether an investment bank is, or is likely to become, unable to pay its debts,
  (b)   on whether the winding up of an investment bank would be fair, or
  (c)   partly on those and partly on other considerations.

(4)   Investment bank insolvency regulations may make provision about the relationship between a procedure established by the regulations and—
  (a)   liquidation or administration under the Insolvency Act 1986,
  (b)   bank insolvency or bank administration under Part 2 or 3 of this Act, and
  (c)   provision made by or under any other enactment in connection with insolvency.

(5)   Regulations by virtue of subsection (4) may, in particular—
  (a)   include provision for temporary or permanent moratoria;
  (b)   amend an enactment.

(6)   Investment bank insolvency regulations may include provision—
  (a)   establishing a mechanism for determining which assets are client assets (subject to section 232);
  (b)   establishing a mechanism for determining that assets are to be, or not to be, treated as client assets (subject to section 232);
  (c)   about the treatment of client assets;
  (d)   about the treatment of unsettled transactions (and related collateral);
  (e)   for the transfer to another financial institution of assets or transactions;
  (f)   for the creation or enforcement of rights (including rights that take preference over creditors' rights) in respect of client assets or other assets;
  (g)   indemnifying a person who is exercising or purporting to exercise functions under or by virtue of the regulations;
  (h)   for recovery of assets transferred in error.

(7)   Provision may be included under subsection (6)(f) only to the extent that the Treasury think it necessary having regard to the desirability of protecting both—
  (a)   client assets, and
  (b)   creditors' rights.

(8)   Investment bank insolvency regulations may confer functions on—
  (a)   a court or tribunal,
  (b)   the Financial Services Authority,
  (c)   the Financial Services Compensation Scheme (established under Part 15 of the Financial Services and Markets Act 2000),
  (d)   the scheme manager of that Scheme, and
  (e)   any other specified person.

(9)   Investment bank insolvency regulations may include provision about institutions that are or were group undertakings (within the meaning of section 1161(5) of the Companies Act 2006) of an investment bank.

(10)   Investment bank insolvency regulations may replicate or apply, with or without modifications, a power to make procedural rules.

(11) Investment bank insolvency regulations may include provision for assigning or apportioning responsibility for the cost of the application of a procedure established or modified by the regulations.

[196]

NOTES

Commencement: 17 February 2009 (in so far as conferring or relating to any power to make subordinate legislation or codes of practice); 21 February 2009 (otherwise).

235 Regulations: procedure

(1) Investment bank insolvency regulations shall be made by statutory instrument.

(2) Investment bank insolvency regulations may not be made unless a draft has been laid before and approved by resolution of each House of Parliament.

(3) The Treasury must consult before laying draft investment bank insolvency regulations before Parliament.

(4) If the power to make investment bank insolvency regulations has not been exercised before the end of the period of 2 years beginning with the date on which this Act is passed, it lapses.

(5) An order under section 232(6)—
    (a)   shall be made by statutory instrument, and
    (b)   may not be made unless a draft has been laid before and approved by resolution of each House of Parliament.

[197]

NOTES

Commencement: 17 February 2009 (in so far as conferring or relating to any power to make subordinate legislation or codes of practice); 21 February 2009 (otherwise).

236 Review

(1) The Treasury shall arrange for a review of the effect of any investment bank insolvency regulations.

(2) The review must be completed during the period of 2 years beginning with the date on which the regulations come into force.

(3) The Treasury shall appoint one or more persons to conduct the review; and a person appointed must have expertise in connection with the law of insolvency or financial services.

(4) The review must consider, in particular—
    (a)   how far the regulations are achieving the objectives specified in section 233(3), and
    (b)   whether the regulations should continue to have effect.

(5) The review must result in a report to the Treasury.

(6) The Treasury shall lay a copy of the report before Parliament.

(7) If a review recommends further reviews—
    (a)   the Treasury may arrange for the further reviews, and
    (b)   subsections (3) to (6) (and this subsection) shall apply to them.

[198]

NOTES

Commencement: 17 February 2009 (in so far as conferring or relating to any power to make subordinate legislation or codes of practice); 21 February 2009 (otherwise).

Banking (Special Provisions) Act 2008

237 Compensation: valuer

Without prejudice to the generality of section 12 of the Banking (Special Provisions) Act 2008 (consequential and supplementary provision), it is declared that the power under section 9 of that Act to make provision for the appointment of a valuer includes power to replicate, or to make provision of a kind that may be made under, section 55(1) to (3) of this Act.

[199]

NOTES

Commencement: 17 February 2009 (in so far as conferring or relating to any power to make subordinate legislation or codes of practice); 21 February 2009 (otherwise).

Bank of England

238–243 *(Amend the Bank of England Act 1998 as follows: s 238 amends s 2 of the 1998 Act at* **[374]** *and inserts ss 2A–2C thereof at* **[375]**–**[377]**; *s 239 amends s 1 of the 1998 Act at* **[373]**; *ss 240, 241(1), 243(1), (2) amend Sch 1 to the 1998 Act at* **[379]**; *s 241(2) amends s 3 of the 1998 Act at* **[378]**; *s 242 amends s 3 of, and Sch 1 to, the 1998 Act at* **[378]**, **[379]**; *s 243(3), (4) amend Sch 3 to the 1998 Act at* **[380]**.)

244 Immunity

(1)   The Bank of England has immunity in its capacity as a monetary authority.

(2)   In this section—
   (a)   a reference to the Bank of England is a reference to the Bank and anyone who acts or purports to act as a director, officer, servant or agent of the Bank,
   (b)   "immunity" means immunity from liability in damages in respect of action or inaction, and
   (c)   a reference to the Bank's capacity as a monetary authority includes a reference to functions exercised by the Bank for the purpose of or in connection with—
      (i)   acting as the central bank of the United Kingdom, or
      (ii)   protecting or enhancing the stability of the financial systems of the United Kingdom.

(3)   The immunity does not extend to action or inaction—
   (a)   in bad faith, or
   (b)   in contravention of section 6(1) of the Human Rights Act 1998.

[200]

NOTES

Commencement: 17 February 2009 (in so far as conferring or relating to any power to make subordinate legislation or codes of practice); 21 February 2009 (otherwise).

245   *(Repeals the Bank Charter Act 1844, s 6 (Bank to produce weekly account).)*

246 Information

(1)   The Bank of England may disclose information that it thinks relevant to the financial stability of—
   (a)   individual financial institutions, or
   (b)   one or more aspects of the financial systems of the United Kingdom.

(2)   Information about the business or other affairs of a specified or identifiable person may be disclosed under subsection (1) only to—
   (a)   the Treasury;
   (b)   the Financial Services Authority;
   (c)   the scheme manager of the Financial Services Compensation Scheme (established under Part 15 of the Financial Services and Markets Act 2000);
   (d)   an authority in a country or territory outside the United Kingdom which exercises functions similar to those of the Treasury, the Bank of England or the Financial Services Authority in relation to financial stability;
   (e)   the European Central Bank.

(3)   This section—
   (a)   overrides a contractual or other requirement to keep information in confidence, and
   (b)   is without prejudice to any other power to disclose information.

[201]

NOTES

Commencement: 17 February 2009 (in so far as conferring or relating to any power to make subordinate legislation or codes of practice); 21 February 2009 (otherwise).

247   Bank of England Act 1946

Nothing in this Act affects the generality of section 4 of the Bank of England Act 1946 (directions and relations with other banks).

[202]

NOTES

Commencement: 17 February 2009 (in so far as conferring or relating to any power to make subordinate legislation or codes of practice); 21 February 2009 (otherwise).

Financial Services Authority

248 *(Amends the Financial Services and Markets Act 2000, s 45 at* **[382]**.*)*

249 Functions

(1) A reference in an enactment to functions conferred on the Financial Services Authority by or under the Financial Services and Markets Act 2000 (or any part of it) includes a reference to functions conferred on the Authority by or under this Act.

(2) A reference in an enactment to functions of the Financial Services Authority includes a reference to functions conferred by or under this Act (irrespective of whether the enactment was passed or made before or after the commencement of this Act).

(3) The Treasury may by order disapply subsection (1) or (2) to a specified extent; and an order—

    (a)   shall be made by statutory instrument, and

    (b)   may not be made unless a draft has been laid before and approved by resolution of each House of Parliament.

(4) *(Adds the Financial Services and Markets Act 2000, s 1(4) at* **[381]**.*)*

[203]

NOTES

Commencement: 17 February 2009 (in so far as conferring or relating to any power to make subordinate legislation or codes of practice); 21 February 2009 (otherwise).

250 Information

(1) The Financial Services Authority shall collect information that it thinks is or may be relevant to the stability of—

    (a)   individual financial institutions, or

    (b)   one or more aspects of the financial systems of the United Kingdom.

(2) The Authority may perform its function under subsection (1) by the exercise of the power in section 165 of the Financial Services and Markets Act 2000 (power to require information—as qualified by section 249 above) or in any other way.

[204]

NOTES

Commencement: 17 February 2009 (in so far as conferring or relating to any power to make subordinate legislation or codes of practice); 21 February 2009 (otherwise).

Central banks

251 Financial assistance to building societies

(1) The Treasury may by order modify the Building Societies Act 1986 for the purpose of facilitating, or in connection with, the provision of financial assistance to building societies by—

    (a)   the Treasury,

    (b)   the Bank of England,

    (c)   another central bank of a Member State of the European Economic Area, or

    (d)   the European Central Bank.

(2) An order may affect any provision of the Building Societies Act 1986 which appears to the Treasury otherwise capable of preventing, impeding or affecting the provision of financial assistance; including, in particular, provision—

    (a)   about the establishment, constitution or powers of building societies,

    (b)   restricting or otherwise dealing with raising funds or borrowing,

    (c)   restricting or otherwise dealing with what may be done by or in relation to building societies,

    (d)   about security, or

    (e)   about the application of insolvency law or other legislation relating to companies.

(3) An order—

    (a)   may disapply or modify a provision;

    (b)   may (but need not) take the form of textual amendment.

(4) Incidental provision of an order (included in reliance on section 259(1)(c)) may, in particular—

    (a)   impose conditions, limits or other restrictions on what may be done in reliance on a provision of the order;

    (b)   confer a discretion on the Treasury, the Bank of England or another person or class of person.

(5)   Incidental or consequential provision of an order (included in reliance on section 259(1)(c)) may disapply or modify an enactment, whether by textual amendment or otherwise.

(6)   An order—
   (a)   shall be made by statutory instrument, and
   (b)   may not be made unless a draft has been laid before and approved by resolution of each House of Parliament.

(7)   The Treasury may by order create exceptions to or otherwise modify the effect of section 9B of the Building Societies Act 1986 (restriction on creation of floating charges); and—
   (a)   the Treasury may make an order only if they think it is likely to help building societies to use, give effect to or take advantage of financial assistance of the kind specified in subsection (1),
   (b)   an order may have effect in relation to transactions between building societies and persons not listed in subsection (1),
   (c)   an order shall be made by statutory instrument, and
   (d)   an order may not be made unless a draft has been laid before and approved by resolution of each House of Parliament.

(8)   In this section, "financial assistance" has the meaning given by section 257.

[205]

NOTES
Commencement: 17 February 2009 (in so far as conferring or relating to any power to make subordinate legislation or codes of practice); 21 February 2009 (otherwise).

252   Registration of charges

(1)   Part 25 of the Companies Act 2006 (registration of charges) does not apply to a charge if the person interested in it is—
   (a)   the Bank of England,
   (b)   the central bank of a country or territory outside the United Kingdom, or
   (c)   the European Central Bank.

(2)   The reference in subsection (1) to Part 25 of the Companies Act 2006 includes a reference to—
   (a)   Part 12 of the Companies Act 1985 (which has effect until the commencement of Part 25 of the 2006 Act),
   (b)   Part 13 of the Companies (Northern Ireland) Order 1986 (which has effect until the commencement of Part 25 of the 2006 Act), and
   (c)   any provision about registration of charges made under section 1052 of the Companies Act 2006 (overseas companies).

[206]

NOTES
Commencement: 17 February 2009 (in so far as conferring or relating to any power to make subordinate legislation or codes of practice); 21 February 2009 (otherwise).

253, 254   (*S 253 amends the Bankruptcy and Diligence etc (Scotland) Act 2007, ss 38, 39, 42–44, 47 at* **[414]**, **[415]**, **[416]–[418]**, **[419]**; *s 254 abolishes the "funds attached" rule in Scotland, amends the Bills of Exchange Act 1882, s 53 at* **[250]** *and repeals s 75A thereof.*)

Financial collateral arrangements

255   Regulations

(1)   The Treasury may make regulations about financial collateral arrangements.

(2)   "Financial collateral arrangements" are arrangements under which financial collateral is used as security in respect of a loan or other liability; and for that purpose—
   (a)   collateral may be in cash, securities or any other form,
   (b)   use as security may involve transfer of the collateral or the creation or transfer of any kind of right, interest or charge (fixed or floating) in respect of it, and
   (c)   in particular, use as security can include use under arrangements of a kind described commercially as "title transfer financial collateral arrangements".

(3)   The regulations—
   (a)   may make any provision that the Treasury think necessary or desirable for the purpose of, or in connection with, implementation of the Financial Collateral Arrangements Directive (2002/47/EC) (or any replacement), but
   (b)   are not restricted to provision required in connection with the Directive, and may make

any provision that the Treasury think necessary or desirable for the purpose of enabling financial collateral arrangements, whether or not with an international element, to be commercially useful and effective.

(4) The regulations may, in particular—
  (a) disapply or modify an enactment or rule of law about formalities or evidence,
  (b) disapply or modify an enactment about insolvency, administration, receivership or any similar procedure,
  (c) disapply or modify an enactment about property law,
  (d) disapply or modify an enactment about companies or other commercial entities or groupings,
  (e) provide for provisions of financial collateral arrangements to have effect despite a reorganisation, winding-up or other process affecting a party to the arrangements,
  (f) make provision for the enforcement of financial collateral arrangements (which may include, in particular, provision—
    (i) about sale, appropriation and set-off,
    (ii) about the use of collateral while subject to the arrangements,
    (iii) about "close out netting arrangements", under which obligations under a number of contracts may be set off against each other in the event of default under a specified contract,
    (iv) permitting a person to foreclose or exercise another right under the arrangements with or without an order of a court,
    (v) permitting or requiring the disclosure of information, and
    (vi) for enforcement after the commencement of, and despite, reorganisation, winding-up or another process),
  (g) make provision for the choice of law according to which, or under which, matters arising under financial collateral arrangements are to be determined, and
  (h) apply to persons whether or not provisions of the Directive apply to them.

(5) The regulations may, in particular—
  (a) do anything done or purported to be done by the Financial Collateral Arrangements (No 2) Regulations 2003,
  (b) provide for those regulations, or a specified provision, to be treated as having had effect despite any lack of vires,
  (c) provide for anything done under or in reliance on those regulations to be treated as having had effect despite any lack of vires, and
  (d) make any provision which the Treasury think necessary or desirable to achieve or restore certainty and stability in connection with the matters to which those regulations relate.
[207]

NOTES
Commencement: to be appointed.

---

256 Supplemental

(1) Regulations under section 255—
  (a) shall be made by statutory instrument, and
  (b) shall lapse unless approved by resolution of each House of Parliament during the period of 28 days (ignoring periods of dissolution, prorogation or adjournment of either House for more than 4 days) beginning with the day on which the regulations are made.

(2) The lapse of regulations under subsection (1)(b)—
  (a) does not invalidate anything done under or in reliance on the regulations before the lapse and at a time when neither House has declined to approve the regulations, and
  (b) does not prevent the making of new regulations (in new terms).
[208]

NOTES
Commencement: to be appointed.

PART 8
GENERAL

257 "Financial assistance"

(1) In this Act "financial assistance" includes giving guarantees or indemnities and any other kind of financial assistance (actual or contingent).

(2) The Treasury may by order provide that a specified activity or transaction, or class of activity or transaction, is to be or not to be treated as financial assistance for a specified purpose of this Act; and subsection (1) is subject to this subsection.

(3) An order—
   (a) shall be made by statutory instrument, and
   (b) shall be subject to annulment in pursuance of a resolution of either House of Parliament.
[209]

NOTES
Commencement: 17 February 2009 (in so far as conferring or relating to any power to make subordinate legislation or codes of practice); 21 February 2009 (otherwise).

258 "Enactment"

In this Act "enactment" includes—
   (a) subordinate legislation,
   (b) an Act of the Scottish Parliament and an instrument under an Act of the Scottish Parliament, and
   (c) Northern Ireland legislation.

[210]

NOTES
Commencement: 17 February 2009 (in so far as conferring or relating to any power to make subordinate legislation or codes of practice); 21 February 2009 (otherwise).

259 Statutory instruments

(1) A statutory instrument under this Act—
   (a) may make provision that applies generally or only for specified purposes, cases or circumstances,
   (b) may make different provision for different purposes, cases or circumstances, and
   (c) may include incidental, consequential or transitional provision.

(2) No statutory instrument under this Act shall be treated as a hybrid instrument under Standing Orders of either House of Parliament.

(3) The Table lists the powers to make statutory instruments under this Act and the arrangements for Parliamentary scrutiny in each case (which are subject to subsections (4) to (6)).

Section	Topic	Parliamentary scrutiny
PART 1—Special resolution regime		
2	Meaning of "bank"	Draft affirmative resolution
25	Share transfer orders	Negative resolution
47	Partial transfers	Draft affirmative resolution
48	Protection of interests	Draft affirmative resolution
55	Independent valuer	Negative resolution
56	Independent valuer: money	Negative resolution
60	Third party compensation	Draft affirmative resolution
62	Compensation orders	Draft affirmative resolution
69	Continuity obligations: consideration and terms	Negative resolution
72	Transfers: enforcement	Negative resolution
74	Tax	Draft affirmative resolution (Commons only)
75	Power to change law	Draft affirmative resolution (except for urgent cases)
78	Public funds	Negative resolution (Commons only)
85	Building societies: orders	Negative resolution
86	Building societies: assets	(As for orders under section 90B of the Building Societies Act 1986)
88	Building societies: consequential	Draft affirmative resolution

Section	Topic	Parliamentary scrutiny
PART 1—Special resolution regime		
89	Credit unions	Draft affirmative resolution
PART 2—Bank insolvency		
91	Meaning of "bank"	Draft affirmative resolution
122	Application of insolvency law	Draft affirmative resolution
125	Rules	(Expansion of power in section 411 of the Insolvency Act 1986)
130	Building societies	Draft affirmative resolution
131	Credit unions	Draft affirmative resolution
132	Partnerships	(As for orders under section 420 of the Insolvency Act 1986)
133	Scottish partnerships	Negative resolution
135	Consequential provision	Draft affirmative resolution
PART 3—Bank administration		
148	Sharing information	Negative resolution
149	Multiple original transfers	Draft affirmative resolution
152	Transfer from temporary public ownership	Draft affirmative resolution
156	Application of other law	Draft affirmative resolution
158	Building societies	Draft affirmative resolution
159	Credit unions	Draft affirmative resolution
160	Rules	(Expansion of power in section 411 of the Insolvency Act 1986)
163	Partnerships	(As for orders under section 420 of the Insolvency Act 1986)
164	Scottish partnerships	Negative resolution
168	Consequential provision	Draft affirmative resolution
PART 4—Financial Services Compensation Scheme		
170	Contingency funding	Draft affirmative resolution
171	Special resolution regime	Draft affirmative resolution
173	Borrowing from National Loans Fund	Negative resolution
PART 5—Inter-bank payment systems		
191	Bank of England directions: immunity	Negative resolution
203	Fees regulations	Negative resolution
204	Information	Negative resolution
PART 6—Banknotes: Scotland and Northern Ireland		
215	Banknote regulations	Draft affirmative resolution
PART 7—Miscellaneous		
230	Financial institution	Negative resolution
232	Investment banks: definition	Draft affirmative resolution
233	Investment banks: insolvency	Draft affirmative resolution
249	FSA—functions	Draft affirmative resolution
251	Central banks: assistance to building societies	Draft affirmative resolution
255	Financial collateral arrangements	Affirmative resolution

Section	Topic	Parliamentary scrutiny
PART 8—General		
257	Financial assistance	Negative resolution
262	Repeal of Banking (Special Provisions) Act 2008	None
263	Commencement	None

(4)   A power listed in subsection (5) may be exercised without a draft being laid before and approved by resolution of each House of Parliament if—

(a)   the power is being exercised for the first time, and

(b)   the person exercising it is satisfied that it is necessary to exercise it without laying a draft for approval.

(5)   The powers are those in—

(a)   section 2 (special resolution regime: meaning of "bank"),

(b)   section 47 (special resolution regime: partial transfers),

(c)   section 48 (special resolution regime: protection of interests),

(d)   section 60 (special resolution regime: third party compensation),

(e)   section 88 (special resolution regime: building societies: consequential),

(f)   section 91 (bank insolvency: meaning of "bank"),

(g)   section 122 (bank insolvency: application of insolvency law),

(h)   section 130 (bank insolvency: building societies),

(i)   section 135 (bank insolvency: consequential provision),

(j)   section 149 (bank administration: multiple original transfers),

(k)   section 152 (bank administration: transfer from temporary public ownership),

(l)   section 156 (bank administration: application of other law),

(m)   section 158 (bank administration: building societies),

(n)   section 168 (bank administration: consequential provision), and

(o)   section 171 (Financial Services Compensation Scheme: special resolution regime).

(6)   Where an instrument is made in reliance on subsection (5)—

(a)   it shall lapse unless approved by resolution of each House of Parliament during the period of 28 days (ignoring periods of dissolution, prorogation or adjournment of either House for more than 4 days) beginning with the day on which the instrument is made,

(b)   the lapse of an instrument under paragraph (a) does not invalidate anything done under or in reliance on it before its lapse and at a time when neither House has declined to approve it, and

(c)   the lapse of an instrument under paragraph (a) does not prevent the making of a new one (in new terms).

[211]

NOTES

Commencement: 17 February 2009 (in so far as conferring or relating to any power to make subordinate legislation or codes of practice); 21 February 2009 (otherwise).

Orders: the Banking Act 2009 (Restriction of Partial Property Transfers) Order 2009, SI 2009/322 at **[543]**; the Building Societies (Insolvency and Special Administration) Order 2009, SI 2009/805 at **[556]**; the Amendments to Law (Resolution of Dunfermline Building Society) Order 2009, SI 2009/814 at **[565]**; the Dunfermline Building Society Compensation Scheme, Resolution Fund and Third Party Compensation Order 2009, SI 2009/1800 at **[580]**; the Amendments to Law (Resolution of Dunfermline Building Society) (No 2) Order 2009, SI 2009/1805 at **[598]**; the Dunfermline Building Society Independent Valuer Order 2009, SI 2009/1810 at **[599]**.

Regulations: the Banking Act 2009 (Bank Administration) (Modification for Application to Banks in Temporary Public Ownership) Regulations 2009, SI 2009/312 at **[504]**; the Banking Act 2009 (Bank Administration) (Modification for Application to Multiple Transfers) Regulations 2009, SI 2009/313 at **[509]**; the Bank Administration (Sharing Information) Regulations 2009, SI 2009/314 at **[513]**; the Banking Act 2009 (Third Party Compensation Arrangements for Partial Property Transfers) Regulations 2009, SI 2009/319 at **[533]**.

260   Money

Expenditure of the Treasury under, by virtue of or in connection with a provision of this Act shall be paid out of money provided by Parliament.

[212]

NOTES

Commencement: 17 February 2009 (in so far as conferring or relating to any power to make subordinate legislation or codes of practice); 21 February 2009 (otherwise).

261 Index of defined terms

The Table sets out expressions defined in this Act for general purposes.

Expression	Section
Action	93 and 166
Bank (Part 1)	2
Bank (Part 2)	91
Bank administration	136
Bank administration order	141
Bank insolvency	90
Bank insolvency order	94
Bridge bank	12
Bridge bank reverse share transfer instrument	31
Bridge bank share transfer instrument	30
Compensation scheme order	49
The court (Part 2)	92
The court (Part 3)	166
Eligible depositors	93
Enactment	258
FSA	3, 93 & 166
FSCS	93
Fair	93
Financial assistance	257
Financial institution	230
Full payment resolution	100
Independent valuer	54
Inter-bank payment system	182
Liquidation committee	100
Objective 1 Achievement Notice	139
Onward bridge bank	12
Onward property transfer instrument	43
Onward share transfer order	28
Partial property transfer	47
Property transfer instrument	33
Property transfer order	45
Resolution fund order	49
Reverse property transfer instrument	44
Reverse property transfer order	46
Reverse share transfer order	29
Securities	14
Share transfer instrument	15
Share transfer order	16
Special resolution regime	1
Special resolution objectives	4
Stabilisation options	1
Stabilisation powers	1

PART I
BANKING ACT 2009

Expression	Section
Supplemental property transfer instrument	42
Supplemental share transfer instrument or order	26 & 27
Third party compensation order	49 & 59
Unable to pay debts	93 & 166

[213]

NOTES
Commencement: 17 February 2009 (in so far as conferring or relating to any power to make subordinate legislation or codes of practice); 21 February 2009 (otherwise).

262 Repeal

(1) The Treasury may by order repeal the Banking (Special Provisions) Act 2008.

(2) An order—
    (a) may include savings, and
    (b) shall be made by statutory instrument.

(3) Subsection (2)(a) is without prejudice to the generality of, or the application to this section of, section 259.

[214]

NOTES
Commencement: 17 February 2009 (in so far as conferring or relating to any power to make subordinate legislation or codes of practice); 21 February 2009 (otherwise).

263 Commencement

(1) The preceding provisions of this Act shall come into force in accordance with provision made by the Treasury by order.

(2) Subsection (1) does not apply to section 254, which comes into force at the end of the period of 2 months beginning with the date of Royal Assent.

(3) An order under subsection (1)—
    (a) may make provision generally or only in relation to specific provisions or purposes,
    (b) may make different provision for different provisions or purposes,
    (c) may include incidental or transitional provision (including savings), and
    (d) shall be made by statutory instrument.

(4) Where the Treasury or another authority are required to consult or take other action before exercising a power or fulfilling a duty to make legislation or to do any other thing under, by virtue of or in connection with this Act, the Treasury or other authority may rely on consultation or other action carried out before the commencement of the relevant provision of this Act.

[215]

NOTES
Commencement: 12 February 2009.
Orders: the Banking Act 2009 (Commencement No 1) Order 2009, SI 2009/296 at **[500]**; the Banking Act 2009 (Commencement No 2) Order 2009, SI 2009/1296 at **[577]**; the Banking Act 2009 (Commencement No 3) Order 2009, SI 2009/2038 at **[626]**.

264 Extent

(1) This Act extends to—
    (a) England and Wales,
    (b) Scotland, and
    (c) Northern Ireland.

(2) But—
    (a) sections 253 and 254 extend to Scotland only, and
    (b) an amendment of an enactment has the same extent as the enactment (or the relevant part).

[216]

NOTES
Commencement: 12 February 2009.

265 Short title

This Act may be cited as the Banking Act 2009.

[217]–[249]

NOTES

Commencement: 12 February 2009.

PART II
OTHER ACTS

BILLS OF EXCHANGE ACT 1882

(45 & 46 Vict c 61)

An Act to codify the law relating to Bills of Exchange, Cheques, and Promissory Notes
[18 August 1882]

NOTES
By the Bills of Exchange (Time of Noting) Act 1917, s 2, the Bills of Exchange Act 1882 and the 1917 Act may be cited by the collective title of the Bills of Exchange Acts 1882 to 1917.

1, 2   *((Pt I) Outside the scope of this work; see Butterworths Banking Law Handbook.)*

PART II
BILLS OF EXCHANGE

3–52   *(Outside the scope of this work; see Butterworths Banking Law Handbook.)*

Liabilities of parties

53   Funds in hands of drawee

(1)   A bill, of itself, does not operate as an assignment of funds in the hands of the drawee available for the payment thereof, and the drawee of a bill who does not accept as required by this Act is not liable on the instrument. This sub-section shall not extend to Scotland.

(2)   [...] in Scotland, where the drawee of a bill [other than a cheque] has in his hands funds available for the payment thereof, the bill operates as an assignment of the sum for which it is drawn in favour of the holder, from the time when the bill is presented to the drawee.

[250]

NOTES
Sub-s (2): words omitted from first pair of square brackets inserted by the Law Reform (Miscellaneous Provisions) (Scotland) Act 1985, s 11 and repealed by the Banking Act 2009, s 254(4)(a)(i), as from 12 April 2009; words in second pair of square brackets inserted by the Banking Act 2009, s 254(4)(a)(ii), as from 12 April 2009.

54–100   *(Outside the scope of this work. For ss 54–75, 76–81A, 83–95, 97, 99 see Butterworths Banking Law Handbook; s 75A inserted by the Law Reform (Miscellaneous Provisions) (Scotland) Act 1985, s 11(b) and repealed by the Banking Act 2009, s 254(4)(b), as from 12 April 2009; s 82 repealed by the Cheques Act 1957, s 6(3), Schedule; s 96 repealed by the Statute Law Revision Act 1898; ss 98, 100 apply to Scotland only.)*

(First Schedule outside the scope of this work; see Butterworths Banking Law Handbook. Second Schedule repealed by the Statute Law Revision Act 1898.)

INSOLVENCY ACT 1986

(1986 c 45)

ARRANGEMENT OF SECTIONS

THE FIRST GROUP OF PARTS
COMPANY INSOLVENCY; COMPANIES WINDING UP

PART I
COMPANY VOLUNTARY ARRANGEMENTS

The proposal

Consideration and implementation of proposal

PART IV
WINDING UP OF COMPANIES REGISTERED
UNDER THE COMPANIES ACTS

CHAPTER VI
WINDING UP BY THE COURT

Grounds and effect of winding-up petition

Appointment of liquidator

Liquidation committees

CHAPTER VII
LIQUIDATORS

Liquidator's powers and duties

CHAPTER VIII
PROVISIONS OF GENERAL APPLICATION IN WINDING UP

Property subject to floating charge

Disclaimer (England and Wales only)

Miscellaneous matters

CHAPTER X
MALPRACTICE BEFORE AND DURING LIQUIDATION;
PENALISATION OF COMPANIES AND COMPANY OFFICERS;
INVESTIGATIONS AND PROSECUTIONS

Penalisation of directors and officers

PART VI
MISCELLANEOUS PROVISIONS APPLYING TO COMPANIES
WHICH ARE INSOLVENT OR IN LIQUIDATION

Management by administrators, liquidators, etc

THE THIRD GROUP OF PARTS
MISCELLANEOUS MATTERS BEARING ON BOTH
COMPANY AND INDIVIDUAL INSOLVENCY;
GENERAL INTERPRETATION;
FINAL PROVISIONS

PART XIII
INSOLVENCY PRACTITIONERS AND THEIR QUALIFICATION

*Restrictions on unqualified persons acting
as liquidator, trustee in bankruptcy, etc*

The requisite qualification, and the means of obtaining it

PART XV
SUBORDINATE LEGISLATION

General insolvency rules

Fees orders

Other order-making powers

PART XVI
PROVISIONS AGAINST DEBT AVOIDANCE
(ENGLAND AND WALES ONLY)

PART XVII
MISCELLANEOUS AND GENERAL

*An Act to consolidate the enactments relating to company insolvency and winding up (including the
winding up of companies that are not insolvent, and of unregistered companies); enactments*

PART II
OTHER ACTS

relating to the insolvency and bankruptcy of individuals; and other enactments bearing on those two subject matters, including the functions and qualification of insolvency practitioners, the public administration of insolvency, the penalisation and redress of malpractice and wrongdoing, and the avoidance of certain transactions at an undervalue

[25 July 1986]

NOTES

Modification in relation to solicitors: the provisions of this Act reproduced in this work (except s 413) are applied, with modifications, in relation to a "recognised body" under the Administration of Justice Act 1985, s 9, by the Solicitors' Incorporated Practices Order 1991, SI 1991/2684, arts 2–5, Sch 1, as amended by SI 2001/645.

Modification in relation to Scotland: by virtue of the Scotland Act 1998, s 125, Sch 8, para 23, (i) anything directed to be done, or which may be done, to or by the registrar of companies in Scotland by virtue of ss 53(1), 54(3), 61(6), 62(5) (so far as relating to the giving of notice), 67(1), 69(2), 84(3), 94(3), 106(3) and (5), 112(3), 130(1), 147(3), 170(2) and 172(8), or the Financial Services Authority by virtue of any of those provisions as applied (with or without modifications) in relation to friendly societies, industrial and provident societies or building societies, shall, or (as the case may be) may, also be done to or by the Accountant in Bankruptcy, and (ii) anything directed to be done, or which may be done, to or by the registrar of companies in Scotland by virtue of ss 89(3), 109(1), 171(5) and 6, 173(2)(a) and 192(1), or the Financial Services Authority by virtue of any of those provisions as applied (with or without modification) in relation to friendly societies, industrial and provident societies or building societies, shall instead be done to or by the Accountant in Bankruptcy.

Modification in relation to insolvent partnerships: this Act is extensively applied and modified in relation to insolvent partnerships; see the Insolvent Partnerships Order 1994, SI 1994/2421.

Modification in relation to limited liability partnerships: the provisions of this Act relating to companies and partnerships are applied with modifications to limited liability partnerships; see the Limited Liability Partnerships (Scotland) Regulations 2001, SSI 2001/128, and the Limited Liability Partnerships Regulations 2001, SI 2001/1090.

Modification in relation to open-ended investment companies: where an open-ended investment company is wound up as an unregistered company under Pt V, the provisions of this Act apply for the purposes of the winding up subject to certain modifications; see the Open-Ended Investment Companies Regulations 2001, SI 2001/1228 at **[865]** et seq.

Application to foreign companies: the Secretary of State may by order provide for this Act to apply, with or without modification, in relation to a company incorporated outside Great Britain; see the Enterprise Act 2002, s 254.

Application to UK insurers: as to the application of this Act to UK insurers, see the Insurers (Reorganisation and Winding Up) Regulations 2004, SI 2004/353.

THE FIRST GROUP OF PARTS
COMPANY INSOLVENCY; COMPANIES WINDING UP

PART I
COMPANY VOLUNTARY ARRANGEMENTS

NOTES

Modification of this Part in relation to building societies: this Part (except s 1A) is applied, with modifications, in respect of the approval of voluntary arrangements in relation to building societies, by the Building Societies Act 1986, s 90A, Sch 15A.

Application to industrial and provident societies and friendly societies: this Part may be applied, with or without modification, in relation to industrial and provident societies and friendly societies by order of the Treasury, with the concurrence of the Secretary of State; see the Enterprise Act 2002, s 255.

The proposal

1 Those who may propose an arrangement

(1)   The directors of a company [(other than one which is in administration or being wound up)] may make a proposal under this Part to the company and to its creditors for a composition in satisfaction of its debts or a scheme of arrangement of its affairs (from here on referred to, in either case, as a "voluntary arrangement").

(2)   A proposal under this Part is one which provides for some person ("the nominee") to act in relation to the voluntary arrangement either as trustee or otherwise for the purpose of supervising its implementation; and the nominee must be a person who is qualified to act as an insolvency practitioner [or authorised to act as nominee, in relation to the voluntary arrangement].

(3)   Such a proposal may also be made—
   [(a)   where the company is in administration, by the administrator,] and
   (b)   where the company is being wound up, by the liquidator.

[(4)   In this Part "company" means—
   (a)   a company within the meaning of section 735(1) of the Companies Act 1985,
   (b)   a company incorporated in an EEA State other than the United Kingdom; or
   (c)   a company not incorporated in an EEA State but having its centre of main interests in a member State other than Denmark.

(5)   In subsection (4), in relation to a company, "centre of main interests" has the same meaning as in the EC Regulation and, in the absence of proof to the contrary, is presumed to be the place of its registered office (within the meaning of that Regulation).

(6)   If a company incorporated outside the United Kingdom has a principal place of business in Northern Ireland, no proposal under this Part shall be made in relation to it unless it also has a principal place of business in England and Wales or Scotland (or both in England and Wales or Scotland).]

[251]

NOTES
Sub-s (1): words in square brackets substituted by the Enterprise Act 2002, s 248(3), Sch 17, paras 9, 10(a), as from 15 September 2003, subject to savings and transitional provisions in the Enterprise Act 2002, s 249 and the Enterprise Act 2002 (Commencement No 4 and Transitional Provisions and Savings) Order 2003, SI 2003/2093, art 3.
Sub-s (2): words in square brackets substituted by the Insolvency Act 2000, s 2, Sch 2, Pt I, paras 1, 2, as from 1 January 2003, subject to transitional provisions in SI 2002/2711, art 3.
Sub-s (3): para (a) substituted by the Enterprise Act 2002, s 248(3), Sch 17, paras 9, 10(b), subject to savings and transitional provisions as noted to sub-s (1) above.
Sub-ss (4)–(6): substituted (for sub-s (4) as originally added by SI 2002/1240, regs 3, 4) by the Insolvency Act 1986 (Amendment) Regulations 2005, SI 2005/879, regs 2(1), (2), 3, as from 13 April 2005 except in relation to a voluntary arrangement under Pt I of this Act or the appointment of an administrator under Pt II of this Act that took effect before that date.

[1A   Moratorium
(1)   Where the directors of an eligible company intend to make a proposal for a voluntary arrangement, they may take steps to obtain a moratorium for the company.

(2)   The provisions of Schedule A1 to this Act have effect with respect to—
   (a)   companies eligible for a moratorium under this section,
   (b)   the procedure for obtaining such a moratorium,
   (c)   the effects of such a moratorium, and
   (d)   the procedure applicable (in place of sections 2 to 6 and 7) in relation to the approval and implementation of a voluntary arrangement where such a moratorium is or has been in force.]

[252]

NOTES
Inserted by the Insolvency Act 2000, s 1, Sch 1, paras 1, 2, as from 1 January 2003.

2   Procedure where nominee is not the liquidator or administrator

(1)   This section applies where the nominee under section 1 is not the liquidator or administrator of the company [and the directors do not propose to take steps to obtain a moratorium under section 1A for the company].

(2)   The nominee shall, within 28 days (or such longer period as the court may allow) after he is given notice of the proposal for a voluntary arrangement, submit a report to the court stating—
   (a)   [whether, in his opinion, the proposed voluntary arrangement has a reasonable prospect of being approved and implemented,
   (aa)]   whether, in his opinion, meetings of the company and of its creditors should be summoned to consider the proposal, and
   (b)   if in his opinion such meetings should be summoned, the date on which, and time and place at which, he proposes the meetings should be held.

(3)   For the purposes of enabling the nominee to prepare his report, the person intending to make the proposal shall submit to the nominee—
   (a)   a document setting out the terms of the proposed voluntary arrangement, and
   (b)   a statement of the company's affairs containing—
      (i)   such particulars of its creditors and of its debts and other liabilities and of its assets as may be prescribed, and
      (ii)   such other information as may be prescribed.

   [(4)   The court may—
   (a)   on an application made by the person intending to make the proposal, in a case where the nominee has failed to submit the report required by this section or has died, or
   (b)   on an application made by that person or the nominee, in a case where it is impracticable or inappropriate for the nominee to continue to act as such,
direct that the nominee be replaced as such by another person qualified to act as an insolvency practitioner, or authorised to act as nominee, in relation to the voluntary arrangement.]

[253]

NOTES
Sub-s (1): words in square brackets added by the Insolvency Act 2000, s 1, Sch 1, paras 1, 3, as from 1 January 2003.
Sub-s (2): words in square brackets inserted by the Insolvency Act 2000, s 2, Sch 2, Pt I, paras 1, 3(a), as from 1 January 2003, subject to transitional provisions in SI 2002/2711, art 3.
Sub-s (4): substituted by the Insolvency Act 2000, s 2, Sch 2, Pt I, paras 1, 3(b), as from 1 January 2003, subject to transitional provisions in SI 2002/2711, art 3.

3 Summoning of meetings

(1)   Where the nominee under section 1 is not the liquidator or administrator, and it has been reported to the court that such meetings as are mentioned in section 2(2) should be summoned, the person making the report shall (unless the court otherwise directs) summon those meetings for the time, date and place proposed in the report.

(2)   Where the nominee is the liquidator or administrator, he shall summon meetings of the company and of its creditors to consider the proposal for such a time, date and place as he thinks fit.

(3)   The persons to be summoned to a creditors' meeting under this section are every creditor of the company of whose claim and address the person summoning the meeting is aware.

[254]

NOTES
See further: in relation to the application of this section, with modifications, in respect of bank insolvency and administration, see the Banking Act 2009, ss 113(6), (7), 154(3), (4) at **[113]**, **[151]**.

Consideration and implementation of proposal

4 Decisions of meetings

(1)   The meetings summoned under section 3 shall decide whether to approve the proposed voluntary arrangement (with or without modifications).

(2)   The modifications may include one conferring the functions proposed to be conferred on the nominee on another person qualified to act as an insolvency practitioner [or authorised to act as nominee, in relation to the voluntary arrangement].

But they shall not include any modification by virtue of which the proposal ceases to be a proposal such as is mentioned in section 1.

(3)   A meeting so summoned shall not approve any proposal or modification which affects the right of a secured creditor of the company to enforce his security, except with the concurrence of the creditor concerned.

(4)   Subject as follows, a meeting so summoned shall not approve any proposal or modification under which—
  (a)   any preferential debt of the company is to be paid otherwise than in priority to such of its debts as are not preferential debts, or
  (b)   a preferential creditor of the company is to be paid an amount in respect of a preferential debt that bears to that debt a smaller proportion than is borne to another preferential debt by the amount that is to be paid in respect of that other debt.

However, the meeting may approve such a proposal or modification with the concurrence of the preferential creditor concerned.

(5)   Subject as above, each of the meetings shall be conducted in accordance with the rules.

(6)   After the conclusion of either meeting in accordance with the rules, the chairman of the meeting shall report the result of the meeting to the court, and, immediately after reporting to the court, shall give notice of the result of the meeting to such persons as may be prescribed.

(7)   References in this section to preferential debts and preferential creditors are to be read in accordance with section 386 in Part XII of this Act.

[255]

NOTES
Sub-s (2): words in square brackets substituted by the Insolvency Act 2000, s 2, Sch 2, Pt I, paras 1, 4, as from 1 January 2003, subject to transitional provisions in SI 2002/2711, art 3.
Modification: this section is modified, in relation to a voluntary arrangement proposed under s 1 of this Act in relation to a UK insurer, where that arrangement includes a composition in satisfaction of any insurance debts and a distribution to creditors of some or all of the assets of that insurer in the course of, or with a view to terminating the whole or any part of the business of that insurer, by the Insurers (Reorganisation and Winding Up) Regulations 2004, SI 2004/353, reg 33(1), (2).

[4A   Approval of arrangement

(1)   This section applies to a decision, under section 4, with respect to the approval of a proposed voluntary arrangement.

(2)   The decision has effect if, in accordance with the rules—
    (a)   it has been taken by both meetings summoned under section 3, or
    (b)   (subject to any order made under subsection (4)) it has been taken by the creditors' meeting summoned under that section.

(3)   If the decision taken by the creditors' meeting differs from that taken by the company meeting, a member of the company may apply to the court.

(4)   An application under subsection (3) shall not bet made after the end of the period of 28 days beginning with—
    (a)   the day on which the decision was taken by the creditors' meeting, or
    (b)   where the decision of the company meeting was taken on a later day, that day.

(5)   Where a member of a regulated company, within the meaning given by paragraph 44 of Schedule A1, applies to the court under subsection (3), the Financial Services Authority is entitled to be heard on the application.

(6)   On an application under subsection (3), the court may—
    (a)   order the decision of the company meeting to have effect instead of the decision of the creditors' meeting, or
    (b)   make such other order as it thinks fit.]

[256]

NOTES
    Inserted by the Insolvency Act 2000, s 2, Sch 2, Pt I, paras 1, 5, as from 1 January 2003, subject to transitional provisions in SI 2002/2711, art 3.

5   Effect of approval

[(1)   This section applies where a decision approving a voluntary arrangement has effect under section 4A.]

(2)   The ... voluntary arrangement—
    (a)   takes effect as if made by the company at the creditors' meeting, and
    [(b)   binds every person who in accordance with the rules—
        (i)   was entitled to vote at that meeting (whether or not he was present or represented at it), or
        (ii)   would have been so entitled if he had had notice of it,
        as if he were a party to the voluntary arrangement.]

[(2A)   If—
    (a)   when the arrangement ceases to have effect any amount payable under the arrangement to a person bound by virtue of subsection (2)(b)(ii) has not been paid, and
    (b)   the arrangement did not come to an end prematurely,
the company shall at that time become liable to pay to that person the amount payable under the arrangement.]

(3)   Subject as follows, if the company is being wound up or [is in administration], the court may do one or both of the following, namely—
    (a)   by order stay or sist all proceedings in the winding up or [provide for the appointment of the administrator to cease to have effect];
    (b)   give such directions with respect to the conduct of the winding up or the administration as it thinks appropriate for facilitating the implementation of the ... voluntary arrangement.

(4)   The court shall not make an order under subsection (3)(a)—
    (a)   at any time before the end of the period of 28 days beginning with the first day on which each of the reports required by section 4(6) has been made to the court, or
    (b)   at any time when an application under the next section or an appeal in respect of such an application is pending, or at any time in the period within which such an appeal may be brought.

[(5)   Where the company is in energy administration, the court shall not make an order or give a direction under subsection (3) unless—
    (a)   the court has given the Secretary of State or the Gas and Electricity Markets Authority a reasonable opportunity of making representations to it about the proposed order or direction; and
    (b)   the order or direction is consistent with the objective of the energy administration.

PART II
OTHER ACTS

(6)   In subsection (5) "in energy administration" and "objective of the energy administration" are to be construed in accordance with Schedule B1 to this Act, as applied by Part 1 of Schedule 20 to the Energy Act 2004.]

[257]

NOTES

Sub-s (1): substituted by the Insolvency Act 2000, s 2, Sch 2, Pt I, paras 1, 6(a), as from 1 January 2003, subject to transitional provisions in SI 2002/2711, art 3.

Sub-s (2): word omitted repealed, and para (b) substituted (together with sub-s (2A)), by the Insolvency Act 2000, ss 2, 15(1), Sch 2, Pt I, paras 1, 6(b), (c), Sch 5, as from 1 January 2003, subject to transitional provisions in SI 2002/2711, art 3.

Sub-s (2A): substituted as noted to sub-s (2) above, as from 1 January 2003, subject to transitional provisions in SI 2002/2711, art 3.

Sub-s (3): first and second words in square brackets substituted by the Enterprise Act 2002, s 248(3), Sch 17, paras 9, 11, as from 15 September 2003, subject to savings and transitional provisions in the Enterprise Act 2002, s 249 and the Enterprise Act 2002 (Commencement No 4 and Transitional Provisions and Savings) Order 2003, SI 2003/2093, art 3; word omitted from para (b) repealed by the Insolvency Act 2000, ss 2, 15(1), Sch 2, Pt I, paras 1, 6(b), Sch 5, as from 1 January 2003, subject to transitional provisions in SI 2002/2711, art 3.

Sub-ss (5), (6): added by the Energy Act 2004, s 159(1), Sch 20, Pt 4, para 43, as from 5 October 2004.

See further: in relation to the application of sub-s (3) above, with modifications, in respect of a proposal made by a bank liquidator or administrator, see the Banking Act 2009, ss 113(6), (8), 154(3), (5) at **[113]**, **[151]**.

6   Challenge of decisions

(1)   Subject to this section, an application to the court may be made, by any of the persons specified below, on one or both of the following grounds, namely—
-   (a)   that a voluntary arrangement [which has effect under section 4A] unfairly prejudices the interests of a creditor, member or contributory of the company;
-   (b)   that there has been some material irregularity at or in relation to either of the meetings.

(2)   The persons who may apply under [subsection (1)] are—
-   (a)   a person entitled, in accordance with the rules, to vote at either of the meetings;
-   [(aa)   a person who would have been entitled, in accordance with the rules, to vote at the creditors' meeting if he had had notice of it]
-   (b)   the nominee or any person who has replaced him under section 2(4) or 4(2); and
-   (c)   if the company is being wound up or [is in administration], the liquidator or administrator.

[(2A)   Subject to this section, where a voluntary arrangement in relation to a company in energy administration is approved at the meetings summoned under section 3, an application to the court may be made—
-   (a)   by the Secretary of State, or
-   (b)   with the consent of the Secretary of State, by the Gas and Electricity Markets Authority,

on the ground that the voluntary arrangement is not consistent with the achievement of the objective of the energy administration.]

(3)   An application under this section shall not be made
-   [(a)]   after the end of the period of 28 days beginning with the first day on which each of the reports required by section 4(6) has been made to the court [or
-   (b)   in the case of a person who was not given notice of the creditors' meeting, after the end of the period of 28 days beginning with the day on which he became aware that the meeting had taken place,

but (subject to that) an application made by a person within subsection (2)(aa) on the ground that the voluntary arrangement prejudices his interests may be made after the arrangement has ceased to have effect, unless it came to an end prematurely.]

(4)   Where on such an application the court is satisfied as to either of the grounds mentioned in subsection (1) [or, in the case of an application under subsection (2A), as to the ground mentioned in that subsection], it may do one or both of the following, namely—
-   (a)   revoke or suspend [any decision approving the voluntary arrangement which has effect under section 4A] or, in a case falling within subsection (1)(b), any [decision taken by the meeting in question which has effect under that section];
-   (b)   give a direction to any person for the summoning of further meetings to consider any revised proposal the person who made the original proposal may make or, in a case falling within subsection (1)(b), a further company or (as the case may be) creditors' meeting to reconsider the original proposal.

(5)   Where at any time after giving a direction under subsection (4)(b) for the summoning of meetings to consider a revised proposal the court is satisfied that the person who made the original proposal does not intend to submit a revised proposal, the court shall revoke the direction and revoke or suspend any [decision approving the voluntary arrangement which has effect under section 4A].

(6)   In a case where the court, on an application under this section with respect to any meeting—

    (a)   gives a direction under subsection (4)(b), or

    (b)   revokes or suspends an approval under subsection (4)(a) or (5),

the court may give such supplemental directions as it thinks fit and, in particular, directions with respect to things done [under the voluntary arrangement since it took effect].

(7)   Except in pursuance of the preceding provisions of this section, [a decision taken] at a meeting summoned under section 3 is not invalidated by any irregularity at or in relation to the meeting.

[(8)   In this section "in energy administration" and "objective of the energy administration" are to be construed in accordance with Schedule B1 to this Act, as applied by Part 1 of Schedule 20 to the Energy Act 2004.]

[258]

NOTES

Sub-s (1): words in square brackets substituted by the Insolvency Act 2000, s 2(a), Sch 2, Pt I, paras 1, 7(1), (2), as from 1 January 2003, subject to transitional provisions in SI 2002/2711, art 3.

Sub-s (2): words in first pair of square brackets substituted by the Energy Act 2004, s 159(1), Sch 20, Pt 4, para 44(1), (2), as from 5 October 2004; para (aa) inserted by the Insolvency Act 2000, s 2, Sch 2, Pt I, paras 1, 7(1), (3), as from 1 January 2003, subject to transitional provisions in SI 2002/2711, art 3; words in square brackets in para (c) substituted by the Enterprise Act 2002, s 248(3), Sch 17, paras 9, 12, as from 15 September 2003, subject to savings and transitional provisions in the Enterprise Act 2002, s 249 and the Enterprise Act 2002 (Commencement No 4 and Transitional Provisions and Savings) Order 2003, SI 2003/2093, art 3.

Sub-s (2A): inserted by the Energy Act 2004, s 159(1), Sch 20, Pt 4, para 44(1), (3), as from 5 October 2004.

Sub-s (3): words in square brackets inserted by the Insolvency Act 2000, s 2, Sch 2, Pt I, paras 1, 7(1), (4), as from 1 January 2003, subject to transitional provisions in SI 2002/2711, art 3.

Sub-s (4): words in first pair of square brackets inserted by the Energy Act 2004, s 159(1), Sch 20, Pt 4, para 44(1), (4), as from 5 October 2004; words in second and third pairs of square brackets substituted by the Insolvency Act 2000, s 2, Sch 2, Pt I, paras 1, 7(1), (5), as from 1 January 2003, subject to transitional provisions in SI 2002/2711, art 3.

Sub-ss (5)–(7): words in square brackets substituted by the Insolvency Act 2000, s 2, Sch 2, Pt I, paras 1, 7(1), (6)–(8), as from 1 January 2003, subject to transitional provisions in SI 2002/2711, art 3.

Sub-s (8): added by the Energy Act 2004, s 159(1), Sch 20, Pt 4, para 44(1), (5), as from 5 October 2004.

[6A   False representations, etc

(1)   If, for the purpose of obtaining the approval of the members or creditors of a company to a proposal for a voluntary arrangement, a person who is an officer of the company—

    (a)   makes any false representation, or

    (b)   fraudulently does, or omits to do, anything,

he commits an offence.

(2)   Subsection (1) applies even if the proposal is not approved.

(3)   For purposes of this section "officer" includes a shadow director.

(4)   A person guilty of an offence under this section is liable to imprisonment or a fine, or both.]

[259]

NOTES

Inserted by the Insolvency Act 2000, s 2, Sch 2, Pt I, paras 1, 8, as from 1 January 2003, subject to transitional provisions in SI 2002/2711, art 3.

7   Implementation of proposal

(1)   This section applies where a voluntary arrangement [has effect under section 4A].

(2)   The person who is for the time being carrying out in relation to the voluntary arrangement the functions conferred—

    [(a)   on the nominee by virtue of the approval given at one or both of the meetings summoned under section 3] or

    (b)   by virtue of section 2(4) or 4(2) on a person other than the nominee,

shall be known as the supervisor of the voluntary arrangement.

(3)   If any of the company's creditors or any other person is dissatisfied by any act, omission or decision of the supervisor, he may apply to the court; and on the application the court may—

    (a)   confirm, reverse or modify any act or decision of the supervisor,

    (b)   give him directions, or

    (c)   make such other order as it thinks fit.

(4)   The supervisor—

    (a)   may apply to the court for directions in relation to any particular matter arising under the voluntary arrangement, and

PART II
OTHER ACTS

(b) is included among the persons who may apply to the court for the winding up of the company or for an administration order to be made in relation to it.

(5) The court may, whenever—

(a) it is expedient to appoint a person to carry out the functions of the supervisor, and

(b) it is inexpedient, difficult or impracticable for an appointment to be made without the assistance of the court,

make an order appointing a person who is qualified to act as an insolvency practitioner [or authorised to act as supervisor, in relation to the voluntary arrangement], either in substitution for the existing supervisor or to fill a vacancy.

(6) The power conferred by subsection (5) is exercisable so as to increase the number of persons exercising the functions of supervisor or, where there is more than one person exercising those functions, so as to replace one or more of those persons.

[260]

NOTES

Sub-s (1): words in square brackets substituted by the Insolvency Act 2000, s 2, Sch 2, Pt I, paras 1, 9(a), as from 1 January 2003, subject to transitional provisions in SI 2002/2711, art 3.

Sub-s (2): para (a) substituted by the Insolvency Act 2000, s 2, Sch 2, Pt I, paras 1, 9(b), as from 1 January 2003, subject to transitional provisions in SI 2002/2711, art 3.

Sub-s (5): words in square brackets substituted by the Insolvency Act 2000, s 2, Sch 2, Pt I, paras 1, 9(c), as from 1 January 2003, subject to transitional provisions in SI 2002/2711, art 3.

[7A Prosecution of delinquent officers of company

(1) This section applies where a moratorium under section 1A has been obtained for a company or the approval of a voluntary arrangement in relation to a company has taken effect under section 4A or paragraph 36 of Schedule A1.

(2) If it appears to the nominee or supervisor that any past or present officer of the company has been guilty of any offence in connection with the moratorium or, as the case may be, voluntary arrangement for which he is criminally liable, the nominee or supervisor shall forthwith—

(a) report the matter to the appropriate authority, and

(b) provide the appropriate authority with such information and give the authority such access to and facilities for inspecting and taking copies of documents (being information or documents in the possession or under the control of the nominee or supervisor and relating to the matter in question) as the authority requires.

In this subsection, "the appropriate authority" means—

(i) in the case of a company registered in England and Wales, the Secretary of State, and

(ii) in the case of a company registered in Scotland, the Lord Advocate.

(3) Where a report is made to the Secretary of State under subsection (2), he may, for the purpose of investigating the matter reported to him and such other matters relating to the affairs of the company as appear to him to require investigation, exercise any of the powers which are exercisable by inspectors appointed under section 431 or 432 of the Companies Act to investigate a company's affairs.

(4) For the purpose of such an investigation any obligation imposed on a person by any provision of the Companies Act to produce documents or give information to, or otherwise to assist, inspectors so appointed is to be regarded as an obligation similarly to assist the Secretary of State in his investigation.

(5) An answer given by a person to a question put to him in exercise of the powers conferred by subsection (3) may be used in evidence against him.

(6) However, in criminal proceedings in which that person is charged with an offence to which this subsection applies—

(a) no evidence relating to the answer may be adduced, and

(b) no question relating to it may be asked,

by or on behalf of the prosecution, unless evidence relating to it is adduced, or a question relating to it is asked, in the proceedings by or on behalf of that person.

(7) Subsection (6) applies to any offence other than—

(a) an offence under section 2 or 5 of the Perjury Act 1911 (false statements made on oath otherwise than in judicial proceedings or made otherwise than on oath), or

(b) an offence under section 44(1) or (2) of the Criminal Law (Consolidation) (Scotland) Act 1995 (false statements made on oath or otherwise than on oath).

(8) Where a prosecuting authority institutes criminal proceedings following any report under subsection (2), the nominee or supervisor, and every officer and agent of the company past and present (other than the defendant or defender), shall give the authority all assistance in connection with the prosecution which he is reasonably able to give.

For this purpose—

"agent" includes any banker or solicitor of the company and any person employed by the company as auditor, whether that person is or is not an officer of the company,
"prosecuting authority" means the Director of Public Prosecutions, the Lord Advocate or the Secretary of State.

(9)   The court may, on the application of the prosecuting authority, direct any person referred to in subsection (8) to comply with that subsection if he has failed to do so.]

[261]

NOTES
Inserted, together with s 7B, by the Insolvency Act 2000, s 2, Sch 2, Pt I, paras 1, 10, as from 1 January 2003, subject to transitional provisions in SI 2002/2711, art 3.

[7B   Arrangements coming to an end prematurely

For the purposes of this Part, a voluntary arrangement the approval of which has taken effect under section 4A or paragraph 36 of Schedule A1 comes to an end prematurely if, when it ceases to have effect, it has not been fully implemented in respect of all persons bound by the arrangement by virtue of section 5(2)(b)(i) or, as the case may be, paragraph 37(2)(b)(i) of Schedule A1.]

[262]

NOTES
Inserted as noted to s 7A at **[261]**.

8–72H   ((*Pts II, III*) *Outside the scope of this work; for s 8 see Butterworths Securities and Financial Services Law Handbook.*)

PART IV
WINDING UP OF COMPANIES REGISTERED UNDER THE COMPANIES ACTS

73–116   ((*Chs I–V*) *Outside the scope of this work.*)

CHAPTER VI
WINDING UP BY THE COURT

117–121   (*Outside the scope of this work.*)

Grounds and effect of winding-up petition

122   (*Outside the scope of this work.*)

123   Definition of inability to pay debts

(1)   A company is deemed unable to pay its debts—
  (a)   if a creditor (by assignment or otherwise) to whom the company is indebted in a sum exceeding £750 then due has served on the company, by leaving it at the company's registered office, a written demand (in the prescribed form) requiring the company to pay the sum so due and the company has for 3 weeks thereafter neglected to pay the sum or to secure or compound for it to the reasonable satisfaction of the creditor, or
  (b)   if, in England and Wales, execution or other process issued on a judgment, decree or order of any court in favour of a creditor of the company is returned unsatisfied in whole or in part, or
  (c)   if, in Scotland, the induciae of a charge for payment on an extract decree, or an extract registered bond, or an extract registered protest, have expired without payment being made, or
  (d)   if, in Northern Ireland, a certificate of unenforceability has been granted in respect of a judgment against the company, or
  (e)   if it is proved to the satisfaction of the court that the company is unable to pay its debts as they fall due.

(2)   A company is also deemed unable to pay its debts if it is proved to the satisfaction of the court that the value of the company's assets is less than the amount of its liabilities, taking into account its contingent and prospective liabilities.

(3)   The money sum for the time being specified in subsection (1)(a) is subject to increase or reduction by order under section 416 in Part XV.

[263]

124   (*Outside the scope of this work.*)

[124A Petition for winding-up on grounds of public interest

(1)   Where it appears to the Secretary of State from—
  (a)   any report made or information obtained under Part XIV [(except section 448A)] of the Companies Act 1985 (company investigations, &c),
  [(b)   any report made by inspectors under—
      (i)   section 167, 168, 169 or 284 of the Financial Services and Markets Act 2000, or
      (ii)   where the company is an open-ended investment company (within the meaning of that Act), regulations made as a result of section 262(2)(k) of that Act;
  (bb)   any information or documents obtained under section 165, 171, 172, 173 or 175 of that Act,]
  (c)   any information obtained under section 2 of the Criminal Justice Act 1987 or section 52 of the Criminal Justice (Scotland) Act 1987 (fraud investigations), or
  (d)   any information obtained under section 83 of the Companies Act 1989 (powers exercisable for purpose of assisting overseas regulatory authorities),

that it is expedient in the public interest that a company should be wound up, he may present a petition for it to be wound up if the court thinks it just and equitable for it to be so.

(2)   This section does not apply if the company is already being wound up by the court.]

[264]

NOTES
  Inserted by the Companies Act 1989, s 60(3).
  Sub-s (1): words in square brackets in para (a) inserted by the Companies (Audit, Investigations and Community Enterprise) Act 2004, s 25(1), Sch 2, Pt 3, para 27, as from 6 April 2005; paras (b), (bb) substituted for original para (b) by the Financial Services and Markets Act 2000 (Consequential Amendments and Repeals) Order 2001, SI 2001/3649, art 305, as from 1 December 2001.

124B–134   (*Outside the scope of this work.*)

Appointment of liquidator

135   Appointment and powers of provisional liquidator

(1)   Subject to the provisions of this section, the court may, at any time after the presentation of a winding-up petition, appoint a liquidator provisionally.

(2)   In England and Wales, the appointment of a provisional liquidator may be made at any time before the making of a winding-up order; and either the official receiver or any other fit person may be appointed.

(3)   In Scotland, such an appointment may be made at any time before the first appointment of liquidators.

(4)   The provisional liquidator shall carry out such functions as the court may confer on him.

(5)   When a liquidator is provisionally appointed by the court, his powers may be limited by the order appointing him.

[265]

NOTES
  Modification: in relation to the notification to the Financial Services Authority of the appointment of a provisional liquidator under sub-s (1) of this section on or after 5 May 2004, see the Credit Institutions (Reorganisation and Winding up) Regulations 2004, SI 2004/1045, reg 9(1)(c), (5).
  See further: in relation to the application of this section, with modifications, in respect of bank insolvency and administration, see the Banking Act 2009, ss 103(3), (4), Table, 145(3), (4), Table 2 at **[103]**, **[142]**.

136–140   (*Outside the scope of this work.*)

Liquidation committees

141   Liquidation committee (England and Wales)

(1)   Where a winding-up order has been made by the court in England and Wales and separate meetings of creditors and contributories have been summoned for the purpose of choosing a person to be liquidator, those meetings may establish a committee ("the liquidation committee") to exercise the functions conferred on it by or under this Act.

(2)   The liquidator (not being the official receiver) may at any time, if he thinks fit, summon separate general meetings of the company's creditors and contributories for the purpose of determining whether such a committee should be established and, if it is so determined, of establishing it.

The liquidator (not being the official receiver) shall summon such a meeting if he is requested, in accordance with the rules, to do so by one-tenth, in value, of the company's creditors.

(3)   Where meetings are summoned under this section, or for the purpose of choosing a person to be liquidator, and either the meeting of creditors or the meeting of contributories decides that a liquidation committee should be established, but the other meeting does not so decide or decides that a committee should not be established, the committee shall be established in accordance with the rules, unless the court otherwise orders.

(4)   The liquidation committee is not to be able or required to carry out its functions at any time when the official receiver is liquidator; but at any such time its functions are vested in the Secretary of State except to the extent that the rules otherwise provide.

(5)   Where there is for the time being no liquidation committee, and the liquidator is a person other than the official receiver, the functions of such a committee are vested in the Secretary of State except to the extent that the rules otherwise provide.

[266]

NOTES
See further: in relation to the application of this section, with modifications, in respect of bank insolvency, see the Banking Act 2009, s 103(3), (4), Table at **[103]**.

142   Liquidation committee (Scotland)

(1)   Where a winding-up order has been made by the court in Scotland and separate meetings of creditors and contributories have been summoned for the purpose of choosing a person to be liquidator or, under section 138(4), only a meeting of creditors has been summoned for that purpose, those meetings or (as the case may be) that meeting may establish a committee ("the liquidation committee") to exercise the functions conferred on it by or under this Act.

(2)   The liquidator may at any time, if he thinks fit, summon separate general meetings of the company's creditors and contributories for the purpose of determining whether such a committee should be established and, if it is so determined, of establishing it.

(3)   The liquidator, if appointed by the court otherwise than under section 139(4)(a), is required to summon meetings under subsection (2) if he is requested, in accordance with the rules, to do so by one-tenth, in value, of the company's creditors.

(4)   Where meetings are summoned under this section, or for the purpose of choosing a person to be liquidator, and either the meeting of creditors or the meeting of contributories decides that a liquidation committee should be established, but the other meeting does not so decide or decides that a committee should not be established, the committee shall be established in accordance with the rules, unless the court otherwise orders.

(5)   Where in the case of any winding up there is for the time being no liquidation committee, the functions of such a committee are vested in the court except to the extent that the rules otherwise provide.

(6)   In addition to the powers and duties conferred and imposed on it by this Act, a liquidation committee has such of the powers and duties of commissioners in a sequestration as may be conferred and imposed on such committees by the rules.

[267]

NOTES
See further: in relation to the application of this section, with modifications, in respect of bank insolvency, see the Banking Act 2009, s 103(3), (4), Table at **[103]**.

143–162   (*Outside the scope of this work.*)

CHAPTER VII
LIQUIDATORS

163, 164   (*Outside the scope of this work.*)

Liquidator's powers and duties

165–167   (*Outside the scope of this work.*)

168   Supplementary powers (England and Wales)

(1)   This section applies in the case of a company which is being wound up by the court in England and Wales.

(2)   The liquidator may summon general meetings of the creditors or contributories for the purpose of ascertaining their wishes; and it is his duty to summon meetings at such times as the creditors or contributories by resolution (either at the meeting appointing the liquidator or otherwise) may direct, or whenever requested in writing to do so by one-tenth in value of the creditors or contributories (as the case may be).

(3)   The liquidator may apply to the court (in the prescribed manner) for directions in relation to any particular matter arising in the winding up.

(4)   Subject to the provisions of this Act, the liquidator shall use his own discretion in the management of the assets and their distribution among the creditors.

(5)   If any person is aggrieved by an act or decision of the liquidator, that person may apply to the court; and the court may confirm, reverse or modify the act or decision complained of, and make such order in the case as it thinks just.

[(5A)   Where at any time after a winding-up petition has been presented to the court against any person (including an insolvent partnership or other body which may be wound up under Part V of the Act as an unregistered company), whether by virtue of the provisions of the Insolvent Partnerships Order 1994 or not, the attention of the court is drawn to the fact that the person in question is a member of an insolvent partnership, the court may make an order as to the future conduct of the insolvency proceedings and any such order may apply any provisions of that Order with any necessary modifications.

(5B)   Any order or directions under subsection (5A) may be made or given on the application of the official receiver, any responsible insolvency practitioner, the trustee of the partnership or any other interested person and may include provisions as to the administration of the joint estate of the partnership, and in particular how it and the separate estate of any member are to be administered.

[(5C)   Where the court makes an order for the winding up of an insolvent partnership under—
    (a)   section 72(1)(a) of the Financial Services Act 1986;
    (b)   section 92(1)(a) of the Banking Act 1987; or
    (c)   section 367(3)(a) of the Financial Services and Markets Act 2000,
the court may make an order as to the future conduct of the winding up proceedings, and any such order may apply any provisions of the Insolvent Partnerships Order 1994 with any necessary modifications.]]

[268]

NOTES

Sub-ss (5A), (5B): added by the Insolvent Partnerships Order 1994, SI 1994/2421, art 14(1).

Sub-s (5C): added, together with sub-ss (5A), (5B), by the Insolvent Partnerships Order 1994, SI 1994/2421, art 14(1); repealed by the Financial Services and Markets Act 2000 (Consequential Amendments and Repeals) Order 2001, SI 2001/3649, art 306, but subsequently substituted by the Financial Services and Markets Act 2000 (Consequential Amendments) Order 2002, SI 2002/1555, art 15, as from 3 July 2002, which further provided that the repeal by SI 2001/3649 is to be treated as if it had not been made.

See further: in relation to the application of this section, with modifications, in respect of bank insolvency and administration, see the Banking Act 2009, ss 103(3), (4), Table, 145(3), (4), Table 2 at **[103]**, **[142]**.

Financial Services Act 1986; Banking Act 1987: repealed by SI 2001/3649, art 3(1)(c), (d).

169   Supplementary powers (Scotland)

(1)   In the case of a winding up in Scotland, the court may provide by order that the liquidator may, where there is no liquidation committee, exercise any of the following powers, namely—
    (a)   to bring or defend any action or other legal proceeding in the name and on behalf of the company, or
    (b)   to carry on the business of the company so far as may be necessary for its beneficial winding up,
without the sanction or intervention of the court.

(2)   In a winding up by the court in Scotland, the liquidator has (subject to the rules) the same powers as a trustee on a bankrupt estate.

[269]

NOTES

See further: in relation to the application of this section, with modifications, in respect of bank insolvency, see the Banking Act 2009, s 103(3), (4), Table at **[103]**.

170–174   (*Outside the scope of this work.*)

CHAPTER VIII
PROVISIONS OF GENERAL APPLICATION IN WINDING UP

175, 176   (*Outside the scope of this work.*)

[Property subject to floating charge]

NOTES

Cross-heading inserted by the Enterprise Act 2002, s 252, as from 15 September 2003.

176ZA (*Outside the scope of this work.*)

[176A Share of assets for unsecured creditors

(1) This section applies where a floating charge relates to property of a company—
  (a) which has gone into liquidation,
  (b) which is in administration,
  (c) of which there is a provisional liquidator, or
  (d) of which there is a receiver.

(2) The liquidator, administrator or receiver—
  (a) shall make a prescribed part of the company's net property available for the satisfaction of unsecured debts, and
  (b) shall not distribute that part to the proprietor of a floating charge except in so far as it exceeds the amount required for the satisfaction of unsecured debts.

(3) Subsection (2) shall not apply to a company if—
  (a) the company's net property is less than the prescribed minimum, and
  (b) the liquidator, administrator or receiver thinks that the cost of making a distribution to unsecured creditors would be disproportionate to the benefits.

(4) Subsection (2) shall also not apply to a company if or in so far as it is disapplied by—
  (a) a voluntary arrangement in respect of the company, or
  (b) a compromise or arrangement agreed under [Part 26 of the Companies Act 2006 (arrangements and reconstructions)].

(5) Subsection (2) shall also not apply to a company if—
  (a) the liquidator, administrator or receiver applies to the court for an order under this subsection on the ground that the cost of making a distribution to unsecured creditors would be disproportionate to the benefits, and
  (b) the court orders that subsection (2) shall not apply.

(6) In subsections (2) and (3) a company's net property is the amount of its property which would, but for this section, be available for satisfaction of claims of holders of debentures secured by, or holders of, any floating charge created by the company.

(7) An order under subsection (2) prescribing part of a company's net property may, in particular, provide for its calculation—
  (a) as a percentage of the company's net property, or
  (b) as an aggregate of different percentages of different parts of the company's net property.

(8) An order under this section—
  (a) must be made by statutory instrument, and
  (b) shall be subject to annulment pursuant to a resolution of either House of Parliament.

(9) In this section—
  "floating charge" means a charge which is a floating charge on its creation and which is created after the first order under subsection (2)(a) comes into force, and
  "prescribed" means prescribed by order by the Secretary of State.

(10) An order under this section may include transitional or incidental provision.]

[270]

NOTES

Inserted by the Enterprise Act 2002, s 252, as from 15 September 2003.

Sub-s (4): words in square brackets substituted by the Companies Act 2006 (Consequential Amendments etc) Order 2008, SI 2008/948, art 3(1)(b), Sch 1, Pt 2, para 103, as from 6 April 2008, subject to transitional provisions and savings in arts 6, 11, 12 thereof.

In relation to the application of this section, with modifications, in respect of bank insolvency and administration, see the Banking Act 2009, ss 103(3), (4), Table, 145(3), (4), Table 2 at **[103]**, **[142]**.

Disapplication: as to the disapplication of this section in relation to any charge created or otherwise arising under a financial collateral arrangement, see the Financial Collateral Arrangements (No 2) Regulations 2003, SI 2003/3226, reg 10(3). This section is also disapplied in respect of regulated covered bonds, by the Regulated Covered Bonds Regulations 2008, SI 2008/346, reg 46, Schedule, Pt 1, para 2(4).

Order: the Insolvency Act 1986 (Prescribed Part) Order 2003, SI 2003/2097.

177 (*Outside the scope of this work.*)

Disclaimer (*England and Wales only*)

178 Power to disclaim onerous property

(1) This and the next two sections apply to a company that is being wound up in England and Wales.

(2) Subject as follows, the liquidator may, by the giving of the prescribed notice, disclaim any onerous property and may do so notwithstanding that he has taken possession of it, endeavoured to sell it, or otherwise exercised rights of ownership in relation to it.

(3)   The following is onerous property for the purposes of this section—
    (a)   any unprofitable contract, and
    (b)   any other property of the company which is unsaleable or not readily saleable or is such that it may give rise to a liability to pay money or perform any other onerous act.

(4)   A disclaimer under this section—
    (a)   operates so as to determine, as from the date of the disclaimer, the rights, interests and liabilities of the company in or in respect of the property disclaimed; but
    (b)   does not, except so far as is necessary for the purpose of releasing the company from any liability, affect the rights or liabilities of any other person.

(5)   A notice of disclaimer shall not be given under this section in respect of any property if—
    (a)   a person interested in the property has applied in writing to the liquidator or one of his predecessors as liquidator requiring the liquidator or that predecessor to decide whether he will disclaim or not, and
    (b)   the period of 28 days beginning with the day on which that application was made, or such longer period as the court may allow, has expired without a notice of disclaimer having been given under this section in respect of that property.

(6)   Any person sustaining loss or damage in consequence of the operation of a disclaimer under this section is deemed a creditor of the company to the extent of the loss or damage and accordingly may prove for the loss or damage in the winding up.

[**271**]

NOTES
    In relation to the application of this section, with modifications, in respect of bank insolvency and administration, see the Banking Act 2009, ss 103(3), (4), Table, 145(3), (4), Table 2 at [**103**], [**142**].
    See further: as to the disapplication of this section, or in Scotland any rule of law having the same effect as this section, in relation to any financial collateral arrangement, where the collateral-provider or collateral-taker under the arrangement is being wound-up, see the Financial Collateral Arrangements (No 2) Regulations 2003, SI 2003/3226, reg 10(4).

179   Disclaimer of leaseholds

(1)   The disclaimer under section 178 of any property of a leasehold nature does not take effect unless a copy of the disclaimer has been served (so far as the liquidator is aware of their addresses) on every person claiming under the company as underlessee or mortgagee and either—
    (a)   no application under section 181 below is made with respect to that property before the end of the period of 14 days beginning with the day on which the last notice served under this subsection was served; or
    (b)   where such an application has been made, the court directs that the disclaimer shall take effect.

(2)   Where the court gives a direction under subsection (1)(b) it may also, instead of or in addition to any order it makes under section 181, make such orders with respect to fixtures, tenant's improvements and other matters arising out of the lease as it thinks fit.

[**272**]

NOTES
    See further: in relation to the application of this section, with modifications, in respect of bank insolvency and administration, see the Banking Act 2009, ss 103(3), (4), Table, 145(3), (4), Table 2 at [**103**], [**142**].

180   Land subject to rentcharge

(1)   The following applies where, in consequence of the disclaimer under section 178 of any land subject to a rentcharge, that land vests by operation of law in the Crown or any other person (referred to in the next subsection as "the proprietor").

(2)   The proprietor and the successors in title of the proprietor are not subject to any personal liability in respect of any sums becoming due under the rentcharge except sums becoming due after the proprietor, or some person claiming under or through the proprietor, has taken possession or control of the land or has entered into occupation of it.

[**273**]

NOTES
    See further: in relation to the application of this section, with modifications, in respect of bank insolvency and administration, see the Banking Act 2009, ss 103(3), (4), Table, 145(3), (4), Table 2 at [**103**], [**142**].

181   Powers of court (general)

(1)   This section and the next apply where the liquidator has disclaimed property under section 178.

(2)   An application under this section may be made to the court by—

(a)   any person who claims an interest in the disclaimed property, or
(b)   any person who is under any liability in respect of the disclaimed property, not being a
       liability discharged by the disclaimer.

(3)   Subject as follows, the court may on the application make an order, on such terms as it
thinks fit, for the vesting of the disclaimed property in, or for its delivery to—
(a)   a person entitled to it or a trustee for such a person, or
(b)   a person subject to such a liability as is mentioned in subsection (2)(b) or a trustee for
       such a person.

(4)   The court shall not make an order under subsection (3)(b) except where it appears to the
court that it would be just to do so for the purpose of compensating the person subject to the liability
in respect of the disclaimer.

(5)   The effect of any order under this section shall be taken into account in assessing for the
purpose of section 178(6) the extent of any loss or damage sustained by any person in consequence
of the disclaimer.

(6)   An order under this section vesting property in any person need not be completed by
conveyance, assignment or transfer.

[274]

NOTES
    See further: in relation to the application of this section, with modifications, in respect of bank insolvency and
administration, see the Banking Act 2009, ss 103(3), (4), Table, 145(3), (4), Table 2 at **[103]**, **[142]**.

182   Powers of court (leaseholds)

(1)   The court shall not make an order under section 181 vesting property of a leasehold nature
in any person claiming under the company as underlessee or mortgagee except on terms making that
person—
(a)   subject to the same liabilities and obligations as the company was subject to under the
       lease at the commencement of the winding up, or
(b)   if the court thinks fit, subject to the same liabilities and obligations as that person would
       be subject to if the lease had been assigned to him at the commencement of the winding
       up.

(2)   For the purposes of an order under section 181 relating to only part of any property
comprised in a lease, the requirements of subsection (1) apply as if the lease comprised only the
property to which the order relates.

(3)   Where subsection (1) applies and no person claiming under the company as underlessee or
mortgagee is willing to accept an order under section 181 on the terms required by virtue of that
subsection, the court may, by order under that section, vest the company's estate or interest in the
property in any person who is liable (whether personally or in a representative capacity, and whether
alone or jointly with the company) to perform the lessee's covenants in the lease.

    The court may vest that estate and interest in such a person freed and discharged from all estates,
incumbrances and interests created by the company.

(4)   Where subsection (1) applies and a person claiming under the company as underlessee or
mortgagee declines to accept an order under section 181, that person is excluded from all interest in
the property.

[275]

NOTES
    See further: in relation to the application of this section, with modifications, in respect of bank insolvency and
administration, see the Banking Act 2009, ss 103(3), (4), Table, 145(3), (4), Table 2 at **[103]**, **[142]**.

183–185   (*Outside the scope of this work.*)

Miscellaneous matters

186, 187   (*Outside the scope of this work.*)

188   Notification that company is in liquidation

[(1)   When a company is being wound up, whether by the court or voluntarily—
(a)   every invoice, order for goods [or services], business letter or order form (whether in
       hard copy, electronic or any other form) issued by or on behalf of the company, or a
       liquidator of the company or a receiver or manager of the company's property, ... and
(b)   all the company's websites,
must contain a statement that the company is being wound up.]

(2)   If default is made in complying with this section, the company and any of the following persons who knowingly and wilfully authorises or permits the default, namely, any officer of the company, any liquidator of the company and any receiver or manager, is liable to a fine.

[276]

NOTES

Sub-s (1): substituted by the Companies (Registrar, Languages and Trading Disclosures) Regulations 2006, SI 2006/3429, reg 7(1), as from 1 January 2007; words in square brackets inserted and words omitted repealed by the Companies (Trading Disclosures) (Insolvency) Regulations 2008, SI 2008/1897, reg 5(1), as from 1 October 2008.

See further: in relation to the application of this section, with modifications, in respect of bank insolvency and administration, see the Banking Act 2009, ss 103(3), (4), Table, 145(3), (4), Table 2 at [103], [142].

189–205   (*Outside the scope of this work.*)

CHAPTER X
MALPRACTICE BEFORE AND DURING LIQUIDATION; PENALISATION OF COMPANIES AND COMPANY OFFICERS; INVESTIGATIONS AND PROSECUTIONS

206–211   (*Outside the scope of this work.*)

Penalisation of directors and officers

212   Summary remedy against delinquent directors, liquidators, etc

(1)   This section applies if in the course of the winding up of a company it appears that a person who—

(a)   is or has been an officer of the company,

(b)   has acted as liquidator ... or administrative receiver of the company, or

(c)   not being a person falling within paragraph (a) or (b), is or has been concerned, or has taken part, in the promotion, formation or management of the company,

has misapplied or retained, or become accountable for, any money or other property of the company, or been guilty of any misfeasance or breach of any fiduciary or other duty in relation to the company.

(2)   The reference in subsection (1) to any misfeasance or breach of any fiduciary or other duty in relation to the company includes, in the case of a person who has acted as liquidator ... of the company, any misfeasance or breach of any fiduciary or other duty in connection with the carrying out of his functions as liquidator ... of the company.

(3)   The court may, on the application of the official receiver or the liquidator, or of any creditor or contributory, examine into the conduct of the person falling within subsection (1) and compel him—

(a)   to repay, restore or account for the money or property or any part of it, with interest at such rate as the court thinks just, or

(b)   to contribute such sum to the company's assets by way of compensation in respect of the misfeasance or breach of fiduciary or other duty as the court thinks just.

(4)   The power to make an application under subsection (3) in relation to a person who has acted as liquidator ... of the company is not exercisable, except with the leave of the court, after [he] has had his release.

(5)   The power of a contributory to make an application under subsection (3) is not exercisable except with the leave of the court, but is exercisable notwithstanding that he will not benefit from any order the court may make on the application.

[277]

NOTES

Sub-s (1): word omitted repealed by the Enterprise Act 2002, ss 248(3), 278(2), Sch 17, paras 9, 18(a), Sch 26, as from 15 September 2003, subject to savings and transitional provisions in the Enterprise Act 2002, s 249 and the Enterprise Act 2002 (Commencement No 4 and Transitional Provisions and Savings) Order 2003, SI 2003/2093, art 3.

Sub-s (2): words omitted repealed by the Enterprise Act 2002, ss 248(3), 278(2), Sch 17, paras 9, 18(b), Sch 26, subject to savings and transitional provisions as noted to sub-s (1) above.

Sub-s (4): words omitted repealed and word in square brackets substituted by the Enterprise Act 2002, ss 248(3), 278(2), Sch 17, paras 9, 18(c), Sch 26, subject to savings and transitional provisions as noted to sub-s (1) above.

See further: in relation to the application of this section, with modifications, in respect of bank insolvency, see the Banking Act 2009, s 103(3), (4), Table at [103].

213 Fraudulent trading

(1)   If in the course of the winding up of a company it appears that any business of the company has been carried on with intent to defraud creditors of the company or creditors of any other person, or for any fraudulent purpose, the following has effect.

(2)   The court, on the application of the liquidator may declare that any persons who were knowingly parties to the carrying on of the business in the manner above-mentioned are to be liable to make such contributions (if any) to the company's assets as the court thinks proper.

[278]

NOTES

See further: in relation to the application of this section, with modifications, in respect of bank insolvency and administration, see the Banking Act 2009, ss 103(3), (4), Table, 145(3), (4), Table 2 at **[103]**, **[142]**.

214 Wrongful trading

(1)   Subject to subsection (3) below, if in the course of the winding up of a company it appears that subsection (2) of this section applies in relation to a person who is or has been a director of the company, the court, on the application of the liquidator, may declare that that person is to be liable to make such contribution (if any) to the company's assets as the court thinks proper.

(2)   This subsection applies in relation to a person if—
    (a)   the company has gone into insolvent liquidation,
    (b)   at some time before the commencement of the winding up of the company, that person knew or ought to have concluded that there was no reasonable prospect that the company would avoid going into insolvent liquidation, and
    (c)   that person was a director of the company at that time; but the court shall not make a declaration under this section in any case where the time mentioned in paragraph (b) above was before 28th April 1986.

(3)   The court shall not make a declaration under this section with respect to any person if it is satisfied that after the condition specified in subsection (2)(b) was first satisfied in relation to him that person took every step with a view to minimising the potential loss to the company's creditors as (assuming him to have known that there was no reasonable prospect that the company would avoid going into insolvent liquidation) he ought to have taken.

(4)   For the purposes of subsections (2) and (3), the facts which a director of a company ought to know or ascertain, the conclusions which he ought to reach and the steps which he ought to take are those which would be known or ascertained, or reached or taken, by a reasonably diligent person having both—
    (a)   the general knowledge, skill and experience that may reasonably be expected of a person carrying out the same functions as are carried out by that director in relation to the company, and
    (b)   the general knowledge, skill and experience that that director has.

(5)   The reference in subsection (4) to the functions carried out in relation to a company by a director of the company includes any functions which he does not carry out but which have been entrusted to him.

(6)   For the purposes of this section a company goes into insolvent liquidation if it goes into liquidation at a time when its assets are insufficient for the payment of its debts and other liabilities and the expenses of the winding up.

(7)   In this section "director" includes a shadow director.

(8)   This section is without prejudice to section 213.

[279]

NOTES

See further: this section is disapplied, in respect of certain specified persons while Northern Rock is wholly owned by the Treasury, by the Northern Rock plc Transfer Order 2008, SI 2008/432, art 17, Schedule, para 3(a). In relation to the disapplication of this section, in respect of certain specified persons while Bradford & Bingley is wholly owned by the Treasury, see the Bradford & Bingley plc Transfer of Securities and Property etc Order 2008, SI 2008/2546, art 13(1), Sch 1, para 3(a) at **[975]**, **[1005]**. In relation to the disapplication of this section, in respect of certain specified persons while Deposits Management (Heritable) is wholly owned by the Treasury, see the Heritable Bank plc Transfer of Certain Rights and Liabilities Order 2008, SI 2008/2644, art 26, Sch 2, para 3(a), at **[1033]**, **[1041]**. In relation to the application of this section, with modifications, in respect of bank insolvency and administration, see the Banking Act 2009, ss 103(3), (4), Table, 145(3), (4), Table 2 at **[103]**, **[142]**.

215–229   (*Ss 215–219, ss 220–229 (Pt V) outside the scope of this work.*)

PART VI
MISCELLANEOUS PROVISIONS APPLYING TO COMPANIES WHICH ARE INSOLVENT OR IN LIQUIDATION

NOTES

Modification of this Part in relation to building societies: this Part is applied with modifications in relation to the winding up, etc, of building societies, by the Building Societies Act 1986, ss 90, 90A, Schs 15, 15A.

Modification of this Part in relation to friendly societies: as to the application, with modifications, of this Part to the winding up of incorporated friendly societies by virtue of the Friendly Societies Act 1992, s 21(1) or 22(2), see s 23 of, and Sch 10 to, the 1992 Act.

230–232   (*Outside the scope of this work.*)

Management by administrators, liquidators, etc

233 Supplies of gas, water, electricity, etc

(1)   This section applies in the case of a company where—
[(a)   the company enters administration,] or
(b)   an administrative receiver is appointed, or
[(ba) a moratorium under section 1A is in force, or]
(c)   a voluntary arrangement [approved under Part I], has taken effect, or
(d)   the company goes into liquidation, or
(e)   a provisional liquidator is appointed;

and "the office-holder" means the administrator, the administrative receiver, [the nominee,] the supervisor of the voluntary arrangement, the liquidator or the provisional liquidator, as the case may be.

(2)   If a request is made by or with the concurrence of the office-holder for the giving, after the effective date, of any of the supplies mentioned in the next subsection, the supplier—
(a)   may make it a condition of the giving of the supply that the office-holder personally guarantees the payment of any charges in respect of the supply, but
(b)   shall not make it a condition of the giving of the supply, or do anything which has the effect of making it a condition of the giving of the supply, that any outstanding charges in respect of a supply given to the company before the effective date are paid.

(3)   The supplies referred to in subsection (2) are—
[(a)   a supply of gas by a gas supplier within the meaning of Part I of the Gas Act 1986;]
[(b)   a supply of electricity by an electricity supplier within the meaning of Part I of the Electricity Act 1989;]
(c)   a supply of water by [a water undertaker] or, in Scotland, [Scottish Water],
[(d)   a supply of communications services by a provider of a public electronic communications service.]

(4)   "The effective date" for the purposes of this section is whichever is applicable of the following dates—
[(a)   the date on which the company entered administration,]
(b)   the date on which the administrative receiver was appointed (or, if he was appointed in succession to another administrative receiver, the date on which the first of his predecessors was appointed),
[(ba) the date on which the moratorium came into force,]
(c)   the date on which the voluntary arrangement [took effect],
(d)   the date on which the company went into liquidation,
(e)   the date on which the provisional liquidator was appointed.

(5)   The following applies to expressions used in subsection (3)—
(a)–(c) ...
(d)   "communications services" do not include electronic communications services to the extent that they are used to broadcast or otherwise transmit programme services (within the meaning of the Communications Act 2003).]

[280]

NOTES

Sub-s (1): para (a) substituted by the Enterprise Act 2002, s 248(3), Sch 17, paras 9, 22(a), as from 15 September 2003, subject to savings and transitional provisions in the Enterprise Act 2002 (Commencement No 4 and Transitional Provisions and Savings) Order 2003, SI 2003/2093, art 3; para (ba) and final words in square brackets inserted, and second words in square brackets substituted, by the Insolvency Act 2000, s 1, Sch 1, paras 1, 8(1), (2), as from 1 January 2003.

Sub-s (3): para (a) substituted by the Gas Act 1995, s 16(1), Sch 4, para 14(1); para (b) substituted by the Utilities Act 2000, s 108, Sch 6, para 47(1), (2)(a), as from 1 October 2001; words in first pair of square brackets in para (c) substituted by the Water Act 1989, s 190(1), Sch 25, para 78(1) and words in second pair of square brackets substituted by the Water Industry (Scotland) Act 2002 (Consequential Modifications) Order 2004, SI 2004/1822, art 2, Schedule, Pt I, para 14(a), as from 14 July 2004; para (d) substituted by the

Communications Act 2003, s 406(1), Sch 17, para 82(1), (2)(a), for the purpose of enabling network and service functions and spectrum functions to be carried out during the transitional period by the Director General of Telecommunications and the Secretary of State respectively (see further s 408 of, and Sch 18 to, the 2003 Act and the Communications Act 2003 (Commencement No 1) Order 2003, SI 2003/1900).

Sub-s (4): para (a) substituted by the Enterprise Act 2002, s 248(3), Sch 17, paras 9, 22(b), as from 15 September 2003, subject to savings and transitional provisions as noted to sub-s (1) above; para (ba) inserted, and words in square brackets substituted by the Insolvency Act 2000, s 1, Sch 1, paras 1, 8(1), (3), as from 1 January 2003.

Sub-s (5): para (a) repealed by the Gas Act 1995, ss 16(1), 17(5), Sch 4, para 14(2), Sch 6; para (b) repealed by the Utilities Act 2000, s 108, Sch 6, para 47(1), (2)(b), Sch 8, as from 1 October 2001; para (c) repealed by SI 2004/1822, art 2, Schedule, Pt I, para 14(b), as from 14 July 2004; para (d) substituted by the Communications Act 2003, s 406(1), Sch 17, para 82(1), (2)(b), for the purpose of enabling network and service functions and spectrum functions to be carried out during the transitional period by the Director General of Telecommunications and the Secretary of State respectively (see further s 408 of, and Sch 18 to, the 2003 Act and SI 2003/1900).

See further: in relation to the application of this section, with modifications, in respect of bank insolvency and administration, see the Banking Act 2009, ss 103(3), (4), Table, 145(3), (4), Table 2 at **[103]**, **[142]**.

234 Getting in the company's property

(1)   This section applies in the case of a company where—
   [(a)   the company enters administration,] or
   (b)   an administrative receiver is appointed, or
   (c)   the company goes into liquidation, or
   (d)   a provisional liquidator is appointed;

and "the office-holder" means the administrator, the administrative receiver, the liquidator or the provisional liquidator, as the case may be.

(2)   Where any person has in his possession or control any property, books, papers or records to which the company appears to be entitled, the court may require that person forthwith (or within such period as the court may direct) to pay, deliver, convey, surrender or transfer the property, books, papers or records to the office-holder.

(3)   Where the office-holder—
   (a)   seizes or disposes of any property which is not property of the company, and
   (b)   at the time of seizure or disposal believes, and has reasonable grounds for believing, that he is entitled (whether in pursuance of an order of the court or otherwise) to seize or dispose of that property,

the next subsection has effect.

(4)   In that case the office-holder—
   (a)   is not liable to any person in respect of any loss or damage resulting from the seizure or disposal except in so far as that loss or damage is caused by the office-holder's own negligence, and
   (b)   has a lien on the property, or the proceeds of its sale, for such expenses as were incurred in connection with the seizure or disposal.

[281]

NOTES

Sub-s (1): para (a) substituted by the Enterprise Act 2002, s 248(3), Sch 17, paras 9, 23, as from 15 September 2003, subject to savings and transitional provisions in the Enterprise Act 2002, s 249 and the Enterprise Act 2002 (Commencement No 4 and Transitional Provisions and Savings) Order 2003, SI 2003/2093, art 3.

See further: in relation to the application of this section, with modifications, in respect of bank insolvency and administration, see the Banking Act 2009, ss 103(3), (4), Table, 145(3), (4), Table 2 at **[103]**, **[142]**.

235 Duty to co-operate with office-holder

(1)   This section applies as does section 234; and it also applies, in the case of a company in respect of which a winding-up order has been made by the court in England and Wales, as if references to the office-holder included the official receiver, whether or not he is the liquidator.

(2)   Each of the persons mentioned in the next subsection shall—
   (a)   give to the office-holder such information concerning the company and its promotion, formation, business, dealings, affairs or property as the office-holder may at any time after the effective date reasonably require, and
   (b)   attend on the office-holder at such times as the latter may reasonably require.

(3)   The persons referred to above are—
   (a)   those who are or have at any time been officers of the company,
   (b)   those who have taken part in the formation of the company at any time within one year before the effective date,
   (c)   those who are in the employment of the company, or have been in its employment (including employment under a contract for services) within that year, and are in the office-holder's opinion capable of giving information which he requires,

   (d)   those who are, or have within that year been, officers of, or in the employment (including employment under a contract for services) of, another company which is, or within that year was, an officer of the company in question, and

   (e)   in the case of a company being wound up by the court, any person who has acted as administrator, administrative receiver or liquidator of the company.

(4)   For the purposes of subsections (2) and (3), "the effective date" is whichever is applicable of the following dates—

   [(a)   the date on which the company entered administration,]

   (b)   the date on which the administrative receiver was appointed or, if he was appointed in succession to another administrative receiver, the date on which the first of his predecessors was appointed,

   (c)   the date on which the provisional liquidator was appointed, and

   (d)   the date on which the company went into liquidation.

(5)   If a person without reasonable excuse fails to comply with any obligation imposed by this section, he is liable to a fine and, for continued contravention, to a daily default fine.

[282]

NOTES

Sub-s (4): para (a) substituted by the Enterprise Act 2002, s 248(3), Sch 17, paras 9, 24, as from 15 September 2003, subject to savings and transitional provisions in the Enterprise Act 2002, s 249 and the Enterprise Act 2002 (Commencement No 4 and Transitional Provisions and Savings) Order 2003, SI 2003/2093, art 3.

See further: in relation to the application of this section, with modifications, in respect of bank insolvency and administration, see the Banking Act 2009, ss 103(3), (4), Table, 145(3), (4), Table 2 at **[103]**, **[142]**.

236 Inquiry into company's dealings, etc

(1)   This section applies as does section 234; and it also applies in the case of a company in respect of which a winding-up order has been made by the court in England and Wales as if references to the office-holder included the official receiver, whether or not he is the liquidator.

(2)   The court may, on the application of the office-holder, summon to appear before it—

   (a)   any officer of the company,

   (b)   any person known or suspected to have in his possession any property of the company or supposed to be indebted to the company, or

   (c)   any person whom the court thinks capable of giving information concerning the promotion, formation, business, dealings, affairs or property of the company.

(3)   The court may require any such person as is mentioned in subsection (2)(a) to (c) to submit an affidavit to the court containing an account of his dealings with the company or to produce any books, papers or other records in his possession or under his control relating to the company or the matters mentioned in paragraph (c) of the subsection.

(4)   The following applies in a case where—

   (a)   a person without reasonable excuse fails to appear before the court when he is summoned to do so under this section, or

   (b)   there are reasonable grounds for believing that a person has absconded, or is about to abscond, with a view to avoiding his appearance before the court under this section.

(5)   The court may, for the purpose of bringing that person and anything in his possession before the court, cause a warrant to be issued to a constable or prescribed officer of the court—

   (a)   for the arrest of that person, and

   (b)   for the seizure of any books, papers, records, money or goods in that person's possession.

(6)   The court may authorise a person arrested under such a warrant to be kept in custody, and anything seized under such a warrant to be held, in accordance with the rules, until that person is brought before the court under the warrant or until such other time as the court may order.

[283]

NOTES

See further: in relation to the application of this section, with modifications, in respect of bank insolvency and administration, see the Banking Act 2009, ss 103(3), (4), Table, 145(3), (4), Table 2 at **[103]**, **[142]**.

237 Court's enforcement powers under s 236

(1)   If it appears to the court, on consideration of any evidence obtained under section 236 or this section, that any person has in his possession any property of the company, the court may, on the application of the office-holder, order that person to deliver the whole or any part of the property to the officer-holder at such time, in such manner and on such terms as the court thinks fit.

(2)   If it appears to the court, on consideration of any evidence so obtained, that any person is indebted to the company, the court may, on the application of the office-holder, order that person to

pay to the office-holder, at such time and in such manner as the court may direct, the whole or any part of the amount due, whether in full discharge of the debt or otherwise, as the court thinks fit.

(3)   The court may, if it thinks fit, order that any person who if within the jurisdiction of the court would be liable to be summoned to appear before it under section 236 or this section shall be examined in any part of the United Kingdom where he may for the time being be, or in a place outside the United Kingdom.

(4)   Any person who appears or is brought before the court under section 236 or this section may be examined on oath, either orally or (except in Scotland) by interrogatories, concerning the company or the matters mentioned in section 236(2)(c).

[284]

NOTES
See further: in relation to the application of this section, with modifications, in respect of bank insolvency and administration, see the Banking Act 2009, ss 103(3), (4), Table, 145(3), (4), Table 2 at **[103]**, **[142]**.

Adjustment of prior transactions (administration and liquidation)

238   Transactions at an undervalue (England and Wales)

(1)   This section applies in the case of a company where—
  [(a)   the company enters administration,] or
  (b)   the company goes into liquidation;
and "the office-holder" means the administrator or the liquidator, as the case may be.

(2)   Where the company has at a relevant time (defined in section 240) entered into a transaction with any person at an undervalue, the office-holder may apply to the court for an order under this section.

(3)   Subject as follows, the court shall, on such an application, make such order as it thinks fit for restoring the position to what it would have been if the company had not entered into that transaction.

(4)   For the purposes of this section and section 241, a company enters into a transaction with a person at an undervalue if—
  (a)   the company makes a gift to that person or otherwise enters into a transaction with that person on terms that provide for the company to receive no consideration, or
  (b)   the company enters into a transaction with that person for a consideration the value of which, in money or money's worth, is significantly less than the value, in money or money's worth, of the consideration provided by the company.

(5)   The court shall not make an order under this section in respect of a transaction at an undervalue if it is satisfied—
  (a)   that the company which entered into the transaction did so in good faith and for the purpose of carrying on its business, and
  (b)   that at the time it did so there were reasonable grounds for believing that the transaction would benefit the company.

[285]

NOTES
Sub-s (1): para (a) substituted by the Enterprise Act 2002, s 248(3), Sch 17, paras 9, 25, as from 15 September 2003, subject to savings and transitional provisions in the Enterprise Act 2002, s 249 and the Enterprise Act 2002 (Commencement No 4 and Transitional Provisions and Savings) Order 2003, SI 2003/2093, art 3.
See further: in relation to the application of this section, with modifications, in respect of bank insolvency and administration, see the Banking Act 2009, ss 103(3), (4), Table, 145(3), (4), Table 2 at **[103]**, **[142]**.

239   Preferences (England and Wales)

(1)   This section applies as does section 238.

(2)   Where the company has at a relevant time (defined in the next section) given a preference to any person, the office-holder may apply to the court for an order under this section.

(3)   Subject as follows, the court shall, on such an application, make such order as it thinks fit for restoring the position to what it would have been if the company had not given that preference.

(4)   For the purposes of this section and section 241, a company gives a preference to a person if—
  (a)   that person is one of the company's creditors or a surety or guarantor for any of the company's debts or other liabilities, and
  (b)   the company does anything or suffers anything to be done which (in either case) has the effect of putting that person into a position which, in the event of the company going into insolvent liquidation, will be better than the position he would have been in if that thing had not been done.

PART II
OTHER ACTS

(5)   The court shall not make an order under this section in respect of a preference given to any person unless the company which gave the preference was influenced in deciding to give it by a desire to produce in relation to that person the effect mentioned in subsection (4)(b).

(6)   A company which has given a preference to a person connected with the company (otherwise than by reason only of being its employee) at the time the preference was given is presumed, unless the contrary is shown, to have been influenced in deciding to give it by such a desire as is mentioned in subsection (5).

(7)   The fact that something has been done in pursuance of the order of a court does not, without more, prevent the doing or suffering of that thing from constituting the giving of a preference.

[286]

NOTES

See further: in relation to the application of this section, with modifications, in respect of bank insolvency and administration: the Banking Act 2009, ss 103(3), (4), Table, 145(3), (4), Table 2 at **[103]**, **[142]**.

240   "Relevant time" under ss 238, 239

(1)   Subject to the next subsection, the time at which a company enters into a transaction at an undervalue or gives a preference is a relevant time if the transaction is entered into, or the preference given—

    (a)   in the case of a transaction at an undervalue or of a preference which is given to a person who is connected with the company (otherwise than by reason only of being its employee), at a time in the period of 2 years ending with the onset of insolvency (which expression is defined below),

    (b)   in the case of a preference which is not such a transaction and is not so given, at a time in the period of 6 months ending with the onset of insolvency, ...

    [(c)   in either case, at a time between the making of an administration application in respect of the company and the making of an administration order on that application, and

    (d)   in either case, at a time between the filing with the court of a copy of notice of intention to appoint an administrator under paragraph 14 or 22 of Schedule B1 and the making of an appointment under that paragraph].

(2)   Where a company enters into a transaction at an undervalue or gives a preference at a time mentioned in subsection (1)(a) or (b), that time is not a relevant time for the purposes of section 238 or 239 unless the company—

    (a)   is at that time unable to pay its debts within the meaning of section 123 in Chapter VI of Part IV, or

    (b)   becomes unable to pay its debts within the meaning of that section in consequence of the transaction or preference;

but the requirements of this subsection are presumed to be satisfied, unless the contrary is shown, in relation to any transaction at an undervalue which is entered into by a company with a person who is connected with the company.

(3)   For the purposes of subsection (1), the onset of insolvency is—

    [(a)   in a case where section 238 or 239 applies by reason of an administrator of a company being appointed by administration order, the date on which the administration application is made,

    (b)   in a case where section 238 or 239 applies by reason of an administrator of a company being appointed under paragraph 14 or 22 of Schedule B1 following filing with the court of a copy of a notice of intention to appoint under that paragraph, the date on which the copy of the notice is filed,

    (c)   in a case where section 238 or 239 applies by reason of an administrator of a company being appointed otherwise than as mentioned in paragraph (a) or (b), the date on which the appointment takes effect,

    (d)   in a case where section 238 or 239 applies by reason of a company going into liquidation either following conversion of administration into winding up by virtue of Article 37 of the EC Regulation or at the time when the appointment of an administrator ceases to have effect, the date on which the company entered administration (or, if relevant, the date on which the application for the administration order was made or a copy of the notice of intention to appoint was filed), and

    (e)   in a case where section 238 or 239 applies by reason of a company going into liquidation at any other time, the date of the commencement of the winding up.]

[287]

NOTES

Sub-s (1): word omitted from para (b) repealed, and paras (c), (d) substituted for original para (c), by the Enterprise Act 2002, ss 248(3), 278(2), Sch 17, paras 9, 26, Sch 26, as from 15 September 2003, subject to savings and transitional provisions in the Enterprise Act 2002, s 249 and the Enterprise Act 2002 (Commencement No 4 and Transitional Provisions and Savings) Order 2003, SI 2003/2093, art 3.

Sub-s (3): paras (a)–(e) substituted for existing paras (a), (aa), (b) (as inserted in the case of para (aa) by SI 2002/1240, regs 3, 11) by the Enterprise Act 2002, s 248(3), Sch 17, paras 9, 26(1), (4), subject to savings and transitional provisions as noted to sub-s (1) above.

See further: in relation to the application of this section, with modifications, in respect of bank insolvency and administration, see the Banking Act 2009, ss 103(3), (4), Table, 145(3), (4), Table 2 at **[103]**, **[142]**.

241   Orders under ss 238, 239

(1)   Without prejudice to the generality of sections 238(3) and 239(3), an order under either of those sections with respect to a transaction or preference entered into or given by a company may (subject to the next subsection)—

(a)   require any property transferred as part of the transaction, or in connection with the giving of the preference, to be vested in the company,

(b)   require any property to be so vested if it represents in any person's hands the application either of the proceeds of sale of property so transferred or of money so transferred,

(c)   release or discharge (in whole or in part) any security given by the company,

(d)   require any person to pay, in respect of benefits received by him from the company, such sums to the office-holder as the court may direct,

(e)   provide for any surety or guarantor whose obligations to any person were released or discharged (in whole or in part) under the transaction, or by the giving of the preference, to be under such new or revived obligations to that person as the court thinks appropriate,

(f)   provide for security to be provided for the discharge of any obligation imposed by or arising under the order, for such an obligation to be charged on any property and for the security or charge to have the same priority as a security or charge released or discharged (in whole or in part) under the transaction or by the giving of the preference, and

(g)   provide for the extent to which any person whose property is vested by the order in the company, or on whom obligations are imposed by the order, is to be able to prove in the winding up of the company for debts or other liabilities which arose from, or were released or discharged (in whole or in part) under or by, the transaction or the giving of the preference.

(2)   An order under section 238 or 239 may affect the property of, or impose any obligation on, any person whether or not he is the person with whom the company in question entered into the transaction or (as the case may be) the person to whom the preference was given; but such an order—

(a)   shall not prejudice any interest in property which was acquired from a person other than the company and was acquired [in good faith and for value], or prejudice any interest deriving from such an interest, and

(b)   shall not require a person who received a benefit from the transaction or preference [in good faith and for value] to pay a sum to the office-holder, except where that person was a party to the transaction or the payment is to be in respect of a preference given to that person at a time when he was a creditor of the company.

[(2A)   Where a person has acquired an interest in property from a person other than the company in question, or has received a benefit from the transaction or preference, and at the time of that acquisition or receipt—

(a)   he had notice of the relevant surrounding circumstances and of the relevant proceedings, or

(b)   he was connected with, or was an associate of, either the company in question or the person with whom that company entered into the transaction or to whom that company gave the preference,

then, unless the contrary is shown, it shall be presumed for the purposes of paragraph (a) or (as the case may be) paragraph (b) of subsection (2) that the interest was acquired or the benefit was received otherwise than in good faith.]

[(3)   For the purposes of subsection (2A)(a), the relevant surrounding circumstances are (as the case may require)—

(a)   the fact that the company in question entered into the transaction at an undervalue; or

(b)   the circumstances which amounted to the giving of the preference by the company in question;

and subsections (3A) to (3C) have effect to determine whether, for those purposes, a person has notice of the relevant proceedings.

[(3A)   Where section 238 or 239 applies by reason of a company's entering administration, a person has notice of the relevant proceedings if he has notice that—

(a)   an administration application has been made,

(b)   an administration order has been made,

(c)   a copy of a notice of intention to appoint an administrator under paragraph 14 or 22 of Schedule B1 has been filed, or

(right margin, vertical text) PART II   OTHER ACTS

(d)   notice of the appointment of an administrator has been filed under paragraph 18 or 29 of that Schedule.]

[(3B)   Where section 238 or 239 applies by reason of a company's going into liquidation at the time when the appointment of an administrator of the company ceases to have effect, a person has notice of the relevant proceedings if he has notice that—

(a)   an administration application has been made,

(b)   an administration order has been made,

(c)   a copy of a notice of intention to appoint an administrator under paragraph 14 or 22 of Schedule B1 has been filed,

(d)   notice of the appointment of an administrator has been filed under paragraph 18 or 29 of that Schedule, or

(e)   the company has gone into liquidation.]

(3C)   In a case where section 238 or 239 applies by reason of the company in question going into liquidation at any other time, a person has notice of the relevant proceedings if he has notice—

(a)   where the company goes into liquidation on the making of a winding-up order, of the fact that the petition on which the winding-up order is made has been presented or of the fact that the company has gone into liquidation;

(b)   in any other case, of the fact that the company has gone into liquidation.]

(4)   The provisions of sections 238 to 241 apply without prejudice to the availability of any other remedy, even in relation to a transaction or preference which the company had no power to enter into or give.

[288]

NOTES

Sub-s (2): in paras (a), (b), words in square brackets substituted by the Insolvency (No 2) Act 1994, s 1(1), in relation to interests acquired and benefits received after 26 July 1994.

Sub-s (2A): inserted by s 1(2) of the 1994 Act, in relation to interests acquired and benefits received after 26 July 1994.

Sub-s (3): substituted, together with sub-ss (3A)–(3C), for sub-s (3) as originally enacted, by s 1(3) of the 1994 Act, in relation to interests acquired and benefits received after 26 July 1994.

Sub-s (3A): substituted, together with sub-ss (3), (3B), (3C), for sub-s (3) as originally enacted, by s 1(3) of the 1994 Act, in relation to interests acquired and benefits received after 26 July 1994; further substituted by the Enterprise Act 2002, s 248(3), Sch 17, paras 9, 27(1), (2), as from 15 September 2003, subject to savings and transitional provisions in the Enterprise Act 2002 (Commencement No 4 and Transitional Provisions and Savings) Order 2003, SI 2003/2093, art 3.

Sub-s (3B): substituted together with sub-ss (3), (3A), (3C), for sub-s (3) as originally enacted, by s 1(3) of the 1994 Act, in relation to interests acquired and benefits received after 26 July 1994; further substituted by the Enterprise Act 2002, s 248(3), Sch 17, paras 9, 27(1), (3), subject to savings and transitional provisions as noted to sub-s (3A) above.

Sub-s (3C): substituted, together with sub-ss (3), (3A), (3B), for sub-s (3) as originally enacted, by s 1(3) of the 1994 Act, in relation to interests acquired and benefits received after 26 July 1994.

See further: in relation to the application of this section, with modifications, in respect of bank insolvency and administration, see the Banking Act 2009, ss 103(3), (4), Table, 145(3), (4), Table 2 at **[103]**, **[142]**.

242   Gratuitous alienations (Scotland)

(1)   Where this subsection applies and—

(a)   the winding up of a company has commenced, an alienation by the company is challengeable by—

(i)   any creditor who is a creditor by virtue of a debt incurred on or before the date of such commencement, or

(ii)   the liquidator;

(b)   [a company enters administration], an alienation by the company is challengeable by the administrator.

(2)   Subsection (1) applies where—

(a)   by the alienation, whether before or after 1st April 1986 (the coming into force of section 75 of the Bankruptcy (Scotland) Act 1985), any part of the company's property is transferred or any claim or right of the company is discharged or renounced, and

(b)   the alienation takes place on a relevant day.

(3)   For the purposes of subsection (2)(b), the day on which an alienation takes place is the day on which it becomes completely effectual; and in that subsection "relevant day" means, if the alienation has the effect of favouring—

(a)   a person who is an associate (within the meaning of the Bankruptcy (Scotland) Act 1985) of the company, a day not earlier than 5 years before the date on which—

(i)   the winding up of the company commences, or

(ii)   as the case may be, [the company enters administration]; or

(b)   any other person, a day not earlier than 2 years before that date.

(4)   On a challenge being brought under subsection (1), the court shall grant decree of reduction or for such restoration of property to the company's assets or other redress as may be appropriate; but the court shall not grant such a decree if the person seeking to uphold the alienation establishes—

(a)   that immediately, or at any other time, after the alienation the company's assets were greater than its liabilities, or

(b)   that the alienation was made for adequate consideration, or

(c)   that the alienation—

  (i)   was a birthday, Christmas or other conventional gift, or

  (ii)   was a gift made, for a charitable purpose, to a person who is not an associate of the company,

which, having regard to all the circumstances, it was reasonable for the company to make:

Provided that this subsection is without prejudice to any right or interest acquired in good faith and for value from or through the transferee in the alienation.

(5)   In subsection (4) above, "charitable purpose" means any charitable, benevolent or philanthropic purpose, whether or not it is charitable within the meaning of any rule of law.

(6)   For the purposes of the foregoing provisions of this section, an alienation in implementation of a prior obligation is deemed to be one for which there was no consideration or no adequate consideration to the extent that the prior obligation was undertaken for no consideration or no adequate consideration.

(7)   A liquidator and an administrator have the same right as a creditor has under any rule of law to challenge an alienation of a company made for no consideration or no adequate consideration.

(8)   This section applies to Scotland only.

[289]

NOTES

Sub-s (1): words in square brackets substituted by the Enterprise Act 2002, s 248(3), Sch 17, paras 9, 28(1), (2), as from 15 September 2003, subject to savings and transitional provisions in the Enterprise Act 2002, s 249 and the Enterprise Act 2002 (Commencement No 4 and Transitional Provisions and Savings) Order 2003, SI 2003/2093, art 3.

Sub-s (3): words in square brackets substituted by the Enterprise Act 2002, s 248(3), Sch 17, paras 9, 28(1), (3), subject to savings as noted to sub-s (1) above.

See further: in relation to the application of this section, with modifications, in respect of bank insolvency and administration, see the Banking Act 2009, ss 103(3), (4), Table, 145(3), (4), Table 2 at **[103]**, **[142]**.

243   Unfair preferences (Scotland)

(1)   Subject to subsection (2) below, subsection (4) below applies to a transaction entered into by a company, whether before or after 1st April 1986, which has the effect of creating a preference in favour of a creditor to the prejudice of the general body of creditors, being a preference created not earlier than 6 months before the commencement of the winding up of the company or [the company enters administration].

(2)   Subsection (4) below does not apply to any of the following transactions—

(a)   a transaction in the ordinary course of trade or business;

(b)   a payment in cash for a debt which when it was paid had become payable, unless the transaction was collusive with the purpose of prejudicing the general body of creditors;

(c)   a transaction whereby the parties to it undertake reciprocal obligations (whether the performance by the parties of their respective obligations occurs at the same time or at different times) unless the transaction was collusive as aforesaid;

(d)   the granting of a mandate by a company authorising an arrestee to pay over the arrested funds or part thereof to the arrester where—

  (i)   there has been a decree for payment or a warrant for summary diligence, and

  (ii)   the decree or warrant has been preceded by an arrestment on the dependence of the action or followed by an arrestment in execution.

(3)   For the purposes of subsection (1) above, the day on which a preference was created is the day on which the preference became completely effectual.

(4)   A transaction to which this subsection applies is challengeable by—

(a)   in the case of a winding up—

  (i)   any creditor who is a creditor by virtue of a debt incurred on or before the date of commencement of the winding up, or

  (ii)   the liquidator; and

(b)   [where the company has entered administration], the administrator.

(5)   On a challenge being brought under subsection (4) above, the court, if satisfied that the transaction challenged is a transaction to which this section applies, shall grant decree of reduction or for such restoration of property to the company's assets or other redress as may be appropriate:

Provided that this subsection is without prejudice to any right or interest acquired in good faith and for value from or through the creditor in whose favour the preference was created.

(6)   A liquidator and an administrator have the same right as a creditor has under any rule of law to challenge a preference created by a debtor.

(7)   This section applies to Scotland only.

[290]

NOTES

Sub-s (1): words in square brackets substituted by the Enterprise Act 2002, s 248(3), Sch 17, paras 9, 29(1), (2), as from 15 September 2003, subject to savings and transitional provisions in the Enterprise Act 2002, s 249 and the Enterprise Act 2002 (Commencement No 4 and Transitional Provisions and Savings) Order 2003, SI 2003/2093, art 3.

Sub-s (4): words in square brackets substituted by the Enterprise Act 2002, s 248(3), Sch 17, paras 9, 29(1), (3), subject to savings as noted to sub-s (1) above.

See further: in relation to the application of this section, with modifications, in respect of bank insolvency and administration, see the Banking Act 2009, ss 103(3), (4), Table, 145(3), (4), Table 2 at **[103]**, **[142]**.

244   Extortionate credit transactions

(1)   This section applies as does section 238, and where the company is, or has been, a party to a transaction for, or involving, the provision of credit to the company.

(2)   The court may, on the application of the office-holder, make an order with respect to the transaction if the transaction is or was extortionate and was entered into in the period of 3 years ending with [the day on which the company entered administration or went into liquidation].

(3)   For the purposes of this section a transaction is extortionate if, having regard to the risk accepted by the person providing the credit—

(a)   the terms of it are or were such as to require grossly exorbitant payments to be made (whether unconditionally or in certain contingencies) in respect of the provision of the credit, or

(b)   it otherwise grossly contravened ordinary principles of fair dealing;

and it shall be presumed, unless the contrary is proved, that a transaction with respect to which an application is made under this section is or, as the case may be, was extortionate.

(4)   An order under this section with respect to any transaction may contain such one or more of the following as the court thinks fit, that is to say—

(a)   provision setting aside the whole or part of any obligation created by the transaction,

(b)   provision otherwise varying the terms of the transaction or varying the terms on which any security for the purposes of the transaction is held,

(c)   provision requiring any person who is or was a party to the transaction to pay to the office-holder any sums paid to that person, by virtue of the transaction, by the company,

(d)   provision requiring any person to surrender to the office-holder any property held by him as security for the purposes of the transaction,

(e)   provision directing accounts to be taken between any persons.

(5)   The powers conferred by this section are exercisable in relation to any transaction concurrently with any powers exercisable in relation to that transaction as a transaction at an undervalue or under section 242 (gratuitous alienations in Scotland).

[291]

NOTES

Sub-s (2): words in square brackets substituted by the Enterprise Act 2002, s 248(3), Sch 17, paras 9, 30, as from 15 September 2003, subject to savings and transitional provisions in the Enterprise Act 2002, s 249 and the Enterprise Act 2002 (Commencement No 4 and Transitional Provisions and Savings) Order 2003, SI 2003/2093, art 3.

See further: in relation to the application of this section, with modifications, in respect of bank insolvency and administration, see the Banking Act 2009, ss 103(3), (4), Table, 145(3), (4), Table 2 at **[103]**, **[142]**.

245   Avoidance of certain floating charges

(1)   This section applies as does section 238, but applies to Scotland as well as to England and Wales.

(2)   Subject as follows, a floating charge on the company's undertaking or property created at a relevant time is invalid except to the extent of the aggregate of—

(a)   the value of so much of the consideration for the creation of the charge as consists of money paid, or goods or services supplied, to the company at the same time as, or after, the creation of the charge,

(b)   the value of so much of that consideration as consists of the discharge or reduction, at the same time as, or after, the creation of the charge, of any debt of the company, and

(c)   the amount of such interest (if any) as is payable on the amount falling within paragraph (a) or (b) in pursuance of any agreement under which the money was so paid, the goods or services were so supplied or the debt was so discharged or reduced.

(3) Subject to the next subsection, the time at which a floating charge is created by a company is a relevant time for the purposes of this section if the charge is created—

(a) in the case of a charge which is created in favour of a person who is connected with the company, at a time in the period of 2 years ending with the onset of insolvency,

(b) in the case of a charge which is created in favour of any other person, at a time in the period of 12 months ending with the onset of insolvency, …

[(c) in either case, at a time between the making of an administration application in respect of the company and the making of an administration order on that application, or

(d) in either case, at a time between the filing with the court of a copy of notice of intention to appoint an administrator under paragraph 14 or 22 of Schedule B1 and the making of an appointment under that paragraph.]

(4) Where a company creates a floating charge at a time mentioned in subsection (3)(b) and the person in favour of whom the charge is created is not connected with the company, that time is not a relevant time for the purposes of this section unless the company—

(a) is at that time unable to pay its debts within the meaning of section 123 in Chapter VI of Part IV, or

(b) becomes unable to pay its debts within the meaning of that section in consequence of the transaction under which the charge is created.

(5) For the purposes of subsection (3), the onset of insolvency is—

[(a) in a case where this section applies by reason of an administrator of a company being appointed by administration order, the date on which the administration application is made,

(b) in a case where this section applies by reason of an administrator of a company being appointed under paragraph 14 or 22 of Schedule B1 following filing with the court of a copy of notice of intention to appoint under that paragraph, the date on which the copy of the notice is filed,

(c) in a case where this section applies by reason of an administrator of a company being appointed otherwise than as mentioned in paragraph (a) or (b), the date on which the appointment takes effect, and

(d) in a case where this section applies by reason of a company going into liquidation, the date of the commencement of the winding up.]

(6) For the purposes of subsection (2)(a) the value of any goods or services supplied by way of consideration for a floating charge is the amount in money which at the time they were supplied could reasonably have been expected to be obtained for supplying the goods or services in the ordinary course of business and on the same terms (apart from the consideration) as those on which they were supplied to the company.

[292]

NOTES

Sub-s (3): word omitted from para (b) repealed, and paras (c), (d) substituted for original para (c), by the Enterprise Act 2002, ss 248(3), 278(2), Sch 17, paras 9, 31(1)–(3), Sch 26, as from 15 September 2003, subject to savings and transitional provisions in the Enterprise Act 2002, s 249 and the Enterprise Act 2002 (Commencement No 4 and Transitional Provisions and Savings) Order 2003, SI 2003/2093, art 3.

Sub-s (5): paras (a)–(d) substituted for original paras (a), (b), by the Enterprise Act 2002, ss 248(3), 278(2), Sch 17, paras 9, 31(1), (4), Sch 26, subject to savings as noted to sub-s (3) above.

See further: as to the disapplication of this section in relation to any charge created or otherwise arising under a security financial collateral arrangement: the Financial Collateral Arrangements (No 2) Regulations 2003, SI 2003/3226, reg 10(5). In relation to the application of this section, with modifications, in respect of bank insolvency and administration, see the Banking Act 2009, ss 103(3), (4), Table, 145(3), (4), Table 2 at **[103]**, **[142]**.

---

246 Unenforceability of liens on books, etc

(1) This section applies in the case of a company where—

[(a) the company enters administration,] or

(b) the company goes into liquidation, or

(c) a provisional liquidator is appointed;

and "the office-holder" means the administrator, the liquidator or the provisional liquidator, as the case may be.

(2) Subject as follows, a lien or other right to retain possession of any of the books, papers or other records of the company is unenforceable to the extent that its enforcement would deny possession of any books, papers or other records to the office-holder.

(3) This does not apply to a lien on documents which give a title to property and are held as such.

[293]

PART II
OTHER ACTS

NOTES

Sub-s (1): para (a) substituted by the Enterprise Act 2002, s 248(3), Sch 17, paras 9, 32, as from 15 September 2003, subject to savings and transitional provisions in the Enterprise Act 2002, s 249 and the Enterprise Act 2002 (Commencement No 4 and Transitional Provisions and Savings) Order 2003, SI 2003/2093, art 3.

See further: in relation to the application of this section, with modifications, in respect of bank insolvency and administration, see the Banking Act 2009, ss 103(3), (4), Table, 145(3), (4), Table 2 at **[103]**, **[142]**.

247–385 *((Pts VII–XI) Outside the scope of this work; for s 264 see Butterworths Securities and Financial Services Law Handbook.)*

THE THIRD GROUP OF PARTS
MISCELLANEOUS MATTERS BEARING ON BOTH COMPANY AND INDIVIDUAL INSOLVENCY; GENERAL INTERPRETATION; FINAL PROVISIONS

386, 387 *((Pt XII) Outside the scope of this work.)*

PART XIII
INSOLVENCY PRACTITIONERS AND THEIR QUALIFICATION

NOTES

Modification of this Part in relation to building societies: this Part is applied, with modifications, in relation to the winding up, etc, of building societies, by the Building Societies Act 1986, ss 90, 90A, Schs 15, 15A.

Friendly societies: as to the application, with modifications, of this Part of this Act to the winding up of incorporated friendly societies by virtue of the Friendly Societies Act 1992, s 21(1) or 22(2), see s 23 of, and Sch 10 to, the 1992 Act.

Restrictions on unqualified persons acting as liquidator, trustee in bankruptcy, etc

388 *(Outside the scope of this work.)*

389 Acting without qualification an offence

(1) A person who acts as an insolvency practitioner in relation to a company or an individual at a time when he is not qualified to do so is liable to imprisonment or a fine, or to both.

[(1A) This section is subject to section 389A.]

(2) This section does not apply to the official receiver [or the Accountant in Bankruptcy (within the meaning of the Bankruptcy (Scotland) Act 1985)].

[294]

NOTES

Sub-s (1A): inserted by the Insolvency Act 2000, s 4(1), (3), as from 1 January 2003.

Sub-s (2): words in square brackets added by the Bankruptcy (Scotland) Act 1993, s 11(2).

See further: in relation to the application of this section, with modifications, in respect of bank insolvency and administration, see the Banking Act 2009, ss 103(3), (4), Table, 145(3), (4), Table 2 at **[103]**, **[142]**.

[389A Authorisation of nominees and supervisors

(1) Section 389 does not apply to a person acting, in relation to a voluntary arrangement proposed or approved under Part I or Part VIII, as nominee or supervisor if he is authorised so to act.

(2) For the purposes of subsection (1) and those Parts, an individual to whom subsection (3) does not apply is authorised to act as nominee or supervisor in relation to such an arrangement if—
   (a) he is a member of a body recognised for the purpose by the Secretary of State, and
   (b) there is in force security (in Scotland, caution) for the proper performance of his functions and that security or caution meets the prescribed requirements with respect to his so acting in relation to the arrangement.

(3) This subsection applies to a person if—
   (a) he has been adjudged bankrupt or sequestration of his estate has been awarded and (in either case) he has not been discharged,
   (b) he is subject to a disqualification order made or a disqualification undertaking accepted under the Company Directors Disqualification Act 1986 or to a disqualification order made under Part II of the Companies (Northern Ireland) Order 1989 [or a disqualification undertaking accepted under the Company Directors Disqualification (Northern Ireland) Order 2002], ...
   (c) he is a patient within the meaning of ... [section 329(1) of the Mental Health (Care and Treatment) (Scotland) Act 2003][, or
   (d) he lacks capacity (within the meaning of the Mental Capacity Act 2005) to act as nominee or supervisor].

(4)   The Secretary of State may by order declare a body which appears to him to fall within subsection (5) to be a recognised body for the purposes of subsection (2)(a).

(5)   A body may be recognised if it maintains and enforces rules for securing that its members—
  (a)   are fit and proper persons to act as nominees or supervisors, and
  (b)   meet acceptable requirements as to education and practical training and experience.

(6)   For the purposes of this section, a person is a member of a body only if he is subject to its rules when acting as nominee or supervisor (whether or not he is in fact a member of the body).

(7)   An order made under subsection (4) in relation to a body may be revoked by a further order if it appears to the Secretary of State that the body no longer falls within subsection (5).

(8)   An order of the Secretary of State under this section has effect from such date as is specified in the order; and any such order revoking a previous order may make provision for members of the body in question to continue to be treated as members of a recognised body for a specified period after the revocation takes effect.]

[295]

NOTES
Inserted by the Insolvency Act 2000, s 4(1), (4), as from 1 January 2003.
Sub-s (3): words in square brackets in para (b) inserted by the Insolvency Act 2000 (Company Directors Disqualification Undertakings) Order 2004, SI 2004/1941, art 3, Schedule, paras 1, 2, as from 1 September 2004, in relation to disqualification undertakings under the Company Directors Disqualification (Northern Ireland) Order 2002, SI 2002/3150, accepted on or after that date; words omitted from paras (b), (c) repealed, and para (d) and the word immediately preceding it inserted by the Mental Capacity Act 2005, s 67(1), (2), Sch 6, para 31(1), (2), Sch 7, as from 1 October 2007; words in square brackets in para (c) substituted in relation to England and Wales by the Mental Health (Care and Treatment) (Scotland) Act 2003 (Consequential Provisions) Order 2005, SI 2005/2078, art 15, Sch 1, para 3(1), (2), as from 5 October 2005, and in relation to Scotland by the Mental Health (Care and Treatment) (Scotland) Act 2003 (Modification of Enactments) Order 2005, SSI 2005/465, art 2, Sch 1, para 18(1), (2), as from 25 September 2005.

[389B   Official receiver as nominee or supervisor

(1)   The official receiver is authorised to act as nominee or supervisor in relation to a voluntary arrangement approved under Part VIII provided that the debtor is an undischarged bankrupt when the arrangement is proposed.

(2)   The Secretary of State may by order repeal the proviso in subsection (1).

(3)   An order under subsection (2)—
  (a)   must be made by statutory instrument, and
  (b)   shall be subject to annulment in pursuance of a resolution of either House of Parliament.]

[296]

NOTES
Inserted by the Enterprise Act 2002, s 264(1), Sch 22, para 3, as from 1 April 2004.

The requisite qualification, and the means of obtaining it

390   Persons not qualified to act as insolvency practitioners

(1)   A person who is not an individual is not qualified to act as an insolvency practitioner.

(2)   A person is not qualified to act as an insolvency practitioner at any time unless at that time—
  (a)   he is authorised so to act by virtue of membership of a professional body recognised under section 391 below, being permitted so to act by or under the rules of that body, or
  (b)   he holds an authorisation granted by a competent authority under section 393.

(3)   A person is not qualified to act as an insolvency practitioner in relation to another person at any time unless—
  (a)   there is in force at that time security or, in Scotland, caution for the proper performance of his functions, and
  (b)   that security or caution meets the prescribed requirements with respect to his so acting in relation to that other person.

(4)   A person is not qualified to act as an insolvency practitioner at any time if at that time—
  (a)   he has been adjudged bankrupt or sequestration of his estate has been awarded and (in either case) he has not been discharged,
  [(aa) a moratorium period under a debt relief order applies in relation of him,]
  (b)   he is subject to a disqualification order made [or a disqualification undertaking accepted] under the Company Directors Disqualification Act 1986 [or to a disqualification order

made under Part II of the Companies (Northern Ireland) Order 1989] [or to a disqualification undertaking accepted under the Company Directors Disqualification (Northern Ireland) Order 2002], ...

  (c) he is a patient within the meaning of ... [section 329(1) of the Mental Health (Care and Treatment) (Scotland) Act 2003] [or has had a guardian appointed to him under the Adults with Incapacity (Scotland) Act 2000 (asp 4)][, or

  (d) he lacks capacity (within the meaning of the Mental Capacity Act 2005) to act as an insolvency practitioner].

[(5) A person is not qualified to act as an insolvency practitioner while a bankruptcy restrictions order [or a debt relief restrictions order] is in force in respect of him.]

[297]

NOTES

  Sub-s (4): para (aa) inserted by the Tribunals, Courts and Enforcement Act 2007, s 108(3), Sch 20, Pt 1, paras 1, 6(1), (2), as from 6 April 2009; in para (b), words in first and second pairs of square brackets inserted by the Insolvency Act 2000, s 8, Sch 4, Pt II, para 16(1), (2), as from 2 April 2001; words in third pair of square brackets inserted by the Insolvency Act 2000 (Company Directors Disqualification Undertakings) Order 2004, SI 2004/1941, art 3, Schedule, paras 1, 3, as from 1 September 2004 in relation to disqualification undertakings under the Company Directors Disqualification (Northern Ireland) Order 2002, SI 2002/3150, accepted on or after that date; words in first pair of square brackets in para (c) substituted in relation to England and Wales by the Mental Health (Care and Treatment) (Scotland) Act 2003 (Consequential Provisions) Order 2005, SI 2005/2078, art 15, Sch 1, para 3(1), (3) as from 5 October 2005 and in relation to Scotland by the Mental Health (Care and Treatment) (Scotland) Act 2003 (Modification of Enactments) Order 2005, SSI 2005/465, art 2, Sch 1, para 18(1), (3), as from 27 September 2005; words in second pair of square brackets in para (c) inserted by the Adults with Incapacity (Scotland) Act 2000, s 88(2), Sch 5, para 18, as from 1 April 2002; words omitted from paras (b), (c) repealed, and para (d) and the word immediately preceding it inserted by the Mental Capacity Act 2005, s 67(1), (2), Sch 6, para 31(1), (3), Sch 7, as from 1 October 2007.

  Sub-s (5): added by the Enterprise Act 2002, s 257(3), Sch 21, para 4, as from 1 April 2004, subject to transitional provisions in s 256(2) of, and Sch 19 to, that Act; words in square brackets inserted by the Tribunals, Courts and Enforcement Act 2007, s 108(3), Sch 20, Pt 1, paras 1, 6(1), (3), as from 6 April 2009.

  See further: in relation to the application of this section, with modifications, in respect of bank insolvency and administration, see the Banking Act 2009, ss 103(3), (4), Table, 145(3), (4), Table 2 at **[103]**, **[142]**.

  Regulations: the Insolvency Practitioners Regulations 1990, SI 1990/439; the Insolvency Practitioners Regulations 2005, SI 2005/524.

391 Recognised professional bodies

  (1) The Secretary of State may by order declare a body which appears to him to fall within subsection (2) below to be a recognised professional body for the purposes of this section.

  (2) A body may be recognised if it regulates the practice of a profession and maintains and enforces rules for securing that such of its members as are permitted by or under the rules to act as insolvency practitioners—

  (a) are fit and proper persons so to act, and

  (b) meet acceptable requirements as to education and practical training and experience.

  (3) References to members of a recognised professional body are to persons who, whether members of that body or not, are subject to its rules in the practice of the profession in question.

  The reference in section 390(2) above to membership of a professional body recognised under this section is to be read accordingly.

  (4) An order made under subsection (1) in relation to a professional body may be revoked by a further order if it appears to the Secretary of State that the body no longer falls within subsection (2).

  (5) An order of the Secretary of State under this section has effect from such date as is specified in the order; and any such order revoking a previous order may make provision whereby members of the body in question continue to be treated as authorised to act as insolvency practitioners for a specified period after the revocation takes effect.

[298]

NOTES

  See further: in relation to the application of this section, with modifications, in respect of bank insolvency and administration, see the Banking Act 2009, ss 103(3), (4), Table, 145(3), (4), Table 2 at **[103]**, **[142]**.

  Order: the Insolvency Practitioners (Recognised Professional Bodies) Order 1986, SI 1986/1764.

392–410   (*Ss 392–398, ss 399–410 (Pt XIV) outside the scope of this work.*)

PART XV
SUBORDINATE LEGISLATION

General insolvency rules

411 Company insolvency rules

(1) Rules may be made—
- (a) in relation to England and Wales, by the Lord Chancellor with the concurrence of the Secretary of State [and, in the case of rules that affect court procedure, with the concurrence of the Lord Chief Justice], or
- (b) in relation to Scotland, by the Secretary of State,

for the purpose of giving effect to Parts I to VII of this Act [or the EC Regulation].

[(1A) Rules may also be made for the purpose of giving effect to Part 2 of the Banking Act 2009 (bank insolvency orders); and rules for that purpose shall be made—
- (a) in relation to England and Wales, by the Lord Chancellor with the concurrence of—
    - (i) the Treasury, and
    - (ii) in the case of rules that affect court procedure, the Lord Chief Justice, or
- (b) in relation to Scotland, by the Treasury.]

[(1B) Rules may also be made for the purpose of giving effect to Part 3 of the Banking Act 2009 (bank administration); and rules for that purpose shall be made—
- (a) in relation to England and Wales, by the Lord Chancellor with the concurrence of—
    - (i) the Treasury, and
    - (ii) in the case of rules that affect court procedure, the Lord Chief Justice, or
- (b) in relation to Scotland, by the Treasury.]

(2) Without prejudice to the generality of subsection (1), [(1A)] [or (1B)] or to any provision of those Parts by virtue of which rules under this section may be made with respect to any matter, rules under this section may contain—
- (a) any such provision as is specified in Schedule 8 to this Act or corresponds to provision contained immediately before the coming into force of section 106 of the Insolvency Act 1985 in rules made, or having effect as if made, under section 663(1) or (2) of the Companies Act (old winding-up rules), and
- (b) such incidental, supplemental and transitional provisions as may appear to the Lord Chancellor or, as the case may be, the Secretary of State [or the Treasury] necessary or expedient.

[(2A) For the purposes of subsection (2), a reference in Schedule 8 to this Act to doing anything under or for the purposes of a provision of this Act includes a reference to doing anything under or for the purposes of the EC Regulation (in so far as the provision of this Act relates to a matter to which the EC Regulation applies).

(2B) Rules under this section for the purpose of giving effect to the EC Regulation may not create an offence of a kind referred to in paragraph 1(1)(d) of Schedule 2 to the European Communities Act 1972.]

[(2C) For the purposes of subsection (2), a reference in Schedule 8 to this Act to doing anything under or for the purposes of a provision of this Act includes a reference to doing anything under or for the purposes of Part 2 of the Banking Act 2009.]

[(2D) For the purposes of subsection (2), a reference in Schedule 8 to this Act to doing anything under or for the purposes of a provision of this Act includes a reference to doing anything under or for the purposes of Part 3 of the Banking Act 2009.]

(3) In Schedule 8 to this Act "liquidator" includes a provisional liquidator [or bank liquidator] [or administrator]; and references above in this section to Parts I to VII of this Act [or Part 2 [or 3] of the Banking Act 2009] are to be read as including [the Companies Acts] so far as relating to, and to matters connected with or arising out of, the insolvency or winding up of companies.

[(3A) In this section references to Part 2 or 3 of the Banking Act 2009 include references to those Parts as applied to building societies (see section 90C of the Building Societies Act 1986).]

(4) Rules under this section shall be made by statutory instrument subject to annulment in pursuance of a resolution of either House of Parliament.

(5) Regulations made by the Secretary of State [or the Treasury] under a power conferred by rules under this section shall be made by statutory instrument and, after being made, shall be laid before each House of Parliament.

(6) Nothing in this section prejudices any power to make rules of court.

[(7) The Lord Chief Justice may nominate a judicial office holder (as defined in section 109(4) of the Constitutional Reform Act 2005) to exercise his functions under this section.]

PART II OTHER ACTS

NOTES

Sub-s (1): words in first pair of square brackets inserted by the Constitutional Reform Act 2005, s 15(1), Sch 4, Pt 1, paras 185, 188(1), (2), as from 3 April 2006; words in second pair of square brackets inserted by the Insolvency Act 1986 (Amendment) Regulations 2002, SI 2002/1037, regs 2, 3(1), as from 3 May 2002.

Sub-ss (1A), (1B): inserted by the Banking Act 2009, ss 125(1), (2), 160(1), (2), as from 21 February 2009.

Sub-s (2): words in square brackets inserted by the Banking Act 2009, ss 125(1), (3), 160(1), (3), as from 21 February 2009.

Sub-ss (2A), (2B): inserted by SI 2002/1037, regs 2, 3(2), as from 3 May 2002.

Sub-ss (2C), (2D): inserted by the Banking Act 2009, ss 125(1), (4), 160(1), (4), as from 21 February 2009.

Sub-s (3): words in first, second, third (outer) and fourth (inner) pairs of square brackets inserted by the Banking Act 2009, ss 125(1), (5), 160(1), (5), as from 21 February 2009; words in fifth pair of square brackets substituted by the Companies Act 2006 (Commencement No 3, Consequential Amendments, Transitional Provisions and Savings) Order 2007, SI 2007/2194, art 10(1), (2), Sch 4, Pt 3, para 44, as from 1 October 2007, subject to savings in art 12 thereof.

Sub-s (3A): inserted by the Building Societies (Insolvency and Special Administration) Order 2009, SI 2009/805, art 13, as from 29 March 2009.

Sub-s (5): words in square brackets inserted by the Banking Act 2009, s 125(1), (6), as from 21 February 2009.

Sub-s (7): added by the Constitutional Reform Act 2005, s 15(1), Sch 4, Pt 1, paras 185, 188(1), (3), as from 3 April 2006.

Extension of the application of the rules. Rules may be made under this section for the purposes of: the Building Societies Act 1986, with respect to the winding up, etc, of building societies (see s 90A of, and Sch 15A, Pt I, para 4(1) to, the 1986 Act); a petition for a special administration order under the Water Industry Act 1991 (see ss 23(3), 24(3) of, and Sch 3, Pt II, para 11(4) to, the 1991 Act); the Friendly Societies Act 1992, with respect to the winding up of incorporated friendly societies (see s 23 of, and Sch 10, Pt IV, para 69(1)(a) to, the 1992 Act); and the Railways Act 1993, with respect to giving effect to the railway administration order provisions of the 1993 Act (see s 59(5) thereof).

Company directors disqualification: this section and ss 414 and 420 are applied by the Company Directors Disqualification Act 1986, s 21(2), (3) at **[346]** for the purposes of certain provisions of that Act.

Rules: the Insurance Companies (Winding-up) Rules 1985, SI 1985/95; the Insolvency (Scotland) Rules 1986, SI 1986/1915; the Insurance Companies (Winding-up) (Scotland) Rules 1986, SI 1986/1918; the Insolvency Rules 1986, SI 1986/1925; the Companies (Unfair Prejudice Applications) Proceedings Rules 1986, SI 1986/2000; the Insolvent Companies (Disqualification of Unfit Directors) Proceedings Rules 1987, SI 1987/2023; the Insolvent Companies (Reports on Conduct of Directors) Rules 1996, SI 1996/1909; the Insolvent Companies (Reports on Conduct of Directors) (Scotland) Rules 1996, SI 1996/1910; the Railway Administration Order Rules 2001, SI 2001/3352; the Insurers (Winding up) Rules 2001, SI 2001/3635; the Insurers (Winding up) (Scotland) Rules 2001, SI 2001/4040; the Insolvency (Amendment) Rules 2003, SI 2003/1730; the Insolvency (Scotland) Amendment Rules 2003, SI 2003/2111; the Energy Administration Rules 2005, SI 2005/2483; the PPP Administration Order Rules 2007, SI 2007/3141; the Bank Administration (Scotland) Rules 2009, SI 2009/350 at **[1261]**; the Bank Insolvency (Scotland) Rules 2009, SI 2009/351 at **[1303]**; the Bank Insolvency (England and Wales) Rules 2009, SI 2009/356 at **[1435]**; the Bank Administration (England and Wales) Rules 2009, SI 2009/357 at **[1729]**; the Building Society Special Administration (Scotland) Rules 2009, SI 2009/806.

Regulations: the Insolvency Regulations 1994, SI 1994/2507.

---

412 (*Outside the scope of this work; see Butterworths Securities and Financial Services Law Handbook.*)

413 Insolvency Rules Committee

(1)   The committee established under section 10 of the Insolvency Act 1976 (advisory committee on bankruptcy and winding-up rules) continues to exist for the purpose of being consulted under this section.

(2)   The Lord Chancellor shall consult the committee before making any rules under section 411 or 412 [other than rules which contain a statement that the only provision made by the rules is provision applying rules made under section 411, with or without modifications, for the purposes of provision made by [any of sections 23 to 26 of the Water Industry Act 1991 or Schedule 3 to that Act]] [or by any of sections 59 to 65 of, or Schedule 6 or 7 to, the Railways Act 1993].

(3)   Subject to the next subsection, the committee shall consist of—
   (a)   a judge of the High Court attached to the Chancery Division;
   (b)   a circuit judge;
   (c)   a registrar in bankruptcy of the High Court;
   (d)   the registrar of a county court;
   (e)   a practising barrister;
   (f)   a practising solicitor; and
   (g)   a practising accountant;

and the appointment of any person as a member of the committee shall be made [in accordance with subsection (3A) or (3B)].

[(3A)   The Lord Chief Justice must appoint the persons referred to in paragraphs (a) to (d) of subsection (3), after consulting the Lord Chancellor.

(3B) The Lord Chancellor must appoint the persons referred to in paragraphs (e) to (g) of subsection (3), after consulting the Lord Chief Justice.]

(4) The Lord Chancellor may appoint as additional members of the committee any persons appearing to him to have qualifications or experience that would be of value to the committee in considering any matter with which it is concerned.

[(5) The Lord Chief Justice may nominate a judicial office holder (as defined in section 109(4) of the Constitutional Reform Act 2005) to exercise his functions under this section.]

[300]

NOTES

Sub-s (2): words in first (outer) pair of square brackets inserted by the Water Act 1989, s 190(1), Sch 25, para 78(2); words in second (inner) pair of square brackets substituted by the Water Consolidation (Consequential Provisions) Act 1991, s 2(1), Sch 1, para 46; words in third pair of square brackets added by the Railways Act 1993, s 152, Sch 12, para 25.

Sub-s (3): words in square brackets substituted by the Constitutional Reform Act 2005, s 15(1), Sch 4, Pt 1, paras 185, 190(1), (2), as from 3 April 2006.

Sub-ss (3A), (3B): inserted by the Constitutional Reform Act 2005, s 15(1), Sch 4, Pt 1, paras 185, 190(1), (3), as from 3 April 2006.

Sub-s (5): added by the Constitutional Reform Act 2005, s 15(1), Sch 4, Pt 1, paras 185, 190(1), (4), as from 3 April 2006.

See further: in relation to the disapplication of sub-s (2) above, to the first set of rules which is made in reliance on the Banking Act 2009, ss 125, 160, see the Banking Act 2009, ss 125(8), 160(6); in relation to the disapplication of sub-s (2) above, to the first set of rules made in relation to building society insolvency or building society special administration, see the Building Societies (Insolvency and Special Administration) Order 2009, SI 2009/805, art 16 at **[558]**.

Fees orders

414 Fees orders (company insolvency proceedings)

(1) There shall be paid in respect of—
    (a) proceedings under any of Parts I to VII of this Act, and
    (b) the performance by the official receiver or the Secretary of State of functions under those Parts,

such fees as the competent authority may with the sanction of the Treasury by order direct.

(2) That authority is—
    (a) in relation to England and Wales, the Lord Chancellor, and
    (b) in relation to Scotland, the Secretary of State.

(3) The Treasury may by order direct by whom and in what manner the fees are to be collected and accounted for.

(4) The Lord Chancellor may, with the sanction of the Treasury, by order provide for sums to be deposited, by such persons, in such manner and in such circumstances as may be specified in the order, by way of security for fees payable by virtue of this section.

(5) An order under this section may contain such incidental, supplemental and transitional provisions as may appear to the Lord Chancellor, the Secretary of State or (as the case may be) the Treasury necessary or expedient.

(6) An order under this section shall be made by statutory instrument and, after being made, shall be laid before each House of Parliament.

(7) Fees payable by virtue of this section shall be paid into the Consolidated Fund.

(8) References in subsection (1) to Parts I to VII of this Act are to be read as including [the Companies Acts] so far as relating to, and to matters connected with or arising out of, the insolvency or winding up of companies.

[(8A) This section applies in relation to Part 2 of the Banking Act 2009 (bank insolvency) as in relation to Parts I to VII of this Act.]

[(8B) This section applies in relation to Part 3 of the Banking Act 2009 (bank administration) as in relation to Parts I to VII of this Act.]

[(8C) In subsections (8A) and (8B) the reference to Parts 2 and 3 of the Banking Act 2009 include references to those Parts as applied to building societies (see section 90C of the Building Societies Act 1986).]

(9) Nothing in this section prejudices any power to make rules of court; and the application of this section to Scotland is without prejudice to section 2 of the Courts of Law Fees (Scotland) Act 1985.

[301]

PART II
OTHER ACTS

NOTES

Sub-s (8): words in square brackets substituted by the Companies Act 2006 (Commencement No 3, Consequential Amendments, Transitional Provisions and Savings) Order 2007, SI 2007/2194, art 10(1), (2), Sch 4, Pt 3, para 44, as from 1 October 2007, subject to savings in art 12 thereof.

Sub-ss (8A), (8B): inserted by the Banking Act 2009, ss 126, 161, as from 21 February 2009.

Sub-s (8C): inserted by the Building Societies (Insolvency and Special Administration) Order 2009, SI 2009/805, art 14, as from 29 March 2009.

Extension of the application of orders: an order made by a competent authority under this section may make provision for fees to be payable in respect of proceedings under the applicable winding up legislation (as defined in the Friendly Societies Act 1992, s 23(3)) and the performance by the official receiver or the Secretary of State of functions under this section; see s 23(2) of, and Sch 10, Pt IV, para 69(2) to, the 1992 Act.

An order made by a competent authority under this section may make provision for fees to be payable in respect of proceedings for the winding up of a building society and the performance by the official receiver or the Secretary of State of functions under this section; see the Building Societies Act 1986, s 90A, Sch 15A, Pt I, para 4(2).

Company directors disqualification: see the note to s 411 at **[299]**.

Orders: the Insolvency Proceedings (Fees) Order 2004, SI 2004/593; the Civil Proceedings Fees Order 2008, SI 2008/1053.

415–419 (*Outside the scope of this work.*)

Other order-making powers

420 Insolvent partnerships

(1) The Lord Chancellor may, by order made with the concurrence of the Secretary of State [and the Lord Chief Justice], provide that such provisions of this Act as may be specified in the order shall apply in relation to insolvent partnerships with such modifications as may be so specified.

[(1A) An order under this section may make provision in relation to the EC Regulation.

(1B) But provision made by virtue of this section in relation to the EC Regulation may not create an offence of a kind referred to in paragraph 1(1)(d) of Schedule 2 to the European Communities Act 1972.]

(2) An order under this section may make different provision for different cases and may contain such incidental, supplemental and transitional provisions as may appear to the Lord Chancellor [and the Lord Chief Justice] necessary or expedient.

(3) An order under this section shall be made by statutory instrument subject to annulment in pursuance of a resolution of either House of Parliament.

[(4) The Lord Chief Justice may nominate a judicial office holder (as defined in section 109(4) of the Constitutional Reform Act 2005) to exercise his functions under this section.]

[302]

NOTES

Sub-ss (1), (2): words in square brackets inserted by the Constitutional Reform Act 2005, s 15(1), Sch 4, Pt 1, paras 185, 191(1)–(3), as from 3 April 2006.

Sub-ss (1A), (1B): inserted by the Insolvency Act 1986 (Amendment) Regulations 2002, SI 2002/1037, regs 2, 3(5), as from 3 May 2002.

Sub-s (4): added by the Constitutional Reform Act 2005, s 15(1), Sch 4, Pt 1, paras 185, 191(1), (4), as from 3 April 2006.

Provisions of this Act: the reference in sub-s (1) to "provisions of this Act" includes the Proceeds of Crime Act 2002, s 311(1)–(3): see s 311(6) of that Act.

Company directors disqualification: see the note to s 411 at **[299]**.

Orders: the Insolvent Partnerships Order 1994, SI 1994/2421.

421, 421A, 422 (*Outside the scope of this work.*)

PART XVI

PROVISIONS AGAINST DEBT AVOIDANCE (ENGLAND AND WALES ONLY)

NOTES

Unfitness of directors: the extent of a director's responsibility for the company entering into any transaction liable to be set aside under this Part is included among the matters to which the court must have regard in determining whether his conduct makes him unfit; see the Company Directors Disqualification Act 1986, s 9, Sch 1, Pt I, para 3 at **[326]**, **[358]**.

423 Transactions defrauding creditors

(1) This section relates to transactions entered into at an undervalue; and a person enters into such a transaction with another person if—

(a)   he makes a gift to the other person or he otherwise enters into a transaction with the other on terms that provide for him to receive no consideration;

(b)   he enters into a transaction with the other in consideration of marriage [or the formation of a civil partnership]; or

(c)   he enters into a transaction with the other for a consideration the value of which, in money or money's worth, is significantly less than the value, in money or money's worth, of the consideration provided by himself.

(2)   Where a person has entered into such a transaction, the court may, if satisfied under the next subsection, make such order as it thinks fit for—

(a)   restoring the position to what it would have been if the transaction had not been entered into, and

(b)   protecting the interests of persons who are victims of the transaction.

(3)   In the case of a person entering into such a transaction, an order shall only be made if the court is satisfied that it was entered into by him for the purpose—

(a)   of putting assets beyond the reach of a person who is making, or may at some time make, a claim against him, or

(b)   of otherwise prejudicing the interests of such a person in relation to the claim which he is making or may make.

(4)   In this section "the court" means the High Court or—

(a)   if the person entering into the transaction is an individual, any other court which would have jurisdiction in relation to a bankruptcy petition relating to him;

(b)   if that person is a body capable of being wound up under Part IV or V of this Act, any other court having jurisdiction to wind it up.

(5)   In relation to a transaction at an undervalue, references here and below to a victim of the transaction are to a person who is, or is capable of being, prejudiced by it; and in the following two sections the person entering into the transaction is referred to as "the debtor".

[303]

NOTES

Sub-s (1): words in square brackets inserted by the Civil Partnership Act 2004, s 261(1), Sch 27, para 121, as from 5 December 2005.

Market contracts: as to limitations on orders made under this section, with regard to adjusting prior transactions in relation to market contracts and certain other transactions relating to default proceedings, see the Companies Act 1989, s 165(1)(c).

See further: in relation to the application of this section, with modifications, in respect of bank insolvency and administration, see the Banking Act 2009, ss 103(3), (4), Table, 145(3), (4), Table 2 at **[103]**, **[142]**.

424   Those who may apply for an order under s 423

(1)   An application for an order under section 423 shall not be made in relation to a transaction except—

(a)   in a case where the debtor has been adjudged bankrupt or is a body corporate which is being wound up or [is in administration], by the official receiver, by the trustee of the bankrupt's estate or the liquidator or administrator of the body corporate or (with the leave of the court) by a victim of the transaction;

(b)   in a case where a victim of the transaction is bound by a voluntary arrangement approved under Part I or Part VIII of this Act, by the supervisor of the voluntary arrangement or by any person who (whether or not so bound) is such a victim; or

(c)   in any other case, by a victim of the transaction.

(2)   An application made under any of the paragraphs of subsection (1) is to be treated as made on behalf of every victim of the transaction.

[304]

NOTES

Sub-s (1): words in square brackets substituted by the Enterprise Act 2002, s 248(3), Sch 17, paras 9, 36, as from 15 September 2003, subject to savings and transitional provisions in the Enterprise Act 2002, s 249 and the Enterprise Act 2002 (Commencement No 4 and Transitional Provisions and Savings) Order 2003, SI 2003/2093, art 3.

See further: in relation to the application of this section, with modifications, in respect of bank insolvency and administration, see the Banking Act 2009, ss 103(3), (4), Table, 145(3), (4), Table 2 at **[103]**, **[142]**.

425   Provision which may be made by order under s 423

(1)   Without prejudice to the generality of section 423, an order made under that section with respect to a transaction may (subject as follows)—

(a)   require any property transferred as part of the transaction to be vested in any person, either absolutely or for the benefit of all the persons on whose behalf the application for the order is treated as made;

(b)   require any property to be so vested if it represents, in any person's hands, the application either of the proceeds of sale of property so transferred or of money so transferred;

(c)   release or discharge (in whole or in part) any security given by the debtor;

(d)   require any person to pay to any other person in respect of benefits received from the debtor such sums as the court may direct;

(e)   provide for any surety or guarantor whose obligations to any person were released or discharged (in whole or in part) under the transaction to be under such new or revived obligations as the court thinks appropriate;

(f)   provide for security to be provided for the discharge of any obligation imposed by or arising under the order, for such an obligation to be charged on any property and for such security or charge to have the same priority as a security or charge released or discharged (in whole or in part) under the transaction.

(2)   An order under section 423 may affect the property of, or impose any obligation on, any person whether or not he is the person with whom the debtor entered into the transaction; but such an order—

(a)   shall not prejudice any interest in property which was acquired from a person other than the debtor and was acquired in good faith, for value and without notice of the relevant circumstances, or prejudice any interest deriving from such an interest, and

(b)   shall not require a person who received a benefit from the transaction in good faith, for value and without notice of the relevant circumstances to pay any sum unless he was a party to the transaction.

(3)   For the purposes of this section the relevant circumstances in relation to a transaction are the circumstances by virtue of which an order under section 423 may be made in respect of the transaction.

(4)   In this section "security" means any mortgage, charge, lien or other security.

[305]

NOTES

See further: in relation to the application of this section, with modifications, in respect of bank insolvency and administration, see the Banking Act 2009, ss 103(3), (4), Table, 145(3), (4), Table 2 at **[103]**, **[142]**.

PART XVII
MISCELLANEOUS AND GENERAL

426 Co-operation between courts exercising jurisdiction in relation to insolvency

(1)   An order made by a court in any part of the United Kingdom in the exercise of jurisdiction in relation to insolvency law shall be enforced in any other part of the United Kingdom as if it were made by a court exercising the corresponding jurisdiction in that other part.

(2)   However, without prejudice to the following provisions of this section, nothing in subsection (1) requires a court in any part of the United Kingdom to enforce, in relation to property situated in that part, any order made by a court in any other part of the United Kingdom.

(3)   The Secretary of State, with the concurrence in relation to property situated in England and Wales of the Lord Chancellor, may by order make provision for securing that a trustee or assignee under the insolvency law of any part of the United Kingdom has, with such modifications as may be specified in the order, the same rights in relation to any property situated in another part of the United Kingdom as he would have in the corresponding circumstances if he were a trustee or assignee under the insolvency law of that other part.

(4)   The courts having jurisdiction in relation to insolvency law in any part of the United Kingdom shall assist the courts having the corresponding jurisdiction in any other part of the United Kingdom or any relevant country or territory.

(5)   For the purposes of subsection (4) a request made to a court in any part of the United Kingdom by a court in any other part of the United Kingdom or in a relevant country or territory is authority for the court to which the request is made to apply, in relation to any matters specified in the request, the insolvency law which is applicable by either court in relation to comparable matters falling within its jurisdiction.

In exercising its discretion under this subsection, a court shall have regard in particular to the rules of private international law.

(6)   Where a person who is a trustee or assignee under the insolvency law of any part of the United Kingdom claims property situated in any other part of the United Kingdom (whether by virtue of an order under subsection (3) or otherwise), the submission of that claim to the court exercising jurisdiction in relation to insolvency law in that other part shall be treated in the same manner as a request made by a court for the purpose of subsection (4).

(7)   Section 38 of the Criminal Law Act 1977 (execution of warrant of arrest throughout the United Kingdom) applies to a warrant which, in exercise of any jurisdiction in relation to insolvency law, is issued in any part of the United Kingdom for the arrest of a person as it applies to a warrant issued in that part of the United Kingdom for the arrest of a person charged with an offence.

(8)   Without prejudice to any power to make rules of court, any power to make provision by subordinate legislation for the purpose of giving effect in relation to companies or individuals to the insolvency law of any part of the United Kingdom includes power to make provisions for the purpose of giving effect in that part to any provision made by or under the preceding provisions of this section.

(9)   An order under subsection (3) shall be made by statutory instrument subject to annulment in pursuance of a resolution of either House of Parliament.

(10)   In this section "insolvency law" means—
- (a)   in relation to England and Wales, provision [extending to England and Wales and] made by or under this Act or sections [1A,] 6 to 10, [12 to 15], 19(c) and 20 (with Schedule 1) of the Company Directors Disqualification Act 1986 [and sections 1 to 17 of that Act as they apply for the purposes of those provisions of that Act];
- (b)   in relation to Scotland, provision extending to Scotland and made by or under this Act, sections [1A,] 6 to 10, [12 to 15], 19(c) and 20 (with Schedule 1) of the Company Directors Disqualification Act 1986 [and sections 1 to 17 of that Act as they apply for the purposes of those provisions of that Act], Part XVIII of the Companies Act or the Bankruptcy (Scotland) Act 1985;
- (c)   in relation to Northern Ireland, provision made by or under [the Insolvency (Northern Ireland) Order 1989] [*or Part II of the Companies* (*Northern Ireland*) *Order 1989*];
- (d)   in relation to any relevant country or territory, so much of the law of that country or territory as corresponds to provisions falling within any of the foregoing paragraphs;

and references in this subsection to any enactment include, in relation to any time before the coming into force of that enactment the corresponding enactment in force at that time.

(11)   In this section "relevant country or territory" means—
- (a)   any of the Channel Islands or the Isle of Man, or
- (b)   any country or territory designated for the purposes of this section by the Secretary of State by order made by statutory instrument.

[(12)   In the application of this section to Northern Ireland—
- (a)   for any reference to the Secretary of State there is substituted a reference to the Department of Economic Development in Northern Ireland;
- (b)   in subsection (3) for the words "another part of the United Kingdom" and the words "that other part" there are substituted the words "Northern Ireland";
- (c)   for subsection (9) there is substituted the following subsection—

"(9)   An order made under subsection (3) by the Department of Economic Development in Northern Ireland shall be a statutory rule for the purposes of the Statutory Rules (Northern Ireland) Order 1979 and shall be subject to negative resolution within the meaning of section 41(6) of the Interpretation Act (Northern Ireland) 1954.".]

[(13)   Section 129 of the Banking Act 2009 provides for provisions of that Act about bank insolvency to be "insolvency law" for the purposes of this section.]

[(14)   Section 165 of the Banking Act 2009 provides for provisions of that Act about bank administration to be "insolvency law" for the purposes of this section.]

[306]

NOTES

Sub-s (10): words in square brackets in paras (a), (b) inserted or substituted by the Insolvency Act 2000, s 8, Sch 4, Pt II, para 16(1), (3), as from 2 April 2001; words in first pair of square brackets in para (c) substituted by the Insolvency (Northern Ireland) Order 1989, SI 1989/2405 (NI 19), art 381(2), Sch 9, Pt II, para 41(a); words in second pair of square brackets in para (c) added by the Companies (Northern Ireland) Order 1989, SI 1989/2404, arts 25(2), 36, Sch 4, Pt I, para 1, and substituted by the words "or the Company Directors Disqualification (Northern Ireland) Order 2002" by the Company Directors Disqualification (Northern Ireland) Order 2002, SI 2002/3150 (NI 4), art 26(2), Sch 3, para 2, as from a day to be appointed.

Sub-s (12): inserted by SI 1989/2405, art 381(2), Sch 9, Pt II, para 41(b).

Sub-ss (13), (14): inserted by the Banking Act 2009, s 129, 165, as from 21 February 2009.

Insolvency law: references to insolvency law in this section include, in relation to a part of the UK, provisions made by or under the Companies Act 1989, Pt VII, and, in relation to a relevant country or territory, so much of the law of that country or territory as corresponds to any such provisions; see the Companies Act 1989, s 183(1). See also, as to insolvency proceedings in other jurisdictions, s 183(2), (3) thereof. See further, the Insolvency Act 2000, s 14, which enables the Secretary of State to give effect to the United Nations Commission on International Trade Law model law on cross-border insolvency by secondary legislation and provides that any such secondary legislation may include amendments to this section.

Orders: the Co-operation of Insolvency Courts (Designation of Relevant Countries and Territories) Order 1986, SI 1986/2123; the Co-operation of Insolvency Courts (Designation of Relevant Countries) Order 1996, SI 1996/253; the Co-operation of Insolvency Courts (Designation of Relevant Country) Order 1998, SI 1998/2766.

426A–429 (*Outside the scope of this work.*)

430 Provision introducing Schedule of punishments

(1) Schedule 10 to this Act has effect with respect to the way in which offences under this Act are punishable on conviction.

(2) In relation to an offence under a provision of this Act specified in the first column of the Schedule (the general nature of the offence being described in the second column), the third column shows whether the offence is punishable on conviction on indictment, or on summary conviction, or either in the one way or the other.

(3) The fourth column of the Schedule shows, in relation to an offence, the maximum punishment by way of fine or imprisonment under this Act which may be imposed on a person convicted of the offence in the way specified in relation to it in the third column (that is to say, on indictment or summarily), a reference to a period of years or months being to a term of imprisonment of that duration.

(4) The fifth column shows (in relation to an offence for which there is an entry in that column) that a person convicted of the offence after continued contravention is liable to a daily default fine; that is to say, he is liable on a second or subsequent conviction of the offence to the fine specified in that column for each day on which the contravention is continued (instead of the penalty specified for the offence in the fourth column of the Schedule).

(5) For the purpose of any enactment in this Act whereby an officer of a company who is in default is liable to a fine or penalty, the expression "officer who is in default" means any officer of the company who knowingly and wilfully authorises or permits the default, refusal or contravention mentioned in the enactment.

[307]

NOTES

See further: in relation to the application of this section, with modifications, in respect of bank insolvency and administration, see the Banking Act 2009, ss 103(3), (4), Table, 145(3), (4), Table 2 at **[103]**, **[142]**.

431 Summary proceedings

(1) Summary proceedings for any offence under any of Parts I to VII of this Act may (without prejudice to any jurisdiction exercisable apart from this subsection) be taken against a body corporate at any place at which the body has a place of business, and against any other person at any place at which he is for the time being.

(2) Notwithstanding anything in section 127(1) of the Magistrates' Courts Act 1980, an information relating to such an offence which is triable by a magistrates' court in England and Wales may be so tried if it is laid at any time within 3 years after the commission of the offence and within 12 months after the date on which evidence sufficient in the opinion of the Director of Public Prosecutions or the Secretary of State (as the case may be) to justify the proceedings comes to his knowledge.

(3) Summary proceedings in Scotland for such an offence shall not be commenced after the expiration of 3 years from the commission of the offence.

Subject to this (and notwithstanding anything in [section 136 of the Criminal Procedure (Scotland) Act 1995]), such proceedings may (in Scotland) be commenced at any time within 12 months after the date on which evidence sufficient in the Lord Advocate's opinion to justify the proceedings came to his knowledge or, where such evidence was reported to him by the Secretary of State, within 12 months after the date on which it came to the knowledge of the latter; and subsection (3) of that section applies for the purpose of this subsection as it applies for the purpose of that section.

(4) For purposes of this section, a certificate of the Director of Public Prosecutions, the Lord Advocate or the Secretary of State (as the case may be) as to the date on which such evidence as is referred to above came to his knowledge is conclusive evidence.

[308]

NOTES

Sub-s (3): words in square brackets substituted by the Criminal Procedure (Consequential Provisions) (Scotland) Act 1995, s 5, Sch 4, para 61.

See further: in relation to the application of this section, with modifications, in respect of bank insolvency and administration, see the Banking Act 2009, ss 103(3), (4), Table, 145(3), (4), Table 2 at **[103]**, **[142]**.

432 Offences by bodies corporate

(1)   This section applies to offences under this Act other than those excepted by subsection (4).

(2)   Where a body corporate is guilty of an offence to which this section applies and the offence is proved to have been committed with the consent or connivance of, or to be attributable to any neglect on the part of, any director, manager, secretary or other similar officer of the body corporate or any person who was purporting to act in any such capacity he, as well as the body corporate, is guilty of the offence and liable to be proceeded against and punished accordingly.

(3)   Where the affairs of a body corporate are managed by its members, subsection (2) applies in relation to the acts and defaults of a member in connection with his functions of management as if he were a director of the body corporate.

(4)   The offences excepted from this section are those under sections 30, 39, 51, 53, 54, 62, 64, 66, 85, 89, 164, 188, 201, 206, 207, 208, 209, 210 and 211 [and those under paragraphs 16(2), 17(3)(a), 18(3)(a), 19(3)(a), 22(1) and 23(1)(a) of Schedule A1].

[309]

NOTES

Sub-s (4): words in square brackets inserted by the Insolvency Act 2000, s 1, Sch 1, paras 1, 11, as from 1 January 2003.

See further: in relation to the application of this section, with modifications, in respect of bank insolvency and administration, see the Banking Act 2009, ss 103(3), (4), Table, 145(3), (4), Table 2 at **[103]**, **[142]**.

433 Admissibility in evidence of statements of affairs, etc

[(1)]   In any proceedings (whether or not under this Act)—

      (a)   a statement of affairs prepared for the purposes of any provision of this Act which is derived from the Insolvency Act 1985,

      [(aa)   a statement made in pursuance of a requirement imposed by or under Part 2 of the Banking Act 2009 (bank insolvency),]

      [(ab)   a statement made in pursuance of a requirement imposed by or under Part 3 of that Act (bank administration),] and

      (b)   any other statement made in pursuance of a requirement imposed by or under any such provision or by or under rules made under this Act,

may be used in evidence against any person making or concurring in making the statement.

[(2)   However, in criminal proceedings in which any such person is charged with an offence to which this subsection applies—

      (a)   no evidence relating to the statement may be adduced, and

      (b)   no question relating to it may be asked,

by or on behalf of the prosecution, unless evidence relating to it is adduced, or a question relating to it is asked, in the proceedings by or on behalf of that person.

(3)   Subsection (2) applies to any offence other than—

      (a)   an offence under section 22(6), 47(6), 48(8), 66(6), 67(8), 95(8), 98(6), 99(3)(a), 131(7), 192(2), 208(1)(a) or (d) or (2), 210, 235(5), 353(1), 354(1)(b) or (3) or 356(1) or (2)(a) or (b) or paragraph 4(3)(a) of Schedule 7;

      (b)   an offence which is—

           (i)   created by rules made under this Act, and

           (ii)   designated for the purposes of this subsection by such rules or by regulations made by the Secretary of State;

      (c)   an offence which is—

           (i)   created by regulations made under any such rules, and

           (ii)   designated for the purposes of this subsection by such regulations;

      (d)   an offence under section 1, 2 or 5 of the Perjury Act 1911 (false statements made on oath or made otherwise than on oath); or

      (e)   an offence under section 44(1) or (2) of the Criminal Law (Consolidation) (Scotland) Act 1995 (false statements made on oath or otherwise than on oath).

(4)   Regulations under subsection (3)(b)(ii) shall be made by statutory instrument and, after being made, shall be laid before each House of Parliament.]

[310]

NOTES

Existing provision renumbered as sub-s (1) and sub-ss (2)–(4) added by the Youth Justice and Criminal Evidence Act 1999, s 59, Sch 3, para 7, as from 14 April 2000 in relation to England and Wales, and as from 1 January 2001 in relation to Scotland.

Sub-s (1): paras (aa), (ab) inserted by the Banking Act 2009, ss 128, 162, as from 21 February 2009.

See further: in relation to the application of this section, with modifications, in respect of bank insolvency and administration, see the Banking Act 2009, ss 103(3), (4), Table, 145(3), (4), Table 2 at **[103]**, **[142]**.

PART II
OTHER ACTS

434–444   (*S 434, ss 434A–444 (Pts XVIIA–XIX) outside the scope of this work; for ss 443, 444 see Butterworths Securities and Financial Services Law Handbook.*)

SCHEDULES

(*Sch A1 outside the scope of this work; see Butterworths Securities and Financial Services Law Handbook.*)

[SCHEDULE B1
ADMINISTRATION
Section 8

ARRANGEMENT OF SCHEDULE

NATURE OF ADMINISTRATION

Administration

1.—(1)   For the purposes of this Act "administrator" of a company means a person appointed under this Schedule to manage the company's affairs, business and property.

(2)   For the purposes of this Act—
   (a)   a company is "in administration" while the appointment of an administrator of the company has effect,
   (b)   a company "enters administration" when the appointment of an administrator takes effect,
   (c)   a company ceases to be in administration when the appointment of an administrator of the company ceases to have effect in accordance with this Schedule, and
   (d)   a company does not cease to be in administration merely because an administrator vacates office (by reason of resignation, death or otherwise) or is removed from office.

2.   A person may be appointed as administrator of a company—
   (a)   by administration order of the court under paragraph 10,
   (b)   by the holder of a floating charge under paragraph 14, or
   (c)   by the company or its directors under paragraph 22.

Purpose of administration

3.—(1)   The administrator of a company must perform his functions with the objective of—
   (a)   rescuing the company as a going concern, or
   (b)   achieving a better result for the company's creditors as a whole than would be likely if the company were wound up (without first being in administration), or
   (c)   realising property in order to make a distribution to one or more secured or preferential creditors.

(2)   Subject to sub-paragraph (4), the administrator of a company must perform his functions in the interests of the company's creditors as a whole.

(3)   The administrator must perform his functions with the objective specified in sub-paragraph (1)(a) unless he thinks either—
   (a)   that it is not reasonably practicable to achieve that objective, or
   (b)   that the objective specified in sub-paragraph (1)(b) would achieve a better result for the company's creditors as a whole.

(4)   The administrator may perform his functions with the objective specified in sub-paragraph (1)(c) only if—
    (a)   he thinks that it is not reasonably practicable to achieve either of the objectives specified in sub-paragraph (1)(a) and (b), and
    (b)   he does not unnecessarily harm the interests of the creditors of the company as a whole.

4.   The administrator of a company must perform his functions as quickly and efficiently as is reasonably practicable.

Status of administrator

5.   An administrator is an officer of the court (whether or not he is appointed by the court).

General restrictions

6.   A person may be appointed as administrator of a company only if he is qualified to act as an insolvency practitioner in relation to the company.

7.   A person may not be appointed as administrator of a company which is in administration (subject to the provisions of paragraphs 90 to 97 and 100 to 103 about replacement and additional administrators).

8.—(1)   A person may not be appointed as administrator of a company which is in liquidation by virtue of—
    (a)   a resolution for voluntary winding up, or
    (b)   a winding-up order.

(2)   Sub-paragraph (1)(a) is subject to paragraph 38.

(3)   Sub-paragraph (1)(b) is subject to paragraphs 37 and 38.

9.—(1)   A person may not be appointed as administrator of a company which—
    (a)   has a liability in respect of a deposit which it accepted in accordance with the Banking Act 1979 (c 37) or 1987 (c 22), but
    (b)   is not an authorised deposit taker.

(2)   A person may not be appointed as administrator of a company which effects or carries out contracts of insurance.

(3)   But sub-paragraph (2) does not apply to a company which—
    (a)   is exempt from the general prohibition in relation to effecting or carrying out contracts of insurance, or
    (b)   is an authorised deposit taker effecting or carrying out contracts of insurance in the course of a banking business.

(4)   In this paragraph—
"authorised deposit taker" means a person with permission under Part IV of the Financial Services and Markets Act 2000 (c 8) to accept deposits, and
"the general prohibition" has the meaning given by section 19 of that Act.

(5)   This paragraph shall be construed in accordance with—
    (a)   section 22 of the Financial Services and Markets Act 2000 (classes of regulated activity and categories of investment),
    (b)   any relevant order under that section, and
    (c)   Schedule 2 to that Act (regulated activities).

APPOINTMENT OF ADMINISTRATOR BY COURT

Administration order

10.   An administration order is an order appointing a person as the administrator of a company.

Conditions for making order

11.   The court may make an administration order in relation to a company only if satisfied—
    (a)   that the company is or is likely to become unable to pay its debts, and
    (b)   that the administration order is reasonably likely to achieve the purpose of administration.

Administration application

12.—(1)   An application to the court for an administration order in respect of a company (an "administration application") may be made only by—
    (a)   the company,
    (b)   the directors of the company,
    (c)   one or more creditors of the company,
    (d)   the [designated officer] for a magistrates' court in the exercise of the power conferred by section 87A of the Magistrates' Courts Act 1980 (c 43) (fine imposed on company), or

(e)　a combination of persons listed in paragraphs (a) to (d).

(2)　As soon as is reasonably practicable after the making of an administration application the applicant shall notify—

(a)　any person who has appointed an administrative receiver of the company,

(b)　any person who is or may be entitled to appoint an administrative receiver of the company,

(c)　any person who is or may be entitled to appoint an administrator of the company under paragraph 14, and

(d)　such other persons as may be prescribed.

(3)　An administration application may not be withdrawn without the permission of the court.

(4)　In sub-paragraph (1) "creditor" includes a contingent creditor and a prospective creditor.

[(5)　Sub-paragraph (1) is without prejudice to section 7(4)(b).]

Powers of court

13.—(1)　On hearing an administration application the court may—

(a)　make the administration order sought;

(b)　dismiss the application;

(c)　adjourn the hearing conditionally or unconditionally;

(d)　make an interim order;

(e)　treat the application as a winding-up petition and make any order which the court could make under section 125;

(f)　make any other order which the court thinks appropriate.

(2)　An appointment of an administrator by administration order takes effect—

(a)　at a time appointed by the order, or

(b)　where no time is appointed by the order, when the order is made.

(3)　An interim order under sub-paragraph (1)(d) may, in particular—

(a)　restrict the exercise of a power of the directors or the company;

(b)　make provision conferring a discretion on the court or on a person qualified to act as an insolvency practitioner in relation to the company.

(4)　This paragraph is subject to paragraph 39.

APPOINTMENT OF ADMINISTRATOR BY HOLDER OF FLOATING CHARGE

Power to appoint

14.—(1)　The holder of a qualifying floating charge in respect of a company's property may appoint an administrator of the company.

(2)　For the purposes of sub-paragraph (1) a floating charge qualifies if created by an instrument which—

(a)　states that this paragraph applies to the floating charge,

(b)　purports to empower the holder of the floating charge to appoint an administrator of the company,

(c)　purports to empower the holder of the floating charge to make an appointment which would be the appointment of an administrative receiver within the meaning given by section 29(2), or

(d)　purports to empower the holder of a floating charge in Scotland to appoint a receiver who on appointment would be an administrative receiver.

(3)　For the purposes of sub-paragraph (1) a person is the holder of a qualifying floating charge in respect of a company's property if he holds one or more debentures of the company secured—

(a)　by a qualifying floating charge which relates to the whole or substantially the whole of the company's property,

(b)　by a number of qualifying floating charges which together relate to the whole or substantially the whole of the company's property, or

(c)　by charges and other forms of security which together relate to the whole or substantially the whole of the company's property and at least one of which is a qualifying floating charge.

Restrictions on power to appoint

15.—(1)　A person may not appoint an administrator under paragraph 14 unless—

(a)　he has given at least two business days' written notice to the holder of any prior floating charge which satisfies paragraph 14(2), or

(b)　the holder of any prior floating charge which satisfies paragraph 14(2) has consented in writing to the making of the appointment.

(2)　One floating charge is prior to another for the purposes of this paragraph if—

(a)　it was created first, or

(b)   it is to be treated as having priority in accordance with an agreement to which the holder of each floating charge was party.

(3)   Sub-paragraph (2) shall have effect in relation to Scotland as if the following were substituted for paragraph (a)—

        "(a)   it has priority of ranking in accordance with section 464(4)(b) of the Companies Act 1985 (c 6),".

16.   An administrator may not be appointed under paragraph 14 while a floating charge on which the appointment relies is not enforceable.

17.   An administrator of a company may not be appointed under paragraph 14 if—

(a)   a provisional liquidator of the company has been appointed under section 135, or
(b)   an administrative receiver of the company is in office.

Notice of appointment

18.—(1)   A person who appoints an administrator of a company under paragraph 14 shall file with the court—

(a)   a notice of appointment, and
(b)   such other documents as may be prescribed.

(2)   The notice of appointment must include a statutory declaration by or on behalf of the person who makes the appointment—

(a)   that the person is the holder of a qualifying floating charge in respect of the company's property,
(b)   that each floating charge relied on in making the appointment is (or was) enforceable on the date of the appointment, and
(c)   that the appointment is in accordance with this Schedule.

(3)   The notice of appointment must identify the administrator and must be accompanied by a statement by the administrator—

(a)   that he consents to the appointment,
(b)   that in his opinion the purpose of administration is reasonably likely to be achieved, and
(c)   giving such other information and opinions as may be prescribed.

(4)   For the purpose of a statement under sub-paragraph (3) an administrator may rely on information supplied by directors of the company (unless he has reason to doubt its accuracy).

(5)   The notice of appointment and any document accompanying it must be in the prescribed form.

(6)   A statutory declaration under sub-paragraph (2) must be made during the prescribed period.

(7)   A person commits an offence if in a statutory declaration under sub-paragraph (2) he makes a statement—

(a)   which is false, and
(b)   which he does not reasonably believe to be true.

Commencement of appointment

19.   The appointment of an administrator under paragraph 14 takes effect when the requirements of paragraph 18 are satisfied.

20.   A person who appoints an administrator under paragraph 14—

(a)   shall notify the administrator and such other persons as may be prescribed as soon as is reasonably practicable after the requirements of paragraph 18 are satisfied, and
(b)   commits an offence if he fails without reasonable excuse to comply with paragraph (a).

Invalid appointment: indemnity

21.—(1)   This paragraph applies where—

(a)   a person purports to appoint an administrator under paragraph 14, and
(b)   the appointment is discovered to be invalid.

(2)   The court may order the person who purported to make the appointment to indemnify the person appointed against liability which arises solely by reason of the appointment's invalidity.

APPOINTMENT OF ADMINISTRATOR BY COMPANY OR DIRECTORS

Power to appoint

22.—(1)   A company may appoint an administrator.

(2)   The directors of a company may appoint an administrator.

Restrictions on power to appoint

23.—(1)   This paragraph applies where an administrator of a company is appointed—

    (a)   under paragraph 22, or

    (b)   on an administration application made by the company or its directors.

    (2)   An administrator of the company may not be appointed under paragraph 22 during the period of 12 months beginning with the date on which the appointment referred to in sub-paragraph (1) ceases to have effect.

24.—(1)   If a moratorium for a company under Schedule A1 ends on a date when no voluntary arrangement is in force in respect of the company, this paragraph applies for the period of 12 months beginning with that date.

    (2)   This paragraph also applies for the period of 12 months beginning with the date on which a voluntary arrangement in respect of a company ends if—

    (a)   the arrangement was made during a moratorium for the company under Schedule A1, and

    (b)   the arrangement ends prematurely (within the meaning of section 7B).

    (3)   While this paragraph applies, an administrator of the company may not be appointed under paragraph 22.

25.   An administrator of a company may not be appointed under paragraph 22 if—

    (a)   a petition for the winding up of the company has been presented and is not yet disposed of,

    (b)   an administration application has been made and is not yet disposed of, or

    (c)   an administrative receiver of the company is in office.

Notice of intention to appoint

26.—(1)   A person who proposes to make an appointment under paragraph 22 shall give at least five business days' written notice to—

    (a)   any person who is or may be entitled to appoint an administrative receiver of the company, and

    (b)   any person who is or may be entitled to appoint an administrator of the company under paragraph 14.

    (2)   A person who proposes to make an appointment under paragraph 22 shall also give such notice as may be prescribed to such other persons as may be prescribed.

    (3)   A notice under this paragraph must—

    (a)   identify the proposed administrator, and

    (b)   be in the prescribed form.

27.—(1)   A person who gives notice of intention to appoint under paragraph 26 shall file with the court as soon as is reasonably practicable a copy of—

    (a)   the notice, and

    (b)   any document accompanying it.

    (2)   The copy filed under sub-paragraph (1) must be accompanied by a statutory declaration made by or on behalf of the person who proposes to make the appointment—

    (a)   that the company is or is likely to become unable to pay its debts,

    (b)   that the company is not in liquidation, and

    (c)   that, so far as the person making the statement is able to ascertain, the appointment is not prevented by paragraphs 23 to 25, and

    (d)   to such additional effect, and giving such information, as may be prescribed.

    (3)   A statutory declaration under sub-paragraph (2) must—

    (a)   be in the prescribed form, and

    (b)   be made during the prescribed period.

    (4)   A person commits an offence if in a statutory declaration under sub-paragraph (2) he makes a statement—

    (a)   which is false, and

    (b)   which he does not reasonably believe to be true.

28.—(1)   An appointment may not be made under paragraph 22 unless the person who makes the appointment has complied with any requirement of paragraphs 26 and 27 and—

    (a)   the period of notice specified in paragraph 26(1) has expired, or

    (b)   each person to whom notice has been given under paragraph 26(1) has consented in writing to the making of the appointment.

    (2)   An appointment may not be made under paragraph 22 after the period of ten business days beginning with the date on which the notice of intention to appoint is filed under paragraph 27(1).

Notice of appointment

29.—(1)   A person who appoints an administrator of a company under paragraph 22 shall file with the court—

    (a)   a notice of appointment, and

(b) such other documents as may be prescribed.

(2) The notice of appointment must include a statutory declaration by or on behalf of the person who makes the appointment—
  (a) that the person is entitled to make an appointment under paragraph 22,
  (b) that the appointment is in accordance with this Schedule, and
  (c) that, so far as the person making the statement is able to ascertain, the statements made and information given in the statutory declaration filed with the notice of intention to appoint remain accurate.

(3) The notice of appointment must identify the administrator and must be accompanied by a statement by the administrator—
  (a) that he consents to the appointment,
  (b) that in his opinion the purpose of administration is reasonably likely to be achieved, and
  (c) giving such other information and opinions as may be prescribed.

(4) For the purpose of a statement under sub-paragraph (3) an administrator may rely on information supplied by directors of the company (unless he has reason to doubt its accuracy).

(5) The notice of appointment and any document accompanying it must be in the prescribed form.

(6) A statutory declaration under sub-paragraph (2) must be made during the prescribed period.

(7) A person commits an offence if in a statutory declaration under sub-paragraph (2) he makes a statement—
  (a) which is false, and
  (b) which he does not reasonably believe to be true.

30. In a case in which no person is entitled to notice of intention to appoint under paragraph 26(1) (and paragraph 28 therefore does not apply)—
  (a) the statutory declaration accompanying the notice of appointment must include the statements and information required under paragraph 27(2), and
  (b) paragraph 29(2)(c) shall not apply.

Commencement of appointment

31. The appointment of an administrator under paragraph 22 takes effect when the requirements of paragraph 29 are satisfied.

32. A person who appoints an administrator under paragraph 22—
  (a) shall notify the administrator and such other persons as may be prescribed as soon as is reasonably practicable after the requirements of paragraph 29 are satisfied, and
  (b) commits an offence if he fails without reasonable excuse to comply with paragraph (a).

33. If before the requirements of paragraph 29 are satisfied the company enters administration by virtue of an administration order or an appointment under paragraph 14—
  (a) the appointment under paragraph 22 shall not take effect, and
  (b) paragraph 32 shall not apply.

Invalid appointment: indemnity

34.—(1) This paragraph applies where—
  (a) a person purports to appoint an administrator under paragraph 22, and
  (b) the appointment is discovered to be invalid.

(2) The court may order the person who purported to make the appointment to indemnify the person appointed against liability which arises solely by reason of the appointment's invalidity.

ADMINISTRATION APPLICATION—SPECIAL CASES

Application by holder of floating charge

35.—(1) This paragraph applies where an administration application in respect of a company—
  (a) is made by the holder of a qualifying floating charge in respect of the company's property, and
  (b) includes a statement that the application is made in reliance on this paragraph.

(2) The court may make an administration order—
  (a) whether or not satisfied that the company is or is likely to become unable to pay its debts, but
  (b) only if satisfied that the applicant could appoint an administrator under paragraph 14.

Intervention by holder of floating charge

36.—(1) This paragraph applies where—
  (a) an administration application in respect of a company is made by a person who is not the holder of a qualifying floating charge in respect of the company's property, and

(b)   the holder of a qualifying floating charge in respect of the company's property applies to the court to have a specified person appointed as administrator (and not the person specified by the administration applicant).

(2)   The court shall grant an application under sub-paragraph (1)(b) unless the court thinks it right to refuse the application because of the particular circumstances of the case.

Application where company in liquidation

37.—(1)   This paragraph applies where the holder of a qualifying floating charge in respect of a company's property could appoint an administrator under paragraph 14 but for paragraph 8(1)(b).

(2)   The holder of the qualifying floating charge may make an administration application.

(3)   If the court makes an administration order on hearing an application made by virtue of sub-paragraph (2)—
(a)   the court shall discharge the winding-up order,
(b)   the court shall make provision for such matters as may be prescribed,
(c)   the court may make other consequential provision,
(d)   the court shall specify which of the powers under this Schedule are to be exercisable by the administrator, and
(e)   this Schedule shall have effect with such modifications as the court may specify.

38.—(1)   The liquidator of a company may make an administration application.

(2)   If the court makes an administration order on hearing an application made by virtue of sub-paragraph (1)—
(a)   the court shall discharge any winding-up order in respect of the company,
(b)   the court shall make provision for such matters as may be prescribed,
(c)   the court may make other consequential provision,
(d)   the court shall specify which of the powers under this Schedule are to be exercisable by the administrator, and
(e)   this Schedule shall have effect with such modifications as the court may specify.

Effect of administrative receivership

39.—(1)   Where there is an administrative receiver of a company the court must dismiss an administration application in respect of the company unless—
(a)   the person by or on behalf of whom the receiver was appointed consents to the making of the administration order,
(b)   the court thinks that the security by virtue of which the receiver was appointed would be liable to be released or discharged under sections 238 to 240 (transaction at undervalue and preference) if an administration order were made,
(c)   the court thinks that the security by virtue of which the receiver was appointed would be avoided under section 245 (avoidance of floating charge) if an administration order were made, or
(d)   the court thinks that the security by virtue of which the receiver was appointed would be challengeable under section 242 (gratuitous alienations) or 243 (unfair preferences) or under any rule of law in Scotland.

(2)   Sub-paragraph (1) applies whether the administrative receiver is appointed before or after the making of the administration application.

EFFECT OF ADMINISTRATION

Dismissal of pending winding-up petition

40.—(1)   A petition for the winding up of a company—
(a)   shall be dismissed on the making of an administration order in respect of the company, and
(b)   shall be suspended while the company is in administration following an appointment under paragraph 14.

(2)   Sub-paragraph (1)(b) does not apply to a petition presented under—
(a)   section 124A (public interest),
[(aa)   section 124B (SEs),] or
(b)   section 367 of the Financial Services and Markets Act 2000 (c 8) (petition by Financial Services Authority).

(3)   Where an administrator becomes aware that a petition was presented under a provision referred to in sub-paragraph (2) before his appointment, he shall apply to the court for directions under paragraph 63.

Dismissal of administrative or other receiver

41.—(1)   When an administration order takes effect in respect of a company any administrative receiver of the company shall vacate office.

(2)   Where a company is in administration, any receiver of part of the company's property shall vacate office if the administrator requires him to.

(3)   Where an administrative receiver or receiver vacates office under sub-paragraph (1) or (2)—
 (a)   his remuneration shall be charged on and paid out of any property of the company which was in his custody or under his control immediately before he vacated office, and
 (b)   he need not take any further steps under section 40 or 59.

(4)   In the application of sub-paragraph (3)(a)—
 (a)   "remuneration" includes expenses properly incurred and any indemnity to which the administrative receiver or receiver is entitled out of the assets of the company,
 (b)   the charge imposed takes priority over security held by the person by whom or on whose behalf the administrative receiver or receiver was appointed, and
 (c)   the provision for payment is subject to paragraph 43.

Moratorium on insolvency proceedings

42.—(1)   This paragraph applies to a company in administration.

(2)   No resolution may be passed for the winding up of the company.

(3)   No order may be made for the winding up of the company.

(4)   Sub-paragraph (3) does not apply to an order made on a petition presented under—
 (a)   section 124A (public interest),
 [(aa)   section 124B (SEs),] or
 (b)   section 367 of the Financial Services and Markets Act 2000 (c 8) (petition by Financial Services Authority).

(5)   If a petition presented under a provision referred to in sub-paragraph (4) comes to the attention of the administrator, he shall apply to the court for directions under paragraph 63.

Moratorium on other legal process

43.—(1)   This paragraph applies to a company in administration.

(2)   No step may be taken to enforce security over the company's property except—
 (a)   with the consent of the administrator, or
 (b)   with the permission of the court.

(3)   No step may be taken to repossess goods in the company's possession under a hire-purchase agreement except—
 (a)   with the consent of the administrator, or
 (b)   with the permission of the court.

(4)   A landlord may not exercise a right of forfeiture by peaceable re-entry in relation to premises let to the company except—
 (a)   with the consent of the administrator, or
 (b)   with the permission of the court.

(5)   In Scotland, a landlord may not exercise a right of irritancy in relation to premises let to the company except—
 (a)   with the consent of the administrator, or
 (b)   with the permission of the court.

(6)   No legal process (including legal proceedings, execution, distress and diligence) may be instituted or continued against the company or property of the company except—
 (a)   with the consent of the administrator, or
 (b)   with the permission of the court.

[(6A)   An administrative receiver of the company may not be appointed.]

(7)   Where the court gives permission for a transaction under this paragraph it may impose a condition on or a requirement in connection with the transaction.

(8)   In this paragraph "landlord" includes a person to whom rent is payable.

Interim moratorium

44.—(1)   This paragraph applies where an administration application in respect of a company has been made and—
 (a)   the application has not yet been granted or dismissed, or
 (b)   the application has been granted but the administration order has not yet taken effect.

(2)   This paragraph also applies from the time when a copy of notice of intention to appoint an administrator under paragraph 14 is filed with the court until—

    (a)   the appointment of the administrator takes effect, or

    (b)   the period of five business days beginning with the date of filing expires without an administrator having been appointed.

(3)   Sub-paragraph (2) has effect in relation to a notice of intention to appoint only if it is in the prescribed form.

(4)   This paragraph also applies from the time when a copy of notice of intention to appoint an administrator is filed with the court under paragraph 27(1) until—

    (a)   the appointment of the administrator takes effect, or

    (b)   the period specified in paragraph 28(2) expires without an administrator having been appointed.

(5)   The provisions of paragraphs 42 and 43 shall apply (ignoring any reference to the consent of the administrator).

(6)   If there is an administrative receiver of the company when the administration application is made, the provisions of paragraphs 42 and 43 shall not begin to apply by virtue of this paragraph until the person by or on behalf of whom the receiver was appointed consents to the making of the administration order.

(7)   This paragraph does not prevent or require the permission of the court for—

    (a)   the presentation of a petition for the winding up of the company under a provision mentioned in paragraph 42(4),

    (b)   the appointment of an administrator under paragraph 14,

    (c)   the appointment of an administrative receiver of the company, or

    (d)   the carrying out by an administrative receiver (whenever appointed) of his functions.

Publicity

[45.—(1)   While a company is in administration, every business document issued by or on behalf of the company or the administrator, and all the company's websites, must state—

    (a)   the name of the administrator, and

    (b)   that the affairs, business and property of the company are being managed by the administrator.

(2)   Any of the following persons commits an offence if without reasonable excuse the person authorises or permits a contravention of sub-paragraph (1)—

    (a)   the administrator,

    (b)   an officer of the company, and

    (c)   the company.

(3)   In sub-paragraph (1) "business document" means—

    (a)   an invoice,

    (b)   an order for goods or services,

    (c)   a business letter, and

    (d)   an order form,

whether in hard copy, electronic or any other form.]

PROCESS OF ADMINISTRATION

Announcement of administrator's appointment

46.—(1)   This paragraph applies where a person becomes the administrator of a company.

(2)   As soon as is reasonably practicable the administrator shall—

    (a)   send a notice of his appointment to the company, and

    (b)   publish a notice of his appointment in the prescribed manner.

(3)   As soon as is reasonably practicable the administrator shall—

    (a)   obtain a list of the company's creditors, and

    (b)   send a notice of his appointment to each creditor of whose claim and address he is aware.

(4)   The administrator shall send a notice of his appointment to the registrar of companies before the end of the period of 7 days beginning with the date specified in sub-paragraph (6).

(5)   The administrator shall send a notice of his appointment to such persons as may be prescribed before the end of the prescribed period beginning with the date specified in sub-paragraph (6).

(6)   The date for the purpose of sub-paragraphs (4) and (5) is—

    (a)   in the case of an administrator appointed by administration order, the date of the order,

    (b)   in the case of an administrator appointed under paragraph 14, the date on which he receives notice under paragraph 20, and

    (c)   in the case of an administrator appointed under paragraph 22, the date on which he receives notice under paragraph 32.

(7) The court may direct that sub-paragraph (3)(b) or (5)—
  (a) shall not apply, or
  (b) shall apply with the substitution of a different period.

(8) A notice under this paragraph must—
  (a) contain the prescribed information, and
  (b) be in the prescribed form.

(9) An administrator commits an offence if he fails without reasonable excuse to comply with a requirement of this paragraph.

Statement of company's affairs

47.—(1) As soon as is reasonably practicable after appointment the administrator of a company shall by notice in the prescribed form require one or more relevant persons to provide the administrator with a statement of the affairs of the company.

(2) The statement must—
  (a) be verified by a statement of truth in accordance with Civil Procedure Rules,
  (b) be in the prescribed form,
  (c) give particulars of the company's property, debts and liabilities,
  (d) give the names and addresses of the company's creditors,
  (e) specify the security held by each creditor,
  (f) give the date on which each security was granted, and
  (g) contain such other information as may be prescribed.

(3) In sub-paragraph (1) "relevant person" means—
  (a) a person who is or has been an officer of the company,
  (b) a person who took part in the formation of the company during the period of one year ending with the date on which the company enters administration,
  (c) a person employed by the company during that period, and
  (d) a person who is or has been during that period an officer or employee of a company which is or has been during that year an officer of the company.

(4) For the purpose of sub-paragraph (3) a reference to employment is a reference to employment through a contract of employment or a contract for services.

(5) In Scotland, a statement of affairs under sub-paragraph (1) must be a statutory declaration made in accordance with the Statutory Declarations Act 1835 (c 62) (and sub-paragraph (2)(a) shall not apply).

48.—(1) A person required to submit a statement of affairs must do so before the end of the period of 11 days beginning with the day on which he receives notice of the requirement.

(2) The administrator may—
  (a) revoke a requirement under paragraph 47(1), or
  (b) extend the period specified in sub-paragraph (1) (whether before or after expiry).

(3) If the administrator refuses a request to act under sub-paragraph (2)—
  (a) the person whose request is refused may apply to the court, and
  (b) the court may take action of a kind specified in sub-paragraph (2).

(4) A person commits an offence if he fails without reasonable excuse to comply with a requirement under paragraph 47(1).

Administrator's proposals

49.—(1) The administrator of a company shall make a statement setting out proposals for achieving the purpose of administration.

(2) A statement under sub-paragraph (1) must, in particular—
  (a) deal with such matters as may be prescribed, and
  (b) where applicable, explain why the administrator thinks that the objective mentioned in paragraph 3(1)(a) or (b) cannot be achieved.

(3) Proposals under this paragraph may include—
  (a) a proposal for a voluntary arrangement under Part I of this Act (although this paragraph is without prejudice to section 4(3));
  (b) a proposal for a compromise or arrangement to be sanctioned under [Part 26 of the Companies Act 2006 (arrangements and reconstructions)].

(4) The administrator shall send a copy of the statement of his proposals—
  (a) to the registrar of companies,
  (b) to every creditor of the company of whose claim and address he is aware, and
  (c) to every member of the company of whose address he is aware.

(5) The administrator shall comply with sub-paragraph (4)—
  (a) as soon as is reasonably practicable after the company enters administration, and

(b)   in any event, before the end of the period of eight weeks beginning with the day on which the company enters administration.

(6)   The administrator shall be taken to comply with sub-paragraph (4)(c) if he publishes in the prescribed manner a notice undertaking to provide a copy of the statement of proposals free of charge to any member of the company who applies in writing to a specified address.

(7)   An administrator commits an offence if he fails without reasonable excuse to comply with sub-paragraph (5).

(8)   A period specified in this paragraph may be varied in accordance with paragraph 107.

Creditors' meeting

50.—(1)   In this Schedule "creditors' meeting" means a meeting of creditors of a company summoned by the administrator—
(a)   in the prescribed manner, and
(b)   giving the prescribed period of notice to every creditor of the company of whose claim and address he is aware.

(2)   A period prescribed under sub-paragraph (1)(b) may be varied in accordance with paragraph 107.

(3)   A creditors' meeting shall be conducted in accordance with the rules.

Requirement for initial creditors' meeting

51.—(1)   Each copy of an administrator's statement of proposals sent to a creditor under paragraph 49(4)(b) must be accompanied by an invitation to a creditors' meeting (an "initial creditors' meeting").

(2)   The date set for an initial creditors' meeting must be—
(a)   as soon as is reasonably practicable after the company enters administration, and
(b)   in any event, within the period of ten weeks beginning with the date on which the company enters administration.

(3)   An administrator shall present a copy of his statement of proposals to an initial creditors' meeting.

(4)   A period specified in this paragraph may be varied in accordance with paragraph 107.

(5)   An administrator commits an offence if he fails without reasonable excuse to comply with a requirement of this paragraph.

52.—(1)   Paragraph 51(1) shall not apply where the statement of proposals states that the administrator thinks—
(a)   that the company has sufficient property to enable each creditor of the company to be paid in full,
(b)   that the company has insufficient property to enable a distribution to be made to unsecured creditors other than by virtue of section 176A(2)(a), or
(c)   that neither of the objectives specified in paragraph 3(1)(a) and (b) can be achieved.

(2)   But the administrator shall summon an initial creditors' meeting if it is requested—
(a)   by creditors of the company whose debts amount to at least 10% of the total debts of the company,
(b)   in the prescribed manner, and
(c)   in the prescribed period.

(3)   A meeting requested under sub-paragraph (2) must be summoned for a date in the prescribed period.

(4)   The period prescribed under sub-paragraph (3) may be varied in accordance with paragraph 107.

Business and result of initial creditors' meeting

53.—(1)   An initial creditors' meeting to which an administrator's proposals are presented shall consider them and may—
(a)   approve them without modification, or
(b)   approve them with modification to which the administrator consents.

(2)   After the conclusion of an initial creditors' meeting the administrator shall as soon as is reasonably practicable report any decision taken to—
(a)   the court,
(b)   the registrar of companies, and
(c)   such other persons as may be prescribed.

(3)   An administrator commits an offence if he fails without reasonable excuse to comply with sub-paragraph (2).

Revision of administrator's proposals

54.—(1) This paragraph applies where—
  (a) an administrator's proposals have been approved (with or without modification) at an initial creditors' meeting,
  (b) the administrator proposes a revision to the proposals, and
  (c) the administrator thinks that the proposed revision is substantial.

(2) The administrator shall—
  (a) summon a creditors' meeting,
  (b) send a statement in the prescribed form of the proposed revision with the notice of the meeting sent to each creditor,
  (c) send a copy of the statement, within the prescribed period, to each member of the company of whose address he is aware, and
  (d) present a copy of the statement to the meeting.

(3) The administrator shall be taken to have complied with sub-paragraph (2)(c) if he publishes a notice undertaking to provide a copy of the statement free of charge to any member of the company who applies in writing to a specified address.

(4) A notice under sub-paragraph (3) must be published—
  (a) in the prescribed manner, and
  (b) within the prescribed period.

(5) A creditors' meeting to which a proposed revision is presented shall consider it and may—
  (a) approve it without modification, or
  (b) approve it with modification to which the administrator consents.

(6) After the conclusion of a creditors' meeting the administrator shall as soon as is reasonably practicable report any decision taken to—
  (a) the court,
  (b) the registrar of companies, and
  (c) such other persons as may be prescribed.

(7) An administrator commits an offence if he fails without reasonable excuse to comply with sub-paragraph (6).

Failure to obtain approval of administrator's proposals

55.—(1) This paragraph applies where an administrator reports to the court that—
  (a) an initial creditors' meeting has failed to approve the administrator's proposals presented to it, or
  (b) a creditors' meeting has failed to approve a revision of the administrator's proposals presented to it.

(2) The court may—
  (a) provide that the appointment of an administrator shall cease to have effect from a specified time;
  (b) adjourn the hearing conditionally or unconditionally;
  (c) make an interim order;
  (d) make an order on a petition for winding up suspended by virtue of paragraph 40(1)(b);
  (e) make any other order (including an order making consequential provision) that the court thinks appropriate.

Further creditors' meetings

56.—(1) The administrator of a company shall summon a creditors' meeting if—
  (a) it is requested in the prescribed manner by creditors of the company whose debts amount to at least 10% of the total debts of the company, or
  (b) he is directed by the court to summon a creditors' meeting.

(2) An administrator commits an offence if he fails without reasonable excuse to summon a creditors' meeting as required by this paragraph.

Creditors' committee

57.—(1) A creditors' meeting may establish a creditors' committee.

(2) A creditors' committee shall carry out functions conferred on it by or under this Act.

(3) A creditors' committee may require the administrator—
  (a) to attend on the committee at any reasonable time of which he is given at least seven days' notice, and
  (b) to provide the committee with information about the exercise of his functions.

PART II
OTHER ACTS

Correspondence instead of creditors' meeting

58.—(1)   Anything which is required or permitted by or under this Schedule to be done at a creditors' meeting may be done by correspondence between the administrator and creditors—
  (a)   in accordance with the rules, and
  (b)   subject to any prescribed condition.

(2)   A reference in this Schedule to anything done at a creditors' meeting includes a reference to anything done in the course of correspondence in reliance on sub-paragraph (1).

(3)   A requirement to hold a creditors' meeting is satisfied by conducting correspondence in accordance with this paragraph.

FUNCTIONS OF ADMINISTRATOR

General powers

59.—(1)   The administrator of a company may do anything necessary or expedient for the management of the affairs, business and property of the company.

(2)   A provision of this Schedule which expressly permits the administrator to do a specified thing is without prejudice to the generality of sub-paragraph (1).

(3)   A person who deals with the administrator of a company in good faith and for value need not inquire whether the administrator is acting within his powers.

60.   The administrator of a company has the powers specified in Schedule 1 to this Act.

61.   The administrator of a company—
  (a)   may remove a director of the company, and
  (b)   may appoint a director of the company (whether or not to fill a vacancy).

62.   The administrator of a company may call a meeting of members or creditors of the company.

63.   The administrator of a company may apply to the court for directions in connection with his functions.

64.—(1)   A company in administration or an officer of a company in administration may not exercise a management power without the consent of the administrator.

(2)   For the purpose of sub-paragraph (1)—
  (a)   "management power" means a power which could be exercised so as to interfere with the exercise of the administrator's powers,
  (b)   it is immaterial whether the power is conferred by an enactment or an instrument, and
  (c)   consent may be general or specific.

Distribution

65.—(1)   The administrator of a company may make a distribution to a creditor of the company.

(2)   Section 175 shall apply in relation to a distribution under this paragraph as it applies in relation to a winding up.

(3)   A payment may not be made by way of distribution under this paragraph to a creditor of the company who is neither secured nor preferential unless the court gives permission.

66.   The administrator of a company may make a payment otherwise than in accordance with paragraph 65 or paragraph 13 of Schedule 1 if he thinks it likely to assist achievement of the purpose of administration.

General duties

67.   The administrator of a company shall on his appointment take custody or control of all the property to which he thinks the company is entitled.

68.—(1)   Subject to sub-paragraph (2), the administrator of a company shall manage its affairs, business and property in accordance with—
  (a)   any proposals approved under paragraph 53,
  (b)   any revision of those proposals which is made by him and which he does not consider substantial, and
  (c)   any revision of those proposals approved under paragraph 54.

(2)   If the court gives directions to the administrator of a company in connection with any aspect of his management of the company's affairs, business or property, the administrator shall comply with the directions.

(3)   The court may give directions under sub-paragraph (2) only if—
  (a)   no proposals have been approved under paragraph 53,
  (b)   the directions are consistent with any proposals or revision approved under paragraph 53 or 54,

(c) the court thinks the directions are required in order to reflect a change in circumstances since the approval of proposals or a revision under paragraph 53 or 54, or

(d) the court thinks the directions are desirable because of a misunderstanding about proposals or a revision approved under paragraph 53 or 54.

Administrator as agent of company

69. In exercising his functions under this Schedule the administrator of a company acts as its agent.

Charged property: floating charge

70.—(1) The administrator of a company may dispose of or take action relating to property which is subject to a floating charge as if it were not subject to the charge.

(2) Where property is disposed of in reliance on sub-paragraph (1) the holder of the floating charge shall have the same priority in respect of acquired property as he had in respect of the property disposed of.

(3) In sub-paragraph (2) "acquired property" means property of the company which directly or indirectly represents the property disposed of.

Charged property: non-floating charge

71.—(1) The court may by order enable the administrator of a company to dispose of property which is subject to a security (other than a floating charge) as if it were not subject to the security.

(2) An order under sub-paragraph (1) may be made only—
   (a) on the application of the administrator, and
   (b) where the court thinks that disposal of the property would be likely to promote the purpose of administration in respect of the company.

(3) An order under this paragraph is subject to the condition that there be applied towards discharging the sums secured by the security—
   (a) the net proceeds of disposal of the property, and
   (b) any additional money required to be added to the net proceeds so as to produce the amount determined by the court as the net amount which would be realised on a sale of the property at market value.

(4) If an order under this paragraph relates to more than one security, application of money under sub-paragraph (3) shall be in the order of the priorities of the securities.

(5) An administrator who makes a successful application for an order under this paragraph shall send a copy of the order to the registrar of companies before the end of the period of 14 days starting with the date of the order.

(6) An administrator commits an offence if he fails to comply with sub-paragraph (5) without reasonable excuse.

Hire-purchase property

72.—(1) The court may by order enable the administrator of a company to dispose of goods which are in the possession of the company under a hire-purchase agreement as if all the rights of the owner under the agreement were vested in the company.

(2) An order under sub-paragraph (1) may be made only—
   (a) on the application of the administrator, and
   (b) where the court thinks that disposal of the goods would be likely to promote the purpose of administration in respect of the company.

(3) An order under this paragraph is subject to the condition that there be applied towards discharging the sums payable under the hire-purchase agreement—
   (a) the net proceeds of disposal of the goods, and
   (b) any additional money required to be added to the net proceeds so as to produce the amount determined by the court as the net amount which would be realised on a sale of the goods at market value.

(4) An administrator who makes a successful application for an order under this paragraph shall send a copy of the order to the registrar of companies before the end of the period of 14 days starting with the date of the order.

(5) An administrator commits an offence if he fails without reasonable excuse to comply with sub-paragraph (4).

Protection for secured or preferential creditor

73.—(1) An administrator's statement of proposals under paragraph 49 may not include any action which—

PART II
OTHER ACTS

(a)   affects the right of a secured creditor of the company to enforce his security,

(b)   would result in a preferential debt of the company being paid otherwise than in priority to its non-preferential debts, or

(c)   would result in one preferential creditor of the company being paid a smaller proportion of his debt than another.

(2)   Sub-paragraph (1) does not apply to—

(a)   action to which the relevant creditor consents,

(b)   a proposal for a voluntary arrangement under Part I of this Act (although this sub-paragraph is without prejudice to section 4(3)), ...

(c)   a proposal for a compromise or arrangement to be sanctioned under [Part 26 of the Companies Act 2006 (arrangements and reconstructions)] [or

(d)   a proposal for a cross-border merger within the meaning of regulation 2 of the Companies (Cross-Border Mergers) Regulations 2007.]

(3)   The reference to a statement of proposals in sub-paragraph (1) includes a reference to a statement as revised or modified.

Challenge to administrator's conduct of company

74.—(1)   A creditor or member of a company in administration may apply to the court claiming that—

(a)   the administrator is acting or has acted so as unfairly to harm the interests of the applicant (whether alone or in common with some or all other members or creditors), or

(b)   the administrator proposes to act in a way which would unfairly harm the interests of the applicant (whether alone or in common with some or all other members or creditors).

(2)   A creditor or member of a company in administration may apply to the court claiming that the administrator is not performing his functions as quickly or as efficiently as is reasonably practicable.

(3)   The court may—

(a)   grant relief;

(b)   dismiss the application;

(c)   adjourn the hearing conditionally or unconditionally;

(d)   make an interim order;

(e)   make any other order it thinks appropriate.

(4)   In particular, an order under this paragraph may—

(a)   regulate the administrator's exercise of his functions;

(b)   require the administrator to do or not do a specified thing;

(c)   require a creditors' meeting to be held for a specified purpose;

(d)   provide for the appointment of an administrator to cease to have effect;

(e)   make consequential provision.

(5)   An order may be made on a claim under sub-paragraph (1) whether or not the action complained of—

(a)   is within the administrator's powers under this Schedule;

(b)   was taken in reliance on an order under paragraph 71 or 72.

(6)   An order may not be made under this paragraph if it would impede or prevent the implementation of—

(a)   a voluntary arrangement approved under Part I,

(b)   a compromise or arrangement sanctioned under [Part 26 of the Companies Act 2006 (arrangements and reconstructions)], ...

[(ba) a cross-border merger within the meaning of regulation 2 of the Companies (Cross-Border Mergers) Regulations 2007, or]

(c)   proposals or a revision approved under paragraph 53 or 54 more than 28 days before the day on which the application for the order under this paragraph is made.

Misfeasance

75.—(1)   The court may examine the conduct of a person who—

(a)   is or purports to be the administrator of a company, or

(b)   has been or has purported to be the administrator of a company.

(2)   An examination under this paragraph may be held only on the application of—

(a)   the official receiver,

(b)   the administrator of the company,

(c)   the liquidator of the company,

(d)   a creditor of the company, or

(e)   a contributory of the company.

(3)   An application under sub-paragraph (2) must allege that the administrator—

(a)   has misapplied or retained money or other property of the company,

(b)   has become accountable for money or other property of the company,

(c)   has breached a fiduciary or other duty in relation to the company, or
(d)   has been guilty of misfeasance.

(4)   On an examination under this paragraph into a person's conduct the court may order him—
(a)   to repay, restore or account for money or property;
(b)   to pay interest;
(c)   to contribute a sum to the company's property by way of compensation for breach of duty or misfeasance.

(5)   In sub-paragraph (3) "administrator" includes a person who purports or has purported to be a company's administrator.

(6)   An application under sub-paragraph (2) may be made in respect of an administrator who has been discharged under paragraph 98 only with the permission of the court.

ENDING ADMINISTRATION

Automatic end of administration

76.—(1)   The appointment of an administrator shall cease to have effect at the end of the period of one year beginning with the date on which it takes effect.

(2)   But—
(a)   on the application of an administrator the court may by order extend his term of office for a specified period, and
(b)   an administrator's term of office may be extended for a specified period not exceeding six months by consent.

77.—(1)   An order of the court under paragraph 76—
(a)   may be made in respect of an administrator whose term of office has already been extended by order or by consent, but
(b)   may not be made after the expiry of the administrator's term of office.

(2)   Where an order is made under paragraph 76 the administrator shall as soon as is reasonably practicable notify the registrar of companies.

(3)   An administrator who fails without reasonable excuse to comply with sub-paragraph (2) commits an offence.

78.—(1)   In paragraph 76(2)(b) "consent" means consent of—
(a)   each secured creditor of the company, and
(b)   if the company has unsecured debts, creditors whose debts amount to more than 50% of the company's unsecured debts, disregarding debts of any creditor who does not respond to an invitation to give or withhold consent.

(2)   But where the administrator has made a statement under paragraph 52(1)(b) "consent" means—
(a)   consent of each secured creditor of the company, or
(b)   if the administrator thinks that a distribution may be made to preferential creditors, consent of—
(i)   each secured creditor of the company, and
(ii)   preferential creditors whose debts amount to more than 50% of the preferential debts of the company, disregarding debts of any creditor who does not respond to an invitation to give or withhold consent.

(3)   Consent for the purposes of paragraph 76(2)(b) may be—
(a)   written, or
(b)   signified at a creditors' meeting.

(4)   An administrator's term of office—
(a)   may be extended by consent only once,
(b)   may not be extended by consent after extension by order of the court, and
(c)   may not be extended by consent after expiry.

(5)   Where an administrator's term of office is extended by consent he shall as soon as is reasonably practicable—
(a)   file notice of the extension with the court, and
(b)   notify the registrar of companies.

(6)   An administrator who fails without reasonable excuse to comply with sub-paragraph (5) commits an offence.

Court ending administration on application of administrator

79.—(1)   On the application of the administrator of a company the court may provide for the appointment of an administrator of the company to cease to have effect from a specified time.

(2)   The administrator of a company shall make an application under this paragraph if—
(a)   he thinks the purpose of administration cannot be achieved in relation to the company,

    (b)   he thinks the company should not have entered administration, or
    (c)   a creditors' meeting requires him to make an application under this paragraph.

(3)   The administrator of a company shall make an application under this paragraph if—
    (a)   the administration is pursuant to an administration order, and
    (b)   the administrator thinks that the purpose of administration has been sufficiently achieved in relation to the company.

(4)   On an application under this paragraph the court may—
    (a)   adjourn the hearing conditionally or unconditionally;
    (b)   dismiss the application;
    (c)   make an interim order;
    (d)   make any order it thinks appropriate (whether in addition to, in consequence of or instead of the order applied for).

Termination of administration where objective achieved

80.—(1)   This paragraph applies where an administrator of a company is appointed under paragraph 14 or 22.

(2)   If the administrator thinks that the purpose of administration has been sufficiently achieved in relation to the company he may file a notice in the prescribed form—
    (a)   with the court, and
    (b)   with the registrar of companies.

(3)   The administrator's appointment shall cease to have effect when the requirements of sub-paragraph (2) are satisfied.

(4)   Where the administrator files a notice he shall within the prescribed period send a copy to every creditor of the company of whose claim and address he is aware.

(5)   The rules may provide that the administrator is taken to have complied with sub-paragraph (4) if before the end of the prescribed period he publishes in the prescribed manner a notice undertaking to provide a copy of the notice under sub-paragraph (2) to any creditor of the company who applies in writing to a specified address.

(6)   An administrator who fails without reasonable excuse to comply with sub-paragraph (4) commits an offence.

Court ending administration on application of creditor

81.—(1)   On the application of a creditor of a company the court may provide for the appointment of an administrator of the company to cease to have effect at a specified time.

(2)   An application under this paragraph must allege an improper motive—
    (a)   in the case of an administrator appointed by administration order, on the part of the applicant for the order, or
    (b)   in any other case, on the part of the person who appointed the administrator.

(3)   On an application under this paragraph the court may—
    (a)   adjourn the hearing conditionally or unconditionally;
    (b)   dismiss the application;
    (c)   make an interim order;
    (d)   make any order it thinks appropriate (whether in addition to, in consequence of or instead of the order applied for).

Public interest winding-up

82.—(1)   This paragraph applies where a winding-up order is made for the winding up of a company in administration on a petition presented under—
    (a)   section 124A (public interest),
    [(aa) section 124B (SEs),] or
    (b)   section 367 of the Financial Services and Markets Act 2000 (c 8) (petition by Financial Services Authority).

(2)   This paragraph also applies where a provisional liquidator of a company in administration is appointed following the presentation of a petition under any of the provisions listed in sub-paragraph (1).

(3)   The court shall order—
    (a)   that the appointment of the administrator shall cease to have effect, or
    (b)   that the appointment of the administrator shall continue to have effect.

(4)   If the court makes an order under sub-paragraph (3)(b) it may also—
    (a)   specify which of the powers under this Schedule are to be exercisable by the administrator, and
    (b)   order that this Schedule shall have effect in relation to the administrator with specified modifications.

Moving from administration to creditors' voluntary liquidation

83.—(1)   This paragraph applies in England and Wales where the administrator of a company thinks—

    (a)   that the total amount which each secured creditor of the company is likely to receive has been paid to him or set aside for him, and

    (b)   that a distribution will be made to unsecured creditors of the company (if there are any).

    (2)   This paragraph applies in Scotland where the administrator of a company thinks—

    (a)   that each secured creditor of the company will receive payment in respect of his debt, and

    (b)   that a distribution will be made to unsecured creditors (if there are any).

    (3)   The administrator may send to the registrar of companies a notice that this paragraph applies.

    (4)   On receipt of a notice under sub-paragraph (3) the registrar shall register it.

    (5)   If an administrator sends a notice under sub-paragraph (3) he shall as soon as is reasonably practicable—

    (a)   file a copy of the notice with the court, and

    (b)   send a copy of the notice to each creditor of whose claim and address he is aware.

    (6)   On the registration of a notice under sub-paragraph (3)—

    (a)   the appointment of an administrator in respect of the company shall cease to have effect, and

    (b)   the company shall be wound up as if a resolution for voluntary winding up under section 84 were passed on the day on which the notice is registered.

    (7)   The liquidator for the purposes of the winding up shall be—

    (a)   a person nominated by the creditors of the company in the prescribed manner and within the prescribed period, or

    (b)   if no person is nominated under paragraph (a), the administrator.

    (8)   In the application of Part IV to a winding up by virtue of this paragraph—

    (a)   section 85 shall not apply,

    (b)   section 86 shall apply as if the reference to the time of the passing of the resolution for voluntary winding up were a reference to the beginning of the date of registration of the notice under sub-paragraph (3),

    (c)   section 89 does not apply,

    (d)   sections 98, 99 and 100 shall not apply,

    (e)   section 129 shall apply as if the reference to the time of the passing of the resolution for voluntary winding up were a reference to the beginning of the date of registration of the notice under sub-paragraph (3), and

    (f)   any creditors' committee which is in existence immediately before the company ceases to be in administration shall continue in existence after that time as if appointed as a liquidation committee under section 101.

Moving from administration to dissolution

84.—(1)   If the administrator of a company thinks that the company has no property which might permit a distribution to its creditors, he shall send a notice to that effect to the registrar of companies.

    (2)   The court may on the application of the administrator of a company disapply sub-paragraph (1) in respect of the company.

    (3)   On receipt of a notice under sub-paragraph (1) the registrar shall register it.

    (4)   On the registration of a notice in respect of a company under sub-paragraph (1) the appointment of an administrator of the company shall cease to have effect.

    (5)   If an administrator sends a notice under sub-paragraph (1) he shall as soon as is reasonably practicable—

    (a)   file a copy of the notice with the court, and

    (b)   send a copy of the notice to each creditor of whose claim and address he is aware.

    (6)   At the end of the period of three months beginning with the date of registration of a notice in respect of a company under sub-paragraph (1) the company is deemed to be dissolved.

    (7)   On an application in respect of a company by the administrator or another interested person the court may—

    (a)   extend the period specified in sub-paragraph (6),

    (b)   suspend that period, or

    (c)   disapply sub-paragraph (6).

    (8)   Where an order is made under sub-paragraph (7) in respect of a company the administrator shall as soon as is reasonably practicable notify the registrar of companies.

(9)   An administrator commits an offence if he fails without reasonable excuse to comply with sub-paragraph (5).

Discharge of administration order where administration ends

85.—(1)   This paragraph applies where—
- (a)   the court makes an order under this Schedule providing for the appointment of an administrator of a company to cease to have effect, and
- (b)   the administrator was appointed by administration order.

(2)   The court shall discharge the administration order.

Notice to Companies Registrar where administration ends

86.—(1)   This paragraph applies where the court makes an order under this Schedule providing for the appointment of an administrator to cease to have effect.

(2)   The administrator shall send a copy of the order to the registrar of companies within the period of 14 days beginning with the date of the order.

(3)   An administrator who fails without reasonable excuse to comply with sub-paragraph (2) commits an offence.

REPLACING ADMINISTRATOR

Resignation of administrator

87.—(1)   An administrator may resign only in prescribed circumstances.

(2)   Where an administrator may resign he may do so only—
- (a)   in the case of an administrator appointed by administration order, by notice in writing to the court,
- (b)   in the case of an administrator appointed under paragraph 14, by notice in writing to the [holder of the floating charge by virtue of which the appointment was made],
- (c)   in the case of an administrator appointed under paragraph 22(1), by notice in writing to the company, or
- (d)   in the case of an administrator appointed under paragraph 22(2), by notice in writing to the directors of the company.

Removal of administrator from office

88.   The court may by order remove an administrator from office.

Administrator ceasing to be qualified

89.—(1)   The administrator of a company shall vacate office if he ceases to be qualified to act as an insolvency practitioner in relation to the company.

(2)   Where an administrator vacates office by virtue of sub-paragraph (1) he shall give notice in writing—
- (a)   in the case of an administrator appointed by administration order, to the court,
- (b)   in the case of an administrator appointed under paragraph 14, to the [holder of the floating charge by virtue of which the appointment was made],
- (c)   in the case of an administrator appointed under paragraph 22(1), to the company, or
- (d)   in the case of an administrator appointed under paragraph 22(2), to the directors of the company.

(3)   An administrator who fails without reasonable excuse to comply with sub-paragraph (2) commits an offence.

Supplying vacancy in office of administrator

90.   Paragraphs 91 to 95 apply where an administrator—
- (a)   dies,
- (b)   resigns,
- (c)   is removed from office under paragraph 88, or
- (d)   vacates office under paragraph 89.

91.—(1)   Where the administrator was appointed by administration order, the court may replace the administrator on an application under this sub-paragraph made by—
- (a)   a creditors' committee of the company,
- (b)   the company,
- (c)   the directors of the company,
- (d)   one or more creditors of the company, or
- (e)   where more than one person was appointed to act jointly or concurrently as the administrator, any of those persons who remains in office.

(2)   But an application may be made in reliance on sub-paragraph (1)(b) to (d) only where—

(a)   there is no creditors' committee of the company,

(b)   the court is satisfied that the creditors' committee or a remaining administrator is not taking reasonable steps to make a replacement, or

(c)   the court is satisfied that for another reason it is right for the application to be made.

92.   Where the administrator was appointed under paragraph 14 the holder of the floating charge by virtue of which the appointment was made may replace the administrator.

93.—(1)   Where the administrator was appointed under paragraph 22(1) by the company it may replace the administrator.

(2)   A replacement under this paragraph may be made only—

(a)   with the consent of each person who is the holder of a qualifying floating charge in respect of the company's property, or

(b)   where consent is withheld, with the permission of the court.

94.—(1)   Where the administrator was appointed under paragraph 22(2) the directors of the company may replace the administrator.

(2)   A replacement under this paragraph may be made only—

(a)   with the consent of each person who is the holder of a qualifying floating charge in respect of the company's property, or

(b)   where consent is withheld, with the permission of the court.

95.   The court may replace an administrator on the application of a person listed in paragraph 91(1) if the court—

(a)   is satisfied that a person who is entitled to replace the administrator under any of paragraphs 92 to 94 is not taking reasonable steps to make a replacement, or

(b)   that for another reason it is right for the court to make the replacement.

Substitution of administrator: competing floating charge-holder

96.—(1)   This paragraph applies where an administrator of a company is appointed under paragraph 14 by the holder of a qualifying floating charge in respect of the company's property.

(2)   The holder of a prior qualifying floating charge in respect of the company's property may apply to the court for the administrator to be replaced by an administrator nominated by the holder of the prior floating charge.

(3)   One floating charge is prior to another for the purposes of this paragraph if—

(a)   it was created first, or

(b)   it is to be treated as having priority in accordance with an agreement to which the holder of each floating charge was party.

(4)   Sub-paragraph (3) shall have effect in relation to Scotland as if the following were substituted for paragraph (a)—

"(a)   it has priority of ranking in accordance with section 464(4)(b) of the Companies Act 1985 (c 6),".

Substitution of administrator appointed by company or directors: creditors' meeting

97.—(1)   This paragraph applies where—

(a)   an administrator of a company is appointed by a company or directors under paragraph 22, and

(b)   there is no holder of a qualifying floating charge in respect of the company's property.

(2)   A creditors' meeting may replace the administrator.

(3)   A creditors' meeting may act under sub-paragraph (2) only if the new administrator's written consent to act is presented to the meeting before the replacement is made.

Vacation of office: discharge from liability

98.—(1)   Where a person ceases to be the administrator of a company (whether because he vacates office by reason of resignation, death or otherwise, because he is removed from office or because his appointment ceases to have effect) he is discharged from liability in respect of any action of his as administrator.

(2)   The discharge provided by sub-paragraph (1) takes effect—

(a)   in the case of an administrator who dies, on the filing with the court of notice of his death,

(b)   in the case of an administrator appointed under paragraph 14 or 22, at a time appointed by resolution of the creditors' committee or, if there is no committee, by resolution of the creditors, or

(c)   in any case, at a time specified by the court.

PART II
OTHER ACTS

(3)   For the purpose of the application of sub-paragraph (2)(b) in a case where the administrator has made a statement under paragraph 52(1)(b), a resolution shall be taken as passed if (and only if) passed with the approval of—
  (a)   each secured creditor of the company, or
  (b)   if the administrator has made a distribution to preferential creditors or thinks that a distribution may be made to preferential creditors—
        (i)   each secured creditor of the company, and
        (ii)   preferential creditors whose debts amount to more than 50% of the preferential debts of the company, disregarding debts of any creditor who does not respond to an invitation to give or withhold approval.

(4)   Discharge—
  (a)   applies to liability accrued before the discharge takes effect, and
  (b)   does not prevent the exercise of the court's powers under paragraph 75.

Vacation of office: charges and liabilities

99.—(1)   This paragraph applies where a person ceases to be the administrator of a company (whether because he vacates office by reason of resignation, death or otherwise, because he is removed from office or because his appointment ceases to have effect).

(2)   In this paragraph—
"the former administrator" means the person referred to in sub-paragraph (1), and
"cessation" means the time when he ceases to be the company's administrator.

(3)   The former administrator's remuneration and expenses shall be—
  (a)   charged on and payable out of property of which he had custody or control immediately before cessation, and
  (b)   payable in priority to any security to which paragraph 70 applies.

(4)   A sum payable in respect of a debt or liability arising out of a contract entered into by the former administrator or a predecessor before cessation shall be—
  (a)   charged on and payable out of property of which the former administrator had custody or control immediately before cessation, and
  (b)   payable in priority to any charge arising under sub-paragraph (3).

(5)   Sub-paragraph (4) shall apply to a liability arising under a contract of employment which was adopted by the former administrator or a predecessor before cessation; and for that purpose—
  (a)   action taken within the period of 14 days after an administrator's appointment shall not be taken to amount or contribute to the adoption of a contract,
  (b)   no account shall be taken of a liability which arises, or in so far as it arises, by reference to anything which is done or which occurs before the adoption of the contract of employment, and
  (c)   no account shall be taken of a liability to make a payment other than wages or salary.

(6)   In sub-paragraph (5)(c) "wages or salary" includes—
  (a)   a sum payable in respect of a period of holiday (for which purpose the sum shall be treated as relating to the period by reference to which the entitlement to holiday accrued),
  (b)   a sum payable in respect of a period of absence through illness or other good cause,
  (c)   a sum payable in lieu of holiday,
  (d)   in respect of a period, a sum which would be treated as earnings for that period for the purposes of an enactment about social security, and
  (e)   a contribution to an occupational pension scheme.

GENERAL

Joint and concurrent administrators

100.—(1)   In this Schedule—
  (a)   a reference to the appointment of an administrator of a company includes a reference to the appointment of a number of persons to act jointly or concurrently as the administrator of a company, and
  (b)   a reference to the appointment of a person as administrator of a company includes a reference to the appointment of a person as one of a number of persons to act jointly or concurrently as the administrator of a company.

(2)   The appointment of a number of persons to act as administrator of a company must specify—
  (a)   which functions (if any) are to be exercised by the persons appointed acting jointly, and
  (b)   which functions (if any) are to be exercised by any or all of the persons appointed.

101.—(1)   This paragraph applies where two or more persons are appointed to act jointly as the administrator of a company.

(2)   A reference to the administrator of the company is a reference to those persons acting jointly.

(3)   But a reference to the administrator of a company in paragraphs 87 to 99 of this Schedule is a reference to any or all of the persons appointed to act jointly.

(4)   Where an offence of omission is committed by the administrator, each of the persons appointed to act jointly—
(a)   commits the offence, and
(b)   may be proceeded against and punished individually.

(5)   The reference in paragraph 45(1)(a) to the name of the administrator is a reference to the name of each of the persons appointed to act jointly.

(6)   Where persons are appointed to act jointly in respect of only some of the functions of the administrator of a company, this paragraph applies only in relation to those functions.

102.—(1)   This paragraph applies where two or more persons are appointed to act concurrently as the administrator of a company.

(2)   A reference to the administrator of a company in this Schedule is a reference to any of the persons appointed (or any combination of them).

103.—(1)   Where a company is in administration, a person may be appointed to act as administrator jointly or concurrently with the person or persons acting as the administrator of the company.

(2)   Where a company entered administration by administration order, an appointment under sub-paragraph (1) must be made by the court on the application of—
(a)   a person or group listed in paragraph 12(1)(a) to (e), or
(b)   the person or persons acting as the administrator of the company.

(3)   Where a company entered administration by virtue of an appointment under paragraph 14, an appointment under sub-paragraph (1) must be made by—
(a)   the holder of the floating charge by virtue of which the appointment was made, or
(b)   the court on the application of the person or persons acting as the administrator of the company.

(4)   Where a company entered administration by virtue of an appointment under paragraph 22(1), an appointment under sub-paragraph (1) above must be made either by the court on the application of the person or persons acting as the administrator of the company or—
(a)   by the company, and
(b)   with the consent of each person who is the holder of a qualifying floating charge in respect of the company's property or, where consent is withheld, with the permission of the court.

(5)   Where a company entered administration by virtue of an appointment under paragraph 22(2), an appointment under sub-paragraph (1) must be made either by the court on the application of the person or persons acting as the administrator of the company or—
(a)   by the directors of the company, and
(b)   with the consent of each person who is the holder of a qualifying floating charge in respect of the company's property or, where consent is withheld, with the permission of the court.

(6)   An appointment under sub-paragraph (1) may be made only with the consent of the person or persons acting as the administrator of the company.

Presumption of validity

104.   An act of the administrator of a company is valid in spite of a defect in his appointment or qualification.

Majority decision of directors

105.   A reference in this Schedule to something done by the directors of a company includes a reference to the same thing done by a majority of the directors of a company.

Penalties

106.—(1)   A person who is guilty of an offence under this Schedule is liable to a fine (in accordance with section 430 and Schedule 10).

(2)   A person who is guilty of an offence under any of the following paragraphs of this Schedule is liable to a daily default fine (in accordance with section 430 and Schedule 10)—
(a)   paragraph 20,
(b)   paragraph 32,
(c)   paragraph 46,
(d)   paragraph 48,

(e)	paragraph 49,
(f)	paragraph 51,
(g)	paragraph 53,
(h)	paragraph 54,
(i)	paragraph 56,
(j)	paragraph 71,
(k)	paragraph 72,
(l)	paragraph 77,
(m)	paragraph 78,
(n)	paragraph 80,
(o)	paragraph 84,
(p)	paragraph 86, and
(q)	paragraph 89.

Extension of time limit

107.—(1)   Where a provision of this Schedule provides that a period may be varied in accordance with this paragraph, the period may be varied in respect of a company—
  (a)   by the court, and
  (b)   on the application of the administrator.

  (2)   A time period may be extended in respect of a company under this paragraph—
  (a)   more than once, and
  (b)   after expiry.

108.—(1)   A period specified in paragraph 49(5), 50(1)(b) or 51(2) may be varied in respect of a company by the administrator with consent.

  (2)   In sub-paragraph (1) "consent" means consent of—
  (a)   each secured creditor of the company, and
  (b)   if the company has unsecured debts, creditors whose debts amount to more than 50% of the company's unsecured debts, disregarding debts of any creditor who does not respond to an invitation to give or withhold consent.

  (3)   But where the administrator has made a statement under paragraph 52(1)(b) "consent" means—
  (a)   consent of each secured creditor of the company, or
  (b)   if the administrator thinks that a distribution may be made to preferential creditors, consent of—
    (i)   each secured creditor of the company, and
    (ii)   preferential creditors whose debts amount to more than 50% of the total preferential debts of the company, disregarding debts of any creditor who does not respond to an invitation to give or withhold consent.

  (4)   Consent for the purposes of sub-paragraph (1) may be—
  (a)   written, or
  (b)   signified at a creditors' meeting.

  (5)   The power to extend under sub-paragraph (1)—
  (a)   may be exercised in respect of a period only once,
  (b)   may not be used to extend a period by more than 28 days,
  (c)   may not be used to extend a period which has been extended by the court, and
  (d)   may not be used to extend a period after expiry.

109.   Where a period is extended under paragraph 107 or 108, a reference to the period shall be taken as a reference to the period as extended.

Amendment of provision about time

110.—(1)   The Secretary of State may by order amend a provision of this Schedule which—
  (a)   requires anything to be done within a specified period of time,
  (b)   prevents anything from being done after a specified time, or
  (c)   requires a specified minimum period of notice to be given.

  (2)   An order under this paragraph—
  (a)   must be made by statutory instrument, and
  (b)   shall be subject to annulment in pursuance of a resolution of either House of Parliament.

Interpretation

111.—(1)   In this Schedule—
    "administrative receiver" has the meaning given by section 251,
    "administrator" has the meaning given by paragraph 1 and, where the context requires, includes a reference to a former administrator,

.....

"correspondence" includes correspondence by telephonic or other electronic means,
"creditors' meeting" has the meaning given by paragraph 50,
"enters administration" has the meaning given by paragraph 1,
"floating charge" means a charge which is a floating charge on its creation,
"in administration" has the meaning given by paragraph 1,
"hire-purchase agreement" includes a conditional sale agreement, a chattel leasing agreement and a retention of title agreement,
"holder of a qualifying floating charge" in respect of a company's property has the meaning given by paragraph 14,
"market value" means the amount which would be realised on a sale of property in the open market by a willing vendor,
"the purpose of administration" means an objective specified in paragraph 3, and "unable to pay its debts" has the meaning given by section 123.

[(1A)   In this Schedule, "company" means—
  (a)   a company within the meaning of section 735(1) of the Companies Act 1985,
  (b)   a company incorporated in an EEA State other than the United Kingdom, or
  (c)   a company not incorporated in an EEA State but having its centre of main interests in a member State other than Denmark.

(1B)   In sub-paragraph (1A), in relation to a company, "centre of main interests" has the same meaning as in the EC Regulation and, in the absence of proof to the contrary, is presumed to be the place of its registered office (within the meaning of that Regulation).]

(2)   A reference in this Schedule to a thing in writing includes a reference to a thing in electronic form.

(3)   In this Schedule a reference to action includes a reference to inaction.

[Non-UK companies

111A.   A company incorporated outside the United Kingdom that has a principal place of business in Northern Ireland may not enter administration under this Schedule unless it also has a principal place of business in England and Wales or Scotland (or both in England and Wales and in Scotland).]

Scotland

112.   In the application of this Schedule to Scotland—
  (a)   a reference to filing with the court is a reference to lodging in court, and
  (b)   a reference to a charge is a reference to a right in security.

113.   Where property in Scotland is disposed of under paragraph 70 or 71, the administrator shall grant to the disponee an appropriate document of transfer or conveyance of the property, and—
  (a)   that document, or
  (b)   recording, intimation or registration of that document (where recording, intimation or registration of the document is a legal requirement for completion of title to the property),
has the effect of disencumbering the property of or, as the case may be, freeing the property from, the security.

114.   In Scotland, where goods in the possession of a company under a hire-purchase agreement are disposed of under paragraph 72, the disposal has the effect of extinguishing as against the disponee all rights of the owner of the goods under the agreement.

115.—(1)   In Scotland, the administrator of a company may make, in or towards the satisfaction of the debt secured by the floating charge, a payment to the holder of a floating charge which has attached to the property subject to the charge.

(2)   In Scotland, where the administrator thinks that the company has insufficient property to enable a distribution to be made to unsecured creditors other than by virtue of section 176A(2)(a), he may file a notice to that effect with the registrar of companies.

(3)   On delivery of the notice to the registrar of companies, any floating charge granted by the company shall, unless it has already so attached, attach to the property which is subject to the charge and that attachment shall have effect as if each floating charge is a fixed security over the property to which it has attached.

116.   In Scotland, the administrator in making any payment in accordance with paragraph 115 shall make such payment subject to the rights of any of the following categories of persons (which rights shall, except to the extent provided in any instrument, have the following order of priority)—
  (a)   the holder of any fixed security which is over property subject to the floating charge and which ranks prior to, or pari passu with, the floating charge,
  (b)   creditors in respect of all liabilities and expenses incurred by or on behalf of the administrator,

(c)   the administrator in respect of his liabilities, expenses and remuneration and any indemnity to which he is entitled out of the property of the company,

(d)   the preferential creditors entitled to payment in accordance with paragraph 65,

(e)   the holder of the floating charge in accordance with the priority of that charge in relation to any other floating charge which has attached, and

(f)   the holder of a fixed security, other than one referred to in paragraph (a), which is over property subject to the floating charge.]

[311]

NOTES

Schedule inserted by the Enterprise Act 2002, s 248(2), Sch 16, as from 15 September 2003, subject to savings and transitional provisions in the Enterprise Act 2002, s 249 and the Enterprise Act 2002 (Commencement No 4 and Transitional Provisions and Savings) Order 2003, SI 2003/2093, art 3.

Para 12: words in square brackets in sub-para (1)(d) substituted by the Courts Act 2003, s 109(1), Sch 8, para 299, as from 1 April 2005, subject to transitional provisions in SI 2005/911, arts 2–5; sub-para (5) added by the Enterprise Act 2002 (Insolvency) Order 2003, SI 2003/2096, art 2(2), as from 15 September 2003.

Para 40: sub-para (2)(aa) inserted by the European Public Limited-Liability Company Regulations 2004, SI 2004/2326, reg 73(4)(c), as from 8 October 2004.

Para 42: sub-para (4)(aa) inserted by SI 2004/2326, reg 73(4)(c), as from 8 October 2004.

Para 43: sub-para (6A) inserted by SI 2003/2096, art 2(3), as from 15 September 2003.

Para 45: substituted by the Companies (Trading Disclosures) (Insolvency) Regulations 2008, SI 2008/1897, reg 4(1), as from 1 October 2008.

Para 49: words in square brackets substituted by the Companies Act 2006 (Consequential Amendments etc) Order 2008, SI 2008/948, art 3(1)(b), Sch 1, Pt 2, para 100(a), as from 6 April 2008, subject to transitional provisions and savings in arts 6, 11, 12 thereof.

Para 73: word omitted from sub-para (2)(b) repealed and sub-para (2)(d), together with word immediately preceding it, inserted by the Companies (Cross-Border Mergers) Regulations 2007, SI 2007/2974, reg 65(1)–(3), as from 15 December 2007; words in square brackets in sub-para (2)(c) substituted by SI 2008/948, art 3(1)(b), Sch 1, Pt 2, para 100(a), as from 6 April 2008, subject to transitional provisions and savings in arts 6, 11, 12 thereof.

Para 74: words in square brackets in sub-para (6)(b) substituted by SI 2008/948, art 3(1)(b), Sch 1, Pt 2, para 100(b), as from 6 April 2008, subject to transitional provisions and savings in arts 6, 11, 12 thereof; word omitted from sub-para (6)(b) repealed and sub-para (6)(ba) inserted by SI 2007/2974, reg 65(1), (4), (5), as from 15 December 2007.

Para 82: sub-para (1)(aa) inserted by SI 2004/2326, reg 73(4)(c), as from 8 October 2004.

Para 87: words in square brackets substituted by SI 2003/2096, art 2(4), as from 15 September 2003.

Para 89: words in square brackets substituted by SI 2003/2096, art 2(5), as from 15 September 2003.

Para 111: in sub-para (1) definition "company" (omitted) repealed, and sub-paras (1A), (1B) inserted by the Insolvency Act 1986 (Amendment) Regulations 2005, SI 2005/879, regs 2(1), (4)(a), (b), 3, as from 13 April 2005, except in relation to a voluntary arrangement under Pt I of this Act or the appointment of an administrator under Pt II of this Act that took effect before that date.

Para 111A: inserted by SI 2005/879, regs 2(1), (4)(c), 3, as from 13 April 2005, except in relation to a voluntary arrangement under Pt I of this Act or the appointment of an administrator under Pt II of this Act that took effect before that date.

Modifications: this Schedule is modified by the Banks (Former Authorised Institutions) (Insolvency) Order 2006, SI 2006/3107, art 3, Schedule. Paras 13, 83 modified, in relation to the notification to the Financial Services Authority of any decision, administration order, appointment of an administrator in an interim order or appointment of a liquidator, on or after 5 May 2004, by the Credit Institutions (Reorganisation and Winding up) Regulations 2004, SI 2004/1045, reg 9(1)(a), (d), (3), (5). Paras 40–44, 46–75, 80, 84–91, 96, 98–104, 106–116 are applied with modifications in respect of bank administration, by the Banking Act 2009, s 145(3), (4), Table 1 at **[142]**. Paras 40, 42 are applied with modifications in respect of a bank insolvency order, by the Banking Act 2009, s 119 at **[119]**. Paras 49–58 are applied with modifications in respect of banks in temporary public ownership, by the Banking Act 2009 (Bank Administration) (Modification for Application to Banks in Temporary Public Ownership) Regulations 2009, SI 2009/312, reg 2(1), (3), Schedule at **[505]**, **[508]**. Paras 59–64, 84 are applied with modifications in respect of building societies, by the Building Societies (Insolvency and Special Administration) Order 2009, SI 2009/805, art 3, Sch 1, Pt 3, paras 29, 30 at **[557]**, **[563]**.

Application: paras 1, 40–50, 54, 59–68, 70–75, 83–91, 98–107, 109–116 are applied, with modifications in relation to the conduct of energy administration, by the Energy Act 2004, s 159(1), Sch 20, Pts 1–3.

Disapplication: para 41(2) is disapplied in relation to a receiver appointed under a charge created or otherwise arising under a financial collateral arrangement, by the Financial Collateral Arrangements (No 2) Regulations 2003, SI 2003/3226, reg 8(2); para 43(2) (including that provision as applied by para 44), paras 70, 71, are disapplied in relation to any security interest created or otherwise arising under a financial collateral arrangement, by SI 2003/3226, reg 8(1).

(*Schs 1–3 outside the scope of this work.*)

SCHEDULE 4
POWERS OF LIQUIDATOR IN A WINDING UP
Sections 165, 167

PART I
POWERS EXERCISABLE WITH SANCTION

1.   Power to pay any class of creditors in full.

2.   Power to make any compromise or arrangement with creditors or persons claiming to be creditors, or having or alleging themselves to have any claim (present or future, certain or contingent, ascertained or sounding only in damages) against the company, or whereby the company may be rendered liable.

3.   Power to compromise, on such terms as may be agreed—

   (a)   all calls and liabilities to calls, all debts and liabilities capable of resulting in debts, and all claims (present or future, certain or contingent, ascertained or sounding only in damages) subsisting or supposed to subsist between the company and a contributory or alleged contributory or other debtor or person apprehending liability to the company, and

   (b)   all questions in any way relating to or affecting the assets or the winding up of the company,

and take any security for the discharge of any such call, debt, liability or claim and give a complete discharge in respect of it.

[3A.   Power to bring legal proceedings under section 213, 214, 238, 239, 242, 243 or 423.]

[312]

NOTES

   Para 3A: inserted by the Enterprise Act 2002, s 253, as from 15 September 2003, subject to transitional provisions in the Enterprise Act 2002 (Commencement No 4 and Transitional Provisions and Savings) Order 2003, SI 2003/2093, art 5.

   See further: in relation to the application of this Part of this Schedule, with modifications, in respect of bank insolvency, see the Banking Act 2009, s 103(3), (4), Table at **[103]**; in relation to the application of this Part of this Schedule, with modifications, in respect of bank administration and applications for bank administration, see the Bank Administration (Scotland) Rules 2009, SI 2009/350, rr 39–42 at **[1299]**–**[1302]**; in relation to the application of this Part of this Schedule, with modifications, in respect of building society special administration and applications for special administration, see the Building Society Special Administration (Scotland) Rules 2009, SI 2009/806, rr 38–41.

PART II
POWERS EXERCISABLE WITHOUT SANCTION IN VOLUNTARY WINDING UP, WITH SANCTION IN WINDING UP BY THE COURT

4.   Power to bring or defend any action or other legal proceeding in the name and on behalf of the company.

5.   Power to carry on the business of the company so far as may be necessary for its beneficial winding up.

[313]

NOTES

   See further: in relation to the application of this Part of this Schedule, with modifications, in respect of bank insolvency, see the Banking Act 2009, s 103(3), (4), Table at **[103]**; in relation to the application of this Part of this Schedule, with modifications, in respect of bank administration and applications for bank administration, see the Bank Administration (Scotland) Rules 2009, SI 2009/350, rr 39–42 at **[1299]**–**[1302]**; in relation to the application of this Part of this Schedule, with modifications, in respect of building society special administration and applications for special administration, see the Building Society Special Administration (Scotland) Rules 2009, SI 2009/806, rr 38–41.

PART III
POWERS EXERCISABLE WITHOUT SANCTION IN ANY WINDING UP

6.   Power to sell any of the company's property by public auction or private contract with power to transfer the whole of it to any person or to sell the same in parcels.

7.   Power to do all acts and execute, in the name and on behalf of the company, all deeds, receipts and other documents and for that purpose to use, when necessary, the company's seal.

8.   Power to prove, rank and claim in the bankruptcy, insolvency or sequestration of any contributory for any balance against his estate, and to receive dividends in the bankruptcy, insolvency or sequestration in respect of that balance, as a separate debt due from the bankrupt or insolvent, and rateably with the other separate creditors.

9.   Power to draw, accept, make and indorse any bill of exchange or promissory note in the name and on behalf of the company, with the same effect with respect to the company's liability as if the bill or note had been drawn, accepted, made or indorsed by or on behalf of the company in the course of its business.

10.   Power to raise on the security of the assets of the company any money requisite.

11.   Power to take out in his official name letters of administration to any deceased contributory, and to do in his official name any other act necessary for obtaining payment of any money due from a contributory or his estate which cannot conveniently be done in the name of the company.

PART II
OTHER ACTS

In all such cases the money due is deemed, for the purpose of enabling the liquidator to take out the letters of administration or recover the money, to be due to the liquidator himself.

12. Power to appoint an agent to do any business which the liquidator is unable to do himself.

13. Power to do all such other things as may be necessary for winding up the company's affairs and distributing its assets.

[314]

NOTES

See further: in relation to the application of this Part of this Schedule, with modifications, in respect of bank insolvency, see the Banking Act 2009, ss 103(3), (4), Table, 145(3), (4), Table 2 at **[103]**, **[142]**; in relation to the application of this Part of this Schedule, with modifications, in respect of bank administration and applications for bank administration, see the Bank Administration (Scotland) Rules 2009, SI 2009/350, rr 39–42 at **[1299]**–**[1302]**; in relation to the application of this Part of this Schedule, with modifications, in respect of building society special administration and applications for special administration, see the Building Society Special Administration (Scotland) Rules 2009, SI 2009/806, rr 38–41.

(Schs 4ZA–7 outside the scope of this work.)

SCHEDULE 8
PROVISIONS CAPABLE OF INCLUSION IN COMPANY INSOLVENCY RULES
Section 411

Courts

1. Provision for supplementing, in relation to the insolvency or winding up of companies, any provision made by or under section 117 of this Act (jurisdiction in relation to winding up).

2.—[(1)] Provision for regulating the practice and procedure of any court exercising jurisdiction for the purposes of Parts I to VII of this Act or [the Companies Acts] so far as relating to, and to matters connected with or arising out of, the insolvency or winding up of companies, being any provision that could be made by rules of court.

[(2) Rules made by virtue of this paragraph about the consequence of failure to comply with practice or procedure may, in particular, include provision about the termination of administration.]

Notices, etc

3. Provision requiring notice of any proceedings in connection with or arising out of the insolvency or winding up of a company to be given or published in the manner prescribed by the rules.

4. Provision with respect to the form, manner of serving, contents and proof of any petition, application, order, notice, statement or other document required to be presented, made, given, published or prepared under any enactment or subordinate legislation relating to, or to matters connected with or arising out of, the insolvency or winding up of companies.

5. Provision specifying the persons to whom any notice is to be given.

Registration of voluntary arrangements

6. Provision for the registration of voluntary arrangements approved under Part I of this Act, including provision for the keeping and inspection of a register.

Provisional liquidator

7. Provision as to the manner in which a provisional liquidator appointed under section 135 is to carry out his functions.

Conduct of insolvency

8. Provision with respect to the certification of any person as, and as to the proof that a person is, the liquidator, administrator or administrative receiver of a company.

9. The following provision with respect to meetings of a company's creditors, contributories or members—
    (a) provision as to the manner of summoning a meeting (including provision as to how any power to require a meeting is to be exercised, provision as to the manner of determining the value of any debt or contribution for the purposes of any such power and provision making the exercise of any such power subject to the deposit of a sum sufficient to cover the expenses likely to be incurred in summoning and holding a meeting);
    (b) provision specifying the time and place at which a meeting may be held and the period of notice required for a meeting;
    (c) provision as to the procedure to be followed at a meeting (including the manner in which decisions may be reached by a meeting and the manner in which the value of any vote at a meeting is to be determined);

(d)   provision for requiring a person who is or has been an officer of the company to attend a meeting;

(e)   provision creating, in the prescribed circumstances, a presumption that a meeting has been duly summoned and held;

(f)   provision as to the manner of proving the decisions of a meeting.

10.—(1)   Provision as to the functions, membership and proceedings of a committee established under [section 49, 68, 101, 141 or 142 of, or paragraph 57 of Schedule B1 to, this Act].

(2)   The following provision with respect to the establishment of a committee under section 101, 141 or 142 of this Act, that is to say—

(a)   provision for resolving differences between a meeting of the company's creditors and a meeting of its contributories or members;

(b)   provision authorising the establishment of the committee without a meeting of contributories in a case where a company is being wound up on grounds including its inability to pay its debts; and

(c)   provision modifying the requirements of this Act with respect to the establishment of the committee in a case where a winding-up order has been made immediately upon the discharge of an administration order.

11.   Provision as to the manner in which any requirement that may be imposed on a person under any of Parts I to VII of this Act by the official receiver, the liquidator, administrator or administrative receiver of a company or a special manager appointed under section 177 is to be so imposed.

12.   Provision as to the debts that may be proved in a winding up, as to the manner and conditions of proving a debt and as to the manner and expenses of establishing the value of any debt or security.

13.   Provision with respect to the manner of the distribution of the property of a company that is being wound up, including provision with respect to unclaimed funds and dividends.

14.   Provision which, with or without modifications, applies in relation to the winding up of companies any enactment contained in Parts VIII to XI of this Act or in the Bankruptcy (Scotland) Act 1985.

[14A.   Provision about the application of section 176A of this Act which may include, in particular—

(a)   provision enabling a receiver to institute winding up proceedings;

(b)   provision requiring a receiver to institute winding up proceedings.]

[Administration

14B.   Provision which—

(a)   applies in relation to administration, with or without modifications, a provision of Parts IV to VII of this Act, or

(b)   serves a purpose in relation to administration similar to a purpose that may be served by the rules in relation to winding up by virtue of a provision of this Schedule.]

Financial provisions

15.   Provision as to the amount, or manner of determining the amount, payable to the liquidator, administrator or administrative receiver of a company or a special manager appointed under section 177, by way of remuneration for the carrying out of functions in connection with or arising out of the insolvency or winding up of a company.

16.   Provision with respect to the manner in which moneys received by the liquidator of a company in the course of carrying out his functions as such are to be invested or otherwise handled and with respect to the payment of interest on sums which, in pursuance of rules made by virtue of this paragraph, have been paid into the Insolvency Services Account.

[16A.   Provision enabling the Secretary of State to set the rate of interest paid on sums which have been paid into the Insolvency Services Account.]

17.   Provision as to the fees, costs, charges and other expenses that may be treated as the expenses of a winding up.

18.   Provision as to the fees, costs, charges and other expenses that may be treated as properly incurred by the administrator or administrative receiver of a company.

19.   Provision as to the fees, costs, charges and other expenses that may be incurred for any of the purposes of Part I of this Act or in the administration of any voluntary arrangement approved under that Part.

Information and records

20.   Provision requiring registrars and other officers of courts having jurisdiction in England and Wales in relation to, or to matters connected with or arising out of, the insolvency or winding up of companies—

(a)   to keep books and other records with respect to the exercise of that jurisdiction, and

PART II
OTHER ACTS

    (b)   to make returns to the Secretary of State of the business of those courts.

21.   Provision requiring a creditor, member or contributory, or such a committee as is mentioned in paragraph 10 above, to be supplied (on payment in prescribed cases of the prescribed fee) with such information and with copies of such documents as may be prescribed.

22.   Provision as to the manner in which public examinations under sections 133 and 134 of this Act and proceedings under sections 236 and 237 are to be conducted, as to the circumstances in which records of such examinations or proceedings are to be made available to prescribed persons and as to the costs of such examinations and proceedings.

23.   Provision imposing requirements with respect to—
    (a)   the preparation and keeping by the liquidator, administrator or administrative receiver of a company, or by the supervisor of a voluntary arrangement approved under Part I of this Act, of prescribed books, accounts and other records;
    (b)   the production of those books, accounts and records for inspection by prescribed persons;
    (c)   the auditing of accounts kept by the liquidator, administrator or administrative receiver of a company, or the supervisor of such a voluntary arrangement; and
    (d)   the issue by the administrator or administrative receiver of a company of such a certificate as is mentioned in section 22(3)(b) of the Value Added Tax Act 1983 (refund of tax in cases of bad debts) and the supply of copies of the certificate to creditors of the company.

24.   Provision requiring the person who is the supervisor of a voluntary arrangement approved under Part I, when it appears to him that the voluntary arrangement has been fully implemented and that nothing remains to be done by him under the arrangement—
    (a)   to give notice of that fact to persons bound by the voluntary arrangement, and
    (b)   to report to those persons on the carrying out of the functions conferred on the supervisor of the arrangement.

25.   Provision as to the manner in which the liquidator of a company is to act in relation to the books, papers and other records of the company, including provision authorising their disposal.

26.   Provision imposing requirements in connection with the carrying out of functions under section 7(3) of the Company Directors Disqualification Act 1986 (including, in particular, requirements with respect to the making of periodic returns).

General

27.   Provision conferring power on the Secretary of State [or the Treasury] to make regulations with respect to so much of any matter that may be provided for in the rules as relates to the carrying out of the functions of the liquidator, administrator or administrative receiver of a company.

28.   Provision conferring a discretion on the court.

29.   Provision conferring power on the court to make orders for the purpose of securing compliance with obligations imposed by or under [section 47, 66, 131, 143(2) or 235 of, or paragraph 47 of Schedule B1 to, this Act] or section 7(4) of the Company Directors Disqualification Act 1986.

30.   Provision making non-compliance with any of the rules a criminal offence.

31.   Provision making different provision for different cases or descriptions of cases, including different provisions for different areas.

[315]

NOTES
    Para 2: sub-para (1) numbered as such and sub-para (2) added by the Enterprise Act 2002, s 248(3), Sch 17, paras 9, 38(1), (2), as from 15 September 2003, subject to savings and transitional provisions in the Enterprise Act 2002, s 249 and the Enterprise Act 2002 (Commencement No 4 and Transitional Provisions and Savings) Order 2003, SI 2003/2093, art 3; words in square brackets in sub-para (1) substituted by the Companies Act 2006 (Commencement No 3, Consequential Amendments, Transitional Provisions and Savings) Order 2007, SI 2007/2194, art 10(1), (2), Sch 4, Pt 3, para 44, as from 1 October 2007, subject to savings in art 12 thereof.
    Para 10: words in square brackets substituted by the Enterprise Act 2002, s 248(3), Sch 17, paras 9, 38(1), (3), as from 15 September 2003, subject to savings as noted to para 2 above.
    Paras 14A, 14B: inserted by the Enterprise Act 2002, s 248(3), Sch 17, paras 9, 38(1), (4), (5), as from 15 September 2003, subject to savings as noted to para 2 above.
    Para 16A: inserted by the Enterprise Act 2002, s 271(1), as from 18 December 2003 in relation to England and Wales, and as from 1 April 2004 in relation to Scotland.
    Para 27: words in square brackets inserted by the Banking Act 2009, s 125(7), as from 21 February 2009.
    Para 29: words in square brackets substituted by the Enterprise Act 2002, s 248(3), Sch 17, paras 9, 38(1), (6), as from 15 September 2003, subject to savings as noted to para 2 above.
    Regulations: the Insolvency Regulations 1994, SI 1994/2507.

(Schs 9–14 outside the scope of this work.)

COMPANY DIRECTORS DISQUALIFICATION ACT 1986

(1986 c 46)

ARRANGEMENT OF SECTIONS

Preliminary

PART II
OTHER ACTS

An Act to consolidate certain enactments relating to the disqualification of persons from being directors of companies, and from being otherwise concerned with a company's affairs

[25 July 1986]

NOTES

Limited liability partnerships: the Limited Liability Partnerships Regulations 2001, SI 2001/1090, reg 4(2) provides that the provisions of this Act shall apply to limited liability partnerships, except where the context otherwise requires, with the general modifications specified in that paragraph. See also Sch 2, Pt II to the 2001 Regulations for specific modifications of Sch 1, Pt II to this Act.

European Economic Interest Groupings: as to the application of ss 1, 2, 4–11, 12(2), 15–17, 20, 22 of, and Sch 1 to, this Act, to European Economic Interest Groupings, see the European Economic Interest Grouping Regulations 1989, SI 1989/638, reg 20.

Insolvent partnerships: as to the application, with modifications, of this Act in relation to insolvent partnerships, see the Insolvent Partnerships Order 1994, SI 1994/2421.

Official Receiver: as to the contracting out of certain functions of the Official Receiver conferred by or under this Act, see the Contracting Out (Functions of the Official Receiver) Order 1995, SI 1995/1386.

Preliminary

1   Disqualification orders: general

(1)   In the circumstances specified below in this Act a court may, and under [sections 6 and 9A] shall, make against a person a disqualification order, that is to say an order that [for a period specified in the order—

  (a)   he shall not be a director of a company, act as receiver of a company's property or in any way, whether directly or indirectly, be concerned or take part in the promotion, formation or management of a company unless (in each case) he has the leave of the court, and

  (b)   he shall not act as an insolvency practitioner.]

(2)   In each section of this Act which gives to a court power or, as the case may be, imposes on it the duty to make a disqualification order there is specified the maximum (and, in section 6, the minimum) period of disqualification which may or (as the case may be) must be imposed by means of the order [and, unless the court otherwise orders, the period of disqualification so imposed shall begin at the end of the period of 21 days beginning with the date of the order].

(3)   Where a disqualification order is made against a person who is already subject to such an order [or to a disqualification undertaking], the periods specified in those orders [or, as the case may be, in the order and the undertaking] shall run concurrently.

(4)   A disqualification order may be made on grounds which are or include matters other than criminal convictions, notwithstanding that the person in respect of whom it is to be made may be criminally liable in respect of those matters.

[316]

NOTES

Sub-s (1): words in first pair of square brackets substituted by the Enterprise Act 2002, s 204(1), (3), as from 20 June 2003; words in second pair of square brackets substituted by the Insolvency Act 2000, s 5(1), as from 2 April 2001.

Sub-ss (2), (3): words in square brackets inserted by the Insolvency Act 2000, ss 5(2), 8, Sch 4, Pt I, paras 1, 2, as from 2 April 2001.

[1A   Disqualification undertakings: general

(1)   In the circumstances specified in sections 7 and 8 the Secretary of State may accept a disqualification undertaking, that is to say an undertaking by any person that, for a period specified in the undertaking, the person—

  (a)   will not be a director of a company, act as receiver of a company's property or in any way, whether directly or indirectly, be concerned or take part in the promotion, formation or management of a company unless (in each case) he has the leave of a court, and

  (b)   will not act as an insolvency practitioner.

(2)   The maximum period which may be specified in a disqualification undertaking is 15 years; and the minimum period which may be specified in a disqualification undertaking under section 7 is two years.

(3)   Where a disqualification undertaking by a person who is already subject to such an undertaking or to a disqualification order is accepted, the periods specified in those undertakings or (as the case may be) the undertaking and the order shall run concurrently.

(4)   In determining whether to accept a disqualification undertaking by any person, the Secretary of State may take account of matters other than criminal convictions, notwithstanding that the person may be criminally liable in respect of those matters.]

[317]

NOTES
Inserted by the Insolvency Act 2000, s 6(1), (2), as from 2 April 2001.

Disqualification for general misconduct in connection with companies

2   Disqualification on conviction of indictable offence

(1)   The court may make a disqualification order against a person where he is convicted of an indictable offence (whether on indictment or summarily) in connection with the promotion, formation, management[, liquidation or striking off] of a company [with the receivership of a company's property or with his being an administrative receiver of a company].

(2)   "The court" for this purpose means—
    (a)   any court having jurisdiction to wind up the company in relation to which the offence was committed, or
    (b)   the court by or before which the person is convicted of the offence, or
    (c)   in the case of a summary conviction in England and Wales, any other magistrates' court acting [in the same local justice] area;
and for the purposes of this section the definition of "indictable offence" in Schedule 1 to the Interpretation Act 1978 applies for Scotland as it does for England and Wales.

(3)   The maximum period of disqualification under this section is—
    (a)   where the disqualification order is made by a court of summary jurisdiction, 5 years, and
    (b)   in any other case, 15 years.

[318]

NOTES
Sub-s (1): words in first pair of square brackets substituted by the Deregulation and Contracting Out Act 1994, s 39, Sch 11, para 6, as from 1 July 1995; words in second pair of square brackets substituted by the Insolvency Act 2000, s 8, Sch 4, Pt I, paras 1, 3, as from 2 April 2001.
Sub-s (2): words in square brackets substituted by the Courts Act 2003, s 109(1), Sch 8, para 300, as from 1 April 2005.

3   Disqualification for persistent breaches of companies legislation

(1)   The court may make a disqualification order against a person where it appears to it that he has been persistently in default in relation to provisions of the companies legislation requiring any return, account or other document to be filed with, delivered or sent, or notice of any matter to be given, to the registrar of companies.

(2)   On an application to the court for an order to be made under this section, the fact that a person has been persistently in default in relation to such provisions as are mentioned above may (without prejudice to its proof in any other manner) be conclusively proved by showing that in the 5 years ending with the date of the application he has been adjudged guilty (whether or not on the same occasion) of three or more defaults in relation to those provisions.

(3)   A person is to be treated under subsection (2) as being adjudged guilty of a default in relation to any provision of that legislation if—
    (a)   he is convicted (whether on indictment or summarily) of an offence consisting in a contravention of or failure to comply with that provision (whether on his own part or on the part of any company), or
    (b)   a default order is made against him, that is to say an order under any of the following provisions—
       (i)   [section 452 of the Companies Act 2006] (order requiring delivery of company accounts),
     [(ia)   [section 456] of that Act (order requiring preparation of revised accounts),]
      (ii)   section 713 of [the Companies Act 1985] (enforcement of company's duty to make returns),
     (iii)   section 41 of the Insolvency Act (enforcement of receiver's or manager's duty to make returns), or
     (iv)   section 170 of that Act (corresponding provision for liquidator in winding up),
    in respect of any such contravention of or failure to comply with that provision (whether on his own part or on the part of any company).

(4)   In this section "the court" means any court having jurisdiction to wind up any of the companies in relation to which the offence or other default has been or is alleged to have been committed.

(5)   The maximum period of disqualification under this section is 5 years.

[319]

NOTES
Sub-s (3): words in square brackets in paras (b)(i), (ia) substituted (for the original words "section 242(4) of the Companies Act" and "section 245B" respectively) by the Companies Act 2006 (Consequential Amendments etc) Order 2008, SI 2008/948, art 3(1), Sch 1, Pt 2, para 106(1), (2)(a), (b), as from 6 April 2008 (for savings see art 6(4) of the 2008 Order which provides that where by virtue of any transitional provision, a provision of the Companies Act 2006 has effect only (a) on or after a specified date, or (b) in relation to matters occurring or arising on or after a specified date, any amendment substituting or inserting a reference to that provision has effect correspondingly); para (b)(ia) inserted by the Companies Act 1989, s 23, Sch 10, para 35(2)(b), as from 7 January 1991; words in square brackets in para (b)(ii) substituted by SI 2008/948, art 3(1), Sch 1, Pt 2, para 106(1), (2)(c), as from 6 April 2008.

4   Disqualification for fraud, etc, in winding up

(1)   The court may make a disqualification order against a person if, in the course of the winding up of a company, it appears that he—
   (a)   has been guilty of an offence for which he is liable (whether he has been convicted or not) under [section 993 of the Companies Act 2006] (fraudulent trading), or
   (b)   has otherwise been guilty, while an officer or liquidator of the company [receiver of the company's property or administrative receiver of the company], of any fraud in relation to the company or of any breach of his duty as such officer, liquidator, [receiver or administrative receiver].

(2)   In this section "the court" means any court having jurisdiction to wind up any of the companies in relation to which the offence or other default has been or is alleged to have been committed; and "officer" includes a shadow director.

(3)   The maximum period of disqualification under this section is 15 years.

[320]

NOTES
Sub-s (1): words in first pair of square brackets substituted by the Companies Act 2006 (Commencement No 3, Consequential Amendments, Transitional Provisions and Savings) Order 2007, SI 2007/2194, art 10(3), Sch 4, Pt 3, para 46, as from 1 October 2007; words in second pair of square brackets substituted by the Insolvency Act 2000, s 8, Sch 4, Pt I, paras 1, 4, as from 2 April 2001.

5   Disqualification on summary conviction

(1)   An offence counting for the purposes of this section is one of which a person is convicted (either on indictment or summarily) in consequence of a contravention of, or failure to comply with, any provision of the companies legislation requiring a return, account or other document to be filed with, delivered or sent, or notice of any matter to be given, to the registrar of companies (whether the contravention or failure is on the person's own part or on the part of any company).

(2)   Where a person is convicted of a summary offence counting for those purposes, the court by which he is convicted (or, in England and Wales, any other magistrates' court acting [in the same local justice] area) may make a disqualification order against him if the circumstances specified in the next subsection are present.

(3)   Those circumstances are that, during the 5 years ending with the date of the conviction, the person has had made against him, or has been convicted of, in total not less than 3 default orders and offences counting for the purposes of this section; and those offences may include that of which he is convicted as mentioned in subsection (2) and any other offence of which he is convicted on the same occasion.

(4)   For the purposes of this section—
   (a)   the definition of "summary offence" in Schedule 1 to the Interpretation Act 1978 applies for Scotland as for England and Wales, and
   (b)   "default order" means the same as in section 3(3)(b).

(5)   The maximum period of disqualification under this section is 5 years.

[321]

NOTES
Sub-s (2): words in square brackets substituted by the Courts Act 2003, s 109(1), Sch 8, para 300, as from 1 April 2005.

Disqualification for unfitness

6 Duty of court to disqualify unfit directors of insolvent companies

(1)   The court shall make a disqualification order against a person in any case where, on an application under this section, it is satisfied—

(a)   that he is or has been a director of a company which has at any time become insolvent (whether while he was a director or subsequently), and

(b)   that his conduct as a director of that company (either taken alone or taken together with his conduct as a director of any other company or companies) makes him unfit to be concerned in the management of a company.

(2)   For the purposes of this section and the next, a company becomes insolvent if—

(a)   the company goes into liquidation at a time when its assets are insufficient for the payment of its debts and other liabilities and the expenses of the winding up,

[(b)   the company enters administration,] or

(c)   an administrative receiver of the company is appointed;

and references to a person's conduct as a director of any company or companies include, where that company or any of those companies has become insolvent, that person's conduct in relation to any matter connected with or arising out of the insolvency of that company.

[(3)   In this section and section 7(2), "the court" means—

(a)   where the company in question is being or has been wound up by the court, that court,

(b)   where the company in question is being or has been wound up voluntarily, any court which has or (as the case may be) had jurisdiction to wind it up,

[(c)   where neither paragraph (a) nor (b) applies but an administrator or administrative receiver has at any time been appointed in respect of the company in question, any court which has jurisdiction to wind it up.]

(3A)   Sections 117 and 120 of the Insolvency Act 1986 (jurisdiction) shall apply for the purposes of subsection (3) as if the references in the definitions of "registered office" to the presentation of the petition for winding up were references—

(a)   in a case within paragraph (b) of that subsection, to the passing of the resolution for voluntary winding up,

[(b)   in a case within paragraph (c) of that subsection, to the appointment of the administrator or (as the case may be) administrative receiver.]

(3B)   Nothing in subsection (3) invalidates any proceedings by reason of their being taken in the wrong court; and proceedings—

(a)   for or in connection with a disqualification order under this section, or

(b)   in connection with a disqualification undertaking accepted under section 7,

may be retained in the court in which the proceedings were commenced, although it may not be the court in which they ought to have been commenced.

(3C)   In this section and section 7, "director" includes a shadow director.]

(4)   Under this section the minimum period of disqualification is 2 years, and the maximum period is 15 years.

[322]

NOTES

Sub-s (2): para (b) substituted by the Enterprise Act 2002, s 248(3), Sch 17, paras 40, 41(a), as from 15 September 2003, subject to savings and transitional provisions.

Sub-s (3): substituted, together with sub-ss (3A), (3B), (3C) for original sub-s (3), by the Insolvency Act 2000, s 8, Sch 4, Pt I, paras 1, 5, as from 2 April 2001; para (c) substituted by the Enterprise Act 2002, s 248(3), Sch 17, paras 40, 41(b), as from 15 September 2003, subject to savings and transitional provisions.

Sub-s (3A): substituted as noted above; para (b) substituted by the Enterprise Act 2002, s 248(3), Sch 17, paras 40, 41(c), as from 15 September 2003, subject to savings and transitional provisions.

Sub-ss (3B), (3C): substituted as noted above.

7   [Disqualification order or undertaking; and reporting provisions]

(1)   If it appears to the Secretary of State that it is expedient in the public interest that a disqualification order under section 6 should be made against any person, an application for the making of such an order against that person may be made—

(a)   by the Secretary of State, or

(b)   if the Secretary of State so directs in the case of a person who is or has been a director of a company which is being [or has been] wound up by the court in England and Wales, by the official receiver.

(2)   Except with the leave of the court, an application for the making under that section of a disqualification order against any person shall not be made after the end of the period of 2 years beginning with the day on which the company of which that person is or has been a director became insolvent.

[(2A)   If it appears to the Secretary of State that the conditions mentioned in section 6(1) are satisfied as respects any person who has offered to give him a disqualification undertaking, he may accept the undertaking if it appears to him that it is expedient in the public interest that he should do so (instead of applying, or proceeding with an application, for a disqualification order).]

(3)   If it appears to the office-holder responsible under this section, that is to say—
    (a)   in the case of a company which is being wound up by the court in England and Wales, the official receiver,
    (b)   in the case of a company which is being wound up otherwise, the liquidator,
    [(c)   in the case of a company which is in administration, the administrator,] or
    (d)   in the case of a company of which there is an administrative receiver, that receiver,

that the conditions mentioned in section 6(1) are satisfied as respects a person who is or has been a director of that company, the officer-holder shall forthwith report the matter to the Secretary of State.

(4)   The Secretary of State or the official receiver may require the liquidator, administrator or administrative receiver of a company, or the former liquidator, administrator or administrative receiver of a company—
    (a)   to furnish him with such information with respect to any person's conduct as a director of the company, and
    (b)   to produce and permit inspection of such books, papers and other records relevant to that person's conduct as such a director,

as the Secretary of State or the official receiver may reasonably require for the purpose of determining whether to exercise, or of exercising, any function of his under this section.

[323]

NOTES

Section heading: substituted by the Insolvency Act 2000, s 8, Sch 4, Pt I, paras 1, 6(b), as from 2 April 2001.
  Sub-s (1): words in square brackets inserted by the Insolvency Act 2000, s 8, Sch 4, Pt I, paras 1, 6(a), as from 2 April 2001.
  Sub-s (2A): inserted by the Insolvency Act 2000, s 6(1), (3), as from 2 April 2001.
  Sub-s (3): para (c) substituted by the Enterprise Act 2002, s 248(3), Sch 17, paras 40, 42, as from 15 September 2003, subject to savings and transitional provisions.

---

8 Disqualification after investigation of company

[(1)   If it appears to the Secretary of State from investigative material that it is expedient in the public interest that a disqualification order should be made against a person who is, or has been, a director or shadow director of a company, he may apply to the court for such an order.

(1A)   "Investigative material" means—
    (a)   a report made by inspectors under—
        (i)   section 437 of the Companies Act 1985;
        (ii)   section 167, 168, 169 or 284 of the Financial Services and Markets Act 2000; or
        (iii)   where the company is an open-ended investment company (within the meaning of that Act) regulations made as a result of section 262(2)(k) of that Act; and
    (b)   information or documents obtained under—
        (i)   section [437, 446E,] 447[, 448[, 451A] or 453A] of the Companies Act 1985;
        (ii)   section 2 of the Criminal Justice Act 1987;
        (iii)   section 28 of the Criminal Law (Consolidation) (Scotland) Act 1995;
        (iv)   section 83 of the Companies Act 1989; or
        (v)   section 165, 171, 172, 173 or 175 of the Financial Services and Markets Act 2000.]

(2)   The court may make a disqualification order against a person where, on an application under this section, it is satisfied that his conduct in relation to the company makes him unfit to be concerned in the management of a company.

[(2A)   Where it appears to the Secretary of State from such report, information or documents that, in the case of a person who has offered to give him a disqualification undertaking—
    (a)   the conduct of the person in relation to a company of which the person is or has been a director or shadow director makes him unfit to be concerned in the management of a company, and
    (b)   it is expedient in the public interest that he should accept the undertaking (instead of applying, or proceeding with an application, for a disqualification order),
he may accept the undertaking.]

(3)   In this section "the court" means the High Court or, in Scotland, the Court of Session.

(4)   The maximum period of disqualification under this section is 15 years.

[324]

NOTES

Sub-s (1): substituted, together with sub-s (1A) for original sub-s (1), by the Financial Services and Markets Act 2000 (Consequential Amendments and Repeals) Order 2001, SI 2001/3649, art 39, as from 1 December 2001.

Sub-s (1A): substituted as noted above; figures in first pair and third (inner) pair of square brackets inserted by the Companies Act 2006, s 1039, as from 1 October 2007; words in second (outer) pair of square brackets substituted by the Companies (Audit, Investigations and Community Enterprise) Act 2004, s 25, Sch 2, Pt 3, para 28, as from 6 April 2005 (for transitional provisions, see the Companies (Audit, Investigations and Community Enterprise) Act 2004 (Commencement) and Companies Act 1989 (Commencement No 18) Order 2004, SI 2004/3322, art 12).

Sub-s (2A): inserted by the Insolvency Act 2000, s 6(1), (4), as from 2 April 2001.

[8A   Variation etc of disqualification undertaking

(1)   The court may, on the application of a person who is subject to a disqualification undertaking—

    (a)   reduce the period for which the undertaking is to be in force, or

    (b)   provide for it to cease to be in force.

(2)   On the hearing of an application under subsection (1), the Secretary of State shall appear and call the attention of the court to any matters which seem to him to be relevant, and may himself give evidence or call witnesses.

[(2A)   Subsection (2) does not apply to an application in the case of an undertaking given under section 9B, and in such a case on the hearing of the application whichever of the OFT or a specified regulator (within the meaning of section 9E) accepted the undertaking—

    (a)   must appear and call the attention of the court to any matters which appear to it or him (as the case may be) to be relevant;

    (b)   may give evidence or call witnesses.]

[(3)   In this section "the court"—

    (a)   in the case of an undertaking given under section 9B means the High Court or (in Scotland) the Court of Session;

    (b)   in any other case has the same meaning as in section 7(2) or 8 (as the case may be).]

[325]

NOTES

Inserted by the Insolvency Act 2000, s 6(1), (5), as from 2 April 2001.

Sub-s (2A): inserted by the Enterprise Act 2002, s 204(1), (4), as from 20 June 2003.

Sub-s (3): substituted by the Enterprise Act 2002, s 204(1), (5), as from 20 June 2003.

9   Matters for determining unfitness of directors

(1)   Where it falls to a court to determine whether a person's conduct as a director ... of any particular company or companies makes him unfit to be concerned in the management of a company, the court shall, as respects his conduct as a director of that company or, as the case may be, each of those companies, have regard in particular—

    (a)   to the matters mentioned in Part I of Schedule 1 to this Act, and

    (b)   where the company has become insolvent, to the matters mentioned in Part II of that Schedule;

and references in that Schedule to the director and the company are to be read accordingly.

[(1A)   In determining whether he may accept a disqualification undertaking from any person the Secretary of State shall, as respects the person's conduct as a director of any company concerned, have regard in particular—

    (a)   to the matters mentioned in Part I of Schedule 1 to this Act, and

    (b)   where the company has become insolvent, to the matters mentioned in Part II of that Schedule;

and references in that Schedule to the director and the company are to be read accordingly.]

(2)   Section 6(2) applies for the purposes of this section and Schedule 1 as it applies for the purposes of sections 6 and 7 [and in this section and that Schedule "director" includes a shadow director].

(3)   Subject to the next subsection, any reference in Schedule 1 to an enactment contained in the Companies Act or the Insolvency Act includes, in relation to any time before the coming into force of that enactment, the corresponding enactment in force at that time.

(4)   The Secretary of State may by order modify any of the provisions of Schedule 1; and such an order may contain such transitional provisions as may appear to the Secretary of State necessary or expedient.

(5)   The power to make orders under this section is exercisable by statutory instrument subject to annulment in pursuance of a resolution of either House of Parliament.

[326]

NOTES
 Sub-s (1): words omitted repealed by the Insolvency Act 2000, ss 8, 15(1), Sch 4, Pt I, paras 1, 7(a), Sch 5, as from 2 April 2001.
 Sub-s (1A): inserted by the Insolvency Act 2000, s 6(1), (6), as from 2 April 2001.
 Sub-s (2): words in square brackets added by the Insolvency Act 2000, s 8, Sch 4, Pt I, paras 1, 7(b), as from 2 April 2001.

[Disqualification for competition infringements

9A   Competition disqualification order

(1)   The court must make a disqualification order against a person if the following two conditions are satisfied in relation to him.

(2)   The first condition is that an undertaking which is a company of which he is a director commits a breach of competition law.

(3)   The second condition is that the court considers that his conduct as a director makes him unfit to be concerned in the management of a company.

(4)   An undertaking commits a breach of competition law if it engages in conduct which infringes any of the following—
   (a)   the Chapter 1 prohibition (within the meaning of the Competition Act 1998) (prohibition on agreements, etc preventing, restricting or distorting competition);
   (b)   the Chapter 2 prohibition (within the meaning of that Act) (prohibition on abuse of a dominant position);
   (c)   Article 81 of the Treaty establishing the European Community (prohibition on agreements, etc preventing, restricting or distorting competition);
   (d)   Article 82 of that Treaty (prohibition on abuse of a dominant position).

(5)   For the purpose of deciding under subsection (3) whether a person is unfit to be concerned in the management of a company the court—
   (a)   must have regard to whether subsection (6) applies to him;
   (b)   may have regard to his conduct as a director of a company in connection with any other breach of competition law;
   (c)   must not have regard to the matters mentioned in Schedule 1.

(6)   This subsection applies to a person if as a director of the company—
   (a)   his conduct contributed to the breach of competition law mentioned in subsection (2);
   (b)   his conduct did not contribute to the breach but he had reasonable grounds to suspect that the conduct of the undertaking constituted the breach and he took no steps to prevent it;
   (c)   he did not know but ought to have known that the conduct of the undertaking constituted the breach.

(7)   For the purposes of subsection (6)(a) it is immaterial whether the person knew that the conduct of the undertaking constituted the breach.

(8)   For the purposes of subsection (4)(a) or (c) references to the conduct of an undertaking are references to its conduct taken with the conduct of one or more other undertakings.

(9)   The maximum period of disqualification under this section is 15 years.

(10)   An application under this section for a disqualification order may be made by the OFT or by a specified regulator.

(11)   Section 60 of the Competition Act 1998 (c 41) (consistent treatment of questions arising under United Kingdom and Community law) applies in relation to any question arising by virtue of subsection (4)(a) or (b) above as it applies in relation to any question arising under Part 1 of that Act.]

[327]

NOTES
 Inserted, together with preceding heading and ss 9B–9E, by the Enterprise Act 2002, s 204(1), (2), as from 20 June 2003.

[9B   Competition undertakings

(1)   This section applies if—
   (a)   the OFT or a specified regulator thinks that in relation to any person an undertaking which is a company of which he is a director has committed or is committing a breach of competition law,

(b)   the OFT or the specified regulator thinks that the conduct of the person as a director makes him unfit to be concerned in the management of a company, and

(c)   the person offers to give the OFT or the specified regulator (as the case may be) a disqualification undertaking.

(2)   The OFT or the specified regulator (as the case may be) may accept a disqualification undertaking from the person instead of applying for or proceeding with an application for a disqualification order.

(3)   A disqualification undertaking is an undertaking by a person that for the period specified in the undertaking he will not—

(a)   be a director of a company;

(b)   act as receiver of a company's property;

(c)   in any way, whether directly or indirectly, be concerned or take part in the promotion, formation or management of a company;

(d)   act as an insolvency practitioner.

(4)   But a disqualification undertaking may provide that a prohibition falling within subsection (3)(a) to (c) does not apply if the person obtains the leave of the court.

(5)   The maximum period which may be specified in a disqualification undertaking is 15 years.

(6)   If a disqualification undertaking is accepted from a person who is already subject to a disqualification undertaking under this Act or to a disqualification order the periods specified in those undertakings or the undertaking and the order (as the case may be) run concurrently.

(7)   Subsections (4) to (8) of section 9A apply for the purposes of this section as they apply for the purposes of that section but in the application of subsection (5) of that section the reference to the court must be construed as a reference to the OFT or a specified regulator (as the case may be).]

[328]

NOTES

Inserted as noted to s 9A at **[327]**.

[9C   Competition investigations

(1)   If the OFT or a specified regulator has reasonable grounds for suspecting that a breach of competition law has occurred it or he (as the case may be) may carry out an investigation for the purpose of deciding whether to make an application under section 9A for a disqualification order.

(2)   For the purposes of such an investigation sections 26 to 30 of the Competition Act 1998 (c 41) apply to the OFT and the specified regulators as they apply to the OFT for the purposes of an investigation under section 25 of that Act.

(3)   Subsection (4) applies if as a result of an investigation under this section the OFT or a specified regulator proposes to apply under section 9A for a disqualification order.

(4)   Before making the application the OFT or regulator (as the case may be) must—

(a)   give notice to the person likely to be affected by the application, and

(b)   give that person an opportunity to make representations.]

[329]

NOTES

Inserted as noted to s 9A at **[327]**.

[9D   Co-ordination

(1)   The Secretary of State may make regulations for the purpose of co-ordinating the performance of functions under sections 9A to 9C (relevant functions) which are exercisable concurrently by two or more persons.

(2)   Section 54(5) to (7) of the Competition Act 1998 (c 41) applies to regulations made under this section as it applies to regulations made under that section and for that purpose in that section—

(a)   references to Part 1 functions must be read as references to relevant functions;

(b)   references to a regulator must be read as references to a specified regulator;

(c)   a competent person also includes any of the specified regulators.

(3)   The power to make regulations under this section must be exercised by statutory instrument subject to annulment in pursuance of a resolution of either House of Parliament.

(4)   Such a statutory instrument may—

(a)   contain such incidental, supplemental, consequential and transitional provision as the Secretary of State thinks appropriate;

(b)   make different provision for different cases.]

[330]

PART II
OTHER ACTS

[9E Interpretation

(1) This section applies for the purposes of sections 9A to 9D.

(2) Each of the following is a specified regulator for the purposes of a breach of competition law in relation to a matter in respect of which he or it has a function—

    [(a) the Office of Communications;]

    (b) the Gas and Electricity Markets Authority;

    [(c) the Water Services Regulation Authority;]

    (d) [the Office of Rail Regulation];

    (e) the Civil Aviation Authority.

(3) The court is the High Court or (in Scotland) the Court of Session.

(4) Conduct includes omission.

(5) Director includes shadow director.]

                                                                      [331]

Other cases of disqualification

10 Participation in wrongful trading

(1) Where the court makes a declaration under section 213 or 214 of the Insolvency Act that a person is liable to make a contribution to a company's assets, then, whether or not an application for such an order is made by any person, the court may, if it thinks fit, also make a disqualification order against the person to whom the declaration relates.

(2) The maximum period of disqualification under this section is 15 years.

                                                                      [332]

11 Undischarged bankrupts

[(1) It is an offence for a person to act as director of a company or directly or indirectly to take part in or be concerned in the promotion, formation or management of a company, without the leave of the court, at a time when—

    (a) he is an undischarged bankrupt,

    [(aa) a moratorium period under a debt relief order applies in relation to him,] or

    (b) a bankruptcy restrictions order [or a debt relief restrictions order] is in force in respect of him.]

(2) "The court" for this purpose is the court by which the person was adjudged bankrupt or, in Scotland, sequestration of his estates was awarded.

(3) In England and Wales, the leave of the court shall not be given unless notice of intention to apply for it has been served on the official receiver; and it is the latter's duty, if he is of opinion that it is contrary to the public interest that the application should be granted, to attend on the hearing of the application and oppose it.

                                                                      [333]

12 *Failure to pay under county court administration order*

(1) *The following has effect where a court under section 429 of the Insolvency Act revokes an administration order under Part VI of the County Courts Act 1984.*

(2)   A person to whom *that section applies by virtue of the order under section 429(2)(b)* shall not, except with the leave of the court which made the order, act as director or liquidator of, or directly or indirectly take part or be concerned in the promotion, formation or management of, a company.

[334]

NOTES

Section heading: for the words in italics there are substituted the words "Disabilities on revocation of administration order" by the Tribunals, Courts and Enforcement Act 2007, s 106, Sch 16, para 5(1), (2), as from a day to be appointed (except in relation to any case in which an administration order was made, or an application for such an order was made, before the day on which s 106 comes into force).

Sub-s (1): repealed by the Tribunals, Courts and Enforcement Act 2007, ss 106, 146, Sch 16, para 5(1), (3), Sch 23, Pt 5, as from a day to be appointed.

Sub-s (2): for the words in italics there are substituted the words "section 429 of the Insolvency Act applies by virtue of an order under subsection (2) of that section" by the Tribunals, Courts and Enforcement Act 2007, s 106, Sch 16, para 5(1), (4), as from a day to be appointed (except in relation to any case in which an administration order was made, or an application for such an order was made, before the day on which s 106 comes into force).

[12A Northern Irish disqualification orders

A person subject to a disqualification order under Part II of the Companies (Northern Ireland) Order 1989—

    (a)   shall not be a director of a company, act as receiver of a company's property or in any way, whether directly or indirectly, be concerned or take part in the promotion, formation or management of a company unless (in each case) he has the leave of the High Court of Northern Ireland, and

    (b)   shall not act as an insolvency practitioner.]

[335]

NOTES

Inserted by the Insolvency Act 2000, s 7(1), as from 2 April 2001, except in relation to a person subject to a disqualification order under the Companies (Northern Ireland) Order 1989, SI 1989/2404, Pt II made before that date.

[12B Northern Irish disqualification undertakings

A person subject to a disqualification undertaking under the Company Directors Disqualification (Northern Ireland) Order 2002—

    (a)   shall not be a director of a company, act as receiver of a company's property or in any way, whether directly or indirectly, be concerned or take part in the promotion, formation or management of a company unless (in each case) he has the leave of the High Court of Northern Ireland, and

    (b)   shall not act as an insolvency practitioner.]

[336]

NOTES

Inserted by the Insolvency Act 2000 (Company Directors Disqualification Undertakings) Order 2004, SI 2004/1941, art 2(1), (2), as from 1 September 2004, in relation to disqualification undertakings under the Company Directors Disqualification (Northern Ireland) Order 2002 accepted on or after that date.

Consequences of contravention

13 Criminal penalties

If a person acts in contravention of a disqualification order or [disqualification undertaking or in contravention] of section 12(2)[, 12A or 12B], or is guilty of an offence under section 11, he is liable—

    (a)   on conviction on indictment, to imprisonment for not more than 2 years or a fine, or both; and

    (b)   on summary conviction, to imprisonment for not more than 6 months or a fine not exceeding the statutory maximum, or both.

[337]

NOTES

Words in first pair of square brackets inserted by the Insolvency Act 2000, s 8, Sch 4, Pt I, paras 1, 8, as from 2 April 2001; words in second pair of square brackets substituted by the Insolvency Act 2000 (Company Directors Disqualification Undertakings) Order 2004, SI 2004/1941, art 2(1), (3), as from 1 September 2004, in relation to disqualification undertakings under the Company Directors Disqualification (Northern Ireland) Order 2002 accepted on or after that date.

PART II
OTHER ACTS

14 Offences by body corporate

(1) Where a body corporate is guilty of an offence of acting in contravention of a disqualification order [or disqualification undertaking or in contravention of section 12A] [or 12B], and it is proved that the offence occurred with the consent or connivance of, or was attributable to any neglect on the part of any director, manager, secretary or other similar officer of the body corporate, or any person who was purporting to act in any such capacity he, as well as the body corporate, is guilty of the offence and liable to be proceeded against and punished accordingly.

(2) Where the affairs of a body corporate are managed by its members, subsection (1) applies in relation to the acts and defaults of a member in connection with his functions of management as if he were a director of the body corporate.

[338]

NOTES

Sub-s (1): words in first pair of square brackets inserted by the Insolvency Act 2000, s 8, Sch 4, Pt I, paras 1, 9, as from 2 April 2001; words in second pair of square brackets inserted by the Insolvency Act 2000 (Company Directors Disqualification Undertakings) Order 2004, SI 2004/1941, art 2(1), (4), as from 1 September 2004, in relation to disqualification undertakings under the Company Directors Disqualification (Northern Ireland) Order 2002 accepted on or after that date.

15 Personal liability for company's debts where person acts while disqualified

(1) A person is personally responsible for all the relevant debts of a company if at any time—
  (a) in contravention of a disqualification order or [disqualification undertaking or in contravention] of section 11[, 12A or 12B] of this Act he is involved in the management of the company, or
  (b) as a person who is involved in the management of the company, he acts or is willing to act on instructions given without the leave of the court by a person whom he knows at that time to be the subject of a disqualification order [or disqualification undertaking or a disqualification order under Part II of the Companies (Northern Ireland) Order 1989] [or disqualification undertaking under the Company Directors Disqualification (Northern Ireland) Order 2002] or to be an undischarged bankrupt.

(2) Where a person is personally responsible under this section for the relevant debts of a company, he is jointly and severally liable in respect of those debts with the company and any other person who, whether under this section or otherwise, is so liable.

(3) For the purposes of this section the relevant debts of a company are—
  (a) in relation to a person who is personally responsible under paragraph (a) of subsection (1), such debts and other liabilities of the company as are incurred at a time when that person was involved in the management of the company, and
  (b) in relation to a person who is personally responsible under paragraph (b) of that subsection, such debts and other liabilities of the company as are incurred at a time when that person was acting or was willing to act on instructions given as mentioned in that paragraph.

(4) For the purposes of this section, a person is involved in the management of a company if he is a director of the company or if he is concerned, whether directly or indirectly, or takes part, in the management of the company.

(5) For the purposes of this section a person who, as a person involved in the management of a company, has at any time acted on instructions given without the leave of the court by a person whom he knew at that time to be the subject of a disqualification order [or disqualification undertaking or a disqualification order under Part II of the Companies (Northern Ireland) Order 1989] [or disqualification undertaking under the Company Directors Disqualification (Northern Ireland) Order 2002] or to be an undischarged bankrupt is presumed, unless the contrary is shown, to have been willing at any time thereafter to act on any instructions given by that person.

[339]

NOTES

Sub-s (1): words in first and third pairs of square brackets inserted by the Insolvency Act 2000, s 8, Sch 4, Pt I, paras 1, 10, as from 2 April 2001; words in second pair of square brackets substituted, and words in final pair of square brackets inserted, by the Insolvency Act 2000 (Company Directors Disqualification Undertakings) Order 2004, SI 2004/1941, art 2(1), (5)(a), as from 1 September 2004, in relation to disqualification undertakings under the Company Directors Disqualification (Northern Ireland) Order 2002 accepted on or after that date.

Sub-s (5): words in first pair of square brackets inserted by the Insolvency Act 2000, s 8, Sch 4, Pt I, paras 1, 10, as from 2 April 2001; words in second pair of square brackets inserted by SI 2004/1941, art 2(1), (5)(b), as from 1 September 2004, in relation to disqualification undertakings under the Company Directors Disqualification (Northern Ireland) Order 2002 accepted on or after that date.

Supplementary provisions

16   Application for disqualification order

(1)   A person intending to apply for the making of a disqualification order by the court having jurisdiction to wind up a company shall give not less than 10 days' notice of his intention to the person against whom the order is sought; and on the hearing of the application the last-mentioned person may appear and himself give evidence or call witnesses.

(2)   An application to a court with jurisdiction to wind up companies for the making against any person of a disqualification order under any of sections 2 to [4] may be made by the Secretary of State or the official receiver, or by the liquidator or any past or present member or creditor of any company in relation to which that person has committed or is alleged to have committed an offence or other default.

(3)   On the hearing of any application under this Act made by [a person falling within subsection (4)], the applicant shall appear and call the attention of the court to any matters which seem to him to be relevant, and may himself give evidence or call witnesses.

[(4)   The following fall within this subsection—
    (a)   the Secretary of State;
    (b)   the official receiver;
    (c)   the OFT;
    (d)   the liquidator;
    (e)   a specified regulator (within the meaning of section 9E).]

                                                      [340]

NOTES

Sub-s (2): figure in square brackets substituted by the Insolvency Act 2000, s 8, Sch 4, Pt I, paras 1, 11, as from 2 April 2001.

Sub-s (3): words in square brackets substituted by the Enterprise Act 2002, s 204(1), (6), as from 20 June 2003.

Sub-s (4): added by the Enterprise Act 2002, s 204(1), (7), as from 20 June 2003.

[17   Application for leave under an order or undertaking

(1)   Where a person is subject to a disqualification order made by a court having jurisdiction to wind up companies, any application for leave for the purposes of section 1(1)(a) shall be made to that court.

(2)   Where—
    (a)   a person is subject to a disqualification order made under section 2 by a court other than a court having jurisdiction to wind up companies, or
    (b)   a person is subject to a disqualification order made under section 5,
any application for leave for the purposes of section 1(1)(a) shall be made to any court which, when the order was made, had jurisdiction to wind up the company (or, if there is more than one such company, any of the companies) to which the offence (or any of the offences) in question related.

(3)   Where a person is subject to a disqualification undertaking accepted at any time under section 7 or 8, any application for leave for the purposes of section 1A(1)(a) shall be made to any court to which, if the Secretary of State had applied for a disqualification order under the section in question at that time, his application could have been made.

[(3A)   Where a person is subject to a disqualification undertaking accepted at any time under section 9B any application for leave for the purposes of section 9B(4) must be made to the High Court or (in Scotland) the Court of Session.]

(4)   But where a person is subject to two or more disqualification orders or undertakings (or to one or more disqualification orders and to one or more disqualification undertakings), any application for leave for the purposes of section 1(1)(a) [1A(1)(a) or 9B(4)] shall be made to any court to which any such application relating to the latest order to be made, or undertaking to be accepted, could be made.

(5)   On the hearing of an application for leave for the purposes of section 1(1)(a) or 1A(1)(a), the Secretary of State shall appear and call the attention of the court to any matters which seem to him to be relevant, and may himself give evidence or call witnesses.

[(6)   Subsection (5) does not apply to an application for leave for the purposes of section 1(1)(a) if the application for the disqualification order was made under section 9A.

(7)   In such a case and in the case of an application for leave for the purposes of section 9B(4) on the hearing of the application whichever of the OFT or a specified regulator (within the meaning of section 9E) applied for the order or accepted the undertaking (as the case may be)—

   (a)   must appear and draw the attention of the court to any matters which appear to it or him (as the case may be) to be relevant;

   (b)   may give evidence or call witnesses.]]

[341]

NOTES

Substituted by the Insolvency Act 2000, s 8, Sch 4, Pt I, paras 1, 12, as from 2 April 2001, subject to transitional provisions in SI 2001/766, art 3.

Sub-ss (3A), (6), (7): inserted and added respectively by the Enterprise Act 2002, s 204(1), (8), (10), as from 20 June 2003.

Sub-s (4): words in square brackets substituted by the Enterprise Act 2002, s 204(1), (9), as from 20 June 2003.

18 [Register of disqualification orders and undertakings]

(1) The Secretary of State may make regulations requiring officers of courts to furnish him with such particulars as the regulations may specify of cases in which—

   (a)   a disqualification order is made, or

   (b)   any action is taken by a court in consequence of which such an order [or a disqualification undertaking] is varied or ceases to be in force, or

   (c)   leave is granted by a court for a person subject to such an order to do any thing which otherwise the order prohibits him from doing; [or

   (d)   leave is granted by a court for a person subject to such an undertaking to do anything which otherwise the undertaking prohibits him from doing]

and the regulations may specify the time within which, and the form and manner in which, such particulars are to be furnished.

(2) The Secretary of State shall, from the particulars so furnished, continue to maintain the register of orders, and of cases in which leave has been granted as mentioned in subsection (1)(c), which was set up by him under section 29 of the Companies Act 1976 and continued under section 301 of the Companies Act 1985.

[(2A) The Secretary of State must include in the register such particulars as he considers appropriate of—

   (a)   disqualification undertakings accepted by him under section 7 or 8;

   (b)   disqualification undertakings accepted by the OFT or a specified regulator under section 9B;

   (c)   cases in which leave has been granted as mentioned in subsection (1)(d).]

(3) When an order [or undertaking] of which entry is made in the register ceases to be in force, the Secretary of State shall delete the entry from the register and all particulars relating to it which have been furnished to him under this section or any previous corresponding provision [and, in the case of a disqualification undertaking, any other particulars he has included in the register].

(4) The register shall be open to inspection on payment of such fee as may be specified by the Secretary of State in regulations.

[(4A) Regulations under this section may extend the preceding provisions of this section, to such extent and with such modifications as may be specified in the regulations, to disqualification orders made under Part II of the Companies (Northern Ireland) Order 1989 [or disqualification undertakings made under the Company Directors Disqualification (Northern Ireland) Order 2002].]

(5) Regulations under this section shall be made by statutory instrument subject to annulment in pursuance of a resolution of either House of Parliament.

[342]

NOTES

Section heading: substituted by the Insolvency Act 2000, s 8, Sch 4, Pt I, paras 1, 13(1), (6), as from 2 April 2001.

Sub-ss (1), (3): words in square brackets inserted by the Insolvency Act 2000, s 8, Sch 4, Pt I, paras 1, 13(1), (2), (4), as from 2 April 2001.

Sub-s (2A): inserted by the Insolvency Act 2000, s 8, Sch 4, Pt I, paras 1, 13(1), (3), as from 2 April 2001; substituted by the Enterprise Act 2002, s 204(1), (11), as from 20 June 2003.

Sub-s (4A): inserted by the Insolvency Act 2000, s 8, Sch 4, Pt I, paras 1, 13(1), (5), as from 2 April 2001; words in square brackets added by the Insolvency Act 2000 (Company Directors Disqualification Undertakings) Order 2004, SI 2004/1941, art 2(1), (6), as from 1 September 2004, in relation to disqualification undertakings under the Company Directors Disqualification (Northern Ireland) Order 2002 accepted on or after that date.

Regulations: the Companies (Disqualification Orders) Regulations 2001, SI 2001/967.

19 Special savings from repealed enactments

Schedule 2 to this Act has effect—

   (a)   in connection with certain transitional cases arising under sections 93 and 94 of the

Companies Act 1981, so as to limit the power to make a disqualification order, or to restrict the duration of an order, by reference to events occurring or things done before those sections came into force,

(b)   to preserve orders made under section 28 of the Companies Act 1976 (repealed by the Act of 1981), and

(c)   to preclude any applications for a disqualification order under section 6 or 8, where the relevant company went into liquidation before 28th April 1986.

[343]

Miscellaneous and general

20 Admissibility in evidence of statements

[(1)]   In any proceedings (whether or not under this Act), any statement made in pursuance of a requirement imposed by or under sections 6 to 10, 15 or 19(c) of, or Schedule 1 to, this Act, or by or under rules made for the purposes of this Act under the Insolvency Act, may be used in evidence against any person making or concurring in making the statement.

[(2)   However, in criminal proceedings in which any such person is charged with an offence to which this subsection applies—

(a)   no evidence relating to the statement may be adduced, and

(b)   no question relating to it may be asked,

by or on behalf of the prosecution, unless evidence relating to it is adduced, or a question relating to it is asked, in the proceedings by or on behalf of that person.

(3)   Subsection (2) applies to any offence other than—

(a)   an offence which is—

    (i)   created by rules made for the purposes of this Act under the Insolvency Act, and

    (ii)   designated for the purposes of this subsection by such rules or by regulations made by the Secretary of State;

(b)   an offence which is—

    (i)   created by regulations made under any such rules, and

    (ii)   designated for the purposes of this subsection by such regulations;

(c)   an offence under section 5 of the Perjury Act 1911 (false statements made otherwise than on oath); or

(d)   an offence under section 44(2) of the Criminal Law (Consolidation) (Scotland) Act 1995 (false statements made otherwise than on oath).

(4)   Regulations under subsection (3)(a)(ii) shall be made by statutory instrument and, after being made, shall be laid before each House of Parliament.]

[344]

NOTES

Sub-s (1) numbered as such, and sub-ss (2)–(4) added, by the Youth Justice and Criminal Evidence Act 1999, s 59, Sch 3, para 8, as from 14 April 2000 (in relation to England and Wales), and 1 January 2001 (in relation to Scotland).

[20A Legal professional privilege

In proceedings against a person for an offence under this Act nothing in this Act is to be taken to require any person to disclose any information that he is entitled to refuse to disclose on grounds of legal professional privilege (in Scotland, confidentiality of communications).]

[345]

NOTES

Commencement: 6 April 2008.

Inserted by the Companies Act 2006 (Consequential Amendments etc) Order 2008, SI 2008/948, art 3(1), Sch 1, Pt 2, para 106(1), (3), as from 6 April 2008.

21 Interaction with Insolvency Act

(1)   References in this Act to the official receiver, in relation to the winding up of a company or the bankruptcy of an individual, are to any person who, by virtue of section 399 of the Insolvency Act, is authorised to act as the official receiver in relation to that winding up or bankruptcy; and, in accordance with section 401(2) of that Act, references in this Act to an official receiver includes a person appointed as his deputy.

(2)   Sections [1A,] 6 to 10, [13, 14,] 15, 19(c) and 20 of, and Schedule 1 to, this Act [and sections 1 and 17 of this Act as they apply for the purposes of those provisions] are deemed included in Parts I to VII of the Insolvency Act for the purposes of the following sections of that Act—

section 411 (power to make insolvency rules);

section 414 (fees orders);

section 420 (orders extending provisions about insolvent companies to insolvent partnerships);

section 422 (modification of such provisions in their application to recognised banks); ...
...

(3) Section 434 of that Act (Crown application) applies to sections [1A,] 6 to 10, [13, 14,] 15, 19(c) and 20 of, and Schedule 1 to, this Act [and sections 1 and 17 of this Act as they apply for the purposes of those provisions] as it does to the provisions of that Act which are there mentioned.

[(4) For the purposes of summary proceedings in Scotland, section 431 of that Act applies to summary proceedings for an offence under section 11 or 13 of this Act as it applies to summary proceedings for an offence under Parts I to VII of that Act.]

[346]

NOTES
Sub-s (2): words in square brackets inserted by the Insolvency Act 2000, s 8, Sch 4, Pt I, paras 1, 14(1), (2), as from 2 April 2001; words omitted repealed by the Companies Act 1989, s 212, Sch 24, as from 1 March 1990.
Sub-s (3): words in square brackets inserted by the Insolvency Act 2000, s 8, Sch 4, Pt I, paras 1, 14(1), (3), as from 2 April 2001.
Sub-s (4): added by the Companies Act 1989, s 208, as from 1 March 1990.
As to Rules and Orders having effect under this section, see the notes to the sections listed in sub-s (2) above.

[21A Bank insolvency

Section 121 of the Banking Act 2009 provides for this Act to apply in relation to bank insolvency as it applies in relation to liquidation.]

[347]

NOTES
Commencement: 21 February 2009.
Inserted by the Banking Act 2009, s 121(4), as from 21 February 2009.

[21B Bank administration

Section 155 of the Banking Act 2009 provides for this Act to apply in relation to bank administration as it applies in relation to liquidation.]

[348]

NOTES
Commencement: 21 February 2009.
Inserted by the Banking Act 2009, s 155(4), as from 21 February 2009.

[21C Building society insolvency and special administration

Section 90E of the Building Societies Act 1986 provides for this Act to apply in relation to building society insolvency and building society special administration as it applies in relation to liquidation.]

[349]

NOTES
Commencement: 30 March 2009.
Inserted by the Building Societies (Insolvency and Special Administration) Order 2009, SI 2009/805, art 12, as from 30 March 2009.

22 Interpretation

(1) This section has effect with respect to the meaning of expressions used in this Act, and applies unless the context otherwise requires.

(2) The expression "company"—
  (a) in section 11, includes an unregistered company and a company incorporated outside Great Britain which has an established place of business in Great Britain, and
  (b) elsewhere, includes any company which may be wound up under Part V of the Insolvency Act.

(3) Section 247 in Part VII of the Insolvency Act (interpretation for the first Group of Parts of that Act) applies as regards references to a company's insolvency and to its going into liquidation; and "administrative receiver" has the meaning given by section 251 of that Act [and references to acting as an insolvency practitioner are to be read in accordance with section 388 of that Act].

(4) "Director" includes any person occupying the position of director, by whatever name called
...

(5) "Shadow director", in relation to a company, means a person in accordance with whose directions or instructions the directors of the company are accustomed to act (but so that a person is not deemed a shadow director by reason only that the directors act on advice given by him in a professional capacity).

(6)   Section 740 of the Companies Act applies as regards the meaning of "body corporate"; and "officer" has the meaning given by section 744 of that Act.

(7)   In references to legislation other than this Act—
    "the Companies Act" means the Companies Act 1985;
    "the Companies Acts" has the meaning given by [section 2 of the Companies Act 2006]; and
    "the Insolvency Act" means the Insolvency Act 1986;
and in section 3(1) and 5(1) of this Act "the companies legislation" means the Companies Acts ... , Parts I to VII of the Insolvency Act and, in Part XV of that Act, sections 411, 413, 414, 416 and 417.

(8)   Any reference to provisions, or a particular provision, of the Companies Acts or the Insolvency Act includes the corresponding provisions or provision of the former Companies Acts (as defined by [section 1171 of the Companies Act 2006]) or, as the case may be, the Insolvency Act 1985.

[(9)   Subject to the provisions of this section, expressions that are defined for the purposes of the Companies Acts have the same meaning in this Act.]

[(10)   Any reference to acting as receiver—
    (a)   includes acting as manager or as both receiver and manager, but
    (b)   does not include acting as administrative receiver;
and "receivership" is to be read accordingly.]

[350]

NOTES
Sub-s (3): words in square brackets added by the Insolvency Act 2000, s 8, Sch 4, Pt I, paras 1, 15(1), (2), as from 2 April 2001.
Sub-s (4): words omitted repealed by the Insolvency Act 2000, ss 8, 15(1), Sch 4, Pt I, paras 1, 15(1), (3), Sch 5, as from 2 April 2001.
Sub-s (7): words in square brackets substituted, and words omitted repealed, by the Companies Act 2006 (Consequential Amendments etc) Order 2008, SI 2008/948, art 3(1), Sch 1, Pt 2, para 106(1), (4)(a), as from 6 April 2008.
Sub-s (8): words in square brackets substituted by SI 2008/948, art 3(1), Sch 1, Pt 2, para 106(1), (4)(b), as from 6 April 2008.
Sub-s (9): substituted by SI 2008/948, art 3(1), Sch 1, Pt 2, para 106(1), (4)(c), as from 6 April 2008.
Sub-s (10): added by the Insolvency Act 2000, s 5(3), as from 2 April 2001.

[22A   Application of Act to building societies
    (1)   This Act applies to building societies as it applies to companies.

    (2)   References in this Act to a company, or to a director or an officer of a company include, respectively, references to a building society within the meaning of the Building Societies Act 1986 or to a director or officer, within the meaning of that Act, of a building society.

    (3)   In relation to a building society the definition of "shadow director" in section 22(5) applies with the substitution of "building society" for "company".

    (4)   In the application of Schedule 1 to the directors of a building society, references to provisions of the Insolvency Act[, the Companies Act 1985 or the Companies Act 2006] include references to the corresponding provisions of the Building Societies Act 1986.]

[351]

NOTES
Inserted by the Companies Act 1989, s 211(3), as from 31 July 1990.
Sub-s (4): words in square brackets substituted by the Companies Act 2006 (Consequential Amendments etc) Order 2008, SI 2008/948, art 3(1), Sch 1, Pt 2, para 106(1), (5), as from 6 April 2008.

[22B   Application of Act to incorporated friendly societies
    (1)   This Act applies to incorporated friendly societies as it applies to companies.

    (2)   References in this Act to a company, or to a director or an officer of a company include, respectively, references to an incorporated friendly society within the meaning of the Friendly Societies Act 1992 or to a member of the committee of management or officer, within the meaning of that Act, of an incorporated friendly society.

    (3)   In relation to an incorporated friendly society every reference to a shadow director shall be omitted.

    (4)   In the application of Schedule 1 to the members of the committee of management of an incorporated friendly society, references to provisions of the Insolvency Act[, the Companies Act 1985 or the Companies Act 2006] include references to the corresponding provisions of the Friendly Societies Act 1992.]

[352]

NOTES
Inserted by the Friendly Societies Act 1992, s 120(1), Sch 21, Pt I, para 8, as from 1 February 1993.
Sub-s (4): words in square brackets substituted by the Companies Act 2006 (Consequential Amendments etc)
Order 2008, SI 2008/948, art 3(1), Sch 1, Pt 2, para 106(1), (6), as from 6 April 2008.

[22C Application of Act to NHS foundation trusts

(1) This Act applies to NHS foundation trusts as it applies to companies within the meaning of this Act.

(2) References in this Act to a company, or to a director or officer of a company, include, respectively, references to an NHS foundation trust or to a director or officer of the trust; but references to shadow directors are omitted.

(3) In the application of Schedule 1 to the directors of an NHS foundation trust, references to the provisions of the Insolvency Act[, the Companies Act 1985 or the Companies Act 2006] include references to the corresponding provisions of [Chapter 5 of Part 2 of the National Health Service Act 2006].]

[353]

NOTES
Inserted by the Health and Social Care (Community Health and Standards) Act 2003, s 34, Sch 4, paras 67, 68, as from 1 April 2004.
Sub-s (3): words in first pair of square brackets substituted by the Companies Act 2006 (Consequential Amendments etc) Order 2008, SI 2008/948, art 3(1), Sch 1, Pt 2, para 106(1), (7), as from 6 April 2008; words in second pair of square brackets substituted by the National Health Service (Consequential Provisions) Act 2006, s 2, Sch 1, paras 91, 92, as from 1 March 2007.

23 Transitional provisions, savings, repeals

(1) The transitional provisions and savings in Schedule 3 to this Act have effect, and are without prejudice to anything in the Interpretation Act 1978 with regard to the effect of repeals.

(2) The enactments specified in the second column of Schedule 4 to this Act are repealed to the extent specified in the third column of that Schedule.

[354]

24 Extent

(1) This Act extends to England and Wales and to Scotland.

(2) Nothing in this Act extends to Northern Ireland.

[355]

25 Commencement

This Act comes into force simultaneously with the Insolvency Act 1986.

[356]

26 Citation

This Act may be cited as the Company Directors Disqualification Act 1986.

[357]

SCHEDULES

SCHEDULE 1
MATTERS FOR DETERMINING UNFITNESS OF DIRECTORS

Section 9

PART I
MATTERS APPLICABLE IN ALL CASES

1. Any misfeasance or breach of any fiduciary or other duty by the director in relation to the company.

2. Any misapplication or retention by the director of, or any conduct by the director giving rise to an obligation to account for, any money or other property of the company.

3. The extent of the director's responsibility for the company entering into any transaction liable to be set aside under Part XVI of the Insolvency Act (provisions against debt avoidance).

[4. The extent of the director's responsibility for any failure by the company to comply with any of the following provisions of the Companies Act 1985, namely—
    (a) section 288 (register of directors and secretaries);
    (b) section 352 (obligation to keep up and enter register of members);
    (c) section 353 (location of register of members);

(d)   section 363 (duty of company to make annual returns); and

(e)   sections 399 and 415 (company's duty to register charges it creates).

4A.   The extent of the director's responsibility for any failure by the company to comply with any of the following provisions of the Companies Act 2006, namely—

(a)   section 386 (companies to keep accounting records); and

(b)   section 388 (where and for how long records to be kept).]

[5.   The extent of the director's responsibility for any failure by the directors of the company to comply with the following provisions of the Companies Act 2006—

(a)   section 394 or 399 (duty to prepare annual accounts);

(b)   section 414 or 450 (approval and signature of abbreviated accounts); or

(c)   section 433 (name of signatory to be stated in published copy of accounts).]

[5A.   In the application of this Part of this Schedule in relation to any person who is a director of an open-ended investment company, any reference to a provision of [the Companies Act 1985 or the Companies Act 2006] is to be taken to be a reference to the corresponding provision of the Open-Ended Investment Companies Regulations 2001 or of any rules made under regulation 6 of those Regulations (Financial Services Authority rules).]

[358]

NOTES

Paras 4, 4A: substituted, for the original para 4 (as amended by the Companies Act 1989), by the Companies Act 2006 (Consequential Amendments etc) Order 2008, SI 2008/948, art 3(1), Sch 1, Pt 2, para 106(1), (8)(a), as from 6 April 2008. Note that art 6(4) of the 2008 Order provides that where by virtue of any transitional provision, a provision of the Companies Act 2006 has effect only (a) on or after a specified date, or (b) in relation to matters occurring or arising on or after a specified date, any amendment substituting or inserting a reference to that provision has effect correspondingly. The references in para 4A to ss 386, 388 of the 2006 Act replace the former references to ss 221, 222 of the 1985 Act contained in the original para 4(a), (b).

Para 5: substituted by SI 2008/948, art 3(1), Sch 1, Pt 2, para 106(1), (8)(b), as from 6 April 2008 (for savings see the para 4 note above). The original para 5 (as substituted by the Companies Act 1989, s 23, Sch 10, para 35(1), (3)) read as follows—

"[5.   The extent of the director's responsibility for any failure by the directors of the company to comply with—

(a)   section 226 or 227 of the Companies Act (duty to prepare annual accounts), or

(b)   section 233 of that Act (approval and signature of accounts).]"

Para 5A: inserted by the Open-Ended Investment Companies (Investment Companies with Variable Capital) Regulations 1996, SI 1996/2827, reg 75, Sch 8, Pt I, para 10, as from 6 January 1997, and substituted by the Open-Ended Investment Companies Regulations 2001, SI 2001/1228, reg 84, Sch 7, para 9, as from 1 December 2001; words in square brackets substituted by SI 2008/948, art 3(1), Sch 1, Pt 2, para 108(1), (8)(c), as from 6 April 2008.

PART II
MATTERS APPLICABLE WHERE COMPANY HAS BECOME INSOLVENT

6.   The extent of the director's responsibility for the causes of the company becoming insolvent.

7.   The extent of the director's responsibility for any failure by the company to supply any goods or services which have been paid for (in whole or in part).

8.   The extent of the director's responsibility for the company entering into any transaction or giving any preference, being a transaction or preference—

(a)   liable to be set aside under section 127 or sections 238 to 240 of the Insolvency Act, or

(b)   challengeable under section 242 or 243 of that Act or under any rule of law in Scotland.

9.   The extent of the director's responsibility for any failure by the directors of the company to comply with section 98 of the Insolvency Act (duty to call creditors' meeting in creditors' voluntary winding up).

10.   Any failure by the director to comply with any obligation imposed on him by or under any of the following provisions of the Insolvency Act—

(a)   [paragraph 47 of Schedule B1] (company's statement of affairs in administration);

(b)   section 47 (statement of affairs to administrative receiver);

(c)   section 66 (statement of affairs in Scottish receivership);

(d)   section 99 (directors' duty to attend meeting; statement of affairs in creditors' voluntary winding up);

(e)   section 131 (statement of affairs in winding up by the court);

(f)   section 234 (duty of any one with company property to deliver it up);

(g)   section 235 (duty to co-operate with liquidator, etc).

[359]

NOTES

Para 10: words in square brackets in sub-para (a) substituted by the Enterprise Act 2002 (Insolvency) Order 2003, SI 2003/2096, arts 4, 6, Schedule, Pt 1, para 12, as from 15 September 2003, except in relation to any case where a petition for an administration order was presented before that date.

Limited liability partnerships: see the introductory notes to this Act.

SCHEDULE 2
SAVINGS FROM COMPANIES ACT 1981 SS 93, 94,
AND INSOLVENCY ACT 1985 SCHEDULE 9

Section 19

1. Sections 2 and 4(1)(b) do not apply in relation to anything done before 15th June 1982 by a person in his capacity as liquidator of a company or as receiver or manager of a company's property.

2. Subject to paragraph 1—
    (a)   section 2 applies in a case where a person is convicted on indictment of an offence which he committed (and, in the case of a continuing offence, has ceased to commit) before 15th June 1982; but in such a case a disqualification order under that section shall not be made for a period in excess of 5 years;
    (b)   that section does not apply in a case where a person is convicted summarily—
        (i)   in England and Wales, if he had consented so to be tried before that date, or
        (ii)   in Scotland, if the summary proceedings commenced before that date.

3. Subject to paragraph 1, section 4 applies in relation to an offence committed or other thing done before 15th June 1982; but a disqualification order made on the grounds of such an offence or other thing done shall not be made for a period in excess of 5 years.

4. The powers of a court under section 5 are not exercisable in a case where a person is convicted of an offence which he committed (and, in the case of a continuing offence, had ceased to commit) before 15th June 1982.

5. For purposes of section 3(1) and section 5, no account is to be taken of any offence which was committed, or any default order which was made, before 1st June 1977.

6. An order made under section 28 of the Companies Act 1976 has effect as if made under section 3 of this Act; and an application made before 15th June 1982 for such an order is to be treated as an application for an order under the section last mentioned.

7. Where—
    (a)   an application is made for a disqualification order under section 6 of this Act by virtue of paragraph (a) of subsection (2) of that section, and
    (b)   the company in question went into liquidation before 28th April 1986 (the coming into force of the provision replaced by section 6),

the court shall not make an order under that section unless it could have made a disqualification order under section 300 of the Companies Act as it had effect immediately before the date specified in sub-paragraph (b) above.

8. An application shall not be made under section 8 of this Act in relation to a report made or information or documents obtained before 28th April 1986.

[360]

SCHEDULE 3
TRANSITIONAL PROVISIONS AND SAVINGS

Section 23(1)

1. In this Schedule, "the former enactments" means so much of the Companies Act, and so much of the Insolvency Act, as is repealed and replaced by this Act; and "the appointed day" means the day on which this Act comes into force.

2. So far as anything done or treated as done under or for the purposes of any provision of the former enactments could have been done under or for the purposes of the corresponding provision of this Act, it is not invalidated by the repeal of that provision but has effect as if done under or for the purposes of the corresponding provision; and any order, regulation, rule or other instrument made or having effect under any provision of the former enactments shall, insofar as its effect is preserved by this paragraph, be treated for all purposes as made and having effect under the corresponding provision.

3. Where any period of time specified in a provision of the former enactments is current immediately before the appointed day, this Act has effect as if the corresponding provision had been in force when the period began to run; and (without prejudice to the foregoing) any period of time so specified and current is deemed for the purposes of this Act—
    (a)   to run from the date or event from which it was running immediately before the appointed day, and
    (b)   to expire (subject to any provision of this Act for its extension) whenever it would have expired if this Act had not been passed;

and any rights, priorities, liabilities, reliefs, obligations, requirements, powers, duties or exemptions dependent on the beginning, duration or end of such a period as above mentioned shall be under this Act as they were or would have been under the former enactments.

4. Where in any provision of this Act there is a reference to another such provision, and the first-mentioned provision operates, or is capable of operating, in relation to things done or omitted, or events occurring or not occurring, in the past (including in particular past acts of compliance with

any enactment, failures of compliance, contraventions, offences and convictions of offences) the reference to the other provision is to be read as including a reference to the corresponding provision of the former enactments.

5. Offences committed before the appointed day under any provision of the former enactments may, notwithstanding any repeal by this Act, be prosecuted and punished after that day as if this Act had not passed.

6. A reference in any enactment, instrument or document (whether express or implied, and in whatever phraseology) to a provision of the former enactments (including the corresponding provision of any yet earlier enactment) is to be read, where necessary to retain for the enactment, instrument or document the same force and effect as it would have had but for the passing of this Act, as, or as including, a reference to the corresponding provision by which it is replaced in this Act.

[361]

(Sch 4 (repeals) outside the scope of this work.)

BUILDING SOCIETIES ACT 1986

(1986 c 53)

ARRANGEMENT OF SECTIONS

PART X
DISSOLUTION, WINDING UP, MERGERS, TRANSFER OF BUSINESS

Dissolution and winding up

An Act to make fresh provision with respect to building societies and further provision with respect to conveyancing services

[25 July 1986]

1–85 *((Pts I–IX) Outside the scope of this work; for s 1 see Butterworths Securities and Financial Services Law Handbook.)*

PART X
DISSOLUTION, WINDING UP, MERGERS, TRANSFER OF BUSINESS
Dissolution and winding up

86 Modes of dissolution and winding up

(1) A building society—
   (a) may be dissolved by consent of the members, or
   (b) may be wound up voluntarily or by the court,

in accordance with this Part; and a building society may not, except where it is dissolved by virtue of section 93(5), 94(10) or 97(9), [or following building society insolvency or building society special administration,] be dissolved or wound up in any other manner.

(2)   A building society which is in the course of dissolution by consent, or is being wound up voluntarily, may be wound up by the court.

[362]

NOTES
Sub-s (1): words in square brackets inserted by the Building Societies (Insolvency and Special Administration) Order 2009, SI 2009/805, art 7, as from 29 March 2009.

87   (*Outside the scope of this work.*)

88   Voluntary winding up

(1)   A building society may be wound up voluntarily under the applicable winding up legislation if it resolves by special resolution that it be wound up voluntarily[, but a resolution may not be passed if—
  (a)   the conditions in section 90D are not satisfied, or
  (b)   the society is in building society insolvency or building society special administration].

[(1A)   A resolution under subsection (1) shall have no effect without the prior approval of the court.]

(2)   A copy of any special resolution passed for the voluntary winding up of a building society shall be sent by the society to the [Authority] within 15 days after it is passed; and the [Authority] shall keep the copy in the public file of the society.

(3)   A copy of any such resolution shall be annexed to every copy of the memorandum or of the rules issued after the passing of the resolution.

(4)   If a building society fails to comply with subsection (2) or (3) above the society shall be liable on summary conviction to a fine not exceeding level 3 on the standard scale and so shall any officer who is also guilty of the offence.

(5)   For the purposes of this section, a liquidator of the society shall be treated as an officer of it.

[363]

NOTES
Sub-s (1): words in square brackets inserted by the Building Societies (Insolvency and Special Administration) Order 2009, SI 2009/805, art 4, as from 29 March 2009.
Sub-s (1A): inserted by SI 2009/805, art 4, as from 29 March 2009.
Sub-s (2): words in square brackets substituted by the Financial Services and Markets Act 2000 (Mutual Societies) Order 2001, SI 2001/2617, art 13(1), Sch 3, Pt II, paras 131, 174(b), as from 1 December 2001.

89   (*Outside the scope of this work.*)

[89A   Building society insolvency as alternative order

(1)   On a petition for a winding up order or an application for an administration order in respect of a building society the court may, instead, make a building society insolvency order (under section 94 of the Banking Act 2009 as applied by section 90C above).

(2)   A building society insolvency order may be made under subsection (1) only—
  (a)   on the application of the Authority made with the consent of the Bank of England, or
  (b)   on the application of the Bank of England.]

[364]

NOTES
Commencement: 29 March 2009.
Inserted by the Building Societies (Insolvency and Special Administration) Order 2009, SI 2009/805, art 5, as from 29 March 2009.

90, 90A   (*Outside the scope of this work.*)

[90B   Power to alter priorities on dissolution and winding up

(1)   The Treasury may by order make provision for the purpose of ensuring that, on the winding up, or dissolution by consent, of a building society, any assets available for satisfying the society's liabilities to creditors or to shareholders are applied in satisfying those liabilities pari passu.

(2)   Liabilities to creditors do not include—
  (a)   liabilities in respect of subordinated deposits;
  (b)   liabilities in respect of preferential debts;
  (c)   any other category of liability which the Treasury specifies in the order for the purposes of this paragraph.

(3)   Liabilities to shareholders do not include liabilities in respect of deferred shares.

(4)   A preferential debt is a debt which constitutes a preferential debt for the purposes of any of the enactments specified in paragraph 1 of Schedule 15 to this Act (or which would constitute such a debt if the society were being wound up).

(5)   An order under this section may—
  (a)   make amendments of this Act;
  (b)   make different provision for different purposes;
  (c)   make such consequential, supplementary, transitional and saving provision as appears to the Treasury to be necessary or expedient.

(6)   The power to make an order under this section is exercisable by statutory instrument but no such order may be made unless a draft of it has been laid before and approved by a resolution of each House of Parliament.]

[365]

NOTES
Commencement: to be appointed.
Inserted by the Building Societies (Funding) and Mutual Societies (Transfers) Act 2007, s 2, as from a day to be appointed.

[90C   Application of bank insolvency and administration legislation to building societies

(1)   Parts 2 (Bank Insolvency) and 3 (Bank Administration) of the Banking Act 2009 shall apply in relation to building societies with any modifications specified in an order made under section 130 or 158 of that Act and with the modifications specified in subsection (2) below.

(2)   In the application of Parts 2 and 3 of that Act to building societies—
  (a)   references to "bank" (except in the term "bridge bank" and the terms specified in paragraphs (b) and (c)) have effect as references to "building society";
  (b)   references to "bank insolvency", "bank insolvency order", "bank liquidation" and "bank liquidator" have effect as references to "building society insolvency", "building society insolvency order", "building society liquidation" and "building society liquidator";
  (c)   references to "bank administration", "bank administration order" and "bank administrator" have effect as references to "building society special administration", "building society special administration order" and "building society special administrator".]

[366]

NOTES
Commencement: 29 March 2009.
Inserted by the Building Societies (Insolvency and Special Administration) Order 2009, SI 2009/805, art 2, as from 29 March 2009.

[90D   Notice to the Authority of preliminary steps

(1)   An application for an administration order in respect of a building society may not be determined unless the conditions below are satisfied.

(2)   A petition for a winding up order in respect of a building society may not be determined unless the conditions below are satisfied.

(3)   A resolution for voluntary winding up of a building society may not be passed unless the conditions below are satisfied.

(4)   An administrator of a building society may not be appointed unless the conditions below are satisfied.

(5)   Condition 1 is that the Authority has been notified—
  (a)   by the applicant for an administration order, that the application has been made,
  (b)   by the petitioner for a winding up order, that the petition has been presented,
  (c)   by the building society, that a resolution for voluntary winding up may be passed, or
  (d)   by the person proposing to appoint an administrator, of the proposed appointment.

(6)   Condition 2 is that a copy of the notice complying with Condition 1 has been filed with the court (and made available for public inspection by the court).

(7)   Condition 3 is that—
  (a)   the period of 2 weeks, beginning with the day on which the notice is received, has ended, or
  (b)   both—
      (i)   the Authority has informed the person who gave the notice that it does not intend to apply for a building society insolvency order (under section 95 of the Banking Act 2009 as applied by section 90C above), and
      (ii)   the Bank of England has informed the person who gave the notice that it does not

intend to apply for a building society insolvency order or to exercise a stabilisation power under Part 1 of the Banking Act 2009.

(8)   Condition 4 is that no application for a building society insolvency order is pending.

(9)   Arranging for the giving of notice in order to satisfy Condition 1 can be a step with a view to minimising the potential loss to a building society's creditors for the purpose of section 214 of the Insolvency Act 1986 (wrongful trading) or Article 178 (wrongful trading) of the Insolvency (Northern Ireland) Order 1989 as applied in relation to building societies by section 90 of, and Schedule 15 to, this Act.

(10)   Where the Authority receives notice under Condition 1—
(a)   the Authority shall inform the Bank of England,
(b)   the Authority shall inform the person who gave the notice, within the period in Condition 3(a), whether it intends to apply for a building society insolvency order, and
(c)   if the Bank of England decides to apply for a building society insolvency order or to exercise a stabilisation power under Part 1 of the Banking Act 2009, the Bank shall inform the person who gave the notice, within the period in Condition 3(a).]

[367]

NOTES
Commencement: 29 March 2009.
Inserted, together with s 90E, by the Building Societies (Insolvency and Special Administration) Order 2009, SI 2009/805, art 6, as from 29 March 2009.

[90E   Disqualification of directors

(1)   In this section "the Disqualification Act" means the Company Directors Disqualification Act 1986.

(2)   In the Disqualification Act—
(a)   a reference to liquidation includes a reference to building society insolvency and a reference to building society special administration,
(b)   a reference to winding up includes a reference to making or being subject to a building society insolvency order and a reference to making or being subject to a building society special administration order,
(c)   a reference to becoming insolvent includes a reference to becoming subject to a building society insolvency order and a reference to becoming subject to a building society special administration order, and
(d)   a reference to a liquidator includes a reference to a building society liquidator and a reference to a building society special administrator.

(3)   For the purposes of the application of section 7(3) of the Disqualification Act (disqualification order or undertaking) to a building society which is subject to a building society insolvency order, the responsible office-holder is the building society liquidator.

(4)   For the purposes of the application of that section to a building society which is subject to a building society special administration order, the responsible office-holder is the building society special administrator.

(5)   In the application of this section to Northern Ireland, references to the Disqualification Act are to the Company Directors Disqualification (Northern Ireland) Order 2002 and the reference in subsection (3) to section 7(3) of the Disqualification Act is a reference to Article 10(4) of that Order (disqualification order or undertaking; and reporting provisions).]

[368]

NOTES
Commencement: 29 March 2009.
Inserted as noted to s 90D at **[367]**.

91   Power of court to declare dissolution of building society void

(1)   Where a building society has been dissolved under section 87 or following a winding up, [building society insolvency or building society special administration,] the High Court or, in relation to a society whose principal office was in Scotland, the Court of Session, may, at any time within 12 years after the date on which the society was dissolved, make an order under this section declaring the dissolution to have been void.

(2)   An order under this section may be made, on such terms as the court thinks fit, on an application by the trustees under section 87 or the liquidator, [building society liquidator or building society special administrator,] as the case may be, or by any other person appearing to the Court to be interested.

(3)   When an order under this section is made, such proceedings may be taken as might have been taken if the society had not been dissolved.

(4)　The person on whose application the order is made shall, within seven days of its being so made, or such further time as the Court may allow, furnish the [Authority] with a copy of the order; and the [Authority] shall keep the copy in the public file of the society.

(5)　If a person fails to comply with subsection (4) above, he shall be liable on summary conviction—

(a)　to a fine not exceeding level 3 on the standard scale, and

(b)　in the case of a continuing offence, to an additional fine not exceeding £40 for every day during which the offence continues.

[369]

NOTES

Sub-ss (1) (2): words in square brackets inserted by the Building Societies (Insolvency and Special Administration) Order 2009, SI 2009/805, art 8, as from 29 March 2009.

Sub-s (4): words in square brackets substituted by the Financial Services and Markets Act 2000 (Mutual Societies) Order 2001, SI 2001/2617, art 13(1), Sch 3, Pt II, paras 131, 174(b), as from 1 December 2001.

[92　Supplementary

Where at any time a building society is being wound up or dissolved by consent, [or is in building society insolvency or building society special administration,] a borrowing member shall not be liable to pay any amount other than one which, at that time, is payable under the mortgage or other security by which his indebtedness to the society in respect of the loan is secured.]

[370]

NOTES

Substituted by the Building Societies Act 1997, s 43, Sch 7, para 40, as from 1 December 1997 or, in the case of an existing building society whose record of alterations takes effect or is registered after 1 December 1997, on the date specified in that record.

Words in square brackets inserted by the Building Societies (Insolvency and Special Administration) Order 2009, SI 2009/805, art 9, as from 29 March 2009.

92A–102D　(*Outside the scope of this work.*)

Cancellation of registration

103　Cancellation of registration

(1)　Where the [Authority] is satisfied, with respect to a building society—

(a)　that the society has been dissolved by virtue of section 93(5), 94(10), 97(9) or 97(10), or

(b)　that the society has been wound up under the applicable winding up legislation and dissolved, [or

(c)　that the society has been dissolved following building society insolvency or building society special administration,]

the [Authority] shall cancel the registration of the society.

(2)　Where the [Authority] is satisfied, with respect to a building society—

(a)　that a certificate of incorporation has been obtained for the society by fraud or mistake and that the society [does not have permission under Part IV of the Financial Services and Markets Act 2000 to accept deposits], or

(b)　that the society has ceased to exist,

the [Authority] may cancel the registration of the society.

(3)　Without prejudice to subsection (2) above, the [Authority] may, if it thinks fit, cancel the registration of a building society at the request of the society, evidenced in such manner as the [Authority] may direct.

(4)　Before cancelling the registration of a building society under subsection (2) above, the [Authority] shall give to the society not less than two months' previous notice, specifying briefly the grounds of the proposed cancellation.

(5)　Where the registration of a building society is cancelled under subsection (2) above, the society may appeal to—

(a)　the High Court, where the principal office of the society is situated in England and Wales or in Northern Ireland, or

(b)　the Court of Session, where that office is situated in Scotland,

and on any such appeal the High Court or the Court of Session, as the case may be, if it thinks it just to do so, may set aside the cancellation.

(6)　Where the registration of a building society is cancelled under subsection (2) or (3) above, then subject to the right of appeal conferred by subsection (5) above, the society, so far as it continues to exist, shall cease to be a society incorporated under this Act (and accordingly shall cease to be a building society within the meaning of this Act).

(7) Subsection (6) above shall have effect in relation to a building society without prejudice to any liability actually incurred by the society; and any such liability may be enforced against the society as if the cancellation had not taken place.

(8) Any cancellation of the registration of a building society under this section shall be effected in writing signed by the [Authority].

(9) As soon as practicable after the cancellation of the registration of a society under this section the [Authority] shall cause notice thereof to be published in the London Gazette, the Edinburgh Gazette or the Belfast Gazette according to the situation of the society's principal office, and if it thinks fit, in one or more newspapers.

[371]

NOTES

Sub-s (1): words in first and third pairs of square brackets substituted by the Financial Services and Markets Act 2000 (Mutual Societies) Order 2001, SI 2001/2617, art 13(1), Sch 3, Pt II, paras 131, 187(a), as from 1 December 2001; para (c) (and word "or" immediately preceding it) inserted by the Building Societies (Insolvency and Special Administration) Order 2009, SI 2009/805, art 10, as from 29 March 2009.

Sub-ss (2)–(4), (8), (9): words in square brackets substituted by SI 2001/2617, art 13(1), Sch 3, Pt II, paras 131, 187, as from 1 December 2001.

PART XI
MISCELLANEOUS AND SUPPLEMENTARY AND CONVEYANCING SERVICES
Miscellaneous and supplementary

104–118 (*Outside the scope of this work.*)

119 Interpretation

(1) In this Act, except where the context otherwise requires—

...

"the applicable winding up legislation" and "the companies winding up legislation" have the meanings given by section 90;

...

["building society insolvency", "building society insolvency order" and "building society liquidator" shall be construed in accordance with Part 2 of the Banking Act 2009 as applied with modifications by section 90C above;
"building society special administration", "building society special administration order" and "building society special administrator" shall be construed in accordance with Part 3 of the Banking Act 2009 as applied with modifications by section 90C above;]

...

["the court", in relation to a building society, means the court which has jurisdiction under the applicable winding up legislation to wind up the society;]

...

["deposit" includes—
  (a) a loan; and
  (b) a subordinated deposit, that is to say, a deposit which, on a winding up, would fall to be repaid only after repayment in full had been made to the holders of shares in the society other than deferred shares,
  and cognate expressions shall be construed accordingly;]

...

["member" shall be construed in accordance with paragraph 5 of Schedule 2 to this Act;]
"memorandum" has the meaning given by paragraph 1 of Schedule 2 to the Act;

...

"mortgage" includes charge;

...

["notice" means written notice but includes a notice in an electronic communication to the extent only that this Act provides for the manner in which the notice may be given electronically, and "notice to" and "notify" shall be construed accordingly;]
"officer", in relation to a building society, means any director, chief executive, secretary or manager of the society; and, in relation to any offence, "officer" also includes any person who purports to act as an officer of the society; and in relation to any other body corporate means the corresponding officers of that body;

...

"the public file", in relation to a building society, means the file relating to the society which the [Authority] is required to maintain under section 106;

...

["share", in relation to a building society, shall be construed in accordance with section 8;]

...

"special resolution" has the meaning given by paragraph 27 of Schedule 2 to this Act;

…

["undertaking" and "subsidiary undertaking" have the same meaning as in the Companies Acts (see sections 1161(1) and 1162 of, and Schedule 7 to, the Companies Act 2006)].

(1A)–(5)   (*Outside the scope of this work*)

[372]

NOTES
Sub-s (1): definitions beginning "building society insolvency" and "building society special administration" inserted by the Building Societies (Insolvency and Special Administration) Order 2009, SI 2009/805, art 11, as from 29 March 2009; definitions "the court", "deposit", "member" and "share" substituted by the Building Societies Act 1997, s 43, Sch 7, para 53(1)(e), (g), (j), (n), as from 1 December 1997 or, in the case of an existing building society whose record of alterations takes effect or is registered after 1 December 1997, on the date specified in that record; definition "notice" substituted by the Building Societies Act 1986 (Electronic Communications) Order 2003, SI 2003/404, art 9(1), (3), as from 20 March 2003; in definition "the public file" word in square brackets substituted by the Financial Services and Markets Act 2000 (Mutual Societies) Order 2001, SI 2001/2617, art 13(1), Sch 3, Pt II, paras 131, 197(a)(ix), as from 1 December 2001; definition ""undertaking" and "subsidiary undertaking"" inserted by the Companies Act 2006 (Consequential Amendments etc) Order 2008, SI 2008/948, arts 3(1)(b), 6, Sch 1, Pt 2, para 108(1), (4), as from 6 April 2008; and definitions omitted are outside the scope of this work.

119A–126   (*Outside the scope of this work; for s 125 see Butterworths Securities and Financial Services Law Handbook.*)

(*Schs 1–21 outside the scope of this work.*)

BANK OF ENGLAND ACT 1998

(1998 c 11)

ARRANGEMENT OF SECTIONS

PART I
CONSTITUTION, REGULATION AND FINANCIAL ARRANGEMENTS

Constitution and regulation

An Act to make provision about the constitution, regulation, financial arrangements and functions of the Bank of England, including provision for the transfer of supervisory functions; to amend the Banking Act 1987 in relation to the provision and disclosure of information; to make provision relating to appointments to the governing body of a designated agency under the Financial Services Act 1986; to amend Schedule 5 to that Act; to make provision relating to the registration of Government stocks and bonds; to make provision about the application of section 207 of the Companies Act 1989 to bearer securities; and for connected purposes

[23 April 1998]

PART I
CONSTITUTION, REGULATION AND FINANCIAL ARRANGEMENTS

Constitution and regulation

1   Court of directors

(1)   There shall continue to be a court of directors of the Bank.

(2)   The court shall consist of a Governor, 2 Deputy Governors and … directors of the Bank, all of whom shall be appointed by Her Majesty.

[(2A)   The number of directors must not exceed 9.]

PART II
OTHER ACTS

(3)   On the day on which this Act comes into force, all persons who are, immediately before that day, holding office as director of the Bank shall vacate their office.

(4)   Schedule 1 shall have effect with respect to the court.

[373]

NOTES
    Sub-s (2): number omitted repealed by the Banking Act 2009, s 239(1), (2), as from 1 June 2009.
    Sub-s (2A): inserted by the Banking Act 2009, s 239(1), (3), as from 1 June 2009.

2   Functions of court of directors

(1)   The court of directors of the Bank shall manage the Bank's affairs, other than the formulation of monetary policy.

(2)   In particular, the court's functions under subsection (1) shall include determining the Bank's objectives (including objectives for its financial management) and strategy.

(3)   In determining the Bank's objectives and strategy, the court's aim shall be to ensure the effective discharge of the Bank's functions.

(4)   Subject to that, in determining objectives for the financial management of the Bank, the court's aim shall be to ensure the most efficient use of the Bank's resources.

[(5)   Sections 2A and 11 set objectives for the Bank in relation to financial stability and monetary policy; and subsections (2) to (4) above are subject to those sections.]

[374]

NOTES
    Sub-s (5): added by the Banking Act 2009, s 238(2), as from 1 June 2009.

[2A   Financial Stability Objective

(1)   An objective of the Bank shall be to contribute to protecting and enhancing the stability of the financial systems of the United Kingdom (the "Financial Stability Objective").

(2)   In pursuing the Financial Stability Objective the Bank shall aim to work with other relevant bodies (including the Treasury and the Financial Services Authority).

(3)   The court of directors shall, consulting the Treasury, determine and review the Bank's strategy in relation to the Financial Stability Objective.]

[375]

NOTES
    Commencement: 1 June 2009.
    Inserted, together with ss 2B, 2C, by the Banking Act 2009, s 238(1), as from 1 June 2009.

[2B   Financial Stability Committee

(1)   There shall be a sub-committee of the court of directors of the Bank (the "Financial Stability Committee") consisting of—
    (a)   the Governor of the Bank, who shall chair the Committee (when present),
    (b)   the Deputy Governors of the Bank, and
    (c)   4 directors of the Bank, appointed by the chair of the court of directors (designated under paragraph 13 of Schedule 1).

(2)   The Committee shall have the following functions—
    (a)   to make recommendations to the court of directors, which they shall consider, about the nature and implementation of the Bank's strategy in relation to the Financial Stability Objective,
    (b)   to give advice about whether and how the Bank should act in respect of an institution, where the issue appears to the Committee to be relevant to the Financial Stability Objective,
    (c)   in particular, to give advice about whether and how the Bank should use stabilisation powers under Part 1 of the Banking Act 2009 in particular cases,
    (d)   to monitor the Bank's use of the stabilisation powers,
    (e)   to monitor the Bank's exercise of its functions under Part 5 of the Banking Act 2009 (inter-bank payment systems), and
    (f)   any other functions delegated to the Committee by the court of directors for the purpose of pursuing the Financial Stability Objective.

(3)   The Treasury may appoint a person to represent the Treasury at meetings of the Committee; and the Treasury's representative—
    (a)   may not vote in proceedings of the Committee,
    (b)   shall in all other respects be a member of the Committee, and
    (c)   may be replaced by the Treasury.

(4)   The Committee may co-opt other non-voting members.

(5)   The chair of the court of directors may replace members of the Committee appointed under subsection (1)(c).]

[376]

NOTES
Commencement: 1 June 2009.
Inserted as noted to s 2A at **[375]**.

[2C   Financial Stability Committee: supplemental

(1)   The Committee shall determine its own procedure (including quorum).

(2)   If a member of the Committee has any direct or indirect interest (including any reasonably likely future interest) in any dealing or business which falls to be considered by the Committee—
   (a)   he shall disclose his interest to the Committee when it considers the dealing or business, and
   (b)   he shall have no vote in proceedings of the Committee in relation to any question arising from its consideration of the dealing or business, unless the Committee has resolved that the interest does not give rise to a conflict of interest.

(3)   The Committee may delegate a function under section 2B(2)(b) to (e) to two or more of its members, excluding—
   (a)   the Treasury representative, and
   (b)   co-opted non-voting members.]

[377]

NOTES
Commencement: 1 June 2009.
Inserted as noted to s 2A at **[375]**.

3   Functions to be carried out by non-executive members

(1)   The functions mentioned in subsection (2) shall stand delegated to a sub-committee of the court of directors of the Bank consisting of the directors of the Bank.

(2)   The functions referred to are—
   (a)   keeping under review the Bank's performance in relation to the objectives and strategy for the time being determined by the court of directors of the Bank,
   (b)   monitoring the extent to which the objectives set by the court of directors of the Bank in relation to the Bank's financial management have been met,
   (c)   keeping under review the internal financial controls of the Bank with a view to securing the proper conduct of its financial affairs, and
   (d)   determining how the functions under paragraph 14 of Schedule 1 (remuneration and pensions etc of executive members of the court) should be exercised.

(3)   …

[(4)   The chair of the court (designated under paragraph 13 of Schedule 1) shall chair meetings of the sub-committee (when present).]

(5)   If a member of the sub-committee has any direct or indirect interest in any dealing or business with the Bank which falls to be considered by the sub-committee—
   (a)   he shall disclose his interest to the sub-committee when it considers the dealing or business, and
   (b)   he shall have no vote in proceedings of the sub-committee in relation to any question arising from its consideration of the dealing or business, unless the sub-committee has resolved that the interest does not give rise to a conflict of interest.

(6)   In any proceedings of the sub-committee, a member shall have no vote in relation to any question arising which touches or concerns him but shall withdraw and be absent during the debate of any matter in which he is concerned.

(7)   Subject to subsections [(4)] to (6), the sub-committee shall determine its own procedure [(including quorum)].

(8)   The sub-committee may delegate any of its functions to two or more of its members.

[378]

NOTES
Sub-s (3): repealed by the Banking Act 2009, s 242(1), (2)(a), as from 1 June 2009.
Sub-s (4): substituted by the Banking Act 2009, s 241(2), as from 1 June 2009.
Sub-s (7): reference in first pair of square brackets substituted and words in second pair of square brackets inserted by the Banking Act 2009, s 242(1), (2)(b), (c), as from 1 June 2009.

4–46 (*Outside the scope of this work; see Butterworths Banking Law Handbook.*)

SCHEDULES

SCHEDULE 1
COURT OF DIRECTORS
Section 1

Terms of office

1.—(1) Appointment as Governor or Deputy Governor of the Bank shall be for a period of 5 years.

(2) A person appointed as Governor or Deputy Governor of the Bank shall work exclusively for the Bank.

[(3) A person may not be appointed as Governor more than twice.

(4) A person may not be appointed as Deputy Governor more than twice.]

2. Appointment as director of the Bank shall be for a period of 3 years, except that initially some appointments may be for shorter and different periods so as to secure that appointments expire at different times.

3. A person appointed as director of the Bank in place of a person who ceased to hold office before the end of the term for which he was appointed shall be appointed for the remainder of that person's term of office.

4. A person appointed as Governor, Deputy Governor or director of the Bank may resign his office by written notice to the Bank.

Qualification for appointment

5.—(1) A person is disqualified for appointment as Governor, Deputy Governor or director of the Bank if he is a Minister of the Crown or a person serving in a government department in employment in respect of which remuneration is payable out of money provided by Parliament.

(2) A person is disqualified for appointment as director of the Bank if he is a servant of the Bank.

6. The fact that a person has held office as Governor, Deputy Governor or director of the Bank does not disqualify him for re-appointment to that office or for appointment to any other of those offices [(subject to paragraph 1(3) and (4))].

Removal from office

7.—(1) A person appointed as Governor or Deputy Governor of the Bank shall vacate office if he becomes a person to whom paragraph 5(1) applies.

(2) A person appointed as director of the Bank shall vacate office if he becomes a person to whom paragraph 5(1) or (2) applies.

8. The Bank may, with the consent of the Chancellor of the Exchequer, remove a person from office as Governor, Deputy Governor or director of the Bank if it is satisfied—
    (a) that he has been absent from meetings of the court for more than 3 months without the consent of the court,
    (b) that he has become bankrupt, that his estate has been sequestrated or that he has made an arrangement with or granted a trust deed for his creditors, or
    (c) that he is unable or unfit to discharge his functions as a member.

Powers

9. The court may act notwithstanding the existence of one or more vacancies among its members.

10. The court may appoint such sub-committees as it thinks fit.

11. The court may delegate such duties and powers as it thinks fit to—
    (a) a member of the court,
    (b) any officer, servant or agent of the Bank,
    (c) a sub-committee consisting of—
        (i) members of the court, or
        (ii) one or more members of the court and one or more of the officers, servants and agents of the Bank.

Meetings

12.—(1) The court shall meet at least [7 times in each calendar year].

[(2) Either of the following may summon a meeting at any time on giving such notice as the circumstances appear to require—

(a)   the Governor of the Bank (or in his absence a Deputy Governor), and

(b)   the chair of the court.]

Proceedings

13.—(1)   At a meeting of the court, the proceedings shall be regulated as follows.

(2)   ...

[(3)   The Chancellor of the Exchequer may designate—

(a)   a member of the court to chair its meetings ("the chair of the court"), and

(b)   one or more members of the court as deputies to chair its meetings in the absence of the chair of the court.]

(4)   If a member of the court has any direct or indirect interest in any dealing or business with the Bank—

(a)   he shall disclose his interest to the court at the time of the dealing or business being negotiated or transacted, and

(b)   he shall have no vote in relation to the dealing or business, unless the court has resolved that the interest does not give rise to a conflict of interest.

(5)   A member of the court shall have no vote in relation to any question arising which touches or concerns him but shall withdraw and be absent during the debate of any matter in which he is concerned.

(6)   Subject to sub-paragraphs [(3)] to (5), the court shall determine its own procedure [(including quorum)].

Remuneration

14.—(1)   A person appointed as Governor or Deputy Governor of the Bank shall be entitled to be paid by the Bank such remuneration as it may determine.

(2)   The Bank may pay, or create and maintain a fund for the payment of, pensions or capital grants to members, or former members, of the court who have rendered exclusive services to the Bank.

15.   A director of the Bank shall be entitled to be paid by the Bank such remuneration as the Bank may determine with the approval of the Chancellor of the Exchequer.

[379]

NOTES

Para 1: sub-paras (3), (4) inserted by the Banking Act 2009, s 243(1), as from 1 June 2009.

Para 6: words in square brackets inserted by the Banking Act 2009, s 243(2), as from 1 June 2009.

Para 12: words in square brackets in sub-para (1), and sub-para (2) substituted by the Banking Act 2009, s 240, as from 1 June 2009.

Para 13: sub-para (2) repealed, sub-para (3) substituted, and in sub-para (6) reference in first pair of square brackets substituted and words in second pair of square brackets inserted by the Banking Act 2009, ss 241(1), 242(1), (3), as from 1 June 2009.

(*Sch 2 outside the scope of this work; see Butterworths Banking Law Handbook.*)

SCHEDULE 3
MONETARY POLICY COMMITTEE

Section 13

Terms of office of appointed members

1.   Appointment as a member of the Committee under section 13(2)(b) or (c) shall be for a period of 3 years, except that initially some appointments may be for shorter and different periods so as to secure that appointments expire at different times.

2.   A person appointed under section 13(2)(b) or (c) in place of a person who ceased to hold office before the end of the term for which he was appointed shall be appointed for the remainder of that person's term of office.

[2A.   A person may not be appointed as a member of the Committee under section 13(2)(c) more than twice.]

3.   A person appointed under section 13(2)(b) or (c) may resign his office by written notice to the Bank.

4.—(1)   A person who holds office as a member of the Committee under section 13(2)(c) shall be a servant of the Bank.

(2)   The terms and conditions of service under sub-paragraph (1) shall be such as the Bank may determine.

(3)   The function of determining terms and conditions of service under sub-paragraph (2) shall stand delegated to the sub-committee constituted by section 3.

Qualification for appointment

5.   A person is disqualified for appointment under section 13(2)(b) or (c) if—
  (a)   he is a Minister of the Crown, or a person serving in a government department in employment in respect of which remuneration is payable out of money provided by Parliament, or
  (b)   he is a member of the court of directors of the Bank.

6.   The fact that a person has held office under section 13(2)(b) or (c) does not disqualify him for further appointment to such office [(subject to paragraph 2A)].

Removal of appointed members

7.   A person appointed under section 13(2)(b) or (c) shall vacate office if he becomes a person to whom paragraph 5(a) or (b) applies.

8.   A person appointed under section 13(2)(b) shall vacate office if he ceases to have executive responsibility within the Bank for monetary policy analysis or, as the case may be, monetary policy operations.

9.—(1)   The Bank may, with the consent of the Chancellor of the Exchequer, remove a member appointed under section 13(2)(b) or (c) if it is satisfied—
  (a)   that he has been absent from the Committee's meetings for more than 3 months without the Committee's consent,
  (b)   that he has become bankrupt, that his estate has been sequestrated or that he has made an arrangement with or granted a trust deed for his creditors, or
  (c)   that he is unable or unfit to discharge his functions as a member.

  (2)   The function of removing a member under sub-paragraph (1) shall stand delegated to the sub-committee constituted by section 3.

Meetings

10.—(1)   The Committee shall meet at least once a month.

  (2)   The Governor of the Bank (or in his absence the Deputy Governor of the Bank with executive responsibility for monetary policy) may summon a meeting at any time on giving such notice as in his judgment the circumstances may require.

Proceedings

11.—(1)   At a meeting of the Committee, the proceedings shall be regulated as follows.

  (2)   The quorum shall be 6, of whom 2 must hold office as Governor or Deputy Governor of the Bank.

  (3)   The chair shall be taken by the Governor of the Bank or, if he is not present, the Deputy Governor of the Bank with executive responsibility for monetary policy.

  (4)   Decisions shall be taken by a vote of all those members present at the meeting.

  (5)   In the event of a tie, the chairman shall have a second casting vote.

  (6)   Subject to sub-paragraphs (2) to (5), the Committee shall determine its own procedure.

12.   The Committee may, in relation to sub-paragraph (2), (3) or (4) of paragraph 11, determine circumstances in which a member who is not present at, but is in communication with, a meeting, is to be treated for the purposes of that sub-paragraph as present at it.

13.   A representative of the Treasury may attend, and speak at, any meeting of the Committee.

Report to court of directors of the Bank

14.   The Committee shall submit a monthly report on its activities to the court of directors of the Bank.

Parliamentary disqualification

15.   ...

[380]

NOTES
  Para 2A: inserted by the Banking Act 2009, s 243(3), as from 1 June 2009.
  Para 6: words in square brackets inserted by the Banking Act 2009, s 243(4), as from 1 June 2009.
  Para 15: amends the House of Commons Disqualification Act 1975, Sch 1, Pt III, and the Northern Ireland Assembly Disqualification Act 1975, Sch 1, Pt III.

(Schs 4–9 outside the scope of this work; see Butterworths Banking Law Handbook.)

FINANCIAL SERVICES AND MARKETS ACT 2000

(2000 c 8)

ARRANGEMENT OF SECTIONS

PART I
THE REGULATOR

PART IV
PERMISSION TO CARRY ON REGULATED ACTIVITIES

Variation and cancellation of Part IV permission

PART XV
THE FINANCIAL SERVICES COMPENSATION SCHEME

The scheme manager

The scheme

Provisions of the scheme

Annual report

Information and documents

Miscellaneous

PART XXIX
INTERPRETATION

PART XXX
SUPPLEMENTAL

An Act to make provision about the regulation of financial services and markets; to provide for the

PART II
OTHER ACTS

transfer of certain statutory functions relating to building societies, friendly societies, industrial and provident societies and certain other mutual societies; and for connected purposes

[14 June 2000]

NOTES

Regulatory functions of the Financial Services Authority: the Legislative and Regulatory Reform Act 2006, s 21 imposes a duty on any person exercising a specified regulatory function to have regard to the five principles of good regulation. The principles provide that regulatory activities should be carried out in a way which is transparent, accountable, proportionate and consistent and should be targeted only at cases in which action is needed. Section 22 of the 2006 Act enables a Minister to issue a Code of Practice relating to the exercise of regulatory functions (the "Regulators' Compliance Code"). Section 22 imposes a duty on any person exercising a specified regulatory function to have regard to the Regulators' Compliance Code when determining general policies or principles by reference to which that person exercises those functions. The Legislative and Regulatory Reform (Regulatory Functions) Order 2007, SI 2007/3544, arts 2–4, Schedule, Pt 1 provide that ss 21, 22 of the 2006 Act apply to the regulatory functions of the FSA.

Application of Act to certain overseas investment exchanges and clearing houses: see the Companies Act 1989, s 170.

Application of Act to payment service providers: see the Payment Services Regulations 2009, SI 2009/209 at **[1127]** et seq. In particular, see Sch 5, Pt 1 to those Regulations at **[1259]** ("Application and Modification of the 2000 Act").

Exemption from requirement for contract for sale etc of land to be in writing: a contract regulated under this Act, other than a regulated mortgage contract, a regulated home reversion plan, a regulated home purchase plan, or a regulated sale and rent back agreement, is exempt from the Law of Property (Miscellaneous Provisions) Act 1989, s 2 (contracts for sale etc of land to be made by writing); see s 2(5) of that Act.

Transfer of functions – mutual societies: The Financial Services and Markets Act 2000 (Mutual Societies) Order 2001, SI 2001/2617, art 4(2) transfers to the Financial Services Authority certain functions which, immediately before 1 December 2001, were functions of: (a) the Chief Registrar of friendly societies, assistant registrars of friendly societies or the central office of the registry of friendly societies; (b) the Friendly Societies Commission; or (c) the Building Societies Commission. Sch 2 to the 2001 Order makes provisions concerning the application of this Act in relation to functions transferred to the Authority by the said art 4(2).

Regulated claims management services: with effect from 23 April 2007 (the day on which the Compensation Act 2006, s 4(1) came into force), a person who provides "regulated claims management services" (i) must be authorised under the 2006 Act to do so, or (ii) be exempted, or (iii) have the benefit of a waiver of the obligation to be authorised, or (iv) be an individual acting otherwise than in the course of business. The Compensation (Regulated Claims Management Services) Order 2006, SI 2006/3319 sets out the kinds of services to be regulated when provided in connection with certain kinds of claim, and this includes claims relating to financial products and services (see art 4(3)(f) of the 2006 Order). The Compensation (Exemptions) Order 2007, SI 2007/209, art 5 exempts a person who is carrying out a regulated claims management service if in providing that service he is carrying on a regulated activity or would be doing so except that he is exempt from the general prohibition under FSMA, or he has the benefit of an exclusion under the Financial Services and Markets Act 2000 (Regulated Activities) Order 2001.

Banking (Special Provisions) Act 2008 and Banking Act 2009: various Orders made under the 2008 and 2009 Acts apply and modify certain provisions of this Act in relation to the banks and building societies that are the subject of the Orders; see:

- the Northern Rock plc Transfer Order 2008, SI 2008/432;
- the Northern Rock plc Compensation Scheme Order 2008, SI 2008/718;
- the Bradford & Bingley plc Transfer of Securities and Property etc Order 2008, SI 2008/2546 at **[963]**;
- the Heritable Bank plc Transfer of Certain Rights and Liabilities Order 2008, SI 2008/2644 at **[1008]**;
- the Transfer of Rights and Liabilities to ING Order 2008, SI 2008/2666 at **[1046]**;
- the Kaupthing Singer & Friedlander Limited Transfer of Certain Rights and Liabilities Order 2008, SI 2008/2674 at **[1078]**;
- the Bradford & Bingley plc Compensation Scheme Order 2008, SI 2008/3249 at **[1113]**;
- the Amendments to Law (Resolution of Dunfermline Building Society) Order 2009, SI 2009/814 at **[565]**.

Application to bank insolvency and administration: as to the application of this Act to bank insolvency and administration, see the Banking Act 2009 (Parts 2 and 3 Consequential Amendments) Order 2009, SI 2009/317 at **[524]** et seq.

Solicitors: references to solicitors, etc: a registered European lawyer may provide professional activities by way of legal advice and assistance or legal aid under this Act and references to a solicitor, counsel or legal representative shall be interpreted accordingly: see the European Communities (Lawyer's Practice) Regulations 2000, SI 2000/1119, reg 14, Sch 3, Pt 1 (as amended by the European Communities (Lawyer's Practice) (Amendment) Regulations 2004, SI 2004/1628).

PART I

THE REGULATOR

1 The Financial Services Authority

(1)   The body corporate known as the Financial Services Authority ("the Authority") is to have the functions conferred on it by or under this Act.

(2)   The Authority must comply with the requirements as to its constitution set out in Schedule 1.

(3)   Schedule 1 also makes provision about the status of the Authority and the exercise of certain of its functions.

[(4) Section 249 of the Banking Act 2009 provides for references to functions of the Authority (whether generally or under this Act) to include references to functions conferred on the Authority by that Act (subject to any order under that section).]

[381]

NOTES
Sub-s (4): added by the Banking Act 2009, s 249, as from 21 February 2009.
Note: the FSA is the same corporate entity as the former Securities and Investments Board and later assumed functions under the Banking Act 1985 and exercised other functions on behalf of the Treasury under other financial services legislation.
The self regulating bodies (the Securities and Futures Authority, the Investment Management Regulatory Organisation and the Personal Investment Authority) established under the Financial Services Act 1986 were constituted as companies limited by guarantee and were wound up on the designated dates specified under the Financial Services and Markets Act 2000 (Transitional Provisions) (Designated Date for The Securities and Futures Authority) Order 2001, SI 2001/2255, and the Financial Services and Markets (Transitional Provisions) (Designated Date for Certain Self-Regulating Organisations) Order 2000, SI 2000/1734.

2–39A (*Ss 2–18, ss 19–39A* (*Pts II, III*) *outside the scope of this work; see Butterworths Banking Law Handbook or Butterworths Securities and Financial Services Law Handbook.*)

PART IV
PERMISSION TO CARRY ON REGULATED ACTIVITIES

NOTES
Transitional provisions: the Financial Services and Markets Act 2000 (Transitional Provisions) (Authorised Persons etc) Order 2001, SI 2001/2636, Pt II, Chapter I provides that persons who are authorised or exempted from the need for authorisation under provisions of the previous regulatory regimes are treated, as from 1 December 2001, as having permission under Pt IV of this Act to carry on the activities they were lawfully able to carry on immediately before that date by reason of that authorisation or exemption. Pt II of SI 2001/2636 applies to: (a) persons authorised or exempted under the Financial Services Act 1986 (repealed by the Financial Services and Markets Act 2000 (Consequential Amendments and Repeals) Order 2001, SI 2001/3649, art 3(1)(c)); (b) persons authorised under the Banking Act 1987 (repealed by SI 2001/3649, art 3(1)(d)); (c) insurance companies; (d) friendly societies; and (e) building societies.
Pt III of SI 2001/2636 provides that restrictions and prohibitions imposed under provisions of the previous regulatory regimes on authorised persons are to have effect after 1 December 2001 as if they were requirements imposed under s 43 (in relation to persons with a permission under Pt IV of this Act). Pt III of SI 2001/2636 applies to: (a) prohibitions and requirements under the Financial Services Act 1986 (repealed as noted above); (b) restrictions and directions under the Banking Act 1987 (repealed as noted above); (c) directions and requirements under the Insurance Companies Act 1982 (repealed by SI 2001/3649, art 3(1)(b)); (d) conditions and directions under the Friendly Societies Act 1992; (e) conditions and directions under the Building Societies Act 1986; and (f) prohibitions and restrictions under the Banking Coordination (Second Council Directive) Regulations 1992, SI 1992/3218 (revoked by SI 2001/3649, art 3(2)(a)) and the Investment Services Regulations 1995, SI 1995/3275 (revoked by SI 2001/3649, art 3(2)(c)).
See also, the Financial Services and Markets Act 2000 (Permission and Applications) (Credit Unions etc) Order 2002, SI 2002/704 (transitional provisions relating to the expiry, on 2 July 2002, of the transitional exemption of credit unions from the general prohibition imposed by s 19 of this Act (see the Financial Services and Markets Act 2000 (Exemption) Order 2001, SI 2001/1201, art 6).
See also, the Financial Services and Markets Act 2000 (Consequential and Transitional Provisions) (Miscellaneous) (No 2) Order 2001, SI 2001/2659 (transitional provisions in consequence of the Financial Services and Markets Act 2000 (Commencement No 5) Order (SI 2001/2632). That Order brings into force the provisions of the Act relating to (among other things) the making of applications under the Act for permission or authorisation coming into force on 1 December 2001).
Interim permissions and interim approvals: see the Financial Services and Markets Act 2000 (Interim Permissions) Order 2001, SI 2001/3374. This Order conferred an interim permission on certain applicants who applied to the FSA for permission under this Part and whose application was pending on the date when the main provisions of the Act come into force (1 December 2001). The scope of the Order is limited by arts 3–5 to those applicants who were lawfully carrying on the activity which was regulated for the first time under this Act. In order to ensure that their business was not disrupted by the fact that the activity became a regulated activity while their application for permission was pending, an applicant who applied for permission before 31 October 2001 and who opted to benefit from the provisions of this Order had an interim permission to enable him to continue to carry on that activity until his application was determined. The Order does not apply to those who were carrying on an activity which was regulated under previous legislation since they benefited from a Part IV permission conferred by the Financial Services and Markets Act 2000 (Transitional Provisions) (Authorised Persons etc) Order 2001, SI 2001/2636 (see above). See also art 8 of this Order (interim permission lapses at the time when it is superseded by the grant of the application or when the application is withdrawn or refused), and art 9 (which conferred interim approval on people who were working for a person who benefited from interim permission if those people would have needed approval under this Part). Article 12 conferred a power on the Authority to modify the rules and guidance it makes under this Act as it applies to persons with interim permission. Article 13 and the Schedule to the Order provided for the application of provisions in this Part and Part V (and various other provisions of this Act and the Regulated Activities Order) to persons who have interim permission under this Order.
As to interim permissions, interim approvals and the application of this Part and Part V (and various other provisions of this Act) to various activities that have become regulated activities following the amendment of the Regulated Activities Order, see the table below:

PART II
OTHER ACTS

Order	Regulated Activity
Financial Services and Markets Act 2000 (Transitional Provisions) (Mortgages) Order 2004, SI 2004/2615	Certain mortgage mediation activities
Financial Services and Markets Act 2000 (Regulated Activities) (Amendment) (No 2) Order 2004, SI 2004/2737	Advice on stakeholder products
Financial Services and Markets Act 2000 (Transitional Provisions) (General Insurance Intermediaries) Order 2004, SI 2004/3351	Certain general insurance mediation activities
Financial Services and Markets Act 2000 (Regulated Activities) (Amendment) Order 2006, SI 2006/1969	Establishing, operating or winding up a personal pension scheme, or activities which relate to the specified investment of rights under a personal pension scheme
Financial Services and Markets Act 2000 (Regulated Activities) (Amendment) (No 2) Order 2006, SI 2006/2383	Administering, arranging or advising on regulated home reversion plans or regulated home purchase plans
Financial Services and Markets Act 2000 (Regulated Activities) (Amendment) (No 2) Order 2007, SI 2007/3510	Provision of travel insurance in certain circumstances
Financial Services and Markets Act 2000 (Regulated Activities) (Amendment) Order 2009, SI 2009/1342	Entering into, administering, arranging and advising on regulated sale and rent back agreements

40–43   (*Outside the scope of this work; see Butterworths Banking Law Handbook or Butterworths Securities and Financial Services Law Handbook.*)

Variation and cancellation of Part IV permission

44   (*Outside the scope of this work; see Butterworths Banking Law Handbook or Butterworths Securities and Financial Services Law Handbook.*)

45   Variation etc on the Authority's own initiative

(1)   The Authority may exercise its power under this section in relation to an authorised person if it appears to it that—

    (a)   he is failing, or is likely to fail, to satisfy the threshold conditions;

    (b)   he has failed, during a period of at least 12 months, to carry on a regulated activity for which he has a Part IV permission; or

    (c)   it is desirable to exercise that power in order to protect the interests of consumers or potential consumers [(whether of the services of the authorised person or of the services of other authorised persons)].

(2)   The Authority's power under this section is the power to vary a Part IV permission in any of the ways mentioned in section 44(1) or to cancel it.

[(2A)   Without prejudice to the generality of subsections (1) and (2), the Authority may, in relation to an authorised person who is an investment firm, exercise its power under this section to cancel the Part IV permission of the firm if it appears to it that—

    (a)   the firm has failed, during a period of at least six months, to carry on a regulated activity which is an investment service or activity for which it has a Part IV permission;

    (b)   the firm obtained the Part IV permission by making a false statement or by other irregular means;

    (c)   the firm no longer satisfies the requirements for authorisation pursuant to Chapter I of Title II of the markets in financial instruments directive, or pursuant to or contained in any Community legislation made under that Chapter, in relation to a regulated activity which is an investment service or activity for which it has a Part IV permission; or

    (d)   the firm has seriously and systematically infringed the operating conditions pursuant to Chapter II of Title II of the markets in financial instruments directive, or pursuant to or contained in any Community legislation made under that Chapter, in relation to a regulated activity which is an investment service or activity for which it has a Part IV permission.

(2B)   For the purposes of subsection (2A) a regulated activity is an investment service or activity if it falls within the definition of "investment services and activities" in section 417(1).]

(3)   If, as a result of a variation of a Part IV permission under this section, there are no longer any regulated activities for which the authorised person concerned has permission, the Authority must, once it is satisfied that it is no longer necessary to keep the permission in force, cancel it.

(4)   The Authority's power to vary a Part IV permission under this section extends to including any provision in the permission as varied that could be included if a fresh permission were being given in response to an application under section 40.

(5)   The Authority's power under this section is referred to in this Part as its own-initiative power.

[382]

NOTES
Sub-s (1): words in square brackets inserted the Banking Act 2009, s 248, as from 21 February 2009.
Sub-ss (2A), (2B): inserted by the Financial Services and Markets Act 2000 (Markets in Financial Instruments) Regulations 2007, SI 2007/126, reg 3(5), Sch 5, paras 1, 4, as from 1 April 2007 (certain purposes (see reg 1(2) thereof), and as from 1 November 2007 (otherwise).

46–211   (*Ss 46–55, ss 56–211 (Pts V–XIV) outside the scope of this work; see Butterworths Banking Law Handbook or Butterworths Securities and Financial Services Law Handbook.*)

PART XV
THE FINANCIAL SERVICES COMPENSATION SCHEME

NOTES
Transitional provisions: see the Financial Services and Markets Act 2000 (Transitional Provisions, Repeals and Savings) (Financial Services Compensation Scheme) Order 2001, SI 2001/2967, which makes transitional provisions in connection with the Financial Services Compensation Scheme. This scheme supersedes eight former compensation schemes; ie, the Policyholders Protection Scheme, the Deposit Protection Scheme, the Building Societies Investor Protection Scheme, the Investor Compensation Scheme, the section 43 Compensation Scheme, the Friendly Societies Protection Scheme, the Personal Investment Authority indemnity scheme, and the arrangements described in the ABI/ICS agreement ("the ABI scheme"). In relation to credit unions, see also the Financial Services and Markets Act 2000 (Consequential Amendments and Transitional Provisions) (Credit Unions) Order 2002, SI 2002/1501, art 5.

The scheme manager

212   The scheme manager

(1)   The Authority must establish a body corporate ("the scheme manager") to exercise the functions conferred on the scheme manager by or under this Part.

(2)   The Authority must take such steps as are necessary to ensure that the scheme manager is, at all times, capable of exercising those functions.

(3)   The constitution of the scheme manager must provide for it to have—
    (a)   a chairman; and
    (b)   a board (which must include the chairman) whose members are the scheme manager's directors.

(4)   The chairman and other members of the board must be persons appointed, and liable to removal from office, by the Authority (acting, in the case of the chairman, with the approval of the Treasury).

(5)   But the terms of their appointment (and in particular those governing removal from office) must be such as to secure their independence from the Authority in the operation of the compensation scheme.

(6)   The scheme manager is not to be regarded as exercising functions on behalf of the Crown.

(7)   The scheme manager's board members, officers and staff are not to be regarded as Crown servants.

[383]

The scheme

213   The compensation scheme

(1)   The Authority must by rules establish a scheme for compensating persons in cases where relevant persons are unable, or are likely to be unable, to satisfy claims against them.

(2)   The rules are to be known as the Financial Services Compensation Scheme (but are referred to in this Act as "the compensation scheme").

(3)   The compensation scheme must, in particular, provide for the scheme manager—
    (a)   to assess and pay compensation, in accordance with the scheme, to claimants in respect of claims made in connection with regulated activities carried on (whether or not with permission) by relevant persons; and
    (b)   to have power to impose levies on authorised persons, or any class of authorised person,

PART II
OTHER ACTS

for the purpose of meeting its expenses (including in particular expenses incurred, or expected to be incurred, in paying compensation, borrowing or insuring risks).

(4)   The compensation scheme may provide for the scheme manager to have power to impose levies on authorised persons, or any class of authorised person, for the purpose of recovering the cost (whenever incurred) of establishing the scheme.

(5)   In making any provision of the scheme by virtue of subsection (3)(b), the Authority must take account of the desirability of ensuring that the amount of the levies imposed on a particular class of authorised person reflects, so far as practicable, the amount of the claims made, or likely to be made, in respect of that class of person.

(6)   An amount payable to the scheme manager as a result of any provision of the scheme made by virtue of subsection (3)(b) or (4) may be recovered as a debt due to the scheme manager.

(7)   Sections 214 to 217 make further provision about the scheme but are not to be taken as limiting the power conferred on the Authority by subsection (1) [(except where limitations are expressly stated)].

(8)   In those sections "specified" means specified in the scheme.

(9)   In this Part (except in sections 219, 220 or 224) "relevant person" means a person who was—

    (a)   an authorised person at the time the act or omission giving rise to the claim against him took place; or

    (b)   an appointed representative at that time.

(10)   But a person who, at that time—

    (a)   qualified for authorisation under Schedule 3, and

    (b)   fell within a prescribed category,

is not to be regarded as a relevant person in relation to any activities for which he had permission as a result of any provision of, or made under, that Schedule unless he had elected to participate in the scheme in relation to those activities at that time.

[384]

NOTES

Sub-s (7): words in square brackets inserted by the Banking Act 2009, s 170(2), as from a day to be appointed.

Note: membership of the scheme is voluntary for those who qualify for authorisation under Sch 3 to this Act (ie, incoming EEA firms authorised under Sch 3). The compensation scheme may provide that incoming EEA firms can elect to participate in relation to some or all the activities for which it has permission under Sch 3 (see s 214(5)). The Financial Services and Markets Act 2000 (Compensation Scheme: Electing Participants) Regulations 2001, SI 2001/1783, reg 3, as amended, prescribes the categories of firms to which this applies, ie, investment firms, relevant management companies under the UCITS management directive, credit institutions with UK branches, and any insurance intermediary which is not an investment firm or a credit institution. The Financial Services Compensation Scheme provides information including a list of those firms that have voluntarily joined the scheme. See http://www.fscs.org.uk/consumer/how_to_claim/deposits/eea_firms_that_have_topped_up.

Regulations: the Financial Services and Markets Act 2000 (Compensation Scheme: Electing Participants) Regulations 2001, SI 2001/1783.

Provisions of the scheme

214   General

(1)   The compensation scheme may, in particular, make provision—

    (a)   as to the circumstances in which a relevant person is to be taken (for the purposes of the scheme) to be unable, or likely to be unable, to satisfy claims made against him;

    (b)   for the establishment of different funds for meeting different kinds of claim;

    (c)   for the imposition of different levies in different cases;

    (d)   limiting the levy payable by a person in respect of a specified period;

    (e)   for repayment of the whole or part of a levy in specified circumstances;

    (f)   for a claim to be entertained only if it is made by a specified kind of claimant;

    (g)   for a claim to be entertained only if it falls within a specified kind of claim;

    (h)   as to the procedure to be followed in making a claim;

    (i)   for the making of interim payments before a claim is finally determined;

    (j)   limiting the amount payable on a claim to a specified maximum amount or a maximum amount calculated in a specified manner;

    (k)   for payment to be made, in specified circumstances, to a person other than the claimant.

[(1A)   Rules by virtue of subsection (1)(h) may, in particular, allow the scheme manager to treat persons who are or may be entitled to claim under the scheme as if they had done so.

(1B)   A reference in any enactment or instrument to a claim or claimant under this Part includes a reference to a deemed claim or claimant in accordance with subsection (1A).

(1C)   Rules by virtue of subsection (1)(j) may, in particular, allow, or be subject to rules which allow, the scheme manager to settle a class of claim by payment of sums fixed without reference to, or by modification of, the normal rules for calculation of maximum entitlement for individual claims.]

(2)   Different provision may be made with respect to different kinds of claim.

(3)   The scheme may provide for the determination and regulation of matters relating to the scheme by the scheme manager.

(4)   The scheme, or particular provisions of the scheme, may be made so as to apply only in relation to—
(a)   activities carried on,
(b)   claimants,
(c)   matters arising, or
(d)   events occurring,
in specified territories, areas or localities.

(5)   The scheme may provide for a person who—
(a)   qualifies for authorisation under Schedule 3, and
(b)   falls within a prescribed category,
to elect to participate in the scheme in relation to some or all of the activities for which he has permission as a result of any provision of, or made under, that Schedule.

(6)   The scheme may provide for the scheme manager to have power—
(a)   in specified circumstances,
(b)   but only if the scheme manager is satisfied that the claimant is entitled to receive a payment in respect of his claim—
    (i)   under a scheme which is comparable to the compensation scheme, or
    (ii)   as the result of a guarantee given by a government or other authority,
to make a full payment of compensation to the claimant and recover the whole or part of the amount of that payment from the other scheme or under that guarantee.

[385]

NOTES
Sub-ss (1A)–(1C): inserted by the Banking Act 2009, s 174(1), as from 21 February 2009.
Regulations: the Financial Services and Markets Act 2000 (Compensation Scheme: Electing Participants) Regulations 2001, SI 2001/1783.

[214A   Contingency funding

(1)   The Treasury may make regulations ("contingency fund regulations") permitting the scheme manager to impose levies under section 213 for the purpose of maintaining contingency funds from which possible expenses may be paid.

(2)   Contingency fund regulations may make provision about the establishment and management of contingency funds; in particular, the regulations may make provision about—
(a)   the number and size of funds;
(b)   the circumstances and timing of their establishment;
(c)   the classes of person from whom contributions to the funds may be levied;
(d)   the amount and timing of payments into and out of funds (which may include provision for different levies for different classes of person);
(e)   refunds;
(f)   the ways in which funds' contents may be invested (including (i) the extent of reliance on section 223A, and (ii) the application of investment income);
(g)   the purposes for which funds may be applied, but only so as to determine whether a fund is to be used (i) for the payment of compensation, (ii) for the purposes of co-operating with a bank liquidator in accordance with section 99 of the Banking Act 2009, or (iii) for contributions under section 214B;
(h)   procedures to be followed in connection with funds, including the keeping of records and the provision of information.

(3)   The compensation scheme may include provision about contingency funds provided that it is not inconsistent with contingency fund regulations.]

[386]

NOTES
Commencement: to be appointed.
Inserted by the Banking Act 2009, s 170(1), as from a day to be appointed.

[214B   Contribution to costs of special resolution regime

(1)   This section applies where—

(a)   a stabilisation power under Part 1 of the Banking Act 2009 has been exercised in respect of a bank, building society or credit union (within the meaning of that Part), and

(b)   the Treasury think that the bank, building society or credit union was, or but for the exercise of the stabilisation power would have become, unable to satisfy claims against it.

(2)   Where this section applies—

(a)   the Treasury may require the scheme manager to make payments in connection with the exercise of the stabilisation power, and

(b)   payments shall be treated as expenditure under the scheme for all purposes (including levies, contingency funds and borrowing).

(3)   The Treasury shall make regulations—

(a)   specifying what expenses the scheme manager may be required to incur under subsection (2),

(b)   providing for independent verification of the nature and amount of expenses incurred in connection with the exercise of the stabilisation power (which may include provision about appointment and payment of an auditor), and

(c)   providing for the method by which amounts to be paid are to be determined.

(4)   The regulations must ensure that payments required do not exceed the amount of compensation that would have been payable under the scheme if the stabilisation power had not been exercised and the bank had been unable to satisfy claims against it; and for that purpose the amount of compensation that would have been payable does not include—

(a)   amounts that would have been likely, at the time when the stabilisation power was exercised, to be recovered by the scheme from the bank, or

(b)   any compensation actually paid to an eligible depositor of the bank.

(5)   The regulations must provide for the appointment of an independent valuer (who may be the person appointed as valuer under section 54 of the Banking Act 2009 in respect of the exercise of the stabilisation power) to calculate the amounts referred to in subsection (4)(a); and the regulations—

(a)   must provide for the valuer to be appointed by the Treasury or by a person designated by the Treasury,

(b)   must include provision enabling the valuer to reconsider a decision,

(c)   must provide a right of appeal to a court or tribunal,

(d)   must provide for payment of the valuer,

(e)   may replicate or apply a provision of section 54 or 55, and

(f)   may apply or include any provision that is or could be made under that section.

(6)   Payments required to be made by the scheme by virtue of section 61 of the Banking Act 2009 (special resolution regime: compensation) shall be treated for the purposes of subsection (4) as if required to be made under this section.

(7)   The regulations may include provision for payments (including payments under those provisions of the Banking Act 2009) to be made—

(a)   before verification in accordance with subsection (3)(b), and

(b)   before the calculation of the limit imposed by subsection (4), by reference to estimates of that limit and subject to any necessary later adjustment.

(8)   The regulations may include provision—

(a)   about timing;

(b)   about procedures to be followed;

(c)   for discretionary functions to be exercised by a specified body or by persons of a specified class;

(d)   about the resolution of disputes (which may include provision conferring jurisdiction on a court or tribunal).

(9)   The compensation scheme may include provision about payments under and levies in connection with this section, provided that it is not inconsistent with this section or regulations under it.]

[387]

NOTES

Commencement: 17 February 2009 (in so far as conferring or relating to any power to make subordinate legislation); 21 February 2009 (otherwise).

Inserted by the Banking Act 2009, s 171(1), as from 17 February 2009 (in so far as conferring or relating to any power to make subordinate legislation), and as from 21 February 2009 (otherwise).

Regulations: the Financial Services and Markets Act 2000 (Contribution to Costs of Special Resolution Regime) Regulations 2009, SI 2009/807.

215   [Rights of the scheme in insolvency]

[(1)   The compensation scheme may make provision—

(a) about the effect of a payment of compensation under the scheme on rights or obligations arising out of matters in connection with which the compensation was paid;

(b) giving the scheme manager a right of recovery in respect of those rights or obligations.]

(2) Such a right of recovery conferred by the scheme does not, in the event of [a person's insolvency], exceed such right (if any) as the claimant would have had in that event.

(3) If a person other than the scheme manager [makes an administration application under Schedule B1 to the 1986 Act or [Schedule B1 to] the 1989 Order] in relation to a company or partnership which is a relevant person, the scheme manager has the same rights as are conferred on the Authority by section 362.

[(3A) In subsection (3) the reference to making an administration application includes a reference to—

(a) appointing an administrator under paragraph 14 or 22 of Schedule B1 to the 1986 Act [or paragraph 15 or 23 of Schedule B1 to the 1989 Order], or

(b) filing with the court a copy of notice of intention to appoint an administrator under [any] of those paragraphs.]

(4) If a person other than the scheme manager presents a petition for the winding up of a body which is a relevant person, the scheme manager has the same rights as are conferred on the Authority by section 371.

(5) If a person other than the scheme manager presents a bankruptcy petition to the court in relation to an individual who, or an entity which, is a relevant person, the scheme manager has the same rights as are conferred on the Authority by section 374.

(6) Insolvency rules may be made for the purpose of integrating any procedure for which provision is made as a result of subsection (1) into the general procedure on the administration of a company or partnership or on a winding-up, bankruptcy or sequestration.

(7) "Bankruptcy petition" means a petition to the court—

(a) under section 264 of the 1986 Act or Article 238 of the 1989 Order for a bankruptcy order to be made against an individual;

(b) under section 5 of the 1985 Act for the sequestration of the estate of an individual; or

(c) under section 6 of the 1985 Act for the sequestration of the estate belonging to or held for or jointly by the members of an entity mentioned in subsection (1) of that section.

(8) "Insolvency rules" are—

(a) for England and Wales, rules made under sections 411 and 412 of the 1986 Act;

(b) for Scotland, rules made by order by the Treasury, after consultation with the Scottish Ministers, for the purposes of this section; and

(c) for Northern Ireland, rules made under Article 359 of the 1989 Order and section 55 of the Judicature (Northern Ireland) Act 1978.

(9) "The 1985 Act", "the 1986 Act", "the 1989 Order" and "court" have the same meaning as in Part XXIV.

[388]

NOTES

Section heading: words in square brackets substituted by the Banking Act 2009, s 175(1), (4), as from 21 February 2009.

Sub-s (1): substituted by the Banking Act 2009, s 175(1), (2), as from 21 February 2009.

Sub-s (2): words in square brackets substituted by the Banking Act 2009, s 175(1), (3), as from 21 February 2009.

Sub-s (3): words in first pair of square brackets substituted by the Enterprise Act 2002, s 248(3), Sch 17, paras 53, 54(1), (2), as from 15 September 2003 (for savings and transitional provisions in relation to a petition for an administration order presented before that date, and in relation to special administration regimes (within the meaning of the Enterprise Act 2002, s 249)); words in second pair of square brackets substituted by the Insolvency (Northern Ireland) Order 2005, SI 2005/1455, art 3(3), Sch 2, paras 56, 57(1), (2), as from 27 March 2006.

Sub-s (3A): inserted by the Enterprise Act 2002, s 248(3), Sch 17, paras 53, 54(1), (3), as from 15 September 2003 (subject to savings and transitional provisions as noted above); words in square brackets in para (a) inserted, and word in square brackets in para (b) substituted, by SI 2005/1455, art 3(3), Sch 2, paras 56, 57(1), (3), as from 27 March 2006.

Limited liability partnerships: this section applies to limited liability partnerships (except where the context otherwise requires and subject to certain modifications); see the Limited Liability Partnerships Regulations 2001, SI 2001/1090, reg 6.

---

216 Continuity of long-term insurance policies

(1) The compensation scheme may, in particular, include provision requiring the scheme manager to make arrangements for securing continuity of insurance for policyholders, or policyholders of a specified class, of relevant long-term insurers.

(2) "Relevant long-term insurers" means relevant persons who—

(a) have permission to effect or carry out contracts of long-term insurance; and

(b)   are unable, or likely to be unable, to satisfy claims made against them.

(3)   The scheme may provide for the scheme manager to take such measures as appear to him to be appropriate—

(a)   for securing or facilitating the transfer of a relevant long-term insurer's business so far as it consists of the carrying out of contracts of long-term insurance, or of any part of that business, to another authorised person;

(b)   for securing the issue by another authorised person to the policyholders concerned of policies in substitution for their existing policies.

(4)   The scheme may also provide for the scheme manager to make payments to the policyholders concerned—

(a)   during any period while he is seeking to make arrangements mentioned in subsection (1);

(b)   if it appears to him that it is not reasonably practicable to make such arrangements.

(5)   A provision of the scheme made by virtue of section 213(3)(b) may include power to impose levies for the purpose of meeting expenses of the scheme manager incurred in—

(a)   taking measures as a result of any provision of the scheme made by virtue of subsection (3);

(b)   making payments as a result of any such provision made by virtue of subsection (4).

[389]

217   Insurers in financial difficulties

(1)   The compensation scheme may, in particular, include provision for the scheme manager to have power to take measures for safeguarding policyholders, or policyholders of a specified class, of relevant insurers.

(2)   "Relevant insurers" means relevant persons who—

(a)   have permission to effect or carry out contracts of insurance; and

(b)   are in financial difficulties.

(3)   The measures may include such measures as the scheme manager considers appropriate for—

(a)   securing or facilitating the transfer of a relevant insurer's business so far as it consists of the carrying out of contracts of insurance, or of any part of that business, to another authorised person;

(b)   giving assistance to the relevant insurer to enable it to continue to effect or carry out contracts of insurance.

(4)   The scheme may provide—

(a)   that if measures of a kind mentioned in subsection (3)(a) are to be taken, they should be on terms appearing to the scheme manager to be appropriate, including terms reducing, or deferring payment of, any of the things to which any of those who are eligible policyholders in relation to the relevant insurer are entitled in their capacity as such;

(b)   that if measures of a kind mentioned in subsection (3)(b) are to be taken, they should be conditional on the reduction of, or the deferment of the payment of, the things to which any of those who are eligible policyholders in relation to the relevant insurer are entitled in their capacity as such;

(c)   for ensuring that measures of a kind mentioned in subsection (3)(b) do not benefit to any material extent persons who were members of a relevant insurer when it began to be in financial difficulties or who had any responsibility for, or who may have profited from, the circumstances giving rise to its financial difficulties, except in specified circumstances;

(d)   for requiring the scheme manager to be satisfied that any measures he proposes to take are likely to cost less than it would cost to pay compensation under the scheme if the relevant insurer became unable, or likely to be unable, to satisfy claims made against him.

(5)   The scheme may provide for the Authority to have power—

(a)   to give such assistance to the scheme manager as it considers appropriate for assisting the scheme manager to determine what measures are practicable or desirable in the case of a particular relevant insurer;

(b)   to impose constraints on the taking of measures by the scheme manager in the case of a particular relevant insurer;

(c)   to require the scheme manager to provide it with information about any particular measures which the scheme manager is proposing to take.

(6)   The scheme may include provision for the scheme manager to have power—

(a)   to make interim payments in respect of eligible policyholders of a relevant insurer;

(b)   to indemnify any person making payments to eligible policyholders of a relevant insurer.

(7)   A provision of the scheme made by virtue of section 213(3)(b) may include power to impose levies for the purpose of meeting expenses of the scheme manager incurred in—
  (a)   taking measures as a result of any provision of the scheme made by virtue of subsection (1);
  (b)   making payments or giving indemnities as a result of any such provision made by virtue of subsection (6).

(8)   "Financial difficulties" and "eligible policyholders" have such meanings as may be specified.

[390]

Annual report

218   Annual report

(1)   At least once a year, the scheme manager must make a report to the Authority [and the Treasury] on the discharge of its functions.

(2)   The report must—
  (a)   include a statement setting out the value of each of the funds established by the compensation scheme; and
  (b)   comply with any requirements specified in rules made by the Authority [or in contingency fund regulations].

(3)   The scheme manager must publish each report in the way it considers appropriate.

[391]

NOTES

Sub-ss (1), (2): words in square brackets inserted by the Banking Act 2009, s 170(3), as from a day to be appointed.

Information and documents

[218A   Authority's power to require information

(1)   The Authority may make rules enabling the Authority to require authorised persons to provide information, which may then be made available to the scheme manager by the Authority.

(2)   A requirement may be imposed only if the Authority thinks the information is of a kind that may be of use to the scheme manager in connection with functions in respect of the scheme.

(3)   A requirement under this section may apply—
  (a)   to authorised persons generally or only to specified persons or classes of person;
  (b)   to the provision of information at specified periods, in connection with specified events or in other ways.

(4)   In addition to requirements under this section, a notice under section 165 may relate to information or documents which the Authority thinks are reasonably required by the scheme manager in connection with the performance of functions in respect of the scheme; and section 165(4) is subject to this subsection.

(5)   Rules under subsection (1) shall be prepared, made and treated in the same way as (and may be combined with) the Authority's general rules.]

[392]

NOTES

Commencement: 21 February 2009.
Inserted by the Banking Act 2009, s 176(1), as from 21 February 2009.

219   Scheme manager's power to require information

(1)   The scheme manager may, by notice in writing [require a person]—
  (a)   to provide specified information or information of a specified description; or
  (b)   to produce specified documents or documents of a specified description.

[(1A)   A requirement may be imposed only—
  (a)   on a person (P) against whom a claim has been made under the scheme,
  (b)   on a person (P) who is unable or likely to be unable to satisfy claims under the scheme against P,
  (c)   on a person ("the Third Party") whom the scheme manager thinks was knowingly involved in matters giving rise to a claim against another person (P) under the scheme, or
  (d)   on a person ("the Third Party") whom the scheme manager thinks was knowingly involved in matters giving rise to the actual or likely inability of another person (P) to satisfy claims under the scheme.

(1B)   For the purposes of subsection (1A)(b) and (d) whether P is unable or likely to be unable to satisfy claims shall be determined in accordance with provision to be made by the scheme (which may, in particular—

(a)   apply or replicate, with or without modifications, a provision of an enactment;

(b)   confer discretion on a specified person).]

(2)   The information or documents must be provided or produced—

(a)   before the end of such reasonable period as may be specified; and

(b)   in the case of information, in such manner or form as may be specified.

(3)   This section applies only to information and documents the provision or production of which the scheme manager considers [to be necessary (or likely to be necessary) for the fair determination of claims which have been or may be made against P].

[(3A)   Where a stabilisation power under Part 1 of the Banking Act 2009 has been exercised in respect of a bank, the scheme manager may by notice in writing require the bank or the Bank of England to provide information that the scheme manager requires for the purpose of applying regulations under section 214B(3) above.]

(4)   If a document is produced in response to a requirement imposed under this section, the scheme manager may—

(a)   take copies or extracts from the document; or

(b)   require the person producing the document to provide an explanation of the document.

(5)   If a person who is required under this section to produce a document fails to do so, the scheme manager may require the person to state, to the best of his knowledge and belief, where the document is.

(6)   If [P] is insolvent, no requirement may be imposed under this section on a person to whom section 220 or 224 applies.

(7)   If a person claims a lien on a document, its production under this Part does not affect the lien.

(8)   ...

(9)   "Specified" means specified in the notice given under subsection (1).

(10)   ...

[393]

NOTES

Sub-s (1): words in square brackets substituted by the Banking Act 2009, s 176(2), (3), as from 21 February 2009.

Sub-ss (1A), (1B), (3A): inserted by the Banking Act 2009, s 176(2), (4), (6), as from 21 February 2009.

Sub-s (3): words in square brackets substituted by the Banking Act 2009, s 176(2), (5), as from 21 February 2009.

Sub-s (6): letter in square brackets substituted by the Banking Act 2009, s 176(2), (7), as from 21 February 2009.

Sub-ss (8), (10): repealed by the Banking Act 2009, s 176(2), (8), (9), as from 21 February 2009.

220   Scheme manager's power to inspect information held by liquidator etc

(1)   For the purpose of assisting the scheme manager to discharge its functions in relation to a claim made in respect of an insolvent relevant person, a person to whom this section applies must permit a person authorised by the scheme manager to inspect relevant documents.

(2)   A person inspecting a document under this section may take copies of, or extracts from, the document.

(3)   This section applies to—

(a)   the administrative receiver, administrator, liquidator[, bank liquidator][, building society liquidator] or trustee in bankruptcy of an insolvent relevant person;

(b)   the permanent trustee, within the meaning of the Bankruptcy (Scotland) Act 1985, on the estate of an insolvent relevant person.

(4)   This section does not apply to a liquidator, administrator or trustee in bankruptcy who is—

(a)   the Official Receiver;

(b)   the Official Receiver for Northern Ireland; or

(c)   the Accountant in Bankruptcy.

(5)   "Relevant person" has the same meaning as in section 224.

[394]

NOTES

Sub-s (3): words in first pair of square brackets inserted by the Banking Act 2009, s 123(3), as from 21 February 2009; words in second pair of square brackets inserted by the Building Societies (Insolvency and Special Administration) Order 2009, SI 2009/805, art 15, as from 30 March 2009.

221 Powers of court where information required

(1)   If a person ("the defaulter")—
  (a)   fails to comply with a requirement imposed under section 219, or
  (b)   fails to permit documents to be inspected under section 220,
the scheme manager may certify that fact in writing to the court and the court may enquire into the case.

(2)   If the court is satisfied that the defaulter failed without reasonable excuse to comply with the requirement (or to permit the documents to be inspected), it may deal with the defaulter (and, in the case of a body corporate, any director or officer) as if he were in contempt[; and "officer", in relation to a limited liability partnership, means a member of the limited liability partnership].

(3)   "Court" means—
  (a)   the High Court;
  (b)   in Scotland, the Court of Session.

[395]

NOTES
Sub-s (2): words in square brackets added by the Limited Liability Partnerships Regulations 2001, SI 2001/1090, reg 9, Sch 5, para 21, as from 6 April 2001.

Miscellaneous

[221A   Delegation of functions

(1)   The scheme manager may arrange for any of its functions to be discharged on its behalf by another person (a "scheme agent").

(2)   Before entering into arrangements the scheme manager must be satisfied that the scheme agent—
  (a)   is competent to discharge the function, and
  (b)   has been given sufficient directions to enable the agent to take any decisions required in the course of exercising the function in accordance with policy determined by the scheme manager.

(3)   Arrangements may include provision for payments to be made by the scheme manager to the scheme agent (which payments are management expenses of the scheme manager).]

[396]

NOTES
Commencement: 21 February 2009.
Inserted by the Banking Act 2009, s 179(1), as from 21 February 2009.

222   Statutory immunity

(1)   Neither the scheme manager nor any person who is, or is acting as, its board member, officer[, scheme agent] or member of staff is to be liable in damages for anything done or omitted in the discharge, or purported discharge, of the scheme manager's functions.

(2)   Subsection (1) does not apply—
  (a)   if the act or omission is shown to have been in bad faith; or
  (b)   so as to prevent an award of damages made in respect of an act or omission on the ground that the act or omission was unlawful as a result of section 6(1) of the Human Rights Act 1998.

[397]

NOTES
Sub-s (1): words in square brackets inserted by the Banking Act 2009, s 179(2), as from 21 February 2009.

223   Management expenses

(1)   The amount which the scheme manager may recover, from the sums levied under the scheme, as management expenses attributable to a particular period may not exceed such amount as may be fixed by the scheme as the limit applicable to that period.

(2)   In calculating the amount of any levy to be imposed by the scheme manager, no amount may be included to reflect management expenses unless the limit mentioned in subsection (1) has been fixed by the scheme.

(3)   "Management expenses" means expenses incurred, or expected to be incurred, by the scheme manager in connection with its functions under this Act other than those incurred—
  (a)   in paying compensation;

(b)   as a result of any provision of the scheme made by virtue of section 216(3) or (4) or 217(1) or (6);

[(c)   under section 214B].

[398]

NOTES
Sub-s (3): para (c) added by the Banking Act 2009, s 171(2), as from 21 February 2009.

[223A   Investing in National Loans Fund

(1)   Sums levied for the purpose of maintaining a contingency fund may be paid to the Treasury.

(2)   The Treasury may receive sums under subsection (1) and may set terms and conditions of receipts.

(3)   Sums received shall be treated as if raised under section 12 of the National Loans Act 1968 (and shall therefore be invested as part of the National Loans Fund).

(4)   Interest accruing on the invested sums may be credited to the contingency fund (subject to any terms and conditions set under subsection (2)).

(5)   The Treasury shall comply with any request of the scheme manager to arrange for the return of sums for the purpose of making payments out of a contingency fund (subject to any terms and conditions set under subsection (2)).]

[399]

NOTES
Commencement: to be appointed.
Inserted by the Banking Act 2009, s 172, as from a day to be appointed.

[223B   Borrowing from National Loans Fund

(1)   The scheme manager may request a loan from the National Loans Fund for the purpose of funding expenses incurred or expected to be incurred under the scheme.

(2)   The Treasury may arrange for money to be paid out of the National Loans Fund in pursuance of a request under subsection (1).

(3)   The Treasury shall determine—
  (a)   the rate of interest on a loan, and
  (b)   other terms and conditions.

(4)   The Treasury may make regulations—
  (a)   about the amounts that may be borrowed under this section;
  (b)   permitting the scheme manager to impose levies under section 213 for the purpose of meeting expenses in connection with loans under this section (and the regulations may have effect despite any provision of this Act);
  (c)   about the classes of person on whom those levies may be imposed;
  (d)   about the amounts and timing of those levies.

(5)   The compensation scheme may include provision about borrowing under this section provided that it is not inconsistent with regulations under this section.]

[400]

NOTES
Commencement: 17 February 2009 (in so far as conferring or relating to any power to make subordinate legislation); 21 February 2009 (otherwise).
Inserted by the Banking Act 2009, s 173, as from 17 February 2009 (in so far as conferring or relating to any power to make subordinate legislation), and as from 21 February 2009 (otherwise).

[223C   Payments in error

(1)   Payments made by the scheme manager in error may be provided for in setting a levy by virtue of section 213, 214A, 214B or 223B.

(2)   This section does not apply to payments made in bad faith.]

[401]

NOTES
Commencement: 21 February 2009.
Inserted by the Banking Act 2009, s 177, as from 21 February 2009.

224   Scheme manager's power to inspect documents held by Official Receiver etc

(1)   If, as a result of the insolvency or bankruptcy of a relevant person, any documents have come into the possession of a person to whom this section applies, he must permit any person authorised by the scheme manager to inspect the documents for the purpose of establishing—

(a) the identity of persons to whom the scheme manager may be liable to make a payment in accordance with the compensation scheme; or

(b) the amount of any payment which the scheme manager may be liable to make.

(2) A person inspecting a document under this section may take copies or extracts from the document.

(3) In this section "relevant person" means a person who was—

(a) an authorised person at the time the act or omission which may give rise to the liability mentioned in subsection (1)(a) took place; or

(b) an appointed representative at that time.

(4) But a person who, at that time—

(a) qualified for authorisation under Schedule 3, and

(b) fell within a prescribed category,

is not to be regarded as a relevant person for the purposes of this section in relation to any activities for which he had permission as a result of any provision of, or made under, that Schedule unless he had elected to participate in the scheme in relation to those activities at that time.

(5) This section applies to—

(a) the Official Receiver;

(b) the Official Receiver for Northern Ireland; and

(c) the Accountant in Bankruptcy.

[402]

NOTES

Regulations: the Financial Services and Markets Act 2000 (Compensation Scheme: Electing Participants) Regulations 2001, SI 2001/1783.

[224A Functions under the Banking Act 2009

A reference in this Part to functions of the scheme manager (including a reference to functions conferred by or under this Part) includes a reference to functions conferred by or under the Banking Act 2009.]

[403]

NOTES

Commencement: 21 February 2009.
Inserted by the Banking Act 2009, s 180, as from 21 February 2009.

225–416 ((*Pts XVI–XXVIII) Outside the scope of this work; see Butterworths Banking Law Handbook or Butterworths Securities and Financial Services Law Handbook.*)

PART XXIX
INTERPRETATION

417 Definitions

(1) In this Act—

"appointed representative" has the meaning given in section 39(2);

"auditors and actuaries rules" means rules made under section 340;

"authorisation offence" has the meaning given in section 23(2);

"authorised open-ended investment company" has the meaning given in section 237(3);

"authorised person" has the meaning given in section 31(2);

"the Authority" means the Financial Services Authority;

"body corporate" includes a body corporate constituted under the law of a country or territory outside the United Kingdom;

"chief executive"—

(a) in relation to a body corporate whose principal place of business is within the United Kingdom, means an employee of that body who, alone or jointly with one or more others, is responsible under the immediate authority of the directors, for the conduct of the whole of the business of that body; and

(b) in relation to a body corporate whose principal place of business is outside the United Kingdom, means the person who, alone or jointly with one or more others, is responsible for the conduct of its business within the United Kingdom;

["claim", in relation to the Financial Services Compensation Scheme under Part XV, is to be construed in accordance with section 214(1B);]

"collective investment scheme" has the meaning given in section 235;

"the Commission" means the European Commission (except in provisions relating to the Competition Commission);

"the compensation scheme" has the meaning given in section 213(2);

"control of information rules" has the meaning given in section 147(1);

"director", in relation to a body corporate, includes—
  (a)   a person occupying in relation to it the position of a director (by whatever name called); and
  (b)   a person in accordance with whose directions or instructions (not being advice given in a professional capacity) the directors of that body are accustomed to act;
"documents" includes information recorded in any form and, in relation to information recorded otherwise than in legible form, references to its production include references to producing a copy of the information in legible form[, or in a form from which it can readily be produced in visible and legible form];
["electronic commerce directive" means Directive 2000/31/EC of the European Parliament and the Council of 8 June 2000 on certain legal aspects of information society services, in particular electronic commerce, in the Internal Market (Directive on electronic commerce);]
"exempt person", in relation to a regulated activity, means a person who is exempt from the general prohibition in relation to that activity as a result of an exemption order made under section 38(1) or as a result of section 39(1) or 285(2) or (3);
"financial promotion rules" means rules made under section 145;
"friendly society" means an incorporated or registered friendly society;
"general prohibition" has the meaning given in section 19(2);
"general rules" has the meaning given in section 138(2);
"incorporated friendly society" means a society incorporated under the Friendly Societies Act 1992;
"industrial and provident society" means a society registered or deemed to be registered under the Industrial and Provident Societies Act 1965 or the Industrial and Provident Societies Act (Northern Ireland) 1969;
["information society service" means an information society service within the meaning of Article 2(a) of the electronic commerce directive;]
["investment services and activities" has the meaning given in Article 4.1.2 of the markets in financial instruments directive, read with—
  (a)   Chapter VI of Commission Regulation 1287/2006 of 10 August 2006, and
  (b)   Article 52 of Commission Directive 2006/73/EC of 10 August 2006;]
"market abuse" has the meaning given in section 118;
"Minister of the Crown" has the same meaning as in the Ministers of the Crown Act 1975;
"money laundering rules" means rules made under section 146;
"notice of control" [(except in Chapter 1A of Part 18)] has the meaning given in section 178(5);
"the ombudsman scheme" has the meaning given in section 225(3);
"open-ended investment company" has the meaning given in section 236;
"Part IV permission" has the meaning given in section 40(4);
"partnership" includes a partnership constituted under the law of a country or territory outside the United Kingdom;
"prescribed" (where not otherwise defined) means prescribed in regulations made by the Treasury;
"price stabilising rules" means rules made under section 144;
"private company" has the meaning given in section 1(3) of the Companies Act 1985 or in Article 12(3) of the Companies (Northern Ireland) Order 1986;
"prohibition order" has the meaning given in section 56(2);
"recognised clearing house" and "recognised investment exchange" have the meaning given in section 285;
"registered friendly society" means a society which is—
  (a)   a friendly society within the meaning of section 7(1)(a) of the Friendly Societies Act 1974; and
  (b)   registered within the meaning of that Act;
"regulated activity" has the meaning given in section 22;
"regulating provisions" has the meaning given in section 159(1);
"regulatory objectives" means the objectives mentioned in section 2;
"regulatory provisions" has the meaning given in section 302;
"rule" means a rule made by the Authority under this Act;
"rule-making instrument" has the meaning given in section 153;
"the scheme manager" has the meaning given in section 212(1);
"the scheme operator" has the meaning given in section 225(2);
"scheme particulars rules" has the meaning given in section 248(1);
"Seventh Company Law Directive" means the European Council Seventh Company Law Directive of 13 June 1983 on consolidated accounts (No 83/349/EEC);
["Takeovers Directive" means Directive 2004/25/EC of the European Parliament and of the Council;]
"threshold conditions", in relation to a regulated activity, has the meaning given in section 41;
"the Treaty" means the treaty establishing the European Community;

"trust scheme rules" has the meaning given in section 247(1);
"UK authorised person" has the meaning given in section 178(4); and
"unit trust scheme" has the meaning given in section 237.

(2)　In the application of this Act to Scotland, references to a matter being actionable at the suit of a person are to be read as references to the matter being actionable at the instance of that person.

(3)　For the purposes of any provision of this Act [(other than a provision of Part 6)] authorising or requiring a person to do anything within a specified number of days no account is to be taken of any day which is a public holiday in any part of the United Kingdom.

[(4)　For the purposes of this Act—
(a)　an information society service is provided from an EEA State if it is provided from an establishment in that State;
(b)　an establishment, in connection with an information society service, is the place at which the provider of the service (being a national of an EEA State or a company or firm as mentioned in Article 48 of the Treaty) effectively pursues an economic activity for an indefinite period;
(c)　the presence or use in a particular place of equipment or other technical means of providing an information society service does not, of itself, constitute that place as an establishment of the kind mentioned in paragraph (b);
(d)　where it cannot be determined from which of a number of establishments a given information society service is provided, that service is to be regarded as provided from the establishment where the provider has the centre of his activities relating to the service.]

[404]

NOTES

Sub-s (1) is amended as follows:

Definition "claim" inserted by the Banking Act 2009, s 174(2), as from 21 February 2009.

Words in square brackets in definition "documents" inserted by the Criminal Justice and Police Act 2001, s 70, Sch 2, Pt 2, para 16(1), (2)(f), as from 1 April 2003.

Definitions "electronic commerce directive" and "information society service" inserted by the Electronic Commerce Directive (Financial Services and Markets) Regulations 2002, SI 2002/1775, reg 13(1), (2)(a), (b), as from 21 August 2002.

Definition "investment services and activities" inserted, and words in square brackets in definition "notice of control" inserted, by the Financial Services and Markets Act 2000 (Markets in Financial Instruments) Regulations 2007, SI 2007/126, reg 3(5), Sch 5, paras 1, 19, as from 1 April 2007 (certain purposes (see reg 1(2) thereof)), and as from 1 November 2007 (otherwise).

Definition "Takeovers Directive" inserted by the Companies Act 2006, s 964(1), (6), as from 6 April 2007.

Sub-s (3): words in square brackets inserted by the Prospectus Regulations 2005, SI 2005/1433, reg 2(1), Sch 1, para 15, as from 1 July 2005.

Sub-s (4): added by SI 2002/1775, reg 13(1), (2)(c), as from 21 August 2002.

Seventh Company Law Directive (83/349/EEC): OJ L193 18.7.1983 p 1.

Companies Act 1985, s 1(3): repealed by the Companies Act 2006 (as from 1 October 2009) and replaced by s 4(1)–(3) of the 2006 Act.

418–425　(*Outside the scope of this work; see Butterworths Banking Law Handbook or Butterworths Securities and Financial Services Law Handbook.*)

PART XXX
SUPPLEMENTAL

426–428　(*Outside the scope of this work; see Butterworths Banking Law Handbook or Butterworths Securities and Financial Services Law Handbook.*)

429　Parliamentary control of statutory instruments

(1)　No order is to be made under—
(a)　section 144(4), 192(b) or (e), 236(5), 404 or 419, or
(b)　paragraph 1 of Schedule 8,

unless a draft of the order has been laid before Parliament and approved by a resolution of each House.

(2)　No regulations are to be made under section [90B[, 214A, 214B] or] 262 unless a draft of the regulations has been laid before Parliament and approved by a resolution of each House.

(3)　An order to which, if it is made, subsection (4) or (5) will apply is not to be made unless a draft of the order has been laid before Parliament and approved by a resolution of each House.

(4)　This subsection applies to an order under section 21 if—
(a)　it is the first order to be made, or to contain provisions made, under section 21(4);
(b)　it varies an order made under section 21(4) so as to make section 21(1) apply in circumstances in which it did not previously apply;

(c)   it is the first order to be made, or to contain provision made, under section 21(5);

(d)   it varies a previous order made under section 21(5) so as to make section 21(1) apply in circumstances in which it did not, as a result of that previous order, apply;

(e)   it is the first order to be made, or to contain provisions made, under section 21(9) or (10);

(f)   it adds one or more activities to those that are controlled activities for the purposes of section 21; or

(g)   it adds one or more investments to those which are controlled investments for the purposes of section 21.

(5)   This subsection applies to an order under section 38 if—

(a)   it is the first order to be made, or to contain provisions made, under that section; or

(b)   it contains provisions restricting or removing an exemption provided by an earlier order made under that section.

(6)   An order containing a provision to which, if the order is made, subsection (7) will apply is not to be made unless a draft of the order has been laid before Parliament and approved by a resolution of each House.

(7)   This subsection applies to a provision contained in an order if—

(a)   it is the first to be made in the exercise of the power conferred by subsection (1) of section 326 or it removes a body from those for the time being designated under that subsection; or

(b)   it is the first to be made in the exercise of the power conferred by subsection (6) of section 327 or it adds a description of regulated activity or investment to those for the time being specified for the purposes of that subsection.

(8)   Any other statutory instrument made under this Act, apart from one made under section 431(2) or to which paragraph 26 of Schedule 2 applies, shall be subject to annulment in pursuance of a resolution of either House of Parliament.

[405]

NOTES

Sub-s (2): words in first (outer) pair of square brackets inserted by the Companies Act 2006, s 1272, Sch 15, Pt 1, paras 1, 12, as from 8 November 2006; words in second (inner) pair of square brackets inserted by the Banking Act 2009, s 178, as from 17 February 2009.

430–433   (*Outside the scope of this work; see Butterworths Banking Law Handbook or Butterworths Securities and Financial Services Law Handbook.*)

SCHEDULES

(*Sch 1 outside the scope of this work; see Butterworths Banking Law Handbook or Butterworths Securities and Financial Services Law Handbook.*)

SCHEDULE 2
REGULATED ACTIVITIES

Section 22(2)

NOTES

The regulated activities for the purposes of s 22 of this Act are set out in the Financial Services and Markets Act 2000 (Regulated Activities) Order 2001, SI 2001/544 at **[700]**.

PART I
[REGULATED ACTIVITIES: GENERAL]

General

1.   The matters with respect to which provision may be made under section 22(1) in respect of activities include, in particular, those described in general terms in this Part of this Schedule.

Dealing in investments

2.—(1)   Buying, selling, subscribing for or underwriting investments or offering or agreeing to do so, either as a principal or as an agent.

(2)   In the case of an investment which is a contract of insurance, that includes carrying out the contract.

Arranging deals in investments

3.   Making, or offering or agreeing to make—

    (a)   arrangements with a view to another person buying, selling, subscribing for or underwriting a particular investment;

    (b)   arrangements with a view to a person who participates in the arrangements buying, selling, subscribing for or underwriting investments.

Deposit taking

4.   Accepting deposits.

Safekeeping and administration of assets

5.—(1)   Safeguarding and administering assets belonging to another which consist of or include investments or offering or agreeing to do so.

(2)   Arranging for the safeguarding and administration of assets belonging to another, or offering or agreeing to do so.

Managing investments

6.   Managing, or offering or agreeing to manage, assets belonging to another person where—

    (a)   the assets consist of or include investments; or

    (b)   the arrangements for their management are such that the assets may consist of or include investments at the discretion of the person managing or offering or agreeing to manage them.

Investment advice

7.   Giving or offering or agreeing to give advice to persons on—

    (a)   buying, selling, subscribing for or underwriting an investment; or

    (b)   exercising any right conferred by an investment to acquire, dispose of, underwrite or convert an investment.

Establishing collective investment schemes

8.   Establishing, operating or winding up a collective investment scheme, including acting as—

    (a)   trustee of a unit trust scheme;

    (b)   depositary of a collective investment scheme other than a unit trust scheme; or

    (c)   sole director of a body incorporated by virtue of regulations under section 262.

Using computer-based systems for giving investment instructions

9.—(1)   Sending on behalf of another person instructions relating to an investment by means of a computer-based system which enables investments to be transferred without a written instrument.

(2)   Offering or agreeing to send such instructions by such means on behalf of another person.

(3)   Causing such instructions to be sent by such means on behalf of another person.

(4)   Offering or agreeing to cause such instructions to be sent by such means on behalf of another person.

[406]

NOTES

Part heading: words in square brackets substituted by the Dormant Bank and Building Society Accounts Act 2008, s 15, Sch 2, para 1(1), (2), as from 12 March 2009.

[PART 1A
REGULATED ACTIVITIES: RECLAIM FUNDS

Activities of reclaim funds

9A.—(1)   The matters with respect to which provision may be made under section 22(1) in respect of activities include, in particular, any of the activities of a reclaim fund.

(2)   "Reclaim fund" has the meaning given by section 5(1) of the Dormant Bank and Building Society Accounts Act 2008.]

[407]

NOTES

Commencement: 12 March 2009.

Inserted by the Dormant Bank and Building Society Accounts Act 2008, s 15, Sch 2, para 1(1), (3), as from 12 March 2009.

PART II
OTHER ACTS

PART II
INVESTMENTS

General

10.   The matters with respect to which provision may be made under section 22(1) in respect of investments include, in particular, those described in general terms in this Part of this Schedule.

Securities

11.—(1)   Shares or stock in the share capital of a company.

(2)   "Company" includes—
    (a)   any body corporate (wherever incorporated), and
    (b)   any unincorporated body constituted under the law of a country or territory outside the United Kingdom,
other than an open-ended investment company.

Instruments creating or acknowledging indebtedness

12.   Any of the following—
    (a)   debentures;
    (b)   debenture stock;
    (c)   loan stock;
    (d)   bonds;
    (e)   certificates of deposit;
    (f)   any other instruments creating or acknowledging a present or future indebtedness.

Government and public securities

13.—(1)   Loan stock, bonds and other instruments—
    (a)   creating or acknowledging indebtedness; and
    (b)   issued by or on behalf of a government, local authority or public authority.

(2)   "Government, local authority or public authority" means—
    (a)   the government of the United Kingdom, of Northern Ireland, or of any country or territory outside the United Kingdom;
    (b)   a local authority in the United Kingdom or elsewhere;
    (c)   any international organisation the members of which include the United Kingdom or another member State.

Instruments giving entitlement to investments

14.—(1)   Warrants or other instruments entitling the holder to subscribe for any investment.

(2)   It is immaterial whether the investment is in existence or identifiable.

Certificates representing securities

15.   Certificates or other instruments which confer contractual or property rights—
    (a)   in respect of any investment held by someone other than the person on whom the rights are conferred by the certificate or other instrument; and
    (b)   the transfer of which may be effected without requiring the consent of that person.

Units in collective investment schemes

16.—(1)   Shares in or securities of an open-ended investment company.

(2)   Any right to participate in a collective investment scheme.

Options

17.   Options to acquire or dispose of property.

Futures

18.   Rights under a contract for the sale of a commodity or property of any other description under which delivery is to be made at a future date.

Contracts for differences

19.   Rights under—
    (a)   a contract for differences; or
    (b)   any other contract the purpose or pretended purpose of which is to secure a profit or avoid a loss by reference to fluctuations in—
        (i)   the value or price of property of any description; or
        (ii)   an index or other factor designated for that purpose in the contract.

Contracts of insurance

20.   Rights under a contract of insurance, including rights under contracts falling within head C of Schedule 2 to the Friendly Societies Act 1992.

Participation in Lloyd's syndicates

21.—(1)   The underwriting capacity of a Lloyd's syndicate.

(2)   A person's membership (or prospective membership) of a Lloyd's syndicate.

Deposits

22.   Rights under any contract under which a sum of money (whether or not denominated in a currency) is paid on terms under which it will be repaid, with or without interest or a premium, and either on demand or at a time or in circumstances agreed by or on behalf of the person making the payment and the person receiving it.

Loans secured on land

23.—(1)   Rights under any contract under which—
   (a)   one person provides another with credit; and
   (b)   the obligation of the borrower to repay is secured on land.

(2)   "Credit" includes any cash loan or other financial accommodation.

(3)   "Cash" includes money in any form.

[Other finance arrangements involving land

23A.—(1)   Rights under any arrangement for the provision of finance under which the person providing the finance either—
   (a)   acquires a major interest in land from the person to whom the finance is provided, or
   (b)   disposes of a major interest in land to that person,
as part of the arrangement.

(2)   References in sub-paragraph (1) to a "major interest" in land are to—
   (a)   in relation to land in England or Wales—
      (i)   an estate in fee simple absolute, or
      (ii)   a term of years absolute,
      whether subsisting at law or in equity;
   (b)   in relation to land in Scotland—
      (i)   the interest of an owner of land, or
      (ii)   the tenant's right over or interest in a property subject to a lease;
   (c)   in relation to land in Northern Ireland—
      (i)   any freehold estate, or
      (ii)   any leasehold estate,
      whether subsisting at law or in equity.

(3)   It is immaterial for the purposes of sub-paragraph (1) whether either party acquires or (as the case may be) disposes of the interest in land—
   (a)   directly, or
   (b)   indirectly.]

Rights in investments

24.   Any right or interest in anything which is an investment as a result of any other provision made under section 22(1).

[408]

NOTES

Para 23A: inserted by the Regulation of Financial Services (Land Transactions) Act 2005, s 1, as from 19 February 2006.

Modifications to para 12(e): (i) a reference to a certificate of deposit includes a reference to uncertificated units of an eligible debt security where the issue of those units corresponds, in accordance with the current terms of issue of the security, to the issue of a certificate of deposit which is a certificate of deposit for the purposes of that enactment; (ii) a reference to an amount stated in a certificate of deposit includes a reference to a principal amount stated in, or determined in accordance with, the current terms of issue of an eligible debt security of the kind referred to in (i) above; see the Uncertificated Securities (Amendment) (Eligible Debt Securities) Regulations 2003, SI 2003/1633, reg 15, Sch 2, para 6 (as from 24 June 2003).

Modifications to para 12(f): the reference to securities, instruments or investments creating or acknowledging indebtedness (or creating or acknowledging a present or future indebtedness) includes a reference to uncertificated units of eligible debt securities; see the Uncertificated Securities (Amendment) (Eligible Debt Securities) Regulations 2003, SI 2003/1633, reg 15, Sch 2, para 8 (as from 24 June 2003).

PART III
SUPPLEMENTAL PROVISIONS

The order-making power

25.—(1)   An order under section 22(1) may—
 (a)   provide for exemptions;
 (b)   confer powers on the Treasury or the Authority;
 (c)   authorise the making of regulations or other instruments by the Treasury for purposes of, or connected with, any relevant provision;
 (d)   authorise the making of rules or other instruments by the Authority for purposes of, or connected with, any relevant provision;
 (e)   make provision in respect of any information or document which, in the opinion of the Treasury or the Authority, is relevant for purposes of, or connected with, any relevant provision;
 (f)   make such consequential, transitional or supplemental provision as the Treasury consider appropriate for purposes of, or connected with, any relevant provision.

(2)   Provision made as a result of sub-paragraph (1)(f) may amend any primary or subordinate legislation, including any provision of, or made under, this Act.

(3)   "Relevant provision" means any provision—
 (a)   of section 22 or this Schedule; or
 (b)   made under that section or this Schedule.

Parliamentary control

26.—(1)   This paragraph applies to the first order made under section 22(1).

(2)   This paragraph also applies to any subsequent order made under section 22(1) which contains a statement by the Treasury that, in their opinion, the effect (or one of the effects) of the proposed order would be that an activity which is not a regulated activity would become a regulated activity.

(3)   An order to which this paragraph applies—
 (a)   must be laid before Parliament after being made; and
 (b)   ceases to have effect at the end of the relevant period unless before the end of that period the order is approved by a resolution of each House of Parliament (but without that affecting anything done under the order or the power to make a new order).

(4)   "Relevant period" means a period of twenty-eight days beginning with the day on which the order is made.

(5)   In calculating the relevant period no account is to be taken of any time during which Parliament is dissolved or prorogued or during which both Houses are adjourned for more than four days.

Interpretation

27.—(1)   In this Schedule—
 "buying" includes acquiring for valuable consideration;
 "offering" includes inviting to treat;
 "property" includes currency of the United Kingdom or any other country or territory; and
 "selling" includes disposing for valuable consideration.

(2)   In sub-paragraph (1) "disposing" includes—
 (a)   in the case of an investment consisting of rights under a contract—
  (i)   surrendering, assigning or converting those rights; or
  (ii)   assuming the corresponding liabilities under the contract;
 (b)   in the case of an investment consisting of rights under other arrangements, assuming the corresponding liabilities under the contract or arrangements;
 (c)   in the case of any other investment, issuing or creating the investment or granting the rights or interests of which it consists.

(3)   In this Schedule references to an instrument include references to any record (whether or not in the form of a document).

[409]

(*Schs 3–22 outside the scope of this work; see Butterworths Banking Law Handbook or Butterworths Securities and Financial Services Law Handbook.*)

COMPANIES ACT 2006

(2006 c 46)

1–153 ((*Pts 1–9*) *Outside the scope of this work; for ss 1–8, 136, 141, 142 see Butterworths Securities and Financial Services Law Handbook.*)

PART 10
A COMPANY'S DIRECTORS

154–226 ((*Chs 1–4*) *Outside the scope of this work.*)

CHAPTER 5
DIRECTORS' SERVICE CONTRACTS

227 Directors' service contracts

(1) For the purposes of this Part a director's "service contract", in relation to a company, means a contract under which—

(a) a director of the company undertakes personally to perform services (as director or otherwise) for the company, or for a subsidiary of the company, or

(b) services (as director or otherwise) that a director of the company undertakes personally to perform are made available by a third party to the company, or to a subsidiary of the company.

(2) The provisions of this Part relating to directors' service contracts apply to the terms of a person's appointment as a director of a company.

They are not restricted to contracts for the performance of services outside the scope of the ordinary duties of a director.

[410]

NOTES
Commencement: 1 October 2007.
See further, in relation to the disapplication of this section, in respect of certain specified persons while Northern Rock is wholly owned by the Treasury: the Northern Rock plc Transfer Order 2008, SI 2008/432, art 17, Schedule, para 2(k); in relation to the disapplication of this section, in respect of certain specified persons while Bradford & Bingley is wholly owned by the Treasury: the Bradford & Bingley plc Transfer of Securities and Property etc Order 2008, SI 2008/2546, art 13(1), Sch 1, para 2(k) at **[975]**, **[1005]**; in relation to the disapplication of this section, in respect of certain specified persons while Deposits Management (Heritable) is wholly owned by the Treasury: the Heritable Bank plc Transfer of Certain Rights and Liabilities Order 2008, SI 2008/2644, art 26, Sch 2, para 2(k) at **[1033]**, **[1041]**.

228–1300 (*Ss 228–259, ss 260–1300 (Pts 11–47) outside the scope of this work. For ss 380–539, 544, 755–828, 895–901, 942–991, 1158–1166, 1170, 1171, 1173, 1209–1263, 1273, 1297–1300 see Butterworths Securities and Financial Services Law Handbook. For ss 860–867, 869–877, 893, 894, 1052 see Butterworths Banking Law Handbook.*)

(*Sch 1 outside the scope of this work.*)

[SCHEDULE 2
SPECIFIED PERSONS, DESCRIPTIONS OF DISCLOSURES ETC FOR THE PURPOSES OF SECTION 948
Section 948

PART 1
SPECIFIED PERSONS

(A) UNITED KINGDOM
1. The Secretary of State.
2. The Department of Enterprise, Trade and Investment for Northern Ireland.
3. The Treasury.
4. The Bank of England.
5. The Financial Services Authority.
6. The Commissioners for Her Majesty's Revenue and Customs.
7. The Lord Advocate.
8. The Director of Public Prosecutions.

9.   The Director of Public Prosecutions for Northern Ireland.

10.   A constable.

11.   A procurator fiscal.

12.   The Scottish Ministers.

(B) JERSEY

1.   The Minister for Economic Development.

2.   The Minister for Treasury and Resources.

3.   The Jersey Financial Services Commission.

4.   The Comptroller of Income Tax.

5.   The Agent of the Impôts.

6.   Her Majesty's Attorney General for Jersey.

7.   The Viscount.

8.   A police officer (within the meaning of the Interpretation (Jersey) Law 1954: see Part 1 of the Schedule to that Law).

(C) GUERNSEY

1.   The Commerce and Employment Department.

2.   The Treasury and Resources Department.

3.   The Guernsey Financial Services Commission.

4.   The Director of Income Tax.

5.   The Chief Officer of Customs and Excise.

6.   Her Majesty's Procureur.

7.   A police officer (within the meaning of the Companies (Guernsey) Law 2008: see section 532 of that Law).

(D) ISLE OF MAN

1.—(1)   The members and officers of each of the Departments constituted by section 1(1) of the Government Departments Act 1987 (an Act of Tynwald: c 13).

(2)   In sub-paragraph (1) "member" has the same meaning as it has by virtue of section 7(1) of that Act.

2.   The Treasury of the Isle of Man.

3.   The Financial Supervision Commission of the Isle of Man.

4.   Her Majesty's Attorney General of the Isle of Man.

5.   A constable (within the meaning of the Interpretation Act 1976 (an Act of Tynwald: c 11): see section 3 of that Act).]

[411]

NOTES
   Commencement: 1 July 2009.
   Schedule substituted by the Companies Act 2006 (Amendment of Schedule 2) (No 2) Order 2009, SI 2009/1208, art 2, Schedule.

[PART 2
SPECIFIED DESCRIPTIONS OF DISCLOSURES

(A) UNITED KINGDOM

1.   A disclosure for the purpose of enabling or assisting a person authorised under section 457 of this Act (revision of defective accounts: persons authorised to apply to court) to exercise their functions.

2.   A disclosure for the purpose of enabling or assisting an inspector appointed under Part 14 of the Companies Act 1985 (c 6) (investigation of companies and their affairs, etc) to exercise their functions.

3.   A disclosure for the purpose of enabling or assisting a person authorised under section 447 of the Companies Act 1985 (power to require production of documents) or section 84 of the Companies Act 1989 (c 40) (exercise of powers by officer etc) to exercise their functions.

4.   A disclosure for the purpose of enabling or assisting a person appointed under section 167 of the Financial Services and Markets Act 2000 (c 8) (general investigations) to conduct an investigation to exercise their functions.

5.   A disclosure for the purpose of enabling or assisting a person appointed under section 168 of the Financial Services and Markets Act 2000 (investigations in particular cases) to conduct an investigation to exercise their functions.

6.   A disclosure for the purpose of enabling or assisting a person appointed under section 169(1)(b) of the Financial Services and Markets Act 2000 (investigation in support of overseas regulator) to conduct an investigation to exercise their functions.

7.   A disclosure for the purpose of enabling or assisting the body corporate responsible for administering the scheme referred to in section 225 of the Financial Services and Markets Act 2000 (the ombudsman scheme) to exercise its functions.

8.   A disclosure for the purpose of enabling or assisting a person appointed under paragraph 4 or 5 of Schedule 17 to the Financial Services and Markets Act 2000 (the panel of ombudsmen or the Chief Ombudsman) to exercise their functions.

9.   A disclosure for the purpose of enabling or assisting a person appointed under regulations made under section 262(1) and (2)(k) of the Financial Services and Markets Act 2000 (investigations into open-ended investment companies) to conduct an investigation to exercise their functions.

10.   A disclosure for the purpose of enabling or assisting a person appointed under section 284 of the Financial Services and Markets Act 2000 (investigations into affairs of certain collective investment schemes) to conduct an investigation to exercise their functions.

11.   A disclosure for the purpose of enabling or assisting the investigator appointed under paragraph 7 of Schedule 1 to the Financial Services and Markets Act 2000 (arrangements for investigation of complaints) to exercise their functions.

12.   A disclosure for the purpose of enabling or assisting a person appointed by the Treasury to hold an inquiry into matters relating to financial services (including an inquiry under section 15 of the Financial Services and Markets Act 2000) to exercise their functions.

13.   A disclosure for the purpose of enabling or assisting the Secretary of State or the Treasury to exercise any of their functions under any of the following—
   (a)   the Companies Acts;
   (b)   the Insolvency Act 1986 (c 45);
   (c)   the Company Directors Disqualification Act 1986 (c 46);
   (d)   Part 3 (investigations and powers to obtain information) or 7 (financial markets and insolvency) of the Companies Act 1989 (c 40);
   (e)   Part 5 of the Criminal Justice Act 1993 (c 36) (insider dealing);
   (f)   the Financial Services and Markets Act 2000;
   (g)   Part 42 of this Act (statutory auditors).

14.   A disclosure for the purpose of enabling or assisting the Scottish Ministers to exercise their functions under the enactments relating to insolvency.

15.   A disclosure for the purpose of enabling or assisting the Department of Enterprise, Trade and Investment for Northern Ireland to exercise any powers conferred on it by the enactments relating to companies or insolvency.

16.   A disclosure for the purpose of enabling or assisting a person appointed or authorised by the Department of Enterprise, Trade and Investment for Northern Ireland under the enactments relating to companies or insolvency to exercise their functions.

17.   A disclosure for the purpose of enabling or assisting an official receiver (including the Accountant in Bankruptcy in Scotland and the Official Assignee in Northern Ireland) to exercise their functions under the enactments relating to insolvency.

18.   A disclosure for the purpose of enabling or assisting the Insolvency Practitioners Tribunal to exercise its functions under the Insolvency Act 1986 (c 45).

19.   A disclosure for the purpose of enabling or assisting a body that is for the time being a recognised professional body for the purposes of section 391 of the Insolvency Act 1986 (recognised professional bodies) to exercise its functions as such.

20.   A disclosure for the purpose of enabling or assisting the Pensions Regulator to exercise the functions conferred on it by or by virtue of any of the following—
   (a)   the Pension Schemes Act 1993 (c 48);
   (b)   the Pensions Act 1995 (c 26);
   (c)   the Welfare Reform and Pensions Act 1999 (c 30);
   (d)   the Pensions Act 2004 (c 35);
   (e)   any enactment in force in Northern Ireland corresponding to any of those enactments.

21.   A disclosure for the purpose of enabling or assisting the Board of the Pension Protection Fund to exercise the functions conferred on it by or by virtue of Part 2 of the Pensions Act 2004 or any enactment in force in Northern Ireland corresponding to that Part.

22.   A disclosure for the purpose of enabling or assisting the Bank of England to exercise its functions.

23.   A disclosure for the purpose of enabling or assisting the Commissioners for Her Majesty's Revenue and Customs to exercise their functions.

24.   A disclosure for the purpose of enabling or assisting organs of the Society of Lloyd's (being organs constituted by or under the Lloyd's Act 1982 (c. xiv)) to exercise their functions under or by virtue of the Lloyd's Acts 1871 to 1982.

25.   A disclosure for the purpose of enabling or assisting the Office of Fair Trading to exercise its functions under any of the following—

(a)   the Fair Trading Act 1973 (c 41);
(b)   the Consumer Credit Act 1974 (c 39);
(c)   the Estate Agents Act 1979 (c 38);
(d)   the Competition Act 1980 (c 21);
(e)   the Competition Act 1998 (c 41);
(f)   the Financial Services and Markets Act 2000 (c 8);
(g)   the Enterprise Act 2002 (c 40);
(h)   the Unfair Terms in Consumer Contracts Regulations 1999 (SI 1999/2083);
(i)   the Business Protection from Misleading Marketing Regulations 2008 (SI 2008/1276);
(j)   the Consumer Protection from Unfair Trading Regulations 2008 (SI 2008/1277).

26.   A disclosure for the purpose of enabling or assisting the Competition Commission to exercise its functions under any of the following—

(a)   the Fair Trading Act 1973;
(b)   the Competition Act 1980;
(c)   the Competition Act 1998;
(d)   the Enterprise Act 2002.

27.   A disclosure with a view to the institution of, or otherwise for the purposes of, proceedings before the Competition Appeal Tribunal.

28.   A disclosure for the purpose of enabling or assisting an enforcer under Part 8 of the Enterprise Act 2002 (enforcement of consumer legislation) to exercise their functions under that Part.

29.   A disclosure for the purpose of enabling or assisting the Charity Commission to exercise its functions.

30.   A disclosure for the purpose of enabling or assisting the Attorney General to exercise their functions in connection with charities.

31.   A disclosure for the purpose of enabling or assisting the National Lottery Commission to exercise its functions under sections 5 to 10 and 15 of the National Lottery etc Act 1993 (c 39) (licensing and power of Secretary of State to require information).

32.   A disclosure by the National Lottery Commission to the National Audit Office for the purpose of enabling or assisting the Comptroller and Auditor General to carry out an examination under Part 2 of the National Audit Act 1983 (c 44) into the economy, effectiveness and efficiency with which the National Lottery Commission has used its resources in discharging its functions under sections 5 to 10 of the National Lottery etc Act 1993.

33.   A disclosure for the purpose of enabling or assisting a qualifying body under the Unfair Terms in Consumer Contracts Regulations 1999 (SI 1999/2083) to exercise its functions under those Regulations.

34.   A disclosure for the purpose of enabling or assisting an enforcement authority under the Consumer Protection (Distance Selling) Regulations 2000 (SI 2000/2334) to exercise its functions under those Regulations.

35.   A disclosure for the purpose of enabling or assisting an enforcement authority under the Financial Services (Distance Marketing) Regulations 2004 (SI 2004/2095) to exercise its functions under those Regulations.

36.   A disclosure for the purpose of enabling or assisting a local weights and measures authority in England and Wales to exercise its functions under section 230(2) of the Enterprise Act 2002 (c 40) (notice of intention to prosecute, etc).

37.   A disclosure for the purpose of enabling or assisting the Financial Services Authority to exercise its functions under any of the following—

(a)   the legislation relating to friendly societies or to industrial and provident societies;
(b)   the Building Societies Act 1986 (c 53);
(c)   Part 7 of the Companies Act 1989 (c 40) (financial markets and insolvency);
(d)   the Financial Services and Markets Act 2000 (c 8).

38.   A disclosure for the purpose of enabling or assisting the competent authority for the purposes of Part 6 of the Financial Services and Markets Act 2000 (official listing) to exercise its functions under that Part.

39.   A disclosure for the purpose of enabling or assisting a body corporate established in accordance with section 212(1) of the Financial Services and Markets Act 2000 (compensation scheme manager) to exercise its functions.

40.—(1)   A disclosure for the purpose of enabling or assisting a recognised investment exchange or a recognised clearing house to exercise its functions as such.

(2)   In sub-paragraph (1) "recognised investment exchange" and "recognised clearing house" have the same meaning as in section 285 of the Financial Services and Markets Act 2000.

41.   A disclosure for the purpose of enabling or assisting a person approved under the Uncertificated Securities Regulations 2001 (SI 2001/3755) as an operator of a relevant system (within the meaning of those Regulations) to exercise their functions.

42.   A disclosure for the purpose of enabling or assisting a body designated under section 326(1) of the Financial Services and Markets Act 2000 (designated professional bodies) to exercise its functions in its capacity as a body designated under that section.

43.   A disclosure with a view to the institution of, or otherwise for the purposes of, civil proceedings arising under or by virtue of the Financial Services and Markets Act 2000.

44.   A disclosure for the purpose of enabling or assisting a body designated by order under section 1252 of this Act (delegation of functions of Secretary of State) to exercise its functions under Part 42 of this Act (statutory auditors).

45.   A disclosure for the purpose of enabling or assisting a recognised supervisory or qualifying body, within the meaning of Part 42 of this Act, to exercise its functions as such.

46.   A disclosure for the purpose of enabling or assisting the Regulator of Community Interest Companies to exercise functions under the Companies (Audit, Investigations and Community Enterprise) Act 2004 (c 27).

47.   A disclosure for the purpose of enabling or assisting a person authorised by the Secretary of State under Part 2, 3 or 4 of the Proceeds of Crime Act 2002 (c 29) to exercise their functions.

48.   A disclosure with a view to the institution of, or otherwise for the purposes of, proceedings on an application under section 6, 7 or 8 of the Company Directors Disqualification Act 1986 (c 46) (disqualification for unfitness).

49.   A disclosure with a view to the institution of, or otherwise for the purposes of, proceedings before the Financial Services and Markets Tribunal.

50.   A disclosure for the purposes of proceedings before the Pensions Regulator Tribunal.

51.   A disclosure for the purpose of enabling or assisting a body appointed under section 14 of the Companies (Audit, Investigations and Community Enterprise) Act 2004 (supervision of periodic accounts and reports of issuers of listed securities) to exercise functions mentioned in subsection (2) of that section.

52.—(1)   A disclosure with a view to the institution of, or otherwise for the purposes of, disciplinary proceedings relating to the performance by a lawyer, auditor, accountant, valuer or actuary of their professional duties.

(2)   In sub-paragraph (1) "lawyer" means—
    (a)   a person who for the purposes of the Legal Services Act 2007 (c 29) is an authorised person in relation to an activity that constitutes a reserved legal activity (within the meaning of that Act),
    (b)   a solicitor or barrister in Northern Ireland,
    (c)   a solicitor or advocate in Scotland, or
    (d)   a person who is a member, and entitled to practise as such, of a legal profession regulated in a jurisdiction outside the United Kingdom.

(3)   Until the coming into force of section 18 of the Legal Services Act 2007, the following is substituted for paragraph (a) of sub-paragraph (2) above—
    "(a)   a solicitor or barrister in England and Wales,".

53.—(1)   A disclosure with a view to the institution of, or otherwise for the purposes of, disciplinary proceedings relating to the performance by a public servant of their duties.

(2)   In sub-paragraph (1) "public servant" means—

    (a)   an officer or employee of the Crown, or
    (b)   an officer or employee of any public or other authority for the time being designated for the purposes of this paragraph by the Secretary of State by order subject to negative resolution procedure.

(B) JERSEY

1.   A disclosure for the purpose of enabling or assisting an inspector appointed under Part 19 of the Companies (Jersey) Law 1991 to exercise their functions.

2.   A disclosure for the purpose of enabling or assisting a person appointed under Article 33 of the Financial Services (Jersey) Law 1998 to exercise their functions.

3.   A disclosure for the purpose of enabling or assisting an inspector appointed under Article 22 of the Collective Investment Funds (Jersey) Law 1988 to exercise their functions.

PART II
OTHER ACTS

4.   A disclosure for the purpose of enabling or assisting the Minister for Economic Development to exercise functions under any of the following—
   (a)   the Bankruptcy Désastre (Jersey) Law 1990;
   (b)   the Companies (Jersey) Law 1991;
   (c)   the Financial Services (Jersey) Law 1998.

5.   A disclosure for the purpose of enabling or assisting the Comptroller of Income Tax to exercise their functions.

6.   A disclosure for the purpose of enabling or assisting the Agent of the Impôts to exercise their functions.

7.   A disclosure for the purpose of enabling or assisting the Jersey Competition Regulatory Authority to exercise its functions.

8.   A disclosure for the purpose of enabling or assisting Her Majesty's Attorney General for Jersey to exercise their functions in connection with charities.

9.   A disclosure for the purpose of enabling or assisting Her Majesty's Attorney General for Jersey to exercise their functions under the Distance Selling (Jersey) Law 2007.

10.   A disclosure for the purpose of enabling or assisting the Viscount to exercise their functions in relation to désastre or in relation to Part 2 of the Proceeds of Crime (Jersey) Law 1999.

11.   A disclosure with a view to the institution of, or otherwise for the purposes of, proceedings on an application under Article 78 of the Companies (Jersey) Law 1991 (disqualification orders).

12.—(1)   A disclosure with a view to the institution of, or otherwise for the purposes of, disciplinary proceedings relating to the performance by a solicitor, advocate, foreign lawyer, auditor, accountant, valuer or actuary of their professional duties.

   (2)   In sub-paragraph (1)—
   (a)   "solicitor" means a person who has been admitted as a solicitor under the Advocates and Solicitors (Jersey) Law 1997;
   (b)   "advocate" means a person who has been admitted to the Bar under that Law; and
   (c)   "foreign lawyer" means a person who has not been admitted as mentioned in paragraph (a) or (b) but is a member, and entitled to practise as such, of a legal profession regulated within a jurisdiction outside Jersey.

13.—(1)   A disclosure with a view to the institution of, or otherwise for the purposes of, disciplinary proceedings relating to the performance by a public servant of their duties.

   (2)   In sub-paragraph (1) "public servant" means—
   (a)   an individual who holds office under, or is employed by, the Crown,
   (b)   a member, officer or employee of the States of Jersey or an officer or employee in an administration of the States of Jersey,
   (c)   a member, officer or employee of the Jersey Financial Services Commission, or
   (d)   any person exercising public functions who is declared by Order of the Minister for Economic Development to be a public servant for the purposes of paragraph 25 of the Schedule to the Companies (Takeovers and Mergers Panel) (Jersey) Law 2009.

(C) GUERNSEY

1.   A disclosure for the purpose of enabling or assisting the Registrar of Companies appointed under the Companies (Guernsey) Law 2008 to exercise their functions under that Law.

2.   A disclosure for the purpose of enabling or assisting a person appointed under—
   (a)   section 27E or 41I of the Protection of Investors (Bailiwick of Guernsey) Law 1987,
   (b)   section 27 of the Banking Supervision (Bailiwick of Guernsey) Law 1994,
   (c)   section 10 of the Company Securities (Insider Dealing) (Bailiwick of Guernsey) Law 1996,
   (d)   section 24 of the Regulation of Fiduciaries, Administration Businesses and Company Directors (Bailiwick of Guernsey) Law 2000,
   (e)   section 69 of the Insurance Business (Bailiwick of Guernsey) Law 2002,
   (f)   section 46 of the Insurance Managers and Insurance Intermediaries (Bailiwick of Guernsey) Law 2002,
   (g)   section 19 of the Registration of Non-Regulated Financial Services Business (Bailiwick of Guernsey) Law 2008,
to exercise their functions.

3.   A disclosure for the purpose of enabling or assisting Her Majesty's Procureur to exercise their functions in connection with charities.

4.   A disclosure for the purpose of enabling or assisting the Guernsey Banking Deposit Compensation Scheme, established under section 46 of the Banking Supervision (Bailiwick of Guernsey) Law 1987 by the Banking Deposit Compensation Scheme (Bailiwick of Guernsey) Ordinance 2008, to exercise its functions.

5.　A disclosure for the purpose of enabling or assisting any supervisory body or professional oversight body to exercise its functions under Part XVIA of the Companies (Guernsey) Law 2008 (regulation of auditors).

6.　A disclosure with a view to the institution of, or otherwise for the purposes of, proceedings on an application under Part XXV of the Companies (Guernsey) Law 2008 (disqualification orders).

7.—(1)　A disclosure with a view to the institution of, or otherwise for the purposes of, disciplinary proceedings relating to the performance by an Advocate of the Royal Court, foreign lawyer, auditor, accountant, valuer or actuary of their professional duties.

(2)　In sub-paragraph (1) "foreign lawyer" means a person who has not been admitted as an Advocate of the Royal Court, but is a member, and entitled to practise as such, of a legal profession regulated within a jurisdiction outside Guernsey.

8.—(1)　A disclosure with a view to the institution of, or otherwise for the purposes of, disciplinary proceedings relating to the performance by a public servant of their duties.

(2)　In sub-paragraph (1) "public servant" means—
    (a)　an officer or employee of the Crown,
    (b)　a member, officer or employee of the States of Guernsey,
    (c)　a member, officer or employee of the Guernsey Financial Services Commission, or
    (d)　any person exercising public functions who is declared by regulations of the Commerce and Employment Department to be a public servant for the purposes of paragraph 17 of Schedule 6 to the Companies (Guernsey) Law 2008.

(D) ISLE OF MAN

1.　A disclosure for the purpose of enabling or assisting an inspector appointed by the High Court of the Isle of Man under the enactments of the Isle of Man relating to companies to discharge their functions.

2.　A disclosure for the purpose of enabling or assisting a person conducting an investigation under—
    (a)　section 16 of the Collective Investment Schemes Act 2008 (an Act of Tynwald: c 7);
    (b)　Schedule 2 to the Financial Services Act 2008 (an Act of Tynwald: c 8); or
    (c)　Schedule 5 to the Insurance Act 2008 (an Act of Tynwald: c 16),
to exercise their functions.

3.　A disclosure for the purpose of enabling or assisting the Financial Supervision Commission of the Isle of Man to exercise any of its functions.

4.　A disclosure for the purpose of enabling or assisting an auditor of a permitted person (within the meaning of the Financial Services Act 2008 (an Act of Tynwald)) to exercise their functions.

5.　A disclosure for the purpose of enabling or assisting the Office of Fair Trading of the Isle of Man to exercise its functions under Schedule 4 to the Financial Services Act 2008 (an Act of Tynwald) in relation to a financial services dispute within the meaning of paragraph 1(1) of that Schedule.

6.　A disclosure for the purpose of enabling or assisting an adjudicator appointed under paragraph 4 of Schedule 4 to the Financial Services Act 2008 (an Act of Tynwald) to exercise their functions.

7.　A disclosure for the purpose of enabling or assisting the body administering a scheme under section 25 of the Financial Services Act 2008 (an Act of Tynwald) (compensation schemes) to exercise its functions under the scheme.

8.　A disclosure with a view to the institution of, or otherwise for the purposes of, civil proceedings arising under or by virtue of the Financial Services Act 2008 (an Act of Tynwald).

9.　A disclosure for the purpose of enabling or assisting—
    (a)　the Insurance and Pensions Authority of the Isle of Man; or
    (b)　the Retirement Benefits Schemes Supervisor of the Isle of Man,
to exercise its functions under the Retirement Benefits Schemes Act 2000 (an Act of Tynwald: c 14).

10.　A disclosure for the purpose of enabling or assisting the Assessor of Income Tax to exercise their functions under enactments of the Isle of Man relating to income tax.

11.　A disclosure for the purpose of enabling or assisting the Office of Fair Trading of the Isle of Man to exercise its functions under any of the following—
    (a)　the Unsolicited Goods and Services (Isle of Man) Act 1974 (an Act of Tynwald: c 5);
    (b)　the Moneylenders Act 1991 (an Act of Tynwald: c 6);
    (c)　the Consumer Protection Act 1991 (an Act of Tynwald: c 11);
    (d)　the Fair Trading Act 1996 (an Act of Tynwald: c 15).

12.　A disclosure for the purpose of enabling or assisting the Department of Local Government and the Environment of the Isle of Man to exercise its functions under the Estate Agents Act 1975 (an Act of Tynwald: c 6) or the Estate Agents Act 1999 (an Act of Tynwald: c 7).

13.   A disclosure for the purpose of enabling or assisting Her Majesty's Attorney General of the Isle of Man to exercise their functions in connection with charities.

14.   A disclosure for the purpose of enabling or assisting the Treasury of the Isle of Man to exercise its functions under the enactments of the Isle of Man relating to companies, insurance companies or insolvency.

15.   A disclosure for the purpose of enabling or assisting an official receiver appointed in the Isle of Man to exercise their functions under the enactments of the Isle of Man relating to insolvency.

16.(1)   A disclosure with a view to the institution of, or otherwise for the purposes of, disciplinary proceedings relating to the performance by an advocate, registered legal practitioner, auditor, accountant, valuer or actuary of their professional duties.

   (2)   In sub-paragraph (1)—
      "advocate" means a person who is qualified to act as an advocate in any court in the Island in
         accordance with section 7 of the Advocates Act 1976 (an Act of Tynwald: c 27);
      "registered legal practitioner" means a legal practitioner within the meaning of section 10 of
         the Legal Practitioners Registration Act 1986 (an Act of Tynwald: c 15) who is registered
         within the meaning of that Act.

17.—(1)   A disclosure with a view to the institution of, or otherwise for the purposes of, disciplinary proceedings relating to the performance by a public servant of their duties.

   (2)   In sub-paragraph (1) "public servant" means—
      (a)   an officer or employee of the Crown, or
      (b)   an officer or employee of any public or other authority for the time being designated for
            the purposes of this paragraph by order made by the Council of Ministers of the Isle of
            Man.

(E) GENERAL

1.   A disclosure for the purpose of enabling or assisting—
      (a)   the European Central Bank, or
      (b)   the central bank of any country or territory outside the British Islands,
to exercise its functions.

2.—(1)   A disclosure for the purpose of enabling or assisting an overseas regulatory authority to exercise its regulatory functions.

   (2)   In sub-paragraph (1) "overseas regulatory authority" and "regulatory functions" have the same meaning as in section 82 of the Companies Act 1989 (assistance for overseas regulatory authorities).

3.   A disclosure with a view to the institution of, or otherwise for the purposes of, criminal proceedings in the British Islands or elsewhere.

4.   A disclosure for the purpose of the provision of a summary or collection of information framed in such a way as not to enable the identity of any person to whom the information relates to be ascertained.

5.   A disclosure in pursuance of any Community obligation.

[412]

NOTES
Commencement: 1 July 2009.
Substituted as noted to Pt 1 of this Schedule at **[411]**.
See further: in relation to the modification of this Part of this Schedule so as to include a reference to the Banking Act 2009, the Banking Act 2009 (Parts 2 and 3 Consequential Amendments) Orders 2009, SI 2009/317, art 6(1), (5) at **[529]**.

[PART 3
OVERSEAS REGULATORY BODIES

1.—(1)   A disclosure is made in accordance with this Part of this Schedule if—
      (a)   it is made to a person or body exercising relevant functions under legislation in a country
            or territory outside the British Islands, and
      (b)   it is made for the purpose of enabling or assisting that person or body to exercise those
            functions.

   (2)   "Relevant functions" for this purpose are functions of a public nature that appear to the Panel to be similar to its own functions or those of the Financial Services Authority.

2.   In determining whether to disclose information to a person or body in accordance with this Part of this Schedule, the Panel must have regard to the following considerations—
      (a)   whether the use that the person or body is likely to make of the information is
            sufficiently important to justify making the disclosure;

(b)   whether the person or body has adequate arrangements to prevent the information from being used or further disclosed, otherwise than—

    (i)   for the purposes of carrying out the functions mentioned in paragraph 1(1)(a), or

    (ii)   for other purposes substantially similar to those for which information disclosed to the Panel could be used or further disclosed.]

        [413]

NOTES

Commencement: 1 July 2009.

Substituted as noted to Pt 1 of this Schedule at **[411]**.

(Schs 3–16 outside the scope of this work; for Schs 6–8, 10–13 see Butterworths Securities and Financial Services Law Handbook.)

BANKRUPTCY AND DILIGENCE ETC (SCOTLAND) ACT 2007

(2007 asp 3)

An Act of the Scottish Parliament to amend the law of sequestration and personal insolvency; to amend the law about floating charges; to establish a Scottish Civil Enforcement Commission and replace officers of court with judicial officers; to amend the law of diligence; and for connected purposes.

        [15 January 2007]

1–36   *((Pt 1) Outside the scope of this work.)*

PART 2
FLOATING CHARGES

Registration and creation etc

37   *(Outside the scope of this work.)*

38   Creation of floating charges

(1)   It continues to be competent, for the purpose of securing any obligation to which this subsection applies, for a company to grant in favour of the creditor in the obligation a charge (known as a "floating charge") over all or any part of the property which may from time to time be comprised in the company's property and undertaking.

(2)   Subsection (1) above applies to any debt or other obligation incurred or to be incurred by, or binding upon, the company or any other person.

(3)   From the coming into force of this section, a floating charge is (subject to [subsection (3A) and] section 39 of this Act) created only when a document—

(a)   granting a floating charge; and

(b)   subscribed by the company granting the charge,

is registered in the Register of Floating Charges.

[(3A)   If a floating charge is granted in favour of a central institution, it is created only when the document granting the floating charge is executed by the company granting the charge.]

(4)   References in this Part to a document which grants a floating charge are to a document by means of which a floating charge is granted.

        [414]

NOTES

Commencement: to be appointed.

Sub-s (3): words in square brackets inserted by the Banking Act 2009, s 253(1), (2)(a), as from 21 February 2009.

Sub-s (3A): inserted by the Banking Act 2009, s 253(1), (2)(b), as from 21 February 2009.

39   Advance notice of floating charges

(1)   Where a company proposes to grant a floating charge, the company and the person in whose favour the charge is to be granted may apply to have joint notice of the proposed charge registered in the Register of Floating Charges.

(2)   Subsection (3) below applies where—

(a)   a notice under subsection (1) above is registered in the Register of Floating Charges; and

    (b)   within 21 days of the notice being so registered, a document—
        (i)   granting a floating charge conforming with the particulars contained in the notice; and
        (ii)   subscribed by the company granting the charge,
is registered in the Register of Floating Charges.

    (3)   Where this subsection applies, the floating charge so created is to be treated as having been created when the notice under subsection (1) above was so registered.

    [(4)   This section does not apply where a company proposes to grant a floating charge in favour of a central institution.]

                                                                       [415]

NOTES

Commencement: to be appointed.
Sub-s (4): inserted by the Banking Act 2009, s 253(1), (3), as from 21 February 2009.

40, 41   *(Outside the scope of this work.)*

42 Assignation of floating charges

    (1)   A floating charge may be assigned (and the rights under it vested in the assignee) by the registration in the Register of Floating Charges of a document of assignation subscribed by the holder of the charge.

    (2)   An assignation under subsection (1) above may be in whole or to such extent as may be specified in the document of assignation.

    (3)   This section is without prejudice to any other enactment, or any rule of law, by virtue of which a floating charge may be assigned.

    [(4)   This section does not apply where a floating charge is assigned (whether in whole or to a specified extent) to or by a central institution.]

                                                                         [416]

NOTES

Commencement: to be appointed.
Sub-s (4): inserted by the Banking Act 2009, s 253(1), (4), as from 21 February 2009.

43 Alteration of floating charges

    (1)   A document of alteration may alter (whether by addition, deletion or substitution of text or otherwise) the terms of a document granting a floating charge.

    (2)   If (and in so far as) an alteration to the terms of a document granting a floating charge concerns—
        (a)   the ranking of the charge with any other floating charge or any fixed security; or
        (b)   the specification of—
            (i)   the property that is subject to the charge; or
            (ii)   the obligations that are secured by the charge,
the alteration is not valid unless subsection (3) below is satisfied.

    (3)   This subsection is satisfied if the alteration is made by a document of alteration which is—
        (a)   subscribed by—
            (i)   the company which granted the charge;
            (ii)   the holder of the charge; and
            (iii)   the holder of any other subsisting floating charge, or any subsisting fixed security, which would be adversely affected by the alteration; and
        (b)   registered in the Register of Floating Charges.

    (4)   [Paragraph] (a)(i) of subsection (3) above does not apply in respect of an alteration which—
        (a)   relates only to the ranking of the floating charge first-mentioned in that subsection with any other floating charge or any fixed security; and
        (b)   does not adversely affect the interests of the company which granted the charge.

    [(4A)   Paragraph (b) of subsection (3) above does not apply in respect of an alteration if—
        (a)   the holder of the floating charge is a central institution, or
        (b)   the holder of the floating charge is not a central institution but the alteration is to be made in connection with a floating charge which is held (or which has been or is to be held) by a central institution.]

    (5)   The granting, by the holder of a floating charge, of consent to the release from the scope of the charge of any particular property, or class of property, which is subject to the charge is to be treated as constituting an alteration—
        (a)   to the terms of the document granting the charge; and

(b)   as to the specification of the property that is subject to the charge.

(6)   For the purpose of subsection (5) above, property is not to be regarded as released from the scope of a floating charge by reason only of its ceasing to be the property of the company which granted the charge.

[417]

NOTES

Commencement: to be appointed.

Sub-s (4): word in square brackets substituted by the Banking Act 2009, s 253(1), (5)(a), as from 21 February 2009.

Sub-s (4A): inserted by the Banking Act 2009, s 253(1), (5)(b), as from 21 February 2009.

44   Discharge of floating charges

(1)   A floating charge may be discharged by the registration in the Register of Floating Charges of a document of discharge subscribed by the holder of the charge.

(2)   A discharge under subsection (1) above may be in whole or to such extent as may be specified in the document of discharge.

(3)   This section is without prejudice to any other means by which a floating charge may be discharged or extinguished.

[(4)   This section does not apply where the floating charge to be discharged (whether in whole or to a specified extent) is or has been held by a central institution.]

[418]

NOTES

Commencement: to be appointed.

Sub-s (4): inserted by the Banking Act 2009, s 253(1), (6), as from 21 February 2009.

45, 46   (*Outside the scope of this work.*)

47   Interpretation

In this Part—

["central institution" means—
    (a)   the Bank of England,
    (b)   the central bank of a country or territory outside the United Kingdom, or
    (c)   the European Central Bank;]

"company" means an incorporated company (whether or not a company within the meaning of the Companies Act 1985 (c 6));

"fixed security", in relation to any property of a company, means any security (other than a floating charge or a charge having the character of a floating charge) which on the winding up of the company in Scotland would be treated as an effective security over that property including, in particular, a heritable security (within the meaning of section 9(8) of the Conveyancing and Feudal Reform (Scotland) Act 1970 (c 35)).

[419]

NOTES

Commencement: to be appointed.

Definition "central institution" inserted by the Banking Act 2009, s 253(1), (7), as from 21 February 2009.

Modification: this section is applied with modifications, in so far as it relates to bank insolvency or administration under the Banking Act 2009, Pts 2, 3, by the Banking Act 2009 (Parts 2 and 3 Consequential Amendments) Order 2009, SI 2009/317, art 3, Schedule, at **[526]**, **[532]**.

48–220   (*Ss 48, 49, ss 50–220 (Pts 3–16) outside the scope of this work.*)

PART 17
GENERAL AND MISCELLANEOUS

221, 222   (*Outside the scope of this work.*)

General

223–226   (*Outside the scope of this work.*)

227   Short title and commencement

(1)   This Act may be cited as the Bankruptcy and Diligence etc (Scotland) Act 2007.

(2)   Section 222 of this Act comes into force on the day after Royal Assent.

(3)   The remaining provisions of this Act, except this section and sections 224 and 225, come into force on such day as the Scottish Ministers may, by order, appoint.

(4)   Different days may, under subsection (3) above, be appointed for different purposes.

[420]

NOTES
Commencement: 15 January 2007.
Orders: the Bankruptcy and Diligence etc (Scotland) Act 2007 (Commencement No 1) Order 2007, SSI 2007/82; the Bankruptcy and Diligence etc (Scotland) Act 2007 (Commencement No 2 and Saving) Order 2008, SSI 2008/45; the Bankruptcy and Diligence etc (Scotland) Act 2007 (Commencement No 3, Savings and Transitionals) Order 2008, SSI 2008/115; the Bankruptcy and Diligence etc (Scotland) Act 2007 (Commencement No 4, Savings and Transitionals) Order 2009, SSI 2009/67.

(*Schs 1–6 outside the scope of this work.*)

BUILDING SOCIETIES (FUNDING) AND MUTUAL SOCIETIES (TRANSFERS) ACT 2007

(2007 c 26)

An Act to make provision in relation to funding limits in respect of building societies; to provide consequential rights to building society members; and to make provision in connection with the transfer of the business of certain mutual societies.

[23 October 2007]

1, 2   (*S 1 amends the Building Societies Act 1986, ss 5, 7 (outside the scope of this work); s 2 inserts the Building Societies Act 1986, s 90B at* **[365]**.)

3   Transfers to subsidiaries of other mutuals

(1)   The Treasury may, by order, make such modifications of the transfer provisions as it thinks appropriate to facilitate, or in consequence of, the transfer of the whole of the business of a mutual society (the transferor) to a subsidiary of a mutual society (whether or not of the same type) (the transferee).

(2)   An order under this section may make provision as to the rights (including rights of and pertaining to membership) in relation to the mutual society of which the transferee is a subsidiary—
    (a)   of the members of the transferor;
    (b)   of persons who, after the transfer, become customers of the transferee.

(3)   An order under this section may confer such functions on the Financial Services Authority as the Treasury think appropriate.

(4)   An order under this section—
    (a)   may make such consequential, saving, supplementary or transitional provision as the Treasury think appropriate;
    (b)   may make different provision for different purposes.

(5)   The power to make an order under this section is exercisable by statutory instrument.

(6)   An order which—
    (a)   makes modifications of a provision mentioned in paragraph (a), (b) or (c) of subsection (11), or
    (b)   amends paragraph (a) or (b) of subsection (13),
(whether or not it contains any other provision) must not be made unless a draft of it has been laid before and approved by resolution of each House of Parliament.

(7)   Otherwise, an order is subject to annulment in pursuance of a resolution of either House of Parliament.

(8)   If a draft of an order mentioned in subsection (6) would, apart from this subsection, be treated for the purposes of the Standing Orders of either House of Parliament as a hybrid instrument it must proceed in that House as if it were not such an instrument.

(9)   Modifications include omissions, additions and alterations.

(10)   A mutual society is—
    (a)   a building society incorporated or deemed to be incorporated under the Building Societies Act 1986 (c 53);
    (b)   a friendly society within the meaning of the Friendly Societies Act 1992 (c 40);
    (c)   an industrial and provident society registered or deemed to be registered under the Industrial and Provident Societies Act 1965 (c 12);

    (d)   an EEA mutual society.

(11)   The transfer provisions are—
    (a)   sections 97 to 102D of the Building Societies Act 1986, paragraph 30 of Schedule 2 to that Act and Schedule 17 to that Act;
    (b)   sections 86 and 88 of and Schedule 15 to the Friendly Societies Act 1992;
    (c)   section 52 of the Industrial and Provident Societies Act 1965;
    (d)   provision contained in subordinate legislation (within the meaning of the Interpretation Act 1978) made under any provision mentioned in paragraph (a), (b) or (c).

(12)   An EEA mutual society is—
    (a)   a body which is a European Cooperative Society for the purposes of Council Regulation (EC) No 1435/2003 (statute for a European Cooperative Society);
    (b)   a body which is established as a cooperative under the law of an EEA state as mentioned in that Regulation;
    (c)   a body which is a cooperative or mutual undertaking of such description as the Treasury specify by order and which is established or operates in accordance with the laws of an EEA state or any of the Channel Islands or the Isle of Man.

(13)   A subsidiary of a mutual society is a relevant company—
    (a)   in which the society holds a majority of the voting rights or of which the society is a member and alone controls, pursuant to an agreement with other shareholders or members, a majority of the voting rights, and
    (b)   in relation to which the society has the right to appoint or remove a majority of the company's board of directors,
but the Treasury may, by order, amend paragraphs (a) and (b) to make the degree of control required more or less onerous.

(14)   A relevant company is—
    (a)   a company within the meaning of the Companies Act 2006 (c 46) (or, before the commencement of Part 1 of that Act, the Companies Act 1985 (c 6));
    (b)   a company within the meaning of the Companies (Northern Ireland) Order 1986 (SI 1986/1032 (NI 6));
    (c)   a body corporate which is incorporated in an EEA state other than the United Kingdom.

(15)   For the purposes of paragraph 17 of Schedule 1 to the Financial Services and Markets Act 2000 (c 8) (power to charge fees) a function conferred on the Financial Services Authority by an order under this section is to be treated as a function conferred under or as a result of that Act.

                                                                         [421]

PART II
OTHER ACTS

NOTES
Commencement: 16 January 2009.
Order: the Mutual Societies (Transfers) Order 2009, SI 2009/509.

4   Transfers to subsidiaries: distribution of funds

(1)   An order under section 3 may provide for this section to have effect.

(2)   Subsection (3) applies if the terms of a transfer to which the order applies include provision for part of the funds of the transferor or the mutual society of which the transferee is a subsidiary (the holding mutual) to be distributed in consideration of the transfer among the members of—
    (a)   the transferor,
    (b)   the holding mutual, or
    (c)   both the transferor and the holding mutual.

(3)   The provision for the distribution must be authorised as follows—
    (a)   it must not exceed the limits prescribed by order under subsection (4), and the distribution must be approved (in the case of the transferor) by the transfer resolution or (in the case of the holding mutual) by a resolution of such description as the Treasury specifies by order;
    (b)   if the provision for a distribution exceeds the prescribed limits, it must be approved by each of the resolutions mentioned in paragraph (a).

(4)   The Treasury must by order authorise distributions of funds to members by mutual societies participating (directly or through a subsidiary) in transfers to which an order mentioned in subsection (1) applies, subject to limits specified by or determined in accordance with the order.

(5)   A transfer resolution is—
    (a)   in relation to a building society, each of the resolutions required pursuant to paragraph 30 of Schedule 2 to the Building Societies Act 1986 (c 53);
    (b)   in relation to a friendly society, the resolution required by section 86(2)(b) of the Friendly Societies Act 1992 (c 40);
    (c)   in relation to an industrial and provident society, the resolution required by section 52 of the Industrial and Provident Societies Act 1965 (c 12).

(6)   Expressions used in this section and in section 3 have the same meaning as in that section.

(7)   Subsections (4) to (7) of that section apply to an order under this section as they apply to an order under that section.

[422]

NOTES
Commencement: 16 January 2009.
Order: the Mutual Societies (Transfers) Order 2009, SI 2009/509.

5   Channel Islands and Isle of Man

Her Majesty may by Order in Council provide for any of the provisions of this Act to extend, with or without modifications, to any of the Channel Islands or to the Isle of Man.

[423]

NOTES
Commencement: 16 January 2009.

6   Short title, commencement and extent

(1)   This Act may be cited as the Building Societies (Funding) and Mutual Societies (Transfers) Act 2007.

(2)   The preceding sections of this Act shall come into force on such day as the Treasury may by order made by statutory instrument appoint, and different days may be appointed for different purposes.

(3)   This Act extends to the whole of the United Kingdom.

[424]

NOTES
Commencement: 23 October 2007.
Order: the Building Societies (Funding) and Mutual Societies (Transfers) Act 2007 (Commencement No 1) Order 2009, SI 2009/36 at **[1125]**.

BANKING (SPECIAL PROVISIONS) ACT 2008

(2008 c 2)

ARRANGEMENT OF SECTIONS

An Act to make provision to enable the Treasury in certain circumstances to make an order relating to the transfer of securities issued by, or of property, rights or liabilities belonging to, an authorised deposit-taker; to make further provision in relation to building societies; and for connected purposes

[21 February 2008]

Introduction

1   Meaning of "authorised UK deposit-taker"

(1)   In this Act "authorised UK deposit-taker" means a UK undertaking that under Part 4 of FSMA 2000 has permission to accept deposits.

(2)   That expression does not, however, include such an undertaking with permission to accept deposits only for the purposes of, or in the course of, an activity other than accepting deposits.

[425]

NOTES

Commencement: 21 February 2008.

2   Cases where Treasury's powers are exercisable

(1)   The power of the Treasury to make an order under—
     (a)   section 3 (transfer of securities issued by an authorised UK deposit-taker), or
     (b)   section 6 (transfer of property, rights and liabilities of an authorised UK deposit-taker),
is exercisable in relation to an authorised UK deposit-taker if (and only if) it appears to the Treasury to be desirable to make the order for either or both of the following purposes.

This is subject to subsection (7).

(2)   The purposes are—
     (a)   maintaining the stability of the UK financial system in circumstances where the Treasury consider that there would be a serious threat to its stability if the order were not made;
     (b)   protecting the public interest in circumstances where financial assistance has been provided by the Treasury to the deposit-taker for the purpose of maintaining the stability of the UK financial system.

(3)   The reference in subsection (2)(b) to the provision of financial assistance by the Treasury to the deposit-taker includes—
     (a)   any case where the Bank of England has provided financial assistance to the deposit-taker and—
         (i)   the Treasury have assumed a liability in respect of the assistance,
         (ii)   the liability is of a kind of which the Treasury are expected to give relevant notice, and
         (iii)   the Treasury have given relevant notice of the liability;
     (b)   any case where the Chancellor of the Exchequer has announced that the Treasury (whether acting alone or with the Bank of England) would, if necessary, put in place relevant guarantee arrangements in relation to the deposit-taker (as well as any case where any such arrangements have been put in place, whether or not following such an announcement).

(4)   For the purposes of subsection (3) the Treasury give "relevant notice" of a liability if—
     (a)   they lay a Minute before the House of Commons containing information about the liability, or
     (b)   they give written notice containing such information to the person who chairs the House of Commons Committee of Public Accounts and the person who chairs the House of Commons Treasury Committee.

(5)   It is immaterial whether the notice or announcement mentioned in subsection (3) is given or made before or after the passing of this Act.

(6)   In this Act "relevant guarantee arrangements", in relation to any authorised UK deposit-taker, means any guarantee arrangements for protecting some or all of the depositors or other creditors of the deposit-taker.

PART II
OTHER ACTS

(7) Where an order has been made under section 3 or 6 in relation to any authorised UK deposit-taker, subsection (1) does not apply in relation to any subsequent exercise of the power to make an order under either of those sections in relation to that deposit-taker.

(8) The power of the Treasury to make an order under section 3 or 6 in relation to an authorised UK deposit-taker may not be exercised after the end of the period of one year beginning with the day on which this Act is passed.

(9) Subsection (8) does not affect the continuation in force or effect of any order made or other thing done by virtue of either of those sections before the end of that period.

(10) In this section "the UK financial system" means the financial system in the United Kingdom.

(11) Section 13 of the National Audit Act 1983 (c 44) (interpretation of references to Committee of Public Accounts) applies for the purposes of this section, but as if—
  (a) the references in that section to that Act were to this Act, and
  (b) the references in that section to the House of Commons Committee of Public Accounts included the House of Commons Treasury Committee.

[426]

NOTES
Commencement: 21 February 2008.

Transfer of securities

3 Transfer of securities

(1) The Treasury may, in relation to all or any securities of a specified description that have been issued by an authorised UK deposit-taker, by order make provision for or in connection with, or in consequence of, the transfer of the securities to any of the following—
  (a) the Bank of England;
  (b) a nominee of the Treasury;
  (c) a company wholly owned by the Bank of England or the Treasury;
  (d) any body corporate not within paragraph (c).

(2) Schedule 1 specifies particular kinds of provisions that may be included in an order under this section.

(3) Where an order providing for the transfer of any securities has been made under this section, the power to make an order under this section may be subsequently exercised so as to make provision in connection with, or in consequence of, the transfer (including provision of a kind specified in Schedule 1) even though the order does not itself provide for the transfer of any securities.

(4) Where an order under this section or section 6 ("the initial order") has been made in relation to an authorised UK deposit-taker, the power to make an order under this section may be subsequently exercised in relation to that deposit-taker whether or not any transfer of securities provided for by the order is to the person to whom any transfer was made by or under the initial order.

(5) For the purposes of this section any provision made by an order under this section in relation to any transaction or event taking place while securities transferred by such an order are held by a person within subsection (1)(a), (b) or (c) is to be regarded as provision made in consequence of the transfer.

[427]

NOTES
Commencement: 21 February 2008.
Orders: the Northern Rock plc Transfer Order 2008, SI 2008/432; the Bradford & Bingley plc Transfer of Securities and Property etc Order 2008, SI 2008/2546 at **[963]**.

4 Extinguishment of subscription rights

(1) This section applies where the Treasury make, or have made, an order under section 3 providing for the transfer of securities issued by an authorised UK deposit-taker.

(2) The Treasury may by order make provision for or in connection with, or in consequence of, the extinguishment of rights of any specified description to subscribe for, or otherwise acquire, securities of—
  (a) the deposit-taker, or
  (b) any of its subsidiary undertakings.

(3) Subsection (2) applies whether the rights have been granted by the deposit-taker or otherwise.

(4)   Where an order providing for the extinguishment of any rights has been made under this section, the power to make an order under this section may be subsequently exercised so as to make provision in connection with, or in consequence of, the extinguishment of those rights even though the order does not itself provide for any rights to be extinguished.

[428]

NOTES

Commencement: 21 February 2008.

Orders: the Northern Rock plc Transfer Order 2008, SI 2008/432; the Bradford & Bingley plc Transfer of Securities and Property etc Order 2008, SI 2008/2546 at **[963]**.

5   Compensation etc for securities transferred etc

(1)   The Treasury must by order—

   (a)   in relation to an order under section 3 that transfers securities only to the public sector, make a scheme for determining the amount of any compensation payable by the Treasury to persons who held the securities immediately before they were so transferred;

   (b)   in relation to an order under section 3 that transfers securities only to a private sector body, make provision for determining the amount of any consideration payable by the body to persons who held the securities immediately before they were so transferred;

   (c)   in relation to an order under section 3 that transfers securities both to the public sector and a private sector body, make provision for determining—

      (i)   the amount of any compensation payable by the Treasury, and

      (ii)   the amount of any consideration payable by the private sector body concerned,

to persons who held the securities immediately before they were so transferred.

(2)   The Treasury must by order make provision for determining the amount of any compensation payable to persons whose rights are extinguished by virtue of an order under section 4 (a "section 4 order") and—

   (a)   in any case where the section 4 order is made in consequence of an order under section 3 that transfers securities only to the public sector, the order must provide for any compensation to be payable by the Treasury;

   (b)   in any case where the section 4 order is made in consequence of an order under section 3 that transfers securities only to a private sector body, the order must provide for any compensation to be payable by the private sector body concerned;

   (c)   in any case where the section 4 order is made in consequence of an order under section 3 that transfers securities both to the public sector and a private sector body, the order must make provision for determining the amount of any compensation payable by the Treasury or the private sector body concerned (or both).

(3)   An order under this section may also make provision for extending provisions of the order, in any specified circumstances, to persons otherwise affected by any provision made in an order under section 3 or 4.

(4)   In determining the amount of any compensation payable by the Treasury by virtue of any provision in an order under this section, it must be assumed—

   (a)   that all financial assistance provided by the Bank of England or the Treasury to the deposit-taker in question has been withdrawn (whether by the making of a demand for repayment or otherwise), and

   (b)   that no financial assistance would in future be provided by the Bank of England or the Treasury to the deposit-taker in question (apart from ordinary market assistance offered by the Bank of England subject to its usual terms).

(5)   For the purposes of subsection (4)—

   (a)   the references to the provision of financial assistance by the Treasury to the deposit-taker include any case where the Chancellor of the Exchequer announces that the Treasury (whether acting alone or with the Bank of England) would, if necessary, put in place relevant guarantee arrangements in relation to the deposit-taker (as well as any case where any such arrangements are put in place, whether or not following such an announcement);

   (b)   "ordinary market assistance" means assistance provided as part of the Bank's standing facilities in the sterling money markets or as part of the Bank's open market operations in those markets.

(6)   It is immaterial whether the announcement mentioned in subsection (5)(a) is made before or after the passing of this Act.

(7)   In this section—

   (a)   any reference to any transfer of securities to the public sector is a reference to the transfer of any securities to any person within paragraphs (a) to (c) of subsection (1) of section 3;

PART II
OTHER ACTS

(b)   any reference to any transfer of securities to a private sector body is a reference to the transfer of any securities to any body corporate within paragraph (d) of that subsection.

(8)   An order under subsection (1) or (2) must be made within the period of 3 months beginning with—

(a)   the day on which the order under section 3 is made (in the case of an order under subsection (1)), or

(b)   the day on which the order under section 4 is made (in the case of an order under subsection (2)).

(9)   But nothing in subsection (8) prevents the making, at any time after the end of that period, of a second or subsequent order under this section in relation to the order under section 3 or 4.

[429]

NOTES
Commencement: 21 February 2008.
Orders: the Northern Rock plc Compensation Scheme Order 2008, SI 2008/718; the Bradford & Bingley plc Compensation Scheme Order 2008, SI 2008/3249 at **[1113]**.

Transfer of property etc

6   Transfer of property, rights and liabilities

(1)   The Treasury may by order make provision for or in connection with, or in consequence of, the transfer of property, rights and liabilities of an authorised UK deposit-taker to either (or each) of the following—

(a)   a company wholly owned by the Bank of England or the Treasury;

(b)   a body corporate not within paragraph (a).

(2)   An order under this section may define the property, rights and liabilities to be transferred in one or more of the following ways—

(a)   by specifying or describing the property, rights and liabilities in question;

(b)   by referring to all the property, rights and liabilities comprised in the whole or a specified part of the deposit-taker's business;

(c)   by identifying the manner in which the property, rights and liabilities to be transferred are to be determined.

(3)   Schedule 2 specifies particular kinds of provisions that may be included in an order under this section.

(4)   Where an order providing for the transfer of any property, rights or liabilities has been made under this section, the power to make an order under this section may be subsequently exercised so as to make provision in connection with, or in consequence of, the transfer (including provision of a kind specified in Schedule 2) even though the order does not itself provide for the transfer of any property, rights or liabilities.

(5)   Where an order under this section or section 3 ("the initial order") has been made in relation to an authorised UK deposit-taker, the power to make an order under this section may be subsequently exercised in relation to that deposit-taker whether or not any transfer of property, rights or liabilities provided for by the order is to the person to whom any transfer was made by or under the initial order.

(6)   A second or subsequent order made under this section in relation to an authorised UK deposit-taker may make provision for any of the property, rights or liabilities transferred by or under a previous order under this section to be transferred back to the deposit-taker.

(7)   The provisions of this section and Schedule 2 apply for the purposes of subsection (6) with any necessary modifications.

(8)   For the purposes of this section any provision made by an order under this section in relation to any transaction or event taking place while property, rights or liabilities transferred by or under such an order are held by a company within subsection (1)(a) is to be regarded as provision made in consequence of the transfer.

[430]

NOTES
Commencement: 21 February 2008.
Orders: the Heritable Bank plc Transfer of Certain Rights and Liabilities Order 2008, SI 2008/2644 at **[1008]**; the Transfer of Rights and Liabilities to ING Order 2008, SI 2008/2666 at **[1046]**; the Kaupthing Singer & Friedlander Limited Transfer of Certain Rights and Liabilities Order 2008, SI 2008/2674 at **[1078]**.

7   Compensation etc for property etc transferred

(1)   The Treasury must by order make provision—

(a)   in relation to an order under section 6 providing for the transfer of property, rights or liabilities to a company within subsection (1)(a) of that section, for determining the amount of any compensation payable by the Treasury to the authorised UK deposit-taker concerned;

    (b)   in relation to an order under section 6 providing for the transfer of property, rights or liabilities to any other body, for determining the amount of any consideration payable by the transferee to the authorised UK deposit-taker concerned.

(2)   An order under this section may also make provision for extending provisions of the order, in any specified circumstances, to persons otherwise affected by any provision made in an order under section 6.

(3)   In determining the amount of any compensation payable by the Treasury by virtue of any provision in an order under this section, it must be assumed—

    (a)   that all financial assistance provided by the Bank of England or the Treasury to the deposit-taker in question has been withdrawn (whether by the making of a demand for repayment or otherwise), and

    (b)   that no financial assistance would in future be provided by the Bank of England or the Treasury to the deposit-taker in question (apart from ordinary market assistance offered by the Bank of England subject to its usual terms).

(4)   For the purposes of subsection (3)—

    (a)   the references to the provision of financial assistance by the Treasury to the deposit-taker include any case where the Chancellor of the Exchequer announces that the Treasury (whether acting alone or with the Bank of England) would, if necessary, put in place relevant guarantee arrangements in relation to the deposit-taker (as well as any case where any such arrangements are put in place, whether or not following such an announcement);

    (b)   "ordinary market assistance" means assistance provided as part of the Bank's standing facilities in the sterling money markets or as part of the Bank's open market operations in those markets.

(5)   It is immaterial whether the announcement mentioned in subsection (4)(a) is made before or after the passing of this Act.

(6)   An order under this section must be made within the period of 3 months beginning with the day on which the order under section 6 is made.

(7)   But nothing in subsection (6) prevents the making, at any time after the end of that period, of a second or subsequent order under this section in relation to the order under section 6.

[431]

NOTES

Commencement: 21 February 2008.
Orders: the Kaupthing Singer & Friedlander Limited (Determination of Compensation) Order 2008, SI 2008/3250 at **[1121]**; the Heritable Bank plc (Determination of Compensation) Order 2008, SI 2008/3251 at **[1123]**.

Further transfers

8 Further transfers following transfer to public sector

(1)   Subsection (2) applies where any securities issued by an authorised UK deposit-taker have been transferred to a person within section 3(1)(a) to (c) by an order under section 3.

(2)   In such a case the Treasury may by order make provision for or in connection with, or in consequence of, the transfer to a specified person of any of the following—

    (a)   any of the securities transferred as mentioned in subsection (1);

    (b)   any securities issued by the deposit-taker at any time after the transfer mentioned in that subsection;

    (c)   any of the property, rights and liabilities of the deposit-taker;

    (d)   any of the property, rights and liabilities of any UK undertaking which is a subsidiary undertaking of the deposit-taker;

    (e)   where the securities so transferred were transferred to a company within section 3(1)(c)—

        (i)   any securities issued by the company;

        (ii)   any property, rights and liabilities of the company.

(3)   Subsection (4) applies where any property, rights or liabilities have been transferred to a company within section 6(1)(a) ("the company") by or under an order under section 6.

(4)   In such a case the Treasury may by order make provision for or in connection with, or in consequence of, the transfer to a specified person of any of the following—

    (a)   any property, rights and liabilities of the company;

    (b)   any property, rights and liabilities of any UK undertaking which is a subsidiary undertaking of the company;

    (c)   any securities issued by the company.

(5)   The following provisions apply in relation to an order under subsection (2) or (4) with any necessary modifications—

    (a)   sections 3(2) to (4) and 4, together with Schedule 1, so apply in relation to an order making provision for or in connection with, or in consequence of, the transfer of any securities;

    (b)   section 6(2) to (5), together with Schedule 2, so apply in relation to an order making provision for or in connection with, or in consequence of, the transfer of any property, rights or liabilities.

(6)   The Treasury may by order make provision, in relation to any description of order under subsection (2) or (4), for determining the amount of any consideration payable by the transferee in respect of any securities, or any property, rights and liabilities, transferred by or under any such order under that subsection.

(7)   A person to whom anything is transferred by or under an order under section 3 or 6 is not to be regarded as precluded by subsection (2) or (4) from making any contractual or other disposition of, or relating to, anything falling within those subsections.

[432]

NOTES

Commencement: 21 February 2008.

Orders: the Bradford & Bingley plc Transfer of Securities and Property etc Order 2008, SI 2008/2546 at **[963]**; the Transfer of Rights and Liabilities to ING Order 2008, SI 2008/2666 at **[1046]**; the Kaupthing Singer & Friedlander Limited Transfer of Certain Rights and Liabilities Order 2008, SI 2008/2674 at **[1078]**.

Supplementary

9 Supplementary provision about compensation schemes etc

(1)   An order under section 5, 7 or 8(6) may in particular make provision—

    (a)   for the manner in which any compensation or consideration is to be assessed, including provision as to methods of calculation, valuation dates and matters to be taken into, or left out of, account in making valuations;

    (b)   for the assessment to be made by an independent valuer appointed by the Treasury;

    (c)   as to the procedure in relation to the assessment of any compensation or consideration, including provision enabling any such valuer to make rules as to that procedure;

    (d)   for decisions relating to the assessment of any compensation or consideration to be reconsidered by the person who made those decisions (including any such provision as to procedure as is mentioned in paragraph (c));

    (e)   for enabling persons to apply for decisions relating to the assessment of any compensation or consideration to be reviewed by the Financial Services and Markets Tribunal or a tribunal appointed by the Treasury for the purposes of the order;

    (f)   as to the powers of a relevant tribunal (that is to say, the Financial Services and Markets Tribunal or a tribunal appointed by the Treasury for the purposes of the order);

    (g)   as to the procedure for applying for any review to a relevant tribunal, including provision enabling the tribunal to make rules as to that procedure;

    (h)   as to remuneration and expenses of any independent valuer, or of any tribunal, appointed by the Treasury for the purposes of the order;

    (i)   as to the appointment of any staff of any such valuer (including provision as to their terms and conditions of employment and as to their pensions, allowances or gratuities).

(2)   The provision that may be made by virtue of subsection (1)(a) includes the making of assumptions as to any matter, including in particular the making of one or more of the following assumptions about the authorised UK deposit-taker in question—

    (a)   that it is unable to continue as a going concern;

    (b)   that it is in administration;

    (c)   that it is being wound up.

(3)   Subsection (1)(a) is subject to sections 5(4) and 7(3), but those subsections do not—

    (a)   prevent the inclusion of provision requiring the making of the assumptions mentioned in those subsections in any case where they are not required to be made by either of those subsections; or

    (b)   otherwise restrict the provision that may be made by virtue of subsection (1)(a).

(4)   In subsection (1)(a) the reference to valuation dates includes—

    (a)   valuation dates falling before the day on which this Act is passed; and

    (b)   valuation dates falling before the day on which the relevant event takes place.

(5)   In subsection (1)(e)—

    (a)   the reference to persons includes the Treasury; and

    (b)   the reference to decisions relating to the assessment of any compensation or consideration includes decisions following any such reconsideration as is mentioned in subsection (1)(d).

(6)   The provision that may be made by virtue of subsection (1)(f)—

    (a)   includes provision enabling a relevant tribunal, where satisfied that the decision in question was not a reasonable decision, to send the matter back to the person who made the decision for reconsideration in accordance with such directions (if any) as it considers appropriate; but

    (b)   does not include provision enabling a relevant tribunal to substitute its own decision for that of the person who made the decision.

(7)   The power of any valuer or tribunal to make provision as to procedure by virtue of subsection (1)(c), (d) or (g) includes power to make different provision for different cases or circumstances.

(8)   In this section "the relevant event" means the transfer or (as the case may be) extinguishment of rights made by or under the order to which the order mentioned in subsection (1) relates.

[433]

NOTES

Commencement: 21 February 2008.

Orders: the Northern Rock plc Compensation Scheme Order 2008, SI 2008/718; the Bradford & Bingley plc Compensation Scheme Order 2008, SI 2008/3249 at **[1113]**.

10   Tax consequences

(1)   The Treasury may by regulations make provision for or in connection with varying the way in which any relevant tax would, apart from the regulations, have effect in relation to, or in connection with, any of the following—

    (a)   anything done for the purpose of, in relation to, or by or under or in consequence of, a relevant order;

    (b)   any securities, or any property, rights or liabilities, which are transferred, extinguished or otherwise affected by any provision made by or under a relevant order;

    (c)   any securities issued by, or any property, rights or liabilities of, any transferee which have not been transferred by or under a relevant order;

    (d)   any securities issued by, or any property, rights or liabilities of, any relevant institution which have not been so transferred.

(2)   The provision that may be made by the regulations includes provision for or in connection with any of the following—

    (a)   a tax provision not to apply, or to apply with modifications, in prescribed cases or circumstances;

    (b)   anything done to have or not to have a specified consequence for the purposes of a tax provision in prescribed cases or circumstances;

    (c)   any securities, or any property, rights or liabilities, to be treated in a specified way for the purposes of a tax provision in prescribed cases or circumstances (whether or not affected by any provision made by or under a relevant order);

    (d)   the withdrawal of relief (whether or not granted by virtue of the regulations), and the charging of any relevant tax, in prescribed cases or circumstances;

    (e)   requiring or enabling the Treasury to determine, or to specify the method to be used for determining, anything (including amounts or values, or times or periods of time) which needs to be determined for the purposes of any tax provision (whether or not modified by the regulations) as it applies in relation to, or in connection with, any of the matters mentioned in subsection (1)(a) to (d).

(3)   In this section—

    "prescribed" means prescribed by or determined in accordance with regulations under this section;

    "relevant institution" means any body in relation to which a relevant order is made;

    "relevant order" means an order under section 3, 4, 6 or 8;

    "relevant tax" means corporation tax, income tax, capital gains tax, stamp duty, stamp duty reserve tax and stamp duty land tax;

    "tax provision" means any enactment relating to any relevant tax;

    "transferee" means any person to whom any securities, or any property, rights or liabilities, are transferred by or under a relevant order.

[434]

NOTES

Commencement: 21 February 2008.

PART II
OTHER ACTS

Building societies

11 Modification of legislation applying in relation to building societies

(1) The Treasury may by order make such modifications of the Building Societies Act 1986 (c 53) as they consider appropriate for or in connection with facilitating the provision of relevant financial assistance by the Bank of England to building societies.

(2) In this section "relevant financial assistance" means any financial assistance provided for the purpose of maintaining the stability of the financial system in the United Kingdom.

(3) An order under this section may in particular make provision for or in connection with modifying the operation of any of the following—
    (a) sections 5, 6 and 7 of, and Schedule 2 to, the Building Societies Act 1986 (c 53) (establishment, constitution and powers, the lending limit and the funding limit);
    (b) any other provision of that Act which might otherwise prevent any relevant financial assistance from being provided by the Bank of England to building societies or affect the amount of any such assistance;
    (c) sections 8, 9A and 9B of the Building Societies Act 1986 (restrictions on raising funds and borrowing, on transactions involving derivative instruments etc and on creation of floating charges);
    (d) any other provision of that Act which might otherwise prevent building societies from entering into any transaction in connection with the provision of financial assistance by the Bank of England to building societies;
    (e) sections 90 and 90A of, and Schedules 15 and 15A to, that Act (application of companies winding up legislation and other companies insolvency legislation to building societies).

(4) An order under this section may in particular disapply (to such extent as is specified) any specified statutory provision.

(5) In this section "building society" means a building society incorporated (or deemed to be incorporated) under the Building Societies Act 1986.

[435]

NOTES
Commencement: 21 February 2008.
Order: the Building Societies (Financial Assistance) Order 2008, SI 2008/1427.

General

12 Consequential and supplementary provision

(1) The Treasury may by order make—
    (a) such supplementary, incidental or consequential provision, or
    (b) such transitory, transitional or saving provision,
as they consider appropriate for the general purposes, or any particular purposes, of this Act or in consequence of any provision made by or under this Act, or for giving full effect to this Act or any such provision.

(2) An order under this section may in particular—
    (a) disapply (to such extent as is specified) any specified statutory provision or rule of law;
    (b) provide for any specified statutory provision to apply (whether or not it would otherwise apply) with specified modifications;
    (c) make provision for or in connection with any of the matters mentioned in subsection (3).

(3) Those matters are—
    (a) imposing a moratorium on the commencement or continuation of proceedings or other legal processes of any specified description in relation to any body or property of any such description;
    (b) providing exceptions from any provision made in pursuance of paragraph (a), whether framed by reference to—
        (i) the leave of the court or the consent of the Treasury or the Bank of England, or
        (ii) instruments or transactions of specified descriptions,
    or otherwise;
    (c) the dissolution of any relevant deposit-taker or of any UK undertaking which is a subsidiary undertaking of any relevant deposit-taker;
    (d) exempting directors of any relevant deposit-taker, or of any group undertaking of any relevant deposit-taker, from liability in connection with acts or omissions in relation to the deposit-taker or undertaking;
    (e) the payment of any compensation by the Treasury to persons affected by an order under this section.

(4)   An order under this section may, in connection with the payment of any such compensation, make provision for any matter for which provision is or may be made by or under section 5, 7 or 9.

(5)   In this section "relevant deposit-taker" means any authorised UK deposit-taker in relation to which an order is being, or has been, made under section 3 or 6.

[436]

NOTES
Commencement: 21 February 2008.
Orders: the Northern Rock plc Transfer Order 2008, SI 2008/432; the Northern Rock plc Compensation Scheme Order 2008, SI 2008/718; the Building Societies (Financial Assistance) Order 2008, SI 2008/1427; the Bradford & Bingley plc Transfer of Securities and Property etc Order 2008, SI 2008/2546 at **[963]**; the Heritable Bank plc Transfer of Certain Rights and Liabilities Order 2008, SI 2008/2644 at **[1008]**; the Transfer of Rights and Liabilities to ING Order 2008, SI 2008/2666 at **[1046]**; the Kaupthing Singer & Friedlander Limited Transfer of Certain Rights and Liabilities Order 2008, SI 2008/2674 at **[1078]**; the Bradford & Bingley plc Compensation Scheme Order 2008, SI 2008/3249 at **[1113]**.

13   Orders and regulations: general

(1)   Orders and regulations under this Act are to be made by statutory instrument.

(2)   Such orders and regulations—
    (a)   may make different provision for different cases or circumstances;
    (b)   may make such supplementary, incidental, consequential, transitory, transitional or saving provision as the Treasury consider appropriate.

(3)   A statutory instrument which contains an order under section 5, 7, 8(6) or 11 (whether alone or with other provision) may not be made unless a draft of the instrument has been laid before, and approved by a resolution of, each House of Parliament.

(4)   If a statutory instrument to which subsection (3) applies would, apart from this subsection, be treated as a hybrid instrument for the purposes of the Standing Orders of either House of Parliament, it is to proceed in that House as if it were not such an instrument.

(5)   A statutory instrument containing an order under this Act to which subsection (3) does not apply is subject to annulment in pursuance of a resolution of either House of Parliament.

(6)   A statutory instrument containing regulations under section 10 is subject to annulment in pursuance of a resolution of the House of Commons.

(7)   Nothing in any provision of this Act that authorises the making of any order or regulations, or the making of any particular kind of provision by any order or regulations, affects the generality of any other such provision of this Act.

[437]

NOTES
Commencement: 21 February 2008.

14   Orders and regulations: retrospective provisions

(1)   Subsections (2) and (3) apply to any order made under section 3, 4, 6 or 12 (a "relevant order").

(2)   A relevant order may—
    (a)   provide for any provision made by the order to have retrospective effect as from any appropriate time or any specified later time;
    (b)   make provision for or in connection with, or in consequence of, nullifying the effect of transactions or events taking place after the time in question.

(3)   "Appropriate time", in relation to a relevant order, means—
    (a)   the specified time on the date of a statement published by the Treasury of their intention to make an order that would have the same general effect as the relevant order;
    (b)   the specified time on the date on which any transfer was effected by or under a previous relevant order.

(4)   It is immaterial whether the statement mentioned in subsection (3)(a) is published before or after the passing of this Act.

(5)   Regulations under section 10 may provide for any of their provisions to have retrospective effect as from any time which is not earlier than 3 months before the day on which this Act is passed.

[438]

NOTES
Commencement: 21 February 2008.

15 Interpretation

(1)   In this Act—

"authorised UK deposit-taker" has the meaning given by section 1;

"body corporate" includes a body incorporated outside the United Kingdom, but does not include the Bank of England;

"company" means a company within the meaning of section 1 of the Companies Act 2006 (c 46);

"director", in relation to a body corporate whose affairs are managed by its members, means a member of the body corporate;

"enactment" includes—

    (a)   an enactment comprised in subordinate legislation within the meaning of the Interpretation Act 1978 (c 30),

    (b)   an enactment contained in, or in an instrument made under, an Act of the Scottish Parliament, and

    (c)   an enactment contained in, or in an instrument made under, Northern Ireland legislation within the meaning of the Interpretation Act 1978;

"financial assistance", in relation to any person, includes—

    (a)   assistance provided by way of loan, guarantee or indemnity,

    (b)   assistance provided by way of any transaction which equates, in substance, to a transaction for lending money at interest (such as a transaction involving the sale and repurchase of securities or other assets), and

    (c)   assistance falling within paragraph (a) or (b) provided indirectly to or otherwise for the benefit of the person (including the provision of assistance within paragraph (a) or (b) to any group undertaking of that person),

    whether provided in pursuance of an agreement or otherwise and whether provided before or after the passing of this Act;

"FSMA 2000" means the Financial Services and Markets Act 2000 (c 8);

"group undertaking" has the meaning given by section 1161 of the Companies Act 2006;

"indemnity" includes any undertaking or other arrangement entered into for the purpose of indemnifying any person or for any similar purpose;

"liabilities" includes obligations;

"modifications" includes omissions, additions and alterations, and "modify" has a corresponding meaning;

"pension scheme" means a scheme or other arrangements for the provision of benefits to or in respect of people—

    (a)   on retirement,

    (b)   on death,

    (c)   on having reached a particular age,

    (d)   on the onset of any serious ill-health or incapacity, or

    (e)   in similar circumstances;

"relevant guarantee arrangements", in relation to any authorised UK deposit-taker, has the meaning given by section 2(6);

"securities" includes—

    (a)   shares and stock,

    (b)   debentures, including debenture stock, loan stock, bonds, certificates of deposit and other instruments creating or acknowledging indebtedness, and

    (c)   warrants or other instruments entitling the holder to subscribe for, or otherwise acquire, securities falling within paragraph (a) or (b),

    and see also subsection (2);

"specified", in relation to any order or regulations under this Act, means specified in the order or regulations;

"statutory provision" means any provision made by or under an enactment (whenever passed or made);

"subsidiary undertaking" has the meaning given by section 1162 of the Companies Act 2006 (c 46);

"UK undertaking" means an undertaking which is incorporated in, or formed under the law of any part of, the United Kingdom;

"undertaking" has the meaning given by section 1161 of the Companies Act 2006 (except in the definition of "indemnity");

"wholly owned", in relation to the Bank of England or the Treasury, is to be construed in accordance with subsection (6);

"wholly-owned subsidiary" has the meaning given by section 1159 of the Companies Act 2006.

(2)   In this Act any reference (however expressed) to securities issued by any authorised UK deposit-taker includes a reference to rights granted by the deposit-taker which form part of its own funds for the purposes of Section 1 of Chapter 2 of Title V of the Banking Consolidation Directive (and which would not otherwise be securities by virtue of subsection (1)).

(3)   In subsection (2) "the Banking Consolidation Directive" means Directive 2006/48/EC of the European Parliament and of the Council of 14 June 2006 relating to the taking up and pursuit of the business of credit institutions (recast).

(4)   For the purposes of this Act any undertaking that was an authorised UK deposit-taker immediately before the making of the first order under section 3 or 6 in relation to the undertaking is to be regarded as continuing to be an authorised UK deposit-taker, whether or not it would be one apart from this subsection.

(5)   For the purposes of this Act any reference (however expressed) to an undertaking which is—

    (a)   a group undertaking of an authorised UK deposit-taker, or

    (b)   a subsidiary undertaking of an authorised UK deposit-taker,

includes, in relation to any time after the making of the first order under section 3 or 6 in relation to the deposit-taker ("the relevant time"), a reference to an undertaking which was a group or subsidiary undertaking of the deposit-taker immediately before the making of that order but is not one at the relevant time.

(6)   For the purposes of this Act—

    (a)   a company is to be regarded as wholly owned by the Bank of England at any time if at that time—

        (i)   it is a company of which no person other than the Bank or a nominee of the Bank is a member, or

        (ii)   it is a wholly-owned subsidiary of a company within sub-paragraph (i); and

    (b)   a company is to be regarded as wholly owned by the Treasury at any time if at that time—

        (i)   it is a company of which no person other than a nominee of the Treasury is a member, or

        (ii)   it is a wholly-owned subsidiary of a company within sub-paragraph (i).

(7)   This subsection makes transitional provision for the purposes of this Act in relation to expressions defined by subsection (1) by reference to provisions of the Companies Act 2006 (c 46) ("the 2006 Act")—

    (a)   in relation to any time before the commencement of section 1 of the 2006 Act, "company" means a company within the meaning of the Companies Act 1985 (c 6) ("the 1985 Act") or the Companies (Northern Ireland) Order 1986 (SI 1986/1032 (NI 6)) ("the 1986 Order");

    (b)   in relation to any time before the commencement of section 1159 of the 2006 Act, "wholly-owned subsidiary" has the meaning given by section 736 of the 1985 Act or Article 4 of the 1986 Order;

    (c)   in relation to any time before the commencement of sections 1161 and 1162 of the 2006 Act, "group undertaking", "subsidiary undertaking" and "undertaking" have the meanings given by sections 258 and 259 of the 1985 Act or Articles 266 and 267 of the 1986 Order.

                                                                          [439]

NOTES

Commencement: 21 February 2008.

16 Financial provision

(1)   There is to be paid out of money provided by Parliament—

    (a)   any expenditure incurred by the Treasury in connection with the provision of financial assistance to any authorised UK deposit-taker in relation to which an order is made under section 3 or 6;

    (b)   any expenditure incurred by the Treasury in connection with the provision of financial assistance to any person to whom any transfer is made under this Act;

    (c)   any expenditure incurred by the Treasury in connection with the giving of any relevant indemnity or the putting in place of relevant guarantee arrangements in relation to any particular authorised UK deposit-taker; and

    (d)   any other expenditure incurred by the Treasury by virtue of this Act.

(2)   In subsection (1)(c) "relevant indemnity" means any indemnity given to—

    (a)   directors of any authorised UK deposit-taker in relation to which an order is made under section 3 or 6,

    (b)   directors of any body to which any transfer is made under this Act,

    (c)   directors of any body which is a group undertaking of any body to which any transfer is made under this Act,

    (d)   the Bank of England in respect of, or in connection with, any financial assistance provided by it to any body within any of paragraphs (a) to (c), or

(e)   any person appointed by the Treasury as an independent valuer for the purposes of any order made under this Act.

(3)   It is immaterial whether the indemnity or arrangements mentioned in subsection (1) are given or put in place before or after the passing of this Act.

[440]

NOTES
Commencement: 21 February 2008.

17   Short title, commencement and extent

(1)   This Act may be cited as the Banking (Special Provisions) Act 2008.

(2)   This Act comes into force on the day on which it is passed.

(3)   This Act extends to England and Wales, Scotland and Northern Ireland.

[441]

NOTES
Commencement: 21 February 2008.

SCHEDULES

SCHEDULE 1
TRANSFER ORDERS UNDER SECTION 3

Section 3

1   Provisions relating to securities transferred: general

(1)   An order under section 3 may make provision—
  (a)   for securities to be transferred free from all trusts, liabilities and incumbrances;
  (b)   for any transfer of securities to take effect despite—
    (i)   the absence of any required consent or concurrence to or with the transfer,
    (ii)   any other restriction relating to the transfer of the securities, or
    (iii)   the absence of the delivery of any instrument representing securities transferable by delivery (a "bearer instrument");
  (c)   for the delivery of any such instruments to a specified person, and the issue to the transferee of instruments representing such securities;
  (d)   for the transferee to be entitled to be entered in any register of securities without the need for delivery of any instrument of transfer;
  (e)   for requiring the person maintaining any such register to register the transferee in the register;
  (f)   for the transferee to be, as from the transfer date, entitled, or subject, to rights, privileges, advantages and liabilities arising from or relating to transferred securities, whether or not the transferee has been so registered or any bearer instrument representing the transferred securities has been delivered to the transferee;
  (g)   for deeming the transferee for any specified purposes to be the holder of the transferred securities at a time when the transferee has yet to be so registered or any such instrument has yet to be so delivered;
  (h)   for securing that rights of holders of securities, and rights relating to securities that are held by persons other than—
    (i)   the holders of the securities, or
    (ii)   the transferee,
    cease to be exercisable by the holders of the securities or (as the case may be) such other persons;
  (i)   for requiring distributions or other relevant amounts payable by the relevant deposit-taker on or after the transfer date to be paid into the Consolidated Fund.

(2)   Sub-paragraph (1)(h) applies to—
  (a)   securities issued by the relevant deposit-taker (whether or not transferred by an order under section 3), or
  (b)   securities issued by any of its group undertakings;
and, in relation to any transferred securities, any references in that provision to holders of securities are to former holders of them.

2   Conversion of form in which securities held etc

(1)   An order under section 3 may make provision—
  (a)   for securities held in one form to be converted, in the specified manner, from that form into another specified form;
  (b)   for converting a specified class of securities into securities of another specified class;
  (c)   for matters consequential on any such conversion as is mentioned in paragraph (a) or (b).

(2)   Sub-paragraph (1) applies to securities issued by the relevant deposit-taker, whether or not transferred by an order under section 3.

3   Delisting of securities

(1)   An order under section 3 may make provision for discontinuing the listing of securities issued by the relevant deposit-taker (whether or not the securities have been transferred by such an order).

(2)   In this paragraph "listing" has the meaning given by section 74(5) of FSMA 2000.

4   Alteration of terms of securities or contracts etc

(1)   An order under section 3 may make provision for varying or nullifying the terms, or the effect of terms, of—
- (a)   securities issued by the relevant deposit-taker (whether or not transferred by such an order),
- (b)   securities issued by any of its group undertakings, or
- (c)   other relevant instruments.

(2)   The provision that may be made by virtue of sub-paragraph (1) includes provision—
- (a)   for securing that transactions or events of any specified description have or do not have (directly or indirectly) such consequences as are specified, or are to be treated in the specified manner for any specified purposes;
- (b)   for discharging persons from further performance of obligations under relevant instruments, and for dealing with the consequences of persons being so discharged.

(3)   In this paragraph "relevant instrument" means any agreement, licence or other instrument to or by which any of the following is a party or bound—
- (a)   the relevant deposit-taker,
- (b)   any of its group undertakings, or
- (c)   any person having a specified connection with the relevant deposit-taker or any of its group undertakings (whether framed by reference to a sale of assets by one to the other, or otherwise).

5   Creation of new rights etc

An order under section 3 may make provision for the creation of new rights and liabilities as between the relevant deposit-taker and any of its group undertakings.

6   Rights etc under pension schemes

(1)   An order under section 3 may make provision—
- (a)   as to the consequences of any transfer, by such an order, in relation to any pension scheme;
- (b)   in relation to any property, rights and liabilities of any relevant occupational pension scheme.

(2)   Such an order may—
- (a)   modify any such rights and liabilities;
- (b)   apportion any such rights and liabilities between different persons;
- (c)   provide for property of, or accrued rights in, any relevant occupational pension scheme to be transferred to another occupational pension scheme without the consent of any person.

(3)   Provision made in pursuance of this paragraph may be made by means of modifications of a relevant occupational pension scheme or otherwise.

(4)   In this paragraph—
"occupational pension scheme" has the meaning given by section 150(5) of the Finance Act 2004 (c 12);
"relevant occupational pension scheme" means an occupational pension scheme in relation to which—
- (a)   the relevant deposit-taker, or
- (b)   any of its group undertakings,
is or has been an employer.

7   Provisions relating to directors of relevant deposit-taker etc

(1)   An order under section 3 may make provision enabling the Treasury—
- (a)   to remove or appoint directors of the relevant deposit-taker or any of its group undertakings;
- (b)   to determine, by agreement with persons so appointed by the Treasury, their remuneration and the other terms and conditions of their service contracts;
- (c)   to terminate, or vary the terms and conditions of, the service contracts of persons who (however appointed) are directors of the relevant deposit-taker or any of its group undertakings.

(2)   An order under section 3 may provide for anything done by the Treasury in accordance with provision made by virtue of sub-paragraph (1) to be treated as done by the relevant deposit-taker.

(3)   In this paragraph "service contract" has the meaning given by section 227 of the Companies Act 2006 (c 46).

8   Supplementary provisions

(1)   An order under section 3 may make provision—
   (a)   for agreements made or other things done by or in relation to former holders of transferred securities to be treated as made or done by or in relation to the transferee;
   (b)   for references to such persons in instruments or documents to have effect with specified modifications;
   (c)   for anything that relates to anything transferred by an order under section 3, and is in the process of being done by or in relation to any such person immediately before it is transferred, to be continued by or in relation to the transferee.

(2)   An order under section 3 may require former holders of transferred securities to provide the transferee with such information and other assistance as is specified.

(3)   An order under section 3 may make provision for disputes as to specified matters arising under or by virtue of an order under that section to be determined in the specified manner.

9   Interpretation

(1)   In this Schedule—
   "distributions or other relevant amounts" includes dividends, payments of interest, principal or capital, premiums and other payments arising in connection with securities transferred by an order under section 3;
   "former holder", in relation to transferred securities, means a person holding the securities before the transfer date;
   "the relevant deposit-taker", in relation to an order under section 3, means the authorised UK deposit-taker in relation to which the order is made;
   "remuneration" includes any benefit in kind;
   "register of securities" means a register of members or any other register of the holders of securities;
   "specified purposes" include the purposes of any specified statutory provision;
   "the transferee" means the person to whom securities are transferred by an order under section 3;
   "the transfer date" means (subject to sub-paragraph (2)) the date on which such a transfer takes place.

(2)   If an order under section 3 provides for any transfer to take place at a particular time on a particular date, then in relation to that transfer, references to the transfer date are to that time on that date.

[442]

NOTES
Commencement: 21 February 2008.
Order: the Bradford & Bingley plc Transfer of Securities and Property etc Order 2008, SI 2008/2546 at **[963]**.

SCHEDULE 2
TRANSFER ORDERS UNDER SECTION 6
Section 6

1   Property, rights and liabilities that may be transferred by or under order

The property, rights and liabilities that may be transferred by or under an order under section 6 include—
   (a)   property, rights and liabilities that would not be capable of being assigned or otherwise transferred by the relevant deposit-taker;
   (b)   property, rights and liabilities acquired or incurred in the period between the making of the order and the transfer date;
   (c)   rights and liabilities arising on or after the transfer date in respect of matters occurring before that date;
   (d)   rights and liabilities under any pension scheme or under any other arrangement for the payment of pensions, allowances and gratuities;
   (e)   property situated outside the United Kingdom and rights and liabilities under the law of a place outside the United Kingdom;
   (f)   rights and liabilities under an enactment or Community instrument.

2   Provisions relating to property, rights and liabilities transferred

(1)   An order under section 6 may make provision—
   (a)   for any transfer of any interests or rights to take effect despite the absence of any required consent or concurrence to or with the transfer;

    (b)   for any transfer of any interests or rights to take effect as if—

        (i)   no associated liability existed in respect of any failure to comply with any other requirement, and

        (ii)   there were no associated interference with the interests or rights;

    (c)   for securing that in any specified circumstances—

        (i)   a person is not entitled to terminate, modify, acquire or claim an interest or right (or to treat an interest or right as terminated or modified) until it is transferred by or under the order, and

        (ii)   the entitlement is subsequently either not enforceable or enforceable only to the specified extent;

    (d)   for rights and liabilities—

        (i)   to be transferred so as to be enforceable by or against both the transferee and the transferor, and

        (ii)   where they are so enforceable, to be enforceable in different or modified respects by or against each of those persons;

    (e)   for interests, rights or liabilities of third parties in relation to anything to which an order under section 6 relates to be modified in the specified manner, including provision—

        (i)   for securing that transactions or events of any specified description do or do not have (directly or indirectly) such consequences as are specified, or are to be treated in the specified manner for any specified purposes;

        (ii)   for persons to be discharged from the further performance of contracts and for dealing with the consequences of persons being so discharged;

    (f)   for the manner in which—

        (i)   any property held in trust by the relevant deposit-taker before the transfer date (whether as sole or joint trustee) is to be held on or after that date, and

        (ii)   any powers, provisions and liabilities relating to any such property are to be exercisable or to have effect on or after that date;

    (g)   for excluding from the transfer specified property, rights and liabilities comprised in the relevant deposit-taker's business or a specified part of it;

    (h)   for the creation of rights, liabilities or interests in relation to property, rights or liabilities transferred from or retained by the relevant deposit-taker;

    (i)   for dealing with cases where securities of a subsidiary undertaking are transferred by or under the order;

    (j)   for enabling the relevant deposit-taker and the transferee (in accordance with the order) to agree on any modification of the order, so long as the order could originally have been made with that modification in accordance with the relevant provisions of this Act;

    (k)   for apportioning liabilities in respect of any tax or duty (in the United Kingdom or elsewhere) between the relevant deposit-taker and the transferee.

(2)   In sub-paragraph (1)(b) "associated liability" and "associated interference" mean respectively any liability or interference that would otherwise exist by virtue of any provision (of an enactment or agreement or otherwise) having effect in relation to the terms on which the relevant deposit-taker is entitled, or subject, to anything to which the transfer relates.

(3)   In sub-paragraph (1)(e) "third parties" means persons other than the relevant deposit-taker or the transferee under an order under section 6.

3 Creation of new rights etc

An order under section 6 may make provision for the creation of new rights and liabilities as between the relevant deposit-taker and any of its group undertakings.

4 Rights etc under pension schemes

(1)   An order under section 6 may make provision—

    (a)   as to the consequences of any transfer, by or under such an order, in relation to any pension scheme;

    (b)   in relation to any property, rights and liabilities of any relevant occupational pension scheme.

(2)   Such an order may—

    (a)   modify any such rights and liabilities;

    (b)   apportion any such rights and liabilities between different persons;

    (c)   provide for property of, or accrued rights in, any relevant occupational pension scheme to be transferred to another occupational pension scheme without the consent of any person.

(3)   Provision made in pursuance of this paragraph may be made by means of modifications of a relevant occupational pension scheme or otherwise.

(4)   In this paragraph—

    "occupational pension scheme" has the meaning given by section 150(5) of the Finance Act 2004 (c 12);

"relevant occupational pension scheme" means an occupational pension scheme in relation to which—
- (a) the relevant deposit-taker, or
- (b) any of its group undertakings,

is or has been an employer.

5 Foreign property etc

(1) An order under section 6 may make provision—
- (a) for requiring or authorising the relevant deposit-taker or the transferee to take any specified steps—
  - (i) for securing the vesting in the transferee under the relevant foreign law of foreign property or foreign rights or liabilities, or
  - (ii) pending any such vesting of such property, rights or liabilities, or
  - (iii) otherwise in relation to such property, rights or liabilities;
- (b) for the payment by a specified person of expenses incurred in connection with such property, rights or liabilities.

(2) In this paragraph—
- (a) "foreign law" means the law of a place outside the United Kingdom; and
- (b) "foreign property" and "foreign rights or liabilities" mean respectively property and rights and liabilities as respects which an issue arising in any proceedings would be determined (in accordance with the rules of private international law) by reference to foreign law.

6 Authorisations and permissions etc

(1) An order under section 6 may make provision for securing that, if on the transfer date the transferee satisfies the specified conditions, it is to be treated for the specified period—
- (a) as an authorised person in relation to any specified regulated activities carried on by the relevant deposit-taker before that date, or
- (b) as an authorised person who has a Part IV permission granted by the Financial Services Authority to carry on any such activities.

(2) Where an order makes provision in accordance with sub-paragraph (1)(b), it may provide that any decision by the Financial Services Authority of a specified description is to have the effect of varying or cancelling (to any specified extent) the Part IV permission which the transferee is to be treated as having by virtue of that provision.

(3) An order under section 6 may make provision—
- (a) for securing that licences, permissions or approvals—
  - (i) relating to anything transferred by or under the order, and
  - (ii) in force or effective immediately before the transfer date,
  are to continue in force or in effect as from that date;
- (b) for apportioning (by means of making modifications of the instruments concerned or otherwise) responsibility between the relevant deposit-taker and the transferee as regards compliance with requirements of licences, permissions or approvals.

(4) In this paragraph "authorised person", "Part IV permission" and "regulated activities" have the same meanings as in FSMA 2000.

7 Supplementary provisions

(1) An order under section 6 may make provision—
- (a) for the transferee to be treated for any purpose connected with the transfer as the same person in law as the relevant deposit-taker;
- (b) for agreements made or other things done by or in relation to any relevant deposit-taker to be treated as made or done by or in relation to the transferee;
- (c) for references in instruments or documents to the relevant deposit-taker, to any combination of bodies that includes that deposit-taker, or to any officer or employee of that deposit-taker, to have effect with specified modifications;
- (d) for securing continuity of employment in the case of contracts of employment transferred by or under the order;
- (e) for anything (including legal proceedings) that relates to anything transferred by or under the order, and is in the process of being done by or in relation to the relevant deposit-taker immediately before it is transferred, to be continued by or in relation to the transferee.

(2) In sub-paragraph (1)(b), (c) and (e) any reference to the relevant deposit-taker includes a reference to any of its group undertakings.

(3) An order under section 6 may require the relevant deposit-taker to provide the transferee with such information and other assistance as is specified.

(4) An order under section 6 may make provision for disputes as to specified matters arising under or by virtue of an order under that section to be determined in the specified manner.

8　Interpretation

(1)　In this Schedule—

"the relevant deposit-taker", in relation to an order under section 6, means the authorised UK deposit-taker in relation to which the order is made;

"specified purposes" include the purposes of any specified statutory provision;

"the transferee" means the person to whom property, rights or liabilities are transferred by or under an order under section 6;

"the transfer date" means (subject to sub-paragraph (2)) the date on which such a transfer takes place.

(2)　If provision is made by or under an order under section 6 for any transfer to take place at a particular time on a particular date, then in relation to that transfer—

(a)　references to the transfer date are to that time on that date; and

(b)　references to things occurring before or on or after the transfer date are references to things occurring before or at or after that time on that date.

(3)　In this Schedule any reference to anything transferred by or under a particular order under section 6 includes a reference to anything transferred by or under any other order under that section.

[443]–[499]

NOTES

Commencement: 21 February 2008.

Orders under section 6: see that section at **[430]**.

PART III
STATUTORY INSTRUMENTS UNDER BANKING ACT 2009

BANKING ACT 2009 (COMMENCEMENT NO 1) ORDER 2009

(SI 2009/296)

NOTES
Made: 16 February 2009.
Authority: Banking Act 2009, s 263(1), (3).

1 Citation and interpretation

(1)   This Order may be cited as the Banking Act 2009 (Commencement No 1) Order 2009.

(2)   In this Order, "the Act" means the Banking Act 2009.

[500]

2 Provisions conferring power to make secondary legislation etc

To the extent that the provisions in the Schedule to this Order confer or relate to the power to make subordinate legislation or codes of practice, those provisions come into force on 17th February 2009 for the purpose of enabling subordinate legislation or codes of practice to be made; but no such subordinate legislation or codes of practice may come into force before 21st February 2009.

[501]

3 Provisions of the Act coming into force on 21st February 2009

The provisions of the Act listed in the Schedule to this Order come into force on 21st February 2009.

[502]

SCHEDULE

1.   Sections 1 to 89 (Part 1 of the Act: the special resolution regime)

2.   Sections 90 to 135 (Part 2 of the Act: bank insolvency)

3.   Sections 136 to 168 (Part 3 of the Act: bank administration)

4.   Sections 169, 171, and 173 to 180 (provisions relating to the Financial Services Compensation Scheme)

5.   Sections 228 to 231 (Treasury support for banks)

6.   Sections 232 to 236 (investment banks)

7.   Section 237 (Banking (Special Provisions) Act 2008, compensation: valuer)

8.   Sections 244 to 247 (provisions relating to the Bank of England)

9.   Sections 248 to 250 (provisions relating to the Financial Services Authority)

10.   Section 251 (financial assistance to building societies)

11.   Sections 252 and 253 (registration of charges and registration of charges: Scotland)

12.   Section 257 (meaning of "financial assistance")

13.   Section 258 (meaning of "enactment")

14.   Section 259 (statutory instruments)

15.   Section 260 (money)

16.   Section 261(index of defined terms)

17.   Section 262 (repeal)

[503]

BANKING ACT 2009 (BANK ADMINISTRATION) (MODIFICATION FOR APPLICATION TO BANKS IN TEMPORARY PUBLIC OWNERSHIP) REGULATIONS 2009

(SI 2009/312)

NOTES
Made: 19 February 2009.
Authority: Banking Act 2009, ss 152(3), 259(1).
Commencement: 21 February 2009.
Modification: these Regulations are applied, with modifications in respect of building societies, by the Building Societies (Insolvency and Special Administration) Order 2009, SI 2009/805, art 18, Sch 2, paras 1(d), 2, 5 at **[560]**, **[564]**.

PART III
SIS UNDER BANKING ACT 2009

1 Citation, commencement and interpretation

(1) These Regulations may be cited as the Banking Act 2009 (Bank Administration) (Modification for Application to Banks in Temporary Public Ownership) Regulations 2009 and come into force on 21st February 2009.

(2) In these Regulations—
"the Act" means the Banking Act 2009;
"onward public sector transferee" means a transferee under a property transfer order by virtue of section 45(2) of the Act who is a company wholly owned by—
    (a)   the Bank of England,
    (b)   the Treasury, or
    (c)   a nominee of the Treasury;
"private sector transferee" means a transferee under a property transfer order by virtue of section 45(2) of the Act who is not an onward public sector transferee.

[504]

NOTES
Commencement: 21 February 2009.

2 Application following transfer of bank etc to temporary public ownership

(1) These Regulations make modifications to Part 3 of the Act (bank administration) as applied by section 152(2) of the Act (which applies Part 3 to banks where the Treasury has made a share transfer order to transfer the securities of a bank or a bank's holding company into temporary public ownership, and makes a property transfer order in respect of that bank to transfer property from the bank to another person).

(2) Regulations 3 and 4 make general modifications.

(3) The Tables in the Schedule make modifications to the specific provisions listed within them.

[505]

NOTES
Commencement: 21 February 2009.

3 General modifications to Part 3 of the Act

In Part 3 of the Act a reference to—
"the Bank of England" is a reference to "the Treasury" (unless otherwise specified in the Schedule);
"a property transfer instrument" is a reference to "a property transfer order".

[506]

NOTES
Commencement: 21 February 2009.

4 General modifications to Tables 1 and 2 of section 145

In Tables 1 and 2 of section 145 of the Act (which apply provisions of the Insolvency Act 1986 in relation to bank administration), in addition to the modifications made by Regulation 3, a reference to "a bridge bank" is a reference to "an onward public sector transferee".

[507]

NOTES
Commencement: 21 February 2009.

SCHEDULE
SPECIFIC MODIFICATIONS

Regulation 2

Table 1: Modifications to sections of Part 3 of the Act

Section and subject	Modification or Comment
136 Overview	For subsection (2)(a) substitute— "(a) it is used where—

Section and subject	Modification or Comment
	(i) a bank or a bank holding company has been transferred into temporary public ownership in accordance with section 13(2) (including as applied by section 82(1)), and
	(ii) the Treasury make a property transfer order in accordance with section 45(2) to transfer part of the business of a bank to a private sector transferee or an onward public sector transferee,
	and it can also be used in certain cases of multiple transfers under Part 1.".
	In subsection (2)(c) for "the commercial purchaser ("private sector purchaser") or the transferee ("the bridge bank")" substitute "the private sector transferee or the onward public sector transferee".
137 Objectives	In subsection (1)(a) for "commercial purchaser or bridge bank" substitute "the private sector transferee or the onward public sector transferee".
138 Objective 1: supporting private sector purchaser or bridge bank	For the heading, substitute "Objective 1: supporting the private sector transferee or onward public sector transferee".
	In subsection (1) for "private sector purchaser or bridge bank" substitute "the private sector transferee or onward public sector transferee".
	In subsection (3) for—
	(a) "a private sector purchase" substitute "a transfer to a private sector transferee";
	(b) "private sector purchaser" substitute "private sector transferee" (in each place).
	In subsection (4) for "bridge bank" substitute "a company wholly owned by the Bank of England".
	Regulation 3 does not apply to subsection (4).
	After subsection (4) insert—
	"(4A) In the case of bank administration following a transfer from a bank in temporary public ownership to a company wholly owned by the Treasury or a nominee of the Treasury ("the company"), the bank administrator must co-operate with any request of the Treasury to enter into an agreement for the residual bank to provide services or facilities to the company; and—
	(a) the bank administrator must avoid action that is likely to prejudice performance by the residual bank of its obligations in accordance with an agreement,
	(b) the bank administrator must ensure that so far as is reasonably practicable an agreement includes provision for consideration at market rate,
	(c) paragraph (b) does not prevent the bank administrator from entering into an agreement on any terms that the bank administrator thinks necessary in pursuit of Objective 1, and
	(d) this subsection does not apply after Objective 1 ceases.".
139 Objective 1: duration	In subsections (1) and (3) for "private sector purchaser or bridge bank" substitute "the private sector transferee or the onward public sector transferee".

PART III
SIS UNDER BANKING ACT 2009

Section and subject	Modification or Comment
140 Objective 2: "normal" administration	In subsection (3) for "bridge bank" substitute "the onward public sector transferee".
143 Grounds for applying	In subsection (2) for "section 11(2) or 12(2)" substitute "section 45(2)".
148 Sharing information	Section 148 is applied following a transfer to a company wholly owned by the Bank of England with the following modifications— (a) for subsection (2) substitute— "(2) Within the period of 5 days beginning with the day on which the bank administrator is appointed, the Bank of England must give the bank administrator information about the financial position of the company wholly owned by the Bank and the Treasury must give the bank administrator information about the financial position of the residual bank."; (b) in subsection (3) for "bridge bank" substitute "company wholly owned by the Bank of England" (in each place); (c) in subsection (4)(a), (b) and (e) after "Bank of England" or "the Bank" add "and the Treasury" (in each place); (d) in subsection (4)(c), (d) and (e) for "bridge bank" substitute "the company wholly owned by the Bank of England and the Treasury" (in each place). Section 148 is applied following a transfer to a company wholly owned by the Treasury or a nominee of the Treasury with the following modifications— (e) for "bridge bank" substitute "a company wholly owned by the Treasury or a nominee of the Treasury" (in each place); (f) for "Bank of England" substitute "the Treasury" (in each place).
150 Bridge bank to private sector purchaser	For the heading, substitute "Onward public sector transferee: company wholly owned by the Treasury or a nominee of the Treasury to private purchaser". Section 150 is applied following a transfer to a company wholly owned by the Treasury or a nominee of the Treasury with the following modifications— (g) for "bridge bank" substitute "a company wholly owned by the Treasury or a nominee of the Treasury" (in each place); (h) for "Bank of England" substitute "the Treasury" (in each place).
151 Property transfer from bridge bank	Ignore.
157 Other processes	For subsection (2)(a) substitute— "(a) "residual bank" means a bank all or part of whose business has been transferred to a private sector transferee or an onward public sector transferee in accordance with section 45(2),".

Table 2: Modifications to Table 1 of Applied Provisions in section 145 of the Act:
Schedule B1 to the Insolvency Act 1986

Provision of Schedule B1	Subject	Modification or comment
Para 49	Administrator's proposals	Ignore paragraph (c) of the Table.
Paras 50–58	Creditors' meeting	For paragraph (d) of the Table substitute— "(d) Until that time a committee shall have the functions of the creditors committee. The committee shall be formed of 3 individuals, one nominated by each of— (i) the Treasury, (ii) the Bank of England, and (iii) the FSA.".

[508]

NOTES
Commencement: 21 February 2009.

BANKING ACT 2009 (BANK ADMINISTRATION) (MODIFICATION FOR APPLICATION TO MULTIPLE TRANSFERS) REGULATIONS 2009

(SI 2009/313)

NOTES
Made: 19 February 2009.
Authority: Banking Act 2009, ss 149(3), 259(1).
Commencement: 21 February 2009.
Modification: these Regulations are applied, with modifications in respect of building societies, by the Building Societies (Insolvency and Special Administration) Order 2009, SI 2009/805, art 18, Sch 2, paras 1(c), 2, 4 at **[560]**, **[564]**.

1   Citation, commencement and interpretation

(1)   These Regulations may be cited as the Banking Act 2009 (Bank Administration) (Modification for Application to Multiple Transfers) Regulations 2009 and come into force on 21st February 2009.

(2)   In these Regulations—
"the Act" means the Banking Act 2009;
"a bank in temporary public ownership" is a reference to a bank wholly owned by the Treasury or a nominee of the Treasury;
"onward public sector transferee" means a transferee under a property transfer order by virtue of section 45(2) of the Act who is a company wholly owned by—
(a)   the Bank of England,
(b)   the Treasury, or
(c)   a nominee of the Treasury;
"private sector transferee" means a transferee under a property transfer order by virtue of section 45(2) of the Act who is not an onward public sector transferee;
"property transfer instrument" has the meaning given by section 149(2) of the Act.

[509]

NOTES
Commencement: 21 February 2009.

2   Modification of Part 3 where more than one property transfer instrument is made (other than in respect of a bank in temporary public ownership)

The modifications of Part 3 of the Act listed in the Table to the Schedule apply where—

(a) the Bank of England makes more than one property transfer instrument in respect of a bank, and

(b) Part 3 applies to the bank by virtue of section 149 of the Act.

[510]

NOTES
Commencement: 21 February 2009.

3 Modification of Part 3 where more than one property transfer instrument is made in respect of a bank in temporary public ownership

(1) The modifications of Part 3 of the Act listed in the Table to the Schedule apply with the general modifications specified in paragraph (2) where—

(a) the Treasury make a share transfer order, in respect of the securities issued by a bank (or a bank's holding company), in accordance with section 13(2) of the Act,

(b) the Treasury make more than one property transfer instrument in respect of the bank under section 45(2) of the Act, and

(c) Part 3 applies to the bank by virtue of section 149 and 152 of the Act.

(2) The general modifications to the Table to the Schedule are—

(a) a reference to "the Bank of England" is a reference to "the Treasury";

(b) a reference to a "private sector purchaser" is a reference to a "private sector transferee";

(c) a reference to a "bridge bank" is a reference to an "onward public sector transferee".

[511]

NOTES
Commencement: 21 February 2009.

SCHEDULES

SCHEDULE 1
MODIFICATIONS

Regulations 2 and 3

Table: Modifications to Part 3 of the Act

Section and subject	Modification or comment
138 Objective 1: supporting private sector purchaser or bridge bank	After section 138, insert—
	"138A Objective 1: Application where more than one property transfer instrument is made—
	(1) Where more than one property transfer instrument is made and business is transferred from a bank to more than one transferee, Objective 1 is to be pursued in relation to each private sector purchaser or bridge bank who, in the opinion of the Bank of England, is to be supplied with such services and facilities as are required to enable it to operate effectively.
	(2) Where the bank administrator considers that the supply to one private sector purchaser or bridge bank of services and facilities may prejudice the supply of services and facilities to another transferee, the bank administrator—
	(a) must consult with the Bank of England, and the Bank of England may give directions to the bank administrator regarding the supply of services and facilities to transferees,
	(b) shall pursue Objective 1 in respect of each transferee in so far as is reasonably practicable in the circumstances, and
	(c) may apply to the court for directions under paragraph 63 of Schedule B1 to the Insolvency Act 1986 (applied by section 145 below) if unsure whether to pursue a proposed action.".

Section and subject	Modification or comment
139 Objective 1: duration	In subsections (1) and (3) for "with the", substitute "with any".
	After subsection (1), insert—
	"(1A) The obligations of Objective 1 cease to apply in respect of a particular private sector purchaser or bridge bank if the Bank of England notifies the bank administrator that the residual bank is no longer required in connection with that private sector purchaser or bridge bank.".
	After subsection (2), add—
	"(2A) A bank administrator who thinks that Objective 1 is no longer required in respect of a particular private sector purchaser or bridge bank may apply to court for directions under paragraph 63 of Schedule B1 to the Insolvency Act (applied by section 145 below); and the court may direct the Bank of England to consider whether to give notice under subsection (1A) above.".
143 Grounds for applying	In subsection (2) for "a property transfer instrument" substitute "one or more property transfer instruments".
	In subsection (3)(b) after "property transfer instrument" add "or instruments".
150 Bridge bank to private sector purchaser	For subsection (1)(a), substitute—
	"(a) notice under section 139(1A) that the residual bank is no longer required in connection with a bridge bank, and".
	In subsection (2) for "An Objective 1 Achievement Notice", substitute "A notice under section 139(1A)".
	For subsection (5), substitute—
	"(5) When the Bank of England gives a notice to the bank administrator that Objective 1 is no longer required to be pursued in respect of a commercial purchaser who has acquired all or part of the business of the bridge bank, the Bank of England may give the bank administrator an Objective 1 Achievement Notice only if the residual bank is no longer required in connection with any private sector purchaser or bridge bank, and section 139 and other provisions of this Part which refer to the giving of an Objective 1 Achievement Notice shall have effect.".

[512]

PART III
SIS UNDER BANKING ACT 2009

NOTES
Commencement: 21 February 2009.
Note: these Regulations are reproduced as per the Queen's Printer's copy, ie, there is no Schedule 2.

BANK ADMINISTRATION (SHARING INFORMATION) REGULATIONS 2009

(SI 2009/314)

NOTES
Made: 19 February 2009.
Authority: Banking Act 2009, ss 148(5), 259(1).
Commencement: 21 February 2009.
Modification: these Regulations are applied, with modifications in respect of building societies, by the Building Societies (Insolvency and Special Administration) Order 2009, SI 2009/805, art 18, Sch 2, paras 1(b), 2 at **[560]**, **[564]**.

ARRANGEMENT OF REGULATIONS

1 Citation and commencement

These Regulations may be cited as the Bank Administration (Sharing Information) Regulations 2009 and come into force on 21st February 2009.

[513]

NOTES
Commencement: 21 February 2009.

2 Interpretation

In these Regulations—
    "the Act" means the Banking Act 2009;
    "HMRC" means Her Majesty's Revenue and Customs;
    "Objective 1" means the first objective of bank administration as defined in sections 137 and
       138 of the Act;
    "order" means a bank administration order (see section 141 of the Act);
    "original bank" means a bank as it existed before a property transfer instrument was made in
       relation to it;
    "residual bank"—
         in Regulations 5 to 10, has the meaning given by section 157(2) of the Act;
         in the Schedule, means a bank in temporary public ownership all or part of whose
         business has been transferred in accordance with a property transfer order made under
         section 45(2) of the Act;
    "transferred business"—
       (a)   in Regulations 5 to 10, means the part of an original bank's business transferred
           under a property transfer instrument;
       (b)   in the Schedule, means the part of the bank in temporary public ownership's
           business transferred in accordance with a property transfer order made under
           section 45(2) of the Act.

[514]

NOTES
Commencement: 21 February 2009.

3 Application to bank administration following transfer to a bridge bank

Regulations 5 to 10 apply to bank administration following a transfer to a bridge bank in accordance with sections 12 and 148(1) of the Act.

[515]

NOTES
Commencement: 21 February 2009.

4 Application to bank administration where Part 3 is applied by section 152 of the Act

(1)   Regulations 5 to 10 apply, with the modifications specified in Tables 1 and 2 of the Schedule, to bank administration following a transfer of business from a bank in temporary public ownership.

(2)   Table 1 applies in cases where section 148 is applied following a transfer from a bank in temporary public ownership to a company wholly owned by the Bank of England.

(3)   Table 2 applies in cases where section 148 is applied following a transfer from a bank in temporary public ownership to a company wholly owned by the Treasury or a nominee of the Treasury.

[516]

NOTES
Commencement: 21 February 2009.

5   Information to be provided to the bank administrator appointed in the first 5 days of the bank administration

(1)   This regulation applies where—

    (a)   the bank administrator has been appointed by the order, or

    (b)   the bank administrator has been appointed to replace the bank administrator appointed by the order (or where joint administrators were appointed, to replace all of them) within 5 days of the order being made.

(2)   The classes of information that must be provided by the Bank of England to the bank administrator under section 148(2) of the Act, within the period of 5 days beginning with the day on which the bank administrator is appointed, are—

    (a)   an estimate of the net value of the original bank,

    (b)   an estimate of the net value of the bridge bank,

    (c)   a list of assets and liabilities of the original bank that have been transferred to the bridge bank, including details of—

        (i)   any charged assets and the creditors holding those charges,

        (ii)   any contingent assets transferred to the bridge bank, and

        (iii)   any liabilities (including contingent liabilities), and

    (d)   details of any supplemental property transfers or reverse property transfers that have been made,

in each case as comprehensive as is reasonably possible and current as at the date it is provided.

                                                                    [517]

NOTES
Commencement: 21 February 2009.

6   Information to be provided to the bank administrator otherwise

(1)   This regulation applies where the bank administrator has been appointed otherwise than as described in regulation 5(1).

(2)   The classes of information that must be provided by the Bank of England to the bank administrator under section 148(2) of the Act, within the period of 5 days beginning with the day on which the bank administrator is appointed, are—

    (a)   details of the net value of the bridge bank, current as at the date on which the information is provided, and

    (b)   an outline of the information provided to a former bank administrator under section 148(2) of the Act, and, where the matters to which that information relates have changed, updated information, current as at the date on which the information is provided.

                                                                    [518]

NOTES
Commencement: 21 February 2009.

7   Information to be provided on request by the bridge bank to the bank administrator

The classes of information that must be provided by the bridge bank to the bank administrator on request under section 148(3) of the Act are—

    (a)   details as to the net value of the bridge bank, management accounts and other information including ledgers, cash books, bank statements, invoices and orders in relation to the transferred business current as at the date on which the information is provided,

    (b)   details of any supplemental property transfers or reverse property transfers that have been made, and

    (c)   details of any amounts of money to be paid to the residual bank from a scheme established by a resolution fund order.

                                                                    [519]

NOTES
Commencement: 21 February 2009.

8   Information to be provided on request by the bank administrator to the Bank of England

The classes of information that must be provided by the bank administrator to the Bank of England on request under section 148(4)(a) of the Act are as follows—

PART III
SIS UNDER BANKING ACT 2009

(a) information required in connection with the Bank of England's role under Part 3 of the Act and under rules made under section 411 of the Insolvency Act 1986 in respect of Part 3,

(b) information regarding the bank administrator's plans for the administration of the residual bank, further to any information provided in the bank administrator's statement of proposals, that may have an impact on the residual bank's ability to meet Objective 1,

(c) information regarding the residual bank's employees, assets and liabilities and its relationships with suppliers that may have an impact on the residual bank's ability to meet Objective 1,

(d) information about—
  (i) wrongful trading (see section 213 of the Insolvency Act 1986),
  (ii) fraudulent trading (see section 214 of the Insolvency Act 1986), or
  (iii) negligence,
  carried out by the directors of the original bank and identified by the bank administrator,

(e) information about any steps taken by the bank administrator in respect of a director of the original bank under the Company Directors Disqualification Act 1986, and

(f) information about any litigation that the bank administrator is pursuing on behalf of the residual bank.

[520]

NOTES
Commencement: 21 February 2009.

9 Information to be provided on request by the bank administrator to the bridge bank

The classes of information that must be provided by the bank administrator to the bridge bank on request under section 148(4)(c) of the Act are—

(a) statutory accounts, management accounts and other information including ledgers, cash books, bank statements, invoices and orders in relation to the transferred business,

(b) the following information relating to the transferred business—
  (i) financial information relating to property, rights and liabilities,
  (ii) personnel records, salary information etc relating to employees, and
  (iii) details of any licenses, permissions, approvals and intellectual property rights.

(c) information in relation to contracts, the rights and obligations of which have been transferred to the bridge bank,

(d) information required by public or regulatory bodies (in the United Kingdom and overseas) including FSA or HMRC,

(e) information about customers and suppliers which are part of the transferred business,

(f) information about target customers, channels to market, distribution networks and other marketing and sales material relating to the transferred business,

(g) information about the original bank's previous trading history required to prepare an investment memorandum,

(h) any other information a potential purchaser asks the bridge bank to provide, and

(i) information in connection with any agreement drawn up between the bank administrator and the bridge bank for the supply by the residual bank of services and facilities to the bridge bank.

[521]

NOTES
Commencement: 21 February 2009.

10 Records to be made accessible by the bank administrator

The class of records that the bank administrator must allow the Bank of England and the bridge bank access to under section 148(4)(b) and (d) of the Act is any records required in connection with the classes of information specified in regulations 8 and 9, whether in hard copy or in electronic form.

[522]

NOTES
Commencement: 21 February 2009.

SCHEDULE

Regulation 4

Table 1: Modifications to Regulations 5 to 10 in cases where section 148 is applied following a transfer from a bank in temporary public ownership to a company wholly owned by the Bank of England

Regulation	Modification or Comment
5	For paragraph (2) substitute—
	"(2) The classes of information that must be provided by the Treasury to the bank administrator under section 148(2) of the Act, within the period of 5 days beginning with the day on which the bank administrator is appointed, are—
	(a) an estimate of the net value of the bank before the transfer of property in accordance with a property transfer order made under section 45(2) of the Act,
	(b) a list of assets and liabilities of the residual bank that have been transferred to the company wholly owned by the Bank of England, including details of—
	(i) any charged assets and the creditors holding those charges,
	(ii) any contingent assets transferred to the company wholly owned by the Bank of England, and
	(iii) any liabilities (including contingent liabilities), and
	(c) details of any supplemental property transfers or reverse property transfers that have been made,
	in each case as comprehensive as is reasonably possible and current as at the date it is provided."
	After paragraph (2) insert—
	"(3) The Bank of England must provide to the bank administrator, within the period of 5 days beginning with the day on which the bank administrator is appointed, an estimate of the net value of the company wholly owned by the Bank of England, as comprehensive as is reasonably possible and current as at the date it is provided."
6	For paragraph (2) substitute—
	"(2) The classes of information that must be provided by the Bank of England to the bank administrator under section 148(2) of the Act, within the period of 5 days beginning with the day on which the bank administrator is appointed, are—
	(a) details of the net value of the company wholly owned by the Bank of England, current as at the date on which the information is provided, and
	(b) an outline of the information provided to a former bank administrator under section 148(2) of the Act, and, where the matters to which that information relates have changed, updated information, current as at the date on which the information is provided.".
	After paragraph (2) insert—
	"(3) The Treasury must provide to the bank administrator, within the period of 5 days beginning with the day on which the bank administrator is appointed, an outline of the information provided to a former bank administrator under section 148(2) of the Act, and, where the matters to which that information relates have changed, updated information, current as at the date on which the information is provided.".
7	For the heading, substitute "Information to be provided on request by the company wholly owned by the Bank of England to the bank administrator".
	For "bridge bank" substitute "company wholly owned by the Bank of England" (in each case).

PART III
SIS UNDER BANKING ACT 2009

Regulation	Modification or Comment
	Ignore sub-paragraph (c).
8	For the heading, substitute "Information to be provided on request by the bank administrator to the Treasury and the Bank of England".
	After "Bank of England" insert "and the Treasury".
	In sub-paragraph (a) after "Bank of England's" insert "or the Treasury's".
	In sub-paragraphs (d) and (e) substitute "original bank" for residual bank".
9	For the heading, substitute "Information to be provided on request by the bank administrator to the Treasury and the company wholly owned by the Bank of England"
	In Regulation 9 (other than in sub-paragraphs (h) and (i)) for "bridge bank" substitute "company wholly owned by the Bank of England and the Treasury".
	In sub-paragraphs (h) and (i) for "bridge bank" substitute "company wholly owned by the Bank of England" (in each place).
	In sub-paragraph (g) for "original bank" substitute "residual bank".
10	For "the Bank of England and the bridge bank" substitute "the Treasury, the Bank of England and the company wholly owned by the Bank of England".

Table 2: Modifications to Regulations 5 to 10 in cases where section 148 is applied following a transfer from a bank in temporary public ownership to a company wholly owned by the Treasury or a nominee of the Treasury

Regulation	Modification or Comment
5 to 10	For "the Bank of England" substitute "the Treasury" (in each place).
	For "bridge bank" substitute "company wholly owned by the Treasury or a nominee of the Treasury" (in each place).
	For "original bank" substitute "residual bank" (within the meaning of sub-paragraph (b) of the definition of "residual bank" in Regulation 2).
7	Ignore sub-paragraph (c).

[523]

NOTES
Commencement: 21 February 2009.

BANKING ACT 2009 (PARTS 2 AND 3 CONSEQUENTIAL AMENDMENTS) ORDER 2009

(SI 2009/317)

NOTES
Made: 19 February 2009.
Authority: Banking Act 2009, ss 135, 168.
Commencement: 21 February 2009.
Modification: this Order is applied, with modifications in respect of building societies, by the Building Societies (Insolvency and Special Administration) Order 2009, SI 2009/805, art 18, Sch 2, paras 1(a), 2, 3 at **[560]**, **[564]**.

ARRANGEMENT OF ARTICLES

PART 1
INTRODUCTION

PART 2
GENERAL MODIFICATIONS TO LEGISLATION

PART 3
SPECIFIC MODIFICATIONS AND AMENDMENTS TO LEGISLATION

PART 1
INTRODUCTION

1   Citation and commencement

This Order may be cited as the Banking Act 2009 (Parts 2 and 3 Consequential Amendments) Order 2009 and comes into force on 21st February 2009.

[524]

NOTES
Commencement: 21 February 2009.

2   Interpretation

In this Order—
    "the 2009 Act" means the Banking Act 2009.

[525]

NOTES
Commencement: 21 February 2009.

PART 2
GENERAL MODIFICATIONS TO LEGISLATION

3.—(1)   So far as the enactments set out in the Schedule ("the listed enactments") apply in relation to liquidation and administration, they apply with the modifications set out in paragraphs (2) to (4).

    (2)   The modifications relating to bank insolvency under Part 2 of the 2009 Act are that references to—
    (a)   "liquidator" include a reference to a bank liquidator under Part 2 of the 2009 Act;
    (b)   "provisional liquidator" include a reference to a provisional bank liquidator under Part 2 of the 2009 Act;
    (c)   "liquidation" or "insolvent liquidation" include a reference to bank insolvency under Part 2 of the 2009 Act;
    (d)   "winding up" or "winding up by the court" include a reference to bank insolvency under Part 2 of the 2009 Act (and a reference to the "commencement of winding up" in this context is to the commencement of bank insolvency);
    (e)   "winding up order" include a reference to a bank insolvency order under Part 2 of the 2009 Act;
    (f)   "wound up" include a reference to a bank having been put into bank insolvency under Part 2 of the 2009 Act; and
    (g)   "winding up petition" or "petition to wind up" include an application for bank insolvency under Part 2 of the 2009 Act.

    (3)   The modifications relating to bank administration under Part 3 of the 2009 Act are that references to—
    (a)   "administrator" include a reference to a bank administrator under Part 3 of the 2009 Act;
    (b)   "administration" or "insolvent administration" include a reference to a bank administration under Part 3 of the 2009 Act;
    (c)   "administration order" include a reference to a bank administration order under Part 3 of the 2009 Act; and
    (d)   "provisional liquidator" include a reference to a provisional bank administrator under Part 3 of the 2009 Act.

    (4)   The modifications relating to bank insolvency or bank administration under Parts 2 and 3 of the 2009 Act are that references to—

(a) "insolvency legislation" or "the law of insolvency" include Parts 2 and 3 of the 2009 Act and the provisions of the Insolvency Act 1986 and the Insolvency (Northern Ireland) Order 1989 as applied by those Parts;

(b) a person acting as an "insolvency practitioner" (as defined in section 388 of the Insolvency Act 1986) include a person acting as a bank liquidator or bank administrator under Parts 2 and 3 of the 2009 Act;

(c) the provisions of the Insolvency Act 1986 and the Insolvency (Northern Ireland) Order 1989, in the context of bank insolvency or bank administration, shall be read to include those provisions as applied and modified by sections 103 and 145 of the 2009 Act; and

(d) the provisions of the Insolvency Rules 1986, the Insolvency Rules (Northern Ireland) 1991 and the Insolvency (Scotland) Rules 1986, in the context of bank insolvency or bank administration, shall be read to include those provisions as applied and modified by rules made under section 411(1A) of the Insolvency Act 1986 in relation to bank insolvency, and under section 411(1B) of the Insolvency Act 1986 in relation to bank administration.

[526]

NOTES
Commencement: 21 February 2009.

PART 3
SPECIFIC MODIFICATIONS AND AMENDMENTS TO LEGISLATION

4 Finance (No 2) Act 1992

(1) The following provision of the Finance (No 2) Act 1992 applies with the modification set out in this article.

(2) Paragraph 2 of Schedule 12 (Banks etc in Compulsory Liquidation) is to be read as if it included the following—

"(3A) Where the company is a bank (as defined in section 91 of the Banking Act 2009), bank insolvency proceedings shall be taken to have commenced against the bank when the application for a bank insolvency order is made to the court under section 95 of the Banking Act 2009.".

[527]

NOTES
Commencement: 21 February 2009.

5 Financial Services and Markets Act 2000

(1) The following provisions of the Financial Services and Markets Act 2000 apply with the modifications set out in this article.

(2) In section 215 (Rights of the scheme in relevant person's insolvency)—
(a) in subsection (3), the reference to making an administration application is to be read as including making an application for a bank administration order under section 142 of the 2009 Act, and
(b) subsection (4) is to be read as if it read the following—

"(4) In the case of a bank insolvency (as defined in Part 2 of the Banking Act 2009), if the scheme manager decides, pursuant to section 100(6)(d) of that Act, not to remain on the liquidation committee, the scheme manager shall retain the rights it usually enjoys in respect of the winding up of a relevant person under section 371(3) and (4).".

(3) In section 355 (Interpretation of Part 24), the definition of "court" is to be read as if ", unless otherwise provided," were inserted after the word "means".

(4) In section 361 (Administrator's duty to report to Authority), references to—
(a) "administration" are to be read as including a reference to bank administration under Part 3 of the 2009 Act; and
(b) "the administrator" are to be read as including the bank administrator under Part 3 of the 2009 Act.

(5) In section 362 (Authority's powers to participate in proceedings)—
(a) references to "court"—
(i) in the context of a bank administration under Part 3 of the 2009 Act in England, Wales or Northern Ireland, are to be read as meaning the High Court, and
(ii) in the context of a bank administration under Part 3 of the 2009 Act in Scotland, are to be read as meaning the Court of Session,

(b)   in subsection (1), the reference to making an administration application is to be read as including making an application for a bank administration order under section 142 of the 2009 Act, and

(c)   in subsections (4) and (4A), references to paragraph 74 of Schedule B1 to the Insolvency Act 1986 and paragraph 75 of Schedule B1 to the Insolvency (Northern Ireland) Order 1989 are to be read as including references to those provisions as applied and modified by section 145 of the 2009 Act.

(6)   In section 370 (Liquidator's duty to report to Authority), references to "liquidator" are to be read as including a reference to a bank liquidator under Part 2 of the 2009 Act.

(7)   In section 375 (Authority's right to apply for an order), references to the provisions of the Insolvency Act 1986 and the Insolvency (Northern Ireland) Order 1989 are to be read as including references to those provisions as applied and modified by section 103 and section 134 of the 2009 Act.

[528]

NOTES
Commencement: 21 February 2009.

6   Companies Act 2006

(1)   The following provisions of the Companies Act 2006 apply with the modifications set out in this article.

(2)   In section 461 (permitted disclosure of information obtained under compulsory powers)—
(a)   subsection (4)(c) is to be read so as to include the 2009 Act in the list of enactments in that subsection;
(b)   in subsection (4)(g) is to be read so as to include the 2009 Act in the list of enactments in that subsection.

(3)   Any references in Part 35 (the registrar of companies) to the Insolvency Act 1986 and the Insolvency (Northern Ireland) Order 1989 are to be read as including a reference to Parts 2 and 3 of the 2009 Act.

(4)   Where an application is made to the court for—
(a)   a bank insolvency order under Part 2 of the 2009 Act,
(b)   the appointment of a provisional bank liquidator under section 135 of the Insolvency Act 1986 or article 115 of the Insolvency (Northern Ireland) Order 1989, as applied by section 103 of the 2009 Act,
(c)   a bank administration order under Part 3 of the 2009 Act, or
(d)   the appointment of a provisional bank administrator under section 135 of the Insolvency Act 1986 or article 115 of the Insolvency (Northern Ireland) Order 1989, as applied by section 145 of the 2009 Act,

sections 1139 and 1140 (service of documents on company, directors, secretaries and others) have effect subject to the provisions for service set out in Parts 2 or 3 of the 2009 Act and in rules made under section 411 of the Insolvency Act 1986 in respect of those Parts.

(5)   In Part 2 of Schedule 2 (Specified Descriptions of Disclosures)—
(a)   paragraph 25 is to be read so as to include the 2009 Act in the list of enactments in that paragraph, and
(b)   paragraph 46 is to be read so as to include the 2009 Act in the list of enactments in that paragraph.

(6)   In Part 2 of Schedule 11A (Specified Descriptions of Disclosures)—
(a)   paragraph 30 is to be read so as to include the 2009 Act in the list of enactments in that paragraph, and
(b)   paragraph 52 is to be read so as to include the 2009 Act in the list of enactments in that paragraph.

[529]

NOTES
Commencement: 21 February 2009.

7   Dormant Bank and Building Society Accounts Act 2008

(1)   This article applies to a reclaim fund established under the Dormant Bank and Building Society Accounts Act 2008 if, under sections 1 or 2 of that Act, the balance of a customer's dormant account is transferred into that reclaim fund from a bank which is a bank within the meaning of section 91 of the 2009 Act.

(2)   Where that reclaim fund is unable, or likely to be unable, to satisfy a claim against it, the fact that it ceases to be authorised does not prevent the operation of the Financial Services

Compensation Scheme under section 213 of the Financial Services and Markets Act 2000 in respect of it; and for that purpose, the reclaim fund is a relevant person within the meaning of section 213(9), despite the lapse of authorisation.

[530]

NOTES
Commencement: 21 February 2009.

8 Pension Protection Fund (Entry Rules) Regulations 2005

(1)   The Pension Protection Fund (Entry Rules) Regulations 2005 are amended as follows.

(2)   In regulation 6 (Circumstances in which insolvency proceedings in relation to the employer are stayed or come to an end), after paragraph (1)(a)(v) insert—
> "(vi)   where the company is a bank (as defined in section 91 of the Banking Act 2009), the bank insolvency procedure is stayed under section 130 of the Insolvency Act 1986 (as applied by section 103 of the Banking Act 2009), or the bank insolvency order is rescinded or discharged, except in circumstances where the court has made an administration order in accordance with section 114 of the Banking Act 2009.".

[531]

NOTES
Commencement: 21 February 2009.

9   (*Amends the Pension Protection Fund (Entry Rules) Regulations (Northern Ireland) 2005* (*outside the scope of this work*).)

SCHEDULE
LEGISLATION SUBJECT TO THE GENERAL MODIFICATIONS IN PART 2
Article 3(1)

Primary Legislation

Taxes Management Act 1970

Prescription and Limitation (Scotland) Act 1973

Companies Act 1985

Companies (Northern Ireland) Order 1986

Debtors (Scotland) Act 1987

Income and Corporation Taxes Act 1988

Companies Act 1989

Companies (No 2) (Northern Ireland) Order 1990

Taxation of Chargeable Gains Act 1992

Finance (No 2) Act 1992

Pension Schemes Act 1993

Pension Schemes (Northern Ireland) Act 1993

Pensions Act 1995

Pensions (Northern Ireland) Order 1995

Proceeds of Crime (Scotland) Act 1995

Finance Act 1996

Employment Rights Act 1996

Employment Rights (Northern Ireland) Order 1996

Terrorism Act 2000

Finance Act 2000

International Criminal Court Act 2001

International Criminal Court (Scotland) Act 2001

Finance Act 2002

Proceeds of Crime Act 2002

Debt Arrangement and Attachment (Scotland) Act 2002

Finance Act 2003

Pensions Act 2004

Pensions (Northern Ireland) Order 2005

Companies Act 2006

Bankruptcy and Diligence (Scotland) Act 2007

Finance Act 2008

Dormant Bank and Building Society Accounts Act 2008

Secondary Legislation

Insolvent Companies (Disqualification of Unfit Directors) Proceedings Rules 1987

Financial Markets and Insolvency Regulations 1991

Financial Markets and Insolvency Regulations (Northern Ireland) 1991

Insolvency Regulations 1994

Non-Domestic Rating (Unoccupied Property) (Scotland) Regulations 1994

Insolvent Companies (Reports on Conduct of Directors) Rules 1996

Financial Markets and Insolvency Regulations 1996

Financial Markets and Insolvency Regulations (Northern Ireland) 1996

Individual Savings Account Regulations 1998

Corporation Tax (Simplified Arrangements for Group Relief) Regulations 1999

Financial Markets and Insolvency (Settlement Finality) Regulations 1999

Financial Collateral Arrangements (No 2) Regulations 2003

Insolvency Practitioners and Insolvency Services Account (Fees) Order 2003

Insolvent Companies (Reports on Conduct of Directors) Rules (Northern Ireland) 2003

Insolvent Companies (Disqualification of Unfit Directors) Proceedings Rules (Northern Ireland) 2003

Land Registration Rules 2003

Credit Institutions (Reorganisation and Winding Up) Regulations 2004

Insolvency Practitioners Regulations 2005

Pension Protection Fund (Entry Rules) Regulations 2005

Pension Protection Fund (Entry Rules) Regulations (Northern Ireland) 2005

Gender Recognition (Disclosure of Information) (England, Wales and Northern Ireland) Order 2005

Gender Recognition (Disclosure of Information) (Scotland) Order 2005

Financial Assistance Scheme Regulations 2005

Insolvency Practitioners Regulations (Northern Ireland) 2006

Insolvency Practitioners and Insolvency Account (Fees) Order (Northern Ireland) 2006

Land Registration (Scotland) Rules 2006

Companies (Cross-Border Mergers) Regulations 2007

Regulated Covered Bonds Regulations 2008

[532]

NOTES

Commencement: 21 February 2009.

BANKING ACT 2009 (THIRD PARTY COMPENSATION ARRANGEMENTS FOR PARTIAL PROPERTY TRANSFERS) REGULATIONS 2009

(SI 2009/319)

NOTES

Made: 19 February 2009.
Authority: Banking Act 2009, ss 60, 259(1).
Commencement: 21 February 2009.

1   Citation, commencement and interpretation

(1)   These Regulations may be cited as the Banking Act 2009 (Third Party Compensation Arrangements for Partial Property Transfers) Regulations 2009.

(2)   These Regulations come into force on 21st February 2009.

(3)   In these Regulations—
"the Act" means the Banking Act 2009;
"the Bank" means the Bank of England;
"banking institution" means—
(a)   a bank (within the meaning of Part 1 of the Act);
(b)   a building society (within the meaning of section 119 of the Building Societies Act 1986); or
(c)   a holding company;
"relevant time" means—
(a)   in relation to Case 1 (as specified in regulation 2(2)), the time at which the partial property transfer took effect;
(b)   in relation to Case 2 (as specified in regulation 2(3)), the time at which the property transfer instrument made in accordance with section 11(2) or 12(2) of the Act took effect;
(c)   in relation to Case 3 (as specified in regulation 2(4)), the time at which the share transfer order made in accordance with section 13(2) of the Act (including that section as applied by section 82 of the Act) took effect;
"third party compensation order in relation to a partial property transfer" has the meaning given in regulation 3(2).

[533]

NOTES
Commencement: 21 February 2009.
Note: the Banking Act 2009 does not define "holding company" but s 82(1) at **[82]** (in relation to temporary public ownership) defines the holding company of a bank as a parent undertaking of a bank.

2   Application of these Regulations

(1)   These Regulations apply in the following cases.

(2)   Case 1 is where a partial property transfer has been made by the Bank in accordance with section 11(2) or 12(2) of the Act.

(3)   Case 2 is where—
(a)   the Bank has made a property transfer instrument in accordance with section 11(2) or 12(2) of the Act which is not a partial property transfer; but
(b)   an onward property transfer instrument has been made by the Bank in accordance with section 43 of the Act which is a partial property transfer.

(4)   Case 3 is where—
(a)   the Treasury have made a share transfer order in accordance with section 13(2) of the Act (including that section as applied by section 82 of the Act); and
(b)   a property transfer order has been made by the Treasury in accordance with section 45(2) of the Act (including that section as modified by section 83 of the Act) which by virtue of section 45(5)(b) of the Act is to be treated as a partial property transfer.

(5)   For the purposes of these Regulations, a property transfer instrument or property transfer order which purports to transfer all property, rights and liabilities of an undertaking shall be treated as having done so effectively (and so shall not be treated as a partial property transfer), notwithstanding the possibility that any of the property, rights or liabilities are foreign property and may not have been effectively transferred by the property transfer instrument or order or by virtue of steps taken under section 39 of the Act.

[534]

NOTES
Commencement: 21 February 2009.

3   Requirement to include a third party compensation order

(1)   A compensation scheme order or a resolution fund order made in the cases in which these Regulations apply must include a third party compensation order.

(2)   Regulations 4 to 9 set out provisions which must be included in a such a third party compensation order ("a third party compensation order in relation to a partial property transfer"); regulation 10 sets out provisions which may be included in such an order.

[535]

NOTES
Commencement: 21 February 2009.

4   Mandatory provisions—appointment of independent valuer

A third party compensation order in relation to a partial property transfer must include provision for a person ("an independent valuer") to be appointed to determine—

   (a)   whether all pre-transfer creditors, a class of pre-transfer creditors or a particular pre-transfer creditor should be paid compensation; and

   (b)   if compensation should be paid, what amount is to be paid,

(and, by virtue of section 59(3)(a) of the Act, sections 54 to 56 (appointment etc of independent valuer) apply to the independent valuer appointed in accordance with this regulation).

[536]

NOTES
Commencement: 21 February 2009.

5   Mandatory provisions—assessment of insolvency treatment

(1)   A third party compensation order in relation to a partial property transfer must include the following provisions (subject to any necessary modifications).

(2)   The independent valuer must assess the treatment ("the insolvency treatment") which pre-transfer creditors would have received had the banking institution in relation to which or in connection with which the partial property transfer has been made entered insolvency immediately before the relevant time.

(3)   The independent valuer must assess the treatment ("the actual treatment") which pre-transfer creditors have received, are receiving or are likely to receive (as specified in the order) if no (or no further) compensation is paid.

(4)   If the independent valuer considers that, in relation to any pre-transfer creditor, the actual treatment assessed under paragraph (3) is less favourable than the insolvency treatment assessed under paragraph (2), the independent valuer must determine that compensation be paid to that pre-transfer creditor.

(5)   The amount of compensation payable by virtue of paragraph (4) must be determined by the independent valuer by reference to the difference in treatment assessed under paragraph (4) and on the basis of the fair and equitable value of that difference in treatment.

[537]

NOTES
Commencement: 21 February 2009.

6   Mandatory provisions—choice of insolvency process

A third party compensation order in relation to a partial property transfer must include either—

   (a)   a provision specifying that the independent valuer must assess the insolvency treatment as required under regulation 5(2) on the basis that the banking institution had entered a particular insolvency process specified in the order; or

   (b)   a provision specifying that the independent valuer must determine what insolvency process it is likely that the banking institution would have entered, had the following instrument or order not been made—

   (i)   in the case of Case 1 (as specified in regulation 2(2)), the partial property transfer;

   (ii)   in the case of Case 2 (as specified in regulation 2(3)), the property transfer instrument made in accordance with section 11(2) or 12(2) of the Act;

(iii) in the case of Case 3 (as specified in regulation 2(4)), the share transfer order made in accordance with section 13(2) of the Act (including that section as applied by section 82 of the Act).

[538]

NOTES
Commencement: 21 February 2009.

7 Mandatory provisions—valuation principles

(1) A third party compensation order in relation to a partial property transfer must include the following provisions (subject to any necessary modifications).

(2) In making the assessment of the insolvency treatment as required under regulation 5(2), the independent valuer must determine the amount of compensation in accordance with the following principles (in addition to the principle which applies by virtue of section 57(3) of the Act)—

    (a) that the banking institution in relation to which or in connection with which the partial property transfer has been made would have entered insolvency immediately before the relevant time;

    (b) that the partial property transfer has not been made and that no other order or instrument under Part 1 of the Act would have been made in relation to or in connection with the banking institution (or, in appropriate cases, any of the banking institutions);

    (c) that no financial assistance would have, after the relevant time, been provided by the Bank or the Treasury.

[539]

NOTES
Commencement: 21 February 2009.

8 Mandatory provisions—interim payments

(1) A third party compensation order in relation to a partial property transfer must include the following provisions (subject to any necessary modifications).

(2) The independent valuer may determine that payments should be made to a pre-transfer creditor, a class of pre-transfer creditors or all pre-transfer creditors on account of compensation to be payable under the third party compensation order ("payments on account").

(3) The independent valuer may make such a determination at any time before the determination required by regulation 5(5) has been made.

(4) Once the determination required by regulation 5(5) has been made, the independent valuer must determine what balancing payments are appropriate to ensure that the pre-transfer creditor receives the amount of compensation determined under regulation 5(5) (and no more than that amount).

(5) Subject to paragraph (6), the independent valuer may make such provision as to payments on account as he thinks fit (including a requirement that payments be made in instalments).

(6) Payments on account must be made subject to the following conditions—

    (a) that the acceptance of such a payment by the pre-transfer creditor reduces any obligation (whether in existence at the time of the payment or not) on the Treasury, the Financial Services Compensation Scheme or any other person (as the case may be) to pay compensation to the pre-transfer creditor by the amount of the payment on account;

    (b) that, where the independent valuer, in accordance with paragraph (4) determines that the pre-transfer creditor should make a balancing payment to the Treasury, the Financial Services Compensation Scheme or any other person (as the case may be), the pre-transfer creditor is liable to pay that amount.

(7) In considering whether to require payments on account to be made in accordance with this regulation, the independent valuer must have regard to the merits of ensuring that pre-transfer creditors receive compensation in a timely manner.

[540]

NOTES
Commencement: 21 February 2009.

9 Mandatory provisions—valuations provided by creditors

A third party compensation order in relation to a partial property transfer must make provision requiring the independent valuer to have regard to any information provided by a pre-transfer creditor which is relevant to the exercise of the independent valuer's functions under the order; in particular, the independent valuer must have regard to any information which relates to the assessment of the insolvency treatment required by regulation 5(2) or the assessment of the actual treatment required by regulation 5(3).

[541]

NOTES
Commencement: 21 February 2009.

10   Optional provisions—valuation principles

(1)   A third party compensation order in relation to a partial property transfer may make any of the following provisions (subject to any necessary modifications).

(2)   In making the assessment of the insolvency treatment required by regulation 5(2), the independent valuer must assume that property specified in the order (or property of a class specified in the order) would have been sold for the price specified in the order or calculated by reference to criteria specified in the order.

(3)   In making the assessment of the insolvency treatment required by regulation 5(2), the independent valuer must assume that property specified in the order (or property of a class specified in the order) would have been treated in the manner specified in order.

[542]

NOTES
Commencement: 21 February 2009.

BANKING ACT 2009 (RESTRICTION OF PARTIAL PROPERTY TRANSFERS) ORDER 2009

(SI 2009/322)

NOTES
Made: 19 February 2009.
Authority: Banking Act 2009, ss 47, 48, 259(1).
Commencement: 21 February 2009.
Note: See Banking Liaison Panel Subgroup advice to HM Treasury (17 June 2009) regarding this Order http://www.hm-treasury.gov.uk/d/bankingliaisonpanel_advice250609.pdf.

ARRANGEMENT OF ARTICLES

PART 1
GENERAL

PART 2
RESTRICTIONS ON PARTIAL PROPERTY TRANSFERS

PART 3
REMEDIES

PART 1
GENERAL

1   Citation, commencement and interpretation

(1)   This Order may be cited as the Banking Act 2009 (Restriction of Partial Property Transfers) Order 2009.

(2)   This Order comes into force on 21st February 2009.

(3)   In this Order—

"the Act" means the Banking Act 2009;

"the Bank" means the Bank of England;

["Banking Consolidation Directive" means Directive 2006/48/EC of the European Parliament and of the Council relating to the taking up and pursuit of the business of credit institutions;]

"banking institution" means—

    (a)   a bank (within the meaning of Part 1 of the Act);

    (b)   an undertaking which was a bank immediately before the making of a share transfer order under section 13(2) of the Act;

    (c)   a bridge bank;

    (d)   a building society (within the meaning of section 119 of the Building Societies Act 1986); or

    (e)   a holding company;

"continuity powers" means the powers conferred by section 64(2) of the Act (including that subsection as applied by sections 65(2) and 83(2)(f) of the Act) and section 67(2) of the Act (including that subsection as applied by sections 68(2) and 83(2)(f) of the Act);

"deposit" has the meaning given by article 5 of the Regulated Activities Order (disregarding the exclusions in articles 6 to 9AA of that Order);

"eligible claimant" has the meaning given by rule 4.2.1 of the Compensation Sourcebook made by the Financial Services Authority under the Financial Services and Markets Act 2000;

"excluded rights" means rights—

    (a)   which relate to a retail deposit made with a banking institution;

    (b)   which relate to a retail liability owed to a banking institution;

    (c)   which relate to a contract which was entered into by or on behalf of a banking institution otherwise than in the course of carrying on of an activity which relates … to relevant financial instruments [or an activity referred to in Annex I to the Banking Consolidation Directive];

    (d)   which relate to a claim for damages, an award of damages or a claim under an indemnity which arose in connection with the carrying on by a banking institution of an activity which relates … to relevant financial instruments [or an activity referred to in Annex I to the Banking Consolidation Directive]; …

    (e)   which relate to subordinated debt; [or

    (f)   which relate to transferable securities (other than transferable securities referred to or described in a set-off arrangement, netting arrangement or title transfer financial collateral arrangement referred to in article 3(1));]

and "excluded liabilities" shall be interpreted accordingly;

"financial instrument" means

    [(a)]   any instrument listed in Section C of Annex I to [the Markets in Financial Instruments Directive], read with Chapter VI of the Commission Regulation 1287/2006/EC;

    [(b)]   any option, future, swap, forward, contract for differences or other derivative contract not falling within paragraph (a); and

    (c)   any combination of any of the foregoing;]

["Markets in Financial Instruments Directive" means Directive 2004/39/EC of the European Parliament and of the Council on markets in financial instruments;]

"Regulated Activities Order" means the Financial Services and Markets Act 2000 (Regulated Activities) Order 2001);

"relevant authority" means—

    [(a)]   in relation to Case 1 or 2 (as specified in article 2(2) and (3)), the Bank;

    [(b)]   in relation to Case 3 (as specified in article 2(4)), the Treasury;

"relevant financial instrument" means—

    [(a)]   a financial instrument;

    [(b)]   a deposit;

    [(c)]   a loan; …

    [(d)]   an instrument which falls within article 77 of the Regulated Activities Order (disregarding the exclusions in article 77(2)(b) to (d)); [or

    (e)   any contract for the sale, purchase or delivery of—

        (i)   transferable securities;

        (ii)   the currency of the United Kingdom or any other country, territory or monetary union;

        (iii)   palladium, platinum, gold, silver or any other precious metal; or

        (iv)   any other commodity;]

"retail deposit" means a deposit in relation to which the condition in paragraph (a) or (b) is satisfied—

[(a)] the depositor is an eligible claimant; or

[(b)] the deposit is held in an account of a particular class or brand provided by a particular banking institution which either—

(i) is mainly used by eligible claimants; or

(ii) has been mainly marketed by the banking institution to eligible claimants;

"retail liability" means a liability which is owed to a banking institution by an eligible claimant;

"title transfer financial collateral arrangements" has the meaning given by regulation 3 of the Financial Collateral Arrangements (No 2) Regulations 2003[;

"transferable securities" has the meaning given by Article 4(18) of the Markets in Financial Instruments Directive].

(4) References in this Order to netting arrangements include—

(a) arrangements which provide for netting (within the meaning given by regulation 2(1) of the Financial Markets and Insolvency (Settlement Finality) Regulations 1999); and

(b) arrangements which include a close-out netting provision (within the meaning given by regulation 3 of the Financial Collateral Arrangements (No 2) Regulations 2003).

[543]

NOTES

Commencement: 21 February 2009.

Para (3): definitions "Banking Consolidation Directive", "Markets in Financial Instruments Directive" and "transferable securities" inserted, in definition "excluded rights" words omitted revoked and words in square brackets inserted, in definition "financial instrument" number "(a)" in square brackets and sub-paras (b), (c) inserted and words in square brackets in sub-para (a) substituted, in definitions "relevant authority" and "retail deposit" numbers in square brackets substituted, and in definition "relevant financial instrument" numbers in square brackets substituted, word omitted revoked and sub-para (e) together with word preceding it inserted, by the Banking Act 2009 (Restriction of Partial Property Transfers) (Amendment) Order 2009, SI 2009/1826, art 3, as from 9 July 2009.

Note: the Banking Act 2009 does not define "holding company" but s 82(1) at **[82]** (in relation to temporary public ownership) defines the holding company of a bank as a parent undertaking of a bank.

2 Application of this Order

(1) This Order applies in the following cases.

(2) Case 1 is where a partial property transfer has been made by the Bank in accordance with section 11(2) or 12(2) of the Act.

(3) Case 2 is where—

(a) the Bank has made a property transfer instrument in accordance with section 11(2) or 12(2) of the Act (whether or not that instrument is a partial property transfer); and

(b) a property transfer instrument under section 42, 43 or 44 of the Act has been made by the Bank which is a partial property transfer.

(4) Case 3 is where—

(a) the Treasury have made a share transfer order in accordance with section 13(2) of the Act (including that section as applied by section 82 of the Act); and

(b) a property transfer instrument has been made by the Treasury under section 45 or 46 of the Act (including those sections as applied and modified by section 83 of the Act) which by virtue of section 45(5)(b) or 46(5)(b) of the Act is to be treated as a partial property transfer.

(5) For the purposes of this Order, a property transfer instrument or order which purports to transfer all of the property, rights and liabilities of a banking institution shall be treated as having done so effectively (and so shall not be treated as a partial property transfer), notwithstanding the possibility that any of the property, rights or liabilities are foreign property and may not have been effectively transferred by the property transfer instrument or order or by virtue of steps taken under section 39 of the Act.

[544]

NOTES

Commencement: 21 February 2009.

PART 2
RESTRICTIONS ON PARTIAL PROPERTY TRANSFERS

3 Set-off and netting

(1) A partial property transfer to which this Order applies may not provide for the transfer of some, but not all, of the protected rights and liabilities between a particular person ("P") and a banking institution under a particular set-off arrangement, netting arrangement or title transfer financial collateral arrangement.

(2)   A partial property transfer to which this Order applies may not include provision under the continuity powers which terminates or modifies the protected rights or liabilities between P and a banking institution.

(3)   For the purposes of paragraphs (1) and (2), rights and liabilities between P and a banking institution are protected if they are rights and liabilities which either P or the banking institution is entitled to set-off or net under a set-off arrangement, netting arrangement or title transfer financial collateral arrangement which P has entered into with the banking institution so long as they are not excluded rights or excluded liabilities.

(4)   For the purposes of paragraph (1), a property transfer instrument or order which purports to transfer all of the protected rights and liabilities between P and a banking institution under a particular set-off arrangement, netting arrangement or title transfer financial collateral arrangement shall be treated as having done so effectively (and so not give rise to a contravention of paragraph (1)), notwithstanding the possibility that any of the protected rights or liabilities are foreign property and may not have been effectively transferred by the property transfer instrument or order or by virtue of steps taken under section 39 of the Act.

(5)   For the purposes of paragraph (3), it is immaterial whether—

(a)   the arrangement which permits P or the banking institution to set-off or net rights and liabilities also permits P or the banking institution to set-off or net rights and liabilities with another person; or

(b)   the right of P or the banking institution to set-off or net is exercisable only on the occurrence of a particular event.

(6)   In this article, "excluded rights" and "excluded liabilities" have the meanings given in article 1 except that the reference to subordinated debt [and the references to transferable securities in paragraph (f) of the definition of "excluded rights" shall be treated as if they were respectively a reference to subordinated debt or transferable securities] issued by P or by the banking institution.

[545]

NOTES

Commencement: 21 February 2009.

Para (6): words in square brackets substituted by the Banking Act 2009 (Restriction of Partial Property Transfers) (Amendment) Order 2009, SI 2009/1826, art 4, as from 9 July 2009.

---

4 Community law

A partial property transfer to which this Order applies may not transfer property, rights or liabilities or include provision under the continuity powers to the extent that to do so would contravene Community law.

[546]

NOTES

Commencement: 21 February 2009.

---

5 Secured liabilities

(1)   Subject to paragraph (5), paragraphs (2), [(2A),] (3) and (4) apply where an arrangement has been entered into under which one party owes a liability to the other and that liability is secured against property or rights; and it is immaterial that—

(a)   the liability is secured against all or substantially all of the property or rights of a person;

(b)   the liability is secured against specified property or rights; or

(c)   the property or rights against which the liability is secured are not owned by the person who owes the liability.

(2)   A partial property transfer to which this Order applies may not transfer the property or rights against which the liability is secured unless that liability and the benefit of the security are also transferred.

[(2A)   A partial property transfer to which this Order applies may not transfer the benefit of the security unless the liability which is secured is also transferred.]

(3)   A partial property transfer to which this Order applies may not transfer the liability unless the benefit of the security is also transferred.

(4)   A partial property transfer to which this Order applies may not include provision under the continuity powers which terminates or modifies the arrangement if the effect of that provision is to provide that the liability is no longer secured against the property or right.

(5)   Paragraphs (2), [(2A),] (3) and (4) do not apply if the arrangement has been entered into by a banking institution in contravention of a rule prohibiting such arrangements made by the Financial Services Authority under the Financial Services and Markets Act 2000 or otherwise than in accordance the Part 4 permission (within the meaning of that Act) of the banking institution.

(6)   For the purposes of paragraphs (2)[, (2A)] and (3), a property transfer instrument or order which purports to transfer any property, rights or liabilities shall be treated as having done so effectively (and so not give rise to a contravention of paragraph (2)[, (2A)] or (3)), notwithstanding the possibility that any of those property, rights or liabilities are foreign property and may not have been effectively transferred by the property transfer instrument or order or by virtue of steps taken under section 39 of the Act.

[547]

NOTES
Commencement: 21 February 2009.
Paras (1), (5), (6): references in square brackets inserted by the Banking Act 2009 (Restriction of Partial Property Transfers) (Amendment) Order 2009, SI 2009/1826, art 5(a), (c), (d), as from 9 July 2009.
Para (2A): inserted by SI 2009/1826, art 5(b), as from 9 July 2009.

---

6   Capital market arrangements

(1)   Subject to paragraph (3), a partial property transfer to which this Order applies may not provide for the transfer of some, but not all, of the property, rights and liabilities which are or form part of a capital market arrangement to which the banking institution is a party.

(2)   Subject to paragraph (3), a partial property transfer to which this Order applies may not include provision under the continuity powers which terminates or modifies property, rights or liabilities which are or form part of a capital market arrangement to which the banking institution is a party.

(3)   Paragraphs (1) and (2) do not apply where the only property, rights and liabilities transferred or not transferred, or terminated or modified (as the case may be) are property, rights and liabilities which relate to deposits.

(4)   For the purposes of paragraph (1), a property transfer instrument or order which purports to transfer all of the property, rights and liabilities which are or form part of a capital market arrangement to which the banking institution is a party shall be treated as having done so effectively (and so not give rise to a contravention of paragraph (1)), notwithstanding the possibility that any of those property, rights or liabilities are foreign property and may not have been effectively transferred by the property transfer instrument or order or by virtue of steps taken under section 39.

(5)   For the purposes of this article, "capital market arrangement" has the meaning given by paragraph 1 of Schedule 2A to the Insolvency Act 1986.

[548]

NOTES
Commencement: 21 February 2009.

---

7   Financial markets

(1)   A property transfer order to which this Order applies may not transfer property, rights or liabilities or include provision under the continuity powers to the extent that to do so would have the effect of modifying, modifying the operation of or rendering unenforceable—
   (a)   a market contract;
   (b)   the default rules of a recognised investment exchange or recognised clearing house; or
   (c)   the rules of a recognised investment exchange or recognised clearing house as to the settlement of market contracts not dealt with under its default rules.

(2)   For the purposes of this article—
   "default rules" has the meaning given by section 188 of the Companies Act 1989;
   "market contract" has the meaning given by section 155 of the Companies Act 1989;
   "recognised clearing house" and "recognised investment exchange" have the meanings given by section 285 of the Financial Services and Markets Act 2000.

[549]

NOTES
Commencement: 21 February 2009.

[7A   Trusts

A partial property transfer to which this Order applies which makes provision under section 34(7)(a) of the Act may remove or alter the terms of the trust (howsoever arising) only to the extent necessary or expedient for the purpose of transferring from the banking institution to the transferee—
   (a)   the legal or beneficial interest of the banking institution in the property held on trust;
   (b)   any powers, rights or obligations of the banking institution in respect of the property held on trust.]

[550]

PART III
SIS UNDER BANKING ACT 2009

NOTES
Commencement: 9 July 2009.
Inserted by the Banking Act 2009 (Restriction of Partial Property Transfers) (Amendment) Order 2009, SI 2009/1826, art 6, as from 9 July 2009.

8 Additional restrictions on reverse transfers

(1)   This article applies to a partial property transfer to which this Order applies which is made—

    (a)   by the Bank under section 44 of the Act; or

    (b)   by the Treasury under section 46 of the Act.

(2)   Subject to paragraph (3), a partial property transfer to which this article applies may not provide for the transfer of—

    (a)   any property, rights or liabilities which were not transferred under the original instrument or order;

    (b)   any liability which was not, at the time immediately before the original instrument or order was made, a liability owed by the banking institution; or

    (c)   rights or liabilities under a [relevant] financial instrument.

(3)   Paragraph (2) does not apply to—

    (a)   a transfer of property, rights or liabilities which have accrued, become or ceased to become payable, changed or lapsed as a result of the application of a default event provision which applies by virtue of the original instrument or order;

    (b)   a transfer of property, rights or liabilities to which consent has been given by the transferee, the transferor and any other person whose consent for the transfer would be required were the transfer not being effected by a property transfer instrument or order;

    (c)   a transfer of a claim for damages or an award of damages against the banking institution which was in existence immediately before the original instrument or order was made;

    (d)   a transfer to an undertaking which has not entered insolvency; or

    (e)   a transfer under article 12(6).

(4)   In this article—

    (a)   "original instrument" has the meaning given by section 44 of the Act and "original order" has the meaning given by section 46 of the Act; and

    (b)   the reference to insolvency includes a reference to (i) liquidation, (ii) bank insolvency, (iii) administration, (iv) bank administration, (v) receivership, (vi) a composition with creditors, and (vii) a scheme of arrangement.

        [551]

NOTES
Commencement: 21 February 2009.
Para (2): word in square brackets inserted by the Banking Act 2009 (Restriction of Partial Property Transfers) (Amendment) Order 2009, SI 2009/1826, art 7, as from 9 July 2009.

9 Termination rights

A partial property transfer to which this Order applies may not make provision for subsection (6) or (7) of section 38 of the Act to apply in relation to—

    (a)   a relevant financial instrument to the extent that it confers rights and liabilities which either party to the instrument is entitled to set-off or net under a set-off arrangement, netting arrangement or title transfer financial collateral arrangement except in so far as those rights and liabilities are excluded rights or excluded liabilities; or

    (b)   a set-off arrangement, netting arrangement or title transfer financial collateral arrangement to the extent that it confers a right to set-off or net rights and liabilities under a relevant financial instrument except in so far as those rights and liabilities are excluded rights or excluded liabilities.

        [552]

NOTES
Commencement: 21 February 2009.

PART 3

REMEDIES

10 Financial markets, termination rights and continuity power

(1)   This article applies where a partial property transfer has been made in contravention of article 7 or 9 or any other provision of this Order which relates to the exercise of the continuity powers.

(2)   The partial property transfer is void in so far as it is made in contravention of those provisions of the Order.

[553]

NOTES
Commencement: 21 February 2009.

11   Set-off and netting

(1)   This article applies where a partial property transfer has been made in contravention of—
(a)   article 3; or
(b)   article 4, to the extent that the contravention relates to set-off arrangements, netting arrangements or title transfer financial collateral arrangements,

unless the contravention relates to the exercise of the continuity powers (in which case article 10 applies).

(2)   The partial property transfer does not affect the exercise of the right to set-off or net.

[554]

NOTES
Commencement: 21 February 2009.

12   Contravention of other provisions of the Order

(1)   Subject to paragraph (2), this article applies where any person ("P") considers that a partial property transfer has been made in contravention of any provision of this Order and that as a result the property, rights or liabilities of P have been affected.

(2)   This article does not apply to the extent that article 10 or 11 applies.

(3)   P may give notice to the relevant authority of the alleged contravention of this Order.

(4)   The notice under paragraph (3) must—
(a)   be given within 60 days of the day on which the partial property transfer took effect;
(b)   be in writing;
(c)   specify the provision of this Order which is alleged to have been contravened and the manner in which that contravention has occurred;
(d)   identify the property, rights or liabilities to which the alleged contravention relates; and
(e)   contain or be accompanied by such information as the relevant authority may reasonably require.

(5)   Subject to paragraph (8), within 60 days of receipt of a notice under paragraph (3), the relevant authority must—
(a)   if it agrees that a provision of this Order has been contravened in the manner specified in the notice given under paragraph (3), take the steps specified in paragraph (6);
(b)   if it does not agree that a provision of this Order has been contravened in the manner specified in the notice given under paragraph (3), take the steps specified in paragraph (7).

(6)   The steps are to remedy the contravention by transferring property, rights or liabilities to the transferee or the transferor under the partial property transfer (whether by means of an onward property transfer instrument under section 43 of the Act, a reverse property transfer under section 44, a property transfer order under section 45, a reverse property transfer under section 46 or by other means).

(7)   The steps are to give reasons to P as to why it considers that no provision of this Order has been contravened in the manner specified in the notice under paragraph (3).

(8)   If the relevant authority considers that the matters raised in the notice under paragraph (3) are of such complexity that it is impracticable to take a decision under paragraph (5) within 60 days of receipt of the notice, the relevant authority may extend the period of 60 days by no more than 60 days; in such cases it must, within 60 days of receipt of the notice under paragraph (3), inform P of the extension and the duration of the extension.

(9)   The property, rights or liabilities which are transferred under paragraph (6) may be the same property, rights or liabilities which were, in contravention of this Order, transferred or not transferred (as the case may be) or, if the transfer of such property, rights or liabilities is not practicable, property, rights or liabilities which, in the opinion of the relevant authority, are equivalent to those property, rights or liabilities.

[555]

PART III
SIS UNDER BANKING ACT 2009

NOTES
Commencement: 21 February 2009.

BUILDING SOCIETIES (INSOLVENCY AND SPECIAL ADMINISTRATION) ORDER 2009

(SI 2009/805)

NOTES
Made: 29 March 2009 (3.06 pm).
Authority: Banking Act 2009, ss 130, 158, 259(1).
Commencement: 29 March 2009.
Note: On 21 July 2009 HM Treasury issued a consultation paper, Special resolution regime: the Building Societies (Insolvency and Special Administration) Order 2009 and related insolvency rules, and financial assistance to building societies to consult fully on the application of the Banking Act 2009 to building societies as the resolution procedures for building societies were not set out on the face of the Banking Act 2009 and time had not previously allowed for consultation before the new regime came into place. The closing date for this consultation paper is 30 October 2009. Following the consultation, HM Treasury will consider whether to bring forward proposals to amend the rules.

1 Citation and interpretation

(1) This Order may be cited as the Building Societies (Insolvency and Special Administration) Order 2009.

(2) In this Order—
"the 1986 Act" means the Building Societies Act 1986;
"the 2009 Act" means the Banking Act 2009.

[556]

NOTES
Commencement: 29 March 2009.

2 *(Inserts the Building Societies Act 1986, s 90C at* **[366]**.)

3 Schedule 1 to this Order specifies modifications to Parts 2 and 3 of the 2009 Act as they apply in relation to building societies.

[557]

NOTES
Commencement: 29 March 2009.

4–15 *(Arts 4–11 amend the Building Societies Act 1986: art 4 amends s 88 at* **[363]***; art 5 inserts s 89A at* **[364]***; art 6 inserts ss 90D, 90E at* **[367]**, **[368]***; art 7 amends s 86(1) at* **[362]***; art 8 amends s 91 at* **[369]***; art 9 amends s 92 at* **[370]***; art 10 inserts s 103(1)(c) at* **[371]***; art 11 amends s 119 at* **[372]**. *Art 12 inserts the Company Directors Disqualification Act 1986, s 21C at* **[349]***; art 13 inserts the Insolvency Act 1986, s 411(3A) at* **[299]***; art 14 inserts the Insolvency Act 1986, s 414(8C) at* **[301]***; art 15 amends the Financial Services and Markets Act 2000, s 220(3)(a) at* **[394]**.)

16 Rules

Section 413(2) of the Insolvency Act 1986 (rules: duty to consult Insolvency Rules Committee) shall not apply to the first set of rules made in relation to building society insolvency or to the first set of rules made in relation to building society special administration.

[558]

NOTES
Commencement: 29 March 2009.

17 Northern Ireland

In the application of this Order to Northern Ireland—
(a) a reference to an enactment is to be treated as a reference to the equivalent enactment having effect in relation to Northern Ireland,
(b) where this Order amends an enactment an equivalent amendment (incorporating any necessary modification) is made to the equivalent enactment having effect in relation to Northern Ireland, and
(c) a reference to the Secretary of State is to be treated as a reference to the Department of Enterprise, Trade and Investment.

[559]

NOTES

Commencement: 29 March 2009.

18   Application of subordinate legislation under Parts 2 and 3 of the 2009 Act

Schedule 2 applies subordinate legislation made under Parts 2 and 3 of the 2009 Act in relation to building societies, with the modifications set out in that Schedule.

[560]

NOTES

Commencement: 29 March 2009.

SCHEDULE 1
MODIFIED APPLICATION OF PARTS 2 AND 3 OF THE BANKING ACT 2009 TO
BUILDING SOCIETIES
Article 3

PART 1
GENERAL MODE OF APPLICATION

General mode of application and interpretation

1.   This Schedule specifies modifications to Part 2 (Bank Insolvency) and Part 3 (Bank Administration) of the 2009 Act as they apply in relation to building societies by virtue of section 90C of the 1986 Act.

2.—(1)   Parts 2 and 3 of the 2009 Act apply to building societies with the following general modifications (in addition to the general modifications set out in section 90C(2) of the 1986 Act)—

(a)   for "company" in each place where it appears (except in section 151) substitute "building society";

(b)   a reference to depositors includes a reference to holders of shares in the society;

(c)   a reference to a provision in Part 1 (Special Resolution Regime) of the 2009 Act is a reference to that provision as applied to building societies with any modifications by section 84 of the 2009 Act (application of Part 1: general);

(d)   a reference to a provision in Part 2 or 3 of the 2009 Act is a reference to that provision as applied in relation to building societies by section 90C of the 1986 Act with any modifications specified in that section or this Schedule.

3.   Where a provision of Part 2 or 3 of the 2009 Act applies a provision of the Insolvency Act 1986 or the Companies Act 2006, the provision so applied has effect in relation to building societies with the following modifications—

(a)   for "articles" substitute "rules";

(b)   for "company" substitute "building society";

(c)   for "registered office" substitute "principal office";

(d)   for "registrar of companies" or "registrar" substitute "FSA";

(e)   for "resolution for voluntary winding up" substitute "resolution passed under section 88(1) of the Building Societies Act 1986";

(f)   every reference to a company registered in Scotland has effect as a reference to a building society whose principal office is situated in Scotland;

(g)   every reference to the officers, or to a particular officer, of a company has effect as a reference to the officers, or to the corresponding officer, of the building society and as including a person holding himself out as such an officer;

(h)   every reference to a voluntary arrangement under Part 1 of the Insolvency Act 1986 has effect as a reference to a voluntary arrangement under that Part as applied in relation to building societies by section 90A of, and Schedule 15A to, the Building Societies Act 1986;

(i)   any requirement to send a notice or other document, or make a report, to the registrar of companies, has effect as a requirement to send that notice or document, or make that report, to the FSA and for the FSA to place it on the public file of the society concerned.

4.   In Parts 2 and 3 of the 2009 Act, and in any provision of the Insolvency Act 1986 applied by those Parts, "contributory", in relation to a building society—

(a)   means every person liable to contribute to the assets of the society in the event of its being wound up, and

(b)   for the purposes of all proceedings for determining, and all proceedings prior to the determination of, the persons who are deemed to be contributories, includes any person alleged to be a contributory, and

(c)   includes persons who are liable to pay or contribute to the payment of—

(i)   any debt or liability of the building society being wound up, or

(ii)   any sum for the adjustment of rights of members among themselves, or

(iii)   the expenses of the winding up,

but does not include persons liable to contribute by virtue of a declaration by the court under section 213 (imputed responsibility for fraudulent trading) or 214 (wrongful trading) of the Insolvency Act 1986.

5.   Expressions used in this Schedule (including in text inserted or substituted by this Schedule) have the same meaning as in the Building Societies Act 1986.

[561]

NOTES
Commencement: 29 March 2009.

PART 2
MODIFIED APPLICATION OF PART 2 OF THE 2009 ACT

6.   This Part sets out modifications to Part 2 of the 2009 Act (Bank Insolvency) as it applies in relation to building societies by virtue of section 90C of the 1986 Act.

Introduction

7.   Ignore section 91 of the 2009 Act (interpretation: "bank").

8.   Subsections (5) and (6) of section 93 of the 2009 Act (interpretation: other expressions) do not apply in relation to any expression defined in this Schedule.

Building society insolvency order

9.   In section 95 of the 2009 Act (application), in subsection (1), ignore paragraph (c).

10.   In section 96 of the 2009 Act (grounds for applying)—
   (a)   in subsection (1), ignore paragraph (b);
   (b)   ignore subsections (4) and (5).

11.   In section 97 of the 2009 Act (grounds for making)—
   (a)   ignore subsection (2);
   (b)   in subsection (3), ignore "or (2)".

12.   In section 98 of the 2009 Act (commencement), in subsection (2)(a), for "section 120" substitute "section 90D of the Building Societies Act 1986".

Process of building society liquidation

13.—(1)   In section 103 of the 2009 Act (general powers, duties and effect), in subsection (4) ignore paragraph (h).

(2)   In that section, the table (Insolvency Act 1986) applies with the modifications set out in this paragraph.

(3)   For the entry for section 154 substitute—

"Section 154	Adjustment of rights of contributories	Any surplus is to be distributed in accordance with the rules of the society.".

(4)   Ignore the entry for section 187 (transfer of assets to employees).

(5)   Ignore the entries for sections 216 (restriction on re-use of names) and 217 (personal liability for debts).

(6)   For the entries for sections 218 and 219 substitute—

"Section 218	Prosecution of officers and members of company	(a)	the section does not apply in relation to offences committed by members of a building society acting in that capacity.
		(b)	In subsection (3), treat the second reference to the official receiver as a reference to the Secretary of State.
		(c)	Ignore subsections (4), (5) and (6).
		(d)	Where a report is made to the Secretary of State under subsection (3), the Secretary of State may refer the matter to the FSA for further enquiry.

		(e)	On such a reference to it the FSA shall exercise its power under section 55(1) of the Building Societies Act 1986 to appoint one or more competent persons to investigate and report on the matter.
Section 219	Obligations under section 218	(a)	The section does not apply in relation to offences committed by members of a building society acting in that capacity.
		(b)	Subsection (1) of section 219 does not apply.
		(c)	Subsections (2), (2A) and (2B) of section 219 apply in relation to the powers referred to in the entry above for section 218.
		(d)	In subsections (3) and (4) of section 219 the references to the Secretary of State shall have effect as references to the FSA.".

(7)   For the entry for sections 423–425 substitute—

"Sections 423–425	Transactions defrauding creditors	(a)	Sections 423–425 apply only where a building society insolvency order is made.
		(b)	Anything done by the building society in connection with the exercise of a stabilisation power under Part 1 of this Act as applied to building societies by section 84 of this Act is not a transaction at an undervalue for the purposes of section 423.".

Termination of process, &c

14.   In section 113 of the 2009 Act (voluntary arrangement)—
    (a)   in subsection (1), at the end insert "as applied in relation to building societies by section 90A of, and Schedule 15A to, the Building Societies Act 1986";
    (b)   in subsection (2), ignore paragraph (b)(v);
    (c)   in subsection (6) at the end insert "and with the modifications made by Schedule 15A to the Building Societies Act 1986".

15.   In section 114 of the 2009 Act (administration)—
    (a)   in subsection (1), for "(under paragraph 38 of Schedule B1 to the Insolvency Act 1986)" substitute "(under section 9 of the Insolvency Act 1986 as applied in relation to building societies by section 90A of, and Schedule 15A to, the Building Societies Act 1986)";
    (b)   in subsection (4), for "the rescue of the bank as a going concern" substitute "the survival of the building society, and the whole or any part of its undertaking, as a going concern".

16.   In section 115 of the 2009 Act (dissolution)—
    (a)   in subsection (2), ignore paragraph (b)(v);
    (b)   in subsection (4), for "registrar of companies" substitute "FSA";
    (c)   in subsection (7), for "the registrar of companies shall register it" substitute "the FSA shall place it on the public file of the society concerned";
    (d)   In subsection (8), for "the day of the registration of the notice" substitute "the day on which the notice is placed on the public file of the society".

17.   In section 116 of the 2009 Act (dissolution: supplemental), in subsections (1) and (2) the references to the Secretary of State have effect as references to the FSA.

18.   Sections 1012 to 1023 and 1034 of the Companies Act 2006 (provisions as to property of dissolved company) apply in relation to the property of a building society dissolved under section 115 of the 2009 Act (as applied by this Schedule) as they apply to the property of a dissolved company.

Other processes

19.   Ignore sections 117 (insolvency as alternative order) and 118 (voluntary winding-up) of the 2009 Act.

20.—(1)   Ignore section 119 of the 2009 Act (exclusion of other procedures); this paragraph, and section 88(1)(b) of the 1986 Act, make equivalent provision.

(2)   A petition for the winding-up of a building society shall be dismissed on the making of a building society insolvency order in respect of the building society.

(3)   Where a building society is in building society insolvency, no order may be made for the winding-up of the building society.

21.   Ignore sections 120 (notice to FSA of preliminary steps) and 121 (disqualification of directors) of the 2009 Act.

Miscellaneous

22.   In section 124 of the 2009 Act (transfer of accounts), after subsection (2) insert—

"(2A)   The arrangements may—
(a)   cancel shares in the building society;
(b)   confer rights and impose liabilities in place of cancelled shares (whether by way of actual or deemed shares in a transferee building society or by way of other rights and liabilities in relation to a transferee bank).".

23.   Ignore sections 130 (building societies), 131 (credit unions), 132 (partnerships) and 133 (Scottish partnerships) of the 2009 Act.

[562]

NOTES

Commencement: 29 March 2009.

PART 3
MODIFIED APPLICATION OF PART 3 OF THE 2009 ACT

24.   This Part sets out modifications to Part 3 of the 2009 Act (Bank Administration) as it applies in relation to building societies by virtue of section 90C of the 1986 Act.

Introduction

25.   In section 140 of the 2009 Act (objective 2: "normal" administration) the references in subsections (1) and (2) to the residual building society's creditors as a whole include references to all holders of shares in the society.

Process

26.   In section 145 of the 2009 Act (general powers, duties and effect), in subsection (4) omit paragraph (d).

27.—(1)   In section 145, table 1 (Schedule B1 to the Insolvency Act 1986) applies with the modifications set out in this paragraph.

(2)   For the entries for paras 59 to 64, see paragraph 29 below;

(3)   For the entry for para 65, substitute—

"Para 65	Distribution	(a)	In sub para (1) the reference to a creditors includes a reference to a shareholding member.
		(b)	In the case of building society special administration following transfer to a bridge bank, until the Bank of England has given an Objective 1 Achievement Notice a bank administrator may make a distribution only with the Bank of England's consent.
		(c)	Ignore sub para (3).".

(4)   For the entry for para 75, substitute—

| "Para 75 | Misfeasance | (a) In addition to applications that may anyway be made under para 75, an application may be made by the building society special administrator or the Bank of England. |
| | | (b) An application may not be made by a borrowing member.". |

(5)   For the entry for para 80 (termination: successful rescue) substitute—

"Para 80	Termination: successful rescue	*See section 153*
		(a) In sub-paragraph (4) the reference to every creditor of whose claim and address he is aware includes a reference to every shareholding member.
		(b) In sub-paragraph (5) the reference to a creditor includes a reference to a shareholding member.".

(6)   Ignore the entry for para 84 (termination: no more assets for distribution): paragraph 30 below makes equivalent provision;

(7)   For the entry for para 111 (interpretation) substitute—

| "Para 111 | Interpretation | Ignore sub-paragraphs (1A) and (1B)".|

28.—(1)   In section 145, table 2 (other provisions of the Insolvency Act 1986) applies with the modifications set out in this paragraph.

(2)   For the entry for section 168(4) (and para 13 of Schedule 4) substitute—

| "Section 168(4) (and para 13 of Schedule 4) | Discretion in managing and distributing assets | (a) In the case of building society special administration following transfer to a bridge bank, until the Bank of England has given an Objective 1 Achievement Notice distribution may be made only (i) with the Bank of England's consent or (ii) out of assets which have been designated as realisable by agreement between the bank administrator and the Bank of England. |
| | | (b) In subsection (4) the references to creditors includes a reference to shareholding members.". |

(3)   For the entry for sections 423–425 substitute—

| "Section 423–425 | Transactions defrauding creditors | (a) Sections 423–425 apply only where a building society special administration order is made. |
| | | (b) In considering granting leave under section 424(1) the court must have regard to Objective 1 of section 134. |

		(c)	In considering making an order in reliance on section 425 the court must have regard to Objective 1 of section 137.".

General powers of administrator

29.—(1) This paragraph modifies the application of paragraphs 59 to 64 of Schedule B1 to the Insolvency Act 1986 (general powers of administrator); the modifications have effect in addition to those set out for those paragraphs in table 1 in section 145 of the 2009 Act.

(2) Subject to sub-paragraph (3), paragraphs 59 to 64 of Schedule B1 have effect as if they required the building society special administrator, in exercising powers under those paragraphs—

  (a) to ensure compliance with the provisions of the Building Societies Act 1986, and
  (b) not to appoint to be a director any person who is not a fit and proper person to hold that position.

(3) Sub-paragraph (2)(a) does not apply in relation to section 5, 6 or 7 of the Building Societies Act 1986.

No more assets for distribution

30.—(1) This paragraph makes provision equivalent to paragraph 84 of Schedule B1 to the Insolvency Act 1986 (termination: no more assets for distribution).

(2) A building society special administrator who thinks that the building society has no property which might permit a distribution to its creditors and shareholding members must send a notice to that effect to the FSA.

(3) The court may on the application of the building society special administrator disapply sub-paragraph (2) in respect of the building society.

(4) On receipt of a notice under sub-paragraph (2) the FSA must place it on the public file of the building society and record in that file the date on which it was placed there.

(5) The appointment of the building society special administrator ceases to have effect on the date on which the notice under sub-paragraph (2) is placed in the public file of the society.

(6) A building society special administrator who sends a notice under sub-paragraph (2) must as soon as is reasonably practicable—

  (a) file a copy of the notice with the court, and
  (b) send a copy of the notice to each creditor and shareholding member whose address is known.

(7) The building society is dissolved at the end of the period of three months beginning with the date on which the notice under sub-paragraph (2) was placed in its public file.

(8) On an application in respect of a building society by the building society special administrator or another interested person the court may—

  (a) extend the period specified in sub-paragraph (7),
  (b) suspend that period, or
  (c) disapply sub-paragraph (7).

(9) Where an order is made under sub-paragraph (8) in respect of a building society the building society special administrator shall as soon as is reasonably practicable notify the FSA.

(10) A building society special administrator who fails without reasonable excuse to comply with sub-paragraph (6) commits an offence.

(11) An offence under sub-paragraph (10) shall be treated for all purposes as an offence under paragraph 84(9) of Schedule B1 to the Insolvency Act 1986.

Property of society dissolved under paragraph 30

31. Sections 1012 to 1023 and 1034 of the Companies Act 2006 (provisions as to property of dissolved company) shall apply in relation to the property of a building society dissolved under paragraph 30 of this Schedule as they apply in relation to the property of a dissolved company.

Multiple transfers

32.—(1) In section 152 of the 2009 Act (property transfer from temporary public ownership), in subsection (1)—

  (a) for paragraph (a) substitute—
    "(a) make an order under section 85 (temporary public ownership) in respect of a building society, and";
  (b) in paragraph (b) for "(or from another bank which is or was in the same group as the bank)" substitute "(or from a bank which is or was in the same group as the building society")".

(2)   Where the Treasury make an order under section 85 in respect of a building society, and later make a property transfer order from a bank which was in the same group as the building society, Part 3 of the 2009 Act, and any subordinate legislation made under that Part, applies to the transferor bank without the modifications made by section 90C of the Building Societies Act 1986 and this Order.

Termination

33.   In section 154 of the 2009 Act (winding-up or voluntary arrangement)—
- (a)   in subsection (2), in paragraph (a), the reference to paragraph 84 of Schedule B1 to the Insolvency Act 1986 has effect as a reference to paragraph 30 of this Schedule;
- (b)   in that subsection, in paragraph (b), at the end insert "as applied in relation to building societies by section 90A of, and Schedule 15A to, the Building Societies Act 1986";
- (c)   in subsection (3), at the end insert "and with the modifications made by Schedule 15A to the Building Societies Act 1986".

Miscellaneous

34.   Ignore section 155 of the 2009 Act (disqualification of directors).

35.—(1)   Ignore section 157 of the 2009 Act (other processes); this paragraph makes equivalent provision.

(2)   Before exercising an insolvency power in respect of a residual building society the FSA must give notice to the Bank of England, which may participate in any proceedings arising out of the exercise of the power.

(3)   In sub-paragraph (2)—
- (a)   "residual building society" means a building society all or part of whose business has been transferred to a commercial purchaser or to a bridge bank in accordance with section 11 or section 12 of the 2009 Act respectively (as applied with modifications by section 84 of the 2009 Act), and
- (b)   "insolvency power" means—
  - (i)   the FSA's power to apply to the court for an administration order (see paragraph 11(1) of Schedule 15A to the Building Societies Act 1986), and
  - (ii)   the FSA's power to present a petition for the winding-up of a building society (see sections 37(1) and 89(2) of the Building Societies Act 1986).

36.   Ignore sections 158 (building societies), 159 (credit unions), 163 (partnerships) and 164 (Scottish partnerships) of the 2009 Act.

37.   Subsections (4) and (5) of section 166 of the 2009 Act (interpretation: general) do not apply to expressions defined in this Schedule.

[563]

NOTES
Commencement: 29 March 2009.

SCHEDULE 2
MODIFIED APPLICATION OF SUBORDINATE LEGISLATION

Article 18

1.   The following instruments apply in relation to building societies as they apply in relation to banks, with the modifications set out in this Schedule—
- (a)   the Banking Act 2009 (Parts 2 and 3 Consequential Amendments) Order 2009;
- (b)   the Bank Administration (Sharing Information) Regulations 2009;
- (c)   the Banking Act 2009 (Bank Administration) (Modification for Application to Multiple Transfers) Regulations 2009;
- (d)   the Banking Act 2009 (Bank Administration) (Modification for Application to Banks in Temporary Public Ownership) Regulations 2009.

2.   The following general modifications apply to all of the instruments referred to in paragraph 1—
- (a)   references to "bank" (except in the term "bridge bank") have effect as references to "building society";
- (b)   references to "bank administration", "bank administration order" and "bank administrator" have effect as references to "building society special administration", "building society special administration order" and "building society special administrator";
- (c)   references to Part 1 of the 2009 Act, or to any provision in that Part, have effect as references to that Part, or that provision, as applied to building societies with any modifications by section 84 of the 2009 Act (application of Part 1: general);
- (d)   references to Part 2 or 3 of the 2009 Act, or to any provision in Part 2 or Part 3, have effect as references to that Part, or that provision, as applied in relation to building societies by section 90C of the 1986 Act with any modifications specified in that section or in Schedule 1 to this Order;

3.   The modifications to the Banking Act 2009 (Parts 2 and 3 Consequential Amendments) Order 2009 (in addition to the modifications set out in paragraph 2) are—

    (a)   references to "bank insolvency", "bank insolvency order" and "bank liquidator" are references to "building society insolvency", "building society insolvency order" and "building society liquidator";

    (b)   ignore article 4 (Finance (No 2) Act 1992);

    (c)   ignore article 5 (Financial Services and Markets Act 2000);

    (d)   ignore article 6 (Companies Act 2006);

    (e)   in article 7 (Dormant Bank and Building Society Accounts Act 2008), for "bank which is a bank within the meaning of section 91 of the 2009 Act" substitute "building society within the meaning of section 119 of the Building Societies Act 1986";

    (f)   in the Schedule, ignore any enactment which does not apply in relation to building societies.

4.   The modifications to the Banking Act 2009 (Bank Administration) (Modification for Application to Multiple Transfers) Regulations 2009 (in addition to the modifications set out in paragraph 2) are—

    (a)   in regulation 1(2), ignore the definition of "a bank in temporary public ownership";

    (b)   in regulation 3(1)(a), for "a share transfer order, in respect of the securities issued by a bank (or a bank's holding company)" substitute "an order under section 85 of the Act (temporary public ownership) in respect of a building society".

5.   The modifications to the Banking Act 2009 (Bank Administration) (Modification for Application to Banks in Temporary Public Ownership) Regulations 2009 (in addition to the modifications set out in paragraph 2) are—

    (a)   in regulation 2(1), for "a share transfer order to transfer the securities of a bank or a bank's holding company into temporary public ownership", substitute "an order under section 85 (temporary public ownership) of the Act in respect of a building society";

    (b)   ignore references to a bank holding company.

[564]

NOTES

Commencement: 29 March 2009.

AMENDMENTS TO LAW (RESOLUTION OF DUNFERMLINE BUILDING SOCIETY) ORDER 2009

(SI 2009/814)

NOTES

Made: 30 March 2009 (9.45 am).

Authority: Banking Act 2009, ss 75, 259(1).

Commencement: 30 March 2009 (8.00 am).

Note: this Order must be read in conjunction with the Dunfermline Building Society Property Transfer Instrument 2009 at **[2011]**, made by the Bank of England under its powers under the Banking Act 2009 and disapplies certain provisions of the Pensions Act 2004 in relation to the Bank of England and a subsidiary of Dunfermline Building Society in connection with the transfer as well as making provisions in relation to the Dunfermline Bridge Bank, in relation to proceedings against directors during the existence of the Dunfermline Bridge Bank, disapplying certain provisions relating to shadow directorship in relation to the Dunfermline Bridge Bank, and providing that the Dunfermline Bridge Bank is not amongst other things a public authority for the purposes of the Freedom of Information Act 2000. The order also modifies the FSA's rule making powers in relation to the Dunfermline Building Society and provides for the treatment of liabilities arising for the purposes of, in connection with and in consequence of the transfer in insolvency proceedings.

ARRANGEMENT OF ARTICLES

PART 1
GENERAL

PART 2
THE TRANSFER

PART 3
THE DUNFERMLINE BRIDGE BANK

PART 4
MISCELLANEOUS

PART 1
GENERAL

1   Citation and commencement

(1)   This order may be cited as the Amendments to Law (Resolution of Dunfermline Building Society) Order 2009.

(2)   This order comes into force on 30th March 2009 at 8 am.

[565]

___

NOTES
    Commencement: 30 March 2009 (8.00 am).

___

2   Interpretation

In this Order—
    "the 2006 Act" means the Companies Act 2006;
    "the 1985 Act" means the Companies Act 1985;
    "the Building Societies Act" means the Building Societies Act 1986;
    "FSMA" means the Financial Services and Markets Act 2000;
    "the Dunfermline Bridge Bank" means PT Shelfco (Scot) Limited, company registered number SC356970, while its only member is the Bank of England;
    "Dunfermline Building Society" means Dunfermline Building Society, a building society incorporated (or deemed to be incorporated) under the Building Societies Act and authorised and regulated by the FSA (Reg no: 158765);
    "Dunfermline Nominees" means Dunfermline BS Nominees Limited, company registered number SC113202;
    "Nationwide" has the meaning given in paragraph 2 of the Property Transfer Instrument;
    "the Nationwide transfer" means made by paragraph 2 of the Property Transfer Instrument;
    "the Property Transfer Instrument" means the Dunfermline Building Society Property Transfer Instrument 2009, made by the Bank of England;
    "subsidiary" has the meaning given in section 1159 of the 2006 Act;
    "the transfer time" has the meaning given in paragraph 2 of the Property Transfer Instrument.

[566]

___

NOTES
    Commencement: 30 March 2009 (8.00 am).

___

PART 2
THE TRANSFER

3   Transfer of shares of Dunfermline Nominees

(1)   This article applies in connection with the transfer, by paragraph 3(1) of the Property Transfer Instrument, of shares owned by Dunfermline Building Society which were issued by Dunfermline Nominees, and references in this article to "the transfer" are to be construed accordingly.

(2)   Nationwide enjoys the entitlement mentioned in paragraph 3(4) of the Property Transfer Instrument whether or not it is entered in the company register of members of Dunfermline Nominees, notwithstanding any provision of the 2006 Act, the 1985 Act, any other enactment or any rule of law.

(3)   Section 776 of the 2006 Act (duty of company as to issue of certificates etc on transfer) has effect in relation to the transfer with the modifications specified in paragraph (4).

(4)   The transfer is to be treated as—
    (a)   a transfer under subsection (2)(a), and

(b)   lodged with Dunfermline Nominees at the transfer time.

(5)   The following provisions of the 2006 Act are disapplied in relation to the transfer—
(a)   section 776(3) and (4) (qualifications as to duty to issue certificates);
(b)   section 777 (issue of certificates etc: cases within the Stock Transfer Act 1982);
(c)   section 778 (issue of certificates etc: allotment or transfer to a financial institution).

[567]

NOTES
Commencement: 30 March 2009 (8.00 am).

4   Employees

(1)   The Transfer of Undertakings (Protection of Employment) Regulations 2006 ("the Transfer Regulations") and sections 257 and 258 of the Pensions Act 2004 apply on the Nationwide transfer as if any individual who is employed by Dunfermline is assigned to the organised grouping of resources or employees that is subject to the relevant transfer.

(2)   Paragraph (1) applies whether or not the Nationwide transfer would otherwise be regarded for the purposes of the Transfer Regulations as giving rise to a relevant transfer.

(3)   In this article—
(a)   "organised grouping of resources or employees" is to be construed in accordance with the Transfer Regulations;
(b)   "relevant transfer" is to be construed in accordance with Regulation 2 of the Transfer Regulations.

[568]

NOTES
Commencement: 30 March 2009 (8.00 am).

5   Pensions

(1)   No relevant person is to be treated as a person connected with, or an associate of, Dunfermline Building Society for the purposes of the following provisions of the Pensions Act 2004—
(a)   section 38 (contribution notices where avoidance of employer debt);
(b)   section 43 (financial support directions).

(2)   Relevant persons are—
(a)   the Bank of England;
(b)   persons employed by or under, or acting on the behalf of, the Bank of England.

(3)   From the transfer time Dunfermline Nominees is to have no liability, including any liability arising by virtue of sections 38 and 43 of the Pensions Act 2004, with regard to the liabilities of the pension scheme by reason of any fact, matter or circumstance occurring or existing prior to the transfer time and accordingly no proceedings may be brought in respect of such matters.

(4)   In paragraph (3), "pension scheme" has the meaning given in paragraph 2 of the Property Transfer Instrument.

[569]

NOTES
Commencement: 30 March 2009 (8.00 am).

PART 3
THE DUNFERMLINE BRIDGE BANK

6   Proceedings against directors

(1)   This article applies in respect of "relevant acts or omissions", which are the acts or omissions of one or more directors (in their capacity as such) of—
(a)   the Dunfermline Bridge Bank, or
(b)   any subsidiary of the Dunfermline Bridge Bank.

(2)   No directors are liable for their relevant acts or omissions or those of other directors.

(3)   No proceedings may (at any time) be brought against directors in respect of their relevant acts or omissions or those of other directors.

(4)   Paragraphs (2) and (3) do not apply—
(a)   in relation to proceedings brought by the FSA;
(b)   to relevant acts or omissions shown to have been fraudulent, dishonest or in bad faith.

(5)   In this article—
(a)   "director" includes an alternate director;

(b)   "proceedings" includes proceedings under Part 11 of the 2006 Act (derivative claims and proceedings by members);

(c)   references to the bringing of proceedings are, in the application of this article to Scotland, references to the raising of proceedings.

(6)   For the purposes of paragraphs (2) and (3) it does not matter that a person later ceases to be a director.

[570]

NOTES

Commencement: 30 March 2009 (8.00 am).

7   Shadow directorship, &c

(1)   A relevant person is not to be treated as—

(a)   a shadow director of the Dunfermline Bridge Bank for the purposes of the provisions listed in the Schedule;

(b)   a person discharging managerial responsibilities in respect of the Dunfermline Bridge Bank for the purposes of the provisions listed in the Schedule (unless that person has been appointed as a director).

(2)   Nor is a relevant person to be treated as a director of the Dunfermline Bridge Bank by virtue of paragraph (b) of the definition of director in section 417(1) of FSMA (certain persons in accordance with whose directions or instructions the directors of the body corporate are accustomed to act).

(3)   Relevant persons are—

(a)   the Bank of England;

(b)   a Minister of the Crown;

(c)   the Treasury;

(d)   UK Financial Investments Limited (company registered number 06720891);

(e)   persons—

(i)   employed by or under, or

(ii)   acting on the behalf of,

any of the persons in paragraph (3)(a) to (d).

(4)   This article applies in relation to any subsidiary of the Dunfermline Bridge Bank as it applies in relation to the Dunfermline Bridge Bank

[571]

NOTES

Commencement: 30 March 2009 (8.00 am).

8   Freedom of information

(1)   The Dunfermline Bridge Bank is not to be treated as—

(a)   a publicly owned company for the purposes of section 3(1)(b) of the Freedom of Information Act 2000;

(b)   holding information on behalf of the Bank of England or the Treasury for the purposes of section 3(2)(b) of that Act.

(2)   Paragraph (1) applies to any subsidiary of the Dunfermline Bridge Bank as it applies to the Dunfermline Bridge Bank.

[572]

NOTES

Commencement: 30 March 2009 (8.00 am).

PART 4

MISCELLANEOUS

9   Modification of the FSA's rule-making power

(1)   Subsections (1) and (1A) of section 138 of FSMA (general rule-making power) have effect as if modified by inserting after "protecting the interests of consumers"—

"or for the purposes of, to facilitate or in consequence of the Dunfermline Building Society Property Transfer Instrument 2009".

(2)   Section 148(2) of FSMA (modification or waiver of rules) is modified so it applies in relation to a relevant person—

(a)   in the absence of an application by the relevant person, and

(b)   without any requirement for consent by the relevant person.

PART III
SIS UNDER BANKING ACT 2009

(3)   Section 148(4) of FSMA is to have effect such that it does not prevent the FSA from modifying or waiving rules in relation to a relevant person under section 148 where the following condition is satisfied.

(4)   The condition is that the FSA is satisfied that the modification or waiver is necessary for the purposes of, to facilitate or in consequence of the Property Transfer Instrument.

(5)   In this article, relevant persons are Dunfermline Building Society and the Dunfermline Bridge Bank.

[573]

NOTES

Commencement: 30 March 2009 (8.00 am).

10   Modification to the FSA's duty to consult on rule changes

(1)   Section 155(7) of FSMA (consultation) has effect as if modified by adding at the end—

"or if it is making rules for the purposes of, to facilitate or in consequence of the Dunfermline Building Society Property Transfer Instrument 2009."

(2)   Section 157 of FSMA (guidance) has effect as if modified by adding after subsection (3)—

"(3A)   Section 155(7) applies to proposed guidance with the modification made by article 10(1) of the Amendments to Law (Resolution of Dunfermline Building Society) Order 2009."

[574]

NOTES

Commencement: 30 March 2009 (8.00 am).

11   Liabilities to Treasury: treatment in insolvency proceedings

(1)   This article makes provision in relation to the treatment in insolvency proceedings of the first and second liabilities assumed by Dunfermline by virtue of paragraph 11 of the Property Transfer Instrument.

(2)   In insolvency proceedings—
    (a)   the first liability ranks pari passu with the claims of unsecured and unsubordinated creditors of Dunfermline;
    (b)   the second liability ranks pari passu with the claims that shareholding members of Dunfermline would have had in respect of the value of their shares but for their transfer.

(3)   The reference in paragraph (2)(b) to shareholding members does not include the holders of deferred shares within the meaning of section 119(1) of the Building Societies Act.

(4)   In this article—
    (a)   the reference to insolvency proceedings is a reference to—
        (i)   liquidation;
        (ii)   administration;
        (iii)   building society special administration (within the meaning of Part 3 of the Banking Act as applied by section 90C of the Building Societies Act);
    (b)   "shareholding member" and the reference to the value of shares are to be construed in accordance with section 119 of the Building Societies Act.

[575]

NOTES

Commencement: 30 March 2009 (8.00 am).

SCHEDULE

Article 7

1.   Section 288 of the 1985 Act (register of directors).

2.   The following provisions of the 2006 Act—
    (a)   section 84 (criminal consequences of failure to make required disclosure);
    (b)   section 162 (register of directors);
    (c)   section 165 (register of directors' residential addresses);
    (d)   section 167 (duty to notify registrar of changes);
    (e)   sections 170 to 177 (general duties of directors);
    (f)   sections 182 to 186 (declaration of interest in existing transactions) as applied to shadow directors by section 187;
    (g)   sections 188 and 189 (directors' service contracts);
    (h)   sections 190 to 196 (substantial property transactions);
    (i)   sections 197 to 214 (loans etc to directors);

(j)   sections 215 to 222 (payments for loss of office) as applied to shadow directors by section 223(2);
(k)   sections 227 to 230 (directors' service contracts);
(l)   section 231 (contracts with sole members who are directors);
(m)   sections 260 to 269 (derivative claims in England and Wales and Northern Ireland);
(n)   sections 854 to 859 (annual return);
(o)   section 1255 (offences by bodies corporate, partnerships and unincorporated associations).

3.   The following provisions of the Insolvency Act 1986—
(a)   section 214 (wrongful trading);
(b)   section 249 ("connected" with a company).

4.   The following provisions of FSMA—
(a)   section 96A (disclosure of information requirements);
(b)   section 96B (disclosure rules: persons responsible for compliance).

[576]

NOTES
Commencement: 30 March 2009 (8.00 am).

BANKING ACT 2009 (COMMENCEMENT NO 2) ORDER 2009

(SI 2009/1296)

NOTES
Made: 20 May 2009.
Authority: Banking Act 2009, s 263(1), (3).

1   Citation and interpretation

(1)   This Order may be cited as the Banking Act 2009 (Commencement No 2) Order 2009.

(2)   In this Order—
"the Act" means the Banking Act 2009;
"the court" means the court of directors of the Bank of England.

[577]

2   Provisions of the Act coming into force on 1st June 2009

The provisions of Part 7 (Miscellaneous) of the Act listed in the Schedule to this Order come into force on 1st June 2009.

[578]

SCHEDULE

1.   Section 238 (UK financial stability)

2.   Section 239 (number of directors of the court)

3.   Section 240 (meetings of the court)

4.   Section 241 (chair of the court)

5.   Section 242 (quorum)

6.   Section 243 (tenure)

[579]

DUNFERMLINE BUILDING SOCIETY COMPENSATION SCHEME, RESOLUTION FUND AND THIRD PARTY COMPENSATION ORDER 2009

(SI 2009/1800)

NOTES
Made: 6 July 2009.
Authority: Banking Act 2009, ss 49, 50, 52, 54, 57–59, 61, 259.
Commencement: 7 July 2009.
Note: this Order must be read in conjunction with the Dunfermline Building Society Property Transfer Instrument 2009 at [2011], made by the Bank of England under its powers under the Banking Act 2009 and it

makes provision for a compensation scheme as required under section 50(2) of the Act as well as making various provisions for an independent valuer to be appointed to perform certain functions under this Order. The Order also makes provision for the Dunfermline Resolution Fund under section 52(2) of the Act where the Bank of England has made a transfer to a bridge bank.

ARRANGEMENT OF ARTICLES

PART 1
GENERAL

PART 2
DUNFERMLINE COMPENSATION SCHEME

PART 3
INDEPENDENT VALUER

PART 4
DUNFERMLINE RESOLUTION FUND

PART 5
THIRD PARTY COMPENSATION

PART 6
FINANCIAL SERVICES COMPENSATION SCHEME

PART 1
GENERAL

1   Citation and commencement

This Order may be cited as the Dunfermline Building Society Compensation Scheme, Resolution Fund and Third Party Compensation Order 2009 and shall come into force on the day after the day on which it is made.

[580]

NOTES
   Commencement: 7 July 2009.

2   Interpretation

In this Order—
   "Account Holder" has the meaning given in paragraph 1(2) of Schedule 1;
   "the Act" means the Banking Act 2009;
   "Bridge Bank" means DBS Bridge Bank Limited, a company with the registered number
      SC356970 whose registered office is Caledonia House, Carnegie Avenue, Dunfermline
      KY11 8PJ;

"Bridge Bank business" means the property, rights and liabilities transferred from Dunfermline to the Bridge Bank by virtue of paragraph 12 of the Transfer Instrument and any property, rights and liabilities transferred from Dunfermline to the Bridge Bank by virtue of a supplemental property transfer instrument;

"Dunfermline" means Dunfermline Building Society, a building society incorporated (or deemed to be incorporated) under the Building Societies Act 1986 and authorised and regulated by the Financial Services Authority (Reg no: 158765);

"Dunfermline Resolution Account" means the account established in accordance with article 6(1);

"Financial Services Compensation Scheme" means the scheme established under Part 15 of the Financial Services and Markets Act 2000;

"financial year" means the twelve months ending with 31st March;

"independent valuer" means the person appointed in accordance with article 5(2);

"Nationwide business" means the property, rights and liabilities transferred from Dunfermline to Nationwide Building Society (incorporated under the Building Societies Act 1986 with registered number 355B) by virtue of paragraph 3 of the Transfer Instrument;

"Transfer Instrument" means the Dunfermline Building Society Property Transfer Instrument 2009.

[581]

NOTES
Commencement: 7 July 2009.

PART 2
DUNFERMLINE COMPENSATION SCHEME

3   Transfer of the Nationwide business: determination of amount of compensation

The amount of compensation payable to Dunfermline in respect of the Nationwide business is determined as nil.

[582]

NOTES
Commencement: 7 July 2009.

PART 3
INDEPENDENT VALUER

4   Functions of the independent valuer

An independent valuer must be appointed to perform the functions specified in—

(a)   article 9 (third party compensation);

(b)   article 11 (assessment of recoveries by the Financial Services Compensation Scheme);

(c)   paragraph 7 of Schedule 1 (certification of costs of the Bank of England or the Treasury to be deducted from the Dunfermline Resolution Account).

[583]

NOTES
Commencement: 7 July 2009.

5   Appointment of the independent valuer

(1)   The Treasury must—

(a)   make arrangements to identify candidates for the office of independent valuer and must publish the details of those arrangements on their website;

(b)   make arrangements for a panel to appoint the independent valuer ("the Appointment Panel").

(2)   The Appointment Panel shall have the function of selecting and appointing an independent valuer from a list of the candidates identified by the Treasury in accordance with paragraph (1)(a).

(3)   The Treasury must ensure that the Appointment Panel comprises no fewer than four members, of which—

(a)   one member is the Chief Executive of the Institute of Chartered Accountants in England and Wales, who must be the chair of the Appointment Panel; and

(b)   one member is a representative of the Treasury, who shall be a non-voting member of the Appointment Panel.

(4)   The independent valuer is to hold and vacate office in accordance with the terms of his or her appointment.

(5)   The independent valuer may be removed from office only—

PART III
SIS UNDER BANKING ACT 2009

    (a)   by the Appointment Panel, excluding the member who is a representative of the Treasury, and

    (b)   on the grounds of incapacity or serious misconduct.

(6)   In the event of the death of the independent valuer, or if the independent valuer is removed from office or resigns, a new independent valuer must be appointed.

(7)   In the event that a member of the Appointment Panel is unable to sit on the Appointment Panel to perform the function in paragraph (5), the Treasury must appoint another member to replace that member of the first Appointment Panel.

(8)   The provisions of this Order apply to the replacement of the independent valuer as to the first independent valuer appointed.

[584]

NOTES

Commencement: 7 July 2009.

PART 4

DUNFERMLINE RESOLUTION FUND

6   Transfer of the Bridge Bank business: resolution fund

(1)   The Treasury must establish an account to be known as the Dunfermline Resolution Account.

(2)   Part 1 of Schedule 1 makes provision for the arrangements for the Dunfermline Resolution Account.

[585]

NOTES

Commencement: 7 July 2009.

---

7   Payments into the resolution fund

Part 2 of Schedule 1 makes provision for the arrangements for paying money into the Dunfermline Resolution Account.

[586]

NOTES

Commencement: 7 July 2009.

---

8   Entitlement to the moneys in the resolution fund and payments out of the resolution fund

Part 3 of Schedule 1 makes provision in respect of—

    (a)   entitlements to the moneys standing to the credit of the Dunfermline Resolution Account; and

    (b)   the arrangements for making payments from the Dunfermline Resolution Account.

[587]

NOTES

Commencement: 7 July 2009.

PART 5

THIRD PARTY COMPENSATION

9   Third party compensation

(1)   Schedule 2 makes provision for the arrangements to be put in place for the assessment of any compensation payable to persons other than Dunfermline.

(2)   The independent valuer must determine, in accordance with Part 2 of Schedule 2, the amount of any compensation payable to any person who was affected by the application of section 38(6) of the Act (termination rights, &c) (by virtue of paragraph 6 of the Transfer Instrument).

(3)   The independent valuer must determine, in accordance with Part 3 of Schedule 2, the amount of any compensation payable to pre-transfer creditors of Dunfermline.

[588]

NOTES

Commencement: 7 July 2009.

10   Payment of compensation

Any compensation determined by an independent valuer to be payable in accordance with this Order must be paid by the Treasury in accordance with paragraph 13 of Schedule 2.

[589]

NOTES
Commencement: 7 July 2009.

PART 6
FINANCIAL SERVICES COMPENSATION SCHEME

11   Assessment of recoveries

The independent valuer must perform the function in regulation 8(1) of the Financial Services and Markets Act 2000 (Contribution to Costs of Special Resolution Regime) Regulations 2009 in order to assess the amount that would have been likely to be recovered by the Financial Services Compensation Scheme from Dunfermline.

[590]

NOTES
Commencement: 7 July 2009.

SCHEDULE 1
THE DUNFERMLINE RESOLUTION FUND

PART 1
ARRANGEMENTS FOR THE DUNFERMLINE RESOLUTION ACCOUNT

The Dunfermline Resolution Account

1.—(1)   The Dunfermline Resolution Account shall be held at the Bank of England and must be an interest bearing account.

(2)   The Dunfermline Resolution Account must be held in the name of an independent person appointed by the Treasury ("the Account Holder").

Annual report and accounts

2.—(1)   The Account Holder must prepare accounts in relation to the operation of the Dunfermline Resolution Account—
  (a)   in such form, and in such manner, as the Treasury specify, and
  (b)   as soon as is reasonably practicable after the end of each financial year in which the Dunfermline Resolution Account is open.

(2)   The accounts must set out the details of each payment from the Dunfermline Resolution Account.

(3)   The Comptroller and Auditor General must examine, certify and report on the accounts.

(4)   The Account Holder must send a copy of the accounts to the Treasury as soon as is reasonably practicable.

(5)   The Treasury shall lay a copy of the accounts before each House of Parliament.

[591]

NOTES
Commencement: 7 July 2009.

PART 2
ARRANGEMENTS FOR MAKING PAYMENTS INTO THE DUNFERMLINE
RESOLUTION ACCOUNT

Payments into the resolution fund

3.—(1)   The Bank of England must pay into the Dunfermline Resolution Account—
  (a)   any distribution made to the Bank of England—
    (i)   by the Bridge Bank (whether made following the disposal of some or all of the business of the Bridge Bank or otherwise);
    (ii)   by a liquidator appointed to wind up the Bridge Bank;
  (b)   any consideration received for shares in the Bridge Bank.

(2)   The Bank of England may require the Bridge Bank, a liquidator of the Bridge Bank or a purchaser of the shares in the Bridge Bank to make payment of amounts under paragraph (1) direct

to the Dunfermline Resolution Account, and any such payment shall constitute a good discharge to the Bridge Bank, liquidator of the Bridge Bank or purchaser as the case may be.

[592]

NOTES
Commencement: 7 July 2009.

PART 3
ARRANGEMENTS FOR MAKING PAYMENTS FROM, AND ENTITLEMENTS TO, THE DUNFERMLINE RESOLUTION ACCOUNT

Payments from the resolution fund

4.—(1)   The Account Holder may only make payments from the Dunfermline Resolution Account in accordance with a direction issued by the Treasury.

(2)   The Treasury may direct the Account Holder to make a payment to—
(a)   Dunfermline;
(b)   the Treasury;
(c)   the Bank of England.

(3)   The Treasury must not direct the Account Holder to make a payment from the Dunfermline Resolution Account if making the payment would cause the balance of the Dunfermline Resolution Account to fall below zero.

(4)   A direction under sub-paragraph (2) must be in writing and the Treasury must send a copy of the direction to—
(a)   Dunfermline, and
(b)   the Bank of England.

Payments to the Treasury and the Bank of England

5.—(1)   The Treasury may direct the Account Holder to make a payment to the Treasury or the Bank of England only where—
(a)   the payment is to be made for the purposes of reimbursing the Treasury or the Bank of England (as the case may be) for any costs (including liability for tax) incurred in relation to, or in consequence of, any of the following—
(i)   the transfer of the Bridge Bank business;
(ii)   the incorporation, authorisation and operation of the Bridge Bank;
(iii)   the sale of the Bridge Bank, or some or all of the property, rights or liabilities of the Bridge Bank, to a purchaser;
(iv)   the winding up of the Bridge Bank;
(b)   the independent valuer has certified, in accordance with paragraph 7, that the costs were properly and reasonably incurred by the Bank of England or the Treasury (as the case may be); and
(c)   the direction is made within 12 months of the date of—
(i)   the completion of the winding up of the Bridge Bank; or
(ii)   if earlier, the sale of shares in the Bridge Bank.

(2)   In the event that the Bank of England (as sole member of the Bridge Bank) passes a resolution to wind up the Bridge Bank, the Bank of England must, as soon as is reasonably practicable after the passing of the resolution, send a copy of the resolution to—
(a)   Dunfermline, and
(b)   the Treasury.

Entitlement to the resolution fund: Dunfermline

6.—(1)   The Treasury must notify the Account Holder when no further (if any) directions are to be made under paragraph (4)(2)(b) or (c) (as the case may be).

(2)   As soon as is reasonably practicable after the notification specified in sub-paragraph (1) has been made the Treasury must direct the Account Holder to pay to Dunfermline any moneys remaining in the Dunfermline Resolution Account.

Certification of costs

7.—(1)   Where the Treasury consider that any costs specified in paragraph 5(1)(a) may be paid from the Dunfermline Resolution Account, the Treasury must supply to the independent valuer—
(a)   any invoices in relation to the costs,
(b)   an explanation of the reasons for the costs, and
(c)   any other information the independent valuer reasonably requests for the purpose of assessing whether the costs were reasonably and properly incurred.

(2)   Within 30 days of receipt of the information specified in sub-paragraph (1), the independent valuer must—

(a) inform the Treasury by notice in writing whether, in the independent valuer's opinion, the costs were reasonably and properly incurred for the purposes specified in paragraph 5(1)(a); or

(b) request further information from the Treasury or the Bank of England (as the case may be).

(3) In the event the independent valuer determines that the costs, or a proportion of the costs, were not properly or reasonably incurred, within 14 days of the receipt of the notification, the Treasury may require, by notice in writing, the independent valuer to reconsider his or her determination.

(4) Where the independent valuer is required to reconsider his or her determination, the independent valuer must issue a revised notice within 14 days of receipt of the notice specified in sub-paragraph (3).

(5) Where the independent valuer determines that only a proportion of the costs were properly and reasonably incurred for the purposes specified in paragraph 5(1)(a), the Treasury may issue a direction, under paragraph 4(2)(b) or (c) (as the case may be), only in relation to that proportion of the costs.

[593]

NOTES
Commencement: 7 July 2009.

SCHEDULE 2
THE DUNFERMLINE THIRD PARTY COMPENSATION SCHEME

PART 1
GENERAL PROVISIONS

Citation

1. This scheme may be cited as the Dunfermline Third Party Compensation Scheme.

Interpretation

2. In this Schedule—
"actual treatment" means the treatment pre-transfer creditors have received, are receiving or are likely to receive if no (or no further) compensation is paid;
"assessment notice" means a notice issued by the independent valuer in accordance with paragraph 4 or 10 of this Schedule;
"insolvency treatment" means the treatment which pre-transfer creditors would have received had Dunfermline entered insolvency immediately before the relevant time;
"relevant time" means 8am on 30 March 2009, which is the time the Transfer Instrument came into force;
"remaining creditors" has the meaning given in paragraph 5(b);
"transferred creditors" has the meaning given in paragraph 5(a).

[594]

NOTES
Commencement: 7 July 2009.

PART 2
DETERMINATION OF AMOUNT OF COMPENSATION: THIRD PARTIES AFFECTED BY THE APPLICATION OF SECTION 38(6) OF THE ACT

Third party compensation: persons affected by the application of section 38(6) of the Act

3.—(1) Subject to sub-paragraph (4), the amount of any compensation payable to persons whose default event provisions were affected by the application of section 38(6) of the Act (by virtue of paragraph 6 of the Transfer Instrument) must be determined by the independent valuer in accordance with this paragraph.

(2) The amount of any compensation payable to a person must be such compensation as may be fair and equitable in respect of the effect on that person's property, rights or liabilities of the application of section 38(6) of the Act.

(3) In determining any compensation payable, the independent valuer must take into account—
(a) any diminution in the value of the person's property or rights; or
(b) any increase in the burden of any liability on that person,
which is attributable to the application of section 38(6) of the Act.

(4) Compensation is payable only if it is required to be paid to comply with the Convention rights (within the meaning of section 1 of the Human Rights Act 1998).

Assessment notice

4.—(1) Where the independent valuer makes a determination in accordance with paragraph 3, the independent valuer must issue an assessment notice to—

    (a)   the person affected by the application of section 38(6) of the Act, and

    (b)   the Treasury.

  (2) An assessment notice must contain the following information—

    (a)   the date on which the assessment notice is issued,

    (b)   the amount of any compensation payable, and

    (c)   the reasons for the independent valuer's decision.

[595]

NOTES

Commencement: 7 July 2009.

PART 3

DETERMINATION OF AMOUNT OF COMPENSATION: PRE-TRANSFER CREDITORS

Third party compensation: pre-transfer creditors of Dunfermline

5.—(1) The amount of any compensation payable to—

    (a)   pre-transfer creditors whose rights were transferred by virtue of the Transfer Instrument ("transferred creditors") shall be determined in accordance with paragraph 7;

    (b)   pre-transfer creditors whose rights were not transferred by virtue of the Transfer Instrument ("remaining creditors") shall be determined in accordance with paragraph 8.

  (2) The independent valuer, in conducting his or her functions in accordance with this Part, may make determinations in respect of all pre-transfer creditors, a class of pre-transfer creditor or a particular pre-transfer creditor as the independent valuer considers appropriate.

  (3) The independent valuer must have regard to any information provided by a pre-transfer creditor which is relevant to the conduct of his or her functions under this Part and in particular must have regard to any information which relates to the assessment of—

    (a)   the insolvency treatment;

    (b)   the actual treatment.

Assessment of insolvency treatment

6.—(1) The independent valuer must assess the insolvency treatment of the pre-transfer creditors of Dunfermline.

  (2) In making the assessment of the insolvency treatment, the independent valuer must determine the insolvency process it is likely Dunfermline would have entered had the Transfer Instrument not been made.

Assessment of compensation: transferred creditors

7.—(1) The independent valuer must assess the actual treatment of transferred creditors (including any payment of compensation to be made in accordance with a determination of the independent valuer under paragraph 3).

  (2) If the independent valuer considers that, in relation to any transferred creditor, the actual treatment is less favourable than the insolvency treatment, the independent valuer must determine the amount of compensation payable to the transferred creditor.

  (3) The independent valuer must assess the compensation payable—

    (a)   by reference to the difference between the insolvency treatment and the actual treatment; and

    (b)   on the basis of the fair and equitable value of that difference in treatment.

Assessment of compensation: remaining creditors

8.—(1) The Treasury must notify the independent valuer as soon as is reasonably practicable after giving the notification under paragraph 6(1) of Schedule 1 that the notification has been made.

  (2) As soon as is reasonably practicable following the receipt of the notification under sub-paragraph (1) the independent valuer must assess the actual treatment of remaining creditors, including by virtue of any payment to be made—

    (a)   to Dunfermline from the Dunfermline Resolution Account; and

    (b)   in accordance with a determination of the independent valuer under paragraph 3.

  (3) If the independent valuer considers that, in relation to any remaining creditor, the actual treatment is less favourable than the insolvency treatment, the independent valuer must determine the amount of compensation payable to the remaining creditor.

  (4) The independent valuer must assess the compensation payable—

    (a)   by reference to the difference between the insolvency treatment and the actual treatment; and

(b)   on the basis of the fair and equitable value of that difference in treatment.

Valuation principles

9.   In making the assessment of the insolvency treatment as required under paragraph 6(1), the independent valuer must determine the amount of compensation payable in accordance with the following valuation principles (in addition to the principle which applies by virtue of section 57(3) of the Act)—

(a)   that Dunfermline was failing, or was likely to fail, to satisfy its threshold conditions (within the meaning of section 41(1) of the Financial Services and Markets Act 2000 (permission to carry on regulated activities));

(b)   that Dunfermline would have entered insolvency immediately before the relevant time;

(c)   the Transfer Instrument has not been made and that no other order or instrument under Part 1 of the Act would have been made in relation to or in connection with Dunfermline; and

(d)   that no financial assistance would have, after the relevant time, been provided to Dunfermline by the Bank of England or the Treasury.

Assessment notice

10.—(1)   Where the independent valuer makes an assessment in accordance with paragraph 7 or 8, the independent valuer must issue an assessment notice to—

(a)   the pre-transfer creditor,

(b)   the building society special administrator of Dunfermline, and

(c)   the Treasury.

(2)   An assessment notice must contain the following information—

(a)   the date on which the notice is issued,

(b)   the amount of any compensation payable, and

(c)   the reasons for the independent valuer's decision.

Interim payments

11.—(1)   The independent valuer may determine that the Treasury must make interim payments to pre-transfer creditors, a class of pre-transfer creditors or all pre-transfer creditors on account of compensation determined to be payable under this Schedule ("payments on account").

(2)   The independent valuer may make a determination under sub-paragraph (1) at any time before the assessment required by paragraph 7(1) or paragraph 8(2) has been made.

(3)   Subject to sub-paragraph (4), the independent valuer may make such provision as to payments on account as he or she thinks fit (including a requirement that payments are to be made in instalments).

(4)   Payments on account must be made subject to the following conditions—

(a)   that the acceptance of such a payment by the pre-transfer creditor reduces any obligation (whether in existence at the time of the payment or not) on the Treasury to pay compensation to the pre-transfer creditor by the amount of the payment on account;

(b)   that, where the independent valuer, in accordance with paragraph 12, determines that the pre-transfer creditor should make a balancing payment to the Treasury, the pre-transfer creditor is liable to pay that amount.

(5)   In considering whether to require payments on account to be made in accordance with this paragraph, the independent valuer must have regard to the merits of ensuring that pre-transfer creditors receive compensation in a timely manner.

Balancing payments

12.—(1)   Where the independent valuer has determined that the Treasury must make interim payments in accordance with paragraph 11, the independent valuer must determine what balancing payments, if any, are appropriate to ensure that each pre-transfer creditor receives the relevant amount of compensation, if any, determined to be payable in accordance with paragraph 7(1) or 8(2) (and no more than that amount).

(2)   The independent valuer must make a determination under sub-paragraph (1) as soon as is reasonably practicable after the assessment required by paragraph 7(1) or 8(2) has been made.

(3)   Where the independent valuer determines that it is necessary for—

(a)   the Treasury to make a balancing payment to a pre-transfer creditor, the independent valuer must notify in writing the Treasury of—

(i)   the need to make that payment, and

(ii)   the amount of the payment to be made;

(b)   the pre-transfer creditor to make a balancing payment to the Treasury, the independent valuer must notify in writing—

(i)   the pre-transfer creditor of—

(aa)   the need to make that payment, and

(bb)   the amount of the payment to be made;

(ii)   the Treasury of the entitlement to receive that payment.

[596]

NOTES
Commencement: 7 July 2009.

PART 4
PAYMENT OF COMPENSATION

Payment of compensation

13.—(1)   The Treasury must, as soon as is reasonably practicable following receipt of an assessment notice, pay to the person entitled the amount of any compensation set out in that assessment notice.

(2)   But where an order under section 55(6) of the Act is in force and a person affected by the determination of the independent valuer—

(a)   requires the reconsideration of the determination;

(b)   appeals to a court or tribunal against a determination of the independent valuer;

the Treasury shall not be required to make payment of the compensation payable (if any) until the matter has been finally disposed of.

[597]

NOTES
Commencement: 7 July 2009.

AMENDMENTS TO LAW (RESOLUTION OF DUNFERMLINE BUILDING SOCIETY) (NO 2) ORDER 2009

(SI 2009/1805)

NOTES
Made: 7 July 2009.
Authority: Banking Act 2009, ss 75, 259(1).
Commencement: see art 1(2).
Note: This order amends the Dunfermline Building Society Property Transfer Instrument 2009, made by the Bank of England in exercise of its powers under the Banking Act 2009. Note that the amendments made by art 2 have retrospective effect and apply as from 30 March 2009 at 08:00am.

1   Citation, commencement, retrospective effect and interpretation

(1)   This Order may be cited as the Amendments to Law (Resolution of Dunfermline Building Society) (No 2) Order 2009.

(2)   This Order comes into force immediately on it being made, but the amendments made by article 2 (including the Schedule introduced by article 2(5)) have effect from 8am on 30th March 2009 (being the time at which the Property Transfer Instrument came into force).

(3)   In this Order, "the Property Transfer Instrument" means the Dunfermline Building Society Property Transfer Instrument 2009.

[598]

NOTES
Commencement: 7 July 2009.

2   (*Amends the Dunfermline Building Society Property Transfer Instrument 2009, paras 2, 3 at* **[2011]**, **[2012]** *and introduces the Schedule to this Order.*)

(*The Schedule inserts the Dunfermline Building Society Property Transfer Instrument 2009, Schedule at* **[2015]**.)

DUNFERMLINE BUILDING SOCIETY INDEPENDENT VALUER ORDER 2009

(SI 2009/1810)

NOTES
Made: 7 July 2009.
Authority: Banking Act 2009, ss 55(2), (3), (5), (6), 56(1)–(3), 259(1).
Commencement: 30 July 2009.

ARRANGEMENT OF ARTICLES

PART 1
GENERAL

PART 1
GENERAL

1 Citation and commencement

This Order may be cited as the Dunfermline Building Society Independent Valuer Order 2009 and shall come into force on 30th July 2009.

[599]

NOTES
Commencement: 30 July 2009.

2 Interpretation

In this Order—
"the Act" means the Banking Act 2009;
"the Dunfermline Compensation Order" means the Dunfermline Building Society Compensation Scheme, Resolution Fund and Third Party Compensation Order 2009;
"independent valuer" means the person appointed in accordance with article 5(2) of the Dunfermline Compensation Order;
"the monitor" has the meaning given in article 3(2);
"the Tribunal" means the Financial Services and Markets Tribunal established under section 132 of the Financial Services and Markets Act 2000.

[600]

PART 2
REMUNERATION, STAFF, RECORDS AND ACCOUNTS

3 Remuneration of the independent valuer

(1)   The Treasury must pay such remuneration and allowances as they must determine to the independent valuer.

(2)   The Treasury must appoint a person to monitor the operation of the arrangements for the remuneration of, and payment of allowances to, the independent valuer ("the monitor").

[601]

4 Remuneration of the Appointment Panel and the monitor

The Treasury may make provision for—
    (a)   the members of the panel appointed under article 5(1)(b) of the Dunfermline Compensation Order; and
    (b)   the monitor,
to be paid such remuneration and allowances as the Treasury may determine.

[602]

5 Staff

(1)   The independent valuer must determine the remuneration, allowances and other conditions of service of any staff appointed by the independent valuer under section 55(4) of the Act.

(2)   The independent valuer may pay such pensions, allowances or gratuities to or in respect of any staff appointed by the independent valuer under section 55(4) of the Act as he or she may determine.

(3)   The references in paragraph (2) to pensions, allowances or gratuities to or in respect of any staff appointed by the independent valuer under section 55(4) of the Act include reference to pensions, allowances or gratuities by way of compensation in respect of any staff who suffer loss of employment.

(4)   Any determination under paragraph (1) or (2) shall require the approval of the Treasury.

[603]

6 Records and accounts

(1)   The independent valuer must maintain reasonable arrangements for—
    (a)   recording decisions made in exercise of his or her functions referred to in article 4 of the Dunfermline Compensation Order; and
    (b)   the safe-keeping of those records.

(2)   The independent valuer must—
    (a)   keep proper accounts and proper records in relation to the accounts, and
    (b)   prepare in respect of each financial year a statement of accounts to be provided to the monitor.

[604]

PART 3
PROCEDURE AND INFORMATION

7 Interpretation

In this Part—
    "court" means the High Court or, in Scotland, the Court of Session;

"specified information" means any information obtained by the independent valuer for the purpose of conducting the functions referred to in article 4(a) or (c) of the Dunfermline Compensation Order.

[605]

NOTES
Commencement: 30 July 2009.

8 Procedure

(1) The independent valuer may make such rules as to the procedure to be applied in conducting his or her functions referred to in article 4 of the Dunfermline Compensation Order as the independent valuer considers appropriate.

(2) The independent valuer may make such rules as to the procedure for the reconsideration of any determination relating to the assessment of compensation under article 12 as the independent valuer considers appropriate.

(3) Rules made under paragraphs (1) and (2) may make different provision for different cases and circumstances.

[606]

NOTES
Commencement: 30 July 2009.

9 Application to the court for information

(1) The court may, on an application by the independent valuer, make an order requiring a person to provide information that is reasonably required by the independent valuer for the purpose of conducting the functions referred to in article 4(a) or (c) of the Dunfermline Compensation Order.

(2) A person required to provide information pursuant to an order under paragraph (1) shall not be required to provide information—
   (a) in respect of which a claim to legal professional privilege (or in Scotland, to confidentiality of communications) could be maintained in legal proceedings;
   (b) if such provision by the person holding it would be prohibited by or under any enactment;
   (c) if it is held by a government department and provision of such information would be contrary to the public interest.

(3) In relation to information recorded otherwise than in legible form, the power to require information to be provided includes a power to require it to be provided in a form from which it can be readily produced in visible and legible form.

[607]

NOTES
Commencement: 30 July 2009.

10 Confidence

A person who provides information to the independent valuer for the purpose of the independent valuer's functions referred to in article 4(a) or (c) of the Dunfermline Compensation Order is not, by reason only of the provision of such information, liable in any proceedings relating to a breach of an obligation of confidence.

[608]

NOTES
Commencement: 30 July 2009.

11 Disclosure

(1) Specified information shall not be disclosed by the independent valuer without the consent of the person from whom the independent valuer obtained the specified information and, if different, the person to whom it relates.

(2) The prohibition in paragraph (1) of the disclosure of specified information is subject to the following exceptions—
   (a) the independent valuer may, for the purpose of conducting the functions referred to in article 4 of the Dunfermline Compensation Order, disclose specified information to any staff appointed by the independent valuer under section 55(4) of the Act or to any person providing advice or assistance to the independent valuer;
   (b) the independent valuer may disclose specified information if and to the extent that he or she considers it necessary to do so for the purpose of conducting the functions referred to in article 4(a) or (c) of the Dunfermline Compensation Order.

PART III SIS UNDER BANKING ACT 2009

(3)   The independent valuer must, before disclosing any specified information in accordance with paragraph (2), have regard to the need to exclude from disclosure (so far as practicable)—

    (a)   commercial information the disclosure of which might significantly harm the legitimate business interests of the person to whom it relates,

    (b)   information relating to the private affairs of an individual, the disclosure of which might significantly harm the individual's interests, or

    (c)   any information the disclosure of which would be contrary to the public interest.

(4)   The independent valuer may disclose specified information in accordance with this article subject to such conditions as the independent valuer thinks appropriate.

(5)   Specified information shall not be disclosed by any person to whom the independent valuer has disclosed such information without the consent of the person from whom the independent valuer obtained the specified information and, if different, the person to whom it relates.

[609]

NOTES

Commencement: 30 July 2009.

PART 4

RECONSIDERATION BY THE INDEPENDENT VALUER

12   Reconsideration of assessment notice

(1)   If—

    (a)   the Treasury, or

    (b)   any person who is affected by the determination of the amount of any compensation payable in accordance with Schedule 2 to the Dunfermline Compensation Order,

are dissatisfied with an assessment notice issued by the independent valuer under paragraph 4 or 10 of Schedule 2 to the Dunfermline Compensation Order, the Treasury or any such person may require the independent valuer to reconsider his or her determination.

(2)   Where the independent valuer is required to reconsider his or her determination in accordance with paragraph (1) he or she must issue a revised assessment notice.

(3)   A revised assessment notice must contain the following information—

    (a)   the date on which the revised assessment notice is issued;

    (b)   either—

        (i)   notification that the independent valuer has upheld the determination specified in the assessment notice; or

        (ii)   notification that the independent valuer has varied the determination specified in the assessment notice;

    (c)   the amount of any compensation determined by the independent valuer as being payable; and

    (d)   the reasons for the independent valuer's decision.

(4)   The independent valuer must send a copy of the revised assessment notice to the Treasury.

[610]

NOTES

Commencement: 30 July 2009.

PART 5

REFERENCES TO THE TRIBUNAL

13   Right to refer to the Tribunal

If—

    (a)   the Treasury, or

    (b)   any person who is affected by the determination set out in a revised assessment notice of the amount of compensation payable,

are dissatisfied with the revised assessment notice, the Treasury or any such person may refer the matter to the Tribunal.

[611]

NOTES

Commencement: 30 July 2009.

14   Application of the Financial Services and Markets Act 2000

(1)   The provisions of—

(a) Part 9 (hearing and appeals) of, and Schedule 13 (the Financial Services and Markets Tribunal) to, the Financial Services and Markets Act 2000; and

(b) the Financial Services and Markets Tribunal Rules 2001;

shall apply in respect of any reference made under article 13, subject to the modifications set out in this Part.

[612]

NOTES
Commencement: 30 July 2009.

15 Modification of the Financial Services and Markets Act 2000
Part 9 of, and Schedule 13 to, the Financial Services and Markets Act 2000 are modified as follows.

[613]

NOTES
Commencement: 30 July 2009.

16 In section 133 (proceedings: general provision) and Schedule 13, for "the Authority" in each place where it occurs substitute "the independent valuer appointed in accordance with article 5(2) of the Dunfermline Building Society Compensation Scheme, Resolution Fund and Third Party Compensation Order 2009".

[614]

NOTES
Commencement: 30 July 2009.

17 In section 133—
(i) in subsection (1)(a) for "the decision notice or supervisory notice in question", substitute "the revised assessment notice issued by the independent valuer under article 12(2) of the Dunfermline Building Society Independent Valuer Order 2009";
(ii) for subsection (4) substitute—

"(4) Where the Tribunal is satisfied that the decision as to the amount of compensation shown in the revised assessment notice was not a reasonable decision the Tribunal must remit the matter to the independent valuer for reconsideration in accordance with such directions (if any) as it considers appropriate.";

(iii) ignore subsections (5) to (9) and (12).

[615]

NOTES
Commencement: 30 July 2009.

18 Ignore sections 134 to 136.

[616]

NOTES
Commencement: 30 July 2009.

19 Modification of Financial Services and Markets Tribunal Rules 2001
The Financial Services and Markets Tribunal Rules 2001 are modified as follows.

[617]

NOTES
Commencement: 30 July 2009.

20 In each place where it occurs (other than in rule 2)—
(a) for "Authority" substitute "respondent";
(b) for "Authority notice" substitute "revised assessment notice";
(c) for "statement of case" substitute "response document".

[618]

NOTES
Commencement: 30 July 2009.

21 In rule 2 (interpretation)—

    (a)   ignore the definitions for "the Authority", "Authority notice", "further material", "protected item", "reply" and "statement of case";

    (b)   in the definition of "party", for "Authority", in both places where it occurs, substitute "respondent";

    (c)   in the definition of "referred action" for "the act (or proposed act) on the part of the Authority" substitute "the revised assessment notice";

    (d)   for the definition of "response document" substitute

    ""response document" means a statement filed by the respondent under rule 5(1);"; and

    (e)   in the appropriate places insert—

    ""respondent" means the independent valuer appointed in accordance with article 5(2) of the Dunfermline Building Society Compensation Scheme, Resolution Fund and Third Party Compensation Order 2009";

    "revised assessment notice" means the revised assessment notice issued by the respondent under article 12(2) of the Dunfermline Building Society Independent Valuer Order 2009,".

[619]

NOTES
Commencement: 30 July 2009.

22 In rule 4(6) (reference notice) ignore ", a direction under rule 10(1)(e) (suspension of Authority's action) or".

[620]

NOTES
Commencement: 30 July 2009.

23 In rule 5 (Authority's statement of case)—

    (a)   for paragraphs (1) and (2) substitute—

    "(1)   The respondent shall file a written statement ("a response document") dealing with any issues arising out of the reference notice that the respondent wishes the Tribunal to consider so that it is received by the Tribunal no later than 28 days after the day on which the respondent received the information sent by the Secretary in accordance with rule 4(9)(b).

    (2)   At the same time as it files the response document, the respondent shall send a copy to the applicant.";

    (b)   ignore paragraphs (3) and (4).

[621]

NOTES
Commencement: 30 July 2009.

24 Ignore rules 6 (applicant's reply), 7 (secondary disclosure by the Authority), 8 (exceptions to disclosure), 11 (filing of subsequent notices in relation to the referred action), 12(2) (summoning of witnesses), 14(3)(c) (withdrawal of reference and unopposed references), 15 (references by third parties) and 23(4) (application for permission to appeal).

[622]

NOTES
Commencement: 30 July 2009.

25 In rule 10 (particular types of directions) ignore paragraphs (1)(e), (2)(a), (6) and (8).

[623]

NOTES
Commencement: 30 July 2009.

26 After rule 10 (particular types of directions) insert—

"10A   Same issues proceedings

    (1)   The President may, of his own motion or on application by a party, direct that a reference is heard as a lead case where—

(a)   two or more references under article 13 of the Dunfermline Building Society Independent Valuer Order 2009 have been made, but have not yet been determined by the Tribunal; and

(b)   it appears to the President that those references give rise to common or related issues of fact or law ("same issues proceedings").

(2)   The President may—

(a)   make such further directions as he or she considers appropriate for determination of the lead case; and

(b)   direct that pending determination of the lead case all other same issues proceedings before the Tribunal shall be stayed.

(3)   All parties in same issue proceedings must be allowed to make representations prior to the President making a direction under paragraph (1) or (2).

(4)   Without prejudice generally to the parties' rights of appeal and to paragraphs (5) to (7), the Tribunal's determination of the same issues in the lead case shall be binding on the parties to each of the same issues proceedings unless the Tribunal or the President directs otherwise.

(5)   Any party to any of the same issues proceedings may apply to the President for a direction that the determination of the same issues in the lead case does not apply to that party's case.

(6)   An application under paragraph (5) must be made not later than 21 days after the date on which that party received notice of the determination of the same issues in the lead case.

(7)   Within 28 days beginning with the date of determination of the same issues in the lead case the President may make further directions in relation to—

(a)   the lead case and each of the same issues proceedings stayed pending the determination of the same issues in the lead case;

(b)   the extent to which the determination of the same issues in the lead case is binding on any subsequent proceedings; and

(c)   any further directions required as a result of an application under paragraph (5), including a direction as to any further hearing required in relation to those proceedings.

(8)   Where a direction has been made for any proceedings to be heard as a lead case and those proceedings are withdrawn or discontinued either before or during the hearing, the President may direct—

(a)   that one of the remaining same issues proceedings be substituted as the lead case; and

(b)   the extent to which any directions made prior to substitution shall be binding in relation to the substituted proceedings.

(9)   The Secretary must send notice of the directions to be made under paragraphs (1) and (2), a copy of the directions made under paragraphs (1), (2), (4), (5), (7) and (8) and the determination of the same issues in the lead case to all the parties to the same issues proceedings.

10B   Joining of parties to proceedings

If it appears to the President or the Chairman, whether on the application of a party or otherwise, that it is desirable that any person other than the respondent be made a party to any proceedings, he or she may direct that such person be joined as a party in the proceedings and may make such further directions for giving effect to, or in connection with, the direction as he or she thinks fit.".

[624]

NOTES

Commencement: 30 July 2009.

27   In rule 19(3) (procedure at hearings) ignore "when taking the referred action".

[625]

NOTES

Commencement: 30 July 2009.

PART III
SIS UNDER BANKING ACT 2009

BANKING ACT 2009 (COMMENCEMENT NO 3) ORDER 2009

(SI 2009/2038)

NOTES
Made: 21 July 2009.
Authority: Banking Act 2009, s 263(1), (3).

1   Citation and interpretation

(1)   This Order may be cited as the Banking Act 2009 (Commencement No 3) Order 2009.

(2)   In this Order "the Act" means the Banking Act 2009.

[626]

2   Provisions of the Act coming into force on 4th August 2009

The provisions of Part 5 of the Act (inter-bank payment systems) listed in the Schedule to this Order come into force on 4th August 2009.

[627]

SCHEDULE

1.   Section 181 (overview)

2.   Sections 182 and 183 (interpretation)

3.   Sections 184 to 187 (recognised systems)

4.   Section 204(1)(a), (2), (3), (4)(a) and (b), (5), (6) and (8) to (11) (information)

5.   Section 205 (pretending to be recognised)

[628]

DRAFT SCOTTISH AND NORTHERN IRELAND BANKNOTES REGULATIONS 2009 (NOTE)

(SI 2009/xxxx)

NOTES
Authority: Banking Act 2009, ss 208–210, 215–220, 222–224, 226, 259(1).

In June 2009 the Treasury issued draft Scottish and Northern Ireland Banknotes Regulations 2009 and a consultation document, which can be accessed at www.hm-treasury.gov.uk. Subject to responses to the consultation document, the regulations will be laid before Parliament in October 2009 and come into force in late 2009.

The Government's aim is to ensure that holders of banknotes issued by authorised commercial banks (Bank of Scotland; Clydesdale Bank; The Royal Bank of Scotland; Bank of Ireland; AIB Group (UK), trading as First Trust Bank; Northern Bank; and Ulster Bank) have a level of protection similar to that of holders of Bank of England notes, and, in the event of an authorised bank failing, can expect to obtain full face value for their notes.

[629]–[699]

PART IV
OTHER STATUTORY INSTRUMENTS

FINANCIAL SERVICES AND MARKETS ACT 2000 (REGULATED ACTIVITIES) ORDER 2001

(SI 2001/544)

NOTES
Made: 26 February 2001.
Authority: Financial Services and Markets Act 2000, ss 22(1), (5), 426, 428(3), Sch 2, para 25.
Commencement: see art 2.
Transitional provisions (interim permissions and interim approvals): for transitional provisions relating to interim permissions and interim approvals and the application of Parts IV, V of FSMA 2000 (and various other provisions of that Act) to various activities that have become regulated activities following the amendment of this Order, see the table below:

Order	Regulated Activity
Financial Services and Markets Act 2000 (Transitional Provisions) (Mortgages) Order 2004, SI 2004/2615	Certain mortgage mediation activities
Financial Services and Markets Act 2000 (Regulated Activities) (Amendment) (No 2) Order 2004, SI 2004/2737	Advice on stakeholder products
Financial Services and Markets Act 2000 (Transitional Provisions) (General Insurance Intermediaries) Order 2004, SI 2004/3351	Certain general insurance mediation activities
Financial Services and Markets Act 2000 (Regulated Activities) (Amendment) Order 2006, SI 2006/1969	Establishing, operating or winding up a personal pension scheme, or activities which relate to the specified investment of rights under a personal pension scheme
Financial Services and Markets Act 2000 (Regulated Activities) (Amendment) (No 2) Order 2006, SI 2006/2383	Administering, arranging or advising on regulated home reversion plans or regulated home purchase plans
Financial Services and Markets Act 2000 (Regulated Activities) (Amendment) (No 2) Order 2007, SI 2007/3510	Provision of travel insurance in certain circumstances
Financial Services and Markets Act 2000 (Regulated Activities) (Amendment) Order 2009, SI 2009/1342	Entering into, administering, arranging and advising on regulated sale and rent back agreements

ARRANGEMENT OF ARTICLES

PART I
GENERAL

PART II
SPECIFIED ACTIVITIES

CHAPTER I

General

CHAPTER II
ACCEPTING DEPOSITS

The activity

Exclusions

CHAPTER VII
MANAGING INVESTMENTS

The activity

Exclusions

CHAPTER VIIA
ASSISTING IN THE ADMINISTRATION AND PERFORMANCE OF A
CONTRACT OF INSURANCE

The Activity

Exclusions

CHAPTER VIII
SAFEGUARDING AND ADMINISTERING INVESTMENTS

The activity

Exclusions

CHAPTER IX
SENDING DEMATERIALISED INSTRUCTIONS

The activities

Exclusions

PART III
SPECIFIED INVESTMENTS

PART V
UNAUTHORISED PERSONS CARRYING ON INSURANCE MEDIATION ACTIVITIES

PART I
GENERAL

1 Citation

This Order may be cited as the Financial Services and Markets Act 2000 (Regulated Activities) Order 2001.

[700]

2 Commencement

(1)   Except as provided by paragraph (2), this Order comes into force on the day on which section 19 of the Act comes into force.

(2)   This Order comes into force—

    (a)   for the purposes of articles 59, 60 and 87 (funeral plan contracts) on 1st January 2002; and

    (b)   for the purposes of articles 61 to 63, 88, 90 and 91 (regulated mortgage contracts) [on such a day as the Treasury may specify].

[(3)   Any day specified under paragraph (2)(b) must be caused to be notified in the London, Edinburgh and Belfast Gazettes published not later than one week before that day.]

[701]

NOTES
Para (2): words in square brackets substituted by the Financial Services and Markets Act 2000 (Commencement of Mortgage Regulation) (Amendment) Order 2002, SI 2002/1777, art 2(1), (2), as from 30 August 2002.
Para (3): added by SI 2002/1777, art 2(1), (3), as from 30 August 2002.
On such a day as the Treasury may specify: 31 October 2004 (see the London Gazette, 14 July 2003).

3   Interpretation

(1)   In this Order—

"the Act" means the Financial Services and Markets Act 2000;

["agreement provider" has the meaning given by article 63J(3);

"agreement seller" has the meaning given by article 63J(3);]

"annuities on human life" does not include superannuation allowances and annuities payable out of any fund applicable solely to the relief and maintenance of persons engaged, or who have been engaged, in any particular profession, trade or employment, or of the dependants of such persons;

"buying" includes acquiring for valuable consideration;

"close relative" in relation to a person means—

    (a)   his spouse [or civil partner];

    (b)   his children and step children, his parents and step-parents, his brothers and sisters and his step-brothers and step-sisters; and

    (c)   the spouse [or civil partner] of any person within sub-paragraph (b);

["the Commission Regulation" means Commission Regulation 1287/2006 of 10 August 2006;]

"contract of general insurance" means any contract falling within Part I of Schedule 1;

"contract of insurance" means any contract of insurance which is a contract of long-term insurance or a contract of general insurance, and includes—

    (a)   fidelity bonds, performance bonds, administration bonds, bail bonds, customs bonds or similar contracts of guarantee, where these are—

        (i)   effected or carried out by a person not carrying on a banking business;

        (ii)   not effected merely incidentally to some other business carried on by the person effecting them; and

        (iii)   effected in return for the payment of one or more premiums;

    (b)   tontines;

    (c)   capital redemption contracts or pension fund management contracts, where these are effected or carried out by a person who—

        (i)   does not carry on a banking business; and

        (ii)   otherwise carries on a regulated activity of the kind specified by article 10(1) or (2);

    (d)   contracts to pay annuities on human life;

    (e)   contracts of a kind referred to in article 1(2)(e) of the first life insurance directive (collective insurance etc); and

    (f)   contracts of a kind referred to in article 1(3) of the first life insurance directive (social insurance);

but does not include a funeral plan contract (or a contract which would be a funeral plan contract but for the exclusion in article 60);

"contract of long-term insurance" means any contract falling within Part II of Schedule 1;

"contractually based investment" means—

    (a)   rights under a qualifying contract of insurance;

    (b)   any investment of the kind specified by any of articles 83, 84, 85 and 87; or

    (c)   any investment of the kind specified by article 89 so far as relevant to an investment falling within (a) or (b);

["credit institution" means—

    (a)   a credit institution authorised under the banking consolidation directive other than an institution to which Article 2.1 of the markets in financial instruments directive (the text of which is set out in Schedule 3) applies, or

    (b)   an institution which would satisfy the requirements for authorisation as a credit institution under that directive (other than an institution to which Article 2.1 of the markets in financial instruments directive would apply) if it had its registered office (or if it does not have a registered office, its head office) in an EEA State;]

"deposit" has the meaning given by article 5;

["electronic money" means monetary value, as represented by a claim on the issuer, which is—

    (a)   stored on an electronic device;

    (b)   issued on receipt of funds; and

    (c)   accepted as a means of payment by persons other than the issuer;]

PART IV
OTHER STATUTORY INSTRUMENTS

["financial instrument" means any instrument listed in Section C of Annex I to the markets in financial instruments directive (the text of which is set out in Part 1 of Schedule 2) read with Chapter VI of the Commission Regulation (the text of which is set out in Part 2 of Schedule 2);]

"funeral plan contract" has the meaning given by article 59;

["home Member State", in relation to an investment firm, has the meaning given by Article 4.1.20 of the markets in financial instruments directive, and in relation to a credit institution, has the meaning given by Article 4.7 of the banking consolidation directive;]

["home purchase provider" has the meaning given by article 63F(3);

"home purchaser" has the meaning given by article 63F(3);]

"instrument" includes any record whether or not in the form of a document;

["investment firm" means a person whose regular occupation or business is the provision or performance of investment services and activities on a professional basis but does not include—

(a)   a person to whom the markets in financial instruments directive does not apply by virtue of Article 2 of that directive (the text of which is set out in Schedule 3);

(b)   a person whose home Member State is an EEA State other than the United Kingdom and to whom, by reason of the fact that the State has given effect to Article 3 of that directive, that directive does not apply by virtue of that Article;

(c)   a person who does not have a home Member State and to whom (if he had his registered office in an EEA State, or, being a person other than a body corporate or a body corporate not having a registered office, if he had his head office in an EEA State) the markets in financial instruments directive would not apply by virtue of Article 2 of that directive;]

["investment services and activities" means—

(a)   any service provided to third parties listed in Section A of Annex I to the markets in financial instruments directive (the text of which is set out in Part 3 of Schedule 2) read with Article 52 of Commission Directive 2006/73/EC of 10 August 2006 (the text of which is set out in Part 4 of Schedule 2), or

(b)   any activity listed in Section A of Annex I to that directive,

        relating to any financial instrument;]

"joint enterprise" means an enterprise into which two or more persons ("the participators") enter for commercial purposes related to a business or businesses (other than the business of engaging in a regulated activity) carried on by them; and, where a participator is a member of a group, each other member of the group is also to be regarded as a participator in the enterprise;

"local authority" means—

(a)   in England and Wales, a local authority within the meaning of the Local Government Act 1972, the Greater London Authority, the Common Council of the City of London or the Council of the Isles of Scilly;

(b)   in Scotland, a local authority within the meaning of the Local Government (Scotland) Act 1973;

(c)   in Northern Ireland, a district council within the meaning of the Local Government Act (Northern Ireland) 1972;

["management company" has the meaning given by Article 1a.2 of the UCITS directive as amended by Directive 2001/107/EC;]

"managing agent" means a person who is permitted by the Council of Lloyd's in the conduct of his business as an underwriting agent to perform for a member of Lloyd's one or more of the following functions—

(a)   underwriting contracts of insurance at Lloyd's;

(b)   reinsuring such contracts in whole or in part;

(c)   paying claims on such contracts;

["market operator" means a market operator within the meaning of Article 4.1.13 of the markets in financial instruments directive, or a person who would be a market operator if he had his registered office, or if he does not have a registered office his head office, in an EEA State, but does not include—

(a)   a person to whom the markets in financial instruments directive does not apply by virtue of Article 2 of that directive (the text of which is set out in Schedule 3);

(b)   a person who does not have a home Member State to whom (if he had his registered office, or if he does not have a registered office his head office, in an EEA State) the markets in financial instruments directive would not apply by virtue of Article 2 of that directive;]

["multilateral trading facility" means—

(a)   a multilateral trading facility (within the meaning of Article 4.1.15 of the markets in financial instruments directive) operated by an investment firm, a credit institution or a market operator, or

(b)   a facility which—

    (i)   is operated by an investment firm, a credit institution or market operator which does not have a home Member State, and

    (ii)   if its operator had a home Member State, would be a multilateral trading facility within the meaning of Article 4.1.15 of the markets in financial instruments directive;]

["occupational pension scheme" has the meaning given by section 1 of the Pension Schemes Act 1993 but with paragraph (b) of the definition omitted;]

"overseas person" means a person who—

    (a)   carries on activities of the kind specified by any of articles 14, 21, 25, [25A,] [25B, 25C,] [25D,] [25E,] 37[, 39A], 40, 45, 51, 52[, 53, 53A [, 53B, 53C, [53D,] 61, 63B and *63F*]] or, so far as relevant to any of those articles, article 64 (or activities of a kind which would be so specified but for the exclusion in article 72); but

    (b)   does not carry on any such activities, or offer to do so, from a permanent place of business maintained by him in the United Kingdom;

"pension fund management contract" means a contract to manage the investments of pension funds (other than funds solely for the benefit of the officers or employees of the person effecting or carrying out the contract and their dependants or, in the case of a company, partly for the benefit of officers and employees and their dependants of its subsidiary or holding company or a subsidiary of its holding company); and for the purposes of this definition, "subsidiary" and "holding company" are to be construed in accordance with section 736 of the Companies Act 1985 or article 4 of the Companies (Northern Ireland) Order 1986;

["personal pension scheme" means a scheme or arrangement which is not an occupational pension scheme or a stakeholder pension scheme and which is comprised in one or more instruments or agreements, having or capable of having effect so as to provide benefits to or in respect of people—

    (a)   on retirement,

    (b)   on having reached a particular age, or

    (c)   on termination of service in an employment;]

["plan provider" has the meaning given by paragraph (3) of article 63B, read with paragraphs (7) and (8) of that article;]

"property" includes currency of the United Kingdom or any other country or territory;

"qualifying contract of insurance" means a contract of long-term insurance which is not—

    (a)   a reinsurance contract; nor

    (b)   a contract in respect of which the following conditions are met—

        (i)   the benefits under the contract are payable only on death or in respect of incapacity due to injury, sickness or infirmity;

        (ii)   ...

        (iii)   the contract has no surrender value, or the consideration consists of a single premium and the surrender value does not exceed that premium; and

        (iv)   the contract makes no provision for its conversion or extension in a manner which would result in it ceasing to comply with any of the above conditions;

["regulated home purchase plan" has the meaning given by article 63F(3);

"regulated home reversion plan" has the meaning given by article 63B(3);]

"regulated mortgage contract" has the meaning given by article 61(3);

["regulated sale and rent back agreement" has the meaning given by article 63J(3);]

["relevant investment" means—

    (a)   rights under a qualifying contract of insurance;

    (b)   rights under any other contract of insurance;

    (c)   any investment of the kind specified by any of articles 83, 84, 85 and 87; or

    (d)   any investment of the kind specified by article 89 so far as relevant to an investment falling within (a) or (c);]

["reversion seller" has the meaning given by article 63B(3);]

"security" means (except where the context otherwise requires) any investment of the kind specified by any of articles 76 to 82 or, so far as relevant to any such investment, article 89;

"selling", in relation to any investment, includes disposing of the investment for valuable consideration, and for these purposes "disposing" includes—

    (a)   in the case of an investment consisting of rights under a contract—

        (i)   surrendering, assigning or converting those rights; or

        (ii)   assuming the corresponding liabilities under the contract;

    (b)   in the case of an investment consisting of rights under other arrangements, assuming the corresponding liabilities under the arrangements; and

    (c)   in the case of any other investment, issuing or creating the investment or granting the rights or interests of which it consists;

"stakeholder pension scheme" has the meaning given by section 1 of the Welfare Reform and Pensions Act 1999 [in relation to Great Britain and has the meaning given by article 3 of the Welfare Reform and Pensions (Northern Ireland) Order 1999 in relation to Northern Ireland];

"syndicate" means one or more persons, to whom a particular syndicate number has been assigned by or under the authority of the Council of Lloyd's, carrying out or effecting contracts of insurance written at Lloyd's;

"voting shares", in relation to a body corporate, means shares carrying voting rights attributable to share capital which are exercisable in all circumstances at any general meeting of that body corporate.

(2) For the purposes of this Order, a transaction is entered into through a person if he enters into it as agent or arranges, in a manner constituting the carrying on of an activity of the kind specified by article 25(1)[, 25A(1), 25B(1) *or 25C(1)*], for it to be entered into by another person as agent or principal.

(3) For the purposes of this Order, a contract of insurance is to be treated as falling within Part II of Schedule 1, notwithstanding the fact that it contains related and subsidiary provisions such that it might also be regarded as falling within Part I of that Schedule, if its principal object is that of a contract falling within Part II and it is effected or carried out by an authorised person who has permission to effect or carry out contracts falling within paragraph I of Part II of Schedule 1.

[702]

NOTES

Para (1) is amended as follows:

Definitions "agreement provider", "agreement seller", and "regulated sale and rent back agreement" inserted by the Financial Services and Markets Act 2000 (Regulated Activities) (Amendment) Order 2009, SI 2009/1342, arts 2, 3(1)(a), (b), as from 1 July 2009 (other than for the purposes of enabling applications to be made for a Part IV permission, or a variation of a Part IV permission, in relation to activities of the kind specified by arts 25E, 53D or 63J or, so far as relevant to any such activity, art 64 of this Order), and as from 30 June 2010 (for those purposes) (for the full commencement details and for transitional provisions etc see arts 1, 32–34 of that Order).

Words in square brackets in the definition "close relative" inserted by the Civil Partnership Act 2004 (Amendments to Subordinate Legislation) Order 2005, SI 2005/2114, art 2(16), Sch 16, Pt 1, para 1(1), (2), as from 5 December 2005.

Definitions "the Commission Regulation", "credit institution", "financial instrument", "home Member State", "investment firm", "investment services and activities", "management company", "market operator", and "multilateral trading facility" inserted by the Financial Services and Markets Act 2000 (Regulated Activities) (Amendment No 3) Order 2006, SI 2006/3384, arts 2, 3(b), as from 1 April 2007 (for the purposes of enabling applications to be made for (i) a Pt IV permission, (ii) a variation of a Pt IV permission, and (iii) the Authority's approval under s 59 of the 2000 Act, in relation to an activity of the kind specified by art 25D of this Order, or in relation to an investment of the kind specified by arts 83, 84 or 85 of this Order), and as from 1 November 2007 (otherwise).

Definition "electronic money" inserted by the Financial Services and Markets Act 2000 (Regulated Activities) (Amendment) Order 2002, SI 2002/682, art 2, as from 27 April 2002 (subject to transitional provisions in relation to persons issuing electronic money immediately before that date contained in art 9).

Definitions "home purchase provider", "home purchaser", "plan provider", "regulated home purchase plan", "regulated home reversion plan", and "reversion seller" inserted by the Financial Services and Markets Act 2000 (Regulated Activities) (Amendment) (No 2) Order 2006, SI 2006/2383, arts 2, 3(1)(a), (c)–(e), as from 6 November 2006 (for the purposes of enabling applications to be made for (i) a Pt IV permission, or a variation of a Pt IV permission, in relation to activities of the kind specified by arts 25B, 25C, 53C, 63B or 63F or, so far as relevant to any such activity, art 64 of this Order; or (ii) the Authority's approval under FSMA 2000, s 59 in relation to any of those activities), and as from 6 April 2007 (otherwise) (for transitional provisions and effect see arts 36–40 of, and the Schedule to, the 2006 Order).

Definition "occupational pension scheme" substituted by the Financial Services and Markets Act 2000 (Regulated Activities) (Amendment) Order 2006, SI 2006/1969, art 2(1), (2)(a), as from 1 October 2006 (for the purposes of enabling applications to be made for Pt IV permission or for a variation of Pt IV permission in relation to the regulated activity specified by art 52(b) of this Order (as amended by SI 2006/1969) or in relation to an investment specified by art 82(2) of this Order (as so amended)), and as from 6 April 2007 (otherwise); for transitional provisions and effect see arts 3–7 of, and the Schedule to, the 2006 Order.

Definition "overseas person" is amended as follows:

Figure "25A," in square brackets inserted by the Financial Services and Markets Act 2000 (Regulated Activities) (Amendment) (No 1) Order 2003, SI 2003/1475, art 3(a), as from 31 October 2004 (for transitional provisions see arts 26–29 thereof).

Figures "25B, 25C," in square brackets inserted by SI 2006/2383, arts 2, 3(1)(b)(i), as from 6 November 2006 (for the purposes of enabling applications to be made for (i) a Pt IV permission, or a variation of a Pt IV permission, in relation to activities of the kind specified by arts 25B, 25C, 53B, 53C, 63B or 63F or, so far as relevant to any such activity, art 64 of this Order; or (ii) the Authority's approval under FSMA 2000, s 59 in relation to any of those activities), and as from 6 April 2007 (otherwise) (for transitional provisions and effect see arts 36–40 of, and the Schedule to, the 2006 Order).

Figure "25D," in square brackets inserted by SI 2006/3384, arts 2, 3(a), as from 1 April 2007 (for the purposes of enabling applications to be made for (i) a Pt IV permission, (ii) a variation of a Pt IV permission, and (iii) the Authority's approval under s 59 of the 2000 Act, in relation to an activity of the kind specified by art 25D of this Order, or in relation to an investment of the kind specified by arts 83, 84 or 85 of this Order), and as from 1 November 2007 (otherwise).

Figure "25E," in square brackets inserted by SI 2009/1342, arts 2, 3(1)(c)(i), as from the same dates and for the same purposes, etc, as mentioned in the note relating to this Order above.

Figure ", 39A" in square brackets inserted by SI 2003/1476, arts 2, 3(1)(a), as from 31 October 2004 (in so far as relating to contracts of long-term care insurance), and as from 14 January 2005 (otherwise) (for transitional provisions see arts 22–27 of that Order).

Words in square brackets beginning with the figures ", 53, 53A" substituted by SI 2003/1475, art 3(b), as from 31 October 2004 (for transitional provisions see arts 26–29 thereof).

Words in square brackets beginning with the figures ", 53B, 53C" substituted by SI 2006/2383, arts 2, 3(1)(b)(ii), as from the same dates and for the same purposes as mentioned in the note relating to this Order above.

Figure "53D," in square brackets inserted by SI 2009/1342, arts 2, 3(1)(c)(ii), as from the same dates and for the same purposes, etc, as mentioned in the note relating to this Order above.

For the words "and 63F" in italics there are substituted the words ", 63F and 63J" by SI 2009/1342, arts 2, 3(1)(c)(iii), as from the same dates and for the same purposes, etc, as mentioned in the note relating to this Order above.

Definition "personal pension scheme" inserted by SI 2006/1969, art 2(1), (2)(a), as from 1 October 2006 (for the purposes of enabling applications to be made for Pt IV permission or for a variation of Pt IV permission in relation to the regulated activity specified by art 52(b) of this Order (as amended by SI 2006/1969) or in relation to an investment specified by art 82(2) of this Order (as so amended)), and as from 6 April 2007 (otherwise); for transitional provisions and effect see arts 3–7 of, and the Schedule to, the 2006 Order.

In definition "qualifying contract of insurance" sub-para (b)(ii) revoked by the Financial Services and Markets Act 2000 (Regulated Activities) (Amendment) Order 2007, SI 2007/1339, arts 2, 3, as from 6 June 2007.

Definition "relevant investment" inserted by SI 2003/1476, art 3(1)(b), as from 31 October 2004 (in so far as relating to contracts of long-term care insurance), and as from 14 January 2005 (otherwise) (for transitional provisions see arts 22–27 of that Order).

Words in square brackets in definition "stakeholder pension scheme" added by SI 2005/593, art 2(1), (2)(b), as from 6 April 2005.

Para (2): words in square brackets inserted by SI 2006/2383, arts 2, 3(2), as from 6 November 2006 (for the purposes of enabling applications to be made for (i) a Pt IV permission, or a variation of a Pt IV permission, in relation to activities of the kind specified by arts 25B, 25C, 53B, 53C, 63B or 63F or, so far as relevant to any such activity, art 64 of this Order; or (ii) the Authority's approval under FSMA 2000, s 59 in relation to any of those activities), and as from 6 April 2007 (otherwise) (for transitional provisions and effect see arts 36–40 of, and the Schedule to, the 2006 Order); for the words in italics there are substituted the words ", 25C(1) or 25E(1)" by SI 2009/1342, arts 2, 3(2), as from the same dates and for the same purposes, etc, as mentioned in the note relating to this Order above.

Step-children, etc: as to the meaning of this and related expressions, see the Civil Partnership Act 2004, s 246 (as applied to this Order by the Civil Partnership Act 2004 (Relationships Arising Through Civil Partnership) Order 2005, SI 2005/3137, art 3, Schedule).

PART II
SPECIFIED ACTIVITIES

CHAPTER I
GENERAL

4   Specified activities: general

(1)   The following provisions of this Part specify kinds of activity for the purposes of section 22 of the Act (and accordingly any activity of one of those kinds, which is carried on by way of business, and relates to an investment of a kind specified by any provision of Part III and applicable to that activity, is a regulated activity for the purposes of the Act).

(2)   The kinds of activity specified by articles [51, 52 and 63N] are also specified for the purposes of section 22(1)(b) of the Act (and accordingly any activity of one of those kinds, when carried on by way of business, is a regulated activity when carried on in relation to property of any kind).

(3)   Subject to paragraph (4), each provision specifying a kind of activity is subject to the exclusions applicable to that provision (and accordingly any reference in this Order to an activity of the kind specified by a particular provision is to be read subject to any such exclusions).

[(4)   Where an investment firm or credit institution—
   (a)   provides or performs investment services and activities on a professional basis, and
   (b)   in doing so would be treated as carrying on an activity of a kind specified by a provision of this Part but for an exclusion in any of articles 15, 16, 19, 22, 23, 29, 38, 67, 68, 69, 70 and 72E,

that exclusion is to be disregarded and, accordingly, the investment firm or credit institution is to be treated as carrying on an activity of the kind specified by the provision in question.]

[(4A)   Where a person, other than a person specified by Article 1.2 of the insurance mediation directive (the text of which is set out in Part 1 of Schedule 4)—
   (a)   for remuneration, takes up or pursues insurance mediation or reinsurance mediation in relation to a risk or commitment located in an EEA State, and
   (b)   in doing so would be treated as carrying on an activity of a kind specified by a provision of this Part but for an exclusion in any of articles 30, 66 and 67,

that exclusion is to be disregarded (and accordingly that person is to be treated as carrying on an activity of the kind specified by the provision in question).]

(5)   In this article—

.....

["insurance mediation" has the meaning given by Article 2.3 of the insurance mediation directive, the text of which is set out in Part II of Schedule 4;]

.....

["reinsurance mediation" has the meaning given by Article 2.4 of the insurance mediation directive, the text of which is set out in Part III of Schedule 4.]

[703]

NOTES

Para (2): words in square brackets substituted by the Financial Services and Markets Act 2000 (Regulated Activities) (Amendment) (No 2) Order 2009, SI 2009/1389, arts 2, 3, as from 13 July 2009.

Para (4): substituted by the Financial Services and Markets Act 2000 (Regulated Activities) (Amendment No 3) Order 2006, SI 2006/3384, arts 2, 4(a), as from 1 April 2007 (for the purposes of enabling applications to be made for (i) a Pt IV permission, (ii) a variation of a Pt IV permission, and (iii) the Authority's approval under s 59 of the 2000 Act, in relation to an activity of the kind specified by art 25D of this Order, or in relation to an investment of the kind specified by arts 83, 84 or 85 of this Order), and as from 1 November 2007 (otherwise).

Para (4A): inserted by the Financial Services and Markets Act 2000 (Regulated Activities) (Amendment) (No 2) Order 2003, SI 2003/1476, art 3(2)(a), as from 31 October 2004 (in so far as relating to contracts of long-term care insurance), and as from 14 January 2005 (otherwise), for transitional provisions see arts 22–27 of that Order.

Para (5): definitions "insurance mediation" and "reinsurance mediation" inserted by SI 2003/1476, art 3(2)(b), as from 31 October 2004 (in so far as relating to contracts of long-term care insurance), and as from 14 January 2005 (otherwise), for transitional provisions see arts 22–27 of that Order; definitions "core investment service" and "investment firm" (omitted) revoked by SI 2006/3384, arts 2, 4(a), as from 1 April 2007 (for the purposes of enabling applications to be made for (i) a Pt IV permission, (ii) a variation of a Pt IV permission, and (iii) the Authority's approval under s 59 of the 2000 Act, in relation to an activity of the kind specified by art 25D of this Order, or in relation to an investment of the kind specified by arts 83, 84 or 85 of this Order), and as from 1 November 2007 (otherwise).

CHAPTER II
ACCEPTING DEPOSITS

The activity

5   Accepting deposits

(1)   Accepting deposits is a specified kind of activity if—
   (a)   money received by way of deposit is lent to others; or
   (b)   any other activity of the person accepting the deposit is financed wholly, or to a material extent, out of the capital of or interest on money received by way of deposit.

(2)   In paragraph (1), "deposit" means a sum of money, other than one excluded by any of [articles 6 to 9A], paid on terms—
   (a)   under which it will be repaid, with or without interest or premium, and either on demand or at a time or in circumstances agreed by or on behalf of the person making the payment and the person receiving it; and
   (b)   which are not referable to the provision of property (other than currency) or services or the giving of security.

(3)   For the purposes of paragraph (2), money is paid on terms which are referable to the provision of property or services or the giving of security if, and only if—
   (a)   it is paid by way of advance or part payment under a contract for the sale, hire or other provision of property or services, and is repayable only in the event that the property or services is or are not in fact sold, hired or otherwise provided;
   (b)   it is paid by way of security for the performance of a contract or by way of security in respect of loss which may result from the non-performance of a contract; or
   (c)   without prejudice to sub-paragraph (b), it is paid by way of security for the delivery up or return of any property, whether in a particular state of repair or otherwise.

[704]

NOTES

Para (2): words in square brackets substituted by the Financial Services and Markets Act 2000 (Regulated Activities) (Amendment) Order 2002, SI 2002/682, art 3(1), as from 27 April 2002, subject to transitional provisions in relation to persons issuing electronic money immediately before that date contained in art 9.

See the Financial Services and Markets Act 2000 (Carrying on Regulated Activities by Way of Business) Order 2001, SI 2001/1177, art 2 in relation to deposit taking business.

Exclusions

6   Sums paid by certain persons

(1)   A sum is not a deposit for the purposes of article 5 if it is—

   (a)   paid by any of the following persons—

     (i) the Bank of England, the central bank of an EEA State other than the United Kingdom, or the European Central Bank;

     (ii) an authorised person who has permission to accept deposits, or to effect or carry out contracts of insurance;

     (iii) an EEA firm falling within paragraph 5(b), (c) or (d) of Schedule 3 to the Act (other than one falling within paragraph (ii) above);

     (iv) the National Savings Bank;

     (v) a municipal bank, that is to say a company which was, immediately before the coming into force of this article, exempt from the prohibition in section 3 of the Banking Act 1987 by virtue of section 4(1) of, and paragraph 4 of Schedule 2 to, that Act;

     (vi) Keesler Federal Credit Union;

     (vii) a body of persons certified as a school bank by the National Savings Bank or by an authorised person who has permission to accept deposits;

     (viii) a local authority;

     (xi) any body which by virtue of any enactment has power to issue a precept to a local authority in England and Wales or a requisition to a local authority in Scotland, or to the expenses of which, by virtue of any enactment, a local authority in the United Kingdom is or can be required to contribute (and in this paragraph, "enactment" includes an enactment comprised in, or in an instrument made under, an Act of the Scottish Parliament);

     (x) the European Community, the European Atomic Energy Community or the European Coal and Steel Community;

     (xi) the European Investment Bank;

     (xii) the International Bank for Reconstruction and Development;

     (xiii) the International Finance Corporation;

     (xiv) the International Monetary Fund;

     (xv) the African Development Bank;

     (xvi) the Asian Development Bank;

     (xvii) the Caribbean Development Bank;

     (xviii) the Inter-American Development Bank;

     (xix) the European Bank for Reconstruction and Development;

     [(xx) the Council of Europe Development Bank;]

   (b)   paid by a person other than one mentioned in sub-paragraph (a) in the course of carrying on a business consisting wholly or to a significant extent of lending money;

   (c)   paid by one company to another at a time when both are members of the same group or when the same individual is a majority shareholder controller of both of them; or

   (d)   paid by a person who, at the time when it is paid, is a close relative of the person receiving it or who is, or is a close relative of, a director or manager of that person or who is, or is a close relative of, a controller of that person.

(2)   For the purposes of paragraph (1)(c), an individual is a majority shareholder controller of a company if he is a controller of the company by virtue of paragraph (a), (c), (e) or (g) of section 422(2) of the Act, and if in his case the greatest percentage of those referred to in those paragraphs is 50 or more.

(3)   In the application of sub-paragraph (d) of paragraph (1) to a sum paid by a partnership, that sub-paragraph is to have effect as if, for the reference to the person paying the sum, there were substituted a reference to each of the partners.

[705]

NOTES

Para (1): sub-para (a)(xx) substituted by the Financial Services and Markets Act 2000 (Financial Promotion and Miscellaneous Amendments) Order 2002, SI 2002/1310, art 4(1), as from 5 June 2002.

---

7   Sums received by solicitors etc

(1)   A sum is not a deposit for the purposes of article 5 if it is received by a practising solicitor acting in the course of his profession.

(2)   In paragraph (1), "practising solicitor" means—

   (a)   a solicitor who is qualified to act as such under section 1 of the Solicitors Act 1974, article 4 of the Solicitors (Northern Ireland) Order 1976 or section 4 of the Solicitors (Scotland) Act 1980;

   (b)   a recognised body;

(c) a registered foreign lawyer in the course of providing professional services as a member of a multi-national partnership;

(d) a registered European lawyer; or

(e) a partner of a registered European lawyer who is providing professional services in accordance with—

    (i) rules made under section 31 of the Solicitors Act 1974;

    (ii) regulations made under article 26 of the Solicitors (Northern Ireland) Order 1976; or

    (iii) rules made under section 34 of the Solicitors (Scotland) Act 1980.

(3) In this article—

(a) "a recognised body" means a body ... recognised by—

    (i) the Council of the Law Society under section 9 of the Administration of Justice Act 1985;

    (ii) the Incorporated Law Society of Northern Ireland under article 26A of the Solicitors (Northern Ireland) Order 1976; or

    (iii) the Council of the Law Society of Scotland under section 34 of the Solicitors (Scotland) Act 1980;

(b) "registered foreign lawyer" has the meaning given by section 89 of the Courts and Legal Services Act 1990 or, in Scotland, section 65 of the Solicitors (Scotland) Act 1980;

(c) "multi-national partnership" has the meaning given by section 89 of the Courts and Legal Services Act 1990 but, in Scotland, is a reference to a "multi-national practice" within the meaning of section 60A of the Solicitors (Scotland) Act 1980; and

(d) "registered European lawyer" has the meaning given by regulation 2(1) of the European Communities (Lawyer's Practice) Regulations 2000 or regulation 2(1) of the European Communities (Lawyer's Practice) (Scotland) Regulation 2000.

[706]

NOTES

Para (3): word omitted from definition "a recognised body" revoked by the Solicitors' Recognised Bodies (Amendment) Order 2009, SI 2009/500, art 3, as from 31 March 2009.

8 Sums received by persons authorised to deal etc

A sum is not a deposit for the purposes of article 5 if it is received by a person who is—

(a) an authorised person with permission to carry on an activity of the kind specified by any of articles 14, 21, 25, 37, 51 and 52, or

(b) an exempt person in relation to any such activity,

in the course of, or for the purpose of, [carrying on any such activity (or any activity which would be such an activity but for any exclusion made by this Part)] with or on behalf of the person by or on behalf of whom the sum is paid.

[707]

NOTES

Words in square brackets substituted by the Financial Services and Markets Act 2000 (Regulated Activities) (Amendment) Order 2001, SI 2001/3544, arts 2, 3, as from 1 December 2001.

9 Sums received in consideration for the issue of debt securities

(1) Subject to paragraph (2), a sum is not a deposit for the purposes of article 5 if it is received by a person as consideration for the issue by him of any investment of the kind specified by article 77 or 78.

(2) The exclusion in paragraph (1) does not apply to the receipt by a person of a sum as consideration for the issue by him of commercial paper unless—

(a) the commercial paper is issued to persons—

    (i) whose ordinary activities involve them in acquiring, holding, managing or disposing of investments (as principal or agent) for the purposes of their businesses; or

    (ii) who it is reasonable to expect will acquire, hold, manage or dispose of investments (as principal or agent) for the purposes of their businesses; and

(b) the redemption value of the commercial paper is not less than £100,000 (or an amount of equivalent value denominated wholly or partly in a currency other than sterling), and no part of the commercial paper may be transferred unless the redemption value of that part is not less than £100,000 (or such an equivalent amount).

[(3) In paragraph (2), "commercial paper" means an investment of the kind specified by article 77 or 78 having a maturity of less than one year from the date of issue.]

[708]

NOTES
    Para (3): substituted by the Financial Services and Markets Act 2000 (Regulated Activities) (Amendment) Order 2002, SI 2002/682, art 12, as from 27 April 2002.

[9A   Sums received in exchange for electronic money

A sum is not a deposit for the purposes of article 5 if it is immediately exchanged for electronic money.]

[709]

NOTES
    Inserted by the Financial Services and Markets Act 2000 (Regulated Activities) (Amendment) Order 2002, SI 2002/682, art 3(2), as from 27 April 2002, subject to transitional provisions in relation to persons issuing electronic money immediately before that date contained in art 9.

[9AA   Information society services

Article 5 is subject to the exclusion in article 72A (information society services).]

[710]

NOTES
    Inserted by the Financial Services and Markets Act 2000 (Regulated Activities) (Amendment) (No 2) Order 2002, SI 2002/1776, art 3(1), (2), as from 21 August 2002.

[9AB   Funds received for payment services

    (1)   A sum is not a deposit for the purposes of article 5 if it is received by an authorised payment institution, an EEA authorised payment institution or a small payment institution from a payment service user with a view to the provision of payment services.

    (2)   For the purposes of paragraph (1), "authorised payment institution", "EEA authorised payment institution", "small payment institution", "payment services" and "payment service user" have the meanings given in the Payment Services Regulations 2009.]

[711]

NOTES
    Commencement: 1 November 2009.
    Inserted by the Payment Services Regulations 2009, SI 2009/209, reg 126, Sch 6, Pt 2, para 4(a), as from 1 November 2009 (for the full commencement details of the 2009 Regulations, see reg 1 of those Regulations at **[1127]**).

[CHAPTER IIA
ELECTRONIC MONEY

The activity

9B   Issuing electronic money

Issuing electronic money is a specified kind of activity.]

[712]

NOTES
    Inserted, together with arts 9C–9K and the preceding heading, by the Financial Services and Markets Act 2000 (Regulated Activities) (Amendment) Order 2002, SI 2002/682, art 4, as from 27 April 2002, subject to transitional provisions in relation to persons issuing electronic money immediately before that date contained in art 9.

[Exclusions

9C   Persons certified as small issuers etc

    (1)   There is excluded from article 9B the issuing of electronic money by a person to whom the Authority has given a certificate under this article (provided the certificate has not been revoked).

    (2)   An application for a certificate may be made by—
        (a)   a body corporate, or
        (b)   a partnership,
(other than a credit institution as defined in [Article 4(1)(a)] of the banking consolidation directive) which has its head office in the United Kingdom.

    (3)   The authority must, on the application of such a person ("A"), give A a certificate if it appears to the Authority that paragraph (4), (5) or (6) applies.

    (4)   This paragraph applies if—

(a)   A does not issue electronic money except on terms that the electronic device on which the monetary value is stored is subject to a maximum storage amount of not more than 150 euro; and

(b)   A's total liabilities with respect to the issuing of electronic money do not (or will not) usually exceed 5 million euro and do not (or will not) ever exceed 6 million euro.

(5)   This paragraph applies if—
(a)   the condition in paragraph (4)(a) is met;
(b)   A's total liabilities with respect to the issuing of electronic money do not (or will not) exceed 10 million euro; and
(c)   electronic money issued by A is accepted as a means of payment only by—
      (i)   subsidiaries of A which perform operational or other ancillary functions related to electronic money issued or distributed by A; or
      (ii)   other members of the same group as A (other than subsidiaries of A).

(6)   This paragraph applies if—
(a)   the conditions in paragraphs (4)(a) and (5)(b) are met; and
(b)   electronic money issued by A is accepted as a means of payment, in the course of business, by not more than one hundred persons where—
      (i)   those persons accept such electronic money only at locations within the same premises or limited local area; or
      (ii)   those persons have a close financial or business relationship with A, such as a common marketing or distribution scheme.

(7)   For the purposes of paragraph (6)(b)(i), locations are to be treated as situated within the same premises or limited local area if they are situated within—
(a)   a shopping centre, airport, railway station, bus station, or campus of a university, polytechnic, college, school or similar educational establishment; or
(b)   an area which does not exceed four square kilometres;

but sub-paragraphs (a) and (b) are illustrative only and are not to be treated as limiting the scope of paragraph (6)(b)(i).

(8)   For the purposes of paragraph (6)(b)(ii), persons are not to be treated as having a close financial or business relationship with A merely because they participate in arrangements for the acceptance of electronic money issued by A.

(9)   In this article, references to amounts in euro include references to equivalent amounts in sterling.

(10)   A person to whom a certificate has been given under this article (and whose certificate has not been revoked) is referred to in this Chapter as a "certified person".]

[713]

NOTES
Inserted as noted to art 9B at **[712]**.
Para (2): words in square brackets substituted the Capital Requirements Regulations 2006, SI 2006/3221, reg 29(4), Sch 6, para 6(1), (2), as from 1 January 2007.

[9D   Applications for certificates
The following provisions of the Act apply to applications to the Authority for certificates under 9C (and the determination of such applications) as they apply to applications for Part IV permissions (and the determination of such applications)—
(a)   section 51(1)(b) and (3) to (6);
(b)   section 52, except subsections (6), (8) and (9)(a) and (b); and
(c)   section 55(1).]

[714]

NOTES
Inserted as noted to art 9B at **[712]**.

[9E   Revocation of certificate on Authority's own initiative
(1)   The Authority may revoke a certificate given to a person ("A") under article 9C if—
(a)   it appears to it that A does not meet the relevant conditions, or has failed to meet the relevant conditions at any time since the certificate was given; or
(b)   the person to whom the certificate was given has contravened any rule or requirement to which he is subject as a result of article 9G.

(2)   For the purposes of paragraph (1), A meets the relevant conditions at any time if, at that time, paragraph (4), (5) or (6) of article 9C applies.

(3)   Sections 54 and 55(2) of the Act apply to the revocation of a certificate under paragraph (1) as they apply to the cancellation of a Part IV permission on the Authority's own initiative, as if references in those sections to an authorised person were references to a certified person.]

[715]

NOTES
Inserted as noted to art 9B at **[712]**.

[9F   Revocation of certificate on request

(1)   A certified person ("B") may apply to the Authority for his certificate to be revoked, and the Authority must then revoke the certificate and give B written notice that it has done so.

(2)   An application under paragraph (1) must be made in such manner as the Authority may direct.

(3)   If—
  (a)   B has made an application under Part IV of the Act for permission to carry on a regulated activity of the kind specified by article 9B (or for variation of an existing permission so as to add a regulated activity of that kind), and
  (b)   on making an application for revocation of his certificate under paragraph (1), he requests that the revocation be conditional on the granting of his application under Part IV of the Act,

the revocation of B's certificate is to be conditional on the granting of his application under Part IV of the Act.]

[716]

NOTES
Inserted as noted to art 9B at **[712]**.

[9G   Obtaining information from certified persons etc

(1)   The Authority may make rules requiring certified persons to provide information to the Authority about their activities so far as relating to the issuing of electronic money, including the amount of their liabilities with respect to the issuing of electronic money.

(2)   Section 148 of the Act (modification or waiver of rules) applies in relation to rules made under paragraph (1) as if references in that section to an authorised person were references to a certified person.

(3)   Section 150 of the Act (actions for damages) applies in relation to a rule made under paragraph (1) as if the reference in subsection (1) of that section to an authorised person were a reference to a certified person.

(4)   The Authority may, by notice in writing given to a certified person, require him—
  (a)   to provide specified information or information of a specified description; or
  (b)   to produce specified documents or documents of a specified description.

(5)   Paragraph (4) applies only to information or documents reasonably required for the purposes of determining whether the certified person meets, or has met, the relevant conditions.

(6)   Subsections (2), (5) and (6) of section 165 of the Act (Authority's power to require information) apply to a requirement imposed under paragraph (4) as they apply to a requirement imposed under that section.

(7)   Section 166 of the Act (reports by skilled persons) has effect as if—
  (a)   the reference in subsection (1) of that section to section 165 included a reference to paragraph (4) above; and
  (b)   the reference in section 166(2)(a) of the Act to an authorised person included a reference to a certified person.

(8)   Subsection (4) of section 168 of the Act (appointment of persons to carry out investigations in particular cases) has effect as if it provided for subsection (5) of that section to apply if it appears to the Authority that there are circumstances suggesting that a certified person may not meet, or may not have met, the relevant conditions.

(9)   Sections 175 (information and documents: supplemental provisions), 176 (entry of premises under warrant) and 177 (offences) of the Act apply to a requirement imposed under paragraph (4) as they apply to a requirement imposed under section 165 of the Act (the reference in section 176(3)(a) to an authorised person being read as a reference to a certified person).

(10)   In this article—
  (a)   "specified", in paragraph (4), means specified in the notice mentioned in that paragraph;
  (b)   a certified person ("A") meets the relevant conditions at any time if, at that time, paragraph (4), (5) or (6) of article 9C applies.]

[717]

NOTES
Inserted as noted to art 9B at **[712]**.

[Supplemental

9H   Rules prohibiting the issue of electronic money at a discount

(1)   The Authority may make rules applying to authorised persons with permission to carry on an activity of the kind specified by article 9B, prohibiting the issue of electronic money having a monetary value greater than the funds received.

(2)   Section 148 of the Act (modification or waiver of rules) applies in relation to rules made under paragraph (1).]

[718]

NOTES
Inserted as noted to art 9B at **[712]**.

[9I   False claims to be a certified person

A person who is not a certified person is to be treated as guilty of an offence under section 24 of the Act (false claims to be authorised or exempt) if he—
   (a)   describes himself (in whatever terms) as a certified person;
   (b)   behaves, or otherwise holds himself out, in a manner which indicates (or which is reasonably likely to be understood as indicating) that he is a certified person.]

[719]

NOTES
Inserted as noted to art 9B at **[712]**.

[9J   Exclusion of electronic money from the compensation scheme

The compensation scheme established under Part XV of the Act is not to provide for the compensation of persons in respect of claims made in connection with any activity of the kind specified by article 9B.]

[720]

NOTES
Inserted as noted to art 9B at **[712]**.

[9K   Record of certified persons

The record maintained by the Authority under section 347 of the Act (public record of authorised persons etc) must include every certified person.]

[721]

NOTES
Inserted as noted to art 9B at **[712]**.

[9L   Funds received for payment services

(1)   Any funds are not to be treated as electronic money for the purposes of this Order if they are received by an authorised payment institution, an EEA authorised payment institution or a small payment institution from a payment service user with a view to the provision of payment services.

(2)   For the purposes of paragraph (1), "authorised payment institution", "EEA authorised payment institution", "small payment institution", "payment services" and "payment service user" have the meanings given in the Payment Services Regulations 2009.]

[722]

NOTES
Commencement: 1 November 2009.
Inserted by the Payment Services Regulations 2009, SI 2009/209, reg 126, Sch 6, Pt 2, para 4(b), as from 1 November 2009 (for the full commencement details of the 2009 Regulations, see reg 1 of those Regulations at **[1127]**).

CHAPTER III
INSURANCE

The activities

10 Effecting and carrying out contracts of insurance

(1)   Effecting a contract of insurance as principal is a specified kind of activity.

(2)   Carrying out a contract of insurance as principal is a specified kind of activity.

[723]

Exclusions

11 Community co-insurers

(1)   There is excluded from article 10(1) or (2) the effecting or carrying out of a contract of insurance by an EEA firm falling within paragraph 5(d) of Schedule 3 to the Act—

    (a)   other than through a branch in the United Kingdom; and

    (b)   pursuant to a Community co-insurance operation in which the firm is participating otherwise than as the leading insurer.

(2)   In paragraph (1), "Community co-insurance operation" and "leading insurer" have the same meaning as in the Council Directive of 30 May 1978 on the co-ordination of laws, regulations and administrative provisions relating to Community co-insurance (No 78/473/EEC).

[724]

12 Breakdown insurance

(1)   There is excluded from article 10(1) or (2) the effecting or carrying out, by a person who does not otherwise carry on an activity of the kind specified by that article, of a contract of insurance which—

    (a)   is a contract under which the benefits provided by that person ("the provider") are exclusively or primarily benefits in kind in the event of accident to or breakdown of a vehicle; and

    (b)   contains the terms mentioned in paragraph (2).

(2)   Those terms are that—

    (a)   the assistance takes either or both of the forms mentioned in paragraph (3)(a) and (b);

    (b)   the assistance is not available outside the United Kingdom and the Republic of Ireland except where it is provided without the payment of additional premium by a person in the country concerned with whom the provider has entered into a reciprocal agreement; and

    (c)   assistance provided in the case of an accident or breakdown occurring in the United Kingdom or the Republic of Ireland is, in most circumstances, provided by the provider's servants.

(3)   The forms of assistance are—

    (a)   repairs to the relevant vehicle at the place where the accident or breakdown has occurred; this assistance may also include the delivery of parts, fuel, oil, water or keys to the relevant vehicle;

    (b)   removal of the relevant vehicle to the nearest or most appropriate place at which repairs may be carried out, or to—

        (i)   the home, point of departure or original destination within the United Kingdom of the driver and passengers, provided the accident or breakdown occurred within the United Kingdom;

        (ii)   the home, point of departure or original destination within the Republic of Ireland of the driver and passengers, provided the accident or breakdown occurred within the Republic of Ireland or within Northern Ireland;

        (iii)   the home, point of departure or original destination within Northern Ireland of the driver and passengers, provided the accident or breakdown occurred within the Republic of Ireland;

    and this form of assistance may include the conveyance of the driver or passengers of the relevant vehicle, with the vehicle, or (where the vehicle is to be conveyed only to the nearest or most appropriate place at which repairs may be carried out) separately, to the nearest location from which they may continue their journey by other means.

(4)   A contract does not fail to meet the condition in paragraph (1)(a) solely because the provider may reimburse the person entitled to the assistance for all or part of any sums paid by him in respect of assistance either because he failed to identify himself as a person entitled to the assistance or because he was unable to get in touch with the provider in order to claim the assistance.

(5)   In this article—

"the assistance" means the benefits to be provided under a contract of the kind mentioned in paragraph (1);

"breakdown" means an event—

   (a)   which causes the driver of the relevant vehicle to be unable to start a journey in the vehicle or involuntarily to bring the vehicle to a halt on a journey because of some malfunction of the vehicle or failure of it to function, and

   (b)   after which the journey cannot reasonably be commenced or continued in the relevant vehicle;

"the relevant vehicle" means the vehicle (including a trailer or caravan) in respect of which the assistance is required.

[725]

[12A   Information society services

Article 10 is subject to the exclusion in article 72A (information society services), as qualified by paragraph (2) of that article.]

[726]

NOTES

Inserted by the Financial Services and Markets Act 2000 (Regulated Activities) (Amendment) (No 2) Order 2002, SI 2002/1776, art 3(1), (3), as from 21 August 2002.

Supplemental

13   Application of sections 327 and 332 of the Act to insurance market activities

(1)   In sections 327(5) and (7) and 332(3)(b) of the Act (exemption from the general prohibition for members of the professions, and rules in relation to such persons), the references to "a regulated activity" and "regulated activities" do not include—

   (a)   any activity of the kind specified by article 10(1) or (2), where—

      (i)   P is a member of the Society; and

      (ii)   by virtue of section 316 of the Act (application of the Act to Lloyd's underwriting), the general prohibition does not apply to the carrying on by P of that activity; or

   (b)   any activity of the kind specified by article 10(2), where—

      (i)   P is a former underwriting member; and

      (ii)   the contract of insurance in question is one underwritten by P at Lloyd's.

(2)   In paragraph (1)—

"member of the Society" has the same meaning as in Lloyd's Act 1982; and

"former underwriting member" has the meaning given by section 324(1) of the Act.

[727]

CHAPTER IV
DEALING IN INVESTMENTS AS PRINCIPAL

The activity

14   Dealing in investments as principal

[(1)]   Buying, selling, subscribing for or underwriting securities or contractually based investments (other than investments of the kind specified by article 87, or article 89 so far as relevant to that article) as principal is a specified kind of activity.

[(2)   Paragraph (1) does not apply to a kind of activity to which article 25D applies.]

[728]

NOTES

Para (1) numbered as such, and para (2) added, by the Financial Services and Markets Act 2000 (Regulated Activities) (Amendment No 3) Order 2006, SI 2006/3384, arts 2, 5, as from 1 April 2007 (for the purposes of enabling applications to be made for (i) a Pt IV permission, (ii) a variation of a Pt IV permission, and (iii) the Authority's approval under s 59 of the 2000 Act, in relation to an activity of the kind specified by art 25D of this Order, or in relation to an investment of the kind specified by arts 83, 84 or 85 of this Order), and as from 1 November 2007 (otherwise).

See the Financial Services and Markets Act 2000 (Carrying on Regulated Activities by Way of Business) Order 2001, SI 2001/1177, art 3 in relation to investment business.

Exclusions

15   Absence of holding out etc

(1)   Subject to paragraph (3), a person ("A") does not carry on an activity of the kind specified by article 14 by entering into a transaction which relates to a security or is the assignment (or, in

Scotland, the assignation) of a qualifying contract of insurance (or an investment of the kind specified by article 89, so far as relevant to such a contract), unless—

    (a)   A holds himself out as willing, as principal, to buy, sell or subscribe for investments of the kind to which the transaction relates at prices determined by him generally and continuously rather than in respect of each particular transaction;

    (b)   A holds himself out as engaging in the business of buying investments of the kind to which the transaction relates, with a view to selling them;

    (c)   A holds himself out as engaging in the business of underwriting investments of the kind to which the transaction relates; or

    (d)   A regularly solicits members of the public with the purpose of inducing them, as principals or agents, to enter into transactions constituting activities of the kind specified by article 14, and the transaction is entered into as a result of his having solicited members of the public in that manner.

(2)   In paragraph (1)(d), "members of the public" means any persons other than—

    (a)   authorised persons or persons who are exempt persons in relation to activities of the kind specified by article 14;

    (b)   members of the same group as A;

    (c)   persons who are or who propose to become participators with A in a joint enterprise;

    (d)   any person who is solicited by A with a view to the acquisition by A of 20 per cent or more of the voting shares in a body corporate;

    (e)   if A (either alone or with members of the same group as himself) holds more than 20 per cent of the voting shares in a body corporate, any person who is solicited by A with a view to—

        (i)   the acquisition by A of further shares in the body corporate; or

        (ii)   the disposal by A of shares in the body corporate to the person solicited or to a member of the same group as the person solicited;

    (f)   any person who—

        (i)   is solicited by A with a view to the disposal by A of shares in a body corporate to the person solicited or to a member of the same group as that person; and

        (ii)   either alone or with members of the same group holds 20 per cent or more of the voting shares in the body corporate;

    (g)   any person whose head office is outside the United Kingdom, who is solicited by an approach made or directed to him at a place outside the United Kingdom and whose ordinary business involves him in carrying on activities of the kind specified by any of articles 14, 21, 25, 37, 40, 45, 51, 52 and 53 or (so far as relevant to any of those articles) article 64, or would do so apart from any exclusion from any of those articles made by this Order.

(3)   This article does not apply where A enters into the transaction as bare trustee or, in Scotland, as nominee for another person and is acting on that other person's instructions (but the exclusion in article 66(1) applies if the conditions set out there are met).

    [(4)   This article is subject to article 4(4).]

[729]

NOTES

Para (4): added by the Financial Services and Markets Act 2000 (Regulated Activities) (Amendment No 3) Order 2006, SI 2006/3384, arts 2, 6, as from 1 April 2007 (for the purposes of enabling applications to be made for (i) a Pt IV permission, (ii) a variation of a Pt IV permission, and (iii) the Authority's approval under s 59 of the 2000 Act, in relation to an activity of the kind specified by art 25D of this Order, or in relation to an investment of the kind specified by arts 83, 84 or 85 of this Order), and as from 1 November 2007 (otherwise).

---

16   Dealing in contractually based investments

    [(1)]   A person who is not an authorised person does not carry on an activity of the kind specified by article 14 by entering into a transaction relating to a contractually based investment—

    (a)   with or through an authorised person, or an exempt person acting in the course of a business comprising a regulated activity in relation to which he is exempt; or

    (b)   through an office outside the United Kingdom maintained by a party to the transaction, and with or through a person whose head office is situated outside the United Kingdom and whose ordinary business involves him in carrying on activities of the kind specified by any of articles 14, 21, 25, 37, 40, 45, 51, 52 and 53 or, so far as relevant to any of those articles, article 64 (or would do so apart from any exclusion from any of those articles made by this Order).

    [(2)   This article is subject to article 4(4).]

[730]

PART IV
OTHER STATUTORY INSTRUMENTS

NOTES

Para (1) numbered as such, and para (2) added, by the Financial Services and Markets Act 2000 (Regulated Activities) (Amendment No 3) Order 2006, SI 2006/3384, arts 2, 7, as from 1 April 2007 (for the purposes of enabling applications to be made for (i) a Pt IV permission, (ii) a variation of a Pt IV permission, and (iii) the Authority's approval under s 59 of the 2000 Act, in relation to an activity of the kind specified by art 25D of this Order, or in relation to an investment of the kind specified by arts 83, 84 or 85 of this Order), and as from 1 November 2007 (otherwise).

17 Acceptance of instruments creating or acknowledging indebtedness

(1) A person does not carry on an activity of the kind specified by article 14 by accepting an instrument creating or acknowledging indebtedness in respect of any loan, credit, guarantee or other similar financial accommodation or assurance which he has made, granted or provided.

(2) The reference in paragraph (1) to a person accepting an instrument includes a reference to a person becoming a party to an instrument otherwise than as a debtor or a surety.

[731]

NOTES
Modification: references in para (1) to securities, instruments or investments creating or acknowledging indebtedness (or creating or acknowledging a present or future indebtedness) includes a reference to uncertificated units of eligible debt securities; see the Uncertificated Securities (Amendment) (Eligible Debt Securities) Regulations 2003, SI 2003/1633, reg 15, Sch 2, para 8 (as from 24 June 2003).
Modification: references in para (2) to a person becoming party to an instrument includes a reference to a person assuming rights and obligations in respect of uncertificated units of an eligible debt security in accordance with its current terms of issue; see the Uncertificated Securities (Amendment) (Eligible Debt Securities) Regulations 2003, SI 2003/1633, reg 15, Sch 2, para 9 (as from 24 June 2003).

18 Issue by a company of its own shares etc

(1) There is excluded from article 14 the issue by a company of its own shares or share warrants, and the issue by any person of his own debentures or debenture warrants.

(2) In this article—
    (a) "company" means any body corporate other than an open-ended investment company;
    (b) "shares" and "debentures" include any investment of the kind specified by article 76 or 77;
    (c) "share warrants" and "debenture warrants" mean any investment of the kind specified by article 79 which relates to shares in the company concerned or, as the case may be, debentures issued by [the person concerned].

[732]

NOTES
Para (2): words in square brackets substituted by the Financial Services and Markets Act 2000 (Regulated Activities) (Amendment) Order 2001, SI 2001/3544, arts 2, 4, as from 1 December 2001.

[18A Dealing by a company in its own shares

(1) A company does not carry on an activity of the kind specified by article 14 by purchasing its own shares where section 162A of the Companies Act 1985 (Treasury shares) applies to the shares purchased.

(2) A company does not carry on an activity of the kind specified by article 14 by dealing in its own shares held as treasury shares, in accordance with section 162D of that Act (Treasury shares: disposal and cancellation).

(3) In this article "shares held as treasury shares" has the same meaning as in that Act.]

[733]

NOTES
Inserted by the Financial Services and Markets Act 2000 (Regulated Activities) (Amendment) (No 3) Order 2003, SI 2003/2822, arts 2, 3, as from 1 December 2003.

19 Risk management

(1) A person ("B") does not carry on an activity of the kind specified by article 14 by entering as principal into a transaction with another person ("C") if—
    (a) the transaction relates to investments of the kind specified by any of articles 83 to 85 (or article 89 so far as relevant to any of those articles);
    (b) neither B nor C is an individual;
    (c) the sole or main purpose for which B enters into the transaction (either by itself or in combination with other such transactions) is that of limiting the extent to which a relevant business will be affected by any identifiable risk arising otherwise than as a result of the carrying on of a regulated activity; and
    (d) the relevant business consists mainly of activities other than—
        (i) regulated activities; or

      (ii)   activities which would be regulated activities but for any exclusion made by this Part.

(2)   In paragraph (1), "relevant business" means a business carried on by—

    (a)   B;

    (b)   a member of the same group as B; or

    (c)   where B and another person are, or propose to become, participators in a joint enterprise, that other person.

[(3)   This article is subject to article 4(4).]

[734]

NOTES

Para (3): added by the Financial Services and Markets Act 2000 (Regulated Activities) (Amendment No 3) Order 2006, SI 2006/3384, arts 2, 8, as from 1 April 2007 (for the purposes of enabling applications to be made for (i) a Pt IV permission, (ii) a variation of a Pt IV permission, and (iii) the Authority's approval under s 59 of the 2000 Act, in relation to an activity of the kind specified by art 25D of this Order, or in relation to an investment of the kind specified by arts 83, 84 or 85 of this Order), and as from 1 November 2007 (otherwise).

20 Other exclusions

Article 14 is also subject to the exclusions in articles 66 (trustees etc), 68 (sale of goods and supply of services), 69 (groups and joint enterprises), 70 (sale of body corporate), 71 (employee share schemes)[, 72 (overseas persons) and 72A (information society services)].

[735]

NOTES

Words in square brackets substituted by the Financial Services and Markets Act 2000 (Regulated Activities) (Amendment) (No 2) Order 2002, SI 2002/1776, art 3(1), (4), as from 21 August 2002.

CHAPTER V
DEALING IN INVESTMENTS AS AGENT

The activity

21 Dealing in investments as agent

[(1)]   Buying, selling, subscribing for or underwriting securities or [relevant investments] (other than investments of the kind specified by article 87, or article 89 so far as relevant to that article) as agent is a specified kind of activity.

[(2)   Paragraph (1) does not apply to a kind of activity to which article 25D applies.]

[736]

NOTES

Para (1) numbered as such, and para (2) added, by the Financial Services and Markets Act 2000 (Regulated Activities) (Amendment No 3) Order 2006, SI 2006/3384, arts 2, 9, as from 1 April 2007 (for the purposes of enabling applications to be made for (i) a Pt IV permission, (ii) a variation of a Pt IV permission, and (iii) the Authority's approval under s 59 of the 2000 Act, in relation to an activity of the kind specified by art 25D of this Order, or in relation to an investment of the kind specified by arts 83, 84 or 85 of this Order), and as from 1 November 2007 (otherwise).

Words in square brackets in para (1) substituted by the Financial Services and Markets Act 2000 (Regulated Activities) (Amendment) (No 2) Order 2003, SI 2003/1476, art 4(1), as from 31 October 2004 (in so far as relating to contracts of long-term care insurance), and as from 14 January 2005 (otherwise), for transitional provisions see arts 22–27 of that Order.

See the Financial Services and Markets Act 2000 (Carrying on Regulated Activities by Way of Business) Order 2001, SI 2001/1177, art 3 in relation to investment business.

Exclusions

22 Deals with or through authorised persons

(1)   A person who is not an authorised person does not carry on an activity of the kind specified by article 21 by entering into a transaction as agent for another person ("the client") with or through an authorised person if—

    (a)   the transaction is entered into on advice given to the client by an authorised person; or

    (b)   it is clear, in all the circumstances, that the client, in his capacity as an investor, is not seeking and has not sought advice from the agent as to the merits of the client's entering into the transaction (or, if the client has sought such advice, the agent has declined to give it but has recommended that the client seek such advice from an authorised person).

[(2)   But the exclusion in paragraph (1) does not apply if—

    (a)   the transaction relates to a contract of insurance; or

(b) the agent receives from any person other than the client any pecuniary reward or other advantage, for which he does not account to the client, arising out of his entering into the transaction.]

[(3) This article is subject to article 4(4).]

[737]

NOTES
Para (2): substituted by the Financial Services and Markets Act 2000 (Regulated Activities) (Amendment) (No 2) Order 2003, SI 2003/1476, art 4(2), as from 31 October 2004 (in so far as relating to contracts of long-term care insurance), and as from 14 January 2005 (otherwise), for transitional provisions see arts 22–27 of that Order.
Para (3): added by the Financial Services and Markets Act 2000 (Regulated Activities) (Amendment No 3) Order 2006, SI 2006/3384, arts 2, 10, as from 1 April 2007 (for the purposes of enabling applications to be made for (i) a Pt IV permission, (ii) a variation of a Pt IV permission, and (iii) the Authority's approval under s 59 of the 2000 Act, in relation to an activity of the kind specified by art 25D of this Order, or in relation to an investment of the kind specified by arts 83, 84 or 85 of this Order), and as from 1 November 2007 (otherwise).

23 Risk management

(1) A person ("B") does not carry on an activity of the kind specified by article 21 by entering as agent for a relevant person into a transaction with another person ("C") if—
  (a) the transaction relates to investments of the kind specified by any of articles 83 to 85 (or article 89 so far as relevant to any of those articles);
  (b) neither B nor C is an individual;
  (c) the sole or main purpose for which B enters into the transaction (either by itself or in combination with other such transactions) is that of limiting the extent to which a relevant business will be affected by any identifiable risk arising otherwise than as a result of the carrying on of a regulated activity; and
  (d) the relevant business consists mainly of activities other than—
    (i) regulated activities; or
    (ii) activities which would be regulated activities but for any exclusion made by this Part.

(2) In paragraph (1), "relevant person" means—
  (a) a member of the same group as B; or
  (b) where B and another person are, or propose to become, participators in a joint enterprise, that other person;
and "relevant business" means a business carried on by a relevant person.

[(3) This article is subject to article 4(4).]

[738]

NOTES
Para (3): added by the Financial Services and Markets Act 2000 (Regulated Activities) (Amendment No 3) Order 2006, SI 2006/3384, arts 2, 11, as from 1 April 2007 (for the purposes of enabling applications to be made for (i) a Pt IV permission, (ii) a variation of a Pt IV permission, and (iii) the Authority's approval under s 59 of the 2000 Act, in relation to an activity of the kind specified by art 25D of this Order, or in relation to an investment of the kind specified by arts 83, 84 or 85 of this Order), and as from 1 November 2007 (otherwise).

24 Other exclusions

Article 21 is also subject to the exclusions in articles 67 (profession or non-investment business), 68 (sale of goods and supply of services), 69 (groups and joint enterprises), 70 (sale of body corporate), 71 (employee share schemes)[, 72 (overseas persons)[, 72A (information society services), 72B (activities carried on by a provider of relevant goods or services) and 72D (large risks contracts where risk situated outside the EEA)]].

[739]

NOTES
Words in first (outer) pair of square brackets substituted by the Financial Services and Markets Act 2000 (Regulated Activities) (Amendment) (No 2) Order 2002, SI 2002/1776, art 3(1), (5), as from 21 August 2002; words in second (inner) pair of square brackets substituted by the Financial Services and Markets Act 2000 (Regulated Activities) (Amendment) (No 2) Order 2003, SI 2003/1476, art 4(3), as from 31 October 2004 (in so far as relating to contracts of long-term care insurance), and as from 14 January 2005 (otherwise), for transitional provisions see arts 22–27 of that Order.

CHAPTER VI
ARRANGING DEALS IN INVESTMENTS

The activities

25   Arranging deals in investments

(1)   Making arrangements for another person (whether as principal or agent) to buy, sell, subscribe for or underwrite a particular investment which is—

(a)   a security,

(b)   a [relevant investment], or

(c)   an investment of the kind specified by article 86, or article 89 so far as relevant to that article,

is a specified kind of activity.

(2)   Making arrangements with a view to a person who participates in the arrangements buying, selling, subscribing for or underwriting investments falling within paragraph (1)(a), (b) or (c) (whether as principal or agent) is also a specified kind of activity.

[(3)   Paragraphs (1) and (2) do not apply to a kind of activity to which article 25D applies.]

[740]

NOTES

Para (1): words in square brackets substituted by the Financial Services and Markets Act 2000 (Regulated Activities) (Amendment) (No 2) Order 2003, SI 2003/1476, art 5(1), as from 31 October 2004 (in so far as relating to contracts of long-term care insurance), and as from 14 January 2005 (otherwise), for transitional provisions see arts 22–27 of that Order.

Para (3): added by the Financial Services and Markets Act 2000 (Regulated Activities) (Amendment No 3) Order 2006, SI 2006/3384, arts 2, 12, as from 1 April 2007 (for the purposes of enabling applications to be made for (i) a Pt IV permission, (ii) a variation of a Pt IV permission, and (iii) the Authority's approval under s 59 of the 2000 Act, in relation to an activity of the kind specified by art 25D of this Order, or in relation to an investment of the kind specified by arts 83, 84 or 85 of this Order), and as from 1 November 2007 (otherwise).

See the Financial Services and Markets Act 2000 (Carrying on Regulated Activities by Way of Business) Order 2001, SI 2001/1177, art 3 in relation to investment business, except in so far as that activity relates to investment of the kind specified by arts 86 or 89 of this order so far as relevant to that article.

[25A   Arranging regulated mortgage contracts

(1)   Making arrangements—

(a)   for another person to enter into a regulated mortgage contract as borrower; or

(b)   for another person to vary the terms of a regulated mortgage contract entered into by him as borrower after the coming into force of article 61, in such a way as to vary his obligations under that contract,

is a specified kind of activity.

(2)   Making arrangements with a view to a person who participates in the arrangements entering into a regulated mortgage contract as borrower is also a specified kind of activity.

(3)   In this article "borrower" has the meaning given by article 61(3)(a)(i).]

[741]

NOTES

Commencement: 31 October 2004.

Inserted by the Financial Services and Markets Act 2000 (Regulated Activities) (Amendment) (No 1) Order 2003, SI 2003/1475, art 4, as from 31 October 2004; for transitional provisions see arts 26–29 thereof.

See the Financial Services and Markets Act 2000 (Carrying on Regulated Activities by Way of Business) Order 2001, SI 2001/1177, art 3A.

[25B   Arranging regulated home reversion plans

(1)   Making arrangements—

(a)   for another person to enter into a regulated home reversion plan as reversion seller or as plan provider; or

(b)   for another person to vary the terms of a regulated home reversion plan, entered into on or after 6th April 2007 by him as reversion seller or as plan provider, in such a way as to vary his obligations under that plan,

is a specified kind of activity.

(2)   Making arrangements with a view to a person who participates in the arrangements entering into a regulated home reversion plan as reversion seller or as plan provider is also a specified kind of activity.]

[742]

NOTES

Commencement: 6 November 2006 (certain purposes); 6 April 2007 (otherwise) (see below).

Inserted, together with art 25C, by the Financial Services and Markets Act 2000 (Regulated Activities) (Amendment) (No 2) Order 2006, SI 2006/2383, arts 2, 4, as from 6 November 2006 (for the purposes of enabling applications to be made for (i) a Pt IV permission, or a variation of a Pt IV permission, in relation to activities of the kind specified by arts 25B, 25C, 53B, 53C, 63B or 63F or, so far as relevant to any such activity, art 64 of this Order; or (ii) the Authority's approval under FSMA 2000, s 59 in relation to any of those activities), and as from 6 April 2007 (otherwise) (for transitional provisions and effect see arts 36–40 of, and the Schedule to, the 2006 Order).

See the Financial Services and Markets Act 2000 (Carrying on Regulated Activities by Way of Business) Order 2001, SI 2001/1177, art 3B.

[25C Arranging regulated home purchase plans

(1) Making arrangements—
  (a) for another person to enter into a regulated home purchase plan as home purchaser; or
  (b) for another person to vary the terms of a regulated home purchase plan, entered into on or after 6th April 2007 by him as home purchaser, in such a way as to vary his obligations under that plan,

is a specified kind of activity.

(2) Making arrangements with a view to a person who participates in the arrangements entering into a regulated home purchase plan as home purchaser is also a specified kind of activity.]

[743]

NOTES

Commencement: 6 November 2006 (certain purposes); 6 April 2007 (otherwise).
Inserted as noted to art 25B at **[742]**.
See the Financial Services and Markets Act 2000 (Carrying on Regulated Activities by Way of Business) Order 2001, SI 2001/1177, art 3C.

[25D Operating a multilateral trading facility

(1) The operation of a multilateral trading facility on which MiFID instruments are traded is a specified kind of activity.

(2) In paragraph (1), "MiFID instrument" means any investment—
  (a) of the kind specified by article 76, 77, 78, 79, 80, 81, 83, 84 or 85; or
  (b) of the kind specified by article 89 so far as relevant to an investment falling within sub-paragraph (a),

that is a financial instrument.]

[744]

NOTES

Commencement: 1 April 2007 (certain purposes); 1 November 2007 (otherwise) (see below).
Inserted by the Financial Services and Markets Act 2000 (Regulated Activities) (Amendment No 3) Order 2006, SI 2006/3384, arts 2, 13, as from 1 April 2007 (for the purposes of enabling applications to be made for (i) a Pt IV permission, (ii) a variation of a Pt IV permission, and (iii) the Authority's approval under s 59 of the 2000 Act, in relation to an activity of the kind specified by art 25D of this Order, or in relation to an investment of the kind specified by arts 83, 84 or 85 of this Order), and as from 1 November 2007 (otherwise).
See the Financial Services and Markets Act 2000 (Carrying on Regulated Activities by Way of Business) Order 2001, SI 2001/1177, art 3 in relation to investment business.

[25E Arranging regulated sale and rent back agreements

(1) Making arrangements—
  (a) for another person to enter into a regulated sale and rent back agreement as an agreement seller or as an agreement provider; or
  (b) for another person ("A") to vary the terms of a regulated sale and rent back agreement, entered into on or after 1st July 2009 by A as agreement seller or agreement provider, in such a way as to vary A's obligations under that agreement,

is a specified kind of activity.

(2) Making arrangements with a view to a person who participates in the arrangements entering into a regulated sale and rent back agreement as agreement seller or agreement provider is also a specified kind of activity.]

[745]

NOTES

Commencement: 1 July 2009 (certain purposes); 30 June 2010 (otherwise) (see below).
Inserted by the Financial Services and Markets Act 2000 (Regulated Activities) (Amendment) Order 2009, SI 2009/1342, arts 2, 4, as from 1 July 2009 (other than for the purposes of enabling applications to be made for a Part IV permission, or a variation of a Part IV permission, in relation to activities of the kind specified by arts 25E, 53D or 63J or, so far as relevant to any such activity, art 64 of this Order), and as from 30 June 2010 (for those purposes) (for the full commencement details and for transitional provisions etc see arts 1, 32–34 of that Order).

Exclusions

26   Arrangements not causing a deal

There are excluded from [articles 25(1), 25A(1), 25B(1) *and 25C(1)*] arrangements which do not or would not bring about the transaction to which the arrangements relate.

[746]

NOTES
   Words in square brackets substituted by the Financial Services and Markets Act 2000 (Regulated Activities) (Amendment) (No 2) Order 2006, SI 2006/2383, arts 2, 5, as from 6 November 2006 (for the purposes of enabling applications to be made for (i) a Pt IV permission, or a variation of a Pt IV permission, in relation to activities of the kind specified by arts 25B, 25C, 53B, 53C, 63B or 63F or, so far as relevant to any such activity, art 64 of this Order; or (ii) the Authority's approval under FSMA 2000, s 59 in relation to any of those activities), and as from 6 April 2007 (otherwise) (for transitional provisions and effect see arts 36–40 of, and the Schedule to, the 2006 Order).
   For the words in italics there are substituted the words ", 25C(1) and 25E(1)" by the Financial Services and Markets Act 2000 (Regulated Activities) (Amendment) Order 2009, SI 2009/1342, arts 2, 5, as from 1 July 2009 (other than for the purposes of enabling applications to be made for a Part IV permission, or a variation of a Part IV permission, in relation to activities of the kind specified by arts 25E, 53D or 63J or, so far as relevant to any such activity, art 64 of this Order), and as from 30 June 2010 (for those purposes) (for the full commencement details and for transitional provisions etc see arts 1, 32–34 of that Order).

27   Enabling parties to communicate

A person does not carry on an activity of the kind specified by [article 25(2), 25A(2), 25B(2) *or 25C(2)*] merely by providing means by which one party to a transaction (or potential transaction) is able to communicate with other such parties.

[747]

NOTES
   Words in square brackets substituted by the Financial Services and Markets Act 2000 (Regulated Activities) (Amendment) (No 2) Order 2006, SI 2006/2383, arts 2, 6, as from 6 November 2006 (for the purposes of enabling applications to be made for (i) a Pt IV permission, or a variation of a Pt IV permission, in relation to activities of the kind specified by arts 25B, 25C, 53B, 53C, 63B or 63F or, so far as relevant to any such activity, art 64 of this Order; or (ii) the Authority's approval under FSMA 2000, s 59 in relation to any of those activities), and as from 6 April 2007 (otherwise) (for transitional provisions and effect see arts 36–40 of, and the Schedule to, the 2006 Order).
   For the words in italics there are substituted the words ", 25C(2) or 25E(2)" by the Financial Services and Markets Act 2000 (Regulated Activities) (Amendment) Order 2009, SI 2009/1342, arts 2, 6, as from 1 July 2009 (other than for the purposes of enabling applications to be made for a Part IV permission, or a variation of a Part IV permission, in relation to activities of the kind specified by arts 25E, 53D or 63J or, so far as relevant to any such activity, art 64 of this Order), and as from 30 June 2010 (for those purposes) (for the full commencement details and for transitional provisions etc see arts 1, 32–34 of that Order).

28   Arranging transactions to which the arranger is a party

   (1)   There are excluded from article 25(1) any arrangements for a transaction into which the person making the arrangements enters or is to enter as principal or as agent for some other person.

   (2)   There are excluded from article 25(2) any arrangements which a person makes with a view to transactions into which he enters or is to enter as principal or as agent for some other person.

   [(3)   But the exclusions in paragraphs (1) and (2) do not apply to arrangements made for or with a view to a transaction which relates to a contract of insurance, unless the person making the arrangements either—
   (a)   is the only policyholder; or
   (b)   as a result of the transaction, would become the only policyholder.]

[748]

NOTES
   Para (3): added by the Financial Services and Markets Act 2000 (Regulated Activities) (Amendment) (No 2) Order 2003, SI 2003/1476, art 5(2), as from 31 October 2004 (in so far as relating to contracts of long-term care insurance), and as from 14 January 2005 (otherwise), for transitional provisions see arts 22–27 of that Order.

[28A   Arranging contracts [*or plans*] to which the arranger is a party

   (1)   There are excluded from [articles 25A(1), 25B(1) *and 25C(1)*] any arrangements—
   (a)   for a [contract *or plan*] into which the person making the arrangements enters or is to enter; or
   (b)   for a variation of a [contract *or plan*] to which that person is (or is to become) a party.

   (2)   There are excluded [articles 25A(2), 25B(2) *and 25C(2)*] any arrangements which a person makes with a view to contracts [*or plans*] into which he enters or is to enter.]

[749]

NOTES
Commencement: 31 October 2004.
Inserted by the Financial Services and Markets Act 2000 (Regulated Activities) (Amendment) (No 1) Order 2003, SI 2003/1475, art 7, as from 31 October 2004; for transitional provisions see arts 26–29 thereof.

Article heading: words in square brackets inserted by the Financial Services and Markets Act 2000 (Regulated Activities) (Amendment) (No 2) Order 2006, SI 2006/2383, arts 2, 7(1), as from 6 November 2006 (for the purposes of enabling applications to be made for (i) a Pt IV permission, or a variation of a Pt IV permission, in relation to activities of the kind specified by arts 25B, 25C, 53B, 53C, 63B or 63F or, so far as relevant to any such activity, art 64 of this Order; or (ii) the Authority's approval under FSMA 2000, s 59 in relation to any of those activities), and as from 6 April 2007 (otherwise) (for transitional provisions and effect see arts 36–40 of, and the Schedule to, the 2006 Order). For those words there are substituted the words ", plans or agreements" by the Financial Services and Markets Act 2000 (Regulated Activities) (Amendment) Order 2009, SI 2009/1342, arts 2, 7(1), as from 1 July 2009 (other than for the purposes of enabling applications to be made for a Part IV permission, or a variation of a Part IV permission, in relation to activities of the kind specified by arts 25E, 53D or 63J or, so far as relevant to any such activity, art 64 of this Order), and as from 30 June 2010 (for those purposes) (for the full commencement details and for transitional provisions etc see arts 1, 32–34 of that Order).

Para (1): words in square brackets substituted by SI 2006/2383, arts 2, 7(1)(a), as from 6 November 2006 (certain purposes), and as from 6 April 2007 (otherwise) (for purposes, transitional provisions, and effect, see the note "Article heading" above); for the first words in italics there are substituted the words ", 25C(1) and 25E(1)", and for the second and third words in italics there are substituted the words ", plan or agreement", by SI 2009/1342, arts 2, 7(2)(a), as from the same dates and for the same purposes, etc, as mentioned in the note relating to this Order above.

Para (2): words in first pair of square brackets substituted, and words in second pair of square brackets inserted, by SI 2006/2383, arts 2, 7(1)(b), as from 6 November 2006 (certain purposes), and as from 6 April 2007 (otherwise) (for purposes, transitional provisions, and effect, see the note "Article heading" above); for the first words in italics there are substituted the words ", 25C(2) and 25E(2)", and for the second words in italics there are substituted the words ", plans or agreements", by SI 2009/1342, arts 2, 7(2)(b), as from the same dates and for the same purposes, etc, as mentioned in the note relating to this Order above.

29 Arranging deals with or through authorised persons

(1) There are excluded from [articles 25(1) and (2), 25A(1) and (2), 25B(1) and (2) *and 25C(1) and* (2)] arrangements made by a person ("A") who is not an authorised person for or with a view to a transaction which is or is to be entered into by a person ("the client") with or though an authorised person if—

    (a)   the transaction is or is to be entered into on advice to the client by an authorised person; or

    (b)   it is clear, in all the circumstances, that the client, in his capacity as an *[investor, borrower, reversion seller, plan provider or (as the case may be) home purchaser]*, is not seeking and has not sought advice from A as to the merits of the client's entering into the transaction (or, if the client has sought such advice, A has declined to give it but has recommended that the client seek such advice from an authorised person).

[(2) But the exclusion in paragraph (1) does not apply if—

    (a)   the transaction relates, or would relate, to a contract of insurance; or

    (b)   A receives from any person other than the client any pecuniary reward or other advantage, for which he does not account to the client, arising out of his making the arrangements.]

[(3) This article is subject to article 4(4).]

[750]

NOTES
Para (1): words in square brackets substituted by the Financial Services and Markets Act 2000 (Regulated Activities) (Amendment) (No 2) Order 2006, SI 2006/2383, arts 2, 8, as from 6 November 2006 (for the purposes of enabling applications to be made for (i) a Pt IV permission, or a variation of a Pt IV permission, in relation to activities of the kind specified by arts 25B, 25C, 53B, 53C, 63B or 63F or, so far as relevant to any such activity, art 64 of this Order; or (ii) the Authority's approval under FSMA 2000, s 59 in relation to any of those activities), and as from 6 April 2007 (otherwise) (for transitional provisions and effect see arts 36–40 of, and the Schedule to, the 2006 Order); for the first words in italics there are substituted the words ", 25C(1) and (2) and 25E(1) and (2)", and for the second words in italics there are substituted the words "investor, borrower, reversion seller, plan provider, home purchaser, agreement provider or (as the case may be) agreement seller", by the Financial Services and Markets Act 2000 (Regulated Activities) (Amendment) Order 2009, SI 2009/1342, arts 2, 8, as from 1 July 2009 (other than for the purposes of enabling applications to be made for a Part IV permission, or a variation of a Part IV permission, in relation to activities of the kind specified by arts 25E, 53D or 63J or, so far as relevant to any such activity, art 64 of this Order), and as from 30 June 2010 (for those purposes) (for the full commencement details and for transitional provisions etc see arts 1, 32–34 of that Order).

Para (2): substituted by the Financial Services and Markets Act 2000 (Regulated Activities) (Amendment) (No 2) Order 2003, SI 2003/1476, art 5(3), as from 31 October 2004 (in so far as relating to contracts of long-term care insurance), and as from 14 January 2005 (otherwise), for transitional provisions see arts 22–27 of that Order.

Para (3): added by the Financial Services and Markets Act 2000 (Regulated Activities) (Amendment No 3) Order 2006, SI 2006/3384, arts 2, 14, as from 1 April 2007 (for the purposes of enabling applications to be made for (i) a Pt IV permission, (ii) a variation of a Pt IV permission, and (iii) the Authority's approval under s 59 of the 2000 Act, in relation to an activity of the kind specified by art 25D of this Order, or in relation to an investment of the kind specified by arts 83, 84 or 85 of this Order), and as from 1 November 2007 (otherwise).

[29A   Arrangements made in the course of administration by authorised person

[(1)]   A person who is not an authorised person ("A") does not carry on an activity of the kind specified by article 25A(1)(b) as a result of—

   (a)   anything done by an authorised person ("B") in relation to a regulated mortgage contract which B is administering pursuant to an arrangement of the kind mentioned in article 62(a); or

   (b)   anything A does in connection with the administration of a regulated mortgage contract in circumstances falling within article 62(b).]

[(2)   A person who is not an authorised person ("A") does not carry on an activity of the kind specified by article 25B(1)(b) as a result of—

   (a)   anything done by an authorised person ("B") in relation to a regulated home reversion plan which B is administering pursuant to an arrangement of the kind mentioned in article 63C(a); or

   (b)   anything A does in connection with the administration of a regulated home reversion plan in circumstances falling within article 63C(b).

(3)   A person who is not an authorised person ("A") does not carry on an activity of the kind specified by article 25C(1)(b) as a result of—

   (a)   anything done by an authorised person ("B") in relation to a regulated home purchase plan which B is administering pursuant to an arrangement of the kind mentioned in article 63G(a); or

   (b)   anything A does in connection with the administration of a regulated home purchase plan in circumstances falling within article 63G(b).]

[(4)   A person who is not an authorised person ("A") does not carry on an activity of the kind specified by article 25E(1)(b) as a result of—

   (a)   anything done by an authorised person ("B") in relation to a regulated sale and rent back agreement which B is administering pursuant to an arrangement of the kind mentioned in article 63K(a); or

   (b)   anything A does in connection with the administration of a regulated sale and rent back agreement in circumstances falling within article 63K(b).]

[751]

NOTES

Commencement: 31 October 2004.

Inserted by the Financial Services and Markets Act 2000 (Regulated Activities) (Amendment) (No 1) Order 2003, SI 2003/1475, art 9, as from 31 October 2004; for transitional provisions see arts 26–29 thereof.

Para (1) numbered as such, and paras (2), (3) added, by the Financial Services and Markets Act 2000 (Regulated Activities) (Amendment) (No 2) Order 2006, SI 2006/2383, arts 2, 9, as from 6 November 2006 (for the purposes of enabling applications to be made for (i) a Pt IV permission, or a variation of a Pt IV permission, in relation to activities of the kind specified by arts 25B, 25C, 53B, 53C, 63B or 63F or, so far as relevant to any such activity, art 64 of this Order; or (ii) the Authority's approval under FSMA 2000, s 59 in relation to any of those activities), and as from 6 April 2007 (otherwise) (for transitional provisions and effect see arts 36–40 of, and the Schedule to, the 2006 Order).

Para (4): added by the Financial Services and Markets Act 2000 (Regulated Activities) (Amendment) Order 2009, SI 2009/1342, arts 2, 9, as from 1 July 2009 (other than for the purposes of enabling applications to be made for a Part IV permission, or a variation of a Part IV permission, in relation to activities of the kind specified by arts 25E, 53D or 63J or, so far as relevant to any such activity, art 64 of this Order), and as from 30 June 2010 (for those purposes) (for the full commencement details and for transitional provisions etc see arts 1, 32–34 of that Order).

---

30   Arranging transactions in connection with lending on the security of insurance policies

(1)   There are excluded from article 25(1) and (2) arrangements made by a money-lender under which either—

   [(a)   a relevant authorised person or a person acting on his behalf will introduce to the money-lender persons with whom the relevant authorised person has entered, or proposes to enter, into a relevant transaction, or will advise such persons to approach the money-lender, with a view to the money-lender lending money on the security of any contract effected pursuant to a relevant transaction;]

   (b)   a relevant authorised person gives an assurance to the money-lender as to the amount which, on the security of any contract effected pursuant to a relevant transaction, will or may be received by the money-lender should the money-lender lend money to a person introduced to him pursuant to the arrangements.

(2)   In paragraph (1)—

"money-lender" means a person who is—

(a)   a money-lending company within the meaning of section 338 of the Companies Act 1985;

(b)   a body corporate incorporated under the law of, or of any part of, the United Kingdom relating to building societies; or

(c)   a person whose ordinary business includes the making of loans or the giving of guarantees in connection with loans;

"relevant authorised person" means an authorised person who has permission to effect [contracts of insurance] or to sell investments of the kind specified by article 89, so far as relevant to such contracts;

"relevant transaction" means the effecting of a [contract of insurance] or the sale of an investment of the kind specified by article 89, so far as relevant to such contracts.

[(3)   This article is subject to article 4(4A).]

[752]

NOTES

Para (1): sub-para (a) substituted by the Financial Services and Markets Act 2000 (Regulated Activities) (Amendment) Order 2001, SI 2001/3544, arts 2, 5, as from 1 December 2001.

Para (2): words in square brackets in definitions "relevant authorised person" and "relevant transaction" substituted by the Financial Services and Markets Act 2000 (Regulated Activities) (Amendment) (No 2) Order 2003, SI 2003/1476, art 5(4), as from 31 October 2004 (in so far as relating to contracts of long-term care insurance), and as from 14 January 2005 (otherwise), for transitional provisions see arts 22–27 of that Order.

Para (3): added by the Financial Services and Markets Act 2000 (Regulated Activities) (Amendment No 3) Order 2006, SI 2006/3384, arts 2, 15, as from 1 April 2007 (for the purposes of enabling applications to be made for (i) a Pt IV permission, (ii) a variation of a Pt IV permission, and (iii) the Authority's approval under s 59 of the 2000 Act, in relation to an activity of the kind specified by art 25D of this Order, or in relation to an investment of the kind specified by arts 83, 84 or 85 of this Order), and as from 1 November 2007 (otherwise).

31   Arranging the acceptance of debentures in connection with loans

(1)   There are excluded from article 25(1) and (2) arrangements under which a person accepts or is to accept, whether as principal or agent, an instrument creating or acknowledging indebtedness in respect of any loan, credit, guarantee or other similar financial accommodation or assurance which is, or is to be, made, granted or provided by that person or his principal.

(2)   The reference in paragraph (1) to a person accepting an instrument includes a reference to a person becoming a party to an instrument otherwise than as a debtor or a surety.

[753]

NOTES

Modification: references in para (1) to securities, instruments or investments creating or acknowledging indebtedness (or creating or acknowledging a present or future indebtedness) includes a reference to uncertificated units of eligible debt securities; see the Uncertificated Securities (Amendment) (Eligible Debt Securities) Regulations 2003, SI 2003/1633, reg 15, Sch 2, para 8 (as from 24 June 2003).

Modification: references in para (2) to a person becoming party to an instrument includes a reference to a person assuming rights and obligations in respect of uncertificated units of an eligible debt security in accordance with its current terms of issue; see the Uncertificated Securities (Amendment) (Eligible Debt Securities) Regulations 2003, SI 2003/1633, reg 15, Sch 2, para 9 (as from 24 June 2003).

32   Provision of finance

There are excluded from article 25(2) arrangements having as their sole purpose the provision of finance to enable a person to buy, sell, subscribe for or underwrite investments.

[754]

33   Introducing

There are excluded from [articles 25(2), 25A(2), 25B(2) *and* 25C(2)] arrangements where—

(a)   they are arrangements under which persons ("clients") will be introduced to another person;

(b)   the person to whom introductions are to be made is—

(i)   an authorised person;

(ii)   an exempt person acting in the course of a business comprising a regulated activity in relation to which he is exempt; or

(iii)   a person who is not unlawfully carrying on regulated activities in the United Kingdom and whose ordinary business involves him in engaging in an activity of the kind specified by any of articles 14, 21, 25, [25A,] [25B, 25C,] [25E,] 37[, 39A], 40, 45, 51, [52, 53[, 53A, 53B *and* 53C]] (or, so far as relevant to any of those articles, article 64), or would do so apart from any exclusion from any of those articles made by this Order; ...

(c)   the introduction is made with a view to the provision of independent advice or the independent exercise of discretion in relation to investments generally or in relation to any class of investments to which the arrangements relate[; and

   (d)   the arrangements are made with a view to a person entering into a transaction which does not relate to a contract of insurance].

[755]

NOTES

Words in first pair of square brackets substituted by the Financial Services and Markets Act 2000 (Regulated Activities) (Amendment) (No 2) Order 2006, SI 2006/2383, arts 2, 10(a), as from 6 November 2006 (for the purposes of enabling applications to be made for (i) a Pt IV permission, or a variation of a Pt IV permission, in relation to activities of the kind specified by arts 25B, 25C, 53B, 53C, 63B or 63F or, so far as relevant to any such activity, art 64 of this Order; or (ii) the Authority's approval under FSMA 2000, s 59 in relation to any of those activities), and as from 6 April 2007 (otherwise) (for transitional provisions and effect see arts 36–40 of, and the Schedule to, the 2006 Order).

For the first words in italics there are substituted the words ", 25C(2) and 25E(2)" by the Financial Services and Markets Act 2000 (Regulated Activities) (Amendment) Order 2009, SI 2009/1342, arts 2, 10(a), as from 1 July 2009 (other than for the purposes of enabling applications to be made for a Part IV permission, or a variation of a Part IV permission, in relation to activities of the kind specified by arts 25E, 53D or 63J or, so far as relevant to any such activity, art 64 of this Order), and as from 30 June 2010 (for those purposes) (for the full commencement details and for transitional provisions etc see arts 1, 32–34 of that Order).

Figure in first pair of square brackets in para (b)(iii) inserted, and words in the penultimate (outer) pair of square brackets in that paragraph substituted, by the Financial Services and Markets Act 2000 (Regulated Activities) (Amendment) (No 1) Order 2003, SI 2003/1475, art 10, as from 31 October 2004, for transitional provisions see arts 26–29 thereof.

Figures in second pair of square brackets in para (b)(iii) inserted, and words in final (inner) pair of square brackets substituted, by SI 2006/2383, arts 2, 10(b), as from 6 November 2006 (certain purposes), and as from 6 April 2007 (otherwise) (for purposes, transitional provisions, and effect, see the note above).

Figure in third pair of square brackets in para (b)(iii) inserted by SI 2009/1342, arts 2, 10(b)(i), as from the same dates and for the same purposes, etc, as mentioned in the note relating to this Order above.

Figure in fourth pair of square brackets in para (b)(iii) inserted, word omitted from that paragraph revoked, and para (d) and the word immediately preceding it added, by the Financial Services and Markets Act 2000 (Regulated Activities) (Amendment) (No 2) Order 2003, SI 2003/1476, art 5(5), as from 31 October 2004 (in so far as relating to contracts of long-term care insurance), and as from 14 January 2005 (otherwise), for transitional provisions see arts 22–27 of that Order.

For the words in italics in para (b)(iii) there are substituted the words ", 53C and 53D" by SI 2009/1342, arts 2, 10(b)(ii), as from the same dates and for the same purposes, etc, as mentioned in the note relating to this Order above.

[33A   Introducing to authorised persons etc

   (1)   There are excluded from article 25A(2) arrangements where—
     (a)   they are arrangements under which a client is introduced to a person ("N") who is—
        (i)   an authorised person who has permission to carry on a regulated activity of the kind specified by any of articles 25A, 53A, and 61(1),
        (ii)   an appointed representative who may carry on a regulated activity of the kind specified by either of articles 25A and 53A without contravening the general prohibition, or
        (iii)   an overseas person who carries on activities specified by any of articles 25A, 53A and 61(1); and
     (b)   the conditions mentioned in paragraph (2) are satisfied.

   [(1A)   There are excluded from article 25B(2) arrangements where—
     (a)   they are arrangements under which a client is introduced to a person ("N") who is—
        (i)   an authorised person who has permission to carry on a regulated activity of the kind specified by any of articles 25B, 53B and 63B(1),
        (ii)   an appointed representative who may carry on a regulated activity of the kind specified by either of articles 25B and 53B without contravening the general prohibition, or
        (iii)   an overseas person who carries on activities specified by any of articles 25B, 53B and 63B(1); and
     (b)   the conditions mentioned in paragraph (2) are satisfied.

   (1B)   There are excluded from article 25C(2) arrangements where—
     (a)   they are arrangements under which a client is introduced to a person ("N") who is—
        (i)   an authorised person who has permission to carry on a regulated activity of the kind specified by any of articles 25C, 53C and 63F(1),
        (ii)   an appointed representative who may carry on a regulated activity of the kind specified by either of articles 25C and 53C without contravening the general prohibition, or
        (iii)   an overseas person who carries on activities specified by any of articles 25C, 53C and 63F(1); and
     (b)   the conditions mentioned in paragraph (2) are satisfied.]

   [(1C)   There are excluded from article 25E(2) arrangements where—
     (a)   they are arrangements under which a client is introduced to a person ("N") who is—

      (i)   an authorised person who has permission to carry on a regulated activity of the kind specified by any of articles 25E, 53D and 63J(1),

      (ii)   an appointed representative who may carry on a regulated activity of the kind specified by either of articles 25E or 53D without contravening the general prohibition, or

      (iii) an overseas person who carries on activities specified by any of articles 25E, 53D and 63J(1); and

(b)   the conditions mentioned in paragraph (2) are satisfied.]

(2)   Those conditions are—

(a)   that the person making the introduction ("P") does not receive any money, other than money payable to P on his own account, paid by the client for or in connection with any transaction which the client enters into with or through N as a result of the introduction; and

(b)   that before making the introduction P discloses to the client such of the information mentioned in paragraph (3) as applies to P.

(3)   That information is—

(a)   that P is a member of the same group as N;

(b)   details of any payment which P will receive from N, by way of fee or commission, for introducing the client to N;

(c)   an indication of any other reward or advantage received or to be received by P that arises out of his introducing clients to N.

[(4)   In this article, "client" means—

(a)   for the purposes of paragraph (1), a borrower within the meaning given by article 61(3)(a)(i), or a person who is or may be contemplating entering into a regulated mortgage contract as such a borrower;

(b)   for the purposes of paragraph (1A), a reversion seller, a plan provider or a person who is or may be contemplating entering into a regulated home reversion plan as a reversion seller or as a plan provider;

(c)   for the purposes of paragraph (1B), a home purchaser or a person who is or may be contemplating entering into a regulated home purchase plan as a home purchaser[;

(d)   for the purposes of paragraph (1C), an agreement provider, an agreement seller or a person who is or may be contemplating entering into a regulated sale and rent back agreement as an agreement provider or agreement seller.]]

[756]

NOTES

Commencement: 31 October 2004.

Inserted by the Financial Services and Markets Act 2000 (Regulated Activities) (Amendment) (No 1) Order 2003, SI 2003/1475, art 11, as from 31 October 2004; for transitional provisions see arts 26–29 thereof.

Paras (1A), (1B): inserted by the Financial Services and Markets Act 2000 (Regulated Activities) (Amendment) (No 2) Order 2006, SI 2006/2383, arts 2, 11(a), as from 6 November 2006 (for the purposes of enabling applications to be made for (i) a Pt IV permission, or a variation of a Pt IV permission, in relation to activities of the kind specified by arts 25B, 25C, 53B, 53C, 63B or 63F or, so far as relevant to any such activity, art 64 of this Order; or (ii) the Authority's approval under FSMA 2000, s 59 in relation to any of those activities), and as from 6 April 2007 (otherwise) (for transitional provisions and effect see arts 36–40 of, and the Schedule to, the 2006 Order).

Para (1C): inserted by the Financial Services and Markets Act 2000 (Regulated Activities) (Amendment) Order 2009, SI 2009/1342, arts 2, 11(a), as from 1 July 2009 (other than for the purposes of enabling applications to be made for a Part IV permission, or a variation of a Part IV permission, in relation to activities of the kind specified by arts 25E, 53D or 63J or, so far as relevant to any such activity, art 64 of this Order), and as from 30 June 2010 (for those purposes) (for the full commencement details and for transitional provisions etc see arts 1, 32–34 of that Order).

Para (4): substituted by SI 2006/2383, arts 2, 11(b), as from 6 November 2006 (certain purposes), and as from 6 April 2007 (otherwise) (for purposes, transitional provisions, and effect, see the note above); sub-para (d) inserted by SI 2009/1342, arts 2, 11(b), as from the same dates and for the same purposes, etc, as mentioned in the note relating to this Order above.

34 Arrangements for the issue of shares etc

(1)   There are excluded from article 25(1) and (2)—

(a)   arrangements made by a company for the purposes of issuing its own shares or share warrants; and

(b)   arrangements made by any person for the purposes of issuing his own debentures or debenture warrants;

and for the purposes of article 25(1) and (2), a company is not, by reason of issuing its own shares or share warrants, and a person is not, by reason of issuing his own debentures or debenture warrants, to be treated as selling them.

(2)   In paragraph (1), "company", "shares", "debentures", "share warrants" and "debenture warrants" have the meanings given by article 18(2).

[757]

35   International securities self-regulating organisations

(1)   There are excluded from article 25(1) and (2) any arrangements made for the purposes of carrying out the functions of a body or association which is approved under this article as an international securities self-regulating organisation, whether the arrangements are made by the organisation itself or by a person acting on its behalf.

(2)   The Treasury may approve as an international securities self-regulating organisation any body corporate or unincorporated association with respect to which the conditions mentioned in paragraph (3) appear to them to be met if, having regard to such matters affecting international trade, overseas earnings and the balance of payments or otherwise as they consider relevant, it appears to them that to do so would be desirable and not result in any undue risk to investors.

(3)   The conditions are that—
   (a)   the body or association does not have its head office in the United Kingdom;
   (b)   the body or association is not eligible for recognition under section 287 or 288 of the Act (applications by investment exchanges and clearing houses) on the ground that (whether or not it has applied, and whether or not it would be eligible on other grounds) it is unable to satisfy the requirements of one or both of paragraphs (a) and (b) of section 292(3) of the Act (requirements for overseas investment exchanges and overseas clearing houses);
   (c)   the body or association is able and willing to co-operate with the Authority by the sharing of information and in other ways;
   (d)   adequate arrangements exist for co-operation between the Authority and those responsible for the supervision of the body or association in the country or territory in which its head office is situated;
   (e)   the body or association has a membership composed of persons falling within any of the following categories, that is to say, authorised persons, exempt persons, and persons whose head offices are outside the United Kingdom and whose ordinary business involves them in engaging in activities which are activities of a kind specified by this Order (or would be apart from any exclusion made by this Part); and
   (f)   the body or association facilitates and regulates the activity of its members in the conduct of international securities business.

(4)   In paragraph (3)(f), "international securities business" means the business of buying, selling, subscribing for or underwriting investments (or agreeing to do so), either as principal or agent, where—
   (a)   the investments are securities or [relevant investments] and are of a kind which, by their nature, and the manner in which the business is conducted, may be expected normally to be bought or dealt in by persons sufficiently expert to understand the risks involved; and
   (b)   either the transaction is international or each of the parties may be expected to be indifferent to the location of the other;
and, for the purposes of this definition, it is irrelevant that the investments may ultimately be bought otherwise than in the course of such business by persons not so expert.

(5)   Any approval under this article is to be given by notice in writing; and the Treasury may by a further notice in writing withdraw any such approval if for any reason it appears to them that it is not appropriate to it to continue in force.

[758]

NOTES
Para (4): words in square brackets in sub-para (a) substituted by the Financial Services and Markets Act 2000 (Regulated Activities) (Amendment) (No 2) Order 2003, SI 2003/1476, art 5(6), as from 31 October 2004 (in so far as relating to contracts of long-term care insurance), and as from 14 January 2005 (otherwise), for transitional provisions see arts 22–27 of that Order.

36   Other exclusions

[(1)]   Article 25 is also subject to the exclusions in articles 66 (trustees etc), 67 (profession or non-investment business), 68 (sale of goods and supply of services), 69 (groups and joint enterprises), 70 (sale of body corporate), 71 (employee share schemes)[, 72 (overseas persons)[, 72A (information society services), 72B (activities carried on by a provider of relevant goods or services), 72C (provision of information about contracts of insurance on an incidental basis) and 72D (large risks contracts where risk situated outside the EEA)]].

[(2)   [Articles 25A, 25B *and 25C* are] also subject to the exclusions in articles 66 (trustees etc), 67 (profession or non-investment business), 72 (overseas persons) and 72A (information society services).]

[(3)   Article 25D is also subject to the exclusion in article 72 (overseas persons).]

[759]

NOTES
Para (1): numbered as such by the Financial Services and Markets Act 2000 (Regulated Activities) (Amendment) (No 1) Order 2003, SI 2003/1475, art 12(a), as from 31 October 2004 (for transitional provisions see arts 26–29 thereof); words in first (outer) pair of square brackets substituted by the Financial Services and Markets Act 2000 (Regulated Activities) (Amendment) (No 2) Order 2002, SI 2002/1776, art 3(1), (6), as from 21 August 2002; words in second (inner) pair of square brackets substituted by the Financial Services and Markets Act 2000 (Regulated Activities) (Amendment) (No 2) Order 2003, SI 2003/1476, art 5(7), as from 31 October 2004 (in so far as relating to contracts of long-term care insurance), and as from 14 January 2005 (otherwise), for transitional provisions see arts 22–27 of that Order.
Para (2): added by SI 2003/1475, art 12(b), as from 31 October 2004, for transitional provisions see arts 26–29 thereof; words in square brackets substituted by the Financial Services and Markets Act 2000 (Regulated Activities) (Amendment) (No 2) Order 2006, SI 2006/2383, arts 2, 12, as from 6 November 2006 (for the purposes of enabling applications to be made for (i) a Pt IV permission, or a variation of a Pt IV permission, in relation to activities of the kind specified by arts 25B, 25C, 53B, 53C, 63B or 63F or, so far as relevant to any such activity, art 64 of this Order; or (ii) the Authority's approval under FSMA 2000, s 59 in relation to any of those activities), and as from 6 April 2007 (otherwise) (for transitional provisions and effect see arts 36–40 of, and the Schedule to, the 2006 Order; for the words in italics there are substituted the words ", 25C and 25E" by the Financial Services and Markets Act 2000 (Regulated Activities) (Amendment) Order 2009, SI 2009/1342, arts 2, 12, as from 1 July 2009 (other than for the purposes of enabling applications to be made for a Part IV permission, or a variation of a Part IV permission, in relation to activities of the kind specified by arts 25E, 53D or 63J or, so far as relevant to any such activity, art 64 of this Order), and as from 30 June 2010 (for those purposes) (for the full commencement details and for transitional provisions etc see arts 1, 32–34 of that Order.
Para (3): added by the Financial Services and Markets Act 2000 (Regulated Activities) (Amendment No 3) Order 2006, SI 2006/3384, arts 2, 16, as from 1 April 2007 (for the purposes of enabling applications to be made for (i) a Pt IV permission, (ii) a variation of a Pt IV permission, and (iii) the Authority's approval under s 59 of the 2000 Act, in relation to an activity of the kind specified by art 25D of this Order, or in relation to an investment of the kind specified by arts 83, 84 or 85 of this Order), and as from 1 November 2007 (otherwise).

CHAPTER VII
MANAGING INVESTMENTS
The activity

37   Managing investments
Managing assets belonging to another person, in circumstances involving the exercise of discretion, is a specified kind of activity if—
   (a)   the assets consist of or include any investment which is a security or a contractually based investment; or
   (b)   the arrangements for their management are such that the assets may consist of or include such investments, and either the assets have at any time since 29th April 1988 done so, or the arrangements have at any time (whether before or after that date) been held out as arrangements under which the assets would do so.

[760]

NOTES
See the Financial Services and Markets Act 2000 (Carrying on Regulated Activities by Way of Business) Order 2001, SI 2001/1177, art 3 in relation to investment business, and art 4 in respect of activities of managing investments where assets in question are held for the purposes of an occupational pension scheme.

Exclusions

38   Attorneys
[(1)]   A person does not carry on an activity of the kind specified by article 37 if—
   (a)   he is a person appointed to manage the assets in question under a power of attorney; and
   (b)   all routine or day-to-day decisions, so far as relating to investments of a kind mentioned in article 37(a), are taken on behalf of that person by—
      (i)   an authorised person with permission to carry on activities of the kind specified by article 37; ...
      (ii)   a person who is an exempt person in relation to activities of that kind[; or
      (iii) an overseas person.]
[(2)   This article is subject to article 4(4).]

[761]

NOTES

Para (1) numbered as such, and para (2) added, by the Financial Services and Markets Act 2000 (Regulated Activities) (Amendment No 3) Order 2006, SI 2006/3384, arts 2, 17, as from 1 April 2007 (for the purposes of enabling applications to be made for (i) a Pt IV permission, (ii) a variation of a Pt IV permission, and (iii) the Authority's approval under s 59 of the 2000 Act, in relation to an activity of the kind specified by art 25D of this Order, or in relation to an investment of the kind specified by arts 83, 84 or 85 of this Order), and as from 1 November 2007 (otherwise). Note that the Queen's Printer's copy of SI 2006/3384 does not actually specify that the words "This article is subject to article 4(4)" should be numbered as paragraph (2) even though it does provide that the original text should be numbered as paragraph (1). It is assumed that this is an error.

Word omitted from para (1)(b)(i) revoked, and para (1)(b)(iii) and the word immediately preceding it added, by the Financial Services and Markets Act 2000 (Regulated Activities) (Amendment) Order 2001, SI 2001/3544, arts 2, 6, as from 1 December 2001.

39   Other exclusions

Article 37 is also subject to the exclusions in articles 66 (trustees etc), 68 (sale of goods and supply of services)[, 69 (groups and joint enterprises)[, 72A (information society services) and 72C (provision of information about contracts of insurance on an incidental basis)]].

[762]

NOTES

Words in first (outer) pair of square brackets substituted by the Financial Services and Markets Act 2000 (Regulated Activities) (Amendment) (No 2) Order 2002, SI 2002/1776, art 3(1), (7), as from 21 August 2002; words in second (inner) pair of square brackets substituted by the Financial Services and Markets Act 2000 (Regulated Activities) (Amendment) (No 2) Order 2003, SI 2003/1476, art 6, as from 31 October 2004 (in so far as relating to contracts of long-term care insurance), and as from 14 January 2005 (otherwise), for transitional provisions see arts 22–27 of that Order.

[CHAPTER VIIA
ASSISTING IN THE ADMINISTRATION AND PERFORMANCE OF A
CONTRACT OF INSURANCE

The Activity

39A   Assisting in the administration and performance of a contract of insurance

Assisting in the administration and performance of a contract of insurance is a specified kind of activity.]

[763]

NOTES

Commencement: 31 October 2004 (in so far as relating to contracts of long-term care insurance); 14 January 2005 (otherwise).

Inserted, together with the preceding headings and arts 39B, 39C, by the Financial Services and Markets Act 2000 (Regulated Activities) (Amendment) (No 2) Order 2003, SI 2003/1476, art 7, as from 31 October 2004 (in so far as relating to contracts of long-term care insurance), and as from 14 January 2005 (otherwise); for transitional provisions see arts 22–27 of that Order.

[Exclusions

39B   Claims management on behalf of an insurer etc

(1)   A person does not carry on an activity of the kind specified by article 39A if he acts in the course of carrying on the activity of—

(a)   expert appraisal;

(b)   loss adjusting on behalf of a relevant insurer; or

(c)   managing claims on behalf of a relevant insurer,

and that activity is carried on in the course of carrying on any profession or business.

(2)   In this article—

(a)   "relevant insurer" means—

(i)   a person who has Part IV permission to carry on an activity of the kind specified by article 10;

(ii)   a person to whom the general prohibition does not apply by virtue of section 316(1)(a) of the Act (members of the Society of Lloyd's);

(iii)   an EEA firm falling within paragraph 5(d) of Schedule 3 to the Act (insurance undertaking); or

(iv)   a relevant reinsurer;

(b)   "relevant reinsurer" means a person whose main business consists of accepting risks ceded by—

(i)   a person falling within sub-paragraph (i), (ii) or (iii) of the definition of "relevant insurer"; ...

[(ii)   an EEA firm falling within paragraph 5(da) of Schedule 3 to the Act (reinsurance undertaking); or

(iii)   a person established outside the United Kingdom and not falling within paragraph (ii) who carries on an activity of the kind specified by article 10 by way of business].]

[764]

NOTES
   Commencement: 31 October 2004 (in so far as relating to contracts of long-term care insurance); 14 January 2005 (otherwise).
   Inserted as noted to art 39A at **[763]**.
   Para (2): word omitted from sub-para (b)(i) revoked, and sub-paras (b)(ii), (iii) substituted (for the original sub-para (b)(ii)) by the Financial Services and Markets Act 2000 (Reinsurance Directive) Order 2007, SI 2007/3254, reg 2, as from 10 December 2007.

[39C Other exclusions

Article 39A is also subject to the exclusions in articles 66 (trustees etc), 67 (profession or non-investment business), 72A (information society services), 72B (activities carried on by a provider of relevant goods or services), 72C (provision of information about contracts of insurance on an incidental basis) and 72D (large risks contracts where risk situated outside the EEA).]

[765]

NOTES
   Commencement: 31 October 2004 (in so far as relating to contracts of long-term care insurance); 14 January 2005 (otherwise).
   Inserted as noted to art 39A at **[763]**.

CHAPTER VIII
SAFEGUARDING AND ADMINISTERING INVESTMENTS

The activity

40 Safeguarding and administering investments

(1)   The activity consisting of both—
   (a)   the safeguarding of assets belonging to another, and
   (b)   the administration of those assets,
or arranging for one or more other persons to carry on that activity, is a specified kind of activity if the condition in sub-paragraph (a) or (b) of paragraph (2) is met.

(2)   The condition is that—
   (a)   the assets consist of or include any investment which is a security or a contractually based investment; or
   (b)   the arrangements for their safeguarding and administration are such that the assets may consist of or include such investments, and either the assets have at any time since 1st June 1997 done so, or the arrangements have at any time (whether before or after that date) been held out as ones under which such investments would be safeguarded and administered.

(3)   For the purposes of this article—
   (a)   it is immaterial that title to the assets safeguarded and administered is held in uncertificated form;
   (b)   it is immaterial that the assets safeguarded and administered may be transferred to another person, subject to a commitment by the person safeguarding and administering them, or arranging for their safeguarding and administration, that they will be replaced by equivalent assets at some future date or when so requested by the person to whom they belong.

[766]

NOTES
   See the Financial Services and Markets Act 2000 (Carrying on Regulated Activities by Way of Business) Order 2001, SI 2001/1177, art 3 in relation to investment business.

Exclusions

41 Acceptance of responsibility by third party

(1)   There are excluded from article 40 any activities which a person carries on pursuant to arrangements which—
   (a)   are ones under which a qualifying custodian undertakes to the person to whom the assets

belong a responsibility in respect of the assets which is no less onerous than the qualifying custodian would have if the qualifying custodian were safeguarding and administering the assets; and

(b)   are operated by the qualifying custodian in the course of carrying on in the United Kingdom an activity of the kind specified by article 40.

(2)   In paragraph (1), "qualifying custodian" means a person who is—

(a)   an authorised person who has permission to carry on an activity of the kind specified by article 40, or

(b)   an exempt person acting in the course of a business comprising a regulated activity in relation to which he is exempt.

[767]

42   Introduction to qualifying custodians

(1)   There are excluded from article 40 any arrangements pursuant to which introductions are made by a person ("P") to a qualifying custodian with a view to the qualifying custodian providing in the United Kingdom a service comprising an activity of the kind specified by article 40, where the qualifying person (or other person who is to safeguard and administer the assets in question) is not connected with P.

(2)   For the purposes of paragraph (1)—

(a)   "qualifying custodian" has the meaning given by article 41(2); and

(b)   a person is connected with P if either he is a member of the same group as P, or P is remunerated by him.

[768]

43   Activities not constituting administration

The following activities do not constitute the administration of assets for the purposes of article 40—

(a)   providing information as to the number of units or the value of any assets safeguarded;

(b)   converting currency;

(c)   receiving documents relating to an investment solely for the purpose of onward transmission to, from or at the direction of the person to whom the investment belongs.

[769]

44   Other exclusions

Article 40 is also subject to the exclusions in articles 66 (trustees etc), 67 (profession or non-investment business), 68 (sale of goods and supply of services), 69 (groups and joint enterprises)[, 71 (employee share schemes)[, 72A (information society services) and 72C (provision of information about contracts of insurance on an incidental basis)]].

[770]

NOTES

Words in first (outer) pair of square brackets substituted by the Financial Services and Markets Act 2000 (Regulated Activities) (Amendment) (No 2) Order 2002, SI 2002/1776, art 3(1), (8), as from 21 August 2002; words in second (inner) pair of square brackets substituted by the Financial Services and Markets Act 2000 (Regulated Activities) (Amendment) (No 2) Order 2003, SI 2003/1476, art 8, as from 31 October 2004 (in so far as relating to contracts of long-term care insurance), and as from 14 January 2005 (otherwise), for transitional provisions see arts 22–27 of that Order.

CHAPTER IX
SENDING DEMATERIALISED INSTRUCTIONS

The activities

45   Sending dematerialised instructions

(1)   Sending, on behalf of another person, dematerialised instructions relating to a security [or a contractually based investment] is a specified kind of activity, where those instructions are sent by means of a relevant system in respect of which an Operator is approved under the [2001] Regulations.

(2)   Causing dematerialised instructions relating to a security [or a contractually based investment] to be sent [on behalf of another person] by means of such a system is also a specified kind of activity where the person causing them to be sent is a system-participant.

(3)   In this Chapter—

[(a)   "the 2001 Regulations" means the Uncertificated Securities Regulations 2001;]

(b)   "dematerialised instruction", "Operator", "settlement bank" and "system-participant" have the meaning given by regulation 3 of the [2001] Regulations.

[771]

Exclusions

46 Instructions on behalf of participating issuers

There is excluded from article 45 the act of sending, or causing to be sent, a dematerialised instruction where the person on whose behalf the instruction is sent or caused to be sent is a participating issuer within the meaning of the [2001] Regulations.

[772]

47 Instructions on behalf of settlement banks

There is excluded from article 45 the act of sending, or causing to be sent, a dematerialised instruction where the person on whose behalf the instruction is sent or caused to be sent is a settlement bank in its capacity as such.

[773]

48 Instructions in connection with takeover offers

(1) There is excluded from article 45 of the act of sending, or causing to be sent, a dematerialised instruction where the person on whose behalf the instruction is sent or caused to be sent is an offeror making a takeover offer.

(2) In this article—
  (a) "offeror" means, in the case of a takeover offer made by two or more persons jointly, the joint offers or any of them;
  (b) "takeover offer" means—
    (i) an offer to acquire shares (which in this sub-paragraph has the same meaning as in [section 974 of the Companies Act 2006]) in a body corporate incorporated in the United Kingdom which is a takeover offer within the meaning of [Chapter 3 of Part 28] of that Act (or would be such an offer if that Part of that Act applied in relation to any body corporate);
    (ii) an offer to acquire all or substantially all the shares, or all the shares of a particular class, in a body corporate incorporated outside the United Kingdom; or
    (iii) an offer made to all the holders of shares, or shares of a particular class, in a body corporate to acquire a specified proportion of those shares;
  but in determining whether an offer falls within paragraph (ii) there are to be disregarded any shares which the offeror or any associate of his (within the meaning of [section 988 of the Companies Act 2006]) holds or has contracted to acquire; and in determining whether an offer falls within paragraph (iii) the offeror, any such associate and any person whose shares the offeror or any such associate has contracted to acquire is not to be regarded as a holder of shares.

[774]

49 Instructions in the course of providing a network

There is excluded from article 45 the act of sending, or causing to be sent, a dematerialised instruction as a necessary part of providing a network, the purpose of which is to carry dematerialised instructions which are at all time properly authenticated (within the meaning of the [2001] Regulations).

[775]

NOTES
Date in square brackets substituted by the Financial Services and Markets Act 2000 (Regulated Activities) (Amendment) Order 2002, SI 2002/682, art 13(4), as from 27 April 2002.

50 Other exclusions

Article 45 is also subject to the exclusions in articles 66 (trustees etc)[, 69 (groups and joint enterprises) and 72A (information society services)].

[776]

NOTES
Words in square brackets substituted by the Financial Services and Markets Act 2000 (Regulated Activities) (Amendment) (No 2) Order 2002, SI 2002/1776, art 3(1), (9), as from 21 August 2002.

CHAPTER X
COLLECTIVE INVESTMENT SCHEMES

The activities

51 Establishing etc a collective investment scheme

(1) The following are specified kinds of activity—
  (a) establishing, operating or winding up a collective investment scheme;
  (b) acting as trustee of an authorised unit trust scheme;
  (c) acting as the depositary or sole director of an open-ended investment company.

(2) In this article, "trustee", "authorised unit trust scheme" and "depositary" have the meaning given by section 237 of the Act.

[777]

NOTES
See the Financial Services and Markets Act 2000 (Carrying on Regulated Activities by Way of Business) Order 2001, SI 2001/1177, art 3 in relation to investment business.

[Exclusion

51A Information society services

Article 51 is subject to the exclusion in article 72A (information society services).]

[778]

NOTES
Inserted, together with the preceding heading by the Financial Services and Markets Act 2000 (Regulated Activities) (Amendment) (No 2) Order 2002, SI 2002/1776, art 3(1), (10), as from 21 August 2002.

CHAPTER XI
… PENSION SCHEMES

The activities

[52 Establishing etc a pension scheme

The following are specified kinds of activity—
  (a) establishing, operating or winding up a stakeholder pension scheme;
  (b) establishing, operating or winding up a personal pension scheme.]

[779]

NOTES
Commencement: 1 October 2006 (certain purposes); 6 April 2007 (otherwise) (see below).
The word omitted from the Chapter heading preceding this article was revoked, and this article was substituted, by the Financial Services and Markets Act 2000 (Regulated Activities) (Amendment) Order 2006, SI 2006/1969, art 2(1), (3), (4), as from 1 October 2006 (for the purposes of enabling applications to be made for Pt IV permission or for a variation of Pt IV permission in relation to the regulated activity specified by art 52(b) of this Order (as so substituted)), and as from 6 April 2007 (otherwise); for transitional provisions and effect see arts 3–7 of, and the Schedule to, the 2006 Order.
See the Financial Services and Markets Act 2000 (Carrying on Regulated Activities by Way of Business) Order 2001, SI 2001/1177, art 3 in relation to investment business.

[Exclusion

52A Information society services

Article 52 is subject to the exclusion in article 72A (information society services).]

[780]

NOTES
Inserted, together with the preceding heading, by the Financial Services and Markets Act 2000 (Regulated Activities) (Amendment) (No 2) Order 2002, SI 2002/1776, art 3(1), (11), as from 21 August 2002.

[CHAPTER XIA
PROVIDING BASIC ADVICE ON STAKEHOLDER PRODUCTS

The Activity

52B Providing basic advice on stakeholder products

(1)   Providing basic advice to a retail consumer on a stakeholder product is a specified kind of activity.

(2)   For the purposes of paragraph (1), a person ("P") provides basic advice when—
    (a)   he asks a retail consumer questions to enable him to assess whether a stakeholder product is appropriate for that consumer; and
    (b)   relying on the information provided by the retail consumer P assesses that a stakeholder product is appropriate for the retail consumer and—
        (i)   describes that product to that consumer;
        (ii)   gives a recommendation of that product to that consumer; and
    (c)   the retail consumer has indicated to P that he has understood the description and the recommendation in sub-paragraph (b).

(3)   In this article—
    "retail consumer" means any person who is advised by P on the merits of opening or buying a stakeholder product in the course of a business carried on by P and who does not receive the advice in the course of a business carried on by him;
    "stakeholder product" means—
        (a)   an account which qualifies as a stakeholder child trust fund within the meaning given by the Child Trust Funds Regulations 2004;
        [(b)   rights under a stakeholder pension scheme;]
        (c)   an investment of a kind specified in regulations made by the Treasury.]

[781]

NOTES
Commencement: 6 April 2005.
Inserted, together with the preceding headings, by the Financial Services and Markets Act 2000 (Regulated Activities) (Amendment) (No 2) Order 2004, SI 2004/2737, arts, 2, 3, as from 6 April 2005. For transitional provisions, see the note below.
Para (3): in definition "stakeholder product", para (b) substituted by the Financial Services and Markets Act 2000 (Regulated Activities) (Amendment) Order 2005, SI 2005/593, art 2(3), as from 6 April 2005.
Transitional provisions: SI 2004/2737, art 4, provides as follows—

"4   Transitional provisions

(1)   Part 4 of the Act shall apply in the case of persons who have permission at the date this Order comes into force to carry out the activity specified in article 53 of the principal Order and who wish to carry out the activity specified in article 52B of that Order as follows.

(2)   Where P is a person to whom paragraph (1) applies—
    (a)   the procedures established under sections 44 and 45 in respect of application for permission shall not apply in respect of permission to carry out the article 52B activity,
    (b)   P shall be deemed to have such a permission if he has notified the Authority in writing of his wish to undertake the activity and the Authority has acknowledged receipt of P's notification in writing from the date of the acknowledgement.".

Regulations: the Financial Services and Markets 2000 (Stakeholder Products) Regulations 2004, SI 2004/2738.

CHAPTER XII
ADVISING ON INVESTMENTS

The activity

53 Advising on investments

Advising a person is a specified kind of activity if the advice is—
    (a)   given to the person in his capacity as an investor or potential investor, or in his capacity as agent for an investor or a potential investor; and
    (b)   advice on the merits of his doing any of the following (whether as principal or agent)—
        (i)   buying, selling, subscribing for or underwriting a particular investment which is a security or a [relevant investment], or

(ii)   exercising any right conferred by such an investment to buy, sell, subscribe for or underwrite such an investment.

[782]

NOTES
Words in square brackets substituted by the Financial Services and Markets Act 2000 (Regulated Activities) (Amendment) (No 2) Order 2003, SI 2003/1476, art 9(1), as from 31 October 2004 (in so far as relating to contracts of long-term care insurance), and as from 14 January 2005 (otherwise); for transitional provisions see arts 22–27 of that Order.
Transitional provisions: see the note to art 52B at **[781]**.
See the Financial Services and Markets Act 2000 (Carrying on Regulated Activities by Way of Business) Order 2001, SI 2001/1177, art 3 in relation to investment business.

[53A   Advising on regulated mortgage contracts
(1)   Advising a person is a specified kind of activity if the advice—
    (a)   is given to the person in his capacity as a borrower or potential borrower; and
    (b)   is advice on the merits of his doing any of the following—
        (i)   entering into a particular regulated mortgage contract, or
        (ii)   varying the terms of a regulated mortgage contract entered into by him after the coming into force of article 61 in such a way as to vary his obligations under that contract.
(2)   In this article, "borrower" has the meaning given by article 61(3)(a)(i).]

[783]

NOTES
Commencement: 31 October 2004.
Inserted by the Financial Services and Markets Act 2000 (Regulated Activities) (Amendment) (No 1) Order 2003, SI 2003/1475, art 13, as from 31 October 2004; for transitional provisions see arts 26–29 thereof.
See the Financial Services and Markets Act 2000 (Carrying on Regulated Activities by Way of Business) Order 2001, SI 2001/1177, art 3A.

[53B   Advising on regulated home reversion plans
Advising a person is a specified kind of activity if the advice—
    (a)   is given to the person in his capacity as—
        (i)   a reversion seller or potential reversion seller, or
        (ii)   a plan provider or potential plan provider; and
    (b)   is advice on the merits of his doing either of the following—
        (i)   entering into a particular regulated home reversion plan, or
        (ii)   varying the terms of a regulated home reversion plan, entered into on or after 6th April 2007 by him, in such a way as to vary his obligations under that plan.]

[784]

NOTES
Commencement: 6 November 2006 (certain purposes); 6 April 2007 (otherwise) (see below).
Inserted, together with art 53C, by the Financial Services and Markets Act 2000 (Regulated Activities) (Amendment) (No 2) Order 2006, SI 2006/2383, arts 2, 13, as from 6 November 2006 (for the purposes of enabling applications to be made for (i) a Pt IV permission, or a variation of a Pt IV permission, in relation to activities of the kind specified by arts 25B, 25C, 53B, 53C, 63B or 63F or, so far as relevant to any such activity, art 64 of this Order; or (ii) the Authority's approval under FSMA 2000, s 59 in relation to any of those activities), and as from 6 April 2007 (otherwise) (for transitional provisions and effect see arts 36–40 of, and the Schedule to, the 2006 Order).
See the Financial Services and Markets Act 2000 (Carrying on Regulated Activities by Way of Business) Order 2001, SI 2001/1177, art 3B.

[53C   Advising on regulated home purchase plans
Advising a person is a specified kind of activity if the advice—
    (a)   is given to the person in his capacity as a home purchaser or potential home purchaser; and
    (b)   is advice on the merits of his doing either of the following—
        (i)   entering into a particular regulated home purchase plan, or
        (ii)   varying the terms of a regulated home purchase plan, entered into on or after 6th April 2007 by him, in such a way as to vary his obligations under that plan.]

[785]

NOTES
Commencement: 6 November 2006 (certain purposes); 6 April 2007 (otherwise).
Inserted as noted to art 53B at **[784]**.
See the Financial Services and Markets Act 2000 (Carrying on Regulated Activities by Way of Business) Order 2001, SI 2001/1177, art 3C.

PART IV   OTHER STATUTORY INSTRUMENTS

[53D Advising on regulated sale and rent back agreements

Advising a person is a specified kind of activity if the advice—
- (a) is given to the person ("A") in A's capacity as—
  - (i) an agreement seller or potential agreement seller, or
  - (ii) an agreement provider or potential agreement provider; and
- (b) is advice on the merits of A doing either of the following—
  - (i) entering into a particular regulated sale and rent back agreement; or
  - (ii) varying the terms of a regulated sale and rent back agreement entered into on or after 1st July 2009 by A as agreement seller or agreement provider, in such a way so as to vary A's obligations under that agreement.]

[786]

NOTES

Commencement: 1 July 2009 (certain purposes); 30 June 2010 (otherwise) (see below).

Inserted by the Financial Services and Markets Act 2000 (Regulated Activities) (Amendment) Order 2009, SI 2009/1342, arts 2, 13, as from 1 July 2009 (other than for the purposes of enabling applications to be made for a Part IV permission, or a variation of a Part IV permission, in relation to activities of the kind specified by arts 25E, 53D or 63J or, so far as relevant to any such activity, art 64 of this Order), and as from 30 June 2010 (for those purposes) (for the full commencement details and for transitional provisions etc see arts 1, 32–34 of that Order).

Exclusions

54 Advice given in newspapers etc

(1) There is excluded from [articles 53, 53A, 53B *and 53C*] the giving of advice in writing or other legible form if the advice is contained in a newspaper, journal, magazine, or other periodical publication, or is given by way of a service comprising regularly updated news or information, if the principal purpose of the publication or service, taken as a whole and including any advertisements or other promotional material contained in it, is neither—
- (a) that of giving advice of a kind mentioned in article 53[, 53A, 53B *or 53C*, as the case may be]; nor
- [(b) that of leading or enabling persons—
  - (i) to buy, sell, subscribe for or underwrite securities or [relevant investments], or (as the case may be),
  - (ii) to enter as borrower into regulated mortgage contracts, or vary the terms of regulated mortgage contracts entered into by them as borrower;
  - [(iii) to enter as reversion seller or plan provider into regulated home reversion plans, or vary the terms of regulated home reversion plans entered into by them as reversion seller or plan provider,
  - (iv) to enter as home purchaser into regulated home purchase plans, or vary the terms of regulated home purchase plans entered into by them as home purchaser][;
  - (v) to enter as agreement seller or agreement provider into regulated sale and rent back agreements, or vary the terms of regulated sale and rent back agreements entered into by them as agreement seller or agreement provider]].

(2) There is also excluded from [articles 53, 53A, 53B *and 53C*] the giving of advice in any service consisting of the broadcast or transmission of television or radio programmes, if the principal purpose of the service, taken as a whole and including any advertisements or other promotional material contained in it, is neither of those mentioned in paragraph (1)(a) and (b).

(3) The Authority may, on the application of the proprietor of any such publication or service as is mentioned in paragraph (1) or (2), certify that it is of the nature described in that paragraph, and may revoke any such certificate if it considers that it is no longer justified.

(4) A certificate given under paragraph (3) and not revoked is conclusive evidence of the matters certified.

[787]

NOTES

Para (1) is amended as follows:

Words in first and second pairs of square brackets substituted by the Financial Services and Markets Act 2000 (Regulated Activities) (Amendment) (No 2) Order 2006, SI 2006/2383, arts 2, 14(a)(i), (ii), as from 6 November 2006 (for the purposes of enabling applications to be made for (i) a Pt IV permission, or a variation of a Pt IV permission, in relation to activities of the kind specified by arts 25B, 25C, 53B, 53C, 63B or 63F or, so far as relevant to any such activity, art 64 of this Order; or (ii) the Authority's approval under FSMA 2000, s 59 in relation to any of those activities), and as from 6 April 2007 (otherwise) (for transitional provisions and effect see arts 36–40 of, and the Schedule to, the 2006 Order).

For the words "and 53C" in italics there are substituted the words ", 53C and 53D", for the words "or 53C," in italics there are substituted the words ", 53C or 53D,", and sub-para (b)(v) is added by the Financial Services and Markets Act 2000 (Regulated Activities) (Amendment) Order 2009, SI 2009/1342, arts 2, 14(a)–(c), as from 1 July 2009 (other than for the purposes of enabling applications to be made for a Part IV permission, or a variation of a Part IV permission, in relation to activities of the kind specified by arts 25E, 53D or 63J or, so far as relevant to any such activity, art 64 of this Order), and as from 30 June 2010 (for those purposes) (for the full commencement details and for transitional provisions etc see arts 1, 32–34 of that Order).

Sub-para (b) substituted, by the Financial Services and Markets Act 2000 (Regulated Activities) (Amendment) (No 1) Order 2003, SI 2003/1475, art 14, as from 31 October 2004 (for transitional provisions see arts 26–29 thereof).

Words in square brackets in sub-para (b)(i) substituted by the Financial Services and Markets Act 2000 (Regulated Activities) (Amendment) (No 2) Order 2003, SI 2003/1476, art 9(2), as from 31 October 2004 (in so far as relating to contracts of long-term care insurance), and as from 14 January 2005 (otherwise) (for transitional provisions see arts 22–27 of that Order).

Sub-paras (b)(iii), (iv) inserted by SI 2006/2383, arts 2, 14(a)(iii), as from 6 November 2006 (certain purposes), and as from 6 April 2007 (otherwise) (for purposes, transitional provisions, and effect, see the note above).

Para (2): words in square brackets substituted by SI 2006/2383, arts 2, 14(b), as from 6 November 2006 (certain purposes), and as from 6 April 2007 (otherwise) (for purposes, transitional provisions, and effect, see the note above); for the words in italics there are substituted the words ", 53C and 53D" by SI 2009/1342, arts 2, 14(d), as from the same dates and for the same purposes, etc, as mentioned in the note relating to this Order above.

[54A   Advice given in the course of administration by authorised person

[(1)]   A person who is not an authorised person ("A") does not carry on an activity of the kind specified by article 53A by reason of—

(a)   anything done by an authorised person ("B") in relation to a regulated mortgage contract which B is administering pursuant to arrangements of the kind mentioned in article 62(a); or

(b)   anything A does in connection with the administration of a regulated mortgage contract in circumstances falling within article 62(b).

[(2)   A person who is not an authorised person ("A") does not carry on an activity of the kind specified by article 53B by reason of—

(a)   anything done by an authorised person ("B") in relation to a regulated home reversion plan which B is administering pursuant to arrangements of the kind mentioned in article 63C(a); or

(b)   anything A does in connection with the administration of a regulated home reversion plan in circumstances falling within article 63C(b).

(3)   A person who is not an authorised person ("A") does not carry on an activity of the kind specified by article 53C by reason of—

(a)   anything done by an authorised person ("B") in relation to a regulated home purchase plan which B is administering pursuant to arrangements of the kind mentioned in article 63G(a); or

(b)   anything A does in connection with the administration of a regulated home purchase plan in circumstances falling within article 63G(b).]]

[(4)   A person who is not an authorised person ("A") does not carry on an activity of the kind specified by article 53D by reason of—

(a)   anything done by an authorised person ("B") in relation to a regulated sale and rent back agreement which B is administering pursuant to arrangements of the kind mentioned in article 63K(a); or

(b)   anything A does in connection with the administration of a regulated sale and rent back agreement in circumstances falling within article 63K(b).]

[788]

NOTES

Commencement: 31 October 2004.

Inserted by the Financial Services and Markets Act 2000 (Regulated Activities) (Amendment) (No 1) Order 2003, SI 2003/1475, art 15, as from 31 October 2004; for transitional provisions see arts 26–29 thereof.

Para (1) numbered as such, and paras (2), (3) added, by the Financial Services and Markets Act 2000 (Regulated Activities) (Amendment) (No 2) Order 2006, SI 2006/2383, arts 2, 15, as from 6 November 2006 (for the purposes of enabling applications to be made for (i) a Pt IV permission, or a variation of a Pt IV permission, in relation to activities of the kind specified by arts 25B, 25C, 53B, 53C, 63B or 63F or, so far as relevant to any such activity, art 64 of this Order; or (ii) the Authority's approval under FSMA 2000, s 59 in relation to any of those activities), and as from 6 April 2007 (otherwise) (for transitional provisions and effect see arts 36–40 of, and the Schedule to, the 2006 Order).

Para (4): added by the Financial Services and Markets Act 2000 (Regulated Activities) (Amendment) Order 2009, SI 2009/1342, arts 2, 15, as from 1 July 2009 (other than for the purposes of enabling applications to be made for a Part IV permission, or a variation of a Part IV permission, in relation to activities of the kind specified by arts 25E, 53D or 63J or, so far as relevant to any such activity, art 64 of this Order), and as from 30 June 2010 (for those purposes) (for the full commencement details and for transitional provisions etc see arts 1, 32–34 of that Order).

55   Other exclusions

[(1)]   Article 53 is also subject to the exclusions in articles 66 (trustees etc), 67, (profession or non-investment business), 68 (sale of goods and supply of services), 69 (groups and joint enterprises), 70 (sale of body corporate)[, 72 (overseas persons)[, 72A (information society services), 72B (activities carried on by a provider of relevant goods or services) and 72D (large risks contracts where risk situated outside the EEA)]].

[(2) [Articles 53A, 53B *and 53C* are] also subject to the exclusions in articles 66 (trustees etc), 67 (profession or non-investment business) and 72A (information society services).]

[789]

NOTES

Para (1): numbered as such by the Financial Services and Markets Act 2000 (Regulated Activities) (Amendment) (No 1) Order 2003, SI 2003/1475, art 16(a), as from 31 October 2004, for transitional provisions see arts 26–29 thereof; words in first (outer) pair of square brackets substituted by the Financial Services and Markets Act 2000 (Regulated Activities) (Amendment) (No 2) Order 2002, SI 2002/1776, art 3(1), (12), as from 21 August 2002; words in second (inner) pair of square brackets substituted by the Financial Services and Markets Act 2000 (Regulated Activities) (Amendment) (No 2) Order 2003, SI 2003/1476, art 9(3), as from 31 October 2004 (in so far as relating to contracts of long-term care insurance), and as from 14 January 2005 (otherwise), for transitional provisions see arts 22–27 of that Order.

Para (2): added by SI 2003/1475, art 16(b), as from 31 October 2004 (for transitional provisions see arts 26–29 thereof); words in square brackets substituted by the Financial Services and Markets Act 2000 (Regulated Activities) (Amendment) (No 2) Order 2006, SI 2006/2383, arts 2, 16, as from 6 November 2006 (for the purposes of enabling applications to be made for (i) a Pt IV permission, or a variation of a Pt IV permission, in relation to activities of the kind specified by arts 25B, 25C, 53B, 53C, 63B or 63F or, so far as relevant to any such activity, art 64 of this Order; or (ii) the Authority's approval under FSMA 2000, s 59 in relation to any of those activities), and as from 6 April 2007 (otherwise) (for transitional provisions and effect see arts 36–40 of, and the Schedule to, the 2006 Order); for the words in italics there are substituted the words ", 53C and 53D" by the Financial Services and Markets Act 2000 (Regulated Activities) (Amendment) Order 2009, SI 2009/1342, arts 2, 16, as from 1 July 2009 (other than for the purposes of enabling applications to be made for a Part IV permission, or a variation of a Part IV permission, in relation to activities of the kind specified by arts 25E, 53D or 63J or, so far as relevant to any such activity, art 64 of this Order), and as from 30 June 2010 (for those purposes) (for the full commencement details and for transitional provisions etc see arts 1, 32–34 of that Order).

CHAPTER XIII
LLOYD'S

The activities

56 Advice on syndicate participation at Lloyd's

Advising a person to become, or continue or cease to be, a member of a particular Lloyd's syndicate is a specified kind of activity.

[790]

57 Managing the underwriting capacity of a Lloyd's syndicate

Managing the underwriting capacity of a Lloyd's syndicate as a managing agent at Lloyd's is a specified kind of activity.

[791]

58 Arranging deals in contracts of insurance written at Lloyd's

The arranging, by the society incorporated by Lloyd's Act 1871 by the name of Lloyd's, of deals in contracts of insurance written at Lloyd's, is a specified kind of activity.

[792]

[Exclusion

58A Information society services

Articles 56 to 58 are subject to the exclusion in article 72A (information society services).]

[793]

NOTES

Inserted, together with the preceding heading, by the Financial Services and Markets Act 2000 (Regulated Activities) (Amendment) (No 2) Order 2002, SI 2002/1776, art 3(1), (13), as from 21 August 2002.

CHAPTER XIV
FUNERAL PLAN CONTRACTS

The activity

59 Funeral plan contracts

(1) Entering as provider into a funeral plan contract is a specified kind of activity.

(2) A "funeral plan contract" is a contract (other than one excluded by article 60) under which—

    (a)   a person ("the customer") makes one or more payments to another person ("the provider"); and

    (b)   the provider undertakes to provide, or secure that another person provides, a funeral in the United Kingdom for the customer (or some other person who is living at the date when the contract is entered into) on his death;

unless, at the time of entering into the contract, the customer and the provider intend or expect the funeral to occur within one month.

[794]

[Exclusions]

60   Plans covered by insurance or trust arrangements

   (1)   There is excluded from article 59 any contract under which—

    (a)   the provider undertakes to secure that sums paid by the customer under the contract will be applied towards a contract of whole life insurance on the life of the customer (or other person for whom the funeral is to be provided), effected and carried out by an authorised person who has permission to effect and carry out such contracts of insurance, for the purpose of providing the funeral; or

    (b)   the provider undertakes to secure that sums paid by the customer under the contract will be held on trust for the purpose of providing the funeral, and that the following requirements are or will be met with respect to the trust—

        (i)   the trust must be established by a written instrument;

        (ii)   more than half of the trustees must be unconnected with the provider;

        (iii) the trustees must appoint, or have appointed, an independent fund manager who is an authorised person who has permission to carry on an activity of the kind specified by article 37, and who is a person who is unconnected with the provider, to manage the assets of the trust;

        (iv) annual accounts must be prepared, and audited by a person who is eligible for appointment as a [statutory auditor under Part 42 of the Companies Act 2006], with respect to the assets and liabilities of the trust; and

        (v)   the assets and liabilities of the trust must, at least once every three years, be determined, calculated and verified by an actuary who is a Fellow of the Institute of Actuaries or of the Faculty of Actuaries.

   (2)   For the purposes of paragraph (1)(b)(ii) and (iii), a person is unconnected with the provider if he is a person other than—

    (a)   the provider;

    (b)   a member of the same group as the provider;

    (c)   a director, other officer or employee of the provider, or of any member of the same group as the provider;

    (d)   a partner of the provider;

    (e)   a close relative of a person falling within sub-paragraph (a), (c) or (d); or

    (f)   an agent of any person falling within sub-paragraphs (a) to (e).

[795]

NOTES

The heading preceding this article was substituted by the Financial Services and Markets Act 2000 (Regulated Activities) (Amendment) (No 2) Order 2002, SI 2002/1776, art 3(1), (14), as from 21 August 2002.

Para (1): words in square brackets substituted (for the original words "company auditor under section 25 of the Companies Act 1989") by the Companies Act 2006 (Consequential Amendments etc) Order 2008, SI 2008/948, art 3(1), Sch 1, Pt 1, para 1(tt), as from 6 April 2008 (for savings see art 6(4) of the 2008 Order which provides that where by virtue of any transitional provision, a provision of the Companies Act 2006 has effect only (a) on or after a specified date, or (b) in relation to matters occurring or arising on or after a specified date, any amendment substituting or inserting a reference to that provision has effect correspondingly).

[60A   Information society services

Article 59 is subject to the exclusion in article 72A (information society services).]

[796]

NOTES

Inserted by the Financial Services and Markets Act 2000 (Regulated Activities) (Amendment) (No 2) Order 2002, SI 2002/1776, art 3(1), (15), as from 21 August 2002.

CHAPTER XV
REGULATED MORTGAGE CONTRACTS

The activities

61 Regulated mortgage contracts

(1) Entering into a regulated mortgage contract as lender is a specified kind of activity.

(2) Administering a regulated mortgage contract is also a specified kind of activity, where the contract was entered into [by way of business] after the coming into force of this article.

(3) In this Chapter—
[(a) a contract is a "regulated mortgage contract" if, at the time it is entered into, the following conditions are met—
(i) the contract is one under which a person ("the lender") provides credit to an individual or to trustees ("the borrower");
(ii) the contract provides for the obligation of the borrower to repay to be secured by a first legal mortgage on land (other than timeshare accommodation) in the United Kingdom;
(iii) at least 40% of that land is used, or is intended to be used, as or in connection with a dwelling by the borrower or (in the case of credit provided to trustees) by an individual who is a beneficiary of the trust, or by a related person;
[but such a contract is not a regulated mortgage contract if it is a regulated home purchase plan;]]
(b) "administering" a regulated mortgage contract means either or both of—
(i) notifying the borrower of changes in interest rates or payments due under the contract, or of other matters of which the contract requires him to be notified; and
(ii) taking any necessary steps for the purposes of collecting or recovering payments due under the contract from the borrower;
but a person is not to be treated as administering a regulated mortgage contract merely because he has, or exercises, a right to take action for the purposes of enforcing the contract (or to require that such action is or is not taken);
(c) "credit" includes a cash loan, and any other form of financial accommodation.

(4) For the purposes of [paragraph 3(a)]—
(a) a "first legal mortgage" means a legal mortgage ranking in priority ahead of all other mortgages (if any) affecting the land in question, where "mortgage" includes charge and (in Scotland) a heritable security;
(b) the area of any land which comprises a building or other structure containing two or more storeys is to be taken to be the aggregate of the floor areas of each of those storeys;
(c) "related person", in relation to the borrower or (in the case of credit provided to trustees) a beneficiary of the trust, means—
(i) that person's spouse [or civil partner];
(ii) a person (whether or not of the opposite sex) whose relationship with that person has the characteristics of the relationship between husband and wife; or
(iii) that person's parent, brother, sister, child, grandparent or grandchild; and
(d) "timeshare accommodation" has the meaning given by section 1 of the Timeshare Act 1992.

[797]

NOTES

Commencement: 31 October 2004.

Para (2): words in square brackets inserted by the Financial Services and Markets Act 2000 (Regulated Activities) (Amendment) Order 2001, SI 2001/3544, arts 2, 8(a), as from 1 September 2002.

Para (3): sub-para (a) substituted by SI 2001/3544, arts 2, 8(b), as from 1 September 2002; words in square brackets inserted by the Financial Services and Markets Act 2000 (Regulated Activities) (Amendment) (No 2) Order 2006, SI 2006/2383, arts 2, 17, as from 6 November 2006 (for the purposes of enabling applications to be made for (i) a Pt IV permission, or a variation of a Pt IV permission, in relation to activities of the kind specified by arts 25B, 25C, 53B, 53C, 63B or 63F or, so far as relevant to any such activity, art 64 of this Order; or (ii) the Authority's approval under FSMA 2000, s 59 in relation to any of those activities), and as from 6 April 2007 (otherwise) (for transitional provisions and effect see arts 36–40 of, and the Schedule to, the 2006 Order).

Para (4): words in first pair of square brackets substituted by SI 2001/3544, arts 2, 8(c), as from 1 September 2002; words in second pair of square brackets inserted by the Civil Partnership Act 2004 (Amendments to Subordinate Legislation) Order 2005, SI 2005/2114, art 2(16), Sch 16, Pt 1, para 1(1), (3), as from 5 December 2005.

Exclusions

62 Arranging administration by authorised person

A person who is not an authorised person does not carry on an activity of the kind specified by article 61(2) in relation to a regulated mortgage contract where he—

(a)   arranges for another person, being an authorised person with permission to carry on an activity of that kind, to administer the contract; or

(b)   administers the contract himself during a period of not more than one month beginning with the day on which any such arrangement comes to an end.

[798]

NOTES
Commencement: 31 October 2004.

63 Administration pursuant to agreement with authorised person

A person who is not an authorised person does not carry on an activity of the kind specified by article 61(2) in relation to a regulated mortgage contract where he administers the contract pursuant to an agreement with an authorised person who has permission to carry on an activity of that kind.

[799]

NOTES
Commencement: 31 October 2004.

[63A Other exclusions

Article 61 is also subject to the exclusions in articles 66 (trustees etc), 72 (overseas persons) and 72A (information society services).]

[800]

NOTES
Commencement: 31 October 2004.
Inserted by the Financial Services and Markets Act 2000 (Regulated Activities) (Amendment) (No 2) Order 2002, SI 2002/1776, art 3(1), (16), as from 21 August 2002; substituted by the Financial Services and Markets Act 2000 (Regulated Activities) (Amendment) (No 1) Order 2003, SI 2003/1475, art 17, as from 31 October 2004 (for transitional provisions see arts 26–29 thereof).

[CHAPTER 15A
REGULATED HOME REVERSION PLANS

The activities

63B Entering into and administering regulated home reversion plans

(1)   Entering into a regulated home reversion plan as plan provider is a specified kind of activity.

(2)   Administering a regulated home reversion plan is also a specified kind of activity where the plan was entered into on or after 6th April 2007.

(3)   In this Chapter—
    (a)   a "regulated home reversion plan" is an arrangement comprised in one or more instruments or agreements, in relation to which the following conditions are met at the time it is entered into—
        (i)   the arrangement is one under which a person (the "plan provider") buys all or part of a qualifying interest in land (other than timeshare accommodation) in the United Kingdom from an individual or trustees (the "reversion seller");
        (ii)   the reversion seller (if he is an individual) or an individual who is a beneficiary of the trust (if the reversion seller is a trustee), or a related person, is entitled under the arrangement to occupy at least 40% of the land in question as or in connection with a dwelling, and intends to do so; and
        (iii)   the arrangement specifies one or more qualifying termination events, on the occurrence of which that entitlement will end;
    (b)   "administering" a regulated home reversion plan means any of—
        (i)   notifying the reversion seller of changes in payments due under the plan, or of other matters of which the plan requires him to be notified;
        (ii)   taking any necessary steps for the purposes of making payments to the reversion seller under the plan; and
        (iii)   taking any necessary steps for the purposes of collecting or recovering payments due under the plan from the reversion seller,
    but a person is not to be treated as administering a regulated home reversion plan merely because he has, or exercises, a right to take action for the purposes of enforcing the plan (or to require that such action is or is not taken).

(4)   For the purposes of paragraph (3)—
    (a)   the reference to a "qualifying interest" in land—

(i) in relation to land in England or Wales, is to an estate in fee simple absolute or a term of years absolute, whether subsisting at law or in equity;

(ii) in relation to land in Scotland, is to the interest of an owner in land or the tenant's right over or interest in a property subject to a lease;

(iii) in relation to land in Northern Ireland, is to any freehold estate or any leasehold estate, whether subsisting at law or in equity;

(b) "timeshare accommodation" has the meaning given by section 1 of the Timeshare Act 1992;

(c) "related person" in relation to the reversion seller or, where the reversion seller is a trustee, a beneficiary of the trust, means—

(i) that person's spouse or civil partner;

(ii) a person (whether or not of the opposite sex) whose relationship with that person has the characteristics of the relationship between husband and wife; or

(iii) that person's parent, brother, sister, child, grandparent or grandchild; and

(d) "qualifying termination event", in relation to a person's entitlement to occupy land, means—

(i) the person becomes a resident of a care home;

(ii) the person dies;

(iii) the end of a specified period of at least twenty years beginning with the day on which the reversion seller entered into the arrangement.

(5) For the purposes of paragraph (3)(a)(ii), the area of any land which comprises a building or other structure containing two or more storeys is to be taken to be the aggregate of the floor areas of each of those storeys.

(6) For the purposes of the definition of "qualifying termination event" in paragraph (4), "care home"—

(a) in relation to England and Wales, has the meaning given by section 3 of the Care Standards Act 2000;

(b) in relation to Scotland, means accommodation provided by a "care home" within the meaning of section 2(3)of the Regulation of Care (Scotland) Act 2001;

(c) in relation to Northern Ireland, means—

(i) a residential care home within the meaning of article 10 of the Health and Personal Social Services (Quality, Improvement and Regulation) (Northern Ireland) Order 2003; or

(ii) a nursing home within the meaning of article 11 of that Order.

(7) In this Order—

(a) references to entering into a regulated home reversion plan as plan provider include acquiring any obligations or rights (including his interest in land) of the plan provider, under such a plan; but

(b) in relation to a person who acquires any such obligations or rights, an activity is a specified kind of activity for the purposes of articles 25B(1)(b) and 53B(b)(ii) and paragraph (2) only if the plan was entered into by the plan provider (rather than the obligations or rights acquired) on or after 6th April 2007.

(8) Accordingly, references in this Order to a plan provider, other than in paragraph (7), include a person who acquires any such obligations or rights.]

[801]

NOTES

Commencement: 6 November 2006 (certain purposes); 6 April 2007 (otherwise) (see below).

Chapters 15A, 15B (arts 63B–63I) inserted by the Financial Services and Markets Act 2000 (Regulated Activities) (Amendment) (No 2) Order 2006, SI 2006/2383, arts 2, 18, as from 6 November 2006 (for the purposes of enabling applications to be made for (i) a Pt IV permission, or a variation of a Pt IV permission, in relation to activities of the kind specified by arts 25B, 25C, 53B, 53C, 63B or 63F or, so far as relevant to any such activity, art 64 of this Order; or (ii) the Authority's approval under FSMA 2000, s 59 in relation to any of those activities), and as from 6 April 2007 (otherwise) (for transitional provisions and effect see arts 36–40 of, and the Schedule to, the 2006 Order).

[Exclusions

63C Arranging administration by authorised person

A person who is not an authorised person does not carry on an activity of the kind specified by article 63B(2) in relation to a regulated home reversion plan where he—

(a) arranges for another person, being an authorised person with permission to carry on an activity of that kind, to administer the plan; or

(b) administers the plan himself during a period of not more than one month beginning with the day on which any such arrangement comes to an end.]

[802]

NOTES
Commencement: 6 November 2006 (certain purposes); 6 April 2007 (otherwise).
Inserted as noted to art 63B at **[801]**.

[63D Administration pursuant to agreement with authorised person

A person who is not an authorised person does not carry on an activity of the kind specified by article 63B(2) in relation to a regulated home reversion plan where he administers the plan pursuant to an agreement with an authorised person who has permission to carry on an activity of that kind.]

[803]

NOTES
Commencement: 6 November 2006 (certain purposes); 6 April 2007 (otherwise).
Inserted as noted to art 63B at **[801]**.

[63E Other exclusions

Article 63B is also subject to the exclusions in articles 66 (trustees etc), 72 (overseas persons) and 72A (information society services).]

[804]

NOTES
Commencement: 6 November 2006 (certain purposes); 6 April 2007 (otherwise).
Inserted as noted to art 63B at **[801]**.

[CHAPTER 15B
REGULATED HOME PURCHASE PLANS

The activities

63F Entering into and administering regulated home purchase plans

(1)　Entering into a regulated home purchase plan as home purchase provider is a specified kind of activity.

(2)　Administering a regulated home purchase plan is also a specified kind of activity where the plan was entered into by way of business on or after 6th April 2007.

(3)　In this Chapter—
    (a)　a "regulated home purchase plan" is an arrangement comprised in one or more instruments or agreements, in relation to which the following conditions are met at the time it is entered into—
        (i)　the arrangement is one under which a person (the "home purchase provider") buys a qualifying interest or an undivided share of a qualifying interest in land (other than timeshare accommodation) in the United Kingdom;
        (ii)　where an undivided share of a qualifying interest in land is bought, the interest is held on trust for the home purchase provider and the individual or trustees mentioned in paragraph (iii) as beneficial tenants in common;
        (iii)　the arrangement provides for the obligation of an individual or trustees (the "home purchaser") to buy the interest bought by the home purchase provider over the course of or at the end of a specified period; and
        (iv)　the home purchaser (if he is an individual) or an individual who is a beneficiary of the trust (if the home purchaser is a trustee), or a related person, is entitled under the arrangement to occupy at least 40% of the land in question as or in connection with a dwelling during that period, and intends to do so;
    (b)　"administering" a regulated home purchase plan means either or both of—
        (i)　notifying the home purchaser of changes in payments due under the plan, or of other matters of which the plan requires him to be notified; and
        (ii)　taking any necessary steps for the purposes of collecting or recovering payments due under the plan from the home purchaser;
    but a person is not to be treated as administering a regulated home purchase plan merely because he has, or exercises, a right to take action for the purposes of enforcing the plan or to require that such action is or is not taken.

(4)　Article 63B(4)(a) to (c) applies for the purposes of paragraph (3)(a) with references to the "reversion seller" being read as references to the "home purchaser".

(5)　Article 63B(5) applies for the purposes of paragraph (3)(a)(iv) with the reference to "paragraph (3)(a)(ii)" being read as a reference to "paragraph (3)(a)(iv)".]

[805]

NOTES
Commencement: 6 November 2006 (certain purposes); 6 April 2007 (otherwise).
Inserted as noted to art 63B at **[801]**.

[Exclusions

63G   Arranging administration by authorised person

A person who is not an authorised person does not carry on an activity of the kind specified by article 63F(2) in relation to a regulated home purchase plan where he—

(a)   arranges for another person, being an authorised person with permission to carry on an activity of that kind, to administer the plan; or

(b)   administers the plan himself during a period of not more than one month beginning with the day on which any such arrangement comes to an end.]

[806]

NOTES
Commencement: 6 November 2006 (certain purposes); 6 April 2007 (otherwise).
Inserted as noted to art 63B at **[801]**.

[63H   Administration pursuant to agreement with authorised person

A person who is not an authorised person does not carry on an activity of the kind specified by article 63F(2) in relation to a regulated home purchase plan where he administers the plan pursuant to an agreement with an authorised person who has permission to carry on an activity of that kind.]

[807]

NOTES
Commencement: 6 November 2006 (certain purposes); 6 April 2007 (otherwise).
Inserted as noted to art 63B at **[801]**.

[63I   Other exclusions

Article 63F is also subject to the exclusions in articles 66 (trustees etc), 72 (overseas persons) and 72A (information society services).]

[808]

NOTES
Commencement: 6 November 2006 (certain purposes); 6 April 2007 (otherwise).
Inserted as noted to art 63B at **[801]**.

[CHAPTER 15C
REGULATED SALE AND RENT BACK AGREEMENTS THE ACTIVITIES

The activities

63J   Entering into and administering regulated sale and rent back agreements

(1)   Entering into a regulated sale and rent back agreement as an agreement provider is a specified kind of activity.

(2)   Administering a regulated sale and rent back agreement is also a specified kind of activity when the agreement was entered into on or after 1st July 2009.

(3)   In this Chapter—

(a)   a "regulated sale and rent back agreement" is an arrangement comprised in one or more instruments or agreements, in relation to which the following conditions are met at the time it is entered into—

(i)   the arrangement is one under which a person (the "agreement provider") buys all or part of the qualifying interest in land (other than timeshare accommodation) in the United Kingdom from an individual or trustees (the "agreement seller "); and

(ii)   the agreement seller (if the agreement seller is an individual) or an individual who is the beneficiary of the trust (if the agreement seller is a trustee), or a related person, is entitled under the arrangement to occupy at least 40% of the land in question as or in connection with a dwelling, and intends to do so;

but such an arrangement is not a regulated sale and rent back agreement if it is a regulated home reversion plan;

(b)   "administering" a regulated sale and rent back agreement means any of—

(i)   notifying the agreement seller of changes in payments due under the agreement, or of other matters of which the agreement requires the agreement seller to be notified;

    (ii)   taking any necessary steps for the purpose of making payments to the agreement seller under the agreement; and

    (iii)   taking any necessary steps for the purposes of collecting or recovering payments due under the agreement from the agreement seller,

but a person is not to be treated as administering a regulated sale and rent back agreement because that person has, or exercises, a right to take action for the purposes of enforcing the agreement (or to require that such action is or is not taken).

(4)   For the purposes of paragraph (3)—
    (a)   the reference to a "qualifying interest" in land—
        (i)   in relation to land in England and Wales, is to an estate in fee simple absolute or a term of years absolute, whether subsisting at law or in equity;
        (ii)   in relation to land in Scotland, is to the interest of an owner in land or the tenant's right over or interest in a property subject to a lease;
        (iii) in relation to land in Northern Ireland, is to any freehold estate or any leasehold estate, whether subsisting at law or in equity;
    (b)   "timeshare accommodation" has the meaning given by section 1 of the Timeshare Act 1992; and
    (c)   "related person" in relation to the agreement seller or, where the agreement seller is a trustee, a beneficiary of the trust, means—
        (i)   that person's spouse or civil partner;
        (ii)   a person (whether or not of the opposite sex) whose relationship with that person has the characteristic of the relationship between husband and wife;
        (iii) that person's parent, brother, sister, child, grandparent or grandchild.

(5)   For the purposes of paragraph (3)(a)(ii), the area of any land which compromises a building or other structure containing two or more storeys is to be taken to be the aggregate of the floor areas of each of those storeys.

(6)   In this Order—
    (a)   references to entering into a regulated sale and rent back agreement as agreement provider include acquiring any obligations or rights of the agreement provider, including the agreement provider's interest in land or interests under one or more of the instruments or agreements referred to in paragraph (3)(a); but
    (b)   in relation to a person who acquires any such obligations or rights, an activity is a specified kind of activity for the purposes of articles 25E(1)(b) and 53D(b)(ii) and paragraph (2) only if the agreement was entered into by the agreement provider (rather than the obligations or rights acquired) on or after 1st July 2009.

(7)   Accordingly, references in this Order to an agreement provider, other than in paragraph (6), include a person who acquires any such obligations or rights.]

[809]

NOTES

Commencement: 1 July 2009 (certain purposes); 30 June 2010 (otherwise) (see below).

Chapter 15C is inserted by the Financial Services and Markets Act 2000 (Regulated Activities) (Amendment) Order 2009, SI 2009/1342, arts 2, 17, as from 1 July 2009 (other than for the purposes of enabling applications to be made for a Part IV permission, or a variation of a Part IV permission, in relation to activities of the kind specified by arts 25E, 53D or 63J or, so far as relevant to any such activity, art 64 of this Order), and as from 30 June 2010 (for those purposes) (for the full commencement details and for transitional provisions etc see arts 1, 32–34 of that Order).

[Exclusions

63K   Arranging administration by authorised person

A person who is not an authorised person does not carry on an activity of the kind specified by article 63J(2) in relation to a regulated sale and rent back agreement where that person—
    (a)   arranges for another person, being an authorised person with permission to carry on an activity of that kind, to administer the agreement; or
    (b)   administers the agreement during a period of not more than one month beginning with the day on which any such arrangement comes to an end.]

[810]

NOTES

Commencement: 1 July 2009 (certain purposes); 30 June 2010 (otherwise) (see art 63J at **[809]**).

Inserted as noted to art 63J at **[809]**.

[63L   Administration pursuant to agreement with authorised person

A person who is not an authorised person does not carry on an activity of the kind specified by article 63J(2) in relation to a regulated sale and rent back agreement where that person administers the agreement pursuant to an agreement with an authorised person who has permission to carry on activity of that kind.]

[811]

NOTES

Commencement: 1 July 2009 (certain purposes); 30 June 2010 (otherwise) (see art 63J at **[809]**).
Inserted as noted to art 63J at **[809]**.

[63M   Other exclusions

Article 63J is also subject to the exclusions in article 66 (trustees etc), 72 (overseas persons) and 72A (information society services).]

[812]

NOTES

Commencement: 1 July 2009 (certain purposes); 30 June 2010 (otherwise) (see art 63J at **[809]**).
Inserted as noted to art 63J at **[809]**.

[CHAPTER 15D
ACTIVITIES OF RECLAIM FUNDS

The activities

63N   Dormant account funds

(1)   The following are specified kinds of activity—
   (a)   the meeting of repayment claims by a reclaim fund;
   (b)   the management of dormant account funds (including the investment of such funds) by a reclaim fund.

(2)   In this article—
   "account", "balance", "dormant" and "reclaim fund" have the same meaning as in Part 1 of the Dormant Bank and Building Society Accounts Act 2008 (transfer of balances in dormant accounts) (see section 6 of that Act);
   "dormant account funds" and "repayment claims" have the same meaning as in section 5 of that Act;
   "management of dormant account funds" means the acceptance of a transfer from a bank or building society of the balance of a dormant account, or a proportion of such a balance, and the management of those funds in such a way as to enable the reclaim fund to meet whatever repayment claims it is prudent to anticipate.]

[813]

NOTES

Commencement: 13 July 2009.
Inserted by the Financial Services and Markets Act 2000 (Regulated Activities) (Amendment) (No 2) Order 2009, SI 2009/1389, arts 2, 4, as from 13 July 2009.

CHAPTER XVI
AGREEING TO CARRY ON ACTIVITIES

The activity

64   Agreeing to carry on specified kinds of activity

Agreeing to carry on an activity of the kind specified by any other provision of this Part (other than article 5, [9B,] 10, [25D,] [51, 52 or 63N]) is a specified kind of activity.

[814]

NOTES

First figure in square brackets inserted by the Financial Services and Markets Act 2000 (Regulated Activities) (Amendment) Order 2002, SI 2002/682, art 5, as from 27 April 2002, subject to transitional provisions in relation to persons issuing electronic money immediately before that date contained in art 9 thereof.
Second figure in square brackets inserted by the Financial Services and Markets Act 2000 (Regulated Activities) (Amendment No 3) Order 2006, SI 2006/3384, arts 2, 18, as from 1 April 2007 (for the purposes of enabling applications to be made for (i) a Pt IV permission, (ii) a variation of a Pt IV permission, and (iii) the Authority's approval under s 59 of the 2000 Act, in relation to an activity of the kind specified by art 25D of this Order, or in relation to an investment of the kind specified by arts 83, 84 or 85 of this Order), and as from 1 November 2007 (otherwise).
Words in third pair of square brackets substituted by the Financial Services and Markets Act 2000 (Regulated Activities) (Amendment) (No 2) Order 2009, SI 2009/1389, arts 2, 4, as from 13 July 2009.

See also the Financial Services and Markets Act 2000 (Carrying on Regulated Activities by Way of Business) Order 2001, SI 2001/1177, arts 3, 3A, 3B, 3C.

[Exclusions

65   Overseas persons etc

Article 64 is subject to the exclusions in articles 72 (overseas persons) and 72A (information society services).]

[815]

NOTES

Substituted, together with the preceding heading, by the Financial Services and Markets Act 2000 (Regulated Activities) (Amendment) (No 2) Order 2002, SI 2002/1776, art 3(1), (17), as from 21 August 2002.

CHAPTER XVII
EXCLUSIONS APPLYING TO SEVERAL SPECIFIED KINDS OF ACTIVITY

66   Trustees, nominees and personal representatives

(1)   A person ("X") does not carry on an activity of the kind specified by article 14 where he enters into a transaction as bare trustee or, in Scotland, as nominee for another person ("Y") and—

    (a)   X is acting on Y's instructions; and

    (b)   X does not hold himself out as providing a service of buying and selling securities or contractually based investments.

(2)   Subject to paragraph (7), there are excluded from [articles 25(1) and (2)[, 25A(1) and (2), 25B(1) and (2) *and 25C(1) and* (2)]] arrangements made by a person acting as trustee or personal representative for or with a view to a transaction which is or is to be entered into—

    (a)   by that person and a fellow trustee or personal representative (acting in their capacity as such); or

    (b)   by a beneficiary under the trust, will or intestacy.

(3)   Subject to paragraph (7), there is excluded from article 37 any activity carried on by a person acting as trustee or personal representative, unless—

    (a)   he holds himself out as providing a service comprising an activity of the kind specified by article 37; or

    (b)   the assets in question are held for the purposes of an occupational pension scheme, and, by virtue of article 4 of the Financial Services and Markets Act 2000 (Carrying on Regulated Activities by Way of Business) Order 2001, he is to be treated as carrying on that activity by way of business.

[(3A)   Subject to paragraph (7), there is excluded from article 39A any activity carried on by a person acting as trustee or personal representative, unless he holds himself out as providing a service comprising an activity of the kind specified by article 39A.]

(4)   Subject to paragraph (7), there is excluded from article 40 any activity carried on by a person acting as trustee or personal representative, unless he holds himself out as providing a service comprising an activity of the kind specified by article 40.

[(4A)   There is excluded from article 40 any activity carried on by a person acting as trustee which consists of arranging for one or more other persons to safeguard and administer trust assets where—

    (a)   that other person is a qualifying custodian; or

    (b)   that safeguarding and administration is also arranged by a qualifying custodian.

In this paragraph, "qualifying custodian" has the meaning given by article 41(2).]

(5)   A person does not, by sending or causing to be sent a dematerialised instruction (within the meaning of article 45), carry on an activity of the kind specified by that article if the instruction relates to an investment which that person holds as trustee or personal representative.

(6)   Subject to paragraph (7), there is excluded from [articles 53[, 53A, 53B *and 53C*]] the giving of advice by a person acting as trustee or personal representative where he gives the advice to—

    (a)   a fellow trustee or personal representative for the purposes of the trust or the estate; or

    (b)   a beneficiary under the trust, will or intestacy concerning his interest in the trust fund or estate.

[(6A)   Subject to paragraph (7), a person acting as trustee or personal representative does not carry on an activity of the kind specified by article 61(1) or (2) where the borrower under the regulated mortgage contract in question is a beneficiary under the trust, will or intestacy.]

[(6B)   Subject to paragraph (7), a person acting as trustee or personal representative does not carry on an activity of the kind specified by article 63B(1) or (2) where the reversion seller under the regulated home reversion plan in question is a beneficiary under the trust, will or intestacy.

PART IV
OTHER STATUTORY INSTRUMENTS

(6C)   Subject to paragraph (7), a person acting as trustee or personal representative does not carry on an activity of the kind specified by article 63F(1) or (2) where the home purchaser under the regulated home purchase plan in question is a beneficiary under the trust, will or intestacy.]

[(6D)   Subject to paragraph (7), a person acting as a trustee or personal representative does not carry on an activity of the kind specified by article 63J(1) or (2) where the agreement seller under the regulated sale and rent back agreement is a beneficiary under the trust, will or intestacy.]

(7)   Paragraphs (2), (3)[, (3A)], [(4), (6)[, (6A), (6B) *and* (6C)]] do not apply if the person carrying on the activity is remunerated for what he does in addition to any remuneration he receives as trustee or personal representative, and for these purposes a person is not to be regarded as receiving additional remuneration merely because his remuneration is calculated by reference to time spent.

[(8)   This article is subject to article 4(4A).]

[816]

NOTES

Para (2) is amended as follows:
Words in first (outer) pair of square brackets substituted by the Financial Services and Markets Act 2000 (Regulated Activities) (Amendment) (No 1) Order 2003, SI 2003/1475, art 18(a), as from 31 October 2004 (for transitional provisions see arts 26–29 thereof).
Words in second (inner) pair of square brackets substituted by the Financial Services and Markets Act 2000 (Regulated Activities) (Amendment) (No 2) Order 2006, SI 2006/2383, arts 2, 19(a), as from 6 November 2006 (for the purposes of enabling applications to be made for (i) a Pt IV permission, or a variation of a Pt IV permission, in relation to activities of the kind specified by arts 25B, 25C, 53B, 53C, 63B or 63F or, so far as relevant to any such activity, art 64 of this Order; or (ii) the Authority's approval under FSMA 2000, s 59 in relation to any of those activities), and as from 6 April 2007 (otherwise) (for transitional provisions and effect see arts 36–40 of, and the Schedule to, the 2006 Order).
For the words in italics there are substituted the words ", 25C(1) and (2) and 25E (1) and (2)" by the Financial Services and Markets Act 2000 (Regulated Activities) (Amendment) Order 2009, SI 2009/1342, arts 2, 18(a), as from 1 July 2009 (other than for the purposes of enabling applications to be made for a Part IV permission, or a variation of a Part IV permission, in relation to activities of the kind specified by arts 25E, 53D or 63J or, so far as relevant to any such activity, art 64 of this Order), and as from 30 June 2010 (for those purposes) (for the full commencement details and for transitional provisions etc see arts 1, 32–34 of that Order).
Para (3A): inserted by the Financial Services and Markets Act 2000 (Regulated Activities) (Amendment) (No 2) Order 2003, SI 2003/1476, art 10(1)(a), as from 31 October 2004 (in so far as relating to contracts of long-term care insurance), and as from 14 January 2005 (otherwise); for transitional provisions see arts 22–27 of that Order.
Para (4A): inserted by the Financial Services and Markets Act 2000 (Regulated Activities) (Amendment) Order 2005, SI 2005/593, art 2(4), as from 6 April 2005.
Para (6): words in first (outer) pair of square brackets substituted by SI 2003/1475, art 18(b), as from 31 October 2004 (for transitional provisions see arts 26–29 thereof); words in second (inner) pair of square brackets substituted by SI 2006/2383, arts 2, 19(b), as from 6 November 2006 (certain purposes), and as from 6 April 2007 (otherwise) (for purposes, transitional provisions, and effect, see the para (2) note above); for the words in italics there are substituted the words ", 53C and 53D" by SI 2009/1342, arts 2, 18(b), as from the same dates and for the same purposes, etc, as mentioned in the note relating to this Order above.
Para (6A): inserted by SI 2003/1475, art 18(c), as from 31 October 2004; for transitional provisions see arts 26–29 thereof.
Paras (6B), (6C): inserted by SI 2006/2383, arts 2, 19(c), as from 6 November 2006 (certain purposes), and as from 6 April 2007 (otherwise) (for purposes, transitional provisions, and effect, see the para (2) note above).
Para (6D): inserted by SI 2009/1342, arts 2, 18(c), as from the same dates and for the same purposes, etc, as mentioned in the note relating to this Order above.
Para (7) is amended as follows:
Figure in first pair of square brackets inserted by SI 2003/1476, art 10(1)(b), as from 31 October 2004 (in so far as relating to contracts of long-term care insurance), and as from 14 January 2005 (otherwise), for transitional provisions see arts 22–27 of that Order.
Words in second (outer) pair of square brackets substituted by SI 2003/1475, art 18(d), as from 31 October 2004, for transitional provisions see arts 26–29 thereof.
Words in third (inner) pair of square brackets substituted by SI 2006/2383, arts 2, 19(d), as from 6 November 2006 (certain purposes), and as from 6 April 2007 (otherwise) (for purposes, transitional provisions, and effect, see the para (2) note above).
For the words in italics there are substituted the words ", (6C) and (6D)" by SI 2009/1342, arts 2, 18(d), as from the same dates and for the same purposes, etc, as mentioned in the note relating to this Order above.
Para (8): added by the Financial Services and Markets Act 2000 (Regulated Activities) (Amendment No 3) Order 2006, SI 2006/3384, arts 2, 19, as from 1 April 2007 (for the purposes of enabling applications to be made for (i) a Pt IV permission, (ii) a variation of a Pt IV permission, and (iii) the Authority's approval under s 59 of the 2000 Act, in relation to an activity of the kind specified by art 25D of this Order, or in relation to an investment of the kind specified by arts 83, 84 or 85 of this Order), and as from 1 November 2007 (otherwise).

67 Activities carried on in the course of a profession or non-investment business

(1)   There is excluded from articles 21, 25(1) and (2)[, 25A], [25B, 25C,] [25E,] [39A, 40], [53 [, 53A, 53B *and* 53C]] any activity which

   (a)   is carried on in the course of carrying on any profession or business which does not otherwise consist of [the carrying on of regulated activities in the United Kingdom]; and

(b)   may reasonably be regarded as a necessary part of other services provided in the course of that profession or business.

(2)   But the exclusion in paragraph (1) does not apply if the activity in question is remunerated separately from the other services.

[(3)   This article is subject to article 4(4) and (4A).]

[817]

NOTES

Para (1) is amended as follows:

Figure in first pair of square brackets inserted, and words in fifth (outer) pair of square brackets substituted, by the Financial Services and Markets Act 2000 (Regulated Activities) (Amendment) (No 1) Order 2003, SI 2003/1475, art 19, as from 31 October 2004, for transitional provisions see arts 26–29 thereof.

Figures in second pair of square brackets inserted by the Financial Services and Markets Act 2000 (Regulated Activities) (Amendment) (No 2) Order 2006, SI 2006/2383, arts 2, 20(a), as from 6 November 2006 (for the purposes of enabling applications to be made for (i) a Pt IV permission, or a variation of a Pt IV permission, in relation to activities of the kind specified by arts 25B, 25C, 53B, 53C, 63B or 63F or, so far as relevant to any such activity, art 64 of this Order; or (ii) the Authority's approval under FSMA 2000, s 59 in relation to any of those activities), and as from 6 April 2007 (otherwise) (for transitional provisions and effect see arts 36–40 of, and the Schedule to, the 2006 Order).

Figure in third pair of square brackets inserted, and for the words in italics there are substituted the words ", 53C and 53D", by the Financial Services and Markets Act 2000 (Regulated Activities) (Amendment) Order 2009, SI 2009/1342, arts 2, 19, as from 1 July 2009 (other than for the purposes of enabling applications to be made for a Part IV permission, or a variation of a Part IV permission, in relation to activities of the kind specified by arts 25E, 53D or 63J or, so far as relevant to any such activity, art 64 of this Order), and as from 30 June 2010 (for those purposes) (for the full commencement details and for transitional provisions etc see arts 1, 32–34 of that Order).

Figures in fourth pair of square brackets substituted by the Financial Services and Markets Act 2000 (Regulated Activities) (Amendment) (No 2) Order 2003, SI 2003/1476, art 10(2), as from 31 October 2004 (in so far as relating to contracts of long-term care insurance), and as from 14 January 2005 (otherwise), for transitional provisions see arts 22–27 of that Order.

Words in sixth (inner) pair of square brackets substituted by SI 2006/2383, arts 2, 20(b), as from 6 November 2006 (certain purposes), and as from 6 April 2007 (otherwise) (for purposes, transitional provisions, and effect, see the note above).

Words in square brackets in sub-para (a) substituted by the Financial Services and Markets Act 2000 (Regulated Activities) (Amendment) Order 2001, SI 2001/3544, arts 2, 9, as from 1 December 2001.

Para (3): added by the Financial Services and Markets Act 2000 (Regulated Activities) (Amendment No 3) Order 2006, SI 2006/3384, arts 2, 20, as from 1 April 2007 (for the purposes of enabling applications to be made for (i) a Pt IV permission, (ii) a variation of a Pt IV permission, and (iii) the Authority's approval under s 59 of the 2000 Act, in relation to an activity of the kind specified by art 25D of this Order, or in relation to an investment of the kind specified by arts 83, 84 or 85 of this Order), and as from 1 November 2007 (otherwise).

---

68 Activities carried on in connection with the sale of goods or supply of services

(1)   Subject to paragraphs (9), (10) and (11), this article concerns certain activities carried on for the purposes of or in connection with the sale of goods or supply of services by a supplier to a customer, where—

   "supplier" means a person whose main business is to sell goods or supply services and not to carry on any activities of the kind specified by any of articles 14, 21, 25, 37[, 39A], 40, 45, 51, 52 and 53 and, where the supplier is a member of a group, also means any other member of that group; and

   "customer" means a person, other than an individual, to whom a supplier sells goods or supplies services, or agrees to do so, and, where the customer is a member of a group, also means any other member of that group;

and in this article "related sale or supply" means a sale of goods or supply of services to the customer otherwise than by the supplier, but for or in connection with the same purpose as the sale or supply mentioned above.

(2)   There is excluded from article 14 any transaction entered into by a supplier with a customer, if the transaction is entered into for the purposes of or in connection with the sale of goods or supply of services, or a related sale or supply.

(3)   There is excluded from article 21 any transaction entered into [by a supplier as agent for a customer], if the transaction is entered into for the purposes of or in connection with the sale of goods or supply of services, or a related sale or supply, and provided that—

   (a)   where the investment to which the transaction relates is a security, the supplier does not hold himself out (other than to the customer) as engaging in the business of buying securities of the kind to which the transaction relates with a view to selling them, and does not regularly solicit members of the public for the purpose of inducing them (as principals or agents) to buy, sell, subscribe for or underwrite securities;

   (b)   where the investment to which the transaction relates is a contractually based investment, the supplier enters into the transaction—

      (i)   with or through an authorised person, or an exempt person acting in the course of a business comprising a regulated activity in relation to which he is exempt; or

(ii) through an office outside the United Kingdom maintained by a party to the transaction, and with or through a person whose head office is situated outside the United Kingdom and whose ordinary business involves him in carrying on activities of the kind specified by any of articles 14, 21, 25, 37, 40, 45, 51, 52 and 53 or, so far as relevant to any of those articles, article 64, or would do so apart from any exclusion from any of those articles made by this Order.

(4) In paragraph (3)(a), "members of the public" has the meaning given by article 15(2), references to "A" being read as references to the supplier.

(5) There are excluded from article 25(1) and (2) arrangements made by a supplier for, or with a view to, a transaction which is or is to be entered into by a customer for the purposes of or in connection with the sale of goods or supply of services, or a related sale or supply.

(6) There is excluded from article 37 any activity carried on by a supplier where the assets in question—
    (a) are those of a customer; and
    (b) are managed for the purposes of or in connection with the sale of goods or supply of services, or a related sale or supply.

(7) There is excluded from article 40 any activity carried on by a supplier where the assets in question are or are to be safeguarded and administered for the purposes of or in connection with the sale of goods or supply of services, or a related sale or supply.

(8) There is excluded from article 53 the giving of advice by a supplier to a customer for the purposes of or in connection with the sale of goods or supply of services, or a related sale or supply, or to a person with whom the customer proposes to enter into a transaction for the purposes of or in connection with such a sale or supply or related sale or supply.

(9) Paragraphs (2), (3) and (5) do not apply in the case of a transaction for the sale or purchase of a [contract of insurance], an investment of the kind specified by article 81, or an investment of the kind specified by article 89 so far as relevant to such a contract or such an investment.

(10) Paragraph (6) does not apply where the assets managed consist of qualifying contracts of insurance, investments of the kind specified by article 81, or investments of the kind specified by article 89 so far as relevant to such contracts or such investments.

(11) Paragraph (8) does not apply in the case of advice in relation to an investment which is a [contract of insurance], is of the kind specified by article 81, or is of the kind specified by article 89 so far as relevant to such a contract or such an investment.

[(12) This article is subject to article 4(4).]

[818]

NOTES

Para (1): figure in square brackets in definition "supplier" inserted by the Financial Services and Markets Act 2000 (Regulated Activities) (Amendment) (No 2) Order 2003, SI 2003/1476, art 10(3)(a), as from 31 October 2004 (in so far as relating to contracts of long-term care insurance), and as from 14 January 2005 (otherwise); for transitional provisions see arts 22–27 of that Order.

Para (3): words in square brackets substituted by the Financial Services and Markets Act 2000 (Regulated Activities) (Amendment) Order 2001, SI 2001/3544, arts 2, 10, as from 1 December 2001.

Paras (9), (11): words in square brackets substituted by SI 2003/1476, art 10(3)(b), (c), as from 31 October 2004 (in so far as relating to contracts of long-term care insurance), and as from 14 January 2005 (otherwise); for transitional provisions see arts 22–27 of that Order.

Para (12): added by the Financial Services and Markets Act 2000 (Regulated Activities) (Amendment No 3) Order 2006, SI 2006/3384, arts 2, 21, as from 1 April 2007 (for the purposes of enabling applications to be made for (i) a Pt IV permission, (ii) a variation of a Pt IV permission, and (iii) the Authority's approval under s 59 of the 2000 Act, in relation to an activity of the kind specified by art 25D of this Order, or in relation to an investment of the kind specified by arts 83, 84 or 85 of this Order), and as from 1 November 2007 (otherwise).

69 Groups and joint enterprises

(1) There is excluded from article 14 any transaction into which a person enters as principal with another person if that other person is also acting as principal and—
    (a) they are members of the same group; or
    (b) they are, or propose to become, participators in a joint enterprise and the transaction is entered into for the purposes of or in connection with that enterprise.

(2) There is excluded from article 21 any transaction into which a person enters as agent for another person if that other person is acting as principal, and the condition in paragraph (1)(a) or (b) is met, provided that—
    (a) where the investment to which the transaction relates is a security, the agent does not hold himself out (other than to members of the same group or persons who are or propose to become participators with him in a joint enterprise) as engaging in the business of buying securities of the kind to which the transaction relates with a view to

selling them, and does not regularly solicit members of the public for the purpose of inducing them (as principals or agents) to buy, sell, subscribe for or underwrite securities;

    (b)   where the investment to which the transaction relates is a contractually based investment, the agent enters into the transaction—

        (i)   with or through an authorised person, or an exempt person acting in the course of a business comprising a regulated activity in relation to which he is exempt; or

        (ii)   through an office outside the United Kingdom maintained by a party to the transaction, and with or through a person whose head office is situated outside the United Kingdom and whose ordinary business involves him in carrying on activities of the kind specified by any of articles 14, 21, 25, 37, 40, 45, 51, 52 and 53 or, so far as relevant to any of those articles, article 64, or would do so apart from any exclusion from any of those articles made by this Order.

(3)   In paragraph (2)(a), "members of the public" has the meaning given by article 15(2), references to "A" being read as references to the agent.

(4)   There are excluded from article 25(1) and (2) arrangements made by a person if—

    (a)   he is a member of a group and the arrangements in question are for, or with a view to, a transaction which is or is to be entered into, as principal, by another member of the same group; or

    (b)   he is or proposes to become a participator in a joint enterprise, and the arrangements in question are for, or with a view to, a transaction which is or is to be entered into, as principal, by another person who is or proposes to become a participator in that enterprise, for the purposes of or in connection with that enterprise.

(5)   There is excluded from article 37 any activity carried on by a person if—

    (a)   he is a member of a group and the assets in question belong to another member of the same group; or

    (b)   he is or proposes to become a participator in a joint enterprise with the person to whom the assets belong, and the assets are managed for the purposes of or in connection with that enterprise.

(6)   There is excluded from article 40 any activity carried on by a person if—

    (a)   he is a member of a group and the assets in question belong to another member of the same group; or

    (b)   he is or proposes to become a participator in a joint enterprise, and the assets in question—

        (i)   belong to another person who is or proposes to become a participator in that joint enterprise; and

        (ii)   are or are to be safeguarded and administered for the purposes of or in connection with that enterprise.

(7)   A person who is a member of a group does not carry on an activity of the kind specified by article 45 where he sends a dematerialised instruction, or causes one to be sent, on behalf of another member of the same group, if the investment to which the instruction relates is one in respect of which a member of the same group is registered as holder in the appropriate register of securities, or will be so registered as a result of the instruction.

(8)   In paragraph (7), "dematerialised instruction" and "register of securities" have the meaning given by regulation 3 of the Uncertificated Securities Regulations [2001].

(9)   There is excluded from article 53 the giving of advice by a person if—

    (a)   he is a member of a group and gives the advice in question to another member of the same group; or

    (b)   he is, or proposes to become, a participator in a joint enterprise and the advice in question is given to another person who is, or proposes to become, a participator in that enterprise for the purposes of or in connection with that enterprise.

[(10)   Paragraph (2) does not apply to a transaction for the sale or purchase of a contract of insurance.

(11)   Paragraph (4) does not apply to arrangements for, or with a view to, a transaction for the sale or purchase of a contract of insurance.

(12)   Paragraph (9) does not apply where the advice relates to a transaction for the sale or purchase of a contract of insurance.]

[(13)   This article is subject to article 4(4).]

[819]

NOTES

    Para (8): date in square brackets substituted by the Financial Services and Markets Act 2000 (Regulated Activities) (Amendment) Order 2002, SI 2002/682, art 13(4), as from 27 April 2002.

Paras (10)–(12): added by the Financial Services and Markets Act 2000 (Regulated Activities) (Amendment) (No 2) Order 2003, SI 2003/1476, art 10(4), as from 31 October 2004 (in so far as relating to contracts of long-term care insurance), and as from 14 January 2005 (otherwise); for transitional provisions see arts 22–27 of that Order.

Para (13): added by the Financial Services and Markets Act 2000 (Regulated Activities) (Amendment No 3) Order 2006, SI 2006/3384, arts 2, 22, as from 1 April 2007 (for the purposes of enabling applications to be made for (i) a Pt IV permission, (ii) a variation of a Pt IV permission, and (iii) the Authority's approval under s 59 of the 2000 Act, in relation to an activity of the kind specified by art 25D of this Order, or in relation to an investment of the kind specified by arts 83, 84 or 85 of this Order), and as from 1 November 2007 (otherwise).

70   Activities carried on in connection with the sale of a body corporate

(1)   A person does not carry on an activity of the kind specified by article 14 by entering as principal into a transaction if—
  (a)   the transaction is one to acquire or dispose of shares in a body corporate other than an open-ended investment company, or is entered into for the purposes of such an acquisition or disposal; and
  (b)   either—
    (i)   the conditions set out in paragraph (2) are met; or
    (ii)   those conditions are not met, but the object of the transaction may nevertheless reasonably be regarded as being the acquisition of day to day control of the affairs of the body corporate.

(2)   The conditions mentioned in paragraph (1)(b) are that—
  (a)   the shares consist of or include 50 per cent or more of the voting shares in the body corporate; or
  (b)   the shares, together with any already held by the person acquiring them, consist of or include at least that percentage of such shares; and
  (c)   in either case, the acquisition or disposal is between parties each of whom is a body corporate, a partnership, a single individual or a group of connected individuals.

(3)   In paragraph (2)(c), "a group of connected individuals" means—
  (a)   in relation to a party disposing of shares in a body corporate, a single group of persons each of whom is—
    (i)   a director or manager of the body corporate;
    (ii)   a close relative of any such director or manager;
    (iii)   a person acting as trustee for any person falling within paragraph (i) or (ii); and
  (b)   in relation to a party acquiring shares in a body corporate, a single group of persons each of whom is—
    (i)   a person who is or is to be a director or manager of the body corporate;
    (ii)   a close relative of any such person; or
    (iii)   a person acting as trustee for any person falling within paragraph (i) or (ii).

(4)   A person does not carry on an activity of the kind specified by article 21 by entering as agent into a transaction of the kind described in paragraph (1).

(5)   There are excluded from article 25(1) and (2) arrangements made for, or with a view to, a transaction of the kind described in paragraph (1).

(6)   There is excluded from article 53 the giving of advice in connection with a transaction (or proposed transaction) of the kind described in paragraph (1).

[(7)   Paragraphs (4), (5) and (6) do not apply in the case of a transaction for the sale or purchase of a contract of insurance.]

[(8)   This article is subject to article 4(4).]

[820]

NOTES
Para (7): added by the Financial Services and Markets Act 2000 (Regulated Activities) (Amendment) (No 2) Order 2003, SI 2003/1476, art 10(5), as from 31 October 2004 (in so far as relating to contracts of long-term care insurance), and as from 14 January 2005 (otherwise); for transitional provisions see arts 22–27 of that Order.

Para (8): added by the Financial Services and Markets Act 2000 (Regulated Activities) (Amendment No 3) Order 2006, SI 2006/3384, arts 2, 23, as from 1 April 2007 (for the purposes of enabling applications to be made for (i) a Pt IV permission, (ii) a variation of a Pt IV permission, and (iii) the Authority's approval under s 59 of the 2000 Act, in relation to an activity of the kind specified by art 25D of this Order, or in relation to an investment of the kind specified by arts 83, 84 or 85 of this Order), and as from 1 November 2007 (otherwise).

71   Activities carried on in connection with employee share schemes

(1)   A person ("C"), a member of the same group as C or a relevant trustee does not carry on an activity of the kind specified by article 14 by entering as principal into a transaction the purpose of which is to enable or facilitate—
  (a)   transactions in shares in, or debentures issued by, C between, or for the benefit of, any of the persons mentioned in paragraph (2); or

(b)   the holding of such shares or debentures by, or for the benefit of, such persons.

(2)   The persons referred to in paragraph (1) are—
    (a)   the bona fide employees or former employees of C or of another member of the same group as C;
    (b)   the wives, husbands, widows, widowers, [civil partners, surviving civil partners,] or children or step-children under the age of eighteen of such employees or former employees.

(3)   C, a member of the same group as C or a relevant trustee does not carry on an activity of the kind specified by article 21 by entering as agent into a transaction of the kind described in paragraph (1).

(4)   There are excluded from article 25(1) or (2) arrangements made by C, a member of the same group as C or a relevant trustee if the arrangements in question are for, or with a view to, a transaction of the kind described in paragraph (1).

(5)   There is excluded from article 40 any activity if the assets in question are, or are to be, safeguarded and administered by C, a member of the same group as C or a relevant trustee for the purpose of enabling or facilitating transactions of the kind described in paragraph (1).

(6)   In this article—
    (a)   "shares" and "debentures" include—
        (i)   any investment of the kind specified by article 76 or 77;
        (ii)   any investment of the kind specified by article 79 or 80 so far as relevant to articles 76 and 77; and
        (iii)   any investment of the kind specified by article 89 so far as relevant to investments of the kind mentioned in paragraph (i) or (ii);
    (b)   "relevant trustee" means a person who, in pursuance of the arrangements made for the purpose mentioned in paragraph (1), holds, as trustee, shares in or debentures issued by C.

[821]

NOTES
Para (2): words in square brackets in sub-para (b) inserted by the Civil Partnership Act 2004 (Amendments to Subordinate Legislation) Order 2005, SI 2005/2114, art 2(16), Sch 16, Pt 1, para 1(1), (4), as from 5 December 2005.
Step-children, etc: as to the meaning of this and related expressions, see the Civil Partnership Act 2004, s 246 (as applied to this Order by the Civil Partnership Act 2004 (Relationships Arising Through Civil Partnership) Order 2005, SI 2005/3137, art 3, Schedule).

72   Overseas persons

(1)   An overseas person does not carry on an activity of the kind specified by article 14 [or 25D] by—
    (a)   entering into a transaction as principal with or though an authorised person, or an exempt person acting in the course of a business comprising a regulated activity in relation to which he is exempt; or
    (b)   entering into a transaction as principal with a person in the United Kingdom, if the transaction is the result of a legitimate approach.

(2)   An overseas person does not carry on an activity of the kind specified by article 21 [or 25D] by—
    (a)   entering into a transaction as agent for any person with or through an authorised person or an exempt person acting in the course of a business comprising a regulated activity in relation to which he is exempt; or
    (b)   entering into a transaction with another party ("X") as agent for any person ("Y"), other than with or through an authorised person or such an exempt person, unless—
        (i)   either X or Y is in the United Kingdom; and
        (ii)   the transaction is the result of an approach (other than a legitimate approach) made by or on behalf of, or to, whichever of X or Y is in the United Kingdom.

(3)   There are excluded from article 25(1) [or 25D] arrangements made by an overseas person with an authorised person, or an exempt person acting in the course of a business comprising a regulated activity in relation to which he is exempt.

(4)   There are excluded from article 25(2) [or 25D] arrangements made by an overseas person with a view to transactions which are, as respects transactions in the United Kingdom, confined to—
    (a)   transactions entered into by authorised persons as principal or agent; and
    (b)   transactions entered into by exempt persons, as principal or agent, in the course of business comprising regulated activities in relation to which they are exempt.

(5)   There is excluded from article 53 the giving of advice by an overseas person as a result of a legitimate approach.

[(5A) An overseas person does not carry on an activity of the kind specified by article 25A(1)(a), 25B(1)(a) *or 25C(1)(a)* if each person who may be contemplating entering into the relevant type of agreement in the relevant capacity is non-resident.

(5B) There are excluded from articles 25A(1)(b), 25B(1)(b) *and 25C(1)(b)* arrangements made by an overseas person to vary the terms of a qualifying agreement.

(5C) There are excluded from articles 25A(2), 25B(2) *and 25C(2)*, arrangements made by an overseas person which are made solely with a view to non-resident persons who participate in those arrangements entering, in the relevant capacity, into the relevant type of agreement.

(5D) An overseas person does not carry on an activity of the kind specified in article 61(1), 63B(1) *or 63F(1)* by entering into a qualifying agreement.

(5E) An overseas person does not carry on an activity of the kind specified in article 61(2), 63B(2) *or 63F(2)* where he administers a qualifying agreement.

(5F) In paragraphs (5A) to (5E)—
  (a) "non-resident" means not normally resident in the United Kingdom;
  (b) "qualifying agreement" means—
    (i) in relation to articles 25A and 61, a regulated mortgage contract where the borrower (or each borrower) is non-resident when he enters into it;
    (ii) in relation to articles 25B and 63B, a regulated home reversion plan where the reversion seller (or each reversion seller) is non-resident when he enters into it;
    (iii) in relation to articles 25C and 63F, a regulated home purchase plan where the home purchaser (or each home purchaser) is non-resident when he enters into it;
    [(iv) in relation to articles 25E and 63J, a regulated sale and rent back agreement where the agreement seller (or each agreement seller) is non-resident when the agreement seller enters into it;]
  (c) "the relevant capacity" means—
    (i) in the case of a regulated mortgage contract, as borrower;
    (ii) in the case of a regulated home reversion plan, as reversion seller or plan provider;
    (iii) in the case of a regulated home purchase plan, as home purchaser;
    [(iv) in the case of a regulated sale and rent back agreement, as agreement seller or agreement provider;]
  (d) "the relevant type of agreement" means—
    (i) in relation to article 25A, a regulated mortgage contract;
    (ii) in relation to article 25B, a regulated home reversion plan;
    (iii) in relation to article 25C, a regulated home purchase plan[;
    (iv) in relation to article 25E, a regulated sale and rent back agreement]].

(6) There is excluded from article 64 any agreement made by an overseas person to carry on an activity of the kind specified by article 25(1) or (2), 37[, 39A], 40 or 45 if the agreement is the result of a legitimate approach.

(7) In this article, "legitimate approach" means—
  (a) an approach made to the overseas person which has not been solicited by him in any way, or has been solicited by him in a way which does not contravene section 21 of the Act; or
  (b) an approach made by or on behalf of the overseas person in a way which does not contravene that section.

[(8) Paragraphs (1) to (5) do not apply where the overseas person is an investment firm or credit institution—
  (a) who is providing or performing investment services and activities on a professional basis; and
  (b) whose home Member State is the United Kingdom.]

[822]

NOTES

Paras (1)–(4): figures in square brackets inserted by the Financial Services and Markets Act 2000 (Regulated Activities) (Amendment No 3) Order 2006, SI 2006/3384, arts 2, 24(a)–(d), as from 1 April 2007 (for the purposes of enabling applications to be made for (i) a Pt IV permission, (ii) a variation of a Pt IV permission, and (iii) the Authority's approval under s 59 of the 2000 Act, in relation to an activity of the kind specified by art 25D of this Order, or in relation to an investment of the kind specified by arts 83, 84 or 85 of this Order), and as from 1 November 2007 (otherwise).

Paras (5A)–(5F): inserted by the Financial Services and Markets Act 2000 (Regulated Activities) (Amendment) (No 1) Order 2003, SI 2003/1475, art 20, as from 31 October 2004; and substituted by the Financial Services and Markets Act 2000 (Regulated Activities) (Amendment) (No 2) Order 2006, SI 2006/2383, arts 2, 21, as from 6 November 2006 (for the purposes of enabling applications to be made for (i) a Pt IV permission, or a variation of a Pt IV permission, in relation to activities of the kind specified by arts 25B, 25C, 53B, 53C, 63B or 63F or, so far as relevant to any such activity, art 64 of this Order; or (ii) the Authority's approval under FSMA 2000, s 59 in relation to any of those activities), and as from 6 April 2007 (otherwise) (for transitional provisions and effect see arts 36–40 of, and the Schedule to, the 2006 Order). These paragraphs have subsequently been amended as follows—

For the words in italics in para (5A) there are substituted the words ", 25C(1)(a) or 25E(1)(a)" by the Financial Services and Markets Act 2000 (Regulated Activities) (Amendment) Order 2009, SI 2009/1342, arts 2, 20(a), as from 1 July 2009 (other than for the purposes of enabling applications to be made for a Part IV permission, or a variation of a Part IV permission, in relation to activities of the kind specified by arts 25E, 53D or 63J or, so far as relevant to any such activity, art 64 of this Order), and as from 30 June 2010 (for those purposes) (for the full commencement details and for transitional provisions etc see arts 1, 32–34 of that Order).

For the words in italics in para (5B) there are substituted the words ", 25C(1)(b) and 25E(1)(b)" by SI 2009/1342, arts 2, 20(b), as from the same dates and for the same purposes, etc, as mentioned in the note relating to this Order above.

For the words in italics in para (5C) there are substituted the words ", 25C(2) and 25E(2)" by SI 2009/1342, arts 2, 20(c), as from the same dates and for the same purposes, etc, as mentioned in the note relating to this Order above.

For the words in italics in para (5D) there are substituted the words ", 63F(1) or 63J(1)" by SI 2009/1342, arts 2, 20(d), as from the same dates and for the same purposes, etc, as mentioned in the note relating to this Order above.

For the words in italics in para (5E) there are substituted the words ", 63F(2) or 63J(2)" by SI 2009/1342, arts 2, 20(e), as from the same dates and for the same purposes, etc, as mentioned in the note relating to this Order above.

In para (5F), sub-paras (b)(iv), (c)(iv), and (d)(iv) are inserted by SI 2009/1342, arts 2, 20(f)–(h), as from the same dates and for the same purposes, etc, as mentioned in the note relating to this Order above.

Para (6): figure in square brackets inserted by the Financial Services and Markets Act 2000 (Regulated Activities) (Amendment) (No 2) Order 2003, SI 2003/1476, art 10(6), as from 31 October 2004 (in so far as relating to contracts of long-term care insurance), and as from 14 January 2005 (otherwise); for transitional provisions see arts 22–27 of that Order.

Para (8): added by SI 2006/3384, arts 2, 24(e), as from 1 April 2007 (for the purposes of enabling applications to be made for (i) a Pt IV permission, (ii) a variation of a Pt IV permission, and (iii) the Authority's approval under s 59 of the 2000 Act, in relation to an activity of the kind specified by art 25D of this Order, or in relation to an investment of the kind specified by arts 83, 84 or 85 of this Order), and as from 1 November 2007 (otherwise).

[72A   Information society services

(1)   There is excluded from this Part any activity consisting of the provision of an information society service from an EEA State other than the United Kingdom.

(2)   The exclusion in paragraph (1) does not apply to the activity of effecting or carrying out a contract of insurance as principal, where—

    (a)   the activity is carried on by an undertaking which has received official authorisation in accordance with [Article 4 of the life assurance consolidation directive] or the first non-life insurance directive, and

    (b)   the insurance falls within the scope of any of the insurance directives.]

[823]

NOTES
Inserted by the Financial Services and Markets Act 2000 (Regulated Activities) (Amendment) (No 2) Order 2002, SI 2002/1776, art 2, as from 21 August 2002.

Para (2): words in square brackets substituted by the Life Assurance Consolidation Directive (Consequential Amendments) Regulations 2004, SI 2004/3379, reg 17, as from 11 January 2005.

[72B   Activities carried on by a provider of relevant goods or services

(1)   In this article—

"connected contract of insurance" means a contract of insurance which—

    (a)   is not a contract of long-term insurance;

    (b)   has a total duration (or would have a total duration were any right to renew conferred by the contract exercised) of five years or less;

    (c)   has an annual premium (or, where the premium is paid otherwise than by way of annual premium, the equivalent of an annual premium) of 500 euro or less, or the equivalent amount in sterling or other currency;

    (d)   covers the risk of—

        (i)   breakdown, loss of, or damage to, non-motor goods supplied by the provider; or

        [(ii)   damage to, or loss of, baggage and other risks linked to the travel booked with the provider ("travel risks") in circumstances where—

            (aa)   the travel booked with the provider relates to attendance at an event organised or managed by that provider and the party seeking insurance is not an individual (acting in his private capacity) or a small business; or

            (bb)   the travel booked with the provider is only the hire of an aircraft, vehicle or vessel which does not provide sleeping accommodation];

PART IV
OTHER STATUTORY INSTRUMENTS

    (e)   does not cover any liability risks (except, in the case of a contract which covers travel risks, where that cover is ancillary to the main cover provided by the contract);

    (f)   is complementary to the non-motor goods being supplied or service being provided by the provider; and

    (g)   is of such a nature that the only information that a person requires in order to carry on an activity of the kind specified by article 21, 25, 39A or 53 in relation to it is the cover provided by the contract;

"non-motor goods" means goods which are not mechanically propelled road vehicles;

"provider" means a person who supplies non-motor goods or provides services related to travel in the course of carrying on a profession or business which does not otherwise consist of the carrying on of regulated activities.

[For these purposes, the transfer of possession of an aircraft, vehicle or vessel under an agreement for hire which is not—

    (a)   a hire-purchase agreement within the meaning of section 189(1) of the Consumer Credit Act 1974, or

    (b)   any other agreement which contemplates that the property in those goods will also pass at some time in the future,

is the provision of a service related to travel, not a supply of goods];

["small business" means—

    (a)   subject to paragraph (b) a sole trader, body corporate, partnership or an unincorporated association which had a turnover in the last financial year of less than £1,000,000;

    (b)   where the business concerned is a member of a group within the meaning of section 262(1) of the Companies Act 1985 (and after the repeal of that section within the meaning of section 474(1) of the Companies Act 2006), reference to its turnover means the combined turnover of the group;

"turnover" means the amounts derived from the provision of goods and services falling within the business's ordinary activities, after deduction of trade discounts, value added tax and any other taxes based on the amounts so derived].

(2)   There is excluded from article 21 any transaction for the sale or purchase of a connected contract of insurance into which a provider enters as agent.

(3)   There are excluded from article 25(1) and (2) any arrangements made by a provider for, or with a view to, a transaction for the sale or purchase of a connected contract of insurance.

(4)   There is excluded from article 39A any activity carried on by a provider where the contract of insurance in question is a connected contract of insurance.

(5)   There is excluded from article 53 the giving of advice by a provider in relation to a transaction for the sale or purchase of a connected contract of insurance.

(6)   For the purposes of this article, a contract of insurance which covers travel risks is not to be treated as a contract of long-term insurance, notwithstanding the fact that it contains related and subsidiary provisions such that it might be regarded as a contract of long-term insurance, if the cover to which those provisions relate is ancillary to the main cover provided by the contract.]

[824]

NOTES

Commencement: 31 October 2004 (in so far as relating to contracts of long-term care insurance); 14 January 2005 (otherwise).

Inserted, together with arts 72C, 72D, by the Financial Services and Markets Act 2000 (Regulated Activities) (Amendment) (No 2) Order 2003, SI 2003/1476, art 11, as from 31 October 2004 (in so far as relating to contracts of long-term care insurance), and as from 14 January 2005 (otherwise); for transitional provisions see arts 22–27 of that Order.

Para (1) is amended as follows:

In definition "connected contract of insurance" sub-para (d)(ii) substituted by the Financial Services and Markets Act 2000 (Regulated Activities) (Amendment) (No 2) Order 2007, SI 2007/3510, art 2(1), (2), as from 30 June 2008 (for the purposes of enabling applications to be made, pursuant to this amendment, for (i) a Pt IV permission, or a variation of a Pt IV permission, in relation to activities of the kind specified by arts 21, 25(1), 25(2), 39A, 53 or, so far as relevant to any such activity, art 64 of this Order, or (ii) the Authority's approval under s 59 of FSMA 2000 in relation to any of those activities), and as from 1 January 2009 (otherwise) (for transitional provisions see arts 3–9 thereof).

Words in square brackets in definition "provider" inserted, and definitions "small business" and "turnover" added, by SI 2007/3510, art 2(1), (3), as from the same dates and for the same purposes as noted above (for transitional provisions see arts 3–9 of thereof).

[72C   Provision of information on an incidental basis

(1)   There is excluded from articles 25(1) and (2) the making of arrangements for, or with a view to, a transaction for the sale or purchase of a contract of insurance or an investment of the kind specified by article 89, so far as relevant to such a contract, where that activity meets the conditions specified in paragraph (4).

(2)   There is excluded from articles 37 and 40 any activity—
  (a)   where the assets in question are rights under a contract of insurance or an investment of the kind specified by article 89, so far as relevant to such a contract; and
  (b)   which meets the conditions specified in paragraph (4).

(3)   There is excluded from article 39A any activity which meets the conditions specified in paragraph (4).

(4)   The conditions specified in this paragraph are that the activity—
  (a)   consists of the provision of information to the policyholder or potential policyholder;
  (b)   is carried on by a person in the course of carrying on a profession or business which does not otherwise consist of the carrying on of regulated activities; and
  (c)   may reasonably be regarded as being incidental to that profession or business.]

[825]

NOTES
  Commencement: 31 October 2004 (in so far as relating to contracts of long-term care insurance); 14 January 2005 (otherwise).
  Inserted as noted to art 72B at **[824]**.

[72D   Large risks contracts where risk situated outside the EEA

(1)   There is excluded from articles 21, 25(1) and (2), 39A and 53 any activity which is carried on in relation to a large risks contract of insurance, to the extent that the risk or commitment covered by the contract is not situated in an EEA State.

(2)   In this article, a "large risks contract of insurance" is a contract of insurance the principal object of which is to cover—
  (a)   risks falling within paragraph 4 (railway rolling stock), 5 (aircraft), 6 (ships), 7 (goods in transit), 11 (aircraft liability) or 12 (liability of ships) of Part 1 of Schedule 1;
  (b)   risks falling within paragraph 14 (credit) or 15 (suretyship) of that Part provided that the risks relate to a business carried on by the policyholder; or
  (c)   risks falling within paragraph 3 (land vehicles), 8 (fire and natural forces), 9 (damage to property), 10 (motor vehicle liability), 13 (general liability) or 16 (miscellaneous financial loss) of that Part provided that the risks relate to a business carried on by the policyholder and that the condition specified in paragraph (3) is met in relation to that business.

(3)   The condition specified in this paragraph is that at least two of the three following criteria were met in the most recent financial year for which information is available—
  (a)   the balance sheet total of the business (within the meaning of section 247(5) of the Companies Act 1985 or article 255(5) of the Companies (Northern Ireland) Order 1986) exceeded 6.2 million euro,
  (b)   the net turnover (within the meaning given to "turnover" by section 262(1) of that Act or article 270(1) of that Order) exceeded 12.8 million euro,
  (c)   the number of employees (within the meaning given by section 247(6) of that Act or article 255(6) of that Order) exceeded 250,

and for a financial year which is a company's financial year but not in fact a year, the net turnover of the policyholder shall be proportionately adjusted.

(4)   For the purposes of paragraph (3), where the policyholder is a member of a group for which consolidated accounts (within the meaning of the Seventh Company Law Directive) are drawn up, the question whether the condition specified by that paragraph is met is to be determined by reference to those accounts.]

[826]

NOTES
  Commencement: 31 October 2004 (in so far as relating to contracts of long-term care insurance); 14 January 2005 (otherwise).
  Inserted as noted to art 72B at **[824]**.

[72E   Business Angel-led Enterprise Capital Funds

(1)   A body corporate of a type specified in paragraph (7) does not carry on the activity of the kind specified by article 21 by entering as agent into a transaction on behalf of the participants of a Business Angel-led Enterprise Capital Fund.

(2)   There are excluded from article 25(1) and (2) arrangements, made by a body corporate of a type specified in paragraph (7), for or with a view to a transaction which is or is to be entered into by or on behalf of the participants in a Business Angel-led Enterprise Capital Fund.

(3)   There is excluded from article 37 any activity, carried on by a body corporate of a type specified in paragraph (7), which consists in the managing of assets belonging to the participants in a Business Angel-led Enterprise Capital Fund.

(4)   There is excluded from article 40 any activity, carried on by a body corporate of a type specified in paragraph (7), in respect of assets belonging to the participants in a Business Angel-led Enterprise Capital Fund.

(5)   A body corporate of a type specified in paragraph (7) does not carry on the activity of the kind specified in article 51(1)(a) where it carries on the activity of establishing, operating or winding up a Business Angel-led Enterprise Capital Fund.

(6)   A body corporate of a type specified in paragraph (7) does not carry on the activity of the kind specified in article 53 where it is advising the participants in a Business Angel-led Enterprise Capital Fund on investments to be made by or on behalf of the participants of that Business Angel-led Enterprise Capital Fund.

(7)   The type of body corporate specified is a limited company—
    (i)   which operates a Business Angel-led Enterprise Capital Fund; and
    (ii) the members of which are participants in the Business Angel-led Enterprise Capital Fund operated by that limited company and between them have invested at least 50 per cent of the total investment in that Business Angel-led Enterprise Capital Fund excluding any investment made by the Secretary of State.

(8)   For the purposes of paragraph (7), "a limited company" means a body corporate with limited liability which is a company or firm formed in accordance with the law of an EEA State and having its registered office, central administration or principal place of business within the territory of an EEA State.

(9)   Nothing in this article has the effect of excluding a body corporate from the application of the Money Laundering Regulations [2007], in so far as those Regulations would have applied to it but for this article.

(10)   Nothing in this article has the effect of excluding a body corporate from the application of section 397 of the Act (misleading statements and practices), in so far as that section would have applied to it but for this article.]

[(11)   This article is subject to article 4(4).]

[827]

NOTES
Commencement: 1 October 2005.
Inserted, together with art 72F, by the Financial Services and Markets Act 2000 (Regulated Activities) (Amendment) (No 2) Order 2005, SI 2005/1518, art 2(1), (3), as from 1 October 2005.
Para (9): date in square brackets substituted by the Money Laundering Regulations 2007, SI 2007/2157, reg 51, Sch 6, Pt 2, para 10, as from 15 December 2007.
Para (11): added by SI 2006/3384, arts 2, 25, as from 1 April 2007 (for the purposes of enabling applications to be made for (i) a Pt IV permission, (ii) a variation of a Pt IV permission, and (iii) the Authority's approval under s 59 of the 2000 Act, in relation to an activity of the kind specified by art 25D of this Order, or in relation to an investment of the kind specified by arts 83, 84 or 85 of this Order), and as from 1 November 2007 (otherwise).

[72F   Interpretation

(1)   For the purposes of this article and of article 72E—
"Business Angel-led Enterprise Capital Fund" means a collective investment scheme which—
    (a)   is established for the purpose of enabling participants to participate in or receive profits or income arising from the acquisition, holding, management or disposal of investments falling within one or more of—
        (i)   article 76, being shares in an unlisted company;
        (ii) article 77, being instruments creating or acknowledging indebtedness in respect of an unlisted company; and
        (iii) article 79, being warrants or other instruments entitling the holder to subscribe for shares in an unlisted company;
    (b)   has only the following as its participants—
        (i)   the Secretary of State;
        (ii) a body corporate of a type specified in article 72E(7); and
        (iii) one or more persons each of whom at the time they became a participant was—
            (aa)   a sophisticated investor;
            (bb)   a high net worth individual;

(cc)   a high net worth company;
(dd)   a high net worth unincorporated association;
(ee)   a trustee of a high value trust; or
(ff)   a self-certified sophisticated investor;

(c)   is prevented, by the arrangements by which it is established, from—

  (i)   acquiring investments, other than those falling within paragraphs (i) to (iii) of sub-paragraph (a); and

  (ii)   acquiring investments falling within paragraphs (i) to (iii) of sub-paragraph (a) in an unlisted company, where the aggregated cost of those investments exceeds £2 million, unless that acquisition is necessary to prevent or reduce the dilution of an existing share-holding in that unlisted company;

"high net worth company" means a body corporate which—

(a)   falls within article 49(2)(a) of the Financial Services and Markets Act 2000 (Financial Promotion) Order 2001 (high net worth companies, unincorporated associations etc); and

(b)   has executed a document [(in a manner which binds the company)] in the following terms:

"This company is a high net worth company and falls within article 49(2)(a) of the Financial Services and Markets Act 2000 (Financial Promotion) Order 2001. We understand that any Business Angel-led Enterprise Capital Fund (within the meaning of article 72F of the Financial Services and Markets Act 2000 (Regulated Activities) Order 2001), in which this company participates, or any person who operates that Business Angel-led Enterprise Capital Fund, in which this company participates, will not be authorised under the Financial Services and Markets Act 2000 (and so will not have to satisfy the threshold conditions set out in Part I of Schedule 6 to that Act and will not be subject to Financial Services Authority rules such as those on holding client money). We understand that this means that redress through the Financial Services Authority, the Financial Ombudsman Scheme or the Financial Services Compensation Scheme will not be available. We also understand the risks associated in investing in a Business Angel-led Enterprise Capital Fund and are aware that it is open to us to seek advice from someone who is authorised under the Financial Services and Markets Act 2000 and who specialises in advising on this kind of investment."

"high net worth individual" means an individual who—

(a)   is a "certified high net worth individual" within the meaning of article 48(2) of the Financial Services and Markets Act 2000 (Financial Promotion) Order 2001 (certified high net worth individuals); and

(b)   has signed a statement in the following terms:

"I declare that I am a certified high net worth individual within the meaning of article 48(2) of the Financial Services and Markets Act 2000 (Financial Promotion) Order 2001 and that I understand that any Business Angel-led Enterprise Capital Fund (within the meaning of article 72F of the Financial Services and Markets Act 2000 (Regulated Activities) Order 2001), in which I participate, or any person who operates that Business Angel-led Enterprise Capital Fund, in which I participate, will not be authorised under the Financial Services and Markets Act 2000 (and so will not have to satisfy the threshold conditions set out in Part I of Schedule 6 to that Act and will not be subject to Financial Services Authority rules such as those on holding client money). I understand that this means that redress through the Financial Services Authority, the Financial Ombudsman Scheme or the Financial Services Compensation Scheme will not be available. I also understand the risks associated in investing in a Business Angel-led Enterprise Capital Fund and am aware that it is open to me to seek advice from someone who is authorised under the Financial Services and Markets Act 2000 and who specialises in advising on this kind of investment.";

"high net worth unincorporated association" means an unincorporated association—

(a)   which falls within article 49(2)(b) of the Financial Services and Markets Act 2000 (Financial Promotion) Order 2001; and

(b)   on behalf of which an officer of that association or a member of its governing body has signed a statement in the following terms:

"This unincorporated association is a high net worth unincorporated association and falls within article 49(2)(b) of the Financial Services and Markets Act 2000 (Financial Promotion) Order 2001. I understand that any Business Angel-led Enterprise Capital Fund (within the meaning of article 72F of the Financial Services and Markets Act 2000 (Regulated Activities) Order 2001), in which this association participates, or any person who operates that Business Angel-led Enterprise Capital Fund, in which this association participates, will not be authorised under the Financial Services and Markets Act 2000 (and so will not have to satisfy the threshold conditions set out in Part I of Schedule 6 to that Act and will not be subject to Financial Services Authority rules such as those on holding client money). I understand that this means that redress through the Financial Services Authority, the Financial Ombudsman Scheme or the Financial Services Compensation Scheme will not be available. I also understand the risks associated in investing in a Business Angel-led Enterprise Capital Fund and am aware that it is open to the association to seek advice from someone who is authorised under the Financial Services and Markets Act 2000 and who specialises in advising on this kind of investment.";

"high value trust" means a trust—

(a) where the aggregate value of the cash and investments which form a part of the trust's assets (before deducting the amount of its liabilities) is £10 million or more;

(b) on behalf of which a trustee has signed a statement in the following terms:

"This trust is a high value trust. I understand that any Business Angel-led Enterprise Capital Fund (within the meaning of article 72F of the Financial Services and Markets Act 2000 (Regulated Activities) Order 2001), in which this trust participates, or any person who operates that Business Angel-led Enterprise Capital Fund, in which this trust participates, will not be authorised under the Financial Services and Markets Act 2000 (and so will not have to satisfy the threshold conditions set out in Part I of Schedule 6 to that Act and will not be subject to Financial Services Authority rules such as those on holding client money). I understand that this means that redress through the Financial Services Authority, the Financial Ombudsman Scheme or the Financial Services Compensation Scheme will not be available. I also understand the risks associated in investing in a Business Angel-led Enterprise Capital Fund and am aware that it is open to the trust to seek advice from someone who is authorised under the Financial Services and Markets Act 2000 and who specialises in advising on this kind of investment.";

"self-certified sophisticated investor" means an individual who—

(a) is a "self-certified sophisticated investor" within the meaning of article 50A of the Financial Services and Markets Act 2000 (Financial Promotion) Order 2001;

(b) has signed a statement in the following terms:

"I declare that I am a self-certified sophisticated investor within the meaning of article 50A of the Financial Services and Markets Act 2000 (Financial Promotion) Order 2001 and that I understand that any Business Angel-led Enterprise Capital Fund (within the meaning of article 72F of the Financial Services and Markets Act 2000 (Regulated Activities) Order 2001), in which I participate, or any person who operates that Business Angel-led Enterprise Capital Fund, in which I participate, will not be authorised under the Financial Services and Markets Act 2000 (and so will not have to satisfy the threshold conditions set out in Part I of Schedule 6 to that Act and will not be subject to Financial Services Authority rules such as those on holding client money). I understand that this means that redress through the Financial Services Authority, the Financial Ombudsman Scheme or the Financial Services Compensation Scheme will not be available. I also understand the risks associated in investing in a Business Angel-led Enterprise Capital Fund and am aware that it is open to me to seek advice from someone who is authorised under the Financial Services and Markets Act 2000 and who specialises in advising on this kind of investment.";

"sophisticated investor" means an individual who—

(a) is a "certified sophisticated investor" within the meaning of article 50(1) of the Financial Services and Markets Act 2000 (Financial Promotion) Order 2001; and

(b) has signed a statement in the following terms:

"I declare that I am a certified sophisticated investor within the meaning of article 50(1) of the Financial Services and Markets Act 2000 (Financial Promotion) Order 2001 and that I understand that any Business Angel-led Enterprise Capital Fund (within the meaning of article 72F of the Financial Services and Markets Act 2000 (Regulated Activities) Order 2001), in which I participate, or any person who operates that Business Angel-led Enterprise Capital Fund, in which I participate, will not be authorised under the Financial Services and Markets Act 2000 (and so will not have to satisfy the threshold conditions set out in Part I of Schedule 6 to that Act and will not be subject to Financial Services Authority rules such as those on holding client money). I understand that this means that redress through the Financial Services Authority, the Financial Ombudsman Scheme or the Financial Services Compensation Scheme will not be available. I also understand the risks associated in investing in a Business Angel-led Enterprise Capital Fund and am aware that it is open to me to seek advice from someone who is authorised under the Financial Services and Markets Act 2000 and who specialises in advising on this kind of investment.";

"unlisted company" has the meaning given by article 3 of the Financial Services and Markets Act 2000 (Financial Promotion) Order 2001.

(2) References in this Article and in Article 72E to a participant in a Business Angel-led Enterprise Capital Fund, doing things on behalf of such a participant and property belonging to such

a participant are, respectively, references to that participant in that capacity, to doing things on behalf of that participant in that capacity or to the property of that participant held in that capacity.]

[828]

NOTES
Commencement: 1 October 2005.
Inserted as noted to art 72E at **[827]**.
Para (1): words in square brackets in definition "high net worth company" substituted by the Financial Services and Markets Act 2000 (Regulated Activities) (Amendment) (No 2) Order 2006, SI 2006/2383, arts 2, 22, as from 6 November 2006 (for the purposes of enabling applications to be made for (i) a Pt IV permission, or a variation of a Pt IV permission, in relation to activities of the kind specified by arts 25B, 25C, 53B, 53C, 63B or 63F or, so far as relevant to any such activity, art 64 of this Order; or (ii) the Authority's approval under FSMA 2000, s 59 in relation to any of those activities), and as from 6 April 2007 (otherwise) (for transitional provisions and effect see arts 36–40 of, and the Schedule to, the 2006 Order).

PART III
SPECIFIED INVESTMENTS

73   Investments: general

The following kinds of investment are specified for the purposes of section 22 of the Act.

[829]

74   Deposits

A deposit.

[830]

[74A   Electronic money

Electronic money.]

[831]

NOTES
Inserted by the Financial Services and Markets Act 2000 (Regulated Activities) (Amendment) Order 2002, SI 2002/682, art 6, as from 27 April 2002, subject to transitional provisions in relation to persons issuing electronic money immediately before that date contained in art 9.

75   Contracts of insurance

Rights under a contract of insurance.

[832]

76   Shares etc

(1)   Shares or stock in the share capital of—
  (a)   any body corporate (wherever incorporated), and
  (b)   any unincorporated body constituted under the law of a country or territory outside the United Kingdom.

(2)   Paragraph (1) includes—
  (a)   any shares of a class defined as deferred shares for the purposes of section 119 of the Building Societies Act 1986; and
  (b)   any transferable shares in a body incorporated under the law of, or any part of, the United Kingdom relating to industrial and provident societies or credit unions, or in a body constituted under the law of another EEA State for purposes equivalent to those of such a body.

(3)   But subject to paragraph (2) there are excluded from paragraph (1) shares or stock in the share capital of—
  (a)   an open-ended investment company;
  (b)   a building society incorporated under the law of, or any part of, the United Kingdom;
  (c)   a body incorporated under the law of, or any part of, the United Kingdom relating to industrial and provident societies or credit unions;
  (d)   any body constituted under the law of an EEA State for purposes equivalent to those of a body falling within sub-paragraph (b) or (c).

[833]

77   Instruments creating or acknowledging indebtedness

(1)   Subject to paragraph (2), such of the following as do not fall within article 78—
  (a)   debentures;
  (b)   debenture stock;
  (c)   loan stock;
  (d)   bonds;

PART IV
OTHER STATUTORY INSTRUMENTS

    (e)   certificates of deposit;

    (f)   any other instrument creating or acknowledging indebtedness.

(2)   If and to the extent that they would otherwise fall within paragraph (1), there are excluded from that paragraph—

    (a)   an instrument acknowledging or creating indebtedness for, or for money borrowed to defray, the consideration payable under a contract for the supply of goods or services;

    (b)   a cheque or other bill of exchange, a banker's draft or a letter of credit (but not a bill of exchange accepted by a banker);

    (c)   a banknote, a statement showing a balance on a current, deposit or savings account, a lease or other disposition of property, or a heritable security; and

    (d)   a contract of insurance.

(3)   An instrument excluded from paragraph (1) of article 78 by paragraph (2)(b) of that article is not thereby to be taken to fall within paragraph (1) of this article.

[834]

NOTES

Modification: references in para (1) to securities, instruments or investments creating or acknowledging indebtedness (or creating or acknowledging a present or future indebtedness) includes a reference to uncertificated units of eligible debt securities; see the Uncertificated Securities (Amendment) (Eligible Debt Securities) Regulations 2003, SI 2003/1633, reg 15, Sch 2, para 8 (as from 24 June 2003).

HM Treasury and the Financial Services Authority have issued a consultation paper, *Consultation on the legislative framework for the regulation of alternative finance investment bonds* (*sukuk*) (*December 2008*) which proposes the insertion of a new art 77A into this Order to make certain alternative finance investment bonds a specified investment for the purposes of the Act. The main effect of the Order (that is set out in draft) would be to regulate a form of Sharia compliant investment bond (known in the plural as 'sukuk' and in the singular as 'sakk') that is, in economic substance, similar to a debt security in an equivalent manner to conventional debt securities, where appropriate. Sukuk arrangements allow assets to be held for the benefit of investors in certificates issued by a company. The benefits may include the payment of a return that is economically equivalent to interest and redemption of the certificates out of the proceeds from the disposal of the assets.

78 Government and public securities

(1)   Subject to paragraph (2), loan stock, bonds and other instruments creating or acknowledging indebtedness, issued by or on behalf of any of the following—

    (a)   the government of the United Kingdom;

    (b)   the Scottish Administration;

    (c)   the Executive Committee of the Northern Ireland Assembly;

    (d)   the National Assembly for Wales;

    (e)   the government of any country or territory outside the United Kingdom;

    (f)   a local authority in the United Kingdom or elsewhere; or

    (g)   a body the members of which comprise—

        (i)   states including the United Kingdom or another EEA State; or

        (ii)   bodies whose members comprise states including the United Kingdom or another EEA State.

(2)   There are excluded from paragraph (1)—

    (a)   so far as applicable, the instruments mentioned in article 77(2)(a) to (d);

    (b)   any instrument creating or acknowledging indebtedness in respect of—

        (i)   money received by the Director of Savings as deposits or otherwise in connection with the business of the National Savings Bank;

        (ii)   money raised under the National Loans Act 1968 under the auspices of the Director of Savings or treated as so raised by virtue of section 11(3) of the National Debt Act 1972.

[835]

NOTES

Modification: references in this article to securities, instruments or investments creating or acknowledging indebtedness (or creating or acknowledging a present or future indebtedness) includes a reference to uncertificated units of eligible debt securities; see the Uncertificated Securities (Amendment) (Eligible Debt Securities) Regulations 2003, SI 2003/1633, reg 15, Sch 2, para 8 (as from 24 June 2003).

79 Instruments giving entitlements to investments

(1)   Warrants and other instruments entitling the holder to subscribe for any investment of the kind specified by article 76, 77 or 78.

(2)   It is immaterial whether the investment to which the entitlement relates is in existence or identifiable.

(3)   An investment of the kind specified by this article is not to be regarded as falling within article 83, 84 or 85.

[836]

80 Certificates representing certain securities

(1) Subject to paragraph (2), certificates or other instruments which confer contractual or property rights (other than rights consisting of an investment of the kind specified by article 83)—

   (a) in respect of any investment of the kind specified by any of articles 76 to 79, being an investment held by a person other than the person on whom the rights are conferred by the certificate or instrument; and

   (b) the transfer of which may be effected without the consent of that person.

(2) There is excluded from paragraph (1) any certificate or other instrument which confers rights in respect of two or more investments issued by different persons, or in respect of two or more different investments of the kind specified by article 78 and issued by the same person.

[837]

81 Units in a collective investment scheme

Units in a collective investment scheme (within the meaning of Part XVII of the Act).

[838]

[82 Rights under a pension scheme

(1) Rights under a stakeholder pension scheme.

(2) Rights under a personal pension scheme.]

[839]

NOTES

Commencement: 1 October 2006 (certain purposes); 6 April 2007 (otherwise) (see below).

Substituted by the Financial Services and Markets Act 2000 (Regulated Activities) (Amendment) Order 2006, SI 2006/1969, art 2(1), (5), as from 1 October 2006 (for the purposes of enabling applications to be made for Pt IV permission or for a variation of Pt IV permission in relation to an investment specified by art 82(2) of this Order (as so substituted)), and as from 6 April 2007 (otherwise); for transitional provisions and effect see arts 3–7 of, and the Schedule to, the 2006 Order.

---

83 Options

[(1)] Options to acquire or dispose of—

   (a) a security or contractually based investment (other than one of a kind specified by this article);

   (b) currency of the United Kingdom or any other country or territory;

   (c) palladium, platinum, gold or silver; ...

   (d) an option to acquire or dispose of an investment of the kind specified by this article by virtue of paragraph (a), (b) or (c);

   [(e) subject to paragraph (4), an option to acquire or dispose of an option to which paragraph 5, 6, 7 or 10 of Section C of Annex I to the markets in financial instruments directive (the text of which is set out in Part I of Schedule 2) applies].

[(2) Subject to paragraph (4), options—

   (a) to which paragraph (1) does not apply;

   (b) which relate to commodities;

   (c) which may be settled physically; and

   (d) either—

      (i) to which paragraph 5 or 6 of Section C of Annex I to the markets in financial instruments directive, the text of which is set out in Part 1 of Schedule 2, applies, or

      (ii) which in accordance with Article 38 of the Commission Regulation (the text of which is set out in Part 2 of Schedule 2) are to be considered as having the characteristics of other derivative financial instruments and not being for commercial purposes, and to which paragraph 7 of Section C of Annex I to the markets in financial instruments directive applies.

(3) Subject to paragraph (4), options—

   (a) to which paragraph (1) does not apply;

   (b) which may be settled physically; and

   (c) to which paragraph 10 of Section C of Annex I to the markets in financial instruments directive (read with the Commission Regulation) applies.

(4) Paragraphs (1)(e), (2) and (3) only apply to options in relation to which—

   (a) an investment firm or credit institution is providing or performing investment services and activities on a professional basis,

   (b) a management company is providing, in accordance with Article 5(3) of the UCITS directive, the investment service specified in paragraph 4 or 5 of Section A, or the ancillary service specified in paragraph 1 of Section B, of Annex I to the markets in financial instruments directive, or

PART IV

OTHER STATUTORY INSTRUMENTS

(c)   a market operator is providing the investment service specified in paragraph 8 of Section A of Annex I to the markets in financial instruments directive.

(5)   Expressions used in paragraphs (1)(e), (2) and (3) and in the markets in financial instruments directive have the same meaning as in that directive.]

[840]

NOTES

Para (1): numbered as such, word omitted from sub-para (c) revoked, and sub-para (e) inserted, by the Financial Services and Markets Act 2000 (Regulated Activities) (Amendment No 3) Order 2006, SI 2006/3384, arts 2, 26(a), (b), as from 1 April 2007 (for the purposes of enabling applications to be made for (i) a Pt IV permission, (ii) a variation of a Pt IV permission, and (iii) the Authority's approval under s 59 of the 2000 Act, in relation to an activity of the kind specified by art 25D of this Order, or in relation to an investment of the kind specified by arts 83, 84 or 85 of this Order), and as from 1 November 2007 (otherwise).

Paras (2)–(5): added by SI 2006/3384, arts 2, 26(c), as from the same dates and for the same purposes as noted above.

84 Futures

(1)   Subject to paragraph (2), rights under a contract for the sale of a commodity or property of any other description under which delivery is to be made at a future date and at a price agreed on when the contract is made.

[(1A)   Subject to paragraph (1D), futures—
    (a)   to which paragraph (1) does not apply;
    (b)   which relate to commodities;
    (c)   which may be settled physically; and
    (d)   to which paragraph 5 or 6 of Section C of Annex I to the markets in financial instruments directive applies.

(1B)   Subject to paragraph (1D), futures and forwards—
    (a)   to which paragraph (1) does not apply;
    (b)   which relate to commodities;
    (c)   which may be settled physically;
    (d)   which in accordance with Article 38 of the Commission Regulation (the text of which is set out in Part 2 of Schedule 2) are to be considered as having the characteristics of other derivative financial instruments and not being for commercial purposes; and
    (e)   to which paragraph 7 of Section C of Annex I to the markets in financial instruments directive applies.

(1C)   Subject to paragraph (1D), futures—
    (a)   to which paragraph (1) does not apply;
    (b)   which may be settled physically; and
    (c)   to which paragraph 10 of Section C of Annex I to the markets in financial instruments directive (read with the Commission Regulation) applies.

(1D)   Paragraph (1A), (1B) and (1C) only apply to futures or forwards in relation to which—
    (a)   an investment firm or credit institution is providing or performing investment services and activities on a professional basis,
    (b)   a management company is providing, in accordance with Article 5(3) of the UCITS directive, the investment service specified in paragraph 4 or 5 of Section A, or the ancillary service specified in paragraph 1 of Section B, of Annex I to the markets in financial instruments directive, or
    (c)   a market operator is providing the investment service specified in paragraph 8 of Section A of Annex I to the markets in financial instruments directive.

(1E)   Expressions used in paragraphs (1A) to (1C) and in the markets in financial instruments directive have the same meaning as in that directive.]

(2)   There are excluded from paragraph (1) rights under any contract which is made for commercial and not investment purposes.

(3)   A contract is to be regarded as made for investment purposes if it is made or traded on a recognised investment exchange, or is made otherwise than on a recognised investment exchange but is expressed to be as traded on such an exchange or on the same terms as those on which an equivalent contract would be made on such an exchange.

(4)   A contract not falling within paragraph (3) is to be regarded as made for commercial purposes if under the terms of the contract delivery is to be made within seven days, unless it can be shown that there existed an understanding that (notwithstanding the express terms of the contract) delivery would not be made within seven days.

(5)   The following are indications that a contract not falling within paragraph (3) or (4) is made for commercial purposes and the absence of them is an indication that it is made for investment purposes—

(a)   one or more of the parties is a producer of the commodity or other property, or uses it in his business;

(b)   the seller delivers or intends to deliver the property or the purchaser takes or intends to take delivery of it.

(6)   It is an indication that a contract is made for commercial purposes that the prices, the lot, the delivery date or other terms are determined by the parties for the purposes of the particular contract and not by reference (or not solely by reference) to regularly published prices, to standard lots or delivery dates or to standard terms.

(7)   The following are indications that a contract is made for investment purposes—

(a)   it is expressed to be as traded on an investment exchange;

(b)   performance of the contract is ensured by an investment exchange or a clearing house;

(c)   there are arrangements for the payment or provision of margin.

(8)   For the purposes of paragraph (1), a price is to be taken to be agreed on when a contract is made—

(a)   notwithstanding that it is left to be determined by reference to the price at which a contract is to be entered into on a market or exchange or could be entered into at a time and place specified in the contract; or

(b)   in a case where the contract is expressed to be by reference to a standard lot and quality, notwithstanding that provision is made for a variation in the price to take account of any variation in quantity or quality on delivery.

[841]

NOTES

Paras (1A)–(1E): inserted by the Financial Services and Markets Act 2000 (Regulated Activities) (Amendment No 3) Order 2006, SI 2006/3384, arts 2, 27, as from 1 April 2007 (for the purposes of enabling applications to be made for (i) a Pt IV permission, (ii) a variation of a Pt IV permission, and (iii) the Authority's approval under s 59 of the 2000 Act, in relation to an activity of the kind specified by art 25D of this Order, or in relation to an investment of the kind specified by arts 83, 84 or 85 of this Order), and as from 1 November 2007 (otherwise).

85   Contracts for differences etc

(1)   Subject to paragraph (2), rights under—

(a)   a contract for differences; or

(b)   any other contract the purpose or pretended purpose of which is to secure a profit or avoid a loss by reference to fluctuations in—

(i)   the value or price of property of any description; or

(ii)   an index or other factor designated for that purpose in the contract.

(2)   There are excluded from paragraph (1)—

(a)   rights under a contract if the parties intend that the profit is to be secured or the loss is to be avoided by one or more of the parties taking delivery of any property to which the contract relates;

(b)   rights under a contract under which money is received by way of deposit on terms that any interest or other return to be paid on the sum deposited will be calculated by reference to fluctuations in an index or other factor;

(c)   rights under any contract under which—

(i)   money is received by the Director of Savings as deposits or otherwise in connection with the business of the National Savings Bank; or

(ii)   money is raised under the National Loans Act 1968 under the auspices of the Director of Savings or treated as so raised by virtue of section 11(3) of the National Debt Act 1972;

(d)   rights under a qualifying contract of insurance.

[(3)   Subject to paragraph (4), derivative instruments for the transfer of credit risk—

(a)   to which neither article 83 nor paragraph (1) applies; and

(b)   to which paragraph 8 of Section C of Annex I to the markets in financial instruments directive applies.

(4)   Paragraph (3) only applies to derivatives in relation to which—

(a)   an investment firm or credit institution is providing or performing investment services and activities on a professional basis,

(b)   a management company is providing, in accordance with Article 5(3) of the UCITS directive, the investment service specified in paragraph 4 or 5 of Section A, or the ancillary service specified in paragraph 1 of Section B, of Annex I to the markets in financial instruments directive, or

(c)   a market operator is providing the investment service specified in paragraph 8 of Section A of Annex I to the markets in financial instruments directive.

PART IV
OTHER STATUTORY INSTRUMENTS

(5)   "Derivative instruments for the transfer of credit risk" has the same meaning as in the markets in financial instruments directive.]

[842]

NOTES
Paras (3)–(5): added by the Financial Services and Markets Act 2000 (Regulated Activities) (Amendment No 3) Order 2006, SI 2006/3384, arts 2, 28, as from 1 April 2007 (for the purposes of enabling applications to be made for (i) a Pt IV permission, (ii) a variation of a Pt IV permission, and (iii) the Authority's approval under s 59 of the 2000 Act, in relation to an activity of the kind specified by art 25D of this Order, or in relation to an investment of the kind specified by arts 83, 84 or 85 of this Order), and as from 1 November 2007 (otherwise).

86   Lloyd's syndicate capacity and syndicate membership
(1)   The underwriting capacity of a Lloyd's syndicate.
(2)   A person's membership (or prospective membership) of a Lloyd's syndicate.

[843]

87   Funeral plan contracts
Rights under a funeral plan contract.

[844]

88   Regulated mortgage contracts
Rights under a regulated mortgage contract.

[845]

NOTES
Commencement: 31 October 2004.

[88A   Regulated home reversion plans
Rights under a regulated home reversion plan.]

[846]

NOTES
Commencement: 6 November 2006 (certain purposes); 6 April 2007 (otherwise) (see below).
Inserted, together with art 88B, by the Financial Services and Markets Act 2000 (Regulated Activities) (Amendment) (No 2) Order 2006, SI 2006/2383, arts 2, 23, as from 6 November 2006 (for the purposes of enabling applications to be made for (i) a Pt IV permission, or a variation of a Pt IV permission, in relation to activities of the kind specified by arts 25B, 25C, 53B, 53C, 63B or 63F or, so far as relevant to any such activity, art 64 of this Order; or (ii) the Authority's approval under FSMA 2000, s 59 in relation to any of those activities), and as from 6 April 2007 (otherwise) (for transitional provisions and effect see arts 36–40 of, and the Schedule to, the 2006 Order).

[88B   Regulated home purchase plans
Rights under a regulated home purchase plan.]

[847]

NOTES
Commencement: 6 November 2006 (certain purposes); 6 April 2007 (otherwise).
Inserted as noted to art 88A at **[846]**.

[88C   Regulated sale and rent back agreements
Rights under a regulated sale and rent back agreement.]

[848]

NOTES
Commencement: 1 July 2009 (certain purposes); 30 June 2010 (otherwise) (see below).
Inserted by the Financial Services and Markets Act 2000 (Regulated Activities) (Amendment) Order 2009, SI 2009/1342, arts 2, 21, as from 1 July 2009 (other than for the purposes of enabling applications to be made for a Part IV permission, or a variation of a Part IV permission, in relation to activities of the kind specified by arts 25E, 53D or 63J or, so far as relevant to any such activity, art 64 of this Order), and as from 30 June 2010 (for those purposes) (for the full commencement details and for transitional provisions etc see arts 1, 32–34 of that Order).

89   Rights to or interests in investments
(1)   Subject to paragraphs (2) to (4), any right to or interest in anything which is specified by any other provision of this Part (other than [article 88, *88A or 88B*]).
(2)   Paragraph (1) does not include interests under the trusts of an occupational pension scheme.
(3)   Paragraph (1) does not include—

   (a)   rights to or interests in a contract of insurance of the kind referred to in paragraph (1)(a) of article 60; or.

   (b)   interests under a trust of the kind referred to in paragraph (1)(b) of that article.

  (4)   Paragraph (1) does not include anything which is specified by any other provision of this Part.

[849]

NOTES

Para (1): words in square brackets substituted by the Financial Services and Markets Act 2000 (Regulated Activities) (Amendment) (No 2) Order 2006, SI 2006/2383, arts 2, 24, as from 6 November 2006 (for the purposes of enabling applications to be made for (i) a Pt IV permission, or a variation of a Pt IV permission, in relation to activities of the kind specified by arts 25B, 25C, 53B, 53C, 63B or 63F or, so far as relevant to any such activity, art 64 of this Order; or (ii) the Authority's approval under FSMA 2000, s 59 in relation to any of those activities), and as from 6 April 2007 (otherwise) (for transitional provisions and effect see arts 36–40 of, and the Schedule to, the 2006 Order); for the words in italics there are substituted the words "88A, 88B or 88C" by the Financial Services and Markets Act 2000 (Regulated Activities) (Amendment) Order 2009, SI 2009/1342, arts 2, 22, as from 1 July 2009 (other than for the purposes of enabling applications to be made for a Part IV permission, or a variation of a Part IV permission, in relation to activities of the kind specified by arts 25E, 53D or 63J or, so far as relevant to any such activity, art 64 of this Order), and as from 30 June 2010 (for those purposes) (for the full commencement details and for transitional provisions etc see arts 1, 32–34 of that Order).

90, 91   *((Pt IV) Reg 90 amends the Consumer Credit Act 1974, ss 16, 43, 52, 53, 137, 151; reg 91 amended the Consumer Credit (Advertisements) Regulations 1989, SI 1989/1125 (revoked) and amends the Consumer Credit (Content of Quotations) and Consumer Credit (Advertisements) (Amendment) Regulations 1999, SI 1999/2725, reg 2.)*

[PART V
UNAUTHORISED PERSONS CARRYING ON INSURANCE MEDIATION ACTIVITIES

92   Interpretation

In this Part—

    "designated professional body" means a body which is for the time being designated by the Treasury under section 326 of the Act (designation of professional bodies);

    "insurance mediation activity" means any regulated activity of the kind specified by article 21, 25(1) or (2), 39A or 53, or, so far as relevant to any of those articles, article 64, which is carried on in relation to a contract of insurance;

    "the record" means the record maintained by the Authority under section 347 of the Act (public record of authorised persons etc);

    "recorded insurance intermediary" has the meaning given by article 93(4);

    "a relevant member", in relation to a designated professional body, means a member (within the meaning of section 325(2) of the Act) of the profession in relation to which that designated professional body is established, or a person who is controlled or managed by one or more such members.]

[850]

NOTES

Commencement: 31 October 2004 (in so far as relating to contracts of long-term care insurance); 14 January 2005 (otherwise).

Inserted, together with the preceding heading and arts 93–96, by the Financial Services and Markets Act 2000 (Regulated Activities) (Amendment) (No 2) Order 2003, SI 2003/1476, art 13, as from 31 October 2004 (in so far as relating to contracts of long-term care insurance), and as from 14 January 2005 (otherwise); for transitional provisions see arts 22–27 of that Order.

[93   Duty to maintain a record of persons carrying on insurance mediation activities

  (1)   Subject to articles 95 and 96, the Authority must include in the record every person who—

   (a)   as a result of information obtained by virtue of its rules or by virtue of a direction given, or requirement imposed, under section 51(3) of the Act (procedure for applications under Part IV), appears to the Authority to fall within paragraph (2); or

   (b)   as a result of information obtained by virtue of article 94, appears to the Authority to fall within paragraph (3).

  (2)   A person falls within this paragraph if he is, or has entered into a contract by virtue of which he will be, an appointed representative who carries on any insurance mediation activity.

  (3)   A person falls within this paragraph if—

   (a)   he is a relevant member of a designated professional body who carries on, or is proposing to carry on, any insurance mediation activity; and

   (b)   the general prohibition does not (or will not) apply to the carrying on of those activities by virtue of section 327 of the Act (exemption from the general prohibition).

PART IV   OTHER STATUTORY INSTRUMENTS

(4)   In this Part, "recorded insurance intermediary" means a person who is included in the record by virtue of paragraph (1).

(5)   The record must include—
   (a)   in the case of any recorded insurance intermediary, its address; and
   (b)   in the case of a recorded insurance intermediary which is not an individual, the name of the individuals who are responsible for the management of the business carried on by the intermediary, so far as it relates to insurance mediation activities.]

[851]

NOTES
Commencement: 31 October 2004 (in so far as relating to contracts of long-term care insurance); 14 January 2005 (otherwise).
Inserted as noted to art 92 at **[850]**.

[94   Members of designated professional bodies
   (1)   A designated professional body must, by notice in writing, inform the Authority of—
   (a)   the name,
   (b)   the address, and
   (c)   in the case of a relevant member which is not an individual, the name of the individuals who are responsible for the management of the business carried on by the member, so far as it relates to insurance mediation activities,
of any relevant member who falls within paragraph (2).

   (2)   A relevant member of a designated professional body falls within this paragraph if, in accordance with the rules of that body, he carries on, or proposes to carry on any insurance mediation activity but does not have, and does not propose to apply for, Part IV permission on the basis that the general prohibition does not (or will not) apply to the carrying on of that activity by virtue of section 327 of the Act.

   (3)   A designated professional body must also, by notice in writing, inform the Authority of any change in relation to the matters specified in sub-paragraphs (a) to (c) of paragraph (1).

   (4)   A designated professional body must inform the Authority when a relevant member to whom paragraph (2) applies ceases, for whatever reason, to carry on insurance mediation activities.

   (5)   The Authority may give directions to a designated professional body as to the manner in which the information referred to in paragraphs (1), (3) and (4) must be provided.]

[852]

NOTES
Commencement: 31 October 2004 (in so far as relating to contracts of long-term care insurance); 14 January 2005 (otherwise).
Inserted as noted to art 92 at **[850]**.

[95   Exclusion from record where not fit and proper to carry on insurance mediation activities
   (1)   If it appears to the Authority that a person who falls within article 93(2) (appointed representatives) ("AR") is not a fit and proper person to carry on insurance mediation activities, it may decide not to include him in the record or, if that person is already included in the record, to remove him from the record.

   (2)   Where the Authority proposes to make a determination under paragraph (1), it must give AR a warning notice.

   (3)   If the Authority makes a determination under paragraph (1), it must give AR a decision notice.

   (4)   If the Authority gives AR a decision notice under paragraph (3), AR may refer the matter to the Tribunal.

   (5)   The Authority may, on the application of AR, revoke a determination under paragraph (1).

   (6)   If the Authority decides to grant the application, it must give AR written notice of its decision.

   (7)   If the Authority proposes to refuse the application, it must give AR a warning notice.

   (8)   If the Authority decides to refuse the application, it must give AR a decision notice.

   (9)   If the Authority gives AR a decision notice under paragraph (8), AR may refer the matter to the Tribunal.

(10)   Sections 393 and 394 of the Act (third party rights and access to Authority material) apply to a warning notice given in accordance with paragraph (2) or (7) and to a decision notice given in accordance with paragraph (3) or (8).]

[853]

NOTES
   Commencement: 31 October 2004 (in so far as relating to contracts of long-term care insurance); 14 January 2005 (otherwise).
   Inserted as noted to art 92 at **[850]**.

[96   Exclusion from the record where Authority has exercised its powers under Part XX of the Act

(1)   If a person who appears to the Authority to fall within article 93(3) (member of a designated professional body) falls within paragraph (2) or (3), the Authority must not include him in the record or, if that person is already included in the record, must remove him from the record.

(2)   A person falls within this paragraph if, by virtue of a direction given by the Authority under section 328(1) of the Act (directions in relation to the general prohibition), section 327(1) of the Act does not apply in relation to the carrying on by him of any insurance mediation activity.

(3)   A person falls within this paragraph if the Authority has made an order under section 329(2) of the Act (orders in relation to the general prohibition) disapplying section 327(1) of the Act in relation to the carrying on by him of any insurance mediation activity.]

[854]

NOTES
   Commencement: 31 October 2004 (in so far as relating to contracts of long-term care insurance); 14 January 2005 (otherwise).
   Inserted as noted to art 92 at **[850]**.

97   ((*Pt VI*) *added by the Financial Services and Markets Act 2000* (*Regulated Activities*) (*Amendment*) *Order 2004, SI 2004/1610, art 3, as from 15 July 2004, and inserts the Financial Services and Markets Act 2000, s 49(2A)*.)

SCHEDULES

SCHEDULE 1
CONTRACTS OF INSURANCE

Article 3(1)

PART I
CONTRACTS OF GENERAL INSURANCE

1   Accident

Contracts of insurance providing fixed pecuniary benefits or benefits in the nature of indemnity (or a combination of both) against risks of the person insured or, in the case of a contract made by virtue of section 140, 140A or 140B of the Local Government Act 1972 (or, in Scotland, section 86(1) of the Local Government (Scotland) Act 1973), a person for whose benefit the contract is made—
   (a)   sustaining injury as the result of an accident or of an accident of a specified class; or
   (b)   dying as a result of an accident or of an accident of a specified class; or
   (c)   becoming incapacitated in consequence of disease or of disease of a specified class,
including contracts relating to industrial injury and occupational disease but excluding contracts falling within paragraph 2 of Part I of, or paragraph IV of Part II of, this Schedule.

2   Sickness

Contracts of insurance providing fixed pecuniary benefits or benefits in the nature of indemnity (or a combination of both) against risks of loss to the persons insured attributable to sickness or infirmity but excluding contracts falling within paragraph IV of Part II of this Schedule.

3   Land vehicles

Contracts of insurance against loss of or damage to vehicles used on land, including motor vehicles but excluding railway rolling stock.

4   Railway rolling stock

Contract of insurance against loss of or damage to railway rolling stock.

5   Aircraft

Contracts of insurance upon aircraft or upon the machinery, tackle, furniture or equipment of aircraft.

6 Ships

Contracts of insurance upon vessels used on the sea or on inland water, or upon the machinery, tackle, furniture or equipment of such vessels.

7 Goods in transit

Contracts of insurance against loss of or damage to merchandise, baggage and all other goods in transit, irrespective of the form of transport.

8 Fire and natural forces

Contracts of insurance against loss of or damage to property (other than property to which paragraphs 3 to 7 relate) due to fire, explosion, storm, natural forces other than storm, nuclear energy or land subsidence.

9 Damage to property

Contracts of insurance against loss of or damage to property (other than property to which paragraphs 3 to 7 relate) due to hail or frost or any other event (such as theft) other than those mentioned in paragraph 8.

10 Motor vehicle liability

Contracts of insurance against damage arising out of or in connection with the use of motor vehicles on land, including third-party risks and carrier's liability.

11 Aircraft liability

Contracts of insurance against damage arising out of or in connection with the use of aircraft, including third-party risks and carrier's liability.

12 Liability of ships

Contracts of insurance against damage arising out of or in connection with the use of vessels on the sea or on inland water, including third party risks and carrier's liability.

13 General liability

Contracts of insurance against risks of the persons insured incurring liabilities to third parties, the risks in question not being risks to which paragraph 10, 11 or 12 relates.

14 Credit

Contracts of insurance against risks of loss to the persons insured arising from the insolvency of debtors of theirs or from the failure (otherwise than through insolvency) of debtors of theirs to pay their debts when due.

15 Suretyship

(1)   Contracts of insurance against the risks of loss to the persons insured arising from their having to perform contracts of guarantee entered into by them.

(2)   Fidelity bonds, performance bonds, administration bonds, bail bonds or customs bonds or similar contracts of guarantee, where these are—
    (a)   effected or carried out by a person not carrying on a banking business;
    (b)   not effected merely incidentally to some other business carried on by the person effecting them; and
    (c)   effected in return for the payment of one or more premiums.

16 Miscellaneous financial loss

Contracts of insurance against any of the following risks, namely—
    (a)   risks of loss to the persons insured attributable to interruptions of the carrying on of business carried on by them or to reduction of the scope of business so carried on;
    (b)   risks of loss to the persons insured attributable to their incurring unforeseen expense (other than loss such as is covered by contracts falling within paragraph 18);
    (c)   risks which do not fall within sub-paragraph (a) or (b) and which are not of a kind such that contracts of insurance against them fall within any other provision of this Schedule.

17 Legal expenses

Contracts of insurance against risks of loss to the persons insured attributable to their incurring legal expenses (including costs of litigation).

18 Assistance

Contracts of insurance providing either or both of the following benefits, namely—
    (a)   assistance (whether in cash or in kind) for persons who get into difficulties while travelling, while away from home or while away from their permanent residence; or

(b)   assistance (whether in cash or in kind) for persons who get into difficulties otherwise than as mentioned in sub-paragraph (a).

[855]

NOTES

Note: see also the FSA Perimeter Guidance Manual, PERG 6, for guidance on the identification of contracts of insurance.

PART II
CONTRACTS OF LONG-TERM INSURANCE

I Life and annuity

Contracts of insurance on human life or contracts to pay annuities on human life, but excluding (in each case) contracts within paragraph III.

II Marriage and birth

Contract of insurance to provide a sum on marriage [or the formation of a civil partnership] or on the birth of a child, being contracts expressed to be in effect for a period of more than one year.

III Linked long term

Contracts of insurance on human life or contracts to pay annuities on human life where the benefits are wholly or party to be determined by references to the value of, or the income from, property of any description (whether or not specified in the contracts) or by reference to fluctuations in, or in an index of, the value of property of any description (whether or not so specified).

IV Permanent health

Contracts of insurance providing specified benefits against risks of persons becoming incapacitated in consequence of sustaining injury as a result of an accident or of an accident of a specified class or of sickness or infirmity, being contracts that—
(a)   are expressed to be in effect for a period of not less than five years, or until the normal retirement age for the persons concerned, or without limit of time; and
(b)   either are not expressed to be terminable by the insurer, or are expressed to be so terminable only in special circumstances mentioned in the contract.

V Tontines

Tontines.

VI Capital redemption contracts

Capital redemption contracts, where effected or carried out by a person who does not carry on a banking business, and otherwise carries on a regulated activity of the kind specified by article 10(1) or (2).

VII Pension fund management
(a)   Pension fund management contracts, and
(b)   pension fund management contracts which are combined with contracts of insurance covering either conservation of capital or payment of a minimum interest,

where effected or carried out by a person who does not carry on a banking business, and otherwise carries on a regulated activity of the kind specified by article 10(1) or (2).

VIII Collective insurance etc

Contracts of a kind referred to in article 1(2)(e) of the first life insurance directive.

IX Social insurance

Contracts of a kind referred to in article 1(3) of the first life insurance directive.

[856]

NOTES

II Marriage and birth: words in square brackets inserted by the Civil Partnership Act 2004 (Amendments to Subordinate Legislation) Order 2005, SI 2005/2114, art 2(16), Sch 16, Pt 1, para 1(1), (5), as from 5 December 2005. Note that it is unclear from the Queen's Printer's copy of the 2005 Order whether these words should also be inserted after the word "Marriage" in the heading to this paragraph.

[SCHEDULE 2
SECTIONS A AND C OF ANNEX I TO THE MARKETS IN FINANCIAL INSTRUMENTS
DIRECTIVE AND RELATED COMMUNITY SUBORDINATE LEGISLATION
Article 3(1)

PART 1
SECTION C OF ANNEX I TO THE MARKETS IN FINANCIAL INSTRUMENTS DIRECTIVE
Financial Instruments

1.   Transferable securities;

2.   Money-market instruments;

3.   Units in collective investment undertakings;

4.   Options, futures, swaps, forward rate agreements and any other derivative contracts relating to securities, currencies, interest rates or yields, or other derivatives instruments, financial indices or financial measures which may be settled physically or in cash;

5.   Options, futures, swaps, forward rate agreements and any other derivative contracts relating to commodities that must be settled in cash or may be settled in cash at the option of one of the parties (otherwise than by reason of a default or other termination event);

6.   Options, futures, swaps, and any other derivative contracts relating to commodities that can be physically settled provided that they are traded on a regulated market and/or an MTF;

7.   Options, futures, swaps, forwards and any other derivative contracts relating to commodities, that can be physically settled not otherwise mentioned in C6 and not being for commercial purposes, which have the characteristics of other derivative financial instruments, having regard to whether, inter alia, they are cleared and settled through recognised clearing houses or are subject to regular margin calls;

8.   Derivative instruments for the transfer of credit risk;

9.   Financial contracts for differences;

10.   Options, futures, swaps, forward rate agreements and any other derivative contracts relating to climatic variables, freight rates, emission allowances or inflation rates or other official economic statistics that must be settled in cash or may be settled in cash at the option of one of the parties (otherwise than by reason of a default or other termination event), as well as any other derivative contracts relating to assets, rights, obligations, indices and measures not otherwise mentioned in this Section, which have the characteristics of other derivative financial instruments, having regard to whether, inter alia, they are traded on a regulated market or an MTF, are cleared and settled through recognised clearing houses or are subject to regular margin calls.]

                                                                                              [857]

NOTES

Commencement: 1 April 2007 (certain purposes); 1 November 2007 (otherwise) (see below).

Substituted by the Financial Services and Markets Act 2000 (Regulated Activities) (Amendment No 3) Order 2006, SI 2006/3384, arts 2, 29, as from 1 April 2007 (for the purposes of enabling applications to be made for (i) a Pt IV permission, (ii) a variation of a Pt IV permission, and (iii) the Authority's approval under s 59 of the 2000 Act, in relation to an activity of the kind specified by art 25D of this Order, or in relation to an investment of the kind specified by arts 83, 84 or 85 of this Order), and as from 1 November 2007 (otherwise).

[PART 2
CHAPTER VI OF THE COMMISSION REGULATION

DERIVATIVE FINANCIAL INSTRUMENTS

Article 38
Characteristics of other derivative financial instruments

1.   For the purposes of Section C(7) of Annex I to Directive 2004/39/EC, a contract which is not a spot contract within the meaning of paragraph 2 of this Article and which is not covered by paragraph 4 shall be considered as having the characteristics of other derivative financial instruments and not being for commercial purposes if it satisfies the following conditions:

   (a)   it meets one of the following sets of criteria:
      (i)   it is traded on a third country trading facility that performs a similar function to a regulated market or an MTF;
      (ii)   it is expressly stated to be traded on, or is subject to the rules of, a regulated market, an MTF or such a third country trading facility;
      (iii)   it is expressly stated to be equivalent to a contract traded on a regulated market, MTF or such a third country trading facility;
   (b)   it is cleared by a clearing house or other entity carrying out the same functions as a central counterparty, or there are arrangements for the payment or provision of margin in relation to the contract;

(c)   it is standardised so that, in particular, the price, the lot, the delivery date or other terms are determined principally by reference to regularly published prices, standard lots or standard delivery dates.

2.   A spot contract for the purposes of paragraph 1 means a contract for the sale of a commodity, asset or right, under the terms of which delivery is scheduled to be made within the longer of the following periods:

(a)   two trading days;

(b)   the period generally accepted in the market for that commodity, asset or right as the standard delivery period.

However, a contract is not a spot contract if, irrespective of its explicit terms, there is an understanding between the parties to the contract that delivery of the underlying is to be postponed and not to be performed within the period mentioned in the first subparagraph.

3.   For the purposes of Section C(10) of Annex I to Directive 2004/39/EC, a derivative contract relating to an underlying referred to in that Section or in Article 39 shall be considered to have the characteristics of other derivative financial instruments if one of the following conditions is satisfied:

(a)   that contract is settled in cash or may be settled in cash at the option of one or more of the parties, otherwise than by reason of a default or other termination event;

(b)   that contract is traded on a regulated market or an MTF;

(c)   the conditions laid down in paragraph 1 are satisfied in relation to that contract.

4.   A contract shall be considered to be for commercial purposes for the purposes of Section C(7) of Annex I to Directive 2004/39/EC, and as not having the characteristics of other derivative financial instruments for the purposes of Sections C(7) and (10) of that Annex, if it is entered into with or by an operator or administrator of an energy transmission grid, energy balancing mechanism or pipeline network, and it is necessary to keep in balance the supplies and uses of energy at a given time.

Article 39
Derivatives Within Section C(10) of Annex I to Directive 2004/39/EC

In addition to derivative contracts of a kind referred to in Section C(10) of Annex I to Directive 2004/39/EC, a derivative contract relating to any of the following shall fall within that Section if it meets the criteria set out in that Section and in Article 38(3):

(a)   telecommunications bandwidth;

(b)   commodity storage capacity;

(c)   transmission or transportation capacity relating to commodities, whether cable, pipeline or other means;

(d)   an allowance, credit, permit, right or similar asset which is directly linked to the supply, distribution or consumption of energy derived from renewable resources;

(e)   a geological, environmental or other physical variable;

(f)   any other asset or right of a fungible nature, other than a right to receive a service, that is capable of being transferred;

(g)   an index or measure related to the price or value of, or volume of transactions in any asset, right, service or obligation.]

[858]

NOTES

Commencement: 1 April 2007 (certain purposes); 1 November 2007 (otherwise).

Substituted as noted to Part 1 at **[857]**.

[PART 3
SECTION A OF ANNEX I TO THE MARKETS IN FINANCIAL INSTRUMENTS DIRECTIVE

INVESTMENT SERVICES AND ACTIVITIES

1.   Reception and transmission of orders in relation to one or more financial instruments.

2.   Execution of orders on behalf of clients.

3.   Dealing on own account.

4.   Portfolio management.

5.   Investment advice.

6.   Underwriting of financial instruments and/or placing of financial instruments on a firm commitment basis.

7.   Placing of financial instruments without a firm commitment basis.

8.   Operation of Multilateral Trading Facilities.]

[859]

PART IV OTHER STATUTORY INSTRUMENTS

NOTES
Commencement: 1 April 2007 (certain purposes); 1 November 2007 (otherwise).
Substituted as noted to Part 1 at **[857]**.

[PART 4
ARTICLE 52 OF COMMISSION DIRECTIVE 2006/73/EC

Article 52
Investment Advice

For the purposes of the definition of "investment advice" in Article 4(1)(4) of Directive 2004/39/EC, a personal recommendation is a recommendation that is made to a person in his capacity as an investor or potential investor, or in his capacity as an agent for an investor or potential investor.

That recommendation must be presented as suitable for that person, or must be based on a consideration of the circumstances of that person, and must constitute a recommendation to take one of the following sets of steps:

(a) to buy, sell, subscribe for, exchange, redeem, hold or underwrite a particular financial instrument;

(b) to exercise or not to exercise any right conferred by a particular financial instrument to buy, sell, subscribe for, exchange, or redeem a financial instrument.

A recommendation is not a personal recommendation if it is issued exclusively through distribution channels or to the public.]

[860]

NOTES
Commencement: 1 April 2007 (certain purposes); 1 November 2007 (otherwise).
Substituted as noted to Part 1 at **[857]**.

[SCHEDULE 3
ARTICLE 2 OF THE MARKETS IN FINANCIAL INSTRUMENTS DIRECTIVE

Article 2
Exemptions

1. This Directive shall not apply to:

(a) insurance undertakings as defined in Article 1 of Directive 73/239/EEC or assurance undertakings as defined in Article 1 of Directive 2002/83/EC or undertakings carrying on the reinsurance and retrocession activities referred to in Directive 64/225/EEC;

(b) persons which provide investment services exclusively for their parent undertakings, for their subsidiaries or for other subsidiaries of their parent undertakings;

(c) persons providing an investment service where that service is provided in an incidental manner in the course of a professional activity and that activity is regulated by legal or regulatory provisions or a code of ethics governing the profession which do not exclude the provision of that service;

(d) persons who do not provide any investment services or activities other than dealing on own account unless they are market makers or deal on own account outside a regulated market or an MTF on an organised, frequent and systematic basis by providing a system accessible to third parties in order to engage in dealings with them;

(e) persons which provide investment services consisting exclusively in the administration of employee-participation schemes;

(f) persons which provide investment services which only involve both administration of employee-participation schemes and the provision of investment services exclusively for their parent undertakings, for their subsidiaries or for other subsidiaries of their parent undertakings;

(g) the members of the European System of Central Banks and other national bodies performing similar functions and other public bodies charged with or intervening in the management of the public debt;

(h) collective investment undertakings and pension funds whether coordinated at Community level or not and the depositaries and managers of such undertakings;

(i) persons dealing on own account in financial instruments, or providing investment services in commodity derivatives or derivative contracts included in Annex I, Section C10 to the clients of their main business, provided this is an ancillary activity to their main business, when considered on a group basis, and that main business is not the provision of investment services within the meaning of this Directive or banking services under Directive 2000/12/EC;

(j) persons providing investment advice in the course of providing another professional activity not covered by this Directive provided that the provision of such advice is not specifically remunerated;

(k) persons whose main business consists of dealing on own account in commodities and/or commodity derivatives. This exception shall not apply where the persons that deal on own account in commodities and/or commodity derivatives are part of a group the main business of which is the provision of other investment services within the meaning of this Directive or banking services under Directive 2000/12/EC;

(l)   firms which provide investment services and/or perform investment activities consisting exclusively in dealing on own account on markets in financial futures or options or other derivatives and on cash markets for the sole purpose of hedging positions on derivatives markets or which deal for the accounts of other members of those markets or make prices for them and which are guaranteed by clearing members of the same markets, where responsibility for ensuring the performance of contracts entered into by such firms is assumed by clearing members of the same markets;

(m)   associations set up by Danish and Finnish pensions funds with the sole aim of managing the assets of pension funds that are members of those associations;

(n)   'agenti di cambio' whose activities and functions are governed by Article 201 of Italian Legislative Decree No 58 of 24 February 1998.

2.   The rights conferred by this Directive shall not extend to the provision of services as counterparty in transactions carried out by public bodies dealing with public debt or by members of the European System of Central Banks performing their tasks as provided for by the Treaty and the Statute of the European System of Central Banks and of the European Central Bank or performing equivalent functions under national provisions.

3.   In order to take account of developments on financial markets, and to ensure the uniform application of this Directive, the Commission, acting in accordance with the procedure referred to in Article 64(2), may, in respect of exemptions (c), (i) and (k) define the criteria for determining when an activity is to be considered as ancillary to the main business on a group level as well as for determining when an activity is provided in an incidental manner.]

[861]

NOTES

Commencement: 1 April 2007 (certain purposes); 1 November 2007 (otherwise) (see below).

Substituted by the Financial Services and Markets Act 2000 (Regulated Activities) (Amendment No 3) Order 2006, SI 2006/3384, arts 2, 30, as from 1 April 2007 (for the purposes of enabling applications to be made for (i) a Pt IV permission, (ii) a variation of a Pt IV permission, and (iii) the Authority's approval under s 59 of the 2000 Act, in relation to an activity of the kind specified by art 25D of this Order, or in relation to an investment of the kind specified by arts 83, 84 or 85 of this Order), and as from 1 November 2007 (otherwise).

[SCHEDULE 4
RELEVANT TEXT OF THE INSURANCE MEDIATION DIRECTIVE

Article 4

PART I
ARTICLE 1.2

This Directive shall not apply to persons providing mediation services for insurance contracts if all the following conditions are met:

(a)   the insurance contract only requires knowledge of the insurance cover that is provided;

(b)   the insurance contract is not a life assurance contract;

(c)   the insurance contract does not cover any liability risks;

(d)   the principal professional activity of the person is other than insurance mediation;

(e)   the insurance is complementary to the product or service supplied by any provider, where such insurance covers:

(i)   the risk of breakdown, loss of or damage to goods supplied by that provider; or

(ii)   damage to or loss of baggage and other risks linked to the travel booked with that provider, even if the insurance covers life assurance or liability risks, provided that the cover is ancillary to the main cover for the risks linked to that travel;

(f)   the amount of the annual premium does not exceed EUR 500 and the total duration of the insurance contract, including any renewals, does not exceed five years.]

[862]

NOTES

Commencement: 31 October 2004 (in so far as relating to contracts of long-term care insurance); 14 January 2005 (otherwise).

Added by the Financial Services and Markets Act 2000 (Regulated Activities) (Amendment) (No 2) Order 2003, SI 2003/1476, art 12, as from 31 October 2004 (in so far as relating to contracts of long-term care insurance), and as from 14 January 2005 (otherwise); for transitional provisions see arts 22–27 of that Order.

[PART II
ARTICLE 2.3

"Insurance mediation" means the activities of introducing, proposing or carrying out other work preparatory to the conclusion of contracts of insurance, or of concluding such contracts, or of assisting in the administration and performance of such contracts, in particular in the event of a claim.

These activities when undertaken by an insurance undertaking or an employee of an insurance undertaking who is acting under the responsibility of the insurance undertaking shall not be considered as insurance mediation.

The provision of information on an incidental basis in the context of another professional activity provided that the purpose of that activity is not to assist the customer in concluding or performing an insurance contract, the management of claims of an insurance undertaking on a professional basis, and loss adjusting and expert appraisal of claims shall also not be considered as insurance mediation.]

[863]

NOTES
Commencement: 31 October 2004 (in so far as relating to contracts of long-term care insurance); 14 January 2005 (otherwise).
Added as noted to Sch 4, Pt I at **[862]**.

[PART III
ARTICLE 2.4

"Reinsurance mediation" means the activities of introducing, proposing or carrying out other work preparatory to the conclusion of contracts of reinsurance, or of concluding such contracts, or of assisting in the administration and performance of such contracts, in particular in the event of a claim.

These activities when undertaken by a reinsurance undertaking or an employee of a reinsurance undertaking who is acting under the responsibility of the reinsurance undertaking are not considered as reinsurance mediation.

The provision of information on an incidental basis in the context of another professional activity provided that the purpose of that activity is not to assist the customer in concluding or performing a reinsurance contract, the management of claims of a reinsurance undertaking on a professional basis, and loss adjusting and expert appraisal of claims shall also not be considered as reinsurance mediation.]

[864]

NOTES
Commencement: 31 October 2004 (in so far as relating to contracts of long-term care insurance); 14 January 2005 (otherwise).
Added as noted to Sch 4, Pt I at **[862]**.

OPEN-ENDED INVESTMENT COMPANIES REGULATIONS 2001

(SI 2001/1228)

NOTES
Made: 27 March 2001.
Authority: Financial Services and Markets Act 2000, ss 262, 428(3).
Commencement: see art 1(2).

ARRANGEMENT OF REGULATIONS

PART I
GENERAL

PART II
FORMATION, SUPERVISION AND CONTROL

General

PART I
GENERAL

1 Citation, commencement and extent

(1)   These Regulations may be cited as the Open-Ended Investment Companies Regulations 2001.

(2)   These Regulations come into force—

    (a)   for the purpose of regulation 6, on the day on which sections 247 and 248 of the Act come into force for the purpose of making rules;

(b)   for the purposes of regulations 7, 12, 13, 18(1) and (3), 74, 77 and 80 to 82, so far as relating to the making of applications for authorisation orders to be made on or after the day mentioned in sub-paragraph (c), on the day on which section 40 of the Act comes into force;

(c)   for all remaining purposes, on the day on which section 19 of the Act comes into force.

(3)   Subject to regulation 20(2)(b) [and paragraphs 4A and 4B of Schedule 4], these Regulations have effect in relation to any open-ended investment company which has its head office situated in Great Britain.

[865]

NOTES

Para (3): words in square brackets inserted by the Open-Ended Investment Companies (Amendment) Regulations 2009, SI 2009/553, reg 2(1), (2), as from 6 March 2009.

---

2   Interpretation

(1)   In these Regulations, except where the context otherwise requires—

"the Act" means the Financial Services and Markets Act 2000;

"the 1985 Act" means the Companies Act 1985;

"the 1986 Act" means the Insolvency Act 1986;

"annual general meeting" has the meaning given in regulation 37(1);

"annual report" has the meaning given in regulation 66(1)(a);

"the appropriate registrar" means—

(a)   the registrar of companies for England and Wales if the company's instrument of incorporation states that its head office is to be situated in England and Wales, or that it is to be situated in Wales;

(b)   the registrar of companies for Scotland if the company's instrument of incorporation states that its head office is to be situated in Scotland;

"authorisation order" means an order made by the Authority under regulation 14;

"bearer shares" has the meaning given in regulation 48;

.....

"court", in relation to any proceedings under these Regulations involving an open-ended investment company the head office of which is situated—

(a)   in England and Wales, means the High Court; and

(b)   in Scotland, means the Court of Session;

"depositary", in relation to an open-ended investment company, has the meaning given in regulation 5(1);

"the designated person" means the person designated in the company's instrument of incorporation for the purposes of paragraph 4 of Schedule 4 to these Regulations;

["electronic communication" has the meaning given in section 15(1) of the Electronic Communications Act 2000;]

"FSA rules" means any rules made by the Authority under regulation 6(1);

"larger denomination share" has the meaning given in regulation 45(5);

"officer", in relation to an open-ended investment company, includes a director or any secretary or manager;

"open-ended investment company" means an body incorporated by virtue of regulation 3(1) or a body treated as if it had been so incorporated by virtue of regulation 85(3)(a);

.....

"prospectus" has the meaning given in regulation 6(2);

"relevant provision" means any requirement imposed by or under the Act;

"register of shareholders" means the register kept under paragraph 1(1) of Schedule 3 to these Regulations;

"scheme property", in relation to an open-ended investment company, means the property subject to the collective investment scheme constituted by the company;

"share certificate" has the meaning given in regulation 46(1);

"smaller denomination share" has the meaning given in regulation 45(5);

"transfer documents" has the meaning given in paragraph 5(3) [and (3A)] of Schedule 4 to these Regulations;

"the Tribunal" means the Financial Services and Markets Tribunal;

.....

"umbrella company" means an open-ended investment company whose instrument of incorporation provides for such pooling as is mentioned in section 235(3)(a) of the Act (collective investment schemes) in relation to separate parts of the scheme property and whose shareholders are entitled to exchange rights in one part for rights in another; and

.....

(2)   In these Regulations any reference to a shareholder of an open-ended investment company is a reference to—

(a) the person who holds the share certificate, or other documentary evidence of title relating to that share mentioned in regulation 48; and

(b) the person whose name is entered on the company's register of shareholders in relation to any share other than a bearer share.

(3) In these Regulations, unless the contrary intention appears, expressions which are also used in [the Companies Acts (as defined in section 2 of the Companies Act 2006)] have the same meaning as in [those Acts].

[866]

NOTES

Para (1) is amended as follows:

Definitions "certificated form", "participating issuer", "participating security", "uncertificated form" and "uncertificated unit of a security" (omitted) revoked by the Uncertificated Securities Regulations 2001, SI 2001/3755, reg 51, Sch 7, Pt 2, para 24(a), as from 26 November 2001.

Definition "electronic communication" inserted, and words in square brackets in definition "transfer documents" inserted, by the Open-Ended Investment Companies (Amendment) Regulations 2009, SI 2009/553, reg 2(1), (3), as from 6 March 2009.

Definition "the UCITS directive" (omitted) revoked by the Collective Investment Schemes (Miscellaneous Amendments) Regulations 2003, SI 2003/2066, reg 13(7)(a), as from 13 February 2004.

Para (3): words in square brackets substituted by the Companies Act 2006 (Consequential Amendments etc) Order 2008, SI 2008/948, art 3(1), Sch 1, Pt 2, para 220, as from 6 April 2008.

PART II
FORMATION, SUPERVISION AND CONTROL
General

3 Open-ended investment company

(1) If the Authority makes an authorisation order then, immediately upon the coming into effect of the order, the body to which the authorisation order relates is to be incorporated as an open-ended investment company (notwithstanding that, at the point of its incorporation by virtue of this paragraph, the body will not have any shareholders or property).

(2) The name of an open-ended investment company is the name mentioned in the authorisation order made in respect of the company or, if it changes its name in accordance with these Regulations and FSA rules, its new name.

[867]

4 Registration by the Authority

(1) Upon making an authorisation order under regulation 14, the Authority must forthwith register—

(a) the instrument of incorporation of the company;

(b) a statement of the address of the company's head office;

(c) a statement, with respect to each person named in the application for authorisation as director of the company, of the particulars set out in regulation 13; and

(d) a statement of the corporate name and registered or principal office of the person named in the application for authorisation as the depositary of the company.

(2) In this regulation any reference to the instrument of incorporation of a company is a reference to the instrument of incorporation supplied for the purposes of regulation 14(1)(c).

[868]

5 Safekeeping of scheme property by depositary

(1) Subject to paragraph (2), all the scheme property of an open-ended investment company must be entrusted for safekeeping to a person appointed for the purpose ("a depositary").

(2) Nothing in paragraph (1)—

(a) applies to any scheme property designated for the purposes of this regulation by FSA rules;

(b) prevents a depositary from—

(i) entrusting to a third party all or some of the assets in its safekeeping; or

(ii) in a case falling within sub-paragraph (i), authorising the third party to entrust all or some of those assets to other specified persons.

(3) Schedule 1 to these Regulations makes provision with respect to depositaries of open-ended investment companies.

[869]

6 FSA rules

(1)   The Authority's powers to make rules under section 247 (trust scheme rules) and section 248 (scheme particulars rules) of the Act in relation to authorised unit trust schemes are, subject to the provisions of these Regulations, exercisable in relation to open-ended investment companies—

(a)   for like purposes; and

(b)   subject to the same conditions.

(2)   In these Regulations any document which a person is required to submit and publish by virtue of rules made by the Authority under paragraph (1) for like purposes to those in section 248 of the Act is referred to as a prospectus.

[870]

7 Modification or waiver of FSA rules

(1)   The Authority may, on the application or with the consent of any person to whom any FSA rules apply, direct that all or any of the FSA rules—

(a)   are not to apply to him as respects a particular open-ended investment company; or

(b)   are to apply to him as respects such a company with such modifications as may be specified in the direction.

(2)   The Authority may, on the application or with the consent of an open-ended investment company and its depositary acting jointly, direct that all or any of the FSA rules—

(a)   are not to apply to the company; or

(b)   are to apply to the company with such modifications as may be specified in the direction.

(3)   Section 148(3) to (9) and (11) of the Act (modification or waiver of rules) have effect in relation to a direction under paragraph (1) as they have effect in relation to a direction under section 148(2) of the Act but with the following modifications—

(a)   ...

(b)   any reference to the [person] is to be read as a reference to the person mentioned in paragraph (1); and

(c)   subsection (7)(b) is to be read, in relation to a shareholder, as if the word "commercial" were omitted.

(4)   Section 148(3) to (9) and (11) of the Act have effect in relation to a direction under paragraph (2) as they have effect in relation to a direction under section 148(2) of the Act but with the following modifications—

(a)   subsection (4)(a) is to be read as if the words "by the ... person" were omitted;

(b)   subsections (7)(b), (8) and (11) are to be read as if the reference to the ... person were a reference to each of the company and its depositary;

(c)   subsection (7)(b) is to be read, in relation to a shareholder, as if the word "commercial" were omitted; and

(d)   subsection (9) is to be read as if the reference to the ... person were a reference to the company and its depositary acting jointly.

[871]

NOTES

Para (3): sub-para (a) revoked, and word in square brackets in sub-para (b) substituted, by the Regulatory Reform (Financial Services and Markets Act 2000) Order 2007, SI 2007/1973, arts 2, 12(a), (b), as from 12 July 2007.

Para (4): words omitted revoked by SI 2007/1973, arts 2, 12(c), as from 12 July 2007.

8 Notices: general

Subject to the provisions of these Regulations—

(a)   section 387 of the Act (warning notices) applies to a warning notice given under any provision of these Regulations in the same way as it applies to a warning notice given under any provision of the Act;

(b)   section 388 of the Act (decision notices) applies to a decision notice given under any provision of these Regulations in the same way as it applies to a decision notice given under any provision of the Act;

(c)   section 389 of the Act (notices of discontinuance) applies to the discontinuance of the action proposed in a warning notice or the action to which a decision notice relates given under any provision of these Regulations in the same way as it applies to a warning notice or decision notice given under any provision of the Act;

(d)   section 390 of the Act (final notices) applies to a decision notice given under any provision of these Regulations in the same way as it applies to a decision notice given under any provision of the Act.

[872]

PART IV OTHER STATUTORY INSTRUMENTS

9 Publication

Section 391 of the Act (publication) applies to the notices mentioned in regulation 8 in the same way as it applies to any such notice given under any provision of the Act.

[873]

10 The Authority's procedures

Section 395 of the Act (the Authority's procedures) applies to the procedure relating to the Authority's functions in relation to supervisory notices, warning notices and decision notices given under any provision of these Regulations.

[874]

11 The Tribunal

Section 133 of the Act (proceedings: general provision) applies to any reference to the Tribunal under these Regulations as it applies to any reference to the Tribunal under the Act.

[875]

Authorisation

12 Applications for authorisation

(1)   Any application for an authorisation order in respect of a proposed open-ended investment company—
   (a)   must be made in such manner as the Authority may direct;
   (b)   must state with respect to each person proposed in the application as a director of the company the particulars set out in regulation 13;
   (c)   must state the corporate name and registered or principal office of the person proposed in the application as depositary of the company; and
   (d)   must contain or be accompanied by such other information as the Authority may reasonably require for the purpose of determining the application.

(2)   At any time after receiving an application and before determining it the Authority may require the applicant to furnish additional information.

(3)   Different directions may be given and different requirements imposed in relation to different applications.

(4)   Any information to be furnished to the Authority under this regulation must be in such form or verified in such manner as it may specify.

(5)   A person commits an offence if—
   (a)   for the purposes of or in connection with any application under this regulation; or
   (b)   in purported compliance with any requirement imposed on him by or under this regulation;
he furnishes information which he knows to be false or misleading in a material particular or recklessly furnishes information which is false or misleading in a material particular.

(6)   A person guilty of an offence under paragraph (5) is liable—
   (a)   on conviction on indictment, to imprisonment for a term not exceeding two years or to a fine or to both;
   (b)   on summary conviction, to imprisonment for a term not exceeding three months or to a fine not exceeding the statutory maximum or to both.

[876]

13 Particulars of directors

(1)   Subject to paragraph (2), an application for an authorisation order must contain the following particulars with respect to each person proposed as a director of the company—
   (a)   in the case of an individual, his present name, any former name, his usual residential address, his nationality, his business occupation (if any), particulars of any other directorships held by him or which have been held by him and his date of birth;
   (b)   in the case of a body corporate of Scottish firm, its corporate or firm name and the address of its registered or principal office.

(2)   The application need not contain particulars of a directorship—
   (a)   which has not been held by a director at any time during the 5 years preceding the date on which the application is delivered to the Authority;
   (b)   which is held by a director in a body corporate which is dormant and, if he also held that directorship for any period during those 5 years, which was dormant for the whole of that period; or
   (c)   which was held by a director for any period during those 5 years in a body corporate which was dormant for the whole of that period.

(3)   For the purposes of paragraph (2), a body corporate is dormant during a period in which no significant transaction occurs; and it ceases to be dormant on the occurrence of such a transaction.

(4) In paragraph (1)(a)—
  (a) name means a person's Christian name (or other forename) and surname, except that in the case of a peer, or an individual usually known by a title, the title may be stated instead of his Christian name (or other forename) and surname or in addition to either or both of them;
  (b) the reference to a former name does not include—
    (i) in the case of a peer, or an individual normally known by a British title, the name by which he was known previous to the adoption of or succession to the title;
    (ii) in the case of any person, a former name which was changed or disused before he attained the age of 18 years or which has been changed or disused for 20 years or more; or
    (iii) in the case of a married woman, the name by which she was known previous to the marriage; and
  (c) the reference to directorships is a reference to directorships in any body corporate whether or not incorporated in Great Britain.

(5) In paragraph (3) the reference to a significant transaction is, in relation to a company within the meaning of section 735(1) of the 1985 Act, a reference to a significant accounting transaction within the meaning of [section 1169(2) of the Companies Act 2006, other than a transaction to which subsection (3) of that section applies].

[877]

NOTES
  Para (5): words in square brackets substituted by the Companies Act 2006 (Consequential Amendments etc) Order 2008, SI 2008/948, art 3(1), Sch 1, Pt 2, para 221, as from 6 April 2008.

14 Authorisation

(1) Where an application is duly made under regulation 12, the Authority may make an authorisation order in respect of an open-ended investment company if—
  (a) it is satisfied that the company will, on the coming into effect of the authorisation order, comply with the requirements in regulation 15;
  (b) it is satisfied that the company will, at that time, comply with the requirements of FSA rules;
  (c) it has been provided with a copy of the proposed company's instrument of incorporation and a certificate signed by a solicitor to the effect that the instrument of incorporation complies with Schedule 2 to these Regulations and with such of the requirements of FSA rules as relate to the contents of that instrument of incorporation; and
  (d) it has received a notification under regulation 18(3) from the appropriate registrar.

(2) If the Authority makes an order under paragraph (1), it must give written notice of the order to the applicant.

(3) In determining whether the requirement referred to in regulation 15(5) is satisfied in respect of any proposed director of a company, the Authority may take into account—
  (a) any matter relating to any person who is or will be employed by or associated with the proposed director, for the purposes of the business of the company;
  (b) if the proposed director is a body corporate, any matter relating to any director or controller of the body, to any other body corporate in the same group or to any director or controller of any such other body corporate;
  (c) if the proposed director is a partnership, any matter relating to any of the partners; and
  (d) if the proposed director is an unincorporated association, any matter relating to any member of the governing body of the association or any officer or controller of the association.

(4) An application must be determined by the Authority before the end of the period of six months beginning with the date on which it receives a completed application.

(5) The Authority may determine an incomplete application if it considers it appropriate to do so and, if it does so, it must determine the application within the period of twelve months beginning with the date on which it first receives the application.

(6) The applicant may withdraw his application, by giving the Authority written notice, at any time before the Authority determines it.

(7) An authorisation order must specify the date on which it is to come into effect.

(8) Schedule 2 to these Regulations makes provision with respect to the contents, alteration and binding nature of the instrument of incorporation of an open-ended investment company.

[878]

15 Requirements for authorisation

(1) The requirements referred to in regulation 14(1)(a) are as follows.

(2)   The company and its instrument of incorporation must comply with the requirements of these regulations and FSA rules.

(3)   The head office of the company must be situated in England and Wales, Wales or Scotland.

(4)   The company must have at least one director.

(5)   The directors of the company must be fit and proper persons to act as such.

(6)   If the company has only one director, that director must be a body corporate which is an authorised person and which has permission under ... the Act to act as sole director of an open-ended investment company.

(7)   If the company has two or more directors, the combination of their experience and expertise must be such as is appropriate for the purposes of carrying on the business of the company.

(8)   The person appointed as the depositary of the company—
  (a)   must be a body corporate incorporated in the United Kingdom or another EEA State;
  (b)   must have a place of business in the United Kingdom;
  (c)   must have its affairs administered in the country in which it is incorporated;
  (d)   must be an authorised person;
  (e)   must have permission under Part IV of the Act to act as the depositary of an open-ended investment company; and
  (f)   must be independent of the company and of the persons appointed as directors of the company.

(9)   The name of the company must not be undesirable or misleading.

(10)   The aims of the company must be reasonably capable of being achieved.

(11)   The company must meet one or both of the following requirements—
  (a)   shareholders are entitled to have their shares redeemed or repurchased upon request at a price related to the net value of the scheme property and determined in accordance with the company's instrument of incorporation and FSA rules; or
  (b)   shareholders are entitled to sell their shares on an investment exchange at a price not significantly different from that mentioned in sub-paragraph (a).

[879]

NOTES
Para (6): words omitted revoked by the Collective Investment Schemes (Miscellaneous Amendments) Regulations 2003, SI 2003/2066, reg 8, as from 13 February 2004.

16   Representations against refusal of authorisation

(1)   If the Authority proposes to refuse an application made under regulation 12, it must give the applicant a warning notice.

(2)   If the Authority decides to refuse the application—
  (a)   it must give the applicant a decision notice; and
  (b)   the applicant may refer the matter to the Tribunal.

[880]

17   Certificates

(1)   If an open-ended investment company which complies with the conditions necessary to enable it to enjoy the rights conferred by [the UCITS directive] so requests, the Authority may issue a certificate to the effect that the company complies with those conditions.

(2)   Such a certificate may be issued on the making of an authorisation order in respect of the company or at any subsequent time.

[881]

NOTES
Para (1): words in square brackets substituted by the Collective Investment Schemes (Miscellaneous Amendments) Regulations 2003, SI 2003/2066, reg 13(7)(b), as from 13 February 2004.

Names

18   Registrar's approval of names

(1)   Where, in respect of a proposed open-ended investment company, it appears to the Authority that the requirements of regulation 14(1)(a) to (c) are or will be met, the Authority must notify the appropriate registrar of the name by which it is proposed that the company should be incorporated.

(2)   Every open-ended investment company must obtain the Authority's approval to any proposed change in the name by which the company is incorporated and the Authority must notify the appropriate registrar of the proposed name.

(3)   If it appears to the appropriate registrar that the provisions of regulation 19(1) are not contravened in relation to the proposed name, he must notify the Authority to that effect.

[882]

19   Prohibition on certain names

(1)   No open-ended investment company is to have a name that—
-   (a)   includes any of the following words or expressions, that is to say—
    -   (i)   limited, unlimited or public limited company, or their Welsh equivalents ("cyfyngedig", "anghyfyngedig" and "cwmni cyfyngedig cyhoeddus" respectively); or
    -   (ii)   European Economic Interest Grouping or any equivalent set out in Schedule 3 to the European Economic Interest Grouping Regulations 1989;
-   (b)   includes an abbreviation of any of the words or expressions referred to in sub-paragraph (a); or
-   (c)   is the same as any other name appearing in the registrar's index of company names.

(2)   In determining for the purposes of paragraph (1)(c) whether one name is the same as another, there are to be disregarded—
-   (a)   the definite article, where it is the first word of the name;
-   (b)   the following word and expressions where they appear at the end of the name—
    "company" or its Welsh equivalent ("cwmni");
    "and company" or its Welsh equivalent ("a'r cwmni");
    "company limited" or its Welsh equivalent ("cwmni cyfyngedig");
    "limited" or its Welsh equivalent ("cyfyngedig");
    "unlimited" or its Welsh equivalent ("anghyfyngedig");
    "public limited company" or its Welsh equivalent ("cwmni cyfyngedig cyhoeddus");
    "European Economic Interest Grouping" or any equivalent set out in Schedule 3 to the European Economic Interest Grouping Regulations 1989;
    "investment company with variable capital" or its Welsh equivalent ("cwmni buddsoddi â chyfalaf newidiol");
    "open-ended investment company" or its Welsh equivalent ("cwmni buddsoddiant penagored");
-   (c)   abbreviations of any of those words or expressions where they appear at the end of the name; and
-   (d)   type and case of letters, accents, spaces between letters and punctuation marks;
and "and" and "&" are to be taken as the same.

[883]

20   Registrar's index of company names

(1)   Upon making an authorisation order in respect of an open-ended investment company or upon approving any change in the name of such a company, the Authority must notify the appropriate registrar of the name by which the company is incorporated or, as the case may be, of the company's new name.

(2)   Section 714 of the 1985 Act (registrar's index of company and corporate names) has effect as if the bodies listed in subsection (1) of that section included—
-   (a)   open-ended investment companies in respect of which an authorisation order has come into effect; and
-   (b)   collective investment schemes which are open-ended investment companies and which have a head office situated in Northern Ireland.

[884]

Alterations

21   The Authority's approval for certain changes in respect of a company

(1)   An open-ended investment company must give written notice to the Authority of—
-   (a)   any proposed alteration to the company's instrument of incorporation;
-   (b)   any proposed alteration to the company's prospectus which, if made, would be significant;
-   (c)   any proposed reconstruction or amalgamation involving the company;
-   (d)   any proposal to wind up the affairs of the company otherwise than by the court;
-   (e)   any proposal to replace a director of the company, to appoint any additional director or to decrease the number of directors in post; and
-   (f)   any proposal to replace the depositary of the company.

(2)   Any notice given under paragraph (1)(a) must be accompanied by a certificate signed by a solicitor to the effect that the change in question will not affect the compliance of the instrument of incorporation with Schedule 2 to these Regulations and with such of the requirements of FSA rules as relate to the contents of that instrument.

(3)   Effect must not be given to any proposal falling within paragraph (1) unless—

(a)   the Authority, by written notice, has given its approval to the proposal; or

(b)   one month, beginning with the date on which notice of the proposal was given, has expired without the company or the depositary having received from the Authority a warning notice under regulation 22 in respect of the proposal.

(4)   No change falling within paragraph (1)(e) may be made if any of the requirements set out in regulation 15(4) to (7) and (8)(f) would not be satisfied if the change were made and no change falling within paragraph (1)(f) may be made if any of the requirements in regulation 15(8) would not be satisfied if the change were made.

[885]

22   Procedure when refusing approval of proposed changes

(1)   If the Authority proposes to refuse approval of a proposal to replace the depositary, or any director, of an open-ended investment company, it must give a warning notice to the company.

(2)   If the Authority proposes to refuse approval of any other proposal falling within regulation 21, it must give separate warning notices to the company and its depositary.

(3)   To be valid the warning notice must be received by that person before the end of one month beginning with the date on which notice of the proposal was given.

(4)   If, having given a warning notice to a person, the Authority decides to refuse approval—

(a)   it must give him a decision notice; and

(b)   he may refer the matter to the Tribunal.

(5)   If, having given a warning notice to a person, the Authority decides to approve the proposal, it must give him a [written] notice.

[886]

NOTES

Para (5): word in square brackets substituted by the Open-Ended Investment Companies (Amendment) Regulations 2005, SI 2005/923, reg 2(1), (2), as from 6 April 2005.

Ending of authorisation

23   Ending of authorisation

(1)   The Authority may revoke an authorisation order if it appears to it that—

(a)   any requirement for the making of the order is no longer satisfied;

(b)   the company, any of its directors or its depositary—

(i)   has contravened any relevant provision; or

(ii)   has, in purported compliance with any such provision, knowingly or recklessly given the Authority information which is false or misleading in a material particular;

(c)   no regulated activity has been carried on in relation to the company for the previous twelve months; or

(d)   it is desirable to revoke the authorisation order in order to protect the interests of shareholders or potential shareholders in the company.

(2)   For the purposes of paragraph (1)(d), the Authority may take into account any matter relating to—

(a)   the company or its depositary;

(b)   any director or controller of the depositary;

(c)   any person employed by or associated, for the purposes of the business of the company, with the company or its depositary;

(d)   any director of the company;

(e)   any person exercising influence over any director of the company or its depositary;

(f)   any body corporate in the same group as any director of the company or its depositary;

(g)   any director of any such body corporate;

(h)   any person exercising influence over any such body corporate;

(i)   any person who would be such a person as is mentioned in regulation 14(3)(a) to (d) were it to apply to a director as it applies to a proposed director.

(3)   Before revoking any authorisation order that has come into effect, the Authority must ensure that such steps as are necessary and appropriate to secure the winding up of the company (whether by the court or otherwise) have been taken.

[887]

24   Procedure

(1)   If the Authority proposes to make an order revoking an authorisation order ("a revoking order"), it must give separate warning notices to the company and its depositary.

(2)   If, having given warning notices, the Authority decides to make a revoking order it must without delay give the company and its depositary a decision notice and either of them may refer the matter to the Tribunal.

(3)   Sections 393 and 394 of the Act apply to a warning notice or a decision notice given in accordance with this regulation.

[888]

Powers of intervention

25   Directions

(1)   The Authority may give a direction under this regulation if it appears to the Authority that—
- (a)   one or more requirements for the making of an authorisation order are no longer satisfied;
- (b)   the company, any of its directors or its depositary—
  - (i)   has contravened or is likely to contravene any relevant provision; or
  - (ii)   has, in purported compliance with any such provision, knowingly or recklessly given the Authority information which is false or misleading in a material particular; or
- (c)   it is desirable to give a direction in order to protect the interests of shareholders or potential shareholders in the company.

(2)   A direction under this regulation may—
- (a)   require the company to cease the issue or redemption, or both the issue and redemption, of shares or any class of shares in the company;
- (b)   in the case of a director of the company who is the designated person, require that director to cease transfers to or from, or both to and from, his own holding of shares, or of any class of shares, in the company;
- (c)   in the case of an umbrella company, require that investments made in respect of one or more parts of the scheme property which are pooled separately be realised and, following the discharge of such liabilities of the company as are attributable to the relevant part or parts of the scheme property, that the resulting funds be distributed to shareholders in accordance with FSA rules;
- (d)   require any director of the company to present a petition to the court to wind up the company; or
- (e)   require that the affairs of the company be wound up otherwise than by the court.

(3)   Subject to paragraph (4), if the authorisation order is revoked, the revocation does not affect the operation of any direction under this regulation which is then in force; and a direction under this regulation may be given in relation to a company in the case of which an authorisation order has been revoked if a direction under this regulation was already in force at the time of revocation.

(4)   Where a winding-up order has been made by the court, no direction under this regulation is to have effect in relation to the company concerned.

(5)   For the purposes of paragraph (1)(c), the Authority may take into account any matter relating to any of the persons mentioned in regulation 23(2).

(6)   If a person contravenes a direction under this regulation, section 150 (actions for damages) applies to the contravention as it applies to a contravention mentioned in that section.

(7)   The Authority may, on its own initiative or on the application of the company or its depositary, revoke or vary a direction given under this regulation if it appears to the Authority—
- (a)   in the case of revocation, that it is no longer necessary for the direction to take effect or continue in force;
- (b)   in the case of variation, that the direction should take effect or continue in force in a different form.

[889]

26   Applications to the court

(1)   This regulation applies if the Authority could give a direction under regulation 25 in relation to an open-ended investment company.

(2)   The Authority may apply to the court for an order removing the depositary or any director of the company and replacing any such person with a person or persons nominated by the Authority.

(3)   The Authority may nominate a person for the purposes of paragraph (2) only if it is satisfied that, if the order were made, the requirements of paragraphs (4) to (7) or, as the case may be, of paragraph (8) of regulation 15 would be met.

(4)   If it appears to the Authority that there is no person whom it may nominate for the purposes of paragraph (2), it may apply to the court for an order removing the director in question or the depositary (or both) and appointing an authorised person to wind up the company.

(5)   On an application under this regulation the court may make such order as it thinks fit.

(6)   The court may, on the application of the Authority, rescind any such order as is mentioned in paragraph (4) and substitute such an order as is mentioned in paragraph (2).

(7)   The Authority must—
- (a)   give written notice of the making of an application under this section to—
  - (i)   the company;
  - (ii)   its depositary; and
  - (iii) where the application seeks the removal of any director of the company, that director; and
- (b)   take such steps as it considers appropriate for bringing the making of the application to the attention of the shareholders of the company.

[890]

27   Procedure on giving directions under regulation 25 and varying them on Authority's own initiative

(1)   A direction takes effect—
- (a)   immediately, if the notice given under paragraph (3) states that that is the case;
- (b)   on such date as may be specified in the notice; or
- (c)   if no date is specified in the notice, when the matter to which it relates is no longer open to review.

(2)   A direction may be expressed to take effect immediately (or on a specified date) only if the Authority, having regard to the ground on which it is exercising its power under regulation 25, considers that it is necessary for the direction to take effect immediately (or on that date).

(3)   If the Authority proposes to give a direction under regulation 25, or gives such a direction with immediate effect, it must give separate written notices to the company and its depositary.

(4)   The notice must—
- (a)   give details of the direction;
- (b)   inform the person to whom it is given of when the direction takes effect;
- (c)   state the Authority's reasons for giving the direction and for its determination as to when the direction takes effect;
- (d)   inform the person to whom it is given that he may make representations to the Authority within such period as may be specified in it (whether or not he has referred the matter to the Tribunal); and
- (e)   inform him of his right to refer the matter to the Tribunal.

(5)   If the direction imposes a requirement under regulation 25(2)(a) or (b), the notice must state that the requirement has effect until—
- (a)   a specified date; or
- (b)   a further direction.

(6)   If the direction imposes a requirement under regulation 25(2)(d) or (e), the petition must be presented (or, as the case may be, the company must be wound up)—
- (a)   by a date specified in the notice; or
- (b)   if no date is specified, as soon as possible.

(7)   The Authority may extend the period allowed under the notice for making representations.

(8)   If, having considered any representations made by a person to whom the notice was given, the Authority decides—
- (a)   to give the direction in the way proposed, or
- (b)   if it has been given, not to revoke the direction,

it must give separate written notices to the company and its depositary.

(9)   If, having considered any representations made by a person to whom the notice was given, the Authority decides—
- (a)   not to give the direction in the way proposed,
- (b)   to give the direction in a way other than that proposed, or
- (c)   to revoke a direction which has effect,

it must give separate written notices to the company and its depositary.

(10)   A notice given under paragraph (8) must inform the person to whom it is given of his right to refer the matter to the Tribunal.

(11)   A notice under paragraph (9)(b) must comply with paragraph (4).

(12)   If a notice informs a person of his right to refer a matter to the Tribunal, it must give an indication of the procedure on such a reference.

(13)   This regulation applies to the variation of a direction on the Authority's own initiative as it applies to the giving of a direction.

(14)   For the purposes of paragraph (1)(c), whether a matter is open to review is to be determined in accordance with section 391(8) of the Act.

(15)   Section 395 of the Act (the Authority's procedures) has effect as if subsection (13) included a reference to a notice given in accordance with paragraph (3), (8) or (9)(b).

[891]

28 Procedure: refusal to revoke or vary direction

(1)   If on an application under regulation 25(7) for a direction to be revoked or varied the Authority proposes—

   (a)   to vary the direction otherwise than in accordance with the application, or

   (b)   to refuse to revoke or vary the direction,

it must give the applicant a warning notice.

(2)   If the Authority decides to refuse to revoke or vary the direction—

   (a)   it must give the applicant a decision notice; and

   (b)   the applicant may refer the matter to the Tribunal.

[892]

29 Procedure: revocation of direction and grant of request for variation

(1)   If the Authority decides on its own initiative to revoke a direction under regulation 25 it must give separate written notices of its decision to the company and its depositary.

(2)   If on an application made under regulation 25(7) for a direction to be revoked or varied, the Authority decides to revoke or vary it in accordance with the application, it must give the applicant written notice of its decision.

(3)   A notice under this regulation must specify the date on which the decision takes effect.

(4)   The Authority may publish such information about the revocation or variation, in such way, as it considers appropriate.

[893]

Investigations

30 Power to investigate

(1)   The Authority or the Secretary of State may appoint one or more competent persons to investigate and report on the affairs of, or of any director or depositary of, an open-ended investment company if it appears to either of them that it is in the interests of shareholders or potential shareholders of the company to do so or that the matter is of public concern.

(2)   A person appointed under paragraph (1) to investigate the affairs of, or of any director or depositary of, a company may also, if he thinks it necessary for the purposes of that investigation, investigate the affairs of (or of the directors, depositary, trustee or operator of)—

   (a)   an open-ended investment company the directors of which include any of the directors of the company whose affairs are being investigated by virtue of that paragraph;

   (b)   an open-ended investment company the directors of which include any of the directors of the depositary whose affairs are being investigated by virtue of that paragraph;

   (c)   an open-ended investment company the depositary of which is—

      (i)   the same as the depositary of the company whose affairs are being investigated by virtue of that paragraph; or

      (ii)   the depositary whose affairs are being investigated by virtue of that paragraph;

   (d)   an open-ended investment company the directors of which include—

      (i)   the director whose affairs are being investigated by virtue of that paragraph; or

      (ii)   any director of a body corporate which is the director whose affairs are being investigated by virtue of that paragraph;

   (e)   a collective investment scheme the manager, depositary or operator of which is a director of the company whose affairs are being investigated by virtue of that paragraph;

   (f)   a collective investment scheme the trustee of which is—

      (i)   the same as the depositary of the company whose affairs are being investigated by virtue of that paragraph; or

      (ii)   the depositary whose affairs are being investigated by virtue of that paragraph; or

   (g)   a collective investment scheme the manager, depositary or operator of which is—

      (i)   the director whose affairs are being investigated by virtue of that paragraph; or

      (ii)   a director of a body corporate which is the director whose affairs are being investigated by virtue of that paragraph.

(3)   If the person ("A") appointed to conduct an investigation under this regulation considers that a person ("B") is or may be able to give information which is relevant to the investigation, A may require B—

   (a)   to produce to A any documents in B's possession or under his control which appear to A to be relevant to that investigation;

   (b)   to attend before A; and

   (c)   otherwise to give A all such assistance in connection with the investigation which B is reasonably able to give;

and it is B's duty to comply with that requirement.

(4)   Subsection (5) to (9) of section 170 of the Act (investigations: general) apply if—

(a)   the Authority appoints a person under this regulation to conduct an investigation on its behalf; or

(b)   the Secretary of State appoints a person under this regulation to conduct an investigation on his behalf;

as they apply in the cases mentioned in subsection (1) of that section.

(5)   Section 174 of the Act (admissibility of statements made to investigators) applies to a statement made by a person in compliance with a requirement imposed on him under this regulation as it applies to a statement mentioned in that section.

(6)   Subsections (2) to (4) and (6) of section 175 (information and documents: supplemental provisions) and section 177 of the Act (offences) have effect as if this regulation were contained in Part XI of the Act (information gathering and investigations).

(7)   Subsections (1) to (9) of section 176 of the Act (entry of premises under warrant) apply in relation to a person appointed under paragraph (1) as if—

(a)   references to an investigator were references to a person so appointed;

(b)   references to an information requirement were references to a requirement imposed under this regulation by a person so appointed;

(c)   the premises mentioned in section 176(3)(a) were the premises of a person whose affairs are the subject of an investigation under this regulation or of an appointed representative of such a person.

(8)   No person may be required under this regulation to disclose information or produce a document in respect of which he owes an obligation of confidence by virtue of carrying on a banking business unless—

(a)   the imposition of the requirement is authorised by the Authority or the Secretary of State (as the case may be) or the person to whom the obligation of confidence is owed; or

(b)   the person to whom it is owed is—

(i)   a director or depositary of any open-ended investment company which is under investigation; or

(ii)   any other person whose own affairs are under investigation.

[894]

Winding up

31   Winding up by the court

(1)   Where an open-ended investment company is wound up as an unregistered company under Part V of the 1986 Act, the provisions of that Act apply for the purposes of the winding up with the following modifications.

(2)   A petition for the winding up of an open-ended investment company may be presented by the depositary of the company as well as by any person authorised under section 124 (application for winding up) or section 124A of the 1986 Act (petition for winding up on grounds of public interest), as those sections apply by virtue of Part V of that Act, to present a petition for the winding up of the company.

(3)   Where a petition for the winding up of an open ended investment company is presented by a person other than the Authority—

(a)   that person must serve a copy of the petition on the Authority; and

(b)   the Authority is entitled to be heard on the petition.

(4)   If, before the presentation of a petition for the winding up by the court of an open-ended investment company as an unregistered company under Part V of the 1986 Act, the affairs of the company are being wound up otherwise than by the court—

(a)   section 129(2) of the 1986 Act (commencement of winding up by the court) is not to apply; and

(b)   any winding up of the company by the court is to be deemed to have commenced—

(i)   at the time at which the Authority gave its approval to a proposal mentioned in paragraph (1)(d) of regulation 21; or

(ii)   in a case falling within paragraph (3)(b) of that regulation, on the day following the end of the one-month period mentioned in that paragraph.

[895]

32   Dissolution on winding up by the court

(1)   Section 172(8) of the 1986 Act (final meeting of creditors and vacation of office by liquidator), as that section applies by virtue of Part V of that Act (winding up of unregistered companies) has effect, in relation to open-ended investment companies, as if the reference to the registrar of companies was a reference to the Authority.

(2)   Where, in respect of an open-ended investment company, the Authority receives—

(a)   a notice given for the purposes of section 172(8) of the 1986 Act (as aforesaid); or

(b)   a notice from the official receiver that the winding up, by the court, of the company is complete;

the Authority must, on receipt of the notice, forthwith register it and, subject to the provisions of this regulation, at the end of the period of three months beginning with the day of the registration of the notice, the company is to be dissolved.

(3)   The Secretary of State may, on the application of the official receiver or any other person who appears to the Secretary of State to be interested, give a direction deferring the date at which the dissolution of the company is to take effect for such period as the Secretary of State thinks fit.

(4)   An appeal to the court lies from any decision of the Secretary of State on an application for a direction under paragraph (3).

(5)   Paragraph (3) does not apply to a case where the winding-up order was made by the court in Scotland, but in such a case the court may, on an application by any person appearing to the court to have an interest, order that the date at which the dissolution of the company is to take effect be deferred for such period as the court thinks fit.

(6)   It is the duty of the person—

(a)   on whose application a direction is given under paragraph (3);

(b)   in whose favour an appeal with respect to an application for such a direction is determined; or

(c)   on whose application an order is made under paragraph (5);

not later than seven days after the giving of the direction, the determination of the appeal or the making of the order, to deliver to the Authority for registration a copy of the direction or determination or, in respect of an order, a certified copy of the interlocutor.

(7)   If a person without reasonable excuse fails to deliver a copy as required by paragraph (6), he is guilty of an offence.

(8)   A person guilty of an offence under paragraph (7) is liable, on summary conviction—

(a)   to a fine not exceeding level 1 on the standard scale; and

(b)   on a second or subsequent conviction instead of the penalty set out in sub-paragraph (a), to a fine of £100 for each day on which the contravention is continued.

[896]

33 Dissolution in other circumstances

(1)   Where the affairs of an open-ended investment company have been wound up otherwise than by the court, the Authority must, as soon as is reasonably practicable after the winding up is complete, register that fact and, subject to the provisions of this regulation, at the end of the period of three months beginning with the day of the registration, the company is to be dissolved.

(2)   The court may, on the application of the Authority or the company, make an order deferring the date at which the dissolution of the company is to take effect for such period as the court thinks fit.

(3)   It is the duty of the company, on whose application an order of the court under paragraph (2) is made, to deliver to the Authority, not later than seven days after the making of the order, a copy of the order for registration.

(4)   Where any company, the head office of which is situated in England and Wales, or Wales, is dissolved by virtue of paragraph (1), any sum of money (including unclaimed distributions) standing to the account of the company at the date of the dissolution must on such date as is determined in accordance with FSA rules, be paid into court.

(5)   Where any company, the head office of which is situated in Scotland, is dissolved by virtue of paragraph (1), any sum of money (including unclaimed dividends and unapplied or undistributable balances) standing to the account of the company at the date of the dissolution must—

(a)   on such date as is determined in accordance with FSA rules, be lodged in an appropriate bank or institution as defined in section 73(1) of the Bankruptcy (Scotland) Act 1985 (interpretation) in the name of the Accountant of the Court; and

(b)   thereafter be treated as if it were a sum of money lodged in such an account by virtue of section 193 of the 1986 Act (unclaimed dividends (Scotland)), as that section applies by virtue of Part V of that Act.

[897]

PART III
CORPORATE CODE

Organs

34 Directors

(1) On the coming into effect of an authorisation order in respect of an open-ended investment company, the persons proposed in the application under regulation 12 as directors of the company are deemed to be appointed as its first directors.

[(2) Subject to regulations 21 and 26, any subsequent appointment as a director of a company must be made by the company in general meeting, save that the directors of the company may appoint a person to act as director to fill any vacancy until such time as the next annual general meeting of the company takes place or, if the company does not hold annual general meetings, the directors of the company may appoint a person to act as director.]

(3) Any act of a director is valid notwithstanding—
    (a) any defect that may thereafter be discovered in his appointment or qualifications; or
    (b) that it is afterwards discovered that his appointment had terminated by virtue of any provision contained in FSA rules which required a director to retire upon attaining a specified age.

(4) The business of a company must be managed—
    (a) where a company has only one director, by that director; or
    (b) where a company has more than one director, by the directors but subject to any provision contained in FSA rules as to the allocation between the directors of responsibilities for the management of the company (including any provision there may be as to the allocation of such responsibility to one or more directors to the exclusion of others).

(5) Subject to the provisions of these Regulations, FSA rules and the company's instrument of incorporation, the directors of a company may exercise all the powers of the company.

[898]

NOTES
Para (2): substituted by the Open-Ended Investment Companies (Amendment) Regulations 2005, SI 2005/923, reg 2(1), (3), as from 6 April 2005.

[34A Removal of certain directors by ordinary resolution

(1) The directors of an open-ended investment company must, on a members' requisition, forthwith proceed duly to convene an extraordinary general meeting of the company and this applies notwithstanding anything in the company's instrument of incorporation.

(2) A members' requisition is a requisition—
    (a) by members of the company holding at the date of the deposit of the requisition not less than one-tenth of such of the paid-up capital of the company as at that date carries the right of voting at general meetings of the company; and
    (b) which states as the object of the meeting the removal of one or more directors appointed in accordance with regulation 34(2) and which must be signed by the requisitionists and deposited at the registered office of the company.

(3) A company may by ordinary resolution at an extraordinary general meeting convened in accordance with paragraph (1) remove any director or directors appointed in accordance with regulation 34(2).

(4) This regulation is not to be treated as depriving a person removed under it of compensation or damages payable to him in respect of the termination of his appointment as director or as derogating from any power to remove a director which exists apart from this regulation.]

[899]

NOTES
Commencement: 6 April 2005.
Inserted by the Open-Ended Investment Companies (Amendment) Regulations 2005, SI 2005/923, reg 2(1), (4), as from 6 April 2005.

35 Directors to have regard to interests of employees

(1) The matters to which a director of an open-ended investment company must have regard in the performance of his functions include the interests of the company's employees in general, as well as the interests of its shareholders.

(2)   The duty imposed by this regulation on a director is owed by him to the company (and the company alone) and is enforceable in the same way as any other fiduciary duty owed to a company by its directors.

[900]

36   Inspection of directors' service contracts

(1)   Every open-ended investment company must keep at an appropriate place—
   (a)   in the case of each director whose contract of service with the company is in writing, a copy of that contract; and
   (b)   in the case of each director whose contract of service with the company is not in writing, a written memorandum setting out its terms.

(2)   All copies and memoranda kept by a company in accordance with paragraph (1) must be kept at the same place.

(3)   The following are appropriate places for the purposes of paragraph (1)—
   (a)   the company's head office;
   (b)   the place where the company's register of shareholders is kept; and
   (c)   where the designated person is a director of the company and is a body corporate, the registered or principal office of that person.

(4)   Every copy and memorandum required by paragraph (1) to be kept must be open to the inspection of any shareholder of the company.

(5)   If such an inspection is refused, the court may by order compel an immediate inspection of the copy or memorandum concerned.

[(6)   Every copy and memorandum required to be kept by paragraph (1) must be made available, for inspection, by the company at the company's annual general meeting or, if the company does not hold annual general meetings, sent to any shareholder at his request within ten days of the company's receipt of such request.]

(7)   Paragraph (1) applies to a variation of a director's contract of service as it applies to the contract.

[901]

NOTES
Para (6): substituted the Open-Ended Investment Companies (Amendment) Regulations 2005, SI 2005/923, reg 2(1), (5), as from 6 April 2005.

37   General meetings

(1)   Subject to paragraph (2) [and regulation 37A], every open-ended investment company [incorporated before 6 April 2005] must in each year hold a general meeting ("annual general meeting") in addition to any other meetings, whether general or otherwise, it may hold in that year.

(2)   If a company holds its first annual general meeting within 18 months of the date on which the authorisation order made by the Authority in respect of the company comes into effect, paragraph (1) does not require the company to hold any other meeting as its annual general meeting in the year of its incorporation or in the following year.

(3)   Subject to paragraph (2) [and regulation 37A], not more than 15 months may elapse between the date of one annual general meeting of a company and the date of the next.

[902]

NOTES
Paras (1), (3): words in square brackets inserted by the Open-Ended Investment Companies (Amendment) Regulations 2005, SI 2005/923, reg 2(1), (6), as from 6 April 2005.

[37A   Election to dispense with annual general meetings

(1)   The directors of an open-ended investment company may elect to dispense with the holding of an annual general meeting by giving sixty days' written notice to all the company's shareholders.

(2)   An election has effect for the year in which it is made and subsequent years, but does not affect any liability already incurred by reason of default in holding an annual general meeting.]

[903]

NOTES
Commencement: 6 April 2005.
Inserted by the Open-Ended Investment Companies (Amendment) Regulations 2005, SI 2005/923, reg 2(1), (7), as from 6 April 2005.

38 Capacity of company

(1) The validity of an act done by an open-ended investment company cannot be called into question on the ground of lack of capacity by reason of anything in these Regulations, FSA rules or the company's instrument of incorporation.

(2) Nothing in paragraph (1) affects the duty of the directors to observe any limitation on their powers.

[904]

39 Power of directors and general meeting to bind the company

(1) In favour of a person dealing in good faith, the following powers, that is to say—
  (a) the power of the directors of an open-ended investment company (whether or not acting as a board) to bind the company, or authorise others to do so; and
  (b) the power of such a company in general meeting to bind the company, or authorise others to do so;
are deemed to be free of any limitation under the company's constitution.

(2) For the purposes of this regulation—
  (a) a person deals with a company if he is party to any transaction or other act to which the company is a party;
  (b) subject to paragraph (4), a person is not to be regarded as acting in bad faith by reason only of his knowing that, under the company's constitution, an act is beyond any of the powers referred to in paragraph (1)(a) or (b); and
  (c) subject to paragraph (4), a person is presumed to have acted in good faith unless the contrary is proved.

(3) The reference in paragraph (1) to any limitation under the company's constitution on the powers therein set out includes any limitation deriving from these Regulations, from FSA rules or from a resolution of the company in general meeting or of a meeting of any class of shareholders.

(4) Sub-paragraphs (b) and (c) of paragraph (2) do not apply where—
  (a) by virtue of a limitation deriving from these Regulations or from FSA rules, an act is beyond any of the powers referred to in paragraph (1)(a) or (b); and
  (b) the person in question—
    (i) has actual knowledge of that fact; or
    (ii) has deliberately failed to make enquiries in circumstances in which a reasonable and honest person would have done so.

(5) Paragraph (1) does not affect any liability incurred by the directors or any other person by reason of the directors exceeding their powers.

[905]

40 No duty to enquire as to capacity etc

Subject to regulation 39(4)(b)(ii), a party to a transaction with an open-ended investment company is not bound to enquire—
  (a) as to whether the transaction is permitted by these Regulations, FSA rules or the company's instrument of incorporation; or
  (b) as to any limitation on the powers referred to in regulation 39(1)(a) or (b).

[906]

41 Exclusion or deemed notice

A person is not to be taken to have notice of any matter merely because of its being disclosed in any document made available by an open-ended investment company for inspection; but this does not affect the question whether a person is affected by notice of any matter by reason of a failure to make such enquiries as ought reasonably to be made.

[907]

42 Restraint and ratification by shareholders

(1) A shareholder of an open-ended investment company may bring proceedings to restrain the doing of an act which but for regulation 38(1) would be beyond the company's capacity.

(2) Paragraph (1) of regulation 39 does not affect any right of a shareholder of an open-ended investment company to bring proceedings to restrain the doing of an act which is beyond any of the powers referred to in that paragraph.

(3) No proceedings may be brought under paragraph (1) in respect of an act to be done in fulfilment of a legal obligation arising from a previous act of the company; and paragraph (2) does not have the effect of enabling proceedings to be brought in respect of any such act.

(4) Any action by the directors of a company—
  (a) which, but for regulation 38(1), would be beyond the company's capacity; or
  (b) which is within the company's capacity but beyond the powers referred to in regulation 39(1)(a);

may only be ratified by a resolution of the company in general meeting.

(5)   A resolution ratifying such action does not affect any liability incurred by the directors or any other person, relief from any such liability requiring agreement by a separate resolution of the company in general meeting.

(6)   Nothing in this regulation affects any power or right conferred by or arising under section 150 (actions for damages) or section 380, 382 or 384 of the Act (injunctions and restitution orders).

[908]

43   Events affecting company status

(1)   Where either of the conditions mentioned in paragraph (2) is satisfied, an open-ended investment company is not entitled to rely against other persons on the happening of any of the following events—
  (a)   any alteration of the company's instrument of incorporation;
  (b)   any change among the directors of the company;
  (c)   as regards service of any document on the company, any change in the situation of the head office of the company; or
  (d)   the making of a winding-up order in respect of the company or, in circumstances in which the affairs of a company are to be wound up otherwise than by the court, the commencement of the winding up.

(2)   The conditions referred to in paragraph (1) are that—
  (a)   the event in question had not been officially notified at the material time and is not shown by the company to have been known at that time by the other person concerned; and
  (b)   if the material time fell on or before the 15th day after the date of official notification (or where the 15th day was a non-business day, on or before the next day that was a business day), it is shown that the other person concerned was unavoidably prevented from knowing of the event at that time.

(3)   In this regulation "official notification" means the notification in the Gazette (by virtue of regulation 78) of any document containing the information referred to in paragraph (1) above, and "officially notified" is to be construed accordingly.

[909]

44   Invalidity of certain transactions involving directors

(1)   This regulation applies where—
  (a)   an open-ended investment company enters into a transaction to which the parties include a director of the company or any person who is an associate of such a director; and
  (b)   in connection with the transaction, the directors of the company (whether or not acting as a board) exceed any limitation on their powers under the company's constitution.

(2)   The transaction is voidable at the instance of the company.

(3)   Whether or not the transaction is avoided, any such party to the transaction as is mentioned in paragraph (1)(a), and any director of the company who authorised the transaction, is liable—
  (a)   to account to the company for any gain which he has made directly or indirectly by the transaction; and
  (b)   to indemnify the company for any loss or damage resulting from the transaction.

(4)   Nothing in paragraphs (1) to (3) is to be construed as excluding the operation of any other enactment or rule of law by virtue of which the transaction may be called into question or any liability to the company may arise.

(5)   The transaction ceases to be voidable if—
  (a)   restitution of any money or other asset which was the subject-matter of the transaction is no longer possible;
  (b)   the company is indemnified for any loss or damage resulting from the transaction;
  (c)   rights which are acquired, bona fide for value and without actual notice of the directors concerned having exceeded their powers, by a person who is not a party to the transaction would be affected by the avoidance; or
  (d)   the transaction is ratified by resolution of the company in general meeting.

(6)   A person other than a director of the company is not liable under paragraph (3) if he shows that at the time the transaction was entered into he did not know that the directors concerned were exceeding their powers.

(7)   This regulation does not affect the operation of regulation 39 in relation to any party to the transaction not within paragraph (1)(a); but where a transaction is voidable by virtue of this regulation and valid by virtue of that regulation in favour of such a person, the court may, on the application of that person or of the company, make such order affirming, severing or setting aside the transaction, on such terms as appear to the court to be just.

PART IV   OTHER STATUTORY INSTRUMENTS

(8) For the purposes of this regulation—

    (a) "associate", in relation to any person who is a director of the company, means that person's spouse, [civil partner,] child or stepchild (if under 18), employee, partner or any body corporate of which that person is a director; and if that person is a body corporate, any subsidiary undertaking or director of that body corporate (including any director or employee of such subsidiary undertaking);

    (b) "transaction" includes any act; and

    (c) the reference in paragraph (1)(b) to any limitation on directors' powers under the company's constitution includes any limitation deriving from these Regulations, from FSA rules or from a resolution of the company in general meeting or of a meeting of any class of shareholders.

[910]

NOTES

Para (8): words in square brackets in sub-para (a) inserted by the Civil Partnership Act 2004 (Amendments to Subordinate Legislation) Order 2005, SI 2005/2114, art 2(16), Sch 16, Pt 1, para 5, as from 5 December 2005.

Stepchild, etc: as to the meaning of this and related expressions, see the Civil Partnership Act 2004, s 246 (as applied to these Regulations by the Civil Partnership Act 2004 (Relationships Arising Through Civil Partnership) Order 2005, SI 2005/3137, art 3, Schedule).

Shares

45 Shares

(1) An open-ended investment company may issue more than one class of shares.

(2) A shareholder may not have any interest in the scheme property of the company.

(3) The rights which attach to each share of any given class are—

    (a) the right, in accordance with the instrument of incorporation, to participate in or receive profits or income arising from the acquisition, holding, management or disposal of the scheme property;

    (b) the right, in accordance with the instrument of incorporation, to vote at any general meeting of the company or at any relevant class meeting; and

    (c) such other rights as may be provided for, in relation to shares of that class, in the instrument of incorporation of the company.

(4) In respect of any class of shares, the rights referred to in paragraph (3) may, if the company's instrument of incorporation so provides, be expressed in two denominations; and in the case of any such class, one (the "smaller") denomination is to be such proportion of the other (the "larger") denomination as is fixed by the instrument of incorporation.

(5) In respect of any class of shares within paragraph (4), any share to which are attached rights expressed in the smaller denomination is to be known as a smaller denomination share; and any share to which are attached rights expressed in the larger denomination is to be known as a larger denomination share.

(6) In respect of any class of shares, the rights which attach to each share of that class are—

    (a) except in respect of a class of shares within paragraph (4), equal to the rights that attach to each other share of that class; and

    (b) in respect of a class of shares within that paragraph, equal to the rights that attach to each other share of that class of the same denomination.

(7) In respect of any class of shares within paragraph (4), the rights that attach to any smaller denomination share of that class are to be a proportion of the rights that attach to any larger denomination share of that class and that proportion is to be the same as the proportion referred to in paragraph (4).

[911]

46 Share certificates

(1) Subject to regulations 47 and 48, an open-ended investment company must prepare documentary evidence of title to its shares ("share certificates") as follows—

    (a) in respect of any new shares issued by it;

    (b) where a shareholder has transferred part only of his holding back to the company, in respect of the remainder of that holding;

    (c) where a shareholder has transferred part only of his holding to the designated person, in respect of the remainder of that holding;

    (d) where a company has registered a transfer of shares made to a person other than the company or a person designated as mentioned in sub-paragraph (c)—

        (i) in respect of the shares transferred to the transferee; and

        (ii) in respect of any shares retained by the transferor which were evidenced by any certificate sent to the company for the purposes of registering the transfer;

    (e) in respect of any holding of bearer shares for which a certificate evidencing title has already been issued but where the certificate has been surrendered to the company for the purpose of being replaced by two or more certificates which between them evidence title to the shares comprising that holding; and

(f)   in respect of any shares for which a certificate has already been issued but where it appears to the company that the certificate needs to be replaced as a result of having been lost, stolen or destroyed or having become damaged or worn out.

(2)   A company must exercise due diligence and take all reasonable steps to ensure that certificates prepared in accordance with paragraph (1)(a) to (e) are ready for delivery as soon as reasonably practicable.

(3)   Certificates need be prepared in the circumstances referred to in paragraph (1)(e) and (f) only if the company has received—

(a)   a request for a new certificate;

(b)   the old certificate (if there is one);

(c)   such indemnity as the company may require; and

(d)   such reasonable sum as the company may require in respect of the expenses incurred by it in complying with the request.

(4)   Each share certificate must state—

(a)   the number of shares the title to which is evidenced by the certificate;

(b)   where the company has more than one class of shares, the class of shares title to which is evidenced by the certificate; and

(c)   except in the case of bearer shares, the name of the holder.

(5)   Where, in respect of any class of shares, the rights that attach to shares of that class are expressed in two denominations, the reference in paragraph (4)(a) (as it applies to shares of that class) to the number of shares is a reference to the total of—

$N + n/p$

(6)   In paragraph (5)—

(a) N is the relevant number of the larger denomination shares of the class in question;

(b) n is the relevant number of the smaller denomination shares of that class; and

(c) p is the number of smaller denomination shares of that class that are equivalent to one larger denomination share of that class.

(7)   Nothing in these Regulations is to be taken as preventing the total arrived at under paragraph (5) being expressed on the certificate as a single entry representing the result derived from the formula set out in that paragraph.

(8)   In England and Wales, a share certificate specifying any shares held by any person which is—

(a)   under the common seal of the company; or

(b)   authenticated in accordance with regulation 59;

is prima facie evidence of that person's title to the shares.

(9)   In Scotland, a share certificate specifying any shares held by any person which is—

(a)   under the common seal of the company; or

(b)   subscribed by the company in accordance with the Requirements of Writing (Scotland) Act 1995;

is, unless the contrary is shown, sufficient evidence of that person's title to the shares.

[912]

47   Exceptions from regulation 46

(1)   …

(2)   Nothing in regulation 46 requires a company to prepare share certificates in the following cases.

(3)   Case 1 is any case where the company's instrument of incorporation states that share certificates will not be issued and contains provision as to other procedures for evidencing a person's entitlement to shares.

(4)   Case 2 is any case where a shareholder has indicated to the company in writing that he does not wish to receive a certificate.

(5)   Case 3 is any case where shares are issued or transferred to the designated person.

(6)   Case 4 is any case where shares are issued or transferred to a nominee of a recognised investment exchange who is designated for the purposes of this paragraph in the rules of the investment exchange in question.

[913]

NOTES
Para (1): revoked by the Uncertificated Securities Regulations 2001, SI 2001/3755, reg 52(4), as from 26 November 2001.

48 Bearer shares

An open-ended investment company may, if its instrument of incorporation so provides, issue shares ("bearer shares") evidenced by a share certificate, or by any other documentary evidence of title for which provision is made in its instrument of incorporation, which indicates—

(a)   that the holder of the document is entitled to the shares specified in it; and

(b)   that no entry will be made on the register of shareholders identifying the holder of those shares.

[914]

49 Register of shareholders

Schedule 3 to these Regulations makes provision with respect to the register of shareholders of an open-ended investment company.

[915]

50 Power to close register

(1)   Subject to paragraph (2), an open-ended investment company may, on giving notice by advertisement in a national newspaper circulating in all the countries in which shares in the company are sold, close the register of shareholders for any time or times not exceeding, in the whole, 30 days in each year.

[(2)   Paragraph (1) has effect subject to any requirements contained in FSA rules].

[916]

NOTES
Para (2): substituted by the Uncertificated Securities Regulations 2001, SI 2001/3755, reg 51, Sch 7, Pt 2, para 24(b), as from 26 November 2001.

51 Power of court to rectify register

(1)   An application to the court may be made under this regulation if—

(a)   the name of any person is, without sufficient cause, entered in or omitted from the register of shareholders of an open-ended investment company;

(b)   default is made as to the details contained in any entry on the register in respect of a person's holding of shares in the company; or

(c)   default is made or unnecessary delay takes place in amending the register so as to reflect the fact of any person having ceased to be a shareholder.

(2)   An application under this regulation may be made by the person aggrieved, by any shareholder of the company or by the company itself.

(3)   The court may refuse the application or may order rectification of the register of shareholders and payment by the company of any damages sustained by any party aggrieved.

(4)   On such an application the court may decide any question necessary or expedient to be decided for rectification of the register of shareholders including, in particular, any question relating to the right of a person who is a party to the application to have his name entered in or omitted from the register (whether the question arises as between shareholders and alleged shareholders or as between shareholders or alleged shareholders on the one hand and the company on the other hand).

[917]

52 Share transfers

Schedule 4 to these Regulations makes provision for the transfer of registered and bearer shares in an open-ended investment company.

[918]

Operation

53 Power incidental to carrying on business

An open-ended investment company has power to do all such things as are incidental or conducive to the carrying on of its business.

[919]

54 Name to appear in correspondence etc

(1)   Every open-ended investment company must have its name mentioned in legible characters in all letters of the company and in all other documents issued by the company in the course of business.

(2)   If an officer of a company or a person on the company's behalf signs or authorises to be signed on behalf of the company any cheque or order for money or goods in which the company's name is not mentioned as required by paragraph (1) he is personally liable to the holder of the cheque or order for money or goods for the amount of it (unless it is duly paid by the company).

[920]

55 Particulars to appear in correspondence etc

(1)   Every open-ended investment company must have the following particulars mentioned in legible characters in all letters of the company and in all other documents issued by the company in the course of business—

(a)   the company's place of registration;
(b)   the number with which it is registered;
(c)   the address of its head office; and
(d)   the fact that it is an investment company with variable capital.

(2)   Where, in accordance with regulation 72, the Authority makes any change of existing registered numbers in respect of any open-ended investment company then, for a period of three years beginning with the date on which the notification of the change is sent to the company by the Authority, the requirement of paragraph (1)(b) is, notwithstanding regulation 72(4), satisfied by the use of either the old number or the new.

[921]

56 Contracts: England and Wales

Under the law of England and Wales a contract may be made—

(a)   by an open-ended investment company by writing under its common seal; or
(b)   on behalf of such a company, by any person acting under its authority (whether expressed or implied);

and any formalities required by law in the case of a contract made by an individual also apply, unless a contrary intention appears, to a contract made by or on behalf of such a company.

[922]

57 Execution of documents: England and Wales

(1)   Under the law of England and Wales the following provisions have effect with respect to the execution of documents by an open-ended investment company.

(2)   A document is executed by a company by the affixing of its common seal.

(3)   A company need not have a common seal, however, and the following provisions of this regulation apply whether it does or not.

(4)   A document that is signed by at least one director and expressed (in whatever form of words) to be executed by the company has the same effect as if executed under the common seal of the company.

(5)   A document executed by a company which makes it clear on its face that it is intended by the person or persons making it to be a deed has effect, upon delivery, as a deed; and it is to be presumed, unless a contrary intention is proved, to be delivered upon its being executed.

(6)   In favour of a purchaser, a document is deemed to have been duly executed by a company if it purports to be signed by at least one director or, in the case of a director which is a body corporate, it purports to be executed by that director; and, where it makes it clear on its face that it is intended by the person or persons making it to be a deed, it is deemed to have been delivered upon its being executed.

(7)   In paragraph (6), "purchaser" means a purchaser in good faith for valuable consideration and includes a lessee, mortgagee or other person who for valuable consideration acquires an interest in property.

[923]

58 Execution of deeds overseas: England and Wales

(1)   Under the law of England and Wales an open-ended investment company may, by writing under its common seal, empower any person, either generally or in respect of any specified matters, as its attorney, to execute deeds on its behalf in any place elsewhere than in the United Kingdom.

(2)   A deed executed by such an attorney on behalf of the company has the same effect as if it were executed under the company's common seal.

[924]

59 Authentication of documents: England and Wales

A document or proceeding requiring authentication by an open-ended investment company is sufficiently authenticated for the purposes of the law of England and Wales—

(a)   by the signature of a director or other authorised officer of the company; or

(b)   in the case of a director which is a body corporate, if it is executed by that director.

[925]

60   Official seal for share certificates

(1)   An open-ended investment company which has a common seal may have, for use for sealing shares issued by the company and for sealing documents creating or evidencing shares so issued, an official seal which is a facsimile of its common seal with the addition on its face of the word "securities".

(2)   The official seal when duly affixed to a document has the same effect as the company's common seal.

(3)   Nothing in this regulation affects the right of an open-ended investment company whose head office is in Scotland to subscribe such shares and documents in accordance with the Requirements of Writing (Scotland) Act 1995.

[926]

61   Personal liability for contracts and deeds

(1)   A contract, which purports to be made by or on behalf of an open-ended investment company at a time before the coming into effect of an authorisation order in relation to that company, has effect (subject to any agreement to the contrary) as a contract made with the person purporting to act for the company or as agent for it, and he is accordingly personally liable under the contract.

(2)   Paragraph (1) applies—
(a)   to the making of a deed under the law of England and Wales; and
(b)   to the undertaking of an obligation under the law of Scotland;
as it applies to the making of a contract.

(3)   If a company enters into a transaction at any time after the authorisation order made in respect of the company has been revoked and the company fails to comply with its obligations in respect of that transaction within 21 days of being called upon to do so, the person who authorised the transaction is liable, and where the transaction was authorised by two or more persons they are jointly and severally liable, to indemnify the other party to the transaction in respect of any loss or damage suffered by him by reason of the company's failure to comply with those obligations.

[927]

62   Exemptions from liability to be void

(1)   This regulation applies to any provision, whether contained in the instrument of incorporation of an open-ended investment company or in any contract with the company or otherwise—
(a)   which exempts any officer of the company or any person (whether or not an officer of the company) employed by the company as auditor from, or indemnifies him against, any liability which by virtue of any rule of law would otherwise attach to him in respect of any negligence, default, breach of duty or breach of trust of which he may be guilty in relation to the company; or
(b)   which exempts the depository of the company from, or indemnifies him against, any liability for any failure to exercise due care and diligence in the discharge of his functions in respect of the company.

(2)   Except as provided by the following paragraph, any such provision is void.

(3)   This regulation does not prevent a company—
(a)   from purchasing and maintaining for any such officer, auditor or depositary insurance against any such liability; or
(b)   from indemnifying any such officer, auditor or depositary against any liability incurred by him—
(i)   in defending any proceedings (whether civil or criminal) in which judgment is given in his favour or he is acquitted; or
(ii)   in connection with any application under regulation 63 in which relief is granted to him by the court.

[928]

63   Power of court to grant relief in certain cases

(1)   This regulation applies to—
(a)   any proceedings for negligence, default, breach of duty or breach of trust against an officer of an open-ended investment company or a person (whether or not an officer of the company) employed by the company as auditor; or
(b)   any proceedings against the depository of such a company for failure to exercise due care and diligence in the discharge of his functions in respect of the company.

(2)   If, in any proceedings to which this regulation applies, it appears to the court hearing the case—

   (a)   that the officer, auditor or depositary is or may be liable in respect of the cause of action in question;

   (b)   that, nevertheless, he has acted honestly and reasonably; and

   (c)   that having regard to all the circumstances of the case (including those connected with his appointment) he ought fairly to be excused from the liability sought to be enforced against him;

the court may relieve him, either wholly or partly, from his liability on such terms as it may think fit.

(3)   If any such officer, auditor or depositary has reason to apprehend that any claim will or might be made against him in proceedings to which this regulation applies, he may apply to the court for relief.

(4)   The court, on an application under paragraph (3), has the same power to relieve the applicant as under this regulation it would have had if it had been a court before which the relevant proceedings against the applicant had been brought.

(5)   Where a case to which paragraph (2) applies is being tried by a judge with a jury, the judge, after hearing the evidence, may, if he is satisfied that the defendant or defender ought in pursuance of that paragraph to be relieved either in whole or in part from the liability sought to be enforced against him, withdraw the case in whole or in part from the jury and forthwith direct judgment to be entered for the defendant or defender on such terms as to costs or otherwise as the judge may think proper.

[929]

64   Punishment for fraudulent trading

(1)   If any business of an open-ended investment company is carried on with intent to defraud creditors of the company or creditors of any other person, or for any fraudulent purpose, every person who was knowingly a party to the carrying on of the business in that manner is guilty of an offence and liable—

   (a)   on conviction on indictment, to imprisonment not exceeding a term of two years or to a fine or to both;

   (b)   on summary conviction, to imprisonment not exceeding a term of three months or to a fine not exceeding the statutory maximum or to both.

(2)   This regulation applies whether or not the company has been, or is in the course of being, wound up (whether by the court or otherwise).

[930]

65   Power to provide for employees on cessation or transfer of business

(1)   The powers of an open-ended investment company include power to make the following provision for the benefit of persons employed or formerly employed by the company, that is to say, provision in connection with the cessation or the transfer to any person of the whole or part of the undertaking of the company.

(2)   The power conferred by paragraph (1) is exercisable notwithstanding that its exercise is not in the best interests of the company.

(3)   The power which a company may exercise by virtue of paragraph (1) may only be exercised by the company—

   (a)   in a case not falling within sub-paragraph (b) or (c), if sanctioned by a resolution of the company in general meeting;

   (b)   if so authorised by the instrument of incorporation—

      (i)   in the case of a company that has only one director, by a resolution of that director; and

      (ii)   in any other case, by such resolution of directors as is required by FSA rules; or

   (c)   if the instrument of incorporation requires the exercise of the power to be sanctioned by a resolution of the company in general meeting for which more than a simple majority of the shareholders voting is necessary, by a resolution of that majority;

and in any case after compliance with any other requirements of the instrument of incorporation applicable to the exercise of the power.

[931]

Reports

66   Reports: preparation

(1)   The directors of an open-ended investment company must—

   (a)   prepare a report ("annual report") for each annual accounting period of the company; and

(b)   subject to paragraph (2), prepare a report ("half-yearly report") for each half-yearly accounting period of the company.

(2)   Where a company's first annual accounting period is a period of less than 12 months, a half-yearly report need not be prepared for any part of that period.

(3)   The directors of a company must lay copies of the annual report before the company in general meeting.

(4)   Nothing in this regulation or in regulation 67 prejudices the generality of regulation 6(1).

(5)   In this regulation any reference to annual and half-yearly accounting periods of a company is a reference to those periods as determined in relation to that company in accordance with FSA rules.

[932]

67   Reports: accounts

(1)   The annual report of an open-ended investment company must, in respect of the annual accounting period to which it relates, contain accounts of the company.

(2)   The company's auditors must make a report to the company's shareholders in respect of the accounts of the company contained in its annual report.

(3)   A copy of the auditor's report must form part of the company's annual report.

[933]

68   Reports: voluntary revision

(1)   If it appears to the directors of an open-ended investment company that any annual report of the company did not comply with the requirements of these Regulations or FSA rules, they may prepare a revised annual report.

(2)   Where copies of the previous report have been laid before the company in general meeting or delivered to the Authority, the revisions must be confined to—
    (a)   the correction of anything in the previous report which did not comply with the requirements of these Regulations or FSA rules; and
    (b)   the making of any necessary consequential alterations.

[934]

69   Auditors

Schedule 5 to these Regulations makes provision with respect to the auditors of open-ended investment companies.

[935]

Mergers and divisions

70   Mergers and divisions

Schedule 6 to these Regulations makes provision with respect to mergers and divisions involving open-ended investment companies.

[936]

PART IV
THE AUTHORITY'S REGISTRATION FUNCTIONS

71   Register of open-ended investment companies

(1)   The Authority must maintain a register of open-ended investment companies.

(2)   The Authority may keep the register in any form it thinks fit provided that it is possible to inspect the information contained on it and to obtain a copy of that information (or any part of it) for inspection.

[937]

72   Companies' registered numbers

(1)   The Authority must allocate to every open-ended investment company a number, which is to be known as the company's registered number.

(2)   Companies' registered numbers must be in such form, consisting of one or more sequences of figures or letters, as the Authority may from time to time determine.

(3)   The Authority may, upon adopting a new form of registered number, make such changes of existing registered numbers (including numbers allocated by the appropriate registrar) as appear to it to be necessary.

(4)   A change in a company's registered number has effect from the date on which the company is notified by the Authority of the change.

[938]

73   Delivery of documents to the Authority

Any document which is required by these Regulations to be delivered to the Authority to be recorded on the register maintained pursuant to regulation 71 must be delivered in such form as the Authority may from time to time specify.

[939]

74   Keeping of company records by the Authority

(1)   The information contained in a document delivered to the Authority under any provision of these Regulations may be recorded and kept by it in any form it thinks fit, provided that it is possible to inspect the information and produce a copy of it in legible form.

(2)   The originals of documents delivered to the Authority under any provision of these Regulations in legible form must be kept by it for ten years after which they may be destroyed.

(3)   Where a company has been dissolved, the Authority may, at any time after the expiration of two years from the date of the dissolution, direct that any records in its custody relating to the company may be removed to the Public Record Office; and records in respect of which such a direction is given must be disposed of in accordance with the enactments relating to that Office and the rules made under them.

(4)   Paragraph (3) does not extend to Scotland.

[940]

75   Inspection etc of records kept by the Authority

(1)   Any person may inspect any records kept by the Authority for the purposes of this Part of these Regulations and may require—

    (a)   a copy, in such form as the Authority considers appropriate, of any information contained in those records; or

    (b)   a certified copy of, or extract from, any such record.

(2)   The right of inspection extends to the originals of documents delivered to the Authority in legible form only where the record kept by the Authority of the contents of the document is illegible or unavailable.

(3)   A copy of or extract from a record kept by the Authority under these Regulations, on which is endorsed a certificate signed by a member of the Authority's staff authorised by it for that purpose certifying that it is an accurate record of the contents of any document delivered to the Authority under these Regulations, is in all legal proceedings admissible in evidence as of equal validity with the original document and as evidence of any fact stated therein of which direct oral evidence would be admissible.

(4)   No process for compelling the production of a document kept by the Authority under these Regulations is to issue from any court except with the leave of the court; and any such process must bear on it a statement that it is issued with the leave of the court.

[941]

76   Provision by the Authority of documents in non-legible form

Any requirement of these Regulations as to the supply by the Authority of a document may, if the Authority thinks fit, be satisfied by the communication by the Authority of the information in any non-legible form it thinks appropriate.

[942]

77   Documents relating to Welsh open-ended investment companies

(1)   This regulation applies to any document which is delivered to the Authority under these Regulations and relates to an open-ended investment company (whether already registered or to be registered) whose instrument of incorporation states that its head office is to be situated in Wales.

(2)   A document to which this regulation applies may be in Welsh but must be accompanied by a certified translation into English.

(3)   The requirement for a translation imposed by paragraph (2) does not apply—

    (a)   to documents of such description as may be specified in FSA rules; or

    (b)   to documents in a form prescribed in Welsh (or partly in Welsh and partly in English) by virtue of section 26 of the Welsh Language Act 1993 (powers to prescribe Welsh forms).

(4)   An open-ended investment company whose instrument of incorporation states that its head office is to be situated in Wales may deliver to the Authority a certified translation into Welsh of any document in English which relates to the company and which is or has been delivered to the Authority.

(5)   In this regulation "certified translation" means a translation which is certified in the manner specified in FSA rules to be a correct translation.

[943]

PART IV   OTHER STATUTORY INSTRUMENTS

78   *(Revoked by the Open-Ended Investment Companies (Amendment) Regulations 2005, SI 2005/923, reg 2(1), (7), as from 6 April 2005.)*

79 Exclusion of deemed notice

A person is not to be taken to have deemed notice of any matter merely because of its being disclosed in any document kept by the Authority (and thus available for inspection) under any provision of these Regulations.

[944]

PART V
MISCELLANEOUS

80 Contraventions

Any of the following persons, that is to say—
  (a)   a person who contravenes any provision of these Regulations; and
  (b)   an open-ended investment company (including any director or depositary of such a company) which contravenes any provision of FSA rules,
is to be treated as having contravened rules made under section 138 of the Act (general rule-making power).

[945]

81 Offences by bodies corporate etc

Section 400 of the Act (offences by bodies corporate etc) applies to an offence under these Regulations as it applies to an offence under the Act.

[946]

82 Jurisdiction and procedure in respect of offences

Section 403 of the Act (jurisdiction and procedure in respect of offences) applies to offences under these Regulations as it applies to offences under the Act.

[947]

83 Evidence of grant of probate etc

The production to a company of any document which is by law sufficient evidence of probate of the will, or letters of administration of the estate, or confirmation as executor, of a deceased person having been granted to some person must be accepted by the company as sufficient evidence of the grant.

[948]

84 Minor and consequential amendments

The provisions mentioned in Schedule 7 to these Regulations (being minor amendments and amendments consequential on the provisions of these Regulations) have effect subject to the amendments specified in that Schedule.

[949]

85 Revocation etc

  (1)   ...

  (2)   Anything done under or in accordance with the 1996 Regulations has effect as if done under or in accordance with these Regulations.

  (3)   Without prejudice to the generality of paragraph (2)—
  (a)   a body incorporated by virtue of regulation 3(1) of the 1996 Regulations is to be treated as if it had been incorporated by virtue of regulation 3(1) of these Regulations;
  (b)   where an application under regulation 7 of the 1996 Regulations had not been determined by the Authority at the time when this regulation comes into force, it is to be treated as if it were an application made under regulation 12 of these Regulations;
  (c)   the Authority's registration functions under Part IV of these Regulations apply to any documents or records delivered to the appropriate registrar pursuant to regulation 4 of, and Schedule 1 to, the 1996 Regulations.

[950]

NOTES
  Para (1): revokes the Open-Ended Investment Companies (Investment Companies with Variable Capital) Regulations 1996, SI 1996/2827.

SCHEDULES

SCHEDULE 1
DEPOSITARIES

Regulation 5

Appointment

1.   On the coming into effect of an authorisation order in respect of an open-ended investment company, the person named in the application under regulation 12 as depositary of the company is deemed to be appointed as its first depositary.

2.   Subject to regulations 21 and 26, any subsequent appointment of the depositary of a company must be made by the directors of the company.

Retirement

3.   The depositary of a company may not retire voluntarily except upon the appointment of a new depositary.

Rights

4.   The depositary of a company is entitled—
    (a)   to receive all such notices of, and other communications relating to, any general meeting of the company as a shareholder of the company is entitled to receive;
    (b)   to attend any general meeting of the company;
    (c)   to be heard at any general meeting which it attends on any part of the business of the meeting which concerns it as depositary;
    (d)   to convene a general meeting of the company when it sees fit;
    (e)   to require from the company's officers such information and explanations as it thinks necessary for the performance of its functions as depositary; and
    (f)   to have access, except in so far as they concern its appointment or removal, to any reports, statements or other papers which are to be considered at any meeting held by the directors of the company (when acting in their capacity as such), at any general meeting of the company or at any meeting of holders of shares of any particular class.

Statement by depositary ceasing to hold office

5.—(1)   Where the depositary of a company ceases, for any reason other than by virtue of a court order made under regulation 26, to hold office, it may deposit at the head office of the company a statement of any circumstances connected with its ceasing to hold office which it considers should be brought to the attention of the shareholders or creditors of the company or, if it considers that there are no such circumstances, a statement that there are none.

(2)   If the statement is of circumstances which the depositary considers should be brought to the attention of the shareholders or creditors of the company, the company must, not later than 14 days after the deposit of the statement, either—
    (a)   send a copy of the statement to each of the shareholders whose name appears on the register of shareholders (other than the designated person) and take such steps as FSA rules may require for the purpose of bringing the fact that the statement has been made to the attention of the holders of any bearer shares; or
    (b)   apply to the court;
and, where an application is made under sub-paragraph (b), the company must notify the depositary.

(3)   Unless the depositary receives notice of an application to the court before the end of the period of 21 days beginning with the day on which it deposited the statement, it must, not later than seven days after the end of that period, send a copy of the statement to the Authority.

(4)   If the court is satisfied that the depositary is using the statement to secure needless publicity for defamatory matter—
    (a)   it must direct that copies of the statement need not be sent out and that the steps required by FSA rules need not be taken; and
    (b)   it may further order the company's costs on the application to be paid in whole or in part by the depositary notwithstanding that the depositary is not a party to the application;
and the company must, not later than 14 days after the court's decision, take such steps in relation to a statement setting out the effect of the order as are required by sub-paragraph (2)(a) in relation to the statement deposited under sub-paragraph (1).

(5)   If the court is not so satisfied, the company must, not later than 14 days after the court's decision, take the steps required by sub-paragraph (2)(a) and notify the depositary of the court's decision.

(6)   The depositary must, not later than seven days after receiving such a notice, send a copy of the statement to the Authority.

(7) Where a notice of appeal is filed not later than 14 days after the court's decision, any reference to that decision in sub-paragraphs (4) and (5) is to be construed as a reference to the final determination or withdrawal of that appeal (as the case may be).

6.—(1) This paragraph applies where copies of a statement have been sent to shareholders under paragraph 5.

(2) The depositary who made the statement has, notwithstanding that it has ceased to hold office, the rights conferred by paragraph 4(a) to (c) in relation to the general meeting of the company next following the date on which the copies were sent out.

(3) The reference in paragraph 4(c) to business concerning the depositary as depositary is to be construed in relation to a depositary who has ceased to hold office as a reference to business concerning it as former depositary.

[951]

SCHEDULE 2
INSTRUMENT OF INCORPORATION

Regulation 14

1. The instrument of incorporation of an open-ended investment company must—
   (a) contain the statements set out in paragraph 2; and
   (b) contain provision made in accordance with paragraphs 3 and 4.

2. The statements referred to in paragraph 1(a) are—
   (a) the head office of the company is situated in England and Wales, Wales or Scotland (as the case may be);
   (b) the company is an open-ended investment company with variable share capital;
   (c) the shareholders are not liable for the debts of the company;
   (d) the scheme property is entrusted to a depositary for safekeeping (subject to any exceptions permitted by FSA rules); and
   (e) charges or expenses of the company may be taken out of the scheme property.

3.—(1) The instrument of incorporation must contain provision as to the following matters—
   (a) the object of the company;
   (b) any matter relating to the procedure for the appointment, retirement and removal of any director of the company for which provision is not made in these Regulations or FSA rules; and
   (c) the currency in which the accounts of the company are to be prepared.

(2) The provision referred to in sub-paragraph (1)(a) as to the object of an open-ended investment company must state clearly the kind of property in which the company is to invest and must state that the object of the company is to invest in property of that kind with the aim of spreading investment risk and giving its shareholders the benefit of the results of the management of that property.

4.—(1) The instrument of incorporation must also contain provision as to the following matters—
   (a) the name of the company;
   (b) the category, as specified in FSA rules, to which the company belongs;
   (c) the maximum and minimum sizes of the company's capital;
   (d) in the case of an umbrella company, the investment objectives applicable to each part of the scheme property that is pooled separately;
   (e) the classes of shares that the company may issue indicating, in the case of an umbrella company, which class or classes of shares may be issued in respect of each part of the scheme property that is pooled separately;
   (f) the rights attaching to shares of each class (including any provision for the expression in two denominations of such rights);
   (g) if the company is to be able to issue bearer shares, a statement to that effect together with details of any limitations on the classes of the company's shares which are to include bearer shares;
   (h) in the case of a company which is a participating issuer, a statement to that effect together with an indication of any class of shares in the company which is a class of participating securities;
   (i) if the company is to dispense with the requirements of regulation 46, the details of any substituted procedures for evidencing title to the company's shares; and
   (j) the form, custody and use of the company's common seal (if any).

(2) For the purposes of sub-paragraph (1)(c), the size at any time of a company's capital is to be taken to be the value at that time, as determined in accordance with FSA rules, of the scheme property of the company less the liabilities of the company.

5.—(1) Once an authorisation order has been made in respect of a company, no amendment may be made to the statements contained in the company's instrument of incorporation which are required by paragraph 2.

(2) Subject to sub-paragraph (1) and to any restriction imposed by FSA rules, a company may amend any provision which is contained in its instrument of incorporation.

(3) No amendment to a provision which is contained in a company's instrument of incorporation by virtue of paragraph 3 may be made unless it has been approved by the shareholders of the company in general meeting.

6.—(1) The provisions of a company's instrument of incorporation are binding on the officers and depositary of the company and on each of its shareholders; and all such persons (but no others) are to be taken to have notice of the provisions of the instrument.

(2) A person is not debarred from obtaining damages or other compensation from a company by reason only of his holding or having held shares in the company.

[952]

SCHEDULE 3
REGISTER OF SHAREHOLDERS

Regulation 49

General

1.—(1) Subject to sub-paragraph (2), every open-ended investment company must keep a register of persons who hold shares in the company.

(2) Except to the extent that the aggregate numbers of shares mentioned in paragraphs 5(1)(b) and 7 include bearer shares, nothing in this Schedule requires any entry to be made in the register in respect of bearer shares.

2.—(1) ... , the register of shareholders is prima facie evidence of any matters which are by these Regulations directed or authorised to be contained in it.

(2) ...

3.—(1) In the case of companies registered in England and Wales, no notice of any trust, express, implied or constructive, is to be entered on the company's register or be receivable by the company.

(2) A company must exercise all due diligence and take all reasonable steps to ensure that the information contained in the register is at all times complete and up to date.

Contents

5.—(1) The register of shareholders must contain an entry consisting of—
    (a) the name of the designated person;
    (b) a statement of the aggregate number of all shares in the company held by that person; ...
    (c) ...

(2) In sub-paragraph (1), for the purposes of sub-paragraph (b), the designated person is to be taken as holding all shares in the company which are in issue and in respect of which no other person's name is entered on the register.

(3) The statements referred to in sub-paragraph (1)(b) and (c) must be up-dated at least once a day.

6.—(1) This paragraph does not apply to any issue or transfer of shares to the designated person.

(2) Where a company issues a share to any person and the name of that person is not already entered on the register, the company must enter his name on the register.

(3) In respect of any person whose name is entered on the register in accordance with sub-paragraph (2) or paragraph 6 of Schedule 4 to these Regulations, the register must contain an entry consisting of—
    (a) the address of the shareholder;
    (b) the date on which the shareholder's name was entered on the register;
    (c) a statement of the aggregate number of shares held by the shareholder, distinguishing each share by its number (if it has one) and, where the company has more than one class of shares, by its class; ...
    (d) ...

7. The register of shareholders must contain a monthly statement of the aggregate number of all the bearer shares in issue except for any bearer shares in issue which, at the time when the statement is made, are held by the designated person.

8.—(1) This paragraph applies where the aggregate number of shares referred to in paragraphs 5 to 7 includes any shares to which attach rights expressed in two denominations.

(2) In respect of each class of shares to which are attached rights expressed in two denominations, the number of shares of that class held by any person referred to in paragraph 5 or 6, or the number of bearer shares of that class referred to in paragraph 7, is to be taken to be the total of—

$N + n/p$

(3) In sub-paragraph (2)—
    (a) N is the relevant number of larger denomination shares of that class;
    (b) n is the relevant number of smaller denomination shares of that class; and
    (c) p is the number of smaller denomination shares of that class that are equivalent to one larger denomination share of that class.

(4) Nothing in these Regulations is to be taken as preventing the total arrived at under sub-paragraph (2) being expressed on the register as a single entry representing the result derived from the formula set out in that sub-paragraph.

Location

9. The register of shareholders of a company must be kept at its head office, except that—
    (a)   if the work of making it up is done at another office of the company, it may be kept there; and
    (b)   if the company arranges with some other person for the making up of the register to be undertaken on its behalf by that other person, it may be kept at the office of the other person at which the work is being done.

Index

10.—(1) Every company must keep an index of the names of the holders of its registered shares.

(2) The index must contain, in respect of each shareholder, a sufficient indication to enable the account of that shareholder in the register to be readily found.

(3) The index must be at all times kept at the same place as the register of shareholders.

(4) Not later than 14 days after the date on which any alteration is made to the register of shareholders, the company must make any necessary alteration in the index.

Inspection

11.—(1) Subject to regulation 50 and to FSA rules, the register of shareholders and the index of names must be open to the inspection of any shareholder (including any holder of bearer shares) without charge.

(2) Any shareholder may require a copy of the entries on the register relating to him and the company must cause any copy so required by a person to be sent to him free of charge.

(3) If an inspection required under this paragraph is refused, or if a copy so required is not sent, the court may by order compel an immediate inspection of the register and index, or direct that the copy required be sent to the person requiring it.

Agent's default

12.—(1) Sub-paragraphs (2) and (4) apply where, in accordance with paragraph 9(b), the register of shareholders is kept at the office of some person other than the company and by reason of any default of his the company fails to comply with any of the requirements of paragraph 10 or 11.

(2) In a case to which this sub-paragraph applies, the person at whose office the register of shareholders is kept is guilty of an offence if he knowingly or recklessly authorises or permits the default in question.

(3) A person guilty of an offence under sub-paragraph (2) is liable in respect of each default on summary conviction to a fine not exceeding level 1 on the standard scale.

(4) The power of the court under paragraph 11(3) extends to the making of orders directed to the person at whose office the register of shareholders is kept and to any officer or employee of his.

[953]

NOTES

Para 2: words omitted from sub-para (1) and the whole of sub-para (2) revoked by the Uncertificated Securities Regulations 2001, SI 2001/3755, regs 51, 52(4), Sch 7, Pt 2, para 24(c), as from 26 November 2001.

Para 5: sub-para (1)(c) and the word immediately preceding it revoked by SI 2001/3755, reg 52(4), as from 26 November 2001.

Para 6: sub-para (3)(d) and the word immediately preceding it revoked by SI 2001/3755, reg 52(4), as from 26 November 2001.

SCHEDULE 4
SHARE TRANSFERS

Regulation 52

General

1. The instrument of incorporation of a company may contain provision as to share transfers in respect of any matter for which provision is not made in these Regulations or FSA rules.

2.   Where any shares are transferred to the company, the company must cancel those shares.

3.   ...

Transfer of registered shares

4.—(1)   Where a transfer of shares is made by the person (if any) who is designated in the company's instrument of incorporation for the purposes of this paragraph, the company may not register the transfer unless such evidence as the company may require to prove that the transfer has taken place has been delivered to the company.

(2)   Where for any reason a person ceases to be designated for the purposes of this paragraph—

   (a)   any shares held by that person which are not disposed of on or before his ceasing to be so designated are to be deemed to be the subject of a new transfer to him which takes effect immediately after he ceases to be so designated; and

   (b)   the company must make such adjustments to the register as are necessary to reflect his change of circumstances.

[4A.—(1)   Subject to sub-paragraph (2), section 136 of the Law of Property Act 1925 (which provides for certain assignments in writing to be effectual in law) applies to an absolute assignment (not purporting to be by way of charge only) of shares by means of electronic communication with the following modifications—

   (a)   the reference in subsection (1) to writing under the hand of the assignor refers to an electronic communication made by the assignor or by his agent authorised in writing, and

   (b)   the reference in that subsection to express notice in writing refers to express notice by electronic communication to the company.

(2)   Sub-paragraph (1) is of no effect in a particular case if the company refuses to register the transfer of shares which would, apart from this sub-paragraph, be made by the assignment in that case.

(3)   Sub-paragraph (1) shall not affect any transfer or assignment which, apart from that sub-paragraph, would be effectual in law.

(4)   This paragraph extends to England and Wales only.

4B.—(1)   Subject to sub-paragraph (3), section 1(2)(a)(ii) of the Requirements of Writing (Scotland) Act 1995 (which requires certain gratuitous unilateral obligations to be in writing) shall not apply (if it would otherwise do so) to any gratuitous unilateral obligation relating to shares where—

   (a)   the obligation is created by means of electronic communication;

   (b)   the electronic communication is made by the debtor in the obligation;

   (c)   such evidence (if any) as the company may require to prove the right of the person referred to in paragraph (b) to create the obligation is provided to it.

(2)   Where section 1(2)(a)(ii) of that Act does not apply by virtue of sub-paragraph (1), the obligation shall not be considered an obligation mentioned in subsection (2)(a) of that section for the purposes of subsection (3).

(3)   Sub-paragraph (1) is of no effect in a particular case if the company refuses to register the transfer of shares which would, apart from this sub-paragraph, by made by the obligation in that case.

(4)   This paragraph extends to Scotland only.

4C.—(1)   Where a transfer of shares is made by means of electronic communication, the company must take reasonable steps to ensure that any electronic communication purporting to be made by the transferor is in fact made by the transferor.

(2)   Failure to take reasonable steps shall not make the transfer void or otherwise affect its validity.]

5.—(1)   Except in the case of any transfer of shares referred to in paragraph 4, the company may not register any transfer unless the transfer documents relating to that transfer have been delivered to the company.

(2)   No share certificate has to be delivered by virtue of sub-paragraph (1) in any case where shares are transferred by a nominee of a recognised investment exchange who is designated for the purposes of regulation 47(6) in the rules of the investment exchange in question.

(3)   In these Regulations "transfer documents", in relation to any transfer of registered shares [except a transfer made by means of electronic communication], means—

   (a)   a stock transfer within the meaning of the Stock Transfer Act 1963 which complies with the requirements of that Act as to the execution and contents of a stock transfer or such other instrument of transfer as is authorised by, and completed and executed in accordance with any requirements in, the company's instrument of incorporation;

   (b)   except in a case falling within paragraph (3) or (4) of regulation 47, a share certificate relating to the shares in question;

    (c)   in a case falling within paragraph (3) of regulation 47, such other evidence of title to those shares as is required by the instrument of incorporation of the company; and

    (d)   such other evidence (if any) as the company may require to prove the right of the transferor to transfer the shares in question.

[(3A)   In these Regulations "transfer documents", in relation to any transfer of registered shares made by means of electronic communication, means—

    (a)   such information in such form and transmitted by such method of electronic communication as is in accordance with any requirements imposed by the company for transfers by electronic communication, or if no such requirements are imposed, evidence of the electronic communication by which the transfer is made; and

    (b)   such evidence (if any) as the company may require to prove the right of the transferor to transfer the shares in question.]

6.—[(1)]   [Subject to sub-paragraph (2),] in the case of any transfer of shares which meets the requirements of paragraph 4 or 5, the company must—

    (a)   register the transfer; and

    (b)   where the name of the transferee is not already entered on the register, enter that name on the register.

[(2)   The company may refuse to register any transfer of shares made by means of electronic communication.]

7.—(1)   A company may, before the end of the period of 21 days commencing with the date of receipt of the transfer documents relating to any transfer of shares, refuse to register the transfer if—

    (a)   there exists a minimum requirement as to the number or value of shares that must be held by any shareholder of the company and the transfer would result in either the transferor or transferee holding less than the required minimum; or

    (b)   the transfer would result in a contravention of any provision of the company's instrument of incorporation or would produce a result inconsistent with any provision of the company's prospectus.

(2)   A company must give the transferee written notice of any refusal to register a transfer of shares.

(3)   Nothing in these Regulations requires a company to register a transfer or give notice to any person of a refusal to register a transfer where registering the transfer or giving the notice would result in a contravention of any provision of law (including any law that is for the time being in force in a country or territory outside the United Kingdom).

8.—(1)   Where, in respect of any transfer of shares, the company certifies that it has received the transfer documents referred to in paragraph 5(3)(b) or (c) (as the case may be), that certification is to be taken as a representation by the company to any person acting on the faith of the certification that there has been produced to the company such evidence as on its face shows a prima facie title to the shares in the transferor named in the instrument of transfer.

(2)   For the purposes of sub-paragraph (1), a certification is made by a company if the instrument of transfer—

    (a)   bears the words "certificate lodged" (or words to the like effect); and

    (b)   is signed by a person acting under authority (whether express or implied) given by the company to issue and sign such certifications.

(3)   A certification under sub-paragraph (1) is not to be taken as a representation that the transferor has any title to the shares in question.

(4)   Where a person acts on the faith of a false certification by a company which is made negligently or fraudulently, the company is liable to pay to that person any damages sustained by him.

Transfer of bearer shares

9.   A transfer of title to any bearer share in a company is effected by the transfer from one person to another of the instrument mentioned in regulation 48 which relates to that share.

10.   Where the holder of bearer shares proposes to transfer to another person a number of shares which is less than the number specified in the instrument relating to those shares, he may only do so if he surrenders the instrument to the company and obtains a new instrument specifying the number of shares to be transferred.

Miscellaneous

11.   Nothing in the preceding provisions of this Schedule prejudices any power of the company to register as shareholder any person to whom the right to any shares in the company has been transmitted by operation of law.

12.   A transfer of registered shares that are held by a deceased person at the time of his death which is made by his personal representative is as valid as if the personal representative had been the holder of the shares at the time of the execution of the instrument of transfer.

13.   On the death of any one of the joint holders of any shares, the survivor is to be the only person recognised by the company as having any title to or any interest in those shares.

[954]

NOTES
   Para 3: revoked by the Uncertificated Securities Regulations 2001, SI 2001/3755, reg 52(4), as from 26 November 2001.
   Paras 4A–4C: inserted by the Open-Ended Investment Companies (Amendment) Regulations 2009, SI 2009/553, reg 2(1), (4)(a), as from 6 March 2009.
   Para 5: words in square brackets in sub-para (3) inserted, and sub-para (3A) inserted, by the Open-Ended Investment Companies (Amendment) Regulations 2009, SI 2009/553, reg 2(1), (4)(b), as from 6 March 2009.
   Para 6: sub-para (1) numbered as such, words in square brackets in that sub-paragraph inserted, and sub-para (2) added, by the Open-Ended Investment Companies (Amendment) Regulations 2009, SI 2009/553, reg 2(1), (4)(c), as from 6 March 2009.

SCHEDULE 5
AUDITORS

Regulation 69

Eligibility

1.   No person is eligible for appointment as auditor of an open-ended investment company unless he is [eligible for appointment as a statutory auditor under Part 42 of the Companies Act 2006].

2.—(1)   A person is ineligible for appointment as auditor of an open-ended investment company if he is—
   (a)   an officer or employee of the company; or
   (b)   a partner or employee of such a person, or a partnership of which such a person is a partner.

   (2)   For the purposes of sub-paragraph (1), an auditor of a company is not to be regarded as an officer or employee of the company.

   [(3)   A person is also ineligible for appointment if there exists between that person, or any associate of that person, and the company a connection of any such description as may be specified by regulations made by the Secretary of State under section 1214(4) of the Companies Act 2006.

   (4)   In sub-paragraph (3) "associate" has the same meaning as in Part 42 of that Act (see section 1260 of that Act).

   (5)   The power of the Secretary of State to make regulations under section 1214(4) of that Act for the purposes of subsection (1) of that section in relation to statutory auditors is exercisable, subject to the same conditions, for the purposes of sub-paragraph (3) above in relation to auditors of open-ended investment companies.]

3.—(1)   No person is to act as auditor of a company if he is ineligible for appointment to the office.

   (2)   If during his term of office an auditor of a company becomes ineligible for appointment to the office, he must thereupon vacate office and give notice in writing to the company concerned that he has vacated it by reason of ineligibility.

   (3)   A person who acts as auditor of a company in contravention of sub-paragraph (1) or fails to give notice of vacating his office as required by sub-paragraph (2) is guilty of an offence and liable—
   (a)   on conviction on indictment, to a fine;
   (b)   on summary conviction, to a fine not exceeding the statutory maximum.

   (4)   In the case of continued contravention he is liable on a second or subsequent summary conviction (instead of the fine mentioned in sub-paragraph (3)(b)) to a fine not exceeding £100 in respect of each day on which the contravention is continued.

   (5)   In proceedings against a person for an offence under this paragraph it is a defence for him to show that he did not know and had no reason to believe that he was, or had become, ineligible for appointment.

Appointment

4.—(1)   Every company must appoint an auditor or auditors in accordance with this paragraph.

   (2)   [Subject to sub-paragraphs (6) and (7), a company] must, at each general meeting at which the company's annual report is laid, appoint an auditor or auditors to hold office from the conclusion of that meeting until the conclusion of the next general meeting at which an annual report is laid.

(3)   [Subject to sub-paragraph (6), the first] auditors of a company may be appointed by the directors of the company at any time before the first general meeting of the company at which an annual report is laid; and auditors so appointed are to hold office until the conclusion of that meeting.

(4)   Where no appointment is made under sub-paragraph (3), the first auditors of any company may be appointed by the company in general meeting.

(5)   No rules made under section 340 of the Act (appointment of auditors) apply in relation to open-ended investment companies.

[(6)   On the date on which the holding of an annual general meeting is dispensed with in accordance with regulation 37A, any auditor or auditors appointed in accordance with sub-paragraph (2) or (3) ceases to hold office and the directors must forthwith re-appoint the auditor or auditors or appoint a new auditor or auditors.]

[(7)   The directors of any company which does not hold annual general meetings must appoint the auditor or auditors.]

5.   If, in any case, no auditors are appointed as required in paragraph 4, the Authority may appoint a person to fill the vacancy.

6.—(1)   The directors of a company, or the company in general meeting, may fill a casual vacancy in the office of auditor.

(2)   While such a vacancy continues, any surviving or continuing auditor or auditors may continue to act.

7.—(1)   Sub-paragraphs (2) to (5) apply to the appointment, as auditor of a company, of a partnership constituted under the law of England and Wales or Northern Ireland, or under the law of any country or territory in which a partnership is not a legal person; and sub-paragraphs (3) to (5) apply to the appointment as such an auditor of a partnership constituted under the law of Scotland, or under the law of any country or territory in which an partnership is a legal person.

(2)   The appointment is, unless the contrary intention appears, an appointment of the partnership as such and not of the partners.

(3)   Where the partnership ceases, the appointment is to be treated as extending to—
  (a)   any partnership which succeeds to the practice of that partnership and is eligible for the appointment; and
  (b)   any person who succeeds to that practice having previously carried it on in partnership and is eligible for the appointment.

(4)   For this purpose a partnership is to be regarded as succeeding to the practice of another partnership only if the members of the successor partnership are substantially the same as those of the former partnership; and a partnership or other person is to be regarded as succeeding to the practice of a partnership only if it or he succeeds to the whole or substantially the whole of the business of the former partnership.

(5)   Where the partnership ceases and no person succeeds to the appointment under sub-paragraph (3), the appointment may with the consent of the company be treated as extending to a partnership or other person eligible for the appointment who succeeds to the business of the former partnership or to such part of it as is agreed by the company to be treated as comprising the appointment.

Rights

8.—(1)   The auditors of a company have a right of access at all times to the company's books, accounts and vouchers and are entitled to require from the company's officers such information and explanations as they think necessary for the performance of their duties as auditors.

(2)   An officer of a company commits an offence if he knowingly or recklessly makes to the company's auditors a statement (whether written or oral) which—
  (a)   conveys or purports to convey any information or explanations which the auditors require, or are entitled to require, as auditors of the company; and
  (b)   is misleading, false or deceptive in a material particular.

(3)   A person guilty of an offence under sub-paragraph (2) is liable—
  (a)   on conviction on indictment, to imprisonment not exceeding a term of two years or to a fine or to both;
  (b)   on summary conviction, to imprisonment not exceeding a term of three months or to a fine not exceeding the statutory maximum or to both.

9.—(1)   The auditors of a company are entitled—
  (a)   to receive all such notices of, and other communications relating to, any general meeting of the company as a shareholder of the company is entitled to receive;
  (b)   to attend any general meeting of the company; and

(c)   to be heard at any general meeting which they attend on any part of the business of the meeting which concerns them as auditors.

(2)   The right to attend and be heard at a meeting is exercisable in the case of a body corporate or partnership by an individual authorised by it in writing to act as its representative at the meeting.

Remuneration

10.—(1)   The remuneration of auditors of a company who are appointed by the company in general meeting must be fixed by the company in general meeting or in such manner as the company in general meeting may decide.

(2)   The remuneration of auditors who are appointed by the directors or the Authority must, as the case may be, be fixed by the directors or the Authority (and be payable by the company even where it is fixed by the Authority).

11.—(1)   Subject to sub-paragraph (2), the power of the Secretary of State to make regulations under [section 494 of the Companies Act 2006] (remuneration of auditors or their associates for non-audit work) in relation to company auditors is to be exercisable in relation to auditors of open-ended investment companies—

(a)   for like purposes; and
(b)   subject to the same conditions.

(2)   For the purposes of the exercise of the power to make regulations under [section 494 of the Companies Act 2006], as extended by sub-paragraph (1), the reference in [section 494(4)] to a note to a company's accounts is to be taken to be a reference to the annual report of an open-ended investment company.

Removal

12.—(1)   A company may by resolution remove an auditor from office notwithstanding anything in any agreement between it and him.

(2)   Where a resolution removing an auditor is passed at a general meeting of a company, the company must, not later than 14 days after the holding of the meeting, notify the Authority of the passing of the resolution.

(3)   Nothing in this paragraph is to be taken as depriving a person removed under it of compensation or damages payable to him in respect of the termination of his appointment as auditor or of any appointment terminating with that as auditor.

Rights on removal or non-reappointment

13.—(1)   A resolution at a general meeting of a company—

(a)   removing an auditor before the expiration of his period of office; or
(b)   appointing as auditor a person other than the retiring auditor;

is not effective unless notice of the intention to move it has been given to the open-ended investment company at least 28 days before the meeting at which it is moved.

(2)   On receipt of notice of such an intended resolution, the company must forthwith send a copy to the person proposed to be removed or, as the case may be, to the person proposed to be appointed and to the retiring auditor.

(3)   The auditor proposed to be removed or, as the case may be, the retiring auditor may make with respect to the intended resolution representations in writing to the company (not exceeding a reasonable length) and request their notification to the shareholders of the company.

(4)   The company must (unless the representations are received by the company too late for it to do so)—

(a)   in any notice of the resolution given to the shareholders of the company, state the fact of the representations having been made;
(b)   send a copy of the representations to each of the shareholders whose name appears on the register of shareholders (other than the designated person) and to whom notice of the meeting is or has been sent;
(c)   take such steps as FSA rules may require for the purpose of bringing the fact that the representations have been made to the attention of the holders of any bearer shares; and
(d)   at the request of any holder of bearer shares, provide a copy of the representations.

(5)   If a copy of any such representations is not sent out as required because they were received too late or because of the company's default or if, for either of those reasons, any steps required by sub-paragraph (4)(c) or (d) are not taken, the auditor may (without prejudice to his right to be heard orally) require that the representations be read out at the meeting.

(6)   Copies of the representations need not be sent out, the steps required by sub-paragraph (4)(c) or (d) need not be taken and the representations need not be read out at the meeting if, on the application of the company or any other person claiming to be aggrieved, the court is satisfied that the rights conferred by this paragraph are being abused to secure needless publicity for

defamatory matter; and the court may order the costs of the company on such an application to be paid in whole or in part by the auditor, notwithstanding that he is not a party to the application.

14.—(1)   An auditor who has been removed from office has, notwithstanding his removal, the rights conferred by paragraph 9 in relation to any general meeting of the company at which his term of office would otherwise have expired or at which it is proposed to fill the vacancy caused by his removal.

(2)   The reference in paragraph 9 to business concerning the auditors as auditors is to be construed in relation to an auditor who has been removed from office as a reference to business concerning him as former auditor.

Resignation

15.—(1)   An auditor of a company may resign his office by depositing a notice in writing to that effect at the company's head office.

(2)   Such a notice is not effective unless it is accompanied by the statement required by paragraph 18.

(3)   An effective notice of resignation operates to bring the auditor's term of office to an end as of the date on which the notice is deposited or on such later date as may be specified in it.

(4)   The company must, not later than 14 days after the deposit of a notice of resignation, send a copy of the notice to the Authority.

16.—(1)   This paragraph applies where a notice of resignation of an auditor is accompanied by a statement of circumstances which he considers ought to be brought to the attention of the shareholders or creditors of the company.

(2)   An auditor may deposit with the notice a signed requisition that a general meeting of the company be convened forthwith for the purpose of receiving and considering such explanation of the circumstances connected with his resignation as he may wish to place before the meeting.

(3)   The company must, not later than 21 days after the date of the deposit of a requisition under this paragraph, proceed to convene a meeting for a day not later than 28 days after the date on which the notice convening the meeting is given.

(4)   The auditor may request the company to circulate a statement in writing (not exceeding a reasonable length) of the circumstances connected with his resignation to each of the shareholders of the company whose name appears on the register of shareholders (other than the designated person)—
    (a)   before the meeting convened on his requisition; or
    (b)   before any general meeting at which his term of office would otherwise have expired or at which it is proposed to fill the vacancy caused by his resignation;
and to take such steps as FSA rules may require for the purpose of bringing the fact that the statement has been made to the attention of the holders of any bearer shares.

(5)   The company must (unless the statement is received by it too late for it to do so)—
    (a)   in any notice or advertisement of the meeting given or made to shareholders of the company, state the fact of the statement having been made;
    (b)   send a copy of the statement to every shareholder of the company to whom notice of the meeting is or has been sent; and
    (c)   at the request of any holder of bearer shares, provide a copy of the statement.

(6)   If a copy of the statement is not sent out or provided as required because it was received too late or because of the company's default the auditor may (without prejudice to his right to be heard orally) require that the statement be read out at the meeting.

(7)   Copies of a statement need not be sent out or provided and the statement need not be read out at the meeting if, on the application of the company or any other person claiming to be aggrieved, the court is satisfied that the rights conferred by this paragraph are being abused to secure needless publicity for defamatory matter; and the court may order the costs of the company on such an application to be paid in whole or in part by the auditor, notwithstanding that he is not a party to the application.

17.—(1)   An auditor who has resigned has, notwithstanding his removal, the rights conferred by paragraph 9 in relation to any such general meeting of the company as is mentioned in paragraph 16(4)(a) or (b).

(2)   The reference in paragraph 9 to business concerning the auditors as auditors is to be construed in relation to an auditor who has resigned as a reference to business concerning him as former auditor.

Statement by auditor ceasing to hold office

18.—(1)   Where an auditor ceases for any reason to hold office, he must deposit at the head office of the company a statement of any circumstances connected with his ceasing to hold office which he considers should be brought to the attention of the shareholders or creditors of the company or, if he considers that there are no such circumstances, a statement that there are none.

(2)   The statement must be deposited—
    (a)   in the case of resignation, along with the notice of resignation;
    (b)   in the case of failure to seek re-appointment, not less than 14 days before the end of the time allowed for next appointing auditors; and
    (c)   in any other case, not later than the end of the period of 14 days beginning with the date on which he ceases to hold office.

(3)   If the statement is of circumstances which the auditor considers should be brought to the attention of the shareholders or creditors of the company, the company must, not later than 14 days after the deposit of the statement, either—
    (a)   send a copy of the statement to each of the shareholders whose name appears on the register of shareholders (other than the designated person) and take such steps as FSA rules may require for the purpose of bringing the fact that the statement has been made to the attention of the holders of any bearer shares; or
    (b)   apply to the court;

and, where an application is made under sub-paragraph (b), the company must notify the auditor.

(4)   Unless the auditor receives notice of an application to the court before the end of the period of 21 days beginning with the day on which he deposited the statement, he must, not later than seven days after the end of that period, send a copy of the statement to the Authority.

(5)   If the court is satisfied that the auditor is using the statement to secure needless publicity for defamatory matter—
    (a)   it must direct that copies of the statement need not be sent out and that the steps required by FSA rules need not be taken; and
    (b)   it may further order the company's costs on the application to be paid in whole or in part by the auditor notwithstanding that he is not a party to the application;

and the company must, not later than 14 days after the court's decision, take such steps in relation to a statement setting out the effect of the order as are required by sub-paragraph (3)(a) in relation to the statement deposited under sub-paragraph (1).

(6)   If the court is not so satisfied, the company must, not later than 14 days after the court's decision, send to each of the shareholders a copy of the auditor's statement and notify the auditor of the court's decision.

(7)   The auditor must, not later than 7 days after receiving such a notice, send a copy of the statement to the Authority.

(8)   Where notice of appeal is filed not later than 14 days after the court's decision, any reference to that decision in sub-paragraphs (5) and (6) is to be construed as a reference to the final determination or withdrawal of that appeal, as the case may be.

19.—(1)   If a person ceasing to hold office as auditor fails to comply with paragraph 18 he is guilty of an offence and liable—
    (a)   on conviction on indictment, to a fine;
    (b)   on summary conviction, to a fine not exceeding the statutory maximum.

(2)   In proceedings for an offence under sub-paragraph (1), it is a defence for the person charged to show that he took all reasonable steps and exercised all due diligence to avoid the commission of the offence.

20.   Section 249(1) of the Act (disqualification of auditor for breach of trust scheme rules) applies to a failure by an auditor to comply with a duty imposed on him by FSA rules as it applies to a breach of trust scheme rules.

[955]

NOTES

Para 1: words in square brackets substituted (for the original words "also eligible under section 25 of the Companies Act 1989 for appointment as a company auditor") by the Companies Act 2006 (Consequential Amendments etc) Order 2008, SI 2008/948, art 3(1), Sch 1, Pt 1, para 28(1), (2), as from 6 April 2008 (for savings see art 6(4) of the 2008 Order which provides that where by virtue of any transitional provision, a provision of the Companies Act 2006 has effect only (a) on or after a specified date, or (b) in relation to matters occurring or arising on or after a specified date, any amendment substituting or inserting a reference to that provision has effect correspondingly).

Para 2: sub-paras (3)–(5) substituted, for original sub-para (3), by SI 2008/948, art 3(1), Sch 1, Pt 1, para 28(1), (3), as from 6 April 2008 (subject to savings as noted in the para 1 note above). The original sub-paragraph read as follows—

"(3)   The power of the Secretary of State to make regulations under section 27 of the Companies Act 1989 (ineligibility on ground of lack of independence) in relation to the appointment of company auditors is to be exercisable in relation to the appointment of auditors of open-ended investment companies—
    (a)   for like purposes; and
    (b)   subject to the same conditions.".

Para 4: words in square brackets in sub-paras (2), (3) substituted, and paras (6), (7) added, by the Open-Ended Investment Companies (Amendment) Regulations 2005, SI 2005/923, reg 2(1), (9), as from 6 April 2005.

Para 11: words in square brackets in sub-para (1), and words in first pair of square brackets in sub-para (2) substituted (for the original words "section 390B of the 1985 Act"), and words in second pair of square brackets in sub-para (2) substituted (for the original words "section 390B(3)"), by SI 2008/948, art 3(1), Sch 1, Pt 2, para 222, as from 6 April 2008 (subject to savings as noted in the para 1 note above).

SCHEDULE 6
MERGERS AND DIVISIONS

Regulation 70

1. This Schedule applies to any reconstruction or amalgamation involving an open-ended investment company which takes the form of a scheme described in paragraph 4.

2. An open-ended investment company may apply to the court under [section 896 or 899 of the Companies Act 2006] (power of company to compromise with creditors and members) [in respect of] a scheme falling within any of sub-paragraphs (a) to (c) of paragraph 4(1) where—

  (a) the scheme in question involves a compromise or arrangement with its shareholders or creditors or any class of its shareholders or creditors; and

  (b) the consideration for the transfer or each of the transfers envisaged by the scheme is to be—

   (i)   shares in the transferee company receivable by shareholders of the transferor company; or

   (ii) where there is more than one transferor company and any one or more of them is a public company, shares in the transferee company receivable by shareholders or members of the transferor companies (as the case may be);

   in each case with or without any cash payment to shareholders.

3. A public company may apply to the court under [section 896 or 899 of the Companies Act 2006] [in respect of] a scheme falling within sub-paragraph (b) or (c) of paragraph 4(1) where—

  (a) the scheme in question involves a compromise or arrangement with its members or creditors or any class of its members or creditors; and

  (b) the consideration for the transfer or each of the transfers envisaged by the scheme is to be—

   (i)   shares in the transferee company receivable by members of the transferor company; or

   (ii) where there is more than one transferor company and any one or more of them is an open-ended investment company, shares in the transferee company receivable by shareholders or members of the transferor companies (as the case may be),

   in each case with or without any cash payment to shareholders.

4.—(1) The schemes falling within this paragraph are—

  (a) any scheme under which the undertaking, property and liabilities of an open-ended investment company are to be transferred to another such company, other than one formed for the purpose of, or in connection with the scheme;

  (b) any scheme under which the undertaking, property and liabilities of two or more bodies corporate, each of which is either—

   (i)   an open-ended investment company; or

   (ii) a public company,

   are to be transferred to an open-ended investment company formed for the purpose of, or in connection with, the scheme;

  (c) any scheme under which the undertaking, property and liabilities of an open-ended investment company or a public company are to be divided among and transferred to two or more open-ended investment companies whether or not formed for the purpose of, or in connection with, the scheme.

  (2) Nothing in this Schedule is to be taken as enabling the court to sanction a scheme under which the whole or any part of the undertaking, property or liabilities of an open-ended investment company may be transferred to any person other than another such company.

[5. An application made by virtue of paragraph 2 or 3 shall be treated as one to which Part 27 of the Companies Act 2006 applies (mergers and divisions of public companies), and the provisions of that Part and Part 26 of that Act have effect accordingly, subject to paragraph 6.]

6.—(1) [The provisions of the Companies Act 2006] referred to in paragraph 5 have effect with such modifications as are necessary or appropriate for the purposes of this Schedule.

  (2) In particular, any reference in those provisions to [a merger by absorption, a merger by formation of a new company or a division] is to be taken to be a reference to a scheme falling within sub-paragraph (a), (b) or (c) of paragraph 4(1).

  (3) Without prejudice to the generality of sub-paragraph (1), the following references in those provisions have effect as follows, unless the context otherwise requires—

(a)   any reference to a scheme is to be taken to be a reference to a scheme falling within any of sub-paragraphs (a) to (c) of paragraph 4(1);

(b)   any reference to a company is to be taken to be a reference to an open-ended investment company;

(c)   any reference to members is to be taken to be a reference to shareholders of an open-ended investment company;

(d)   any reference to the registered office of a company is to be taken to be a reference to the head office of an open-ended investment company;

(e)   any reference to the memorandum and articles of a company is to be taken to be a reference to the instrument of incorporation of an open-ended investment company;

(f)   any reference to a report under section 103 of the 1985 Act (non-cash consideration to be valued before allotment) is to be taken to be a reference to any report with respect to the valuation of any non-cash consideration given for shares in an open-ended investment company which may be required by FSA rules;

(g)   any reference to annual accounts is to be taken to be a reference to the accounts contained in the annual report of an open-ended investment company;

(h)   ...

(i)   any reference to the requirements of [the Companies Act 2006] as to balance sheets forming part of a company's annual accounts is to be taken to be a reference to any requirements arising by virtue of FSA rules as to balance sheets drawn up for the purposes of the accounts contained in the annual report of an open-ended investment company;

(j)   any reference to paid up capital is to be taken to be a reference to the share capital of an open-ended investment company.

[956]

NOTES

Paras 2, 3: words in square brackets substituted by the Companies Act 2006 (Consequential Amendments etc) Order 2008, SI 2008/948, art 3(1), Sch 1, Pt 2, para 223(1)–(3), as from 6 April 2008.

Para 5: substituted by SI 2008/948, art 3(1), Sch 1, Pt 2, para 223(1), (4), as from 6 April 2008.

Para 6: words in square brackets substituted, and words omitted revoked by SI 2008/948, art 3(1), Sch 1, Pt 2, para 223(1), (5), as from 6 April 2008.

(Sch 7 (Minor and Consequential Amendments) amends the Trustee Investments Act 1961, Sch 1, Pt III (repealed subject to savings), the Stock Transfer Act 1963, s 1, the Companies Act 1985, ss 26, 199, 209, 220, 718, and amended s 716 of that Act (repealed), the Company Directors Disqualification Act 1986, Sch 1, the Pension Schemes Act 1993, s 38, the Limited Liability Partnerships Act 2000, Schedule, and amended the Uncertificated Securities Regulations 1995, SI 1995/3272, regs 3, 19 (revoked).)

FINANCIAL SERVICES AND MARKETS ACT 2000 (CONTROL OF BUSINESS TRANSFERS) (REQUIREMENTS ON APPLICANTS) REGULATIONS 2001

(SI 2001/3625)

NOTES

Made: 7 November 2001.

Authority: Financial Services and Markets Act 2000, ss 108, 417(1), 428(3), Sch 12, para 6(2).

Commencement: 1 December 2001.

1   Citation, commencement and interpretation

(1)   These Regulations may be cited as the Financial Services and Markets Act 2000 (Control of Business Transfers) (Requirements on Applicants) Regulations 2001 and come into force on 1st December 2001.

(2)   In these Regulations—

"the Act" means the Financial Services and Markets Act 2000;

"the parties" means the authorised person concerned and the transferee (within the meaning of section 105(2) or, as the case may be, section 106(2) of the Act);

["reclaim fund business transfer scheme" has the meaning given by section 106A(1) of the Act;]

"the report" means the scheme report mentioned in section 109(1) of the Act;

"State of the commitment" has the meaning given by paragraph 6(1) of Schedule 12 to the Act;

"State in which the risk is situated" has the meaning given by paragraph 6(3) of Schedule 12 to the Act;

"a summary of the report" means a summary of the report sufficient to indicate the opinion of the person making the report of the likely effects of the insurance business transfer scheme on the policyholders of the parties.

[957]

NOTES
Definition "reclaim fund business transfer scheme" inserted by the Financial Services and Markets Act 2000 (Control of Business Transfers) (Requirements on Applicants) (Amendment) Regulations 2009, SI 2009/1390, reg 2(a), as from 13 July 2009.

2 Meaning of "commitment"

There is prescribed for the purposes of paragraph 6(2) of Schedule 12 to the Act any contract of insurance of a kind referred to in [Article 2 of the life assurance consolidation directive].

[958]

NOTES
Words in square brackets substituted by the Life Assurance Consolidation Directive (Consequential Amendments) Regulations 2004, SI 2004/3379, reg 20, as from 11 January 2005.

3 Transfer of an insurance business

(1) An applicant under section 107 of the Act for an order sanctioning an insurance business transfer scheme ("the scheme") must comply with the following requirements.

(2) A notice stating that the application has been made must be—
  (a) published—
      (i) in the London, Edinburgh and Belfast Gazettes;
      (ii) in two national newspapers in the United Kingdom; ...
      (iii) where, as regards any policy [(other than a policy which evidences a contract of reinsurance)] included in the proposed transfer, an EEA State other than the United Kingdom is the State of the commitment or the State in which the risk is situated, in two national newspapers in that EEA State; and
      [(iv) where, as regards any policy included in the proposed transfer which evidences a contract of reinsurance, an EEA State other than the United Kingdom is the State in which the establishment of the policyholder to which the policy relates is situated at the date when the contract was entered into, in one business newspaper which is published or circulated in that EEA State; ...]
  (b) sent to every policyholder of the parties[; and
  (c) sent—
      (i) to every reinsurer of the authorised person concerned (within the meaning of section 105(2) of the Act) any of whose contracts of reinsurance (in whole or part) are to be transferred by the scheme; or
      (ii) in a case where such a contract has been placed with or through a person authorised to act on behalf of the reinsurer, then to that person; or
      (iii) in a case where such a contract has been placed with more than one reinsurer, then to the person or persons authorised to act on behalf of those reinsurers or groups of reinsurers].

(3) The notices mentioned in paragraph (2) must—
  (a) be approved by the Authority prior to publication (or, as the case may be, being sent); and
  (b) contain the address from which the documents mentioned in paragraph (4) may be obtained.

(4) A copy of the report and a statement setting out the terms of the scheme and containing a summary of the report must be given free of charge to any person who requests them.

(5) A copy of the application, the report and the statement mentioned in paragraph (4) must be given free of charge to the Authority.

(6) In the case of any such scheme as is mentioned in section 105(5) of the Act, copies of the documents listed in paragraph 6(1) of Schedule 15B to the Companies Act 1985 or in paragraph 6(1) of Schedule 15B to the Companies (Northern Ireland) Order 1986 (application of provisions about compromises and arrangements to mergers and divisions of public companies) must be given to the Authority by the beginning of the period referred to in paragraph 3(e) of that Schedule.

[959]

NOTES
Para (2): word omitted from sub-para (a)(ii) revoked, words in square brackets in sub-para (a)(iii) inserted, and sub-para (a)(iv) inserted, by the Financial Services and Markets Act 2000 (Reinsurance Directive) Regulations 2007, SI 2007/3255, reg 2(1), (2), as from 10 December 2007; word omitted from sub-para (a)(iv)

revoked, and sub-para (c) (and the word immediately preceding it) added, by the Financial Services and Markets Act 2000 (Control of Business Transfers) (Requirements on Applicants) (Amendment) Regulations 2008, SI 2008/1467, reg 2(a), (b), as from 30 June 2008.

4—(1)   Subject to paragraph (2) [or (3)], the court may not determine an application under section 107 for an order sanctioning an insurance business transfer scheme—
   (a)   where the applicant has failed to comply with the requirements in regulation 3(2), (3) or (6); and
   (b)   until a period of not less than twenty-one days has elapsed since the Authority was given the documents mentioned in regulation 3(5).

   (2)   The requirements in regulation 3(2)(a)(ii)[, (iii) and (iv)][, (b) and (c)] may be waived by the court in such circumstances and subject to such conditions as the court considers appropriate.

   [(3)   The requirement in regulation 3(2)(a)(iv) must be waived where an applicant demonstrates that he has notified all policyholders of contracts of reinsurance.]

[960]

NOTES
   Para (1): words in square brackets inserted by the Financial Services and Markets Act 2000 (Reinsurance Directive) Regulations 2007, SI 2007/3255, reg 2(1), (3), as from 10 December 2007.
   Para (2): words in first pair of square brackets substituted by SI 2007/3255, reg 2(1), (4), as from 10 December 2007; words in second pair of square brackets substituted by the Financial Services and Markets Act 2000 (Control of Business Transfers) (Requirements on Applicants) (Amendment) Regulations 2008, SI 2008/1467, reg 2(c), as from 30 June 2008.
   Para (3): added by SI 2007/3255, reg 2(1), (5), as from 10 December 2007.

5   [Transfer of a banking business or a reclaim fund business]

   (1)   An applicant under section 107 of the Act for an order sanctioning a banking business transfer scheme [or reclaim fund business transfer scheme] ("the scheme") must comply with the following requirements.

   (2)   A notice stating that the application has been made must be published—
   (a)   in the London, Edinburgh and Belfast Gazettes; and
   (b)   in two national newspapers in the United Kingdom.

   (3)   The notice mentioned in paragraph (2) must—
   (a)   be approved by the Authority prior to its publication; and
   (b)   contain the address from which the statement mentioned in paragraph (4) may be obtained.

   (4)   A statement setting out the terms of the scheme must be given free of charge to any person who requests it.

   (5)   Copies of the application and the statement mentioned in paragraph (4) must be given free of charge to the Authority.

[961]

NOTES
   Regulation heading: words in square brackets substituted by the Financial Services and Markets Act 2000 (Control of Business Transfers) (Requirements on Applicants) (Amendment) Regulations 2009, SI 2009/1390, reg 2(b), as from 13 July 2009.
   Para (1): words in square brackets inserted by SI 2009/1390, reg 2(c), as from 13 July 2009.

6—(1)   Subject to paragraph (2), the court may not determine an application under section 107 for an order sanctioning a banking business transfer scheme [or reclaim fund business transfer scheme]—
   (a)   where the applicant has failed to comply with the requirements in regulation 5(2) or (3); and
   (b)   until a period of not less than twenty-one days has elapsed since the Authority was given the documents mentioned in regulation 5(5).

   (2)   The requirement in regulation 5(2)(b) may be waived by the court in such circumstances and subject to such conditions as the court considers appropriate.

[962]

NOTES
   Para (1): words in square brackets inserted by the Financial Services and Markets Act 2000 (Control of Business Transfers) (Requirements on Applicants) (Amendment) Regulations 2009, SI 2009/1390, reg 2(d), as from 13 July 2009.

PART IV
OTHER STATUTORY INSTRUMENTS

BRADFORD & BINGLEY PLC TRANSFER OF SECURITIES AND PROPERTY ETC ORDER 2008

(SI 2008/2546)

NOTES
Made: 29 September 2008 (7.30 am).
Authority: Banking (Special Provisions) Act 2008, ss 3, 4, 8, 12, 13(2), Sch 1.
Commencement: 29 September 2008 (8.00 am).

ARRANGEMENT OF ARTICLES

PART 1
GENERAL

PART 2
THE FIRST TRANSFER AND RELATED PROVISIONS

PART 3
MEMBERS, MEETINGS, DIRECTORS AND PROCEEDINGS

PART 4
DE-LISTING, APPROVAL ETC

PART 5
THE SECOND TRANSFER

PART 6
FINANCIAL SERVICES COMPENSATION SCHEME

PART 7
TRANSITIONAL PROVISIONS

PART 1
GENERAL

1   Citation and commencement

(1)   This Order may be cited as the Bradford & Bingley plc Transfer of Securities and Property etc Order 2008.

(2)   This Order comes into force at 8.00 am on 29th September 2008.

[963]

NOTES

Commencement: 29 September 2008 (at 8.00 am).

2   Interpretation: general

In this Order—

"the 1985 Act" means the Companies Act 1985;

"the 2000 Act" means the Financial Services and Markets Act 2000;

"the 2006 Act" means the Companies Act 2006;

"Abbey" means Abbey National plc, company registered number 2294747;

"the Act" means the Banking (Special Provisions) Act 2008;

"the Authority" means the Financial Services Authority;

"the Bank" means the Governor and Company of the Bank of England;

"Bradford & Bingley" means Bradford & Bingley plc, company registered number 3938288;

"Bradford & Bingley International" means Bradford & Bingley International Limited, a company registered in the Isle of Man, company number 052221C;

"Bradford & Bingley's registrar" means the person appointed by Bradford & Bingley, as its agent, among other things to maintain its register of members;

"the COMP Sourcebook" means the Compensation Sourcebook made by the Authority under the 2000 Act;

"the Companies Acts" has the meaning given by section 2 of the 2006 Act;

"the dated subordinated notes" means the following debt issued by Bradford & Bingley—

    (a)   the £125,000,000 7.625 per cent subordinated notes due February 2010;

    (b)   the £125,000,000 6.625 per cent subordinated notes due 16 June 2023;

    (c)   the £200,000,000 fixed-rate step-up subordinated notes due 2022;

    (d)   the £150,000,000 floating rate dated subordinated notes due March 2054;

    (e)   the £250,000,000 fixed rate/floating rate callable step-up subordinated notes due January 2018; and

    (f)   any further subordinated debt which ranks or is expressed to rank *pari passu* with any of the notes referred to in (a) to (e);

"eligible claimant" has the meaning given in rule 4.2.1 of the COMP Sourcebook;

"the FEES 6 Chapter" means Chapter 6 (Financial Services Compensation Scheme Funding) of the Fees Manual made by the Authority under the 2000 Act;

"the Financial Services Compensation Scheme" means the scheme established by the Authority under Part 15 (the financial services compensation scheme) of the 2000 Act;

"the first transfer" means the transfer effected by article 3;

"the first transfer time" has the meaning given by article 3(2);

"FSCS" means the body corporate established by the Authority under section 212 (the scheme manager) of the 2000 Act;

"protected deposit" has the meaning given in rule 5.3.1 of the COMP Sourcebook;

"qualifying claimant" means an eligible claimant who immediately before the first transfer time had a claim against Bradford & Bingley for a protected deposit;

"relevant undertaking" means Bradford & Bingley or any of its UK subsidiary undertakings;

"retail deposits" means liabilities represented by amounts standing to the credit of retail deposit accounts including instant access accounts, fixed term and notice savings accounts, savings bonds and individual savings accounts, together with interest and other sums accruing to the benefit of such accounts;

"the second transfer" means the transfer effected by article 16;

"the second transfer time" has the meaning given by article 16(2);

"shares in Bradford & Bingley" means the ordinary shares issued by Bradford & Bingley;

"the transitional period" means the period of 18 months beginning with the date of this Order;

"the Treasury Solicitor" has the same meaning as in the Treasury Solicitor Act 1876 and whose address is One Kemble Street, London WC2B 4TS;

"UK subsidiary undertaking" means a subsidiary undertaking of Bradford & Bingley that is a body corporate incorporated, or a partnership established, under the law of any part of the United Kingdom; and

"the USRs" means the Uncertificated Securities Regulations 2001.

[964]

NOTES
Commencement: 29 September 2008 (at 8.00 am).

PART 2
THE FIRST TRANSFER AND RELATED PROVISIONS

3 The first transfer

(1)   By virtue of this Order, the shares in Bradford & Bingley are transferred to the Treasury Solicitor as nominee of the Treasury.

(2)   The transfer under paragraph (1) takes place at the time this Order comes into force ("the first transfer time").

(3)   The transfer of the shares effected under paragraph (1) shall vest title in the Treasury Solicitor—

    (a)   free from all trusts, liabilities and incumbrances; and

    (b)   together with all rights, benefits or privileges which attach or accrue to or arise from such shares on or after the first transfer time.

[965]

NOTES
Commencement: 29 September 2008 (at 8.00 am).

4 Registration of shares and issue of certificates

(1)   The Treasury Solicitor is entitled with effect from the first transfer time to be entered in the register of members of Bradford & Bingley as holder of the shares in Bradford & Bingley without the need for delivery of any instrument of transfer or other instrument or document and notwithstanding—

    (a)   the absence of any required consent or concurrence to or with the transfer; and

    (b)   any other restriction relating to the transfer.

(2)   The operator of a relevant system in which any shares in Bradford & Bingley are held immediately prior to the first transfer time ("relevant shares") shall forthwith after the first transfer time—

    (a)   withdraw his permission for title to the relevant shares to be transferred by means of the relevant system with effect from the first transfer time; and

    (b)   inform all the system-members and Bradford & Bingley's registrar of the date and time the relevant shares ceased to be securities participating in the system.

(3)   Bradford & Bingley shall procure that Bradford & Bingley's registrar shall forthwith after the first transfer time—

    (a)   take such action as the operator of a relevant system may require to convert any relevant shares held in such a system immediately prior to the first transfer time into certificated form; and

    (b)   register in Bradford & Bingley's register of members (including its issuer register of members) the Treasury Solicitor as the holder of shares in Bradford & Bingley.

(4)   The operator of a relevant system in which any relevant shares are held immediately prior to the first transfer time, Bradford & Bingley and Bradford & Bingley's registrar shall each—

    (a)   provide each other with such information as shall be necessary to comply with this article; and

(b)   co-operate to ensure that the issuer register of members of Bradford & Bingley reconciles with the operator register of members of Bradford & Bingley immediately prior to the first transfer time.

(5)   From the first transfer time and until the Treasury Solicitor is entered in Bradford & Bingley's register of members (including its issuer register of members)—

(a)   he is deemed for all purposes (including for the purposes of the Companies Acts and the USRs) to be—
   (i)   the sole member of Bradford & Bingley; and
   (ii)   entered as holder on the operator register of members of Bradford & Bingley and in Bradford & Bingley's register of members (including its issuer register of members); and

(b)   no other person may exercise or purport to exercise in respect of Bradford & Bingley any right deriving from any shares in Bradford & Bingley.

(6)   The Treasury Solicitor is entitled from the first transfer time to all the rights and advantages of a member of Bradford & Bingley to the exclusion of all other persons, notwithstanding that he is not entered in either Bradford & Bingley's register of members (including its issuer register of members) or the operator register of members of Bradford & Bingley.

(7)   Part 21 of the 2006 Act (certification and transfer of securities) applies to Bradford & Bingley with the following modifications—

(a)   the transfer effected by article 3(1) is deemed to be a transfer falling within section 776(2)(a) (duty of company as to issue of certificates etc on transfer); and

(b)   sections 776(3) and (4), 777 (issue of certificates etc: cases within the Stock Transfer Act 1982) and 778 (issue of certificates etc: allotment or transfer to financial institution) do not apply.

(8)   In this article "certificated", "issuer register of members", "operator", "operator register of members", "relevant system" and "system-member" have the meanings given in the USRs.

[966]

NOTES
Commencement: 29 September 2008 (at 8.00 am).

5 Extinguishment of rights in relation to shares in Bradford & Bingley

By virtue of this Order, with effect from the first transfer time, any right or entitlement of a person to receive shares in Bradford & Bingley (whether by subscription, conversion or otherwise) is extinguished if the right or entitlement was granted by—

(a)   a relevant undertaking; or

(b)   a person not within sub-paragraph (a) and is enjoyed by reason of or in connection with—
   (i)   any person's office or employment with a relevant undertaking; or
   (ii)   the services provided by any person to a relevant undertaking.

[967]

NOTES
Commencement: 29 September 2008 (at 8.00 am).

6 Modification of interests, rights and liabilities associated with the dated subordinated notes

(1)   This article applies, with effect from the first transfer time, in respect of the dated subordinated notes.

(2)   By virtue of this Order, the rights and liabilities associated with the dated subordinated notes shall be modified in accordance with paragraph (3).

[(3)   The principal and interest due in respect of a dated subordinated note shall not become due and payable except to the extent that condition 1 or 2 (as specified in paragraphs (4) and (5)) is met and paragraph (6) applies.

(4)   Condition 1 is that Bradford & Bingley notifies the holder of a dated subordinated note that the principal or interest (or any part of either) is to be due and payable (whereupon the payment is due on the date specified by Bradford & Bingley).

(5)   Condition 2 is that Bradford & Bingley has satisfied in full its liability to the FSCS under article 30(1); that liability shall not be regarded as satisfied in full for the purposes of this paragraph if article 30(4) applies.

(6)   Principal or interest in respect of a dated subordinated note shall become due or payable only to the extent that Bradford & Bingley could make the payment and continue to be solvent thereafter.

(7)   Any interest in respect of a dated subordinated note which, by virtue of paragraph (3), has not become due and payable, shall bear interest calculated at the same rate and in the same manner as provided for in the dated subordinated note.

(8)   In a winding-up of, or on a distribution by an administrator appointed in respect of, Bradford & Bingley there shall be payable in respect of each dated subordinated note such amount as would be payable to a holder of a preference share in Bradford & Bingley ranking ahead of all other issued shares of Bradford & Bingley (including any other preference shares or any notional shares), on the assumption that such preference share was entitled to an amount equal to the principal amount of such dated subordinated note together any interest which has accrued up to the date of repayment.

(9)   For the purposes of paragraph (6), Bradford & Bingley is not solvent if it would be deemed unable to pay its debts within the meaning given by section 123 of the Insolvency Act 1986.]

[968]

NOTES
Commencement: 29 September 2008 (at 8.00 am).
Paras (3)–(9): substituted for original para (3) by the Bradford & Bingley plc Transfer of Securities and Property etc (Amendment) Order 2009, SI 2009/320, art 2(1), (2), as from 20 February 2009.
Note: for terms of reference of the independent valuer of the Bradford & Bingley Compensation Scheme see http://www.hm-treasury.gov.uk/d/bbappointmentletter_240609.pdf. The independent valuer has his own website at: http://www.bandbvaluer.org.uk.

7   Modification of rights in relevant instruments

(1)   The consequences specified in paragraph (3) shall not arise in respect of any relevant instrument as a result of the first transfer, or any other thing done, or matter arising, by virtue of or in connection with the first transfer.

(2)   Any circumstances which, but for paragraph (1), would give rise to the consequences specified in paragraph (3) shall be taken not to have arisen for the purposes of any relevant instrument.

(3)   The consequences are—
   (a)   the termination of the relevant instrument or any rights or obligations under it;
   (b)   any right to terminate the relevant instrument or any right or obligation under it becoming exercisable;
   (c)   any amount becoming due and payable or capable of being declared due and payable;
   (d)   any other change in the amount or timing of any payment falling to be made or due to be received by any person;
   (e)   any right to withhold, net or set off any payment becoming exercisable;
   (f)   any event of default or breach of any right arising;
   (g)   any right not to advance any amount becoming exercisable;
   (h)   any obligation to provide or transfer any deposit or collateral;
   (i)   any right to give or withhold any consent or approval; or
   (j)   any other right or remedy (whether or not similar in kind to those referred to in paragraphs (a) to (i)) arising or becoming exercisable.

(4)   Without prejudice to paragraph (3), any provision in a relevant instrument that, as a result of the first transfer or any other thing done, or matter arising, by virtue of or in connection with the first transfer, provides for an obligation not to be created, suspends or extinguishes (in whole or in part) such an obligation or renders such an obligation subject to conditions, shall be of no effect.

(5)   This article does not apply to any action taken by the Treasury under article 10.

(6)   In this article, "relevant instrument" has the meaning given in paragraph 4(3) of Schedule 1 to the Act and the specified connection referred to in paragraph 4(3)(c) of that Schedule is between Bradford & Bingley and those undertakings whose assets and liabilities, profits and losses are consolidated in the consolidated accounts of Bradford & Bingley.

[969]

NOTES
Commencement: 29 September 2008 (at 8.00 am).

PART 3
MEMBERS, MEETINGS, DIRECTORS AND PROCEEDINGS

8   Minimum membership for carrying on business

(1)   While Bradford & Bingley is wholly owned by the Treasury, section 24 of the 1985 Act (minimum membership for carrying on business) shall not apply in relation to Bradford & Bingley or any member of Bradford & Bingley.

(2)   While Bradford & Bingley is wholly owned by the Treasury, no petition shall be presented for the winding up of Bradford & Bingley on the ground that the number of its members is less than the number required by law, nor shall any person be liable on that ground as a member of the company for the payment of any of its debts.

[970]

NOTES

Commencement: 29 September 2008 (at 8.00 am).

9   Resolutions and meetings

(1)   While Bradford & Bingley is wholly owned by the Treasury, any meeting of members of Bradford & Bingley shall, if the Treasury Solicitor is present in person, by proxy or authorises a corporate representative to attend, be deemed to be a duly constituted general meeting of the company notwithstanding that it may not have been properly called, or notice of it may not have been properly given, or any quorum required by Bradford & Bingley's articles of association may not be present.

(2)   Notwithstanding any provision in the articles of association of Bradford & Bingley, an appointment of a proxy for the Treasury Solicitor—
  (a)   may be in any written form (including in an electronic communication);
  (b)   need not be given with any period of notice;
  (c)   shall not require the approval of the board of Bradford & Bingley; and
  (d)   is deemed to be given in accordance with the articles of association.

(3)   A resolution of the company adopted after the first transfer time is effective notwithstanding that special notice (notice of intention to move it given to company at least 28 days before the meeting at which it is moved) of the resolution is required by any provision of the 1985 Act or 2006 Act but has not been given.

[971]

NOTES

Commencement: 29 September 2008 (at 8.00 am).

10   Removal of directors

(1)   While Bradford & Bingley is wholly owned by the Treasury, the Treasury may in accordance with this article—
  (a)   remove any person as a director of a relevant undertaking;
  (b)   terminate a director's service contract with any relevant undertaking.

(2)   For the purposes of any contract or arrangement between a person and a relevant undertaking, action taken under paragraph (1) shall be treated as having been carried out by the relevant undertaking and, in the case of paragraph (1)(a), under and in accordance with its articles of association.

(3)   The Treasury may remove a person as a director of a relevant undertaking and may terminate his service contract by written notice to the relevant undertaking.

(4)   Any notice given in accordance with paragraph (3) shall take effect from the date specified in the notice.

(5)   A relevant undertaking which receives notice under paragraph (3) shall notify the person to whom the notice relates of that fact as soon as reasonably practicable.

(6)   A person—
  (a)   removed as director of a relevant undertaking, or
  (b)   whose service contract with a relevant undertaking is terminated,
in accordance with this article shall not have any right or claim against the Treasury or any company wholly owned by the Treasury (other than a relevant undertaking) in consequence of the Treasury's actions under this article.

(7)   This article does not—
  (a)   deprive any person removed under it of compensation or damages payable to him by a relevant undertaking in respect of—
    (i)   the termination of his appointment as director or of any appointment terminating with that as director; or
    (ii)   the termination of his service contract; or
  (b)   derogate from any power to remove a director or to terminate a director's service contract that may exist apart from this article.

(8)   In this article and in article 11, "service contract" has the meaning given by section 227 of the 2006 Act (directors' service contracts).

[972]

NOTES
Commencement: 29 September 2008 (at 8.00 am).

11 Appointment of directors

(1)   While Bradford & Bingley is wholly owned by the Treasury, the Treasury may appoint one or more directors of a relevant undertaking in accordance with this article and notwithstanding any provision in the articles of association of the relevant undertaking.

(2)   The Treasury may appoint a director of a relevant undertaking by written notice to the relevant undertaking provided the appointee has agreed to act in such a capacity.

(3)   The appointment shall take effect from the date specified in the notice.

(4)   The Treasury may determine the terms (including remuneration) of the service contract of a person appointed as a director under this article in whatever written form they see fit.

(5)   Any appointment, contract or arrangement which is made or the terms of which are determined under this article is to be treated as made or entered into by the relevant undertaking in question.

(6)   This article does not derogate from any power to appoint a director or determine the remuneration and other terms and conditions of a director's service contract that may exist apart from this article.

[973]

NOTES
Commencement: 29 September 2008 (at 8.00 am).

12 Proceedings against directors

(1)   No director of a relevant undertaking shall be liable for any act or omission of the director, acting in such capacity, which occurs while Bradford & Bingley is wholly owned by the Treasury and accordingly no proceedings may be brought (or in Scotland, raised) against any such director in respect of such matters.

(2)   The Treasury may in writing—
   (a)   disapply paragraph (1), and
   (b)   give consent to bring (or in Scotland, raise) such proceedings against such directors.

(3)   Where paragraph (1) applies, section 232 of the 2006 Act (provisions protecting directors from liability) shall not apply to a relevant undertaking.

(4)   In this article—
   "proceedings" includes proceedings under Part 11 of the 2006 Act (derivative claims and proceedings by members);
   "director" means—
      (a)   a person who is appointed as a director while Bradford & Bingley is wholly owned by the Treasury, whether or not he has ceased to be a director when proceedings in respect of that liability commenced;
      (b)   a person who was a director immediately before the first transfer time and whose continuing appointment as director while Bradford & Bingley is wholly owned by the Treasury, the Treasury approves in writing, whether or not he has ceased to be a director at the time when proceedings in respect of that liability commenced; and
      (c)   an alternate director of a person falling within sub-paragraph (a) or (b).

[974]

NOTES
Commencement: 29 September 2008 (at 8.00 am).

13 Shadow directorship

(1)   While Bradford & Bingley is wholly owned by the Treasury, for the purposes of the provisions listed in Schedule 1 to this Order, none of the persons listed in paragraph (3) shall be regarded as a shadow director of or (unless otherwise appointed as a director) a person discharging managerial responsibilities of a relevant undertaking.

(2)   For the purposes of the definition of "director" in section 417 of the 2000 Act (definitions), while Bradford & Bingley is wholly owned by the Treasury, none of the persons listed in paragraph (3) shall be regarded as a person in accordance with whose directions or instructions (not being advice given in a professional capacity) the directors of a relevant undertaking are accustomed to act.

(3)   The persons are—

(a)   a Minister of the Crown;
(b)   the Treasury;
(c)   the Treasury Solicitor;
(d)   the Bank;
(e)   persons—
        (i)   employed by or under; or
        (ii) acting on behalf of,
      any of the persons specified in sub-paragraphs (a) to (d).

[975]

NOTES
Commencement: 29 September 2008 (at 8.00 am).

PART 4
DE-LISTING, APPROVAL ETC

14   De-listing

(1)   By virtue of this Order, the listing of any shares of Bradford & Bingley is discontinued with effect from the first transfer time without the need for any notice to, or consent of, Bradford & Bingley or any other person.

(2)   In paragraph (1), "listing" has the meaning given in section 74 of the 2000 Act (the official list).

[976]

NOTES
Commencement: 29 September 2008 (at 8.00 am).

15   Approved persons

(1)   While Bradford & Bingley is wholly owned by the Treasury, the requirements imposed on a relevant undertaking by section 59 of the 2000 Act (approval for particular arrangements) in relation to directors (including non-executive directors) and the chief executive officer shall be deemed to be satisfied in relation to the relevant undertaking, provided that at all material times the Authority is satisfied that at least two individuals who effectively direct the business of the relevant undertaking are of sufficiently good repute and have sufficient experience to perform controlled functions in that respect.

(2)   The Treasury may give written notice to the Authority that paragraph (1) is no longer to apply in respect of a relevant undertaking.

(3)   At least one month prior to giving a notice under paragraph (2) the Treasury shall give written notice to the relevant undertaking of their intention to give a notice to the Authority under that paragraph.

(4)   In paragraph (1), "controlled functions" has the meaning given in section 59(3) of the 2000 Act.

[977]

NOTES
Commencement: 29 September 2008 (at 8.00 am).

PART 5
THE SECOND TRANSFER

16   The second transfer

(1)   By virtue of this Order—
    (a)   the rights and liabilities of Bradford & Bingley specified in paragraph 1 of Schedule 2;
    (b)   the property specified in paragraph 3 of Schedule 2;
    (c)   the contracts, agreements and other arrangements specified in paragraph 4 of Schedule 2;
    (d)   the personal property specified in paragraph 5 of Schedule 2; and
    (e)   the intellectual property specified in paragraph 6 of Schedule 2,
are transferred to Abbey.

(2)   The transfer under paragraph (1) takes place immediately after the first transfer time ("the second transfer time").

[978]

NOTES
Commencement: 29 September 2008 (at 8.00 am).

17 Isle of Man deposits

(1)   Subject to the prior approval of the Financial Services Commission of the Isle of Man of the proposed change of control of Bradford & Bingley International, as soon as practicable after the second transfer time, Bradford & Bingley shall—

(a)   transfer the Bradford & Bingley International shares to Abbey; and

(b)   take such steps as are reasonably necessary to ensure that—

(i)   the transfer in sub-paragraph (a) is effective under Manx law (including but not limited to duly executing requisite transfers, paying related Manx taxes such as stamp duty and delivering the relevant share certificates to Abbey);

(ii)   the Bradford & Bingley International shares are transferred to Abbey free from all trusts, liabilities and incumbrances;

(iii)   any right or other entitlement to receive shares in Bradford & Bingley International (whether by subscription, conversion or otherwise) is extinguished with effect from the relevant time; and

(iv)   Abbey is entered in the register of members of Bradford & Bingley International.

(2)   By virtue of this Order—

(a)   the intercompany undertaking is terminated from the relevant time, except in relation to liabilities arising from or in respect of a breach of contract or other duty or of any legal or regulatory requirement occurring before the relevant time; and

(b)   subject to sub-paragraph (a) any interests, rights, entitlements or claims that have accrued in connection with the intercompany undertaking are extinguished.

(3)   Articles 18 to 22 apply to any transfer made under this article as they apply to the second transfer.

(4)   In this article—

"the Bradford & Bingley International shares" means all shares in Bradford & Bingley International held by or on behalf of Bradford & Bingley at the relevant time;

"the intercompany undertaking" means the undertaking by Bradford & Bingley, dated 4 December 2000, to discharge the liabilities of Bradford & Bingley International;

"the relevant time" means the time at which the transfer under paragraph (1) is effected.

[979]

NOTES
Commencement: 29 September 2008 (at 8.00 am).

18 No consent or concurrence required

The second transfer is effective despite the absence of any required consent or concurrence to or with the transfer.

[980]

NOTES
Commencement: 29 September 2008 (at 8.00 am).

19 Associated liability and interference

(1)   The second transfer takes effect as if—

(a)   no associated liability existed in respect of any failure to comply with any requirement in respect of the transfer; and

(b)   there were no associated interference with the property, rights and liabilities transferred.

(2)   In this article, "associated liability" and "associated interference" have the meanings given in paragraph 2(2) of Schedule 2 to the Act.

[981]

NOTES
Commencement: 29 September 2008 (at 8.00 am).

20 Termination etc of interest or right

(1)   Subject to paragraph (2)—

(a)   from the coming into force of this Order until the second transfer time, no person is entitled to terminate, modify, acquire or claim any interest or right to be transferred by article 16, or to treat such an interest or right as terminated or modified; and

(b)   any purported termination, modification, acquisition or claim in contravention of sub-paragraph (a), and any action taken in consequence of a contravention of that sub-paragraph, shall have no effect.

(2)   This article shall not apply to the ordinary course of dealings by a depositor in relation to his retail deposit.

[982]

NOTES
Commencement: 29 September 2008 (at 8.00 am).

21 Interests, rights and liabilities of third parties relating to property, rights and liabilities transferred

(1)   No interest or right of any third party relating to any property, right or liability of Bradford & Bingley, whether or not it is transferred by article 16, shall arise or become exercisable by virtue of or in connection with the second transfer.

(2)   Save as otherwise provided in this Order, no third party shall, by virtue of or in connection with the second transfer, incur any liability or be subject to any obligation relating to any property, right or liability of Bradford & Bingley, whether or not it is transferred by article 16.

(3)   Without prejudice to the generality of paragraphs (1) and (2)—
(a)   the consequences specified in paragraph (4) shall not arise in respect of any relevant instrument as a result of the second transfer or any other thing done, or matter arising, by virtue of or in connection with that transfer; and
(b)   any circumstances which, but for sub-paragraph (a), would give rise to the consequences specified in paragraph (4) shall be taken not to have arisen for the purposes of any relevant instrument.

(4)   The consequences are—
(a)   the termination of a relevant instrument or any rights or obligations under it;
(b)   any right to terminate a relevant instrument or any right or obligation under it becoming exercisable;
(c)   any amount becoming due and payable or capable of being declared due and payable;
(d)   any other change in the amount or timing of any payment falling to be made or due to be received by any person;
(e)   any right to withhold, net or set off any payment becoming exercisable;
(f)   any event of default or breach of any right arising;
(g)   any right not to advance any amount becoming exercisable;
(h)   any obligation to provide or transfer any deposit or collateral;
(i)   any right to give or withhold any consent or approval; or
(j)   any other right or remedy (whether or not similar in kind to those referred to in sub-paragraphs (a) to (i)) arising or becoming exercisable.

(5)   Without prejudice to paragraph (4), any provision in a relevant instrument that, as a result of the second transfer or any other thing done, or matter arising, by virtue of or in connection with that transfer, provides for an obligation not to be created, suspends or extinguishes (in whole or in part) such an obligation or renders such an obligation subject to conditions, shall be of no effect.

(6)   In this article—
"relevant instrument" has the same meaning as in paragraph 4(3) of Schedule 1 to the Act and the specified connection referred to in paragraph 4(3)(c) of that Schedule is between Bradford & Bingley and those undertakings whose assets and liabilities, profits and losses are consolidated in the consolidated accounts of Bradford & Bingley; and
"third party" shall be construed in accordance with paragraph 2(3) of Schedule 2 to the Act.

[983]

NOTES
Commencement: 29 September 2008 (at 8.00 am).

22 Modification of rights and liabilities transferred

(1)   Where a transferred obligation conflicts with an obligation of Abbey existing at the second transfer time, the transferred obligation is modified to the extent required to avoid that conflict.

(2)   No person shall be entitled to acquire, claim, modify or terminate any interest or right by virtue of or in connection with paragraph (1).

(3)   In this article a "transferred obligation" means an obligation, covenant, undertaking or restriction under a contract, agreement or arrangement transferred to Abbey under article 16(1)(c) or treated as made or done by or in relation to Abbey in accordance with article 25(a).

[984]

NOTES
Commencement: 29 September 2008 (at 8.00 am).

23 Foreign property etc

Bradford & Bingley must take such steps as are reasonably requested by Abbey for securing the vesting in Abbey under the relevant foreign law of any foreign property, foreign rights or liabilities expressed to be transferred by article 16.

[985]

NOTES
Commencement: 29 September 2008 (at 8.00 am).

24 Subsequent transactions

(1) To the extent that any property, rights or liabilities—
    (a) transferred by Bradford & Bingley to Abbey in connection with the second transfer do not relate mainly to the retail deposit business or to any property, rights or liabilities transferred to Abbey by article 16(1)(b) or (d); or
    (b) retained by Bradford & Bingley after the second transfer time relate mainly to the retail deposit business or to any property, rights or liabilities transferred to Abbey by article 16(1)(b) or (d),

the Treasury Solicitor and Abbey shall procure that such property, rights and liabilities are promptly transferred for no further consideration to Bradford & Bingley or Abbey as appropriate.

(2) This article shall not apply to any contract of employment or qualifying financial contract.

(3) Articles 18 to 22 apply to any transfer made under this article as they apply to the second transfer.

(4) For the purposes of this article "qualifying financial contract" means any agreement entered into either with the purpose of borrowing or lending money (not being a retail deposit), or in connection with a transaction on the financial markets, including (howsoever documented) any loan agreement, securities contract, derivative contract, commodities contract, forward contract, repurchase contract, swap agreement, margin lending agreement and master agreement.

[986]

NOTES
Commencement: 29 September 2008 (at 8.00 am).

25 Construction of documents etc

As from the second transfer time, and save as otherwise provided in this Order—
    (a) agreements made or other things done by or in relation to Bradford & Bingley shall be treated, so far as may be necessary for the purposes of or in connection with the second transfer, but not otherwise, as made or done by or in relation to Abbey, as the case may be; and
    (b) references to Bradford & Bingley, or to any officer or employee of Bradford & Bingley, in instruments or documents relating to the property, rights and liabilities transferred by or under article 16 shall have effect as if they were references to Abbey, or to any officer or employee of Abbey, as the case may be.

[987]

NOTES
Commencement: 29 September 2008 (at 8.00 am).

26 Pensions

Schedule 3 shall have effect.

[988]

NOTES
Commencement: 29 September 2008 (at 8.00 am).

27 Employees

(1) The Transfer of Undertakings (Protection of Employment) Regulations 2006 (the "transfer regulations") and sections 257 and 258 of the Pensions Act 2004 shall apply upon the second transfer on the basis that any individual other than a director of Bradford & Bingley who is employed by a relevant undertaking and—
    (a) whose work relates wholly or mainly to—

  (i)   the retail deposit business of Bradford and Bingley; or
  (ii) any property, rights or liabilities transferred to Abbey by article 16(1)(b) or (d); or
  (b)   whose normal place of work is any real property transferred by article 16(1)(b),

is assigned to the organised grouping of resources or employees that is subject to the relevant transfer.

(2)   Paragraph (1) is without prejudice to the application of the transfer regulations or sections 257 and 258 of the Pensions Act 2004 in respect of any individual not referred to in that paragraph.

                                                                                                              [989]

NOTES
Commencement: 29 September 2008 (at 8.00 am).

PART 6
FINANCIAL SERVICES COMPENSATION SCHEME

28   Sums to be paid to Abbey following the second transfer

(1)   The following liabilities arise on the occurrence of the second transfer—
  (a)   the FSCS is liable to pay, as soon as practicable, to Abbey an amount equal to the amount that qualifying claimants would, immediately before the first transfer time, have been entitled to claim from the FSCS in respect of claims against Bradford & Bingley for protected deposits; and
  (b)   the Treasury are liable to pay, as soon as practicable, to Abbey an amount equal to the aggregate amount of the liabilities transferred to Abbey under article 16(1)(a) less the amount specified in sub-paragraph (a) and less £612,000,000,

and the Treasury shall subsequently make the necessary adjustments such that Bradford & Bingley obtains the benefit of the reduction of £612,000,000 referred to in sub-paragraph (b).

(2)   For the purposes of paragraph (1)(a), if the quantification date for a claim would have been a date other than the date on which Bradford & Bingley was determined to be in default for the purposes of section 6.3 of the COMP Sourcebook, the amount that a qualifying claimant would have been entitled to claim from the FSCS is the lesser of—
  (a)   the amount which the FSCS quantifies as being the value of that claim as at immediately before the first transfer time; and
  (b)   the amount that would have been payable at the quantification date, if different, for that claim.

(3)   In paragraph (2), "quantification date" has the meaning given in rule 12.3.1 of the COMP Sourcebook.

(4)   Immediately after the second transfer time—
  (a)   Bradford & Bingley shall estimate the aggregate amount of the liabilities transferred to Abbey under article 16(1)(a);
  (b)   the FSCS shall pay to Abbey the amount it is liable to pay under paragraph (1)(a) as estimated by the Authority; and
  (c)   the Treasury shall pay to Abbey an amount equal to the amount estimated by Bradford & Bingley in accordance with sub-paragraph (a) less the amount estimated by the Authority in accordance with sub-paragraph (b) and less £612,000,000.

(5)   From time to time—
  (a)   the FSCS may revise the estimate of its liability under paragraph (1)(a); and
  (b)   Bradford & Bingley may revise the estimate of the aggregate amount of the liabilities transferred to Abbey under article 16(1)(a),

and the FSCS, the Treasury and Abbey shall make such corresponding payments to each other as are necessary to ensure that the FSCS and the Treasury have each paid to Abbey the amount required to meet their liability under paragraph (1) (and no more than such amount).

(6)   The liability referred to in paragraph (1)(a) shall be assessed by the FSCS and, in doing so, the FSCS may calculate, by any methodology or approach it considers appropriate, the total amounts of compensation that would have been paid to all qualifying claimants, if (and to the extent that) it considers that the costs of ascertaining the entitlement to and amount of compensation by reference to each qualifying claimant would exceed or be disproportionate to the benefit of doing so.

                                                                                                              [990]

NOTES
Commencement: 29 September 2008 (at 8.00 am).

PART IV
OTHER STATUTORY INSTRUMENTS

29 Payment to Abbey to constitute payment of compensation for the purposes of the Financial Services Compensation Scheme

For the purposes of Part 15 (the financial services compensation scheme) of the 2000 Act, the COMP Sourcebook and the FEES 6 Chapter (including, without limitation, the power of the FSCS to impose levies)—

(a) all payments by the FSCS to Abbey under article 28 shall constitute the payment of compensation to each qualifying claimant under the Financial Services Compensation Scheme in accordance with their respective entitlements in respect of claims against Bradford & Bingley for protected deposits;

(b) each qualifying claimant—

(i) is deemed to have made an application for compensation for the purposes of rule 3.2.1(1) of the COMP Sourcebook; and

(ii) is deemed to have accepted an offer of compensation made by the FSCS and to have received payment of such compensation for the purposes of rule 11.2.1 of the COMP Sourcebook,

and, accordingly, a qualifying claimant has no right to claim, and the FSCS has no obligation to pay, for a protected deposit any further compensation under the Financial Services Compensation Scheme in respect of the default of Bradford & Bingley determined by the Authority under section 6.3 of the COMP Sourcebook.

[991]

NOTES

Commencement: 29 September 2008 (at 8.00 am).

30 Liability of Bradford & Bingley to the FSCS and the Treasury

(1) Bradford & Bingley is liable to the FSCS in respect of an amount equal to the aggregate of—

(a) the amount which the FSCS is liable to pay under article 28(1)(a); and

(b) the amount which the Treasury are liable to pay under article 28(1)(b).

(2) Bradford & Bingley, the FSCS and the Treasury shall agree terms on which, subject to paragraph (6), the amount of Bradford & Bingley's liability to the FSCS under paragraph (1) is to be reduced out of excess cash flow and other proceeds.

(3) The FSCS shall determine the proportion of any amount which it receives or recovers from Bradford & Bingley which is properly attributable to each type of liability described below and shall promptly on receipt account to the Treasury as follows—

(a) in full, where the liability is a liability which has been transferred under article 16(1)(a) and the person to whom such transferred liability is owed would not have been entitled to make a claim for compensation from the FSCS immediately before the first transfer time; and

(b) up to the amount of the excess, where the liability is a liability owed by Bradford & Bingley to a qualifying claimant and the amount of such liability exceeds the maximum compensation that the qualifying claimant would have been entitled to claim from the FSCS immediately before the first transfer time,

and, where the liability is a liability owed by Bradford and Bingley to a qualifying claimant and the amount of such liability is equal to or less than the maximum compensation that the qualifying claimant would have been entitled to claim from the FSCS immediately before the first transfer time, that amount shall be for the account of the FSCS.

(4) Once all the assets of Bradford & Bingley have been realised and distributed, if the claim of the FSCS against Bradford & Bingley has not been satisfied in full, Bradford & Bingley's liability for the shortfall shall be extinguished, without prejudice to any claim the FSCS may have against any other party.

(5) The FSCS shall not take or join in any corporate action or other steps or legal proceedings for the winding-up, dissolution or re-organisation or for the appointment of an administrator, liquidator or similar appointment in respect of Bradford & Bingley, or any analogous step or proceeding in any other jurisdiction.

(6) Nothing in this Part shall have the effect that the FSCS recovers less than it would have recovered if this Order had not been made and Bradford and Bingley had gone into liquidation following the declaration of default by the Authority in relation to Bradford and Bingley for the purposes of section 6.3 of the COMP Sourcebook.

[992]

NOTES

Commencement: 29 September 2008 (at 8.00 am).

31   Co-operation with the FSCS

(1)   Bradford & Bingley and Abbey must each—

(a)   comply with any request of the FSCS for the provision of information; and

(b)   provide the FSCS with any other information which Bradford & Bingley or Abbey, as the case may be, considers may be useful for the purpose of co-operating in the fulfilment of the FSCS's functions under the COMP Sourcebook and the FEES 6 Chapter.

(2)   Nothing in this article affects the power of the FSCS to require information under section 219 of the 2000 Act (scheme manager's power to require information).

[993]

NOTES

Commencement: 29 September 2008 (at 8.00 am).

32   Statutory immunity

For the purposes of section 222 (statutory immunity) of the 2000 Act the scheme manager's functions shall include any acts or omissions carried out by the FSCS pursuant to or in connection with this Order.

[994]

NOTES

Commencement: 29 September 2008 (at 8.00 am).

PART 7
TRANSITIONAL PROVISIONS

33   Services and facilities

The agreement dated 29th September [2008] between the Treasury and Abbey relating to the provision of transitional services by Bradford & Bingley and Abbey to one another shall bind Bradford & Bingley as if it were a party.

[995]

NOTES

Commencement: 29 September 2008 (at 8.00 am).
Year in square brackets substituted by the Bradford & Bingley plc Transfer of Securities and Property etc (Amendment) Order 2009, SI 2009/320, art 2(1), (3), as from 20 February 2009.

34   Use of the Bradford & Bingley brand by Abbey

Bradford & Bingley shall grant to Abbey a non-exclusive royalty-free licence for a period of three years to use the Bradford & Bingley brand for the purposes of carrying on the business transferred to Abbey by the second transfer.

[996]

NOTES

Commencement: 29 September 2008 (at 8.00 am).

35   Termination etc of interest or right

(1)   Except with the consent of the Treasury or the permission of the court, during the transitional period—

(a)   no person is entitled—

(i)   to terminate or modify any contract or agreement, or any right or obligation under any contract or agreement where such contract or agreement is for the services and facilities reasonably required by—

(aa)   Bradford & Bingley to carry on the business retained by it after the second transfer; or

(bb)   Abbey to carry on the retail deposit business, or

(ii)   to treat such a contract, agreement, right, obligation or interest as terminated or modified,

by virtue of or in connection with the first or second transfer; and

(b)   any counterparty to such contract or agreement must perform their obligations in accordance with that contract or agreement.

(2)   Any purported termination or modification of any contract, agreement, right, obligation or interest in contravention of paragraph (1), and any action taken in consequence of any such purported termination or modification, shall have no effect.

(3)   Paragraph (1) does not apply where—

    (a)   Bradford & Bingley or Abbey, as the case may be, has failed to perform its payment obligations under the relevant contract or agreement and such non-payment is not remedied within 7 days of Bradford & Bingley becoming aware of the non-performance; or

    (b)   Bradford & Bingley or Abbey, as the case may be, fails to notify the counterparty to the relevant contract or agreement within 14 days of his becoming aware of the request for consent to such termination, modification or non-performance of an obligation, that such consent has been withheld.

(4)   Without prejudice to the generality of paragraph (1), neither the first nor second transfer shall have the effect of terminating or otherwise changing the terms of Bradford & Bingley's membership of any payment system, including, in particular, BACS, CHAPS and the LINK payments systems.

(5)   This article is subject to any requirement of Community law.

[997]

NOTES
Commencement: 29 September 2008 (at 8.00 am).

36 Provision of information

Bradford & Bingley shall provide Abbey with such information as is reasonably requested by Abbey in relation to anything transferred by or under article 16.

[998]

NOTES
Commencement: 29 September 2008 (at 8.00 am).

PART 8
SUPPLEMENTARY

37 Modification to Authority's rule-making power

(1)   Subsections (1) and (1A) of section 138 of the 2000 Act (general rule-making power) have effect as if modified by inserting after "protecting the interests of consumers"—
      "or for the purposes of, to facilitate or in consequence of, a transfer under section 3 or 8 of the Banking (Special Provisions) Act 2008".

(2)   Section 148(2) of the 2000 Act (modification or waiver of rules) shall also apply in relation to a relevant undertaking—
    (a)   in the absence of an application by a person subject to rules made by the Authority; and
    (b)   without any requirement for the consent of such a person.

(3)   Section 148(4) of the 2000 Act shall not prevent the Authority from modifying or waiving rules in relation to a relevant undertaking under section 148 of that Act provided that the Authority is satisfied that the modification or waiver is necessary for the purposes of, to facilitate or in consequence of the first or second transfer.

[999]

NOTES
Commencement: 29 September 2008 (at 8.00 am).

38 Modification to Authority's duty to consult on rule changes

(1)   Section 155(7) of the 2000 Act (consultation) has effect as if modified by adding at the end—
      "or if it is making rules for the purposes of, or to facilitate or in consequence of, a transfer under section 3 or 8 of the Banking (Special Provisions) Act 2008."

(2)   Section 157 of the 2000 Act (guidance) has effect as if modified by adding after subsection (3)—

    "(3A) Section 155(7) applies to proposed guidance as it applies to proposed rules with the modification made by article 39(1) of the Bradford & Bingley plc Transfer of Securities and Property etc Order 2008.".

[1000]

NOTES
Commencement: 29 September 2008 (at 8.00 am).

39   Modification of provision on liability in relation to operator's functions

(1)   Section 291 of the 2000 Act (liability in relation to recognised body's regulatory functions) shall have effect for the purposes of this Order as if the following modifications are made.

(2)   In subsection (1)—
    (a)   after "its officers and staff" add "and an operator and its officers and staff";
    (b)   after "recognised body's" add "or the operator's".

(3)   In subsection (3) at the end add—

"and the functions of the operator so far as relating to, or matters arising out of, the obligations to which the operator is subject under the Bradford & Bingley plc Transfer of Securities and Property etc Order 2008.

    (4)   In this section, "operator" has the meaning given in the Uncertificated Securities Regulations 2001.".

[1001]

NOTES
Commencement: 29 September 2008 (at 8.00 am).

40   Enterprise Act 2002

Part 3 of the Enterprise Act 2002 (mergers) shall not apply to the first or second transfer save insofar as it gives effect to an obligation under Community law.

[1002]

NOTES
Commencement: 29 September 2008 (at 8.00 am).

41   Freedom of information

For the purposes of section 3 of the Freedom of Information Act 2000 (public authorities), while Bradford & Bingley is wholly owned by the Treasury, a relevant undertaking shall be deemed—
    (a)   not to be a publicly-owned company for the purposes of subsection (1)(b);
    (b)   not to hold information on behalf of the Treasury for the purposes of subsection (2)(b).

[1003]

NOTES
Commencement: 29 September 2008 (at 8.00 am).

42   Notification requirement

(1)   The Treasury must notify the Authority of the making of this Order.

(2)   A notification under paragraph (1)—
    (a)   may be given by such means as the Treasury consider appropriate;
    (b)   must be given to the Authority as soon as reasonably practicable after the first transfer time.

[1004]

NOTES
Commencement: 29 September 2008 (at 8.00 am).

SCHEDULES

SCHEDULE 1
SHADOW DIRECTORSHIP

Article 13

1.   The following provisions of the Insolvency Act 1986—
    (a)   section 288 (register of directors);
    (b)   section 305 (directors' names on correspondence, etc);
    (c)   section 317 (disclosure of interests in contracts).

2.   The following provisions of the 2006 Act—
    (a)   section 84 (criminal consequences of failure to make required disclosure);
    (b)   section 162 (register of directors);
    (c)   section 165 (register of directors' residential addresses);
    (d)   section 167 (duty to notify registrar of changes);
    (e)   sections 170 to 177 (general duties of directors);
    (f)   sections 182 to 186 (declaration of interest in existing transaction) as applied to shadow directors by section 187;

(g)   sections 188 and 189 (directors' service contracts);
(h)   sections 190 to 196 (substantial property transactions);
(i)   sections 197 to 214 (loans etc to directors);
(j)   sections 215 to 222 (payments for loss of office) as applied to shadow directors by section 223(2);
(k)   sections 227 to 230 (directors' service contracts);
(l)   section 231 (contracts with sole members who are directors);
(m)   sections 260 to 269 (derivative claims in England and Wales and Northern Ireland);
(n)   sections 854 to 859 (annual return).

3.   The following provisions of the 1986 Act—
(a)   section 214 (wrongful trading);
(b)   section 249 ("connected" with a company).

4.   The following provisions of the 2000 Act—
(a)   section 96A (disclosure of information requirements);
(b)   section 96B (disclosure rules: persons responsible for compliance).

[1005]

NOTES
Commencement: 29 September 2008 (at 8.00 am).
Note: paras 1, 3 above have been reproduced in accordance with the Queen's Printer's copy. It is understood that there is a drafting error and that the references in paras 1 and 3 are to the Companies Act 1985 and the Insolvency Act 1986 respectively.

SCHEDULE 2
PROPERTY, RIGHTS AND LIABILITIES OF BRADFORD & BINGLEY TRANSFERRED TO ABBEY
Article 16

1.   Subject to paragraph 2, all rights and liabilities in respect of retail deposits with Bradford & Bingley.

2.   The liabilities referred to in paragraph 1 shall not include any liability in respect of any breach of a contract with or other duty in relation to any customer of the retail deposit business arising before the second transfer time.

3.   All freehold and leasehold real property of a relevant undertaking relating to—
(a)   all retail deposit branches of Bradford & Bingley;
(b)   the operation of any branch-type agency of Bradford & Bingley; and
(c)   any other properties, including call-centres, which mainly relate to the operation of the retail deposit business of Bradford & Bingley.

4.   All contracts, agreements and other arrangements of Bradford & Bingley or a relevant undertaking which relate mainly to—
(a)   the retail deposit business of Bradford & Bingley; or
(b)   any property, rights or liabilities transferred to Abbey by article 16(1)(b) or (d), but excluding any contract of employment,
but excluding any qualifying financial contract within the meaning of article 24(4).

5.   Any personal property of a relevant undertaking—
(a)   situated within any real property transferred by article 16(1)(b); or
(b)   relating mainly to the retail deposit business of Bradford & Bingley.

6.   All intellectual property which relate to the operation of the retail deposit business of Bradford & Bingley except the Bradford & Bingley brand.

[1006]

NOTES
Commencement: 29 September 2008 (at 8.00 am).

SCHEDULE 3
PENSIONS
Article 26

1.   With effect from the segregation time the provisions of the pension scheme shall be modified so as to include a section ("the international section") which is divided from the remainder of the pension scheme ("the remaining section") such that—
(a)   the only employer in the international section shall be Bradford & Bingley International;
(b)   all members of the pension scheme who are in pensionable service with Bradford & Bingley International at the segregation time shall become members of the international section immediately following the segregation time;

(c) the contributions payable by Bradford & Bingley International and the members of the international section to the pension scheme shall be allocated to the international section; and

(d) the assets attributable to the international section cannot be used for the purposes of, or to meet any liabilities arising under, any other part of the pension scheme.

2. The liabilities of the international section shall be—

(a) the liabilities of the pension scheme existing at the segregation time that are attributable to pensionable service with Bradford & Bingley International including any liabilities attributable to a transfer received by the pension scheme during that pensionable service; and

(b) any liabilities arising after the segregation time by reason of—

(i) the continued pensionable service of the active members referred to in paragraph 1(b); or

(ii) the admission of new members after the segregation time in accordance with the terms of the international section from time to time.

3. At the segregation time, the following assets shall be allocated to the international section—

(a) the assets representing the value of any rights to money purchase benefits which are comprised within the liabilities mentioned in paragraph 2(a); and

(b) a proportion of the assets of the pension scheme determined in accordance with paragraph 4 at the segregation time.

4. The proportion shall be—

(a) comprised of a selection of assets of the pension scheme (excluding any assets representing the value of any rights to money purchase benefits) that the actuary reasonably considers to be representative of those assets; and

(b) equal in value to such proportion of the pension scheme's assets as the amount of the liabilities in paragraph 2(a) bears to the total amount of the pension scheme's liabilities.

5. For the purposes of paragraph 4(b)—

(a) any liabilities or assets representing the value of any rights to money purchase benefits under the pension scheme are to be left out of account;

(b) the value of any other liabilities is to be determined by the actuary—

(i) using the method and assumptions used to calculate the pension scheme's technical provisions for the purposes of Part 3 of the Pensions Act 2004; and

(ii) updating any economic and financial assumptions which are based on yields, rates or indices to take account of those yields, rates or indices as at the segregation time (or the latest practicable time prior to the segregation time); and

(c) the value of any asset is to be determined by such method as the actuary reasonably considers to be a proper means of providing a market value of that asset at the segregation time.

6. At the segregation time—

(a) Bradford & Bingley International shall cease to be an employer in the remaining section; and

(b) if it would otherwise apply, section 75 of the Pensions Act 1995 shall not apply to that cessation.

7.—(1) Following the segregation time Bradford & Bingley International shall have no liability, including any liability arising by virtue of sections 38 and 43 of the Pensions Act 2004, with regard to the liabilities of any part of the pension scheme (other than the international section) by reason of any fact, matter or circumstance occurring or existing prior to the second transfer time and accordingly no proceedings may be brought in respect of such matters.

(2) The Treasury may in writing—

(a) disapply sub-paragraph (1); and

(b) give consent to bring such proceedings.

8. Subject to this Schedule, the provisions of the international section (including any provisions as to amendment or termination) at the segregation time shall be identical to those of the remaining section, save that any reference in the pension scheme to Bradford & Bingley shall, in relation only to the international section, be taken to be a reference to Bradford & Bingley International.

9. No provision of the pension scheme shall apply if it would otherwise have the effect of requiring Bradford & Bingley International to cease participation in the scheme when it ceases to be associated with Bradford & Bingley.

10. The Treasury shall give a guarantee or make other arrangements for the purposes of securing that the assets of the remaining section are sufficient to meet its liabilities.

11. Unless otherwise stated or provided in the guarantee or arrangements mentioned in paragraph 10—

(a) that guarantee or those arrangements shall for the purposes of determining the application of any provision of pensions legislation be deemed to have been given or made at the guarantee time; and

(b) from the guarantee time until the time that such guarantee or arrangements have been given or made the following provisions shall not apply to the remaining section—
(i) section 75 of the Pensions Act 1995;
(ii) sections 38, 43 and 52 of the Pensions Act 2004; and
(iii) Part 3 (scheme funding) of the Pensions Act 2004.

12. Except as expressly provided in this Schedule, or to the extent necessary to give effect to article 27, or to the extent necessary to give effect to the Transfer of Undertakings (Protection of Employment) Regulations 2006—
(a) nothing in Part 7 transfers to Abbey, or to any party associated or connected with Abbey, any rights or liabilities in connection with any occupational pension scheme operated by any relevant undertaking; and
(b) article 23 shall not apply to any agreements, instruments, documents or other things related to any such scheme.

13. In this Schedule—
"the actuary" means the actuary appointed for the pension scheme in pursuance of subsection (1)(b) of section 47 of the Pensions Act 1995;
"the guarantee time" means the time immediately before the second transfer time;
"money purchase benefits" shall have the meaning given in section 181 of the Pension Schemes Act 1993;
"pensions legislation" shall have the meaning given in section 13 of the Pensions Act 2004;
"the pension scheme" means the Bradford & Bingley Staff Pension Scheme established by a trust deed and rules dated 24 April 1967;
"the segregation time" means the time immediately before the guarantee time.

[1007]

NOTES
Commencement: 29 September 2008 (at 8.00 am).

HERITABLE BANK PLC TRANSFER OF CERTAIN RIGHTS AND LIABILITIES ORDER 2008

(SI 2008/2644)

NOTES
Made: 7 October 2008 (9.27 am).
Authority: Banking (Special Provisions) Act 2008, ss 6, 12, 13(2), Sch 2.
Commencement: 7 October 2008 (9.30 am).
See also the Transfer of Rights and Liabilities to ING Order 2008, SI 2008/2666 at **[1046]**. That Order is also made under the Banking (Special Provisions) Act 2008 and provides for certain rights and liabilities to be transferred to ING. The transferred rights and liabilities are those, relating to certain accounts, which were transferred to Deposits Management (Holding) by virtue of this Order.

ARRANGEMENT OF ARTICLES

PART 1
GENERAL

PART 2
THE TRANSFER

PART 3
FINANCIAL SERVICES COMPENSATION SCHEME

PART 1
GENERAL

1 Citation and commencement

(1)   This Order may be cited as the Heritable Bank plc Transfer of Certain Rights and Liabilities Order 2008.

(2)   This Order comes into force at 9.30 am on 7 October 2008.

               [1008]

NOTES
    Commencement: 7 October 2008 (9.30 am).

---

2 Interpretation

In this Order—
    "the Act" means the Banking (Special Provisions) Act 2008;
    "the 1986 Act" means the Insolvency Act 1986;
    "the 2000 Act" means the Financial Services and Markets Act 2000;
    "administrator" means—
        (a)   an administrator appointed under paragraph 14 or 22 of Schedule B1 (Administration) to the 1986 Act or on an administration application made to the court (and if more than one administrator is appointed, the reference to "the administrator" is to any administrator so appointed); or
        (b)   any person on whom a discretion is conferred under an interim order made under paragraph 13(1)(d) of Schedule B1 to the 1986 Act;
    "the Authority" means the Financial Services Authority;
    "the Bank" means the Bank of England;
    "Community law" means—
        (c)   all the rights, powers, liabilities, obligations and restrictions from time to time created or arising by or under the Community Treaties; and
        (d)   all the remedies and procedures from time to time provided for by or under the Community Treaties;
    "the COMP Sourcebook" means the Compensation Sourcebook made by the Authority under the 2000 Act;
    "Deposits Management (Heritable)" means Deposits Management (Heritable) Limited, company registered number 6690442, a company which is for the purposes of the Act wholly owned by the Treasury;
    "the effective time" means the time this Order comes into force;

"eligible claimant" has the meaning given in rule 4.2.1 of the COMP Sourcebook;

"the FEES 6 Chapter" means Chapter 6 (Financial Services Compensation Scheme Funding) of the Fees Manual made by the Authority under the 2000 Act;

"the Financial Services Compensation Scheme" means the scheme established by the Authority under Part 15 of the 2000 Act (The Financial Services Compensation Scheme);

"FSCS" means the body corporate established by the Authority under section 212 of the 2000 Act (the Scheme Manager);

"Heritable" means Heritable Bank plc, company registered in Scotland number SC000717;

"protected deposit" has the meaning given in rule 5.3.1 of the COMP Sourcebook;

"relevant protected deposit" means a protected deposit which relates to a transferred account;

"the transfer" means the transfer effected by article 3;

"transferred accounts" means the accounts to which the transferred rights and liabilities relate;

"transferred liabilities" means the liabilities transferred by article 3(1);

"transferred rights" means the rights transferred by article 3(2);

"the transitional period" means the period of 6 months following the effective time.

[1009]

NOTES
Commencement: 7 October 2008 (9.30 am).

PART 2
THE TRANSFER

3 Transfer

(1)   Subject to paragraph (3), by virtue of this Order the liabilities of Heritable to depositors in respect of the principal of, and accrued interest on, relevant deposit accounts are transferred to Deposits Management (Heritable).

(2)   From the effective time, Deposits Management (Heritable) shall have the same rights in relation to depositors in relation to the transferred accounts as it would have if Heritable's relevant terms of business applied.

(3)   Paragraph (1) does not apply to any liability in respect of any breach of contract or other duty which arose before the effective time.

(4)   In paragraph (1), "relevant deposit accounts" means any of the following accounts operated by Heritable—
    (a)   1 Year Fixed Rate Bond;
    (b)   2 Year Fixed Rate Bond;
    (c)   3 Year Fixed Rate Bond;
    (d)   4 Year Fixed Rate Bond;
    (e)   5 Year Fixed Rate Bond;
    (f)   50 Plus Saver;
    (g)   60 Day Notice;
    (h)   90 Day Notice;
    (i)   120 Day Notice;
    (j)   Easy Access;
    (k)   Online Saver;
    (l)   Direct Saver.

(5)   The transfer under paragraph (1) takes place at the time this Order comes into force.

[1010]

NOTES
Commencement: 7 October 2008 (9.30 am).

4 No consent or concurrence required

The transfer is effective despite the absence of any required consent or concurrence to, or in connection with, the transfer.

[1011]

NOTES
Commencement: 7 October 2008 (9.30 am).

5 Associated liability and interference

(1)   The transfer takes effect as if—
    (a)   no associated liability existed in respect of any failure to comply with any requirement in respect of the transfer; and
    (b)   there were no associated interference with the transferred rights and liabilities.

(2)   In this article "associated liability" and "associated interference" have the meanings given in paragraph 2(2) of Schedule 2 to the Act.

[1012]

NOTES
Commencement: 7 October 2008 (9.30 am).

6   Interests, rights and liabilities of third parties relating to transferred rights and liabilities

(1)   No interest or right of any third party relating to any of the transferred rights and liabilities shall arise or become exercisable by virtue of or in connection with this Order.

(2)   Save as otherwise provided in this Order, no third party shall incur any liability, or be subject to any obligation, relating to any of the transferred rights and liabilities, by virtue of or in connection with this Order.

(3)   Without prejudice to the generality of paragraphs (1) and (2)—
    (a)   the consequences specified in paragraph (4) shall not arise in respect of any relevant instrument as a result of the transfer or any other thing done, or matter arising, by virtue of or in connection with article 3 of this Order;
    (b)   any circumstances which, but for sub-paragraph (a), would give rise to the consequences specified in paragraph (4) shall not be taken to have arisen for the purposes of any relevant instrument.

(4)   The consequences are—
    (a)   the termination of a relevant instrument or any rights or obligations under it;
    (b)   any right to terminate a relevant instrument or any right or obligation under it becoming exercisable;
    (c)   any amount becoming due and payable or capable of being declared due and payable;
    (d)   any other change in the amount or timing of any payment falling to be made or due to be received by any person;
    (e)   any right to withhold, net or set off any payment becoming exercisable;
    (f)   any event of default or breach of any right arising;
    (g)   any right not to advance any amount becoming exercisable;
    (h)   any obligation to provide or transfer any deposit or collateral;
    (i)   any right to give or withhold any consent or approval; or
    (j)   any other right or remedy (whether or not similar in kind to those referred to in paragraphs (a) to (i)) arising or becoming exercisable.

(5)   Without prejudice to paragraph (4), any provision in a relevant instrument that, as a result of the transfer or any other thing done, or matter arising, by virtue of or in connection with article 3 of this Order, provides for an obligation not to be created, suspends or extinguishes (in whole or in part) such an obligation or renders such an obligation subject to conditions, shall be of no effect.

(6)   In this article—
    "relevant instrument" has same meaning as in paragraph 4(3) of Schedule 1 to the Act and the specified connection referred to in paragraph 4(3)(c) of that Schedule is between Heritable and those undertakings whose assets and liabilities, profits and losses are consolidated in the consolidated accounts of Heritable;
    "third party" shall be construed in accordance with paragraph 2(3) of Schedule 2 to the Act.

[1013]

NOTES
Commencement: 7 October 2008 (9.30 am).

7   Payment of transferred liabilities

(1)   Deposits Management (Heritable) may without penalty or other charge pay any transferred liability prior to the due date for payment.

(2)   Where Deposits Management (Heritable), in pursuance of paragraph (1), pays a transferred liability prior to the due date for payment, Deposits Management (Heritable) may not rely on any transferred right or any other term of business of Heritable to reduce or modify the transferred liability by reason of the fact that payment is being made prior to the due date for payment.

(3)   Deposits Management (Heritable) shall not be obliged to pay any transferred liability sooner than is reasonably practicable.

[1014]

NOTES
Commencement: 7 October 2008 (9.30 am).

8   Construction of documents etc

As from the effective time and save as otherwise provided in this Order—

(a)   agreements made or other things done by or in relation to Heritable shall be treated, so far as may be necessary for the purposes of or in connection with the transfer (but not otherwise) as made or done by or in relation to Deposits Management (Heritable), as the case may be;

(b)   references to Heritable or to any officer or employee of Heritable in instruments or documents relating to the transferred rights and liabilities, shall have effect as if they were references to Deposits Management (Heritable), or to any officer or employee of Deposits Management (Heritable), as the case may be.

[1015]

NOTES

Commencement: 7 October 2008 (9.30 am).

9   Validity of acts done by Deposits Management (Heritable)

Anything done by or in relation to Deposits Management (Heritable) after the effective time for the purposes of or in connection with this Order which would have been effective had it been done by or in relation to Heritable prior to the effective time shall be effective.

[1016]

NOTES

Commencement: 7 October 2008 (9.30 am).

10   Exemption of Deposits Management (Heritable) Limited

Deposits Management (Heritable) is an exempt person for the purposes of the 2000 Act in respect of any regulated activity of the kind specified by article 5 of the Financial Services and Markets Act 2000 (Regulated Activities) Order 2001(accepting deposits).

[1017]

NOTES

Commencement: 7 October 2008 (9.30 am).

11   Provision of information and assistance

(1)   Heritable shall provide Deposits Management (Heritable) with such information and assistance as is reasonably requested by Deposits Management (Heritable)—

(a)   in relation to the transferred rights and liabilities;

(b)   for any purpose relating to this Order; or

(c)   for any purpose relating to any other function of Deposits Management (Heritable) which relate to its functions under this Order.

(2)   Heritable shall provide the Treasury with such information and assistance as is requested by the Treasury for any purposes relating to this Order.

[1018]

NOTES

Commencement: 7 October 2008 (9.30 am).

PART 3
FINANCIAL SERVICES COMPENSATION SCHEME

12   Application of Part 3

This Part applies where, before the effective time, Heritable is in default for the purposes of rule 6.3.1 of the COMP Sourcebook.

[1019]

NOTES

Commencement: 7 October 2008 (9.30 am).

13   Sums to be paid to Deposits Management (Heritable) following the transfer

(1)   The following liabilities arise at the effective time—

(a)   the FSCS is liable to pay (as soon as practicable) to Deposits Management (Heritable) an amount equal to the amount that eligible claimants would, immediately before the effective time, have been entitled to claim from the FSCS in respect of claims against Heritable in relation to relevant protected deposits; and

(b)   the Treasury are liable to pay (as soon as practicable) to Deposits Management

(Heritable) an amount equal to the aggregate amount of the liabilities transferred to Deposits Management (Heritable) under article 3 less the amount specified in sub-paragraph (a).

(2)   For the purposes of paragraph (1)(a), if the quantification date for a claim would have been a date other than the date on which Heritable was determined to be in default for the purposes of section 6.3 of the COMP Sourcebook, the amount that an eligible claimant would have been entitled to claim from the FSCS is the lesser of—

(a)   the amount which the FSCS quantifies as being the value of that claim as at immediately before the effective time; and

(b)   the amount that would have been payable at the quantification date, if different, for that claim.

(3)   In paragraph (2), "quantification date" has the meaning given in rule 12.3.1 of the COMP Sourcebook.

(4)   As soon as practicable after the effective time—

(a)   Heritable shall estimate the aggregate amount of the transferred liabilities;

(b)   the FSCS shall pay to Deposits Management (Heritable) the amount it is liable to pay under paragraph (1)(a) as estimated by the Authority; and

(c)   the Treasury shall pay to Deposits Management (Heritable) an amount equal to the amount estimated by Heritable in accordance with sub-paragraph (a) less the amount estimated by the Authority in accordance with sub-paragraph (b).

(5)   From time to time—

(a)   the FSCS may revise the estimate of its liability under paragraph (1)(a); and

(b)   Heritable may revise the estimate of the aggregate amount of the transferred liabilities,

and the FSCS, the Treasury and Deposits Management (Heritable) shall make such corresponding payments to each other as are necessary to ensure that the FSCS and the Treasury have each paid to Deposits Management (Heritable) the amount required (and no more than the required amount) to meet their liability under paragraph (1).

(6)   If at any time after the effective time Heritable is placed into administration or an interim order is made in relation to Heritable under paragraph 13(1)(d) of Schedule B1 to the 1986 Act, the references to Heritable in paragraphs (4) and (5) are to be treated as references to the administrator.

[(7)   The liability referred to in paragraph (1)(a) shall be assessed by the FSCS and, in so doing, the FSCS may calculate, by any methodology or approach it considers appropriate, the total amounts of compensation that would have been paid to all eligible claimants, if (and to the extent that) it considers that the costs of ascertaining the entitlement to and amount of compensation by reference to each qualifying claimant would exceed or be disproportionate to the benefit of doing so.]

[1020]

NOTES

Commencement: 7 October 2008 (9.30 am).

Para (7): added by the Transfer of Rights and Liabilities to ING Order 2008, SI 2008/2666, art 10(1), (2), as from 10.10 am on 8 October 2008.

See further, the Heritable Bank plc Transfer of Certain Rights and Liabilities (Amendment) Order 2009, SI 2009/310, art 2 which provides that if the Treasury, the FSCS, Heritable and ING agree that it is not appropriate or reasonable to make (or to continue to make) the revisions specified in paras (5)(a), (b) above, no revision (or no further revision) may be made under those provisions.

14   Payment to Deposits Management (Heritable) to constitute payment of compensation for the purposes of the Financial Services Compensation Scheme

For the purposes of Part 15 (the financial services compensation scheme) of the 2000 Act, the COMP Sourcebook and the FEES 6 Chapter (including, without limitation, the power of the FSCS to impose levies)—

(a)   all payments by the FSCS to Deposits Management (Heritable) under article 13 shall constitute the payment of compensation to each eligible claimant under the Financial Services Compensation Scheme in accordance with their respective entitlements in respect of claims against Heritable for relevant protected deposits;

(b)   each eligible claimant—

(i)   is deemed to have made an application for compensation for the purposes of rule 3.2.1(1) of the COMP Sourcebook; and

(ii)   is deemed to have accepted an offer of compensation made by the FSCS and to have received payment of such compensation for the purposes of rule 11.2.1 of the COMP Sourcebook,

and, accordingly, an eligible claimant has no right to claim, and the FSCS has no obligation to pay, for a relevant protected deposit any further compensation under the

Financial Services Compensation Scheme in respect of the default of Heritable determined by the Authority under section 6.3 of the COMP Sourcebook.

[1021]

NOTES
Commencement: 7 October 2008 (9.30 am).

15 Liability of Heritable to the FSCS and the Treasury

(1)   Heritable is liable to the FSCS in respect of an amount equal to the amount which would have been provable in the administration of Heritable in respect of the transferred liabilities had this Order not been made and had Heritable been placed in administration immediately before the [effective time].

(2)   The FSCS shall pursue recoveries from Heritable in respect of the liability incurred under paragraph (1) to the extent reasonably practicable.

(3)   Subject to paragraph (4), if an eligible claimant had, in relation to a relevant protected deposit, a liability to Heritable which would have been capable of being set-off against a liability of Heritable to that claimant in an administration [or liquidation] of Heritable (if that liability had not been transferred), the amount which [the FSCS is entitled to recover] in the administration [or liquidation] shall for the purposes of paragraph (1) be taken to be the sum of—
  (a)   the amount of the reduction in the depositor's liability to Heritable as a result of the application of set-off; and
  (b)   the amount which would have been recovered in respect of the balance of the claim (if any) provable in the administration [or liquidation] of Heritable.

(4)   Paragraph (3) applies only to the extent that its application does not have the effect that the other creditors of Heritable are in a worse position than they would have been had the set-off been applied.

(5)   The FSCS shall determine the proportion of any amount which it receives or recovers from Heritable which is properly attributable to each type of liability described below and shall promptly on receipt account for that receipt or recovery as follows—
  (a)   in full to the Treasury, to the extent that—
    (i)   the receipt is attributable to a transferred liability; and
    (ii)   the person to whom such transferred liability is owed would not have been entitled to make a claim for compensation from the FSCS immediately before the effective time;
  (b)   to the Treasury by reference to the relevant proportion, to the extent that—
    (i)   the receipt is attributable to a transferred liability;
    (ii)   the person to whom such transferred liability is owed is an eligible claimant; and
    (iii) the amount of such liability exceeds the maximum compensation that the eligible claimant would have been entitled to claim from the FSCS immediately before the effective time;
  (c)   for the account of the FSCS, to the extent that—
    (i)   the receipt is attributable to a transferred liability owed to an eligible claimant; and
    (ii)   the amount of such liability is equal to or less than the maximum compensation that the eligible claimant would have been entitled to claim from the FSCS immediately before the effective time.

(6)   In paragraph (5), the "relevant proportion" is the proportion of the total liabilities which arise under article 13(1) for which the Treasury are liable.

(7)   If Heritable is in administration or an interim order has been made in relation to Heritable under paragraph 13(1)(d) of Schedule B1 to the 1986 Act, the liability incurred under paragraph (1) shall not be treated as an expense of the administration under paragraph 99(3) of Schedule B1 of the 1986 Act, rule 2.67 of the Insolvency Rules 1986 or any analogous provision of the Insolvency (Scotland) Rules 1986.

(8)   Nothing in this Part shall have the effect that the FSCS recovers less than it would have recovered if this Order had not been made.

[1022]

NOTES
Commencement: 7 October 2008 (9.30 am).
Para (1): words in square brackets substituted by the Heritable Bank plc Transfer of Certain Rights and Liabilities (Amendment) Order 2009, SI 2009/310, art 4(1)(a), as from 20 February 2009.
Para (3): words in first, third and final pairs of square brackets inserted, and words in second pair of square brackets substituted, by the Transfer of Rights and Liabilities to ING Order 2008, SI 2008/2666, art 10(1), (3), as from 10.10 am on 8 October 2008.

16 FSCS's power to require information

(1)   The FSCS may, by notice in writing given to Deposits Management (Heritable), require it—
   (a)   to provide specified information or information of a specified description; or
   (b)   to produce specified documents or documents of a specified description.

(2)   Paragraph (1) only applies to information and documents the provision or production of which the FSCS considers to be necessary (or likely to be necessary) for the exercise of its functions under or by virtue of this Order.

(3)   Subsections (2), (4), (5) and (7) of section 219 of the 2000 Act (scheme manager's power to require information) apply to a requirement imposed under paragraph (1) as if it were a requirement imposed under that section.

[1023]

NOTES
   Commencement: 7 October 2008 (9.30 am).

17 Statutory immunity

For the purposes of section 222 (statutory immunity) of the 2000 Act the scheme manager's functions shall include any acts or omissions carried out by the FSCS pursuant to or in connection with this Order.

[1024]

NOTES
   Commencement: 7 October 2008 (9.30 am).

PART 4
THE ADMINISTRATOR AND TRANSITIONAL PROVISIONS

18 Application of this Part

This Part applies if after the effective time—
   (a)   Heritable is placed into administration; or
   (b)   an interim order in made in relation to Heritable under paragraph 13(1)(d) of Schedule B1 to the 1986 Act.

[1025]

NOTES
   Commencement: 7 October 2008 (9.30 am).

19 The administration

The relevant provisions of the 1986 Act, the Insolvency Rules 1986 and the Insolvency (Scotland) Rules 1986 shall apply to Heritable subject to the provisions of this Part.

[1026]

NOTES
   Commencement: 7 October 2008 (9.30 am).

20 Objectives etc of the administrator

(1)   This article only applies during the transitional period.

(2)   The administrator must perform his or her functions with the objectives ("the overriding objectives") of—
   (a)   ensuring that Heritable provides, and managing the affairs, business and property of Heritable to enable it to provide, the services and facilities reasonably required by Deposits Management (Heritable) to carry on its functions in relation to the transferred rights and liabilities; and
   (b)   ensuring that Heritable performs the other obligations imposed on it by or under this Order.

(3)   The administrator shall only perform his or her functions with the objective determined in accordance with paragraph 3 of Schedule B1 to the 1986 Act to the extent that such objective is not inconsistent with and does not interfere with the achievement of the overriding objectives.

(4)   Paragraph 3(2) of Schedule B1 to the 1986 Act only applies to the performance of the functions of the administrator to the extent that it is not inconsistent with and does not interfere with the achievement of the overriding objectives.

(5)   The Treasury may, by notice in writing, give a direction to the administrator specifying that an act (or omission) is required for the overriding objectives.

PART IV
OTHER STATUTORY INSTRUMENTS

(6)   The Treasury may also, by notice in writing, give a direction to the administrator requiring him or her to act (or not act) if the Treasury consider that it is necessary to give such a direction for the purposes of—

(a)   protecting or enhancing the stability of the financial systems of the United Kingdom;

(b)   protecting or enhancing public confidence in the stability of the banking system of the United Kingdom; or

(c)   protecting depositors.

(7)   The administrator must comply with any directions given under paragraph (5) or (6).

(8)   The services and facilities to which paragraph (2)(a) applies include (but are not limited to) the services and facilities specified in Schedule 1.

(9)   The administrator shall not be required to include any proposals for achieving the overriding objectives in any statement he or she makes under paragraph 49 (administrator's proposals) or paragraph 54 (revision of administrator's proposals) of Schedule B1 to the 1986 Act or to obtain approval of such proposals at any creditors' meeting or from the court.

(10)   The administrator shall not enter into a transaction or a series of transactions (whether related or not) to sell, lease, transfer or otherwise dispose of any property or right of Heritable having a value of more than £50 million at any time unless—

(a)   the court orders otherwise;

(b)   the Treasury gives its consent to the transaction; or

(c)   the sale, lease, transfer or disposal has been specifically approved at a meeting of creditors summoned under paragraph 51(1), 54(2) or 62 of Schedule B1 to the 1986 Act or by a creditors' committee constituted in accordance with rule 2.50 of the Insolvency Rules 1986 or any analogous provision of the Insolvency (Scotland) Rules 1986.

(11)   In this article, "court" means—

(a)   in England and Wales, the High Court;

(b)   in Scotland, the Court of Session;

(c)   in Northern Ireland, the High Court.

[1027]

NOTES

Commencement: 7 October 2008 (9.30 am).

21   Insolvency rules etc

Nothing in the 1986 Act, the Insolvency Rules 1986, the Insolvency (Scotland) Rules 1986 or any other enactment or rule of law shall operate to invalidate or prejudice any act or omission done under or pursuant to this Order or give rise to a claim against or impose any liability on Heritable or the administrator for any act or omission so done.

[1028]

NOTES

Commencement: 7 October 2008 (9.30 am).

22   Use of the Heritable brand

Heritable shall grant to Deposits Management (Heritable) a licence to use the Heritable brand during the transitional period for the purposes of Deposits Management (Heritable) carrying on its business in relation to the transferred rights and liabilities.

[1029]

NOTES

Commencement: 7 October 2008 (9.30 am).

23   Compensation payable to Heritable

(1)   The Treasury shall reimburse Heritable for the costs and expenses (including fees) properly incurred by the administrator during the transitional period in fulfilling his or her obligations under [article 20].

(2)   Paragraph (1) does not apply to any cost or expense which would have been incurred even if this Order had not been made.

[1030]

NOTES

Commencement: 7 October 2008 (9.30 am).

Para (1): words in square brackets substituted by the Heritable Bank plc Transfer of Certain Rights and Liabilities (Amendment) Order 2009, SI 2009/310, art 4(1)(b), (2), as from 9.30 am on 7 October 2008.

See further, the Heritable Bank plc Transfer of Certain Rights and Liabilities (Amendment) Order 2009, SI 2009/310, art 3 which provides that the reference to the Treasury in para (1) above shall, from the effective time (within the meaning of the Transfer of Rights and Liabilities to ING Order 2008, SI 2008/2666), have effect as if it was a reference to ING.

24 Continuity

(1)   During the transitional period, any person wishing to terminate or modify (or treat as terminated or modified) any contract or agreement with Heritable for services and facilities or any right or obligation under such a contract or agreement must give not less than 14 days prior written notice to the administrator and to Deposits Management (Heritable).

(2)   Except with the consent of the Treasury or the permission of the court, during the transitional period—
   (a)   no person is entitled—
      (i)   to terminate or modify any contract or agreement with Heritable for services and facilities, or any right or obligation under such a contract or agreement, where the contract or agreement or right or obligation relates to services or facilities which are reasonably required by—
         (aa)   Heritable to perform its duties under or pursuant to this Order;
         (bb)   the administrator to perform his or her duties under or pursuant to this Order; or
         (cc)   Deposits Management (Heritable) to carry on its functions in relation to the transferred rights and liabilities, or
      (ii)   to treat such a contract, agreement, right or obligation as terminated or modified, by virtue of or in connection with the transfer, the commencement of the administration in relation to Heritable or the making of an interim order in relation to Heritable under paragraph 13(1)(d) of Schedule B1 to the 1986 Act; and
   (b)   any counterparty to such a contract or agreement must perform his or her obligations in accordance with that contract or agreement.

(3)   The services and facilities to which paragraphs (1) and (2) apply include (but are not limited to) the services and facilities specified in Schedule 1.

(4)   Any purported termination or modification of any contract, agreement, right or obligation in contravention of paragraph (1) or (2), and any action taken in consequence of any such purported termination or modification, shall have no effect.

(5)   Paragraph (2) does not apply where—
   (a)   Heritable, Deposits Management (Heritable) or the administrator, as the case may be, has failed to perform its payment obligations under the relevant contract or agreement and such non-payment is not remedied within 14 days of that person becoming aware of the non-performance; or
   (b)   Heritable, Deposits Management (Heritable) or the administrator, as the case may be, fails to notify the counterparty to the relevant contract or agreement within 14 days of its becoming aware of the request for consent to such termination, modification or non-performance of an obligation, that such consent has been withheld.

(6)   Without prejudice to the generality of paragraph (2), the transfer shall not have the effect of terminating or otherwise changing the terms of Heritable's membership (if any) of any payment system, including, in particular, BACS, CHAPS and the LINK payments systems.

(7)   This article is subject to any requirement of Community law.

[1031]

NOTES
Commencement: 7 October 2008 (9.30 am).

25 Financial Ombudsman Scheme

For the purposes of section 227(2) (voluntary jurisdiction) of the 2000 Act, Deposits Management (Heritable) is deemed to be carrying on an activity to which the voluntary jurisdiction rules apply and is deemed to be participating in the ombudsman scheme.

[1032]

NOTES
Commencement: 7 October 2008 (9.30 am).

PART 5
MISCELLANEOUS

26 Shadow directorship

(1)   While Deposits Management (Heritable) is wholly owned by the Treasury (or to be regarded as wholly owned by the Treasury for the purposes of the Act), for the purposes of the provisions listed in Schedule 2 to this Order, none of the persons listed in paragraph (3) shall be regarded as a shadow director or (unless otherwise appointed as a director) a person discharging managerial responsibilities of Deposits Management (Heritable).

(2)   For the purposes of the definition of "director" in section 417 of the 2000 Act (definitions), none of the persons listed in paragraph (3) shall be regarded as a person in accordance with whose directions or instructions (not being advice given in a professional capacity) the directors of a relevant undertaking are accustomed to act while Deposits Management (Heritable) is wholly owned by the Treasury.

(3)   The persons are—
  (a)   a Minister of the Crown;
  (b)   the Treasury;
  (c)   the Treasury Solicitor;
  (d)   the Bank;
  (e)   persons—
        (i)   employed by or under; or
        (ii)   acting on behalf of,
        any of the persons listed in sub-paragraph (a) to (d).

[1033]

NOTES

Commencement: 7 October 2008 (9.30 am).

27 Modification to Authority's rule-making power

(1)   Subsections (1) and (1A) of section 138 of the 2000 Act (general rule-making power) have effect as if modified by inserting after "protecting the interests of consumers"—

"or for the purposes of, to facilitate or in consequence of, a transfer under section 6 of the Banking (Special Provisions) Act 2008".

(2)   Section 148(2) of the 2000 Act (modification or waiver of rules) shall also apply in relation to Heritable—
  (a)   in the absence of an application by a person subject to rules made by the Authority; and
  (b)   without any requirement for the consent of such a person.

(3)   Section 148(4) of the 2000 Act shall not prevent the Authority from modifying or waiving rules in relation to Heritable under section 148 of that Act provided that the Authority is satisfied that the modification or waiver is necessary for the purposes of, to facilitate or in consequence of the transfer.

[1034]

NOTES

Commencement: 7 October 2008 (9.30 am).

28 Modification to Authority's duty to consult on rule changes

(1)   Section 155(7) of the 2000 Act (consultation) has effect as if modified by adding at the end—

"or if it is making rules for the purposes of, or to facilitate or in consequence of, a transfer under section 6 of the Banking (Special Provisions) Act 2008."

(2)   Section 157 of the 2000 Act (guidance) has effect as if modified by adding after subsection (3)—

"(3A)   Section 155(7) applies to proposed guidance as it applies to proposed rules with the modification made by article 28 of the Heritable Bank plc Transfer of Certain Rights and Liabilities Order 2008.".

[1035]

NOTES

Commencement: 7 October 2008 (9.30 am).

29 Freedom of information

For the purposes of section 3 of the Freedom of Information Act 2000 (public authorities), Deposits Management (Heritable) shall be deemed—

    (a)   not to be a publicly-owned company for the purposes of subsection (1)(b);

    (b)   not to hold information on behalf of the Treasury or Treasury Solicitor for the purpose of subsection (2)(b).

[1036]

NOTES

Commencement: 7 October 2008 (9.30 am).

30   Proceedings against directors

(1)   No director of—

    (a)   Heritable; or

    (b)   Deposits Management (Heritable),

shall be liable in connection with the transfer or any other provisions of this Order and accordingly no proceedings may be brought (or, in Scotland, raised) against any such director in respect of such matters.

(2)   The Treasury may in writing—

    (a)   waive the effect of paragraph (1), and

    (b)   give consent to bring (or, in Scotland, raise) such proceedings against such directors.

(3)   Where paragraph (1) applies, section 232 of the Companies Act 2006 (provisions protecting directors from liability) shall not apply to a relevant undertaking.

(4)   In this article—

"director" means a person who was a director immediately before the effective time, whether or not he has ceased to be a director at the time when proceedings in respect of that liability commenced;

"proceedings" includes proceedings under Part 11 of the Companies Act 2006 (derivative claims and proceedings by members).

[1037]

NOTES

Commencement: 7 October 2008 (9.30 am).

31   Notification requirement

(1)   The Treasury must notify the Authority of the making of this Order.

(2)   A notification under paragraph (1)—

    (a)   may be given by such means as the Treasury consider appropriate;

    (b)   must be given to the Authority as soon as reasonably practicable after the effective time.

(3)   On receiving a notification under paragraph (1), the Authority must in turn notify any relevant EEA authority of the making of the Order.

(4)   A notification under paragraph (3)—

    (a)   may be given by such means as the Authority considers appropriate;

    (b)   must be given to the relevant EEA authority as soon as reasonably practicable after the Authority is notified under paragraph (1).

(5)   "Relevant EEA authority" means any regulatory authority in an EEA state that exercises functions in relation to any office or branch of the authorised deposit-taker in question in that state.

[1038]

NOTES

Commencement: 7 October 2008 (9.30 am).

32   Transfer of data

Any transfer of data under this Order is not to be taken to breach any restriction on disclosure of information, however imposed.

[1039]

NOTES

Commencement: 7 October 2008 (9.30 am).

SCHEDULES

SCHEDULE 1
SERVICES AND FACILITIES

Article 20

1.   Website hosting services or facilities.

2. Information technology services or facilities.

3. Back office processing services or facilities.

4. Call centre services or facilities.

5. Payment and clearing services or facilities.

[1040]

NOTES
Commencement: 7 October 2008 (9.30 am).

SCHEDULE 2
SHADOW DIRECTORSHIP

Article 26

1. The following provisions of the Companies Act 1985—
   (a)   section 317 of the (disclosure of interests in contracts);
   (b)   section 733 (offences by bodies corporate).

2. The following provisions of the Companies Act 2006—
   (a)   section 84 (criminal consequences of failure to make required disclosure);
   (b)   section 162 (register of directors);
   (c)   section 165 (register of directors' residential addresses);
   (d)   section 167 (duty to notify registrar of changes);
   (e)   sections 170 to 177 (general duties of directors);
   (f)   sections 182 to 186 (declaration of interest in existing transaction) as applied to shadow directors by section 187;
   (g)   sections 188 and 189 (directors' service contracts);
   (h)   sections 190 to 196 (substantial property transactions);
   (i)   sections 197 to 214 (loans etc to directors);
   (j)   sections 215 to 222 (payments for loss of office) as applied to shadow directors by section 223(2);
   (k)   sections 227 to 230 (directors' service contracts);
   (l)   section 231 (contracts with sole members who are directors);
   (m)   sections 260 to 269 (derivative claims in England and Wales and Northern Ireland);
   (n)   sections 854 to 859 (annual return).

3. The following provisions of the Insolvency Act 1986—
   (a)   section 214 (wrongful trading);
   (b)   section 249 ("connected" with a company).

4. The following provisions of the 2000 Act—
   (a)   section 96A (disclosure of information requirements);
   (b)   section 96B (disclosure rules: persons responsible for compliance).

[1041]

NOTES
Commencement: 7 October 2008 (9.30 am).

ENTERPRISE ACT 2002 (SPECIFICATION OF ADDITIONAL SECTION 58 CONSIDERATION) ORDER 2008

(SI 2008/2645)

NOTES
Made: 6 October 2008.
Authority: Enterprise Act 2002, ss 58(3), (4), 124(2), (4).
Commencement: 24 October 2008.

1   Citation, commencement and transitional provision

(1)   This Order may be cited as the Enterprise Act 2002 (Specification of Additional Section 58 Consideration) Order 2008 and shall come into force on 24th October 2008.

(2)   This Order shall apply in relation to cases under consideration by the OFT, OFCOM, the Commission or the Secretary of State before the making of this Order as well as cases under consideration on or after the making of this Order.

[1042]

NOTES
Commencement: 24 October 2008.

2 Amendment of section 58 of the Enterprise Act 2002

In section 58 of the Enterprise Act 2002 (specified considerations), after subsection (2C) insert—

"(2D) The interest of maintaining the stability of the UK financial system is specified in this section (other than for the purposes of sections 67 and 68 or references made, or deemed to be made, by the European Commission to the OFT under article 4(4) or 9 of the EC Merger Regulation)."

[1043]

NOTES
Commencement: 24 October 2008.

3 Amendment of sections 129 and 130 of the Enterprise Act 2002

(1) In section 129(1) of that Act (definitions), after the definition of "supply" and before the word "and" which follows it insert—
""the UK financial system" means the financial system in the United Kingdom;".

(2) In section 130 of that Act (index of defined expressions), in the table, after the entry for "The turnover in the United Kingdom of an enterprise" insert the following entry—
(a) in the first column, "The UK financial system", and
(b) in the second column "Section 129(1)".

[1044]

NOTES
Commencement: 24 October 2008.

4 Amendment of Schedule 8 to the Enterprise Act 2002

In Schedule 8 of that Act (provision that may be contained in certain enforcement orders), after paragraph 20A insert—

"Maintaining the stability of the UK financial system

20B.—(1) This paragraph applies for the purposes of a relevant order under paragraph 5, 10 or 11 of Schedule 7 (enforcement orders in cases relating to the stability of the UK financial system) but not for any other purposes of Part 3 or 4 or any other enactment.

(2) The order may make such provision as the person making the order considers to be appropriate in the interest of maintaining the stability of the UK financial system.

(3) Such provision may, in particular, include provision requiring a person to do, or not to do, particular things.

(4) This paragraph is without prejudice to the operation of the other paragraphs of this Schedule in relation to the order.

(5) In this paragraph "relevant order" means an order—
(a) which is to be made following the giving of an intervention notice or special intervention notice which mentions the consideration specified in section 58(2D) (including, in the case of a notice given before the consideration was so specified, an intervention notice which mentions the consideration as a consideration which ought to be specified in section 58); and
(b) to which the consideration is still relevant.".

[1045]

NOTES
Commencement: 24 October 2008.

TRANSFER OF RIGHTS AND LIABILITIES TO ING ORDER 2008

(SI 2008/2666)

NOTES
Made: 8 October 2008 (10.00 am).
Authority: Banking (Special Provisions) Act 2008, ss 6, 8, 12, 13(2), Sch 2.
Commencement: 8 October 2008 (10.10 am).

ARRANGEMENT OF ARTICLES

PART 1
GENERAL

PART 2
THE TRANSFER

PART 3
FINANCIAL SERVICES COMPENSATION SCHEME

PART 4
MISCELLANEOUS

PART 1
GENERAL

1 Citation and commencement

(1)   This Order may be cited as the Transfer of Rights and Liabilities to ING Order 2008.

(2)   This Order comes into force at 10.10 am on 8th October 2008.

[1046]

NOTES

Commencement: 8 October 2008 (10.10 am).

2 Interpretation: general

In this Order—

"the 2000 Act" means the Financial Services and Markets Act 2000;

"the Act" means the Banking (Special Provisions) Act 2008;

"the Authority" means the Financial Services Authority;

"the Companies Acts" has the meaning given by section 2 of the Companies Act 2006;

"Deposits Management (Heritable)" means Deposits Management (Heritable) Limited, company registered number 6690442, a company which is for the purposes of the Act wholly owned by the Treasury;

"the effective time" means the time this Order comes into force;

"the Financial Services Compensation Scheme" means the scheme established by the Authority under Part 15 (the financial services compensation scheme) of the 2000 Act;

"the first Order" means the Heritable Bank plc Transfer of Certain Rights and Liabilities Order 2008;

"FSCS" means the body corporate established by the Authority under section 212 (the scheme manager) of the 2000 Act;

"Heritable" means Heritable Bank plc, company registered in Scotland number SC000717;

"ING" means ING Direct NV, incorporated in the Netherlands and acting through its branch in the United Kingdom, branch reference number BR 7357;

"the transfer" means the transfer effected under article 3(1);

"the transitional period" means the period of 6 months beginning with the date of this Order.

[1047]

NOTES
Commencement: 8 October 2008 (10.10 am).

PART 2
THE TRANSFER

3   The transfer

(1)   By virtue of this Order all the rights and liabilities transferred to Deposits Management (Heritable) by article 3 of the first Order are transferred to ING.

(2)   From the effective time, ING shall—

   (a)   have the same rights and obligations in relation to depositors in relation to the transferred accounts as it would have if Heritable's relevant terms of business applied; and

   (b)   be liable to pay to depositors any accrued interest on the transferred accounts as at the time of coming into force of the first Order and any interest accruing after that time on those accounts.

(3)   In paragraph (2) "transferred accounts" has the same meaning as in the first Order.

(4)   Paragraph (1) does not apply to any liability in respect of any breach of contract or other duty which arose before the effective time.

(5)   The transfer under paragraph (1) takes place at the effective time.

[1048]

NOTES
Commencement: 8 October 2008 (10.10 am).

4   No consent or concurrence required

The transfer is effective despite the absence of any required consent or concurrence to or with the transfer.

[1049]

NOTES
Commencement: 8 October 2008 (10.10 am).

5   Associated liability and interference

(1)   The transfer takes effect as if—

   (a)   no associated liability existed in respect of any failure to comply with any requirement in respect of the transfer; and

   (b)   there were no associated interference with the rights and liabilities transferred.

(2)   In this article, "associated liability" and "associated interference" have the meanings given in paragraph 2(2) of Schedule 2 to the Act.

[1050]

NOTES
Commencement: 8 October 2008 (10.10 am).

6   Interests, rights and liabilities of third parties relating to property, rights and liabilities transferred

(1)   No interest or right of any third party relating to any right or liability transferred by article 3, shall arise or become exercisable by virtue of or in connection with this Order.

(2)   Save as otherwise provided in this Order, no third party shall, by virtue of or in connection with this Order, incur any liability or be subject to any obligation relating to any right or liability transferred by article 3.

(3)   Without prejudice to the generality of paragraphs (1) and (2)—

   (a)   the consequences specified in paragraph (4) shall not arise in respect of any relevant instrument as a result of the transfer or any other thing done, or matter arising, by virtue of or in connection with the transfer; and

   (b)   any circumstances which, but for sub-paragraph (a), would give rise to the consequences specified in paragraph (4) shall be taken not to have arisen for the purposes of any relevant instrument.

(4)   The consequences are—

   (a)   the termination of a relevant instrument or any rights or obligations under it;

   (b)   any right to terminate a relevant instrument or any right or obligation under it becoming exercisable;

   (c)   any amount becoming due and payable or capable of being declared due and payable;

   (d)   any other change in the amount or timing of any payment falling to be made or due to be received by any person;

   (e)   any right to withhold, net or set off any payment becoming exercisable;

   (f)   any event of default or breach of any right arising;

   (g)   any right not to advance any amount becoming exercisable;

   (h)   any obligation to provide or transfer any deposit or collateral;

   (i)   any right to give or withhold any consent or approval; or

   (j)   any other right or remedy (whether or not similar in kind to those referred to in sub-paragraphs (a) to (i)) arising or becoming exercisable.

   (5)   Without prejudice to paragraph (4), any provision in a relevant instrument that, as a result of the transfer or any other thing done, or matter arising, by virtue of or in connection with the transfer, provides for an obligation not to be created, suspends or extinguishes (in whole or in part) such an obligation or renders such an obligation subject to conditions, shall be of no effect.

   (6)   In this article—

   "relevant instrument" has the same meaning as in paragraph 4(3) of Schedule 1 to the Act and the specified connection referred to in paragraph 4(3)(c) of that Schedule is between Heritable and those undertakings whose assets and liabilities, profits and losses are consolidated in the consolidated accounts of Heritable; and

   "third party" shall be construed in accordance with paragraph 2(3) of Schedule 2 to the Act.

[1051]

NOTES
Commencement: 8 October 2008 (10.10 am).

7 Construction of documents etc

As from the effective time, and save as otherwise provided in this Order—

   (a)   agreements made or other things done by or in relation to Heritable shall be treated, so far as may be necessary for the purposes of or in connection with the transfer, but not otherwise, as made or done by or in relation to ING, as the case may be; and

   (b)   references to Heritable, or to any officer or employee of Heritable, in instruments or documents relating to the rights and liabilities transferred by or under article 3 shall have effect as if they were references to ING, or to any officer or employee of ING, as the case may be.

[1052]

NOTES
Commencement: 8 October 2008 (10.10 am).

8 Provision of information and assistance

Heritable shall provide ING with such information and assistance as is reasonably requested by ING—

   (a)   in relation to the rights and liabilities transferred by article 3;

   (b)   for any purpose relating to this Order;

   (c)   for any purpose relating to any other function of ING which relates to its functions under this Order.

[1053]

NOTES
Commencement: 8 October 2008 (10.10 am).

PART 3
FINANCIAL SERVICES COMPENSATION SCHEME

9 Sum to be paid to ING following the transfer

   (1)   Deposits Management (Heritable) is liable to pay (as soon as practicable after the effective time) to ING an amount equal to the aggregate amount of the liabilities transferred to ING under article 3 less £1,000,000.

   (2)   The Treasury shall subsequently make the necessary adjustments such that Heritable obtains the benefit of the reduction of £1,000,000 referred to in paragraph (1) less the total of all costs and liabilities incurred by Deposits Management (Heritable) in performing its obligations under this Order or the first Order.

[1054]

10   (*Amends the Heritable Bank plc Transfer of Certain Rights and Liabilities Order 2008, SI 2008/2644, arts 13, 15 at* **[1020]**, **[1022]**.)

11 Balancing payments

(1)   Any payment which is required to be made pursuant to article 13(5) of the first Order by or to Deposits Management (Heritable) after the effective time shall be made by or, as the case may be, to ING.

(2)   Deposits Management (Heritable) shall have no obligation to make or, as the case may be, right to receive any such payment.

[1055]

NOTES
Commencement: 8 October 2008 (10.10 am).

12 Payment by the FSCS to ING

Any payment by the FSCS to ING pursuant to article 11 shall for the purposes of article 14(a) of the first Order be deemed to be a payment by the FSCS to Deposits Management (Heritable) under article 13(5) of the first Order.

[1056]

NOTES
Commencement: 8 October 2008 (10.10 am).

13 FSCS power to require information

(1)   The FSCS may, by notice in writing given to ING, require it—
    (a)   to provide specified information or information of a specified description; or
    (b)   to produce specified documents or documents of a specified description.

(2)   Paragraph (1) only applies to information and documents the provision or production of which the FSCS considers to be necessary (or likely to be necessary) for the exercise of its functions under or by virtue of this Order or the first Order.

(3)   Subsections (2), (4), (5) and (7) of section 219 of the 2000 Act (scheme manager's power to require information) apply to a requirement imposed under paragraph (1) as if it were a requirement imposed under that section.

[1057]

NOTES
Commencement: 8 October 2008 (10.10 am).

14 Statutory immunity

For the purposes of section 222 (statutory immunity) of the 2000 Act the scheme manager's functions shall include any acts or omissions carried out by the FSCS pursuant to or in connection with this Order.

[1058]

NOTES
Commencement: 8 October 2008 (10.10 am).

PART 4
MISCELLANEOUS

15 Transitional provisions

Part 4 of the first Order (except for article 22) shall apply from the effective time with the substitution for references to Deposits Management (Heritable) of references to ING.

[1059]

NOTES
Commencement: 8 October 2008 (10.10 am).

16 Services and facilities

The agreement dated 8th October 2008 between the Treasury and ING relating to the provision of transitional services by Heritable to ING shall bind Heritable as if it were a party.

[1060]

NOTES
Commencement: 8 October 2008 (10.10 am).

17 Business continuity

(1) During the transitional period, any person who provides to Heritable, pursuant to any contract or agreement, services or facilities which are reasonably required by Heritable to perform its duties under or pursuant to this Order or the agreement referred to in article 16 shall—

(a) provide such services to Heritable for the benefit of ING; or

(b) if so requested by Heritable, provide such services direct to ING.

(2) No such person shall, without the consent of the Treasury or permission of the Court, during the transitional period, terminate or modify any such contract or agreement, or treat it as terminated or modified, by virtue or in connection with the requirement under this article to provide services or facilities to or for the benefit of ING.

[1061]

NOTES
Commencement: 8 October 2008 (10.10 am).

18 Modification to Authority's rule-making power

(1) Subsections (1) and (1A) of section 138 of the 2000 Act (general rule-making power) have effect as if modified by inserting after "protecting the interests of consumers"—

"or for the purposes of, to facilitate or in consequence of, a transfer under section 6 or 8 of the Banking (Special Provisions) Act 2008".

(2) Section 148(2) of the 2000 Act (modification or waiver of rules) shall also apply in relation to ING—

(a) in the absence of an application by a person subject to rules made by the Authority; and

(b) without any requirement for the consent of such a person.

(3) Section 148(4) of the 2000 Act shall not prevent the Authority from modifying or waiving rules in relation to ING under section 148 of that Act provided that the Authority is satisfied that the modification or waiver is necessary for the purposes of, to facilitate or in consequence of the transfer.

[1062]

NOTES
Commencement: 8 October 2008 (10.10 am).

19 Modification to Authority's duty to consult on rule changes

(1) Section 155(7) of the 2000 Act (consultation) has effect as if modified by adding at the end—

"or if it is making rules for the purposes of, or to facilitate or in consequence of, a transfer under section 6 or 8 of the Banking (Special Provisions) Act 2008."

(2) Section 157 of the 2000 Act (guidance) has effect as if modified by adding after subsection (3)—

"(3A) Section 155(7) applies to proposed guidance as it applies to proposed rules with the modification made by article 19 of the Transfer of Rights and Liabilities to ING Order 2008.".

[1063]

NOTES
Commencement: 8 October 2008 (10.10 am).

20 Transfer of data

Any transfer of data under this Order is not to be taken to breach any restriction on disclosure of information, however imposed.

[1064]

NOTES
Commencement: 8 October 2008 (10.10 am).

LANDSBANKI FREEZING ORDER 2008

(SI 2008/2668)

NOTES
Made: 8 October 2008 (10.00 am).
Authority: Anti-terrorism, Crime and Security Act 2001, ss 4, 14, Sch 3.

Commencement: 8 October 2008 (10.10 am).
This Order was revoked by the Landsbanki Freezing (Revocation) Order 2009, SI 2009/1392, art 2(a) at
[1829], as from 15 June 2009.

1   Citation, commencement, extent and application

*(1)   This Order may be cited as the Landsbanki Freezing Order 2008 and comes into force
at 10.10 am on 8th October 2008.*

(2)   [Subject to paragraph (3),] this Order extends to the United Kingdom.

(3)   [The prohibitions imposed by article 4 apply to the following persons]—
(a)   any person in the United Kingdom;
(b)   any person elsewhere who is—
*(i)   a British citizen, a British overseas territories citizen, a British National
(Overseas) or a British Overseas citizen;*
(ii)   a person who under the British Nationality Act 1981 is a British subject;
(iii)   a British protected person within the meaning of that Act;
(iv)   a body incorporated under the law of any part of the United Kingdom.

[1065]

NOTES
Commencement: 8 October 2008 (10.10 am).
Revoked as noted at the beginning of this Order.
Para (2): words in square brackets inserted by the Landsbanki Freezing (Amendment) Order 2008,
SI 2008/2766, arts 2, 3(a), as from 21 October 2008.
Para (3): words in square brackets substituted by SI 2008/2766, arts 2, 3(b), as from 21 October 2008.

---

2   Interpretation

(1)   In this Order—
"the 2000 Act" means the Financial Services and Markets Act 2000;
"the Authorities" means—
(a)   the Central Bank of Iceland, Kalkofnsvegi 1, 150 Reykjavik;
(b)   the Icelandic Financial Services Authority (the Fjármálaeftirlitid); and
*(c)   the Landsbanki receivership committee established by the Icelandic Financial
Services Authority;*
*"body corporate" includes a Scottish partnership and "a body incorporated under the law of
any part of the United Kingdom" is to be interpreted accordingly;*
"frozen funds" has the meaning given in article 4(1);
*"funds" means financial assets and economic benefits of any kind, including (but not limited
to)—*
*(a)   gold, cash, cheques, claims on money, drafts, money orders and other payment
instruments;*
*(b)   deposits with relevant institutions or other persons, balances on accounts, debts
and debt obligations;*
*(c)   publicly and privately traded securities and debt instruments, including stocks
and shares, certificates representing securities, bonds, notes, warrants,
debentures and derivative products;*
*(d)   interest, dividends or other income on or value accruing from or generated by
assets;*
*(e)   credit, rights of set-off, guarantees, performance bonds or other financial
commitments;*
(f)   letters of credit, bills of lading, bills of sale; and
(g)   documents providing evidence of an interest in funds or financial resources;

"*Landsbanki*" means Landsbanki Íslands hf, a public limited company incorporated under the law of Iceland;

"*relevant institution*" means—

    (h)   a person who has permission under Part 4 of the 2000 Act; and

    (i)   an EEA firm of the kind mentioned in paragraph 5(b) of Schedule 3 to the 2000 Act which has permission under paragraph 15 of that Schedule as a result of qualifying for authorisation under paragraph 12 of that Schedule to accept deposits.

(2)   *The definition of "relevant institution" in paragraph (1) must be read with—*

    (a)   section 22 of the 2000 Act;

    (b)   any relevant order under that section; and

    (c)   Schedule 2 to that Act.

[1066]

NOTES

Commencement: 8 October 2008 (10.10 am).
Revoked as noted at the beginning of this Order.

3 Specified persons

(1)   *The following are specified persons for the purposes of this Order [(being persons believed by the Treasury to have taken or be likely to take action to the detriment of the United Kingdom's economy (or part of it))]—*

    (a)   Landsbanki;

    (b)   the Authorities; and

    (c)   the Government of Iceland.

(2)   *If a specified person makes a written request, the Treasury must[, as soon as is practicable,] give it written reasons why it has been specified.*

[1067]

NOTES

Commencement: 8 October 2008 (10.10 am).
Revoked as noted at the beginning of this Order.
Words in square brackets inserted by the Landsbanki Freezing (Amendment) Order 2008, SI 2008/2766, arts 2, 4, as from 21 October 2008.

4 Freezing prohibitions

(1)   *The provisions of this article apply in relation to the following funds ("frozen funds")—*

    (a)   funds owned, held or controlled by Landsbanki; and

    (b)   funds relating to Landsbanki and owned, held or controlled by—

        (i)   any of the Authorities; or

        (ii)   the Government of Iceland.

(2)   *A person must not make frozen funds available to or for the benefit of a specified person.*

(3)   *A person must not make frozen funds available at the direction or instruction of a specified person.*

(4)   *A person must not deal with frozen funds.*

(5)   *For the purposes of this article, making funds available to or for the benefit of a specified person includes—*

    (a)   allowing it to withdraw from an account;

    (b)   honouring a cheque payable to it;

    (c)   crediting its account with interest;

    (d)   releasing documents of title (such as share certificates) held on its behalf;

    (e)   making available the proceeds of realisation of its property; and

    (f)   making a payment to or for its benefit.

(6)   *In this article, "deal with" means—*

    (a)   use, alter, move, allow access to or transfer;

    (b)   deal with in any other way that would result in any change in volume, amount, location, ownership, possession, character or destination; or

    (c)   make any other change that would enable use, including portfolio management.

[1068]

NOTES

Commencement: 8 October 2008 (10.10 am).
Revoked as noted at the beginning of this Order.

5 Freezing prohibitions: offences

(1)   A person [referred to in article 1(3)] who fails to comply with a prohibition imposed by article 4 commits an offence.

(2)   A person who engages in an activity knowing or intending that it will enable or facilitate the commission by another person of an offence under paragraph (1) commits an offence.

(3)   It is a defence to the offences in this article for a person to prove that he or she did not know and had no reason to suppose that—

- *(a)   in relation to the prohibition in article 4(2) the person to whom or for whose benefit frozen funds were made available, or were to be made available;*
- *(b)   in relation to the prohibition in article 4(3), the person at the direction or instruction of whom frozen funds were made available, or were to be made available;*
- *(c)   in relation to the prohibition in article 4(4), the person who owned, held or controlled the frozen funds,*

was a specified person.

[1069]

NOTES
Commencement: 8 October 2008 (10.10 am).
Revoked as noted at the beginning of this Order.
Para (1): words in square brackets inserted by the Landsbanki Freezing (Amendment) Order 2008, SI 2008/2766, arts 2, 5, as from 21 October 2008.

6 Licensing

(1)   The Treasury may, by licence, authorise frozen funds to be made available.

(2)   A licence may authorise a person to deal with frozen funds.

(3)   A licence granted under this article disapplies the prohibitions in article 4 in respect of frozen funds made available or dealt with in accordance with the licence.

(4)   A licence may be—

- *(a)   of indefinite duration or subject to an expiry date;*
- *(b)   subject to conditions;*
- *(c)   granted generally or to a person or persons named or described in the licence;*
- *(d)   granted in relation to frozen funds generally or to funds of a description specified in the licence.*

(5)   A licence may authorise frozen funds to be made available—

- *(a)   generally or for purposes specified in the licence;*
- *(b)   to or for the benefit of persons generally or a person or persons named or described in the licence.*

(6)   The Treasury may vary or revoke a licence at any time.

(7)   The Treasury, where they grant, vary or revoke a licence, must—

- *(a)   in the case of a licence granted to a particular person, give written notice of the licence, variation or revocation to that person, and*
- *(b)   in the case of a general licence or a licence granted to a category of persons, take such steps as the Treasury consider appropriate to publicise the licence, variation or revocation.*

[1070]

NOTES
Commencement: 8 October 2008 (10.10 am).
Revoked as noted at the beginning of this Order.

7 Licensing procedure

(1)   A person applying for a licence must—

- *(a)   apply in writing; and*
- *(b)   include such documentation and information that may be required for taking the relevant licensing decision.*

(2)   The Treasury—

- *(a)   are not required to consider an application which is incomplete; but*
- *(b)   if an application is incomplete, must inform the applicant of the further documentation or information required.*

(3)   The Treasury may grant a licence without an application having been made.

(4)   The Treasury may authorise a person to grant licences on their behalf.

(5)   A person who provides information, or produces a document, which he or she knows is false in a material particular with a view to obtaining a licence is guilty of an offence.

(6)   *A person who recklessly provides information, or produces a document, which is false in a material particular with a view to obtaining a licence is guilty of an offence.*

[1071]

NOTES
Commencement: 8 October 2008 (10.10 am).
Revoked as noted at the beginning of this Order.

8 Information

The Schedule (which contains provisions about information and documents, and their disclosure) has effect.

[1072]

NOTES
Commencement: 8 October 2008 (10.10 am).
Revoked as noted at the beginning of this Order.

9 Penalties

(1)   *A person guilty of an offence under article 5 is liable—*
  (a)   *on summary conviction, to imprisonment for a term not exceeding 6 months or to a fine not exceeding the statutory maximum or to both;*
  (b)   *on conviction on indictment, to imprisonment for a term not exceeding 2 years or to a fine or to both.*

(2)   *A person guilty of an offence under article 7 or under [the Schedule] is liable on summary conviction to imprisonment for a term not exceeding 6 months or to a fine not exceeding level 5 on the standard scale or to both.*

[1073]

NOTES
Commencement: 8 October 2008 (10.10 am).
Revoked as noted at the beginning of this Order.
Para (2): words in square brackets substituted by the Landsbanki Freezing (Amendment) Order 2008, SI 2008/2766, arts 2, 6, as from 21 October 2008.

10 Offences: procedure

(1)   *Proceedings for an offence under this Order are not to be instituted in England and Wales except by or with the consent of the Treasury or the Director of Public Prosecutions.*

(2)   *Proceedings for an offence under this Order are not to be instituted in Northern Ireland except by or with the consent of the Treasury or the Director of Public Prosecutions for Northern Ireland.*

(3)   *Despite anything in section 127(1) of the Magistrates' Courts Act 1980(information to be laid within 6 months of offence) an information relating to an offence under this Order which is triable by a magistrates' court in England and Wales may be so tried if it is laid at any time in the period of one year starting with the date of the commission of the offence.*

(4)   *In Scotland summary proceedings for an offence under this Order may be commenced at any time in the period of one year starting with the date of the commission of the offence.*

(5)   *In its application to an offence under this Order Article 19(1)(a) of the Magistrates' Courts (Northern Ireland) Order 1981 (time limit within which complaint charging offence must be made) is to have effect as if the reference to six months were a reference to twelve months.*

[1074]

NOTES
Commencement: 8 October 2008 (10.10 am).
Revoked as noted at the beginning of this Order.

11 Offences by bodies corporate etc

(1)   *If an offence under this Order—*
  (a)   *is committed by a body corporate, and*
  (b)   *is proved to have been committed with the consent or connivance of an officer, or to be attributable to any neglect on his or her part,*
he or she as well as the body corporate is guilty of the offence and liable to be proceeded against and punished accordingly.

(2)   *For the purpose of paragraph (1) these are officers of a body corporate—*
  (a)   *a director, manager, secretary or other similar officer of the body;*

    (*b*)   *any person purporting to act in any such capacity;*

    (*c*)   *in the case of a Scottish partnership, a partner.*

    (*3*)   *If the affairs of a body corporate are managed by its members, paragraph (1) applies in relation to the acts and defaults of a member in connection with his or her functions of management as if he or she were an officer of the body.*

[1075]

NOTES

Commencement: 8 October 2008 (10.10 am).
Revoked as noted at the beginning of this Order.

---

12 Notices

    (*1*)   *This article has effect in relation to any notice to be given to a person by the Treasury under article 6.*

    (*2*)   *Any such notice may be given—*

    (*a*)   *by posting it to his or her last known address; or*

    (*b*)   *where the person is a body corporate, by posting it to the registered or principal office of the body corporate.*

    (*3*)   *Where the Treasury do not have an address for the person, they must make arrangements for the notice to be given to him or her at the first available opportunity.*

[1076]

NOTES

Commencement: 8 October 2008 (10.10 am).
Revoked as noted at the beginning of this Order.

---

13   *(Revoked by the Landsbanki Freezing (Amendment) Order 2008, SI 2008/2766, arts 2, 7, as from 21 October 2008.)*

SCHEDULE

Article 8

1.—(1)   *The Treasury may, in writing, request a person to provide information or produce documentation to them which they may reasonably need for the purpose of ascertaining whether an offence has been committed under this Order.*

    (*2*)   *The request may be made by the Treasury or by a person authorised by the Treasury.*

    (*3*)   *Any person to whom a request is made under sub-paragraph (1) must comply with it within 14 days and in such manner as may be specified in the request.*

2.   *A relevant institution must disclose [to the Treasury] information as soon as practicable if the conditions in paragraph 16 are satisfied.*

3.—[(1)]   *The conditions are that—*

    (*a*)   *the relevant institution knows or suspects, or has grounds for knowing or suspecting, that a specified person—*

        (*i*)   *is a customer or has been a customer of the institution at any time since this Order came into force, or*

        (*ii*)   *is a person with whom it has dealings in the course of its business or has had such dealings at any time since this Order came into force.*

    (*b*)   *the information—*

        (*i*)   *on which the knowledge or suspicion of the [relevant institution] required to disclose is based, or*

        (*ii*)   *which gives grounds for the knowledge or suspicion,*

    came to the [relevant institution] in the course of a business in the regulated sector.

    (*2*)   *For the purposes of this paragraph, Schedule 3A to the Terrorism Act 2000 is to have effect for the purpose of determining what is a business in the regulated sector.*

4.   *Disclosure of information in accordance with this Schedule is not to be taken to breach any restriction on the disclosure of information (however imposed).*

5.—(1)   *This Schedule does not require any person to provide information or produce documentation which is privileged.*

    (*2*)   *Information and documentation is privileged if the person asked to provide or produce it would be entitled to refuse to do so on grounds of legal professional privilege in proceedings in the High Court or (in Scotland) on grounds of confidentiality of communications in proceedings in the Court of Session.*

    (*3*)   *But information or documentation held with the intention of furthering a criminal purpose is not privileged.*

6.   ... *A person who—*

   (a)   *fails without reasonable excuse to provide information, or to produce a document, in response to a requirement in or under this Schedule;*

   (b)   *provides information, or produces a document, which he or she knows is false in a material particular in [response] to a requirement in or under this Schedule;*

   (c)   *recklessly provides information, or produces a document, which is false in a material particular in response to a requirement in or under this Schedule;*

   (d)   *fails without reasonable excuse to disclose information as required under paragraph 15,*

is guilty of an offence.

7.   *The Treasury may only disclose information given or documentation produced under this Order (including any copy or extract made of any such document)—*

   (a)   *to a police officer;*

   (b)   *to any person holding or acting in any office under or in the service of—*

      (i)   *the Crown in respect of the Government of the United Kingdom;*

      (ii)   *the Government of the Isle of Man;*

      (iii) *the States of Guernsey or Alderney or the Chief Pleas of Sark;*

      (iv)   *the State of Jersey;*

      (v)   *any British overseas territory;*

   (c)   *for the purpose of giving assistance or cooperation to the Government of any country;*

   (d)   *to the Financial Services Authority;*

   (e)   *with a view to instituting, or otherwise for the purposes of, any proceedings—*

      (i)   *in the United Kingdom, for an offence under this Order; or*

      (ii)   *in any of the Channel Islands, the Isle of Man or any British overseas territory, for an offence under a similar provision in any such jurisdiction; or*

   (f)   *with the consent of a person who, in his or her own right (and not merely in the capacity of servant or agent), is entitled to the information or to the possession of the document, to any third party.*

8.   *Where a person is convicted of an offence under paragraph 19 of this Schedule the court may make an order requiring that person, within such period as may be specified in the order, to give the requested information or to produce the requested document.*

[1077]

NOTES

Commencement: 8 October 2008 (10.10 am).

Revoked as noted at the beginning of this Order.

Para 2: words in square brackets inserted by the Landsbanki Freezing (Amendment) Order 2008, SI 2008/2766, arts 2, 8(a), as from 21 October 2008.

Para 3: number "(1)" in square brackets inserted (to correct a drafting error), and words "relevant institution" in square brackets substituted, by SI 2008/2766, arts 2, 8(b), as from 21 October 2008.

Para 6: figure "(1)" (omitted) revoked (to correct a drafting error), and word "response" in square brackets substituted, by SI 2008/2766, arts 2, 8(c), as from 21 October 2008.

Note: in the original Queen's Printer's copy of this Order, the paragraphs in this Schedule were numbered as paragraphs 14–21. It is assumed that this was a drafting error made because the provision before this Schedule in the original Order was article 13 (now revoked). The Landsbanki Freezing (Amendment) Order 2008, SI 2008/2766 does not renumber the paragraphs of this Schedule, but it does specify that the amendments made to this Schedule are to paragraphs 2, 3 and 6 (and not paragraphs 14, 16 and 19). On this basis, this Schedule has been renumbered so that it begins at paragraph 1 and not paragraph 14 as in the original.

KAUPTHING SINGER & FRIEDLANDER LIMITED TRANSFER OF CERTAIN RIGHTS AND LIABILITIES ORDER 2008

(SI 2008/2674)

NOTES

Made: 8 October 2008 (12.05 pm).

Authority: Banking (Special Provisions) Act 2008, ss 6, 8, 12, 13(2), Sch 2.

Commencement: 8 October 2008 (12.15 pm).

ARRANGEMENT OF ARTICLES

PART 1
GENERAL

PART 2
THE FIRST TRANSFER

PART 3
THE SECOND TRANSFER

PART 4
FINANCIAL SERVICES COMPENSATION SCHEME

PART 5
THE ADMINISTRATOR AND TRANSITIONAL PROVISIONS

PART 6
MISCELLANEOUS

PART 1
GENERAL

1   Citation and commencement

(1)   This Order may be cited as the Kaupthing Singer & Friedlander Limited Transfer of Certain Rights and Liabilities Order 2008.

(2)   This Order comes into force at 12.15 pm on 8th October 2008.

[1078]

NOTES

Commencement: 8 October 2008 (12.15 pm).

---

2   Interpretation

In this Order—

        "the 1986 Act" means the Insolvency Act 1986;
        "the 2000 Act" means the Financial Services and Markets Act 2000;
        "the Act" means the Banking (Special Provisions) Act 2008;

"administrator" means an administrator appointed under paragraph 13, 14 or 22 of Schedule B1 (Administration) to the 1986 Act or on an administration application made to the court (and if more than one administrator is appointed, the reference to "the administrator" is to any administrator so appointed);

"the Authority" means the Financial Services Authority;

"the Bank" means the Governor and Company of the Bank of England;

"Community law" means—

(a) all the rights, powers, liabilities, obligations and restrictions from time to time created or arising by or under the Community Treaties; and

(b) all the remedies and procedures from time to time provided for by or under the Community Treaties;

"the COMP Sourcebook" means the Compensation Sourcebook made by the Authority under the 2000 Act;

"Deposits Management (Edge)" means Frontpedal Limited (in the process of changing its name to Deposits Management (Edge) Limited), company registered number 6690432, a company which is for the purposes of the Act wholly owned by the Bank;

"Edge account" has the meaning given in article 3(4);

"the effective time" means the time this Order comes into force;

"eligible claimant" has the meaning given in rule 4.2.1 of the COMP Sourcebook;

"the FEES 6 Chapter" means Chapter 6 (Financial Services Compensation Scheme Funding) of the Fees Manual made by the Authority under the 2000 Act;

"the Financial Services Compensation Scheme" means the scheme established by the Authority under Part 15 of the 2000 Act (The Financial Services Compensation Scheme);

"the first transfer" means the transfer effected by article 3;

"FSCS" means the body corporate established by the Authority under section 212 of the 2000 Act (the Scheme Manager);

"ING" means ING Direct N.V., a limited liability company incorporated in the Netherlands acting through its branch in the United Kingdom with branch reference number BR7357;

"the Insolvency Rules" means the Insolvency Rules 1986;

"Kaupthing" means Kaupthing Singer & Friedlander Limited, company registered number 875947;

"protected deposit" has the meaning given in rule 5.3.1 of the COMP Sourcebook;

"relevant protected deposit" means a protected deposit which relates to a transferred right or liability;

"the second transfer" means the transfer effected by article 8;

"the second transfer time" has the meaning given in article 8(2);

"transferred accounts" means the accounts to which the transferred rights and liabilities relate;

"transferred liabilities" means the liabilities transferred by article 3(1);

"transferred rights" means the rights transferred by article 3(2);

"the transitional period" means the period of 6 months following the effective time.

[1079]

NOTES

Commencement: 8 October 2008 (12.15 pm).

PART 2
THE FIRST TRANSFER

3 The first transfer

(1) Subject to paragraph (2), by virtue of this Order the liabilities of Kaupthing to holders of Edge accounts in respect of principal and accrued interest are transferred to Deposits Management (Edge).

(2) From the effective time, Deposits Management (Edge) shall have the same rights in relation to each holder of an Edge account as it would have if Kaupthing's relevant terms of business applied.

(3) Paragraph (1) does not apply to any liability in respect of any breach of contract or other duty which arose before the effective time.

(4) In this article, "Edge account" means any of the following accounts held with Kaupthing—

(a) the accounts known as Kaupthing Edge Savings Accounts; and

(b) the accounts known as Kaupthing Edge fixed term deposit accounts.

(5) The transfer under paragraph (1) takes place at the time this Order comes into force.

[1080]

NOTES

Commencement: 8 October 2008 (12.15 pm).

4   No consent or concurrence required

The first transfer is effective despite the absence of any required consent or concurrence to, or in connection with, the transfer.

[1081]

NOTES
Commencement: 8 October 2008 (12.15 pm).

5   Associated liability and interference

(1)   The first transfer takes effect as if—
    (a)   no associated liability existed in respect of any failure to comply with any requirement in respect of the transfer; and
    (b)   there were no associated interference with the transferred rights and liabilities.

(2)   In this article "associated liability" and "associated interference" have the meanings given in paragraph 2(2) of Schedule 2 to the Act.

[1082]

NOTES
Commencement: 8 October 2008 (12.15 pm).

6   Interests, rights and liabilities of third parties relating to transferred rights and liabilities

(1)   No interest or right of any third party relating to any of the transferred rights and liabilities shall arise or become exercisable by virtue of or in connection with this Order.

(2)   Save as otherwise provided in this Order, no third party shall incur any liability, or be subject to any obligation, relating to any of the transferred rights and liabilities, by virtue of or in connection with this Order.

(3)   Without prejudice to the generality of paragraphs (1) and (2)—
    (a)   the consequences specified in paragraph (4) shall not arise in respect of any relevant instrument as a result of the first transfer or any other thing done, or matter arising, by virtue of or in connection with the transfer;
    (b)   any circumstances which, but for sub-paragraph (a), would give rise to the consequences specified in paragraph (4) shall not be taken to have arisen for the purposes of any relevant instrument.

(4)   The consequences are—
    (a)   the termination of a relevant instrument or any rights or obligations under it;
    (b)   any right to terminate a relevant instrument or any right or obligation under it becoming exercisable;
    (c)   any amount becoming due and payable or capable of being declared due and payable;
    (d)   any other change in the amount or timing of any payment falling to be made or due to be received by any person;
    (e)   any right to withhold, net or set off any payment becoming exercisable;
    (f)   any event of default or breach of any right arising;
    (g)   any right not to advance any amount becoming exercisable;
    (h)   any obligation to provide or transfer any deposit or collateral;
    (i)   any right to give or withhold any consent or approval; or
    (j)   any other right or remedy (whether or not similar in kind to those referred to in paragraphs (a) to (i)) arising or becoming exercisable.

(5)   Without prejudice to paragraph (4), any provision in a relevant instrument that, as a result of the first transfer or any other thing done, or matter arising, by virtue of or in connection with the transfer or this Order, provides for an obligation not to be created, suspends or extinguishes (in whole or in part) such an obligation or renders such an obligation subject to conditions, shall be of no effect.

(6)   In this article—
    "relevant instrument" means an instrument which provides for interests or rights of third parties and in relation to which Kaupthing is a party or is bound;
    "third party" shall be construed in accordance with paragraph 2(3) of Schedule 2 to the Act.

[1083]

NOTES
Commencement: 8 October 2008 (12.15 pm).

PART IV   OTHER STATUTORY INSTRUMENTS

7 Exemption of Deposits Management (Edge)

Deposits Management (Edge) is an exempt person for the purposes of the 2000 Act in respect of any regulated activity of the kind specified by article 5 of the Financial Services and Markets Act 2000 (Regulated Activities) Order 2001(accepting deposits).

[1084]

NOTES

Commencement: 8 October 2008 (12.15 pm).

PART 3
THE SECOND TRANSFER

8 The second transfer

(1)   By virtue of this Order the transferred rights and liabilities are transferred to ING.

(2)   The second transfer takes place immediately after the first transfer ("the second transfer time").

(3)   From the second transfer time, ING shall—
    (a)   be liable to pay depositors any accrued interest on the transferred accounts and any interest accruing at or after that time on those accounts;
    (b)   have the same rights in relation to each holder of an Edge account as it would have if Kaupthing's relevant terms of business applied.

(4)   Paragraph (1) does not apply to any liability in respect of any breach of contract or other duty which arose before the second transfer time.

[1085]

NOTES

Commencement: 8 October 2008 (12.15 pm).

9 Provision of information and assistance

(1)   Kaupthing shall provide Deposits Management (Edge) and ING with such information and assistance as is reasonably requested by each of them, respectively—
    (a)   in relation to the transferred rights and liabilities;
    (b)   for any purpose relating to this Order; or
    (c)   for any purpose relating to any other function of Deposits Management (Edge) or ING, as the case may be, which relates to its functions under this Order.

(2)   Kaupthing shall provide the Treasury with such information and assistance as is requested by the Treasury for any purposes relating to this Order.

[1086]

NOTES

Commencement: 8 October 2008 (12.15 pm).

10 No consent or concurrence required

The second transfer is effective despite the absence of any required consent or concurrence to, or in connection with, the transfer.

[1087]

NOTES

Commencement: 8 October 2008 (12.15 pm).

11 Associated liability and interference

(1)   The second transfer takes effect as if—
    (a)   no associated liability existed in respect of any failure to comply with any requirement in respect of the transfer; and
    (b)   there were no associated interference with the rights and liabilities transferred under the transfer.

(2)   In this article "associated liability" and "associated interference" have the meanings given in paragraph 2(2) of Schedule 2 to the Act.

[1088]

NOTES

Commencement: 8 October 2008 (12.15 pm).

12   Interests, rights and liabilities of third parties relating to transferred rights and liabilities

(1)   No interest or right of any third party relating to any of the rights and liabilities transferred under the second transfer shall arise or become exercisable by virtue of or in connection with this Order.

(2)   Save as otherwise provided in this Order, no third party shall incur any liability, or be subject to any obligation, relating to any of the rights and liabilities transferred under the second transfer, by virtue of or in connection with this Order.

(3)   Without prejudice to the generality of paragraphs (1) and (2)—

    (a)   the consequences specified in paragraph (4) shall not arise in respect of any relevant instrument as a result of the second transfer or any other thing done, or matter arising, by virtue of or in connection with the second transfer;

    (b)   any circumstances which, but for sub-paragraph (a), would give rise to the consequences specified in paragraph (4) shall not be taken to have arisen for the purposes of any relevant instrument.

(4)   The consequences are—

    (a)   the termination of a relevant instrument or any rights or obligations under it;

    (b)   any right to terminate a relevant instrument or any right or obligation under it becoming exercisable;

    (c)   any amount becoming due and payable or capable of being declared due and payable;

    (d)   any other change in the amount or timing of any payment falling to be made or due to be received by any person;

    (e)   any right to withhold, net or set off any payment becoming exercisable;

    (f)   any event of default or breach of any right arising;

    (g)   any right not to advance any amount becoming exercisable;

    (h)   any obligation to provide or transfer any deposit or collateral;

    (i)   any right to give or withhold any consent or approval; or

    (j)   any other right or remedy (whether or not similar in kind to those referred to in paragraphs (a) to (i)) arising or becoming exercisable.

(5)   Without prejudice to paragraph (4), any provision in a relevant instrument that, as a result of the second transfer or any other thing done, or matter arising, by virtue of or in connection with the second transfer or this Order, provides for an obligation not to be created, suspends or extinguishes (in whole or in part) such an obligation or renders such an obligation subject to conditions, shall be of no effect.

(6)   In this article—

    "relevant instrument" means an instrument which provides for interests or rights of third parties and in relation to which Kaupthing is a party or is bound;

    "third party" shall be construed in accordance with paragraph 2(3) of Schedule 2 to the Act.

                                                [1089]

NOTES

Commencement: 8 October 2008 (12.15 pm).

PART 4
FINANCIAL SERVICES COMPENSATION SCHEME

13   Application of Part 3

This Part applies where, before the effective time, Kaupthing is in default for the purposes of rule 6.3.1 of the COMP Sourcebook.

                                              [1090]

NOTES

Commencement: 8 October 2008 (12.15 pm).

14   Sums to be paid to ING following the second transfer

(1)   The following liabilities arise at the second transfer time—

    (a)   the FSCS is liable to pay (as soon as practicable) to ING an amount equal to the amount that eligible claimants would, immediately before the effective time, have been entitled to claim from the FSCS in respect of claims against Kaupthing in relation to relevant protected deposits; and

    (b)   the Treasury are liable to pay (as soon as practicable) to ING an amount equal to the aggregate amount of the liabilities transferred to ING under the second transfer less the amount specified in sub-paragraph (a) and less £5,000,000, and the Treasury shall subsequently make the necessary adjustment such that Kaupthing obtains the benefit [(net of all costs and liabilities incurred by Deposits Management (Edge) in connection with the first or second transfer or its obligations under this Order)] of the reduction of £5,000,000 referred to in sub-paragraph (b).

(2)   For the purposes of paragraph (1)(a), if the quantification date for a claim would have been a date other than the date on which Kaupthing was determined to be in default for the purposes of section 6.3 of the COMP Sourcebook, the amount that an eligible claimant would have been entitled to claim from the FSCS is the lesser of—

    (a)   the amount which the FSCS quantifies as being the value of that claim as at immediately before the effective time; and

    (b)   the amount which would have been payable at the quantification date, if different, for that claim.

(3)   In paragraph (2), "quantification date" has the meaning given in rule 12.3.1 of the COMP Sourcebook.

(4)   As soon as practicable after the second transfer time—

    (a)   Kaupthing shall estimate the aggregate amount of the transferred liabilities;

    (b)   the FSCS shall pay to ING the amount it is liable to pay under paragraph (1)(a) as estimated by the Authority; and

    (c)   the Treasury shall pay to ING an amount equal to the amount estimated by Kaupthing in accordance with sub-paragraph (a) less the amount estimated by the Authority in accordance with sub-paragraph (b) and less £5,000,000.

(5)   From time to time—

    (a)   the FSCS may revise the estimate of its liability under paragraph (1)(a); and

    (b)   Kaupthing may revise the estimate of the aggregate amount of the transferred liabilities.

[(5A)   If the Treasury, the FSCS, Kaupthing and ING agree that it is not appropriate or reasonable to make (or to continue to make) the revisions specified in paragraph (5)(a) and (b), no revision (or no further revision) may be made under those provisions.]

(6)   In consequence of paragraph (5), the FSCS, the Treasury and ING shall make such corresponding payments to each other as are necessary to ensure that the FSCS and the Treasury have each paid to ING the amount required (and no more than the required amount) to meet their liability under paragraph (1).

(7)   If at any time after the effective time Kaupthing is placed into administration, the references to Kaupthing in paragraphs (4) and (5) are to be treated as references to the administrator.

(8)   The liability referred to in paragraph (1)(a) shall be assessed by the FSCS and, in doing so, the FSCS may calculate, by any methodology or approach it considers appropriate, the total amounts of compensation that would have been paid to all eligible claimants if (and to the extent that) it considers that the costs of ascertaining the entitlement to and the amount of compensation by reference to each eligible claimant would exceed or be disproportionate to the benefit of doing so.

[1091]

NOTES

Commencement: 8 October 2008 (12.15 pm).

Para (1): words in square brackets substituted by the Kaupthing Singer & Friedlander Limited Transfer of Certain Rights and Liabilities (Amendment) Order 2009, SI 2009/308, art 2(a)(i), as from 20 February 2009.

Para (5A): inserted by SI 2009/308, art 2(a)(ii), as from 20 February 2009.

---

15 Payment to ING to constitute payment of compensation for the purposes of the Financial Services Compensation Scheme

For the purposes of Part 15 of the 2000 Act (the financial services compensation scheme), the COMP Sourcebook and the FEES 6 Chapter (including, without limitation, the power of the FSCS to impose levies)—

    (a)   all payments by the FSCS to ING under article 14 shall constitute the payment of compensation to each eligible claimant under the Financial Services Compensation Scheme in accordance with their respective entitlements in respect of claims against Kaupthing for relevant protected deposits;

    (b)   in relation to a relevant protected deposit, each eligible claimant—

        (i)   is deemed to have made an application for compensation for the purposes of rule 3.2.1(1) of the COMP Sourcebook; and

        (ii)   is deemed to have accepted an offer of compensation made by the FSCS and to have received payment of such compensation for the purposes of rule 11.2.1 of the COMP Sourcebook,

and, accordingly, an eligible claimant has no right to claim, and the FSCS has no obligation to pay, for a relevant protected deposit any further compensation under the

Financial Services Compensation Scheme in respect of the default of Kaupthing determined by the Authority under section 6.3 of the COMP Sourcebook.

[1092]

NOTES
Commencement: 8 October 2008 (12.15 pm).

16 Liability of Kaupthing to the FSCS and the Treasury

(1)   Kaupthing is liable to the FSCS in respect of an amount equal to the amount which would have been provable in the administration of Kaupthing in respect of the transferred liabilities had this Order not been made and had Kaupthing been placed in administration immediately before the effective time.

(2)   The FSCS shall pursue recoveries from Kaupthing in respect of the liability under paragraph (1) to the extent reasonably practicable.

(3)   Subject to paragraph (4), if an eligible claimant had, in relation to a relevant protected deposit, a liability to Kaupthing which would have been capable of being set-off against a liability of Kaupthing to that claimant in an administration or liquidation of Kaupthing (if that liability had not been transferred), the amount which the FSCS is entitled to recover in the administration or liquidation shall be taken to be the sum of—

    (a)   the amount of the reduction in the depositor's liability to Kaupthing as a result of the application of the set-off; and

    (b)   the amount which would have been recovered in respect of the balance of the claim (if any) provable in the administration or liquidation of Kaupthing.

(4)   Paragraph (3) applies only to the extent that its application does not have the effect that the other creditors of Kaupthing are in a worse position than they would have been had the set-off been applied.

(5)   The FSCS shall determine the proportion of any amount which it receives or recovers from Kaupthing which is properly attributable to each type of liability described below and shall promptly, on receipt, account for that receipt or recovery as follows—

    (a)   in full to the Treasury, to the extent that—

        (i)   the receipt is attributable to a transferred liability; and

        (ii)   the person to whom such a transferred liability is owed would not have been entitled to make a claim for compensation from the FSCS immediately before the effective time;

    (b)   by reference to the relevant proportion, to the extent that—

        (i)   the receipt is attributable to a transferred liability;

        (ii)   the person to whom such a transferred liability is an eligible claimant; and

        (iii)   the amount of such liability exceeds the maximum compensation that the eligible claimant would have been entitled to claim from the FSCS immediately before the effective time;

    and where the receipt is attributable to a transferred liability owed to an eligible claimant in relation to a [relevant protected deposit] and the amount of such liability is equal to or less than the maximum compensation that the eligible claimant would have been entitled to claim from the FSCS immediately before the effective time that amount shall be for the account of the FSCS.

(6)   In paragraph (5), the "relevant proportion" is the proportion of the total liabilities which arise under article 14(1) for which the Treasury are liable.

(7)   If Kaupthing is in administration, the liability incurred under paragraph (1) shall not be treated as an expense of the administration under paragraph 99(3) of Schedule B1 of the 1986 Act or rule 2.67 of the Insolvency Rules.

(8)   Nothing in this Part shall have the effect that the FSCS recovers less than it would have recovered if this Order had not been made.

[1093]

NOTES
Commencement: 8 October 2008 (12.15 pm).
Para (5): words in square brackets substituted by the Kaupthing Singer & Friedlander Limited Transfer of Certain Rights and Liabilities (Amendment) Order 2009, SI 2009/308, art 2(b), as from 20 February 2009.

17 FSCS's power to require information

(1)   The FSCS may, by notice in writing given to ING, require it—

    (a)   to provide specified information or information of a specified description; or

    (b)   to produce specified documents or documents of a specified description.

PART IV   OTHER STATUTORY INSTRUMENTS

(2)   Paragraph (1) only applies to information and documents the provision or production of which the FSCS considers to be necessary (or likely to be necessary) for the exercise of its functions under or by virtue of this Order.

(3)   Subsections (2), (4), (5) and (7) of section 219 of the 2000 Act (scheme manager's power to require information) apply to a requirement imposed under paragraph (1) as if it were a requirement imposed under that section.

[1094]

NOTES
Commencement: 8 October 2008 (12.15 pm).

18   Statutory immunity

For the purposes of section 222 of the 2000 Act (statutory immunity) the scheme manager's functions shall include any acts or omissions carried out by the FSCS pursuant to or in connection with this Order.

[1095]

NOTES
Commencement: 8 October 2008 (12.15 pm).

PART 5
THE ADMINISTRATOR AND TRANSITIONAL PROVISIONS

19   Application of this Part

This Part applies if Kaupthing is placed into administration after the effective time.

[1096]

NOTES
Commencement: 8 October 2008 (12.15 pm).

20   The administration

The relevant provisions of the 1986 Act and the Insolvency Rules shall apply to the administration of Kaupthing subject to the modifications set out in this Part.

[1097]

NOTES
Commencement: 8 October 2008 (12.15 pm).

21   Objectives etc of the administrator

(1)   This article only applies during the transitional period.

(2)   The administrator must perform his or her functions with the objectives ("the overriding objectives") of—
  (a)   ensuring that Kaupthing provides, and managing the affairs, business and property of Kaupthing to enable it to provide, the services and facilities reasonably required by ING to discharge its obligations in respect of the rights and liabilities under the second transfer; and
  (b)   ensuring that Kaupthing performs the other obligations imposed on it by or under this Order.

(3)   The administrator shall only perform his or her functions with the objective determined in accordance with paragraph 3 of Schedule B1 to the 1986 Act to the extent that to do so is not inconsistent with and does not interfere with the achievement of the overriding objectives.

(4)   Paragraph 3(2) of Schedule B1 to the 1986 Act only applies to the performance of the functions of the administrator to the extent that it is not inconsistent with and does not interfere with the achievement of the overriding objectives.

(5)   The Treasury may, by notice in writing, give a direction to the administrator specifying that an act (or omission) is required for the overriding objectives.

(6)   The Treasury may also, by notice in writing, give a direction to the administrator requiring him or her to act (or not act) if the Treasury consider that it is necessary to give such a direction for the purposes of—
  (a)   protecting or enhancing the stability of the financial systems of the United Kingdom;
  (b)   protecting or enhancing public confidence in the stability of the banking system of the United Kingdom; or
  (c)   protecting depositors.

(7) The Treasury may also, by notice in writing, give a direction to the administrator that he or she need not perform his or her functions in accordance with the overriding objectives, either in relation to a particular matter or generally.

(8) The administrator must comply with any directions given under paragraph (5), (6) or (7).

(9) The services and facilities to which paragraph (2)(a) applies include (but are not limited to) the services and facilities specified in the Schedule.

(10) The administrator shall not be required to include any proposals for achieving the overriding objectives in any statement he or she makes under paragraph 49 (administrator's proposals) or paragraph 54 (revision of administrator's proposals) of Schedule B1 to the 1986 Act or to obtain approval of such proposals at any creditors' meeting or from the court.

(11) The administrator shall not enter into a transaction or a series of transactions (whether related or not) to sell, lease, transfer or otherwise dispose of any property or right of Kaupthing having in aggregate a value of more than £50 million at any time unless—

 (a) the court orders otherwise;
 (b) the Treasury gives its consent to the transaction; or
 (c) the sale, lease, transfer or disposal has been specifically approved at a meeting of creditors summoned under paragraph 51(1), 54(2) or 62 of Schedule B1 to the 1986 Act or by a creditors' committee constituted in accordance with rule 2.50 of the Insolvency Rules …

(12) In this article, "court" means—

 (a) in England and Wales, the High Court;
 (b) in Scotland, the Court of Session;
 (c) in Northern Ireland, the High Court.

[1098]

NOTES
Commencement: 8 October 2008 (12.15 pm).
Para (11): words omitted from sub-para (c) revoked by the Kaupthing Singer & Friedlander Limited Transfer of Certain Rights and Liabilities (Amendment) Order 2009, SI 2009/308, art 2(c), as from 20 February 2009.

22 Insolvency Act and Insolvency Rules etc

Nothing in the 1986 Act, the Insolvency Rules or any other enactment or rule of law shall operate to invalidate or prejudice any act or omission done under or pursuant to this Order or give rise to a claim against or impose any liability on Kaupthing or the administrator for any act or omission so done.

[1099]

NOTES
Commencement: 8 October 2008 (12.15 pm).

23 Services and facilities

The agreement dated 8th October 2008 between the Treasury and ING relating to the provision of transitional services by Kaupthing to ING shall bind Kaupthing as if it were a party.

[1100]

NOTES
Commencement: 8 October 2008 (12.15 pm).

24 Use of the Kaupthing brand

Kaupthing shall grant to ING a non-exclusive royalty-free licence to use the Kaupthing brand and the Edge brand and any relevant brands and sub-brands of Kaupthing during the transitional period for the purposes of ING carrying on its activities in relation to the rights and liabilities transferred under the second transfer.

[1101]

NOTES
Commencement: 8 October 2008 (12.15 pm).

25 Compensation payable to Kaupthing

(1) ING shall reimburse Kaupthing for the costs and expenses (including fees) properly incurred by the administrator during the transitional period in fulfilling his or her obligations under article 21.

(2)   Paragraph (1) does not apply to any cost or expense which would have been incurred in the administration if this Order had not been made.

[1102]

NOTES
Commencement: 8 October 2008 (12.15 pm).

26   Continuity

(1)   During the transitional period, any person wishing to terminate or modify (or treat as terminated or modified) any contract or agreement with Kaupthing for services and facilities or any right or obligation under such a contract or agreement must give not less than 14 days' prior written notice to the administrator and to ING.

(2)   During the transitional period, any person who provides to Kaupthing, pursuant to any contract or agreement, services or facilities which are reasonably required by Kaupthing to perform its duties under or pursuant to this Order or the agreement dated 8th October 2008 between the Treasury and ING relating to the provision of transitional services by Kaupthing to ING shall, whether or not required pursuant to such contract or agreement, provide such services to Kaupthing for the benefit of ING or, at Kaupthing's request, directly to ING.

(3)   Except with the consent of the Treasury or the permission of the court, during the transitional period—

(a)   no person is entitled—

    (i)   to terminate or modify any contract or agreement with Kaupthing for services and facilities, or any right or obligation under such a contract or agreement, where the contract or agreement or right or obligation relates to services or facilities which are reasonably required by—

        (aa)   Kaupthing to perform its duties under or pursuant to this Order;

        (bb)   the administrator to perform his or her duties under or pursuant to this Order; or

        (cc)   ING to carry on its functions in relation to the transferred rights and liabilities, or

    (ii)   to treat such a contract, agreement, right or obligation as terminated or modified, by virtue of, or in connection with, the first transfer or the second transfer, the requirement to provide services or facilities to or for the benefit of ING under paragraph (2) or the commencement of the administration in relation to Kaupthing; and

(b)   any counterparty to such a contract or agreement must perform his or her obligations in accordance with that contract or agreement.

(4)   The services and facilities to which paragraphs (1), (2) and (3) apply include (but are not limited to) the services and facilities specified in the Schedule.

(5)   Any purported termination or modification of any contract, agreement, right or obligation in contravention of paragraph (1), (2) or (3), and any action taken in consequence of any such purported termination or modification, shall have no effect.

(6)   Paragraph (2) does not apply where—

(a)   Kaupthing, ING or the administrator, as the case may be, has failed to perform its payment obligations under the relevant contract or agreement and such non-payment is not remedied within 14 days of that person becoming aware of the non-performance; or

(b)   Kaupthing, ING or the administrator, as the case may be, fails to notify the counterparty to the relevant contract or agreement within 14 days of its becoming aware of the request for consent to such termination, modification or non-performance of an obligation, that such consent has been withheld.

(7)   Without prejudice to the generality of paragraph (3), the first transfer or the second transfer shall not have the effect of terminating or otherwise changing the terms of Kaupthing's membership (if any) of any payment system, including, in particular, BACS, CHAPS and the LINK payments systems.

(8)   "Court" has the meaning given by article 21(12).

(9)   This article is subject to any requirement of Community law.

[1103]

NOTES
Commencement: 8 October 2008 (12.15 pm).

27   Moratorium on payment to related companies

(1)   Kaupthing shall not make any payment, dispose of any property or modify or release any right or liability to or for the benefit of a related party without the prior consent of the Treasury, and any such purported payment, disposal, modification or release shall be void.

(2)   No related party shall exercise any right of set-off or combination of accounts in respect of any debt owing by Kaupthing without the consent of the Treasury, and any such purported exercise shall be void.

(3)   In this article, "related party" means any member of the same group as Kaupthing that is not a subsidiary undertaking of Kaupthing.

(4)   In paragraph (1), if Kaupthing is in administration, the reference to Kaupthing is to be treated as a reference to the administrator.

(5)   In paragraph (3), "group" has the meaning given by section 421 of the 2000 Act.

[1104]

NOTES
Commencement: 8 October 2008 (12.15 pm).

PART 6
MISCELLANEOUS

28   Construction of documents etc

As from the effective time and save as otherwise provided in this Order—
  (a)   agreements made or other things done by or in relation to Kaupthing shall be treated, so far as may be necessary for the purposes of or in connection with the first transfer or the second transfer (but not otherwise) as made or done by or in relation to Deposits Management (Edge) or ING or both, as the case may be and as the context requires;
  (b)   references to Kaupthing or to any officer or employee of Kaupthing in instruments or documents relating to the transferred rights and liabilities and rights and liabilities transferred under the second transfer, shall have effect as if they were references to Deposits Management (Edge) or ING or both, or to any officer or employee of Deposits Management (Edge) or ING, as the case may be and as the context requires.

[1105]

NOTES
Commencement: 8 October 2008 (12.15 pm).

29   Modification to Authority's rule-making power

(1)   Subsections (1) and (1A) of section 138 of the 2000 Act (general rule-making power) have effect as if modified by inserting after "protecting the interests of consumers"—

"or for the purposes of, to facilitate or in consequence of, a transfer under section 6 or section 8 of the Banking (Special Provisions) Act 2008".

(2)   Section 148(2) of the 2000 Act (modification or waiver of rules) shall also apply in relation to Kaupthing—
  (a)   in the absence of an application by a person subject to rules made by the Authority; and
  (b)   without any requirement for the consent of such a person.

(3)   Section 148(4) of the 2000 Act shall not prevent the Authority from modifying or waiving rules in relation to Kaupthing under section 148 of that Act provided that the Authority is satisfied that the modification or waiver is necessary for the purposes of, to facilitate or in consequence of the first transfer or the second transfer.

[1106]

NOTES
Commencement: 8 October 2008 (12.15 pm).

30   Modification to Authority's duty to consult on rule changes

(1)   Section 155(7) of the 2000 Act (consultation) has effect as if modified by adding at the end—

"or if it is making rules for the purposes of, or to facilitate or in consequence of, a transfer under section 6 or section 8 of the Banking (Special Provisions) Act 2008."

(2)   Section 157 of the 2000 Act (guidance) has effect as if modified by adding after subsection (3)—

"(3A)   Section 155(7) applies to proposed guidance as it applies to proposed rules with the modification made by article 30 of the Kaupthing Singer & Friedlander Limited Transfer of Certain Rights and Liabilities Order 2008.".

[1107]

PART IV   OTHER STATUTORY INSTRUMENTS

NOTES
Commencement: 8 October 2008 (12.15 pm).

31 Freedom of information

For the purposes of section 3(2)(b) of the Freedom of Information Act 2000 (public authorities), Deposits Management (Edge) shall be deemed not to hold information on behalf of the Bank.

[1108]

NOTES
Commencement: 8 October 2008 (12.15 pm).

32 Proceedings against directors

(1) No director of—
    (a) Kaupthing; or
    (b) Deposits Management (Edge),
shall be liable in connection with the first transfer or the second transfer or any other provisions of this Order and accordingly no proceedings may be brought (or, in Scotland, raised) against any such director in respect of such matters.

(2) The Treasury may in writing—
    (a) waive the effect of paragraph (1), and
    (b) give consent to bring (or, in Scotland, raise) such proceedings against such directors.

(3) Where paragraph (1) applies, section 232 of the Companies Act 2006 (provisions protecting directors from liability) shall not apply to a relevant undertaking.

(4) In this article—
    "director" means a person who was a director immediately before the effective time, whether or not he has ceased to be a director at the time when proceedings in respect of that liability commenced;
    "proceedings" includes proceedings under Part 11 of the Companies Act 2006 (derivative claims and proceedings by members).

[1109]

NOTES
Commencement: 8 October 2008 (12.15 pm).

33 Immunity of Bank

(1) The Bank has immunity in relation to action or inaction in relation to or pursuant to this Order.

(2) In this article—
    (a) a reference to the Bank is a reference to the Bank and anyone who acts or purports to act as a director, officer, servant or agent of the Bank;
    (b) "immunity" means immunity from liability in damages.

(3) The immunity does not extend to action taken—
    (a) in bad faith, or
    (b) in contravention of section 6(1) of the Human Rights Act 1998.

[1110]

NOTES
Commencement: 8 October 2008 (12.15 pm).

34 Transfer of data

Any transfer of data under this Order is not to be taken to breach any restriction on disclosure of information, however imposed.

[1111]

NOTES
Commencement: 8 October 2008 (12.15 pm).

SCHEDULE
SERVICES AND FACILITIES

Article 21

1. Website hosting services or facilities.

2. Information technology services or facilities.

3.   Back office processing services or facilities.

4.   Call centre services or facilities.

5.   Payment and clearing services or facilities.

[1112]

NOTES
   Commencement: 8 October 2008 (12.15 pm).

BRADFORD & BINGLEY PLC COMPENSATION SCHEME ORDER 2008

(SI 2008/3249)

NOTES
   Made: 18 December 2008.
   Authority: Banking (Special Provisions) Act 2008, ss 5, 9, 12, 13(2).
   Commencement: 19 December 2008.

ARRANGEMENT OF ARTICLES

1—(1)   This Order may be cited as the Bradford & Bingley plc Compensation Scheme Order 2008.

   (2)   This Order comes into force on the day after the day on which it is made.

[1113]

NOTES
   Commencement: 19 December 2008.

---

2   The Bradford & Bingley plc Compensation Scheme set out in the Schedule to this Order shall have effect.

[1114]

NOTES
   Commencement: 19 December 2008.

SCHEDULE
THE BRADFORD & BINGLEY PLC COMPENSATION SCHEME
Article 2

PART 1
GENERAL PROVISIONS

Citation

1.   This Scheme may be cited as the Bradford & Bingley plc Compensation Scheme.

Interpretation

2.   In this Scheme—
   "the Act" means the Banking (Special Provisions) Act 2008;
   "assessment notice" means a notice issued under paragraph 10;
   "Bradford & Bingley" means Bradford & Bingley plc, company registered number 3938288;
   "revised assessment notice" means a notice issued under paragraph 11;
   "shares in Bradford & Bingley" means the ordinary shares issued by Bradford & Bingley;
   "the Transfer Order" means the Bradford & Bingley plc Transfer of Securities and Property etc Order 2008;

"the transfer time" means 8.00 a.m. on 29th September 2008;

"the Tribunal" means the Financial Services and Markets Tribunal;

"valuer" means the independent valuer appointed by the Treasury in accordance with paragraph 6.

[1115]

NOTES

Commencement: 19 December 2008.

PART 2

DETERMINATION OF AMOUNT OF COMPENSATION

Transfer of Bradford & Bingley shares

3.—(1)   The amount of any compensation payable by the Treasury to persons who held shares in Bradford & Bingley immediately before they were transferred by the Transfer Order shall be determined in accordance with this paragraph.

(2)   The amount of compensation payable to a person shall be an amount equal to the value immediately before the transfer time of all shares in Bradford & Bingley held immediately before the transfer time by that person.

(3)   For the purposes of this Scheme, the holders of shares in Bradford & Bingley, and the class and number of shares held by them, shall be identified by reference to—

   (a)   the Operator register of members of Bradford & Bingley; and

   (b)   the issuer register of members of Bradford & Bingley,

following the reconciliation required by article 4(4) of the Transfer Order.

(4)   In sub-paragraph (3) "issuer register of members" and "Operator register of members" have the meanings given in the Uncertificated Securities Regulations 2001.

Extinguishment of subscription rights

4.—(1)   The amount of any compensation payable by the Treasury to persons whose subscription rights were extinguished by virtue of article 5 of the Transfer Order shall be determined in accordance with this paragraph.

(2)   The amount of compensation payable to a person shall be an amount equal to the value immediately before the transfer time of that person's subscription rights.

(3)   In this paragraph "subscription rights" means any right or other entitlement to receive shares in Bradford & Bingley (whether by subscription, conversion or otherwise) granted by—

   (a)   a relevant undertaking; or

   (b)   a person not within paragraph (a), where the right or entitlement is enjoyed by reason of or in connection with—

      (i)   any individual's office or employment with a relevant undertaking; or

      (ii)   the services provided by any individual to a relevant undertaking.

(4)   In sub-paragraph (3) "relevant undertaking" means Bradford & Bingley or any of its UK subsidiary undertakings that is a body corporate incorporated, or a partnership established, under the law of any part of the United Kingdom.

Modification of interests, rights and liabilities in relevant instruments

5.—(1)   Subject to sub-paragraph (4), the amount of any compensation payable by the Treasury to persons whose rights were extinguished by virtue of the provision made in article 6 or 7 of the Transfer Order (referred to in this paragraph as "consequential rights") shall be determined in accordance with this paragraph.

(2)   The amount of compensation payable to a person shall be such compensation as may be just in respect of that person's consequential rights.

(3)   The determination of any compensation in respect of consequential rights shall take into account—

   (a)   any diminution in the value of property; or

   (b)   any increase in the burden of any liability,

which is attributable to the consequences specified in article 7(3) of the Transfer Order not arising.

(4)   Compensation is payable in respect of a person's consequential rights only if such compensation is required to be paid to comply with the Convention rights (within the meaning given by section 1 of the Human Rights Act 1998).

[(5)   In sub-paragraph (1) the reference to article 6 of the Transfer Order is a reference to that article as amended by article 2(2) of the Bradford & Bingley plc Transfer of Securities and Property etc (Amendment) Order 2009.]

[1116]

NOTES
Commencement: 19 December 2008.
Para 5: sub-para (5) inserted by the Bradford & Bingley plc Compensation Scheme (Amendment) Order 2009, SI 2009/790, arts 2, 3, as from 26 March 2009.

PART 3
INDEPENDENT VALUER

Appointment of independent valuer

6.—(1)   The Treasury shall appoint an independent valuer for the purposes of this Scheme.

(2)   The valuer so appointed shall determine the amount of any compensation payable by the Treasury in accordance with Part 2 of this Scheme.

(3)   The valuer is to hold and vacate office in accordance with the terms of his appointment.

(4)   The Treasury may remove the valuer only on the ground of incapacity or serious misbehaviour.

(5)   Before making any appointment under sub-paragraph (1) the Treasury must consult the Institute of Chartered Accountants in England and Wales.

Remuneration

7.   The valuer shall be—
    (a)   paid such remuneration; and
    (b)   reimbursed such expenses;
as the Treasury may determine.

Appointment of staff

8.—(1)   The valuer may appoint such staff as he or she may determine.

(2)   The valuer shall determine the remuneration and other conditions of service of the persons appointed under this paragraph.

(3)   The valuer may pay such pensions, allowances or gratuities to or in respect of the persons appointed under this paragraph as he or she may determine.

(4)   The references in sub-paragraph (3) to pensions, allowances or gratuities to or in respect of the persons appointed under this paragraph include reference to pensions, allowances or gratuities by way of compensation in respect of any of those persons who suffer loss of employment.

(5)   Any determination under sub-paragraphs (2) to (4) shall require the approval of the Treasury.

[1117]

NOTES
Commencement: 19 December 2008.

[PART 3A
INFORMATION

8A.—(1)   The court may, on an application by the valuer, make an order requiring the provision of information that is reasonably required for the purpose of assessing the amount of any compensation payable by the Treasury.

(2)   A person required to provide information pursuant to an order under sub-paragraph (1) shall not be required to provide information—
    (a)   in respect of which a claim to legal professional privilege (in Scotland, to confidentiality of communications) could be maintained in legal proceedings;
    (b)   if such provision by the person holding it would be prohibited by or under any enactment;
    (c)   if it is held by a government department and such provision would be contrary to the public interest.

(3)   In relation to information recorded otherwise than in legible form, the power to require it to be provided includes power to require it to be provided in a form from which it can readily be produced in visible and legible form.

8B.   A person who provides information to the valuer for the purpose of the assessment by the valuer of the amount of any compensation payable by the Treasury is not, by reason only of the provision of such information, liable in any proceedings relating to a breach of an obligation of confidence.

PART IV
OTHER STATUTORY INSTRUMENTS

8C. Specified information shall not be disclosed by the valuer (or any person to whom the valuer has disclosed such information in accordance with paragraph 8D(2)) without the consent of the person from whom the valuer obtained the specified information and, if different, the person to whom it relates.

8D.—(1) The prohibition in paragraph 8C of the disclosure of specified information is subject to the following exceptions.

(2) The valuer may, for the purpose of assessing the amount of any compensation payable, disclose specified information to any staff appointed under paragraph 8 or to any person providing advice or assistance to the valuer.

(3) The valuer may disclose specified information if and to the extent that the valuer considers it necessary to do so for the purpose of exercising the functions of the office.

(4) The valuer must, before disclosing any specified information in accordance with sub-paragraph (3), have regard to the need to exclude from disclosure (so far as practicable)—

(a) commercial information, the disclosure of which might significantly harm the legitimate business interests of the person to whom it relates,

(b) information relating to the private affairs of an individual, the disclosure of which might significantly harm the individual's interests, or

(c) any information the disclosure of which would be contrary to the public interest.

(5) The valuer may disclose specified information in accordance with this paragraph subject to such conditions as the valuer thinks appropriate.

8E. In this Part—

"court" means the High Court or the Court of Session;

"specified information" means any information obtained by the valuer for the purpose of assessing the amount of any compensation payable by the Treasury.]

[1118]

NOTES

Commencement: 26 March 2009.

Inserted by the Bradford & Bingley plc Compensation Scheme (Amendment) Order 2009, SI 2009/790, arts 2, 4.

PART 4
ASSESSMENT OF COMPENSATION BY VALUER

Procedure

9.—(1) The valuer may make such rules as to the procedure in relation to the assessment of any compensation (including the procedure for the reconsideration of any decisions relating to the assessment of compensation) as he or she considers appropriate.

(2) Rules made under sub-paragraph (1) may make different provision for different cases or circumstances.

Assessment notice

10.—(1) Where the valuer has assessed the amount of any compensation payable by the Treasury—

(a) to any person; or

(b) in respect of a class or description of shares or rights,

the valuer shall issue an assessment notice.

(2) An assessment notice shall contain the following information—

(a) the date on which the notice is issued;

(b) the amount of any compensation determined by the valuer as being payable; and

(c) the reasons for the valuer's decision.

(3) The valuer shall send a copy of the assessment notice to the Treasury.

Reconsideration of assessment notice

11.—(1) If—

(a) the Treasury; or

(b) any person who is affected by the determination of the amount of any compensation which is contained in an assessment notice,

are dissatisfied with the assessment notice, the Treasury or any such person may require the valuer to reconsider the determination.

(2) Where the valuer is required to reconsider a determination in accordance with sub-paragraph (1) he or she shall issue a revised assessment notice.

(3) A revised assessment notice shall contain the following information—

(a) the date on which the notice is issued;

(b) either—

(i)   notification that the valuer has upheld the assessment notice; or

(ii)   notification that the valuer has varied the assessment notice;

(c)   the amount of any compensation determined by the valuer as being payable; and

(d)   the reasons for the valuer's decision.

(4)   The valuer shall send a copy of the revised assessment notice to the Treasury.

Right to refer to the Tribunal

12.   If—

(a)   the Treasury; or

(b)   any person who is affected by the determination of the amount of any compensation which is contained in the revised assessment notice,

are dissatisfied with the revised assessment notice, the Treasury or any such person may refer the matter to the Tribunal.

Payment of compensation

13.—(1)   The Treasury shall pay the amount of any compensation determined by the valuer to be payable—

(a)   to any person; or

(b)   in respect of a class or description of shares or rights.

(2)   The Treasury shall not be required to make a payment in accordance with sub-paragraph (1) until—

(a)   they have received a copy of the assessment notice or revised assessment notice, as the case may be; or

(b)   if there is a reference to the Tribunal, the matter has been finally disposed of.

[1119]

NOTES
Commencement: 19 December 2008.

PART 5
REFERENCES TO THE TRIBUNAL

Application of FSMA 2000

14.—(1)   The provisions of—

(a)   Part 9 (hearing and appeals) of, and Schedule 13 (the Financial Services and Markets Tribunal) to, FSMA 2000; and

(b)   the Financial Services and Markets Tribunal Rules 2001;

shall apply in respect of any reference made under paragraph 12, subject to the modifications set out in this Part.

Modification of FSMA 2000

15.   Part 9 of, and Schedule 13 to, FSMA 2000 are modified as follows.

16.   In section 133 (proceedings: general provisions) and Schedule 13, for "the Authority" in each place it occurs substitute "the independent valuer appointed under paragraph 6 of the Schedule to the Bradford & Bingley plc Compensation Scheme Order 2008".

17.   In section 133—

(i)   in subsection (1)(a) for "the decision notice or supervisory notice in question", substitute " the revised assessment notice issued by the valuer under paragraph 11(2) of the Schedule to the Bradford & Bingley plc Compensation Scheme Order 2008";

(ii)   for subsection (4) substitute—

"(4)   Where the Tribunal is satisfied that the decision as to the amount of compensation shown in the revised assessment notice was not a reasonable decision the Tribunal must remit the matter to the valuer for reconsideration in accordance with such directions (if any) as they consider appropriate.";

(iii)   omit subsections (5) to (9) and (12).

18.   Omit sections 134 to 136.

Modification of Financial Services and Markets Tribunal Rules 2001

19.   The Financial Services and Markets Tribunal Rules 2001 are modified as follows.

20.   In each place where it occurs (other than in rule 2)—

(a)   for "Authority" substitute "respondent";

(b)   for "Authority notice" substitute "revised assessment notice";

(c)   for "statement of case" substitute "response document".

21.   In rule 2 (interpretation)—

(a)   omit the definitions for "the Authority", "Authority notice", "further material", "protected item", "reply" and "statement of case";

   (b)   in the definition of "party", for "Authority", in both places where it occurs, substitute "respondent";

   (c)   in the definition of "referred action" for "the act (or proposed act) on the part of the Authority" substitute "the revised assessment notice";

   (d)   for the definition of "response document" substitute ""response document" means a statement filed by the respondent under rule 5(1);"; and

   (e)   in the appropriate place insert—
        ""respondent" means the independent valuer appointed under paragraph 6 of the Schedule to the Bradford & Bingley plc Compensation Scheme Order 2008;";
        "revised assessment notice" means the revised assessment notice issued by the respondent under paragraph 11 of the Schedule to the Bradford & Bingley plc Compensation Scheme Order 2008;".

22.   In rule 4(6) (reference notice) omit ", a direction under rule 10(1)(e) (suspension of Authority's action) or".

23.   In rule 5 (Authority's statement of case)—

   (a)   for paragraphs (1) and (2) substitute—

      "(1)   The respondent shall file a written statement ("a response document") dealing with any issues arising out of the reference notice that the respondent wishes the Tribunal to consider so that it is received by the Tribunal no later than 28 days after the day on which the respondent received the information sent by the Secretary in accordance with rule 4(9)(b).

      (2)   At the same time as it files the response document, the respondent shall send a copy to the applicant.";

   (b)   omit paragraphs (3) and (4).

24.   Omit rules 6 (applicant's reply), 7 (secondary disclosure by the Authority), 8 (exceptions to disclosure), 11 (filling of subsequent notices in relation to the referred action), 12(2) (summoning of witnesses), 14(3)(c) (withdrawal of reference and unopposed references), 15 (references by third parties) and 23(4) (application for permission to appeal).

25.   In rule 10 (particular types of directions) omit paragraphs (1)(e), (2)(a), (6) and (8).

26.   After rule 10 (particular types of directions) insert—

"10A   Same issues proceedings

    (1)   The President may, of his own motion or on application by a party, direct that a reference is heard as a lead case where—

   (a)   two or more references under paragraph 12 of the Schedule to the Bradford & Bingley plc Compensation Scheme Order 2008 have been made, but have not yet been determined by the Tribunal; and

   (b)   it appears to the President that those references give rise to common or related issues of fact or law ("same issues proceedings").

    (2)   The President may—

   (a)   make such further directions as he considers appropriate for determination of the lead case; and

   (b)   direct that pending determination of the lead case all other same issues proceedings before the Tribunal shall be stayed.

    (3)   All parties in same issue proceedings must be allowed to make representations prior to the President making a direction under paragraph (1) or (2).

    (4)   Without prejudice generally to the parties' rights of appeal and to paragraphs (5) to (7), the Tribunal's determination of the same issues in the lead case shall be binding on the parties to each of the same issues proceedings unless the Tribunal or the President directs otherwise.

    (5)   Any party to any of the same issues proceedings may apply to the President for a direction that the determination of the same issues in the lead case does not apply to that party's case.

    (6)   An application under paragraph (5) must be made not later than 21 days after the date on which that party received notice of the determination of the same issues in the lead case.

    (7)   Within 28 days beginning with the date of determination of the same issues in the lead case the President may make further directions in relation to—

   (a)   the lead case and each of the same issues proceedings stayed pending the determination of the same issues in the lead case;

   (b)   the extent to which the determination of the same issues in the lead case is binding on any subsequent proceedings; and

   (c)   any further directions required as a result of an application under paragraph (5), including a direction as to any further hearing required in relation to those proceedings.

(8)   Where a direction has been made for any proceedings to be heard as a lead case and those proceedings are withdrawn or discontinued either before or during the hearing, the President may direct—

(a)   that one of the remaining same issues proceedings be substituted as the lead case; and

(b)   the extent to which any directions made prior to substitution shall be binding in relation to the substituted proceedings.

(9)   The Secretary must send notice of the directions to be made under paragraphs (1) and (2), a copy of the directions made under paragraphs (1), (2), (4), (5), (7) and (8) and the determination of the same issues in the lead case to all the parties to the same issues proceedings.

10B   Joining of parties to proceedings

If it appears to the President or the Chairman, whether on the application of a party or otherwise, that it is desirable that any person other than the respondent be made a party to any proceedings, he may direct that such person be joined as a party in the proceedings and may make such further directions for giving effect to, or in connection with, the direction as he thinks fit.".

27.   In rule 19(3) (procedure at hearings) omit "when taking the referred action".

[1120]

NOTES
Commencement: 19 December 2008.

KAUPTHING SINGER & FRIEDLANDER LIMITED (DETERMINATION OF COMPENSATION) ORDER 2008

(SI 2008/3250)

NOTES
Made: 18 December 2008.
Authority: Banking (Special Provisions) Act 2008, s 7(1)(a).
Commencement: 19 December 2008.

1—(1)   This Order may be cited as the Kaupthing Singer & Friedlander Limited (Determination of Compensation) Order 2008.

(2)   This Order comes into force on the day after the day on which it is made.

[1121]

NOTES
Commencement: 19 December 2008.

2—(1)   The amount of any compensation payable by the Treasury to Kaupthing in respect of the rights and liabilities transferred by the Kaupthing Singer & Friedlander Limited Transfer of Certain Rights and Liabilities Order 2008 is determined as nil.

(2)   In paragraph (1) "Kaupthing" means Kaupthing Singer & Friedlander Limited, company registered number 875947.

[1122]

NOTES
Commencement: 19 December 2008.

HERITABLE BANK PLC (DETERMINATION OF COMPENSATION) ORDER 2008

(SI 2008/3251)

NOTES
Made: 18 December 2008.
Authority: Banking (Special Provisions) Act 2008, s 7(1)(a).

Commencement: 19 December 2008.

1—(1)   This Order may be cited as the Heritable Bank plc (Determination of Compensation) Order 2008.

(2)   This Order comes into force on the day after the day on which it is made.

[1123]

NOTES
Commencement: 19 December 2008.

2—(1)   The amount of any compensation payable by the Treasury to Heritable in respect of the rights and liabilities transferred by the Heritable Bank plc Transfer of Certain Rights and Liabilities Order 2008 is determined as nil.

(2)   In paragraph (1) "Heritable" means Heritable Bank plc, company registered in Scotland number SC000717.

[1124]

NOTES
Commencement: 19 December 2008.

BUILDING SOCIETIES (FUNDING) AND MUTUAL SOCIETIES (TRANSFERS) ACT 2007 (COMMENCEMENT NO 1) ORDER 2009

(SI 2009/36)

NOTES
Made: 15 January 2009.
Authority: Building Societies (Funding) and Mutual Societies (Transfers) Act 2007, s 6(2).

1   Citation and interpretation

(1)   This Order may be cited as the Building Societies (Funding) and Mutual Societies (Transfers) Act 2007 (Commencement No 1) Order 2009.

(2)   In this Order "the Act" means the Building Societies (Funding) and Mutual Societies (Transfers) Act 2007.

[1125]

2   Provisions coming into force

The 16th January 2009 is the appointed day for the coming into force of sections 3, 4 and 5 of the Act.

[1126]

PAYMENT SERVICES REGULATIONS 2009

(SI 2009/209)

NOTES
Made: 9 February 2009.
Authority: European Communities Act 1972, s 2(2).
Commencement: see reg 1(2).

ARRANGEMENT OF REGULATIONS

PART 1
INTRODUCTORY PROVISIONS

PART 2
REGISTRATION

The register

Authorisation as a payment institution

Registration as a small payment institution

Common provisions

PART 3
AUTHORISED PAYMENT INSTITUTIONS

Exercise of passport rights

PART 4
PROVISIONS APPLICABLE TO AUTHORISED PAYMENT INSTITUTIONS AND SMALL PAYMENT INSTITUTIONS

PART 5
INFORMATION REQUIREMENTS FOR PAYMENT SERVICES

Application

Single payment service contracts

Framework contracts

PART 6
RIGHTS AND OBLIGATIONS IN RELATION TO THE PROVISION OF PAYMENT SERVICES

Application

Charges

Authorisation of payment transactions

Execution of payment transactions

Execution time and value date

Liability

PART 7
THE AUTHORITY

The functions of the Authority

Supervision and enforcement

PART 8
ACCESS TO PAYMENT SYSTEMS

General

Supervision and enforcement

Miscellaneous

PART 9
GENERAL

Criminal Offences

Duties of the Authority, the Commissioners and the OFT to cooperate

Actions for breach of requirements

Transitional provisions

Amendments to primary and secondary legislation

Schedules:

PART IV
OTHER STATUTORY INSTRUMENTS

PART 1
INTRODUCTORY PROVISIONS

1 Citation and commencement

(1)   These Regulations may be cited as the Payment Services Regulations 2009.

(2)   These Regulations come into force—

  (a)   on 2nd March 2009 for the purposes of regulations 25, 80, 92 to 94, 95 in respect of paragraphs 5 and 10 of Schedule 5, 119 and 126 in respect of paragraphs 1 and 6(g) of Schedule 6;

  (b)   on 1st May 2009 for the purposes of—

   (i)   enabling applications for authorisation as a payment institution and the variation of an authorisation to be made under regulation 5 and the Authority to determine such applications in accordance with regulations 6 to 9;

   (ii)   enabling applications for registration as a small payment institution and the variation of a registration to be made under regulation 12 and the Authority to determine such applications in accordance with regulation 13 and regulations 7 to 9 (as applied by regulation 14);

   (iii)   enabling applications for an agent to be included on the register under regulation 29 and the Authority to determine such applications in accordance with that regulation;

   (iv)   enabling the Authority to give directions as to the manner in which an application under regulation 5(1) or (2), 12(1) or (2) or 29(3) is to be made and enabling the Authority to require the applicant to provide further information in accordance with regulation 5(4), 12(4) or 29(3)(a)(iv), as the case may be;

   (v)   enabling the Authority to cancel an authorisation or registration or vary an authorisation or registration on its own initiative in accordance with regulation 10 or 11 (as applied, in the case of a registration, by regulation 14);

   (vi)   requiring a person who has made an application under regulation 5(1) or (2) or 12(1) or (2) to provide information to the Authority in accordance with regulation 16 and enabling the Authority to give directions under that regulation;

   (vii)   enabling a person to make a reference to the Tribunal under regulation 9(9), 10(4), 11(5), 24(4) or 29(11);

   (viii)   enabling an applicant for authorisation as a payment institution to give the Authority a notice of intention under regulation 23(1) and the Authority to give directions as to the manner in which such a notice is to be given and to inform the host state competent authority in accordance with regulation 23(2);

   (ix)   enabling the Authority to decide whether to register an EEA branch, or to cancel such a registration, under regulation 24(1);

   (x)   enabling the Authority to give directions under regulation 82 to a person whose application under regulation 5(1) or 12(1) has been granted before 1st November 2009 in respect of—

    (aa)   its provision as from that date of payment services; and

    (bb)   its compliance as from that date with requirements imposed by or under Parts 2 to 6 of these Regulations;

   (xi)   enabling the Authority to give directions under paragraph 7, 11, 12 or 16(3) of Schedule 3 to a person whose application under regulation 5(1) has been granted before 1st November 2009;

   (xii)   requiring a person whose application under regulation 5(1), 12(1) or 29(3) has been granted before 1st November 2009 to provide information to the Authority in accordance with regulation 32 and enabling the Authority to give directions under that regulation;

   (xiii)   regulations 95 in respect of paragraphs 2 and 7 to 9 of Schedule 5, 114 to 118, and 121, 124 and 125; and

  (c)   for all other purposes on 1st November 2009.

NOTES
Commencement: these Regulations come into force on 2 March 2009 (for the purposes specified in reg 1(2)(a)), 1 May 2009 (for the purposes specified in reg 1(2)(b)), and 1 November 2009 (otherwise). See above.

2 Interpretation

(1)   In these Regulations—

"the 2000 Act" means the Financial Services and Markets Act 2000;

"agent" means a person who acts on behalf of an authorised payment institution or a small payment institution in the provision of payment services;

"authorised payment institution" means—

(a)   a person included by the Authority in the register as an authorised payment institution pursuant to regulation 4(1)(a); or

(b)   a person deemed to have been granted authorisation by the Authority by virtue of regulation 121;

"the Authority" means the Financial Services Authority;

"the banking consolidation directive" means Directive 2006/48/EC of the European Parliament and of the Council of 14th June 2006 relating to the taking up and pursuit of the business of credit institutions;

"branch" means a place of business of an authorised payment institution, a small payment institution, or an EEA authorised payment institution, other than its head office, which forms a legally dependent part of the institution and which carries out directly all or some of the transactions inherent in its business; and, for the purposes of these Regulations, all places of business set up in the same EEA State other than the United Kingdom by an authorised payment institution are to be regarded as a single branch;

"business day" means any day on which the relevant payment service provider is open for business as required for the execution of a payment transaction;

"charity" means a body whose annual income is less than £1 million and is—

(c)   in England and Wales, a charity as defined by section 1(1) of the Charities Act 2006;

(d)   in Scotland, a charity as defined by section 106 of the Charities and Trustee Investment (Scotland) Act 2005;

(e)   in Northern Ireland, a charity as defined by section 1(1) of the Charities Act (Northern Ireland) 2008 or, until that section comes into force, a body which is recognised as a charity for tax purposes by Her Majesty's Revenue and Customs;

"the Commissioners" means the Commissioners for Her Majesty's Revenue and Customs;

"consumer" means an individual who, in contracts for payment services to which these Regulations apply, is acting for purposes other than a trade, business or profession;

"credit institution" has the meaning given in Article 4(1)(a) of the banking consolidation directive;

"direct debit" means a payment service for debiting the payer's payment account where a payment transaction is initiated by the payee on the basis of consent given by the payer to the payee, to the payee's payment service provider or to the payer's own payment service provider;

"durable medium" means any instrument which enables the payment service user to store information addressed personally to them in a way accessible for future reference for a period of time adequate for the purposes of the information and which allows the unchanged reproduction of the information stored;

"the EEA" means the European Economic Area;

"EEA agent" means an agent through which an authorised payment institution, in the exercise of its passport rights, provides payment services in an EEA State other than the United Kingdom;

"EEA authorised payment institution" means a person authorised in an EEA State other than the United Kingdom to provide payment services in accordance with the payment services directive;

"EEA branch" means a branch established by an authorised payment institution, in the exercise of its passport rights, to carry out payment services in an EEA State other than the United Kingdom;

"the electronic money directive" means Directive 2000/46/EC of the European Parliament and of the Council of 18th September 2000 on the taking up, pursuit and prudential supervision of the business of electronic money institutions;

"electronic money institution" has the meaning given in Article 1(3)(a) of the electronic money directive;

"framework contract" means a contract for payment services which governs the future execution of individual and successive payment transactions and which may contain the obligation and conditions for setting up a payment account;

PART IV   OTHER STATUTORY INSTRUMENTS

"funds" means banknotes and coins, scriptural money, and electronic money as defined in Article 1(3)(b) of the electronic money directive;

"group" means a group of undertakings which consists of a parent undertaking, its subsidiary undertakings and the entities in which the parent undertaking or its subsidiary undertakings have a holding, as well as undertakings linked to each other by a relationship referred to in Article 12(1) of the Seventh Council Directive 83/349/EEC of 13th June 1983 based on Article 54(3)(g) of the Treaty on consolidated accounts;

"home state competent authority" means the competent authority designated in accordance with Article 20 of the payment services directive as being responsible for the authorisation and prudential supervision of an EEA authorised payment institution which is exercising (or intends to exercise) its passport rights in the United Kingdom;

"host state competent authority" means the competent authority designated in accordance with Article 20 of the payment services directive in an EEA State in which an authorised payment institution exercises (or intends to exercise) its passport rights;

"means of distance communication" means any means which, without the simultaneous physical presence of the payment service provider and the payment service user, may be used for the conclusion of a contract for payment services between those parties;

"micro-enterprise" means an enterprise which, at the time at which the contract for payment services is entered into, is an enterprise as defined in Article 1 and Article 2(1) and (3) of the Annex to Recommendation 2003/361/EC;

"the money laundering directive" means Directive 2005/60/EC of the European Parliament and of the Council of 26th October 2005 on the prevention of the use of the financial system for the purpose of money laundering and terrorist financing;

"money remittance" means a service for the transmission of money (or any representation of monetary value), without any payment accounts being created in the name of the payer or the payee, where—

    (a)   funds are received from a payer for the sole purpose of transferring a corresponding amount to a payee or to another payment service provider acting on behalf of the payee; or

    (b)   funds are received on behalf of, and made available to, the payee;

"notice" means a notice in writing;

"the OFT" means the Office of Fair Trading;

"parent undertaking" has the same meaning as in the Companies Acts (see section 1162 of, and Schedule 7 to, the Companies Act 2006);

"passport right" (except for the purposes of regulation 26(1)) means the entitlement of a person to establish a branch or provide services in an EEA State other than that in which they are authorised to provide payment services—

    (a)   in accordance with the Treaty establishing the European Community as applied in the EEA; and

    (b)   subject to the conditions of the payment services directive;

"payee" means a person who is the intended recipient of funds which have been the subject of a payment transaction;

"payer" means—

    (a)   a person who holds a payment account and initiates, or consents to the initiation of, a payment order from that payment account; or

    (b)   where there is no payment account, a person who gives a payment order;

"payment account" means an account held in the name of one or more payment service users which is used for the execution of payment transactions;

"payment instrument" means any—

    (a)   personalised device; or

    (b)   personalised set of procedures agreed between the payment service user and the payment service provider,

used by the payment service user in order to initiate a payment order;

"payment order" means any instruction by—

    (a)   a payer; or

    (b)   a payee,

to their respective payment service provider requesting the execution of a payment transaction;

"payment services" means any of the activities specified in Part 1 of Schedule 1 when carried out as a regular occupation or business activity, other than any of the activities specified in Part 2 of that Schedule;

"payment services directive" means Directive 2007/64/EC of the European Parliament and of the Council of 13th November 2007 on payment services in the internal market;

"payment service provider" means any of the following persons when they carry out payment services—

    (a)   authorised payment institutions;

    (b)   small payment institutions;

    (c)   EEA authorised payment institutions;

    (d)   credit institutions;

    (e)   electronic money institutions;

    (f)   the Post Office Limited;

    (g)   the Bank of England, the European Central Bank and the national central banks of EEA States other than the United Kingdom, other than when acting in their capacity as a monetary authority or carrying out other functions of a public nature; and

    (h)   government departments and local authorities, other than when carrying out functions of a public nature;

"payment service user" means a person when making use of a payment service in the capacity of either payer or payee, or both;

"payment system" means a funds transfer system with formal and standardised arrangements and common rules for the processing, clearing and settlement of payment transactions;

"payment transaction" means an act, initiated by the payer or payee, of placing, transferring or withdrawing funds, irrespective of any underlying obligations between the payer and payee;

"qualifying holding" has the meaning given in article 4(11) of the banking consolidation directive;

"reference exchange rate" means the exchange rate which is used as the basis to calculate any currency exchange and which is made available by the payment service provider or comes from a publicly available source;

"reference interest rate" means the interest rate which is used as the basis for calculating any interest to be applied and which comes from a publicly available source which can be verified by both parties to a contract for payment services;

"the register" means the register maintained by the Authority under regulation 4;

"regulated agreement" has the meaning given by section 189(1) of the Consumer Credit Act 1974 (definitions);

"single payment service contract" means a contract for a single payment transaction not covered by a framework contract;

"small payment institution" means a person included by the Authority in the register pursuant to regulation 4(1)(b);

"subsidiary undertaking" has the same meaning as in the Companies Acts (see section 1162 of, and Schedule 7 to, the Companies Act 2006);

"the Tribunal" means the Financial Services and Markets Tribunal;

"unique identifier" means a combination of letters, numbers or symbols specified to the payment service user by the payment service provider and to be provided by the payment service user in relation to a payment transaction in order to identify unambiguously one or both of—

    (a)   the other payment service user who is a party to the payment transaction;

    (b)   the other payment service user's payment account;

"value date" means a reference time used by a payment service provider for the calculation of interest on the funds debited from or credited to a payment account.

(2)   In these Regulations references to amounts in euro include references to equivalent amounts in another currency.

(3)   Unless otherwise defined, expressions used in these Regulations which are also used in the payment services directive have the same meaning as in that directive.

(4)   Expressions used in these Regulations and in a modification to a provision in primary or secondary legislation applied by these Regulations have the same meaning as in these Regulations.

[1128]

NOTES

Commencement: these Regulations come into force on 2 March 2009 (for the purposes specified in reg 1(2)(a)), 1 May 2009 (for the purposes specified in reg 1(2)(b)), and 1 November 2009 (otherwise). See reg 1 at **[1127]**.

---

3 Exemption for certain bodies

(1)   Subject to paragraph (2) and regulation 4(1)(d), these Regulations do not apply to the following persons—

    (a)   credit unions;

    (b)   municipal banks; and

    (c)   the National Savings Bank.

(2)   Where municipal banks provide or propose to provide payment services they must give notice to the Authority.

(3)   In this regulation—

"credit union" means a credit union within the meaning of—

    (a)   the Credit Unions Act 1979;

(b)   the Credit Unions (Northern Ireland) Order 1985;
"municipal bank" means a company which, immediately before 1st December 2001, fell within the definition in section 103 of the Banking Act 1987.

[1129]

NOTES
Commencement: these Regulations come into force on 2 March 2009 (for the purposes specified in reg 1(2)(a)), 1 May 2009 (for the purposes specified in reg 1(2)(b)), and 1 November 2009 (otherwise). See reg 1 at **[1127]**.

PART 2
REGISTRATION
The register

4 The register of certain payment service providers

(1)   The Authority must maintain a register of—
  (a)   authorised payment institutions and their EEA branches;
  (b)   small payment institutions;
  (c)   agents of authorised payment institutions and small payment institutions required to be registered under regulation 29; and
  (d)   the persons specified in regulation 3(1) where they provide payment services.

(2)   The Authority may include on the register any of the persons mentioned in paragraphs (c) to (h) of the definition of a payment service provider in regulation 2(1) where such persons provide payment services.

(3)   Where a person mentioned in paragraph (f), (g) or (h) of the definition of a payment service provider in regulation 2(1)—
  (a)   is not included on the register; and
  (b)   provides, or proposes to provide, payment services,
the person must give notice to the Authority.

(4)   The Authority may—
  (a)   keep the register in any form it thinks fit;
  (b)   include on it such information as the Authority considers appropriate, provided that the register identifies the payment services for which an institution is authorised or registered under this Part; and
  (c)   exploit commercially the information contained in the register, or any part of that information.

(5)   The Authority must—
  (a)   publish the register online and make it available for public inspection;
  (b)   update the register on a regular basis; and
  (c)   provide a certified copy of the register, or any part of it, to any person who asks for it—
    (i)   on payment of the fee (if any) fixed by the Authority; and
    (ii)   in a form (either written or electronic) in which it is legible to the person asking for it.

[1130]

NOTES
Commencement: these Regulations come into force on 2 March 2009 (for the purposes specified in reg 1(2)(a)), 1 May 2009 (for the purposes specified in reg 1(2)(b)), and 1 November 2009 (otherwise). See reg 1 at **[1127]**.

Authorisation as a payment institution

5 Application for authorisation as a payment institution or variation of an existing authorisation

(1)   An application for authorisation as a payment institution must contain or be accompanied by the information specified in Schedule 2.

(2)   An application for the variation of an authorisation as a payment institution must—
  (a)   contain a statement of the proposed variation;
  (b)   contain a statement of the payment services which the applicant proposes to carry on if the authorisation is varied; and
  (c)   contain, or be accompanied by, such other information as the Authority may reasonably require.

(3)   An application under paragraph (1) or (2) must be made in such manner as the Authority may direct.

(4)   At any time after receiving an application and before determining it, the Authority may require the applicant to provide it with such further information as it reasonably considers necessary to enable it to determine the application.

(5)   Different directions may be given, and different requirements imposed, in relation to different applications or categories of application.

[1131]

NOTES

Commencement: these Regulations come into force on 2 March 2009 (for the purposes specified in reg 1(2)(a)), 1 May 2009 (for the purposes specified in reg 1(2)(b)), and 1 November 2009 (otherwise). See reg 1 at **[1127]**.

6 Conditions for authorisation as a payment institution

(1)   The Authority may refuse to grant all or part of an application for authorisation as a payment institution only if any of the conditions set out in paragraphs (2) to (8) is not met.

(2)   The application must comply with the requirements of, and any requirements imposed under, regulation 5.

(3)   The applicant must immediately before the time of authorisation hold the amount of initial capital required in accordance with Part 1 of Schedule 3.

(4)   The applicant must be a body corporate constituted under the law of a part of the United Kingdom having—

    (a)   its head office, and

    (b)   if it has a registered office, that office,

in the United Kingdom.

(5)   The applicant must satisfy the Authority that, taking into account the need to ensure the sound and prudent conduct of the affairs of the institution, it has—

    (a)   robust governance arrangements for its payment service business, including a clear organisational structure with well-defined, transparent and consistent lines of responsibility;

    (b)   effective procedures to identify, manage, monitor and report any risks to which it might be exposed;

    (c)   adequate internal control mechanisms, including sound administrative, risk management and accounting procedures,

which are comprehensive and proportionate to the nature, scale and complexity of the payment services to be provided by the institution.

(6)   The applicant must satisfy the Authority that—

    (a)   any persons having a qualifying holding in it are fit and proper persons having regard to the need to ensure the sound and prudent conduct of the affairs of an authorised payment institution;

    (b)   the directors and persons responsible for the management of the institution and, where relevant, the persons responsible for the management of payment services, are of good repute and possess appropriate knowledge and experience to provide payment services;

    (c)   it has a business plan (including, for the first three years, a forecast budget calculation) under which appropriate and proportionate systems, resources and procedures will be employed by the institution to operate soundly; and

    (d)   it has taken adequate measures for the purpose of safeguarding payment service users' funds in accordance with regulation 19.

(7)   The applicant must comply with a requirement of the Money Laundering Regulations 2007 to be included in a register maintained under those Regulations where such a requirement applies to the applicant.

(8)   If the applicant has close links with another person ("CL") the applicant must satisfy the Authority—

    (a)   that those links are not likely to prevent the Authority's effective supervision of the applicant; and

    (b)   if it appears to the Authority that CL is subject to the laws, regulations or administrative provisions of a territory which is not an EEA State ("the foreign provisions"), that neither the foreign provisions, nor any deficiency in their enforcement, would prevent the Authority's effective supervision of the applicant.

(9)   For the purposes of paragraph (8), an applicant has close links with CL if—

    (a)   CL is a parent undertaking of the applicant;

    (b)   CL is a subsidiary undertaking of the applicant;

    (c)   CL is a parent undertaking of a subsidiary undertaking of the applicant;

    (d)   CL is a subsidiary undertaking of a parent undertaking of the applicant;

    (e)   CL owns or controls 20% or more of the voting rights or capital of the applicant; or

(f)   the applicant owns or controls 20% or more of the voting rights or capital of CL.

[1132]

NOTES
Commencement: these Regulations come into force on 2 March 2009 (for the purposes specified in reg 1(2)(a)), 1 May 2009 (for the purposes specified in reg 1(2)(b)), and 1 November 2009 (otherwise). See reg 1 at **[1127]**.

7   Imposition of requirements

(1)   The Authority may include in an authorisation such requirements as it considers appropriate.

(2)   A requirement may, in particular, be imposed so as to require the person concerned to—
(a)   take a specified action;
(b)   refrain from taking a specified action.

(3)   A requirement may be imposed by reference to the person's relationship with its group or other members of its group.

(4)   Where—
(a)   an applicant for authorisation as a payment institution intends to carry on business activities other than the provision of payment services; and
(b)   the Authority considers that the carrying on of such other business activities will impair, or is likely to impair—
(i)   the financial soundness of the applicant, or
(ii)   the Authority's effective supervision of the applicant,
the Authority may require the applicant to establish a separate body corporate to carry on the payment service business.

(5)   A requirement expires at the end of such period as the Authority may specify in the authorisation.

(6)   Paragraph (5) does not affect the Authority's powers under regulation 8 or 11.

[1133]

NOTES
Commencement: these Regulations come into force on 2 March 2009 (for the purposes specified in reg 1(2)(a)), 1 May 2009 (for the purposes specified in reg 1(2)(b)), and 1 November 2009 (otherwise). See reg 1 at **[1127]**.

8   Variation etc at request of authorised payment institution

The Authority may, on the application of an authorised payment institution, vary that person's authorisation by—
(a)   adding a payment service to those for which it has granted authorisation;
(b)   removing a payment service from those for which it has granted authorisation;
(c)   imposing a requirement such as may, under regulation 7, be included in an authorisation;
(d)   cancelling a requirement included in the authorisation or previously imposed under paragraph (c); or
(e)   varying such a requirement,
provided that the conditions set out in regulation 6(4) to (8) and, if applicable, the requirement in regulation 18(1) to maintain own funds, will continue to be met.

[1134]

NOTES
Commencement: these Regulations come into force on 2 March 2009 (for the purposes specified in reg 1(2)(a)), 1 May 2009 (for the purposes specified in reg 1(2)(b)), and 1 November 2009 (otherwise). See reg 1 at **[1127]**.

9   Determination of application for authorisation or variation of authorisation

(1)   The Authority must determine an application for authorisation or the variation of an authorisation before the end of the period of three months beginning with the date on which it received the completed application.

(2)   The Authority may determine an incomplete application if it considers it appropriate to do so, and it must in any event determine any such application within 12 months beginning with the date on which it received the application.

(3)   The applicant may withdraw its application, by giving the Authority notice, at any time before the Authority determines it.

(4)   The Authority may grant authorisation to carry out the payment services to which the application relates or such of them as may be specified in the grant of the authorisation.

(5)   If the Authority decides to grant an application for authorisation, or for the variation of an authorisation, it must give the applicant notice of its decision specifying—
  (a)   the payment services for which authorisation has been granted; or
  (b)   the variation granted,
described in such manner as the Authority considers appropriate.

(6)   The notice must state the date on which the authorisation or variation takes effect.

(7)   If the Authority proposes to refuse an application or to impose a requirement it must give the applicant a warning notice.

(8)   The Authority must, having considered any representations made in response to the warning notice—
  (a)   if it decides to refuse the application or to impose a requirement, give the applicant a decision notice; or
  (b)   if it grants the application without imposing a requirement, give the applicant notice of its decision, stating the date on which the authorisation or variation takes effect.

(9)   If the Authority decides to refuse the application or to impose a requirement the applicant may refer the matter to the Tribunal.

(10)   If the Authority decides to authorise the applicant, or vary its authorisation, it must update the register as soon as practicable.

[1135]

NOTES
Commencement: these Regulations come into force on 2 March 2009 (for the purposes specified in reg 1(2)(a)), 1 May 2009 (for the purposes specified in reg 1(2)(b)), and 1 November 2009 (otherwise). See reg 1 at **[1127]**.

10   Cancellation of authorisation

(1)   The Authority may cancel a person's authorisation and remove the person from the register where—
  (a)   the person does not provide payment services within 12 months beginning with the date on which the authorisation took effect;
  (b)   the person requests, or consents to, the cancellation of the authorisation;
  (c)   the person ceases to engage in business activity for more than six months;
  (d)   the person has obtained authorisation through false statements or any other irregular means;
  (e)   the person no longer meets, or is unlikely to continue to meet, any of the conditions set out in regulation 6(4) to (8) or, if applicable, the requirement in regulation 18(1) to maintain own funds;
  (f)   the person has provided payment services other than in accordance with the authorisation granted to it;
  (g)   the person would constitute a threat to the stability of a payment system by continuing its payment services business;
  (h)   the cancellation is desirable in order to protect the interests of consumers; or
  (i)   the person's provision of payment services is otherwise unlawful.

(2)   Where the Authority proposes to cancel a person's authorisation, other than at the person's request, it must give the person a warning notice.

(3)   The Authority must, having considered any representations made in response to the warning notice—
  (a)   if it decides to cancel the authorisation, give the person a decision notice; or
  (b)   if it decides not to cancel the authorisation, give the person notice of its decision.

(4)   If the Authority decides to cancel the authorisation, other than at the person's request, the person may refer the matter to the Tribunal.

(5)   Where the period for a reference to the Tribunal has expired without a reference being made, the Authority must as soon as practicable update the register accordingly.

[1136]

NOTES
Commencement: these Regulations come into force on 2 March 2009 (for the purposes specified in reg 1(2)(a)), 1 May 2009 (for the purposes specified in reg 1(2)(b)), and 1 November 2009 (otherwise). See reg 1 at **[1127]**.

11   Variation of authorisation on Authority's own initiative

(1)   The Authority may vary a person's authorisation in any of the ways mentioned in regulation 8 if it appears to the Authority that—

PART IV   OTHER STATUTORY INSTRUMENTS

(a)   the person no longer meets, or is unlikely to continue to meet, any of the conditions set out in regulation 6(4) to (8) or, if applicable, the requirement in regulation 18(1) to maintain own funds;

(b)   the person has provided a particular payment service or payment services other than in accordance with the authorisation granted to it;

(c)   the person would constitute a threat to the stability of a payment system by continuing to provide a particular payment service or payment services;

(d)   the variation is desirable in order to protect the interests of consumers; or

(e)   the person's provision of a particular payment service or payment services is otherwise unlawful.

(2)   A variation under this regulation takes effect—

(a)   immediately, if the notice given under paragraph (6) states that that is the case;

(b)   on such date as may be specified in the notice; or

(c)   if no date is specified in the notice, when the matter to which the notice relates is no longer open to review.

(3)   A variation may be expressed to take effect immediately or on a specified date only if the Authority, having regard to the ground on which it is exercising the power under paragraph (1), reasonably considers that it is necessary for the variation to take effect immediately or, as the case may be, on that date.

(4)   The Authority must as soon as practicable after the variation takes effect update the register accordingly.

(5)   A person who is aggrieved by the variation of their authorisation under this regulation may refer the matter to the Tribunal.

(6)   Where the Authority proposes to vary a person's authorisation under this regulation, it must give the person notice.

(7)   The notice must—

(a)   give details of the variation;

(b)   state the Authority's reasons for the variation and for its determination as to when the variation takes effect;

(c)   inform the person that they may make representations to the Authority within such period as may be specified in the notice (whether or not the person has referred the matter to the Tribunal);

(d)   inform the person of the date on which the variation takes effect; and

(e)   inform the person of their right to refer the matter to the Tribunal and the procedure for such a reference.

(8)   The Authority may extend the period allowed under the notice for making representations.

(9)   If, having considered any representations made by the person, the Authority decides—

(a)   to vary the authorisation in the way proposed, or

(b)   if the authorisation has been varied, not to rescind the variation,

it must give the person notice.

(10)   If, having considered any representations made by the person, the Authority decides—

(a)   not to vary the authorisation in the way proposed,

(b)   to vary the authorisation in a different way, or

(c)   to rescind a variation which has taken effect,

it must give the person notice.

(11)   A notice given under paragraph (9) must inform the person of their right to refer the matter to the Tribunal and the procedure for such a reference.

(12)   A notice under paragraph (10)(b) must comply with paragraph (7).

(13)   For the purposes of paragraph (2)(c), paragraphs (a) to (d) of section 391(8) of the 2000 Act (publication) apply to determine whether a matter is open to review.

[1137]

NOTES

Commencement: these Regulations come into force on 2 March 2009 (for the purposes specified in reg 1(2)(a)), 1 May 2009 (for the purposes specified in reg 1(2)(b)), and 1 November 2009 (otherwise). See reg 1 at **[1127]**.

Registration as a small payment institution

12 Application for registration as a small payment institution or variation of an existing registration

(1)   An application for registration as a small payment institution must contain, or be accompanied by, such information as the Authority may reasonably require.

(2)   An application for the variation of a registration as a small payment institution must—
    (a)   contain a statement of the proposed variation;
    (b)   contain a statement of the payment services which the applicant proposes to carry on if the registration is varied; and
    (c)   contain, or be accompanied by, such other information as the Authority may reasonably require.

(3)   An application under paragraph (1) or (2) must be made in such manner as the Authority may direct.

(4)   At any time after receiving an application and before determining it, the Authority may require the applicant to provide it with such further information as it reasonably considers necessary to enable it to determine the application.

(5)   Different directions may be given, and different requirements imposed, in relation to different applications or categories of application.

[1138]

NOTES

Commencement: these Regulations come into force on 2 March 2009 (for the purposes specified in reg 1(2)(a)), 1 May 2009 (for the purposes specified in reg 1(2)(b)), and 1 November 2009 (otherwise). See reg 1 at **[1127]**.

13   Conditions for registration as a small payment institution

(1)   The Authority may refuse to register an applicant as a small payment institution only if any of the conditions set out in paragraphs (2) to (6) is not met.

(2)   The application must comply with the requirements of, and any requirements imposed under, regulation 12.

(3)   The monthly average over the period of 12 months preceding the application of the total amount of payment transactions executed by the applicant, including any of its agents in the United Kingdom, must not exceed 3 million euros.

(4)   None of the individuals responsible for the management or operation of the business has been convicted of—
    (a)   an offence under Part 7 of the Proceeds of Crime Act 2002 (money laundering) or under the Money Laundering Regulations 2007;
    (b)   an offence under section 15 (fund-raising), 16 (use and possession), 17 (funding arrangements), 18 (money laundering) or 63 (terrorist finance: jurisdiction) of the Terrorism Act 2000;
    (c)   an offence under the 2000 Act;
    (d)   an offence under article 7, 8 or 10 of the Terrorism (United Nations Measures) Order 2006 or article 7, 8 or 10 of the Al-Qaida and Taliban (United Nations Measures) Order 2006;
    (e)   an offence under these Regulations; or
    (f)   any other financial crimes.

(5)   The applicant's head office, registered office or place of residence, as the case may be, must be in the United Kingdom.

(6)   The applicant must comply with a requirement of the Money Laundering Regulations 2007 to be included in a register maintained under those Regulations where such a requirement applies to the applicant.

(7)   For the purposes of paragraph (3), where the applicant has yet to commence the provision of payment services, or has been providing payment services for less than 12 months, the monthly average may be based on the projected total amount of payment transactions over a 12 month period.

(8)   In paragraph (4) "financial crime" includes any offence involving fraud or dishonesty and, for this purpose, "offence" includes any act or omission which would be an offence if it had taken place in the United Kingdom.

[1139]

NOTES

Commencement: these Regulations come into force on 2 March 2009 (for the purposes specified in reg 1(2)(a)), 1 May 2009 (for the purposes specified in reg 1(2)(b)), and 1 November 2009 (otherwise). See reg 1 at **[1127]**.

14   Supplementary provisions

Regulations 7 to 11 apply to registration as a small payment institution as they apply to authorisation as a payment institution with the following modifications—
    (a)   references to authorisation are to be treated as references to registration;

(b)   omit regulation 7(4);

(c)   in regulation 8 for "an authorised payment institution" substitute "small payment institution" and for "provided that" to the end substitute—

"provided that the conditions set out in regulation 13(4) to (6) will continue to be met and that the monthly average over any period of 12 months of the total amount of payment transactions executed by the institution, including any of its agents in the United Kingdom, continues not to exceed 3 million euro ("the financial limit").";

(d)   in regulation 10 for paragraph (1)(e) substitute—
"(e)   the person no longer meets, or is unlikely to continue to meet, any of the conditions set out in regulation 13(4) to (6) or the financial limit referred to in regulation 8;"; and

(e)   in regulation 11 for paragraph (1)(a) substitute—
"(a)   the person no longer meets, or is unlikely to continue to meet, any of the conditions set out in regulation 13(4) to (6) or the financial limit referred to in regulation 8;".

[1140]

NOTES
Commencement: these Regulations come into force on 2 March 2009 (for the purposes specified in reg 1(2)(a)), 1 May 2009 (for the purposes specified in reg 1(2)(b)), and 1 November 2009 (otherwise). See reg 1 at **[1127]**.

15 Application for authorisation as a payment institution where the financial limit is exceeded

Where the financial limit referred to in regulation 8 (as applied by regulation 14(c)) is exceeded, the institution concerned must, within 30 days of becoming aware of the change in circumstances, apply for authorisation as a payment institution under regulation 5 if it intends to continue providing payment services in the United Kingdom.

[1141]

NOTES
Commencement: these Regulations come into force on 2 March 2009 (for the purposes specified in reg 1(2)(a)), 1 May 2009 (for the purposes specified in reg 1(2)(b)), and 1 November 2009 (otherwise). See reg 1 at **[1127]**.

Common provisions

16 Duty to notify changes

(1)   If at any time after an applicant has provided the Authority with any information under regulation 5(1), (2), or (4), or 12(1), (2) or (4) and before the Authority has determined the application—

(a)   there is, or is likely to be, a material change affecting any matter contained in that information; or

(b)   it becomes apparent to the applicant that the information is incomplete or contains a material inaccuracy,

the applicant must provide the Authority with details of the change, the complete information or a correction of the inaccuracy (as the case may be) without undue delay, or, in the case of a material change which has not yet taken place, the applicant must provide details of the likely change as soon as the applicant is aware of such change.

(2)   The obligation in paragraph (1) also applies to material changes or significant inaccuracies affecting any matter contained in any supplementary information provided pursuant to that paragraph.

(3)   Any information to be provided to the Authority under this regulation must be in such form or verified in such manner as it may direct.

[1142]

NOTES
Commencement: these Regulations come into force on 2 March 2009 (for the purposes specified in reg 1(2)(a)), 1 May 2009 (for the purposes specified in reg 1(2)(b)), and 1 November 2009 (otherwise). See reg 1 at **[1127]**.

17 Authorised payment institutions and small payment institutions acting without permission

If an authorised payment institution or a small payment institution carries on a payment service in the United Kingdom, or purports to do so, other than in accordance with an authorisation or registration granted, or deemed to be granted under regulation 121, to it by the Authority under these Regulations, it is to be taken to have contravened a requirement imposed on it under these Regulations.

[1143]

NOTES
Commencement: these Regulations come into force on 2 March 2009 (for the purposes specified in reg 1(2)(a)), 1 May 2009 (for the purposes specified in reg 1(2)(b)), and 1 November 2009 (otherwise). See reg 1 at **[1127]**.

PART 3
AUTHORISED PAYMENT INSTITUTIONS

18 Capital requirements

(1) Subject to paragraph (2), an authorised payment institution must maintain at all times own funds as defined for the purposes of Part 2 of Schedule 3 equal to or in excess of—
   (a) the amount of initial capital specified in Part 1 of Schedule 3, or
   (b) the amount of the own funds requirement calculated in accordance with paragraph 11 of Schedule 3 subject to any adjustment directed by the Authority under paragraph 12 of that Schedule,
whichever is greater.

(2) Paragraph (1) does not apply to an authorised payment institution—
   (a) which is included in the consolidated supervision of a parent credit institution pursuant to the banking consolidation directive; and
   (b) in respect of which all of the conditions specified in Article 69(1) of the banking consolidation directive are met.

[1144]

NOTES
Commencement: these Regulations come into force on 2 March 2009 (for the purposes specified in reg 1(2)(a)), 1 May 2009 (for the purposes specified in reg 1(2)(b)), and 1 November 2009 (otherwise). See reg 1 at **[1127]**.

19 Safeguarding requirements

(1) For the purposes of this regulation "relevant funds" comprise the following—
   (a) sums received from, or for the benefit of, a payment service user for the execution of a payment transaction; and
   (b) sums received from a payment service provider for the execution of a payment transaction on behalf of a payment service user.

(2) Where—
   (a) only a portion of the sums referred to in paragraph (1)(a) or (b) is to be used for the execution of a payment transaction (with the remainder being used for non-payment services); and
   (b) the precise portion attributable to the execution of the payment transaction is variable or unknown in advance,
the relevant funds are such amount as may be reasonably estimated, on the basis of historical data and to the satisfaction of the Authority, to be representative of the portion attributable to the execution of the payment transaction.

(3) Where the relevant funds in respect of a payment transaction exceed £50, an authorised payment institution must safeguard such funds in accordance with either—
   (a) paragraphs (4) to (8); or
   (b) paragraphs (9) and (10).

(4) An authorised payment institution must keep relevant funds segregated from any other funds that it holds.

(5) Where the authorised payment institution continues to hold the relevant funds at the end of the business day following the day on which they were received it must—
   (a) place them in a separate account that it holds with an authorised credit institution; or
   (b) invest the relevant funds in such secure, liquid assets as the Authority may approve ("relevant assets") and place those assets in a separate account with an authorised custodian.

(6) An account in which relevant funds or relevant assets are placed under paragraph (5) must—
   (a) be designated in such a way as to show that it is an account which is held for the purpose of safeguarding relevant funds or relevant assets in accordance with this regulation; and
   (b) be used only for holding those funds or assets.

(7)   No person other than the authorised payment institution may have any interest in or right over the relevant funds or relevant assets placed in an account in accordance with paragraph (5)(a) or (b) except as provided by this regulation.

(8)   The authorised payment institution must keep a record of—
    (a)   any relevant funds segregated in accordance with paragraph (4);
    (b)   any relevant funds placed in an account in accordance with paragraph (5)(a); and
    (c)   any relevant assets placed in an account in accordance with paragraph (5)(b).

(9)   The authorised payment institution must ensure that—
    (a)   any relevant funds are covered by—
        (i)   an insurance policy with an authorised insurer;
        (ii)   a guarantee from an authorised insurer; or
        (iii) a guarantee from an authorised credit institution; and
    (b)   the proceeds of any such insurance policy or guarantee are payable upon an insolvency event into a separate account held by the authorised payment institution which must—
        (i)   be designated in such a way as to show that it is an account which is held for the purpose of safeguarding relevant funds in accordance with this regulation; and
        (ii)   be used only for holding such proceeds.

(10)   No person other than the authorised payment institution may have any interest in or right over the proceeds placed in an account in accordance with paragraph (9)(b) except as provided by this regulation.

(11)   Subject to paragraph (12), where there is an insolvency event—
    (a)   the claims of payment service users are to be paid from the asset pool in priority to all other creditors; and
    (b)   until all the claims of payment service users have been paid, no right of set-off or security right may be exercised in respect of the asset pool except to the extent that the right of set-off relates to fees and expenses in relation to operating an account held in accordance with paragraph (5)(a) or (b) or (9)(b).

(12)   The claims referred to in paragraph (11)(a) shall not be subject to the priority of expenses of an insolvency proceeding except in respect of the costs of distributing the asset pool.

(13)   Paragraphs (11) and (12) shall apply to any relevant funds which a small payment institution (or an authorised payment institution in relation to relevant funds of £50 or less) voluntarily safeguards in accordance with either paragraphs (4) to (8) or paragraphs (9) and (10).

(14)   An authorised payment institution (and any small payment institution which voluntarily safeguards relevant funds) must maintain organisational arrangements sufficient to minimise the risk of the loss or diminution of relevant funds or relevant assets through fraud, misuse, negligence or poor administration.

(15)   In this regulation—
    "asset pool" means—
        (a)   any relevant funds segregated in accordance with paragraph (4);
        (b)   any relevant funds held in an account in accordance with paragraph (5)(a);
        (c)   any relevant assets held in an account in accordance with paragraph (5)(b); and
        (d)   any proceeds of an insurance policy or guarantee held in an account in accordance with paragraph (9)(b);
    "authorised insurer" means a person authorised for the purposes of the 2000 Act to effect and carry out a contract of general insurance as principal or otherwise authorised in accordance with Article 6 of the First Council Directive 73/239/EEC of 24th July 1973 on the business of direct insurance other than life insurance, other than a person in the same group as the authorised payment institution;
    "authorised credit institution" means a person authorised for the purposes of the 2000 Act to accept deposits or otherwise authorised as a credit institution in accordance with Article 6 of the banking consolidation directive other than a person in the same group as the authorised payment institution;
    "authorised custodian" means a person authorised for the purposes of the 2000 Act to safeguard and administer investments or authorised as an investment firm under Article 5 of Directive 2004/39/EC of 12th April 2004 on markets in financial instruments which holds those investments under regulatory standards at least equivalent to those set out under Article 13 of that directive;
    "insolvency event" means any of the following procedures in relation to an authorised payment institution or small payment institution—
        (e)   the making of a winding-up order;
        (f)   the passing of a resolution for voluntary winding-up;
        (g)   the entry of the institution into administration;
        (h)   the appointment of a receiver or manager of the institution's property;
        (i)   the approval of a proposed voluntary arrangement (being a composition in satisfaction of debts or a scheme of arrangement);

(j)   the making of a bankruptcy order;
(k)   in Scotland, the award of sequestration;
(l)   the making of any deed of arrangement for the benefit of creditors or, in Scotland, the execution of a trust deed for creditors;
(m)   the conclusion of any composition contract with creditors; or
(n)   the making of an insolvency administration order or, in Scotland, sequestration, in respect of the estate of a deceased person;

"insolvency proceeding" means—
(o)   winding-up, administration, receivership, bankruptcy or, in Scotland, sequestration;
(p)   a voluntary arrangement, deed of arrangement or trust deed for the benefit of creditors; or
(q)   the administration of the insolvent estate of a deceased person;

"security right" means—
(r)   security for a debt owed by an authorised payment institution or a small payment institution and includes any charge, lien, mortgage or other security over the asset pool or any part of the asset pool; and
(s)   any charge arising in respect of the expenses of a voluntary arrangement.

[1145]

NOTES
Commencement: these Regulations come into force on 2 March 2009 (for the purposes specified in reg 1(2)(a)), 1 May 2009 (for the purposes specified in reg 1(2)(b)), and 1 November 2009 (otherwise). See reg 1 at **[1127]**.

20 Accounting and statutory audit

(1)   Where an authorised payment institution carries on activities other than the provision of payment services, it must provide to the Authority separate accounting information in respect of its provision of payment services.

(2)   Such accounting information must be subject, where relevant, to an auditor's report prepared by the institution's statutory auditors or an audit firm (within the meaning of Directive 2006/43/EC of the European Parliament and of the Council of 17th May 2006 on statutory audits of annual accounts and consolidated accounts).

(3)   A statutory auditor or audit firm ("the auditor") must, in any of the circumstances referred to in paragraph (4), communicate to the Authority information on, or its opinion on, matters—
(a)   of which it has become aware in its capacity as auditor of an authorised payment institution or of a person with close links to an authorised payment institution; and
(b)   which relate to payment services provided by that institution.

(4)   The circumstances are that—
(a)   the auditor reasonably believes that—
    (i)   there is or has been, or may be or may have been, a contravention of any requirement imposed on the authorised payment institution by or under these Regulations; and
    (ii)   the contravention may be of material significance to the Authority in determining whether to exercise, in relation to that institution, any functions conferred on the Authority by these Regulations;
(b)   the auditor reasonably believes that the information on, or his opinion on, those matters may be of material significance to the Authority in determining whether the institution meets or will continue to meet the conditions set out in regulation 6(4) to (8) and, if applicable, the requirement in regulation 18(1) to maintain own funds;
(c)   the auditor reasonably believes that the institution is not, may not be or may cease to be, a going concern;
(d)   the auditor is precluded from stating in his report that the annual accounts have been properly prepared in accordance with the Companies Act 2006;
(e)   the auditor is precluded from stating in his report, where applicable, that the annual accounts give a true and fair view of the matters referred to in section 495 of the Companies Act 2006 (auditor's report on company's annual accounts) including as it is applied and modified by regulation 39 of the Limited Liability Partnerships (Accounts and Audit) (Application of Companies Act 2006) Regulations 2008 ("the LLP Regulations"); or
(f)   the auditor is required to state in his report in relation to the person concerned any of the facts referred to in subsection (2), (3) or (5) of section 498 of the Companies Act 2006 (duties of auditor) or, in the case of limited liability partnerships, subsection (2), (3) or (4) of section 498 as applied and modified by regulation 40 of the LLP Regulations.

(5)   In this regulation a person has close links with an authorised payment institution ("A") if that person is—

(a)   a parent undertaking of A;
(b)   a subsidiary undertaking of A;
(c)   a parent undertaking of a subsidiary undertaking of A; or
(d)   a subsidiary undertaking of a parent undertaking of A.

[1146]

NOTES
Commencement: these Regulations come into force on 2 March 2009 (for the purposes specified in reg 1(2)(a)), 1 May 2009 (for the purposes specified in reg 1(2)(b)), and 1 November 2009 (otherwise). See reg 1 at **[1127]**.

21 Outsourcing

(1)   An authorised payment institution must notify the Authority of its intention to enter into a contract with another person under which that other person will carry out any operational function relating to its provision of payment services ("outsourcing").

(2)   Where an authorised payment institution intends to outsource any important operational function, all of the following conditions must be met—
(a)   the outsourcing is not undertaken in such a way as to impair—
      (i)   the quality of the authorised payment institution's internal control; or
      (ii)   the ability of the Authority to monitor the authorised payment institution's compliance with these Regulations;
(b)   the outsourcing does not result in any delegation by the senior management of the authorised payment institution of responsibility for complying with the requirements imposed by or under these Regulations;
(c)   the relationship and obligations of the authorised payment institution towards its payment service users under these Regulations is not substantially altered;
(d)   compliance with the conditions which the authorised payment institution must observe in order to be authorised and remain so is not adversely affected; and
(e)   none of the conditions of the payment institution's authorisation requires removal or variation.

(3)   For the purposes of paragraph (2), an operational function is important if a defect or failure in its performance would materially impair—
(a)   compliance by the authorised payment institution with these Regulations and any requirements of its authorisation;
(b)   the financial performance of the authorised payment institution; or
(c)   the soundness or continuity of the authorised payment institution's payment services.

[1147]

NOTES
Commencement: these Regulations come into force on 2 March 2009 (for the purposes specified in reg 1(2)(a)), 1 May 2009 (for the purposes specified in reg 1(2)(b)), and 1 November 2009 (otherwise). See reg 1 at **[1127]**.

22 Record keeping

(1)   An authorised payment institution must maintain relevant records and keep them for at least five years from the date on which the record was created.

(2)   For the purposes of paragraph (1), records are relevant where they relate to the authorised payment institution's compliance with this Part and, in particular, would enable the Authority to supervise effectively such compliance.

[1148]

NOTES
Commencement: these Regulations come into force on 2 March 2009 (for the purposes specified in reg 1(2)(a)), 1 May 2009 (for the purposes specified in reg 1(2)(b)), and 1 November 2009 (otherwise). See reg 1 at **[1127]**.

Exercise of passport rights

23 Notice of intention

(1)   Where an authorised payment institution intends to exercise its passport rights for the first time in a particular EEA State it must give the Authority, in such manner as the Authority may direct, notice of its intention to do so ("a notice of intention") which—
(a)   identifies the payment services which it seeks to carry on in exercise of those rights in that State;
(b)   gives the names of those responsible for the management of a proposed EEA branch, if any; and

(c)   provides details of the organisational structure of a proposed EEA branch, if any.

(2)   The Authority must, within one month beginning with the date on which it receives the notice of intention, inform the host state competent authority of—
   (a)   the name and address of the authorised payment institution; and
   (b)   the information contained in the notice of intention.

(3)   Where an authorised payment institution intends to exercise its passport rights through an EEA agent, the provisions of regulation 29 apply.

[1149]

NOTES
   Commencement: these Regulations come into force on 2 March 2009 (for the purposes specified in reg 1(2)(a)), 1 May 2009 (for the purposes specified in reg 1(2)(b)), and 1 November 2009 (otherwise). See reg 1 at **[1127]**.

24   Registration of EEA branch

(1)   If the Authority, taking into account any information received from the host state competent authority, has reasonable grounds to suspect that, in connection with the establishment of an EEA branch by an authorised payment institution—
   (a)   money laundering or terrorist financing within the meaning of the money laundering directive is taking place, has taken place, or has been attempted; or
   (b)   the risk of such activities taking place would be increased,
the Authority may refuse to register the EEA branch or cancel any such registration already made and remove the branch from the register.

(2)   If the Authority proposes to refuse to register, or cancel the registration of, an EEA branch, it must give the relevant authorised payment institution a warning notice.

(3)   The Authority must, having considered any representations made in response to the warning notice—
   (a)   if it decides not to register the branch, or to cancel its registration, give the authorised payment institution a decision notice; or
   (b)   if it decides to register the branch, or not to cancel the registration, give the authorised payment institution notice of its decision.

(4)   If the Authority decides not to register the branch, or to cancel its registration, the authorised payment institution may refer the matter to the Tribunal.

(5)   If the Authority decides to register an EEA branch, it must update the register as soon as practicable.

(6)   If the Authority decides to cancel the registration, the Authority must, where the period for a reference to the Tribunal has expired without a reference being made, as soon as practicable update the register accordingly.

[1150]

NOTES
   Commencement: these Regulations come into force on 2 March 2009 (for the purposes specified in reg 1(2)(a)), 1 May 2009 (for the purposes specified in reg 1(2)(b)), and 1 November 2009 (otherwise). See reg 1 at **[1127]**.

25   Supervision of firms exercising passport rights

(1)   Without prejudice to the generality of regulation 119, the Authority must co-operate with the relevant host state competent authority or home state competent authority, as the case may be, in relation to the exercise of passport rights by any authorised payment institution or EEA authorised payment institution.

(2)   The Authority must, in particular—
   (a)   notify the host state competent authority whenever it intends to carry out an on-site inspection in the host state competent authority's territory; and
   (b)   provide the host state competent authority or home state competent authority, as the case may be—
      (i)   on request, with all relevant information; and
      (ii)   on its own initiative, with all essential information,
relating to the exercise of passport rights by an authorised payment institution or EEA authorised payment institution, including where there is an infringement or suspected infringement of these Regulations or of the provisions of the payment services directive by an agent, branch or entity carrying out activities on behalf of such an institution.

(3)   Where the Authority and the home state competent authority agree, the Authority may carry out on-site inspections on behalf of the home state competent authority in respect of payment services provided by an EEA authorised payment institution exercising its passport rights.

PART IV   OTHER STATUTORY INSTRUMENTS

(4)   If the Authority has reasonable grounds to suspect that, in connection with the proposed establishment of a branch or the proposed provision of services by an EEA authorised payment institution—

(a)   money laundering or terrorist financing within the meaning of the Money Laundering Regulations 2007 is taking place, has taken place, or has been attempted; or

(b)   the risk of such activities taking place would be increased,

it must inform the relevant home state competent authority of its grounds for suspicion.

[1151]

NOTES

Commencement: these Regulations come into force on 2 March 2009 (for the purposes specified in reg 1(2)(a)), 1 May 2009 (for the purposes specified in reg 1(2)(b)), and 1 November 2009 (otherwise). See reg 1 at **[1127]**.

26   Carrying on of Consumer Credit Act business by EEA authorised payment institutions

(1)   Sections 203 (power to prohibit the carrying on of Consumer Credit Act business) and 204 (power to restrict the carrying on of Consumer Credit Act business) of, and Schedule 16 (prohibitions and restrictions imposed by OFT) to, the 2000 Act apply in relation to EEA authorised payment institutions exercising passport rights in the United Kingdom under these Regulations as they apply in relation to EEA firms exercising passport rights under Part 2 of Schedule 3 to the 2000 Act (EEA passport rights) with the following modifications—

(a)   in section 203(10)—

(i)   for the definition of "a consumer credit EEA firm" substitute—

""a consumer credit EEA firm" means an EEA authorised payment institution (as defined by regulation 2(1) of the Payment Services Regulations 2009) which is exercising passport rights in the United Kingdom and is carrying on any Consumer Credit Act business;" and

(ii)   for the definition of "listed activity" substitute—

""listed activity" means an activity listed in the Annex to the payment services directive and any activity carried on in accordance with Article 16 of that directive;";

(b)   in paragraph 2(5)(b) of Schedule 16, for "the firm's home state regulator" substitute "the home state competent authority (as defined by regulation 2(1) of the Payment Services Regulations 2009)".

(2)   Sections 21 (businesses needing a licence) and 39(1) (offences against Part 3) of the Consumer Credit Act 1974 do not apply in relation to the carrying on by an EEA authorised payment institution of a payment service which is Consumer Credit Act business, unless the OFT has exercised the power conferred on it by section 203 of the 2000 Act, as applied with modifications by paragraph (1), in relation to that institution.

(3)   In this regulation "Consumer Credit Act business" has the same meaning as in section 203 of the 2000 Act.

[1152]

NOTES

Commencement: these Regulations come into force on 2 March 2009 (for the purposes specified in reg 1(2)(a)), 1 May 2009 (for the purposes specified in reg 1(2)(b)), and 1 November 2009 (otherwise). See reg 1 at **[1127]**.

PART 4
PROVISIONS APPLICABLE TO AUTHORISED PAYMENT INSTITUTIONS AND SMALL PAYMENT INSTITUTIONS

27   Additional activities

(1)   Authorised payment institutions and small payment institutions may, in addition to providing payment services, engage in the following activities—

(a)   the provision of operational and closely related ancillary services, including—

(i)   ensuring the execution of payment transactions;

(ii)   foreign exchange services;

(iii)   safe-keeping activities; and

(iv)   the storage and processing of data;

(b)   the operation of payment systems; and

(c)   business activities other than the provision of payment services, subject to any relevant Community or national law.

(2)   Authorised payment institutions and small payment institutions may grant credit in relation to the provision of the payment services specified in paragraph 1(d), (e) and (g) of Schedule 1 only if—

(a)   such credit is ancillary and granted exclusively in connection with the execution of a payment transaction;

(b)   such credit is not granted from the funds received or held for the purposes of executing payment transactions;

(c)   in cases where such credit is granted by an authorised payment institution exercising its passport rights, there is an obligation upon the payment service user to repay the credit within a period not exceeding 12 months; and

(d)   in relation to an authorised payment institution, in the opinion of the Authority the institution's own funds (comprising the items specified in paragraph 3(a) to (j) of Schedule 3) are, and continue to be, adequate in the light of the overall amount of credit granted.

[1153]

NOTES

Commencement: these Regulations come into force on 2 March 2009 (for the purposes specified in reg 1(2)(a)), 1 May 2009 (for the purposes specified in reg 1(2)(b)), and 1 November 2009 (otherwise). See reg 1 at **[1127]**.

28   Payment accounts and sums received for the execution of payment transactions

Any payment account held by an authorised payment institution or a small payment institution must be used only in relation to payment transactions.

[1154]

NOTES

Commencement: these Regulations come into force on 2 March 2009 (for the purposes specified in reg 1(2)(a)), 1 May 2009 (for the purposes specified in reg 1(2)(b)), and 1 November 2009 (otherwise). See reg 1 at **[1127]**.

29   Use of agents

(1)   Authorised payment institutions and small payment institutions may not provide payment services in the United Kingdom through an agent unless the agent is included on the register.

(2)   Authorised payment institutions may not provide payment services in the exercise of their passport rights through an EEA agent unless the agent is included on the register.

(3)   An application for an agent to be included on the register must—
  (a)   contain, or be accompanied by, the following information—
    (i)   the name and address of the agent;
    (ii)   where relevant, a description of the internal control mechanisms that will be used by the agent—
      (aa) in the case of an agent in the United Kingdom, to comply with the Money Laundering Regulations 2007; and
      (bb) in the case of an EEA agent, to comply with provisions of the money laundering directive; and
    (iii) in the case of an agent of an authorised payment institution, the identity of the directors and persons responsible for the management of the agent and evidence that they are fit and proper persons; and
    (iv)   such other information as the Authority may reasonably require; and
  (b)   be made in such manner as the Authority may direct.

(4)   Different directions may be given, and different requirements imposed, in relation to different applications or categories of application.

(5)   At any time after receiving an application and before determining it, the Authority may require the applicant to provide it with such further information as it reasonably considers necessary to enable it to determine the application.

(6)   The Authority may refuse to include the agent on the register only if—
  (a)   it has not received the information referred to in paragraph (3)(a), or is not satisfied that such information is correct;
  (b)   it is not satisfied that the directors and persons responsible for the management of the agent are fit and proper persons;
  (c)   it has reasonable grounds to suspect that, in connection with the provision of services through the agent—
    (i)   money laundering or terrorist financing within the meaning of the money laundering directive (or, in the United Kingdom, the Money Laundering Regulations 2007) is taking place, has taken place, or has been attempted; or
    (ii)   the risk of such activities taking place would be increased.

(7)   Where—

(a) an authorised payment institution intends to provide payment services through an EEA agent; and

(b) the Authority proposes to include the EEA agent on the register,

the Authority must inform the host state competent authority and take account of its opinion (if provided within such reasonable period as the Authority specifies) on any of the matters referred to in paragraph (6)(b) or (c).

(8) The Authority must decide whether to include the agent on the register within a reasonable period of it having received a completed application.

(9) If the Authority proposes to refuse to include the agent on the register, it must give the authorised payment institution or the small payment institution, as the case may be, a warning notice.

(10) The Authority must, having considered any representations made in response to the warning notice—

(a) if it decides not to include the agent on the register, give the applicant a decision notice; or

(b) if it decides to include the agent on the register, give the applicant notice of its decision, stating the date on which the registration takes effect.

(11) If the Authority decides not to include the agent on the register the applicant may refer the matter to the Tribunal.

(12) If the Authority decides to include the agent on the register, it must update the register as soon as practicable.

(13) An application under paragraph (3) may be combined with an application under regulation 5 or 12, in which case the application must be determined in the manner set out in regulation 9 (if relevant, as applied by regulation 14).

(14) An authorised payment institution or a small payment institution must ensure that agents acting on its behalf inform payment service users of the agency arrangement.

[1155]

NOTES

Commencement: these Regulations come into force on 2 March 2009 (for the purposes specified in reg 1(2)(a)), 1 May 2009 (for the purposes specified in reg 1(2)(b)), and 1 November 2009 (otherwise). See reg 1 at **[1127]**.

30 Removal of agent from register

(1) The Authority may remove an agent of an authorised payment institution or small payment institution from the register where—

(a) the authorised payment institution or small payment institution requests, or consents to, the agent's removal from the register;

(b) the authorised payment institution or small payment institution has obtained registration through false statements or any other irregular means;

(c) regulation 29(6)(b) or (c) applies;

(d) the removal is desirable in order to protect the interests of consumers; or

(e) the agent's provision of payment services is otherwise unlawful.

(2) Where the Authority proposes to remove an agent from the register, other than at the request of the authorised payment institution or small payment institution, it must give the authorised payment institution or small payment institution a warning notice.

(3) The Authority must, having considered any representations made in response to the warning notice—

(a) if it decides to remove the agent, give the authorised payment institution or small payment institution a decision notice; or

(b) if it decides not to remove the agent, give the authorised payment institution or small payment institution notice of its decision.

(4) If the Authority decides to remove the agent, other than at the request of the authorised payment institution or small payment institution, the institution concerned may refer the matter to the Tribunal.

(5) Where the period for a reference to the Tribunal has expired without a reference being made, the Authority must as soon as practicable update the register accordingly.

[1156]

NOTES

Commencement: these Regulations come into force on 2 March 2009 (for the purposes specified in reg 1(2)(a)), 1 May 2009 (for the purposes specified in reg 1(2)(b)), and 1 November 2009 (otherwise). See reg 1 at **[1127]**.

31 Reliance

(1)   Where an authorised payment institution or a small payment institution relies on a third party for the performance of operational functions it must take all reasonable steps to ensure that these Regulations are complied with.

(2)   Without prejudice to paragraph (1), an authorised payment institution or a small payment institution is responsible, to the same extent as if it had expressly permitted it, for anything done or omitted by any of its employees, any agent or branch providing payment services on its behalf, or any entity to which activities are outsourced.

[1157]

NOTES

Commencement: these Regulations come into force on 2 March 2009 (for the purposes specified in reg 1(2)(a)), 1 May 2009 (for the purposes specified in reg 1(2)(b)), and 1 November 2009 (otherwise). See reg 1 at **[1127]**.

32 Duty to notify change in circumstance

(1)   Where it becomes apparent to an authorised payment institution or a small payment institution that there is, or is likely to be, a significant change in circumstances which is relevant to—

    (a)   in the case of an authorised payment institution—

        (i)   its fulfilment of any of the conditions set out in regulation 6(4) to (8) and, if applicable, the requirement in regulation 18(1) to maintain own funds;

        (ii)   the payment services which it seeks to carry on in exercise of its passport rights;

    (b)   in the case of a small payment institution, its fulfilment of any of the conditions set out in regulation 13(4) to (6) and compliance with the financial limit referred to in regulation 8 (as applied by regulation 14(c)); and

    (c)   in the case of the use of an agent to provide payment services, the matters referred to in regulation 29(6)(b) and (c),

it must provide the Authority with details of the change without undue delay, or, in the case of a substantial change in circumstances which has not yet taken place, details of the likely change a reasonable period before it takes place.

(2)   Any information to be provided to the Authority under this regulation must be in such form or verified in such manner as it may direct.

[1158]

NOTES

Commencement: these Regulations come into force on 2 March 2009 (for the purposes specified in reg 1(2)(a)), 1 May 2009 (for the purposes specified in reg 1(2)(b)), and 1 November 2009 (otherwise). See reg 1 at **[1127]**.

PART 5

INFORMATION REQUIREMENTS FOR PAYMENT SERVICES

Application

33 Application of Part 5

(1)   This Part applies to a contract for payment services where—

    (a)   the services are provided from an establishment maintained by a payment service provider or its agent in the United Kingdom;

    (b)   the payment service providers of both the payer and the payee are located within the EEA; and

    (c)   the payment services are carried out either in euro or in the currency of an EEA State that has not adopted the euro as its currency.

(2)   Regulations 36 to 39 apply to payment services provided under a single payment service contract.

(3)   Regulations 40 to 46 apply to payment services provided under a framework contract.

(4)   Except where the payment service user is—

    (a)   a consumer,

    (b)   a micro-enterprise, or

    (c)   a charity,

the parties may agree that any or all of the provisions of this Part do not apply to a contract for payment services.

[1159]

NOTES
Commencement: these Regulations come into force on 2 March 2009 (for the purposes specified in reg 1(2)(a)), 1 May 2009 (for the purposes specified in reg 1(2)(b)), and 1 November 2009 (otherwise). See reg 1 at **[1127]**.

34 Disapplication of certain regulations in the case of consumer credit agreements

Where the contract under which a payment service is provided is, or would be, when entered into, a regulated agreement—
- (a) regulations 41, 42 and 43 do not apply;
- (b) the payment service provider is only required under regulation 40(1) to provide the information specified in paragraph 3(b) of Schedule 4; and
- (c) the payment service provider is only required under regulation 45(1) to provide the information specified in paragraph (2)(d) of regulation 45.

[1160]

NOTES
Commencement: these Regulations come into force on 2 March 2009 (for the purposes specified in reg 1(2)(a)), 1 May 2009 (for the purposes specified in reg 1(2)(b)), and 1 November 2009 (otherwise). See reg 1 at **[1127]**.

35 Disapplication of certain regulations in the case of low-value payment instruments

(1) This regulation applies in respect of payment instruments which, under the framework contract governing their use—
- (a) can be used only to execute individual payment transactions of 30 euro or less, or in relation to payment transactions executed wholly within the United Kingdom, 60 euro or less;
- (b) have a spending limit of 150 euro, or where payment transactions must be executed wholly within the United Kingdom, 300 euro; or
- (c) store funds that do not exceed 500 euro at any time.

(2) Where this regulation applies—
- (a) regulations 40 and 44 do not apply and the payment service provider is only required to provide the payer with information about the main characteristics of the payment service, including—
  - (i) the way in which the payment instrument can be used;
  - (ii) the liability of the payer, as set out in regulation 62;
  - (iii) charges levied;
  - (iv) any other material information the payer might need to take an informed decision; and
  - (v) an indication of where the information specified in Schedule 4 is made available in an easily accessible manner;
- (b) the parties may agree that regulations 45 and 46 do not apply and instead—
  - (i) the payment service provider must provide or make available a reference enabling the payment service user to identify—
    - (aa) the payment transaction;
    - (bb) the amount of the payment transaction;
    - (cc) any charges payable in respect of the payment transaction;
  - (ii) in the case of several payment transactions of the same kind made to the same payee, the payment service provider must provide or make available to the payment service user information about the total amount of the payment transactions and any charges for those payment transactions; or
  - (iii) where the payment instrument is used anonymously or the payment service provider is not otherwise technically able to provide or make available the information specified in paragraph (i) or (ii), the payment service provider must enable the payer to verify the amount of funds stored; and
- (c) the parties may agree that regulation 47(1) does not apply to information provided or made available in accordance with regulation 42.

[1161]

NOTES
Commencement: these Regulations come into force on 2 March 2009 (for the purposes specified in reg 1(2)(a)), 1 May 2009 (for the purposes specified in reg 1(2)(b)), and 1 November 2009 (otherwise). See reg 1 at **[1127]**.

Single payment service contracts

36 Information required prior to the conclusion of a single payment service contract

(1) A payment service provider must provide or make available to the payment service user the information specified in paragraph (2), whether by supplying a copy of the draft single payment service contract or supplying a copy of the draft payment order or otherwise, either—

    (a) before the payment service user is bound by the single payment service contract; or

    (b) immediately after the execution of the payment transaction, where the contract is concluded at the payment service user's request using a means of distance communication which does not enable provision of such information in accordance with sub-paragraph (a).

(2) The information referred to in paragraph (1) is—

    (a) the information or unique identifier that has to be provided by the payment service user in order for a payment order to be properly executed;

    (b) the maximum time in which the payment service will be executed;

    (c) the charges payable by the payment service user to the user's payment service provider and, where applicable, a breakdown of the amounts of such charges;

    (d) where applicable, the actual or reference exchange rate to be applied to the payment transaction; and

    (e) such of the information specified in Schedule 4 as is relevant to the single payment service contract in question.

[1162]

NOTES

Commencement: these Regulations come into force on 2 March 2009 (for the purposes specified in reg 1(2)(a)), 1 May 2009 (for the purposes specified in reg 1(2)(b)), and 1 November 2009 (otherwise). See reg 1 at **[1127]**.

37 Information required after receipt of the payment order

(1) The payer's payment service provider must, immediately after receipt of the payment order, provide or make available to the payer the information specified in paragraph (2).

(2) The information referred to in paragraph (1) is—

    (a) a reference enabling the payer to identify the payment transaction and, where appropriate, information relating to the payee;

    (b) the amount of the payment transaction in the currency used in the payment order;

    (c) the amount of any charges for the payment transaction payable by the payer and, where applicable, a breakdown of the amounts of such charges;

    (d) where an exchange rate is used in the payment transaction and the actual rate used in the payment transaction differs from the rate provided in accordance with regulation 36(2)(d), the actual rate used or a reference to it, and the amount of the payment transaction after that currency conversion; and

    (e) the date on which the payment service provider received the payment order.

[1163]

NOTES

Commencement: these Regulations come into force on 2 March 2009 (for the purposes specified in reg 1(2)(a)), 1 May 2009 (for the purposes specified in reg 1(2)(b)), and 1 November 2009 (otherwise). See reg 1 at **[1127]**.

38 Information for the payee after execution

(1) The payee's payment service provider must, immediately after the execution of the payment transaction, provide or make available to the payee the information specified in paragraph (2).

(2) The information referred to in paragraph (1) is—

    (a) a reference enabling the payee to identify the payment transaction and, where appropriate, the payer and any information transferred with the payment transaction;

    (b) the amount of the payment transaction in the currency in which the funds are at the payee's disposal;

    (c) the amount of any charges for the payment transaction payable by the payee and, where applicable, a breakdown of the amount of such charges;

    (d) where applicable, the exchange rate used in the payment transaction by the payee's payment service provider, and the amount of the payment transaction before that currency conversion; and

    (e) the credit value date.

[1164]

NOTES
Commencement: these Regulations come into force on 2 March 2009 (for the purposes specified in reg 1(2)(a)), 1 May 2009 (for the purposes specified in reg 1(2)(b)), and 1 November 2009 (otherwise). See reg 1 at **[1127]**.

39 Avoidance of duplication of information

Where a payment order for a single payment transaction is transmitted by way of a payment instrument issued under a framework contract, the payment service provider in respect of that single payment transaction need not provide or make available under regulations 36 to 38 information which has been provided or made available, or will be provided or made available, under regulations 40 to 45 by another payment service provider in respect of the framework contract.

[1165]

NOTES
Commencement: these Regulations come into force on 2 March 2009 (for the purposes specified in reg 1(2)(a)), 1 May 2009 (for the purposes specified in reg 1(2)(b)), and 1 November 2009 (otherwise). See reg 1 at **[1127]**.

Framework contracts

40 Prior general information for framework contracts

(1) A payment service provider must provide to the payment service user the information specified in Schedule 4, either—
  (a) in good time before the payment service user is bound by the framework contract; or
  (b) where the contract is concluded at the payment service user's request using a means of distance communication which does not enable provision of such information in accordance with sub-paragraph (a), immediately after the conclusion of the contract.

(2) The payment service provider may discharge the duty under paragraph (1) by supplying a copy of the draft framework contract provided that such contract includes the information specified in Schedule 4.

[1166]

NOTES
Commencement: these Regulations come into force on 2 March 2009 (for the purposes specified in reg 1(2)(a)), 1 May 2009 (for the purposes specified in reg 1(2)(b)), and 1 November 2009 (otherwise). See reg 1 at **[1127]**.

41 Information during period of contract

If the payment service user so requests at any time during the contractual relationship, the payment service provider must provide the information specified in Schedule 4 and the terms of the framework contract.

[1167]

NOTES
Commencement: these Regulations come into force on 2 March 2009 (for the purposes specified in reg 1(2)(a)), 1 May 2009 (for the purposes specified in reg 1(2)(b)), and 1 November 2009 (otherwise). See reg 1 at **[1127]**.

42 Changes in contractual information

(1) Subject to paragraph (4), any proposed changes to—
  (a) the existing terms of the framework contract; or
  (b) the information specified in Schedule 4,
must be communicated by the payment service provider to the payment service user no later than two months before the date on which they are to take effect.

(2) The framework contract may provide for any such proposed changes to be made unilaterally by the payment service provider where the payment service user does not, before the proposed date of entry into force of the changes, notify the payment service provider to the contrary.

(3) Where paragraph (2) applies, the payment service provider must inform the payment service user that—
  (a) the payment service user will be deemed to have accepted the changes in the circumstances referred to in that paragraph; and
  (b) the payment service user has the right to terminate the framework contract immediately and without charge before the proposed date of their entry into force.

(4) Changes in the interest or exchange rates may be applied immediately and without notice where—

(a)   such a right is agreed under the framework contract and the changes are based on the reference interest or exchange rates information on which has been provided to the payment service user in accordance with this Part; or

(b)   the changes are more favourable to the payment service user.

(5)   The payment service provider must inform the payment service user of any change to the interest rate as soon as possible unless the parties have agreed on a specific frequency or manner in which the information is to be provided or made available.

(6)   Any change in the interest or exchange rate used in payment transactions must be implemented and calculated in a neutral manner that does not discriminate against payment service users.

[1168]

NOTES

Commencement: these Regulations come into force on 2 March 2009 (for the purposes specified in reg 1(2)(a)), 1 May 2009 (for the purposes specified in reg 1(2)(b)), and 1 November 2009 (otherwise). See reg 1 at **[1127]**.

43   Termination of framework contract

(1)   The payment service user may terminate the framework contract at any time unless the parties have agreed on a period of notice not exceeding one month.

(2)   Subject to paragraph (3), any charges for the termination of the contract must reasonably correspond to the actual costs to the payment service provider of termination.

(3)   The payment service provider may not charge the payment service user for the termination, after the expiry of 12 months, of a framework contract concluded for a fixed period of more than 12 months or for an indefinite period.

(4)   The payment service provider may terminate a framework contract concluded for an indefinite period by giving at least two months' notice, if the contract so provides.

(5)   Notice of termination given in accordance with paragraph (4) must be provided in the same way as information is required by regulation 47(1) to be provided or made available.

(6)   Where charges for the payment service are levied on a regular basis, such charges must be apportioned up until the time of the termination of the contract and any charges paid in advance must be reimbursed proportionally.

(7)   This regulation does not affect any right of a party to the framework contract to treat it as unenforceable or void (including any right arising out of a breach of the contract).

[1169]

NOTES

Commencement: these Regulations come into force on 2 March 2009 (for the purposes specified in reg 1(2)(a)), 1 May 2009 (for the purposes specified in reg 1(2)(b)), and 1 November 2009 (otherwise). See reg 1 at **[1127]**.

44   Information prior to execution of individual payment transaction

Where an individual payment transaction under a framework contract is initiated by the payer, at the payer's request the payer's payment service provider must inform the payer of—

(a)   the maximum execution time;

(b)   the charges payable by the payer in respect of the payment transaction; and

(c)   where applicable, a breakdown of the amounts of such charges.

[1170]

NOTES

Commencement: these Regulations come into force on 2 March 2009 (for the purposes specified in reg 1(2)(a)), 1 May 2009 (for the purposes specified in reg 1(2)(b)), and 1 November 2009 (otherwise). See reg 1 at **[1127]**.

45   Information for the payer on individual payment transactions

(1)   The payer's payment service provider under a framework contract must provide to the payer the information specified in paragraph (2) as soon as reasonably practicable either—

(a)   after the amount of an individual payment transaction is debited from the payer's payment account; or

(b)   where the payer does not use a payment account, after receipt of the payment order.

(2)   The information referred to in paragraph (1) is—

(a)   a reference enabling the payer to identify each payment transaction and, where appropriate, information relating to the payee;

PART IV   OTHER STATUTORY INSTRUMENTS

(b)   the amount of the payment transaction in the currency in which the payer's payment account is debited or in the currency used for the payment order;

(c)   the amount of any charges for the payment transaction and, where applicable, a breakdown of the amounts of such charges, or the interest payable by the payer;

(d)   where applicable, the exchange rate used in the payment transaction by the payer's payment service provider and the amount of the payment transaction after that currency conversion; and

(e)   the debit value date or the date of receipt of the payment order.

(3)   A framework contract may include a condition that the information specified in paragraph (2) be provided or made available periodically at least once a month and in an agreed manner which enables the payer to store and reproduce the information unchanged.

[1171]

NOTES

Commencement: these Regulations come into force on 2 March 2009 (for the purposes specified in reg 1(2)(a)), 1 May 2009 (for the purposes specified in reg 1(2)(b)), and 1 November 2009 (otherwise). See reg 1 at **[1127]**.

46 Information for the payee on individual payment transactions

(1)   As soon as reasonably practicable after the execution of an individual payment transaction under a framework contract, the payee's payment service provider must provide to the payee the information specified in paragraph (2).

(2)   The information referred to in paragraph (1) is-

(a)   a reference enabling the payee to identify the payment transaction and, where appropriate, the payer, and any information transferred with the payment transaction;

(b)   the amount of the payment transaction in the currency in which the payee's payment account is credited;

(c)   the amount of any charges for the payment transaction and, where applicable, a breakdown of the amounts of such charges, or the interest payable by the payee;

(d)   where applicable, the exchange rate used in the payment transaction by the payee's payment service provider, and the amount of the payment transaction before that currency conversion; and

(e)   the credit value date.

(3)   A framework contract may include a condition that the information specified in paragraph (2) is to be provided or made available periodically at least once a month and in an agreed manner which enables the payee to store and reproduce the information unchanged.

[1172]

NOTES

Commencement: these Regulations come into force on 2 March 2009 (for the purposes specified in reg 1(2)(a)), 1 May 2009 (for the purposes specified in reg 1(2)(b)), and 1 November 2009 (otherwise). See reg 1 at **[1127]**.

Common provisions

47 Communication of information

(1)   Subject to regulation 35(2)(c), any information provided or made available in accordance with this Part must be provided or made available—

(a)   in an easily accessible manner;

(b)   if the payment service user so requests, on paper or on another durable medium;

(c)   in easily understandable language and in a clear and comprehensible form; and

(d)   in English or in the language agreed by the parties.

(2)   Paragraph (1)(b) is subject to any agreement in accordance with regulation 45(3) or 46(3) as to the manner in which information is to be provided or made available.

[1173]

NOTES

Commencement: these Regulations come into force on 2 March 2009 (for the purposes specified in reg 1(2)(a)), 1 May 2009 (for the purposes specified in reg 1(2)(b)), and 1 November 2009 (otherwise). See reg 1 at **[1127]**.

48 Charges for information

(1)   A payment service provider may not charge for providing or making available information which is required to be provided or made available by this Part.

(2)   The payment service provider and the payment service user may agree on charges for any information which is provided at the request of the payment service user where such information is—

(a)   additional to the information required to be provided or made available by this Part;

(b)   provided more frequently than is specified in this Part; or

(c)   transmitted by means of communication other than those specified in the framework contract.

(3)   Any charges imposed under paragraph (2) must reasonably correspond to the payment service provider's actual costs.

[1174]

NOTES

Commencement: these Regulations come into force on 2 March 2009 (for the purposes specified in reg 1(2)(a)), 1 May 2009 (for the purposes specified in reg 1(2)(b)), and 1 November 2009 (otherwise). See reg 1 at **[1127]**.

49   Currency and currency conversion

(1)   Payment transactions must be executed in the currency agreed between the parties.

(2)   Where a currency conversion service is offered before the initiation of the payment transaction—

(a)   at the point of sale; or

(b)   by the payee,

the party offering the currency conversion service to the payer must disclose to the payer all charges as well as the exchange rate to be used for converting the payment transaction.

[1175]

NOTES

Commencement: these Regulations come into force on 2 March 2009 (for the purposes specified in reg 1(2)(a)), 1 May 2009 (for the purposes specified in reg 1(2)(b)), and 1 November 2009 (otherwise). See reg 1 at **[1127]**.

50   Information on additional charges or reductions

(1)   The payee must inform the payer of any charge requested or reduction offered by the payee for the use of a particular payment instrument before the initiation of the payment transaction.

(2)   The payment service provider, or any relevant third party, must inform the payment service user of any charge requested by the payment service provider or third party, as the case may be, for the use of a particular payment instrument before the initiation of the payment transaction.

[1176]

NOTES

Commencement: these Regulations come into force on 2 March 2009 (for the purposes specified in reg 1(2)(a)), 1 May 2009 (for the purposes specified in reg 1(2)(b)), and 1 November 2009 (otherwise). See reg 1 at **[1127]**.

PART 6
RIGHTS AND OBLIGATIONS IN RELATION TO THE PROVISION OF
PAYMENT SERVICES

Application

51   Application of Part 6

(1)   This Part applies to a contract for payment services where—

(a)   the services are provided from an establishment maintained by a payment service provider or its agent in the United Kingdom;

(b)   subject to paragraph (2), the payment service providers of both the payer and the payee are located within the EEA; and

(c)   where the payment services are carried out in euro or in the currency of an EEA State that has not adopted the euro as its currency.

(2)   Regulation 73 applies whether or not the payment service providers of both the payer and the payee are located within the EEA.

(3)   Except where the payment service user is a consumer, a micro-enterprise or a charity, the parties may agree that—

(a)   any or all of regulations 54(1), 55(2), 60, 62, 63, 64, 67, 75, 76 and 77 do not apply;

(b)   a different time period applies for the purposes of regulation 59(1).

[1177]

NOTES
Commencement: these Regulations come into force on 2 March 2009 (for the purposes specified in reg 1(2)(a)), 1 May 2009 (for the purposes specified in reg 1(2)(b)), and 1 November 2009 (otherwise). See reg 1 at **[1127]**.

52 Disapplication of certain regulations in the case of consumer credit agreements

The following provisions of the Consumer Credit Act 1974 shall apply in relation to contracts for the provision of payment services which are regulated agreements for the purposes of that Act in place of the following provisions of these Regulations—

(a) section 51 (prohibition of unsolicited credit tokens) in place of regulation 58(1)(b);

(b) sections 66 (acceptance of credit tokens) and 84 (misuse of credit tokens) in place of regulations 59, 61 and 62;

(c) section 83 (liability for misuse of credit facilities) in place of regulations 59, 61 and 62;

(d) sections 76 (duty to give notice before taking certain action) and 87 (need for default notice) in relation to the grounds mentioned in regulation 56(2) in place of regulation 56(3) to (6).

[1178]

NOTES
Commencement: these Regulations come into force on 2 March 2009 (for the purposes specified in reg 1(2)(a)), 1 May 2009 (for the purposes specified in reg 1(2)(b)), and 1 November 2009 (otherwise). See reg 1 at **[1127]**.

53 Disapplication of certain regulations in the case of low value payment instruments

(1) This regulation applies in respect of payment instruments which, under the framework contract governing their use—

(a) can be used only to execute individual payment transactions of 30 euro or less, or in relation to payment transactions executed wholly within the United Kingdom, 60 euro or less;

(b) have a spending limit of 150 euro, or where payment transactions must be executed wholly within the United Kingdom, 300 euro; or

(c) store funds that do not exceed 500 euro at any time.

(2) Where this regulation applies the parties may agree that—

(a) regulations 57(1)(b), 58(1)(c), (d) and (e) and 62(3) do not apply where the payment instrument does not allow for the stopping or prevention of its use;

(b) regulations 60, 61 and 62(1) and (2) do not apply where the payment instrument is used anonymously or the payment service provider is not in a position, for other reasons concerning the payment instrument, to prove that a payment transaction was authorised;

(c) the payment service provider is not required under regulation 66(1) to notify the payment service user of the refusal of a payment order if the non-execution is apparent from the context;

(d) the payer may not revoke the payment order under regulation 67 after transmitting the payment order or giving their consent to execute the payment transaction to the payee;

(e) execution periods other than those provided by regulations 70 and 71 apply.

(3) Subject to paragraph (2)(b), regulations 61 and 62(1) and (2) apply to electronic money as defined in Article 1(3)(b) of the electronic money directive unless the payer's payment service provider does not have the ability under the contract to—

(a) freeze the payment account; or

(b) stop the use of the payment instrument.

[1179]

NOTES
Commencement: these Regulations come into force on 2 March 2009 (for the purposes specified in reg 1(2)(a)), 1 May 2009 (for the purposes specified in reg 1(2)(b)), and 1 November 2009 (otherwise). See reg 1 at **[1127]**.

Charges

54 Charges

(1) The payment service provider may only charge the payment service user for the fulfilment of any of its obligations under this Part—

(a) in accordance with regulation 66(3), 67(6) or 74(2)(b);

(b) where agreed between the parties; and

(c) where such charges reasonably correspond to the payment service provider's actual costs.

(2)   Where a payment transaction does not involve any currency conversion, the respective payment service providers must ensure that—
  (a)   the payee pays any charges levied by the payee's payment service provider; and
  (b)   the payer pays any charges levied by the payer's payment service provider.

(3)   The payee's payment service provider may not prevent the payee from—
  (a)   requiring payment of a charge by; or
  (b)   offering a reduction to,
the payer for the use of a particular payment instrument.

[1180]

NOTES

Commencement: these Regulations come into force on 2 March 2009 (for the purposes specified in reg 1(2)(a)), 1 May 2009 (for the purposes specified in reg 1(2)(b)), and 1 November 2009 (otherwise). See reg 1 at **[1127]**.

Authorisation of payment transactions

55   Consent and withdrawal of consent

(1)   A payment transaction is to be regarded as having been authorised by the payer for the purposes of this Part only if the payer has given its consent to—
  (a)   the execution of the payment transaction; or
  (b)   the execution of a series of payment transactions of which that payment transaction forms part.

(2)   Such consent—
  (a)   may be given before or, if agreed between the payer and its payment service provider, after the execution of the payment transaction; and
  (b)   must be given in the form, and in accordance with the procedure, agreed between the payer and its payment service provider.

(3)   The payer may withdraw its consent to a payment transaction at any time before the point at which the payment order can no longer be revoked under regulation 67.

(4)   Subject to regulation 67(3) to (5), the payer may withdraw its consent to the execution of a series of payment transactions at any time with the effect that any future payment transactions are not regarded as authorised for the purposes of this Part.

[1181]

NOTES

Commencement: these Regulations come into force on 2 March 2009 (for the purposes specified in reg 1(2)(a)), 1 May 2009 (for the purposes specified in reg 1(2)(b)), and 1 November 2009 (otherwise). See reg 1 at **[1127]**.

56   Limits on the use of payment instruments

(1)   Where a specific payment instrument is used for the purpose of giving consent to the execution of a payment transaction, the payer and its payment service provider may agree on spending limits for any payment transactions executed through that payment instrument.

(2)   A framework contract may provide for the payment service provider to have the right to stop the use of a payment instrument on reasonable grounds relating to—
  (a)   the security of the payment instrument;
  (b)   the suspected unauthorised or fraudulent use of the payment instrument; or
  (c)   in the case of a payment instrument with a credit line, a significantly increased risk that the payer may be unable to fulfil its liability to pay.

(3)   The payment service provider must, in the manner agreed between the payment service provider and the payer and before carrying out any measures to stop the use of the payment instrument—
  (a)   inform the payer that it intends to stop the use of the payment instrument; and
  (b)   give its reasons for doing so.

(4)   Where the payment service provider is unable to inform the payer in accordance with paragraph (3) before carrying out any measures to stop the use of the payment instrument, it must do so immediately after.

(5)   Paragraphs (3) and (4) do not apply where provision of the information in accordance with paragraph (3) would compromise reasonable security measures or is otherwise unlawful.

(6)   The payment service provider must allow the use of the payment instrument or replace it with a new payment instrument as soon as practicable after the reasons for stopping its use cease to exist.

[1182]

NOTES
Commencement: these Regulations come into force on 2 March 2009 (for the purposes specified in reg 1(2)(a)), 1 May 2009 (for the purposes specified in reg 1(2)(b)), and 1 November 2009 (otherwise). See reg 1 at **[1127]**.

57 Obligations of the payment service user in relation to payment instruments

(1) A payment service user to whom a payment instrument has been issued must—
  (a) use the payment instrument in accordance with the terms and conditions governing its issue and use; and
  (b) notify the payment service provider in the agreed manner and without undue delay on becoming aware of the loss, theft, misappropriation or unauthorised use of the payment instrument.

(2) The payment service user must on receiving a payment instrument take all reasonable steps to keep its personalised security features safe.

[1183]

NOTES
Commencement: these Regulations come into force on 2 March 2009 (for the purposes specified in reg 1(2)(a)), 1 May 2009 (for the purposes specified in reg 1(2)(b)), and 1 November 2009 (otherwise). See reg 1 at **[1127]**.

58 Obligations of the payment service provider in relation to payment instruments

(1) A payment service provider issuing a payment instrument must—
  (a) subject to regulation 57, ensure that the personalised security features of the payment instrument are not accessible to persons other than the payment service user to whom the payment instrument has been issued;
  (b) not send an unsolicited payment instrument, except where a payment instrument already issued to a payment service user is to be replaced;
  (c) ensure that appropriate means are available at all times to enable the payment service user to notify the payment service provider in accordance with regulation 57(1)(b) or to request that the use of the payment instrument is no longer stopped in accordance with regulation 56(6);
  (d) on request, provide the payment service user at any time during a period of 18 months after the alleged date of notification under regulation 57(1)(b) with the means to prove that such notification to the payment service provider was made;
  (e) prevent any use of the payment instrument once notification has been made under regulation 57(1)(b).

(2) The payment service provider bears the risk of sending a payment instrument or any of its personalised security features to the payment service user.

[1184]

NOTES
Commencement: these Regulations come into force on 2 March 2009 (for the purposes specified in reg 1(2)(a)), 1 May 2009 (for the purposes specified in reg 1(2)(b)), and 1 November 2009 (otherwise). See reg 1 at **[1127]**.

59 Notification of unauthorised or incorrectly executed payment transactions

(1) A payment service user is entitled to redress under regulation 61, 75, 76 or 77 only if it notifies the payment service provider without undue delay, and in any event no later than 13 months after the debit date, on becoming aware of any unauthorised or incorrectly executed payment transaction.

(2) Where the payment service provider has failed to provide or make available information concerning the payment transaction in accordance with Part 5 of these Regulations, the payment service user is entitled to redress under the regulations referred to in paragraph (1) notwithstanding that the payment service user has failed to notify the payment service provider as mentioned in that paragraph.

[1185]

NOTES
Commencement: these Regulations come into force on 2 March 2009 (for the purposes specified in reg 1(2)(a)), 1 May 2009 (for the purposes specified in reg 1(2)(b)), and 1 November 2009 (otherwise). See reg 1 at **[1127]**.

60 Evidence on authentication and execution of payment transactions

(1) Where a payment service user—

(a) denies having authorised an executed payment transaction; or

(b) claims that a payment transaction has not been correctly executed,

it is for the payment service provider to prove that the payment transaction was authenticated, accurately recorded, entered in the payment service provider's accounts and not affected by a technical breakdown or some other deficiency.

(2) In paragraph (1) "authenticated" means the use of any procedure by which a payment service provider is able to verify the use of a specific payment instrument, including its personalised security features.

(3) Where a payment service user denies having authorised an executed payment transaction, the use of a payment instrument recorded by the payment service provider is not in itself necessarily sufficient to prove either that—

(a) the payment transaction was authorised by the payer; or

(b) the payer acted fraudulently or failed with intent or gross negligence to comply with regulation 57.

[1186]

NOTES

Commencement: these Regulations come into force on 2 March 2009 (for the purposes specified in reg 1(2)(a)), 1 May 2009 (for the purposes specified in reg 1(2)(b)), and 1 November 2009 (otherwise). See reg 1 at **[1127]**.

61 Payment service provider's liability for unauthorised payment transactions

Subject to regulations 59 and 60, where an executed payment transaction was not authorised in accordance with regulation 55, the payment service provider must immediately—

(a) refund the amount of the unauthorised payment transaction to the payer; and

(b) where applicable, restore the debited payment account to the state it would have been in had the unauthorised payment transaction not taken place.

[1187]

NOTES

Commencement: these Regulations come into force on 2 March 2009 (for the purposes specified in reg 1(2)(a)), 1 May 2009 (for the purposes specified in reg 1(2)(b)), and 1 November 2009 (otherwise). See reg 1 at **[1127]**.

62 Payer's liability for unauthorised payment transaction

(1) Subject to paragraphs (2) and (3), the payer is liable up to a maximum of £50 for any losses incurred in respect of unauthorised payment transactions arising—

(a) from the use of a lost or stolen payment instrument; or

(b) where the payer has failed to keep the personalised security features of the payment instrument safe, from the misappropriation of the payment instrument.

(2) The payer is liable for all losses incurred in respect of an unauthorised payment transaction where the payer—

(a) has acted fraudulently; or

(b) has with intent or gross negligence failed to comply with regulation 57.

(3) Except where the payer has acted fraudulently, the payer is not liable for any losses incurred in respect of an unauthorised payment transaction—

(a) arising after notification under regulation 57(1)(b);

(b) where the payment service provider has failed at any time to provide, in accordance with regulation 58(1)(c), appropriate means for notification; or

(c) where the payment instrument has been used in connection with a distance contract (other than an excepted contract).

(4) In paragraph (3)(c) "distance contract" and "excepted contract" have the meanings given in the Consumer Protection (Distance Selling) Regulations 2000.

[1188]

NOTES

Commencement: these Regulations come into force on 2 March 2009 (for the purposes specified in reg 1(2)(a)), 1 May 2009 (for the purposes specified in reg 1(2)(b)), and 1 November 2009 (otherwise). See reg 1 at **[1127]**.

63 Refunds for payment transactions initiated by or through a payee

(1) Where the conditions in paragraph (2) and the requirement in regulation 64(1) are satisfied, the payer is entitled to a refund from its payment service provider of the full amount of any authorised payment transaction initiated by or through the payee.

(2) The conditions are that—

PART IV OTHER STATUTORY INSTRUMENTS

(a)   the authorisation did not specify the exact amount of the payment transaction when the authorisation was given in accordance with regulation 55; and

(b)   the amount of the payment transaction exceeded the amount that the payer could reasonably have expected taking into account the payer's previous spending pattern, the conditions of the framework contract and the circumstances of the case.

(3)   The payer and payment service provider may agree in the framework contract, in respect of direct debits, that the conditions in paragraph (2) need not be satisfied in order for the payer to be entitled to a refund.

(4)   For the purposes of paragraph (2)(b), the payer cannot rely on currency exchange fluctuations where the reference exchange rate provided under regulation 36(2)(d) or paragraph 3(b) of Schedule 4 was applied.

(5)   The payer and payment service provider may agree in the framework contract that the right to a refund does not apply where—

(a)   the payer has given consent directly to the payment service provider for the payment transaction to be executed; and

(b)   if applicable, information on the payment transaction was provided or made available in an agreed manner to the payer for at least four weeks before the due date by the payment service provider or by the payee.

[1189]

NOTES

Commencement: these Regulations come into force on 2 March 2009 (for the purposes specified in reg 1(2)(a)), 1 May 2009 (for the purposes specified in reg 1(2)(b)), and 1 November 2009 (otherwise). See reg 1 at **[1127]**.

64   Requests for refunds for payment transactions initiated by or through a payee

(1)   The payer must request a refund under regulation 63 from its payment service provider within 8 weeks from the date on which the funds were debited.

(2)   The payment service provider may require the payer to provide such information as is reasonably necessary to ascertain whether the conditions in regulation 63(2) are satisfied.

(3)   Subject to paragraph (4), the payment service provider must either—

(a)   refund the full amount of the payment transaction; or

(b)   provide justification for refusing to refund the payment transaction, indicating the bodies to which the payer may refer the matter if the payer does not accept the justification provided.

(4)   Where an agreement in accordance with regulation 63(3) applies, the payment service provider must, notwithstanding that a condition in regulation 63(2) is not satisfied, refund the full amount of the payment transaction.

(5)   Any refund or justification for refusing a refund must be provided within 10 business days of receiving a request for a refund or, where applicable, within 10 business days of receiving any further information requested under paragraph (2).

[1190]

NOTES

Commencement: these Regulations come into force on 2 March 2009 (for the purposes specified in reg 1(2)(a)), 1 May 2009 (for the purposes specified in reg 1(2)(b)), and 1 November 2009 (otherwise). See reg 1 at **[1127]**.

Execution of payment transactions

65   Receipt of payment orders

(1)   Subject to paragraphs (2) to (5), for the purposes of these Regulations the time of receipt of a payment order is the time at which the payment order, given directly by the payer or indirectly by or through a payee, is received by the payer's payment service provider.

(2)   If the time of receipt of a payment order does not fall on a business day for the payer's payment service provider, the payment order is deemed to have been received on the first business day thereafter.

(3)   The payment service provider may set a time towards the end of a business day after which any payment order received will be deemed to have been received on the following business day.

(4)   Where the payment service user initiating a payment order agrees with its payment service provider that execution of the payment order is to take place—

(a)   on a specific day;

(b)   on the last day of a certain period; or

(c)   on the day on which the payer has put funds at the disposal of its payment service provider,

the time of receipt is deemed to be the day so agreed.

(5)   If the day agreed under paragraph (4) is not a business day for the payer's payment service provider, the payment order is deemed to have been received on the first business day thereafter.

[1191]

NOTES

Commencement: these Regulations come into force on 2 March 2009 (for the purposes specified in reg 1(2)(a)), 1 May 2009 (for the purposes specified in reg 1(2)(b)), and 1 November 2009 (otherwise). See reg 1 at **[1127]**.

66   Refusal of payment orders

(1)   Subject to paragraph (4), where a payment service provider refuses to execute a payment order, it must notify the payment service user of—

(a)   the refusal;

(b)   if possible, the reasons for such refusal; and

(c)   the procedure for rectifying any factual errors that led to the refusal.

(2)   Any notification under paragraph (1) must be given or made available in an agreed manner and at the earliest opportunity, and in any event within the periods specified in regulation 70.

(3)   The framework contract may provide for the payment service provider to charge the payment service user for such notification where the refusal is reasonably justified.

(4)   The payment service provider is not required to notify the payment service user under paragraph (1) where such notification would be otherwise unlawful.

(5)   Where all the conditions set out in the payer's framework contract have been satisfied, the payment service provider may not refuse to execute an authorised payment order irrespective of whether the payment order is initiated by the payer or by or through a payee, unless such execution is otherwise unlawful.

(6)   For the purposes of regulations 70, 75 and 76 a payment order of which execution has been refused is deemed not to have been received.

[1192]

NOTES

Commencement: these Regulations come into force on 2 March 2009 (for the purposes specified in reg 1(2)(a)), 1 May 2009 (for the purposes specified in reg 1(2)(b)), and 1 November 2009 (otherwise). See reg 1 at **[1127]**.

67   Revocation of a payment order

(1)   Subject to paragraphs (2) to (5), a payment service user may not revoke a payment order after it has been received by the payer's payment service provider.

(2)   In the case of a payment transaction initiated by or through the payee, the payer may not revoke the payment order after transmitting the payment order or giving consent to execute the payment transaction to the payee.

(3)   In the case of a direct debit, the payer may not revoke the payment order after the end of the business day preceding the day agreed for debiting the funds.

(4)   Where a day is agreed under regulation 65(4), the payment service user may not revoke a payment order after the end of the business day preceding the agreed day.

(5)   At any time after the time limits for revocation set out in paragraphs (1) to (4), the payment order may only be revoked if the revocation is—

(a)   agreed between the payment service user and its payment service provider; and

(b)   in the case of a payment transaction initiated by or through the payee, including in the case of a direct debit, also agreed with the payee.

(6)   A framework contract may provide for the payment service provider to charge for revocation under this regulation.

[1193]

NOTES

Commencement: these Regulations come into force on 2 March 2009 (for the purposes specified in reg 1(2)(a)), 1 May 2009 (for the purposes specified in reg 1(2)(b)), and 1 November 2009 (otherwise). See reg 1 at **[1127]**.

PART IV   OTHER STATUTORY INSTRUMENTS

68 Amounts transferred and amounts received

(1)   Subject to paragraph (2), the payment service providers of the payer and payee must ensure that the full amount of the payment transaction is transferred and that no charges are deducted from the amount transferred.

(2)   The payee and its payment service provider may agree for the payment service provider to deduct its charges from the amount transferred before crediting it to the payee provided that the full amount of the payment transaction and the amount of the charges are clearly stated in the information provided to the payee.

(3)   If charges other than those provided for by paragraph (2) are deducted from the amount transferred—

(a)   in the case of a payment transaction initiated by the payer, the payer's payment service provider must ensure that the payee receives the full amount of the payment transaction;

(b)   in the case of a payment transaction initiated by the payee, the payee's payment service provider must ensure that the payee receives the full amount of the payment transaction.

[1194]

NOTES
Commencement: these Regulations come into force on 2 March 2009 (for the purposes specified in reg 1(2)(a)), 1 May 2009 (for the purposes specified in reg 1(2)(b)), and 1 November 2009 (otherwise). See reg 1 at **[1127]**.

Execution time and value date

69 Application of regulations 70 to 72

(1)   Regulations 70 to 72 apply to any transaction—

(a)   in euro;

(b)   in sterling; or

(c)   involving only one currency conversion between the euro and sterling, provided that—

(i)   the currency conversion is carried out in the United Kingdom; and

(ii)   in the case of cross-border payment transactions, the cross-border transfer takes place in euro.

(2)   In respect of any other transaction, the payment service user may agree with the payment service provider that regulations 70 (other than regulation 70(4)) to 72 do not apply.

[1195]

NOTES
Commencement: these Regulations come into force on 2 March 2009 (for the purposes specified in reg 1(2)(a)), 1 May 2009 (for the purposes specified in reg 1(2)(b)), and 1 November 2009 (otherwise). See reg 1 at **[1127]**.

70 Payment transactions to a payment account

(1)   Subject to paragraphs (2), (3) and (4), the payer's payment service provider must ensure that the amount of the payment transaction is credited to the payee's payment service provider's account by the end of the business day following the time of receipt of the payment order.

(2)   Until 1st January 2012, the payer and their payment service provider may agree that the amount of the payment transaction is to be credited to the payee's payment service provider's account by the end of the third business day following the time of receipt of the payment order.

(3)   Where a payment transaction is initiated by way of a paper payment order—

(a)   the reference in paragraph (1) to the end of the business day following the time of receipt of the payment order is to be treated as a reference to the end of the second business day following the time of receipt of the payment order; and

(b)   the reference in paragraph (2) to the end of the third business day following the time of receipt of the payment order is to be treated as a reference to the end of the fourth business day following the time of receipt of the payment order.

(4)   Where a payment transaction—

(a)   does not fall within paragraphs (a) to (c) of regulation 69(1); but

(b)   is to be executed wholly within the EEA,

the payer's payment service provider must ensure that the amount of the payment transaction is credited to the payee's payment service provider's account by the end of the fourth business day following the time of receipt of the payment order.

(5)   The payee's payment service provider must value date and credit the amount of the payment transaction to the payee's payment account following its receipt of the funds.

(6)   The payee's payment service provider must transmit a payment order initiated by or through the payee to the payer's payment service provider within the time limits agreed between the payee and its payment service provider, enabling settlement in respect of a direct debit to occur on the agreed due date.

[1196]

NOTES
Commencement: these Regulations come into force on 2 March 2009 (for the purposes specified in reg 1(2)(a)), 1 May 2009 (for the purposes specified in reg 1(2)(b)), and 1 November 2009 (otherwise). See reg 1 at **[1127]**.

71 Absence of payee's payment account with the payment service provider

(1)   Paragraph (2) applies where a payment service provider accepts funds on behalf of a payee who does not have a payment account with that payment service provider.

(2)   The payment service provider must make the funds available to the payee immediately after the funds have been credited to that payment service provider's account.

[1197]

NOTES
Commencement: these Regulations come into force on 2 March 2009 (for the purposes specified in reg 1(2)(a)), 1 May 2009 (for the purposes specified in reg 1(2)(b)), and 1 November 2009 (otherwise). See reg 1 at **[1127]**.

72 Cash placed on a payment account

Where a payment service user places cash on its payment account with a payment service provider in the same currency as that payment account, the payment service provider must—

    (a)   if the user is a consumer, micro-enterprise or charity, ensure that the amount is made available and value dated immediately after the receipt of the funds;

    (b)   in any other case, ensure that the amount is made available and value dated no later than the end of the business day after the receipt of the funds.

[1198]

NOTES
Commencement: these Regulations come into force on 2 March 2009 (for the purposes specified in reg 1(2)(a)), 1 May 2009 (for the purposes specified in reg 1(2)(b)), and 1 November 2009 (otherwise). See reg 1 at **[1127]**.

73 Value date and availability of funds

(1)   The credit value date for the payee's payment account must be no later than the business day on which the amount of the payment transaction is credited to the account of the payee's payment service provider.

(2)   The payee's payment service provider must ensure that the amount of the payment transaction is at the payee's disposal immediately after that amount has been credited to that payment service provider's account.

(3)   The debit value date for the payer's payment account must be no earlier than the time at which the amount of the payment transaction is debited to that payment account.

[1199]

NOTES
Commencement: these Regulations come into force on 2 March 2009 (for the purposes specified in reg 1(2)(a)), 1 May 2009 (for the purposes specified in reg 1(2)(b)), and 1 November 2009 (otherwise). See reg 1 at **[1127]**.

Liability

74 Incorrect unique identifiers

(1)   Where a payment order is executed in accordance with the unique identifier, the payment order is deemed to have been correctly executed by each payment service provider involved in executing the payment order with respect to the payee specified by the unique identifier.

(2)   Where the unique identifier provided by the payment service user is incorrect, the payment service provider is not liable under regulation 75 or 76 for non-execution or defective execution of the payment transaction, but the payment service provider—

    (a)   must make reasonable efforts to recover the funds involved in the payment transaction; and

    (b)   may, if agreed in the framework contract, charge the payment service user for any such recovery.

(3)   Where the payment service user provides information additional to that specified in regulation 36(2)(a) or paragraph 2(b) of Schedule 4, the payment service provider is liable only for the execution of payment transactions in accordance with the unique identifier provided by the payment service user.

[1200]

NOTES

Commencement: these Regulations come into force on 2 March 2009 (for the purposes specified in reg 1(2)(a)), 1 May 2009 (for the purposes specified in reg 1(2)(b)), and 1 November 2009 (otherwise). See reg 1 at **[1127]**.

75   Non-execution or defective execution of payment transactions initiated by the payer

(1)   This regulation applies where a payment order is initiated by the payer.

(2)   The payer's payment service provider is liable to the payer for the correct execution of the payment transaction unless it can prove to the payer and, where relevant, to the payee's payment service provider, that the payee's payment service provider received the amount of the payment transaction in accordance with regulation 70.

(3)   The payer's payment service provider must, on request, make immediate efforts to trace the payment transaction and notify the payer of the outcome.

(4)   Where the payer's payment service provider is liable under paragraph (2), it must without undue delay refund to the payer the amount of the non-executed or defective payment transaction and, where applicable, restore the debited payment account to the state in which it would have been had the defective payment transaction not taken place.

(5)   Where the payer's payment service provider can prove (as set out in paragraph (2)) that the payee's payment service provider received the amount of the payment transaction in accordance with regulation 70, the payee's payment service provider is liable to the payee for the correct execution of the payment transaction and must—
   (a)   immediately make available the amount of the payment transaction to the payee; and
   (b)   where applicable, credit the corresponding amount to the payee's payment account.

[1201]

NOTES

Commencement: these Regulations come into force on 2 March 2009 (for the purposes specified in reg 1(2)(a)), 1 May 2009 (for the purposes specified in reg 1(2)(b)), and 1 November 2009 (otherwise). See reg 1 at **[1127]**.

76   Non-execution or defective execution of payment transactions initiated by the payee

(1)   This regulation applies where a payment order is initiated by the payee.

(2)   The payee's payment service provider is liable to the payee for the correct transmission of the payment order to the payer's payment service provider in accordance with regulation 70(6).

(3)   Where the payee's payment service provider is liable under paragraph (2), it must immediately re-transmit the payment order in question to the payer's payment service provider.

(4)   The payee's payment service provider must, on request, make immediate efforts to trace the payment transaction and notify the payee of the outcome.

(5)   Where the payee's payment service provider can prove to the payee and, where relevant, to the payer's payment service provider, that it is not liable under paragraph (2) in respect of a non-executed or defectively executed payment transaction, the payer's payment service provider is liable to the payer and must, as appropriate and without undue delay—
   (a)   refund to the payer the amount of the payment transaction; and
   (b)   restore the debited payment account to the state in which it would have been had the defective payment transaction not taken place.

[1202]

NOTES

Commencement: these Regulations come into force on 2 March 2009 (for the purposes specified in reg 1(2)(a)), 1 May 2009 (for the purposes specified in reg 1(2)(b)), and 1 November 2009 (otherwise). See reg 1 at **[1127]**.

77   Liability of payment service provider for charges and interest

A payment service provider is liable to its payment service user for—
   (a)   any charges for which the payment service user is responsible; and
   (b)   any interest which the payment service user must pay,
as a consequence of the non-execution or defective execution of the payment transaction.

[1203]

NOTES
Commencement: these Regulations come into force on 2 March 2009 (for the purposes specified in reg 1(2)(a)), 1 May 2009 (for the purposes specified in reg 1(2)(b)), and 1 November 2009 (otherwise). See reg 1 at **[1127]**.

78 Right of recourse

Where the liability of a payment service provider ("the first provider") under regulation 75 or 76 is attributable to another payment service provider or an intermediary, the other payment service provider or intermediary must compensate the first provider for any losses incurred or sums paid pursuant to those regulations.

[1204]

NOTES
Commencement: these Regulations come into force on 2 March 2009 (for the purposes specified in reg 1(2)(a)), 1 May 2009 (for the purposes specified in reg 1(2)(b)), and 1 November 2009 (otherwise). See reg 1 at **[1127]**.

79 Force majeure

(1) A person is not liable for any contravention of a requirement imposed on it by or under this Part where the contravention is due to abnormal and unforeseeable circumstances beyond the person's control, the consequences of which would have been unavoidable despite all efforts to the contrary.

(2) A payment service provider is not liable for any contravention of a requirement imposed on it by or under this Part where the contravention is due to the obligations of the payment service provider under other provisions of Community or national law.

[1205]

NOTES
Commencement: these Regulations come into force on 2 March 2009 (for the purposes specified in reg 1(2)(a)), 1 May 2009 (for the purposes specified in reg 1(2)(b)), and 1 November 2009 (otherwise). See reg 1 at **[1127]**.

PART 7
THE AUTHORITY

The functions of the Authority

80 Functions of the Authority

(1) The Authority is to have the functions conferred on it by these Regulations.

(2) In discharging its function of determining the general policy and principles by reference to which it performs particular functions under these Regulations, the Authority must have regard to—
  (a) the need to use its resources in the most efficient and economic way;
  (b) the responsibilities of those who manage the affairs of payment service providers;
  (c) the principle that a burden or restriction which is imposed on a person, or on the carrying on of an activity, should be proportionate to the benefits, considered in general terms, which are expected to result from the imposition of that burden or restriction;
  (d) the desirability of facilitating innovation in connection with payment services;
  (e) the international character of financial services and markets and the desirability of maintaining the competitive position of the United Kingdom;
  (f) the need to minimise the adverse effects on competition that may arise from anything done in the discharge of those functions; and
  (g) the desirability of facilitating competition in relation to payment services.

[1206]

NOTES
Commencement: these Regulations come into force on 2 March 2009 (for the purposes specified in reg 1(2)(a)), 1 May 2009 (for the purposes specified in reg 1(2)(b)), and 1 November 2009 (otherwise). See reg 1 at **[1127]**.

Supervision and enforcement

81 Monitoring and enforcement

(1) The Authority must maintain arrangements designed to enable it to determine whether—
  (a) persons on whom requirements are imposed by or under Part 2, 3 or 4 of these Regulations are complying with them;
  (b) there has been any contravention of regulation 110(1), 111(1) or 114(1)(a) or (2).

(2)   The Authority may maintain arrangements designed to enable it to determine whether persons on whom requirements are imposed by or under Part 5 or 6 of these Regulations are complying with them.

(3)   The arrangements referred to in paragraphs (1) and (2) may provide for functions to be performed on behalf of the Authority by any body or person who is, in its opinion, competent to perform them.

(4)   The Authority must also maintain arrangements for enforcing the provisions of these Regulations.

(5)   Paragraph (3) does not affect the Authority's duty under paragraph (1).

[1207]

NOTES

Commencement: these Regulations come into force on 2 March 2009 (for the purposes specified in reg 1(2)(a)), 1 May 2009 (for the purposes specified in reg 1(2)(b)), and 1 November 2009 (otherwise). See reg 1 at **[1127]**.

82   Reporting requirements

(1)   A payment service provider must give the Authority such information in respect of its provision of payment services and its compliance with requirements imposed by or under Parts 2 to 6 of these Regulations as the Authority may direct.

(2)   Information required under this regulation must be given at such times and in such form, and verified in such manner, as the Authority may direct.

[1208]

NOTES

Commencement: these Regulations come into force on 2 March 2009 (for the purposes specified in reg 1(2)(a)), 1 May 2009 (for the purposes specified in reg 1(2)(b)), and 1 November 2009 (otherwise). See reg 1 at **[1127]**.

83   Entry, inspection without a warrant etc

(1)   Paragraph (2) applies where an officer has reasonable cause to believe that any premises are being used by—
> (i)   an authorised payment institution, an EEA authorised payment institution or a small payment institution (including any of its branches) in connection with its business activities;
> (ii)   an agent providing payment services on behalf of an authorised payment institution, an EEA authorised payment institution or a small payment institution; or
> (iii)   an entity to which an authorised payment institution or an EEA authorised payment institution has outsourced any of its business activities.

(2)   The officer may on producing evidence of authority at any reasonable time—
> (a)   enter the premises;
> (b)   inspect the premises;
> (c)   observe the carrying on of business activities by the authorised payment institution, the EEA authorised payment institution or the small payment institution, as the case may be;
> (d)   inspect any document found on the premises;
> (e)   require any person on the premises to provide an explanation of any document or to state where it may be found.

(3)   An officer may take copies of, or make extracts from, any document found under paragraph (2).

(4)   An officer may exercise powers under this regulation only if the information or document sought to be obtained as a result is reasonably required in connection with the exercise by the Authority of its functions under these Regulations.

(5)   An officer may not exercise powers under this regulation in relation to information or documents in respect of which a claim to legal professional privilege (in Scotland, to confidentiality of communications) could be maintained in legal proceedings.

(6)   In this regulation—
> "document" includes information recorded in any form;
> "officer" means an officer of the Authority and includes a member of the Authority's staff or an agent of the Authority;
> "premises" means any premises other than premises used only as a dwelling.

[1209]

NOTES
Commencement: these Regulations come into force on 2 March 2009 (for the purposes specified in reg 1(2)(a)), 1 May 2009 (for the purposes specified in reg 1(2)(b)), and 1 November 2009 (otherwise). See reg 1 at **[1127]**.

84 Public censure

If the Authority considers that a payment service provider has contravened a requirement imposed on them by or under these Regulations the Authority may publish a statement to that effect.

[1210]

NOTES
Commencement: these Regulations come into force on 2 March 2009 (for the purposes specified in reg 1(2)(a)), 1 May 2009 (for the purposes specified in reg 1(2)(b)), and 1 November 2009 (otherwise). See reg 1 at **[1127]**.

85 Financial penalties

(1) The Authority may impose a penalty of such amount as it considers appropriate on—

    (a) a payment service provider who has contravened a requirement imposed on them by or under these Regulations; or

    (b) a person who has contravened regulation 110(1), 111(1) or 114(1)(a) or (2).

(2) The Authority may not in respect of any contravention both require a person to pay a penalty under this regulation and cancel their authorisation as a payment institution or their registration as a small payment institution (as the case may be).

(3) A penalty under this regulation is a debt due from that person to the Authority, and is recoverable accordingly.

[1211]

NOTES
Commencement: these Regulations come into force on 2 March 2009 (for the purposes specified in reg 1(2)(a)), 1 May 2009 (for the purposes specified in reg 1(2)(b)), and 1 November 2009 (otherwise). See reg 1 at **[1127]**.

86 Proposal to take disciplinary measures

(1) Where the Authority proposes to publish a statement under regulation 84 or to impose a penalty under regulation 85, it must give the person concerned a warning notice.

(2) The warning notice must set out the terms of the proposed statement or state the amount of the proposed penalty.

(3) If, having considered any representations made in response to the warning notice, the Authority decides to publish a statement under regulation 84 or to impose a penalty under regulation 85, it must without delay give the person concerned a decision notice.

(4) The decision notice must set out the terms of the statement or state the amount of the penalty.

(5) If the Authority decides to publish a statement under regulation 84 or impose a penalty on a person under regulation 85, the person concerned may refer the matter to the Tribunal.

(6) Sections 210 (statements of policy) and 211 (statements of policy: procedure) of the 2000 Act apply in respect of the imposition of penalties under regulation 85 and the amount of such penalties as they apply in respect of the imposition of penalties under Part 14 of the 2000 Act (disciplinary measures) and the amount of penalties under that Part of that Act.

(7) After a statement under regulation 84 is published, the Authority must send a copy of it to the person concerned and to any person to whom a copy of the decision notice was given under section 393(4) of the 2000 Act (third party rights) (as applied by paragraph 7 of Schedule 5 to these Regulations).

[1212]

NOTES
Commencement: these Regulations come into force on 2 March 2009 (for the purposes specified in reg 1(2)(a)), 1 May 2009 (for the purposes specified in reg 1(2)(b)), and 1 November 2009 (otherwise). See reg 1 at **[1127]**.

87 Injunctions

(1) If, on the application of the Authority, the court is satisfied—

    (a) that there is a reasonable likelihood that any person will contravene a requirement imposed by or under these Regulations; or

(b)   that any person has contravened such a requirement and that there is a reasonable likelihood that the contravention will continue or be repeated,

the court may make an order restraining (or in Scotland an interdict prohibiting) the contravention.

(2)   If, on the application of the Authority, the court is satisfied—
    (a)   that any person has contravened a requirement imposed by or under these Regulations, and
    (b)   that there are steps which could be taken for remedying the contravention,

the court may make an order requiring that person, and any other person who appears to have been knowingly concerned in the contravention, to take such steps as the court may direct to remedy it.

(3)   If, on the application of the Authority, the court is satisfied that any person may have—
    (a)   contravened a requirement imposed by or under these Regulations, or
    (b)   been knowingly concerned in the contravention of such a requirement,

it may make an order restraining (or in Scotland an interdict prohibiting) them from disposing of, or otherwise dealing with, any assets of theirs which it is satisfied they are reasonably likely to dispose of or otherwise deal with.

(4)   The jurisdiction conferred by this regulation is exercisable by the High Court and the Court of Session.

(5)   In paragraph (2), references to remedying a contravention include references to mitigating its effect.

[1213]

NOTES

Commencement: these Regulations come into force on 2 March 2009 (for the purposes specified in reg 1(2)(a)), 1 May 2009 (for the purposes specified in reg 1(2)(b)), and 1 November 2009 (otherwise). See reg 1 at **[1127]**.

88   Power of Authority to require restitution

(1)   The Authority may exercise the power in paragraph (2) if it is satisfied that a payment service provider (referred to in this regulation and regulation 89 as "the person concerned") has contravened a requirement imposed by or under these Regulations, or been knowingly concerned in the contravention of such a requirement, and that—
    (a)   profits have accrued to the person concerned as a result of the contravention; or
    (b)   one or more persons have suffered loss or been otherwise adversely affected as a result of the contravention.

(2)   The power referred to in paragraph (1) is a power to require the person concerned, in accordance with such arrangements as the Authority considers appropriate, to pay to the appropriate person or distribute among the appropriate persons such amount as appears to the Authority to be just having regard—
    (a)   in a case within sub-paragraph (a) of paragraph (1), to the profits appearing to the Authority to have accrued;
    (b)   in a case within sub-paragraph (b) of that paragraph, to the extent of the loss or other adverse effect;
    (c)   in a case within both of those paragraphs, to the profits appearing to the Authority to have accrued and to the extent of the loss or other adverse effect.

(3)   In paragraph (2) "appropriate person" means a person appearing to the Authority to be someone—
    (a)   to whom the profits mentioned in paragraph (1)(a) are attributable; or
    (b)   who has suffered the loss or adverse effect mentioned in paragraph (1)(b).

[1214]

NOTES

Commencement: these Regulations come into force on 2 March 2009 (for the purposes specified in reg 1(2)(a)), 1 May 2009 (for the purposes specified in reg 1(2)(b)), and 1 November 2009 (otherwise). See reg 1 at **[1127]**.

89   Proposal to require restitution

(1)   If the Authority proposes to exercise the power under regulation 88(2), it must give the person concerned a warning notice.

(2)   The warning notice must state the amount which the Authority propose to require the person concerned to pay or distribute as mentioned in regulation 88(2).

(3)   If, having considered any representations made in response to the warning notice, the Authority decides to exercise the power under regulation 88(2), it must without delay give the person concerned a decision notice.

(4)   The decision notice must—

(a) state the amount that the person concerned is to pay or distribute;
(b) identify the person or persons to whom that amount is to be paid or among whom that amount is to be distributed; and
(c) state the arrangements in accordance with which the payment or distribution is to be made.

(5) If the Authority decides to exercise the power under regulation 88(2), the person concerned may refer the matter to the Tribunal.

[1215]

NOTES
Commencement: these Regulations come into force on 2 March 2009 (for the purposes specified in reg 1(2)(a)), 1 May 2009 (for the purposes specified in reg 1(2)(b)), and 1 November 2009 (otherwise). See reg 1 at **[1127]**.

90 Restitution orders

(1) The court may, on the application of the Authority, make an order under paragraph (2) if it is satisfied that a payment service provider has contravened a requirement imposed by or under these Regulations, or been knowingly concerned in the contravention of such a requirement, and that—
(a) profits have accrued to them as a result of the contravention; or
(b) one or more persons have suffered loss or been otherwise adversely affected as a result of the contravention.

(2) The court may order the person concerned to pay to the Authority such sum as appears to the court to be just having regard—
(a) in a case within sub-paragraph (a) of paragraph (1), to the profits appearing to the court to have accrued;
(b) in a case within sub-paragraph (b) of that paragraph, to the extent of the loss or other adverse effect;
(c) in a case within both of those sub-paragraphs, to the profits appearing to the court to have accrued and to the extent of the loss or other adverse effect.

(3) Any amount paid to the Authority in pursuance of an order under paragraph (2) must be paid by it to such qualifying person or distributed by it among such qualifying persons as the court may direct.

(4) In paragraph (3), "qualifying person" means a person appearing to the court to be someone—
(a) to whom the profits mentioned in paragraph (1)(a) are attributable; or
(b) who has suffered the loss or adverse effect mentioned in paragraph (1)(b).

(5) On an application under paragraph (1) the court may require the person concerned to supply it with such accounts or other information as it may require for any one or more of the following purposes—
(a) establishing whether any and, if so, what profits have accrued to them as mentioned in sub-paragraph (a) of that paragraph;
(b) establishing whether any person or persons have suffered any loss or adverse effect as mentioned in sub-paragraph (b) of that paragraph; and
(c) determining how any amounts are to be paid or distributed under paragraph (3).

(6) The court may require any accounts or other information supplied under paragraph (5) to be verified in such manner as it may direct.

(7) The jurisdiction conferred by this regulation is exercisable by the High Court and the Court of Session.

(8) Nothing in this regulation affects the right of any person other than the Authority to bring proceedings in respect of the matters to which this regulation applies.

[1216]

NOTES
Commencement: these Regulations come into force on 2 March 2009 (for the purposes specified in reg 1(2)(a)), 1 May 2009 (for the purposes specified in reg 1(2)(b)), and 1 November 2009 (otherwise). See reg 1 at **[1127]**.

91 Complaints

(1) The Authority must maintain arrangements designed to enable payment service users and other interested parties to submit complaints to it that a requirement imposed by or under Parts 2 to 6 of these Regulations has been breached by a payment service provider.

(2)   Where it considers it appropriate, the Authority must include in any reply to a complaint under paragraph (1) details of the ombudsman scheme established under Part 16 of the 2000 Act (the ombudsman scheme).

[1217]

NOTES
Commencement: these Regulations come into force on 2 March 2009 (for the purposes specified in reg 1(2)(a)), 1 May 2009 (for the purposes specified in reg 1(2)(b)), and 1 November 2009 (otherwise). See reg 1 at **[1127]**.

Miscellaneous

92   Costs of supervision

(1)   The functions of the Authority under these Regulations are to be treated for the purposes of paragraph 17 (fees) of Part 3 of Schedule 1 to the 2000 Act as functions conferred on the Authority under that Act with the following modifications—

(a)   section 2(3) of the 2000 Act (the Authority's general duties) does not apply to the making of rules under paragraph 17 by virtue of this regulation;

(b)   rules made under paragraph 17 by virtue of this regulation are not to be treated as regulating provisions for the purposes of section 159(1) of the 2000 Act (competition scrutiny);

(c)   paragraph 17(2) and (3) are omitted.

(2)   The Authority must apply amounts paid to it by way of penalties imposed under regulation 85 towards expenses incurred in carrying out its functions under these Regulations or for any incidental purpose.

[1218]

NOTES
Commencement: these Regulations come into force on 2 March 2009 (for the purposes specified in reg 1(2)(a)), 1 May 2009 (for the purposes specified in reg 1(2)(b)), and 1 November 2009 (otherwise). See reg 1 at **[1127]**.

93   Guidance

(1)   The Authority may give guidance consisting of such information and advice as it considers appropriate with respect to—

(a)   the operation of these Regulations;

(b)   any matters relating to the functions of the Authority under these Regulations;

(c)   any other matters about which it appears to the Authority to be desirable to give information or advice in connection with these Regulations.

(2)   The Authority may—

(a)   publish its guidance;

(b)   offer copies of its published guidance for sale at a reasonable price;

(c)   if it gives guidance in response to a request made by any person, make a reasonable charge for that guidance.

[1219]

NOTES
Commencement: these Regulations come into force on 2 March 2009 (for the purposes specified in reg 1(2)(a)), 1 May 2009 (for the purposes specified in reg 1(2)(b)), and 1 November 2009 (otherwise). See reg 1 at **[1127]**.

94   Authority's exemption from liability in damages

The functions of the Authority under these Regulations are to be treated for the purposes of paragraph 19 (exemption from liability in damages) of Part 4 of Schedule 1 to the 2000 Act as functions conferred on the Authority under that Act.

[1220]

NOTES
Commencement: these Regulations come into force on 2 March 2009 (for the purposes specified in reg 1(2)(a)), 1 May 2009 (for the purposes specified in reg 1(2)(b)), and 1 November 2009 (otherwise). See reg 1 at **[1127]**.

95   Application and modification of primary and secondary legislation

The provisions of primary and secondary legislation set out in Schedule 5 apply in respect of the Authority's functions under these Regulations with the modifications set out in that Schedule.

[1221]

NOTES
Commencement: these Regulations come into force on 2 March 2009 (for the purposes specified in reg 1(2)(a)), 1 May 2009 (for the purposes specified in reg 1(2)(b)), and 1 November 2009 (otherwise). See reg 1 at **[1127]**.

PART 8
ACCESS TO PAYMENT SYSTEMS

General

96 Application of Part 8

(1)   This Part does not apply to the following kinds of payment systems—
   (a)   a designated system;
   (b)   a payment system consisting solely of payment service providers belonging to the same group where one of the payment service providers enjoys effective control over the others;
   (c)   a payment system where the sole payment service provider (whether as a single entity or a group)—
      (i)   acts or is able to act as the payment service provider for both the payer and the payee and is solely responsible for the management of the system; and
      (ii)   licenses other payment service providers to participate in the system subject to their having no right to negotiate fees in respect of the system between or amongst themselves (although they may establish their own pricing in relation to payers and payees).

(2)   In paragraph (1)(a), "designated system" means a system which is declared by a designation order for the time being in force under regulation 4 of the Financial Markets and Insolvency (Settlement Finality) Regulations 1999 to be a designated system for the purposes of those Regulations.

[1222]

NOTES
Commencement: these Regulations come into force on 2 March 2009 (for the purposes specified in reg 1(2)(a)), 1 May 2009 (for the purposes specified in reg 1(2)(b)), and 1 November 2009 (otherwise). See reg 1 at **[1127]**.

97 Prohibition on restrictive rules on access to payment systems

(1)   Rules or conditions governing access to, or participation in, a payment system by authorised payment institutions, EEA authorised payment institutions and small payment institutions must—
   (a)   be objective, proportionate and non-discriminatory; and
   (b)   not prevent, restrict or inhibit access or participation more than is necessary to—
      (i)   safeguard against specific risks such as settlement risk, operational risk or business risk; or
      (ii)   protect the financial and operational stability of the payment system.

(2)   Paragraph (1) applies only to such small payment institutions as are legal persons.

(3)   Rules or conditions governing access to, or participation in, a payment system which, in respect of payment service providers, payment service users or other payment systems—
   (a)   restrict effective participation in other payment systems;
   (b)   discriminate (whether directly or indirectly) between—
      (i)   different authorised payment institutions, or
      (ii)   different small payment institutions,
      in relation to the rights, obligations or entitlements of participants in the payment system; or
   (c)   impose any restrictions on the basis that a person is not of a particular institutional status,
are prohibited.

[1223]

NOTES
Commencement: these Regulations come into force on 2 March 2009 (for the purposes specified in reg 1(2)(a)), 1 May 2009 (for the purposes specified in reg 1(2)(b)), and 1 November 2009 (otherwise). See reg 1 at **[1127]**.

PART IV OTHER STATUTORY INSTRUMENTS

Supervision and enforcement

98 Power of OFT to investigate

(1)   The OFT may conduct an investigation where there are reasonable grounds for suspecting that any rule or condition governing access to, or participation in, a payment system contravenes regulation 97(1) or (3).

(2)   Where the investigation relates to a possible breach of regulation 97(1)(b)(ii), the OFT must consult the Bank of England and the Authority.

[1224]

NOTES
Commencement: these Regulations come into force on 2 March 2009 (for the purposes specified in reg 1(2)(a)), 1 May 2009 (for the purposes specified in reg 1(2)(b)), and 1 November 2009 (otherwise). See reg 1 at **[1127]**.

99   OFT power to require information

(1)   For the purposes of an investigation under regulation 98 the OFT may require any person—
  (a)   to produce to it or to a person appointed by it, at a specified time and place, any specified document, or
  (b)   to provide to it or to a person appointed by it, at a specified time and place, any specified information,
which the OFT considers relates to any matter relevant to the investigation.

(2)   The power conferred by paragraph (1) is to be exercised by a notice indicating the subject matter and purpose of the investigation.

(3)   Information required to be provided under paragraph (1) must be provided in the specified manner and form, or, if that is not possible, in the nearest equivalent manner and form.

(4)   The power conferred by paragraph (1) to require a person to produce a document includes power—
  (a)   to require them to provide an explanation of the document, or
  (b)   if the document is not produced, to require them to state, to the best of their knowledge and belief, where it is.

(5)   In this regulation—
  "document" includes information recorded in any form;
  "information" includes estimates and forecasts;
  "specified" means—
      (a)   specified, or described, in the notice referred to in paragraph (2), or
      (b)   falling within a category which is specified, or described, in such notice.

[1225]

NOTES
Commencement: these Regulations come into force on 2 March 2009 (for the purposes specified in reg 1(2)(a)), 1 May 2009 (for the purposes specified in reg 1(2)(b)), and 1 November 2009 (otherwise). See reg 1 at **[1127]**.

100   Failure to comply with information requirement

(1)   If, on an application made by the OFT, it appears to the court that a person (the "information defaulter") has failed to do something that they were required to do under regulation 99, the court may make an order under this regulation.

(2)   An order under this regulation may require the information defaulter—
  (a)   to do the thing that they failed to do within such period as may be specified in the order;
  (b)   otherwise to take such steps to remedy the consequence of the failure as may be so specified.

(3)   In this regulation, "the court" means—
  (a)   in England and Wales and Northern Ireland, the High Court or the county court;
  (b)   in Scotland, the Court of Session or the sheriff court.

[1226]

NOTES
Commencement: these Regulations come into force on 2 March 2009 (for the purposes specified in reg 1(2)(a)), 1 May 2009 (for the purposes specified in reg 1(2)(b)), and 1 November 2009 (otherwise). See reg 1 at **[1127]**.

101   Privileged communications

(1)   A person is not required under regulation 99 to produce or disclose a privileged communication.

(2) In paragraph (1) "privileged communication" means a communication—
   (a) between a professional legal adviser and their client, or
   (b) made in connection with, or in contemplation of, legal proceedings and for the purposes of those proceedings,
which in proceedings in the High Court would be protected from disclosure on grounds of legal professional privilege.

(3) In the application of this regulation to Scotland the reference in paragraph (2) to—
   (a) proceedings in the High Court is to be read as a reference to legal proceedings generally; and
   (b) an entitlement on grounds of legal professional privilege is to be read as a reference to an entitlement on the grounds of confidentiality of communications.

[1227]

NOTES
Commencement: these Regulations come into force on 2 March 2009 (for the purposes specified in reg 1(2)(a)), 1 May 2009 (for the purposes specified in reg 1(2)(b)), and 1 November 2009 (otherwise). See reg 1 at **[1127]**.

102 Notice of OFT decision

Before the OFT, as the result of an investigation under regulation 98, makes a decision that any rules or conditions governing access to, or participation in, a payment system contravene regulation 97(1) or (3), the OFT must—
   (a) give notice to the person (or persons) who the OFT considers are responsible for the contravention, and
   (b) give that person (or those persons) an opportunity to make representations.

[1228]

NOTES
Commencement: these Regulations come into force on 2 March 2009 (for the purposes specified in reg 1(2)(a)), 1 May 2009 (for the purposes specified in reg 1(2)(b)), and 1 November 2009 (otherwise). See reg 1 at **[1127]**.

103 Publication of OFT decision

Where the OFT makes a decision after an investigation under regulation 98, the OFT must publish its decision, together with its reasons for making it.

[1229]

NOTES
Commencement: these Regulations come into force on 2 March 2009 (for the purposes specified in reg 1(2)(a)), 1 May 2009 (for the purposes specified in reg 1(2)(b)), and 1 November 2009 (otherwise). See reg 1 at **[1127]**.

104 Enforcement of decisions

(1) If the OFT makes a decision that any rules or conditions governing access to, or participation in, a payment system contravene regulation 97(1) or (3), the OFT may give such directions as the OFT considers appropriate to such person or persons as it considers appropriate.

(2) A direction under paragraph (1) may (in particular)—
   (a) require the person concerned to change any rule or condition so that it no longer contravenes regulation 97(1) or (3); and
   (b) relate to the conduct of the person in implementing any rule or condition.

(3) A direction under paragraph (1) must be given in writing.

(4) If a person fails, without reasonable excuse, to comply with a direction under paragraph (1), the OFT may apply to the High Court (or, in Scotland, the Court of Session) for an order requiring that person to comply with the direction within a time specified in the order.

(5) An order under paragraph (4) may provide for all of the costs of, or incidental to, the application for the order to be borne by the person in default.

[1230]

NOTES
Commencement: these Regulations come into force on 2 March 2009 (for the purposes specified in reg 1(2)(a)), 1 May 2009 (for the purposes specified in reg 1(2)(b)), and 1 November 2009 (otherwise). See reg 1 at **[1127]**.

105 Power of OFT to impose financial penalties

(1)   Where the OFT is satisfied that any rules or conditions governing access to, or participation in, a payment system contravene regulation 97(1) or (3), the OFT may impose a penalty of such amount as it considers appropriate on such persons as it considers appropriate.

(2)   The OFT may impose a penalty on a person under paragraph (1) only if the OFT is satisfied that the infringement has been committed intentionally or negligently by that person.

(3)   Notice of a penalty under this regulation must—
    (a)   be in writing; and
    (b)   specify the date before which the penalty is required to be paid.

(4)   The date specified must not be earlier than the end of the period within which an appeal against the notice may be brought under regulation 106.

(5)   Any sums received by the OFT under this regulation are to be paid into the Consolidated Fund.

[1231]

NOTES
    Commencement: these Regulations come into force on 2 March 2009 (for the purposes specified in reg 1(2)(a)), 1 May 2009 (for the purposes specified in reg 1(2)(b)), and 1 November 2009 (otherwise). See reg 1 at **[1127]**.

Miscellaneous

106 Appeal to the Competition Appeal Tribunal

(1)   A person may appeal to the Competition Appeal Tribunal from a decision by the OFT to give a direction under regulation 104(1) to that person or to impose a penalty under regulation 105 on that person.

(2)   In determining an appeal under paragraph (1) the Competition Appeal Tribunal shall apply the same principles as would be applied by a court on an application for judicial review.

(3)   Sections 14 (constitution of tribunal) and 15 (tribunal rules) of the Enterprise Act 2002 apply in respect of appeals to the Competition Appeal Tribunal under paragraph (1) as they apply in respect of appeals to the Competition Appeal Tribunal under that Act.

[1232]

NOTES
    Commencement: these Regulations come into force on 2 March 2009 (for the purposes specified in reg 1(2)(a)), 1 May 2009 (for the purposes specified in reg 1(2)(b)), and 1 November 2009 (otherwise). See reg 1 at **[1127]**.

107 Disclosure of information by OFT

Subject to regulation 119(2) and (3), Part 9 of the Enterprise Act 2002 (information) applies in respect of information which comes to the OFT by virtue of these Regulations as it applies in respect of information which is specified information for the purposes of Part 9.

[1233]

NOTES
    Commencement: these Regulations come into force on 2 March 2009 (for the purposes specified in reg 1(2)(a)), 1 May 2009 (for the purposes specified in reg 1(2)(b)), and 1 November 2009 (otherwise). See reg 1 at **[1127]**.

108 Defamation

For the purposes of the law relating to defamation, absolute privilege attaches to any decision made or notice given by the OFT in the exercise of any of its functions under this Part.

[1234]

NOTES
    Commencement: these Regulations come into force on 2 March 2009 (for the purposes specified in reg 1(2)(a)), 1 May 2009 (for the purposes specified in reg 1(2)(b)), and 1 November 2009 (otherwise). See reg 1 at **[1127]**.

109 Guidance

(1)   The OFT may give guidance consisting of such information and advice as it considers appropriate with respect to the exercise of its functions under this Part.

(2)   The OFT may—
    (a)   publish its guidance;

(b)   if it gives guidance in response to a request made by any person, make a reasonable charge for that guidance.

[1235]

NOTES
Commencement: these Regulations come into force on 2 March 2009 (for the purposes specified in reg 1(2)(a)), 1 May 2009 (for the purposes specified in reg 1(2)(b)), and 1 November 2009 (otherwise). See reg 1 at **[1127]**.

PART 9
GENERAL

Criminal Offences

110   Prohibition on provision of payment services by persons other than payment service providers

(1)   A person may not provide a payment service in the United Kingdom, or purport to do so, unless the person is—
    (a)   an authorised payment institution;
    (b)   a small payment institution;
    (c)   an EEA authorised payment institution exercising its passport rights;
    (d)   a person mentioned in any of paragraphs (d) to (h) of the definition in regulation 2(1) of a payment service provider, including, where relevant, such a person exercising an EEA right in accordance with Part 2 of Schedule 3 to the 2000 Act (exercise of passport rights by EEA firms); or
    (e)   exempt under regulation 3.

(2)   A person who contravenes paragraph (1) is guilty of an offence and is liable—
    (a)   on summary conviction, to imprisonment for a term not exceeding three months or to a fine not exceeding the statutory maximum, or both;
    (b)   on conviction on indictment, to imprisonment for a term not exceeding two years or to a fine, or both.

[1236]

NOTES
Commencement: these Regulations come into force on 2 March 2009 (for the purposes specified in reg 1(2)(a)), 1 May 2009 (for the purposes specified in reg 1(2)(b)), and 1 November 2009 (otherwise). See reg 1 at **[1127]**.

111   False claims to be a payment service provider or exempt

(1)   A person who does not fall within any of sub-paragraphs (a) to (e) of regulation 110(1) may not—
    (a)   describe themselves (in whatever terms) as a person falling within any of those sub-paragraphs; or
    (b)   behave, or otherwise hold themselves out, in a manner which indicates (or which is reasonably likely to be understood as indicating) that they are such a person.

(2)   A person who contravenes paragraph (1) is guilty of an offence and is liable on summary conviction to imprisonment for a term not exceeding three months or to a fine not exceeding level 5 on the standard scale, or both.

[1237]

NOTES
Commencement: these Regulations come into force on 2 March 2009 (for the purposes specified in reg 1(2)(a)), 1 May 2009 (for the purposes specified in reg 1(2)(b)), and 1 November 2009 (otherwise). See reg 1 at **[1127]**.

112   Defences

In proceedings for an offence under regulation 110 or 111 it is a defence for the accused to show that they took all reasonable precautions and exercised all due diligence to avoid committing the offence.

[1238]

NOTES
Commencement: these Regulations come into force on 2 March 2009 (for the purposes specified in reg 1(2)(a)), 1 May 2009 (for the purposes specified in reg 1(2)(b)), and 1 November 2009 (otherwise). See reg 1 at **[1127]**.

113   Contravention of regulations 49 and 50

(1)   A person (not being a payment service provider) who contravenes regulation 49(2) or 50(2) is guilty of an offence and liable on summary conviction to a fine not exceeding level 5 on the standard scale.

(2)   No offence is committed if the person took all reasonable steps and exercised all due diligence to ensure that the requirement imposed on the person by regulation 49(2) or 50(2), as the case may be, would be complied with.

[1239]

NOTES
Commencement: these Regulations come into force on 2 March 2009 (for the purposes specified in reg 1(2)(a)), 1 May 2009 (for the purposes specified in reg 1(2)(b)), and 1 November 2009 (otherwise). See reg 1 at **[1127]**.

114   Misleading the Authority or the OFT

(1)   A person may not, in purported compliance with any requirement imposed by or under these Regulations, knowingly or recklessly give—
   (a)   the Authority; or
   (b)   the OFT,
information which is false or misleading in a material particular.

(2)   A person may not—
   (a)   provide any information to another person, knowing the information to be false or misleading in a material particular, or
   (b)   recklessly provide to another person any information which is false or misleading in a material particular,
knowing that the information is to be used for the purpose of providing information to the Authority in connection with its functions under these Regulations.

(3)   A person may not—
   (a)   provide any information to another person, knowing the information to be false or misleading in a material particular, or
   (b)   recklessly provide to another person any information which is false or misleading in a material particular,
knowing that the information is to be used for the purpose of providing information to the OFT in connection with their functions under these Regulations.

(4)   A person who knows or suspects that an investigation by the OFT under regulation 98 is being or is likely to be conducted may not—
   (a)   intentionally or recklessly destroy or otherwise dispose of, falsify or conceal a document (as defined by regulation 99(5)) which may be relevant to such an investigation; or
   (b)   cause or permit its destruction, disposal, falsification or concealment.

(5)   A person who contravenes paragraph (1), (2), (3) or (4) is guilty of an offence and is liable—
   (a)   on summary conviction, to a fine not exceeding the statutory maximum;
   (b)   on conviction on indictment, to a fine.

[1240]

NOTES
Commencement: these Regulations come into force on 2 March 2009 (for the purposes specified in reg 1(2)(a)), 1 May 2009 (for the purposes specified in reg 1(2)(b)), and 1 November 2009 (otherwise). See reg 1 at **[1127]**.

115   Restriction on penalties

A person who is convicted of an offence under these Regulations is not liable to a penalty under regulation 85 or 105 in respect of the same contravention of a requirement imposed by or under these Regulations.

[1241]

NOTES
Commencement: these Regulations come into force on 2 March 2009 (for the purposes specified in reg 1(2)(a)), 1 May 2009 (for the purposes specified in reg 1(2)(b)), and 1 November 2009 (otherwise). See reg 1 at **[1127]**.

116   Liability of officers of bodies corporate etc

(1)   If an offence under these Regulations committed by a body corporate is shown—
   (a)   to have been committed with the consent or connivance of an officer, or

(b)   to be attributable to any neglect on their part,
the officer as well as the body corporate is guilty of the offence and liable to be proceeded against and punished accordingly.

(2)   If the affairs of a body corporate are managed by its members, paragraph (1) applies in relation to the acts and defaults of a member in connection with such member's functions of management as if the member were a director of the body.

(3)   If an offence under these Regulations committed by a partnership is shown—
(a)   to have been committed with the consent or connivance of a partner, or
(b)   to be attributable to any neglect on their part,
the partner as well as the partnership is guilty of the offence and liable to be proceeded against and punished accordingly.

(4)   If an offence under these Regulations committed by an unincorporated association (other than a partnership) is shown—
(a)   to have been committed with the consent or connivance of an officer, or
(b)   to be attributable to any neglect of such officer,
the officer as well as the association is guilty of the offence and liable to be proceeded against and punished accordingly.

(5)   In this regulation—
"officer"—
(a)   in relation to a body corporate, means a director, manager, secretary, chief executive, member of the committee of management, or a person purporting to act in such a capacity; and
(b)   in relation to an unincorporated association, means any officer of the association or any member of its governing body, or a person purporting to act in such capacity; and
"partner" includes a person purporting to act as a partner.

[1242]

NOTES
Commencement: these Regulations come into force on 2 March 2009 (for the purposes specified in reg 1(2)(a)), 1 May 2009 (for the purposes specified in reg 1(2)(b)), and 1 November 2009 (otherwise). See reg 1 at **[1127]**.

---

117   Prosecution of offences

(1)   Proceedings for an offence under these Regulations may be instituted only—
(a)   in respect of an offence under regulation 110, 111, 113, or 114(1)(a) or (2), by the Authority;
(b)   in respect of an offence under regulation 114(1)(b), (3) or (4), by the OFT; or
(c)   by or with the consent of the Director of Public Prosecutions.

(2)   Paragraph (1) does not apply to proceedings in Scotland.

[1243]

NOTES
Commencement: these Regulations come into force on 2 March 2009 (for the purposes specified in reg 1(2)(a)), 1 May 2009 (for the purposes specified in reg 1(2)(b)), and 1 November 2009 (otherwise). See reg 1 at **[1127]**.

---

118   Proceedings against unincorporated bodies

(1)   Proceedings for an offence alleged to have been committed by a partnership or an unincorporated association must be brought in the name of the partnership or association (and not in that of its members).

(2)   A fine imposed on the partnership or association on its conviction of an offence is to be paid out of the funds of the partnership or association.

(3)   Rules of court relating to the service of documents are to have effect as if the partnership or association were a body corporate.

(4)   In proceedings for an offence brought against the partnership or association—
(a)   section 33 of the Criminal Justice Act 1925 (procedure on charge of offence against corporation) and section 46 of and Schedule 3 to the Magistrates' Courts Act 1980 (corporations) apply as they do in relation to a body corporate;
(b)   section 70 of the Criminal Procedure (Scotland) Act 1995 (proceedings against bodies corporate) applies as it does in relation to a body corporate;
(c)   section 18 of the Criminal Justice (Northern Ireland) Act 1945 (procedure on charge) and Schedule 4 to the Magistrates' Courts (Northern Ireland) Order 1981 (corporations) apply as they do in relation to a body corporate.

PART IV   OTHER STATUTORY INSTRUMENTS

(5) Summary proceedings for an offence under these Regulations may be taken—
  (a) against a body corporate or unincorporated association at any place at which it has a place of business;
  (b) against an individual at any place where they are for the time being.

(6) Paragraph (5) does not affect any jurisdiction exercisable apart from this regulation.

[1244]

NOTES
Commencement: these Regulations come into force on 2 March 2009 (for the purposes specified in reg 1(2)(a)), 1 May 2009 (for the purposes specified in reg 1(2)(b)), and 1 November 2009 (otherwise). See reg 1 at **[1127]**.

Duties of the Authority, the Commissioners and the OFT to cooperate

119 Duty to co-operate and exchange of information

(1) The Authority, the Commissioners and the OFT must take such steps as they consider appropriate to co-operate with each other and—
  (a) the competent authorities designated under Article 20(1), or referred to in Article 82(1), of the payment services directive, of EEA States other than the United Kingdom;
  (b) the European Central Bank, the Bank of England and the national central banks of EEA States other than the United Kingdom; and
  (c) any other relevant competent authorities designated under Community law or the law of the United Kingdom or any other EEA State which is applicable to payment service providers,

for the purposes of the exercise by those bodies of their functions under the payment services directive and other relevant Community or national legislation.

(2) Subject to the requirements of the Data Protection Act 1998, sections 348 and 349 of the 2000 Act (as applied with modifications by paragraph 5 of Schedule 5 to these Regulations), regulation 49A of the Money Laundering Regulations 2007 (as inserted by paragraph 6(g) of Schedule 6 to these Regulations) and any other applicable restrictions on the disclosure of information, the Authority, the Commissioners and the OFT may provide information to each other and—
  (a) the bodies mentioned in paragraph (1)(a) and (c);
  (b) the European Central Bank, the Bank of England and the national central banks of EEA States other than the United Kingdom when acting in their capacity as monetary and oversight authorities;
  (c) where relevant, other public authorities responsible for the oversight of payment and settlement systems;

for the purposes of the exercise by those bodies of their functions under the payment services directive and other relevant Community or national legislation.

(3) Part 9 of the Enterprise Act 2002 does not prohibit disclosure by the OFT under paragraph (2) but the OFT must have regard to the considerations mentioned in section 244 of that Act (specified information: considerations relevant to disclosure) before making any such disclosure.

[1245]

NOTES
Commencement: these Regulations come into force on 2 March 2009 (for the purposes specified in reg 1(2)(a)), 1 May 2009 (for the purposes specified in reg 1(2)(b)), and 1 November 2009 (otherwise). See reg 1 at **[1127]**.

Actions for breach of requirements

120 Right to bring actions

(1) A contravention—
  (a) which is to be taken to have occurred by virtue of regulation 17;
  (b) of a requirement imposed by regulation 19; or
  (c) of a requirement imposed by or under Part 5 or 6,

is actionable at the suit of a private person who suffers loss as a result of the contravention, subject to the defences and other incidents applying to actions for breach of statutory duty.

(2) A person acting in a fiduciary or representative capacity may bring an action under paragraph (1) on behalf of a private person if any remedy—
  (a) will be exclusively for the benefit of the private person; and
  (b) cannot be obtained by way of an action brought otherwise than at the suit of the fiduciary or representative.

(3) In this regulation "private person" means—

(a)   any individual, except where the individual suffers the loss in question in the course of providing payment services; and

(b)   any person who is not an individual, except where that person suffers the loss in question in the course of carrying on business of any kind;

but does not include a government, a local authority (in the United Kingdom or elsewhere) or an international organisation.

[1246]

NOTES

Commencement: these Regulations come into force on 2 March 2009 (for the purposes specified in reg 1(2)(a)), 1 May 2009 (for the purposes specified in reg 1(2)(b)), and 1 November 2009 (otherwise). See reg 1 at **[1127]**.

Transitional provisions

121   Transitional provisions: deemed authorisation

(1)   Any financial institution (within the meaning of the banking consolidation directive) which—

(a)   is constituted under the law of a part of the United Kingdom and has its head office and, if it has a registered office, that office, in the United Kingdom; and

(b)   before 25th December 2007 had—

(i)   lawfully provided payment services in the United Kingdom; and

(ii)   met the condition in Article 24(1)(e) of the banking consolidation directive;

shall be deemed to have been granted authorisation by the Authority under regulation 9.

(2)   An institution which is deemed to have been granted authorisation by virtue of paragraph (1) shall continue on or after 25th December 2009 to be deemed to have been granted authorisation only if it has by that date—

(a)   notified the Authority of the payment services referred to in sub-paragraph (b)(i); and

(b)   provided the Authority with the information specified in paragraph 1, 4, 7 to 9 and 12 of Schedule 2 ("the required information").

(3)   Authorisation which continues on or after 25th December 2009 to be deemed to have been granted by virtue of paragraph (2) shall continue to be so deemed until such time as the Authority decides whether to include the institution in the register as an authorised payment institution.

(4)   If the Authority decides to include the institution in the register as an authorised payment institution—

(a)   it must as soon as practicable update the register accordingly; and

(b)   the institution shall cease to be deemed to have been granted authorisation by virtue of paragraph (1) or (2).

(5)   The Authority may decide that an institution is not to be included in the register as an authorised payment institution only if—

(a)   it has not received the required information; or

(b)   any of the conditions in regulation 6(4) to (6) (other than the condition that a person must be a body corporate) ("the required conditions") are not met in respect of that institution.

(6)   If the Authority is satisfied that—

(a)   it has received the required information; and

(b)   the required conditions are met,

it must give the institution notice of its decision.

(7)   If the Authority proposes to decide that—

(a)   it has not received the required information; or

(b)   any of the required conditions is not met,

it must give the institution a warning notice.

(8)   The Authority must, having considered any representations in response to the warning notice—

(a)   if it decides that it has not received the required information or that any of the required conditions is not met, give the institution a decision notice; or

(b)   if it decides that it has received the required information and that the required conditions have been met, give the institution notice of its decision.

(9)   If the Authority gives the institution a decision notice, the institution may refer the matter to the Tribunal.

(10)   Where the period for a reference to the Tribunal has expired without a reference being made, the institution shall cease to be deemed to have been granted authorisation by virtue of paragraph (1) or (2).

(11)   Where an institution is deemed to have been granted authorisation by virtue of paragraph (1) or (2)—

    (a)   the duty to which the Authority is subject under regulation 4(1)(a) to maintain a register shall not apply in respect of it; and

    (b)   Parts 3 and 4 shall not apply to it.

[1247]

NOTES

Commencement: these Regulations come into force on 2 March 2009 (for the purposes specified in reg 1(2)(a)), 1 May 2009 (for the purposes specified in reg 1(2)(b)), and 1 November 2009 (otherwise). See reg 1 at **[1127]**.

122   Transitional provisions: requirement to be authorised as a payment institution

(1)   Any person which—

    (a)   is a body corporate constituted under the law of a part of the United Kingdom and has its head office and, if it has a registered office, that office, in the United Kingdom;

    (b)   is not a body—

        (i)   mentioned in any of paragraphs (d) to (h) of the definition in regulation 2(1) of a payment service provider; or

        (ii)   which is deemed to have been granted authorisation by virtue of regulation 121(1) or (2); and

    (c)   immediately before 25th December 2007, was lawfully providing payment services in the United Kingdom,

may continue until 1st May 2011 to provide payment services in the United Kingdom notwithstanding that the person has not been granted authorisation by the Authority under regulation 9.

(2)   Parts 5 to 8 and regulation 110(1) apply to a person falling within paragraph (1) as if the person were an authorised payment institution.

[1248]

NOTES

Commencement: these Regulations come into force on 2 March 2009 (for the purposes specified in reg 1(2)(a)), 1 May 2009 (for the purposes specified in reg 1(2)(b)), and 1 November 2009 (otherwise). See reg 1 at **[1127]**.

123   Transitional provisions: requirement to be registered as a small payment institution

(1)   Any person who—

    (a)   immediately before 25th December 2007, was lawfully providing payment services in the United Kingdom;

    (b)   is not a body—

        (i)   mentioned in any of paragraphs (d) to (h) of the definition in regulation 2(1) of a payment service provider; or

        (ii)   which is deemed to have been granted authorisation by virtue of regulation 121(1) or (2) or which falls within regulation 122(1); and

    (c)   meets the conditions set out in regulation 13(4) to (6) and complies with the financial limit referred to in regulation 8 (as applied by regulation 14(c)),

may continue until 25th December 2010 to provide payment services in the United Kingdom notwithstanding that the person has not been granted registration by the Authority under regulation 9 (as applied by regulation 14).

(2)   Parts 5 to 8 and regulation 110(1) apply to a person falling within paragraph (1) as if the person were a small payment institution.

[1249]

NOTES

Commencement: these Regulations come into force on 2 March 2009 (for the purposes specified in reg 1(2)(a)), 1 May 2009 (for the purposes specified in reg 1(2)(b)), and 1 November 2009 (otherwise). See reg 1 at **[1127]**.

124   Transitional provisions: early applications

(1)   Where an application is made under regulation 5(1) or (2) or 12(1) or (2) before 1st August 2009 and is a completed application, the Authority must determine it before 1st November 2009.

(2)   The requirement under regulation 23(2) for information to be given to the host state competent authority within one month of receipt by the Authority of a notice of intention does not apply where the notice of intention is received by the Authority before 1st November 2009.

(3) Any requirement under these Regulations to update the register does not apply until 1st November 2009.

[1250]

NOTES
Commencement: these Regulations come into force on 2 March 2009 (for the purposes specified in reg 1(2)(a)), 1 May 2009 (for the purposes specified in reg 1(2)(b)), and 1 November 2009 (otherwise). See reg 1 at **[1127]**.

125 Transitional provisions: the ombudsman scheme

Part 16 of, and Schedule 17 to, the 2000 Act (the ombudsman scheme) shall apply as if persons who fall within regulation 122(1) or 123(1) were payment service providers within the meaning of these Regulations.

[1251]

NOTES
Commencement: these Regulations come into force on 2 March 2009 (for the purposes specified in reg 1(2)(a)), 1 May 2009 (for the purposes specified in reg 1(2)(b)), and 1 November 2009 (otherwise). See reg 1 at **[1127]**.

Amendments to primary and secondary legislation

126 Amendments to primary and secondary legislation

Schedule 6, which contains amendments to primary and secondary legislation, has effect.

[1252]

NOTES
Commencement: these Regulations come into force on 2 March 2009 (for the purposes specified in reg 1(2)(a)), 1 May 2009 (for the purposes specified in reg 1(2)(b)), and 1 November 2009 (otherwise). See reg 1 at **[1127]**.

SCHEDULES

SCHEDULE 1
PAYMENT SERVICES

Regulation 2(1)

PART 1
PAYMENT SERVICES

1. Subject to Part 2, the following activities, when carried out as a regular occupation or business activity, are payment services—
  (a) services enabling cash to be placed on a payment account and all of the operations required for operating a payment account;
  (b) services enabling cash withdrawals from a payment account and all of the operations required for operating a payment account;
  (c) the execution of the following types of payment transaction—
    (i) direct debits, including one-off direct debits;
    (ii) payment transactions executed through a payment card or a similar device;
    (iii) credit transfers, including standing orders;
  (d) the execution of the following types of payment transaction where the funds are covered by a credit line for the payment service user—
    (i) direct debits, including one-off direct debits;
    (ii) payment transactions executed through a payment card or a similar device;
    (iii) credit transfers, including standing orders;
  (e) issuing payment instruments or acquiring payment transactions;
  (f) money remittance;
  (g) the execution of payment transactions where the consent of the payer to execute the payment transaction is given by means of any telecommunication, digital or IT device and the payment is made to the telecommunication, IT system or network operator acting only as an intermediary between the payment service user and the supplier of the goods or services.

[1253]

NOTES
Commencement: these Regulations come into force on 2 March 2009 (for the purposes specified in reg 1(2)(a)), 1 May 2009 (for the purposes specified in reg 1(2)(b)), and 1 November 2009 (otherwise). See reg 1 at **[1127]**.

PART IV OTHER STATUTORY INSTRUMENTS

PART 2
ACTIVITIES WHICH DO NOT CONSTITUTE PAYMENT SERVICES

2.   The following activities do not constitute payment services—
   (a)   payment transactions executed wholly in cash and directly between the payer and the payee, without any intermediary intervention;
   (b)   payment transactions between the payer and the payee through a commercial agent authorised to negotiate or conclude the sale or purchase of goods or services on behalf of the payer or the payee;
   (c)   the professional physical transport of banknotes and coins, including their collection, processing and delivery;
   (d)   payment transactions consisting of non-professional cash collection and delivery as part of a not-for-profit or charitable activity;
   (e)   services where cash is provided by the payee to the payer as part of a payment transaction for the purchase of goods or services following an explicit request by the payer immediately before the execution of the payment transaction;
   (f)   money exchange business consisting of cash-to-cash operations where the funds are not held on a payment account;
   (g)   payment transactions based on any of the following documents drawn on the payment service provider with a view to placing funds at the disposal of the payee—
      (i)   paper cheques of any kind, including traveller's cheques;
      (ii)   bankers' drafts;
      (iii)   paper-based vouchers;
      (iv)   paper postal orders;
   (h)   payment transactions carried out within a payment or securities settlement system between payment service providers and settlement agents, central counterparties, clearing houses, central banks or other participants in the system;
   (i)   payment transactions related to securities asset servicing, including dividends, income or other distributions, or redemption or sale, carried out by persons referred to in sub-paragraph (h) or by investment firms, credit institutions, collective investment undertakings or asset management companies providing investment services or by any other entities allowed to have the custody of financial instruments;
   (j)   services provided by technical service providers, which support the provision of payment services, without the provider entering at any time into possession of the funds to be transferred, including—
      (i)   the processing and storage of data;
      (ii)   trust and privacy protection services;
      (iii)   data and entity authentication;
      (iv)   information technology;
      (v)   communication network provision; and
      (vi)   the provision and maintenance of terminals and devices used for payment services;
   (k)   services based on instruments that can be used to acquire goods or services only—
      (i)   in or on the issuer's premises; or
      (ii)   under a commercial agreement with the issuer, either within a limited network of service providers or for a limited range of goods or services,
      and for these purposes the "issuer" is the person who issues the instrument in question;
   (l)   payment transactions executed by means of any telecommunication, digital or IT device, where the goods or services purchased are delivered to and are to be used through a telecommunication, digital or IT device, provided that the telecommunication, digital or IT operator does not act only as an intermediary between the payment service user and the supplier of the goods and services;
   (m)   payment transactions carried out between payment service providers, or their agents or branches, for their own account;
   (n)   payment transactions between a parent undertaking and its subsidiary or between subsidiaries of the same parent undertaking, without any intermediary intervention by a payment service provider other than an undertaking belonging to the same group;
   (o)   services by providers to withdraw cash by means of automated teller machines acting on behalf of one or more card issuers, which are not party to the framework contract with the customer withdrawing money from a payment account, where no other payment service is conducted by the provider.

[1254]

NOTES

Commencement: these Regulations come into force on 2 March 2009 (for the purposes specified in reg 1(2)(a)), 1 May 2009 (for the purposes specified in reg 1(2)(b)), and 1 November 2009 (otherwise). See reg 1 at [1127].

SCHEDULE 2
INFORMATION TO BE INCLUDED IN OR WITH AN APPLICATION
FOR AUTHORISATION

Regulation 5(1)

1.   A programme of operations setting out, in particular, the type of payment services envisaged.

2.   A business plan including a forecast budget calculation for the first three financial years which demonstrates that the applicant is able to employ appropriate and proportionate systems, resources and procedures to operate soundly.

3.   Evidence that the applicant holds initial capital for the purposes of regulation 6(3).

4.   Where regulation 19 applies, a description of the measures taken for safeguarding payment service users' funds in accordance with that regulation.

5.   A description of the applicant's governance arrangements and internal control mechanisms, including administrative risk management and accounting procedures, which demonstrates that such arrangements, mechanisms and procedures are proportionate, appropriate, sound and adequate.

6.   A description of the internal control mechanisms which the applicant has established in order to comply with the Money Laundering Regulations 2007 and Regulation (EC) No 1781/2006 of the European Parliament and of the Council of 15 November 2006 on information on the payer accompanying transfers of funds.

7.   A description of the applicant's structural organisation, including, where applicable, a description of the intended use of agents and branches and a description of outsourcing arrangements, and of its participation in a national or international payment system.

8.—(1)   In relation to each person holding, directly or indirectly, a qualifying holding in the applicant—

    (a)   the size and nature of their qualifying holding; and

    (b)   evidence of their suitability taking into account the need to ensure the sound and prudent management of a payment institution.

9.—(1)   The identity of directors and persons who are or will be responsible for the management of the applicant and, where relevant, persons who are or will be responsible for the management of the payment services activities of the applicant.

    (2)   Evidence that the persons described in sub-paragraph (1) are of good repute and that they possess appropriate knowledge and experience to perform payment services.

10.   The identity of the auditors of the applicant, if any.

11.—(1)   The legal status of the applicant and, where the applicant is a limited company, its articles.

    (2)   In this paragraph "articles" has the meaning given in section 7 of the Companies Act 1985 (articles prescribing regulations for companies) until the coming into force of section 18 of the Companies Act 2006 (articles of association) when it will have the meaning given by that section.

12.   The address of the head office of the applicant.

13.   For the purposes of paragraphs 4, 5 and 7, a description of the audit arrangements of the applicant and of the organisational arrangements the applicant has set up with a view to taking all reasonable steps to protect the interests of its payment service users and to ensure continuity and reliability in the performance of payment services.

[1255]

NOTES

Commencement: these Regulations come into force on 2 March 2009 (for the purposes specified in reg 1(2)(a)), 1 May 2009 (for the purposes specified in reg 1(2)(b)), and 1 November 2009 (otherwise). See reg 1 at **[1127]**.

Note: para 8 above is reproduced as it appears in the Queen's Printer's copy of these Regulations, ie, there is no sub-paragraph (2).

SCHEDULE 3
CAPITAL REQUIREMENTS

Regulations 6(3), 18

PART 1
INITIAL CAPITAL

1.   For the purposes of this Part, "initial capital" comprises the items specified in paragraph 3(a), (b) and (c) of this Schedule.

2.—(1)   An applicant for authorisation as a payment institution must hold the amount of initial capital specified in the second column of the table, corresponding to the payment services provided or to be provided (as specified in the first column).

(2)   Where more than one initial capital requirement applies, the applicant must hold initial capital of whichever is the greater amount.

Payment services	Initial capital requirement (euro)
Payment services specified in paragraph 127(f) of Schedule 1	20,000
Payment services specified in paragraph 127(g) of Schedule 1	50,000
Any of the payment services specified in paragraph 127(a) to (e) of Schedule 1	125,000

[1256]

NOTES
Commencement: these Regulations come into force on 2 March 2009 (for the purposes specified in reg 1(2)(a)), 1 May 2009 (for the purposes specified in reg 1(2)(b)), and 1 November 2009 (otherwise). See reg 1 at **[1127]**.

PART 2
OWN FUNDS

Qualifying items

3.   For the purposes of this Part, "own funds" means the following items, subject to the deductions specified in paragraph 147 and to the limits specified in paragraph 149—
  (a)   paid up capital, including share premium accounts but excluding amounts arising in respect of cumulative preference shares;
  (b)   reserves other than—
      (i)   revaluation reserves;
      (ii)   fair value reserves related to gains or losses on cash flow hedges of financial instruments measured at amortised cost; and
      (iii) that part of profit and loss reserves that arises from any gains on liabilities valued at fair value that are due to changes in the authorised payment institution's credit standing;
  (c)   profit or loss brought forward as a result of the application of the final profit or loss, provided that—
      (i)   interim profits may only be included if they are—
          (aa)   verified by persons responsible for the auditing of the authorised payment institution's accounts;
          (bb)   shown to the satisfaction of the Authority that the amount has been evaluated in accordance with the principles set out in directive 86/635/EEC of the Council of the 8th December 1986 on the annual accounts and consolidated accounts of banks and other financial institutions; and
          (cc)   net of any foreseeable charge or dividend;
      (ii)   in the case of an authorised payment institution which is the originator of a securitisation, net gains arising from the capitalisation of future income from the securitised assets and providing credit enhancement to positions in the securitisation are excluded;
  (d)   revaluation reserves;
  (e)   general or collective provisions if—
      (i)   they are freely available to the authorised payment institution to cover normal payment services risks where revenue or capital losses have not yet been identified;
      (ii)   their existence is disclosed in internal accounting records; and
      (iii) their amount is determined by the management of the authorised payment institution, verified by a statutory auditor or audit firm (as defined by regulation 20(2)) and notified to the Authority;
  (f)   securities of indeterminate duration and other instruments that fulfil the following conditions—
      (i)   they may not be reimbursed on the bearer's initiative or without the prior agreement of the Authority;
      (ii)   the debt agreement provides for the authorised payment institution to have the option of deferring the payment of interest on the debt;
      (iii) the lender's claim on the authorised payment institution is wholly subordinated to those of all non-subordinated creditors;
      (iv)   the documents governing the issue of the securities provide for debt and unpaid

interest to be such as to absorb losses, whilst leaving the authorised payment institution in a position to continue trading;

provided that only fully paid-up amounts are to be taken into account;

(g)   cumulative preferential shares, other than fixed-term cumulative preference shares referred to in paragraph (j);

(h)   the commitments of the members of an authorised payment institution set up as a cooperative, comprising—

    (i)   that institution's uncalled capital; and

    (ii)   the legal commitments of the members of that institution to make additional non-refundable payments should the institution incur a loss provided that such payments can be demanded without delay;

(i)   the joint and several commitments of the borrower in the case of an authorised payment institution organised as a fund, comprising—

    (i)   that institution's uncalled capital; and

    (ii)   the legal commitments of the borrowers of that institution to make additional non-refundable payments should the institution incur a loss provided that such payments can be demanded without delay;

(j)   fixed-term cumulative preferential shares and subordinated loan capital if—

    (i)   binding agreements exist under which, in the event of the winding-up of the authorised payment institution, they rank after the claims of all other creditors and are not to be repaid until all other debts outstanding at the time have been settled; and

    (ii)   in the case of subordinated loan capital—

        (aa)   only fully paid-up funds are taken into account;

        (bb)   the loans involved have an original maturity of at least five years, after which they may be repaid;

        (cc)   the extent to which they may rank as own funds is gradually reduced during at least the last five years before the repayment date; and

        (dd)   the loan agreement does not include any clause providing that in specified circumstances, other than the winding-up of the authorised payment institution, the debt will become repayable before the agreed repayment date.

4.   The items specified in paragraph 144(a) to (d) must be—

(a)   available to the authorised payment institution for unrestricted and immediate use to cover risks or losses as soon as these occur; and

(b)   net of any foreseeable tax charge at the moment of their calculation or be suitably adjusted in so far as such tax charges reduce the amount up to which these items may be applied to cover risks or losses.

5.   Own funds are not to include guarantees provided by the Crown or a local authority to a payment institution which is a public sector entity for the purposes of the banking consolidation directive.

Deductions from own funds

6.   The deductions from own funds are—

(a)   own shares at book value held by the authorised payment institution;

(b)   intangible assets;

(c)   material losses of the current financial year;

(d)   holdings of shares in credit institutions and financial institutions exceeding 10% of their capital;

(e)   if sub-paragraph (d) applies, the items specified in paragraph 144(f), (g) and (j) held in the relevant credit institution or financial institution;

(f)   holdings of shares or of the items specified in paragraph 3(f), (g) and (j) held in other credit institutions or financial institutions where—

    (i)   the holding has not been deducted in accordance with sub-paragraph (d) or (e) of this paragraph; and

    (ii)   the total amount of such holdings exceeds 10% of the authorised payment institution's own funds calculated before deduction of the items specified in this sub-paragraph and sub-paragraphs (d), (e), (g) and (h);

(g)   participations which the authorised payment institution holds in an insurance undertaking, reinsurance undertaking or insurance holding company; and

(h)   the following instruments held in an insurance undertaking, reinsurance undertaking or insurance holding company in which the authorised payment institution holds a participation—

    (i)   instruments referred to in article 16(3) of directive 73/239/EEC of the Council on the coordination of laws, regulations and administrative provisions relating to the taking-up and pursuit of the business of direct insurance other than life assurance;

    (ii)   instruments referred to in article 27(3) of directive 2002/83/EC of the European Parliament and of the Council of 5th November 2002 concerning life assurance.

PART IV

OTHER STATUTORY INSTRUMENTS

7.   Where shares in another credit institution, financial institution, insurance undertaking, reinsurance undertaking or insurance holding company are held temporarily for the purposes of a financial assistance operation designed to reorganise and save that entity, the Authority may direct that any or all of the items specified in paragraph 147(d) to (h) are not to be deducted from own funds.

Limits on qualifying items

8.—(1)   The limits referred to in paragraph 144 are—

   (a)   that A must not exceed B; and

   (b)   that C must not exceed 50% of B.

   (2)   After applying such limits—

   (a)   50% of the total of the items specified in paragraph 6(d) to (h) must be deducted from A and the remaining 50% must be deducted from B; and

   (b)   the amount, if any, by which the amount to be deducted from A exceeds A must be deducted from B.

   (3)   In this paragraph—

   (a)   "A" means the total of the items specified in paragraph 144(d) to (j);

   (b)   "B" means the total of the items specified in paragraph 144(a) to (c) less the total of the items specified in paragraph 147(a) to (c); and

   (c)   "C" means the total of the items specified in paragraph 144(h) to (j).

9.   The Authority may in temporary and exceptional circumstances direct that an authorised payment institution may exceed one or more of the limits described in paragraph 8(1).

10.   An authorised payment institution must not include in its own funds calculation any item—

   (a)   used in an equivalent calculation by an authorised payment institution, credit institution, investment firm, asset management company or insurance undertaking in the same group; or

   (b)   in the case of an authorised payment institution which carries out activities other than providing payment services, is used in carrying out those activities.

Own funds requirement

11.   An authorised payment institution must hold own funds calculated in accordance with such of Method A, Method B or Method C as the Authority may direct.

Adjustment by the Authority

12.   The Authority may direct that an authorised payment institution must hold own funds up to 20% higher, or up to 20% lower, than the amount which would result from paragraph 152.

13.   A direction made under paragraph 153 must be on the basis of an evaluation of the relevant authorised payment institution including, if available and where the Authority considers it appropriate, any risk-management processes, risk loss database or internal control mechanisms of the authorised payment institution.

14.   The Authority may make a reasonable charge for making an evaluation required under paragraph 154.

Provision for start-up payment institutions

15.   If an authorised payment institution has not completed a full financial year's business, references to a figure for the preceding financial year are to be read as the equivalent figure projected in the business plan provided in the payment institution's application for authorisation, subject to any adjustment to that plan required by the Authority.

Method A

16.—(1)   "Method A" means the calculation method set out in this paragraph.

   (2)   The own funds requirement is 10% of the authorised payment institution's fixed overheads for the preceding financial year.

   (3)   If a material change has occurred in an authorised payment institution's business since the preceding financial year, the Authority may direct that the own funds requirement is to be a higher or lower amount than that calculated in accordance with sub-paragraph (2).

Method B

17.—(1)   "Method B" means the calculation method set out in this paragraph.

   (2)   The own funds requirement is the sum of the following elements multiplied by the scaling factor—

   (a)   4% of the first 5,000,000 euro of payment volume;

   (b)   2.5% of the next 5,000,000 euro of payment volume;

    (c)   1% of the next 90,000,000 euro of payment volume;

    (d)   0.5% of the next 150,000,000 euro of payment volume; and

    (e)   0.25% of any remaining payment volume.

    (3)   "Payment volume" means the total amount of payment transactions executed by the authorised payment institution in the preceding financial year divided by the number of months in that year.

    (4)   The "scaling factor" is—

    (a)   0.5 for a payment institution that is authorised to provide the payment service specified in paragraph 127(f) of Schedule 1;

    (b)   0.8 for a payment institution that is authorised to provide the payment service specified in paragraph 127(g) of Schedule 1; and

    (c)   1 for a payment institution that is authorised to provide any other payment service.

Method C

18.—(1)   "Method C" means the calculation method set out in this paragraph.

    (2)   The own funds requirement is the relevant indicator multiplied by—

    (a)   the multiplication factor; and

    (b)   the scaling factor;

subject to the proviso in sub-paragraph (7).

    (3)   The "relevant indicator" is the sum of the following elements—

    (a)   interest income;

    (b)   interest expenses;

    (c)   gross commissions and fees received; and

    (d)   gross other operating income.

    (4)   For the purpose of calculating the relevant indicator—

    (a)   each element must be included in the sum with its positive or negative sign;

    (b)   income from extraordinary or irregular items may not be used;

    (c)   expenditure on the outsourcing of services rendered by third parties may reduce the relevant indicator if the expenditure is incurred from a payment service provider;

    (d)   the relevant indicator is calculated on the basis of the twelve-monthly observation at the end of the previous financial year;

    (e)   the relevant indicator must be calculated over the previous financial year; and

    (f)   audited figures must be used unless they are not available in which case business estimates may be used.

    (5)   The "multiplication factor" is the sum of—

    (a)   10% of the first 2,500,000 euro of the relevant indicator;

    (b)   8% of the next 2,500,000 euro of the relevant indicator;

    (c)   6% of the next 20,000,000 euro of the relevant indicator;

    (d)   3% of the next 25,000,000 euro of the relevant indicator; and

    (e)   1.5% of any remaining amount of the relevant indicator.

    (6)   "Scaling factor" has the meaning given in paragraph 158(4).

    (7)   The proviso is that the own funds requirement must not be less than 80 % of the average of the previous three financial years for the relevant indicator.

Application of accounting standards

19.   Except where this Schedule provides for a different method of recognition, measurement or valuation, whenever a provision in this Schedule refers to an asset, liability, equity or income statement item, an authorised payment institution must, for the purpose of that provision, recognise the asset, liability, equity or income statement item and measure its value in accordance with whichever of the following are applicable for the purpose of the institution's external financial reporting—

    (a)   Financial Reporting Standards and Statements of Standard Accounting Practice issued or adopted by the Accounting Standards Board;

    (b)   Statements of Recommended Practice, issued by industry or sectoral bodies recognised for this purpose by the Accounting Standards Board;

    (c)   International Financial Reporting Standards and International Accounting Standards issued or adopted by the International Accounting Standards Board;

    (d)   International Standards on Auditing (United Kingdom and Ireland) issued by the Auditing Practices Board; and

    (e)   the Companies Act 2006.

[1257]

PART IV   OTHER STATUTORY INSTRUMENTS

NOTES
Commencement: these Regulations come into force on 2 March 2009 (for the purposes specified in reg 1(2)(a)), 1 May 2009 (for the purposes specified in reg 1(2)(b)), and 1 November 2009 (otherwise). See reg 1 at **[1127]**.

SCHEDULE 4
PRIOR GENERAL INFORMATION FOR FRAMEWORK CONTRACTS
Regulations 36(2), 40(1)

1. The following information about the payment service provider—
    (a) the name of the payment service provider;
    (b) the address and contact details of the payment service provider's head office;
    (c) if different from the information under sub-paragraph (b), the address and contact details of the branch or agent from which the payment service is being provided;
    (d) details of the payment service provider's regulators, including any reference or registration number of the payment service provider.

2. The following information about the payment service—
    (a) a description of the main characteristics of the payment service to be provided;
    (b) the information or unique identifier that must be provided by the payment service user in order for a payment order to be properly executed;
    (c) the form and procedure for giving consent to the execution of a payment transaction and for the withdrawal of consent in accordance with regulation 55;
    (d) a reference to the time of receipt of a payment order, as defined in regulation 65, and the cut-off time, if any, established by the payment service provider;
    (e) the maximum execution time for the payment services to be provided;
    (f) whether spending limits for the use of a payment instrument may be agreed in accordance with regulation 56(1).

3. The following information about charges, interest and exchange rates—
    (a) details of all charges payable by the payment service user to the payment service provider and, where applicable, a breakdown of the amounts of any charges;
    (b) where relevant, details of the interest and exchange rates to be applied or, if reference interest and exchange rates are to be used, the method of calculating the actual interest and the relevant date and index or base for determining such reference interest or exchange rates;
    (c) if agreed, the immediate application of changes in reference interest or exchange rates and information requirements relating to the changes in accordance with regulation 42(4).

4. The following information about communication—
    (a) the means of communication agreed between the parties for the transmission of information or notifications under these Regulations including, where relevant, any technical requirements for the payment service user's equipment for receipt of the information or notifications;
    (b) the manner in which and frequency with which information under these Regulations is to be provided or made available;
    (c) the language or languages in which the framework contract will be concluded and in which any information or notifications under these Regulations will be communicated;
    (d) the payment service user's right to receive the terms of the framework contract and information in accordance with regulation 41.

5. The following information about safeguards and corrective measures—
    (a) where relevant, a description of the steps that the payment service user is to take in order to keep safe a payment instrument and how to notify the payment service provider for the purposes of regulation 57(1)(b);
    (b) where relevant, the conditions under which the payment service provider proposes to reserve the right to stop or prevent the use of a payment instrument in accordance with regulation 56;
    (c) the payer's liability under regulation 62, including details of any limits on such liability;
    (d) how and within what period of time the payment service user is to notify the payment service provider of any unauthorised or incorrectly executed payment transaction under regulation 59, and the payment service provider's liability for unauthorised payment transactions under regulation 61;
    (e) the payment service provider's liability for the execution of payment transactions under regulation 75 or 76;
    (f) the conditions for the payment of any refund under regulation 63.

6. The following information about changes to and termination of the framework contract—
    (a) where relevant, the proposed terms under which the payment service user will be deemed to have accepted changes to the framework contract in accordance with

regulation 42(2), unless they notify the payment service provider that they do not accept such changes before the proposed date of their entry into force;
   (b)   the duration of the framework contract;
   (c)   the right of the payment service user to terminate the framework contract and any agreements relating to termination in accordance with regulation 43.

7.   The following information about redress—
   (a)   any contractual clause on—
       (i)   the law applicable to the framework contract;
      (ii)   the competent courts;
   (b)   the availability of out-of-court complaint and redress procedures for the payment service user and the methods for having access to them.

[1258]

NOTES

Commencement: these Regulations come into force on 2 March 2009 (for the purposes specified in reg 1(2)(a)), 1 May 2009 (for the purposes specified in reg 1(2)(b)), and 1 November 2009 (otherwise). See reg 1 at **[1127]**.

SCHEDULE 5
APPLICATION AND MODIFICATION OF LEGISLATION

Regulation 95

PART 1
APPLICATION AND MODIFICATION OF THE 2000 ACT

Disciplinary powers

1.   Sections 66 (disciplinary powers) to 70 (statements of policy: procedure) of the 2000 Act apply with the following modifications to section 66—
   (a)   for subsection (2) substitute—

"(2)   A person is guilty of misconduct if, while a relevant person, he has been knowingly concerned in a contravention of the Payment Services Regulations 2009 by an authorised payment institution or a small payment institution.";
   (b)   for subsection (6) substitute—

"(6)   "Relevant person" means any person responsible for the management of the authorised payment institution or small payment institution or, where relevant, any person responsible for the management of the institution's payment services activities."; and
   (c)   omit subsection (7).

The Tribunal

2.   Part 9 of the 2000 Act (hearings and appeals) applies in respect of references to the Tribunal made under these Regulations as it applies in respect of references made to the Tribunal under that Act, with the following modifications to section 133 (proceedings: general provision)—
   (a)   in subsection (6) omit ", or as a result of section 338(2),";
   (b)   omit subsection (8); and
   (c)   in subsection (12) for "has the same meaning as in section 395" substitute "means a notice given under regulation 11(6), (9) or (10)(b) (including as applied by regulation 14) of the Payment Services Regulations 2009".

Information gathering and investigations

3.   Part 11 of the 2000 Act (information gathering and investigations) applies with the following modifications—
   (a)   in section 165 (Authority's power to require information)—
       (i)   for references to "an authorised person" substitute "an authorised payment institution, an EEA authorised payment institution or a small payment institution";
      (ii)   in subsection (4), for "this Act" substitute "the Payment Services Regulations 2009"; and
      (iii) in subsection (7) omit paragraphs (b) and (c);
   (b)   in subsection (2)(a) of section 166 (reports by skilled persons), for "an authorised person" substitute "an authorised payment institution, an EEA authorised payment institution or a small payment institution";
   (c)   in section 167 (appointment of persons to carry out general investigations)—
       (i)   in subsection (1)—
          (aa)   omit "or the Secretary of State";
          (bb)   in paragraph (a) for "a recognised investment exchange or an authorised

person or of an appointed representative" substitute "an authorised payment institution, an EEA authorised payment institution or a small payment institution";

    (cc) in paragraph (c) for "a recognised investment exchange or an authorised person" substitute "an authorised payment institution, an EEA authorised payment institution or a small payment institution";

  (ii) in subsection (4)—

    (aa) for "in relation to a former authorised person (or appointed representative)" substitute "in relation to a former authorised payment institution, former EEA authorised payment institution or former small payment institution";

    (bb) in paragraph (a) for "he was an authorised person (or appointed representative)" substitute "it was an authorised payment institution, EEA authorised payment institution or small payment institution";

    (cc) for paragraph (b) substitute—

"(b) the ownership or control of a former authorised payment institution, former EEA authorised payment institution or former small payment institution at any time when it was an authorised payment institution, EEA authorised payment institution or small payment institution, as the case may be.";

  (iii) in subsection (5) for "regulated activities" substitute "payment services"; and

  (iv) omit subsection (6);

(d) in section 168 (appointment of persons to carry out investigations in particular cases)—

  (i) in subsection (1)—

    (aa) in paragraph (a) for "any regulation made under section 142" substitute "any requirement of or imposed under the Payment Services Regulations 2009";

    (bb) in paragraph (b) for "191" to the end substitute "or under regulation 110, 111, 113 or 114 of the Payment Services Regulations 2009";

  (ii) for subsection (2) substitute—

"(2) Subsection (3) also applies if it appears to an investigating authority that there are circumstances suggesting that a person may be guilty of an offence under, or has contravened a requirement of, the Money Laundering Regulations 2007.";

  (iii) omit subsections (4) and (5); and

  (iv) in subsection (6) omit "or the Secretary of State";

(e) in section 169 (investigations etc in support of overseas regulator)—

  (i) in subsection (8) for "Part XXIII" substitute "sections 348, 349, 351 and 352, as applied with modifications by the Payment Services Regulations 2009"; and

  (ii) in subsection (13) for "has the same meaning as in section 195" substitute "means a competent authority designated in accordance with Article 20 of the payment services directive";

(f) in section 170 (investigations: general)—

  (i) in subsection (1) omit "or (5)";

  (ii) in subsection (3)(a) omit "or (4)"; and

  (iii) for subsection (10) substitute—

"(10) "Investigating authority" in relation to an investigator means the Authority.";

(g) in section 171 (powers of persons appointed under section 167), omit subsections (3A) and (7);

(h) in subsection (4) of section 172 (additional power of persons appointed as a result of section 168(1) or (4)), omit "or (4)";

(i) in section 174 (admissibility of statements made to investigators)—

  (i) in subsection (2) omit "or in proceedings in relation to action to be taken against that person under section 123";

  (ii) in subsection (3)(a) for "398" substitute "regulation 114 of the Payment Services Regulations 2009"; and

  (iii) in subsection (4) omit "or (5)";

(j) in subsection (8) of section 175 (information and documents: supplemental provisions) omit "or (5)";

(k) in section 176 (entry of premises under warrant)—

  (i) in subsection (1)—

    (aa) omit "the Secretary of State,"; and

    (bb) for "the first, second or third" substitute "the first or second";

  (ii) in subsection (3)(a) for "an authorised person or an appointed representative" substitute "an authorised payment institution, a small payment institution or an EEA authorised payment institution";

  (iii) omit subsection (4);

  (iv) in subsection (10) omit "or (5)";

  (v) in subsection (11)(a) omit "87C, 87J,"; and

(1) in subsection (5)(a) of section 177 (offences), for "six months" substitute "three months".

Auditors and actuaries

4. Sections 341 (access to books etc) to 346 (provision of false or misleading information to auditor or actuary) of the 2000 Act apply as though in sections 341(1), 342(1) to (3) and (7), 343(1) to (3), (7) and (8), 344(2), 345(1) and 346(1) and (2) the references to "an authorised person" were to "an authorised payment institution".

Restriction on disclosure of information

5. Sections 348 (restrictions on disclosure of confidential information by Authority etc), 349 (exceptions from section 348), 351 (competition information) and 352 (offences) of the 2000 Act apply with the following modifications—
    (a) in section 348—
        (i) in subsection (2)(b) for the words from ", the competent authority" to the end substitute "under the Payment Services Regulations 2009";
        (ii) in subsection (3)(a) for "this Act" substitute "the Payments Services Regulations 2009";
        (iii) in subsection (5)—
            (aa) for "this Part", substitute "the Payment Services Regulations 2009";
            (bb) omit paragraphs (b) and (c);
            (cc) in paragraph (e) for "paragraphs (a) to (c)" substitute "paragraph (a)";
        (iv) in subsection (6)—
            (aa) omit paragraphs (a) and (b); and
            (bb) in paragraph (c) for "paragraph 6 of Schedule 1" substitute "regulation 81 of the Payment Services Regulations 2009"; and
    (b) in section 349 omit subsections (3A) and (3B).

Insolvency

6. Sections 359 (administration order), 367 (winding-up petitions) and 368 (winding-up petitions: EEA and Treaty firms) of the 2000 Act apply with the following modifications—
    (a) for references to "an authorised person" substitute "an authorised payment institution or an EEA authorised payment institution";
    (b) in section 359—
        (i) omit subsections (1)(b), (3)(b) and (5);
        (ii) for subsection (1)(c) substitute—
    "(c) is providing or has provided payment services in contravention of regulation 110(1) of the Payment Services Regulations 2009.";
        (iii) in subsection (3)(a) omit "or partnership" and for "an agreement" substitute "a contract for payment services"; and
        (iv) in subsection (4) omit the definitions of "agreement", "authorised deposit taker" and "relevant deposit";
    (c) in section 367—
        (i) omit subsections (1)(b), (2), (5), (6) and (7);
        (ii) for subsection (1)(c) substitute—
    "(c) is providing or has provided payment services in contravention of regulation 110(1) of the Payment Services Regulations 2009."; and
        (iii) in subsection (4) for "an agreement" substitute "a contract for payment services"; and
    (d) in section 368 for the words from "winding up" to the end substitute "winding up of an EEA authorised payment institution unless it has been asked to do so by the home state competent authority.".

Warning notices and decision notices

7. Part 26 of the 2000 Act (notices) applies with the following modifications—
    (a) omit section 388(2) (decision notices);
    (b) in section 390 (final notices)—
        (i) omit subsections (6) and (10); and
        (ii) in subsection (8) omit "or (6)(c)";
    (c) in section 391 (publication), in subsection (10) for "has the same meaning as in section 395" substitute "means a notice given under regulation 11(6), (9) or (10)(b) (including as applied by regulation 14) of the Payment Services Regulations 2009";
    (d) for section 392 (application of sections 393 and 394) substitute—
    "**392.** Sections 393 and 394 apply to—
        (a) a warning notice given in accordance with regulations 10(2) (including as applied

by regulation 14), 24(2) (in relation to the cancellation of a registration), 30(2), 86(1) or 89(1) of the Payment Services Regulations 2009;
  (b) a decision notice given in accordance with regulations 10(3)(a) (including as applied by regulation 14), 24(3)(a) (in relation to the cancellation of a registration), 30(3)(a), 86(3) or 89(3) of the Payment Services Regulations 2009."; and

(e) in section 395 (the Authority's procedures) in subsection (13) for "in accordance with" to the end substitute "under regulation 11(6), (9) or (10)(b) (including as applied by regulation 14) of the Payment Services Regulations 2009".

Limitation on power to require documents

8.   Section 413 of the 2000 Act (protected items) applies for the purposes of these Regulations as it applies for the purposes of that Act.

[1259]

NOTES

Commencement: these Regulations come into force on 2 March 2009 (for the purposes specified in reg 1(2)(a)), 1 May 2009 (for the purposes specified in reg 1(2)(b)), and 1 November 2009 (otherwise). See reg 1 at **[1127]**.

PART 2
APPLICATION AND MODIFICATION OF SECONDARY LEGISLATION

The Financial Services and Markets Act 2000 (Service of Notices) Regulations 2001

9.   The Financial Services and Markets Act 2000 (Service of Notices) Regulations 2001 applies to any notice, direction or document of any kind given by or to the Authority under these Regulations as it applies to any notice, direction or document of any kind under the 2000 Act.

The Financial Services and Markets Act 2000
(Disclosure of Confidential Information) Regulations 2001

10. The Financial Services and Markets Act 2000 (Disclosure of Confidential Information) Regulations 2001 applies with the following modifications—
  (a) in regulation 2—
    (i) in the definition of "directive restrictions" for "and article 9 of the insurance mediation directive" substitute ", article 9 of the insurance mediation directive and Article 22 of the payment services directive";
    (ii) in paragraph (a) of the definition of "overseas regulatory authority" after "of the Act" insert "or any function conferred under national legislation in implementation of the payment services directive"; and
    (iii) after the definition of "overseas regulatory authority" insert—
""payment services directive" means Directive 2007/64/EC of the European Parliament and of the Council of 13th November 2007 on payment services in the internal market;
"payment services directive information" means confidential information received by the Authority in the course of discharging its functions as the competent authority under the payment services directive;";
  (b) in regulation 5(4)(a) for "an authorised person, former authorised person or former regulated person" substitute "an authorised payment institution, former authorised payment institution, small payment institution or former small payment institution";
  (c) in regulation 5(6)(e) for "an authorised person, former authorised person or former regulated person" substitute "an authorised payment institution, former authorised payment institution, small payment institution or former small payment institution";
  (d) in regulation 8 after sub-paragraph (b) insert—
"(c) payment services directive information.";
  (e) in regulation 9—
    (i) in paragraph (1) for "(3) and (3A)" substitute "(3), (3A) and (4)"; and
    (ii) after paragraph (3B) insert—
"(4) Paragraph (1) does not permit disclosure to the persons specified in the first column in Part 5 of Schedule 1 unless the disclosure is of payment services directive information.";
  (f) in regulation 11 after sub-paragraph (d) insert—
"(e) payment services directive information.";
  (g) in the second column in Part 1 of Schedule 1, in the list of functions beside—
    (i) "An official receiver appointed under section 399 of the Insolvency Act 1986, or an official receiver for Northern Ireland appointed under article 355 of the Insolvency (Northern Ireland) Order 1989", after paragraph (ii) insert—
      "or
      (iii) payment service providers or former payment service providers";

(ii)   "The Department of Enterprise, Trade and Investment in Northern Ireland", after paragraph (c)(ii) insert—

"or

(iii)   payment service providers or former payment service providers";

(iii)   "The Pensions Regulator", after paragraph (ii) insert—

"or

(iii)   payment service providers or former payment service providers";

(iv)   "The Charity Commissioners for England and Wales", after paragraph (ii) insert—

"or

(iii)   payment service providers or former payment service providers"; and

(h)   in Schedule 1, after Part 4 insert—

"PART 5

Person	Functions
The Commissioners for Her Majesty's Revenue and Customs	Their functions under the Money Laundering Regulations 2007"

[1260]

NOTES

Commencement: these Regulations come into force on 2 March 2009 (for the purposes specified in reg 1(2)(a)), 1 May 2009 (for the purposes specified in reg 1(2)(b)), and 1 November 2009 (otherwise). See reg 1 at **[1127]**.

*(Sch 6 amends the Financial Services and Markets Act 2000, ss 226, 234, Sch 17, revokes the Cross-Border Credit Transfers Regulations 1999, SI 1999/1876, and the Consumer Protection (Distance Selling) Regulations 2000, SI 2000/2334, reg 21, adds the Financial Services and Markets Act 2000 (Regulated Activities) Order 2001, SI 2001/544, arts 9AB, 9L (at **[711]**, **[722]**), amends the Financial Services (Distance Marketing) Regulations 2004, SI 2004/2095, regs 7, 8 and revokes reg 14 of those Regulations, and contain various amendments to the Money Laundering Regulations 2007, SI 2007/2157.)*

BANK ADMINISTRATION (SCOTLAND) RULES 2009

(SI 2009/350)

NOTES

Made: 23 February 2009.
Authority: Insolvency Act 1986, s 411(1B)(b), (2), (2D), (3).
Commencement: 25 February 2009.

ARRANGEMENT OF RULES

PART 1
INTRODUCTION

PART 2
APPLICATION FOR BANK ADMINISTRATION ORDER

PART 3
PROCESS OF BANK ADMINISTRATION

PART 4
APPLICATION OF INSOLVENCY (SCOTLAND) RULES 1986

PART 1
INTRODUCTION

1 Citation

These Rules may be cited as the Bank Administration (Scotland) Rules 2009.

[1261]

NOTES
　　Commencement: 25 February 2009.

2 Commencement

These Rules come into force on 25th February 2009.

[1262]

NOTES
　　Commencement: 25 February 2009.

3 Extent

These Rules extend to Scotland only.

[1263]

NOTES
　　Commencement: 25 February 2009.

Interpretation

4—(1)　The following expressions used in these Rules take their meaning from the Banking Act 2009 (in accordance with section 11 of the Interpretation Act 1978—construction of subordinate legislation) or are as expressly defined below—
　　(a)　"bank" (s 2);
　　(b)　"bank administration" (s 141(4)(a));
　　(c)　"bank administration order" (s 141(1));
　　(d)　"bank administrator" (s 141(1));
　　(e)　"the court" (the Court of Session)—s 166(1));
　　(f)　"the FSA" (the Financial Services Authority—s 166(2));
　　(g)　"Objective 1" (support for commercial purchaser or bridge bank—s 138(1));
　　(h)　"Objective 1 Achievement Notice" (s 139(4));
　　(i)　"Objective 2" (normal administration—s 140(1));
　　(j)　"residual bank" (s 136(2));
　　(k)　"resolution fund order" (s 49(3));
　　(l)　"the 1986 Act" means the Insolvency Act 1986;
　　(m)　"the 1986 Rules" means the Insolvency (Scotland) Rules 1986; and
　　(n)　"the 2009 Act" means the Banking Act 2009.

　　(2)　Any notice or document sent electronically pursuant to these Rules shall be treated as having been sent or given to the person if—

(a)   it is sent by email to the person's last known email address; and
(b)   the email contains a prompt asking the person for an electronic receipt saying that the email has been read.

[1264]

NOTES
Commencement: 25 February 2009.

5   In these Rules—
(a)   "the FSCS" means the scheme manager of the Financial Services Compensation Scheme (established under Part 15 of the Financial Services and Markets Act 2000);
(b)   "the Objective 1 Stage" means the period during which a bank administration order is in force before the Bank of England gives an Objective 1 Achievement Notice; and
(c)   "the Objective 2 Stage" means the period during which a bank administration order is in force after the Bank of England gives an Objective 1 Achievement Notice.

[1265]

NOTES
Commencement: 25 February 2009.

6 Overview
The purpose of these Rules is to prescribe a procedure in Scotland for the appointment of a bank administrator, and the operation of bank administration, under Part 3 of the 2009 Act.

[1266]

NOTES
Commencement: 25 February 2009.

7 Forms
(1)   This rule applies where a provision of these Rules—
(a)   applies a provision of the 1986 Rules which requires the use of a prescribed form; or
(b)   makes provision similar to that made by a provision of the 1986 Rules which requires the use of a prescribed form.

(2)   The form prescribed for the purposes of the 1986 Rules is to be used, with any modification that the person using the form thinks desirable to reflect the nature of bank administration.

[1267]

NOTES
Commencement: 25 February 2009.

PART 2
APPLICATION FOR BANK ADMINISTRATION ORDER

8 Introduction
This Part makes specific provision for a number of aspects of applications for bank administration orders. Part 4 applies a number of provisions of the 1986 Rules to applications for bank administration orders (with specified modifications).

[1268]

NOTES
Commencement: 25 February 2009.

Content of application

9   An application by the Bank of England for a bank administration order in respect of a bank must specify—
(a)   the full name of the bank;
(b)   any other trading names of the bank;
(c)   the address of the bank's registered office;
(d)   an email address for the bank;
(e)   the address of the Bank of England; and
(f)   the identity of the person (or persons) nominated for appointment as bank administrator.

[1269]

NOTES
Commencement: 25 February 2009.

10   If the bank has notified the Bank of England of an address for service which is, because of special circumstances, to be used in place of the registered office, that address shall be specified under rule 9(c).

[1270]

NOTES
Commencement: 25 February 2009.

11   Statement of proposed bank administrator
An application must be accompanied by a statement by each proposed bank administrator—
  (a)   specifying the name and address of the person proposed to be appointed;
  (b)   giving that person's consent to act;
  (c)   giving details of that person's qualification to act as an insolvency practitioner; and
  (d)   giving details of any prior professional relationship that person (or any other proposed bank administrator) has had with the bank.

[1271]

NOTES
Commencement: 25 February 2009.

12   Lodging
The application, and its accompanying documents, must be lodged with the court.

[1272]

NOTES
Commencement: 25 February 2009.

Service

13   The Bank of England shall serve the application—
  (a)   on the bank;
  (b)   on the person (or each of the persons) nominated for appointment as bank administrator;
  (c)   on any person whom the Bank of England knows to be entitled to appoint an administrator under paragraph 14 of Schedule B1 to the 1986 Act or a receiver of the whole (or substantially the whole) of the bank's property;
  (d)   on any person who has given notice to the FSA in respect of the bank under section 120 of the 2009 Act (bank insolvency: notice of preliminary steps of other insolvency procedures); and
  (e)   if a property transfer instrument was made or is to be made under section 11(2)(b) of the 2009 Act (transfer to commercial purchaser), on each transferee as referred to in that instrument.

[1273]

NOTES
Commencement: 25 February 2009.

14   Service must be effected as soon as is reasonably practicable, having regard in particular to the need to give the bank's representatives a reasonable opportunity to attend the hearing of the application.

[1274]

NOTES
Commencement: 25 February 2009.

15   Other notification
As soon as is reasonably practicable after lodging the application the Bank of England must notify—
  (a)   any enforcement officer or other officer whom the Bank of England knows to be charged with effecting an execution, any diligence or other legal process against the bank or its property;

(b)   any person whom the Bank of England knows to have executed diligence against the bank or its property; and

(c)   the FSA.

[1275]

NOTES

Commencement: 25 February 2009.

Notice of order

16   If the court makes a bank administration order, it shall send four certified copies of it to the Bank of England.

[1276]

NOTES

Commencement: 25 February 2009.

17   The Bank of England shall as soon as is reasonably practicable send—

(a)   one certified copy to the bank administrator;

(b)   one certified copy to the FSA; and

(c)   one certified copy to the FSCS.

[1277]

NOTES

Commencement: 25 February 2009.

18   Expenses

If the court makes a bank administration order, the following are payable as an expense of the bank administration:—

(a)   the Bank of England's expenses of making the application and complying with the requirements of these Rules; and

(b)   any other expenses allowed by the court.

[1278]

NOTES

Commencement: 25 February 2009.

PART 3

PROCESS OF BANK ADMINISTRATION

19   Introduction

This Part makes specific provision for a number of aspects of bank administration. Part 4 applies a number of provisions of the 1986 Rules to bank administration (with specified modifications).

[1279]

NOTES

Commencement: 25 February 2009.

20   Bank administrator's proposals: Objective 1 Stage

(1)   This rule makes provision about the statement of proposals which the bank administrator is required to make in the Objective 1 Stage under section 147 of the 2009 Act.

(2)   In addition to the information required by section 147 the statement must include—

(a)   details of the court where the proceedings are and the court reference number;

(b)   the full name, any other trading names, the registered office and registered number of the bank;

(c)   details of the appointment of the bank administrator (including the date);

(d)   in the case of joint bank administrators, details of the apportionment of functions;

(e)   the names of the directors and secretary of the bank and details of any shareholdings in the bank they have;

(f)   an account of the circumstances giving rise to the application for the appointment of the bank administrator;

(g)   if a statement of the bank's affairs has been submitted, a copy or summary of it with the comments of the bank administrator, if any;

(h) if an order limiting the disclosure of the statement of affairs has been made under rule 2.22 of the 1986 Rules (as applied by rule 39 below), a statement of that fact, as well as—
    (i) details of who provided the statement of affairs;
    (ii) the date of the order for limited disclosure; and
    (iii) the details or a summary of the details that are not subject to that order;
(i) if a full statement of affairs is not provided, the names, addresses and debts of the creditors including details of any security held (or, in the case of depositors, a single statement of their aggregate debt);
(j) if no statement of affairs has been provided, details of the financial position of the bank at the latest practicable date (which must, unless the court otherwise orders, be a date not earlier than that on which the bank entered bank administration), a list of the bank's creditors including their names, addresses and details of their debts, including any security held, and an explanation as to why there is no statement of affairs;
(k) the basis upon which it is proposed that the remuneration of the bank administrator(s) should be fixed under rule 2.39 of the 1986 Rules (as applied by rule 39 below);
(l) how the bank administrator proposes to pursue Objective 1;
(m) whether the bank administrator proposes to pursue Objective 2(a) or Objective 2(b);
(n) if the bank administrator proposes to pursue Objective 2(a), how it is envisaged the purpose of the bank administration will be achieved in the Objective 2 Stage;
(o) if the bank administrator proposes to pursue Objective 2(b)—
    (i) how it is envisaged the purpose of the bank administration will be achieved in the Objective 2 Stage; and
    (ii) how it is proposed that the bank administration shall end (winding-up or voluntary arrangement, in accordance with section 154 of the 2009 Act);
(p) the manner in which the affairs and business of the bank have been managed and financed since the date of the appointment of the bank administrator (including the reasons for and terms of any disposal of assets); and
(q) the manner in which the affairs and business of the bank will be managed and financed if the proposals of the bank administrator are approved.

(3) The statement—
(a) may exclude information, the disclosure of which could seriously prejudice the commercial interests of the bank; and
(b) must include a statement of any exclusion.

[1280]

NOTES
Commencement: 25 February 2009.

Bank administrator's proposals: Objective 2 Stage

21—(1) This rule makes provision about the statement of proposals which the bank administrator is required to make under paragraph 49 of Schedule B1 to the 1986 Act as it applies during the Objective 2 Stage (in accordance with Table 1 in section 145 of the 2009 Act).

(2) The statement must include—
(a) details of the court where the proceedings are and the court reference number;
(b) the full name, any other trading names, the registered office and registered number of the bank;
(c) details of the appointment of the bank administrator (including the date);
(d) in the case of joint bank administrators, details of the apportionment of functions;
(e) the names of the directors and secretary of the bank and details of any shareholdings in the bank they have;
(f) an account of the circumstances giving rise to the application for the appointment of the bank administrator;
(g) if a statement of the bank's affairs has been submitted, a copy or summary of it with the comments of the bank administrator, if any;
(h) if an order limiting the disclosure of the statement of affairs has been made under rule 2.22 of the 1986 Rules (as applied by rule 39 below), a statement of that fact, as well as—
    (i) details of who provided the statement of affairs;
    (ii) the date of the order for limited disclosure; and
    (iii) the details or a summary of the details that are not subject to that order;
(i) if a full statement of affairs is not provided, the names, addresses and debts of the creditors including details of any security held (or, in the case of depositors, a single statement of their aggregate debt);
(j) if no statement of affairs has been provided, details of the financial position of the bank

at the latest practicable date (which must, unless the court otherwise orders, be a date not earlier than that on which the bank entered bank administration), a list of the bank's creditors including their names, addresses and details of their debts, including any security held, and an explanation as to why there is no statement of affairs;

(k) the basis upon which it is proposed that the remuneration of the bank administrator should be fixed under rule 2.39 of the 1986 Rules (as applied by rule 39 below);

(l) details of whether (and why) the bank administrator proposes to apply to the court under section 176A(5) of the 1986 Act (omission of distribution to unsecured creditors: as applied by Table 2 in section 145 of the 2009 Act)(unless the bank administrator intends to propose a company voluntary arrangement);

(m) an estimate of the value of the prescribed part for the purposes of section 176A of the 1986 Act (unless the bank administrator intends to propose a company voluntary arrangement) certified as being made to the best of the bank administrator's knowledge and belief;

(n) an estimate of the value of the bank's net property (unless the bank administrator intends to propose a company voluntary arrangement) certified as being made to the best of the bank administrator's knowledge and belief;

(o) whether the bank administrator proposes to pursue Objective 2(a) or Objective 2(b);

(p) if the bank administrator proposes to pursue Objective 2(a), how it is envisaged the purpose of the bank administration will be achieved;

(q) if the bank administrator proposes to pursue Objective 2(b)—
    (i) how it is envisaged the purpose of the bank administration will be achieved; and
    (ii) how it is proposed that the bank administration shall end (winding-up or voluntary arrangement, in accordance with section 154 of the 2009 Act);

(r) if the bank administrator has decided not to call a meeting of creditors, the reasons for that decision;

(s) the manner in which the affairs and business of the bank have been managed and financed since the date of the appointment of the bank administrator (including the reasons for and terms of any disposal of assets);

(t) the manner in which the affairs and business of the bank will be managed and financed if the proposals of the bank administrator are approved; and

(u) any other information which the bank administrator thinks necessary to enable creditors to decide whether or not to vote for the approval of the proposals.

(3) In the case of bank administration following transfer to a bridge bank under section 12(2) of the 2009 Act—

(a) the statement under paragraph 49 of Schedule B1 must state whether any payment is to be made to the bank from a scheme under a resolution fund order; or

(b) if that information is unavailable when the statement under paragraph 49 of Schedule B1 is made, the bank administrator must issue a supplemental statement as soon as reasonably practicable after the information becomes available.

(4) The statement—

(a) may exclude information, the disclosure of which could seriously prejudice the commercial interests of the bank; and

(b) must include a statement of any exclusion.

[1281]

NOTES
Commencement: 25 February 2009.

---

22 If the bank administrator thinks that the statement made under section 147 of the 2009 Act in accordance with rule 20 contains information required by rule 21(2), the statement under paragraph 49 of Schedule B1 to the 1986 Act (as applied by Table 1 in section 145 of the 2009 Act) may consist of the statement under section 147, with such additions, modifications and supplemental information as the bank administrator thinks necessary—

(a) to comply with rule 21(2); and

(b) to bring the statement under section 147 up to date.

[1282]

NOTES
Commencement: 25 February 2009.

---

23 Where the court orders an extension of the period of time under paragraph 49(5) of Schedule B1 on an application by the bank administrator under paragraph 107 (as applied by Table 1 in section 145 of the 2009 Act), the bank administrator must notify the persons set out in paragraph 49(4) as soon as is reasonably practicable after the making of the order.

[1283]

NOTES
Commencement: 25 February 2009.

24 Where the bank administrator has made a statement under paragraph 52(1) of Schedule B1 to the 1986 Act (as applied by Table 1 in section 145 of the 2009 Act) and has not called an initial meeting of creditors, the proposals issued in accordance with rule 21 above will be deemed to have been approved by the creditors (if no meeting has been requisitioned under paragraph 52(2) within the period set out in rule 7.6 of the 1986 Rules—as applied by rule 39 below).

[1284]

NOTES
Commencement: 25 February 2009.

25 Where the bank administrator intends to apply to the court (or file or lodge a notice under paragraph 80(2) of Schedule B1 to the 1986 Act in accordance with section 153 of the 2009 Act) for the bank administration to cease before the statement of proposals is sent to creditors in accordance with paragraph 49 of Schedule B1 to the 1986 Act, the bank administrator(s) must, at least 10 days before making the application (or filing or lodging the notice), send to all known creditors of the bank a report containing the information required by rule 21(2).

[1285]

NOTES
Commencement: 25 February 2009.

26—(1) Any bank administrator who wishes to publish a notice under paragraph 49(6) of Schedule B1 to the 1986 Act must publish the notice once in a newspaper which the bank administrator thinks most appropriate for ensuring that the notice comes to the attention of the bank's members.

    (2)   The notice must—
      (a)   state the full name of the bank;
      (b)   state the full name and address of each bank administrator of the bank;
      (c)   give details of the appointment of the bank administrator; and
      (d)   specify an address to which members can write for a copy of the statement of proposals.

    (3)   The notice must be published as soon as is reasonably practicable after the bank administrator sends the statement of proposals to the bank's creditors but no later than 8 weeks (or such other period as may be agreed by the creditors or as the court may order) from the date that the bank entered bank administration.

[1286]

NOTES
Commencement: 25 February 2009.

Reports to creditors

27—(1)   "A progress report" means a report which includes—
      (a)   details of the court where the proceedings are and the relevant court reference number;
      (b)   full details of the bank's name, address of registered office and registered number;
      (c)   full details of the name and address and date of appointment of the bank administrator, including any changes in office-holder;
      (d)   in the case of joint bank administrators, details of the apportionment of functions;
      (e)   details of any extensions of the initial period of appointment;
      (f)   details of progress during the period of the report, including a receipts and payments account (as detailed in paragraph (2) below);
      (g)   details of any assets that remain to be realised;
      (h)   details of any amounts received from a scheme under a resolution fund order; and
      (i)   any other information likely to be relevant to the creditors.

    (2)   A receipts and payments account must state what assets of the bank have been realised, for what value, and what payments have been made to creditors or others.

    (3)   The account must be in the form of an abstract showing receipts and payments during the period of the report; and where the bank administrator has ceased to act, the receipts and payments

account shall include a statement as to the amount paid to unsecured creditors by virtue of the application of section 176A of the 1986 Act (prescribed part).

(4)   During the Objective 1 Stage, a progress report must include details of—
- (a)   the extent of the business of the bank that has been transferred;
- (b)   any property, rights or liabilities that have been transferred, or which the bank administrator expects to be transferred, under a power in Part 1 of the 2009 Act (special resolution regime);
- (c)   any requirements imposed on the residual bank, for the purpose of the pursuit of Objective 1, under a power under that Part; and
- (d)   the arrangements for managing and financing the bank during the Objective 1 Stage.

(5)   In complying with paragraph (4)(c) and (d) a report—
- (a)   may exclude information, the disclosure of which could seriously prejudice the commercial interests of the bank; and
- (b)   must include a statement of any exclusion.

[1287]

NOTES
Commencement: 25 February 2009.

28   A progress report must be produced for—
- (a)   the first period of 6 months of the bank administration;
- (b)   every subsequent period of 6 months; and
- (c)   when the bank administrator ceases to act, the period from the date of the previous report (or, if there was none, from the beginning of the bank administration) until the administrator ceases to act.

[1288]

NOTES
Commencement: 25 February 2009.

29—(1)   The bank administrator must send a copy of each progress report within 28 days of the end of the period covered by that report, to—
- (a)   the creditors of the bank;
- (b)   the court;
- (c)   the Bank of England;
- (d)   the FSA;
- (e)   the FSCS; and
- (f)   the registrar of companies.

(2)   Instead of complying with paragraph (1)(a) the bank administrator may publish the progress report on its internet website (and take appropriate steps to draw attention to it).

(3)   The court may, on the application of the bank administrator—
- (a)   extend the period specified in paragraph (1) above;
- (b)   make any other order about the content of a progress report.

[1289]

NOTES
Commencement: 25 February 2009.

30—(1)   A bank administrator who fails to comply with rule 28 or 29 is liable to a fine and, for continued contravention, to a daily default fine.

(2)   For that purpose, failure to comply with rule 28 or 29 shall be treated in the same way as failure to comply with rule 2.38 of the 1986 Rules.

[1290]

NOTES
Commencement: 25 February 2009.

31   Removal of bank administrator in Objective 1 Stage

(1)   With regard to any application for removal of a bank administrator made by the Bank of England during the Objective 1 Stage (in accordance with the modifications for the application of paragraph 91 of Schedule B1 to the 1986 Act in Table 1 in section 145 of the 2009 Act), the rules for service of notice of the application shall be as for the application to appoint a bank administrator under Part 2 of these Rules.

(2)   Both the person proposed to be appointed as a replacement and the existing bank administrator are entitled to be served and heard.

[1291]

NOTES
Commencement: 25 February 2009.

Appointment of provisional bank administrator

32   If the court makes an order appointing one or more provisional bank administrators the court shall—
  (a)   notify the Bank of England;
  (b)   send a copy of the order to the person appointed (by email if possible); and
  (c)   send a copy of the order to any administrative receiver of the bank.

[1292]

NOTES
Commencement: 25 February 2009.

33—(1)   As soon as is reasonably practicable after appointment any provisional bank administrator must send a copy of the order of appointment—
  (a)   the bank;
  (b)   the FSA; and
  (c)   the registrar of companies (in Form 4.9(Scot), with such variations, if any, as the circumstances may require).
  (2)   Notice to the bank must be given by effecting service to its registered office.

[1293]

NOTES
Commencement: 25 February 2009.

34   The Bank of England may disclose the fact and terms of an order appointing any provisional bank administrator to any person whom the Bank of England thinks has a sufficient business interest.

[1294]

NOTES
Commencement: 25 February 2009.

35   Additional joint bank administrator

  (1)   The process for the appointment of an additional joint bank administrator is the same as for the initial appointment of a bank administrator.
  (2)   The existing bank administrator (or each of them) is entitled to a copy of the application and may—
  (a)   lodge written answers; and
  (b)   be heard at any hearing fixed by the court.
  (3)   An application for the appointment of an additional joint bank administrator may be made during the Objective 1 Stage only by the Bank of England.
  (4)   Rule 39 below applies rules 2.19 and 2.55 of the 1986 Rules.

[1295]

NOTES
Commencement: 25 February 2009.

36   End of administration: successful rescue

  (1)   This rule supplements section 153 of the 2009 Act (end of bank administration where bank administrator satisfied that Objective 2(a) has been achieved).
  (2)   The notice of the bank administrator under paragraph 80 of Schedule B1 to the 1986 Act (as applied by section 153 of the 2009 Act)—
  (a)   must be lodged with the court in Form 2.23B (subject to rule 7(2) above); and
  (b)   must be accompanied by a final progress report.
  (3)   The notice takes effect when the court discharges the bank administration order on the application of the bank administrator.

(4)   Before applying for discharge the bank administrator must send a copy of the notice under paragraph 80 of Schedule B1 to the 1986 Act and the progress report to—

    (a)   the Bank of England;

    (b)   the FSA;

    (c)   the FSCS; and

    (d)   the registrar of companies.

(5)   Notice under paragraph (4)(b) and (c) above must be given at least 7 days' before the hearing of the application for approval of the notice.

(6)   The bank administrator shall be taken to have complied with the requirements of paragraph 80(5) of Schedule B1 to the 1986 Act if, within 5 business days of lodging the notice under paragraph 80 of Schedule B1 to the 1986 Act with the court, the bank administrator publishes once in the same newspaper in which the bank administrator's notice of appointment was published, and once in the Edinburgh Gazette, a notice specifying—

    (a)   the full name of the bank and any other trading names;

    (b)   the name and address of the bank administrator;

    (c)   the date of the notice under paragraph 80 of Schedule B1 to the 1986 Act; and

    (d)   an address to which creditors of the bank can write for a copy of the notice under paragraph 80 of Schedule B1 to the 1986 Act and the final progress report.

(7)   The application of the bank administrator for discharge must certify compliance with the requirements of paragraph 80 of Schedule B1 to the 1986 Act and of the preceding paragraphs of this rule.

(8)   If the court is satisfied that the conditions in section 153(1) of the 2009 Act have been met it shall—

    (a)   discharge the bank administration order; and

    (b)   notify the bank administrator who shall notify the registrar of companies.

[1296]

NOTES

Commencement: 25 February 2009.

End of administration: dissolution

37—(1)   This rule supplements section 154(2)(a) of the 2009 Act (bank administrator giving notice under paragraph 84 of Schedule B1 to the 1986 Act that there are no more assets for distribution, and moving to dissolution).

(2)   The notice of the bank administrator under paragraph 84 of Schedule B1 to the 1986 Act—

    (a)   must be lodged with the court in Form 2.26B (subject to rule 7(2) above); and

    (b)   must be accompanied by a final progress report.

(3)   The notice shall not take effect until the court discharges the bank administration order on the application of the bank administrator.

(4)   Before applying for discharge the bank administrator must send a copy of the notice under paragraph 84 of Schedule B1 to the 1986 Act and the final progress report to—

    (a)   the registrar of companies; and

    (b)   each person who received notice of the appointment of the bank administrator.

(5)   After the expiry of the period mentioned in paragraph 84(6) of Schedule B1 to the 1986 Act (and subject to extension under paragraph 84(7) of Schedule B1 to the 1986 Act) if the court discharges the bank administration order under paragraph 84 of Schedule B1 to the 1986 Act—

    (a)   the notice takes effect as specified in paragraph 84(6) of Schedule B1 to the 1986 Act and;

    (b)   the court shall notify the bank administrator, who shall notify the registrar of companies.

(6)   If the court makes an order under paragraph 84(7) of Schedule B1 to the 1986 Act it shall notify the bank administrator in Form 2.27 (subject to rule 7(2) above), who shall notify the registrar of companies.

[1297]

NOTES

Commencement: 25 February 2009.

---

38   Proceedings under sections 213 and 214 of the Insolvency Act 1986 (fraudulent and wrongful trading) shall be conducted in accordance with section 215 of that Act subject to the modifications specified in section 145 of the 2009 Act.

[1298]

NOTES
Commencement: 25 February 2009.

PART 4
APPLICATION OF INSOLVENCY (SCOTLAND) RULES 1986

General application

39 The provisions of the 1986 Rules listed in the Table in rule 42 apply for the purposes of bank administration and applications for bank administration.

[1299]

NOTES
Commencement: 25 February 2009.

40 For that purpose the rules apply with—
   (a)   the general modifications set out in rule 41;
   (b)   any specific modification set out in the Table in rule 42; and
   (c)   any other necessary modification.

[1300]

NOTES
Commencement: 25 February 2009.

41 General modifications

The general modifications are that—
   (a)   a reference to an administrator or a liquidator is to be treated as a reference to a bank administrator;
   (b)   a reference to administration or liquidation is to be treated as a reference to bank administration;
   (c)   a reference to a provisional liquidator is to be treated as a reference to a provisional bank administrator;
   (d)   a reference to a winding-up order is to be treated as a reference to a bank administration order;
   (e)   a reference to a petition for a winding-up order is to be treated as a reference to an application for a bank administration order;
   (f)   a reference to insolvency proceedings is to be treated as a reference to bank administration (or proceedings for bank administration);
   (g)   a reference to the responsible insolvency practitioner is to be treated as a reference to the bank administrator or provisional bank administrator;
   (h)   all references to the EC Regulation or to the appointment of a member State liquidator are to be ignored;
   (i)   a reference to the company is to be treated as a reference to the bank;
   (j)   a reference in the rules to a paragraph of Schedule B1 to the 1986 Act is to be treated as a reference to that paragraph as applied and modified by section 145 of the 2009 Act; and
   (k)   a reference to the 1986 Act includes a reference to Part 3 of the 2009 Act.

[1301]

NOTES
Commencement: 25 February 2009.

42 Table of applications and specific modifications

This rule contains the Table of applied 1986 Rules.

Rule	*Subject*	*Specific Modifications*
2.19	Notification and advertisement of administrator's appointment	Ignore paragraphs 2(a), (b), and (c).

Rule	Subject	Specific Modifications
2.20	Notice requiring statement of affairs	
2.21	Statements of affairs and statements of concurrence	
2.22	Limited disclosure	On an application for disclosure under paragraph (4) any of the following may appear and be heard, or make representations:— (a) the bank administrator; (b) the Bank of England; (c) the FSA.
2.23	Release from duty to submit statement of affairs; extension of time	On an application under paragraph (2) for release or extension of time any of the following may appear and be heard, or make written representations:— (a) the bank administrator; (b) the Bank of England; (c) the FSA.
2.24	Expenses of statement of affairs	
2.25	*Administrator's proposals*	*Rule 2.25 is not applied. Equivalent provision is made in Part 3 of these Rules.*
2.26	General (Meetings)	In the application of paragraph (1) of rule 7.2, the FSA and the FSCS shall be treated as entitled to attend the meeting. Ignore the application of rules 7.1 and 7.4.
2.27	Meetings to consider administrator's proposals	(1) Rule 2.27 applies in the Objective 2 Stage. (2) The bank administrator shall give the FSA and the FSCS at least 14 days notice of any meeting referred to in paragraph (1) of rule 2.27.
2.28	Correspondence instead of creditors meetings	
2.29	Applicable law	
2.31	Meetings requisitioned by creditors	Treat the reference to the administrator's statement of proposals as a reference to the bank administrator's statement of proposals in accordance with rule 24 above.
2.33	Hire-purchase, conditional sale and hiring agreements	
2.34	Revision of administrator's proposals	In paragraph 1(c) ignore the reference to the person making the appointment.
2.35	Notices to creditors	
2.36	Application of provisions in Part 3 (Receivers)	*(A creditors' committee cannot be established until the Objective 2 Stage – see the modifications for the application of paragraphs 50 to 58 of Schedule B1 of the Insolvency Act 1986 in Table 1 in section 145 of the 2009 Act).* In the application of paragraph (2) of rule 3.8— (a) notice of the application must be given to the FSA and the FSCS; and (b) the FSA and the FSCS may appear and be heard.

Rule	Subject	Specific Modifications
2.37	Disposal of secured property, etc	If an application is made during the Objective 1 Stage, then in addition to the requirements of rule 2.37— (a) the bank administrator must notify the Bank of England of the time and place of the hearing; (b) the Bank of England may appear; and (c) if an order is made the bank administrator must send a copy of the order to the Bank of England as soon as reasonably practicable.
2.38	*Progress reports*	*Rule 2.38 is not applied. Equivalent provision is made in Part 3 of these Rules.*
2.39	Determination of outlays and remuneration	(1) In the Objective 1 Stage the Bank of England shall fix the bank administrators' remuneration in accordance with rule 2.39(4). (2) In the Objective 2 Stage, rule 2.39 shall apply (but pending action under paragraphs (2), (3) and (6) arrangements established by the Bank of England in the Objective 1 Stage shall continue to apply).
2.39A	Appeal against fixing of remuneration	(1) In respect of remuneration fixed by the Bank of England— (a) Rule 2.39A applies as if references to the creditors' committee and creditors were references to the Bank of England; and (b) the court shall have regard to Objective 1. (2) In respect of any application under rule 2.39A— (a) notice of the application must be given to the FSA; and (b) the FSA may appear and be heard. Rule 2.39A (5), (6) and (7) applies only during the Objective 2 Stage.
2.39B	Expenses of the administration	In addition to the matters listed in rule 2.39B, expenses in connection with a provisional bank administration are payable in the following order of priority— (a) the cost of any security provided by the provisional bank administrator takes priority equally with security provided by the bank administrator; (b) the remuneration of the provisional bank administrator ranks next; and (c) any deposit lodged on an application for the appointment of a provisional bank administrator ranks next.
2.40	Distributions to creditors	(*Distributions in the case of bank administration following transfer to a bridge bank under section 12(2) of the 2009 Act and during the Objective 1 Stage require the Bank of England's consent—see the modification for the application of paragraph 65 of Schedule B1 to the Insolvency Act 1986 in Table 1 in section 145 of the 2009 Act.*)

Rule	Subject	Specific Modifications
2.41	Distributions to creditors	(*Distributions in the case of bank administration following transfer to a bridge bank under section 12(2) of the 2009 Act and during the Objective 1 Stage require the Bank of England's consent—see the modification for the application of paragraph 65 of Schedule B1 to the Insolvency Act 1986 in Table 1 in section 145 of the 2009 Act.*) (1) In respect of an application under s.49(6) of the Bankruptcy (Scotland) Act 1985 (as applied)— (a) notice of the application must be given to the FSA and the FSCS and, during the Objective 1 Stage, the Bank of England; and (b) the FSA, the FSCS and the Bank of England during the Objective 1 Stage, may appear and be heard. (2) The bank administrator shall give 28 days notice of any proposed payment of distribution or dividend and notice of any payment of distribution or dividend to— (a) the FSA and the FSCS; and (b) during the Objective 1 Stage of a bank administration following transfer to a bridge bank under section 12(2) of the 2009 Act, the Bank of England. (3) In the case of notice of any payment of distribution or dividend in a bank administration following transfer to a bridge bank under section 12(2) of the 2009 Act and during the Objective 1 Stage, the notice shall include details of any payment made from a scheme under a resolution fund order. (4) If the bank administrator is unable to declare any dividend or any further dividend, the bank administrator must, in addition to notifying the creditors of this fact, notify— (a) the FSA; (b) the FSCS; and (c) the Bank of England; in a case where it consented to a distribution under these Rules.
2.41A	Payments of Dividends	(*Distributions in the case of bank administration following transfer to a bridge bank under section 12(2) of the 2009 Act and during the Objective 1 Stage require the Bank of England's consent—see the modification for the application of paragraph 65 of Schedule B1 to the Insolvency Act 1986 in Table 1 in section 145 of the 2009 Act*).
2.42	Final progress report	In the case of a bank administration following transfer to a bridge bank under section 12(2) of the 2009 Act the final progress report— (1) must not be made until the bank administrator is satisfied that any payment to be made to the bank from a scheme under a resolution fund order has been made; and (2) must state whether any payment has been received and, if so, its amount.

Rule	Subject	Specific Modifications
2.45	*Notice of end of administration*	*Rule 2.45 is not applied. Equivalent provision is made by Part 3 of these Rules.*
2.46	Application to court	The references to paragraph 79 are to be treated as references to paragraph 80 of Schedule B1 to the 1986 Act (as applied by section 153(2) of the 2009 Act).
2.48	*Moving from administration to dissolution*	*Rule 2.48 is not applied. Equivalent provision is made by Part 3 of these Rules.*
2.49	Grounds for resignation	During the Objective 1 Stage the Bank of England's consent, as well as the court's leave, is required for resignation under paragraph (2).
2.50	Notice of intention to resign	The Bank of England and the FSA are added to the list of those entitled to notice under paragraph (1).
2.51	Notice of resignation	
2.52	Administrator deceased	
2.53	Application to replace	Rule 2.53 is applied during the Objective 2 Stage only (and ignoring references to paragraph 95 of Schedule B1). *(For equivalent provisions about application for removal by the Bank of England during the Objective 1 Stage (in accordance with the modifications for the application of paragraph 91 of Schedule B1 to the Insolvency Act 1986 in Table 1 in section 145 of the 2009 Act) see Part 3 of these Rules.*
2.54	Application to replace	
2.55	Joint or concurrent appointments	
2.56	Application to court to remove administrator from office	An application may be made during the Objective 1 Stage only with the consent of the Bank of England —see the modifications for the application of paragraph 88 of Schedule B1 to the Insolvency Act 1986 in Table 1 in section 145 of the 2009 Act. (1) An application must state either— (a) that the Bank of England has consented to its being made; or (b) that the Objective 1 Stage has ended. (2) The FSA is added to the list of those on whom an application under paragraph (1) must be served.
4.1	*Appointment of provisional liquidator*	*Rule 4.1 is not applied. Equivalent provision is made by Part VII of Chapter 74 of Schedule 2 to the Act of Sederunt (Rules of the Court of Session 1994)1994.*
4.2	*Order of Appointment*	*Rule 4.2 is not applied. Equivalent provision is made by Part 3 of these Rules.*
4.3	Caution	
4.4	Failure to find or to maintain caution	
4.5	Remuneration	
4.6	Termination of Appointment	An application for termination may be made by— the provisional bank administrator, or the Bank of England only.

Rule	Subject	Specific Modifications
7.13A	Application under section 176A(5) to disapply section 176A	
7.13B	Notice of order under section 176A(5)	
7.14 to 7.20	Proxies	(*In rule 7.20, the reference to section 375 of the Companies Act 1985 is now a reference to section 323 of the Companies Act 2006*) For rule 7.20(2), substitute— "The copy resolution must be signed or subscribed by or on behalf of the bank in accordance with the provisions of the Requirements of Writing (Scotland) Act 1995 or certified by the secretary or director of the bank to be a true copy."
7.21	Giving of notices, etc	
7.22	Sending by post	Rule 7.22 applies subject to express provision about service made in these Rules.
7.23	Certificate of giving notice, etc	
7.24	Validity of proceedings	
7.25	Evidence of proceedings at meetings	
7.26	Right to list of creditors and copy documents	(1) The following have the right, at all reasonable times, to inspect documents in respect of bank administration proceedings:— (a) a person who is or was a director or officer of the bank; (b) a member of the bank; (c) any person stating himself in writing to be a creditor of the bank; (d) any person stating himself in writing to be a contributor in respect of the bank; (e) the Bank of England, and (f) the FSA; and (g) the FSCS. (2) A right of inspection may be exercised on a person's behalf by anyone authorised by him in writing. (3) A right of inspection in terms of paragraph 1 is not exercisable in the case of documents, or parts of documents, as to which the court directs (either generally or specifically) that they are not to be made open to inspection without the court's leave; and an application for such leave may be made by— (a) the bank administrator(s) or provisional bank administrator(s); or (b) any party appearing to the court to have an interest. (4) References to "a creditor who has a right to inspect documents" in rule 7.26(2) shall include a reference to the persons listed in paragraph (1) above.

Rule	Subject	Specific Modifications
7.27	Confidentiality of documents	
7.28	Insolvency practitioner's caution	
7.29 and Sch 4 of the Insolvency Act 1986	Punishment of offences	
7.31	Fees, expenses, etc	
7.32	Power of court to cure defects in procedure	
7.33	Sederunt book	
7.34	Disposal of company's books, papers and other records	
7.35	Information about time spent on a case-administration and company voluntary arrangements	

[1302]

NOTES
Commencement: 25 February 2009.

BANK INSOLVENCY (SCOTLAND) RULES 2009

(SI 2009/351)

NOTES
Made: 23 February 2009.
Authority: Insolvency Act 1986, s 411(1A)(b), (2), (2C), (3).
Commencement: 25 February 2009.

ARRANGEMENT OF RULES

PART 1
INTRODUCTORY PROVISIONS

PART 2
APPLICATION FOR ORDER

PART 3
PROVISIONAL LIQUIDATION

PART 9
THE LIQUIDATION COMMITTEE

PART 10
DISTRIBUTION OF BANK ASSETS

PART 11
SPECIAL MANAGER

PART 12
MISCELLANEOUS

PART 13
COMPANY WITH PROHIBITED NAME

PART 14
MEETINGS

PART 15
GENERAL PROVISIONS

PART 1
INTRODUCTORY PROVISIONS

1   Citation and commencement

These Rules may be cited as the Bank Insolvency (Scotland) Rules 2009 and come into force on 25th February 2009.

[1303]

NOTES
Commencement: 25 February 2009.

2   Extent

These rules extend to Scotland only.

[1304]

NOTES
Commencement: 25 February 2009.

3   Application of rules, construction and interpretation

(1)   These Rules apply in relation to a bank undergoing the procedure in Part 2 of the Banking Act 2009 known as bank insolvency.

(2)   In these Rules—
"the 1986 Act" means the Insolvency Act 1986 as applied by section 103 of the 2009 Act;
"the 1986 Rules" means the Insolvency (Scotland) Rules 1986;
"the 2009 Act" means the Banking Act 2009;
"bank" means a bank within the meaning of section 91 of the 2009 Act;
"Bankruptcy Act" means the Bankruptcy (Scotland) Act 1985;
"court" means the Court of Session;
"eligible depositor" has the meaning given by section 93(3) of the 2009 Act;
"the FSA" means the Financial Services Authority;
"the FSA Rules" means the FSA's Compensation Sourcebook (made under section 213 of the Financial Services and Markets Act 2000);
"the FSCS" means the Financial Services Compensation Scheme (established under Part 15 of the Financial Services and Markets Act 2000) or, where appropriate, the scheme manager of that scheme;
"the liquidation committee" means the committee established pursuant to section 100 of the 2009 Act;
"protected deposits" means a protected deposit within the meaning given in the FSA Rules;

"registered address" has the meaning given by section 1140 of the Companies Act 2006 ;
"Rules of the Court of Session" means Schedule 2 to the Act of Sederunt (Rules of the Court of Session 1994) 1994;
"set off" includes (without limitation) claims of compensation, rights of retention and rights of balancing accounts on insolvency; and
"sums held by the bank" includes amounts due by the bank to the relevant eligible depositor.

(3)   These Rules consist of—
   (a)   the rules set out in full;
   (b)   in the case of a rule applying a rule of the 1986 Rules, the rules as applied with—
         (i)   the modifications set out in paragraph (4);
         (ii)   the modifications contained in the rule applying it; and
         (iii) any other necessary modification.

(4)   The modifications are that—
   (a)   a reference to the liquidator is a reference to the bank liquidator;
   (b)   a reference to the provisional liquidator is a reference to the provisional bank liquidator;
   (c)   a reference to winding up is a reference to bank insolvency;
   (d)   a reference to winding up by the court is a reference to a bank being placed into insolvency by the court;
   (e)   a reference to the commencement of winding up is a reference to the commencement of bank insolvency;
   (f)   a reference to going into liquidation is a reference to entering bank insolvency;
   (g)   a reference to a winding-up order is a reference to a bank insolvency order;
   (h)   a reference to the chairman is a reference to the chair;
   (i)   a reference to insolvency proceedings is a reference to bank insolvency proceedings;
   (j)   a reference to a company is a reference to a bank;
   (k)   a reference to a petition is a reference to an application under section 95 of the 2009 Act;
   (l)   a reference to a petitioner is a reference to an applicant; and
   (m)   a reference to a responsible insolvency practitioner is a reference to a bank liquidator.

(5)   Expressions used—
   (a)   both in a rule set out in full and in Part 2 of the Banking Act 2009; or
   (b)   both in a modification to a rule of the 1986 Rules applied by these Rules and in Part 2 of the 2009 Act,
have the same meaning as in Part 2 of the 2009 Act.

(6)   Where a rule applies a rule of the 1986 rules and modifies that rule by inserting or substituting text—
   (a)   any reference in the modified rule to the 2009 Rules is a reference to these Rules;
   (b)   expressions inserted or substituted have the same meaning as in these Rules.

(7)   Where a rule in the 1986 Rules (Rule A) contains a reference to another such rule (Rule B) and—
   (a)   both Rule A and Rule B are applied by these Rules; or
   (b)   Rule A is applied by and the provision in Rule B to which Rule A refers is substantially repeated in these Rules;
the reference in Rule A shall be treated, for the purpose of these Rules, as being, respectively, to the rule in these Rules that applies Rule B or the provision in these Rules that substantially repeats the provision in Rule B.

(8)   Where a rule (Rule A) refers to another rule (Rule B) and Rule B applies a rule of the 1986 Rules (Rule C) with or without modifications, the reference in Rule A includes a reference to Rule C as applied to Rule B.

(9)   Any notice or document sent electronically pursuant to these Rules shall be treated as having been sent or given to the person if—
   (a)   it is sent by email to the person's last known email address; and
   (b)   the email contains a prompt asking the person for an electronic receipt saying that the email has been read.

(10)   The 1986 Rules apply to bank insolvency, to the extent that these Rules do not make express provision, but only so far as consistent with Part 2 of the 2009 Act, these Rules, the Rules of the Court of Session, and any other rule of law relating to bank insolvency.

[1305]

NOTES

Commencement: 25 February 2009.

4   Time limits

(1)   Where by any provision of the 1986 Act, the 2009 Act or these Rules, the time for doing anything is limited, the court may extend the time, either before or after it has expired, on such terms, if any, as it thinks fit.

(2)   If the court's consideration of whether to extend the time for doing anything takes place before a full payment resolution has been passed, the court shall only extend the time if it considers that the resulting delay will not significantly prejudice the achievement of Objective 1.

[1306]

NOTES
Commencement: 25 February 2009.

5   Overview

The purpose of these Rules is to provide a procedure for the appointment of a bank liquidator and the operation of bank insolvency under Part 2 of the 2009 Act in Scotland.

[1307]

NOTES
Commencement: 25 February 2009.

PART 2
APPLICATION FOR ORDER

6   Application for bank insolvency order

An application for a bank insolvency order under section 95 of the 2009 Act shall be in accordance with Part 2 of these Rules and Part VII of Chapter 74 of the Rules of the Court of Session.

[1308]

NOTES
Commencement: 25 February 2009.

7   Persons entitled to copy of application

(1)   Every contributory or creditor of the bank is entitled to a copy of the application on request from the applicant.

(2)   The applicant shall respond to any request for a copy of the application as soon as reasonably practicable after the application has been made on payment of the appropriate fee.

(3)   In paragraph (2), "the appropriate fee" means 15 pence per A4 or A5 page, and 30 pence per A3 page.

[1309]

NOTES
Commencement: 25 February 2009.

8   Appointment of bank liquidator by the court

(1)   This rule applies where an application for a bank insolvency order is made to the court under section 95 of the 2009 Act.

(2)   The court shall not make the order unless there is lodged in court a statement to the effect that—
    (a)   the person proposed to be appointed as the bank liquidator is qualified to act as an insolvency practitioner in accordance with section 390 of the 1986 Act; and
    (b)   that person consents so to act.

(3)   When the bank insolvency order has been made the court shall immediately send a certified copy of the order to—
    (a)   the bank liquidator who shall also, where practicable, be sent an electronic copy of the certified copy order; and
    (b)   the applicant.

(4)   The bank liquidator shall immediately—
    (a)   serve a copy of the order on the bank at its registered office and, where the bank liquidator has received an electronic copy of the order and knows the bank 's email address, send an electronic copy to the bank;
    (b)   give notice of the appointment to the Accountant in Bankruptcy;
    (c)   forward a copy of the order to the registrar of companies in accordance with section 130(1) of the 1986 Act (as applied by section 103 of the 2009 Act);

(d)   advertise the appointment once in the Edinburgh Gazette and such newspaper as the bank liquidator may select or as the court may otherwise direct; and

(e)   send (electronically or otherwise) a copy of the order to—

(i)   the FSA, if it is not the applicant;

(ii)   the Bank of England, if it is not the applicant; and

(iii) the FSCS.

[1310]

NOTES

Commencement: 25 February 2009.

9 Initial duties of bank liquidation committee

(1)   As soon as reasonably practicable after the making of a bank insolvency order the liquidation committee will meet the bank liquidator for the purpose of discussing which of the Objectives, or combination of Objectives, mentioned in section 102(1) of the 2009 Act the committee should recommend the bank liquidator pursue.

(2)   If the bank liquidator and every individual on the liquidation committee agree, the meeting may be held by audio or video conference.

(3)   The liquidation committee will make its recommendation to the bank liquidator at the meeting.

(4)   The Bank of England will confirm the liquidation committee's recommendation in writing as soon as reasonably practicable after the meeting.

(5)   As soon as reasonably practicable after the making of a bank insolvency order, the liquidation committee shall also pass a resolution as to the terms on which, in accordance with rule 45 the bank liquidator is to be remunerated.

(6)   Until a full payment resolution has been passed, the liquidation committee—

(a)   shall take decisions and pass resolutions by a simple majority; and

(b)   for the purpose of taking decisions and passing resolutions, may communicate by any means that its members consider convenient.

[1311]

NOTES

Commencement: 25 February 2009.

10 Authentication of bank liquidator's appointment

Apply rule 4.20 of the 1986 Rules.

[1312]

NOTES

Commencement: 25 February 2009.

PART 3
PROVISIONAL LIQUIDATION

11 Appointment of provisional bank liquidator

(1)   This rule applies after an application for a bank insolvency order has been made under Part 2 of these Rules and Part VII of Chapter 74 of the Court of Session Rules and before that order is made.

(2)   Apply rule 4.1 of the 1986 Rules.

(3)   For rule 4.1(1) substitute—

"(1)   An application to the court for the appointment of a provisional bank liquidator under section 135 of the 1986 Act may be made—

(a)   by the Bank of England;

(b)   by the FSA, with the consent of the Bank of England; or

(c)   by the Secretary of State.".

[1313]

NOTES

Commencement: 25 February 2009.

12 Order of appointment of provisional bank liquidator

(1)   The order of appointment of the provisional bank liquidator shall specify the functions to be carried out by the provisional bank liquidator in relation to the bank's affairs.

(2)   The applicant shall, immediately after the order is made, send a certified copy of the order to—

    (a)   the provisional bank liquidator;

    (b)   the Bank of England, if the Bank of England is not the applicant;

    (c)   the FSA, if the FSA is not the applicant; and

    (d)   the FSCS,

and may also send to those persons an electronic copy of the certified copy order.

(3)   The provisional bank liquidator shall immediately after the order appointing him is made—

    (a)   serve a certified copy of the order on the bank and each director of the bank;

    (b)   give notice of his appointment to the registrar of companies and the Accountant in Bankruptcy;

    (c)   give notice of his appointment to any receiver of the whole or any part of the property of the bank; and

    (d)   advertise the appointment in accordance with the directions of the court.

(4)   Service on a director may be effected electronically by sending it to his work email address.

[1314]

NOTES

Commencement: 25 February 2009.

---

13   Caution

Apply rule 4.3 of the 1986 Rules.

[1315]

NOTES

Commencement: 25 February 2009.

---

14   Failure to find or to maintain caution

Apply rule 4.4 of the 1986 Rules.

[1316]

NOTES

Commencement: 25 February 2009.

---

15   Remuneration

Apply rule 4.5 of the 1986 Rules.

[1317]

NOTES

Commencement: 25 February 2009.

---

16   Termination of appointment

(1)   Apply rule 4.6(1) and (2) of the 1986 Rules.

(2)   In rule 4.6(1) ignore "Except in relation to winding up petitions under section 124A".

(3)   After rule 4.6(2) insert—

    "(3)   On the making of a bank insolvency order, the appointment of the provisional bank liquidator shall terminate.".

[1318]

NOTES

Commencement: 25 February 2009.

PART 4
STATEMENT OF AFFAIRS

17   Notice requiring statement of affairs

(1)   Apply rule 4.7 of the 1986 Rules.

(2)   Insert new rule 4.7(5)—

    "(5)   The bank liquidator shall, at the same time as sending a notice under paragraph (3), send a copy of such notice, to the registrar of companies.".

[1319]

NOTES
Commencement: 25 February 2009.

18 Form of the statement of affairs

(1) Apply rule 4.8 of the 1986 Rules.

[1320]

NOTES
Commencement: 25 February 2009.
This rule is reproduced as it appears in the original Queen's Printer's copy; there is no paragraph (2).

19 Expenses of statement of affairs

Apply rule 4.9 of the 1986 Rules.

[1321]

NOTES
Commencement: 25 February 2009.

20 Limited disclosure

Without prejudice to any other means of restricting disclosure, the Bank of England may also apply to the court for an order limiting disclosure of the names, addresses and claims of persons who were depositors of the bank and who, at the time of making the statement of affairs, still have a claim against the bank in respect of those deposits.

[1322]

NOTES
Commencement: 25 February 2009.

PART 5
INFORMATION TO CREDITORS AND CONTRIBUTORIES

21 Report by bank liquidator

(1) The bank liquidator shall, at least once after the making of the bank insolvency order, make a report with respect to the proceedings in the bank insolvency and the state of the bank's affairs.

(2) Regardless of whether the liquidation committee has passed a full payment resolution, the first report under paragraph (1) shall be, within 8 weeks of the commencement of the bank insolvency, made publicly available on the bank's website.

(3) The bank liquidator shall include in the report under paragraph (1)—
   (a) a statement that a petition has been presented to the court and the relevant court number;
   (b) the full name, registered address, registered number and any other trading names of the bank;
   (c) details relating to the bank liquidator's appointment, including the date of appointment, and where there are joint liquidators, details of—
      (i) which functions (if any) are to be exercised by the persons appointed acting jointly, and
      (ii) which functions (if any) are to be exercised by any of all of the persons appointed.
   (d) the names of the directors and secretary of the bank and details of any shareholdings in the bank that they have;
   (e) an account of the circumstances giving rise to the bank insolvency;
   (f) if a statement of affairs has been submitted, a copy of that statement;
   (g) if a statement of affairs has yet to be submitted—
      (i) subject to sub-paragraph (ii) the names, addresses and details of any debts of the creditors, including details of any security held (or in the case of depositors who still are creditors of the bank at the time the report is made, a single statement of their aggregate debt); and
      (ii) details of the financial position of the bank at the latest practicable date (which must, unless the court orders otherwise, be a date not earlier than the commencement of bank insolvency);
   (h) the basis upon which it has been proposed under rule 24, or, if the full payment resolution has yet to be passed, rule 9, that the bank liquidator's remuneration has been fixed;
   (i) to the best of the bank liquidator's knowledge and belief—
      (i) an estimate of the value of the prescribed part (within the meaning of section 176A of the 1986 Act) regardless of whether—

            (aa)   the bank liquidator proposes to make an application to the court under section 176A(5) of that Act; or

            (bb)   section 176A(3) of that Act applies);

        (ii)   an estimate of the value of the company's net property;

(j)   whether, and if so, why, the bank liquidator proposes to make an application to the court under section 176A(5) of the 1986 Act;

(k)   a summary of—

        (i)   how Objective 1 is being or has been achieved and an estimate of the costs to the bank liquidator of achieving it;

        (ii)   the manner in which the affairs and business of the bank not involved in the achievement of Objective 1 have, since the commencement of the bank insolvency, been managed and financed, including, where any assets have been disposed of, the reasons for such disposals and the terms upon which such disposals were made; and

        (iii)   how the affairs and business of the bank will continue to be managed and financed; and

(l)   an explanation of how it is envisaged the purpose of the bank liquidation will be achieved, including whether a dividend will be paid and an estimate as to the amount of this dividend and how it is proposed that the bank liquidation shall end.

(4)   Nothing in this rule is to be taken as requiring either estimate mentioned in paragraph (3)(i) to include any information, the disclosure of which could seriously prejudice the commercial interests of the bank. If such information is excluded from the calculation, the estimate shall be accompanied by a statement to that effect.

(5)   Any reference in this rule to creditors is to persons known to the bank liquidator to be creditors of the bank.

(6)   Where a statement of affairs has been submitted to him, the bank liquidator may send out to creditors and contributories with the next convenient report to be made under paragraph (1) a summary of the statement and such observations (if any) as he thinks fit to make with respect to it.

(7)   The bank liquidator shall insert a copy of any report sent under this rule in the sederunt book.

                                                           [1323]

NOTES

Commencement: 25 February 2009.

22   Information as to pending liquidations

(1)   Apply rule 4.11 of the 1986 Rules.

(2)   In rule 4.11(1) after "the Accountant in Bankruptcy" insert "and the registrar of companies".

                                                           [1324]

NOTES

Commencement: 25 February 2009.

PART 6
MEETINGS OF CREDITORS AND CONTRIBUTORIES

23   First meetings in the bank liquidation

(1)   Once the liquidation committee passes a full payment resolution the bank liquidator shall—

    (a)   immediately summon a meeting of the bank's creditors and contributories; and

    (b)   fix a venue, date and time for the meeting,

and the date must be within three months of the date on which the full payment resolution was passed.

(2)   When the venue, date and time of the meeting have been fixed, the bank liquidator shall give notice of the meeting to—

    (a)   every creditor who is known to the bank liquidator or is identified in the bank's statement of affairs, and

    (b)   each member of the liquidation committee,

and shall advertise the venue, date and time of the meeting in such manner as the bank liquidator thinks fit.

(3)   In giving the notice mentioned in paragraph (2), the bank liquidator shall, if practicable, indicate whether the present intention of the FSCS is to resign from the liquidation committee at the meeting.

(4)   Notice to the members of the liquidation committee shall be given immediately.

PART IV   OTHER STATUTORY INSTRUMENTS

(5)   Notice to creditors shall be given, and the advertisements placed to appear, at least 21 days before the date fixed for the meeting.

(6)   The notice to creditors shall specify a time and date, not more than 4 days before the date fixed for the meeting, by which they must lodge claims and (if applicable) proxies, in order to be entitled to vote at the meeting.

(7)   The FSCS is entitled to be represented at the meeting and Schedule 3 to the 1986 Rules has effect with respect to its voting rights at such a meeting.

(8)   Meetings summoned under this rule are known respectively as "the first meeting of creditors" and "the first meeting of contributories", and jointly as "the first meetings in the bank liquidation".

[1325]

NOTES
Commencement: 25 February 2009.

24   Business at the first meeting of creditors and contributories

(1)   At the first meeting of creditors the FSCS shall state whether or not it is resigning from the liquidation committee.

(2)   At the meeting those creditors present or represented by proxy may—
(a)   where the FSCS has not resigned, elect 2 or 4 individuals as new members of the liquidation committee;
(b)   where the FSCS has resigned, elect 3 or 5 individuals as new members of the liquidation committee,
in place of members nominated by the Bank of England and the FSA.

(3)   In accordance with section 100(6)(e) of the 2009 Act, the liquidation committee ceases to exist at the end of the meeting if no individuals are elected as mentioned or if the resulting committee would have fewer than 3 members or an even number of members. The maximum number of committee members will be 5.

(4)   At the first meeting of the creditors, no resolutions shall be taken other than the following—
(a)   if an application has been made to the court by creditors under rule 39 for the court to direct the bank liquidator to summon a meeting of creditors for the purpose of removing him, and the court has directed that a resolution may be passed at the first meeting of creditors to that effect—
(i)   a resolution to remove the bank liquidator (or a resolution to remove one or more of the bank liquidators if joint liquidators were originally appointed); and
(ii)   a resolution to appoint a named insolvency practitioner to be bank liquidator or two or more insolvency practitioners as joint bank liquidators;
(b)   if no individuals have been elected to form a liquidation committee under paragraph (2), a resolution specifying the terms on which the liquidator is to be remunerated, or to defer consideration of that matter;
(c)   where two or more persons are appointed jointly to act as bank liquidator, a resolution specifying which acts are to be done by both of them, all of them or by only one;
(d)   a resolution to adjourn the meeting for not more than 3 weeks;
(e)   any other resolution which the chair considers it right to allow for special reason.

(5)   At the first meeting of contributories, no resolutions shall be taken other than the following—
(a)   if no individuals have been elected to form a liquidation committee under paragraph (2), a resolution to form a liquidation committee (and rule 57 shall then apply);
(b)   a resolution to adjourn the meeting for not more than 3 weeks;
(c)   any other resolutions which the chair thinks it right to allow for special reason.

[1326]

NOTES
Commencement: 25 February 2009.

25   Other meetings

Apply rule 4.13 of the 1986 Rules.

[1327]

NOTES
Commencement: 25 February 2009.

26 Attendance at meetings of bank's personnel

Apply rule 4.14 of the 1986 Rules.

[1328]

NOTES
Commencement: 25 February 2009.

PART 7
CLAIMS IN LIQUIDATION

27 Submission of claims

Apply rule 4.15 of the 1986 Rules.

[1329]

NOTES
Commencement: 25 February 2009.

28 Application of the Bankruptcy Act

(1) Apply rule 4.16 of the 1986 Rules.

(2) Ignore rule 4.16(3).

[1330]

NOTES
Commencement: 25 February 2009.

29 Claims in foreign currency

(1) Apply rule 4.17 of the 1986 Rules.

(2) In rule 4.17(2) omit from "or, if" to the end.

[1331]

NOTES
Commencement: 25 February 2009.

30 Rights of eligible depositor and set-off

(1) This rule applies if the FSA Rules allow the FSCS to make gross payments of compensation.

(2) In determining the sums due from the bank to an eligible depositor or from the eligible depositor to the bank for the purpose of any right or claim of set off available to the bank against the eligible depositor—

    (a) where the total of the sums held by the bank for any eligible depositor in respect of protected deposits is no more than the amount prescribed as the maximum compensation payable in respect of protected deposits under Part 15 of the Financial Services and Markets Act 2000, paragraph (3) applies; and

    (b) where the sums held by the bank exceed that limit, paragraph (4) applies.

(3) Where paragraph (2)(a) applies, regardless of whether there are any sums due from the eligible depositor to the bank, the bank shall not be entitled to exercise or claim any right of set off available to it against or in respect of those sums held by the bank for the eligible depositor in respect of the protected deposits; and the sum due to the eligible depositor from the bank will be the total of the sums held by the bank for that eligible depositor in respect of protected deposits which sum shall be deemed free from any right or claim of set off by the bank.

(4) Where paragraph (2)(b) applies—

    (a) the bank shall be entitled to exercise any right or claim of set off available to it only in respect of any sums held by the bank for that eligible depositor in excess of that limit, which sums shall be subject to any right or claim of set off available to the bank; and

    (b) the sums due from the bank to the eligible depositor will be—

        (i) the amount by which the total amount exceeds that limit subject to any right or claim of set off available to the bank; and

        (ii) the sums held by the bank for the eligible depositor in respect of protected deposits up to the limit of the amount prescribed as the maximum compensation payable in respect of protected deposits under Part 15 of the Financial Services and Markets Act 2000.

(5) Any arrangements with regard to set off between the bank and the eligible depositor in existence before the commencement of bank insolvency shall be subject to this rule.

[1332]

NOTES
Commencement: 25 February 2009.

PART 8
THE LIQUIDATOR

SECTION A—APPOINTMENT BY CREDITORS AND FUNCTIONS OF LIQUIDATOR

31 Appointment by creditors

(1)   This rule applies where a person is appointed as bank liquidator by a meeting of creditors.

(2)   The chair of the meeting shall certify the appointment of a person as bank liquidator by the meeting but not until the person to be appointed has provided him with a written statement to the effect that he is qualified to act as an insolvency practitioner in accordance with section 390 of the 1986 Act, and that he consents so to act.

(3)   The appointment of the bank liquidator takes effect upon the passing of the resolution for the appointment and the date of the appointment shall be stated in the certificate.

(4)   The chair of the meeting shall send the certificate to the new bank liquidator who shall send a copy of the certificate to the Bank of England (if the Bank of England was the applicant for the bank insolvency order), or the FSA, (if the FSA was that applicant).

[1333]

NOTES
Commencement: 25 February 2009.

32 Appointment to be advertised and registered

(1)   This rule applies where the bank liquidator is appointed by a meeting of the creditors under rule 31 or by the Bank of England under rule 50.

(2)   The bank liquidator shall, after receiving the certificate of appointment, give notice of the appointment in such newspapers as the bank liquidator thinks most appropriate for ensuring that it comes to the notice of the bank's creditors and contributories.

(3)   The expense of giving notice under this rule shall be borne in the first instance by the bank liquidator and such expense shall be treated as an expense of the bank insolvency.

(4)   The bank liquidator shall immediately notify the appointment to the court, the registrar of companies and the Accountant in Bankruptcy.

[1334]

NOTES
Commencement: 25 February 2009.

33 Hand-over of assets to bank liquidator

Apply rule 4.21 of the 1986 Rules.

[1335]

NOTES
Commencement: 25 February 2009.

34 Taking possession and realisation of the company's assets

Apply rule 4.22 of the 1986 Rules.

[1336]

NOTES
Commencement: 25 February 2009.

35 General qualification on powers

In exercising any power conferred on the bank liquidator by these Rules before a full payment resolution has been passed, the bank liquidator shall exercise it consistently with Objective 1.

[1337]

NOTES
Commencement: 25 February 2009.

SECTION B—REMOVAL AND RESIGNATION

36 Summoning of meeting for removal of bank liquidator

(1) This rule applies where—

    (a)   the court has made an order under rule 39 directing the bank liquidator to summon a meeting of creditors for the purpose of his removal; and

    (b)   the liquidation committee has passed a full payment resolution.

(2) A copy of the notice summoning the meeting shall be sent to the Bank of England and the FSA.

(3) Where a meeting of creditors is summoned especially for the purpose of removing the bank liquidator, the notice summoning it shall draw attention to section 109 of the 2009 Act with respect to the bank liquidator's release.

(4) At the meeting, a person other than the bank liquidator or his nominee may be elected to act as chair; but if the bank liquidator or his nominee is chair and a resolution has been proposed for the bank liquidator's removal, the chair shall not adjourn the meeting without the consent of at least one-half (in value) of the creditors present (in person or by proxy) and entitled to vote.

(5) Where a meeting is to be held or is proposed to be summoned for the purpose of removal of the bank liquidator, the court may, on the application of any creditor, give directions as to the mode of summoning it, the sending out and return of forms of proxy, the conduct of the meeting, and any other matter which appears to the court to require regulation or control under this rule.

(6) The Bank of England and FSA shall have the opportunity to make representations at the meeting.

(7) Where, at a meeting held under this rule, the bank liquidator is removed, another bank liquidator may be appointed in accordance with rule 31.

[1338]

NOTES

Commencement: 25 February 2009.

37 Procedure on bank liquidator's removal

(1) Apply rule 4.24 of the 1986 Rules.

(2) At the end of rule 4.24(1)(a) and (b) after "Accountant in Bankruptcy" where it appears insert "the registrar of companies and the Bank of England.".

[1339]

NOTES

Commencement: 25 February 2009.

38 Release of bank liquidator on removal

Where the bank liquidator has been removed by a creditors' meeting which has not resolved against the bank liquidator's release, the fact of that release shall be stated in the certificate of removal before a copy of it is sent, in accordance with rule 37, to the court, the Accountant in Bankruptcy, the registrar of companies and the Bank of England.

[1340]

NOTES

Commencement: 25 February 2009.

39 Removal of bank liquidator by the court

(1) This rule applies where application is made to the court for the removal of the bank liquidator, or for an order directing the bank liquidator to summon a meeting of creditors for the purpose of removing him.

(2) If the liquidation committee has not yet passed a full payment resolution, the court shall dismiss any application under paragraph (1) where the application is made by a person other than the Bank of England, the FSA or the liquidation committee.

(3) The court may require the applicant to make a deposit or give caution for the expenses to be incurred by the bank liquidator on the application.

(4) Subject to paragraph (2) and (3), the applicant shall send to the bank liquidator a notice of the hearing, stating date, time and place and accompanied by a copy of the application, and of any evidence which he intends to adduce in support of it.

(5) The notice and copies mentioned in paragraph (4) shall be sent—

(a)   if the application is made before the passing of a full payment resolution, so as to give the bank liquidator such notice of the hearing as is reasonable in all the circumstances; and

(b)   if the application is made after the passing of a full payment resolution, at least 14 days before the hearing.

(6)   Subject to any contrary order of the court, the expenses of the application are not payable as an expense of the bank liquidation.

(7)   Where the court removes the bank liquidator—
(a)   it shall send three copies of the order of removal to him;
(b)   the order may include such provision as the court thinks fit with respect to matters arising in connection with the removal; and
(c)   if the court appoints a new liquidator, rule 8 of these Rules applies.

(8)   The bank liquidator, on receipt of the three copies of the court orders under paragraph (7), shall send one copy of the order to each of the registrar of companies, Accountant in Bankruptcy and the Bank of England, together with a notice of his ceasing to act as a bank liquidator.

[1341]

NOTES
Commencement: 25 February 2009.

40   Advertisement of removal

(1)   Apply rule 4.27 of the 1986 Rules.

[1342]

NOTES
Commencement: 25 February 2009.
This rule is reproduced as it appears in the original Queen's Printer's copy; there is no paragraph (2).

41   Resignation of liquidator

(1)   Before resigning office in accordance with section 109 of the 2009 Act, the bank liquidator must call a meeting of creditors to notify them of the proposed resignation and, where the bank liquidator was appointed by the Bank of England or by the court, obtain the consent of the Bank of England.

(2)   The notice summoning the meeting shall—
(a)   indicate that this is the purpose, or one of the purposes of the meeting;
(b)   draw the creditors' attention to section 111 of the 2009 Act and rule 43 with respect to the bank liquidator's release and shall also be accompanied by an account of the bank liquidator's administration of the bank insolvency, including a summary of his receipts and payments and a statement as to the amount paid to unsecured creditors by virtue of the application of section 176A of the 1986 Act (prescribed part); and
(c)   where the bank liquidator was appointed by the Bank of England or by the court, enclose a copy of the Bank of England's consent.

(3)   Copies of the notice and of the account mentioned in paragraph (2) shall be sent to the court, the Bank of England and the FSA.

(4)   Subject to paragraph (5), the bank liquidator may only proceed under this rule on the grounds of ill health or because—
(a)   he intends ceasing to be in practice as an insolvency practitioner; or
(b)   there has been some conflict of interest or change of personal circumstances which precludes or makes impracticable the further discharge by him of the duties of the bank liquidator.

(5)   Where two or more persons are acting as the bank liquidator jointly, any one of them may resign (without prejudice to the continuation in office of the other or others) on the ground that, in his opinion and that of the other or others, it is no longer expedient that there should continue to be the present number of joint bank liquidators.

[1343]

NOTES
Commencement: 25 February 2009.

42   Action following acceptance of bank liquidator's resignation

(1)   This rule applies where a meeting is summoned to notify the creditors of the bank liquidator's resignation.

(2)   The meeting will resolve whether to give the bank liquidator his release.

(3)   If the meeting decides not to give the bank liquidator his release, the bank liquidator will be given a copy of that resolution and rule 43 applies.

(4)   After the meeting the bank liquidator shall lodge the notice of his resignation in court and shall send copies of it to the Bank of England and registrar of companies.

(5)   The bank liquidator's resignation is effective as from the date on which the court receives notice of his resignation, and the court shall endorse that date on the notice.

(6)   Where the creditors have resolved to appoint a new bank liquidator in place of the one who has resigned, rules 4.19 to 4.21 of the 1986 Rules shall apply to the appointment of the new bank liquidator, except that the notice to be given by the new bank liquidator under rules 4.19(4) of the 1986 Rules shall also state that his predecessor as bank liquidator has resigned and whether he has been released.

(7)   If there is no quorum present at the meeting summoned to notify the creditors of the bank liquidator's resignation, the meeting is deemed to have been held, a resolution is deemed to have been passed that the bank liquidator's resignation be accepted, and the creditors are deemed not to have resolved against the bank liquidator having his release.

[1344]

NOTES
Commencement: 25 February 2009.

43   Release of resigning or removed bank liquidator

(1)   Where the liquidator's resignation is notified to a meeting of creditors which has not resolved against his release, he has his release from when his resignation is effective under rule 42.

(2)   Where—
   (a)   the bank liquidator is removed by the court following an application under rule 39;
   (b)   the Bank of England has refused to consent to the bank liquidator's proposed resignation;
   (c)   the meeting of creditors held under rule 36 resolves against giving him release;
   (d)   the bank liquidator ceases to be qualified to act as an insolvency practitioner; or
   (e)   the meeting of the liquidation committee held under rule 44 resolves against the bank liquidator being released,

he must apply to the Accountant of Court for his release.

(3)   Where the Accountant of Court gives release under this rule, he shall certify it accordingly, and send the certificate to the Accountant in Bankruptcy, registrar of companies and the Bank of England.

(4)   A copy of the certificate shall be sent by the Accountant of Court to the former liquidator, whose release is effective from the date of the certificate.

[1345]

NOTES
Commencement: 25 February 2009.

SECTION C—RELEASE ON COMPLETION OF WINDING UP

44   Final meeting

(1)   The bank liquidator shall give at least 14 days' notice of the final meeting of the liquidation committee to be held under section 115 of the 2009 Act to the following—
   (a)   the FSA;
   (b)   the FSCS;
   (c)   the Bank of England;
   (d)   the Treasury;
   (e)   the registrar of companies; and
   (f)   the members of the liquidation committee.

(2)   The bank liquidator's final report to be laid before the meeting under section 115 of the 2009 Act shall contain an account of the liquidator's administration of the winding up, including—
   (a)   details as to how Objective 1 was achieved having regard, in particular, to the expenses of the bank liquidator in connection with that Objective;
   (b)   a summary of the bank liquidator's receipts and payments;
   (c)   a statement that the bank liquidator has reconciled his account with that which is held by the Secretary of State in respect of the winding up; and
   (d)   a statement as to the amount paid to unsecured creditors by virtue of the application of section 176A (prescribed part) of the 1986 Act.

(3)   At the same time that notice of the final meeting is sent out, the bank liquidator shall lodge the final report in court and send it to the registrar of companies and the Accountant in Bankruptcy.

(4)   The bank liquidator shall give notice that the final report is available to all creditors and contributories, either on request to the bank liquidator or the registrar of companies, and shall cause that notice to be advertised in the Edinburgh Gazette at least 14 days before the final meeting is held.

(5)   At the final meeting, the liquidation committee may question the bank liquidator with respect to any matter contained in the final report, and may resolve against the bank liquidator being released.

(6)   The bank liquidator shall give notice to the court, the registrar of companies and the Accountant in Bankruptcy that the final meeting has been held and the notice shall state whether or not he has been given his release.

(7)   Where the liquidation committee does not resolve against the bank liquidator's release, the bank liquidator vacates office and has his release when the notice in paragraph (6) is lodged in court.

(8)   If there is no quorum present at the final meeting, the bank liquidator shall report to the court that a final meeting was summoned in accordance with section 115 of the 2009 Act, but there was no quorum present; and the final meeting is then deemed to have been held, and the liquidation committee not to have resolved against the bank liquidator being released.

(9)   If the liquidation committee resolves against the bank liquidator having his release then rule 43 of these Rules applies.

[1346]

NOTES
Commencement: 25 February 2009.

SECTION D—OUTLAYS AND REMUNERATION

45   Determination of amount of outlays and remuneration
Apply rule 4.32 of the 1986 Rules.

[1347]

NOTES
Commencement: 25 February 2009.

46   Recourse of liquidator to meeting of creditors
Apply rule 4.33 of the 1986 Rules.

[1348]

NOTES
Commencement: 25 February 2009.

47   Recourse to the court
Apply rule 4.34 of the 1986 Rules.

[1349]

NOTES
Commencement: 25 February 2009.

48   Creditors' claim that remuneration is excessive
Apply rule 4.35 of the 1986 Rules.

[1350]

NOTES
Commencement: 25 February 2009.

49   Primacy of Objective 1
Nothing done under this section of the Rules may prejudice the achievement of Objective 1.

[1351]

NOTES
Commencement: 25 February 2009.

SECTION E—SUPPLEMENTARY PROVISIONS

50 Replacement bank liquidator

(1)   Where the bank liquidator vacates his office for any reason (including death) other than by removal by a meeting of creditors in accordance with rule 36, the Bank of England shall appoint a new bank liquidator as soon as practicable.

(2)   Where a bank liquidator has been removed by a meeting of creditors but 1 month has passed and there has been no resolution passed by a meeting of creditors to appoint a new bank liquidator, the Bank of England shall appoint a new bank liquidator as soon as practicable.

(3)   The Bank of England shall lodge in court the document appointing the new bank liquidator ("the appointment document") together with statements to the effect that the new bank liquidator—

     (a)   is qualified to act as an insolvency practitioner in accordance with section 390 of the 1986 Act; and

     (b)   consents to act as the bank liquidator.

(4)   The Bank of England shall send a copy of the appointment document to the bank.

(5)   The bank liquidator shall forward a copy of the appointment document to the registrar of companies and the Accountant in Bankruptcy.

(6)   The bank liquidator shall as soon as reasonably practicable—

     (a)   advertise the appointment in the Edinburgh Gazette; and

     (b)   advertise the appointment in such manner as the bank liquidator thinks fit.

     [1352]

NOTES

Commencement: 25 February 2009.

51 Bank liquidator deceased

(1)   Apply rule 4.36 of the 1986 Rules.

(2)   In rule 4.36(1) after "court" insert "the Bank of England and liquidation committee".

     [1353]

NOTES

Commencement: 25 February 2009.

52 Loss of qualification as insolvency practitioner

(1)   Apply rule 4.37 paragraphs (1) and (2) of the 1986 Rules.

(2)   In rule 4.37(2) after "Accountant in Bankruptcy" insert "and the Bank of England".

     [1354]

NOTES

Commencement: 25 February 2009.

53 Resignation of the bank liquidator

(1)   This rule applies where the bank liquidator was appointed by the court or by the Bank of England under rule 50.

(2)   The bank liquidator can only resign—

     (a)   after the liquidation committee has passed a full payment resolution; and

     (b)   with the consent of the Bank of England.

(3)   Before calling a meeting of creditors under rule 41 to receive notice of the bank liquidator's resignation, the bank liquidator must write to the Bank of England notifying it of the intention to resign.

(4)   The Bank of England shall notify the bank liquidator in writing within 21 days as to whether it consents to the resignation. If the Bank of England does not consent to the resignation, it will set out its reasons in writing.

(5)   The bank liquidator, if not content with the Bank of England's response above, may apply to the court for directions in relation to any particular matter in the bank insolvency.

     [1355]

NOTES

Commencement: 25 February 2009.

54 Notice to Bank of England of intention to vacate office

(1)   This rule applies where the bank liquidator was appointed by a meeting of creditors.

PART IV
OTHER STATUTORY INSTRUMENTS

(2)   Where the bank liquidator intends to vacate office, whether by resignation or otherwise, he shall give notice of his intention to the Bank of England together with notice of any creditors' meeting to be held in respect of his vacation of office, including any meeting to be notified of his resignation.

(3)   The Bank of England must be given at least 21 days before any such creditors' meeting.

(4)   Where there remains any property of the bank which has not been realised, applied, distributed or otherwise fully dealt with in the bank insolvency, the bank liquidator shall include in his notice to the Bank of England details of the nature of that property, its value (or the fact that it has no value), its location, any action taken by the bank liquidator to deal with that property or any reason for his not dealing with it, and the current position in relation to it.

[1356]

NOTES

Commencement: 25 February 2009.

55   Power of court to set aside certain transactions

(1)   Apply rule 4.38 of the 1986 Rules.

(2)   In rule 4.38(2) of that Rule—
    (a)   leave out "either";
    (b)   leave out "or" at the end of sub-paragraph (a); and
    (c)   after sub-paragraph (b) insert—

", or (c) it is shown to the court's satisfaction that the transaction was entered into by the bank liquidator for the purpose of achieving Objective 1.".

[1357]

NOTES

Commencement: 25 February 2009.

56   Rule against solicitation

Apply rule 4.39 of the 1986 Rules.

[1358]

NOTES

Commencement: 25 February 2009.

PART 9
THE LIQUIDATION COMMITTEE

57   Application of rules

The rules in this Part apply only in relation to the liquidation committee established under rule 23 after a full payment resolution has been passed.

[1359]

NOTES

Commencement: 25 February 2009.

58   Membership of committee

(1)   Apply rule 4.41 of the 1986 Rules.

(2)   For rule 4.41(1) substitute—

"(1)   Subject to rule 4.43 of the 1986 Rules as applied by rule 56 of the 2009 Rules, the liquidation committee shall consist of either 3 or 5 creditors of the bank, elected by the meeting of creditors held under rule 23 of those Rules.".

(3)   Ignore paragraphs (3) and (6) and in paragraph (5) ignore any reference to contributory members.

[1360]

NOTES

Commencement: 25 February 2009.

59   Formalities of establishment

(1)   Apply rule 4.42 of the 1986 Rules.

[1361]

NOTES
Commencement: 25 February 2009.
This rule is reproduced as it appears in the original Queen's Printer's copy; there is no paragraph (2).

60 Committee established by contributories

(1) Apply rule 4.43 of the 1986 Rules.

(2) For rule 4.43(1) of that rule substitute—

"(1) This rule applies where the outcome of the creditors' meeting summoned by the bank liquidator under rule 23 of the 2009 Rules is, by virtue of rule 24(3), that the liquidation committee ceases to exist at the end of the meeting".

(3) In rule 4.43(2) omit "Section 138 or".

(4) In rule 4.43(4) omit "at least 3 and not more than 5" and substitute "3 or 5".

[1362]

NOTES
Commencement: 25 February 2009.

61 Obligations of liquidator to committee

Apply rule 4.44 of the 1986 Rules.

[1363]

NOTES
Commencement: 25 February 2009.

62 Meetings of the committee

Apply rule 4.45 of the 1986 Rules.

[1364]

NOTES
Commencement: 25 February 2009.

63 The chair at meetings

Apply rule 4.46 of the 1986 Rules.

[1365]

NOTES
Commencement: 25 February 2009.

64 Quorum

Apply rule 4.47 of the 1986 Rules.

[1366]

NOTES
Commencement: 25 February 2009.

65 Committee members' representatives

Apply rule 4.48 of the 1986 Rules.

[1367]

NOTES
Commencement: 25 February 2009.

66 Resignation

Apply rule 4.49 of the 1986 Rules.

[1368]

NOTES
Commencement: 25 February 2009.

67 Termination of membership

Apply rule 4.50 of the 1986 Rules.

[1369]

NOTES
Commencement: 25 February 2009.

68 Removal

Apply rule 4.51 of the 1986 Rules.

[1370]

NOTES
Commencement: 25 February 2009.

69 Vacancy (creditor members)

Apply rule 4.52 of the 1986 Rules.

[1371]

NOTES
Commencement: 25 February 2009.

70 Vacancy (contributory members)

Apply rule 4.53 of the 1986 Rules.

[1372]

NOTES
Commencement: 25 February 2009.

71 Voting rights and resolutions

Apply rule 4.54 of the 1986 Rules.

[1373]

NOTES
Commencement: 25 February 2009.

72 Resolutions by post

(1) Apply rule 4.55 of the 1986 Rules.

(2) Ignore rule 4.55(3) and (4).

[1374]

NOTES
Commencement: 25 February 2009.

73 Liquidator's reports

(1) Apply rule 4.56 of the 1986 Rules.

(2) At the end of rule 4.56(1) insert "but does not apply to the FSCS".

[1375]

NOTES
Commencement: 25 February 2009.

74 Expenses of members, etc

Apply rule 4.57(1) of the 1986 Rules.

[1376]

NOTES
Commencement: 25 February 2009.

75 Dealings by committee-members and others

Apply rule 4.58 of the 1986 Rules.

[1377]

NOTES
Commencement: 25 February 2009.

76 Composition of committee when creditors paid in full

(1) Apply rule 4.59 of the 1986 Rules.

(2)   For rule 4.59(4) substitute "The members of the liquidation committee will cease to be members at the end of the final meeting held under rule 44 of the 2009 Rules."

[1378]

NOTES
Commencement: 25 February 2009.

77   Formal defects

Apply rule 4.59A of the 1986 Rules.

[1379]

NOTES
Commencement: 25 February 2009.

PART 10
DISTRIBUTION OF BANK ASSETS

78   Order of priority in distribution

Apply rule 4.66 of the 1986 Rules.

[1380]

NOTES
Commencement: 25 February 2009.

79   Order of priority of expenses of liquidation

Apply rule 4.67 of the 1986 Rules.

[1381]

NOTES
Commencement: 25 February 2009.

80   Application of the Bankruptcy Act

Apply rule 4.68 of the 1986 Rules.

[1382]

NOTES
Commencement: 25 February 2009.

PART 11
SPECIAL MANAGER

81   Appointment and remuneration

Apply rule 4.69 of the 1986 Rules.

[1383]

NOTES
Commencement: 25 February 2009.

82   Caution

Apply rule 4.70 of the 1986 Rules.

[1384]

NOTES
Commencement: 25 February 2009.

83   Failure to find or maintain caution

Apply rule 4.71 of the 1986 Rules.

[1385]

NOTES
Commencement: 25 February 2009.

84   Accounting

Apply rule 4.72 of the 1986 Rules.

[1386]

NOTES
Commencement: 25 February 2009.

85 Termination of appointment

Apply rule 4.73 of the 1986 Rules.

[1387]

NOTES
Commencement: 25 February 2009.

PART 12
MISCELLANEOUS

86 Secretary of State's directions under section 116 of the 2009 Act

(1)   Where the Secretary of State gives a direction under section 116 of the 2009 Act (application by an interested person for postponement of dissolution) the Secretary of State shall send two copies of the direction to that applicant for it.

(2)   Of those copies, one shall be sent by the applicant to the registrar of companies to comply with section 116(4) of the 2009 Act.

[1388]

NOTES
Commencement: 25 February 2009.

87 Procedure following appeal under section 116 of the 2009 Act

Following an appeal under section 116(2) of the 2009 Act (against a decision of the Secretary of State under the applicable section) the court shall send two certified copies of its order to the person in whose favour the appeal was determined; and that party shall send one of the copies to the registrar of companies.

[1389]

NOTES
Commencement: 25 February 2009.

88 Limitation

Apply rule 4.76 of the 1986 Rules.

[1390]

NOTES
Commencement: 25 February 2009.

89 Dissolution after winding up

Apply rule 4.77 of the 1986 Rules.

[1391]

NOTES
Commencement: 25 February 2009.

PART 13
COMPANY WITH PROHIBITED NAME

90 Preliminary

(1)   Apply rule 4.78 of the 1986 Rules.

(2)   In paragraph (c) of that rule, omit the words from "whether" to the end.

[1392]

NOTES
Commencement: 25 February 2009.

91 Application for leave under section 216(3) before passing of full payment resolution

Where an application for leave under section 216 of the 1986 Act is made before a full payment resolution has been passed, it may only be made with the consent of the bank liquidator.

[1393]

NOTES
Commencement: 25 February 2009.

92 Application for leave under section 216(3)

Apply rule 4.79 of the 1986 Rules.

[1394]

NOTES
Commencement: 25 February 2009.

93 First excepted case

(1)   Apply rule 4.80 of the 1986 Rules.

(2)   In rule 4.80(1)(b)(ii) ignore the reference to Administrator.

[1395]

NOTES
Commencement: 25 February 2009.

94 Second excepted case

Apply rule 4.81 of the 1986 Rules.

[1396]

NOTES
Commencement: 25 February 2009.

95 Third excepted case

(1)   Apply rule 4.82 of the 1986 Rules.

(2)   In rule 4.82(a), for the words "liquidating company went into liquidation", substitute "bank went into bank insolvency".

(3)   In rule 4.82(b), for the words "section 252(5) of the Companies Act", substitute "section 1169 of the Companies Act 2006".

[1397]

NOTES
Commencement: 25 February 2009.

96 Further exception

The court's leave under section 216(3) of the 1986 Act is not required in respect of anything done by a person in connection with the exercise of a stabilisation power under Part 1 of the 2009 Act.

[1398]

NOTES
Commencement: 25 February 2009.

PART 14
MEETINGS

97 Summoning of meetings

Apply rule 7.2 of the 1986 Rules.

[1399]

NOTES
Commencement: 25 February 2009.

98 Notice of meeting

(1)   Apply rule 7.3 of the 1986 Rules.

(2)   Ignore rule 7.3(2) and (7).

(3)   For rule 7.3(3) substitute "The convenor may also publish notice of the date, time and place of the meeting in such newspaper as he thinks most appropriate for ensuring that it comes to the notice of the persons who are entitled to attend the meeting.".

(4)   In rule 7.3(3A) omit "or, in cases" to the end.

PART IV OTHER STATUTORY INSTRUMENTS

(5)   In rule 7.3(4), for the words "section 171(2) or 172(2)", substitute "section 108 of the 2009 Act".

[1400]

NOTES
Commencement: 25 February 2009.

99   Chair of meetings

(1)   Meetings shall be chaired by the bank liquidator or a person nominated in writing by the bank liquidator.

(2)   A person nominated under paragraph (1) must be—
    (a)   qualified to act as an insolvency practitioner in accordance with section 390 of the 1986 Act; or
    (b)   an employee of the bank liquidator or of the bank liquidator's firm who is experienced in insolvency matters.

[1401]

NOTES
Commencement: 25 February 2009.

100   Meetings requisitioned

(1)   Apply rule 7.6(1) to (8) of the 1986 Rules.

(2)   For rule 7.6(1) substitute "Subject to paragraph (8), this rule applies to any request by a creditor or creditors to a bank liquidator for a meeting of creditors, separate meetings of creditors or contributories or for any other meeting under any other provision of the 1986 Act as applied by the 2009 Act, or these rules.".

(3)   In rule 7.6(3), (4) and (5) ignore "the administrator, or, as the case may be".

[1402]

NOTES
Commencement: 25 February 2009.

101   Requisitioned meetings reforming the liquidation committee

(1)   Rule 7.6 of the 1986 Act also applies where—
    (a)   the liquidation committee has ceased to exist at the end of the first meeting of creditors under rule 24 and no further steps have been taken to re-establish that committee; and
    (b)   the bank liquidator has been requested by no less than one-tenth in value of the bank's creditors to summon a meeting for the purpose of re-establishing the liquidation committee.

(2)   Where a meeting is requisitioned to reform the liquidation committee, the time periods set out in rule 7.6 of the 1986 Rules may be expedited by the bank liquidator on request of the bank's creditors.

(3)   The bank liquidator shall give notice of the meeting to the FSA and the Bank of England.

(4)   Rule 24(1), (2) and (3) shall then apply at this meeting as it were the first meeting of the creditors.

[1403]

NOTES
Commencement: 25 February 2009.

102   Quorum

Apply rule 7.7 of the 1986 Rules.

[1404]

NOTES
Commencement: 25 February 2009.

103   Adjournment

Apply rule 7.8(1) to (6) of the 1986 Rules.

[1405]

NOTES
Commencement: 25 February 2009.

104   Entitlement to vote (creditors)

Apply rule 7.9(1) to (3) of the 1986 Rules.

[1406]

NOTES
Commencement: 25 February 2009.

105   Entitlement to vote (members and contributories)

Apply rule 7.10 of the 1986 Rules.

[1407]

NOTES
Commencement: 25 February 2009.

106   Chair of meeting as proxy holder

Apply rule 7.11(1) of the 1986 Rules.

[1408]

NOTES
Commencement: 25 February 2009.

107   Resolutions

Apply rule 7.12 of the 1986 Rules.

[1409]

NOTES
Commencement: 25 February 2009.

108   Report of meeting

Apply rule 7.13 of the 1986 Rules.

[1410]

NOTES
Commencement: 25 February 2009.

109   Application under section 176A(5) to disapply section 176A

Apply rule 7.13A of the 1986 Rules.

[1411]

NOTES
Commencement: 25 February 2009.

110   Notice of order under section 176A(5)

(1)   Apply rule 7.13B of the 1986 Rules.

(2)   In rule 7.13B(1)(b) omit the words "receiver or".

[1412]

NOTES
Commencement: 25 February 2009.

111   Definition of "proxy"

Apply rule 7.14 of the 1986 Rules.

[1413]

NOTES
Commencement: 25 February 2009.

112   Form of proxy

Apply rule 7.15 of the 1986 Rules.

[1414]

NOTES
Commencement: 25 February 2009.

113 Use of proxy at meeting

Apply rule 7.16 of the 1986 Rules.

[1415]

NOTES
Commencement: 25 February 2009.

114 Retention of proxies

Apply rule 7.17 of the 1986 Rules.

[1416]

NOTES
Commencement: 25 February 2009.

115 Right of inspection

(1) Apply rule 7.18 of the 1986 Rules.

(2) In rule 7.18(1)(b) for the words "a company's members or", substitute "the company's".

(3) For rule 7.18 (2) substitute—

"(2) The reference in paragraph (1) to creditors is to those creditors whose claims have been accepted in whole or in part but does not include a person whose claim has been wholly rejected for purposes of voting, dividend or otherwise.".

[1417]

NOTES
Commencement: 25 February 2009.

116 Proxy holder with financial interest

Apply rule 7.19 of the 1986 Rules.

[1418]

NOTES
Commencement: 25 February 2009.

117 Representation of corporations

(1) Apply rule 7.20 of the 1986 Rules.

(2) In rule 7.20(1) the reference to section 375 of the Companies Act should be read as section 323 of the Companies Act 2006.

(3) For rule 7.20(2), substitute "The copy resolution must be signed or subscribed by or on behalf of the bank in accordance with the provisions of the Requirements of Writing (Scotland) Act 1995 or certified by the secretary or director of the bank to be a true copy.".

[1419]

NOTES
Commencement: 25 February 2009.

PART 15
GENERAL PROVISIONS

118 Giving of notices, etc

(1) Apply rule 7.21 of the 1986 Rules.

(2) In rule 7.21(1) for the words "the Act or the Rules" substitute "the Act as applied by the 2009 Act or these Rules".

[1420]

NOTES
Commencement: 25 February 2009.

119 Service outside the United Kingdom

Where, for the purposes of bank insolvency proceedings, there is a requirement to effect service on a person outwith the United Kingdom, the court may, on application, order service to be effected in such manner as it thinks fit.

[1421]

NOTES
Commencement: 25 February 2009.

120   Sending by post
Apply rule 7.22 of the 1986 Rules.

[1422]

NOTES
Commencement: 25 February 2009.

121   Certificate of giving notice, etc
Apply rule 7.23 of the 1986 Rules.

[1423]

NOTES
Commencement: 25 February 2009.

122   Validity of proceedings
(1)   Apply rule 7.24 of the 1986 Rules.

(2)   For the words "the Act or the Rules", substitute "the Act as applied by the 2009 Act or these Rules".

[1424]

NOTES
Commencement: 25 February 2009.

123   Evidence of proceedings at meetings
Apply rule 7.25 of the 1986 Rules.

[1425]

NOTES
Commencement: 25 February 2009.

124   Right to list of creditors and copy documents
(1)   Apply rule 7.26 of the 1986 Rules.

(2)   Apply rule 7.26 of the 1986 Rules.

(3)   For rule 7.26(1) substitute "Paragraph (2) applies to bank insolvency proceedings.".

(4)   Ignore rule 7.26(2A) where it first occurs referring to Member State Liquidator.

[1426]

NOTES
Commencement: 25 February 2009.

125   Confidentiality of documents
Apply rule 7.27 of the 1986 Rules.

[1427]

NOTES
Commencement: 25 February 2009.

126   Insolvency practitioner's caution
(1)   Apply rule 7.28 of the 1986 Rules.

(2)   For rule 7.28(2) substitute "It is the duty of the liquidation committee in a bank insolvency to review from time to time the adequacy of the bank liquidator's caution.".

[1428]

NOTES
Commencement: 25 February 2009.

PART IV   OTHER STATUTORY INSTRUMENTS

127   Forms for use in insolvency proceedings

The forms contained in Schedule 5 to the 1986 Rules shall be used, with such variations as circumstances require.

[1429]

NOTES

Commencement: 25 February 2009.

128   Fees, expenses, etc

Apply rule 7.31 of the 1986 Rules.

[1430]

NOTES

Commencement: 25 February 2009.

129   Power of court to cure defects in procedure

Apply rule 7.32 of the 1986 Rules.

[1431]

NOTES

Commencement: 25 February 2009.

130   Sederunt book

(1)   Apply rule 7.33 of the 1986 Rules.

(2)   In rule 7.33 for the words "the Act or of the Rules", substitute "the Act as applied by the 2009 Act and these Rules".

[1432]

NOTES

Commencement: 25 February 2009.

131   Disposal of company's books, papers and other records

Apply rule 7.34(1) and (3) of the 1986 Rules.

[1433]

NOTES

Commencement: 25 February 2009.

132   Information about time spent on a case

Apply rule 7.36 of the 1986 Rules.

[1434]

NOTES

Commencement: 25 February 2009.

BANK INSOLVENCY (ENGLAND AND WALES) RULES 2009

(SI 2009/356)

NOTES

Made: 23 February 2009.
Authority: Insolvency Act 1986, s 411(1A)(a), (2), (2C), (3).
Commencement: 25 February 2009.

ARRANGEMENT OF RULES

PART 1
INTRODUCTORY PROVISIONS

PART 7
PROOF OF DEBTS

PART 8
SECURED CREDITORS

PART 9
THE BANK LIQUIDATOR

CHAPTER 1
GENERAL

CHAPTER 2
RESIGNATION AND REMOVAL

CHAPTER 3
RELEASE ON COMPLETION OF WINDING UP

CHAPTER 4
REMUNERATION

PART 20
EXAMINATION OF PERSONS CONCERNED IN BANK INSOLVENCY

PART 21
DECLARATION AND PAYMENT OF DIVIDEND

PART 22
MISCELLANEOUS AND GENERAL

PART 23
INTERPRETATION

PART 1
INTRODUCTORY PROVISIONS

1 Citation and commencement

These Rules may be cited as the Bank Insolvency (England and Wales) Rules 2009 and come into force on 25th February 2009.

[1435]

NOTES
Commencement: 25 February 2009.

2 Extent

These Rules extend to England and Wales only.

[1436]

NOTES
Commencement: 25 February 2009.

3 Application of rules, construction and interpretation

(1)   These Rules apply in relation to a bank undergoing the procedure in Part 2 of the Banking Act 2009 known as bank insolvency.

(2)   In these Rules—
"the 1985 Act" means the Companies Act 1985;
"the 1986 Act" means the Insolvency Act 1986 (and includes those provisions as applied by section 103 of the 2009 Act);
"the 1986 Rules" means the Insolvency Rules 1986;
"the 2006 Act" means the Companies Act 2006;
"the 2009 Act" means the Banking Act 2009;
"bank" means the bank (as defined by section 91(1) of the 2009 Act) which is or is to be the subject of the bank insolvency order;
"CPR" means the Civil Procedure Rules 1998;
"the FSA" means the Financial Services Authority;
"the FSCS" means the Financial Services Compensation Scheme (established under Part 15 of the Financial Services and Markets Act 2000) or, where appropriate, the scheme manager of that scheme;
"the insolvent" means the bank that has been put into bank insolvency;
"liquidation committee" means the committee established pursuant to section 100 of the 2009 Act;
"personal service" has the meaning given in Part 6 of the CPR;
"registered address" has the meaning given by section 1140 of the 2006 Act;
"sealed" means sealed with the seal of the court under which the application was made: and
"statement of truth" has the meaning set out in Part 22 of the CPR.

(3)   These Rules consist of—
(a)   the rules set out in full;
(b)   in the case of a rule applying a rule in Part 4, 7, 8, 9, 11, 12 or 13 of the 1986 Rules, the rule so applied with—
(i)   the modifications set out in paragraph (4),
(ii)   the modifications contained in the rule applying it, and
(iii)   any other necessary modification;
(c)   the Schedule, which applies the relevant schedules of the 1986 Rules.

(4)   The modifications are that where applicable, a reference to—
(a)   the 1986 Act (or to "the Act") is a reference to that Act as applied, with modifications, by the 2009 Act, (and includes, where appropriate, a reference to Part 2 of the 2009 Act.)
(b)   the 1986 Rules (or to "the Rules") is a reference to these Rules,
(c)   an affidavit is a reference to a witness statement,
(d)   the commencement of winding up is a reference to the commencement of bank insolvency,
(e)   the chairman is a reference to the chair,
(f)   a reference to a company is a reference to a bank,
(g)   going into liquidation is a reference to entering bank insolvency,
(h)   insolvency proceedings is a reference to bank insolvency proceedings,
(i)   the official receiver should be ignored unless otherwise stated,
(j)   a petition for winding up is a reference to an application for bank insolvency under section 95 of the 2009 Act,
(k)   a petitioner is a reference to an applicant,
(l)   the provisional liquidator is a reference to the provisional bank liquidator,

(m) winding up is a reference to bank insolvency,

(n) winding up by the court is a reference to a bank being placed into bank insolvency by the court, and

(o) a winding-up order is a reference to a bank insolvency order.

(5) Expressions used—

(a) both in a rule set out in full and in Part 2 of the 2009 Act, or

(b) both in a modification to a rule from the 1986 Rules applied by these Rules and in Part 2 of the 2009 Act,

have the same meaning as in Part 2 of the 2009 Act.

(6) Where a rule applies a rule of the 1986 Rules and modifies that rule by inserting or substituting text—

(a) any reference in the modified rule to the 2009 Rules is a reference to these rules;

(b) expressions inserted or substituted have the same meaning as in these rules.

(7) Where a rule in the 1986 Rules (Rule A) contains a reference to another such rule (Rule B) and—

(a) both Rule A and Rule B are applied by these Rules, or

(b) Rule A is applied by and the provision in Rule B to which Rule A refers is substantially repeated in these Rules,

the reference in Rule A shall be treated, for the purpose of these Rules, as being, respectively, to the rule in these Rules that applies Rule B or the provision in these Rules that substantially repeats the provision in Rule B.

(8) Where a rule (Rule A) refers to another rule (Rule B), and Rule B applies a rule of the 1986 Rules (Rule C) with or without modifications, the reference in Rule A includes a reference to Rule C as applied to Rule B.

(9) Any notice or document required to sent electronically by these Rules shall be treated as having been sent to the person if—

(a) it is sent by email to the person's last known email address, and

(b) the email contains a prompt asking the person for an electronic receipt saying that the email has been read.

(10) Where the rules provide for a witness statement (either expressly, or through the application of the 1986 Rules as modified above)—

(a) that statement is a reference to a witness statement verified by a statement of truth in accordance with Part 22 of the CPR, and

(b) if the statement is made by the bank liquidator or provisional bank liquidator, the statement should state as such and should include the address at which that person works.

[1437]

NOTES

Commencement: 25 February 2009.

4 Overview

The purpose of these Rules is to provide a procedure for the appointment of a bank liquidator and the operation of bank insolvency under Part 2 of the 2009 Act in England and Wales.

[1438]

NOTES

Commencement: 25 February 2009.

5 Forms

(1) This Rule applies where a provision of these Rules—

(a) applies a provision of the Insolvency Rules 1986 which requires the use of a prescribed form, or

(b) makes provision similar to that made by a provision of those Rules which requires the use of a prescribed form.

(2) The form prescribed for the purposes of those Rules is to be used with any modification that the person using the form thinks desirable to reflect the nature of bank insolvency (whether or not the modification is set out in a Practice Form issued by the Treasury for that purpose).

[1439]

NOTES

Commencement: 25 February 2009.

6   Time Limits

(1)   Where by any provision of the 1986 Act, the 2009 Act or these Rules, the time for doing anything is limited, the court may extend the time, either before or after it has expired, on such terms, if any, as it thinks fit.

(2)   If the court's consideration of whether to extend the time for doing anything takes place before a full payment resolution has been passed, the court shall only extend the time if it considers that the resulting delay will not significantly prejudice the achievement of Objective 1.

[1440]

NOTES

Commencement: 25 February 2009.

PART 2
APPLICATION FOR ORDER

7   Filing of application

(1)   The application for a bank insolvency order, verified by witness statement in accordance with rule 11, shall be filed in court.

(2)   There shall be filed with the application—
    (a)   1 copy for service on the bank,
    (b)   1 copy to be attached to the proof of service, and
    (c)   further copies to be sent to those persons under rule 10.

(3)   The court shall fix the venue, date and time for the hearing of the application and in doing so shall have regard to—
    (a)   the desirability of the application being heard as soon as is reasonably practicable, and
    (b)   the need to give the bank a reasonable opportunity to attend.

(4)   Each of the copies issued to the applicant shall be sealed and be endorsed with the venue, date and time for the hearing.

(5)   Any application filed in relation to a bank in respect of which there is in force a voluntary arrangement under Part 1 of the 1986 Act shall be filed in accordance with this rule, but a copy of that application shall also be sent to the court to which the nominee's report under section 2 of the 1986 Act was submitted, if that is not the same court.

[1441]

NOTES

Commencement: 25 February 2009.

8   Service of application

(1)   The applicant shall serve the bank with a sealed copy of the application.

(2)   The application shall be served on the bank by personal service at its registered office.

(3)   In paragraph (2) "registered office" means—
    (a)   the place which is specified, in the bank's statement delivered under section 9 of the 2006 Act or, before that section comes into force, section 10 of the 1985 Act as the intended situation of its registered office on incorporation, or
    (b)   if notice has been given by the bank to the registrar of companies under section 87 of the 2006 Act or, before that section comes into force, section 287 of the 1985 Act, the place specified in that notice or, as the case may be, in the last such notice.

(4)   Service of the application at the registered office may be effected in any of the following ways—
    (a)   it may be handed to a person who there and then acknowledges that they are , or to the best of the server's knowledge, information and belief are, a director or other officer, or employee, of the bank, or
    (b)   it may be handed to a person who there and then acknowledges that they are authorised to accept service documents on the company's behalf, or
    (c)   in the absence of such person as is mentioned in sub-paragraphs (a) and (b), it may be deposited at or about the registered office in such a way that it is likely to come to the notice of a person attending the office.

(5)   If for any reason it is impracticable to effect service as provided by paragraph (2) or (4), the application may be served in such other manner as the court may approve or direct.

(6)   Application for permission of the court under paragraph (5) may be made without notice to the bank, stating in a witness statement what steps have been taken to comply with paragraph (2) or (4), and the reasons why it is impracticable to effect service as there provided.

PART IV
OTHER STATUTORY INSTRUMENTS

(7)   If the bank or its legal representatives fail to attend the hearing, the court may make the bank insolvency order in its absence if satisfied that the application has been served in accordance with this rule.

[1442]

NOTES
Commencement: 25 February 2009.

9   Proof of service
Apply rule 4.9 of the 1986 Rules.

[1443]

NOTES
Commencement: 25 February 2009.

10   Other persons to receive copy of application
(1)   The applicant shall send a sealed copy of the application to—
   (a)   the proposed bank liquidator,
   (b)   the Bank of England, (if it is not the applicant,)
   (c)   the FSA, (if it is not the applicant,)
   (d)   the FSCS,
   (e)   on any person who has given notice to the FSA in respect of the bank under section 120 of the Banking Act 2009,
   (f)   if there is in force for the bank a voluntary arrangement under Part 1 of the 1986 Act, the supervisor of that arrangement, and
   (g)   if an administrative receiver has been appointed in relation to the bank, that receiver,
in accordance with paragraph (2).

(2)   1 copy shall be sent electronically as soon as practicable and the other shall be sent by first class post on the business day on which the application is served on the bank.

(3)   Any of the persons in sub-paragraph (1) will have the right to attend and be heard at the hearing of the application.

[1444]

NOTES
Commencement: 25 February 2009.

11   Verification of application
(1)   This applies where an application has been filed at the court under rule 7 above.

(2)   A witness statement shall be attached to the application to state that the statements in the application are true, or are true to the best of the applicant's knowledge, information and belief.

(3)   The witness statement should identify the person making the statement and should include the capacity in which that person makes the statement and the basis for that person's knowledge of the matters set out in the application.

(4)   The witness statement is, unless proved otherwise, evidence of the statements in the application.

[1445]

NOTES
Commencement: 25 February 2009.

12   Persons entitled to copy of application
(1)   Every contributory or creditor of the bank is entitled to a copy of the application on request from the applicant.

(2)   The applicant shall respond to any request for a copy of the application as soon as reasonably practicable after the application has been made on payment of the appropriate fee.

[1446]

NOTES
Commencement: 25 February 2009.

13   Certificate of compliance
(1)   Apply rule 4.14 of the 1986 Rules.

(2)   In paragraph (1) the period for filing shall be as soon as reasonably practicable before the hearing of the application.

(3)   In paragraph (2), leave out the words "a copy of the advertisement" to the end, and insert—

"A witness statement made by the proposed bank liquidator to the effect that—

    (c)   the person is qualified to act as an insolvency practitioner in accordance with section 390 of the 1986 Act, and

    (d)   the person consents to act as the bank liquidator,

shall be filed in court with the certificate."

[1447]

NOTES
Commencement: 25 February 2009.

14   Leave for the applicant to withdraw

Apply rule 4.15 of the 1986 Rules. Leave out "at least 5 days" and ignore sub-paragraph (a).

[1448]

NOTES
Commencement: 25 February 2009.

15   Witness statement in opposition

(1)   If the bank intends to oppose an application, the bank or a director of the bank may (but need not) file a witness statement in opposition in court.

(2)   A statement under paragraph (1) must be filed before the hearing of the application and a copy must be served on the applicant, before the hearing.

(3)   The statement may be served on the applicant by personal service or by electronic means.

(4)   The statement should also be sent to the persons in rule 10(1) before the hearing by personal service or by electronic means.

(5)   The fact that the neither the bank nor its directors have filed a statement under this rule shall not prevent any of those persons or their legal representatives from being heard at the hearing.

[1449]

NOTES
Commencement: 25 February 2009.

16   Making, transmission and advertisement of order

(1)   The court shall not make a bank insolvency order unless the person nominated to be appointed as the bank liquidator in the application for the order has filed in court a witness statement under rule 13.

(2)   When the bank insolvency order has been made the court shall immediately send 5 sealed copies (or such larger number as the bank liquidator may have requested) to the bank liquidator.

(3)   The court shall also, if practicable, immediately send a sealed copy of the order to the bank liquidator electronically.

(4)   The bank liquidator shall serve a sealed copy of the order on the bank at its registered office and, where the bank liquidator knows the bank's email address, will send an electronic copy to the bank.

(5)   The bank liquidator shall send a sealed copy of the order—

    (a)   to the Bank of England, the FSA and the FSCS (electronically or otherwise), and

    (b)   to the registrar of companies in accordance with section 130(1) of the 1986 Act (as applied by the 2009 Act).

(6)   The bank liquidator shall as soon as reasonably practicable—

    (a)   cause the order to be gazetted, and

    (b)   advertise the order in such other manner as the bank liquidator thinks fit.

[1450]

NOTES
Commencement: 25 February 2009.

17 Authentication of bank liquidator's appointment

A sealed copy of the court's order may in any proceedings be adduced as proof that the person appointed is duly authorised to exercise the powers and perform the duties of the bank liquidator in the bank insolvency.

[1451]

NOTES
Commencement: 25 February 2009.

18 Initial duties of bank liquidation committee

(1)   As soon as reasonably practicable after the making of a bank insolvency order, the liquidation committee will meet the bank liquidator for the purpose of discussing which of the objectives, or combination of objectives, mentioned in section 102(1) of the 2009 Act, the committee should recommend the bank liquidator to pursue.

(2)   If the bank liquidator and every individual on the liquidation committee agree, the meeting may be held by audio or video conference.

(3)   The liquidation committee will make its recommendation to the bank liquidator at the meeting.

(4)   The Bank of England will confirm the liquidation committee's recommendation in writing as soon as practicable after the meeting.

(5)   As soon as practicable after the making of a bank insolvency order, the liquidation committee shall also pass a resolution as to the terms on which, in accordance with rule 98, the bank liquidator is to be remunerated.

(6)   Until a full payment resolution has been passed, the bank liquidation committee—
    (a)   shall take decisions and pass resolutions by a simple majority, and
    (b)   for the purpose of taking decisions and passing resolutions, may communicate by any means that its members consider convenient.

[1452]

NOTES
Commencement: 25 February 2009.

19 Expenses of voluntary arrangement

Apply rule 4.21A of the 1986 Rules.

[1453]

NOTES
Commencement: 25 February 2009.

PART 3
PROVISIONAL BANK LIQUIDATOR

20 Appointment of provisional bank liquidator

(1)   The rule applies after an application for a bank insolvency order has been filed under rule 7 and before that order is made.

(2)   An application to the court for the appointment of a provisional bank liquidator under section 135 of the Act may be made—
    (a)   by the Bank of England,
    (b)   by the FSA, (with the consent of the Bank of England), or
    (c)   by the Secretary of State.

(3)   The application must be supported by a witness statement stating—
    (a)   the grounds upon which it is proposed that the provisional bank liquidator should be appointed;
    (b)   that the person to be appointed has consented to act,
    (c)   that the person to be appointed is qualified to act as an insolvency practitioner,
    (d)   whether to the applicant's knowledge—
        (i)   there has been proposed or is in force for the bank a company voluntary arrangement under Part 1 of the 1986 Act, or
        (ii)   an administrative receiver is acting in relation to the bank.
    (e)   the applicant's estimate of the value of the assets in respect of which the provisional bank liquidator is to be appointed, and
    (f)   the functions the applicant wishes to be carried out by the provisional bank liquidator in relation to the bank's affairs.

(4)   The court may on the application, if satisfied that sufficient grounds are shown for the appointment, make it on such terms as it thinks fit.

    [1454]

NOTES
Commencement: 25 February 2009.

21 Notice of appointment

Where a provisional bank liquidator has been appointed, the court shall notify the applicant and the person appointed.

    [1455]

NOTES
Commencement: 25 February 2009.

22 Order of appointment

(1)   The order of appointment shall specify the functions to be carried out by the provisional bank liquidator in relation to the bank's affairs.

(2)   The court shall, immediately after the order is made, send 4 sealed copies of the order (or such larger number as the provisional bank liquidator may have requested), to the provisional bank liquidator.

(3)   The court shall also, if practicable, immediately send a sealed copy of the order to the provisional bank liquidator electronically.

(4)   The provisional bank liquidator shall serve a sealed copy of the order on the bank at its registered office and, where the provisional bank liquidator knows the bank's email address, will send an electronic copy to the bank.

(5)   The bank liquidator shall send a sealed copy of the order—
    (a)   to the Bank of England, the FSA, and the FSCS (electronically or otherwise), and
    (b)   to the registrar of companies, and
    (c)   (if applicable) to any administrative receiver of the bank.

    [1456]

NOTES
Commencement: 25 February 2009.

23 Security

Apply rule 4.28 of the 1986 Rules.

    [1457]

NOTES
Commencement: 25 February 2009.

24 Failure to give or keep up security

Apply rule 4.29 of the 1986 Rules.

    [1458]

NOTES
Commencement: 25 February 2009.

25 Remuneration

Apply rule 4.30 of the 1986 Rules. Ignore paragraph (4).

    [1459]

NOTES
Commencement: 25 February 2009.

26 Termination of appointment

(1)   Apply rule 4.31 of the 1986 Rules.

(2)   At the end insert—

    "(3)   On the making of a bank insolvency order the appointment of the provisional bank liquidator shall terminate.".

    [1460]

NOTES
Commencement: 25 February 2009.

PART 4
STATEMENT OF AFFAIRS AND OTHER INFORMATION

27 Notice requiring statement of affairs

(1) Apply rule 4.32 of the 1986 Rules. For "official receiver", substitute "Bank of England".

(2) In paragraph (3), for "Chapter" substitute "Part".

[1461]

NOTES
Commencement: 25 February 2009.

28 Verification and filing

(1) Apply rule 4.33 of the 1986 Rules.

(2) For paragraph (6), substitute—

"(6) The bank liquidator shall file the statement of affairs in court and shall send a copy of it to the registrar of companies."

(3) Ignore paragraph (7).

[1462]

NOTES
Commencement: 25 February 2009.

29 Limited disclosure

(1) Apply rule 4.35 of the 1986 Rules. In paragraph (1), for "official receiver", substitute "Bank of England".

(2) After paragraph (1), insert—

"(1A) The Bank of England may also apply to the court for an order of limited disclosure in respect of those depositors of the bank who, at the time of the making of the statement of affairs, still have a claim against the bank in respect of their deposits."

[1463]

NOTES
Commencement: 25 February 2009.

30 Release from duty to submit statement of affairs; extension of time

Apply rule 4.36 of the 1986 Rules. For "official receiver" substitute "bank liquidator."

[1464]

NOTES
Commencement: 25 February 2009.

31 Expenses of statement of affairs

Apply rule 4.37 of the 1986 Rules. For "official receiver", substitute "Bank of England".

[1465]

NOTES
Commencement: 25 February 2009.

32 Submission of accounts

Apply rule 4.39 of the 1986 Rules. For "official receiver", substitute "Bank of England".

[1466]

NOTES
Commencement: 25 February 2009.

33 Further disclosure

Apply rule 4.42 of the 1986 Rules. For "official receiver", substitute "Bank of England".

[1467]

NOTES
Commencement: 25 February 2009.

PART 5
INFORMATION TO CREDITORS AND CONTRIBUTORIES

34 Report by bank liquidator

(1)   The bank liquidator shall, at least once after the making of the bank insolvency order, make a report with respect to the proceedings in the bank insolvency and the state of the bank's affairs.

(2)   Regardless of whether the liquidation committee has passed a full payment resolution, the first report under paragraph (1) shall be, within 8 weeks of the commencement of the bank insolvency, made publicly available on the bank's website.

(3)   The bank liquidator shall include in the report under paragraph (1)—

(a)   a statement that the proceedings are being held in the High Court and the relevant court reference number;

(b)   the full name, registered office address, registered companies house number and any other trading names of the bank;

(c)   details relating to the bank liquidator's appointment, including the date of appointment, and where there are joint liquidators, details of—

(i)   which functions (if any) are to be exercised by the persons appointed acting jointly, and

(ii)   which functions (if any) are to be exercised by any of all of the persons appointed.

(d)   the names of the directors and secretary of the bank and details of any shareholdings in the bank that they have;

(e)   an account of the circumstances giving rise to the bank insolvency;

(f)   if a statement of affairs has been submitted, a copy of that statement;

(g)   if a statement of affairs has yet to be submitted—

(i)   subject to sub paragraph (ii), the names, addresses and details of any debts of the creditors, including details of any security held (or, in the case of depositors who still are creditors of the bank at the time the report is made, a single statement of their aggregate debt),

(ii)   details of the financial position of the bank at the latest practicable date (which must, unless the court orders otherwise, be a date not earlier than the commencement of bank insolvency);

(h)   the basis upon it has been proposed under rule 41, or, if the full payment resolution has yet to be passed, rule 18, that the bank liquidator's remuneration has been fixed;

(i)   to the best of the bank liquidator's knowledge and belief—

(i)   an estimate of the value of the prescribed part (within the meaning of section 176A of the 1986 Act) regardless of whether—

(aa)   the bank liquidator proposes to make an application to the court under section 176A(5) of that Act, or

(bb)   section 176A(3) of that Act applies, and

(ii)   an estimate of the value of the company's net property;

(j)   whether, and if so, why, the bank liquidator proposes to make an application to court under section 176A(5) of the 1986 Act;

(k)   a summary of—

(i)   how Objective 1 is being or has been achieved and an estimate of the costs to the bank liquidator of achieving it,

(ii)   the manner in which the affairs and business of the bank not involved in the achievement of Objective 1 have, since the commencement of the bank insolvency; been managed and financed, including, where any assets have been disposed of, the reasons for such disposals and the terms upon which such disposals were made, and

(iii)   how the affairs and business of the bank will continue to be managed and financed; and

(l)   an explanation of how it is envisaged the purpose of the bank liquidation will be achieved, including whether a dividend will be paid and an estimate as to the amount of this dividend and how it is proposed that the bank liquidation shall end.

(4)   Nothing in this rule is to be taken as requiring either estimate mentioned in paragraph (3) to include any information the disclosure of which could seriously prejudice the commercial interests of the company. If such information is excluded from the calculation the estimate shall be accompanied by a statement to that effect.

(5)   The bank liquidator shall file with the court a copy of any report sent under this rule.

PART IV
OTHER STATUTORY INSTRUMENTS

NOTES
Commencement: 25 February 2009.

35 Meaning of "creditors"
Apply rule 4.44 of the 1986 Rules.

[1469]

NOTES
Commencement: 25 February 2009.

36 Report where statement of affairs lodged
Apply rule 4.45 of the 1986 Rules. For "official receiver", substitute "Bank of England".

[1470]

NOTES
Commencement: 25 February 2009.

37 Statement of affairs dispensed with
Apply rule 4.46 of the 1986 Rules.

[1471]

NOTES
Commencement: 25 February 2009.

38 General rule as to reporting
(1) Apply rule 4.47 of the 1986 Rules.
(2) In paragraph (1), for "Chapter" substitute "Part".
(3) In paragraph (2), for "official receiver", substitute "Bank of England".

[1472]

NOTES
Commencement: 25 February 2009.

39 Bank insolvency stayed
(1) Apply rule 4.48 of the 1986 Rules.
(2) In paragraph (1), for "Chapter" substitute "Part".
(3) In paragraph (2), for "official receiver", substitute "Bank of England".

[1473]

NOTES
Commencement: 25 February 2009.

PART 6
MEETINGS OF CREDITORS AND CONTRIBUTORIES
RULES OF GENERAL APPLICATION

40 First meeting
(1) Once the liquidation committee passes a full payment resolution the bank liquidator shall—
    (a) immediately summon a meeting of the bank's creditors and a meeting of the bank's contributories, and
    (b) fix a venue, date and time for the meetings,
and the date must be within 3 months of the date on which the full payment resolution was passed.

(2) When the venue, date and time of the meetings have been fixed the bank liquidator shall give notice of the meetings to—
    (a) the court,
    (b) every creditor who is known to the bank liquidator or is identified in the bank's statement of affairs,
    (c) every person appearing (by the bank's books or otherwise) to be a contributory of the bank, and
    (d) each member of the liquidation committee,
and shall advertise the venue, date and time of the meetings in such manner as the bank liquidator thinks fit.

(3)   In giving the notice mentioned in paragraph (2) the bank liquidator shall, if practicable, indicate whether the present intention of the FSCS is to resign from the liquidation committee at the meeting.

(4)   Notice to the court and the members of the liquidation committee shall be given immediately; notice to creditors and contributories shall be given, and the advertisements placed to appear, at least 21 days before the date fixed for the meeting.

(5)   The notice to creditors shall specify a time and date, not more than 4 days before the date fixed for the meeting, by which they must lodge proofs and (if applicable) proxies, in order to be entitled to vote at the meeting.

(6)   The FSCS is entitled to be represented at the meeting and Schedule 1 to the 1986 Rules, as applied by rule 293, has effect with respect to its voting rights at such a meeting.

(7)   Meetings summoned under this rule are known respectively as "the first meeting of creditors" and "the first meeting of contributories", and jointly as "the first meetings in the bank liquidation."

[1474]

NOTES
Commencement: 25 February 2009.

41   Business at first meetings of creditors and contributories

(1)   At the first meeting of creditors the FSCS shall state whether or not it is resigning from the liquidation committee.

(2)   At that meeting those creditors present (or represented by proxy) may—
    (a)   where the FSCS has not resigned, elect 2 or 4 individuals as new members of the liquidation committee,
    (b)   where the FSCS has resigned, elect 3 or 5 individuals as new members of the liquidation committee,

in place of the members nominated by the Bank of England and the FSA. In accordance with section 100(6)(d) of the 2009 Act, the liquidation committee ceases to exist at the end of the meeting if no individuals are elected as mentioned or if the resulting committee would have fewer than 3 members or an even number of members. The maximum number of committee members will be 5.

(3)   At the first meeting of creditors no resolutions shall be taken other than the following—
    (a)   if an application has been made to the court by the creditors under rule 94 for the court to direct the bank liquidator to summon a meeting of creditors for the purpose of removing him, and the court has directed that a resolution may be passed to that effect at the first meeting of creditors,—
        (i)   a resolution to remove the bank liquidator (or a resolution to remove 1 or more of the bank liquidators if joint liquidators were originally appointed), and
        (ii)   a resolution to appoint a named insolvency practitioner to be bank liquidator or 2 or more insolvency practitioners as joint liquidators;
    (b)   if no individuals have been elected to form a liquidation committee under paragraph (2), a resolution specifying the terms on which the liquidator is to be remunerated, or to defer consideration of that matter;
    (c)   where 2 or more persons are appointed jointly to act as bank liquidator, a resolution specifying which acts are to be done by both of them, all of them or by only 1;
    (d)   a resolution to adjourn the meeting for not more than 3 weeks; and
    (e)   any other resolutions which the chair thinks it right to allow for special reasons.

(4)   At the first meeting of contributories, no resolutions shall be taken other than the following—
    (a)   if no individuals have been elected to form a liquidation committee under paragraph (2), a resolution to form a liquidation committee (and rule 117 shall then apply);
    (b)   a resolution to adjourn the meeting for not more than 3 weeks;
    (c)   any other resolutions which the chair thinks it right to allow for special reasons.

[1475]

NOTES
Commencement: 25 February 2009.

42   General power to call meetings

(1)   Apply rule 4.54 of the 1986 Rules.

(2)   Where the bank liquidator has been directed to summon a meeting of creditors under section 195 of the Act (as applied by section 109 of the 2009 Act) for the purpose of removing the bank liquidator, the bank liquidator shall give notice of the meeting to the Bank of England and the FSA.

[1476]

NOTES
Commencement: 25 February 2009.

43   The chair at meetings

(1)   Meetings shall be chaired by the bank liquidator or a person nominated in writing by the bank liquidator.

(2)   A person nominated under paragraph (1) must be—
   (a)   qualified to act as an insolvency practitioner in accordance with section 390 of the 1986 Act, or
   (b)   an employee of the bank liquidator or of the bank liquidator's firm who is experienced in insolvency matters.

[1477]

NOTES
Commencement: 25 February 2009.

44   Requisitioned meetings: general

(1)   Apply rule 4.57 of the 1986 Rules.

[1478]

NOTES
Commencement: 25 February 2009.
This rule is reproduced as it appears in the original Queen's Printer's copy; there is no paragraph (2).

45   Requisitioned meetings: reforming the liquidation committee

(1)   Rule 4.57 of the 1986 Rules also applies where—
   (a)   the liquidation committee has ceased to exist at the end of the first meeting of creditors under rule 41 and no further steps have been taken to re establish that committee; and
   (b)   the bank liquidator has been requested, by no less than one-tenth in value of the bank's creditors, to summon a meeting for the purpose of re-establishing the liquidation committee.

(2)   Where a meeting is requisitioned to re-establish the liquidation committee, the time periods set out in rule 4.57 of the 1986 Rules may be expedited by the bank liquidator on the request of the bank's creditors.

(3)   The bank liquidator shall give notice of the meeting to the FSA and Bank of England.

(4)   Rule 41(1) and (2) shall apply at this meeting as if it were the first meeting of creditors.

[1479]

NOTES
Commencement: 25 February 2009.

46   Attendance at meetings of bank's personnel

Apply rule 4.58 of the 1986 Rules.

[1480]

NOTES
Commencement: 25 February 2009.

47   Notice of meetings by advertisement only

Apply rule 4.59 of the 1986 Rules.

[1481]

NOTES
Commencement: 25 February 2009.

48   Venue

Apply rule 4.60 of the 1986 Rules.

[1482]

NOTES
Commencement: 25 February 2009.

49   Expenses of summoning meetings
Apply rule 4.61 of the 1986 Rules.

[1483]

NOTES
Commencement: 25 February 2009.

50   Resolutions
Apply rule 4.63 of the 1986 Rules.

[1484]

NOTES
Commencement: 25 February 2009.

51   Chair of meeting as proxy-holder
Apply rule 4.64 of the 1986 Rules.

[1485]

NOTES
Commencement: 25 February 2009.

52   Suspension and adjournment
(1)   Apply rule 4.65 of the 1986 Rules.
(2)   In paragraph (3), leave out "or, as the case may be, 4.114—CVL(3)".

[1486]

NOTES
Commencement: 25 February 2009.

53   Entitlement to vote (creditors)
(1)   Apply rule 4.67 of the 1986 Rules.
(2)   Ignore paragraph (ii) of paragraph (1)(a) and paragraph (8).
(3)   In paragraph (9), ignore the reference to paragraph (8).

[1487]

NOTES
Commencement: 25 February 2009.

54   Entitlement to vote (contributories)
Apply rule 4.69 of the 1986 Rules.

[1488]

NOTES
Commencement: 25 February 2009.

55   Admission and rejection of proof (creditors' meetings)
Apply rule 4.70 of the 1986 Rules. For paragraph (5) substitute—
    "(5)   The chair is not personally liable for costs incurred by any person in respect of an application under this rule unless the court makes an application to that effect.".

[1489]

NOTES
Commencement: 25 February 2009.

56   Record of proceedings
Apply rule 4.71 of the 1986 Rules.

[1490]

PART IV
OTHER STATUTORY INSTRUMENTS

NOTES
Commencement: 25 February 2009.

PART 7
PROOF OF DEBTS

57 Meaning of "prove"

(1) Apply rule 4.73 of the 1986 Rules.

(2) In paragraph (5), for "or a Government Department" substitute ", a Government Department or the FSCS".

(3) Ignore paragraphs (2), and (8).

[1491]

NOTES
Commencement: 25 February 2009.

58 Supply of forms

Apply rule 4.74 of the 1986 Rules.

[1492]

NOTES
Commencement: 25 February 2009.

59 Contents of proof

Apply rule 4.75 of the 1986 Rules.

[1493]

NOTES
Commencement: 25 February 2009.

60 Claim established by affidavit

Apply rule 4.77 of the 1986 Rules. Ignore paragraph (3).

[1494]

NOTES
Commencement: 25 February 2009.

61 Cost of proving

(1) Apply rule 4.78 of the 1986 Rules.

(2) In paragraph (1), leave out "or 4.76—CVL".

[1495]

NOTES
Commencement: 25 February 2009.

62 Bank liquidator to allow inspection of proofs

Apply rule 4.79 of the 1986 Rules.

[1496]

NOTES
Commencement: 25 February 2009.

63 New bank liquidator appointed

Apply rule 4.81 of the 1986 Rules.

[1497]

NOTES
Commencement: 25 February 2009.

64 Admission and rejection of proofs for dividend

Apply rule 4.82 of the 1986 Rules.

[1498]

NOTES
  Commencement: 25 February 2009.

65   Appeal against decision on proof

(1)   Apply rule 4.83 of the 1986 Rules.

(2)   For paragraph (6) substitute—

"(6)   The bank liquidator is not personally liable for costs incurred by any person in respect of an application under this rule unless the court makes an order to that effect.".

[1499]

NOTES
  Commencement: 25 February 2009.

66   Withdrawal or variation of proof

Apply rule 4.84 of the 1986 Rules.

[1500]

NOTES
  Commencement: 25 February 2009.

67   Expunging of proof by the court

Apply rule 4.85 of the 1986 Rules.

[1501]

NOTES
  Commencement: 25 February 2009.

68   Estimate of quantum

Apply rule 4.86 of the 1986 Rules.

[1502]

NOTES
  Commencement: 25 February 2009.

69   Negotiable instruments, etc

Apply rule 4.87 of the 1986 Rules.

[1503]

NOTES
  Commencement: 25 February 2009.

70   Secured creditors

Apply rule 4.88 of the 1986 Rules.

[1504]

NOTES
  Commencement: 25 February 2009.

71   Discounts

Apply rule 4.89 of the 1986 Rules.

[1505]

NOTES
  Commencement: 25 February 2009.

72   Mutual credits and set-off

This rule applies where, before the bank goes into bank insolvency, there have been mutual credits, mutual debts or other mutual dealings between the company and any creditor of the bank proving or claiming to prove for a debt in the bank insolvency.

(1)   The reference in paragraph (1) to mutual credits, mutual debts or other mutual dealings does not include—

PART IV   OTHER STATUTORY INSTRUMENTS

(a)   any debt arising out of an obligation incurred at a time when the creditor had notice that—
   (i)   a meeting of creditors had been summoned under section 98 of the 1986 Act,
   (ii) a petition for the winding up of the bank was pending, or
   (iii) an application for a bank insolvency order in respect of the bank was pending;
(b)   any debt which has been acquired by a creditor on assignment or otherwise, pursuant to an agreement between the creditor and any other party where that agreement was entered into—
   (i)   after the commencement of bank insolvency,
   (ii) at a time when the creditor had notice that a meeting of creditors had been summoned under section 98,
   (iii) at a time when the creditor had notice that a winding up petition was pending, or
   (iv) at a time when the creditor had notice that an application for a bank insolvency order in respect of the bank was pending.

(2)   An account shall be taken of what is due from each party to the other in respect of the mutual dealings, and the sums due from 1 party shall be set off against the sums due from the other.

(3)   A sum shall be regarded as being due to or from the bank for the purposes of paragraph (2) whether—
(a)   it is payable at present or in the future;
(b)   the obligation by virtue of which it is payable is certain or contingent; or
(c)   its amount is fixed or liquidated, or is capable of being ascertained by fixed rules or as a matter of opinion.

(4)   Rule 4.86 of the 1986 Rules shall apply for the purposes of this Rule to any obligation to or from the bank which, by reason of its being subject to any contingency or for any other reason, does not bear a certain value.

(5)   Rules 74 to 76 shall apply for the purposes of this Rule in relation to any sums due to the bank which—
(a)   are payable in a currency other than sterling,
(b)   are of a periodical nature, or
(c)   bear interest.

(6)   Rule 259 shall apply for the purposes of this rule to any sum due to or from the bank which is payable in the future.

(7)   Subject to rule 73, only the balance (if any) of the account owed to the creditor is provable in the liquidation. Alternatively the balance (if any) owed to the company shall be paid to the bank liquidator as part of the assets except where all or part of the balance result from a contingent or prospective debt owed by the creditor and in such a case the balance (or that part of it which results from the contingent or prospective debt) shall be paid if and when that debt becomes due and payable.

(8)   In this rule, "obligation" means an obligation however arising, whether by virtue of an agreement, rule of law or otherwise.

[1506]

NOTES
   Commencement: 25 February 2009.

73 Disapplication of set off for eligible depositors

(1)   This rule applies if the FSA Rules allow the FSCS to make gross payments of compensation. .

(2)   Rule 72 shall apply but, for the purpose of determining the sums due from the bank to an eligible depositor and from an eligible depositor to the bank for the purpose of rule 72(2)—
(a)   where the total of the sums held by the bank for the eligible depositor in respect of protected deposits is no more than the amount prescribed as the maximum compensation payable in respect of protected deposits under Part 15 of the Financial Services and Markets Act 2000, then paragraph (3) applies; and
(b)   where the sums held exceeds that limit, then paragraph (4) applies.

(3)   Where paragraph (2)(a) applies, there shall be deemed to have been no mutual dealings, regardless of whether there are any sums due from the depositor to the bank, and the sum due to the eligible depositor from the bank will be the total of the sums held by the bank for that depositor in respect of the protected deposits.

(4)   Where paragraph (2)(b) applies then—
(a)   any mutual dealings shall be treated as being mutual dealings only in relation to the amount by which that total exceeds that limit, and
(b)   the sums due from the bank to the eligible depositor will be—

     (i)   the amount by which that total exceeds that limit, set off in accordance with rule 72(2); and

     (ii)   the sums held by the bank for the eligible depositor in respect of protected deposits up to the limit of the amount prescribed as the maximum compensation payable.

(5)   Any arrangements with regard to set off between the bank and the eligible depositor in existence before the commencement of bank insolvency shall be subject to this rule.

(6)   "Protected deposit" means a protected deposit within the meaning given by the Compensation Sourcebook.

[1507]

NOTES
    Commencement: 25 February 2009.

74 Debt in foreign currency

Apply rule 4.91 of the 1986 Rules. In paragraph (1), leave out from "or, if" to the end.

[1508]

NOTES
    Commencement: 25 February 2009.

75 Payments of a periodical nature

Apply rule 4.92 of the 1986 Rules. In paragraph (1), leave out from "or, if" to the end.

[1509]

NOTES
    Commencement: 25 February 2009.

76 Interest

Apply rule 4.93 of the 1986 Rules. In paragraph (1), leave out from "or, if" to the end.

[1510]

NOTES
    Commencement: 25 February 2009.

77 Debt payable at future time

(1)   Apply rule 4.94 of the 1986 Rules.

(2)   Leave out from "or, if" to "entered administration".

[1511]

NOTES
    Commencement: 25 February 2009.

PART 8
SECURED CREDITORS

78 Value of security

Apply rule 4.95 of the 1986 Rules.

[1512]

NOTES
    Commencement: 25 February 2009.

79 Surrender for non-disclosure

Apply rule 4.96 of the 1986 Rules. Ignore paragraph (3).

[1513]

NOTES
    Commencement: 25 February 2009.

80 Redemption by liquidator

Apply rule 4.97 of the 1986 Rules.

[1514]

NOTES
Commencement: 25 February 2009.

81 Test of security's value
Apply rule 4.98 of the 1986 Rules.

[1515]

NOTES
Commencement: 25 February 2009.

82 Realisation of security by creditor
Apply rule 4.99 of the 1986 Rules.

[1516]

NOTES
Commencement: 25 February 2009.

PART 9
THE BANK LIQUIDATOR

CHAPTER 1
GENERAL

83 Remuneration of bank liquidator
(1)   This rule applies where—
    (a)   the liquidation committee has ceased to exist as mentioned in rule 41(1),
    (b)   the committee has not been reformed at a meeting of creditors held under either rule 41 rules 44 and 45, and
    (c)   the committee has not been reformed at a meeting of contributories held under rule 117.

(2)   Where this rule applies the creditors may, at the first or any subsequent meeting of creditors, pass a resolution as to the terms on which, in accordance with rule 98, the bank liquidator is to be remunerated.

(3)   Where such a resolution is passed—
    (a)   it supersedes any resolution as to the remuneration of the bank liquidator passed by the liquidation committee before the first meeting of creditors, and
    (b)   the bank liquidator shall be paid under the resolution passed by the bank liquidation committee under rule 18(5) in respect of the performance of his functions before the day on which the creditors' resolution is passed and under the creditors' resolution in respect of the performance of his functions on and after that day.

[1517]

NOTES
Commencement: 25 February 2009.

84 Replacement of bank liquidator by creditors
(1)   Apply rule 4.100 of the 1986 Rules.
(2)   For paragraph (1) substitute—

    "(1)   This rule applies where a person is appointed as bank liquidator by a meeting of creditors."

(3)   For paragraph (4) substitute—

    "(4)   The chairman of the meeting shall—
        (a)   send the certificate to the new bank liquidator,
        (b)   send a copy of the certificate to the Bank of England and the FSA, and
        (c)   file a copy of the certificate in court ."

[1518]

NOTES
Commencement: 25 February 2009.

85 Authentication of bank liquidator's appointment
Apply rule 4.105 of the 1986 Rules). Leave out from "or (as" to "the Act".

[1519]

NOTES
Commencement: 25 February 2009.

86   Appointment to be advertised and registered

(1)   This rule applies where the bank liquidator is appointed by a meeting of the creditors or by the Bank of England under rule 106.

(2)   The bank liquidator shall, after receiving the certificate of appointment, give notice of his appointment in such manner as the bank liquidator thinks fit for ensuring that it comes to the notice of the bank's creditors and contributories.

(3)   The expense of giving notice under this rule shall be borne in the first instance by the bank liquidator; but he is entitled to be reimbursed as an expense of the bank insolvency.

(4)   The bank liquidator shall immediately notify his appointment to the registrar of companies.

[1520]

NOTES
Commencement: 25 February 2009.

CHAPTER 2
RESIGNATION AND REMOVAL

87   Creditors' meeting to be notified of the bank liquidator's resignation

(1)   Apply rule 4.108 of the 1986 Rules.

(2)   For paragraph (1), substitute—

"(1)   Before resigning office, the bank liquidator must obtain the consent of the Bank of England and must call a meeting of creditors to notify them of this.

(1A)   The notice summoning the meeting shall indicate that this is the purpose, or one of the purposes, of the meeting and shall draw the attention of the creditors to rule 95 with respect to the bank liquidator's release.

(1B)   The notice in (1A) shall enclose a copy of the Bank of England's consent."

(3)   For paragraph (2) substitute—

"(2)   Copies of the notice and of the account mentioned in paragraph (3) shall be sent to the court, the Bank of England and the FSA.".

[1521]

NOTES
Commencement: 25 February 2009.

88   Action following acceptance of resignation

(1)   This rule applies where a meeting is summoned to notify the creditors of the bank liquidator's resignation

(2)   The meeting will resolve whether to give the bank liquidator their release.

(3)   If the meeting decides to not give the bank liquidator his release, the bank liquidator will be given a copy of that resolution and rule 95 applies.

(4)   After the meeting the bank liquidator shall file the notice of his resignation in court and will send copies of the notice to the Bank of England, the FSA and the registrar of companies.

(5)   The bank liquidator's resignation is effective as from the date on which the court receives the notice of his resignation, and the court will endorse that date on the notice.

[1522]

NOTES
Commencement: 25 February 2009.

89   Advertisement of resignation

Apply rule 4.112 of the 1986 Rules.

[1523]

NOTES
Commencement: 25 February 2009.

90 Meeting of creditors to remove bank liquidator

(1) Apply rule 4.113 of the 1986 Rules.

(2) In paragraph (1), for "section 174(4)" substitute "section 109 of the Banking Act 2009".

(3) In paragraph (2), for "official receiver" substitute "Bank of England and the FSA".

(4) In paragraph (4) substitute—

"(4) Where the meeting passes a resolution that—
(a) the bank liquidator be removed;
(b) a new bank liquidator be appointed, or
(c) the bank liquidator not to be given their release

the bank liquidator will be given a copy of that resolution and if it has been resolved to remove the bank liquidator, the bank liquidator will be given a certificate to that effect."

(5) For paragraph (5) substitute—

"(5) If the creditors have resolved to appoint a new bank liquidator, the certificate of his appointment shall also be sent to the registrar of companies within that time and rule 4.100 shall apply."

[1524]

NOTES
Commencement: 25 February 2009.

91 Court's power to regulate meetings under rule 90

Apply rule 4.115 of the 1986 Rules. Leave out "or 4.114—CVL".

[1525]

NOTES
Commencement: 25 February 2009.

92 Procedure on removal

(1) Apply rule 4.116 of the 1986 Rules.

(2) For "official receiver", wherever it appears, substitute "out-going bank liquidator".

(3) For paragraph (3) substitute—

"(3) A copy of the certificate so endorsed shall be sent by the court to the outgoing bank liquidator and, if a new liquidator has been appointed, to him."

(4) Ignore paragraph (4).

[1526]

NOTES
Commencement: 25 February 2009.

93 Advertisement of removal

Apply rule 4.118 of the 1986 Rules.

[1527]

NOTES
Commencement: 25 February 2009.

94 Removal of bank liquidator by the court

(1) Apply rule 4.119 of the 1986 Rules.

(2) After paragraph (1) insert—

"(2A) If the liquidation committee has not yet passed a full payment resolution, the court shall dismiss any application under paragraph (1) where the application is made by someone other than the Bank of England, the FSA or the liquidation committee."

(3) In paragraph (2), for "at least 7 days' notice" substitute—
"(a) if the application is made before the passing of a full payment resolution, such notice as is reasonable in all the circumstances, and
(b) if the application is made after the passing of a full payment resolution, at least 7 days' notice.".

(4) In paragraph (4), leave out ", at least 14 days before the hearing,".

(5) After paragraph (4) insert—

"(4A) The notice and copies mentioned in paragraph (4) shall be sent—

    (a)   if the application is made before the passing of a full payment resolution, within such time so as to give the bank liquidator notice of the hearing as is reasonable in all the circumstances, and

    (b)   if the application is made after the passing of a full payment resolution, at least 14 days before the hearing.".

(6)   In paragraph (6)—

    (a)   in sub-paragraph (a), for "official receiver" substitute "Bank of England and the FSA" and at the end insert "and", and

    (b)   leave out "and" at the end of sub-paragraph (b), and sub-paragraph (c).

    [1528]

NOTES

Commencement: 25 February 2009.

---

95 Release of resigning or removed bank liquidator

(1)   Apply rule 4.121 of the 1986 Rules.

(2)   In paragraph (1), for "accepted by" substitute "notified to".

(3)   For rule 4.109 substitute "rule 88 of the Bank Insolvency Rules 2009".

(4)   In paragraph (3)—

    (a)   in sub paragraph (a) for "receive his resignation" substitute "be notified of his resignation"; and

    (b)   leave out "or" at the end of sub-paragraph (a) and at the end of sub-paragraph (b) insert—

", or

    (c)   the bank liquidator resigns, and the Bank of England has refused his release,".

(5)   For paragraph (4) substitute—

"(4)   When the Secretary of State gives the release, he shall certify it accordingly, file the certificate in court and send a copy to the registrar of companies."

    [1529]

NOTES

Commencement: 25 February 2009.

CHAPTER 3
RELEASE ON COMPLETION OF WINDING UP

96 Final meeting

(1)   The bank liquidator shall give at least 14 days' notice of the final meeting of the liquidation committee to be held under section 115 of the 2009 Act to the following—

    (a)   the FSA,

    (b)   the FSCS,

    (c)   the Bank of England,

    (d)   the Treasury,

    (e)   the registrar of companies, and

    (f)   the members of the liquidation committee.

(2)   The bank liquidator's final report to be laid before the meeting under that section shall contain an account of the liquidator's administration of the winding up, including—

    (a)   details as to how Objective 1 was achieved having regard, in particular, to the expenses of the bank liquidator in connection with that Objective,

    (b)   a summary of the bank liquidator's receipts and payments,

    (c)   a statement that the bank liquidator has reconciled his account with that which is held by the Secretary of State in respect of the winding up, and

    (d)   a statement as to the amount paid to unsecured creditors by virtue of the application of section 176A (prescribed part) of the 1986 Act.

(3)   At the same time that notice of the final meeting is sent out, the bank liquidator shall file the final report in court and send it to the registrar of companies.

(4)   The bank liquidator shall give notice that the final report is available to all creditors and contributories, either on request to the bank liquidator or at Companies House, and shall cause that notice to be gazetted at least 14 days before the final meeting is held.

(5)   At the final meeting, the liquidation committee may question the bank liquidator with respect to any matter contained in the final report, and may resolve against the bank liquidator being released.

(6) The bank liquidator shall give notice to the court that the final meeting has been held and the notice shall state whether or not he has been given his release.

(7) Where the liquidation committee does not resolve against the bank liquidator's release, the bank liquidator vacates office at the end of the meeting and has his release when the notice in paragraph (6) is filed in court.

(8) If there is no quorum present at the final meeting, the bank liquidator shall report to the court that a final meeting was summoned in accordance with section 115 of the 2009 Act, but there was no quorum present; and the final meeting is then deemed to have been held, and the liquidation committee not to have resolved against the bank liquidator being released.

(9) If the liquidation committee resolves against the bank liquidator having his release then rule 95 applies.

[1530]

NOTES
Commencement: 25 February 2009.

97 Rule as to reporting
Apply rule 4.125A of the 1986 Rules. Ignore the reference to rule 4.124.

[1531]

NOTES
Commencement: 25 February 2009.

CHAPTER 4
REMUNERATION

98 Fixing of remuneration
(1) Apply rule 4.127 of the 1986 Rules.

(2) In paragraph (3), leave out from the beginning to "receiver".

(3) For paragraph (5) substitute—

"(5) If, under rule 41(2), the liquidation committee ceases to exist at the end of the first meeting of creditors, the remuneration of the bank liquidator fixed by the initial liquidation committee under rule 18 can be redetermined by a resolution of a meeting of creditors, and paragraph (4) applies to the determination of the creditors as it does to the determination of the liquidation committee."

(4) In paragraph (6), for the words from the beginning to "his" substitute "Where the bank liquidator's".

[1532]

NOTES
Commencement: 25 February 2009.

99 Bank liquidator's entitlement to remuneration where it is not fixed under rule 98
(1) Apply rule 4.127A of the 1986 Rules.

(2) In paragraph (1), for the words from "liquidator" to "his" substitute "bank liquidator's".

(3) In paragraph (2), after "Schedule 6" add "to the 1986 Rules as applied by Schedule 1 to the Bank Insolvency Rules 2009 ".

[1533]

NOTES
Commencement: 25 February 2009.

100 Bank liquidator's remuneration where he realises assets on behalf of chargeholder
(1) Apply rule 4.127B of the 1986 Rules.

(2) In paragraph (1), for the words from "liquidator" to "and" substitute "bank liquidator".

(3) In paragraphs (2) and (3), after "Schedule 6" add "to the 1986 Rules as applied by Schedule 1 to the Bank Insolvency Rules 2009 ".

[1534]

NOTES
Commencement: 25 February 2009.

101   Other matters affecting remuneration

Apply rule 4.128 of the 1986 Rules.

[1535]

NOTES
Commencement: 25 February 2009.

102   Recourse of bank liquidator to meeting of creditors

Apply rule 4.129 of the 1986 Rules.

[1536]

NOTES
Commencement: 25 February 2009.

103   Recourse to the court

Apply rule 4.130 of the 1986 Rules.

[1537]

NOTES
Commencement: 25 February 2009.

104   Creditors' claim that remuneration is excessive

Apply rule 4.131 of the 1986 Rules.

[1538]

NOTES
Commencement: 25 February 2009.

105   Primacy of Objective 1

Nothing done under a rule in this chapter may prejudice the achievement of Objective 1.

[1539]

NOTES
Commencement: 25 February 2009.

CHAPTER 5
SUPPLEMENTARY PROVISIONS

106   Replacement Bank liquidator

(1)   Where the bank liquidator vacates his office for any reason (including death) other than by removal by a meeting of creditors in accordance with rule 90, the Bank of England shall appoint a new bank liquidator as soon as practicable.

(2)   Where a bank liquidator has been removed by a meeting of creditors but 1 month has passed and there has been no resolution passed by a meeting of creditors to appoint a new bank liquidator, the Bank of England shall appoint a new bank liquidator as soon as practicable.

(3)   The Bank of England shall file in court the document appointing the new bank liquidator ("the appointment document") together with statements to the effect that the new bank liquidator—
  (a)   is qualified to act as an insolvency practitioner in accordance with section 390 of the 1986 Act, and
  (b)   consents to act as the bank liquidator.

(4)   The bank liquidator shall send a copy of the appointment document to the FSA and registrar of companies.

(5)   The bank liquidator shall as soon as reasonably practicable—
  (a)   cause the appointment to be gazetted, and
  (b)   advertise the appointment in such manner as the bank liquidator thinks fit.

[1540]

NOTES
Commencement: 25 February 2009.

107 Bank liquidator deceased

(1)   Unless notice of the death of the bank liquidator has been given under paragraph (2) or (3), it is the duty of the bank liquidator's personal representatives, where the bank liquidator has died, to give notice of that fact to the Bank of England and the liquidation committee, specifying the date of the death.

(2)   If the deceased bank liquidator was a partner in a firm, notice may be given to the Bank of England, the FSA and liquidation committee by a partner in the firm who is qualified to act as an insolvency practitioner, or is a member of any body recognised by the Secretary of State for the authorisation of insolvency practitioners.

(3)   Notice of the death may also be given by any person producing the relevant death certificate or a copy of it to the Bank of England, the FSA and the liquidation committee.

(4)   The Bank of England shall give notice to the court, for the purpose of fixing the date of the deceased bank liquidator's release.

[1541]

NOTES
Commencement: 25 February 2009.

108 Loss of qualification as insolvency practitioner

(1)   Apply rule 4.134 of the 1986 Rules. For paragraph (2) substitute—

"(2)   The bank liquidator shall immediately give notice of his doing to the Bank of England.

(3)   The Bank of England shall file a copy of this notice in court."

[1542]

NOTES
Commencement: 25 February 2009.
This rule is reproduced as it appears in the original Queen's Printer's copy; there is no paragraph (2).

109 Resignation of the bank liquidator

(1)   This rule applies where the bank liquidator was appointed by the bank insolvency order or by the Bank of England.

(2)   The bank liquidator can only resign—
    (a)   after the liquidation committee have passed a full payment resolution, and
    (b)   with the consent of the Bank of England.

(3)   Before calling a meeting of creditors under rule 87 to receive notice of the bank liquidator's resignation, the bank liquidator must write to the Bank of England notifying it of the intention to resign.

(4)   The Bank of England shall notify the bank liquidator in writing within 21 days as to whether it consents to the resignation; if the Bank of England does not consent to the resignation, it shall set out its reasons in writing.

(5)   The bank liquidator, if not content with the Bank of England's response, may apply to the Court for directions under section 168(3) of the 1986 Act.

[1543]

NOTES
Commencement: 25 February 2009.

110 Notice to Bank of England of intention to vacate office

(1)   This rule applies where the bank liquidator was appointed by a meeting of creditors.

(2)   Apply rule 4.137 of the 1986 Rules.

(3)   For "official receiver", wherever it appears, substitute "Bank of England" and for "receive his resignation" substitute "be notified of his resignation".

[1544]

NOTES
Commencement: 25 February 2009.

111 Bank liquidator's duties on vacating office

Apply rule 4.138 of the 1986 Rules. Ignore paragraph (3).

[1545]

NOTES
Commencement: 25 February 2009.

112   Power of court to set aside certain transactions

(1)   Apply rule 4.149 of the 1986 Rules.

(2)   In paragraph (2)—
  (a)   leave out "either", and
  (b)   leave out "or" at the end of sub-paragraph (a), and after sub-paragraph (b) insert—
", or
      (c)   it is shown to the court's satisfaction that the transaction was entered into by the
      liquidator for the purpose of achieving Objective 1.".

[1546]

NOTES
Commencement: 25 February 2009.

113   Rule against solicitation

(1)   Apply rule 4.150 of the 1986 Rules.

[1547]

NOTES
Commencement: 25 February 2009.
This rule is reproduced as it appears in the original Queen's Printer's copy; there is no paragraph (2).

PART 10
THE LIQUIDATION COMMITTEE

114   Application of rules in this Part

The rules in this Part apply only in relation to the liquidation committee established under rule 41
after a full payment resolution has been passed.

[1548]

NOTES
Commencement: 25 February 2009.

115   Membership of committee

(1)   Apply rule 4.152 of the 1986 Rules.

(2)   For paragraph (1) substitute—

"(1)   Subject to rule 4.154 as applied by rule 117 of the Bank Insolvency Rules 2009, the
liquidation committee shall consist of either 3 or 5 creditors of the company, elected by the
meeting of creditors held under rule 41 of those Rules."

(3)   Ignore paragraphs (2), (4) and (7) and ignore any reference to contributory members in
paragraph (6).

[1549]

NOTES
Commencement: 25 February 2009.

116   Formalities of establishment

Apply rule 4.153 of the 1986 Rules. In paragraph (3), the reference to section 375 of the 1985 Act,
shall, after that section is repealed, be to section 323 of the 2006 Act.

[1550]

NOTES
Commencement: 25 February 2009.

117   Committee established by contributories

(1)   Apply rule 4.154 of the 1986 Rules.

(2)   For paragraph (1) substitute—

"(1)   This rule applies where the outcome of the creditors' meeting summoned by the bank
liquidator under rule 41 of the Bank Insolvency 2009 Rules is, (by virtue of rule 41 (2)), that
the liquidation committee ceases to exist at the end of the meeting.".

(3) In paragraph (2), for "that section" substitute "section 141 of the Act".

(4) In paragraph (4) for "at least 3 and not more than 5", substitute "3 or 5".

[1551]

NOTES
Commencement: 25 February 2009.

118 Obligations of liquidator to committee

Apply rule 4.155 of the 1986 Rules.

[1552]

NOTES
Commencement: 25 February 2009.

119 Meetings of the committee

Apply rule 4.156 of the 1986 Rules.

[1553]

NOTES
Commencement: 25 February 2009.

120 The chair at meetings

Apply rule 4.157 of the 1986 Rules.

[1554]

NOTES
Commencement: 25 February 2009.

121 Quorum

A meeting of the committee is duly constituted if due notice of it has been given to all the members, and at least 2 members are present or represented.

[1555]

NOTES
Commencement: 25 February 2009.

122 Committee-members' representatives

Apply rule 4.159 of the 1986 Rules. In paragraph (2), the reference to section 375 of the 1985 Act, shall, after that section is repealed, be to section 323 of the 2006 Act.

[1556]

NOTES
Commencement: 25 February 2009.

123 Resignation

Apply rule 4.160 of the 1986 Rules.

[1557]

NOTES
Commencement: 25 February 2009.

124 Termination of membership

Apply rule 4.161 of the 1986 Rules.

[1558]

NOTES
Commencement: 25 February 2009.

125 Removal

Apply rule 4.162 of the 1986 Rules.

[1559]

NOTES
Commencement: 25 February 2009.

126   Vacancy (creditor members)

Apply rule 4.163 of the 1986 Rules.

[1560]

NOTES
Commencement: 25 February 2009.

127   Vacancy (contributory members)

Apply rule 4.164 of the 1986 Rules.

[1561]

NOTES
Commencement: 25 February 2009.

128   Voting rights and resolutions

Apply rule 4.165 of the 1986 Rules.

[1562]

NOTES
Commencement: 25 February 2009.

129   Resolutions by post

Apply rule 4.167 of the 1986 Rules.

[1563]

NOTES
Commencement: 25 February 2009.

130   Liquidator's reports

Apply rule 4.168 of the 1986 Rules.

[1564]

NOTES
Commencement: 25 February 2009.

131   Expenses of members, etc

Apply rule 4.169 of the 1986 Rules.

[1565]

NOTES
Commencement: 25 February 2009.

132   Dealings by committee-members and others

Apply rule 4.170 of the 1986 Rules.

[1566]

NOTES
Commencement: 25 February 2009.

133   Composition of committee when creditors paid in full

(1)   Apply rule 4.171 of the 1986 Rules.

(2)   For paragraph (4) substitute—

"(4)   The members of the liquidation committee will cease to be members at the end of the final meeting held under rule 96 of the Bank Insolvency Rules 2009."

[1567]

NOTES
Commencement: 25 February 2009.

134   Committee's functions vested in the Secretary of State

Apply rule 4.172 of the 1986 Rules. Ignore paragraph (2).

[1568]

PART IV
OTHER STATUTORY INSTRUMENTS

NOTES
Commencement: 25 February 2009.

135 Formal defects

Apply rule 4.172A of the 1986 Rules.

[1569]

NOTES
Commencement: 25 February 2009.

PART 11
COLLECTION AND DISTRIBUTION OF BANK'S ASSETS BY BANK LIQUIDATOR

136 General duties of bank liquidator

Apply rule 4.179 of the 1986 Rules.

[1570]

NOTES
Commencement: 25 February 2009.

137 General qualification on powers

In exercising any power conferred on the bank liquidator by this Part before a full payment resolution has been passed, the bank liquidator shall exercise it consistently with Objective 1.

[1571]

NOTES
Commencement: 25 February 2009.

138 Manner of distributing assets

Apply rule 4.180 of the 1986 Rules.

[1572]

NOTES
Commencement: 25 February 2009.

139 Debts of insolvent company to rank equally

Apply rule 4.181 of the 1986 Rules.

[1573]

NOTES
Commencement: 25 February 2009.

140 Supplementary provisions as to dividend

Apply rule 4.182 of the 1986 Rules.

[1574]

NOTES
Commencement: 25 February 2009.

141 Division of unsold assets

Apply rule 4.183 of the 1986 Rules.

[1575]

NOTES
Commencement: 25 February 2009.

142 General powers of the liquidator

Apply rule 4.184 of the 1986 Rules. In paragraph (1) leave out "section 165(2) or".

[1576]

NOTES
Commencement: 25 February 2009.

143 Enforced delivery up of company's property

Apply rule 4.185 of the 1986 Rules.

[1577]

NOTES
Commencement: 25 February 2009.

144 Final distribution

Apply rule 4.186 of the 1986 Rules. For "Part 11 of the Rules", substitute "Part 21 of the 2009 Rules".

[1578]

NOTES
Commencement: 25 February 2009.

PART 12
DISCLAIMER

145 Liquidator's notice of disclaimer

Apply rule 4.187 of the 1986 Rules.

[1579]

NOTES
Commencement: 25 February 2009.

146 Communication of disclaimer to persons interested

Apply rule 4.188 of the 1986 Rules.

[1580]

NOTES
Commencement: 25 February 2009.

147 Additional notices

Apply rule 4.189 of the 1986 Rules.

[1581]

NOTES
Commencement: 25 February 2009.

148 Duty to keep court informed

Apply rule 4.190 of the 1986 Rules.

[1582]

NOTES
Commencement: 25 February 2009.

149 Application by interested party under s 178(5)

Apply rule 4.191 of the 1986 Rules.

[1583]

NOTES
Commencement: 25 February 2009.

150 Interest in property to be declared on request

Apply rule 4.192 of the 1986 Rules.

[1584]

NOTES
Commencement: 25 February 2009.

151 Disclaimer presumed valid and effective

Apply rule 4.193 of the 1986 Rules. For "Chapter" substitute "Part".

[1585]

NOTES
Commencement: 25 February 2009.

152   Application for exercise of court's powers under s 181

Apply rule 4.194 of the 1986 Rules.

[1586]

NOTES
Commencement: 25 February 2009.

PART 13
SETTLEMENT OF LIST OF CONTRIBUTORIES

153   Preliminary

Apply rule 4.195 of the 1986 Rules.

[1587]

NOTES
Commencement: 25 February 2009.

154   Primacy of Objective 1

Where the bank liquidator considers that the carrying out of a duty imposed by a rule in this Part would prejudice the achievement of Objective 1, the bank liquidator shall postpone the carrying out of that duty until he considers that the carrying out of the duty would no longer be likely to prejudice the achievement of that Objective.

[1588]

NOTES
Commencement: 25 February 2009.

155   Duty of liquidator to settle list

Apply rule 4.196 of the 1986 Rules.

[1589]

NOTES
Commencement: 25 February 2009.

156   Form of list

Apply rule 4.197 of the 1986 Rules.

[1590]

NOTES
Commencement: 25 February 2009.

157   Procedure for settling list

Apply rule 4.198 of the 1986 Rules.

[1591]

NOTES
Commencement: 25 February 2009.

158   Application to court for variation of the list

Apply rule 4.199 of the 1986 Rules.

[1592]

NOTES
Commencement: 25 February 2009.

159   Variation of, or addition to, the list

Apply rule 4.200 of the 1986 Rules. For "Chapter", substitute "Part".

[1593]

NOTES
Commencement: 25 February 2009.

160   Costs not to fall on bank liquidator

The bank liquidator is not personally liable for any costs incurred by a person in respect of an application to set aside or vary the bank liquidator's act or decision in settling the list of contributories, or varying or adding to the list, unless the court makes an order to that effect.

[1594]

NOTES
Commencement: 25 February 2009.

PART 14
CALLS

161   Calls by liquidator

Apply rule 4.202 of the 1986 Rules.

[1595]

NOTES
Commencement: 25 February 2009.

162   Control by bank liquidation committee

Apply rule 4.203 of the 1986 Rules.

[1596]

NOTES
Commencement: 25 February 2009.

163   Application to court for leave to make a call

Apply rule 4.204 of the 1986 Rules.

[1597]

NOTES
Commencement: 25 February 2009.

164   Making and enforcement of the call

Apply rule 4.205 of the 1986 Rules.

[1598]

NOTES
Commencement: 25 February 2009.

PART 15
SPECIAL MANAGER

165   Appointment and remuneration

Apply rule 4.206 of the 1986 Rules.

[1599]

NOTES
Commencement: 25 February 2009.

166   Security

Apply rule 4.207 of the 1986 Rules.

[1600]

NOTES
Commencement: 25 February 2009.

167   Failure to give or keep up security

Apply rule 4.208 of the 1986 Rules.

[1601]

NOTES
Commencement: 25 February 2009.

168   Accounting

Apply rule 4.209 of the 1986 Rules.

[1602]

NOTES

Commencement: 25 February 2009.

169   Termination of appointment

Apply rule 4.210 of the 1986 Rules.

[1603]

NOTES

Commencement: 25 February 2009.

PART 16

ORDER OF PAYMENT AS TO COSTS, ETC OUT OF ASSETS

170   General rule as to priority

(1)   Apply rule 4.218 of the 1986 Rules.

(2)   In paragraph (3)—

   (a)   ignore sub-paragraphs (a)(iii) and (iv), (b), and (d),

   (b)   in sub-paragraph (c) leave out the words from "or section 415A" to the end, and

   (c)   in sub-paragraph (1a), leave out the words from "in any case" to the end.

[1604]

NOTES

Commencement: 25 February 2009.

171   Litigation expenses and property subject to a floating charge—general application

Apply rule 4.218A of the 1986 Rules.

[1605]

NOTES

Commencement: 25 February 2009.

172   Litigation expenses and property subject to a floating charge—requirement for approval or authorisation

Apply rule 4.218B of the 1986 Rules.

[1606]

NOTES

Commencement: 25 February 2009.

173   Litigation expenses and property subject to a floating charge—request for approval or authorisation

Apply rule 4.218C of the 1986 Rules.

[1607]

NOTES

Commencement: 25 February 2009.

174   Litigation expenses and property subject to a floating charge—grant of approval or authorisation

Apply rule 4.218D of the 1986 Rules.

[1608]

NOTES

Commencement: 25 February 2009.

175   Litigation expenses and property subject to a floating charge—application to court by the bank liquidator

Apply rule 4.218E of the 1986 Rules.

[1609]

NOTES
Commencement: 25 February 2009.

176   Saving for powers of the court

Apply rule 4.220 of the 1986 Rules.

[1610]

NOTES
Commencement: 25 February 2009.

PART 17
MISCELLANEOUS RULES

CHAPTER 1
RETURN OF CAPITAL

177   Application to court for order authorising return of capital

Apply rule 4.221 of the 1986 Rules.

[1611]

NOTES
Commencement: 25 February 2009.

178   Procedure for return of capital

Apply rule 4.222 of the 1986 Rules.

[1612]

NOTES
Commencement: 25 February 2009.

CHAPTER 2
CONCLUSION OF BANK INSOLVENCY

179   Secretary of State's directions under s 116 of the 2009 Act

(1)   Where the Secretary of State gives a direction under section 116 of the 2009 Act (application by an interested person for postponement of dissolution) the Secretary of State shall send 2 copies of the direction to that applicant.

(2)   Of those copies, 1 shall be sent by the applicant to the registrar of companies to comply with section 116(4) of the 2009 Act.

[1613]

NOTES
Commencement: 25 February 2009.

180   Procedure following appeal under s 116 of the 2009 Act

Following an appeal under section 116 (2) of the 2009 Act (against a decision of the Secretary of State under that section) the court shall send 2 sealed copies of its order to the person in whose favour the appeal was determined, and that party shall send 1 of the copies to the registrar of companies.

[1614]

NOTES
Commencement: 25 February 2009.

CHAPTER 3
LEAVE TO ACT AS DIRECTOR, ETC OF BANK WITH PROHIBITED NAME

181   Preliminary

Apply rule 4.226 of the 1986 Rules. In paragraph (c), leave out the words from "whether" to the end.

[1615]

NOTES
Commencement: 25 February 2009.

182 Application for leave under s 216(3) before passing of full payment resolution

Where an application for leave under section 216 of the 1986 Act is made before a full payment resolution has been passed, it may only be made with the consent of the bank liquidator.

[1616]

NOTES
Commencement: 25 February 2009.

183 Consideration of application for leave under s 216(3)

Apply rule 4.227 of the 1986 Rules.

[1617]

NOTES
Commencement: 25 February 2009.

184 First excepted case

Apply rule 4.228 of the 1986 Rules. In paragraph (1)(b)(ii) ignore the reference to administrator.

[1618]

NOTES
Commencement: 25 February 2009.

185 Second excepted case

Apply rule 4.229 of the 1986 Rules. In paragraph (b), the reference to section 242(5) of the 1985 Act should, after that section is repealed, be to section 451 of the 2006 Act.

[1619]

NOTES
Commencement: 25 February 2009.

186 Third excepted case

Apply rule 4.230 of the 1986 Rules. In paragraph (a), for "liquidating company went into liquidation" substitute "bank went into bank insolvency".

[1620]

NOTES
Commencement: 25 February 2009.

187 Further exception

The court's leave under section 216(3) of the Act is not required in respect of anything done by a person in connection with the exercise of a stabilisation power under Part 1 of the 2009 Act.

[1621]

NOTES
Commencement: 25 February 2009.

PART 18
COURT PROCEDURE AND PRACTICE

CHAPTER 1
APPLICATIONS (GENERAL)

188 Preliminary

This Part applies to any application made to the court under the 2009 Act or these Rules except an application under section 95 of the 2009 Act for a bank insolvency order.

[1622]

NOTES
Commencement: 25 February 2009.

189 Interpretation

Apply rule 7.2 of the 1986 Rules.

[1623]

NOTES
  Commencement: 25 February 2009.

190 Form and contents of application
Apply rule 7.3 of the 1986 Rules.

[1624]

NOTES
  Commencement: 25 February 2009.

191 Application under section 176A(5) to disapply section 176A
(1)   Apply rule 7.3A of the 1986 Rules.

(2)   In paragraph (1), ignore "administrator or receiver."

(3)   Ignore paragraph (2)(a).

[1625]

NOTES
  Commencement: 25 February 2009.

192 Filing and service of application
Apply rule 7.4 of the 1986 Rules.

[1626]

NOTES
  Commencement: 25 February 2009.

193 Notice of application under section 176A(5)
Apply rule 7.4A of the 1986 Rules. Leave out the words from "save that notice" to the end.

[1627]

NOTES
  Commencement: 25 February 2009.

194 Other hearings without notice
Apply rule 7.5 of the 1986 Rules.

[1628]

NOTES
  Commencement: 25 February 2009.

195 Hearing of application
Apply rule 7.6 of the 1986 Rules.

[1629]

NOTES
  Commencement: 25 February 2009.

196 Use of evidence
Apply rule 7.7 of the 1986 Rules.

[1630]

NOTES
  Commencement: 25 February 2009.

197 Filing and service of witness statements
Apply rule 7.8 of the 1986 Rules. Ignore paragraph (2).

[1631]

NOTES
  Commencement: 25 February 2009.

198 Use of reports

(1)   Unless the application involves other parties, or the court orders otherwise, a report may be filed in court instead of a witness statement by—

(a)   the bank liquidator,

(b)   the provisional bank liquidator, or

(c)   the special manager.

(2)   In any case where a report is filed instead of a witness statement, the report shall be treated for the purposes of rule 197, and any hearing before the court, as if it were a witness statement.

[1632]

NOTES

Commencement: 25 February 2009.

199 Adjournment of hearings: directions

Apply rule 7.10 of the 1986 Rules.

[1633]

NOTES

Commencement: 25 February 2009.

CHAPTER 3
SHORTHAND WRITERS

200 Nomination and appointment of shorthand writers

(1)   Apply rule 7.16 of the 1986 Rules.

(2)   In paragraph (1) leave out "and, in a county court, the registrar".

(3)   In paragraph (2) leave out "133" and "290 or 366".

(4)   Ignore paragraph (3).

[1634]

NOTES

Commencement: 25 February 2009.

201 Remuneration

Apply rule 7.17 of the 1986 Rules.

[1635]

NOTES

Commencement: 25 February 2009.

CHAPTER 4
ENFORCEMENT PROCEDURES

202 Enforcement of court orders

(1)   Apply rule 7.19 of the 1986 Rules.

(2)   Ignore paragraph (2).

[1636]

NOTES

Commencement: 25 February 2009.

203 Orders enforcing compliance with the rules

(1)   The court may, on the application of the bank liquidator (or the provisional bank liquidator as the case may be,) make such orders as it thinks necessary for the enforcement of obligations falling on any person in accordance with—

(a)   section 143(2) (liquidator to furnish information, books, papers etc) of the 1986 Act or

(b)   section 235 (duty to cooperate with liquidator) of that Act.

(2)   An order of the court under this rule may provide that all the costs of and incidental to the application for it shall be borne by the person against whom the order is made.

[1637]

NOTES

Commencement: 25 February 2009.

204   Warrants (general provisions)

(1)   A warrant issued by the court under any provision of the 1986 Act shall be addressed to such officer of the High Court as the warrant specifies, or to any constable.

(2)   The person described in section 236(5) of the 1986 Act as the prescribed officer of the court is the tipstaff and his assistants of the court.

(3)   In this Chapter, references to property include books, papers and records.

[1638]

NOTES

Commencement: 25 February 2009.

205   Warrants under section 236

Apply rule 7.23 of the 1986 Rules. In paragraph (1), leave out "or 366 (the equivalent in bankruptcy)".

[1639]

NOTES

Commencement: 25 February 2009.

CHAPTER 5
COURT RECORDS AND RETURNS

206   Title of proceedings

Every proceeding under Part 2 of the 2009 Act shall, with any necessary additions, be titled "IN THE MATTER OF .... (naming the bank to which the proceedings relate) AND IN THE MATTER OF THE BANKING ACT 2009".

[1640]

NOTES

Commencement: 25 February 2009.

207   Court records

Apply rule 7.27 of the 1986 Rules.

[1641]

NOTES

Commencement: 25 February 2009.

208   Inspection of records

Apply rule 7.28 of the 1986 Rules.

[1642]

NOTES

Commencement: 25 February 2009.

209   File of court proceedings and inspection

(1)   The Court shall open and maintain a file for each bank insolvency and (subject to the direction of the registrar) all documents relating to that bank insolvency shall be placed on that file.

(2)   Where a file has been opened under paragraph (1), the following have the right, at all reasonable times, to inspect that file—
   (a)   the bank liquidator,
   (b)   any person stating in writing that they are a creditor of the bank to which the bank insolvency relates,
   (c)   a member of the bank,
   (d)   any person who is, or at any time has been, a director or officer of the bank to which the bank insolvency relates,
   (e)   any person who is a contributory of the bank to which the bank insolvency relates, and
   (f)   the Bank of England, the FSA and the FSCS.

(3)   The right of inspection conferred on any person by paragraph (2) may be exercised on their behalf by a person properly authorised by them.

(4)   Any person may, with permission of the court, inspect the file.

(5)   The right of inspection conferred by this rule is not exercisable in respect of documents, or parts of documents, which the court has directed (either generally or specially) are not to be open to inspection without the court's permission.

(6)   An application for a direction of the court under paragraph (5) may be made by the bank liquidator or by any party appearing to the court to have an interest in the bank insolvency.

(7)   If, for the purposes of powers conferred by the 1986 Act, the 2009 Act or these rules, the Secretary of State wishes to inspect the file on a bank insolvency and requests the court to transmit the file, the court shall comply with the request or, if the file is for the time being in use for the court's own purposes, as soon as the file is no longer in such use.

(8)   Rule 208 applies in respect of the court's records on any bank insolvency as they apply in respect of court records of general insolvency proceedings.

[1643]

NOTES
Commencement: 25 February 2009.

210   Filing of Gazette notices and advertisements
Apply rule 7.32 of the 1986 Rules. For "an officer of the court" substitute "the bank liquidator".

[1644]

NOTES
Commencement: 25 February 2009.

CHAPTER 6
COSTS AND DETAILED ASSESSMENT

211   Application of the CPR
Apply rule 7.33 of the 1986 Rules.

[1645]

NOTES
Commencement: 25 February 2009.

212   Requirement to assess costs by the detailed procedure
(1)   Apply rule 7.34 of the 1986 Rules.

(2)   In paragraph (1)—
  (a)   for "company insolvency" and "liquidation" substitute "bank insolvency",
  (b)   ignore sub-paragraph (b), and
  (c)   for the words from "court to which" to the end substitute "High Court".

(3)   In paragraph (2), leave out "or creditors".

(4)   In paragraph (5), for "trustee in bankruptcy or a liquidator" substitute "bank liquidator."

(5)   Ignore paragraph (6).

[1646]

NOTES
Commencement: 25 February 2009.

213   Procedure where detailed assessment required
Apply rule 7.35 of the 1986 Rules. Ignore paragraph (6).

[1647]

NOTES
Commencement: 25 February 2009.

214   Costs of officers charged with executions of writs or other process
(1)   Apply rule 7.36 of the 1986 Rules.

(2)   In paragraph (1)(a), leave out "or 346(2)".

(3)   In paragraph (1)(b), leave out "or 346(3)".

[1648]

NOTES
Commencement: 25 February 2009.

215   Costs paid otherwise than out of the insolvent estate
Apply rule 7.38 of the 1986 Rules.

[1649]

NOTES
Commencement: 25 February 2009.

216 Award of costs against responsible insolvency practitioner
(1) Apply rule 7.39 of the 1986 Rules.

(2) Leave out from the beginning to "expenses" and "the official receiver or".

[1650]

NOTES
Commencement: 25 February 2009.

217 Application for costs
(1) Apply rule 7.40 of the 1986 Rules.

(2) In paragraph (1) for "insolvency" substitute "bank insolvency".

(3) In paragraph (2), leave out the words from ", and, in winding up" to the end.

(4) In paragraph (3), leave out "and, where appropriate, the official receiver".

[1651]

NOTES
Commencement: 25 February 2009.

218 Costs and expenses of witnesses
(1) Apply rule 7.41 of the 1986 Rules.

(2) In paragraph (1), leave out "the bankrupt or".

(3) Ignore paragraph (2).

[1652]

NOTES
Commencement: 25 February 2009.

219 Final costs certificate
Apply rule 7.42 of the 1986 Rules.

[1653]

NOTES
Commencement: 25 February 2009.

CHAPTER 7
PERSONS INCAPABLE OF MANAGING THEIR AFFAIRS

220 Introductory
Apply rule 7.43 of the 1986 Rules. In paragraph (1), for (a), substitute "by reason of being a protected person within the meaning of Part 21 of the CPR or".

[1654]

NOTES
Commencement: 25 February 2009.

221 Appointment of another person to act
Apply rule 7.44 of the 1986 Rules. Ignore paragraph (3)(c).

[1655]

NOTES
Commencement: 25 February 2009.

222 Witness statement in support of application
(1) Apply rule 7.45 of the 1986 Rules.

(2) In paragraph (1) leave out from the beginning to "receiver".

(3) Ignore paragraph (2).

[1656]

PART IV
OTHER STATUTORY INSTRUMENTS

NOTES
Commencement: 25 February 2009.

223 Service of notices following appointment

Apply rule 7.46 of the 1986 Rules.

[1657]

NOTES
Commencement: 25 February 2009.

CHAPTER 8
APPEALS IN BANK INSOLVENCY PROCEEDINGS

224 Appeals and review of court orders

(1)   The High Court may review, rescind or vary any order made by it in the exercise of its jurisdiction under Part 2 of the Banking Act 2009.

(2)   An appeal from a decision of a registrar of the High Court lies, with the permission of the registrar or a judge of the High Court, to a single judge of the High Court, and a second appeal lies, with the permission of the Court of Appeal to the Court of Appeal.

(3)   An appeal of a decision of first instance of a judge of the High Court lies, with the permission of the judge or the Court of Appeal, to the Court of Appeal.

(4)   A bank insolvency order made under rule 16 cannot be appealed under this rule.

[1658]

NOTES
Commencement: 25 February 2009.

225 Procedure on appeal

Part 52 of the CPR applies with regard to the procedure for appeals.

[1659]

NOTES
Commencement: 25 February 2009.

226 Appeal against a decision of the Secretary of State

Apply rule 7.50 of the 1986 Rules. Ignore the reference to the official receiver and paragraph (2).

[1660]

NOTES
Commencement: 25 February 2009.

CHAPTER 9
GENERAL

227 Principal court rules and practice to apply

(1)   The CPR and the practice and procedure of the High Court (including any practice direction) apply to bank insolvency proceedings in the High Court, with any necessary modifications, except so far as inconsistent with these Rules.

(2)   All bank insolvency proceedings shall be allocated to the multi-track for which CPR Part 29 makes provision and, accordingly those provisions of the CPR which provide for allocation questionnaires and track allocation do not apply.

[1661]

NOTES
Commencement: 25 February 2009.

228 Right of attendance

Apply rule 7.53 of the 1986 Rules. In paragraph (1) for "company insolvency proceedings" substitute "bank insolvency proceedings".

[1662]

NOTES
Commencement: 25 February 2009.

229   Restriction on concurrent proceedings and remedies

Where in a bank insolvency, the court makes an order staying any action, execution or legal process against the property of the bank, service of the order may be effected by delivering a sealed copy by personal service to the applicant for the bank insolvency order.

[1663]

NOTES
Commencement: 25 February 2009.

230   Security in court

Apply rule 7.58 of the 1986 Rules.

[1664]

NOTES
Commencement: 25 February 2009.

231   Payment into court

Apply rule 7.59 of the 1986 Rules.

[1665]

NOTES
Commencement: 25 February 2009.

232   Further information and disclosure

(1)   Apply rule 7.60 of the 1986 Rules.

(2)   After paragraph (2) insert—

"(3)   Before the passing of a full payment resolution the court shall only grant an order on an application under paragraph (1)(b) if satisfied that granting the order is unlikely to prejudice the achievement of Objective 1."

[1666]

NOTES
Commencement: 25 February 2009.

233   Office copies of documents

Apply rule 7.61 of the 1986 Rules.

[1667]

NOTES
Commencement: 25 February 2009.

PART 19
PROXIES AND COMPANY REPRESENTATION

234   Definition of "proxy"

(1)   Apply rule 8.1 of the 1986 Rules.

(2)   In paragraph (2) leave out "company".

(3)   In paragraph (4), after "the meeting", add "or the bank liquidator" and ignore the rest of the sentence.

[1668]

NOTES
Commencement: 25 February 2009.

235   Issue and use of forms

Apply rule 8.2 of the 1986 Rules.

[1669]

NOTES
Commencement: 25 February 2009.

236   Use of proxies at meetings

Apply rule 8.3 of the 1986 Rules. Ignore paragraph (2).

[1670]

PART IV
OTHER STATUTORY INSTRUMENTS

NOTES
Commencement: 25 February 2009.

237 Retention of proxies

Apply rule 8.4 of the 1986 Rules.

[1671]

NOTES
Commencement: 25 February 2009.

238 Right of inspection

(1) Apply rule 8.5 of the 1986 Rules.

(2) In paragraph (1)(b), for " a company's members or" substitute "of the company's".

(3) For paragraph (2) substitute—

"(2) The reference in paragraph (1) to creditors is to those creditors who have proved their debts, but this does not include a person whose proof has been wholly rejected for purposes of voting, dividend or otherwise.".

(4) Ignore paragraph (3)(b).

[1672]

NOTES
Commencement: 25 February 2009.

239 Proxy-holder with financial interest

Apply rule 8.6 of the 1986 Rules.

[1673]

NOTES
Commencement: 25 February 2009.

240 Company representation

Apply rule 8.7 of the 1986 Rules. In paragraph (1), the reference to section 375 of the 1985 Act should, after that section is repealed, be to section 323 of the 2006 Act.

[1674]

NOTES
Commencement: 25 February 2009.

PART 20
EXAMINATION OF PERSONS CONCERNED IN BANK INSOLVENCY

241 Preliminary

(1) The rules in this Part relate to applications to the court for an order under section 236 of the 1986 Act (inquiry into company's dealings when it is, or is alleged to be, insolvent).

(2) The following definitions apply—
   (a) the person in respect of whom an order is applied for is "the respondent",
   (b) "the applicable section" is section 236 of the 1986 Act, and
   (c) the bank is "the insolvent".

[1675]

NOTES
Commencement: 25 February 2009.

242 Form and contents of application

Apply rule 9.2 of the 1986 Rules.

[1676]

NOTES
Commencement: 25 February 2009.

243 Order for examination, etc

Apply rule 9.3 of the 1986 Rules.

[1677]

NOTES
Commencement: 25 February 2009.

244   Procedure for examination

Apply rule 9.4 of the 1986 Rules.

[1678]

NOTES
Commencement: 25 February 2009.

245   Record of examination

Apply rule 9.5 of the 1986 Rules.

[1679]

NOTES
Commencement: 25 February 2009.

246   Costs of proceedings

(1)   Apply rule 9.6 of the 1986 Rules.
(2)   In paragraph (2)(a) leave out "or 367(1)" and in paragraph (2)(b) leave out "or 367(2)".
(3)   In paragraph (3)(a), for "company insolvency" substitute "bank insolvency".
(4)   Ignore paragraph (3)(b).
(5)   Ignore paragraph (5).

[1680]

NOTES
Commencement: 25 February 2009.

PART 21
DECLARATION AND PAYMENT OF DIVIDEND

247   Preliminary

(1)   The rules in this Part relate to the declaration and payment of dividends in a bank insolvency.
(2)   In this Part—
"creditors" means those creditors of the bank of whom the bank liquidator is aware, or who are identified in the bank's statement of affairs and
"the insolvent" means the bank.

[1681]

NOTES
Commencement: 25 February 2009.

248   Notice of intended dividend

Apply rule 11.2 of the 1986 Rules. Ignore paragraph (1)(b).

[1682]

NOTES
Commencement: 25 February 2009.

249   Final admission/rejection of proofs

Apply rule 11.3 of the 1986 Rules. Ignore paragraph (4).

[1683]

NOTES
Commencement: 25 February 2009.

250   Postponement or cancellation of dividend

Apply rule 11.4 of the 1986 Rules.

[1684]

PART IV
OTHER STATUTORY INSTRUMENTS

NOTES
Commencement: 25 February 2009.

251 Decision to declare dividend
Apply rule 11.5 of the 1986 Rules.

[1685]

NOTES
Commencement: 25 February 2009.

252 Notice of declaration
(1) Apply rule 11.6 of the 1986 Rules.
(2) Ignore paragraph (1)(b).
(3) In paragraph (2), after (b), add—
    "(ba) expenses incurred by the bank liquidator in the achievement of objective 1 under section 99 of the Banking Act 2009."

[1686]

NOTES
Commencement: 25 February 2009.

253 Notice of no, or no further, dividend
Apply rule 11.7 of the 1986 Rules.

[1687]

NOTES
Commencement: 25 February 2009.

254 Proof altered after payment of dividend
Apply rule 11.8 of the 1986 Rules.

[1688]

NOTES
Commencement: 25 February 2009.

255 Secured creditors
Apply rule 11.9 of the 1986 Rules.

[1689]

NOTES
Commencement: 25 February 2009.

256 Disqualification from dividend
Apply rule 11.10 of the 1986 Rules.

[1690]

NOTES
Commencement: 25 February 2009.

257 Assignment of right to dividend
Apply rule 11.11 of the 1986 Rules.

[1691]

NOTES
Commencement: 25 February 2009.

258 Preferential creditors
Apply rule 11.12 of the 1986 Rules.

[1692]

NOTES
Commencement: 25 February 2009.

259 Debt payable at future time

Apply rule 11.13 of the 1986 Rules. For paragraph (3) substitute "In paragraph (2), "relevant date" means the date of the commencement of bank insolvency."

[1693]

NOTES
Commencement: 25 February 2009.

PART 22
MISCELLANEOUS AND GENERAL

260 Power of Secretary of State or Treasury to regulate certain matters

(1)   As provided for in paragraph 27 of Schedule 8 to the 1986 Act, either the Secretary of State or the Treasury may, subject to the Act and to these Rules, make regulations with respect to any matter provided for in these Rules relating to the carrying out of the functions of a bank liquidator or provisional bank liquidator, including, without prejudice to the generality of the above, provision with respect to the following matters arising in bank insolvency—

(a)   the preparation and keeping by bank liquidators and provisional bank liquidators of books, accounts and other records, and their production to such persons as may be authorised or required to inspect them;

(b)   the auditing of bank liquidators' accounts;

(c)   the manner in which bank liquidators are to act in relation to the bank's books, papers and other records, and the manner of their disposal by the bank liquidator or others;

(d)   the supply by the bank liquidator to creditors and contributories and to the liquidation committee of copies of documents relating to the bank insolvency and the affairs of the bank (on payment, in such cases as may be specified in the regulations, of a fee.);

(e)   the manner in which insolvent estates are to be distributed by the bank liquidator, including provision with respect to unclaimed funds and dividends;

(f)   the manner in which monies coming into the hands of the bank liquidator are to be handled and invested and the payment of interest on sums which, in pursuance of regulations made under this sub-paragraph, have been paid into the Insolvency Services Account;

(2)   Regulations made under paragraph (1) may—

(a)   confer a discretion on the court,

(b)   make non-compliance with any of the regulations a criminal offence,

(c)   make different provision for different cases, including different provision for different areas, and

(d)   contain such incidental, supplemental and transitional provisions as may appear to the Secretary of State or the Treasury as necessary or expedient.

[1694]

NOTES
Commencement: 25 February 2009.

261 Costs, expenses, etc

(1)   All fees, costs, charges and other expenses incurred in the course of bank insolvency, except for any money paid by the FSCS to eligible depositors in pursuance of objective 1, and any expense incurred by the FSCS in this process, are to be regarded as expenses of the bank insolvency.

(2)   The costs associated with the Prescribed Part shall be paid out of that Prescribed Part.

[1695]

NOTES
Commencement: 25 February 2009.

262 Provable debts

(1)   Subject to paragraphs (2) and (3) in a bank insolvency all claims by creditors are provable as debts against the bank, whether they are present or future, certain or contingent, ascertained or sounding only in damages.

(2)   Any obligation arising under a confiscation order made under Parts 2, 3 or 4 of the Proceeds of Crime Act 2002 is not provable.

(3)   The following are not provable except at a time when all other claims of creditors in the insolvency proceedings (other than any of a kind mentioned in this paragraph) have been paid in full with interest under section 189(2) of the 1986 Act—

(a)   any claim arising by virtue of section 382(1)(a) of the Financial Services and Markets Act 2000, not being a claim arising by virtue of section 382(1)(b) of that Act; or

PART IV   OTHER STATUTORY INSTRUMENTS

(b)   any claim which by virtue of the 1986 Act or any enactment is a claim the payment of which in the bank insolvency is to be postponed.

(4)   Nothing in this rule prejudices any enactment or rule of law under which a particular kind of debt is not provable, whether on grounds of public policy or otherwise.

[1696]

NOTES
Commencement: 25 February 2009.

263 Notices

(1)   Apply rule 12.4 of the 1986 Rules.

(2)   Ignore references to the official receiver.

[1697]

NOTES
Commencement: 25 February 2009.

264 Quorum at meeting of creditors or contributories

(1)   Apply rule 12.4A of the 1986 Rules.

(2)   For paragraph (3) substitute—

"(3)   For the purposes of this rule, the reference to the creditor or contributories necessary to constitute a quorum is to those persons present or represented by proxy by any person (including the chair) including persons duly represented under section 375 of the 1985 Act (or, after that section is repealed, by section 323 of the 2006 Act."

[1698]

NOTES
Commencement: 25 February 2009.

265 Evidence of proceedings at meetings

Apply rule 12.5 of the 1986 Rules.

[1699]

NOTES
Commencement: 25 February 2009.

266 Documents issuing from Secretary of State

Apply rule 12.6 of the 1986 Rules. In paragraph (1) ignore the reference to "members of a company".

[1700]

NOTES
Commencement: 25 February 2009.

267 Insolvency practitioner's security

(1)   Apply rule 12.8 of the 1986 Rules.

(2)   For paragraph (2) substitute—

"(2)   It is the duty of the liquidation committee in a bank insolvency to review from time to time the adequacy of the bank liquidator's security.".

[1701]

NOTES
Commencement: 25 February 2009.

268 Time limits

Apply rule 12.9(1) of the 1986 Rules as regards time limits for anything required or authorised to be done by these Rules.

[1702]

NOTES
Commencement: 25 February 2009.

269   Service by post

Apply rule 12.10 of the 1986 Rules.

[1703]

NOTES
Commencement: 25 February 2009.

270   General provisions as to service

CPR Part 6 (service of documents) applies as regards any matter relating to the service of documents and the giving of notice in bank insolvency proceedings except in cases where a rule makes provision as to the service of a document or the giving of a notice.

[1704]

NOTES
Commencement: 25 February 2009.

271   Service outside the jurisdiction

(1)   CPR Part 6 applies as regards any matter relating to the service of documents in Scotland and Northern Ireland except in cases where a rule makes provision as to the service of a document or the giving of a notice.

(2)   Where for the purposes of bank insolvency proceedings any process or order of the court, or other document, is required to be served on a person who is not in the United Kingdom—
    (a)   with regard to the service of documents to which a rule makes provision, the court may order service to be effected within such time, on such person, at such place and in such manner as it thinks fit, and may also require such proof of service as it thinks fit,
    (b)   with regard to the service of documents otherwise, CPR Rules 6.41 to 6.4 apply.

(3)   An application under paragraph (2)(a) shall be supported by a witness statement stating—
    (a)   the grounds on which the application is made, and
    (b)   in what place or country the person to be served is, or probably may be found.

[1705]

NOTES
Commencement: 25 February 2009.

272   Confidentiality of documents

(1)   Apply rule 12.13 of the 1986 Rules.

(2)   In paragraph (2) ignore the reference to a creditors' committee.

[1706]

NOTES
Commencement: 25 February 2009.

273   Notices sent simultaneously to the same person

Apply rule 12.14 of the 1986 Rules.

[1707]

NOTES
Commencement: 25 February 2009.

274   Right to copy documents

Apply rule 12.15 of the 1986 Rules.

[1708]

NOTES
Commencement: 25 February 2009.

275   Charge for copy documents

Apply rule 12.15A of the 1986 Rules.

[1709]

NOTES
Commencement: 25 February 2009.

PART IV   OTHER STATUTORY INSTRUMENTS

276 Non-receipt of notice of meeting

Apply rule 12.16 of the 1986 Rules.

[1710]

NOTES
Commencement: 25 February 2009.

277 Right to have list of creditors

(1) Where a creditor has the right under these Rules to inspect documents on the court file, the creditor may require the bank liquidator to send them a list of the bank's creditors and the amounts of their respective debts.

(2) Paragraph (1) does not apply if a statement of the bank's affairs has been filed in court or filed with the registrar of companies.

(3) The bank liquidator must respond to a request in paragraph (1) but may charge the appropriate fee for doing so.

[1711]

NOTES
Commencement: 25 February 2009.

278 False claim of status as creditor, etc

Apply rule 12.18 of the 1986 Rules.

[1712]

NOTES
Commencement: 25 February 2009.

279 Execution overtaken by judgement debtor's insolvency

(1) This rule applies where execution has been taken out against property of a judgment debtor, and notice is given to the enforcement officer or other officer charged with the execution under section 184(1) of the 1986 Act (that a bank insolvency order has been made against the debtor, or that a provisional bank liquidator has been appointed).

(2) The notice shall be in writing and be delivered by personal service at, or sent by recorded delivery to, the office of the enforcement officer or (as the case may be) of the officer charged with the execution.

[1713]

NOTES
Commencement: 25 February 2009.

280 The Gazette

Apply rule 12.20 of the 1986 Rules.

[1714]

NOTES
Commencement: 25 February 2009.

281 Punishment of offences

Apply rule 12.21 of the 1986 Rules. For "Schedule 3" substitute "Schedule 5".

[1715]

NOTES
Commencement: 25 February 2009.

282 Notice of order under section 176A(5)

(1) Apply rule 12.22 of the 1986 Rules. For references to "the liquidator, administrator or receiver" read "bank liquidator".

[1716]

NOTES
Commencement: 25 February 2009.
This rule is reproduced as it appears in the original Queen's Printer's copy; there is no paragraph (2).

PART 23
INTERPRETATION

283   Introductory

This Part of the Rules has effect for their interpretation and application; and any definition given in this Part (and in any provision of the 1986 Rules applied by this Part) applies except, and in so far as, the context requires otherwise.

[1717]

NOTES
Commencement: 25 February 2009.

284   "The court"; "the registrar"

(1)   Apply rule 13.2 of the 1986 Rules.

(2)   Ignore paragraphs (3) and (5).

(3)   In paragraph (4), for "company insolvency proceedings" substitute "bank insolvency proceedings."

[1718]

NOTES
Commencement: 25 February 2009.

285   "Give notice", etc

Apply rule 13.3 of the 1986 Rules.

[1719]

NOTES
Commencement: 25 February 2009.

286   Notice, etc to solicitors

Apply rule 13.4 of the 1986 Rules.

[1720]

NOTES
Commencement: 25 February 2009.

287   Notice to joint bank liquidators

Where 2 or more persons are acting jointly as the bank liquidator, delivery of a document to 1 of them is to be treated as delivery to them all.

[1721]

NOTES
Commencement: 25 February 2009.

288   "Insolvent estate"

References to "the insolvent estate" are to the assets of the bank.

[1722]

NOTES
Commencement: 25 February 2009.

289   "Responsible insolvency practitioner", etc

In relation to a bank insolvency, "the responsible insolvency practitioner" means the person acting in the bank insolvency as the bank liquidator or provisional bank liquidator.

[1723]

NOTES
Commencement: 25 February 2009.

290   "The appropriate fee"

"The appropriate fee" means 15 pence per A4 or A5 page, and 30 pence per A3 page.

[1724]

NOTES
Commencement: 25 February 2009.

291 "Debt", "liability"

(1)   Apply rule 13.12 of the 1986 Rules.

(2)   Ignore paragraph (5).

[1725]

NOTES
Commencement: 25 February 2009.

292 Expressions used generally

(1)   Apply rule 13.13 of the 1986 Rules.

(2)   In paragraph (1) for "Rules 1.7" to "6.23" substitute "rule 10 of the Bank Insolvency Rules 2009".

(3)   In paragraph (5), after "Secretary of State" insert "or the Treasury".

(4)   In paragraph (7), for "Chapter 20 of Part 4 of these Rules, or Chapter 23 of Part 6" substitute "Part 16 of the Bank Insolvency Rules 2009".

(5)   Ignore paragraphs (8) to (14).

(6)   In paragraph (15), after "section 176A(2)(a)" insert "as applied by section 103 of the Banking Act 2009".

[1726]

NOTES
Commencement: 25 February 2009.

293 The Schedule

The Schedule, which applies relevant schedules to the 1986 Rules to these rules with modifications, has effect.

[1727]

NOTES
Commencement: 25 February 2009.

SCHEDULE

1.   The following schedules to the 1986 Rules are applied to these Rules—
   (a)   Schedule 1. Ignore all references to rule 4.72 and for paragraph (1) substitute—

   "1.   This Schedule applies where a bank insolvency order (as defined under Part 2 of the Banking Act 2009) has been made in respect of a bank".

   (b)   Schedule 5; and
   (c)   Schedule 6.

[1728]

NOTES
Commencement: 25 February 2009.
This Schedule is reproduced as it appears in the original Queen's Printer's copy; there is no paragraph 2.

BANK ADMINISTRATION (ENGLAND AND WALES) RULES 2009

(SI 2009/357)

NOTES
Made: 23 February 2009.
Authority: Insolvency Act 1986, s 411(1B)(a), (2), (2D), (3).
Commencement: 25 February 2009.

ARRANGEMENT OF RULES

PART 1
INTRODUCTION

PART 2
APPLICATION FOR BANK ADMINISTRATION ORDER

PART 3
PROCESS OF BANK ADMINISTRATION

PART 4
COURT PROCEDURE AND PRACTICE

PART 5
APPLICATION OF INSOLVENCY RULES 1986

PART 1
INTRODUCTION

1   Citation

These Rules may be cited as the Bank Administration (England and Wales) Rules 2009.

[1729]

NOTES
Commencement: 25 February 2009.

2   Commencement

These Rules come into force on 25th February 2009.

[1730]

NOTES
Commencement: 25 February 2009.

3   Extent

These Rules extend to England and Wales only.

[1731]

NOTES
Commencement: 25 February 2009.

Interpretation

4—(1)   The following expressions used in these Rules take their meaning from the Banking Act 2009 (in accordance with section 11 of the Interpretation Act 1978—construction of subordinate legislation)—

    (a)   "bank" (s 2),
    (b)   "bank administration" (s 141(4)(a)),
    (c)   "bank administration order" (s 141(1)),
    (d)   "bank administrator" (s 141(1)),
    (e)   "bridge bank" (s 136(2)),
    (f)   "the court" (the High Court—s 166(1)),
    (g)   "the FSA" (the Financial Services Authority—s 166(2)),
    (h)   "Objective 1" (support for commercial purchaser or bridge bank—ss 137 & 138),
    (i)   "Objective 1 Achievement Notice" (s 139(4)),
    (j)   "Objective 2" (normal administration—ss 137 & 140),
    (k)   "private sector purchaser" (s 136(2)),
    (l)   "property transfer instrument" (s 33),
    (m)   "residual bank" (s 136(2)), and
    (n)   "resolution fund order" (s 49(3)).

    (2)   Expressions used in the Companies Act 2006 have the same meaning as in these rules.

[1732]

NOTES

Commencement: 25 February 2009.

5   In these Rules—

    (a)   "the FSCS" means the scheme manager of the Financial Services Compensation Scheme (established under Part 15 of the Financial Services and Markets Act 2000),
    (b)   "the Objective 1 Stage" means the period during which a bank administration order is in force before the Bank of England gives an Objective 1 Achievement Notice,
    (c)   "the Objective 2 Stage" means the period during which a bank administration order is in force after the Bank of England gives an Objective 1 Achievement Notice,
    (d)   a reference to personal service is a reference to personal service in accordance with Part 6 of the Civil Procedure Rules 1998,
    (e)   a reference to the CPR is to the Civil Procedure Rules 1998, and
    (f)   a reference to a witness statement (including a reference implied by the application of an enactment) is a reference to a witness statement—
        (i)   verified by a statement of truth in accordance with Part 22 of the CPR, and
        (ii)   if made by a bank administrator, stating that the statement is made in that capacity and giving the address at which the bank administrator works.

[1733]

NOTES

Commencement: 25 February 2009.

6 Overview

The purpose of these Rules is to prescribe a procedure for the appointment of a bank administrator, and the operation of bank administration, under Part 3 of the Banking Act 2009 in England and Wales.

[1734]

NOTES

Commencement: 25 February 2009.

7 Forms

    (1)   This Rule applies where a provision of these Rules—

    (a)   applies a provision of the Insolvency Rules 1986 which requires the use of a prescribed form, or
    (b)   makes provision similar to that made by a provision of those Rules which requires the use of a prescribed form.

    (2)   The form prescribed for the purposes of those Rules is to be used, with any modification that the person using the form thinks desirable to reflect the nature of bank administration (whether or not the modification is set out in a Practice Form issued by the Treasury for that purpose).

[1735]

NOTES
Commencement: 25 February 2009.

PART 2
APPLICATION FOR BANK ADMINISTRATION ORDER

8　Introduction

This Part makes specific provision for a number of aspects of applications for bank administration orders; Part 5 applies a number of provisions of the Insolvency Rules 1986 to applications for bank administration orders (with specified modifications).

[1736]

NOTES
Commencement: 25 February 2009.

Content of application

9　An application by the Bank of England for a bank administration order in respect of a bank must specify—
  (a)　the full name of the bank,
  (b)　any other trading names,
  (c)　the address of the bank's registered office,
  (d)　an email address for the bank,
  (e)　the address of the Bank of England, and
  (f)　the identity of the person (or persons) nominated for appointment as bank administrator.

[1737]

NOTES
Commencement: 25 February 2009.

10　If the bank has notified the Bank of England of an address for service which is, because of special circumstances, to be used in place of the registered office, that address shall be specified under Rule 9(c).

[1738]

NOTES
Commencement: 25 February 2009.

11　Statement of proposed bank administrator

An application must be accompanied by a statement by the proposed bank administrator—
  (a)　specifying the name and address of the person (or of each person) proposed to be appointed,
  (b)　giving that person's (or each person's) consent to act,
  (c)　giving details of the person's (or each person's) qualification to act as an insolvency practitioner, and
  (d)　giving details of any prior professional relationship that the person (or any of them) has had with the bank.

[1739]

NOTES
Commencement: 25 February 2009.

12　Bank of England witness statement

　(1)　An application for a bank administration order in respect of a bank must be accompanied by a witness statement made on behalf of the Bank of England—
  (a)　certifying that the conditions for applying for a bank administration order, set out in section 143 of the Banking Act 2009, are met in respect of the bank,
  (b)　stating the bank's current financial position to the best of the Bank of England's knowledge and belief (including actual, contingent and prospective assets and liabilities),
  (c)　specifying any security which the Bank of England knows or believes to be held by a creditor of the bank,
  (d)　specifying whether any security confers power to appoint an administrator under

paragraph 14 of Schedule B1 to the Insolvency Act 1986 (holder of qualifying floating charge) or an administrative receiver (and whether an administrative receiver has been appointed),

(e)   specifying any insolvency proceedings which have been instituted in respect of the bank (including any process notified to the FSA under section 120 of the Banking Act 2009),

(f)   giving details of the property transfer instrument which the Bank of England has made or intends to make in respect of the bank,

(g)   where the property transfer instrument has not yet been made, explaining what effect it is likely to have on the bank's financial position,

(h)   specifying how functions are to be apportioned where more than one person is to be appointed as bank administrator (stating, in particular, whether functions are to be exercisable jointly or concurrently), and

(i)   including any other material which the Bank of England thinks may help the court to decide whether to make the bank administration order.

(2)   The statement should identify the person maker the statement and should include the capacity in which that person makes the statement and the basis for that person's knowledge of the matters set out in the statement.

[1740]

NOTES
Commencement: 25 February 2009.

Filing

13   The application, and its accompanying documents, must be filed with the court, together with enough copies of the application and accompanying documents for service under Rule 15.

[1741]

NOTES
Commencement: 25 February 2009.

14   Each filed copy—
(a)   shall have the seal of the court applied to it,
(b)   shall be endorsed with the date and time of filing,
(c)   shall be endorsed with the venue for the hearing of the application (fixed by the court under Rule 21), and
(d)   shall be issued to the Bank of England.

[1742]

NOTES
Commencement: 25 February 2009.

Service

15   The Bank of England shall serve the application—
(a)   on the bank,
(b)   on the person (or each of the persons) nominated for appointment as bank administrator,
(c)   on any person whom the Bank of England knows to be entitled to appoint an administrator under paragraph 14 of Schedule B1 to the Insolvency Act 1986 or an administrative receiver,
(d)   on any person who has given notice to the FSA in respect of the bank under section 120 of the Banking Act 2009 (bank insolvency: notice of preliminary steps of other insolvency procedures), and
(e)   if the property transfer instrument was made or is to be made under section 11(2)(b) of the Banking Act 2009 (transfer to commercial purchaser), on each transferee.

[1743]

NOTES
Commencement: 25 February 2009.

16   Service under rule 15 must be service of a sealed and endorsed copy of the application and its accompanying documents issued under Rule 14.

[1744]

NOTES
Commencement: 25 February 2009.

17   Service must be effected as soon as is reasonably practicable, having regard in particular to the need to give the bank's representatives a reasonable opportunity to attend the hearing.

[1745]

NOTES
Commencement: 25 February 2009.

18—(1)   Service must be effected—
   (a)   by personal service to an address that the person has notified to the Bank of England as an address for service,
   (b)   by personal service to the person's registered office (where no address for service has been notified),
   (c)   by personal service to the person's usual or last known principal place of business in England and Wales (where there is no registered office and no address for service has been notified), or
   (d)   in such other manner and at such a place as the court may direct.

(2)   If the Bank of England knows of an email address that is habitually used for business purposes by a person on whom service is required, the Bank must (in addition to personal service) as soon as is reasonably practicable send by email an electronic copy of a sealed and endorsed copy of the application and its accompanying documents.

[1746]

NOTES
Commencement: 25 February 2009.

19—(1)   Service of the application shall be verified by a witness statement specifying the date on which, and the manner in which, service was effected.

(2)   The witness statement, with a sealed copy of the application exhibited to it, shall be filed with the court—
   (a)   as soon as is reasonably practicable, and
   (b)   in any event, before the hearing of the application.

[1747]

NOTES
Commencement: 25 February 2009.

20   Other notification
As soon as is reasonably practicable after filing the application the Bank of England must notify—
   (a)   any enforcement officer or other officer whom the Bank of England knows to be charged with effecting an execution or other legal process against the bank or its property,
   (b)   any person whom the Bank of England knows to have distrained against the bank or its property, and
   (c)   the FSA.

[1748]

NOTES
Commencement: 25 February 2009.

21   Venue
(1)   The court shall fix the venue for the hearing when the application is filed.

(2)   In fixing the venue the court shall have regard to—
   (a)   the desirability of the application being heard as soon as is reasonably practicable, and
   (b)   the need for the bank's representatives to be able to reach the venue in time for the hearing.

[1749]

NOTES
Commencement: 25 February 2009.

PART IV   OTHER STATUTORY INSTRUMENTS

22 Hearing

At the hearing of the application, any of the following may appear or be represented—
- (a) the Bank of England,
- (b) the FSA,
- (c) the bank,
- (d) a director of the bank,
- (e) the person (or a person) nominated for appointment as bank administrator,
- (f) any person who has given notice to the FSA in respect of the bank under section 120 of the Banking Act 2009 (bank insolvency: notice of preliminary steps of other insolvency procedures), and
- (g) with the permission of the court, any other person who appears to have an interest.

[1750]

NOTES
Commencement: 25 February 2009.

23 The order

A bank administration order must be in the form specified in Rule 2.12(2) of the Insolvency Rules 1986, with such variations, if any, as the circumstances may require.

[1751]

NOTES
Commencement: 25 February 2009.

Notice of order

24 If the court makes a bank administration order, it shall send 4 sealed copies to the Bank of England.

[1752]

NOTES
Commencement: 25 February 2009.

25 The Bank of England shall as soon as is reasonably practicable send—
- (a) one sealed copy to the bank administrator,
- (b) one sealed copy to the FSA, and
- (c) one sealed copy to the FSCS.

[1753]

NOTES
Commencement: 25 February 2009.

26 Costs

If the court makes a bank administration order, the following are payable as an expense of the bank administration—
- (a) the Bank of England's costs of making the application, and
- (b) any other costs allowed by the court.

[1754]

NOTES
Commencement: 25 February 2009.

PART 3
PROCESS OF BANK ADMINISTRATION

27 Introduction

This Part makes specific provision for a number of aspects of bank administration; Part 5 applies a number of provisions of the Insolvency Rules 1986 to bank administration (with specified modifications).

[1755]

NOTES
Commencement: 25 February 2009.

28   Bank administrator's proposals: Objective 1 Stage

(1)   This Rule makes provision about the statement of proposals which the bank administrator is required to make in the Objective 1 Stage under section 147 of the Banking Act 2009.

(2)   In addition to the information required by section 147 the statement must include—
- (a)   details of the court where the proceedings are and the court reference number,
- (b)   the full name, any other trading names, the registered address and registered number of the bank,
- (c)   details of the bank administrator's appointment (including the date),
- (d)   in the case of joint bank administrators, details of the apportionment of functions,
- (e)   the names of the directors and secretary of the bank and details of any shareholdings in the bank they have,
- (f)   an account of the circumstances giving rise to the application for the appointment of the bank administrator,
- (g)   if a statement of the bank's affairs has been submitted, a copy or summary of it with the bank administrator's comments, if any,
- (h)   if an order limiting the disclosure of the statement of affairs has been made under Rule 2.30 of the Insolvency Rules 1986 (as applied by Rule 58 below), a statement of that fact, as well as—
  - (i)   details of who provided the statement of affairs,
  - (ii)   the date of the order for limited disclosure, and
  - (iii)   the details or a summary of the details that are not subject to that order,
- (i)   if a full statement of affairs is not provided, the names, addresses and debts of the creditors including details of any security held (or, in the case of depositors, a single statement of their aggregate debt),
- (j)   if no statement of affairs has been submitted, details of the financial position of the bank at the latest practicable date (which must, unless the court otherwise orders, be a date not earlier than that on which the bank entered bank administration), a list of the bank's creditors including their names, addresses and details of their debts, including any security held, (or, in the case of depositors, a single statement of their aggregate debt), and an explanation as to why there is no statement of affairs,
- (k)   the basis upon which it is proposed that the bank administrator's remuneration should be fixed under Rule 2.106 of the Insolvency Rules 1986 (as applied by Rule 58),
- (l)   how the bank administrator proposes to pursue Objective 1,
- (m)   whether the bank administrator proposes to pursue Objective 2(a) or Objective 2(b),
- (n)   if the bank administrator proposes to pursue Objective 2(a), how it is envisaged the purpose of the bank administration will be achieved in the Objective 2 Stage,
- (o)   if the bank administrator proposes to pursue Objective 2(b)—
  - (i)   how it is envisaged the purpose of the bank administration will be achieved in the Objective 2 Stage, and
  - (ii)   how it is proposed that the bank administration shall end (winding-up or voluntary arrangement, in accordance with section 154 of the Banking Act 2009),
- (p)   the manner in which the affairs and business of the bank have been managed and financed since the date of the bank administrator's appointment (including the reasons for and terms of any disposal of assets), and
- (q)   the manner in which the affairs and business of the bank will be managed and financed if the bank administrator's proposals are approved.

(3)   The statement—
- (a)   may exclude information, the disclosure of which could seriously prejudice the commercial interests of the bank or of the bridge bank or private sector purchaser, and
- (b)   must include a statement of any exclusion.

[1756]

NOTES

Commencement: 25 February 2009.

Bank administrator's proposals: Objective 2 Stage

29—(1)   This Rule makes provision about the statement of proposals which the bank administrator is required to make under paragraph 49 of Schedule B1 to the Insolvency Act 1986 as it applies during the Objective 2 Stage (in accordance with Table 1 in section 145(6) of the Banking Act 2009).

(2)   The statement must include—
- (a)   details of the court where the proceedings are and the court reference number,
- (b)   the full name, any other trading names, the registered address and registered number of the bank,
- (c)   details of the bank administrator's appointment (including the date),

(d)   in the case of joint bank administrators, details of the apportionment of functions,

(e)   the names of the directors and secretary of the bank and details of any shareholdings in the bank they have,

(f)   an account of the circumstances giving rise to the application for the appointment of the bank administrator,

(g)   if a statement of the bank's affairs has been submitted, a copy or summary of it with the bank administrator's comments, if any,

(h)   if an order limiting the disclosure of the statement of affairs has been made under Rule 2.30 of the Insolvency Rules 1986 (as applied by Rule 58 below), a statement of that fact, as well as—

    (i)   details of who provided the statement of affairs,

    (ii)   the date of the order for limited disclosure, and

    (iii)   the details or a summary of the details that are not subject to that order,

(i)   if a full statement of affairs is not provided, the names, addresses and debts of the creditors including details of any security held (or, in the case of depositors, a single statement of their aggregate debt),

(j)   if no statement of affairs has been submitted, details of the financial position of the bank at the latest practicable date (which must, unless the court otherwise orders, be a date not earlier than that on which the bank entered bank administration), a list of the bank's creditors including their names, addresses and details of their debts including any security held, (or, in the case of depositors, a single statement of their aggregate debt), and an explanation as to why there is no statement of affairs,

(k)   the basis upon which it is proposed that the bank administrator's remuneration should be fixed under Rule 2.106 of the Insolvency Rules 1986 (as applied by Rule 58 below),

(l)   details of whether (and why) the bank administrator proposes to apply to the court under section 176A(5) of the Insolvency Act 1986 (omission of distribution to unsecured creditors: as applied by Table 2 in section 145(6) of the Banking Act 2009) (unless the bank administrator intends to propose a company voluntary arrangement),

(m)   an estimate of the value of the prescribed part for the purposes of section 176A (unless the bank administrator intends to propose a company voluntary arrangement) certified as being made to the best of the bank administrator's knowledge and belief,

(n)   an estimate of the value of the bank's net property (unless the bank administrator intends to propose a company voluntary arrangement) certified as being made to the best of the bank administrator's knowledge and belief,

(o)   whether the bank administrator proposes to pursue Objective 2(a) or Objective 2(b),

(p)   if the bank administrator proposes to pursue Objective 2(a), how it is envisaged the purpose of the bank administration will be achieved,

(q)   if the bank administrator proposes to pursue Objective 2(b)—

    (i)   how it is envisaged the purpose of the bank administration will be achieved, and

    (ii)   how it is proposed that the bank administration shall end (winding-up or voluntary arrangement, in accordance with section 154 of the Banking Act 2009),

(r)   if the bank administrator has decided not to call a meeting of creditors, the reasons,

(s)   the manner in which the affairs and business of the bank have been managed and financed since the date of the bank administrator's appointment (including the reasons for and terms of any disposal of assets),

(t)   the manner in which the affairs and business of the bank will be managed and financed if the bank administrator's proposals are approved, and

(u)   any other information which the bank administrator thinks necessary to enable creditors to decide whether or not to vote for the approval of the proposals.

(3)   In the case of bank administration following transfer to a bridge bank under section 12(2) of the Banking Act 2009—

(a)   the statement under paragraph 49 of Schedule B1 must state whether any payment is to be made to the bank from a scheme under a resolution fund order, or

(b)   if that information is unavailable when the statement under paragraph 49 is made, the bank administrator must issue a supplemental statement when the information is available.

(4)   The statement—

(a)   may exclude information, the disclosure of which could seriously prejudice the commercial interests of the bank, and

(b)   must include a statement of any exclusion.

[1757]

NOTES

Commencement: 25 February 2009.

---

30 If the bank administrator thinks that the statement made under section 147 of the Banking Act 2009 in accordance with Rule 28 contains information required by Rule 29(2), the statement under paragraph 49 of Schedule B1 to the Insolvency Act 1986 (as applied by Table 1 in section 145(6) of the Banking Act 2009) may consist of the statement under section 147, with such additions, modifications and supplemental information as the bank administrator thinks necessary—
    (a)   to comply with Rule 29(2), and
    (b)   to bring the statement under section 147 up to date.

[1758]

NOTES
    Commencement: 25 February 2009.

31 Where the court orders an extension of the period of time under paragraph 49(5) of Schedule B1 on an application by the bank administrator under paragraph 107 (as applied by Table 1 in section 145(6) of the Banking Act 2009), the bank administrator must notify the persons set out in paragraph 49(4) as soon as is reasonably practicable after the making of the order.

[1759]

NOTES
    Commencement: 25 February 2009.

32 Where the bank administrator has made a statement under paragraph 52(1) of Schedule B1 (as applied by Table 1 in section 145(6) of the Banking Act 2009) and has not called an initial meeting of creditors, the proposals issued in accordance with Rule 29 above will be deemed to have been approved by the creditors (if no meeting has been requisitioned under paragraph 52(2) within the period set out in Rule 2.37(1) of the Insolvency Rules 1986—as applied by Rule 58 below).

[1760]

NOTES
    Commencement: 25 February 2009.

33 Where the bank administrator intends to apply to the court (or file a notice under paragraph 80(2) of Schedule B1 in accordance with section 153 of the Banking Act 2009) for the bank administration to cease before the statement of proposals is sent to creditors in accordance with paragraph 49 of Schedule B1, the bank administrator must, at least 10 days before making the application (or filing the notice), send to all known creditors of the bank a report containing the information required by Rule 29(2).

[1761]

NOTES
    Commencement: 25 February 2009.

34—(1) A bank administrator who wishes to publish a notice under paragraph 49(6) of Schedule B1 (as applied by Table 1 in section 145(6) of the Banking Act 2009) must publish the notice in such manner that the bank administrator thinks most appropriate for ensuring that the notice comes to the attention of the bank's members.
    (2)   The notice must—
        (a)   state the full name of the bank,
        (b)   state the full name and address of the bank administrator,
        (c)   give details of the bank administrator's appointment, and
        (d)   specify an address to which members can write for a copy of the statement of proposals.
    (3)   The notice must be published as soon as is reasonably practicable after the bank administrator sends the statement of proposals to the bank's creditors but no later than 8 weeks (or such other period as may be agreed by the creditors or as the court may order) from the date that the bank entered bank administration.

[1762]

NOTES
    Commencement: 25 February 2009.

Reports to creditors

35—(1)   "Progress report" means a report which includes—
    (a)   details of the court where the proceedings are and the relevant court reference number,

(b)   full details of the bank's name, address of registered office and companies house registered number, and other trading names of the bank,

(c)   full details of the bank administrator's name and address and date of appointment, including any changes in office-holder,

(d)   in the case of joint bank administrators, details of the apportionment of functions,

(e)   details of any extensions of the initial period of appointment,

(f)   details of progress during the period of the report, including a receipts and payments account (as detailed in paragraph (2) below),

(g)   details of any assets that remain to be realised,

(h)   details of any amounts received from a scheme under a resolution fund order, and

(i)   any other information likely to be relevant to the creditors.

(2)   A receipts and payments account must state what assets of the bank have been realised, for what value, and what payments have been made to creditors or others.

(3)   The account must be in the form of an abstract showing receipts and payments during the period of the report; and where the bank administrator has ceased to act, the receipts and payments account shall include a statement as to the amount paid to unsecured creditors by virtue of the application of section 176A of the Insolvency Act 1986 (prescribed part).

(4)   During the Objective 1 Stage, a progress report must include details of—

(a)   the extent of the business of the bank that has been transferred,

(b)   any property, rights or liabilities that have been transferred, or which the bank administrator expects to be transferred, under a power in Part 1 of the Banking Act 2009 (special resolution regime),

(c)   any requirements imposed on the residual bank, for the purpose of the pursuit of Objective 1, under a power in that Part, and

(d)   the arrangements for managing and financing the bank during the Objective 1 Stage.

(5)   In complying with paragraph (4)(c) and (d) a report—

(a)   may exclude information, the disclosure of which could seriously prejudice the commercial interests of the bank or of the bridge bank or private sector purchaser, and

(b)   must include a statement of any exclusion.

[1763]

NOTES

Commencement: 25 February 2009.

36   A progress report must be produced for—

(a)   the first period of 6 months of the bank administration,

(b)   every subsequent period of 6 months, and

(c)   when the bank administrator ceases to act, the period from the date of the previous report (or, if there was none, from the beginning of the bank administration) until the administrator ceases to act.

[1764]

NOTES

Commencement: 25 February 2009.

37—(1)   The bank administrator must send a copy of each progress report within 28 days of the end of the period covered by the report, to—

(a)   the creditors,

(b)   the court,

(c)   the Bank of England,

(d)   the FSA,

(e)   the FSCS, and

(f)   the registrar of companies.

(2)   Instead of complying with paragraph (1)(a) the bank administrator may publish the progress report on its internet website (and take appropriate steps to draw attention to it).

(3)   The court may, on the bank administrator's application—

(a)   extend the period specified in paragraph (1),

(b)   make any other order about the content of a progress report.

[1765]

NOTES

Commencement: 25 February 2009.

38—(1)   A bank administrator who fails to comply with Rules 36 and 37 is liable to a fine and, for continued contravention, to a daily default fine.

(2)   For that purpose, failure to comply with Rules 36 and 37 shall be treated in the same way as failure to comply with Rule 2.47 of the Insolvency Rules 1986.

[1766]

NOTES
Commencement: 25 February 2009.

39   Removal of bank administrator in Objective 1 Stage

(1)   This Rule is about an application for removal of a bank administrator made by the Bank of England during the Objective 1 Stage (in accordance with the modifications for the application of paragraph 91 of Schedule B1 to the Insolvency Act 1986 in Table 1 in section 145(6) of the Banking Act 2009).

(2)   The rules for service of notice of the application, other notification of the application and for the hearing shall be as for the application to appoint a bank administrator under Part 2 of these Rules.

(3)   But both the person proposed to be appointed as a replacement and the existing bank administrator are entitled to be served and heard.

[1767]

NOTES
Commencement: 25 February 2009.

Appointment of provisional bank administrator

40   An application to the court for the appointment of a provisional bank administrator under section 135 of the Insolvency Act 1986 (as applied by Table 2 in section 145(6) of the Banking Act 2009) may be made by the Bank of England.

[1768]

NOTES
Commencement: 25 February 2009.

41   The application must be supported by a witness statement stating—
  (a)   why the Bank of England thinks that a provisional bank administrator should be appointed,
  (b)   that the person to be appointed has consented to act,
  (c)   that the person to be appointed is qualified to act as an insolvency practitioner,
  (d)   whether, to the Bank of England's knowledge, a company voluntary arrangement under Part 1 of the Insolvency Act 1986 has been proposed or is in force in respect of the bank,
  (e)   whether, to the Bank of England's knowledge, an administrative receiver is acting in respect of the bank, and
  (f)   the Bank of England's estimate of the value of the assets in respect of which the provisional bank administrator is to be appointed.

[1769]

NOTES
Commencement: 25 February 2009.

42   If satisfied that sufficient grounds are shown for the appointment, the court may make it on such terms as it thinks fit.

[1770]

NOTES
Commencement: 25 February 2009.

43   An order appointing a provisional bank administrator must specify the functions to be carried out in relation to the bank's affairs.

[1771]

NOTES
Commencement: 25 February 2009.

44   If the court makes an order appointing a provisional bank administrator the court shall—
  (a)   notify the Bank of England,
  (b)   send 4 copies of the order to the person appointed (by email if possible), and
  (c)   send a copy of the order to any administrative receiver of the bank.

[1772]

NOTES
Commencement: 25 February 2009.

45—(1)   As soon as is reasonably practicable after appointment a provisional bank administrator must send a copy of the order of appointment to—
  (a)   the bank,
  (b)   the FSA, and
  (c)   the registrar of companies (together with the form specified in Rule 4.26(3)(ii) of the Insolvency Rules 1986, with such variations, if any, as the circumstances may require).

  (2)   Notice to the bank must be given by service in accordance with Rule 18 above.

[1773]

NOTES
Commencement: 25 February 2009.

46   The Bank of England may disclose the fact and terms of an order appointing a provisional bank administrator to any person whom the Bank thinks has a sufficient business interest.

[1774]

NOTES
Commencement: 25 February 2009.

47   Additional joint bank administrator

  (1)   The process for the appointment of an additional joint bank administrator is the same as for the initial appointment of a bank administrator.

  (2)   The existing bank administrator (or each of them) is entitled to a copy of the application and may—
  (a)   file written representations, and
  (b)   be heard at the hearing.

  (3)   An application for the appointment of an additional joint bank administrator may be made during the Objective 1 Stage only by the Bank of England.

  (4)   Rule 58 below applies Rules 2.127 and 2.128 of the Insolvency Rules 1986 (notification and advertisement of the appointment of an additional joint administrator).

[1775]

NOTES
Commencement: 25 February 2009.

48   End of administration: successful rescue

  (1)   This Rule supplements section 153 of the Banking Act 2009 (end of bank administration where bank administrator satisfied that Objective 2(a) has been achieved).

  (2)   The bank administrator's notice under paragraph 80 of Schedule B1 to the Insolvency Act 1986 (as applied by section 153)—
  (a)   must be filed with the court in Form 2.32B (the form specified in rule 2.113 of the Insolvency Rules 1986 subject to Rule 7(2) above), and
  (b)   must be accompanied by a final progress report.

  (3)   The notice takes effect when the court discharges the bank administration order on the application of the bank administrator.

  (4)   Before applying for discharge the bank administrator must send a copy of the notice under paragraph 80 of Schedule B1 and the progress report to—
  (a)   the Bank of England,
  (b)   the FSA,
  (c)   the FSCS, and
  (d)   the registrar of companies.

  (5)   Notice under paragraph (4)(b) and (c) must be given at least 7 days' before the hearing of the application for approval of the notice.

(6)   The bank administrator shall be taken to have complied with the requirements of paragraph 80(5) if, within 5 business days of filing the notice under paragraph 80 with the court, he publishes in the same manner as he published his notice of appointment, and in the Gazette, a notice specifying—

(a)   the full name of the bank and any other trading names,

(b)   the name and address of the bank administrator,

(c)   the date of the notice under paragraph 80, and

(d)   an address to which creditors can write for a copy of the notice under paragraph 80 and the final progress report.

(7)   The bank administrator's application for discharge must certify compliance with the requirements of paragraph 80 and of the preceding paragraphs of this Rule.

(8)   If the court is satisfied that the conditions in section 153(1) of the Banking Act 2009 have been met it shall—

(a)   discharge the bank administration order, and

(b)   notify the bank administrator, who shall notify the registrar of companies.

[1776]

NOTES
Commencement: 25 February 2009.

49   End of administration: dissolution

(1)   This Rule supplements section 154(2)(a) of the Banking Act 2009 (bank administrator giving notice under paragraph 84 of Schedule B1 to the Insolvency Act 1986 that there are no more assets for distribution, and moving to dissolution).

(2)   The bank administrator's notice under paragraph 84—

(a)   must be filed with the court in Form 2.35B (the form specified in rule 2.118 of the Insolvency Rules 1986 subject to Rule 7(2) above), and

(b)   must be accompanied by a final progress report.

(3)   The notice shall not take effect until the court discharges the bank administration order on the application of the bank administrator.

(4)   Before applying for discharge the bank administrator must send a copy of the notice under paragraph 84 and the progress report to—

(a)   the registrar of companies, and

(b)   each person who received notice of the bank administrator's appointment.

(5)   After the expiry of the period mentioned in paragraph 84(6) (and subject to extension under paragraph 84(7)) if the court discharges the bank administration order—

(a)   the notice takes effect as specified in paragraph 84(6),

(b)   the court shall notify the bank administrator, who shall notify the registrar of companies.

(6)   If the court makes an order under paragraph 84(7) it shall notify the bank administrator in Form 2.36B (the form specified in rule 2.118 of the Insolvency Rules 1986 subject to Rule 7(2) above), who shall notify the registrar of companies.

[1777]

NOTES
Commencement: 25 February 2009.

PART 4
COURT PROCEDURE AND PRACTICE

50   Introduction

This Part makes specific provision for a number of aspects of proceedings under Part 3 of the Banking Act 2009 (bank administration); Part 5 of these Rules applies a number of provisions of the Insolvency Rules 1986 to proceedings under the 2009 Act (with specified modifications).

[1778]

NOTES
Commencement: 25 February 2009.

51   Title of proceedings

Proceedings under Part 3 of the Banking Act 2009 shall be entitled "IN THE MATTER OF … (naming the bank to which the proceedings relate) AND IN THE MATTER OF PART 3 OF THE BANKING ACT 2009".

[1779]

NOTES
Commencement: 25 February 2009.

Right to inspect file

52—(1)   The court must open and maintain a file for each set of bank administration proceedings.

(2)   All documents relating to the bank administration are to be placed on the file, subject to any direction of the registrar.

(3)   The following have the right, at all reasonable times, to inspect the court's file in respect of bank administration proceedings—

    (a)   the bank administrator or provisional bank administrator,

    (b)   a person who is or was a director or officer of the bank,

    (c)   a member of the bank,

    (d)   any person stating himself in writing to be a creditor of the bank,

    (e)   any person stating himself in writing to be a contributory in respect of the bank,

    (f)   the Bank of England,

    (g)   the FSA, and

    (h)   the FSCS.

[1780]

NOTES
Commencement: 25 February 2009.

53   A right of inspection may be exercised on a person's behalf by anyone authorised by him in writing.

[1781]

NOTES
Commencement: 25 February 2009.

54   Any person may, with permission of the court, inspect the court's file in respect of bank administration proceedings.

[1782]

NOTES
Commencement: 25 February 2009.

55   A right of inspection is not exercisable in the case of documents, or parts of documents, as to which the court directs that they are not to be made open to inspection without the court's permission; and an application for a direction may be made by—

    (a)   the bank administrator or provisional bank administrator, or

    (b)   any person appearing to the court to have an interest.

[1783]

NOTES
Commencement: 25 February 2009.

56   Rule 7.28(2) and (3) of the Insolvency Rules 1986 (as applied by Rule 58 below) apply in respect of the court's file of bank administration proceedings as they apply in respect of court records.

[1784]

NOTES
Commencement: 25 February 2009.

57   Proceedings under sections 213 and 214 of the Insolvency Act 1986 (fraudulent and wrongful trading) shall be conducted in accordance with section 215 of that Act subject to the modifications specified in section 145 of the Banking Act 2009.

[1785]

NOTES
Commencement: 25 February 2009.

PART 5
APPLICATION OF INSOLVENCY RULES 1986

General application

58 The provisions of the Insolvency Rules 1986 listed in the Table in Rule 61 apply for the purposes of bank administration and applications for bank administration.

[1786]

NOTES
Commencement: 25 February 2009.

59 For that purpose the rules apply with—
(a)   the general modifications set out in Rule 60,
(b)   any specific modification set out in the Table in Rule 61, and
(c)   any other necessary modification.

[1787]

NOTES
Commencement: 25 February 2009.

60   General modifications
The general modifications are that—
(a)   a reference to an administrator or liquidator is to be treated as a reference to the bank administrator,
(b)   a reference to administration or liquidation is to be treated as a reference to bank administration,
(c)   a reference to a provisional liquidator is to be treated as a reference to a provisional bank administrator,
(d)   a reference to a winding-up order is to be treated as a reference to a bank administration order,
(e)   a reference to a petition for a winding-up order is to be treated as a reference to an application for a bank administration order,
(f)   a reference to insolvency proceedings is to be treated as a reference to bank administration (or proceedings for bank administration),
(g)   a reference to the responsible insolvency practitioner is to be treated as a reference to the bank administrator or provisional bank administrator,
(h)   all references to the Official Receiver are to be ignored,
(i)   all references to the county courts are to be ignored,
(j)   all references to the EC regulation or to the appointment of a member State liquidator are to be ignored,
(k)   a reference to the company is to be treated as a reference to the bank,
(l)   a reference to an affadavit is to be treated as to a witness statement verified by a statement of truth in accordance with Part 22 of the CPR,
(m)   a reference in the rules to a paragraph of Schedule B1 to the Insolvency Act 1986 is to be treated as a reference to that paragraph as applied and modified by section 145 of the Banking Act 2009, and
(n)   a reference to the Insolvency Act 1986 includes a reference to Part 3 of the Banking Act 2009.

[1788]

NOTES
Commencement: 25 February 2009.

61   Table of applications and specific modifications
This Rule contains the Table of applied provisions of the Insolvency Rules 1986.

RULE	SUBJECT	SPECIFIC MODIFICATIONS
Preparatory steps		
2.27	Notification and advertisement of administrator's appointment	In paragraph (1), ignore "and once in such newspaper". Ignore paragraph (2)(a) and (b).

RULE	SUBJECT	SPECIFIC MODIFICATIONS
Preparatory steps		
2.28	Notice requiring statement of affairs	
2.29	Verification and filing	
2.30	Limited disclosure	On an application for disclosure under paragraph (4) any of the following may appear and be heard, or make written representations— (a) the bank administrator, (b) the Bank of England, and (c) the FSA.
2.31	Release from duty to submit statement of affairs; extension of time	On an application under paragraph (2) for release or extension of time any of the following may appear and be heard, or make written representations— (a) the bank administrator, (b) the Bank of England, and (c) the FSA.
2.32	Expenses of statement of affairs	
Bank administrator's proposals and creditors' meetings		
2.33	*Administrator's proposals*	*Rule 2.33 is not applied—but equivalent provision is made by Part 3 of these Rules.*
2.34	Meetings to consider administrator's proposals	(1) Rule 2.34 applies in the Objective 2 Stage. (2) The FSA and the FSCS are added to the list in paragraph (2) of persons entitled to notice.
2.35	Creditors' meetings generally	The FSA and the FSCS are added to the list in paragraph (3) of persons to whose convenience the bank administrator is to have regard.
2.36	Chairman at meetings	
2.37	Meeting requisitioned by creditors	Treat the reference to the administrator's statement of proposals as a reference to the bank administrator's statement of proposals in accordance with Rule 29 above.
2.38	Entitlement to vote	
2.39	Admission and rejection of claims	
2.40	Secured creditors	
2.41	Holders of negotiable instruments	
2.42	Hire-purchase, conditional sale and chattel leasing agreements	
2.43	Resolutions	
2.44	Minutes	
2.45	Revision of the administrator's proposals	In paragraph (2)(c) ignore the reference to the person making the appointment.
2.46	Notice to creditors	
2.47	*Reports to creditors*	*Rule 2.47 is not applied—but equivalent provision is made by Part 3 of these Rules.*

RULE	SUBJECT	SPECIFIC MODIFICATIONS
Bank administrator's proposals and creditors' meetings		
2.48	Correspondence instead of creditors' meetings	
2.49	Venue and conduct of company meeting	
Creditors' committee		
2.50	Constitution of committee	*(A creditors' committee cannot be established until the Objective 2 Stage—see the modifications for the application of paragraphs 50 to 58 of Schedule B1 to the Insolvency Act 1986 in Table 1 in section 145 of the Banking Act 2009.)*
2.51	Formalities of establishment	
2.52	Functions and meetings of the committee	
2.53	The chairman at meetings	
2.54	Quorum	
2.55	Committee-members' representatives	
2.56	Resignation	
2.57	Termination of membership	
2.58	Removal	
2.59	Vacancies	
2.60	Procedure at meetings	
2.61	Resolutions of creditors' committee by post	
2.62	Information from administrator	
2.63	Expenses of members	
2.64	Members dealing with the company	In respect of any application to set aside a transaction under paragraph (2)— (a) notice of the application must be given to the FSA, and (b) the FSA may appear and be heard.
2.65	Formal defects	
Process of administration		
2.66	Application to court to dispose of charged property	If an application is made during the Objective 1 Stage, then in addition to the requirements of Rule 2.66— (a) the bank administrator must notify the Bank of England of the time and place of the hearing, (b) the Bank of England may appear, and (c) if an order is made the bank administrator must send a copy to the Bank of England as soon as is reasonably practicable.
2.67	Priority of expenses of administration	In addition to the matters listed in Rule 2.67(1), expenses in connection with provisional bank administration are payable in the following order of priority— (a) the cost of any security provided by the provisional bank administrator takes priority equally with security provided by the bank administrator, and

PART IV
OTHER STATUTORY INSTRUMENTS

RULE	SUBJECT	SPECIFIC MODIFICATIONS
Process of administration		
		(b) the remuneration of the provisional bank administrator ranks next, and
		(c) any deposit lodged on an application for the appointment of a provisional bank administrator ranks next.
2.68	Distributions to creditors: introduction	(*Distributions in the case of bank administration following transfer to a bridge bank under section 12(2) of the Banking Act 2009 and during the Objective 1 Stage require the Bank of England's consent—see the modification for the application of paragraph 65 of Schedule B1 to the Insolvency Act 1986 in Table 1 in section 145 of the Banking Act 2009.*)
2.69	Debts of insolvent company to rank equally	
2.70	Dividends: supplementary	
2.71	Division of unsold assets	
2.72	Proving a debt	
2.73	Claim established by witness statement	
2.74	Costs of proving	
2.75	Administrator to allow inspection of proofs	
2.76	New administrator: transfer of proofs	
2.77	Admission and rejection of proofs for dividend	
2.78	Appeal against decision on proof	In respect of any application under Rule 2.78(1) or (2)— (a) notice of the application must be given to the FSA and (b) the FSA
2.79	Withdrawal or variation of proof	
2.80	Expunging of proof by the court	In respect of any application under Rule 2.80(1)(b)— (a) notice of the application must be given to the FSA and (b) the FSA
2.81	Estimate of quantum of claims	
2.82	Negotiable instruments etc	
2.83	Secured creditors	
2.84	Discounts	
2.85	Mutual credit and set-off	
2.86	Debt in foreign currency	
2.87	Periodical payments	
2.88	Interest	
2.89	Debt payable in future	
2.90	Value of security	

RULE	SUBJECT	SPECIFIC MODIFICATIONS
Process of administration		
2.91	Surrender for non-disclosure	
2.92	Redemption by administrator	
2.93	Test of security's value	
2.94	Realisation of security by creditor	
2.95	Notice of proposed distribution	The following are added to the list of those entitled to receive notice under Rule 2.95(2)— (a) the FSA (b) the FSCS (c) during the Objective 1 Stage of a bank administration following transfer to a bridge bank under section 12(2) of the Banking Act 2009
2.96	Admission or rejection of proofs	
2.97	Declaration of dividend	
2.98	Notice of declaration of dividend	(1) The following are added to the list of those entitled to receive notice under Rule 2.98(1)— (a) the FSA (b) the FSCS (c) during the Objective 1 Stage of a bank administration following transfer to a bridge bank under section 12(2) of the Banking Act 2009 (2) In the case of bank administration following transfer to a bridge bank under section 12(2) of the Banking Act 2009 and during the Objective 1 Stage
2.99	Payment of dividends etc	
2.100	Notice of no dividend or no further dividend	The bank administrator must copy any notice under Rule 2.100 to— (a) the FSA (b) the FSCS (c) the Bank of England
2.101	Proof altered after payment of dividend	
2.102	Secured creditors	
2.103	Disqualification from dividend	In respect of any application for disqualification under Rule 2.103— (a) notice of the application must be given to the FSA, and (b) the FSA may appear and be heard.
2.104	Assignment of right to dividend	
2.105	Debt payable in future	The "relevant date" is the date of the bank administration order.
The bank administrator		
2.106	Fixing of remuneration	(1) In the Objective 1 Stage the Bank of England shall fix the bank administrator's remuneration in accordance with Rule 2.106(2)(a) or (b).

RULE	SUBJECT	SPECIFIC MODIFICATIONS
The bank administrator		
		(2) In the Objective 2 Stage, Rule 2.106 applies (but pending action under paragraphs (3) or (5) arrangements established by the Bank of England in the Objective 1 Stage shall continue to apply).
2.107	Recourse to meeting of creditors	
2.108	Recourse to the court	(1) In respect of remuneration fixed by the Bank of England—
		(a) Rule 2.108 applies as if references to the creditors' committee were references to the Bank of England, and
		(b) the court shall have regard to Objective 1.
		(2) In respect of any application under Rule 2.108—
		(a) notice of the application must be given to the FSA, and
		(b) the FSA may appear and be heard.
2.109	Creditors' claim that remuneration is excessive	Rule 2.109 applies only during the Objective 2 Stage.
4.127B and Sch 6	Remuneration where assets realised on behalf of chargeholder	
Ending administration		
2.110	Final progress report	(1) The reference to Rule 2.47 is to be treated as a reference to Rule 35 above.
		(2) In the case of bank administration following transfer to a bridge bank under section 12(2) of the Banking Act 2009 the final progress report—
		(a) must not be made until the bank administrator is satisfied that any payment likely to be made to the bank from a scheme under a resolution fund order has been made, and
		(b) must state whether any payment has been received and, if so, its amount.
2.113	*Notice of end of administration*	*Rule 2.113 is not applied—but equivalent provision is made by Part 3 of these Rules.*
2.114	Application to court by administrator	The reference to an application to the court under paragraph 79 of Schedule B1 to the Insolvency Act 1986 is to be treated as a reference to a notice under paragraph 80 (as applied by section 153(2) of the Banking Act 2009).
2.118	Moving from administration to dissolution	*Rule 2.118 is not applied—but equivalent provision is made by Part 3 of these Rules.*
Replacing bank administrator		
2.119	Grounds for resignation	During the Objective 1 Stage the Bank of England's consent, as well as the court's permission, is required for resignation under paragraph (2).
2.120	Notice of intention to resign	The Bank of England and the FSA are added to the list of those entitled to notice under paragraph (1).
2.121	Notice of resignation	

RULE	SUBJECT	SPECIFIC MODIFICATIONS
Replacing bank administrator		

2.122	Application to court to remove administrator	*(An application may be made during the Objective 1 Stage only with the Bank of England's consent —see the modifications for the application of paragraph 88 of Schedule B1 to the Insolvency Act 1986 in Table 1 in section 145 of the Banking Act 2009.)*
		
		(1) An application must state either—
		
		    (a) that the Bank of England has consented to its being made, or
		
		    (b) that the Objective 1 Stage has ended.
		
		(2) The FSA is added to the list of those entitled to notice under paragraph (2).

2.123	Notice of vacation of office on ceasing to be qualified	
2.124	Death of administrator	
2.125	Application to replace	Rule 2.125 is applied during the Objective 2 Stage only (and ignoring references to paragraph 95 of Schedule B1). *(For equivalent provision about application for removal by the Bank of England during the Objective 1 Stage (in accordance with the modifications for the application of paragraph 91 of Schedule B1 to the Insolvency Act 1986 in Table 1 in section 145 of the Banking Act 2009) see Part 3 of these Rules.*
2.126	Notification and advertisement of replacement	
2.127	Notification and advertisement of appointment of joint administrator	
2.128	Notice to registrar of companies of replacement or addition	
2.129	Duties on vacating office	
Provisional bank administrator (see application of section 135 of the Insolvency Act 1986 in Table 2 in section 145 of the Banking Act 2009)		
4.25	*Appointment*	*Rule 4.25 is not applied—but equivalent provision is made by Part 3 of these Rules.*
4.25A	*Notice of appointment*	*Rule 4.25A is not applied—but equivalent provision is made by Part 3 of these Rules.*
4.26	*Order of appointment*	*Rule 4.26 is not applied—but equivalent provision is made by Part 3 of these Rules.*
4.28	Security	
4.29	Failure to give or keep up security	
4.30	Remuneration	Ignore paragraph (4).

4.31	Termination of appointment	(1) An application for termination may be made by—
		
		    (a) the provisional bank administrator, or
		
		    (b) the Bank of England.

RULE	SUBJECT	SPECIFIC MODIFICATIONS

Provisional bank administrator (see application of section 135 of the Insolvency Act 1986 in Table 2 in section 145 of the Banking Act 2009)

| | | (2) A provisional bank administrator's appointment terminates on the making of a bank administration order. |

Disclaimer

4.187	Notice of disclaimer	(*In the case of bank administration following transfer to a bridge bank under section 12(2) of the Banking Act 2009 notice may be given during the Objective 1 Stage only with the Bank of England's consent —see the modifications for the application of section 178 of the Insolvency Act 1986 in Table 2 in section 145 of the Banking Act 2009.*)
4.188	Communication to interested persons	
4.189	Additional notices	
4.190	Duty to keep court informed	
4.191	Application by interested party	
4.192	Interest in property to be declared on request	
4.193	Disclaimer presumed valid and effective	
4.194	Application for exercise of court's powers under section 181 of the Insolvency Act 1986	(*Section 181 is applied by Table 2 in section 145 of the Banking Act 2009.*)

Court procedure and practice

7.1	Application of Chapter 1 of Part 7	Chapter 1 does not apply to an application for a bank administration order (which is addressed in Part 2 of these Rules).
7.2	Interpretation	
7.3	Form and contents of application	
7.3A	Application to disapply section 176A of the Insolvency Act 1986	
7.4	Filing and service of application	
7.4A	Notice of application under section 176A of the Insolvency Act 1986	
7.5	Other hearings *ex parte*	
7.6	Hearing of application	
7.7	Use of witness statement evidence	
7.8	Filing and service of witness statements	
7.9	Use of reports	
7.10	Adjournment of hearings; directions	

RULE	SUBJECT	SPECIFIC MODIFICATIONS
Court procedure and practice		
7.16	Nomination and appointment of shorthand writers	
7.17	Remuneration of shorthand writers	
7.19	Enforcement of court orders	
7.20	Orders enforcing compliance with Rules	
7.21	Warrants	
7.23	Warrants under section 236	
7.27	Court records	
7.28	Inspection of records	
7.30	File of court proceedings	
7.31	*Right to inspect court file*	*Rule 7.31 is not applied—but equivalent provision is made in Part 4 of these Rules.*
7.32	Filing of Gazette notices and advertisements	
7.33	Costs: application of the Civil Proceedings Rules	
7.34	Requirement to assess costs by the detailed procedure	
7.35	Procedure where detailed assessment required	
7.36	Costs of execution or other process	
7.38	Costs paid otherwise than out of the insolvent estate	
7.39	Award of costs against responsible insolvency practitioner	
7.40	Application for costs	
7.41	Costs and expenses of witnesses	
7.42	Final costs certificate	
7.43	Persons who lack capacity to manage their affairs: introductory	
7.44	Appointment of another person to act	
7.45	Witness statement in support of application	
7.46	Services of notices following appointment	
7.47	Appeals and reviews of court orders	*(Rule 7.47 is not applied so as to permit an appeal against the making of a bank administration order.)*
7.49	Procedure on appeal	
7.51	Principal court rules and practice to apply	*(The reference to the CPR, the practice and procedure of the High Court and of the county court is to be treated as a reference to the CPR (Part 52).)*

PART IV
OTHER STATUTORY INSTRUMENTS

RULE	SUBJECT	SPECIFIC MODIFICATIONS
Court procedure and practice		
7.53	Right of attendance	
7.54	Insolvency practitioner's solicitor	
7.55	Formal defects	
7.56	Restriction on concurrent proceedings and remedies	
7.58	Security in court	
7.59	Payment into court	
7.60	Further information and disclosure	
7.61	Office copies of documents	
Proxies		
8.1	Definition of proxy	
8.2	Issue and use of forms	
8.3	Use of proxies at meetings	
8.4	Retention of proxies	
8.5	Right of inspection of proxies	
8.6	Proxy-holder with financial interest	
8.7	Company representation	*(The reference to section 375 of the Companies Act 1985 becomes a reference to section 323 of the Companies Act 2006.)*
Examination of persons		
9.1	Preliminary	(1) *Part 9 applies to applications under section 236 of the Insolvency Act 1986 (inquiry into company's dealings) as applied by Table 2 in section 145 of the Banking Act 2009.* (2) Treat a reference to "the insolvent" as a reference to the bank.
9.2	Form and contents of application	
9.3	Order for examination	
9.4	Procedure for examination	
9.5	Record of examination	
9.6	Costs of proceedings	
Declaration and payment of dividend		
11.1	Preliminary	
11.2	Notice of intended dividend	
11.3	Final admission or rejection of proofs	
11.4	Postponement or cancellation of dividend	
11.5	Decision to declare dividend	
11.6	Notice of declaration	
11.7	Notice of no dividend or no further dividend	

RULE	SUBJECT	SPECIFIC MODIFICATIONS
Declaration and payment of dividend		
11.8	Proof altered after payment of dividend	
11.9	Secured creditors	
11.10	Disqualification from dividend	
11.11	Assignment of right to dividend	
11.12	Preferential creditors	
11.13	Debt payable in future	The "relevant date" is the date of the bank administration order.
Miscellaneous and general		
12.1	Regulation of specified administrative matters	A reference to the Secretary of State includes a reference to the Treasury.
12.2	Costs and expenses	
12.3	Provable debts	
12.4	Notices	
12.4A	Quorum at meetings	*(The reference to section 375 of the Companies Act 1985 becomes a reference to section 323 of the Companies Act 2006.)*
12.5	Evidence of proceedings at meeting	
12.6	Documents issued by Secretary of State	
12.8	Insolvency practitioner's security	
12.9	Time-limits	
12.10	Service by post	*(Rule 12.10 applies subject to express provision about service made in these Rules.)*
12.11	Service and notice: general	Part 6 of the CPR applies subject to any provision of these rules.
12.12	Service outside jurisdiction	Part 6 of the CPR applies with regard to service in Scotland or Northern Ireland, subject to any provision of these rules. Where service is to take place outside the United Kingdom, where these rules provide for service, the court may direct how that service is to be effect. With regard to service otherwise, Part 6 of the CPR applies.
12.13	Confidentiality of documents	
12.14	Notices sent simultaneously to same person	
12.15	Right to copy documents	
12.15A	Charge for copy documents	
12.16	Non-receipt of notice of meeting	
12.17	Right to have list of creditors	
12.18	False claim of status as creditor	
12.20	Gazette	

RULE	SUBJECT	SPECIFIC MODIFICATIONS
Miscellaneous and general		
12.21 and Sch 5	Punishment of offences	
12.22	Notice of order under section 176A of the Insolvency Act 1986	
13.1 to 13.13	Interpretation and application	

[1789]

NOTES
Commencement: 25 February 2009.

INSOLVENCY (AMENDMENT) REGULATIONS 2009

(SI 2009/482)

NOTES
Made: 4 March 2009.
Authority: Insolvency Act 1986, ss 411(7), 412(4), Sch 8, para 27, Sch 9, para 30; Insolvency Rules 1986, SI 1986/1925, r 12.1(g).
Commencement: 6 April 2009.

1 Citation and commencement

These Regulations may be cited as the Insolvency (Amendment) Regulations 2009 and come into force on 6th April 2009.

[1790]

NOTES
Commencement: 6 April 2009.

2 Amendment of the Insolvency Regulations 1994

For Table 2 and Table 3 in Schedule 2 to the Insolvency Regulations 1994, substitute—

"Table 2

London Rates

Grade according to the Insolvency Service grading structure/Status of Official	Total hourly rate £
D2/Official Receiver	75
C2/Deputy or Assistant Official Receiver	63
C1/Senior Examiner	58
L3/Examiner	46
L2 Examiner	42
B2/Administrator	46
L1/Examiner	40
B1/Administrator	46
A2/Administrator	40
A1/Administrator	35

Table 3

Provincial Rates

Grade according to the Insolvency Service grading structure/Status of Official	Total hourly rate £
D2/Official Receiver	69
C2/Deputy or Assistant Official Receiver	58
C1/Senior Examiner	52
L3/Examiner	46
L2 Examiner	40
B2/Administrator	43
L1/Examiner	38
B1/Administrator	42
A2/Administrator	36
A1/Administrator	31"

[1791]

NOTES
Commencement: 6 April 2009.

INSOLVENCY PRACTITIONERS AND INSOLVENCY SERVICES ACCOUNT (FEES) (AMENDMENT) ORDER 2009

(SI 2009/487)

NOTES
Made: 2 March 2009.
Authority: Insolvency Act 1986, ss 414(5), 415A(1), (2), (3), (4)(b).
Commencement: 6 April 2009.

1 Citation, commencement and revocation

(1)   This Order may be cited as the Insolvency Practitioners and Insolvency Services Account (Fees) (Amendment) Order 2009 and comes into force on 6th April 2009.

(2)   The Insolvency Practitioners and Insolvency Services Account (Fees) (Amendment) (No 2) Order 2005 and the Insolvency Practitioners and Insolvency Services Account (Fees) (Amendment) Order 2008 are revoked.

[1792]

NOTES
Commencement: 6 April 2009.

2 Amendment to the Insolvency Practitioners and Insolvency Services Account (Fees) Order 2003

The Insolvency Practitioners and Insolvency Services Account (Fees) Order 2003 ("the principal Order") is amended as set out below.

[1793]

NOTES
Commencement: 6 April 2009.

3   In article 2 of the principal Order, for paragraph (2), substitute—

"(2)   On or before 6th April 2009 and on or before 6th April in each subsequent year, there shall be paid to the Secretary of State by each body recognised pursuant to section 391 in respect of the maintenance of that body's recognition pursuant to that section, a fee calculated

PART IV   OTHER STATUTORY INSTRUMENTS

by multiplying £300 by the number of persons who as at the 1st January in that year were authorised to act as insolvency practitioners by virtue of membership of that body.".

[1794]

NOTES
Commencement: 6 April 2009.

4—(1) This article applies to a body recognised pursuant to section 391 of the Insolvency Act 1986 that—

(a) pursuant to article 2(2) of the principal Order (as it stood before the coming into force of this Order) makes a payment by reference to the number of persons who as at 1st January 2009 were authorised to act as insolvency practitioners by virtue of membership of that body; and

(b) makes that payment in the period commencing on 1st January 2009 and ending immediately before 6th April 2009.

(2) The substitution of article 2(2) of the principal Order by article 3 of this Order shall not require a body to which this article applies to make any further payment by reference to the number of persons who as at 1st January 2009 were authorised to act as insolvency practitioners by virtue of membership of that body.

[1795]

NOTES
Commencement: 6 April 2009.

5 In each of paragraphs (3), (4) and (5) of article 3 of the principal Order, for "£2,550" substitute "£3,250".

[1796]

NOTES
Commencement: 6 April 2009.

6 In the Table of fees in paragraph 2 of the Schedule to the principal Order—

(a) in relation to fee No 1 (banking fee: winding up by the court and bankruptcy), for the amount of the fee in the third column, substitute "£18";

(b) in relation to fee No 2 (banking fee: voluntary winding up), for the amount of the fee in the third column, substitute "£23";

(c) in the first column, between the reference to fee No 2B and the reference to fee No 3, insert a reference to fee No 2C;

(d) for the description of fee No 2C in the second column and the circumstances in which it is payable, insert—

"Payment of unclaimed dividends or other money—voluntary winding up

Where any money is paid into the Insolvency Services Account pursuant to regulation 18(2)(a), that payment shall be accompanied by a fee in respect of each company to which it relates of—";

(e) for the amount of fee No 2C in the third column, insert "£25.00";

(f) in relation to fee No 3 (cheque etc issue fee), for the amount of the fee in the third column payable in respect of item (ii), substitute "£1".

[1797]

NOTES
Commencement: 6 April 2009.

UNIT TRUSTS (ELECTRONIC COMMUNICATIONS) ORDER 2009

(SI 2009/555)

NOTES
Made: 5 March 2009.
Authority: Electronic Communications Act 2000, ss 8, 9.
Commencement: 6 March 2009.

1   Citation and commencement

This Order may be cited as the Unit Trusts (Electronic Communications) Order 2009 and comes into force on the day after the day on which it is made.

[1798]

NOTES
Commencement: 6 March 2009.

2   Interpretation

In this Order—

"the 2001 instrument" means the General Provisions and Glossary Instrument 2001 (2001/7) made by the Authority under the Act on 21st June 2001;

"the Act" means the Financial Services and Markets Act 2000;

"authorised unit trust scheme" has the meaning given in section 237(3) of the Act;

"the Authority" means the Financial Services Authority;

"manager" has the meaning given in that part of its definition in the Glossary contained in the 2001 instrument which relates to an authorised unit trust scheme;

"register" has the meaning given in that part of its definition in the Glossary contained in the 2001 instrument which relates to unitholders of an authorised unit trust scheme;

"trust deed" has the meaning given in that part of its definition in the Glossary contained in the 2001 instrument which relates to an authorised unit trust scheme;

"trustee" has the meaning given in section 237(2) of the Act;

"unit" has the meaning given in that part of its definition in the Glossary contained in the 2001 instrument which relates to an authorised unit trust scheme; and

"unitholder" has the meaning given in that part of its definition in the Glossary contained in the 2001 instrument .

[1799]

NOTES
Commencement: 6 March 2009.

3   Dispositions of units in authorised unit trust schemes by electronic communication

(1)   This article extends to England and Wales only.

(2)   Subject to paragraph (4), section 53(1)(c) of the Law of Property Act 1925 (which imposes requirements for certain dispositions to be in writing) shall not apply (if it would otherwise do so) to any disposition of units in an authorised unit trust scheme where—

    (a)   the disposition is by means of electronic communication;

    (b)   the electronic communication is made by the person disposing of the units or by his agent authorised in writing or by will; and

    (c)   such evidence (if any) as the trustee or manager of the scheme, being the person responsible for the register of unitholders in accordance with the trust deed, may require to prove the right of the person referred to in sub-paragraph (b) to dispose of the units is provided to the trustee or manager.

(3)   The trustee or manager mentioned in paragraph (2)(c) may refuse to register a transfer of units by means of electronic communication.

(4)   This article shall be of no effect in a particular case if the trustee or manager mentioned in paragraph (2)(c) refuses to register the transfer of units which would, apart from paragraph (3), be made by the disposition in that case.

[1800]

NOTES
Commencement: 6 March 2009.

4   Gratuitous unilateral obligations relating to units in authorised unit trust schemes

(1)   This article extends to Scotland only.

(2)   Subject to paragraph (5), section 1(2)(a)(ii) of the Requirements of Writing (Scotland) Act 1995 (which requires certain gratuitous unilateral obligations to be in writing) shall not apply (if it would otherwise do so) to any gratuitous unilateral obligation relating to units in an authorised unit trust scheme where—

    (a)   the obligation is created by means of electronic communication;

    (b)   the electronic communication is made by the debtor in the obligation; and

    (c)   such evidence (if any) as the trustee or manager of the scheme, being the person responsible for the register of unitholders in accordance with the trust deed, may require to prove the right of the person referred to in sub-paragraph (b) to create the obligation is provided to the trustee or manager.

(3)   Where section 1(2)(a)(ii) of that Act does not apply by virtue of paragraph (2), the obligation shall not be considered an obligation mentioned in subsection (2)(a) of that section for the purposes of subsection (3).

(4)   The trustee or manager mentioned in paragraph (2)(c) may refuse to register a transfer of units by means of electronic communication.

(5)   This article shall be of no effect in a particular case if the trustee or manager mentioned in paragraph (2)(c) refuses to register the transfer of units which would, apart from paragraph (4), be made by the creation of the obligation in that case.

                                                                                           [1801]

NOTES
Commencement: 6 March 2009.

5   Grants or assignments of any trust or confidence

(1)   This article extends to Northern Ireland only.

(2)   Subject to paragraph (4), section 6 of the Statute of Frauds (Ireland) 1695 (which requires all grants and assignments of any trust or confidence to be in writing) shall not apply (if it would otherwise do so) to any grant or assignment of units in an authorised unit trust scheme where—
   (a)   the grant or assignment is by means of electronic communication;
   (b)   the electronic communication is made by the person granting or assigning the units; and
   (c)   such evidence (if any) as the trustee or manager of the scheme, being the person responsible for the register of unitholders in accordance with the trust deed, may require to prove the right of the person referred to in sub-paragraph (b) to grant or assign the units is provided to the trustee or manager.

(3)   The trustee or manager mentioned in paragraph (2)(c) may refuse to register a transfer of units by means of electronic communication.

(4)   This article shall be of no effect in a particular case if the trustee or manager mentioned in paragraph (2)(c) refuses to register the transfer of units which would, apart from paragraph (3), be made by the grant or assignment in that case.

                                                                                           [1802]

NOTES
Commencement: 6 March 2009.

INSOLVENCY (SCOTLAND) AMENDMENT RULES 2009

(SI 2009/662)

NOTES
Made: 12 March 2009.
Authority: Insolvency Act 1986, s 411.
Commencement: 6 April 2009.

1   Citation, commencement and interpretation

(1)   These Rules may be cited as the Insolvency (Scotland) Amendment Rules 2009 and come into force on 6th April 2009.

(2)   In these Rules—
   "the principal Rules" means the Insolvency (Scotland) Rules 1986.

                                                                                           [1803]

NOTES
Commencement: 6 April 2009.

2   Amendments to the principal Rules

The principal Rules shall be amended in the manner provided for in the Schedule.

                                                                                           [1804]

NOTES
Commencement: 6 April 2009.

3   Transitional provisions

The amendments to the principal Rules contained in the Schedule shall not apply—

(a)   where a moratorium under a company voluntary arrangement comes into force; or
(b)   in an administration, where the company enters administration;
before 6th April 2009.

[1805]

NOTES
Commencement: 6 April 2009.

SCHEDULE
AMENDMENTS TO THE PRINCIPAL RULES
Rule 2

PART 1

1.   In Part 1 (Company Voluntary Arrangements) of the Rules, wherever "forthwith" appears, substitute with "as soon as is reasonably practicable".

2.   For Rule 1.30(2) substitute—

"On receipt of the copies of the schedule pursuant to paragraph (1), the nominee—
  (a)   as soon as is reasonably practicable, shall advertise the coming into force of the moratorium once in the Edinburgh Gazette; and
  (b)   may advertise the coming into force of the moratorium in such other manner as the nominee thinks fit."

3.   For Rule 1.32(1) substitute—

"After the moratorium comes to an end, the nominee—

  (a)   as soon as is reasonably practicable, shall advertise its coming to an end once in the Edinburgh Gazette; and
  (b)   may advertise its coming to an end in such other manner as the nominee thinks fit;
and such notice shall specify the date on which the moratorium came to an end."

4.   For Rule 2.19(1) substitute—

"The notice of appointment, which an administrator must publish as soon as is reasonably practicable after his appointment by virtue of paragraph 46(2)(b), shall be advertised in the Edinburgh Gazette and may be advertised in such other manner as the administrator thinks fit."

5.   For Rule 2.25(6) substitute—

"Where the administrator wishes to publish a notice under paragraph 49(6), the notice shall be advertised in such manner as the administrator thinks fit."

6.   After Rule 2.25(6) insert—

"(6A)   A notice published under Rule 2.25(6) shall—

  (a)   state the full name of the company;
  (b)   state the full name and address of the administrator;
  (c)   give details of the administrator's appointment; and
  (d)   specify an address to which any member of the company can write to request that a copy of the statement of proposals be provided free of charge."

7.   After Rule 2.26 insert—

"2.26A   Notice of meetings

(1)   The administrator shall publish notice of an initial creditors' meeting under paragraph 51 in the Edinburgh Gazette and the notice may be advertised in such other manner as the administrator thinks fit.

(2)   An administrator may publish notice of any other meeting, in such manner as the administrator thinks fit to ensure the meeting comes to the notice of any persons who are entitled to attend.

(3)   A notice published under paragraphs (1) or (2) shall include—
  (a)   the name, registered number and address of the registered office of the company in administration;
  (b)   the venue fixed for the meeting;
  (c)   the date and time of the meeting; and
  (d)   the full name and address of the administrator.

(4)   Rule 7.3(3) (notice of meeting) shall not apply to a meeting of creditors summoned by the administrator."

8.   For Rule 2.34(3) substitute—

"Where the administrator wishes to publish a notice under paragraph 54(3), the notice shall be advertised in such manner as the administrator thinks fit."

PART IV   OTHER STATUTORY INSTRUMENTS

9.   After Rule 2.34(3) insert—

"(4)   The notice referred to in paragraph (3) shall—
   (a)   state the full name of the company;
   (b)   state the name and address of the administrator;
   (c)   specify an address to which any member of the company can write to request that a copy of the statement be provided free of charge; and
   (d)   be published as soon as is reasonably practicable after the administrator sends the statement to the creditors."

10.   For Rule 2.45(3) substitute—

"Where the administrator wishes to publish a notice under paragraph 80(5), the notice
   (a)   shall be published in the Edinburgh Gazette; and
   (b)   may be advertised in such other manner as the administrator thinks fit."

11.   For Rule 2.45(4) substitute—

"A notice published under Rule 2.45(3) shall—
   (a)   state the full name of the company;
   (b)   state the name and address of the administrator;
   (c)   state the date when the administrator's appointment ceased to have effect;
   (d)   specify an address to which any creditor of the company can write to request that a copy of the notice be provided; and
   (e)   be published within five business days of filing the notice of the end of administration with the court."

12.   In Rule 7.3(3) omit the words "In the case of a creditors' meeting" to "shall publish such a notice.".

13.   In Rule 7.3(3A) after the words "this paragraph" insert—

"or Rule 2.26A (1) or (2)".

14.   For Form 1.10 (Scot) (Advertisement of coming into force or ending of moratorium) in Schedule 5, Part 1, substitute Form 1.10 (Scot) set out in Part 2 of the Schedule to these Rules.

15.   For Form 2.10B (Scot) (Notification of appointment of administrator) in Schedule 5, Part 2, substitute Form 2.10B (Scot) set out in Part 2 of the Schedule to these Rules.

[1806]

NOTES

Commencement: 6 April 2009.

PART 2
FORMS FOR INSERTION INTO SCHEDULE 5 TO THE PRINCIPAL RULES

Rule 1.30/1.32	Form 1.10 (Scot)

Advertisement of coming into force or ending of moratorium (for Edinburgh Gazette and other advertising)

The Insolvency Act 1986

(a) Insert full name of company

In matter of (a) _____

_____

_____ Limited

(b) Give details of nature of business carried on by the company

Nature of business (b) _____

A moratorium under section 1A of the Insolvency Act 1986 came into force

(c) Insert date

on (c) _____

OR (d)

(d) Delete as applicable

The moratorium under section 1A of the Insolvency Act 1986 which came into force on (c) _____ came to an end on (c)

_____

Signed _____ Nominee

Rule 2.19

The Insolvency Act 1986   Form 2.10B (Scot)

Notification of appointment of administrator (for Edinburgh Gazette and other advertising)

Pursuant to paragraph 46(2)(b) of Schedule B1 to the Insolvency Act 1986 and Rule 2.19 of the Insolvency (Scotland) Rules 1986

Name of company	Company number

Name of business _____

Registered office of company _____

_____

(a) Insert date

*Delete as applicable

(b) Insert full name of court

Appointment of administrator made on (a) _____ 20

by *order of/*notice of appointment lodged in (b) _____

_____

Name(s) and address(es) of administrator(s) _____

_____

_____

Administrator/Joint administrator (IP No(s) _____)

[1807]

NOTES
Commencement: 6 April 2009.

FINANCIAL SERVICES AND MARKETS ACT 2000 (CONTRIBUTION TO COSTS OF SPECIAL RESOLUTION REGIME) REGULATIONS 2009

(SI 2009/807)

NOTES
Made: 29 March 2009.
Authority: Financial Services and Markets Act 2000, ss 214B, 428.
Commencement: 29 March 2009.
Note: On 21 July 2009 HM Treasury issued a consultation paper, Special resolution regime: the FSMA (Contribution to Costs of Special Resolution Regime) Regulations 2009 to consult fully on the Regulations (the effect of which is to require the FSCS to contribute towards the costs of the resolution of the Dunfermline Building Society) as time had not previously allowed for consultation before the regulations came into effect. The closing date for this consultation paper is 30 October 2009. Following the consultation, HM Treasury will consider whether to bring forward proposals to amend the regulations.

ARRANGEMENT OF REGULATIONS

1 Citation

These Regulations may be cited as the Financial Services and Markets Act 2000 (Contribution to Costs of Special Resolution Regime) Regulations 2009.

[1808]

NOTES
Commencement: 29 March 2009.

2 Interpretation

In these Regulations—

"the Act" means the Financial Services and Markets Act 2000;

"the 2009 Act" means the Banking Act 2009;

"Amount A" has the meaning set out in regulation 4(2)(a)(vii)(aa);

"Amount B" has the meaning set out in regulation 5(2);

"amount of recovery" has the meaning set out in regulation 8(1);

"banking institution" means—

(a) a bank (within the meaning of section 2 of the 2009 Act);

(b) a building society (within the meaning of section 119 of the Building Societies Act 1986);

(c) a holding company (within the meaning of section 82 of the 2009 Act); or

(d) if an order has been made under section 89 of the 2009 Act applying Part 1 of that Act to credit unions (within the meaning of section 31 of the Credit Unions Act 1979 or, in Northern Ireland, Article 2 of the Credit Unions (Northern Ireland) Order 1985), a credit union;

"compensation scheme order" has the meaning set out in section 49(2) of the 2009 Act;

"COMP Sourcebook" means the Authority's Compensation Sourcebook as amended from time to time, made by the Authority under the Act;

"court" means the High Court or the Court of Session;

"determination notice" has the meaning set out in regulation 8(6);

"eligible claimant" means a person who is eligible to make a claim under the scheme in respect of a deposit at a banking institution (see rule 4.2.1 of the COMP Sourcebook);

"end of the resolution" means the time at which the scheme manager receives the final notification under regulation 5 or 6;

"FEES 6 Chapter" means Chapter 6 (Financial Services Compensation Scheme Funding) of the Fees Manual as amended from time to time, made by the Authority under the Act;

"protected deposit" means a protected deposit under the scheme (see rule 5.3.1 of the COMP Sourcebook);

"qualifying claimant" means an eligible claimant who, if the banking institution were to have been in default for the purposes of the COMP Sourcebook immediately before the relevant time, would have had a claim against the banking institution in respect of a protected deposit;

"relevant time" means the time at which a stabilisation power takes effect in respect of a banking institution and, if more than one stabilisation power is exercised, means the time at which the first stabilisation power so exercised takes effect;

"resolution fund order" has the meaning set out in section 49(3) of the 2009 Act;

"revised determination notice" has the meaning set out in regulation 9(3);

"scheme" means the compensation scheme;

"stabilisation power" means one of the stabilisation powers referred to in section 1(4) of the 2009 Act and a reference to the exercise of a stabilisation power includes the exercise of more than one stabilisation power in respect of or in connection with the same banking institution;

"third party compensation scheme order" has the meaning set out in section 49(4) of the 2009 Act; and

"total liability" has the meaning set out in regulation 5(6).

[1809]

NOTES
Commencement: 29 March 2009.

3 Liability of the scheme

(1) The scheme manager may be required under section 214B of the Act to make payments—

(a) in connection with the transfer of rights and liabilities in respect of protected deposits,

(b) in connection with the transfer of any other property, rights and liabilities of the banking institution,

(c)   to a bank administrator in connection with the pursuit of Objective 1 (and "bank administrator" and "Objective 1" have the meanings given in sections 141 and 138 of the 2009 Act respectively), and

(d)   in connection with taking the banking institution into temporary public ownership in accordance with section 13 of the 2009 Act.

(2)   Those payments include payments in respect of expenses incurred by the Bank of England or the Treasury in connection with the activities in paragraph (1).

[1810]

NOTES
Commencement: 29 March 2009.

4   Notification

(1)   Where section 214B applies, and the Treasury requires the scheme manager to make payments under regulation 3, the Treasury will notify the scheme manager as soon as practicable.

(2)   The notification under paragraph (1)—
  (a)   shall include—
    (i)   the name and address of the banking institution in respect of which, or in connection with which, the stabilisation power has been exercised,
    (ii)   a statement that the Treasury think that the banking institution was or, but for the exercise of the stabilisation power, would have become unable to satisfy claims against it,
    (iii)   details of the stabilisation power exercised,
    (iv)   details of when it was exercised,
    (v)   details of the transferee (if any),
    (vi)   the activities in regulation 3 in connection with which the scheme manager is required to make payments,
    (vii)   subject to regulation 6(2), either—

      (aa)   a calculation of the provisional amount ("Amount A") of the scheme's liability in respect of the activities in sub-paragraph (vi) and any information and assumptions upon which this calculation is based, or

      (bb)   (if insufficient information is known at the time the notification is made), an estimate of Amount A,
    (viii)   details as to any payments to be made by the scheme manager in respect of Amount A and when those payments are to be made,
    (ix)   details of the person to whom any payments are to be made; and
  (b)   may also include—
    (i)   any relevant conditions to be satisfied before payments are to be made, and
    (ii)   any further information that the Treasury consider necessary in respect of payments to be made.

(3)   Amount A, and any other information contained in a notification may be adjusted from time to time by the Treasury sending a revised notification to the scheme manager.

(4)   A notification under this regulation may be given by such means as the Treasury consider appropriate.

[1811]

NOTES
Commencement: 29 March 2009.

5   Payment after the end of the resolution

(1)   This regulation applies when the notification under regulation 4(1) requires the scheme manager to make payments after the end of the resolution.

(2)   Following receipt of the notification, the scheme manager will, by any methodology or approach it considers appropriate, make an assessment of the amount of compensation ("Amount B") that qualifying claimants would, immediately before the relevant time, have been entitled to claim from the scheme in respect of protected deposits if—
  (a)   the banking institution was in default (see rule 6.3.1 of the COMP Sourcebook) immediately before the relevant time, and
  (b)   the stabilisation power had not been exercised and no other order or instrument under Parts 1 to 3 of the 2009 Act would have been made in relation to or in connection with the banking institution,

and the scheme manager will notify Amount B, together with any calculations or assumptions made in carrying out the assessment, to the Treasury.

(3)   For the purposes of paragraph (2), if the quantification date for a claim would have been a date other than the date upon which the banking institution would have been in default, the amount that a qualifying claimant would have been entitled to claim from the scheme is the lesser of—

    (a)   the amount which the scheme manager quantifies as being the value of that claim as at the time immediately before the relevant time, and

    (b)   the amount that would have been payable at the quantification date, if different, for that claim,

and in this paragraph, "quantification date" means the date the banking institution would have been in default or the day the protected deposit would have been due and payable (if later) (see rule 12.3.1 of the COMP Sourcebook).

(4)   Amount B may be adjusted from time to time by the scheme manager and any such adjustment shall be notified to the Treasury by the scheme manager as soon as reasonably practicable after the adjustment is made.

(5)   If, at any time, Amount A is greater than Amount B then, subject to paragraph (6), the scheme's liability will be reduced to Amount B and the scheme manager will notify this to the Treasury.

(6)   The scheme's liability will be further reduced by—

    (a)   the amount of recovery set out in the determination notice or in the revised determination notice under regulations 8 or 9,

    (b)   the amount of compensation (if any) actually paid out under the scheme to eligible claimants in respect of protected deposits held with the banking institution, and

    (c)   the amount of any other compensation which the scheme has become liable to pay under a provision made under section 61(2) of the 2009 Act,

to give the scheme's total liability ("the total liability").

(7)   When the Treasury have received sufficient information to calculate the scheme's total liability and consider that no further revised notifications are to be made, the Treasury will—

    (a)   calculate the scheme's total liability, and

    (b)   appoint a person to carry out an independent verification of the total liability,

and the costs of the appointment will be borne jointly by the Treasury and the scheme.

(8)   After the independent verification has taken place, the Treasury will—

    (a)   make any adjustments to the total liability as a result of the verification, and

    (b)   send a final notification to the scheme manager that a payment is required, setting out the scheme's total liability and the date by which the payment is to be made.

(9)   The Treasury and the scheme manager may agree that it is neither appropriate nor reasonable to make further revised notifications under regulations 4(3) or 5(4), and, following such an agreement, paragraphs (7) and (8) will apply.

[1812]

NOTES
Commencement: 29 March 2009.

---

6 Payment before the end of the resolution

(1)   This regulation applies when the notification under regulation 4(1) or a revised notification under 4(3) requires the scheme manager to make payments before the end of the resolution.

(2)   The notification or revised notification must also contain an estimate of the total liability, to the best of the Treasury's knowledge in the circumstances at the time the notification is made and for the purpose of this regulation, this estimate shall constitute Amount A.

(3)   The scheme manager will pay Amount A in accordance with the timetable for payments set out in the notification.

(4)   Regulations 5(2) to (7) and (9) will then apply.

(5)   After the independent verification has taken place, the Treasury will—

    (a)   make any adjustments to the total liability as a result of the verification, and

    (b)   send a final notification to the scheme manager setting out the scheme's total liability, a summary of the amounts paid or to be paid by the scheme, and the date when any outstanding payments (if any) are to be made.

(6)   If the scheme's total liability is less than the aggregate amount already paid by the scheme manager in accordance with the notification, the scheme manager will notify the Treasury and the Treasury will refund the difference.

(7)   The Treasury will pay any refund within 28 days of the final notification.

(8)   The Treasury will pay interest on the refunded amount at such a rate as may be agreed between the Treasury and the scheme manager.

(9)   For the purposes of paragraph (8)—

(a)   interest shall be calculated from the date on which the amount paid by the scheme manager under the notification or a revised notification first exceeded the total liability, and

(b)   where the notification or a revised notification required several payments to be made, interest shall be calculated on each amount paid by the scheme manager after the date referred to in paragraph (a) from the date on which the relevant amount was paid.

[1813]

NOTES

Commencement: 29 March 2009.

7   Independent valuer

(1)   After making a notification under regulation 4(1), the Treasury must make arrangements for an independent valuer to perform the function in regulation 8(1).

(2)   Where section 54 of the 2009 Act applies and the Treasury makes provision for the appointment of an independent valuer in a compensation scheme order, a resolution fund order or a third party compensation scheme order, the Treasury may specify that the independent valuer may perform the function in regulation 8(1).

(3)   Where the Treasury do not make the specification in paragraph (2), Part 1 of the Schedule to these Regulations shall apply.

[1814]

NOTES

Commencement: 29 March 2009.

8   Function of the independent valuer

(1)   The independent valuer must calculate the amount that would have been likely to be recovered by the scheme from the banking institution ("the amount of recovery") if immediately before the relevant time—

(a)   the banking institution was in default (see rule 6.3.1 of the COMP Sourcebook),

(b)   the institution had entered into insolvency, and

(c)   the scheme manager had paid the amount of compensation that qualifying claimants would have been entitled to receive.

(2)   For the purposes of paragraph (1)(b), where regulation 7(2) applies and a valuation principle specified in the compensation scheme order, resolution fund order or third party compensation scheme order requires the independent valuer to assume the banking institution is in a specified insolvency procedure, in sub-paragraph (1)(b), for "insolvency", substitute a reference to the specified insolvency procedure.

(3)   The independent valuer may do anything necessary or desirable for the purposes of or in connection with calculating the amount of recovery.

(4)   The independent valuer may apply to the court for an order requiring the provision of information reasonably required for the purposes of calculating the amount of recovery and in that event paragraph 12 of the Schedule shall apply.

(5)   Paragraphs 13 to 16 of the Schedule apply to information obtained by the independent valuer in connection with the function specified in paragraph (1).

(6)   When the amount of recovery has been calculated, the independent valuer will give the scheme manager and the Treasury notice in writing of the determination ("the determination notice").

(7)   The determination notice shall contain the following information—

(a)   the date on which it is issued,

(b)   the amount of recovery, and

(c)   assumptions and calculations relevant to the determination.

(8)   The scheme manager may publish the determination notice on the scheme's website.

[1815]

NOTES

Commencement: 29 March 2009.

9   Appeal against the amount of recovery

(1)   If the scheme manager or the Treasury are dissatisfied with the determination notice, the Treasury or the scheme manager may require the independent valuer to reconsider his or her determination.

(2)   The request must be made within 3 months of the date of the determination notice and must—

(a)   set out the reasons for disputing the amount of recovery, and

(b)   be in writing.

(3)   Where the independent valuer is required to reconsider the determination made under regulation 8, he or she must give the Treasury and the scheme manger notice in writing of his or her revised determination ("the revised determination notice").

(4)   The revised determination notice must contain the information specified in regulation 8(7).

(5)   If the Treasury or the scheme manager is dissatisfied with the revised determination notice, either may apply to the court.

(6)   On receiving an application under paragraph (5), the court may require the independent valuer to redetermine his or her revised determination and may give directions, including directions as to costs (in Scotland, expenses).

(7)   Where paragraph (6) applies, paragraphs (3), (4) and (8) will apply to any re-determination in accordance with a direction of the court.

(8)   The scheme manager may publish the revised determination notice on the scheme's website.

[1816]

NOTES

Commencement: 29 March 2009.

10   Application to the court

(1)   An application may be made to the court by the Treasury or the scheme manager for the resolution of disputes arising under these Regulations.

(2)   An application may concern—

(a)   a calculation or assumption made, or

(b)   the timing or any issue relating to the making of payments,

but no application may be made under this regulation in respect of any determination or revised determination made by the independent valuer under regulations 8 or 9.

(3)   On receipt of an application the court may give directions as to—

(a)   the revising of a calculation,

(b)   the assumptions to be made when revising that calculation,

(c)   the independent verification of a revised calculation,

(d)   the timing or any issue relating to the making of payments, and

(e)   any other such matters, including directions as to the adjustment of the total liability as a result of any revised calculations as the court thinks fit.

(4)   The court shall give directions as to costs (in Scotland, expenses) of the application.

[1817]

NOTES

Commencement: 29 March 2009.

11   Payments made under these Regulations to constitute payment of compensation under the scheme

(1)   For the purposes of Part 15 of the Act, the COMP Sourcebook and the FEES 6 Chapter—

(a)   any payments made by the scheme manager under these Regulations in respect of protected deposits shall constitute payment of compensation to each qualifying claimant in respect of claims under the scheme against the banking institution for protected deposits;

(b)   on the scheme manager receiving the notification from the Treasury under regulation 4(1)—

(i)   the banking institution shall be deemed to be in default for purposes of section 213, the COMP Sourcebook and the FEES 6 Chapter,

(ii)   each qualifying claimant shall be deemed to have made an application for compensation for the purpose of the COMP Sourcebook and the FEES 6 Chapter, and

(iii)   each qualifying claimant shall be deemed to have accepted an offer of compensation made by the scheme and to have received payment for such compensation for the purposes of the COMP Sourcebook and the FEES 6 Chapter,

and, accordingly, a qualifying claimant has no right to claim, and the scheme has no obligation to pay, any further compensation in respect of a protected deposit with that banking institution.

(2)   For the purposes of this regulation—

(a)   where all or part of the business of a banking institution has been transferred to a bridge bank under section 12 of the 2009 Act, the bridge bank is to be treated as being the same banking institution as the institution in respect of which the stabilisation power was exercised;

(b)   where the banking institution has been taken into temporary public ownership under section 13 of the 2009 Act, when that institution ceases to be publicly owned, it shall be treated as a new banking institution; and

(c)   a "qualifying claimant" means a qualifying claimant whose protected deposit has been dealt with by the exercise of the stabilisation power.

[1818]

NOTES
Commencement: 29 March 2009.

SCHEDULE
Regulations 7 and 8

PART 1
THE APPOINTMENT AND REMUNERATION OF THE INDEPENDENT VALUER

1.   The Treasury must appoint, or appoint a panel to appoint, an independent valuer to perform the function in regulation 8(1).

2.   The independent valuer is to hold and vacate office in accordance with the terms of his or her appointment.

3.   The Treasury may remove the independent valuer only on the ground of incapacity or serious misbehaviour.

4.   In the event of the death of the independent valuer, or if the valuer is removed from office or resigns, the Treasury (or panel appointed by the Treasury) shall appoint a new independent valuer as soon as possible.

5.   The independent valuer shall be—

(a)   paid such remuneration, and

(b)   reimbursed such expenses,

as the Treasury may determine.

6.   The Treasury may appoint a person to verify the remuneration and expenses of the independent valuer.

7.   The independent valuer may appoint staff.

8.   The independent valuer shall determine the remuneration and other conditions of service of persons appointed under paragraph 7.

9.   Any determination under paragraph 8 shall require the approval of the Treasury.

10.   Independent valuers (and their staff) are neither servants nor agents of the Crown (and in particular are not civil servants).

11.   Records of an independent valuer in relation to his or her functions in connection with an appointment under these Regulations are public records for the purposes of the Public Records Act 1958.

[1819]

NOTES
Commencement: 29 March 2009.

PART 2
APPLICATION TO THE COURT FOR INFORMATION

12.—(1)   The court may, on an application by the independent valuer, make an order requiring a person to provide information that is reasonably required for the purpose of assessing the amount of recovery.

(2)   A person required to provide information pursuant to an order under sub-paragraph (1) shall not be required to provide information—

(a)   in respect of which a claim to legal professional privilege (in Scotland, to confidentiality of communications) could be maintained in legal proceedings,

(b)   if such provision by the person holding it would be prohibited by or under any enactment, or

(c)   if it is held by a government department and provision of such information would be contrary to the public interest.

(3)   In relation to information recorded otherwise than in legible form, the power to require it to be provided includes power to require it to be provided in a form from which it can be readily produced in visible and legible form.

13.   A person who provides information to the independent valuer for the purposes of the assessment by the valuer of the amount of recovery is not, by reason only of the provision of such information, liable in any proceedings relating to a breach of confidence.

14.   Specified information shall not be disclosed by the independent valuer (or any person to whom the independent valuer has disclosed such information in accordance with paragraph 15(2)) without the consent of the person from whom the independent valuer obtained the specified information and, if different, the person to whom it relates.

15.—(1)   The prohibition in paragraph 14 of the disclosure of specified information is subject to the following exceptions.

(2)   The independent valuer may, for the purpose of assessing the amount of recovery, disclose specified information to any staff appointed by the independent valuer or to any person providing advice or assistance to the independent valuer.

(3)   The independent valuer may disclose specified information if and to the extent that the independent valuer considers it necessary to do so for the purposes of exercising the functions of the office.

(4)   The independent valuer must, before disclosing any specified information in accordance with sub-paragraph (3), have regard to the need to exclude from disclosure (so far as practicable)—

(a)   commercial information the disclosure of which might significantly harm the legitimate business interests of the person to whom it relates,

(b)   information relating to the private affairs of an individual, the disclosure of which might significantly harm the individual's interests, or

(c)   any information the disclosure of which would be contrary to the public interest.

(5)   The independent valuer may disclose specified information in accordance with this paragraph subject to such conditions as the independent valuer thinks appropriate.

16.   In this Part, "specified information" means any information obtained by the independent valuer for the purpose of assessing the amount of recovery.

[1820]

NOTES
Commencement: 29 March 2009.

NATIONAL SAVINGS (UNCLAIMED MONEYS) REGULATIONS 2009

(SI 2009/1263)

NOTES
Made: 19 May 2009.
Authority: National Debt Act 1972, ss 3(1)(a), (bb), 3(2)(c), (e), 10(2A), 11(1)(a), (2)(a).
Commencement: 15 June 2009 (regs 1–3); 1 September 2009 (otherwise).

ARRANGEMENT OF REGULATIONS

1   Citation, commencement and interpretation

(1)   These Regulations may be cited as the National Savings (Unclaimed Moneys) Regulations 2009.

(2)   Regulations 1, 2 and 3 shall come into force on 15th June 2009 and all other regulations shall come into force on 1st September 2009.

(3)   In these Regulations—
"the 1955 Act" means the Miscellaneous Financial Provisions Act 1955;
"the 1972 Regulations" means the Premium Savings Bonds Regulations 1972;

"the 1976 Regulations" means the National Savings Stock Register Regulations 1976;

"the Commissioners" means the National Debt Commissioners; and

"special Director's account" has the same meaning as in section 8(4) of the National Savings Bank Act 1971.

[1821]

NOTES

Commencement: 15 June 2009.

2 National savings stamps and gift tokens

(1)   The Commissioners shall repay to the National Loans Fund out of their account of unclaimed redemption moneys a sum equal to the balance held by the Commissioners in respect of sums paid to them under section 10(2) of the National Debt Act 1972 (unclaimed sums in relation to national savings stamps and gift tokens).

(2)   Section 120(1), (2), (3) and (6) of the Finance Act 1980 shall apply to the sum repaid as if it were a sum received by the Director of Savings as an investment deposit and paid by the Director into the National Loans Fund.

(3)   The Director of Savings shall credit an amount equal to the sum repaid in respect of national savings stamps to a special Director's account in the National Savings Bank.

(4)   The Director of Savings shall credit an amount equal to the sum repaid in respect of national savings gift tokens to a special Director's account in the National Savings Bank.

[1822]

NOTES

Commencement: 15 June 2009.

3 British Savings Bonds

(1)   The Commissioners shall repay to the Director of Savings out of their account of unclaimed redemption moneys and their account of unclaimed dividends a sum equal to the balance held by the Commissioners in respect of sums paid to them under regulation 43 of the 1976 Regulations in respect of British Savings Bonds.

(2)   The Director of Savings shall apply the sum repaid by a transfer by way of investment deposit to a special Director's account in the National Savings Bank.

(3)   Regulations 43 and 44 of the 1976 Regulations shall cease to apply to British Savings Bonds.

[1823]

NOTES

Commencement: 15 June 2009.

4 Premium savings bonds

(1)   The Commissioners shall repay to the Director of Savings out of their account of unclaimed dividends a sum equal to the balance held by the Commissioners in respect of sums paid to them under regulation 15 of the 1972 Regulations.

(2)   The Director of Savings shall apply that sum by transferring, by way of investment deposit to an investment account in the National Savings Bank in the name of each person entitled, an amount equal to each amount deemed to be unclaimed under regulation 15 of the 1972 Regulations on a bond held by that person.

(3)   Where the Director of Savings is unable, for any reason, to apply sums in accordance with paragraph (2), the Director of Savings shall apply those sums by transfer to a special Director's account in the National Savings Bank.

[1824]

NOTES

Commencement: 1 September 2009.

5   The 1972 Regulations are amended as follows—

    (a)   omit regulation 15; and

    (b)   after regulation 15 insert:

PART IV
OTHER STATUTORY INSTRUMENTS

"15A Transfer of unclaimed moneys to the National Savings Bank

(1) The Director of Savings shall transfer sums equal to moneys due on a bond which, having been entrusted to the Director of Savings for repayment, remain unclaimed, to an investment account in the National Savings Bank in the name of the person in whose name the bond is held.

(2) Where the Director of Savings is unable, for any reason, to transfer sums in accordance with paragraph (1), the Director of Savings shall transfer those sums to a special Director's account in the National Savings Bank and the sums shall be held on behalf of the persons entitled to them.

(3) For the purposes of this regulation, moneys due on a bond shall be deemed to be unclaimed if a period of five years has elapsed since the due date, but the Director of Savings may treat any such moneys as unclaimed before the expiration of that period.".

[1825]

NOTES
Commencement: 1 September 2009.

6 Stock in the register

(1) The Commissioners shall repay to the Director of Savings out of their account of unclaimed dividends a sum equal to the balance held by the Commissioners in respect of sums paid to them under regulation 43 of the 1976 Regulations.

(2) The Director of Savings shall apply that sum by transferring by way of investment deposit to an investment account in the National Savings Bank in the name of each person entitled an amount equal to each amount deemed to be unclaimed under regulation 43 of the 1976 Regulations.

(3) Where the Director of Savings is unable, for any reason, to apply sums in accordance with paragraph (2), the Director of Savings shall apply those sums by transfer to a special Director's account in the National Savings Bank.

[1826]

NOTES
Commencement: 1 September 2009.

7 The 1976 Regulations are amended as follows—
    (a)   omit regulations 43;
    (b)   after regulation 43 insert:

"43A Transfer of unclaimed moneys to the National Savings Bank

(1) The Director of Savings may transfer sums equal to all moneys due on stock which, having been entrusted to the Director of Savings for payment, remain unclaimed, to an investment account in the National Savings Bank in the name of the person in whose name the stock is held.

(2) Where the Director of Savings is unable, for any reason, to transfer sums in accordance with paragraph (1) above, the Director of Savings may transfer those sums to a special Director's account and the sums shall be held on behalf of the persons entitled to them.

(3) For the purposes of this regulation, moneys due on stock shall be deemed to be unclaimed if a period of five years, or in the case of redemption moneys two years, has elapsed since the due date, but the Director of Savings may treat any such moneys as unclaimed before the expiration of that period."; and

    (c)   omit regulation 44.

[1827]

NOTES
Commencement: 1 September 2009.

LANDSBANKI FREEZING (REVOCATION) ORDER 2009

(SI 2009/1392)

NOTES
Made: 10 June 2009.
Authority: Anti-terrorism, Crime and Security Act 2001, ss 4, 14, Sch 3.

Commencement: 15 June 2009.

1   Citation and commencement

This Order may be cited as the Landsbanki Freezing (Revocation) Order 2009 and comes into force on 15th June 2009.

[1828]

NOTES
Commencement: 15 June 2009.

2   Revocations

The following Orders are revoked—
    (a)   the Landsbanki Freezing Order 2008;
    (b)   the Landsbanki Freezing (Amendment) Order 2008.

[1829]

NOTES
Commencement: 15 June 2009.

FINANCIAL MARKETS AND INSOLVENCY (SETTLEMENT FINALITY) (AMENDMENT) REGULATIONS 2009

(SI 2009/1972)

NOTES
Made: 20 July 2009.
Authority: European Communities Act 1972, s 2(2).
Commencement: 1 October 2009.

1   Citation, commencement and interpretation

These Regulations may be cited as the Financial Markets and Insolvency (Settlement Finality) (Amendment) Regulations 2009, and come into force on 1st October 2009.

[1830]

NOTES
Commencement: 1 October 2009.

2   Amendment of the Regulations

The Financial Markets and Insolvency (Settlement Finality) Regulations 1999 are amended as follows.

[1831]

NOTES
Commencement: 1 October 2009.

3   In paragraph (2) of regulation 6 (certain bodies deemed to satisfy requirements for designation) for "the 1986 Act" substitute "the 2000 Act".

[1832]

NOTES
Commencement: 1 October 2009.

4   In regulation 14 (proceedings of designated system take precedence over insolvency proceedings)
    (a)   in paragraph (1), after "winding up," insert "administration,"
    (b)   in paragraph (2), omit the words from "This does not prevent the court" to the end of the paragraph;
    (c)   in paragraph (4), for "or bankruptcy" substitute ", bankruptcy, or administration,"
    (d)   in paragraph (5)—
        (i)   in sub-paragraph (a), for "section 735 of the Companies Act 1985 or Article 3 of

the Companies (Northern Ireland) Order 1986" substitute "section 1 of the Companies Act 2006) or by a building society (within the meaning of section 119 of the Building Societies Act 1986)";

 (ii) for sub-paragraph (a)(i), substitute—

  "(i) sections 175, 176ZA and 176A of, and paragraph 65(2) of Schedule B1 to, the Insolvency Act 1986 or Articles 149, 150ZA, and 150A of, and paragraph 66(2) of Schedule B1 to, the Insolvency (Northern Ireland) Order 1989;

  (ii) Rules 4.30(3) and 4.218(2)(b) of the Insolvency Rules 1986, Rules 4.033(3) and 4.228(2)(b) of the Insolvency Rules (Northern Ireland) 1991 and rule 4.5(3) of the Insolvency (Scotland) Rules 1986;";

 (iii) for sub-paragraph (a)(ii), substitute—

  "(iii) section 40 (or in Scotland, section 59 and 60(1)(e)) of the Insolvency Act 1986, paragraph 99(3) of Schedule B1 to that Act and section 19(4) of that Act as that section has effect by virtue of section 249(1) of the Enterprise Act 2002;

  (iv) paragraph 100(3) of Schedule B1 to, and Article 31(4) of that Order, as that Article has effect by virtue of Article 4(1) of the Insolvency (Northern Ireland) Order 2005; and

  (v) section 754 of the Companies Act 2006; and"

 (e) in paragraph (6)—

  (i) in sub-paragraph (a)—

   (aa) after "paragraph 99(3) of Schedule B1 to that Act" insert "and in section 19(4) of that Act as that section has effect by virtue of section 249(1) of the Enterprise Act 2002";

   (bb) after "paragraph 100(3) to Schedule B1 to that Order" insert "and Article 31(4) of that Order, as that Article has effect by virtue of Article 4(1) of the Insolvency (Northern Ireland) Order 2005";

  (ii) after sub-paragraph (b), insert—

"and

  (c) the debts or liabilities arising or incurred under contracts mentioned in—

   (i) paragraph 99(4) of Schedule B1 to the Insolvency Act 1986 and section 19(5) of that Act, as that section has effect by virtue of section 249(1) of the Enterprise Act 2002, or

   (ii) paragraph 100(4) of Schedule B1 to, the Insolvency (Northern Ireland) Order 1989 and Article 31(5) of that Order as that article has effect by virtue of Article 4(1) of the Insolvency (Northern Ireland) Order 2005,".

[1833]

NOTES

Commencement: 1 October 2009.

5 In regulation 15 (net sum payable on completion of action taken under default arrangements)—

 (a) in paragraph (2)

  (i) for the words "or winding-up" each time they occur, substitute ", winding-up or administration";

  (ii) in sub-paragraph (b)—

   (aa) after "(Northern Ireland) Order 1989" insert "or Rule 2.85 of the Insolvency Rules 1986 or Rule 2.086 of the Insolvency Rules (Northern Ireland) 1991";

   (bb) after "the case of winding-up" insert "or administration";

  (iii) after the words "Article 6 of the Insolvency (Northern Ireland) Order 1989) or" insert "enters into administration (within the meaning of paragraph 1 of Schedule B1 to the Insolvency Act 1986 or paragraph 2 of Schedule B1 to the Insolvency (Northern Ireland) Order 1989) or";

 (b) after paragraph (3), insert—

 "(4) A reference in this regulation to "administration order" shall include—

  (a) the appointment of an administrator under paragraph 14 or 22 of Schedule B1 to the Insolvency Act 1986 or under paragraph 15 or 23 of Schedule B1 to the Insolvency (Northern Ireland) Order 1989;

  (b) the making of an order under section 8 of that Act as it has effect by virtue of section 249(1) of the Enterprise Act 2002; and

(c)   the making of an order under Article 21 of that Order as it has effect by virtue of Article 4(1) of the Insolvency (Northern Ireland) Order 2005;

and "administration" shall be construed accordingly."

[1834]

NOTES
Commencement: 1 October 2009.

6   In regulation 16(3) (disclaimer of property, rescission of contracts &c)—

(a)   for the words "Sections 127 and 284 of the Insolvency Act 1986" substitute "Sections 88, 127, 245 and 284 of the Insolvency Act 1986";

(b)   for the words "Articles 107 and 257 of the Insolvency (Northern Ireland) Order 1989" substitute "Articles 74, 107, 207 and 257 of the Insolvency (Northern Ireland) Order 1989".

[1835]

NOTES
Commencement: 1 October 2009.

7   In regulation 19 (administration orders, &c)—

(a)   after paragraph (1) insert—

"(1ZA)   The following provisions of the Insolvency Act 1986 (which relate to administration orders and administrators), as they have effect by virtue of section 249(1) of the Enterprise Act 2002, do not apply in relation to a collateral security charge—

(a)   sections 10(1)(b) and 11(3)(c) (restriction on enforcement of security while petition for administration order pending or order in force); and

(b)   sections 15(1) and (2) (power of administrator to deal with charged property);

and section 11(2) (receiver to vacate office when so required by administrator) does not apply to a receiver appointed under such a charge.";

(b)   after paragraph (1A) insert—

"(1B)   The following provisions of the Insolvency (Northern Ireland) Order 1989 (administration), as they have effect by virtue of Article 4(1) of the Insolvency (Northern Ireland) Order 2005, do not apply in relation to a collateral security charge—

(a)   Article 23(1)(b) and Article 24(3)(c) (restriction on enforcement of security while petition for administration order pending or order in force); and

(b)   Article 28(1) and (2) (power of administrator to deal with charged property);

and Article 24(2) of that Order (receiver to vacate office at request of administrator) shall not apply to a receiver appointed under such a charge.";

(c)   after paragraph (3) insert—

"(4)   Paragraph 20 and paragraph 12(1)(g) of Schedule A1 to the Insolvency Act 1986, and paragraph 31 and paragraph 23(1)(g) of Schedule A1 to the Insolvency (Northern Ireland) Order 1989 (effect of moratorium on creditors) shall not apply (if they would otherwise do so) to any collateral security charge.".

[1836]–[1899]

NOTES
Commencement: 1 October 2009.

PART V
EU MATERIALS

COMMUNICATION FROM THE COMMISSION

European financial supervision
(Text with EEA relevance)

{SEC (2009) 715}
{SEC (2009) 716}

NOTES
  Brussels, 27.5.2009; COM(2009) 252 final. Notes are as per the original.
  As of 1 August 2009 this document had not been amended.

1. INTRODUCTION

Experience of the financial crisis has exposed important failures in financial supervision, both in particular cases and in relation to the financial system as a whole. Current supervisory arrangements proved incapable of preventing, managing and resolving the crisis. Nationally-based supervisory models have lagged behind the integrated and interconnected reality of today's European financial markets, in which many financial firms operate across borders. The crisis exposed serious failings in the cooperation, coordination, consistency and trust between national supervisors.

The Commission has been closely involved in coordinating the substantial interventions by Member States to restore confidence in financial institutions through guarantee schemes, injection of additional capital and measures to relieve balance sheets of impaired assets, while ensuring that beneficiary institutions take the necessary steps to return to viability. This effort should be complemented by steps to address the failures in supervision revealed by the crisis.

In November 2008, the Commission mandated a High Level Group chaired by Mr Jacques de Larosière to propose recommendations to the Commission on how to strengthen European supervisory arrangements to better protect its citizens and rebuild trust in the financial system. As one of the two largest financial markets in the world, the EU also has a clear responsibility to promote global financial stability and security – a role that it can only perform if it has a strong supervisory and regulatory framework itself.

The final report presented by the de Larosière Group on 25 February 2009 set out a balanced and pragmatic vision for a new system of European financial supervision. At the core of this vision are proposals to strengthen cooperation and coordination between national supervisors including through the creation of new European Supervisory Authorities, and, for the first time, a European level body charged with overseeing risk in the financial system as a whole.

In the Communication *"Driving European Recovery"* of 4 March 2009[1], the Commission welcomed and supported the main thrust of these recommendations[2]. Building on the recommendations of the de Larosière report, the Communication set out an action plan for reforming the way financial markets are regulated and supervised. The Commission has already taken a series of measures to implement the regulatory reform, including important initiatives on alternative investment funds, including hedge funds, and executive remuneration. Further measures on capital requirements for banks will follow in June.

Given the urgent need for parallel action on supervision, the Commission proposed an accelerated timetable for delivering on the reform of EU financial supervision. Discussions in the European Council, the Council and the European Parliament, as well as a public consultation, have demonstrated a broad consensus about the need for reform and the objectives to be achieved in line with the de Larosière report and the Commission's proposals for its follow-up.

This Communication is a key milestone and sets out the basic architecture for a new European financial supervisory framework. The Commission invites the European Council to endorse this architecture, as set out in the conclusions. It is envisaged that the legislative changes to give effect to the framework for EU supervision set out in this document will follow in the autumn of this year, after further consultation of stakeholders, and should be adopted in time for the renewed supervisory framework to be up and running during 2010.

The Commission welcomes reactions from stakeholders to this Communication by 15 July 2009 at the latest.

[1900]

NOTES
¹   Commission Communication of 4 March 2009 to the Spring European Council, "Driving European Recovery" – COM(2009) 114.
²   See the report of the High-Level Group on Financial Supervision in the EU published on 25 February 2009. The Group was chaired by Mr Jacques de Larosière.

2. A NEW SUPERVISORY FRAMEWORK FOR THE EU

As announced in the Communication of 4 March 2009, the Commission will propose that an enhanced European financial supervisory framework should be composed of two new pillars (see the figure in the Annex):

— **a European Systemic Risk Council (ESRC)** which will monitor and assess potential threats to financial stability that arise from macro-economic developments and from developments within the financial system as a whole ("macro-prudential supervision"). To this end, the ESRC would provide an early warning of system-wide risks that may be building up and, where necessary, issue recommendations for action to deal with these risks. The creation of the ESRC will address one of the fundamental weaknesses highlighted by the crisis, which is the vulnerability of the financial system to interconnected, complex, sectoral and cross-sectoral systemic risks; and

— **a European System of Financial Supervisors (ESFS)** consisting of a robust network of national financial supervisors working in tandem with new European Supervisory Authorities to safeguard financial soundness at the level of individual financial firms and protect consumers of financial services ("micro-prudential supervision"). The new European network will be built on shared and mutually reinforcing responsibilities, combining nationally based supervision of firms with centralisation of specific tasks at the European level so as to foster harmonised rules as well as coherent supervisory practice and enforcement. This network should be based on the principles of partnership, flexibility and subsidiarity. It would aim to enhance trust between national supervisors by ensuring, inter alia, that host supervisors have an appropriate say in setting policies relating to financial stability and consumer protection, thereby allowing cross-border risks to be addressed more effectively.

Implementing both pillars of the new supervisory system is essential: to achieve valuable synergies; to mutually reinforce the impact on financial stability; to ensure a fully connected macro-micro supervisory framework. It would be inefficient to reinforce EU financial services regulation, while preserving a supervisory system that has showed multiple deficiencies in this crisis. In parallel, differences in the national transposition of Community law stemming from exceptions, derogations, additions or ambiguities in current directives must be identified and removed, so that one harmonised core set of standards (a single rulebook) can be defined and applied throughout the EU by all supervisors. This process could be strengthened by introducing more directly applicable rules at the EU level, where possible.

The new European financial supervisory framework must be fully accountable to political authorities in the EU. It must develop a common supervisory culture; be sensitive to the interests of all Member States – and the need for a balanced, strengthened confidence building relationship between home and host authorities. It must be a system that is based on high supervisory standards, applied equivalently, fairly and consistently to all market actors, while respecting the independence of supervisors to carry out their work.

With this initiative, the EU is not just responding to its calls in the G20 framework for international action to build a stronger, more globally consistent, regulatory and supervisory system for the future financial sector[3], but also setting out a modern and comprehensive regional framework, whose principles should be taken up at international level.

[1901]

NOTES

3   See the London Summit Statement of 2 April 2009.

---

3. EUROPEAN SYSTEMIC RISK COUNCIL (ESRC)

3.1. THE CASE FOR REFORM OF MACRO-PRUDENTIAL SUPERVISION

The weaknesses of the present arrangements for macro-prudential supervision have had dramatic consequences across the global financial system. Many of the imbalances that accumulated in the global financial system before the crisis can be attributed to excessive credit expansion and surging asset price inflation, amid a generalised under-pricing of financial risk in a period of sustained non-inflationary economic growth. Against this background, the G20 has decided to reinforce the global arrangements for safeguarding financial stability at the global level, with the newly established Financial Stability Board (FSB)[4] expected to collaborate closely with the International Monetary Fund (IMF) to provide early warnings of macro-prudential risks at the global level. Meanwhile, the US Government plans to put in place a powerful body with responsibility for macro-prudential supervision of its domestic financial system.

Similarly, the EU needs a specific body responsible for macro-prudential supervision across the EU financial system, which would identify risks to financial stability and, where necessary, issue risk warnings and/or recommendations for action to address such risks. The present EU arrangements place too little emphasis on the macro-prudential side. Macro-prudential analysis is fragmented, executed by different authorities at different levels with no mechanism to ensure that macro-prudential risk warnings and/or recommendations are followed up and translated into action. In the run-up to this crisis, interconnected complex market risks were not properly analysed, nor were the consequences drawn for regulatory and supervisory policy. These fragmented arrangements must change because the economic costs of failure in macro-prudential supervision, as this crisis has shown, can be heavy.

3.2. ROLE AND RESPONSIBILITIES OF THE ESRC

The Commission will propose that the ESRC should be established as a new independent body, responsible for safeguarding financial stability by conducting macro-prudential supervision at the European level. In order to perform this role, the ESRC should:

Role of ESRC

— collect and analyse all information relevant for monitoring and assessing potential threats to financial stability that arise from macro-economic developments and developments within the financial system as a whole;
— identify and prioritise such risks;
— issue risk warnings where risks appear to be significant;
— where necessary give recommendations on the measures to be taken in reaction to the risks identified;
— monitor the required follow-up to warnings and recommendations, and
— liaise effectively with the IMF, the FSB and third country counterparts.

The main task of the ESRC would be assessments of stability across the EU financial system in the context of macro-economic developments and general trends in financial markets. If significant stability risks are foreseen, the ESRC would provide early warnings and, where appropriate, issue recommendations for remedial action. The warnings and recommendations issued by the ESRC could be of a general nature or could concern individual Member States and there would be a specified timeline for the relevant policy response. These warnings and/or recommendations would be channelled through the ECOFIN Council and/or the new European Supervisory Authorities. The ESRC would also be responsible for monitoring compliance with its recommendations, based on reports from the addressees.

The ESRC would not have any legally binding powers. However, the ESRC would be expected to exert major influence on the addressees of warnings/recommendations through the high quality of its analysis and the participation in its work of all EU central bank governors and supervisors and the Commission. The addressees of warnings and recommendations would therefore be expected to act on them unless inaction could be adequately justified. In short, the follow-up to warnings and recommendations would be ensured by an "act or explain" mechanism. The ESRC would decide in each case whether a recommendation should be kept confidential or made public, on the basis of its own judgement. However, bearing in mind that the recommendations by the ESRC would not be binding, public disclosure would be expected to increase their effectiveness.

The ESRC would be fully accountable to the Council and the European Parliament. Accountability would take the form of regular (ie, at least bi-annual) reporting to these institutions. More frequent reporting would be likely in the event of widespread financial distress, although it should be noted that the ESRC would not have any direct crisis management responsibilities.

3.3. COMPOSITION AND FUNCTIONING OF THE ESRC

Central banks should have a leading role in macro-prudential supervision. The main responsibilities of central banks relate to the maintenance of monetary and financial stability. Indeed, the analysis necessary for carrying out macro-prudential tasks can partly be based on the economic and monetary analyses undertaken by central banks for the formulation of monetary policy, although additional information and analysis of vulnerabilities in the financial system would also be required. Furthermore, central banks have a crucial financial safety net function through their role as lenders of last resort. As safeguarding financial stability is a fundamental responsibility of central banks, the Commission will propose that the ESRC would include the central bank governors of the 27 Member States and the President of the ECB. Participation in the ESRC will not prejudice any existing financial stability responsibilities.

The participation of micro-prudential supervisors in the work of the ESRC is also indispensable. The interconnectedness of financial institutions and markets clearly implies that the monitoring and assessment of potential systemic risks should be based on a broad set of relevant macro-economic and micro-financial data and indicators. Micro-prudential supervisors have detailed knowledge of developments in financial markets and in major firms and will have critical information to assess stability risks. For these reasons, the chairpersons of the three European Supervisory Authorities of the ESFS as well as senior representatives of the national supervisory authorities should be involved. To ensure that the ESRC can work efficiently, the membership of supervisors in the ESRC would be limited to the three chairpersons of the European Supervisory Authorities. However, each central

PART V
EU MATERIALS

bank governor should be accompanied by one senior representative of the national supervisory authorities as observer (ie, a 1+1 formula). The representative accompanying the central bank governor could vary from meeting to meeting, depending on the issues to be discussed by the ESRC, in particular in those Member States where there are several supervisory authorities.

A member of the Commission would also have membership in the ESRC, notably because of the Commission's Treaty-based responsibilities for macro-economic surveillance. It regularly monitors and analyses macroeconomic developments and policies and identifies macro-financial risks. It has both the necessary country-specific expertise and an EU-wide perspective and so would be well placed to contribute to the work of the ESRC.

Participation of Finance Ministries in the ESRC could be perceived as blurring its role in providing independent technical analysis of macro-prudential risks. However, as budgetary and/or taxation policies can contribute to or mitigate financial-stability risks, the Economic and Financial Committee (EFC) chairperson would represent the finance ministries by participating as an observer in ESRC meetings. This would also reflect the role of finance ministries in crisis management and resolution and ensure a smooth flow of information between the ESRC and the political authorities.

Meetings of the ESRC would be held at least quarterly, with more frequent meetings held in times of stress in the financial system. All ESRC members and observers would have the right to attend and to speak at these meetings. In order to streamline the decision-making process, however, only ESRC members would have the right to vote, ie only the President of the ECB, national central bank governors, the chairmen of the European Supervisory Authorities and the Commission member. Votes would not be weighted and decisions would be taken by a simple majority.

In line with the recommendation made in the de Larosière report, the chairperson of the ESRC should be the ECB President (in which case, the chairperson of the ESRC being independent, the ECB Vice-President should also be a member). As the chairperson comes from a central bank within the Eurosystem, it would seem appropriate that a vice-chairperson should be elected from among those Member States outside of the euro area.

A small steering committee – consisting of the ESRC chairperson and vice-chairperson, five additional central bank members of the ESRC, the chairpersons of the new European Supervisory Authorities and the Commission member – should be established to prepare and ensure efficient ESRC meetings. In addition, an advisory technical committee should be established to support the ESRC, including preparing detailed technical analysis of financial stability issues. In performing its duties, it would seem advisable that the ESRC should also seek the advice of private-sector stakeholders, including consumer representatives. The ECB will provide the Secretariat to the ESRC as well as analytical, administrative and logistic support.

The ESRC would closely collaborate with the IMF, the FSB and third country counterparts in the context of an early warning system at the global level, for example by drawing attention to potential risks in the global financial system outside of the EU. In this way, the ESRC would be expected to increase the influence of the EU in any global risk warning system.

Composition of the European Systemic Risk Council (ESRC)

Members:
— Chairperson: President of the ECB;
— Vice-Chairperson (elected by ESRC members);
— Governors of the 27 national central banks;
— Vice-President of the ECB;
— Chairpersons of the three European Supervisory Authorities;
— Member of the European Commission.

Observers:
— A representative of the national supervisory authorities, accompanying the central bank Governor in a 1+1 formula;
— Chairperson of the EFC.

3.4. LEGAL BASIS FOR THE ESRC

Only with arrangements in place that properly acknowledge the interdependence between micro- and macro-prudential risks can all stakeholders, eg financial institutions, investors and consumers, have sufficient confidence to engage in cross-border financial activities. Too often in the past, the focus of prudential supervision has been exclusively at the micro-level, with supervisors assessing the balance sheets of individual financial institutions without due consideration for interactions between institutions and between institutions and the broader financial system. Providing this broader perspective is the responsibility of macro-prudential supervisors. These supervisors shall monitor and assess potential financial-stability risks arising from developments that can impact on a sectoral level or at the level of the financial system as a whole. By addressing such risks, the ESRC would be an essential building block for an integrated EU supervisory structure necessary to promote timely and consistent policy responses among the Member States thus preventing diverging approaches and so improve the functioning of the Internal Market. In addition, as an integral part of the legal and institutional framework, the ESRC will facilitate the consistent, coherent and effective implementation and application of Community rules for cross-border financial services.

Having considered a range of possible options, the Commission considers it appropriate that the ESRC should be established on the basis of Article 95 of the EC Treaty as a body without legal personality. This legal basis would allow the ESRC to have the core features outlined above and to have a mandate covering the whole financial sector without exceptions, including insurance. Moreover, it would allow the ESRC, together with the ESFS, to form a common innovative framework for financial supervision, while maintaining a clear distinction of responsibilities between the ESRC and the other institutions. This choice of legal base does not prevent the conferring of responsibilities on the ECB in respect of tasks in respect of the ESRC by means of an act adopted on the basis of Article 105(6) of the EC Treaty.

[1902]

NOTES

4   The successor to the Financial Stability Forum (FSF).

---

4. EUROPEAN SYSTEM OF FINANCIAL SUPERVISORS (ESFS)

4.1. THE CASE FOR MICRO-PRUDENTIAL REFORMS

On micro-prudential supervision, the EU has reached the limits of what can be done with the present status of the Committees of European Supervisors[5] (Level 3 Committees) – which remain advisory bodies to the Commission. In spite of a number of improvements to these Committees, the EU cannot remain in a situation where there is no mechanism to ensure that national supervisors arrive at the best possible supervisory decisions for cross-border institutions; where there is insufficient cooperation and information exchange between national supervisory authorities; where joint action by national authorities requires a tour de force to take account of the patchwork of regulatory and supervisory requirements; where national solutions are most often the only feasible option in responding to European problems, where different interpretations of the same legal text abound. The new ESFS will be designed to overcome these deficiencies and provide a system that is in line with the objective of a stable and single EU financial market for financial services – linking national supervisors into a strong Community network.

4.2. ROLE AND RESPONSIBILITIES OF THE ESFS

The ESFS should become therefore an operational European network with shared and mutually reinforcing responsibilities. At the EU-level, the three existing Committees of Supervisors would be replaced by three new European Supervisory Authorities, ie, a European Banking Authority (EBA), a European Insurance and Occupational Pensions Authority (EIOPA), and a European Securities Authority (ESA), which would each have legal personality. These new European Supervisory Authorities will take on all the missions of the current Committees of Supervisors[6], but in addition have increased responsibilities, defined legal powers and greater authority (see below). They would also contribute to the development of a single set of harmonised rules, improve the supervision of cross-border institutions by developing common supervisory requirements and approaches and help settle possible disputes between national supervisors.

The focal point for day to day supervision would remain at the national level, with national supervisors remaining responsible for the supervision of individual entities, for example with respect to capital adequacy. This reflects, for the time being, that the financial means for rescuing financial institutions remains at the Member State level and with national tax payers, as the current crisis has demonstrated. For cross-border institutions, the colleges of supervisors which are being set up[7] will be the lynchpin of the supervisory system and should play an important role in ensuring a balanced flow of information between home and host authorities. The European Supervisory Authorities should participate in meetings of the colleges of supervisors, as observers, so as to contribute to the emergence of a common supervisory culture and consistent supervisory practices. Set up in this way, the ESFS will combine the advantages of an overarching European framework for financial supervision with the expertise of local supervisory bodies that are closest to the institutions operating in their jurisdictions.

In order for the ESFS to work effectively, flanking measures and changes to the sectoral legislation will be needed to ensure a more harmonised set of financial regulations. The goal will be to bring about more harmonisation in the rules that have to be applied by supervisors as well as greater consistency in the national powers and sanctions available to them. On the latter, the Commission will come forward with proposals in the autumn.

To achieve its objectives, the new European Supervisory Authorities will need to be equipped to fulfil the following functions:

(1) Ensure a single set of harmonised rules

The Authorities will:

— develop binding technical standards in specific areas and on the basis of criteria which will be specified in Community legislation (eg supervisory standards for colleges of supervisors and technical standards for internal model validation). Such standards shall apply within a fixed period of time, provided the Commission endorses by non-opposition, and

— draw up interpretative guidelines, which the competent national authorities would apply in taking individual decisions, notably as regards the licensing and supervision of financial institutions.

(2) Ensure consistent application of EU rules

Even with a single set of harmonised rules, the application of these rules may, in occasional cases, lead to differences of opinion on the application of Community legislation. The European Supervisory Authorities should therefore have, in cases clearly specified in Community legislation, the means to ensure coherent application of Community legislation.

— *Disagreement between national supervisors*

In the case of diverging opinions between national supervisory authorities, the European Supervisory Authorities should facilitate a dialogue and assist the supervisors in reaching a joint agreement. If, after a phase of conciliation, the latter have not been able to reach an agreement, the European Supervisory Authorities should, through a decision, settle the matter. However, this would clearly be a last resort option as in most cases the respective national authorities should be able to come to an agreement in the preceding conciliation procedure.

— *Manifest breach of Community Law*

A mechanism should also be put in place to address behaviour by a national supervisory authority which is considered to be manifestly diverging from the existing Community legislation. The European Supervisory Authorities, on their own initiative or upon request from one or more national supervisors or from the Commission, would investigate the issue and, if necessary, adopt a recommendation for action addressed to the relevant national supervisor.

Within the general duty of compliance with Community legislation the national authority would be called to comply with the recommendation within a fixed period of time. On the rare occasion that the situation would pertain, the European Supervisory Authorities would inform the Commission of the particular case. The Commission could, shortly after the adoption of the European Supervisory Authorities' recommendation, take a decision, requiring the national supervisory authority to either take specific action or to refrain from action in order to ensure full compliance with the acquis communautaire in the area of financial services.

In order to overcome inaction in relation to the implementation of Community law or delaying of action by national supervisors or in case of need for urgent action, the European Supervisory Authorities could also be empowered to adopt decisions directly applicable to financial institutions in relation to requirements stemming from EU Regulations relating to the prudential supervision of financial institutions and markets as well as the stability of the financial system. These decisions would be without prejudice to the initiation of infringement proceedings by the Commission against Member States.

(3) Ensure a common supervisory culture and consistent supervisory practices

The new European Supervisory Authorities will build a common European supervisory culture and consistent supervisory practices, for example by developing common training programmes and participating in meetings of the colleges of supervisors as an observer. They could also promote the use of delegation of tasks and responsibilities from one national supervisory authority to the other.

(4) Full supervisory powers for some specific entities

The European Supervisory Authorities shall be given the responsibility for the authorisation and supervision of certain entities with pan-European reach, eg, credit rating agencies and EU central counterparty clearing houses. These responsibilities could include such powers as those of investigation, on-site inspections and supervisory decisions. These responsibilities would be defined in sectoral legislation (eg, the Regulation on Credit Rating Agencies). Apart from reinforcing the effectiveness of supervision, this could enhance efficiency by creating a 'one-stop shop' for these supervised institutions. The European Supervisory Authorities could also be involved in the prudential assessment of European mergers and acquisitions throughout the financial sector[8].

(5) Ensure a coordinated response in crisis situations

The European Supervisory Authorities should have a strong coordinating role in crisis situations: they should facilitate cooperation and exchange of information between the competent authorities, act as mediator when needed, verify the reliability of the information that should be available to all parties and help the relevant authorities to define and implement the right decisions. As for the latter, the introduction of a European mandate by mid-2009 will allow national authorities to consider financial stability concerns in other Member States when exercising their duties. In this respect progress on burden sharing and resolution mechanisms is critical to reinforcing trust between national authorities and strengthening the functioning of the ESFS, work which must advance as soon as possible. In specific crisis situations, the European Supervisory Authorities could have the power to adopt some emergency decisions (e g on short-selling) – the scope of these emergency procedures should be defined in Community legislation.

(6) Collect micro-prudential information

The European Supervisory Authorities should be responsible for the aggregation of all relevant micro-prudential information emanating from national supervisors. To this end a central European database should be established and managed by the European Supervisory Authorities. The information would be available for the relevant authorities in colleges of supervisors and may be forwarded in aggregated and/or anonymous format to the ESRC (see section 5). To this end, existing sectoral legislation may need to be amended.

(7) Undertake an international role

Without prejudice to the institutional competences of the European Institutions, the European Supervisory Authorities could be given a certain role as regards international activities, including technical arrangements with international organisations and with the administrations of third countries at its level. The European Supervisory Authorities could also assist the Commission in preparing equivalence decisions pertaining to supervisory regimes in third countries.

(8) Safeguards

The framework for the exercise of the above competences will be specified exhaustively and in precise detail in the relevant sectoral legislation. The conferring of these competences will be in full conformity with Articles 226 and 228 of the Treaty. Without prejudice to the application of Community law, and recognising the potential liabilities that may be involved for Member States, decisions under the above mechanisms shall not directly impinge on the fiscal responsibilities of the Member States. Moreover, any decision by the European Supervisory Authorities or the Commission must be subject to review by the Community Courts.

4.3. COMPOSITION AND OPERATIONAL STRUCTURE OF THE ESFS

The network approach to supervision described above, with the new European Supervisory Authorities working in tandem with the national financial supervisors, is proposed in line with the de Larosière report, as opposed to solutions such as full centralisation of supervision at the EU level, on which there is no consensus. However, given the urgency to improve the quality and coherence of supervision in Europe, the Commission considers it necessary to accelerate the preparatory work proposed by the de Larosière Group, so that the strengthened framework will be up and running in 2010.

The Commission recognises that there is a vigorous – and so far inconclusive – debate within many countries in the world on the most appropriate supervisory structure, with options including: (i) one single supervisor for all sectors, (ii) separate supervisors for prudential and conduct-of-business supervision for all financial institutions combined (the so-called "twin peaks" model), and (iii) a sectoral approach (ie, separate supervisors for banking, insurance companies and securities activities). However, in the Commission's view, at this point in time it is preferable to maintain the latter approach at European level, building upon the existing structures given that there is no persuasive evidence to suggest that other structures would be more efficient for the specific competences which are proposed for the European Supervisory Authorities. These competences are not mainly composed of direct supervision, and therefore the arguments and evidence adduced in national debates on supervisory structure cannot necessarily be applied to them. For these reasons, the Commission will propose to build on the existing structure and, when necessary, allow it to evolve over time, with a review after a fixed number of years.

Within the proposed structure, cross-sectoral cooperation will however be fundamental so as to reflect the relevant market trends and realities. To the extent that the degree of convergence between sectors will continue, the three European Supervisory Authorities and a representative of the Commission would increasingly need to evaluate the respective sectoral regimes to identify common principles and understanding possible differences. An overarching steering committee should therefore be formally introduced in the structure to ensure mutual understanding, cooperation and consistent supervisory approaches between the three new European Supervisory Authorities in addressing cross-sectoral challenges, including financial conglomerates, and ensuring a level playing field. In addition, each European Supervisory Authority should have the possibility to participate in meetings of the other European Supervisory Authorities as an observer.

Each new Authority would have a Board of Supervisors comprised of the highest-level representatives from the appropriate national supervisory authorities and chaired by the chairperson of the respective European Supervisory Authority. Representatives from the Commission, the ESRC and the relevant supervisory authorities from EFTA-EEA countries should take part in the Board of Supervisors as observers. However, they would not be able to attend any discussions pertaining to individual institutions. In line with current practice, a Management Board should also be set up to deal with general operational issues (budget etc) and would include the Commission. The chairpersons and secretary generals of the European Supervisory Authorities should be full-time independent professionals. The chairperson will be nominated after an open competition. Appointment would be confirmed by the European Parliament and should be valid for a period of 5 years.

Composition of the European System of Financial Supervisors

I. Steering Committee:
— Representatives of the three European Supervisory Authorities and the Commission.

II. Three European Supervisory Authorities [the European Banking Authority (EBA), the European Insurance and Occupational Pensions Authority (EIOPA), and the European Securities Authority (ESA)]:
Board of Supervisors of each European Supervisory Authority:
— Chairperson of the European Supervisory Authorities, and
— Chairpersons from the appropriate national supervisory authorities.

Observers:
— A Commission representative;
— A representative of the ESRC, and
— A representative from the appropriate national supervisory authority of each EFTA-EEA country.

Management Board of each European Supervisory Authority:
— Representatives from the appropriate national supervisory authorities and the Commission.

III. National supervisory authorities

The Board of Supervisors should meet on a regular basis, with additional meetings held in times of stress. The European Supervisory Authorities' decisions on technical rules would be taken, through the board structure, by qualified majority based on the Treaty weighting for Member States. Separate arrangements should be considered for dealing with other functions of the European Supervisory Authorities. For example, decisions on the application of existing laws should be taken by simple majority on the basis of "one person, one vote".

The European Supervisory Authorities would each have their own budget, subject to discharge by the European Parliament. Their resources could stem from the EU budget as well other sources such as contributions by the national authorities. Any budgets would have to be commensurate with their responsibilities, and ensure independence. The European Supervisory Authorities should liaise in a structured way with all relevant stakeholders, including consumers.

Ensuring the independence of these European Supervisory Authorities will be crucial. They would need the highest degree of independence vis-à-vis national authorities other than supervisors and vis-à-vis the European Institutions, which should not interfere in the decisions of the European Supervisory Authorities. The European Supervisory Authorities would however be fully accountable to the Council, the European Parliament and the Commission. Transparency would be a key instrument to make this work and the European Supervisory Authorities would have to report formally to the European Institutions on a frequent basis (eg, at least bi-annually).

4.4. LEGAL BASIS FOR THE ESFS

The legal basis for establishing the European Supervisory Authorities should be the provision of the EC Treaty which constitutes the specific legal basis for the policy they will be called upon to implement.

The financial and economic crisis has created risks to the stability of the internal market. Restoring and maintaining a stable and reliable financial system is an absolute prerequisite to preserving trust and coherence in the internal market, hence to preserve and improve the conditions for the establishment of a fully integrated and functioning internal market in the field of financial services. Moreover, deeper and more integrated financial markets offer better opportunities for financing and risk diversification, and thus help to improve the capacity of the economies to absorb shocks. Financial integration and stability are therefore mutually reinforcing.

The establishment of the ESFS, and the three European Supervisory Authorities, will be accompanied by the development of a single rule book which will ensure uniform application of rules in the EU and thus contribute to the functioning of the internal market. The task of the European Supervisory Authorities will be to assist the national authorities in the consistent interpretation and application of the Community rules.

The Court of Justice has acknowledged[9] that Article 95 of the EC Treaty relating to the adoption of measures for the approximation of legislation for the establishment and functioning of the internal market provides an appropriate legal basis for setting up a "*Community body responsible for contributing to the implementation of a process of harmonisation*", when the tasks conferred on such a body are closely linked to the subject-matter of the acts approximating the national legislations.

The tasks to be conferred on the European Supervisory Authorities being thus closely linked to the measures put in place as a response to the financial crisis and to those announced in the Communication on "*Driving European recovery*", they can, thus, in line with the Court's case law, be established on the basis of Article 95 of the EC Treaty.

[1903]

NOTES

5   Committee of European Banking Supervisors (CEBS), Committee of European Insurance and Occupational Pensions Committee (CEIOPS) and the Committee of European Securities Regulators (CESR), also often known as the "Lamfalussy level 3 Committees".
6   eg, giving technical advice to the European Commission.
7   Regarding the major financial groups in the EU, colleges already exist or are being set up in 2009.
8   The Commission would remain exclusively competent to apply the EU State aid rules and, for Community dimension mergers, to assess the competition aspects of such transaction in line with the EC Merger Regulation.
9   See CJCE, C-217/04, pt 44.

5. COOPERATION BETWEEN THE ESFS AND THE ESRC

The proposed framework for EU supervision can only work if the ESRC and ESFS cooperate efficiently. Indeed, the objective of the reform is to ensure a smoother interaction of supervision at the macro-prudential and micro-prudential levels. In fulfilling its role as macro-prudential supervisor, the ESRC would need a timely flow of harmonised micro-level data, while micro-prudential supervision by national authorities would benefit from the ESRC's insights into the macro-prudential environment. Binding cooperation and information sharing procedures between the "micro" and the "macro" levels would be of fundamental importance, if the pitfalls from the past are to be avoided.

In order to identify and prioritise risks to the stability of the EU financial system, the ESRC would need to: (i) receive relevant micro-prudential data – notably on large and complex cross-border groups- from the ESFS, and (ii) have the possibility to launch ad-hoc surveys on specific issues requiring direct input from national supervisors and/or the market operators. The Commission will propose that the necessary information would be passed to the European Supervisory Authorities by the national supervisory authorities in application of the rules establishing the new European Supervisory Authorities. The powers to receive all information relevant for financial stability could be attributed to the ESRC by a combination of the legal instrument establishing the ESRC and the legal instruments establishing the new European Supervisory Authorities. Meanwhile, the Regulations establishing the new European Supervisory Authorities would require them to periodically (eg, on a monthly basis) provide the ESRC with aggregated and relevant anonymous disaggregated data on all financial institutions and markets, but notably on large and complex cross-border groups. Given the sensitivity of the data and information, ensuring necessary confidentiality in the cooperation between the ESRC and the ESFS would be crucial and adequate legal safeguards should be in place. In addition, for the colleges to receive up-to-date information on the macro-prudential environment in which individual institutions operate, the participation of ESRC representatives as observers could be envisaged.

[1904]

6. CONCLUSION

The Commission invites the European Council to:
— endorse the creation of a new European Systemic Risk Council (ESRC), chaired by the ECB President and including governors of national central banks, the chairpersons of the three European Supervisory Authorities and a member of the European Commission. There should also be close involvement of national supervisory authorities and the chair of the Economic and Financial Committee in the work of the ESRC;
— agree that the ESRC will be charged with continuously assessing the stability of the financial system as a whole and be given the necessary authority to issue timely warnings/recommendations for remedial action and to monitor responses;
— agree on the establishment of a new European System of Financial Supervisors (ESFS) composed of 3 new European Supervisory Authorities working in a network with national supervisory authorities to develop common supervisory approaches to the supervision of all financial firms, to protect consumers of financial services and to contribute to the development of a single set of harmonized rules. Inter alia, the ESFS should draw up technical standards, help ensure the consistent application of Community law and resolve disputes between supervisors;

— underline the importance of a truly integrated approach to European financial supervision: the need for strong interaction between the ESRC and the ESFS including the exchange of micro-prudential information relevant for macro-prudential analysis; the willingness of the relevant parties to act upon risk warnings and/or recommendations; and the need for the ESRC to act as an interface with international institutions notably the FSB and IMF;

— welcome the Commission's intention to bring forward, as soon as possible, the legislative changes to put in place the new framework for EU supervision, on the basis of the orientations set out in this Communication and after further consultation of stakeholders, so that the necessary measures are adopted in time for the renewed framework to be up and running during 2010;

— in addition, support the acceleration of work to build a comprehensive cross border framework to strengthen the European Union's financial crisis management/resolution systems, including guarantee schemes and burden sharing.

[1905]

ANNEX:

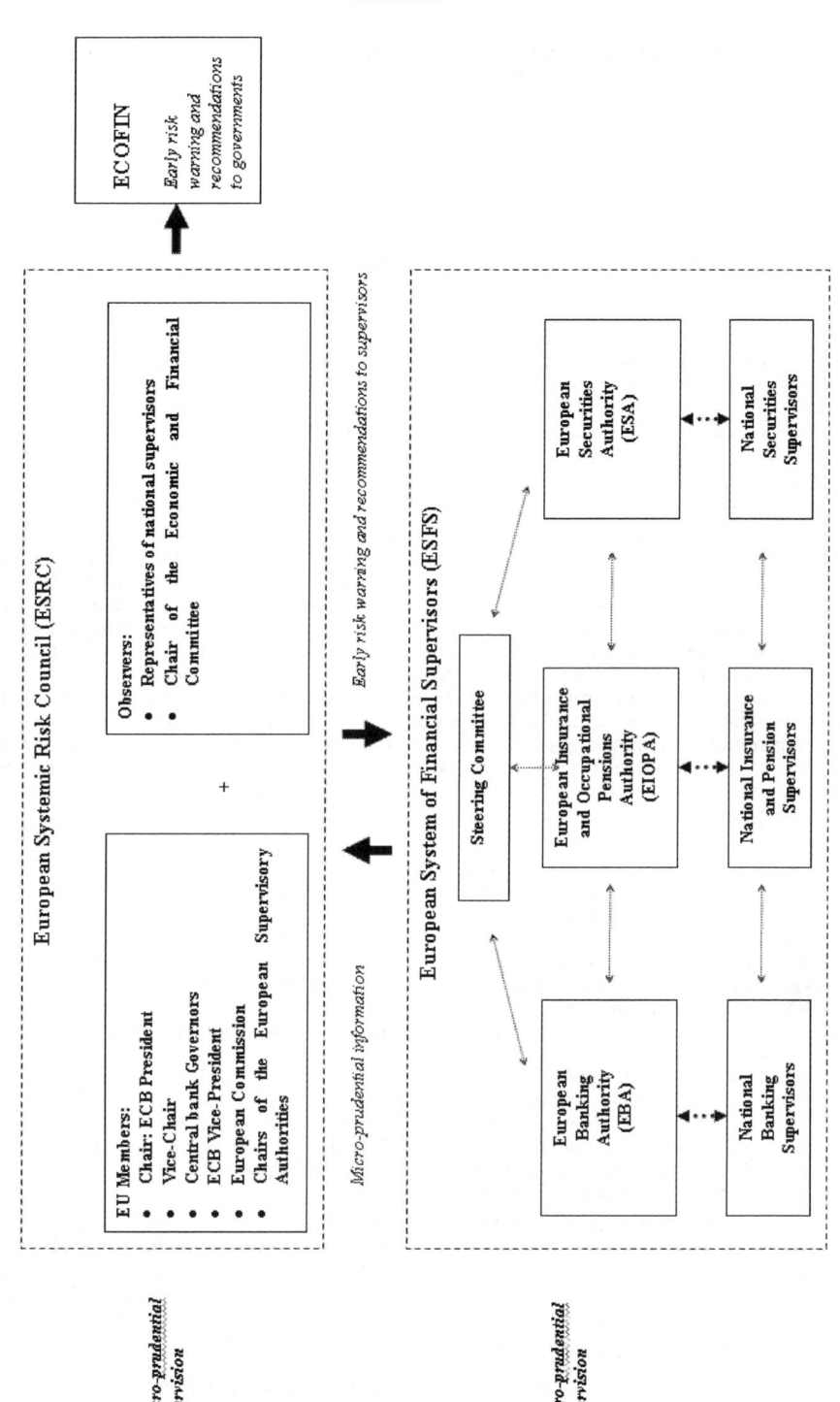

COMMISSION STAFF WORKING DOCUMENT

**Accompanying document to the Communication from the Commission
'European financial supervision'
IMPACT ASSESSMENT**

{SEC (2009) 715}
{SEC (2009) 716}

NOTES
Brussels, 27.5.2009; COM(2009) 252 final. Notes are as per the original.
As of 1 August 2009 this document had not been amended.

1. INTRODUCTION

In its Communication "Driving European recovery" of 4 March 2009, the European Commission committed itself to come forward with proposals for reform of the EU framework for financial supervision. It was specifically highlighted that the Commission would present a Communication on European financial supervision before the end of May 2009, for discussion at the June European Council. This initiative is part of a broader programme for financial market reform announced in that Communication, consisting of a series of initiatives for adjusting the EU regulatory framework for financial services to address the problems revealed by the recent financial crisis.

In the absence of adequate EU-action, there is a risk that the financial integration process in Europe will slow down as a result of fragmented national responses to the financial and economic crisis. The other initiatives undertaken by the Commission – apart from the work on financial supervision – include improving and removing gaps in regulation (eg concerning alternative investment funds and capital requirements for banks), protecting consumers and SMEs (eg, initiatives to foster responsible lending and borrowing), improving incentives to reduce excessive short-term risk-taking (eg, initiatives on remuneration in financial services) and strengthening sanctions for infringements of the rules. The Commission is also working to ensure that appropriate crisis intervention tools are available in all Member States to allow early intervention in ailing banks or insurance firms, in order to guarantee the continuity of key financial services, whilst minimising costs to the taxpayer. Specific regulatory issues related to large and complex financial groups are being addressed in the context of the review of the Financial Conglomerates Directive (FCD).

The Commission's action in the area of supervision takes due account of and builds on the findings and recommendations of the High Level Group on financial supervision in the EU, created by President Barroso in October 2008 and chaired by J. de Larosière. The de Larosière report[1], which cannot be quoted in extenso here, examines in detail the causes of the crisis. These were numerous, often with a global dimension. The report subsequently covers the issues of how to organise the supervision of financial institutions and markets in the EU; how to strengthen European co-operation on financial stability oversight, early warning and crisis mechanisms; and how EU supervisors should co-operate globally. The Group brought forward a number of recommendations on regulation of financial markets. However, it is the recommendations regarding the building blocks for a new European financial supervisory framework which are relevant here. They are based on two pillars:

- a *European System of Financial Supervisors (ESFS)*, for the supervision of individual financial institutions ("micro-prudential supervision") consisting of new European Supervisory Authorities working in tandem with the national financial supervisors, and
- a *European Systemic Risk Council (ESRC)* to oversee the stability of the financial system as a whole ("macro-prudential supervision") and provide early warning of systemic risks and recommendations where necessary.

The Spring European Council agreed on the need to improve both regulation and supervision of financial institutions in the EU and concluded that the de Larosière report is indeed the basis for action. At the informal Ecofin Council in Prague on 4 April 2009, EU Finance Ministers and Central Bank Governors discussed the key principles for the reform of financial market supervision, including establishing a European body responsible for the oversight on the stability of the financial system and the transformation of the existing Committees of Supervisors into three new European Supervisory Authorities. These discussions demonstrated that there was a large agreement on the objectives that should be achieved. The informal Ecofin confirmed that the June European Council wishes to analyse this issue again, on the basis of a document from the Commission.

Parallel efforts to strengthening financial supervision in the international context have also been undertaken at the global level by the G-20. At the summit in London on 2 April, the heads of state agreed to "take action to build a stronger, more globally consistent, supervisory and regulatory framework for the future financial sector, which will support sustainable growth and serve the needs of business and citizens"[2]. The Action Plan agreed at the first G-20 summit in Washington in November 2008 includes as objectives the creation of supervisory colleges for all international banks and strengthening international and regional crisis management. The leaders have also agreed on reshaping their regulatory systems to strengthen macro-prudential supervision, both at the national and international level. The newly established Financial Stability Board (FSB)[3] will collaborate with the International Monetary Fund (IMF) to provide early warning of macro-economic and financial risks at the global level. The US is putting in place a powerful financial stability body as well. The EU should also act and establish a new body responsible for identifying financial stability risks at European level and, where necessary, issue risk warnings. Being the two largest financial markets in the world, the EU and the US must closely work together to contribute to global stability and security.

This impact assessment provides an analysis of the rationale, the alternatives and the impact of the Commission proposals for reform of financial supervision in the EU presented in the Communication on European financial supervision[4]. It will be followed by a more comprehensive and detailed impact assessment for the envisaged legislative proposals to implement the reform.

[1907]

NOTES
1	"Report of the high-level group on financial supervision in the EU", chaired by J. de Larosière, Brussels 25/2/2009. Available at: http://ec.europa.eu/internal_market/finances/docs/de_larosiere_report_en.pdf. The report has also been endorsed by the Spring European Council as a basis for action to reform financial supervision. See annex for a summary of the deviations from the de Larosière report in the options retained in this Impact Assessment.
2	London Summit – Leaders' Statement, 2 April 2009, §13.
3	The successor to the Financial Stability Forum (FSF).
4	COM(2009)XXX of 13 May 2009.

2. CONSULTATIONS AND PROCEDURAL ISSUES

In preparing its report in the period November 2008 – February 2009, the de Larosière Group organised a number of hearings with experts representing the supervisory and regulatory authorities at the EU and international level as well as various segments of the financial services industry[5]. Their input has been reflected in the conclusions of the final report.

The Commission conducted a public written consultation on the de Larosière report between 10 March and 10 April 2009. A list and summary of contributions received is included in annex.

An Impact Assessment Steering Group was constituted in order to steer the preparation of this Impact Assessment, comprising representatives from DGs: MARKT, ECFIN, SG, SJ, ENTR, EMPL, COMP, SANCO. The Steering Group met twice on 25 March and 6 April 2009 and there was a written consultation on the last draft of the text. The Impact Assessment was submitted on 15 April 2009 and discussed by the Impact Assessment Board on 22 April 2009.

The IAB opinion was delivered on 24 April 2009, endorsing the report with several suggestions for improvement, including the recommendation to delimit more clearly the scope of the initiative, better define the options analysed, strengthen the analysis of the impacts of the preferred options, and highlight the specific case of cross-border banks and financial conglomerates. The respective parts of the report have been revised accordingly.

The Impact Assessment Steering Group agreed to inform the sectoral social dialogue committees in the financial services sectors (banking, insurance) about the initiative and impact assessment and to consult them, with the assistance of unit EMPL/F1, on the impact assessments for the upcoming legislative proposals.

[1908]

NOTES
5	The list of consulted parties is included in Annex II of the de Larosière report.

3. PROBLEM DEFINITION

3.1. GENERAL PROBLEMS

As the de Larosière report stated, although the way in which the financial sector has been supervised in the EU has not been one of the primary causes of the crisis, there have been real and important failures, both of micro- and macro-prudential supervision[6].

As highlighted by recent events, it is very difficult to achieve simultaneously a single financial market and stability in the financial system, while preserving fragmented nationally-based supervision and crisis management[7].

Financial stability is clearly a common good. It refers to a condition in which the financial system is capable of withstanding shocks and the unravelling of financial imbalances, thereby mitigating the likelihood of disruptions in the financial intermediation process which may significantly impair the allocation of savings to profitable investment opportunities and exert unsustainable pressure on public budgets and automatic stabilisers to cope with the real economy effects of the crisis[8]. This has certainly not been the case amid the current financial crisis, where problems in the banking sector have disrupted the flow of credit at both wholesale and retail levels.

From an Internal Market perspective, the ambition is to create an efficiently functioning internal market in financial services. Financial markets are crucial to the functioning of efficient economies. The more integrated these markets are, the more efficient allocation of capital and the higher long-run economic growth will be. Completing the single market for financial services is therefore a crucial part of the overriding objective of delivering stronger, lasting growth, and creating more and better jobs.

EU financial markets are increasingly integrated, especially at the wholesale level. The banking and insurance markets are dominated by pan-European groups, whose risk management functions are centralised in the group's headquarters. There has been an increase in cross-border M&A transactions in terms of value since 2003. This trend was particularly strong in 2005, when several large-value cross-border transactions were conducted, amounting to over 50% of the total M&A value in the euro area banking system. EU banks have become more international than ever, expanding into foreign markets both in Europe and beyond. Currently around 70% of EU banking assets is in the hands of some 40 banking groups with substantial cross-border activities. Especially in the EU-12, banking markets are dominated by foreign (mostly Western European) financial groups (see figure 1). In these countries, on average 65% of banking assets are in foreign-owned banks. In countries like Estonia, the Czech Republic and Slovakia over 92% of banking assets are in foreign-owned banks.

Figure 1. Market share of foreign-owned banks (% of total assets)

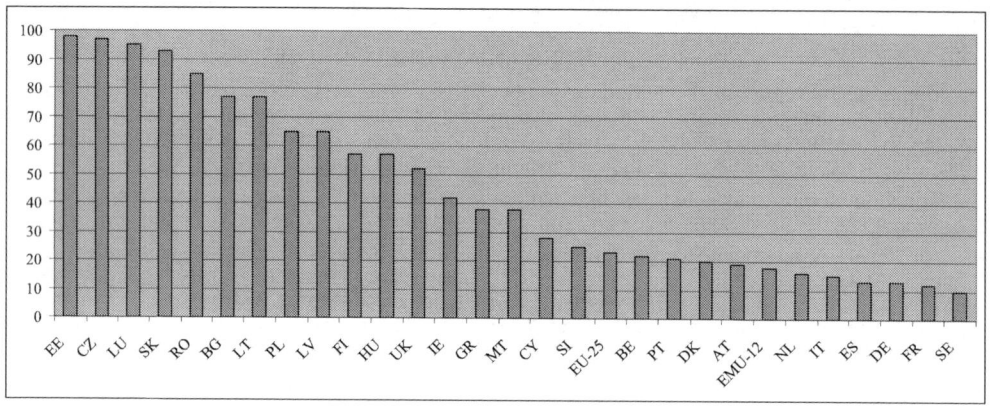

As for financial markets, the available evidence suggests that integration has progressed considerably, but varies depending on the market segment, and is to a large extent correlated with the degree of integration of the underlying financial infrastructure. Table 1 provides an overview of the level of integration of the various segments. It should be noted that due to intensive cross-border consolidation of stock exchanges, concentration of the underlying infrastructures is increasing (ie the market share of the five largest stock exchanges in Europe exceeded 90% in 2006).

Table 1. Integration of various market segments

Market segment	Degree of integration
Money market	High degree
Bond markets	
• government bonds	Considerable degree
• corporate bonds	Considerable degree
Equity markets	Increasing integration
Banking markets	
• interbank/wholesale activities	Increasing integration
• capital market related activities	Increasing integration
• retail banking activities	Fragmented

Whilst the Lamfalussy process has since 2001 contributed to a closer co-operation between national supervisors, the EU is still in a situation where the supervision of the EU markets and financial groups is fragmented and exercised at the national level, both with respect to prudential and conduct of business supervision (e g disagreements between national supervisors regarding the prudential assessment of cross-border mergers of financial institutions in the cases of ABN AMRO/Antonveneta in 2005 and Unicredit/Bank BPH in 2006).

The crisis which in 2008 hit the European financial sector as a whole has brought into sharp focus the weaknesses of the present arrangements to guarantee adequate protection for depositors, policy-holders and investors, as well as financial stability in the EU. Even though, at national/regional level, small groups of Member States took urgent and coordinated decisions to rescue cross-border institutions, overall the response was characterised by decisions which were ad hoc and mainly informed by national interests. Supervisors were unable to adopt rapid common decisions to tackle the most imminent cross-border problems (e g various unco-ordinated national bans on short selling of different durations). Some Member States took unilateral decisions which had the potential of undermining the soundness of other Member States' financial institutions (e g difficulties of collaboration between national supervisors in the case of Fortis). Member States have appeared strongly divided in the search for urgent and radical measures which could rebuild confidence and stabilise the situation. All this contributed to further weaken confidence and render the financial sector even more fragile.

On the other hand, the Commission intervened in October 2008 to facilitate the agreement of a framework for intervention in the financial sector, including respect for the state aid rules and prevention of distortions of competition. Overall, the EU can do much better, both in preventing and managing future financial crises. In this respect it should also be stressed that variations between national rules in member States continue to cause incoherencies in the internal market (examples include the wide variety of definitions of "own funds", impediments to asset transfers and temporary bans on short selling in some Member States but not others).

Another serious challenge highlighted by the crisis is the fact that the present EU arrangements – like arrangements at national and global level – place too much emphasis on the supervision of individual firms, and too little on risks to the stability of the financial system as a whole. Such analyses were fragmented and executed by different authorities at different levels. To the extent to which risks were identified there was no EU mechanism to ensure that this assessment of risk was translated into action. If Europe is serious about building a stable and truly integrated market, it will be necessary to make progress in resolving these weaknesses by developing a new concept for the supervision of the EU financial sector.

In summary, the crisis exposed that the arrangements for financial supervision in the EU can create risks to stability through the **mismatch between the level of European integration of EU financial markets and the national organisation of supervisory responsibilities.**

The seriousness of this problem is magnified given the other weaknesses exposed by the crisis:

- **Increased risks of cross-border contagion for EU financial markets linked with the increased integration, both throughout the EU and with global financial markets.**
- **Undermined confidence of consumers, employees, pensioners, small business and retail investors contributing to the economic recession.**
- **Reduced global competitiveness of the European financial industry, compared with what would have been the case with better supervisory practices.**
- **Risks of unco-ordinated policies driven by national interest with negative impact on the Single Market.**

These **general problems** are common to both micro-prudential supervision and macro-prudential supervision.

3.2. AFFECTED STAKEHOLDERS

Both theoretical and empirical research confirms that there is a strong positive link between the functioning of the financial system and (long-run) economic growth[9]. Better functioning financial systems ease the external financing constraints that impede expansion of firms and institutions and offer individuals and firms the possibility to trade, diversify, and manage risk. Financial instability can therefore have a significant negative impact on the real economy and lead to substantial output losses. It can seriously impair the lending of funds from savers to borrowers, resulting in a sharp reduction in the ability of the financial system to allocate credit. It can severely reduce the possibilities for individuals to diversify risks and smooth their consumption over time.

Given the fact that – especially in advanced economies – total financial assets often represent multiples of GDP, the fiscal costs of financial crises can be substantial. A study by the IMF[10] of 40 financial crisis episodes puts the fiscal costs associated with resolving financial crises in the average country at 16% of GDP. Although this average includes some small and emerging economies, the fiscal cost is equally high among industrialised economies – at 15% of GDP on average. About half (or 8% of GDP) of these fiscal outlays relate to costs associated with government-assisted recapitalisation of banks. The remainder relate mainly to costs associated with government asset purchase and debtor relief programs.

Up to now, EU governments have pledged around EUR 3 trillion in recapitalisation obligations and different guarantee schemes (ie, 28–30% of GDP). While not all of these obligations and guarantees will actually be used, the fiscal costs of the current crisis are likely to be substantial.

Due to their broad impact on the financial sector and the whole economy, financial instability will affect a very wide range of stakeholders, ie:

- Financial institutions, including their shareholders and employees;
- Users of financial services, including depositors, investors, pensioners, and non-financial companies, and
- Public authorities, including supervisors, central banks and finance ministries.

To the extent that financial instability damages the economy, a whole range of stakeholders will be affected (eg, employees and consumers) and to the extent that public intervention is required, taxpayers will also be affected.

3.3. MICRO- AND MACRO-PRUDENTIAL SUPERVISION: DEFINITIONS

In analysing the problems related to organisation of financial supervision in the EU, the de Larosière Group distinguished between micro-prudential supervision and macro-prudential supervision (see table 2). This division also holds throughout the subsequent analysis, so it is important to define these concepts at the outset.

The main objective of **micro-prudential supervision** is to supervise and limit the risk of distress in individual financial institutions. By preventing the failure of individual financial institutions, micro-prudential supervision attempts to protect the clients of the institutions and prevent (or at least mitigate) the risk of contagion and the subsequent negative externalities in terms of confidence in the overall financial system. However, the fact that the financial system as a whole may be exposed to common risks is not always fully taken into account.

Macro-prudential supervision focuses on limiting risks to the financial system as a whole that may arise from broad developments in the economy (eg, excessive domestic credit expansion). While risks to the financial system can in principle arise from the failure of one financial institution alone if it is large enough in relation to the country concerned and/or with multiple branches/ subsidiaries in other countries, the much more important systemic risk arises from a common exposure of many financial institutions to the same risk factors. Macro-prudential analysis therefore must pay particular attention to common or correlated shocks and to shocks to those parts of the financial system that trigger contagious knock-on or feedback effects. Obviously it should also focus on any other contagion mechanisms that could be a source of systemic risk, like interlinkages between financial institutions and overreactions provoked by imperfect information.

Micro-prudential supervision and macro-prudential supervision are interlinked. In this respect the de Larosière report stresses that macro-prudential supervision cannot be meaningful unless it can somehow impact supervision at the micro-level; whilst micro-prudential supervision cannot effectively safeguard financial stability without adequately taking account of macro-level developments.

Table 2. Micro- and macro-prudential supervision

	Micro-prudential supervision	**Macro-prudential supervision**
Immediate Objective	Limit risk of distress in individual institutions	Limit risk of financial system-wide stress due to macro-economic developments
Ultimate Objective	Consumer and user protection	Avoid correlated negative shocks that may threaten system stability and trigger output (GDP) costs

3.4. MICRO-PRUDENTIAL SUPERVISION

The current system of prudential supervision in the EU is based on the principle of home country control combined with minimum prudential standards and mutual recognition. A financial institution is thus authorised and supervised in its home country and can expand throughout the EU (by offering cross-border services in other EU member States or establishing branches in those States) without additional supervision. The host country has to recognise supervision from the home country authorities on most prudential issues.

In practice, however, financial institutions can also choose to operate through subsidiaries (separate legal entities) in other countries. These subsidiaries are separately licensed and supervised by the host country authorities. The scope for control by host countries of these subsidiaries is limited in practice, as key decisions are often taken at the parent company in the home country and the financial health of the subsidiary is closely linked to the well-being of the financial group as a whole. The primary effective control of large financial groups as a whole is therefore essentially in the hands of the consolidated supervisor in the home country. The latter may create tensions as decisions by home country authorities to preserve the stability of their national financial system can affect outcomes in host countries.

The cross-border nature of many financial institutions requires close co-operation between national supervisory authorities. This co-operation takes place in three main ways:

- Within the Lamfalussy framework[11] national supervisors are grouped in three committees (known as the Lamfalussy level 3 Committees): the Committee of European Banking Supervisors (CEBS), the Committee of European Insurance and Occupational Pension Supervisors (CEIOPS) and the Committee of European Securities Regulators (CESR). These Committees of Supervisors have been established with the aim of: ensuring convergence of supervisory practices; agreeing on common application of EU rules with non-binding guidelines; and fostering greater mutual trust. Supervision of financial conglomerates is carried out jointly by the Committees in the Joint Committee on Financial Conglomerates (JCFC). These committees are institutionally part of the Commission and have no regulatory or executive powers.
- Recently, colleges of supervisors have started to be created for the larger financial institutions in the EU. Within these colleges co-operation and information exchange between home and host authorities is reinforced.
- Ad hoc bilateral Memoranda of Understandings (MoUs) between respective supervisory authorities.

As highlighted in the de Larosière report, the situation nevertheless remains sub-optimal, as these co-operation mechanisms do not have the potential of removing the most serious inefficiencies of the present supervisory set-up. Supervisors are still not able to take binding decisions at the EU level. National supervisors will tend to take decisions on the basis of domestic considerations, even when the problems at hand have a European dimension and would require coordinated decisions and actions in order to achieve the best possible outcome for all.

Against this background, the main issues in the area of micro-prudential supervision can be aggregated in the following **problems**:

- **Imbalance of interests of the home and host countries in the current supervisory model (resulting in a misalignment of incentives in cross-border crisis management),**
- **Risks of competitive distortions in the Internal Market and of regulatory arbitrage by financial companies (arising in part from differing supervisory rules and practices),**
- **Lack of co-operation and information exchange between national supervisors,**
- **Excessive costs and administrative burden to cross-border companies due to fragmented and inconsistent financial supervision.**

They are linked with a number of particular **problem drivers** encountered in day to day practice of co-operation between national supervisors from various Member States, including:

- *Failure to challenge supervisory practices on a cross-border basis.* Home country authorities are given powers over branches but may well be unable or unwilling to use them, while host countries are losing powers that they have been willing to use. This gap may become a real problem once there is a banking group or bank that is systemically relevant in a host country. As national authorities are merely accountable to their national Parliaments and taxpayers, there is no guarantee that host authorities will take the interests of host countries into account in the event of a crisis with a cross-border dimension. The imbalance between home and host countries may be further deepened by differences in size between countries. The present processes and practices for challenging the decisions of a national supervisor on a cross-border basis have proven to be inadequate to address this (eg conflict between the Polish and Italian banking supervisors concerning minimum capital ratios of Pekao, the Polish subsidiary of Unicredit);
- *Lack of consistent rules, powers and sanctions across Member States,* mainly due to a lack of harmonisation in certain areas (eg national discretion under the Capital Requirements Directive) or differences in transposition (eg "gold plating" in transposition of the Transparency Directive, different interpretation of the Insurance Mediation Directive etc)[12];
- *Differences in supervisory practices,* eg in areas where the host supervisor of a branch has supervisory discretion (such as in the area of liquidity supervision), or in cases where supervisors take different perspectives (like an accounting perspective, which induces a focus on reporting, or a risk perspective, which induces a focus on group risk assessments with supervisory risk methodologies);
- *Fragmented responsibilities* (or lack of legal certainty regarding responsibilities) for

supervision of the same European financial group complicate co-ordination, cause incomplete oversight of group-wide risks and of growing risks, but also cause insufficient liability for decisions regarding group-wide risk management and capital allocation. There is no single entity which has the complete overview of the financial situation of a cross-border group or a market and which is in a position to take the often extremely urgent decisions which need to be taken in potential crisis situations;

— *Absence of legal arrangements allowing for EU-wide supervision of specific institutions* (eg, credit rating agencies and post-trading infrastructures);

As a consequence of fragmented responsibilities, incomplete co-ordination, and national mandates/interests, actors in the financial sector can exploit loopholes and arbitrage opportunities in the European financial system, causing risky activities to fall outside scope of supervision. The relations between the general problems and the problems specific to the areas of micro-prudential as well as their drivers can be visualised in this problem tree:

Figure 2. Problem tree: micro prudential supervision

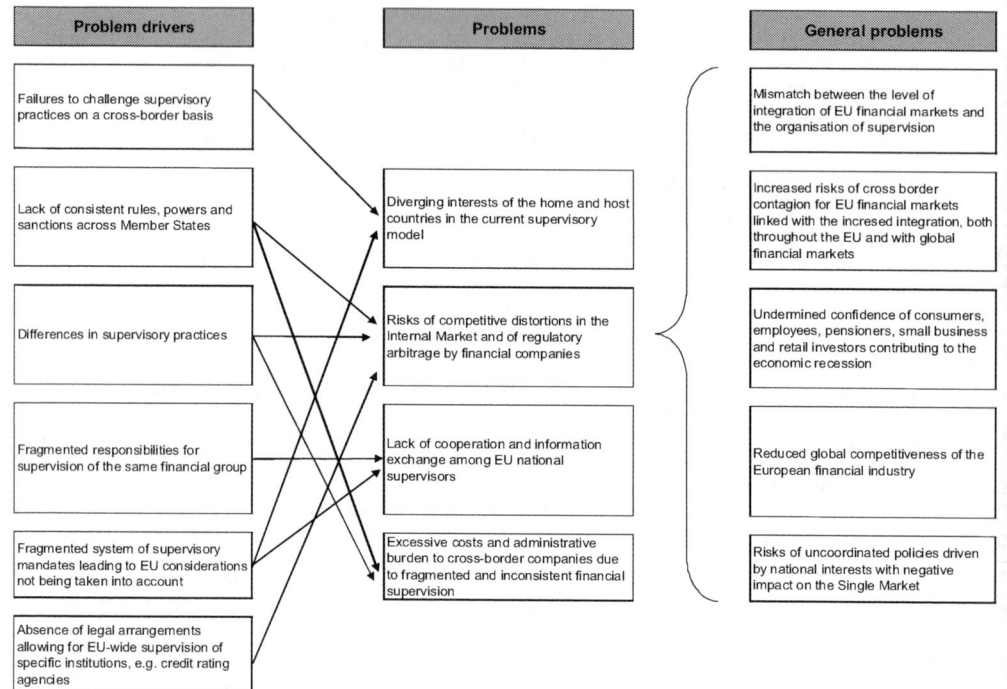

3.5. MACRO-PRUDENTIAL SUPERVISION

Macro-prudential supervision aims to identify risks in the economy (including macro-economic imbalances) and in the financial system which may have implications for the stability of the financial system as a whole, and, where necessary, advise on measures which could be taken to address these risks. In this respect, the de Larosière report concludes that there has been a lack of adequate macro-prudential supervision in Europe. In particular the report notes the following phenomena, which can be identified as problem drivers:

- *the present EU supervisory arrangements place too much emphasis on the supervision of individual firms, and too little on the macro-prudential side.* The soundness of individual firms was often supervised in isolation and there was little or no awareness of the degree of "interdependence" or "interconnectedness" between financial institutions and between markets;
- *early warning systems in the EU were largely ineffective,* insofar as macro-prudential risks were identified (there was no shortage of comments about worrying developments in both macro-economic imbalances and the lowering price of risk for example) but *there was no EU mechanism to ensure that this assessment of risk was translated into action.*

Another problem driver is the *fragmented approach to macro-prudential supervision.* At present, a great number of different authorities are in one way or another involved in macro-prudential analysis as well as the identification of possible policy measures, including the following bodies: The Economic and Financial Committee (EFC), The Joint Committee on Financial Conglomerates, the European System of Central Banks (ESCB) and the European Central Bank (ECB), including its

The Banking Supervision Committee (BSC). The role of the EU Committees of Supervisors ("level 3 Committees", CEBS, CEIOPS, CESR) as regards the safeguarding of financial stability has recently also been enhanced. All of these bodies are described elsewhere in this report[13].

As a result of the problem drivers described above, the specific problems affecting the current EU arrangements for the safeguard of financial stability can be summarised as follows (see figure 2 below):

- **Lack of appropriate analysis of macro-prudential risks at EU level, including risks stemming from macro-economic imbalances;**
- **Lack of interaction between micro- and macro-prudential analysis. The soundness of individual firms' was often supervised in isolation and there was little or no awareness of the degree of "interdependence" or "interconnectedness";**
- **Lack of adequate corrective action, cooperation and co-ordination by competent authorities during the building up and in the course of financial crisis.**

These conclusions are confirmed by the ECB (2009)[14] which argues that the present crisis has revealed that micro-prudential supervision in many cases proved inadequate to identify, in a timely manner, the nature and size of accumulating risks and to impose appropriate remedial action. Moreover, although the build-up of financial imbalances, the underpricing and lack of internalisation of risk and the rise in the degree of leverage in the financial system had been identified as sources of potential instability by international institutions and central banks, it did not trigger appropriate responses either by market participants or by the authorities responsible for the oversight of individual financial institutions or specific market segments.

It is therefore argued that there is a manifest need to strengthen both the macro-prudential and micro-prudential supervision of the financial system and to do so in a way that achieves valuable synergies and has a mutually reinforcing impact on the stability of the financial system as a whole. In particular, the role of macro-financial factors, of the interconnectedness of markets and institutions and of cross-border financial integration in determining the size, nature and propagation of systemic risk calls for the strengthening of macro-prudential supervision in Europe and globally. This should help prevent the recurrence of similar episodes of externalisation of risks, market excesses and corrections in the future, with disruptive effects on the real economy and unsustainable pressures on public budgets and social policy instruments to cope with these effects, and it should help ensure that the financial system is socially responsible, dynamically stable and resilient to shocks.

Against this background, the G20 has decided to reinforce the global arrangements: the newly established Financial Stability Board (FSB)[15] will collaborate with the International Monetary Fund (IMF) to provide early warning of macro-economic and financial risks at the global level. The US is putting in place a financial stability body as well. Further streamlining in the EU is therefore critical as well, as macro-prudential analysis is currently fragmented and executed by different authorities at different levels. Once the crisis spread, this fragmented approach posed real challenges in terms of getting a timely and reliable overview of developments in the economy and in the financial system relevant for the stability of the financial system. The latter is also related to legal and practical obstacles to information sharing between the relevant authorities.

PART V
EU MATERIALS

Figure 3. Problem tree: macro-prudential supervision

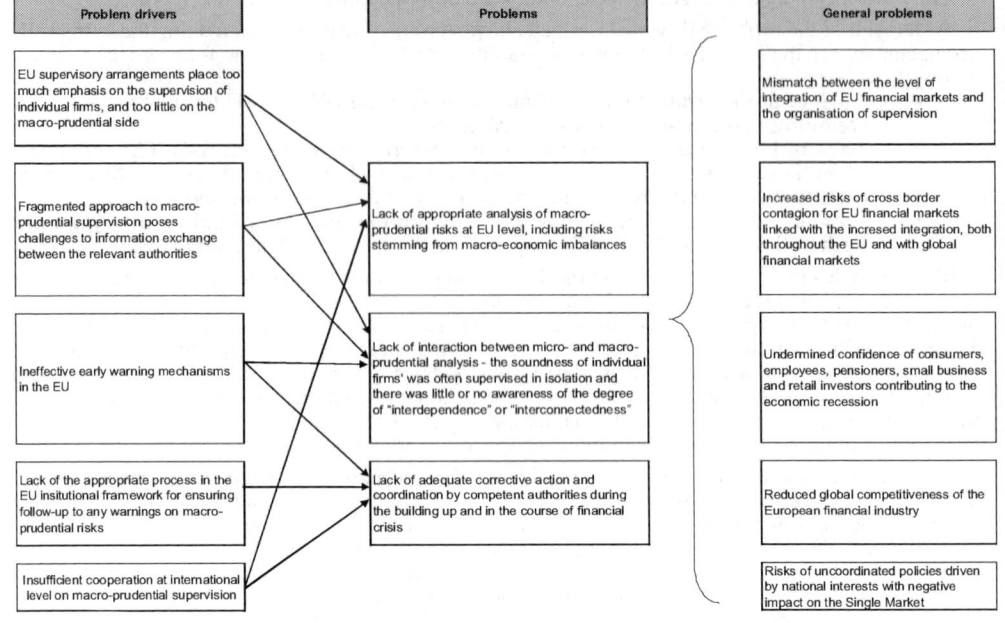

3.6. BASELINE SCENARIO

The baseline scenario would be one in which the EU would continue to build on its existing framework and continue to rely on the existing Committees of Supervisors, which are merely advisory bodies to the Commission, and the recently-established colleges of supervisors. Recent reforms of the three Committees of Supervisors, which are currently being implemented, will reinforce the functioning of these bodies to a certain extent. In particular, the fact that the Committees will be able to take decisions by qualified majority should help accelerate the process of convergence in the implementation of EU Law. Moreover, once all colleges of supervisors are up and running, co-operation and information exchange between national supervisory authorities should be improved. This scenario nevertheless remains sub-optimal, as these co-operation mechanisms do not have the potential of removing the most serious inefficiencies of the present supervisory set-up (see section 3.4).

Within this scenario the EU would also retain its fragmented approach to macro-prudential oversight, without introducing a mechanism ensuring follow-up to warnings and recommendations. While the recent lessons of the crisis would probably lead to an increased awareness of direct and indirect linkages in the financial system, it is questionable whether in the absence of a proper institutional framework the EU would be effective in pooling and analysing all relevant information and be able to trigger corrective action.

The baseline scenario is presented as a "dynamic" status-quo option for both micro- and macro-prudential supervision.

3.7. CASE FOR EU ACTION

Against the background of what is possibly the worst economic and financial crisis since the 1930s, an overhaul of the European regulatory and supervisory system is needed. If Europe is serious about building a stable and integrated financial market, it must put in place a supervisory framework that acknowledges this.

On micro-prudential supervision, the EU has reached the limits of what can be done with the present status of the EU Committees of Supervisors – which are merely advisory bodies to the Commission. The EU cannot remain in a situation where there is no mechanism to ensure that national supervisors arrive at the best possible supervisory decisions for cross-border institutions; where there is insufficient co-operation and information exchange between national supervisory authorities; where all the technical details of financial regulation have to go through slow and cumbersome procedures; where joint action by national authorities needs to take account of the patchwork of regulatory and supervisory requirements; where only national solutions can be implemented in the face of European problems.

The weaknesses of the present macro-prudential arrangements clearly have had dramatic consequences. Like the G20 and the US, the EU should establish a new body responsible for identifying financial stability risks at European level and, where necessary, issue risk warnings. The present EU arrangements place too little on the macro-prudential side of supervision; macro-prudential analysis is fragmented and executed by different authorities at different levels; there is no mechanism in the EU to ensure that macro-prudential risk warnings and/or recommendations are translated into action.

The analysis of the principles of subsidiarity and proportionality is included in the comparative assessment of options (Chapter 6).

[1909]

NOTES

6   De Larosière report §152.
7   See Thygesen, Niels (2003) 'Comments on the political economy of financial harmonisation in Europe', in Jeroen Kremers, Dirk Schoenmaker and Peter Wierts (eds) Financial Supervision in Europe, Cheltenham: Edward Elgar.
8   "A condition whereby the financial system is able to withstand shocks without giving way to cumulative processes, which impair the allocation of savings to investment opportunities and the processing of payments in the economy". See T.P. Schioppa, Central banks and financial stability.
9   Levine, R. (2005), Finance and Growth: Theory and Evidence, in: P. Aghion and S. Derlauf (eds), Handbook of Economic Growth, chapter 12, 865–934, North-Holland: Elesevier.
10   Laeven, L. and F. Valencia, 2008. "Systemic Banking Crises: A New Database", Working Paper No 08/224, International Monetary Fund.
11   The Lamfalussy framework is a four-level legislative procedure. It divides the legislation into high-level framework provisions and implementing measures. Under the Lamfalussy arrangements, the Commission proposes framework legislation and it is adopted under the 'co-decision' procedure by Council and Parliament (Level 1). It is supplemented at Level 2 by more detailed implementation measures, adopted by the Commission and endorsed by a qualified majority of Member States. The detailed Level 2 legislation is prepared by the Commission on the basis of advice provided by representatives of national supervisory authorities, acting through the 'Level 3' committees (CEBS, CEIOPS and CESR). The Level 3 committees also aim to foster supervisory convergence and best practice, principally through the creation of (non legally binding) guidance. Finally, at Level 4, the Commission ensures that Member States are complying with applicable legislation and it pursues enforcement action where required.
12   The Communication of 4 March "Driving European Recovery" announced a programme to review differences between national rules and achieve greater convergence.
13   See section 5.2. This JCFC, not described in that section, includes CEBS and CEIOPS, and focuses exclusively on prudential issues in relation to the Financial Conglomerates Directive and on the identification/assessment of the potential risks of financial conglomerates.
14   Speech by Mr Lucas Papademos, Vice President of the European Central Bank, at the conference on "After The Storm: The Future Face of Europe's Financial System", organised by Bruegel, National Bank of Belgium and the International Monetary Fund, Brussels, 24 March 2009.
15   The successor to the Financial Stability Forum (FSF).

4. OBJECTIVES

The reform of EU financial supervision has general, specific and operational objectives. At each level, they correspond to the identified problems (the general problems, the problem drivers, and the specific problems).

The **general objectives** are the same for the reform of the EU supervisory framework:
1.   **Establish a more effective framework for financial supervision in the EU, adapted to the level of financial market integration;**
2.   **Enhance financial stability in the EU (and thereby contain potential risks to the real economy and to the public finances);**
3.   **Safeguard interests of consumers, investors, other users of financial services and other relevant stakeholders, notably employees;**
4.   **Increase competitiveness of EU financial markets, and**
5.   **Foster integration of EU financial markets supportive of sustainable development.**

These objectives are in line with the initiatives described in the Commission Communication 'Driving European Recovery' of 4 March 2009. The specific objectives set in the areas of micro-prudential supervision and macro-prudential supervision (see below) are aimed at contributing to achieving these general objectives.

4.1. MICRO-PRUDENTIAL SUPERVISION

The **specific objectives** in the area of micro-prudential supervision are to:
1.   **Balance home and host supervisor interests, ie, reinforce processes and practices for challenging the decisions of national supervisors on a cross-border basis;**
2.   **Ensure a level playing field for financial institutions operating in various Member States;**
3.   **Improve crisis prevention and crisis management on the European scale, and**
4.   **Improve effectiveness and cost efficiency of supervision for supervised companies.**

The table below links the problem drivers for micro-prudential supervision with the operational and specific objectives in this area.

Table 3. Problem drivers and objectives: micro-prudential supervision

Problem drivers	Operational objectives	Specific objectives			
		Home-host balance	Level playing field	Crisis prevention and management	Cost efficiency
Failure to challenge supervisory practices on a cross-border basis	Ensure adequate process for challenging decisions of national supervisors to balance home and host interests	v	v		
Lack of consistent rules, powers and sanctions across Member States	Provide for a possibility to adopt binding technical standards at EU level		v	v	v
Differences in supervisory practices	Increase consistency of supervisory practices in the EU	v	v	v	v
Fragmented responsibilities for supervision of the same financial group	Ensure effective functioning of colleges of supervisors	v		v	v
Fragmented system of supervisory mandates leading to EU considerations not being taken into account	Create framework for pooling relevant information on supervised companies at EU level		v	v	
	Strengthen EU dimension in prudential assessment of cross-border mergers and acquisitions	v	v	v	
	Provide for strong coordination at EU level in crisis situations	v	v	v	v
	Ensure effective cooperation with 3rd countries on supervisory issues	v	v	v	

Problem drivers	Operational objectives	Specific objectives			
		Home-host balance	Level playing field	Crisis prevention and management	Cost efficiency
Absence of legal arrangements allowing for EU-wide supervision of specific institutions, e g credit rating agencies	Grant to an EU-level authority responsibility for licensing and supervision of specific EU-wide institutions	v	v	v	v

4.2. MACRO-PRUDENTIAL SUPERVISION

The **specific objectives** in the area of macro-prudential supervision are to:

1.   **Develop European macro-prudential risk assessment;**
2.   **Enhance effectiveness of Early Warning mechanisms, and**
3.   **Allow for risk assessments to be translated into action by the relevant authorities.**

The table below links the problem drivers for macro-prudential supervision with the operational and specific objectives in this area.

Table 4. Problem drivers and objectives: macro-prudential supervision

Problem drivers	Operational objectives	Specific objectives		
		Developing a European risk assessment framework	Enhance effectiveness of Early warning mechanisms	Ensuring follow-up
Current EU supervisory arrangements are quasi-exclusively focused on micro-prudential supervision	Identify macro-prudential risks in Europe and analyse the interconnection with individual financial institutions' soundness	v	v	
Legal and practical obstacles to information sharing between supervisors, central banks and finance ministers	Establish adequate procedures to pool information about macro-economic risks for financial stability	v	v	
Absence of adequate, EU-wide early warning mechanisms	Issue warnings to the relevant actors and recommend the appropriate actions	v	v	v

Problem drivers	Operational objectives	Specific objectives		
		Developing a European risk assessment framework	Enhance effectiveness of Early warning mechanisms	Ensuring follow-up
Lack of the appropriate process in the EU institutional framework for ensuring follow-up to any warnings on macro-prudential risks	Ensure follow-up to warnings and recommendations	v	v	v
Insufficient cooperation at international on macro-prudential supervision	Ensuring effective interfacing with international organization dealing with financial stability	v	v	v

5. IDENTIFICATION OF POLICY OPTIONS

To address the identified problems – and fulfil the objectives – two separate sets of options have to be considered: one for micro-prudential supervision and one for macro-prudential supervision. These options have been identified by the Commission services on the basis of general ongoing debate on financial supervision among various stakeholders in the EU.

5.1. MICRO-PRUDENTIAL SUPERVISION

The options for organising micro-prudential supervision in the EU may be considered in two stages:

- Stage 1 considers the various options with regard to the solutions for organising micro-prudential supervision at the Community level;
- Stage 2 analyses the various institutional structures possible for bodies tasked with financial supervision activities at the EU level.

Stage 1: Supervisory system

1. Dynamic status quo: home country model and the Lamfalussy framework

This option implies a situation in which the room to improve the European supervisory framework is limited by the constraints presented in the description of problems in the current framework for micro-prudential supervision (section 3.4).

2. Step back: host country model

Under this option the model of host country supervision adopted in the 1970s would be restored. The First Banking Directive (1977) granted full responsibility for supervision of banks operating in a given country to national supervisors. It also stipulated that national supervisors should co-operate and that foreign identity could not be a ground for refusing a banking licence. It allowed for cross-border branching under the host-country rule, which meant that a bank had to obtain permission to operate in a foreign country by the supervisory agencies of that country. The foreign branches were required to compete on equivalent standards with the host country's own banks. The range of activities deployed by the branch was also limited by the host country's legislation. The advantage of this model would be that the relevant authorities would have full control over the activities in their territory and to an extent, fiscal and supervisory responsibilities would be clearer (although it should be noted that there is an increasing mismatch between the legal and operational structures of firms). However, it would be inefficient as every branch would have to pledge (additional) capital and it would not solve the problem of inadequate co-operation among supervisors in the context of cross-border banks. Furthermore, over time divergence of supervisory approaches might lead to increased risks to financial stability.

3. Lead supervisor model

The lead supervisor model, involving extended powers for the supervisor of the parent company of a number of cross-border subsidiaries (already the case for branches), would be one option for evolution of the existing supervisory framework. There are different versions of this model foreseeable: the lead supervisor could be responsible for supervision merely on a consolidated level, or also on the solo and sub-consolidated level. In its most radical form, it would grant full powers for supervision of cross-border financial groups to the home state supervisor. Under this model, the lead supervisor would be the single point of contact for the financial institution and would be the sole authority for all matters of prudential supervision at the level of the group and its constituents, including model validations and authorisations, capital allocation etc. However, strengthening the role of the lead supervisor seems to be unrealistic as Member States remain reluctant to transfer powers to other Member States (as shown in Council discussions on the proposed changes to the Capital Requirements Directive for banks and Solvency II for insurance). Furthermore, over time divergence of supervisory approaches might lead to increased risks to financial stability – particularly as different approaches may be applied within the same jurisdiction.

4. de Larosière proposal: European System of Financial Supervisors (ESFS)

The de Larosière report recommended that the EU should establish an integrated European System of Financial Supervisors (ESFS) by transforming the existing EU Committees of Supervisors into three European Supervisory Authorities: a European Banking Authority (EBA), a European Insurance and Occupational Pension Authority (EIOPA) and a European Securities Authority (ESA). The three new European Supervisory Authorities (whose role is essentially coordination rather than supervision) would work in a close network with the national financial supervisors, who would continue to be responsible for executing day-to-day supervision. They could also have the legal possibility to delegate supervisory tasks upwards to the EU-level authorities if they choose to do so, and not only between each other.

At the EU-level, the new European Supervisory Authorities, at the centre of the new network, would fulfil all the missions of the current Committees of Supervisors, but with more power and authority. They would, in addition, make a greater contribution than at present to the emergence of a true harmonised rulebook (for example by issuing guidelines and recommendations, and adopting technical standards and rules) and improve the supervision of cross-border institutions by developing common supervisory approaches settling possible disputes between home and host supervisors, and acting as direct supervisors for certain pan-European institutions (such as credit rating agencies or Central Counterparty Clearing infrastructures). They would thus act as guarantors of a consistent application of EU law. They could also exercise a role in crisis management, and could represent the EU in international supervisory fora (participating in global colleges of supervisors, liaising with multilateral bodies on micro-prudential supervision etc). Flexibility and a network arrangement would be at the heart of the arrangement, and the EU and national authorities would constitute a network within which tasks could be shared.

As a follow up, the supervisory set-up chosen should be evaluated after three years the and consideration of whether any further changes are necessary made.

5. A single EU-level supervisor

As for the option of establishing a single EU supervisor the following questions need to be addressed:
- a single supervisor for all financial institutions or only the pan-European groups?, and
- should pan-European groups be supervised directly by the central EU agency or would it built on the existing network of national supervisors (ie, a hub and spokes model)?

As for the first, there are many small and medium-sized financial institutions which operate mainly within national borders. For these institutions there is no need for any direct supervisory powers at the EU level (ie, the existing national supervisors are best placed to supervise domestically oriented institutions). So the single EU supervisor should focus its attention on pan-European institutions.

As for the second, there are two options for the architecture of the European supervisor:
- (i) a single EU supervisor which would replace national supervisors for supervision of cross-border entities and would leave no role for national supervisors in monitoring cross-border groups, and
- (ii) a single EU supervisor which would build on the existing network of national supervisors, so as to preserve experience, expertise and continuity (ie, a "hub and spokes" model). In this particular case, the Authorities could for example ask national authorities to perform on-site inspections on its behalf (as they are closer to the firm and more familiar with local market conditions).

The further discussion is valid for both options, focussing on powers and responsibilities of a single EU supervisor. These would be the same (centralised at the EU level), irrespective of the chosen organisation: a single central entity or a "hub and spokes" model.

Under this scenario all supervisory competences for institutions with cross-border activities would be consolidated at the Community level. The single EU supervisor would bear the full responsibility for day-to-day supervision of the biggest cross-border institutions in the EU (and not rely on the existing network of national supervisors). It would also be responsible for creating a regulatory and supervisory level playing field between pan-European banks and domestically oriented banks, as both are competing in the same markets.

Stage 2: Institutional structure

Once the preferred option at stage one has been identified, one can consider the best option in terms of institutional structure. The options listed below may in principle apply to any of the options proposed at stage one. However, we assume that for Options 1, 2 and 3 presented above the Committees of Supervisors at level 3 of the current Lamfalussy framework would be maintained, to continue their current role, even though merging the existing committees or adding a new independent committee for financial conglomerates could be potentially considered. The consideration of the institutional structure is clearly of direct relevance for Options 4 and 5, which imply the creation of new institutions at the EU level.[16]

A. One body, ie, the integrated approach

One body could cover the whole financial sector (banking, insurance and securities markets) and all aspects of financial supervision (prudential oversight as well as conduct-of-business supervision).[17]

B. Two bodies, the approach by objective

This approach (often referred to as "twin peaks") would be based on the principle of supervision by objective not by sector. It refers to a separation of supervisory functions between two supervisors: one that performs prudential supervision and the other focuses on conduct-of-business supervision.[18] A Steering Committee could co-ordinate between the two bodies.

C. Three bodies, ie, the sectoral approach

Under this approach each supervisory body covers a particular sector, ie, a banking supervisor, an insurance and pensions supervisor, and a securities supervisor[19]. This is for example the case of the current framework with the three EU Committees of Supervisors (CESR, CEBS and CEIOPS), in line with the sectorally-based EU financial legislation[20]. The three-body model could in particular benefit from an overarching steering committee to co-ordinate the supervisory activities across sectors, incorporating the Joint Committee on Financial Conglomerates (JCFC), in which CEBS and CEIOPS meet to discuss issues related to the supervision of financial conglomerates.

D. Four bodies, ie, the institutional approach

In addition to the three bodies responsible for supervision of banking, insurance and securities sectors, a distinct fourth body, replacing the JCFC, could be created for supervision of financial conglomerates (groups including banking and insurance activities), following the Financial Conglomerates Directive, supplementary to CRD and Solvency II.

5.2. MACRO-PRUDENTIAL SUPERVISION

A. Status quo

This scenario implies no or hardly any change of the existing EU arrangements, ie, the EU would retain its fragmented approach to macro-prudential oversight, without introducing a mechanism ensuring follow-up to warnings and recommendations (see section 3.6).

B. Build on existing or proposed structures

This option would involve one of the following existing or proposed bodies being tasked with the same macro-prudential responsibilities proposed in the de Larosière report for the suggested ESRC.

● The Economic and Financial Committee (EFC)

This body of the ECOFIN Council includes representatives of ministries of finance, the European Commission, the ECB, and central banks. It provides high-level assessments of developments in financial markets and services and advises ECOFIN and the European Commission. Twice a year the EFC meets as the "Financial Stability Table" in a configuration including the Chairs of the Banking Supervision Committee (BSC – see below) and the EU Committees of Supervisors. Discussions are based on input from various sources, eg, ECB, the Financial Services Committee (FSC), CEBS, CEIOPS, CESR, BSC, and the Commission. The FST brings together the broadest group of actors in matters of financial stability (prudential, monetary and fiscal authorities) and is a forum that can provide policy co-ordination.

- **The European System of Central Banks (ESCB)/European Central Bank (ECB)**

The ESCB contributes to the smooth conduct of policies pursued by the competent authorities relating to the prudential supervision of credit institutions and the stability of the financial system. The ECB and the ESCB have three tasks in the field of financial stability:

— Financial stability monitoring: the ECB, together with the ESCB, systematically monitors cyclical and structural developments in the euro-area/EU banking sector and in other financial sectors. The purpose is to assess the possible vulnerabilities in the EU financial sector, and its resilience to potential shocks. The assessment is undertaken in collaboration with the EU national central banks and supervisory agencies. They are all represented in the ESCB Banking Supervision Committee (BSC)[21],

— Provision of advice: the ECB is frequently asked by the competent authorities at EU level and national level to contribute its technical expertise to the design and definition of financial rules and supervisory requirements. The ECB can also make a contribution on its own initiative, and

— Promotion of co-operation: the ECB, together with the ESCB, promotes co-operation between central banks and supervisory authorities in the EU. This is primarily done through the BSC (see above).

Under this option, the ECB would be entrusted with the task of carrying out macro-prudential supervision in the EU. In so far as compatible with the Treaty and the Statute of the ECB, the new tasks and related powers could be implemented by the ECB or with the support of an "enlarged and empowered" Banking Supervision Committee (including for instance the Chairs of the Committees of Supervisors).

- **The ESFS**

Under this option, the new European authority or authorities as recommended by the de Larosière report to strengthen EU micro-prudential supervision could be entrusted with the task of macro-prudential supervision. They would be supported by the network of national supervisors.

The institutional structure of the EFSF – among the 4 options possible (see "stage 2" above) – would impact on the (hypothetical) practical feasibility of this option. Indeed, while a single body could also be tasked with the responsibility for monitoring macro-economic risks, it would be challenging to attribute this responsibility to the ESFS comprising several authorities. In that case one could imagine giving the functions related to macro-prudential supervision to the overarching ESFS Steering Committee including the chairs of the different authorities (see description of ESFS above, "stage 1", point 4).

C. Establish a new body (European Systemic Risk Council, ESRC)[22]

This option foresees, in line with the recommendations of the de Larosière Group, the establishment of a new body, the European Systemic Risk Council (ESRC). For such a new body to be effective, it would need to: (a) identify macro-prudential risks (risks to financial stability) sufficiently in advance; (b) competently identify appropriate measures to reduce these risks; and (c) trigger corrective action to address the identified risks. The effective functioning of the ESRC would be determined by a range of factors, including its status, composition, operational and technical support, status, mandate, and operating procedures. Moreover, choices made in respect of these various factors would be crucial in ensuring that the ESRC would enjoy the necessary legitimacy to assure corrective action in response to its warnings.

Under the proposal of the de Larosière report, the ESRC would be an independent body placed outside the ECB, but chaired by the President of the ECB. Operational and technical support would primarily be provided by the ECB/ESCB. The Council would therefore not be built from scratch, so as to preserve experience, expertise and continuity.

In order to perform this role, the ESRC would carry out all the tasks of an EU macro-prudential supervisor, that is:

— collect and analyse all information relevant for financial stability, pertaining to macro-economic conditions and macro-prudential developments in all the financial sectors;

— identify and prioritise risks to the stability of the EU financial system;

— issue macro-prudential risk warnings;

— give recommendations on the appropriate measures to be taken in reaction to the risks identified;

— ensure follow-up to warnings and recommendations, and

— be the interface with the IMF, the FSB and third country counterparts.

The composition of the ESRC is reflected in the box below. To ensure that the ESRC can work efficiently, the membership of supervisors in the ESRC would be limited to the three chairmen of the European Supervisory Authorities. However, each central bank governor should be accompanied by one senior representative of the national supervisory authorities as observer (ie, a 1+1 formula). In those Member States where there are several supervisory authorities, the representative accompanying the central bank governor could vary from meeting to meeting, depending on the issues to be discussed by the ESRC.

All ESRC members and observers would have the right to attend and to speak at these meetings. In order to streamline the decision-making process, however, only ESRC members would have the right to vote, i e only central bank governors, the chairmen of the European Supervisory Authorities and the Commission member would be voting members.

Box 1. Composition of the European Systemic Risk Council (ESRC)

Members:
— Chairperson: President of the ECB (or alternatively a Governor elected by ESRC members);
— Vice-Chairperson (elected by ESRC members);
— Governors of the 27 national central banks;
— President of the ECB (if the latter is the chairperson of the ESRC, the ECB would be represented by its Vice-President);
— Chairpersons of the three European Supervisory Authorities;
— Member of the European Commission.

Observers:
— A representative of the national supervisory authorities, accompanying the central bank Governor in a 1+1 formula;
— Chairperson of the Economic and Financial Committee;
— A representative of each national central bank of the EFTA-EEA countries.

[1910]

NOTES

[16] For a detailed discussion of different supervisory structures, see the G30 report "the structure of financial supervision: approaches and challenges in a global marketplace", G30 6/10/2008.

[17] Member States with a single supervisory model separate from central banks: BE, DK, EE, FI, IE (with a separate supervisor for pensions), HU, LA, MT, PL, UK, SE. Member States with a single supervisory model with a link to (or integrated within) central banks: AT, CZ, DE, SK.

[18] In the EU this model is adopted only by NL.

[19] Member States with a sectoral model: BG, CY, ES, FR, GR, IT, LT, LU, PT, RO, SI.

[20] For example, the Markets in Financial Instruments Directive for securities sector; the Capital Requirements Directive for banking sector and the Solvency II Directive (not yet adopted) for the insurance sector.

[21] The Banking Supervision Committee (BSC), which was set up in 1999, is a committee of ESCB. Its members include representatives of the ECB, the national central banks and the banking supervisory authorities. The Committee supports banking supervision and helps forge financial stability, for example, by providing advice to the banking supervisory authorities. It focuses on macroeconomic issues, such as developments in the banking and financial system. Its activities also focus on providing advice to the European Central Bank on issues relating to national and EU law where these issues affect banking supervision and the stability of the financial system. It also promotes co-operation and exchange of information between central banks and supervisory authorities on issues of common interest, including the prevention and effective handling of financial crises.

[22] Further discussions between DG ECFIN and DG MARKT are needed on the functioning of the ESRC.

6. PRELIMINARY ANALYSIS OF IMPACTS AND COMPARISON OF OPTIONS

This section examines the effectiveness of the identified options in achieving the set objectives. We are looking in particular at the Specific Objectives which have been set separately for the areas of micro- and macro-prudential supervision. The options will also be compared with regard to the criteria of effectiveness, efficiency and coherence, according to the following definitions:

- **Effectiveness:** The extent to which options achieve the objectives of the proposal with sufficient legal certainty;
- **Efficiency:** The extent to which objectives can be achieved for a given level of resources/at least cost (cost-effectiveness);
- **Coherence:** The extent to which options are coherent with the overarching objectives of EU policy, and the extent to which they are likely to limit trade-offs across the economic, social, and environmental domain.[23]

6.1. MICRO-PRUDENTIAL SUPERVISION

There are four Specific Objectives defined for the reform of the EU framework for micro-prudential supervision, as presented in chapter 4:

1. **Balance the home and host supervisor interests: reinforce processes and practices for challenging supervisory practices on a cross-border basis;**
2. **Ensure a level playing field for financial institutions operating in various Member States;**

3.   **Improve crisis prevention and management on the European scale;**
4.   **Improve cost efficiency of supervision for supervised companies.**

Stage 1 – Options for Supervision

At stage 1 of the assessment, we shall analyse how effective the proposed options can be in achieving the above objectives.

1. Dynamic status quo: home country model and the Lamfalussy framework

The current supervisory framework in the EU, based on the proposals of the Lamfalussy committee, was a step forward in the evolutionary process of enhancing co-ordination of financial supervision in the Internal Market. It introduced the notion of close co-operation of national supervisors to harmonise rules and practices and build mutual trust, as well as an institutional framework to achieve that. Recently, the system has been strengthened by improvement of decision making procedures, formalising supervisory cooperation on financial conglomerates and additional funding from the EU budget. Colleges of supervisors have been being set up for all major cross-border groups. However, during seven years of supervisory co-operation in the securities area and four years in the banking and insurance sectors the progress has turned out to be much slower and more limited than expected.

In terms of achieving a **balance between home and host** supervisor interest in the supervision of cross-border financial groups, the current system is clearly lacking a mechanism for solving conflicts between participating supervisors. As national authorities are merely accountable to their national Parliaments/national taxpayers, host authorities can only hope that home authorities will take their situation into account in the event of a crisis. The imbalance between home and host countries may be further deepened by differences in size between countries.

The Lamfalussy framework has proved suboptimal in ensuring consistent implementation and enforcement of EU rules. Diverging national interpretations of supervisory rules remain the common problem. In some cases, even slight differences in the approach may favour national companies or act to the detriment of foreign competitors. Without legal powers to set binding supervisory standards and decisions on individual firms, CESR, CEBS and CEIOPS have not been able to move forward much in this area. The existing situation cannot achieve a **level playing field**. The lack of progress in harmonisation of supervision also causes higher **compliance costs** for companies.

The existing mechanisms have proved to be ineffective in ensuring a co-ordinated reaction during the recent financial **crisis**. Prudential supervision, as well as the capacity to manage the stability of the financial system, is highly dependent on the quality of co-operation and information exchange between supervisors. Problems of communication, or a lack of trust between supervisors, can severely endanger the effective control of the institutions or financial systems concerned.

In summary, it is likely that the EU has reached the limits of what can be done with the present status of the Committees of European Supervisors as advisory bodies to the Commission. If serious progress is to be made on building a stable and integrated financial market, the costs of this option clearly outweigh the benefits.

2. Step back: host country model

By granting full powers to the host country supervisor, this model would not fulfil the objective of ensuring the appropriate **balance between home and host** supervisors. Concerning **crisis management**, full control by national supervisors over companies operating in their domestic market would likely be beneficial from the perspective of consumer protection and financial stability. On the other hand, taking into account the prevention aspect, the main deficiency of this model is the lack of any kind of oversight of big cross-border financial groups. Moreover, the scope for control of cross-border groups by host countries would be limited in practice, as key decisions are often taken by the parent company in the home country and the financial health of the subsidiary is closely linked to that of the financial group as a whole. The effective control of large financial groups would therefore be primarily in the hands of the supervisor in the home country, but it would not take account of subsidiaries and branches in other countries. Furthermore, from the Internal Market point of view, the host country model would not fulfil the objective of creating a **level playing field**. It would also be ineffective in terms of **reducing costs**, as companies wishing to operate cross-border would have to comply with various national sets of supervisory requirements and practices, incurring significant compliance costs. In other words, host country control could not work without significant financial disintermediation and removal of many of the benefits of the internal market in terms of income and welfare. For example, a complete legal and operational alignment of branches and subsidiaries with the domestic legislation of the host country would lead to a complete unbundling of cross-border groups, which would damage efficiency.

3. Lead supervisor model

This model entails significant reallocation of responsibilities to home country supervisors from host country supervisors (in the case of branches) and from home country supervisors of subsidiaries to home country supervisors of the parent company. In a college of supervisors, the lead (home) supervisor would make use of the expertise and knowledge of local supervisors and delegate to them tasks and, where possible, responsibilities. But in the end decisions would be made by the home authority. This raises serious questions with respect to ensuring an appropriate balance between **home and host** interests, as reflected by the reluctance of a vast number of Member States to move towards stronger group-wide supervision[24].

While home country supervisors would be fully responsible for oversight of cross-border financial groups, national (host) supervisors would remain responsible for financial stability in their own jurisdiction. As for **crisis management**, this option would result in a misalignment between the accountability of host authorities to their taxpayers and their (decreasing) competencies in terms of prudential requirements. In this respect, this option could have a particularly negative impact on the new Member States, where on average 65% of banking assets are in foreign-owned banks, while in countries like Estonia, the Czech Republic and Slovakia over 92% of banking assets are foreign-owned.

Also in terms of ensuring a **level playing field**, the lead supervisor model would not accomplish the objective of the reform. Under this model, each financial group operating on a cross-border basis would indeed have to comply with only one set of supervisory standards and practices, as required by the lead supervisor. However, supervisors in different countries could still have differing requirements. This would create an increasing risk of situations where in a given country companies operate according to various supervisory regimes: that of the local supervisor – for domestic firms, and those of various lead supervisors – for subsidiaries of financial groups based in other countries. Moreover, this model would create the risk of supervisory arbitrage in which lead supervisors could compete by easing the rules to favour their domestic undertakings. Another possibility would be that cross-border groups will choose to establish themselves in the Member State with the lightest prudential regime.

Concerning **cost reduction for financial institutions**, the lead supervisor concept would allow for minimising supervisory costs at a company level as there would be a 'one stop shop'. However, supervisory competition between lead supervisors could entail significant costs for companies and society in case of a failure linked with too lenient supervision.

4. de Larosière proposal: European System of Financial Supervisors (ESFS)

The proposal for a European System of Financial Supervisors (ESFS) addresses the specific problems identified in the area of supervision in the EU. It ensures the necessary co-ordination at the Community level while preserving Member States' primary competence in the area of supervision. The decision-making powers of the Authorities are primarily related to ensuring a correct and coherent application of EU law.

To ensure the **balance between the different** supervisory interests, the Authorities would be granted certain powers. Specifically in case of conflicts between home and host authorities on the application of EU rules, the European Supervisory Authorities/y could be called in by the respective national authorities to settle disputes. With regard to institutions for which global colleges of supervisors exist (in line with recent G20 conclusions), such interventions of the new Authorities could have the role of good examples.

In order to ensure a **level playing field** for all financial companies in the EU, the European Supervisory Authorities would be called on to develop technical standards and interpretative guidelines which would be applied by national supervisory authorities. This would bring about more harmonisation in the rules to be applied by supervisors as well as greater consistency in the execution of day-to-day supervisory tasks.

They could also have **direct decision-making** powers with regard to certain specific situations pertaining to their exercise of ensuring consistent application of EU law and with regard to certain pan-European financial institutions which are regulated at a European level (Credit Rating Agencies, Central Clearing Counterparties, etc).

The powers of the new Authorities would also allow them to be more effective in **crisis prevention and management**. They would: have a strong co-ordinating role in crisis situations; facilitate co-operation and exchange of information between the competent authorities; act as mediator when that is needed; verify the reliability of the information that should be available to all parties; and help the relevant authorities to define and implement the right decisions. In specific crisis situations, the Authorities would adopt emergency decisions based on specific parameters set by legislation. For example, they could have played this role in the Fortis case quoted in chapter 3.

The ESFS would improve **cost efficiency** of supervision for supervised companies, as they would benefit from (more) harmonised prudential and reporting rules.

5. Full supervisory centralisation: a single EU Supervisor

As explained above in 5.1, the working hypothesis for this option assumes that a single EU supervisor (organised either as a single central unit or as a 'hub and spokes' model with the central unit and national branches, which could be based on the existing national supervisory authorities) would replace national supervisors for supervision of cross-border entities. This would practically eliminate the issue of **balance between the home and host** supervisory authorities, as all cross-border institutions would be supervised by one central authority. Thus, it would completely fulfil one of the objectives of the reform. In the same way, supervision at the EU level would guarantee a **level playing field** across the Internal Market, with a fully uniform set of rules, standards and practices for cross-border groups applied in each Member State. The creation of a two-tier system, with an EU supervisor for cross-border institutions and national supervision for institutions with domestic activities only, could however risk creating an un-level playing field in supervision between pan-European banks and banks operating within one Member State only, while both would be competing on the same market for customers. To address this, the EU Supervisor could exercise co-ordination powers to ensure harmonised supervisory approaches in each national market.

The full harmonisation of supervisory standards and practices would also clearly lead to the reduction of **compliance costs** of cross-border financial groups.

Centralised supervision at the EU level would also be effective in co-ordination of **crisis prevention and management mechanisms**. However, this would need to be coordinated with burden-sharing arrangements given that certain decisions could have fiscal consequences.

Conclusion

In light of the above analysis, options 1 (Status quo), 2 (a step back) and 3 (Lead supervisor) are rejected (as they fail to meet the specific objectives). This means that option 4 (ESFS, leaving responsibility for day-to-day supervision with national supervisors as described above) and option 5 (EU Supervisor, with EU-responsibility for cross border groups) are retained for further comparative assessment.

Table 5. Effectiveness in achieving the Specific Objectives (Level 1)

(0 baseline; + positive; – negative; / difficult to establish)

Options	Specific Objectives			
Level 1: Supervisory system	Home-host balance	Level playing field	Crisis prevention and management	Cost effectiveness
1. Status quo: Lamfalussy framework	0	0	0	0
2. Stage back: host country model	–	–	–	–
3. Lead supervisor model	–	–	–	++
4. De Larosière proposal: ESFS	++	++	++	++
5. Full centralisation: single EU supervisor	++	++	++	++

Comparison of the selected options (4 & 5)

Effectiveness

Any future structure should obviously have as its prime objective to ensure the greatest possible *effectiveness* of supervision and, thereby, guarantee adequate protection for depositors, policy-holders and investors, as well as financial stability in the EU.

There is a strong case for decentralisation. First, there are many small and medium-sized financial institutions which operate exclusively within national borders. There is no need for direct supervisory involvement at the European level for these institutions. Second, prudential supervision should be executed at the local level where the financial institutions are based. The use of field inspections is an important tool of prudential supervision. By being close to the actual activities of the firm, supervisors would get a feeling for what is going on in an institution and would also be more familiar with the local market conditions in which an institution is operating. The proposed ESFS recognises this by building on the existing decentralised structure and preserving experience, expertise and continuity. The focal point would remain at the national level, as the national supervisors would conduct day-to-day supervision. One drawback of a single EU supervisor would be that the distance between this body and the supervised institutions may be too large – both physically and in terms of familiarity with local circumstances. So the single EU supervisor could not fully replace national supervisors, which would still need to deliver a local element of supervision. This could be partly alleviated by having branches within the Member States, but this would increase cost. Furthermore, an EU body would not have the legal power to apply rules made at national level within the Member States.

While the single EU supervisor option would practically eliminate the home-host issue, the ESFS option would also grant the necessary powers to the EU Authorities to enforce solutions balancing the interests of home and host authorities and avoid decision-making deadlocks. Both the ESFS and the single EU Supervisor would possess the competences to issue technical standards and interpretations, thus fostering a level playing field in the Internal Market.

Concerning crisis prevention and management, in both options the authorities would have access to the relevant information at the EU, individual country, and individual company level. While the preferred route to solving a failure of a financial institution is a private sector solution, recent events have shown that in extreme situations governments may be forced to step in so as to secure the stability of the financial system. As such, EU-level supervision could raise complicated issues with respect to the fiscal costs of a possible bail-out (as highlighted before, over the past months, EU governments have already pledged around EUR 3 trillion in recapitalisation obligations and different guarantee schemes). However, the proposed ESFS addresses this by ensuring that the focal point remains at the national level (see the foregoing description in section 6.1). In the absence of an EU-level mechanism for financing cross-border crisis resolution efforts, transferring additional supervisory responsibilities to the EU level, would need to be accompanied by more detailed criteria for burden sharing.

In terms of legal feasibility, the competences proposed for the ESFS raise a number of challenges and specific solutions would have to be sought within the current EU legal framework.

In conclusion, both the ESFS and the EU Supervisor options would fulfil well the specific objectives of the reform. However, in contrast to the single EU supervisor, the proposed ESFS clearly recognises the need for decentralisation and would create a network of EU financial supervisors, based on the principles of partnership and flexibility within a network arrangement. This is also in line with the existing responsibilities in the field of crisis prevention and management. However, in line with the recommendations of the de Larosière Group, the functioning of the ESFS should be reviewed after some time, among other things to examine the case for wider supervisory duties at the EU level (eg, examine the case for transferring supervisory responsibilities for cross-border institutions to the proposed Authorities).

Efficiency

The criterion of efficiency helps assess the extent to which objectives can be achieved for a given level of resources/at least cost. We shall take into account the impact on the supervised financial companies, both operating cross-border and local (firms); supervisors, regulators and other public authorities (supervisors); and other stakeholders including consumers, employees, pensioners etc (taxpayers).

In terms of cost effectiveness for **supervised companies**, both models would lead to potential reduction of compliance cost for cross-border groups thanks to a harmonised set of supervisory rules. Both options would also entail no significant change of the compliance costs of domestic companies (ie, small and medium-sized financial institutions which operate within national borders).

Looking at the impact on **supervisors**, both options would enhance cost-efficiency. The ESFS would foster greater efficiency through the promotion of consistency and arbitration between national authorities, and by taking over responsibility for a number of decisions pertaining to EU-wide groups or firms. A single EU supervisory authority for cross-border groups could be a way of making some economies of scale in comparison to the present situation (although this would be limited by the fact that national authorities would remain in place to oversee firms active in one Member State only). However, the detailed cost and staffing of the European Supervisory Agencies would depend on the specific tasks delegated to these bodies. It is evident that enhanced resources are needed, both in personnel and budget, but at this stage it is not possible to specify the exact numbers. This requires a detailed management plan linked to the specific functions of these Authorities.

In terms of impact on **taxpayers**, both proposals should strengthen the resilience of the EU financial system, thereby lowering the risk of financial crises that could imply high fiscal costs. Both bodies would require their own budget, which could be financed by industry and/or contributions from the public sector (including the EU budget). While the EU Supervisory Authorities within the ESFS would primarily rely on the execution of supervisory tasks at the national level, their resources would be relatively limited in comparison with the resources needed for the single EU supervisor (as the latter would replace national supervisors for the supervision of cross-border groups). From the perspective of the Community budget, the ESFS should at this stage be a better option as it would allow for achievement of the same objectives as the single EU supervisor, but at lower cost. Yet, looking from the perspective of EU taxpayers in the long-term, it is not possible to establish the differences in terms of general efficiency of the two models at this stage.

Coherence

Under the criterion of coherence we shall examine the extent to which options match the overarching objectives of EU policy, and the extent to which they are likely to limit trade-offs across the economic, social, and environmental domain.

Both options are consistent with the overall objectives of the EU to contribute to sustainable economic growth and job creation, to foster the Single Market and to promote EU industry globally. Numerous studies have shown the positive impact of well-functioning financial markets and intermediaries on the real economy[25.] The financial sector in the EU is also an important employer, not only in a few financial centres in Europe but practically in all Member States. A number of other studies, including Commission analyses[26], have pointed to the interplay between the level of financial integration and the increased risk of cross-border contagion. So, effective cross-border arrangements for supervision are an essential element in fostering stable and integrated financial markets. By fostering a sound and prosperous financial sector, both options would also contribute to increasing international competitiveness of EU industry.

Subsidiarity and proportionality

Another important aspect of comparative assessment is testing the options with regard to the EU principles of **proportionality** and **subsidiarity**. The former requires that Community action does not go beyond what is necessary to achieve the objectives satisfactorily. The latter requires that any action at EU level is justified by the added value as compared to action at the Member State level.

The ESFS would be largely based on experience with the current supervisory framework. The proposed system consists of one or more new European Supervisory Authorities working in tandem with the national financial supervisors. Key elements of the ESFS would be: decentralised day-to-day supervision by national supervisors, centralisation of specific tasks to foster harmonised rules and coherent enforcement, and enhanced co-operation and information exchange at all levels. The ESFS option therefore meets both the criteria of proportionality, by presenting targeted solutions to the identified problems, and of subsidiarity, by transferring at the Community level only the minimum of necessary competences.

The above cannot be said of a single EU supervisor, which – apart from the competences necessary to address the problems identified – would transfer to the Community level all responsibility for financial supervision of cross-border groups in the EU. Full centralisation of supervisory responsibilities for cross-border groups can only be considered when there are strong arguments in favour of such a proposal. At this stage, the complexities entailed by such a proposal are such that creating a single EU supervisor would be disproportionate to the current problems and therefore out of keeping with the subsidiarity principle.

Conclusion

In light of the assessment criteria, the ESFS is the preferred option for reform of the EU financial supervisory system. Especially with respect to effectiveness, it is questionable whether a single EU supervisor would be sufficiently close to the activities of a financial group to guarantee adequate protection for depositors, policy-holders and investors as well as financial stability in the EU. Within the ESFS, the focal point would remain at the national level, as the national supervisors would conduct day-to-day supervision. It builds on the existing decentralised structure and therefore preserves experience, expertise and continuity. It is also an evolutionary model, allowing if needed for the transfer of additional supervisory responsibilities to the EU-level over time. As for the efficiency condition, the ESFS should at this stage be a better option as it would allow for achievement of the same objectives as the single EU supervisor, but at lower cost. Another key point is that at present there is no EU-level financing mechanism for use when intervention is needed to assist an institution in difficulty. Therefore, it will be important to also make progress on burden sharing and crisis management and resolution arrangements in the cross-border context.

Table 6. Micro-prudential supervision: comparison of options (Level 1)

(+ positive; – negative; / difficult to establish)

Options	Assessment criteria			
Level 1: Supervisory system	Effectiveness	Efficiency	Coherence	Subsidiarity and proportionality
4. De Larosière proposals: ESFS	++	++	++	++
5. Single EU supervisor	++	++	++	–

Stage 2 – Institutional set-up

We may pass to assessing the institutional set-up for the new Authority or Authorities, a question which is valid regardless of whether the ESFS or a single EU supervisor is chosen. Four options exist, involving establishment of one, two, three or four bodies (see the description in the previous section). These options must be analysed according to the criteria of effectiveness, efficiency and coherence. We shall treat the option C with three Authorities as the baseline as it corresponds to the current Lamfalussy framework.

Firstly, with regard to **effectiveness,** the empirical evidence which exists as to the different supervisory models is inconclusive and is in any case drawn from different regulatory environments around the world, as noted by the G30.[27] The ESFS would have as its main tasks activities other than direct supervision (co-ordination, harmonisation of rules etc), and therefore evidence related to national supervisors, whose main task is day-to-day supervision of individual entities, cannot be directly applied. We can however note that the current structure of the Committees of Supervisors involves a sectoral approach with three committees and a Joint Committee for Financial Conglomerates, so any move towards a different structure would probably involve a short-term drop in effectiveness during a transitional period. Furthermore, if a non-sectoral approach were to be adopted (single supervisor or "twin peaks" for example), the effectiveness for each sector would depend on a good representation of that sector in the oversight management staff and work plan of the authority(ies) in question. We can therefore only conclude that there is no decisive evidence as to the effectiveness of the different models as regards the tasks proposed for the ESFS at EU level.

As to **efficiency**, it would seem a priori logical to suppose that the smaller the number of authorities, the lower the level of duplication of administrative resources and expenses would be, and the higher the cost-efficiency. This would point towards a single authority as the most efficient set-up, then a two-authority structure, and so forth. As mentioned above, the detailed costs and staff requirements for the different supervisory options is something that would need to be set out in the impact assessments accompanying the legislative proposals in the autumn. The efficiency of a "twin-peaks" option would depend on the balance of work at ESFS level between prudential matters and conduct-of-business matters, which will be clearer after a few years of ESFS existence.

Coming to **coherence**, the most coherent structure would be that which best reflects the nature of financial regulation in the EU and the structure of financial institutions in the EU. Here, it must first be observed that EU regulation is currently organised on a sectoral basis, with separate legislative acts and separate prudential and conduct of business requirements, for the banking insurance and securities sectors, and there is no sign that this will change in the foreseeable future. The current structure of the Committees of Supervisors reflects this fact, and a similar sectoral structure for the ESFS would seem therefore to be the most coherent with current legislation. Secondly, although many EU financial institutions are financial conglomerates, this trend may not continue and may even reverse[28].

Given the fact that no one option emerges as a clear leader under the above analysis, it is considered at this stage that the most proportional solution, involving the minimum of necessary change, is to retain the current sectoral structure of the three Committees of Supervisors by creating three European Authorities with the same sectoral mandates as these Committees, combined with a review clause which commits to an analysis of the functioning of the new structures three years after the entry into being of the ESFS. The proposed Steering Committee could ensure cross-fertilisation and interlinkage between the three Authorities and also replace the current Joint Committee on Financial Conglomerates. If the future review were to decide that effectiveness, efficiency and coherence could be better achieved by passing to a different supervisory model, taking account of the evolution of market structure in the meantime, then the existence of the Steering Committee could facilitate any changes.

Table 7. Micro-prudential supervision: comparison of options (Level 2)

(+ positive; – negative; / difficult to establish)

Options	Assessment criteria		
Level 2: Institutional set-up	**Effectiveness**	**Efficiency**	**Coherence**
A. One body	/ (–)*	+	0
B. Two bodies	/ (–)	+	0
C. Three bodies	**0**	**0**	**0**
D. Four bodies	/ (–)	–	–

* (–) marks the drop of effectiveness in the short term due to transition to a new set-up

6.2. MACRO-PRUDENTIAL SUPERVISION

The assessment will be carried out in relation to the specific objectives (see section 4.2.) according to the usual criteria of effectiveness, efficiency and coherence. If not specified differently, the assessment of the single criterion is deemed to be referred to all of these objectives at the same time.

As regards the criterion of **coherence** all options (except for A – dynamic status quo), as regards all the specific objectives referred above, are consistent with the overall objectives of the EU to contribute to economic growth and create jobs, to foster the Single Market and to promote the competitiveness of EU enterprises. The setting-up of an EU framework for macro-prudential supervision will contribute to preserving financial stability, thus providing for one of the essential pre-conditions for the achievement of the goals mentioned above. The objective of a macro-prudential approach is indeed to limit the risk of episodes of financial distress with significant losses in terms of real output for the economy as a whole.

A. Dynamic status quo

As highlighted in section 3.5, the present EU arrangements are not effective as they place too little emphasis on the macro-prudential side. Moreover, there is no mechanism in the EU to ensure that macro-prudential risk warnings and/or recommendations are translated into action. Nor are the present arrangements efficient, as macro-prudential analysis is fragmented and executed by different authorities at different levels.

B. Build on existing or proposed structures

● **The EFC**

As regards **effectiveness** it could be argued that the role of this committee in preparing political discussion within the ECOFIN Council tends to discourage a candid assessment of risks and specific recommendations for corrective action as a search for consensus could lead to dilution in the messages coming from the committee. Such drawbacks are heightened by the fact that Finance Ministers could be direct addressees of risk warnings.

In terms of powers and resources, two main drawbacks can be highlighted with regard to the option of giving the EFC lead responsibility for macro-prudential assessment. First, the EFC Secretariat, as currently stands, would not provide the adequate level of expertise to effectively undertake the operational tasks required for such a body. It is common understanding that central bank representatives would be better placed to provide the right level of analytical support, including the development of methodology (macro-systemic stress testing), and management of a complex and wide set of early warning indicators at EU and Member State level[29]. The latter also requires substantial resources (both in terms of staff and budget).

As concerns pooling of information, the composition of the EFC (ie its political dimension due to the presence of ministries of finance) could induce national supervisors to adopt a quite conservative approach, particularly on information which may raise confidentiality issues (ie concerning individual systemically relevant institutions). Supervisory authorities might be reluctant to disseminate sensitive data to a body having not exclusively a technical dimension.

In terms of **cost efficiency** this option would lead to substantial cost (and duplication) if the necessary expertise and technical infrastructure would have to be built up from scratch (and not be based on existing experience and expertise of for example the ESCB).

● **The ECB/ESCB**

In terms of effectiveness it would make sense to give central banks a leading role in macro-prudential supervision. Historically, the two main objectives of central banks relate to the maintenance of monetary and financial stability. Both objectives are closely interlinked; monetary policy has significant implications for financial stability, while financial stability is an essential pillar for effective monetary policy. Identifying vulnerabilities in the financial and non-financial sectors and potential shocks in these markets is therefore a vital part of the work of central banks. Moreover, central banks have a clear financial safety net function through their role as lender of last resort. Safeguarding financial stability has therefore been and always will be a fundamental objective of central banks.

The European Central Bank (ECB)/European System of Central Banks (ESCB) has wide-ranging macro-prudential expertise and is at the heart of the EU monetary system. It has also demonstrated its effectiveness in times of crisis management. The ECB/ESCB therefore seems to be uniquely placed to have a prominent position in macro-prudential supervision. In view of the integrated financial market in the EU and the geographical distribution of financial activities, it is however essential that all EU central banks be associated, not merely those in the euro area.

On the other hand, three arguments can be presented against the attribution of the macro-prudential supervision to the ECB/ESCB. First, there may be a conflict of interest between financial and monetary stability, in connection with concerns that the ECB/ESCB for reasons of financial stability would pursue a more accommodating monetary policy than warranted for the pursuance of price stability. On the other hand, in the light of the primary task of maintaining price stability, it can also be argued that the ECB/ESCB might be induced to take account of financial instability mainly to the extent that the latter is relevant for the prospects of inflation.

Second, there would be a reputational risk linked to the conduct of macro-prudential supervision. A perceived failure in fulfilling the task of early warning or in advising on the most effective measures to react to risks identified might prove detrimental to the reputation of the ECB/ESCB, thereby jeopardising their credibility as a monetary authority as well.

Third, the **concentration of power argument** could also be mentioned; attributing to the ESCB/ECB the powers linked to macro-prudential supervision might be considered detrimental to the system of checks and balances within the framework for managing the EU economy and financial sector.

Having regard to the **efficiency** criterion, giving to the ECB/ESCB the mandate of undertaking the macro-prudential supervision would allow to fully benefit from the available qualified resources to carry out the analytical and statistical work. Therefore the costs linked to implementation of this option would be reduced.

● **The ESFS**

This option would imply giving the leading role in macro-prudential supervision to the new Authorities with the support of the network of national supervisors.

As highlighted before, the scope of macro-prudential supervision differs considerably from micro-prudential supervision. The former aims at limiting the risk of episodes of widespread financial distress with significant losses in terms of the real output for the economy as a whole. This differs from the objective of micro-prudential supervision, which is to limit the risk of episodes of financial distress at individual institutions, independently of their impact on the overall economy. Given this considerable difference in scope, it would not be effective to transfer this task to the ESFS.

As for cost efficiency, this option would lead to substantial cost (and duplication) if the necessary expertise and technical infrastructure would have to be built up from scratch (and not be based on existing experience and expertise of for example the ESCB).

C. Establish a new body, ie, a European Systemic Risk Council (ESRC)

The envisaged composition of the ESRC should attain high level of effectiveness and provide the ESRC with an adequate level of legitimacy. In this respect, the de Larosière report argues that membership of any body responsible for macro-prudential supervision should be at the highest level. Having both central bankers and supervisory authorities around the table would create valuable synergies and have a mutually reinforcing impact on the stability of the financial system. As indicated, it is vital to give **central banks** a leading role in macro-prudential supervision. Within the EU, the ESCB is uniquely placed to provide the analytical and statistical support for the functioning of the ESRC.

Central banks' focus on system stability puts them in a position to better assess not only the likelihood and the potential of macro-shocks or disturbances in domestic and international capital markets, but also the operation of common factors affecting the stability of groups and intermediaries.

The involvement of **micro-prudential supervisors** through the *3L3 Committees* (or through the future European Authorities) as full members and the presence of national supervisors as observers, would ensure a close cooperation and efficient and timely exchange of information. As a result the synergies between supervisors and central banks will be enhanced. This is essential particularly for the detailed knowledge in financial markets micro-prudential supervisors hold and because they play a crucial role in early intervention mechanisms in case of a financial crisis.

Participation of the **Commission** would provide an essential contribution to the ESRC work. Indeed, the Commission plays a key role in macro-economic surveillance[30]; it would therefore be in position to confirm, complement or challenge the risks identified and provide a broader perspective of risks to the financial system. Furthermore, on its own initiative or upon invitation by the Council, the Commission could intervene in the follow-up to risk warnings and recommendations issued by the ESRC, for example proposing legislation.

The technical profile of members should avoid any major risk of interference of political stances in carrying out the analysis and providing advice on corrective actions. Moreover, the level of members will provide the ESRC with the adequate legitimacy to perform its duties, in particular to ensure adequate follow-up to its advice. Involvement of the EFC Chair, albeit with observer status, is advisable as it would ease the information exchange process with political authorities. Indeed, the latter will in many cases play a relevant role in the follow-up to the warnings, particularly in connection with their prominent responsibilities in the crisis prevention and management. Giving the EFC (through its Chair) the possibility to attend meetings of the ESRC would enhance the commitment of Finance ministries in ensuring proper follow-up when their action is requested. This would also reflect the role of finance ministries in crisis management and resolution and ensure a smooth flow of information between the ESRC and the political authorities.

As regards the decision-making mechanism, various options can be envisaged at this stage: giving voting powers to ESCB Members only, extending these powers to the new European Supervisory Authorities and the Commission too, or even more widely also to (national) supervisors. The option of giving votes to all the parties involved would be too unwieldy, as it would seriously hamper the effectiveness of the body. The first option would mean for ESRC activities to benefit from light and fast procedures, thereby potentially increasing its effectiveness and preventing a potential blurring of responsibilities. This would stem, inter alia, from the level of homogeneity of voting Authorities. As a possible negative effect this mechanism could impact on the commitment of supervisors within the ESRC. Moreover giving voting power to the central bankers only might blur the distinction between the ESRC and the ECB/ESCB, thereby involving for EU Central Banks the same drawbacks as placing the ESCR within the ESCB, ie a "reputational risk" in connection to their participation in the ESRC. Letting European Supervisory Authorities supervisors and the Commission participate in the decision-making process, might be an acceptable intermediate way which would increase the willingness of the EU Authorities to act more proactively within the ESRC and might reduce the reputational risk for individual Members for any potential failure of the new body and fully preserve their credibility in fulfilling their own specific mandates.

The ESRC would introduce an effective mechanism for addressees of warnings and recommendations to act on them. Proper follow-up to warnings and recommendations would be ensured by introducing a "comply or explain" mechanism. As far as the addressees of its recommendations are concerned, there are two main options:

- the ESRC could interact directly with any relevant Authority or Institution at all levels (national and supranational). This would increase its effectiveness as the recommendations would be immediately transmitted to those that should implement the corrective measures suggested. On the other hand, interfacing with a wide range of Institutions and Authorities of different nature and level could imply setting-up a quite complex network of institutional relationships, with a numerous and varied group of interlocutors;
- the alternative option would be to have a rather limited number of counterparts at EU level, like the ECOFIN Council and the 3 new European Authorities (which would then forward the recommendations to the final addressees) and at global level, like the FSB and the IMF This would ensure better coordination and a proper overview of ongoing activities, reduce the administrative actions (and burden) for the ESRC and heavily simplify and speed-up its activities, offsetting in several cases the additional time needed for the transmission to the final recipients. This second option would seem to be the best one.

The ESRC would decide in each case whether a recommendation should be kept confidential or made public, on the basis of its own judgement. However, bearing in mind that the recommendations by the ESRC would not be binding, public disclosure would be expected to increase their effectiveness.

As regards the **cost efficiency** criterion the ERSC would be supported by a Secretariat staffed with officials working in the ECB[31] with rather limited costs mainly related to the equipment and running costs.

Conclusion

Based on the previous assessment, the ESRC emerges clearly as the best solution for the EU framework for macro-prudential supervision. The envisaged architecture, status and operating procedures should allow this body to meet the three objectives in the most effective way. It would be effective as having sole responsibility for macro-prudential risk warnings and a composition which would: create valuable synergies, ensure an appropriate level of representation, and have a mutually reinforcing impact on the stability of the financial system. As for efficiency, it would build on operational and technical support from the ECB/ESCB.

Subsidiarity and Proportionality

Concerning the **subsidiarity** principle it can be observed that only Community action would provide an effective solution to the problems identified with the existing arrangements for macro-prudential supervision. Macro-prudential supervision requires, in addition to the judgement made by individual Member States, a judgement to be taken at the EU level. The "interconnectedness" of macro-prudential risks reflects a variety of direct and indirect linkages in the financial system and involves in-depth analysis across national and sectoral borders.

Regarding the principle of **proportionality**, the establishment of the ESRC, as explained above, would not involve excessive administrative and financial costs, as it would obtain logistical support from the ECB. Moreover the proposed solution would achieve the right balance between the sovereignty of national authorities and the need to ensure an appropriate macro-prudential supervision at EU level. Other options would entail a sub-optimal representation of national/EU authorities.

Table 8. Macro-prudential supervision: comparison of options

Options	Assessment criteria			
	Effectiveness	**Efficiency**	**Coherence**	**Proportionality**
Status quo	0	0	0	0
EFC	+	+	+	+
Tasking the ESFS	+	+	+	+
ECB/ESCB	+++	++	+	+
ESRC	++++	++	+	++

[1911]

NOTES

23   Impact Assessment Guidelines.

24   For example, the Member States rejected the Commission proposals to strengthen home country control for capital add-ons in subsidiaries in other Member States under the banking Capital Requirements Directive. Likewise, they also vetoed Commission proposal under the insurance Solvency II directive to allow the home based firm to allocate capital throughout the group in an efficient way, subject to safeguards to protect the financial soundness of all the legal entities belonging to the group.

25   London Economics (in association with PricewaterhouseCoopers and Oxford Economic Forecasting), *Quantification of the Macro-Economic Impact of Integration of EU Financial Markets*, Report to European Commission, November 2002.

26   European Financial Integration Report 2007–2008, Financial Integration Monitor 2004–2006.

27   See the G30 report, "The Structure of Financial Supervision – approaches and challenges in a global marketplace" G30, 9/10/2008, which states "In general, no one model has proven unambiguously superior in achieving all the objectives of regulation."

28   For example, ING announced on 9/4/2009 that it will separate out its banking and insurance businesses.

29   These must encompass Aggregate capital adequacy ratios; financial gaps: liquidity, interest rate, funding and foreign exchange rate gaps; household indebtedness; balance sheet growth rate; level of provisions; non-performing loans; risk concentration ratios; growth rate of domestic credit, rate of growth of house and other asset prices.

30   See Art. 99, §3 and 4 of the EC Treaty:

"3.   In order to ensure closer co-ordination of economic policies and sustained convergence of the economic performances of the Member States, the Council shall, on the basis of reports submitted by the Commission, monitor economic developments in each of the Member States and in the Community as well as the consistency of economic policies with the broad guidelines referred to in paragraph 2, and regularly carry out an overall assessment. For the purpose of this multilateral surveillance, Member States shall forward information to the Commission about important measures taken by them in the field of their economic policy and such other information as they deem necessary.

4.   Where it is established, under the procedure referred to in paragraph 3, that the economic policies of a Member State are not consistent with the broad guidelines referred to in paragraph 2 or that they risk jeopardising the proper functioning of economic and monetary union, the Council may, acting by a qualified majority on a recommendation from the Commission, make the necessary recommendations to the Member State concerned. The Council may, acting by a qualified majority on a proposal from the Commission, decide to make its recommendations public. The President of the Council and the Commission shall report to the European Parliament on the results of

multilateral surveillance. The President of the Council may be invited to appear before the competent committee of the European Parliament if the Council has made its recommendations public."

31   The ESRC Secretariat could be also strengthened with personnel seconded from national Central banks or from national supervisors.

7. IMPACT OF THE SELECTED OPTIONS

The selected options should achieve the objectives of the reform by giving effect to a number of immediate changes to the organisation of micro-prudential and macro-prudential supervision in the EU, subject to the appropriate legal framework. These changes will be achieved by work of the newly established ESFS and the ESRC, fulfilling the operational objectives listed in Chapter 4.

It is important to emphasise that the preferred options are neutral as to the organisation of supervision at the national level. They will be consistent with any of the models currently adopted in Member States. Secondly, regarding the competencies of the new Authorities, they will not include decisions with direct fiscal consequences.

The table below presents the comparison of the impact of the ESFS and ESRC on various groups of stakeholders, including consumers, employees, industry, supervisors etc, as identified in the problem description.

Table 9. Impact of the selected options on the stakeholders

	Micro-prudential supervision ESFS (3 Authorities)	Macro-prudential supervision ESRC
Financial industry: cross-border	+ Prevent failure of financial institutions through better co-ordinated supervision. Ensure level playing field and reduce compliance costs thanks to harmonised standards and supervisory practices. Improve business environment thanks to financial stability and more effective crisis prevention in the EU	+ Prevention of failure of financial institutions through systemic contagion from other financial institutions in difficulty. Improved business environment due to financial stability and crisis prevention in the EU
Financial industry: local	= No significant changes, possible adaptation to the EU standards and improved business environment due to more effective financial stability and crisis prevention in the EU	+ Prevention of failure of financial institutions through systemic contagion from other financial institutions in difficulty. Improved business environment due to financial stability and crisis prevention in the EU
Financial industry: 3rd countries	+ Attracting investments to Internal Market thanks to harmonised business environment and high quality supervision	+ Attracting investments to Internal Market thanks to increased financial stability
Consumers and users of financial services (including retail investors)	+ Greater convergence of conduct-of-business supervision in Europe	+ Increase confidence by strengthening financial stability

	Micro-prudential supervision ESFS (3 Authorities)	Macro-prudential supervision ESRC
Employees	+ Preventing job losses in individual financial institutions by better detecting and remedying prudential-related difficulties	+ Preventing job losses in the economy as a whole arising from spill-over of financial sector difficulties to the real economy
Pensioners	+ Providing incentives for development of cross-border occupational pension funds and strengthening their oversight. Improve stability of pension funds	+ Strengthened confidence of pensioners by strengthening financial stability. Improve stability of pension funds.
Corporations from non-financial sector and SMEs	+ Facilitating access to finance by better preventing failure of individual institutions (e g European Authorities in oversight of credit ratings, approval of prospectuses)	+ Preventing major financial crises with damaging impacts on corporate equity value. Preventing major economic recessions linked with reduction of trade and demand.
Supervisors	+ Ensuring more effective cooperation by clarifying the roles and responsibilities of supervisors at the national and Community level and establishing an effective framework for conflict resolution between supervisors. Indirect strengthening of supervisory independence.	+ Creating a framework linking micro-prudential supervision with macro-prudential supervision. Facilitating exchange of information and leading to creation of a common information pool.
National governments	+ Establishing EU supervisory arrangements that are more consistent with European financial integration. Less risks of having to inject public money in the financial system.	+ Providing governments with recommendations for actions needed to protect macro-economic stability in the EU and individual Member States
Central banks	+ Establishing EU supervisory arrangements that are more consistent with European financial integration.	+ Giving effectiveness to the analysis of macro prudential developments carried out in the central banks. Facilitating exchange of information and leading to creation of a common information pool.

In general, by contributing to safeguarding financial stability and more effective control over conduct of financial companies, the ESFS and the ESRC would increase the welfare of most stakeholder groups in the Internal Market.

[1912]

8. MONITORING AND EVALUATION

A number of indicators are applied to monitor the trends related to the General Objectives of the reform: financial stability, consumer and business confidence, international competitiveness of EU financial industry, financial integration (see the European Financial Integration Report[32]). However, it is difficult to establish the degree to which the EU policies, in particular the reform of financial supervision, influence the evolution of these indicators.

To monitor effectively the impact of the EU action in the area of micro- and macro-prudential supervisions, specific indicators should be matched with the specific objectives and – where possible – also with the operational objectives. These indicators should serve to evaluate the performance of the ESFS and the ESRC in fulfilling their tasks. As for the functioning of the ESFS, one could examine the progress in moving towards harmonised rules, powers and sanctions, measure confidence among supervisory authorities, and verify the effectiveness of processes and practices to challenge supervisory practices on a cross-border basis. For the ESRC to be effective it would need to fulfil three key conditions: (i) it should be effective in identifying macro-prudential risks sufficiently in advance; (ii) it should be able to competently identify appropriate measures to reduce these risks; and (c) it should be able to effectively trigger corrective action to address the identified risks. These indicators should be developed in more detail in the impact assessment of legislative proposals implementing the supervisory reform.

[1913]

NOTES
   [32]   SEC(2009)19 final.

ANNEX 1 – COMPARISON OF THE RETAINED OPTIONS WITH THE DE LAROSIÈRE REPORT

Major differences between the options retained by the Commission and the proposals of the de Larosière report

Micro-prudential supervision:
*   Timing: implementation in one phase not two
*   Sectoral coverage: European Insurance Authority to cover also occupational pensions

Macro-prudential supervision
*   Composition of the ESRC: national supervisors would always be represented
*   Voting in the ESRC: one vote per national delegation
*   Addressee of ESRC warnings: only through ECOFIN Council and ESFS and not directly to national Central Banks and Supervisors (in addition to the EFC)

[1914]

ANNEX 2 – SUMMARY OF PUBLIC SUBMISSIONS RECEIVED

The total number of submissions received to date in reply to the public consultation on financial supervision is 116 (including those which arrived after the deadline of 10 April 2009, which were accepted). The breakdown is as follows (NB all submissions not containing a registration number for the submitting organisation have been classified as individual replies):

Public authorities:	26
Registered organisations:	16
Individuals:	74

Many of the submissions covered not only supervisory issues from the de Larosière report but also regulatory ones. A few did not touch on supervisory issues at all. Most congratulated the de Larosière group and broadly supported its conclusions, but some noted the lack of representativity of the group (being composed only of bankers with no representatives of other financial sectors nor of consumers or employees). The majority of contributions noted that more details are needed on the powers and composition of both macro- and micro-supervisors in order to reach definitive positions.

Submissions were received from public authorities in 18 EU and EFTA Member States and international bodies such as the IMF and the existing "Level Three committees" (for some Member States more than one submission was received from different public bodies – see annex).

On *micro-supervision*, all submissions from public authorities strongly or cautiously support the principle of the ESFS, with one exception, which withheld its support. But most submissions have issues of detail to express. Three submissions explicitly oppose binding powers for new ESFS authorities over national authorities. Most submissions highlight the need to resolve issues of governance independence and answerability in the ESFS, notably with regard to fiscal responsibility and burden-sharing arrangements. Most responses do not explicitly refer to the structure of the new authorities; of those that did, one favour "twin peaks" and four favour a unitary authority.

On *macro-supervision*, none of the responses from public authorities opposes the proposed ESRC but while some replies strongly support the proposal others support it conditionally upon further details being provided. Some favour an ESRC within the European System of Central Banks while others prefer it to be outside the ESCB.

The three EFTA submissions are supportive of the de Larosière proposals. They all support a unitary authority for micro-prudential supervision, and all advocate for observer representation of EFTA-EEA countries on both the ESFS and the ESRC.

The joint response of the existing level 3 committees is supportive of the de Larosière report (with the exception of one national delegation). On micro-prudential supervision, they emphasise the need for independence and accountability, and adequate legal powers (while recognising the legal challenges). They are open on the question of the number of authorities. Colleges of supervisors should remain at the core of supervision of cross-border groups in their view. On macro-prudential supervision, they support the ESRC proposal, while emphasising that information should be fed in by micro-supervisors not individual institutions. The IMF supports a "twin-peaks" model for micro-supervision, with some direct supervisory powers at EU-level. It strongly supports the ESRC, advocating mandatory follow-up to ESRC recommendations and co-ordination with global bodies such as the IMF. Both responses argue in favour of strong participation by micro-prudential supervisors in the macro-prudential body.

The bulk of the contributions received are from financial sector associations and institutions, whether or not registered as representative interest groups, and views are diverse.

As a broad generalisation, those responses which refer to the *macro-prudential* proposals of the de Larosière report either cautiously or more openly support them, subject to further clarifications on the exact powers and composition of the ESRC. There is no explicit opposition to the ESRC proposal expressed in sectoral submissions. Many replies emphasise the importance of good linkage between the ESRC and micro-prudential supervisors, including exchange of information; others question the mechanism which will be used for ensuring follow-up to ESRC recommendations. A number of replies emphasise the importance of avoiding double reporting requirements and of confidential treatment of information received.

On *micro-prudential supervision*, a majority of sectoral submissions express cautious support for the proposal for an ESFS. A number note that in their view colleges of supervisors should be the heart of supervision for cross-border groups, with lead supervision by the home country supervisor (and EU level oversight). Views differed on the issue of binding powers for the ESFS authorities, and on the question of direct EU-level supervision of cross-border groups. Regarding supervisory structure (one, two or three bodies), the majority of contributions either do not refer to this question or favour three bodies. Contributions from insurance associations all oppose merging banking and insurance into one supervisory body. A small number of sectoral submissions favour "twin peaks" or a single supervisor.

One contribution from the pensions sector criticises the absence of any reference to pensions in the de Larosière report and argues in favour of a separate mandate for pensions in any new supervisory structure.

On timing, a number of sectoral submissions argue for a cautious, two-stage approach, as proposed by the de Larosière report. Very few of them explicitly favour a rapid approach.

Of the nine submissions from consumer and end-user associations, only four cover the issue of supervision. One opposes the ESRC because of lack of clarity as to its competences, and on micro-supervision supports a single EU supervisor for cross-border institutions, with strengthened national supervisors for other institutions. Another emphasises the general goals of equality and sustainability for financial supervision, and favours global level (not EU-level) macro-prudential supervision. A third agrees with the need for a macro-prudential supervision body, and on micro-supervision argues that co-operation between colleges of supervisors needs to be strengthened. Another argues in favour of European Agencies for both macro- and micro-supervision, with rule-making powers in the case of micro-supervision, while leaving day-to-day supervision at national level. All consumer contributions emphasise the need for independence and transparency of supervisory bodies, and for involvement of stakeholders including consumers (possibly via an advisory panel).

All of the three trades unions which responded argue for the need for consultation of employees by both micro- and macro-level supervisors, via a consultative panel. All support the principle of the ESRC, though one favours global-level co-ordination of macro-prudential supervision. Two of the three union responses support direct EU-level supervision of cross-border financial groups.

[1915]

ANNEX 3 – LIST OF PUBLIC SUBMISSIONS RECEIVED

Public Authorities
3L3 committees (joint response)
Austria (finance ministry, financial market authority, central bank joint response)
Autorité des Marchés Financiers (FR)
Bulgarian finance ministry
Comisión Nacional del Mercado de Valores (ES)
Czech Central bank
Danish Financial Services Authority
EFTA EEA Standing Committee
Estonia finance ministry
Hungarian Financial Supervisory Authority
Hungarian Ministry of Finance
Hungarian National Bank
Iceland government
IMF
Ireland Ministry of Finance
Irish Financial Regulator
Latvian finance ministry
Netherlands Finance Ministry
NL Central Bank
NL Financial Market Authority
Norway (finance ministry, Central Bank & Supervisory authority joint submission)
Polish Financial Supervision Authority
Portugal Finance Ministry
Slovak Republic
Swedish FSA and Central Bank
UK (government and FSA)
Registered Organisations
Association fédérative internationale des porteurs d'emprunts russes (AFIPER)
Association of British Insurers (ABI)
Bundesverband Investment und Asset Management (BVI)
Comité Européen des Assurances (CEA)
Eumedion (NL corporate governance forum)
European Fund and Asset Management Association (EFAMA)
Fédération des Associations Indépendantes de Défense des Epargnants pour la Retraite (FAIDER)
Federation of Enterprises in Belgium (FEB)
Forum of European Asset Managers (FEAM)
German Insurance Federation (GDV)
Investment & Life Assurance Group (ILAG)
La Voix des Emprunts Russes
Luxembourg Banking association (ABBL)
Nordic Finance Trade Union (NFU)
Royal Institution of Chartered Surveyors (RICS)
UK Investment Management Association (IMA)

Individuals
Alternative investment management association
Association Française des entreprises privées
Association Française des Marchés Financiers
Association of Chartered Certified Accountants
Association of international life offices
Associazione Bancaria Italiana
Aviva
Banco Santander
Bank Track
Barclays
Baxter Fianncial Services
Bundesverband Deutscher Banken
German Association of Energy and Water Industries (BDEW)
BEUC (Bureau Européen des Unions des Consommateurs)
BIPAR (European Federation of Insurance Intermediaries)
BNP-Paribas
Business Reporting – Advisory Group
British Bankers' Association
Building Societies Association
BVR-DSG-VÖB-VDP (German Banking Associations)
Confederation of British Industry
Caisse des Dépôts and Cassa Depositi e Prestiti
Confédération Européenne des Associations de Petites et Moyennes Entreprises
CFA Institute Centre for Financial Market Integrity
Consumers International
European Association of Co-operative Banks
European Association of Public Banks
European Banking Industry Committee
European Financial Services Round Table
European Federation for Retirement Provision
European Savings Banks Group
Euroclear
European Banking Federation
European Contact Group
European issuers
F Roels
Fédération Bancaire Française
Fédération Européenne des Conseils et Intermédiaires Financiers
Federation of European Stock Exchanges (not for publication)
Fédération des experts comptables européens
Fédération française des sociétés d'assurance
Fédération française des sociétés d'assurance mutuelles
FIN USE
Futures and Options Association
Financial Services Consumer Panel

Groupe Consultatif Actuariel Europeen
HSBC
Institute of Chartered Accountants of Scotland
International Capital Market Association
ING
Irish Stock Exchange
J P Marin Arrese
LIBA, SIFMA, and ISDA
M Wendschlag
MAF, SMABTP, MACSF
Managed Funds Association
M Grinover
NASDAQ OMX
Nederlandse Vereininging van Banken
NYSE-Euronext
Omgeo
Pan-European Insurance Forum
PriceWaterhouseCoopers
Quoted Companies Alliance
R K Associates
S Walby
Transparency International
UNI Europa
Unicredit
Unite the Union
Verbraucherzentrale Bundesverband
Which?
XBRL Europe
Zentraler Kreditausschuss

[1916]–[1999]

PART VI
OTHER MATERIALS

BANKING ACT 2009
SPECIAL RESOLUTION REGIME: CODE OF PRACTICE

February 2009
Presented to Parliament pursuant to sections 5 and 6 of the Banking Act 2009

1 INTRODUCTION

1.1   The Banking Act 2009 (the Act), covering England, Scotland, Northern Ireland and Wales, strengthens the UK's statutory framework for financial stability and depositor protection.

1.2   The Act puts in place a permanent special resolution regime (SRR), providing the Financial Services Authority (FSA), Bank of England and the Her Majesty's Treasury (the Authorities) with tools to protect financial stability by effectively resolving banks and building societies that are failing, while protecting depositors, taxpayers and the wider economy.

1.3   This Code of Practice, issued in accordance with sections 5 and 6 of the Act, supports the legal framework of the SRR, and provides guidance as to how and in what circumstances the Authorities will use the special resolution tools. In particular, it sets out guidance on the use of:
- the **three stabilisation options**: transfer to a private sector purchaser, transfer to a bridge bank and transfer to temporary public sector ownership;
- the **bank insolvency procedure**, which facilitates the Financial Services Compensation Scheme (FSCS) in providing prompt payout to depositors; and
- the **bank administration procedure**, for use where there has been a partial transfer of business from a failing institution.

1.4   The Treasury has issued this Code having consulted the FSA, the Bank of England and the FSCS in accordance with section 6 of the Act. The Code is laid before Parliament on 23 February 2009.

[2000]

2 OVERVIEW OF THE CODE

2.1   This Code of Practice provides guidance on the use of the SRR set out in Parts 1–3 of the Act. The SRR provides the Authorities with a permanent set of tools to deal with banks and building societies in circumstances in which their failure has become highly likely, and a threat is posed to the public interest. It consists of:
- the **three stabilisation options**: transfer to a private sector purchaser, transfer to a bridge bank and transfer to temporary public sector ownership;
- the **bank insolvency procedure**; and
- the **bank administration procedure**.

2.2   The special resolution tools may be used by the Authorities to resolve a failing banking institution, and include powers to take bank holding companies into temporary public ownership, if necessary.

Contents of the Code

2.3   In accordance with section 5 of the Act, this Code sets out:
- how the special resolution objectives are to be understood and achieved;
- the choice between different resolution options;
- the information to be provided in the course of a consultation under this Part (i e information to be provided as part of any consultation between the Authorities and the giving of advice between one authority and another);
- the giving of advice by one relevant Authority to another about whether, when and how the stabilisation powers are to be used;
- how to determine whether Condition 2 in section 7 is met (this condition stipulates that, before a banking institution can be placed in the SRR, the FSA must have determined that it is not reasonably likely that action will be taken by or in respect of the institution that will enable it to satisfy its threshold conditions);
- how to determine whether the test for the use of stabilisation powers in section 8 is satisfied (i e how the Bank of England will determine the public interest test for the use of the bridge bank and private sector purchaser stabilisation options will be satisfied);
- sections 63 and 66 (general continuity obligations); and
- compensation.

2.4   Sections 12 and 13 require the inclusion in the Code of certain matters relating to the governance of bridge banks and temporary public ownership.

2.5   In describing the use of the statutory powers under the SRR (Chapters 3–10), the Code uses the general term 'banking institution' to refer to a bank, building society or bank holding company, except where otherwise stated.

PART VI
OTHER MATERIALS

The Authorities' regard to the Code

2.6   The Authorities are legally obliged to have regard to the Code under section 5(4) of the Act.

2.7   The Treasury considers that one of the primary purposes of the Code is to provide a clear guide, for banking institutions and the financial markets, to how the Authorities will seek to achieve the special resolution objectives.

Revising and maintaining the Code

2.8   The Treasury will update the Code on a periodic basis, in the light of evolving experience. The Treasury will consult the Bank of England, FSA and the FSCS on any changes. In making material changes to the Code the Treasury will also consult the Banking Liaison Panel, which has a statutory remit to advise the Treasury on the Code of Practice under section 10(2)(b) of the Act.

2.9   When a new Code is issued, the Treasury will lay a copy before Parliament as soon as is practicable.

Banking Liaison Panel

2.10   The Banking Liaison Panel will advise the Treasury on certain matters relating to the SRR. The remit and terms of reference of the panel will be published, and will include advising the Treasury on the effect of the SRR on banking institutions, persons with whom they do business, and the financial markets.

2.11   The Treasury expects the Panel to take a particular interest in providing advice in relation to the operation of the safeguards provided by and under the Act in relation to partial property transfers and on this Code.

2.12   Summaries of the proceedings of meetings of the Banking Liaison Panel will be published, subject to considerations of commercial and market confidentiality.

[2001]

3 SPECIAL RESOLUTION OBJECTIVES

3.1   Section 4 of the Act provides for the special resolution objectives, as follows:
- objective 1 is to protect and enhance the stability of the financial systems of the UK;
- objective 2 is to protect and enhance public confidence in the stability of the banking systems of the UK;
- objective 3 is to protect depositors;
- objective 4 is to protect public funds; and
- objective 5 is to avoid interfering with property rights in contravention of a Convention Right (within the meaning of the Human Rights Act 1998).

Matters to be considered in having regard to the objectives

3.2   Specific terms used within the objectives are not generally defined by the Act. The objectives set out in the Act are context-specific and neither they nor the terms within them can be defined in an exhaustive or definitive manner. In addition, the specific relevance and application of the objectives may change over time (for example, as the threats to financial stability change over time).

3.3   Therefore, this Code provides further explanation as to how the objectives may be achieved by outlining the factors that the Authorities may consider to be relevant in applying them.

Stability of the financial systems of the UK

3.4   The term "stability of the financial systems of the UK" refers to the stable functioning of the systems and institutions (including trading, payment and settlement infrastructure) supporting the efficient operation of financial services and markets for purposes including capital-raising, risk-transfer, and the facilitation of domestic and international commerce in addition to day-to-day banking operations.

3.5   By virtue of section 4(9) of the Act, the reference to the stability of the financial systems of the UK includes in particular a reference to the continuity of banking services. Continuity of banking services is relevant not only for the protection of depositors under objective 2, but has wider relevance to the stability of the financial systems of the UK.

3.6   The intention of the first objective is to (a) recognise the wider systemic risks posed by the potential or actual failure of a banking institution or group of companies containing a banking institution; and (b) require the Authorities to have regard to the likely systemic impact of their actions (including a decision not to act) when considering whether to use a SRR tool.

3.7   The Authorities will have regard to ensuring that the transfer powers are not exercised in a manner that is likely to harm financial stability. As part of this, in transferring rights and obligations that confer a particular status (for example, as a settlement or clearance bank), the Authorities will seek to ensure that this status is not transferred to an unsuitable entity.

Public confidence in the stability of the banking systems

3.8   The term "public confidence in the stability of the banking systems" refers to the crucial role that public confidence has in maintaining the stable and efficient operation of financial services and markets. The confidence of the general public is of particular significance in maintaining stability in a banking system based on a fractional reserve model, whereby institutions' deposit liabilities exceed the liquid assets they hold at any one time.

3.9   Public confidence has a number of dimensions. For example, it refers to the expectation that (a) deposits will be repaid in accordance with their terms; (b) normal banking services will continue to be available; (c) problems (or perceived problems) in one institution will not extend to other institutions (contagion); and (d) if an institution does fail, systems exist to protect the interests of depositors.

3.10   The intention of the second objective is to provide that the Authorities have regard to the need to act so that a failing institution will be resolved in a manner that protects and enhances public confidence in the banking system as a whole.

Protection of depositors

3.11   The term "protection of depositors" refers specifically to the objective of protecting depositors from the effects of the failure of an institution, as an end in itself. This objective goes beyond the need to ensure public confidence in the banking systems (although, as noted above, depositor protection may be an important element of such confidence), and recognises the important public policy objective of ensuring that depositors in a failed institution are adequately protected.

3.12   Under the Act such protection can be delivered in different ways. For example by (a) facilitating fast payout to eligible depositors up to the compensation limit under the FSCS (or arranging a bulk transfer of accounts) through the bank insolvency procedure; or (b) facilitating continuity of banking services through the stabilisation options provided in the SRR.

3.13   Effective depositor protection is particularly important in the case of deposits protected by the FSCS. Protection of these deposits, including prompt access to them, is also likely to be conducive to the realisation of a number of other SRR objectives such as protecting and enhancing public confidence in the banking systems. However, the use of the SRR may also offer protection to other types of depositor and non-depositor creditors if necessary to meet the special resolution objectives.

Protection of public funds

3.14   The term "protection of public funds" refers primarily to the protection of taxpayers' interest in the effective expenditure of public money. The intention of the fourth objective is to recognise the strong duty of the Authorities, and particularly the Treasury, to protect public funds in taking decisions with implications for public funds.

Avoiding interference with property rights

3.15   The term "avoiding interfering with property rights in contravention of a Convention right" refers in particular to holders of property rights in a failing banking institution. This can include the institution itself, its shareholders (or, in the case of a building society, members), creditors, counterparties, or other third parties. Such persons may hold property in the failing institution, or have a right of control over such property, or both. The primary Convention right at issue is Article 1 of Protocol 1 to the Convention (right to property). Other Convention rights (including Article 6, the right to a fair trial and Article 14, prohibition of discrimination) may also be relevant. The inclusion of this objective acknowledges the importance ensuring that any interference with the Convention rights is in the public interest and proportionate.

Balancing the objectives

3.16   Neither the Act, nor this Code, ranks the SRR objectives. Under section 4(10) of the Act, the objectives are to be balanced as appropriate in each case. This provision recognises that the relative weighting and balancing of objectives will vary according to the particular circumstances of each failure, including both (a) circumstances specific to the failing institution; and (b) general circumstances relating to the wider financial system.

Authorities' regard to objectives

3.17   The special resolution objectives in the Act serve two purposes:
- they reflect the purpose of the SRR measures in the Act; and
- they set out the objectives to which the Authorities must have regard when using or considering the use of their powers under the SRR.

3.18   This means that the Authorities must consider the effect of their likely actions (including inaction) and assess them in light of the objectives. This applies to the exercise of all powers under Parts 1, 2 and 3 of the Act.

3.19   The sole exception to this requirement relates to a determination made by the FSA, under section 7(2) and (3) of the Act, that an institution is failing or is likely to fail to satisfy the threshold conditions within the meaning of the Financial Services and Markets Act 2000 (FSMA) that that it is not reasonably likely that action will be taken to enable the bank to satisfy those conditions. These decisions will be taken in the context of the FSA's objectives under FSMA.

3.20   In exercising the powers under Parts 1, 2 and 3, the Authorities will also, as is the case with any public body in the exercise of its functions, necessarily have regard to restrictions and conventions of public law, in particular the requirement for the Authorities to act reasonably and to have respect for the rule of law and principle of legal certainty. The Authorities must also act in accordance with common law principles of procedural fairness when exercising the SRR tools.

3.21   Following actions taken under the SRR, the Authorities shall make a public statement explaining (a) how they have acted with regard to the special resolution objectives; and (b) how they have balanced the objectives against each other. The form that such an explanation will take will depend on the circumstances.

3.22   However, it should be noted that it may not be possible to divulge certain information; for example, information the release of which would threaten financial stability or confidence in the banking systems will not be made available by the Authorities in any public statement.

[2002]

4 ROLES OF THE AUTHORITIES

4.1   The resolution of failing banking institutions will involve intensive coordination, cooperation and information sharing between the Authorities at each stage of the decision-making process. Each of the Authorities will take lead responsibility for specified aspects of the resolution.

4.2   As set out in section 7 of the Act, the FSA will be responsible for making the determination that a banking institution is failing (or is likely to fail) to satisfy its threshold conditions, and that it is not reasonably likely that action will be taken by or in respect of the institution that will enable the institution to meet those conditions. The FSA will also be responsible for the authorisation of a bridge bank and ongoing supervision of institutions in the SRR.

4.3   The Bank of England will be responsible for the operation of the SRR, including the decision on which of the SRR tools to use, and its implementation (with the exception of the power to take an institution into temporary public ownership). The Bank of England will also remain responsible for the provision of liquidity support, which uses the Bank of England's balance sheet.

4.4   The Treasury will be responsible for decisions with implications for public funds, for ensuring the UK's ongoing compliance with its international obligations, and for matters relating to the wider public interest. The Treasury will also be responsible for the temporary public ownership tool. The Treasury will also exercise a number of the ancillary powers under the SRR (particularly those where Parliamentary scrutiny is required), including the power to modify the law and powers in relation to compensation.

4.5   The FSCS will also work closely with the Authorities. Under the compensation scheme, triggered in the insolvency procedure, the FSCS has the role of delivering payout to eligible depositors. Further, under section 171 of the Act the FSCS may be a contributor to the cost of the SRR.

4.6   The FSCS will need to assess and prepare for the payout, and its assessment of the possibilities for payout, or account transfer, will be a relevant factor in the selection of the SRR tool by the Bank of England. For both a depositor payout or account transfer, or for any contribution to SRR costs, information-sharing protocols will be put in place to ensure that the FSCS has access to information relating to the failing institution and its systems at the appropriate time.

4.7   A revised Memorandum of Understanding between the Authorities will outline how the Authorities will coordinate with each other before and during the resolution of an institution, including through the operation of the Tripartite Standing Committee.

[2003]

5 GENERAL AND SPECIFIC CONDITIONS FOR CHOOSING THE SRR TOOLS

SRR tools

5.1   The Act provides the Bank of England and the Treasury with the following stabilisation options for resolving a failing institution:

- in the case of bank or building society, transfer by the Bank of England of the banking institution or some or all of its business to a private sector purchaser;
- in the case of a bank or building society, transfer by the Bank of England of some or all of its business to a bridge bank; and
- in the case of a bank, building society or holding company of a bank, transfer by the Treasury of the institution into temporary public ownership.

5.2   As set out below, bringing a bank holding company into temporary public ownership is only likely to occur when other options are considered to be inadequate. Temporary public ownership is the only tool that can be used in respect of bank holding companies.

5.3   Each of the three stabilisation options is achieved through the exercise of one or more of the "stabilisation powers", which are the powers to effect the transfer of shares and other securities or property, rights and liabilities, by operation of law. These stabilisation powers include the onward and supplemental transfer powers, which are discussed in paragraphs 6.2–6.12 of this Code.

5.4   The Act also provides the FSA and the Bank of England with the ability to apply to the court for a bank insolvency order to wind up a banking institution in the interests of creditors as a whole, and to facilitate a rapid FSCS payout to eligible depositors or transfer of their accounts to another institution.

5.5   The Bank of England can also apply for a bank administration order to facilitate the transfer of part of a failing banking institution's business to a private sector purchaser or bridge bank.

Determining that the regulatory pre-conditions are satisfied

5.6   A stabilisation power may be exercised in respect of a banking institution only if the FSA is satisfied that the conditions set out in section 7 of the Act have been met. The first condition is that the FSA determines that the institution is failing, or is likely to fail, to satisfy the threshold conditions.

5.7   The second condition is that the FSA must also determine that, having regard to timing and other relevant circumstances it is not reasonably likely that (ignoring the stabilisation powers that are available to exercise the stabilisation options) action will be taken by or in respect of the banking institution that would enable it to satisfy the threshold conditions.

5.8   This determination is a regulatory matter for the FSA, which will be undertaken in line with its existing statutory objectives under FSMA 2000. Before determining whether it is reasonably likely that action will be taken by or in respect of the institution that will enable it to satisfy the threshold conditions, the FSA must consult the Bank of England and the Treasury.

5.9   The threshold conditions represent the minimum conditions that a firm is required to satisfy, and continue to satisfy, in order to have permission to undertake regulated activities. In making this determination, the FSA are required to discount financial assistance provided by the Treasury or Bank of England disregarding ordinary market assistance offered by the Bank on its usual terms. The concept of 'ordinary market assistance' contained in section 7(4)(b) does not create a new 'hard-edged' legal definition. The Bank of England provides banks with a spectrum of assistance in all types of different circumstances. Whether or not financial assistance from the Bank of England constitutes "ordinary market assistance ... on its usual terms" will depend on a combination of factors, including the terms of the Bank's operation, the circumstances of the bank receiving liquidity from the Bank, and conditions in the relevant markets in which the firm was, or would otherwise be, seeking to access funding. Furthermore, these factors may vary during the period that any assistance is given. The provision does not imply whether a particular facility is, for all banks using it, "ordinary market assistance" or not.

5.10   The FSA Handbook contains rules and guidance relevant to an authorised firm.[1] In particular, the "COND" sourcebook contains rules and guidance on the threshold conditions. There are a range of conditions, including: legal status and location of offices; the adequacy of the firm's resources (financial and non financial) in relation to the regulated activities which the firm undertakes; and suitability issues (for example competent and prudent management, conducting business with integrity and in compliance with proper standards). The FSA is currently updating its handbook to provide further guidance on its actions under section 7 of the Act.

Determining that the specific conditions for exercising the SRR tools are met

5.11   Under section 8 of the Act, the Bank of England may only exercise a stabilisation power if satisfied that the exercise of the power is necessary having regard to the public interest in:
- the stability of the financial systems of the United Kingdom;
- the maintenance of public confidence in the stability of the banking systems of the United Kingdom; or
- the protection of depositors.

5.12   The Bank of England must consult the Treasury and the FSA before making this determination and deciding how to proceed. In determining whether to proceed with the bank insolvency procedure, the Bank of England will also consult with the FSCS.

5.13   The three public interest conditions may overlap (to a greater or lesser degree) depending on the particular circumstances of the banking institution and the wider circumstances of the financial system as a whole.

5.14   The test of "necessity" is a high one, and the Bank of England and the Treasury will necessarily have regard to public law restrictions, the Authorities regard to the special resolution objectives and the duty to act compatibly with the Convention rights.

5.15   The assessment must seek to balance the short and long-term effects on financial stability, public confidence and depositor protection of different resolution options. When considering the need to protect depositors, the Bank of England will take into account not only the implications of losses but also the consequences of lack of continuity of depositor services. While particular importance is attached to the protection of FSCS eligible depositors, at times of heightened systemic risk greater emphasis may be placed on protecting a wider range of depositors of a failing institution. At other times, the preferred option might be to use the bank insolvency procedure to facilitate rapid FSCS payout to eligible depositors, or a transfer of their accounts to another institution.

5.16   If, having had regard to the public interest test, the Bank of England determines that it is necessary to exercise one of the SRR tools, the Bank of England will need to consider as a practical matter which of the tools it will be possible to use; and further, whether use of the tool would be compatible with the Bank of England's legal obligations and the special resolution objectives.

The choice between the tools

5.17   In choosing between the resolution tools, the Bank of England will consider the relative merits of the stabilisation options and the bank insolvency procedure given the circumstances. There are, however, some general considerations that may be taken into account. Some of these are detailed below.

5.18   Resolution by way of the bank insolvency procedure may be the option that best meets the special resolution objectives where the most appropriate outcome would be the winding up of the failed institution's affairs in the interests of creditors as a whole, and prompt FSCS payouts to eligible depositors or the bulk transfer of their accounts to another institution. It is also generally important for market discipline that firms – including banks and building societies – should not be immune from failure.

5.19   Resolution by way of a transfer to a private sector purchaser is generally likely to be the resolution option that best meets the special resolution objectives if it can be effected in a cost effective way. It provides the flexibility for both whole-bank and part-bank solutions, and for a swift and certain transfer. It does, however, require a willing purchaser in order for it to be effective.

5.20   Resolution by way of a transfer to a bridge bank may be appropriate where an immediate private sector sale is not possible, and where a stable platform is needed to prepare for and effect the onward sale of all or part of the bank to a private sector purchaser.

5.21   Temporary public ownership is generally likely to be the least preferred option, and involves the Treasury taking control and ownership of a failing banking institution through the transfer of shares, in order to provide a stable platform for restructuring. Temporary public ownership may be the most suitable resolution option if, for example, the Treasury has provided a failing institution with a significant amount of public money in order to stabilise it prior to its entry into the SRR. The option may also be exercised where it is necessary to resolve or reduce a serious threat to the stability of the UK's financial systems. This is the only option available in relation to a holding company of a bank.

5.22   A key determinant of the practicality of implementation will be the amount and quality of information available to the Authorities on the balance sheet and operations of the banking institution and on any interests of third parties.

5.23   Further issues which the Authorities will need to take into account in determining the feasibility of different tools include:

- the existence of, or likelihood of finding, a private sector purchaser;
- the likely saleability of assets and liabilities of the failing banking institution, including whether a whole institution sale is viable;
- the likely speed of FSCS payout to eligible depositors, and the method by which this would be achieved under the bank insolvency procedure;
- the feasibility of effecting a partial transfer in compliance with the safeguards set out in primary and secondary legislation;
- the operational risks of managing a bridge bank, and the amount of public funding that may be required to keep it operational, including consideration of State Aid issues; and
- the time available to implement a private sector sale, including for due diligence by potential purchasers.

5.24   Before determining which of the stabilisation options to use, the Bank of England must consult the FSA and the Treasury.

5.25   If the Treasury notifies the Bank of England that they have provided financial assistance in respect of a banking institution for the purpose of resolving or reducing a serious threat to financial stability, a different public interest condition must be satisfied before the Bank of England can exercise its stabilisation powers. This test is that the exercise of the power is necessary to protect the public interest. The Treasury will lead in judging that this public interest condition is met but the Bank of England will still lead in deciding that an exercise of a particular stabilisation option best protects that public interest.

Specific conditions for temporary public ownership

5.26   Under section 9, if the Treasury believe that an institution should be taken into temporary public ownership, specific conditions for this tool must be met in addition to the general condition relating to the failure to meet the threshold conditions. The specific condition is that the Treasury must be satisfied that such action is necessary to:

- resolve or reduce a serious threat to the stability of the financial systems of the UK; or
- protect the public interest, where the Treasury have provided financial assistance in respect of the banking institution for the purpose of resolving or reducing a serious threat to the stability of the financial systems of the UK.

5.27   Temporary public ownership is the only tool that can be used in respect of bank holding companies. There are specific considerations relevant to bank holding companies, which are outlined in paragraphs 5.35–5.41 of this Code.

Specific conditions for entering the bank insolvency procedure

5.28   Under section 96, an application to the court for a bank insolvency order may be made on one of three grounds:

- that a banking institution is insolvent, i e it is unable, or is likely to become unable, to pay its debts;
- that winding up the banking institution would be 'fair' (this has the same legal meaning as the phrase "just and equitable" in the Insolvency Act 1986); or
- that winding up the affairs of the banking institution would be fair and in the public interest (Secretary of State only).

5.29   The general conditions also apply to the bank insolvency procedure. Therefore, before the Bank of England or the FSA makes an application to the court for a bank insolvency order, the FSA must be satisfied that the conditions set out in section 7 of the Act have been met.

Specific considerations relevant to building societies

5.30   Under sections 84–88, the stabilisation options can also be applied to building societies.

5.31   Building societies have different corporate structures to banks. Individuals who have a share account or a mortgage with a building society are members and therefore have certain rights including rights to vote (with some limited exceptions) and receive information.[2] Each member of a building society has one vote, regardless of how much money they have invested or borrowed, or how many accounts they hold. Further, building society shares are not like company shares. Generally, shares in a building society can be withdrawn by investors in line with the society's rules and terms of issue. So, they are more like deposits. For these reasons, some of the SRR tools need to be tailored to building societies.

5.32   The private sector purchaser and bridge bank stabilisation options are broadly the same for building societies as they are for banks. However, the temporary public sector ownership stabilisation option for building societies is different to that for banks. This is because, given the ownership structure for building societies, it would not be possible to effect public ownership of a building society through a share transfer.

5.33   The Act therefore provides the Treasury with the power to take a building society into temporary public ownership through cancelling private membership rights and becoming a member of the society in question either by transferring all deferred shares, such as PIBS (Permanent Interest Bearing Shares, a special type of long-term, interest-bearing investment in a building society) to the Government or by issuing new deferred shares to Government on the building society's behalf.

5.34   The effect of taking a building society into temporary public ownership will be that customers lose voting and other membership rights but their savings and mortgages will be unaffected. Under section 86 these "former members" may be given a right to participate in the distribution of any surplus on the winding up of the society, once all creditors and any remaining members of the society had been paid in respect of their liabilities and shares.

Specific considerations relevant to bank holding companies

5.35   Under section 82, where it is necessary, the Treasury may bring the holding company of a banking institution into temporary public ownership.

5.36   A bank holding company may only be taken into temporary public ownership if the FSA is satisfied that a bank in the group satisfies the general conditions set out in section 7. The Treasury must also be satisfied that it is necessary to take action for the purposes specified in the specific conditions for temporary public ownership set out in section 9, to resolve or reduce a serious threat to the stability of the financial systems of the UK or to protect the public interest where financial assistance has been provided.

PART VI
OTHER MATERIALS

5.37   In determining whether it is necessary to take action in relation to the holding company, the Treasury will consider whether action in relation to the bank alone would be sufficient for the purposes specified in section 9.

5.38   Only the Treasury is able to exercise the power to take a bank holding company into temporary public ownership. In taking a decision to exercise the temporary public ownership tool in relation to a holding company, the Treasury will balance the interests of relevant parties against the public interest in resolving the difficulties caused by the failing bank.

5.39   Although holding company temporary public ownership is an option involving the whole of the holding company, partial transfers of the company's property may be carried out by the Treasury in onwards or other subsequent transfers to private sector purchasers. The limitations on partial property transfers provided for in sections 47, 48 and 60 of the Act, and secondary legislation made under them (and described in Chapter 7 of this Code), will also apply to bank holding companies.

5.40   The Treasury's legislative powers with respect to non-bank entities within the group are restricted. The full range of onward transfer powers (including the partial transfer powers discussed above) only apply to banks in the group and the holding company itself.

5.41   It is considered highly unlikely that circumstances would arise under which it would be possible or desirable for the Treasury to take a holding company into public ownership, where that holding company did not have a close connection with the operation of the bank or where the primary activities of the holding company were not closely related to financial services.

Announcement of tools

5.42   When publicly announcing any action to exercise the stabilisation options or initiate the bank insolvency procedure, the Bank of England will explain the grounds on which it considers that the conditions for the exercise of the tool (set out in section 8 or, for the bank insolvency procedure, section 96) are met.

5.43   When publicly announcing any action to take a banking institution into temporary public ownership the Treasury will explain the grounds on which it considers that the one of the conditions set out in section 9 (or, in the case of a holding company, the conditions in section 82) are met.

5.44   It should be noted that it may not be possible to divulge certain information where, for example, its release would threaten financial stability or confidence in the banking systems.

[2004]

---

[1]   Available in the FSA Handbook. The Threshold Conditions section of the handbook sets out the minimum standards for becoming and remaining authorised (reference code: COND). (http://fsahandbook.info)

[2]   Minors do not have voting rights, and societies can require shareholding members to hold at least £100 in shares to enjoy voting rights. Mortgage holders in subsidiaries of a building society will not have membership rights in the society itself, unless they also have a share account or mortgage directly with the society.

---

6 ENSURING THAT RESOLUTIONS ARE EFFECTIVE

6.1   There are a number of supplementary and ancillary powers that may be needed to ensure that resolutions are effective. This Code provides further information on powers are covered by sections 63–70 (continuity obligations), 26–31 (supplemental, reverse and onward share transfers), 42–46 (supplemental, reverse and onward property transfers) and 75 (power to change law).

Bridge Bank and Private Sector Purchaser: Supplemental, reverse and onwards transfers

6.2   The Bank of England may make supplemental, reverse or onward transfer instruments in relation to property or securities. Supplemental transfers allow further transfers of property or securities from the original owner to a bridge bank or private sector purchaser. Reverse transfers provide for property to be moved back from a bridge bank to the previous owner, subject to certain restrictions. Onward transfers allow for the bridge bank's property or shares in the bridge bank to be transferred to a private sector purchaser or a Treasury-or Bank of England-owned company. These powers increase the chances of a private-sector solution, reducing the barriers to an onwards sale.

6.3   This may become necessary, for example, if additional details come to light about the nature of the transferred securities, property or business, after the initial transfer, which would effect the saleability of the bridge bank, or the achievement of the SRR objectives more widely. The Bank of England must consult with the Treasury and the FSA before making any of these types of transfer instrument.

6.4   The general and specific conditions of SRR intervention do not apply to these transfer instruments as they form part of the continuing resolution, and the Authorities will already have determined that the conditions have been met by the failing banking institution on its entry into the SRR.

6.5 However, these tools can only be used in a manner consistent with the SRR objectives, and the general public law responsibilities governing the action of public bodies. In particular, where these further transfers interfere with property rights, the Bank of England must be satisfied that the action is in the public interest and is proportionate to the public interest aim being pursued.

6.6 Furthermore, such transfers can only be conducted in accordance with the safeguards for partial property transfers provided for in secondary legislation made under sections 47, 48 and 60 of the Act.

6.7 These considerations also apply to the Treasury, in its exercise of supplemental, reverse and onwards transfers, as described in the next sections.

TPO: Supplemental, reverse and onwards transfers

6.8 Where a banking institution has been taken into temporary public ownership, the Treasury may make supplemental and reverse transfers of securities. Supplemental transfers provide for transfers of further classes of securities from the holders of those securities to public ownership. Reverse transfers provide for property to be moved back from public ownership to the original holders.

6.9 The Treasury may also effect an onward transfer of the shares or business of a bank in temporary public ownership. These powers increase the chances of a private-sector solution, reducing the barriers to an onwards sale of a bridge bank or a bank in temporary public ownership.

6.10 These subsequent transfers may become necessary, for example, if additional details come to light about the nature of the transferred securities or business after the initial transfer. As with all other forms of transfer, the Treasury must consult with the Bank of England and the FSA before making the order.

Powers in relation to holding companies in temporary public ownership

6.11 Under section 82, the Act provides for powers in relation to holding companies in temporary public ownership, similar to those for banks in temporary public ownership. These are limited in important respects. In particular, the Treasury's powers in respect of non-bank entities within the group are limited in that the full range of onward transfer powers only applies to deposit-takers in the group and the holding company itself. The Treasury may:

- make an onwards share transfer or reverse share transfer of the securities issued by the failing bank or another bank within the group;
- make an onward share transfer or reverse share transfer of the securities of the bank holding company; and
- make an onwards property transfer of the property of the bank holding company, a bank or another bank within the group (including property which takes the form of securities, for example shares held in a subsidiary undertaking).

6.12 However, it is not otherwise possible under the Act for the Treasury to transfer the shares or property of any non-bank subsidiaries within the group. Resolution of these parts of the group (ie their return to the private sector) will therefore need to be undertaken via normal commercial routes.

Continuity obligations

6.13 Where it is necessary to use a stabilisation option in respect of an individual banking institution that forms part of a group of companies, the general continuity obligations will apply.

6.14 Group companies will be obliged under the continuity obligations to provide services and facilities that the Bank of England or Treasury considers are required to enable the acquirer of the transferred business to operate it effectively. A general continuity obligation will arise following a transfer automatically, by operation of law.

6.15 In addition, it may be appropriate to impose special continuity obligations. These obligations will be restricted to ensuring that necessary services and facilities continue to be provided to the business transferred.

6.16 The special obligations provide powers to create, modify or cancel contracts and confer or impose rights and obligations between a transferee and the group companies of a residual bank and the residual bank itself – but only in relation to services and facilities required to operate the banking business effectively. Providers will be due reasonable consideration for any services provided.

6.17 The Bank of England may only exercise these powers with Treasury consent, and Ministers will assess the broad public interest of the particular situation.

Power to change law

6.18   Where necessary for the purpose of enabling the powers of Part 1 of the Act to be used effectively, the Treasury may exercise its power under section 75 of the Act to modify legislation. This power may be used in respect of both primary and secondary legislation, and the provisions of common law.

6.19   The power may only be used to facilitate or in connection with the use of one the stabilisation options. The power may be used in two ways:

- to make a specific amendment to a piece of legislation for the purposes of making the resolution of a specific banking institution effective. Generally, such an amendment would only apply to that banking institution or a related institution (eg a group company). It would not generally apply to any other banks, or any other banking institutions; or
- to make an amendment to legislation that is applied to all resolutions or a class of resolutions carried out under the SRR. This would then apply in each resolution where the Bank of England or the Treasury used a stabilisation tool.

6.20   The power can be used retrospectively if this is necessary or desirable for giving effect to the particular exercise of a power under the Act. However in using the power, the Treasury must have regard to the fact that it is in the public interest to avoid retrospection. The Treasury will also necessarily have regard to existing public law restrictions, in particular the requirement on the Treasury to have respect for the rule of law and legal certainty. In addition the Treasury must have regard to the special resolution objectives and act compatibly with the Convention rights. Thus the power could not be used for purposes unconnected with the use of the powers under the Act, for example to change the law for wider public policy objectives.

6.21   The power cannot be used to amend the Act itself, or any standing secondary legislation made under it. The power can be used in relation to an instrument or order made in the exercise of a stabilisation power, including transfer orders and instruments.

6.22   In general, exercise of the power to change law will be approved in advance by Parliament under the draft affirmative resolution procedure. Where the Treasury consider it to be necessary to make an order without prior Parliamentary approval, the 28-day procedure will be used. Under this procedure, the order can be made and brought into force immediately but will cease to have effect 28 days later unless approved by both Houses of Parliament.

6.23   The Banking Liaison Panel has a statutory right to provide advice on use of the power to change law. However, this does not include a right to provide advice on an exercise of this power that is carried out in connection with or to facilitate a particular use (proposed or actual) of a stabilisation power.

[2005]

7 PARTIAL TRANSFERS AND SAFEGUARDS

Partial transfers

7.1   The property transfer powers (sections 33–48) provide the flexibility to transfer just some, but not necessarily all, of the property of a failing institution. The Bank of England (or following temporary public ownership, the Treasury) will exercise the power to effect a partial transfer when they believe that this approach will best meet the special resolution objectives.

7.2   The most likely use for this power is to transfer the 'good' part of an institution's business to a new entity – either a private sector purchaser or a bridge bank – with a 'residual bank' left behind, containing any assets and liabilities that are not transferred.

7.3   It is also possible to exercise the power to move 'bad' assets to a bridge bank leaving the residual company solvent.

7.4   The Authorities recognise the significant potential for partial property transfers to interfere with vital market interests including set-off and netting arrangements and security interests. The Act provides that limits may be placed on the ability of the Bank of England or the Treasury to make partial property transfers. Such limits are set out in secondary legislation, as set out in Chapter 7 of this Code.

Bank administration procedure

7.5   Part 3 of the Act provides for a bank administration procedure to be applied following a partial property transfer. This procedure may be required in the event of a partial transfer of a banking institution's business to a bridge bank or private sector purchaser. Where a partial transfer of property takes place, the 'residual bank' (the part left behind) may be insolvent. Despite being insolvent, it may be vital that the residual bank continues to provide services and facilities to the purchaser or bridge bank where these are required to enable the transferred business to be operated effectively. For example, it might be impossible to transfer certain business assets or service contracts as part of the initial arrangements. These items may be vital for the successful operation of the transferred business.

7.6   Therefore, the Act provides that the Bank of England may make an application to the court for a bank administration order.

7.7   The bank administration procedure is a new insolvency procedure created to deal with an insolvent residual bank following a partial transfer. It is largely based on existing insolvency provisions, specifically the administration procedure as set out in Schedule B1 to the Insolvency Act 1986. It is designed to ensure that any essential services and facilities that cannot be immediately transferred to a bridge bank or private sector purchaser will continue to be provided, for a period of time.

7.8   The bank administration procedure imposes on the bank administrator an objective to ensure the supply of essential services and facilities to the transferee. To this end, the bank administrator will have unique statutory objectives: firstly, to provide support to a private sector purchaser or bridge bank in relation to the transferred business; and secondly to rescue the residual bank as a going concern or wind up its affairs in the best interests of creditors.

7.9   By obliging the residual bank to continue to provide services to the transferee, the bank administration procedure is intended to increase the likelihood of a successful resolution of a failing banking institution's business.

7.10   Once the Bank of England considers that it is no longer necessary for the residual bank to continue to provide support services, the procedure will continue in a similar way to an ordinary administration although to keep down costs, maximise returns to creditors, and to protect the interests of creditors by providing for a full-range range of outcomes, some of the existing powers of a liquidator have been built in to the procedure.

Safeguards for partial property transfers

7.11   Partial property transfers under the Act are subject to restrictions imposed by secondary legislation, to ensure that banking institution creditors and counterparties are adequately protected, thereby mitigating any negative market consequences. These legislative safeguards are intended to continue to allow the flexibility to execute a bank partial transfer where necessary. The Treasury will keep the safeguards under review.

7.12   The safeguards, which are established in secondary legislation[1] (the safeguard order), are:
- a broad safeguard for set-off and netting arrangements;
- a broad protection for secured liabilities;
- protection for structured finance arrangements (such as covered bonds and securitisations);
- a requirement to establish a compensation scheme which has regard to ensuring that no pre-transfer creditor is "worse off" than they would have been had the institution gone into an insolvency process;
- restrictions on reverse partial transfers, which prevent the Bank of England or the Treasury from transferring certain types of financial contract from the solvent 'newco' back to an insolvent 'resco', in the interests of ensuring those transferred to 'newco' can have confidence in their position;
- protection for default rules of clearing houses and investment exchanges and market contracts, reflecting protections under Part VII of the Companies Act 1989;
- an express bar on action in contravention of Community law;
- prohibition on use of the powers to provide for continuity of intra-group services and facilities in a way which would contravene the key safeguards provided for in the Safeguards Order; and
- targeted protections for termination rights under financial contracts (that are relevant for set-off and netting).

7.13   Remedies in the event of a breach of a safeguard are set out in the secondary legislation. The Authorities are under a statutory duty to comply with the safeguards, and this duty is unaffected by the existence of such remedies. The remedy provisions exist to provide certainty to the market as to the outcome should the safeguards be inadvertently contravened.

7.14   The Authorities consider that the provision of certainty is relevant to achievement of special resolution objectives 1, 2 and 5. And further, the Authorities will necessarily have regard to restrictions and conventions of public law, in particular the requirement on Government of respect for the rule of law and legal certainty.

[2006]

---

[1]   Available from the Office of Public Sector Information website, in the section covering Statutory Instruments (2009) numbers 300–399 (www.opsi.gov.uk).

8 GOVERNANCE ARRANGEMENTS FOR BRIDGE BANKS

8.1   Bridge banks are defined in section 12 of the Act.

Bridge bank objectives

8.2   A bridge bank is intended to be a short-term operation, until appropriate private sector solutions can be arranged and implemented.

8.3   To this end, the primary bridge bank objective shall be to facilitate the sale of a bridge bank – in whole or in part – to one or more private sector purchasers.

8.4   Insofar as the pursuance of that objective is not compromised, the Bank of England shall take steps to manage its relationship with the bridge bank at arm's length. However, an arm's length arrangement may not be appropriate if a bridge bank is only in existence for a short period of time (as is intended and envisaged). Paragraphs 8.11–8.14 of this Code provide further guidance on this point.

8.5   In some circumstances, it may not be feasible for some or all of a bridge bank's business to be transferred to a private sector purchaser. In these circumstances, the bridge bank will either be wound up, in a manner that meets the special resolution objectives and is in the interests of the remaining creditors of the bridge bank, or taken into temporary public ownership.

8.6   It should be noted that the bridge bank objectives are subordinate to the special resolution objectives. In situations where there is a conflict between the two sets of objectives, the special resolution objectives take precedence.

Contents of property transfer instruments

8.7   Section 33 of the Act describes the provisions that a property transfer instrument may make. There are a number of options for how an instrument may describe which property, rights and liabilities have been transferred. Section 33(2) provides that "a property transfer instrument may relate to– (a) all property, rights and liabilities of the specified bank, (b) all its property, rights and liabilities subject to specified exceptions, (c) specified property, rights or liabilities, or (d) property, rights or liabilities of a specified description."

8.8   The Bank of England shall take steps to specify appropriately in the given circumstances which property, rights and liabilities of a failing banking institution have been transferred.

8.9   Once a property transfer instrument is made, the Treasury shall lay a copy in the Houses of Parliament.

Establishment

8.10   The Bank of England shall establish or acquire an incorporated company to which property, rights and liabilities will be transferred. The Bank will work with the FSA to arrange appropriate authorisations where necessary to carry on the relevant regulated activities. The company will need to comply with authorisation requirements on an ongoing basis and will be subject to FSA supervision.

Nature of the shareholder relationship

8.11   A bridge bank when it is established or acquired will be a company limited by shares that is wholly owned by the Bank of England.

8.12   The nature of the shareholder relationship with a bridge bank will vary depending on the nature of each resolution and the particular 'phase' of the resolution. In broad terms, a bridge bank might go through a number of phases, and the key phases include:

- the stabilisation phase, immediately following the transfer; and
- the sale / purchase phase, where the Bank works with one or more private sector purchaser to transfer the business while managing the bridge bank on a conservative basis.

8.13   In many cases the purchase phase may immediately follow the stabilisation phase. In these situations, it is likely that arm's length management may not be appropriate. The Bank would be expected to take an active role in managing the affairs of the bank, first to ensure stabilisation, and second to ensure a successful transaction.

8.14   However, in situations where there is expected to be a lengthy period of time prior to a sale, the Bank shall put in place an appropriate governance structure. This structure shall be based on the objective of taking steps to manage the relationship with the bridge bank at arm's length.

8.15   Arm's length is defined as leaving the day-to-day management of the bridge bank to its board of directors and keeping shareholder involvement at a strategic level (for example, the Bank shall have an oversight role to ensure that its objectives continue to be met in the face of changing circumstances).

Articles of association

8.16   The articles of association of a bridge bank will provide for the company regulations governing the relationship between the Bank of England (in its capacity as shareholder) and the directors of the company. These articles will be based on the model articles prescribed by the Secretary of State for a limited liability company but with such modifications as are necessary or appropriate. Such modifications shall be based on what best meets the bridge bank objectives.

Directors

8.17   The Bank of England shall take steps to put in place appropriate arrangements for the management of a bridge bank.

8.18   As noted above, the nature of the management structure put in place will depend on the particular circumstances of the resolution. Over the period of stabilisation, the management arrangements may involve a relatively small core of directors with appropriate skills and experience. If a bridge bank is, as intended, only in existence for a short period of time, then this arrangement may remain suitable.

8.19   In circumstances where the bridge bank exists for a longer period of time, the Bank shall take steps to ensure the composition of the board of directors continues to remain appropriate. This may include appointing additional directors. The composition of the board will be decided by the Bank on a case-by-case basis, and having regard to relevant regulation and legislation.

8.20   At any time over the course of the resolution, the bridge bank's board of directors may or may not include employees of the Bank of England.

8.21   In addition, board members and senior managers performing key functions will need to be approved persons for the purposes of the FSA's regime, although there may be transitional arrangements in appropriate cases.

Operating strategy

8.22   The operating strategy for a bridge bank shall be decided by what best meets the bridge bank objectives. This is likely to involve the bridge bank operating on a conservative basis, to protect the franchise value of the business, and provide continuity of banking services.

8.23   The Bank of England shall take steps to ensure that the bridge bank meets it regulatory requirements for its relevant regulated activities, including taking necessary steps to comply with relevant FSA requirements.

8.24   In its role as shareholder, the Bank of England shall work with the board of directors to decide on how the bridge bank should be operated. A business plan will be required for authorisation purposes. Where appropriate, the board shall produce a business plan setting out how the directors intend to operate the bridge bank in a manner pursuant to meeting the objectives. This business plan shall be presented to the Bank of England, who shall ensure that it meets the Bank of England's objectives for the resolution. If a bridge bank exists for only a short amount of time it may be unnecessary to go through this process.

Reporting

8.25   Bridge banks are covered by a number of reporting requirements. These are:
- the provision of section 80(1) of the Act (a "bridge bank report");
- the provision of section 80(5) of the Act (a "specific report"); and
- any other reports as agreed between the directors of the bridge bank and the Bank of England.

Bridge bank report

8.26   It is envisaged that a bridge bank will typically exist for less than one year: It is intended to be a short-term operation. While a bridge bank report is not required in these circumstances, the Bank of England shall report appropriately about the resolution to the Chancellor.

8.27   In the event that a bridge bank continues to exist after one year, the Bank of England must report to the Chancellor about the activities of the bridge bank. The first report must be made as soon as is reasonably practicable after the end of one year beginning with the date of the first transfer to the bridge bank. A similar report must also be made as soon as is reasonably practicable after the end of each subsequent year. Such reports shall include:
- an account of the activities of the bridge bank over the year; and
- how the Bank of England is intending to achieve the bridge bank objectives.

8.28   When compiling the report, the Bank of England may choose to not reveal market-sensitive information.

8.29   These reports to the Chancellor are supplementary to the reporting arrangements that the Bank of England in its role as shareholder will put in place to ensure it receives appropriate management information from a bridge bank.

PART VI
OTHER MATERIALS

Specific report

8.30   The contents of specific reports will be determined on a case-by-case basis, dependent on the specific request of the Treasury.

Other reports

8.31   In addition to bridge bank reports and specific reports, and the reporting requirements imposed on the bridge bank pursuant to the Companies Act 2006, the Bank of England shall consider, in each case, whether the bridge bank should have regard to any additional reporting requirements to which similar commercial banks may be subject. In addition, the Bank of England shall make arrangements to provide for regulatory reporting appropriate to the activities undertaken by the bridge bank.

Disposal and onward transfer

8.32   The primary bridge bank objective is to facilitate the sale of a bridge bank – in whole or in part – to one or more private sector purchasers. It is envisaged that a sale of business should follow as soon as possible after the initial transfer of property to a bridge bank.

8.33   In each case, the Bank of England shall establish an appropriate mechanism for selecting a preferred purchaser and agreeing on a price for the business of the bridge bank. In its assessment the Bank of England shall take account of the special resolution objectives (section 4 of the Act). It shall also work with the FSA to ensure that the acquiring party is suitable for taking on the bridge bank's business.

8.34   Following this process, the Bank of England shall complete the transaction. This may be achieved through a standard commercial agreement (for example, a sale of securities, or an asset sale using the Part 7 process of FSMA) or by exercising the onward transfer powers provided in the Act, either by making a bridge bank share transfer instrument (section 28) or an onward property transfer instrument (section 40).

8.35   In some circumstances it may be appropriate to transfer some or all of a bridge bank's business to a public-sector transferee, either a company wholly owned by the Treasury or an onward bridge bank (defined in section 12). However, this would only occur if it best met the bridge bank objectives.

[2007]

9 GOVERNANCE ARRANGEMENTS FOR INSTITUTIONS IN TEMPORARY PUBLIC OWNERSHIP

9.1   Temporary public ownership is described in section 13 of the Act.

Temporary public ownership objectives

9.2   The objectives of an institution in temporary public ownership will reflect the special resolution objectives. Where possible, the intention shall be to return the business of the bank to the private sector in a manner that maintains financial stability and protects depositors and the taxpayer while acting in a way that promotes competition.

Contents of share transfer orders

9.3   Section 16 of the Act describes the provision a share transfer order may make. A share transfer order may relate to either specified securities or securities of a specified description.

9.4   The Treasury shall take steps to specify appropriately which securities of a failing institution have been transferred.

The nature of institutions in temporary public ownership

9.5   The securities of a bank in temporary public ownership shall either be held by a nominee of the Treasury (for example, the Treasury Solicitor) or by a company wholly owned by the Treasury.

9.6   Provision will be made as to the relationship between the Treasury (in its capacity as shareholder) and the directors of the company. As shareholder, the Treasury will have the power to exercise normal shareholder rights.

9.7   Immediately following the transfer of securities and for the initial period of stabilisation, the Treasury may take a 'hands on' role in managing the affairs of the bank. However, once stabilised, the Treasury shall seek to introduce corporate governance arrangements in line with best practice, as soon as is reasonably practicable. The nature of these arrangements will depend on how likely the bank is to remain in public ownership. If a bank is likely to remain in public ownership for longer than a short period (to be determined on a case by case basis), the Treasury shall set out for the directors objectives as to how the bank should be operated. Based on these objectives, the board shall produce a business plan setting out how the directors intend to operate the bank.

9.8   The plan may include:
- a commercial strategy;

- a funding plan, including arrangements for repaying any public money that has been provided;
- a risk management strategy; and
- an approach for complying with competition issues, state aid and regulatory requirements.

9.9   This business plan shall be presented to the Treasury, who shall ensure that it meets the Treasury's objectives for the banking institution.

9.10   The Treasury shall then take an oversight role to ensure that the plan continues to meet its objectives in the face of changing circumstances.

9.11   In many cases, it will be appropriate for the Treasury to develop and implement an investment strategy for disposing of the investments in an orderly way.

9.12   Insofar as the banking institution carries on relevant regulated activities, the FSA shall continue to authorise and regulate it where appropriate.

Arm's length management of institutions in temporary public ownership

9.13   In circumstances where an institution is likely to remain in public ownership for longer than a short period, the Treasury may seek to put in place arrangements to operate the bank at arm's length, for example through UK Financial Investments Limited (UKFI), which is an arm's length company wholly owned by the Government.[1]

9.14   In such circumstances, the Treasury may set out objectives for the directors as to how the bank should be operated. It is likely that these objectives would include protecting and creating value with due regard to the special resolution objectives, and maintaining and promoting competition in the banking sector.

Disposal of institutions in temporary public ownership

9.15   Sale of the institution in temporary public ownership may be carried out through normal commercial means, or existing statutory mechanisms. However, the Treasury may alternatively make an onward share transfer, by order (under section 28), or onward property transfer, by order (under section 45). These may be more expeditious and therefore command more confidence than a transfer through existing commercial or statutory processes. The powers to make such orders provide for swift and effective transfer to a private sector purchaser, maximising the commercial opportunities and minimising risks to the purchaser.

9.16   Where an institution in temporary public ownership is being managed at arm's length by a separate body, it will be the responsibility of the arm's-length body, with appropriate consultation with the Treasury, to develop and execute an investment strategy for disposing of the investments in an orderly and active way.

Reporting

9.17   The Treasury shall make arrangements to ensure that a bank in temporary public ownership reports on a similar basis to other commercial banks. This includes regulatory reporting appropriate to the activities undertaken by the bank. In addition section 81 of the Act requires the Chancellor of the Exchequer to report to Parliament on an annual basis about the activities of a bank in temporary public ownership.

[2008]

---

[1]   Further information is available from the UKFI website (www.ukfi.gov.uk).

---

10 COMPENSATION

10.1   Sections 49–62 of the Act make provision for the assessment of any compensation which may be due to those affected by an exercise of the stabilisation options, or where onward and reverse transfers are made. Provision is made for three types of orders, which may be made for the purposes of assessing or providing compensation:

- **compensation scheme orders**, which establish a scheme to determine whether compensation should be paid to transferors;[1] or provide for transferors to be paid compensation, and establish a scheme for this purpose;
- **resolution fund orders**, which establish a scheme under which the transferors become entitled to the proceeds of resolution in specified circumstances, and to a specified extent; and
- **third party compensation orders**, which establish a scheme for paying compensation to third parties (persons who are not transferors), for example counterparties of a bank who suffer compensatable interferences in their property rights as a result of an exercise of the powers under Part 1 of the Act.

Bank resolution fund and the associated management duty

10.2   The purpose of a bank resolution fund is to provide the failing bank or its former shareholders, as the case may be, with a contingent economic interest in the proceeds of the resolution of a failing bank. These proceed may include, for example, the proceeds from the sale of property transferred from a failing bank into a bridge bank.

10.3   A resolution fund order (under section 49) may make provision establishing who will be entitled to a share of the proceeds, and the manner in which the shares of the proceeds will be calculated.

10.4   The proceeds may be calculated net of any resolution costs. These could include the costs of financial assistance – including loans or guarantees provided from or backed by public funds or administrative expenses incurred by the Authorities during the course of the resolution. This is to ensure that the taxpayer receives a suitable return for public funds that have been invested or put at risk during the course of the resolution.

10.5   The Treasury may specify in a resolution fund order that the resolution authority, the Bank of England or the Treasury, is required to maximise the proceeds available for distribution (a "management duty"). However, the management duty must be complied with only in so far as compatible with the pursuit of the special resolution objectives, and the compliance with the Code of Practice under section 5.

10.6   In determining whether to impose such a management duty, the Treasury will have regard to a number of factors, including the length of time the resolution is likely to take.

10.7   The resolution fund order may also include provision for the determination of any disputes about the application of its provisions.

Independent valuer

10.8   A compensation scheme order may provide for an independent valuer to be appointed to determine the amount of compensation, if any, due to those persons affected by an exercise of the stabilisation options. Alternatively, a compensation scheme order may provide for transferors (i e the former shareholders in the case of a share transfer, or the failing bank in the case of a property transfer) to be paid compensation. This may be achieved by the deeming of the amount paid by a private sector purchaser for the property of a bank to be the compensation due to the transferors.

10.9   A person appointed to determine the amount of compensation, if any, payable under a compensation scheme order or a third party compensation order must be independent and impartial. Sections 54–56 make extensive provision for providing for and safeguarding the independence and impartiality of the valuer. For example:

- the valuer must be appointed by a person appointed by the Treasury; and
- an independent monitor must be appointed to oversee the arrangements for the remuneration and allowances of the valuer.

10.10   The Act provides that in conducting his or her valuation exercise, the independent valuer must:

- disregard actual or potential financial assistance provided by the Bank of England or the Treasury (other than ordinary market assistance offered by the Bank on its usual terms), and
- have regard to any valuation principles specified by the Treasury in the compensation scheme order.

Appointment of the valuer and criteria for independence

10.11   The Treasury is required to appoint a person to appoint the independent valuer. It is possible that the Treasury might appoint more than one person for this function, in order to form an appointment panel. The appointing person or panel will appoint the valuer through a competitive and fair process. The following criteria will be relevant for an applicant to be considered for appointment as valuer:

- **Demonstrable independence** from Government and interested parties; and
- **Freedom from conflicts of interest**: potential candidates may be ruled out because of actual or potential conflicts of interest.

10.12   In considering which person to appoint, the following additional criteria will be relevant:

1   **Professional skills and experience**: the primary qualification for the valuer is that he or she must have extensive professional financial company valuation skills. The valuer is likely to need to draw on a range of professional expertise, notably accountancy, investment banking and legal expertise in performing the function of valuation

2   **Experience and ability to carry out a high profile public process**: in addition to being able to carry out the professional task of assessing any compensation, the valuer will need to have the capacity, resources, and robustness to—

    a.   manage a high-profile, potentially multi-stage, public process; and

    b.   explain his or her assessment to a range of different audiences (for example, affected individuals, corporate stakeholder, or potentially a tribunal or court in the event of a legal challenge) in writing, in person and through professional intermediaries such as lawyers if necessary.

3   **Track record of timely delivery**: applicants will need to demonstrate by reference to an existing track record that they will be adequately resourced and capable of discharging the function of independent valuer in a timely and efficient manner in the absence of conventional contract performance management by a client.

4   **Value for money** is also an important criterion against which candidates will be assessed.

Valuer's remuneration and role of the monitor

10.13   Under section 56, the Treasury shall pay the remuneration and expenses of the independent valuer.

10.14   The Treasury will put in place a monitor to oversee the remuneration and any allowances for the independent valuer, including his or her pension arrangements. As part of this role, the monitor may be required to approve certain actions or to authorise certain expenditures. The Treasury will remunerate and reimburse the expenses of the monitor.

Valuation principles

10.15   The Treasury may establish principles for the conduct of the valuation in addition to the mandatory valuation assumption. For example, the Treasury could:

- specify certain methods or matters to be taken into account; and
- require certain assumptions to be made as to the status of the bank had it not entered the SRR.

[2009]

---

¹   For example, the former shareholders of a bank where the securities transfer powers are exercised, or a failing bank where the property transfer powers are exercised.

A LIST OF ABBREVIATIONS

the Act	the Banking Act 2009
the Authorities	the Financial Service Authority, the Bank of England and the Treasury
the Code	the Banking Act 2009 special resolution regime Code of Practice
Convention Right	a right under the European Convention of Human Rights, within the meaning of the Human Rights Act 1998
FSA	Financial Service Authority
FSCS	Financial Services Compensation Scheme
FSMA	Financial Services and Markets Act 2000
PIBS	Permanent Interest Bearing Shares
SRR	special resolution regime
the stabilisation options	transfer to a private sector purchaser, transfer to a bridge bank and transfer to temporary public sector ownership
UKFI	UK Financial Investments Limited

[2010]

DUNFERMLINE BUILDING SOCIETY PROPERTY TRANSFER INSTRUMENT 2009

NOTES

© Bank of England

Note: this Instrument is reproduced as amended by the Amendments to Law (Resolution of the Dunfermline Building Society) (No 2) Order 2009, SI 2009/1805 at **[598]**; the amendments have been taken in by LexisNexis editors and do not appear in the original version of this document which can be found at www.bankofengland.co.uk.

PART VI
OTHER MATERIALS

Made: 30 March 2009

Coming into force: 30 March 2009

This Instrument is made by the Bank of England in the exercise of the powers conferred by sections 11(2), 12(2), 34, 35, 36, 37, 38, 39, 40 and 84 of the Banking Act.

In accordance with section 7 of that Act (as applied by section 84), the FSA is satisfied that—
> Dunfermline is failing, or is likely to fail, to satisfy the threshold conditions (within the meaning of section 41(1) of the Financial Services and Markets Act 2000 (c. 8)); and
> having regard to timing and other relevant circumstances it is not reasonably likely that (ignoring the stabilisation powers) action will be taken by or in respect of Dunfermline that will enable it to satisfy the threshold conditions.

In accordance with section 7(5) of that Act (as applied by section 84), the FSA has consulted the Bank of England and the Treasury.

In accordance with section 8 of that Act (as applied by section 84), the Bank of England is satisfied that it is necessary to make this Instrument having regard to the public interest considerations specified in section 8(2).

In accordance with section 8(3) of that Act (as applied by section 84), the Bank of England has consulted the FSA and the Treasury and has obtained the consent of the Treasury to the use of public funds under section 78(1) of that Act.

In accordance with section 4(2) of that Act the Bank of England has had regard to the special resolution objectives.

In accordance with section 5(4) of that Act, the Bank of England has had regard to the code of practice published by the Treasury under section 5 of that Act.

The Treasury have notified the Bank of England that, for the purposes of making the transfer to be effected by this Instrument possible and in connection with the transfer, the Treasury have agreed to pay to the Nationwide a sum in respect of the liabilities that are to be transferred to it from Dunfermline, by virtue of the transfer effected by paragraph 3 of this Instrument and to be determined in accordance with the Nationwide payment agreement.

Accordingly, the Bank of England makes the following Instrument —

PART 1
GENERAL

Citation and commencement

1.—(1)   This Instrument may be cited as the Dunfermline Building Society Property Transfer Instrument 2009.

(2)   This Instrument comes into force at the transfer time.

Interpretation: general

2.   In this Instrument:
> "acquired mortgage loan" means a mortgage loan which Dunfermline has acquired from a third party;
> "the Banking Act" means the Banking Act 2009, (c 1);
> "Bridge Bank" means PT Shelfco (Scot) Limited, a company with the registered number 356970 incorporated in Scotland under Scots law whose registered office is at 24 Great King Street, Edinburgh EH 3 6QN;
> "Bridge Bank transfer" means the transfer effected by paragraph 12;
> "Bridge Bank business" means the property, rights and liabilities transferred by paragraph 12;
> "Bridge Bank excluded property, rights and liabilities" has the meaning given in paragraph 14;
> "Building Societies Act" means the Building Societies Act 1986 (c 53);
> ["commercial loan" means—
>> (a)   a loan, including a mortgage loan, made or agreed to be made by or on behalf of Dunfermline and which at the transfer time is designated in Dunfermline's books and records with one of the reference numbers set out in the Schedule;
>> (b)   the loans acquired by Dunfermline on 15th April 2004 from DB UK Bank Limited (company registered number 00315841) and Morgan Grenfell (Local Authority Finance) Limited (company registered number 01672903) and identified in Dunfermline's books and records as "Dortmund" loans;]
>
> ...
>
> association; "deposit" has the meaning given by article 5 of the Regulated Activities Order (disregarding the exclusions in articles 6 to 9AA of that Order);
> "Dunfermline" means Dunfermline Building Society, incorporated under the Building Societies Act with registered number 9B(S);

"Dunfermline Nominees" means Dunfermline BS Nominees Limited (company number SC113202);

"eligible claimant" has the meaning given by rule 4.2.1 of the Compensation Sourcebook made by the FSA under the Financial Services and Markets Act 2000 (c 8);

"excluded property, rights and liabilities" has the meaning given in paragraph 3(3);

"the FSA" means the Financial Services Authority;

"FRNs" means the £250,000,000 Floating Rate Notes issued by Dunfermline due 30th March 2009;

"housing association" means a society, body of trustees, or company, which is established for the purpose of, or amongst whose objects or powers are included those of providing, constructing, improving or managing, or facilitating or encouraging the construction or improvement of housing accommodation, and which does not trade for profit or whose constitution or rules prohibit the issue of capital with interest or dividend exceeding such rate as may be described by the Treasury, whether with or without differentiation as between share and loan capital and including a registered social landlord under the Housing (Scotland) Act 2001;

"housing association deposit" means any deposit made by a housing association with Dunfermline; "housing association loan" means any loan or mortgage loan made by Dunfermline to a housing association;

"membership rights" means constitutional and ownership rights and obligations, and include—

    (a)   voting rights;

    (b)   the right to participate in the distribution of any surplus assets;

    (c)   rights to requisition meetings;

    (d)   rights in relation to the appointment of directors;

    (e)   the right to receive information;

    (f)   rights and obligations arising from a charitable assignment declaration of Nationwide; and

    (g)   all other rights of a similar nature;

"mortgage loan" means a loan which is fully or substantially secured on heritable, leasehold or other real property;

"Nationwide" means Nationwide Building Society, incorporated under the Building Societies Act with registered number 355B;

"Nationwide business" means the property, rights and liabilities transferred by paragraph 3;

"Nationwide payment agreement" means the agreement entered into between the Treasury and the Nationwide relating to the payment to be made to Nationwide by the Treasury in connection with the transfer (as mentioned in the ninth recital to this instrument);

"Nationwide transfer" means the transfer effected by paragraph 3;

"Partial Property Transfers Order" means The Banking Act 2009 (Restrictions of Partial Property Transfers) Order 2009;

"pension scheme" means the Dunfermline Building Society 1974 Pension and Life Assurance Scheme established by deeds dated 19th and 21st November 1960 and currently governed by a deed of amendment attaching rules, which is effective on and from 6 April 2006;

"Regulated Activities Order" means The Financial Services and Markets Act 2000 (Regulated Activities) Order 2001 (as amended);

"relevant loan account" means an account opened by the Nationwide in respect of any loan fully secured on land which was outstanding to Dunfermline and was transferred to the Nationwide upon the transfer;

"relevant undertaking" means Dunfermline or any of its subsidiary undertakings within the meaning of section 1159 of the Companies Act 2006;

"security rights" means any standard security, mortgages, charges, pledges, liens or other security rights or interests granted in order to secure an obligation and any reference to property, rights and liabilities in this Instrument shall be considered to include a reference to security rights;

"share" (other than in sub-paragraph 3(3)(f)); "shareholding member" and references to the value of shares are to be construed in accordance with section 119 of the Building Societies Act;

"share account" means any share account with Dunfermline;

"tax" means all taxes, whether of the United Kingdom or otherwise, including those taxes listed in section 74(2) of the Banking Act and value added tax; and "the transfer time" is 8 a.m. on 30th March 2009 (and is used in the Instrument to denote the time that the Nationwide transfer and the Bridge Bank transfer take place in pursuance of paragraphs 3 and 12 respectively from which other things take effect).

[2011]

NOTES

    Para 2: definition "commercial loan" substituted and definition "commercial mortgage loan" (omitted) repealed by the Amendments to Law (Resolution of the Dunfermline Building Society) (No 2) Order 2009, SI 2009/1805, art 2(1)–(3), with effect from 30 March 2009 at 8.00 am (see art 1(2) of the 2009 Order at **[598]**).

The amendments have been taken in by LexisNexis editors and do not appear in the original version of this document which can be found at www.bankofengland.co.uk.

PART 2
THE NATIONWIDE TRANSFER

Nationwide Transfer

3.—(1)   By virtue of this Instrument, all property, rights and liabilities (including the Dunfermline brand name and all property, rights and liabilities that fall within any of the descriptions specified in section 35(1) of the Banking Act) of Dunfermline are transferred to the Nationwide other than excluded property, rights and liabilities.

(2)   The transfer takes place at the transfer time.

(3)   "excluded property, rights and liabilities" means—
    (a)   the Bridge Bank business;
    (b)   all medium term notes and residential mortgage-backed securities held by Dunfermline as treasury assets;
    (c)   all property, rights and liabilities in respect of the £50,000,000 6 per cent. Subordinated Notes due 2015 issued by Dunfermline;
    (d)   all property, rights and liabilities in respect of acquired mortgage loans and all other property, rights and liabilities which relate solely to the acquired mortgage loans or which relate to the acquired mortgage loans to a greater extent than to the other property, rights and liabilities of Dunfermline;
    (e)   all property, rights and liabilities in respect of commercial loans … and all other property, rights and liabilities which relate solely to the commercial loans … or which relate to the commercial loans … to a greater extent than to the other property, rights and liabilities of Dunfermline;
    (f)   the shares held by Dunfermline in Dunfermline Solutions Limited (company number SC113203), Dunfermline Commercial Finance Limited (company number SC113201) and Dunfermline Development Services Limited (company number SC113429) and any rights (including membership rights) and liabilities of Dunfermline in respect of Funds Transfer Sharing Limited (company number 01850222);
    (g)   the rights and liabilities of Dunfermline in respect of shares held by shareholding members, other than the aggregate liabilities that Dunfermline would have owed to shareholding members if shareholding members had given notice of withdrawal effective immediately before the transfer time;
    (h)   any liability specified in sub-paragraph 7(8);
    (i)   any liability in respect of (i) any award of damages or any fine imposed on or against Dunfermline by any court, tribunal or public body where the proceedings or investigations giving rise to that liability commenced before the transfer time and (ii) any legal or other costs incurred by Dunfermline in connection with the defence of the proceedings or investigations that gave rise to that liability except that this subparagraph 3(3)(i) does not apply to the extent that it would be incompatible with the Transfer of Undertakings (Protection of Employment) Regulations 2006 or article 4 of the Amendments to Law (Resolution of Dunfermline Building Society) Order 2009;
    (j)   all rights and liabilities in respect of tax;
    (k)   any property, rights and liabilities the transfer of which would constitute a contravention of articles 3 to 7 of the Partial Property Transfers Order; and
    (l)   all rights, obligations and liabilities under or in respect of the pension scheme and any other occupational pension schemes operated by any relevant undertaking except that this sub-paragraph 3(3)(l) does not apply to the extent that it would be incompatible with the Transfer of Undertakings (Protection of Employment) Regulations 2006 or section 257 or 258 of the Pensions Act 2004 or article 4 of the Amendments to Law (Resolution of Dunfermline Building Society) Order 2009.

(4)   For the purposes of, in connection with, and in consequence of the transfer of shares of Dunfermline Nominees by this paragraph, Nationwide is entitled as from the transfer time to all the rights, benefits and privileges of a member of Dunfermline Nominees.

Shares of shareholding members: further provision

4.—(1)   The following provision is made in respect of the shares held by the shareholding members of Dunfermline.

(2)   At the transfer time all shares held by shareholding members of Dunfermline are cancelled.

(3)   The liabilities transferred to Nationwide by paragraph 3 are, subject to sub-paragraph (5), on the same terms that existed between the shareholding member and Dunfermline before the transfer.

(4)   The rights of shareholding members in relation to the liabilities transferred by paragraph 3 are, subject to sub-paragraph (5), on the same terms that existed between the shareholding member and Dunfermline before the transfer.

(5)   The membership rights of each shareholding member in relation to the liabilities transferred by paragraph 5 are the same as the membership rights of existing shareholding members of the Transferee.

Non-application of sections 93 to 102D of the Building Societies Act

5.   This Instrument is to have effect without causing sections 93 to 102D (mergers and transfers) of the Building Societies Act to apply.

Termination rights

6.—(1)   Section 38(6) of the Banking Act (which makes provision in respect of "default event provisions") is applied by this Instrument.

(2)   But section 38(6) does not apply to the extent that it would be incompatible with —

(a)   Directive 1998/26/EC (on settlement finality in payment and securities settlement systems), Directive 2002/47/EC (on financial collateral arrangements) or any other enforceable European Community right; or

(b)   article 9 of the Partial Property Transfers Order.

Continuity

7.—(1)   As from the transfer time, the Nationwide is to be treated for all purposes necessary to give effect to the Nationwide transfer as the same person as Dunfermline except in relation to the excluded property, rights and liabilities or relevant loan accounts referred to in subparagraph (6).

(2)   Agreements or other things done by or in relation to Dunfermline are, if they relate to the Nationwide business (including the shareholding accounts held by the shareholding members of Dunfermline) immediately prior to the transfer time, to be treated as made or done by or in relation to the Nationwide.

(3)   Without limiting sub-paragraph (2)—

(a)   any payment received after the transfer time by or in relation to Dunfermline that relates to any account held by or with Dunfermline immediately before the transfer time other than an account that relates to any excluded property, rights and liabilities is to be treated as received by or in relation to the Nationwide;

(b)   any payment made or other things done by or in relation to Dunfermline that relate to the FRNs is to be treated as made or done by or in relation to the Nationwide.

(4)   Subject to sub-paragraph 3(3)(i), anything (including legal proceedings)—

(a)   that relates to some or all of the Nationwide business or to the share accounts held by the shareholding members of Dunfermline immediately prior to the transfer time; and

(b)   which is in the process of being done by or in relation to Dunfermline immediately before the transfer time, shall be continued by or in relation to the Nationwide on the same terms and subject to the same discretions.

(5)   Subject to sub-paragraph (6), a reference (express or implied) in a relevant instrument or document relating to Dunfermline is to have effect as if it were a reference to the Nationwide if the reference is in connection with rights and obligations that relate to the Nationwide business and nothing in this sub-paragraph (5) shall preclude the application of, in particular, sub-paragraph 17(5).

(6)   Sub-paragraph (5) does not have effect so far as it would modify the basis for calculation of any standard variable rates of interest in respect of any relevant loan account.

(7)   A relevant instrument or document is one which relates to some or all of the Nationwide business.

(8)   Where any breach of contract or breach of duty in connection with some or all of the Nationwide business occurs before the transfer time, any liability of Dunfermline in connection with that breach (whenever that liability may arise) remains that of Dunfermline.

(9)   Sub-paragraph (8) does not apply to the extent that it would be incompatible with the Transfer of Undertakings (Protection of Employment) Regulations 2006 or article 4 of the Amendments to Law (Resolution of Dunfermline Building Society) Order 2009.

(10)   Dunfermline and the Nationwide may by agreement modify paragraphs 6 or 7 to the extent permitted by section 36(7) of the Banking Act.

Provision of assistance

8.   Dunfermline must provide Nationwide with such information and assistance as is reasonably requested by Nationwide in writing—

(i)   in relation to the transferred business or to the operation of the transferred business; and

PART VI
OTHER MATERIALS

    (ii)   for any other purpose relating to, in connection with or in consequence of this Instrument.

[2012]

NOTES

Para 3: words omitted from sub-para (3)(e) repealed by the Amendments to Law (Resolution of the Dunfermline Building Society) (No 2) Order 2009, SI 2009/1805, art 2(1), (4), with effect from 30 March 2009 at 8.00 am (see art 1(2) of the 2009 Order at **[598]**). The amendments have been taken in by LexisNexis editors and do not appear in the original version of this document which can be found at www.bankofengland.co.uk.

PART 3
MISCELLANEOUS

Pensions

9.   Nothing in this Instrument will operate to transfer any rights, obligations or liabilities under or in respect of the pension scheme or any other occupational pension scheme operated by a relevant undertaking to the Nationwide or the Bridge Bank. Nationwide shall have no liability in relation to any early retirement benefits to which any employee may become entitled following the transfer as a consequence of any rights or entitlements to such benefits under the pension scheme, any other occupational pension scheme operated by a relevant undertaking or any contract of employment with a relevant undertaking in relation to service prior to the Nationwide transfer.

10.   Paragraph 9 does not apply to the extent that it would be incompatible with the Transfer of Undertakings (Protection of Employees) Regulations 2006, sections 257 or 258 of the Pensions Act 2004 or article 4 of the Amendments to Law (Resolution of Dunfermline Building Society) Order 2009.

Liabilities of Dunfermline arising in connection with the Nationwide transfer

11.—(1)   Sub-paragraph (2) applies where the Treasury pays to the Nationwide all or any part of the sum payable under the Nationwide payment agreement.

(2)   For the purposes of, in connection with, and in consequence of the transfer of liabilities under paragraph 3, Dunfermline assumes the following liabilities to the Treasury (subject to the limitation of sub-paragraph (7)).

(3)   The first liability is a liability in an amount equal to the aggregate liabilities transferred under paragraph 3 that Dunfermline would have owed to any person in respect of—
    (a)   a deposit (other than a deposit which comprises a liability specified in sub-paragraph (4)), and
    (b)   any other unsecured and unsubordinated liability (other than a liability specified in sub-paragraph (4)),
if those liabilities of Dunfermline had not been transferred by paragraph 3.

(4)   The second liability is a liability in an amount equal to the aggregate liabilities that Dunfermline would have owed to shareholding members if—
    (a)   shareholding members had given notice of withdrawal effective immediately before the transfer time, and
    (b)   the liabilities of Dunfermline in respect of their share accounts had not been transferred by paragraph 3.

(5)   Dunfermline is to calculate the first and second liabilities as follows—
    (a)   Dunfermline must, immediately after the transfer time, estimate the amount of the first and second liabilities, and
    (b)   Dunfermline may revise its estimate from time to time, and must do so on the written request of the Treasury.

(6)   Dunfermline must notify the Treasury and the Nationwide of estimates and revisions.

(7)   Where the aggregate of the first and second liabilities would exceed the relevant amount, any claim made in respect of the first and second liabilities shall be limited to their respective proportions of the relevant amount.

(8)   The relevant amount is the amount ultimately to be paid by the Treasury to the Nationwide in accordance with the Nationwide payment agreement.

(9)   Sub-paragraph (10) applies where a building society special administration order has been made in respect of Dunfermline (under section 144 of the Banking Act as applied by section 90C of the Building Societies Act).

(10)   References in sub-paragraphs (5) and (6) to Dunfermline are to the special administrator.

(11)   For the purposes of calculating the amount specified in sub-paragraph (3)(b) and the proportions referred to in sub-paragraph (7), the amount of any contingent liability is to be disregarded.

[2013]

PART 4
BRIDGE BANK TRANSFER

Bridge Bank Transfer

12.   By virtue of this Instrument, the property, rights and liabilities of Dunfermline specified in paragraphs 15 and 16 below (including relevant property, rights and liabilities that fall within any of the descriptions specified in section 35(1) of the Banking Act) are transferred to the Bridge Bank other than the Bridge Bank excluded property, rights and liabilities.

13.   The Bridge Bank transfer takes place at the transfer time.

14.   "the Bridge Bank excluded property, rights and liabilities" means—
   (1)   any liability specified in sub-paragraph 17(7);
   (2)   any liability in respect of (i) any award of damages or any fine imposed on or against Dunfermline by any court, tribunal or public body where the proceedings or investigations giving rise to that liability commenced before the transfer time and (ii) any legal or other costs incurred by Dunfermline in connection with the defence of the proceedings or investigations that gave rise to that liability except that this sub-paragraph (2) does not apply to the extent that it would be incompatible with the Transfer of Undertakings (Protection of Employment) Regulations 2006;
   (3)   all rights and liabilities in respect of tax; and
   (4)   any property, rights and liabilities the transfer of which would constitute a contravention of paragraphs 3 to 7 of the Partial Property Transfers Order.

Housing Association Loans and Deposits

15.   All property, rights and liabilities in respect of the housing association loans together with the housing association deposits held by a housing association which has a housing association loan.

16.   All property, rights and liabilities in respect of any customer databases owned by Dunfermline relating exclusively to the property, rights and liabilities referred to in paragraph 15.

Bridge Bank Continuity

17.—(1)   As from the transfer time, Bridge Bank is to be treated for all purposes necessary to give effect to the transfer as the same person as Dunfermline except in relation to the Bridge Bank excluded property, rights and liabilities.

(2)   Agreements or other things done by or in relation to Dunfermline are, if they relate to the Bridge Bank business immediately prior to the transfer time, to be treated as made or done by or in relation to Bridge Bank.

(3)   Without limiting sub-paragraph (2) any payment received after the transfer time by or in relation to Dunfermline that relates to any account held by or with Dunfermline in relation to the Bridge Bank business immediately before the transfer time other than an account that relates to any Bridge Bank excluded property, rights and liabilities is to be treated as received by or in relation to Bridge Bank;

(4)   Subject to sub-paragraph 14(2), anything (including legal proceedings)—
   (a)   that relates to some or all of the Bridge Bank business immediately prior to the transfer time; and
   (b)   which is in the process of being done by or in relation to Dunfermline immediately before the transfer time,

shall be continued by or in relation to Bridge Bank on the same terms and subject to the same discretions.

(5)   A reference (express or implied) in a relevant instrument or document relating to Dunfermline is to have effect as if it were a reference to the Bridge Bank if the reference is in connection with rights and obligations that relate to the Bridge Bank business and nothing in this sub-paragraph (5) shall preclude the application of, in particular, subparagraph 7(5).

(6)   A relevant instrument or document is one which relates to some or all of the Bridge Bank business.

(7)   Where any breach of contract or breach of duty in connection with some or all of the Bridge Bank business occurs before the transfer time, any liability of Dunfermline in connection with that breach (whenever that liability may arise) remains that of Dunfermline.

PART VI
OTHER MATERIALS

(8) Sub-paragraph (7) does not apply to the extent that it would be incompatible with the Transfer of Undertakings (Protection of Employment) Regulations 2006 or article 4 of the Amendments to Law (Resolution of Dunfermline Building Society) Order 2009.

(9) Dunfermline and Bridge Bank may by agreement modify any provision of this Instrument to the extent permitted by section 36(7) of the Banking Act.

[2014]

The Governor and Company of the Bank of England

[SCHEDULE
COMMERCIAL LOANS: REFERENCE NUMBERS

Paragraph 2

Reference no	Reference no	Reference no	Reference no	Reference no
20346	522341	797065	842052	892998
25844	525294	797073	842648	893552
26158	525481	797081	845817	893749
36323	527351	797090	846473	895482
87254	659703	797448	846589	895563
93068	661341	801470	849502	895954
93416	688541	802361	850641	896233
96270	700037	802930	852414	896845
105694	702714	803871	852716	897060
147923	703214	804649	852741	897736
155942	723151	805572	853208	898074
177270	726737	805874	854727	899950
178152	726818	805882	855073	900532
185051	730416	806641	874477	900966
187551	737712	807303	874647	901491
211401	738280	807656	876518	901709
227684	739405	807800	877778	902144
229504	745227	808431	878669	902306
234087	758183	816795	879673	904163
250180	763918	817007	880973	904465
274089	768693	818551	881023	904562
277142	776661	818950	882372	904571
277151	780201	819042	882402	905178
310689	780707	819221	886378	905828
313874	783935	819361	886998	905925
318213	784087	819654	887552	906867
358819	787281	819671	887633	907901
360805	788481	820172	888150	909238
364690	789861	824836	888532	909246
365734	789887	825751	889083	909998
368709	790842	826839	889105	910139
383945	790869	828246	889121	910341
427292	790877	828769	889431	910821
428205	790893	829854	889806	910899
456586	791458	832251	889814	910911

Reference no	Reference no	Reference no	Reference no	Reference no
475203	793621	832693	890111	911186
477681	796301	839876	891193	912344
487511	797014	840564	891312	912671
513962	797022	840858	892505	912689
518069	797031	841188	892661	913120
913341	928135	940356	948284	956333
916706	928143	940917	948420	956422
917231	928364	940925	948837	957101
919209	928691	941484	948985	957518
919802	928941	941565	949175	957941
920401	929735	942251	949329	958867
920479	931179	942260	949663	958972
920711	931543	942413	949752	960349
921564	931781	944025	949787	960381
924032	932213	944084	949795	960756
924156	933368	944114	950319	960934
924326	933503	944602	950785	960951
924385	933619	944611	951056	961329
924393	933627	944645	951153	961701
924598	933635	944742	952346	961914
924768	936715	944751	952630	962929
926833	936723	944858	952729	967327
926841	937517	944891	953326	967335
927139	937835	944904	953946	967343
927449	939188	945463	953954	967840
927759	939480	946770	955124	970476]

[2015]

NOTES
Schedule inserted by the Amendments to Law (Resolution of the Dunfermline Building Society) (No 2) Order 2009, SI 2009/1805, art 2(1), (5), Schedule, with effect from 30 March 2009 at 8.00 am (see art 1(2) of the 2009 Order at **[598]**). The amendments have been taken in by LexisNexis editors and do not appear in the original version of this document which can be found at www.bankofengland.co.uk.

DBS BRIDGE BANK LIMITED SUPPLEMENTAL AND ONWARD PROPERTY TRANSFER INSTRUMENT 2009

NOTES
© Bank of England
The original version of this document can be found at www.bankofengland.co.uk.

Made: 30 June 2009

Coming into force: 1 July 2009

This Instrument is made by the Bank of England in the exercise of the powers conferred by sections 34, 35, 36, 37, 38, 40, 42(2), 43(2) and 84 of the Banking Act.

In accordance with section 2B of the Bank of England Act 1998, the Bank of England has obtained advice from the Financial Stability Committee.

In accordance with sections 42(5) and 43(7) of the Banking Act, the Bank of England has consulted the FSA and the Treasury.

In accordance with section 4(2) of the Banking Act the Bank of England has had regard to the special resolution objectives.

In accordance with section 5(4) of the Banking Act, the Bank of England has had regard to the code of practice issued by the Treasury under section 5 of the Banking Act.

Accordingly, the Bank of England makes the following Instrument—

PART 1
GENERAL

Citation and commencement

1.—(1) This Instrument may be cited as the DBS Bridge Bank Limited Supplemental and Onward Property Transfer Instrument 2009.

(2)   This Instrument comes into force at the first supplemental transfer time.

Non-application of sections 93 to 102D of the Building Societies Act

2. This Instrument is to have effect without causing sections 93 to 102D (mergers and transfers) of the Building Societies Act to apply.

Termination rights

3.—(1) Section 38(6) of the Banking Act (which makes provision in respect of "default event provisions") is applied by this Instrument.

(2)   But section 38(6) does not apply to the extent that it would be incompatible with—
   (a)   Directive 1998/26/EC (on settlement finality in payment and securities settlement systems), Directive 2002/47/EC (on financial collateral arrangements) or any other enforceable European Community right; or
   (b)   article 9 of the Partial Property Transfers Order.

Interpretation: general

4. In this Instrument:
   "the Banking Act" means the Banking Act 2009, (c 1);
   "Bridge Bank" means DBS Bridge Bank Limited, a company with the registered number SC356970 incorporated in Scotland whose registered office is at Caledonia House, Carnegie Avenue, Dunfermline KY11 8PJ;
   "Building Societies Act" means the Building Societies Act 1986 (c 53);
   "deposit" has the meaning given by article 5 of the Regulated Activities Order (disregarding the exclusions in articles 6 to 9AA of that Order);
   "Dunfermline" means Dunfermline Building Society (in building society special administration procedure), incorporated under the Building Societies Act with register number 9B(S);
   "Dunfermline additional loan" means any loan or mortgage loan made by Dunfermline and which at 8am on 30 March 2009 (being the time at which the Dunfermline Building Society Property Transfer Instrument 2009 came into force) was designated in Dunfermline's books and records with a reference number set out in Schedule 1 to this Instrument;
   "first onward transfer" means the transfer effected by paragraph 12;
   "first onward transfer time" is the time immediately after the first supplemental transfer time;
   "first supplemental transfer" means the transfer effected by paragraph 5;
   "first supplemental transfer time" is 00:01am on 1 July 2009;
   "FSA" means the Financial Services Authority;
   "housing association" means a society, body of trustees, or company, which is established for the purpose of, or amongst whose objects or powers are included those of providing, constructing, improving or managing, or facilitating or encouraging the construction or improvement of housing accommodation, and which does not trade for profit or whose constitution or rules prohibit the issue of capital with interest or dividend exceeding such rate as may be described by the Treasury, whether with or without differentiation as between share and loan capital and including a registered social landlord under the Housing (Scotland) Act 2001;
   "housing association deposit" means any deposit made by a housing association and vested in Bridge Bank immediately prior to the first onward transfer time (including any such deposit at the first onward transfer time that is designated in Bridge Bank's books and records with a reference number set out in Schedule 3 to this Instrument);
   "housing association loan" means:
      (a)   any loan or mortgage loan (including, for the avoidance of doubt, any committed but unfunded loan or mortgage loan) made to a housing association and vested in Bridge Bank immediately prior to the first onward transfer time (including any

such loan or mortgage loan at the first onward transfer time that is designated in Bridge Bank's books and records with a reference number set out in Schedule 4 to this Instrument); and

    (b)   any pipeline loan;

"initial bridge bank business" means the property, rights and liabilities transferred by paragraph 12;

"mortgage loan" means a loan which is fully or substantially secured on heritable, leasehold or other real property;

"Nationwide" means Nationwide Building Society, incorporated under the Building Societies Act with register number 355B;

"Nationwide additional loan" means any loan or mortgage loan made by Dunfermline and which at 8am on 30 March 2009 (being the time at which the Dunfermline Building Society Property Transfer Instrument 2009 came into force) was designated in Dunfermline's books and records with a reference number set out in Schedule 2 to this Instrument;

"Partial Property Transfers Order" means The Banking Act 2009 (Restriction of Partial Property Transfers) Order 2009 (SI 2009/322);

"pipeline loan" means any future potential loan classified as a category 2 pipeline loan by Bridge Bank in connection with the initial bridge bank business immediately prior to the first onward transfer time (including any such future potential loan at the first onward transfer time that is designated in Bridge Bank's books and records with a reference number set out in Schedule 5 to this Instrument);

"Regulated Activities Order" means The Financial Services and Markets Act 2000 (Regulated Activities) Order 2001 (SI 2001/544);

"second onward transfer" means the transfer effected by paragraph 27;

"second onward transfer time" is the time immediately after the second supplemental transfer time;

"second supplemental transfer" means the transfer effected by paragraph 20;

"second supplemental transfer time" is the later of the first supplemental transfer time and the time immediately after the time at which the draft Amendments to Law (Resolution of Dunfermline Building Society) (No 2) Order 2009 laid before Parliament by Her Majesty's Treasury under section 75(7)(b) of the Banking Act, if approved by resolution of each House of Parliament in accordance with section 75(7) of the Banking Act, comes into force;

"subsequent bridge bank business" means the property, rights and liabilities transferred by paragraph 27;

"tax" means all taxes, whether of the United Kingdom or otherwise, including those taxes listed in section 74(2) of the Banking Act and value added tax; and

"TUPE" means the Transfer of Undertakings (Protection of Employment) Regulations 2006 (SI 2006/246).

[2016]

PART 2
FIRST SUPPLEMENTAL TRANSFER

First supplemental transfer

5. By virtue of this Instrument, all property, rights and liabilities of Dunfermline specified in paragraphs 8 and 9 (including relevant property, rights and liabilities specified in paragraphs 8 and 9 that fall within any of the descriptions specified in section 35(1) of the Banking Act) are transferred to Bridge Bank, other than the Dunfermline additional loans excluded property, rights and liabilities.

6. The first supplemental transfer takes place at the first supplemental transfer time.

7. "Dunfermline additional loans excluded property, rights and liabilities" means—
    (1)   any liability specified in paragraph 10(7);
    (2)   any liability in respect of (i) any award of damages or any fine imposed on or against Dunfermline by any court, tribunal or public body where the proceedings or investigations giving rise to that liability commenced before the first supplemental transfer time and (ii) any legal or other costs incurred by Dunfermline in connection with the defence of the proceedings or investigations that gave rise to that liability except that this sub-paragraph (2) does not apply to the extent that it would be incompatible with TUPE;
    (3)   all rights and liabilities in respect of tax; and
    (4)   any property, rights and liabilities the transfer of which would constitute a contravention of articles 3 to 7 of the Partial Property Transfers Order.

Dunfermline additional loans property, rights and liabilities

8. All property, rights and liabilities in respect of the Dunfermline additional loans.

9. All property, rights and liabilities in respect of any customer databases owned by Dunfermline relating exclusively to the property, rights and liabilities referred to in paragraph 8.

Dunfermline additional loans continuity

10.—(1) As from the first supplemental transfer time, Bridge Bank is to be treated for all purposes necessary to give effect to the first supplemental transfer as the same person as Dunfermline except in relation to the Dunfermline additional loans excluded property, rights and liabilities.

(2)   Agreements or other things done by or in relation to Dunfermline are, if they relate to the Dunfermline additional loans immediately prior to the first supplemental transfer time, to be treated as made or done by or in relation to Bridge Bank.

(3)   Without limiting sub-paragraph (2), any payment received after the first supplemental transfer time by or in relation to Dunfermline that relates to the Dunfermline additional loans immediately before the first supplemental transfer time other than a payment that relates to any Dunfermline additional loans excluded property, rights and liabilities is to be treated as received by or in relation to Bridge Bank.

(4)   Subject to paragraph 7(2), anything (including legal proceedings)—
  (a)   that relates to some or all of the Dunfermline additional loans immediately prior to the first supplemental transfer time; and
  (b)   which is in the process of being done by or in relation to Dunfermline immediately before the first supplemental transfer time,
shall be continued by or in relation to Bridge Bank.

(5)   Save in respect of the Dunfermline additional loans excluded property, rights and liabilities, any reference (express or implied) to Dunfermline in a relevant Dunfermline additional loans instrument or document is to have effect as if it were a reference to Bridge Bank.

(6)   For the purposes of sub-paragraph (5), "a relevant Dunfermline additional loans instrument or document" is one which relates to some or all of the Dunfermline additional loans.

(7)   Where any breach of contract or breach of duty in connection with some or all of the Dunfermline additional loans occurs before the first supplemental transfer time, any liability of Dunfermline in connection with that breach (whenever that liability may arise) remains that of Dunfermline.

(8)   Sub-paragraph (7) does not apply to the extent that it would be incompatible with TUPE.

(9)   Dunfermline and Bridge Bank may by agreement modify any provision of this Instrument to the extent permitted by section 36(7) of the Banking Act.

Provision of assistance

11. Dunfermline must provide Bridge Bank with such information and assistance as is reasonably requested by Bridge Bank in writing—
  (1)   in relation to the Dunfermline additional loans; and
  (2)   for any other purpose relating to, in connection with or in consequence of this Instrument.

[2017]

PART 3
FIRST ONWARD TRANSFER

First onward transfer

12. By virtue of this Instrument, the property, rights and liabilities of Bridge Bank specified in paragraphs 15 to 17 (including relevant property, rights and liabilities specified in paragraphs 15 to 17 that fall within any of the descriptions specified in section 35(1) of the Banking Act) are transferred to Nationwide, other than the initial bridge bank excluded property, rights and liabilities.

13. The first onward transfer takes place at the first onward transfer time.

14. "initial bridge bank excluded property, rights and liabilities" means—
  (1)   any property, rights and liabilities the transfer of which would constitute a contravention of articles 3 to 7 of the Partial Property Transfers Order;
  (2)   all rights and liabilities in respect of tax;
  (3)   any liability specified in paragraph 18(7); and
  (4)   any liability in respect of (i) any award of damages or any fine imposed on or against Bridge Bank by any court, tribunal or public body where the proceedings or investigations giving rise to that liability commenced before the first onward transfer time and (ii) any legal or other costs incurred by Bridge Bank in connection with the defence of the proceedings or investigations that gave rise to that liability except that this sub-paragraph (4) does not apply to the extent that it would be incompatible with TUPE.

Initial bridge bank property, rights and liabilities

15. All property, rights and liabilities of Bridge Bank in respect of the housing association loans and the housing association deposits.

16. All property, rights and liabilities in respect of any customer databases owned by Bridge Bank relating exclusively to the property, rights and liabilities referred to in paragraph 15.

17. All property, rights and liabilities of Bridge Bank transferred to it by the first supplemental transfer by paragraph 5 of this Transfer Instrument.

Initial bridge bank continuity

18.—(1) As from the first onward transfer time, Nationwide is to be treated for all purposes necessary to give effect to the first onward transfer as the same person as Bridge Bank except in relation to the initial bridge bank excluded property, rights and liabilities.

(2)   Agreements or other things done by or in relation to Bridge Bank or treated as made or done by or in relation to Bridge Bank are, if they relate to the initial bridge bank business immediately prior to the first onward transfer time, to be treated as made or done by or in relation to Nationwide.

(3)   Without limiting sub-paragraph (2), any payment received, or treated as received, after the first onward transfer time by or in relation to Bridge Bank that relates to the initial bridge bank business immediately before the first onward transfer time other than a payment that relates to any initial bridge bank excluded property, rights and liabilities is to be treated as received by or in relation to Nationwide.

(4)   Subject to paragraph 14(4), anything (including legal proceedings)—
   (a)   that relates to some or all of the initial bridge bank business immediately prior to the first onward transfer time; and
   (b)   which is in the process of being done by or in relation to Bridge Bank or continued by or in relation to Bridge Bank immediately before the first onward transfer time,
shall be continued by or in relation to Nationwide.

(5)   Save in respect of the initial bridge bank excluded property, rights and liabilities, any reference (express or implied) to Bridge Bank in a relevant bridge bank instrument or document (including by virtue of paragraph 10(5)) is to have effect as if it were a reference to Nationwide.

(6)   For the purposes of sub-paragraph (5), "a relevant bridge bank instrument or document" is one which relates to some or all of the initial bridge bank business.

(7)   Where any breach of contract or breach of duty in connection with some or all of the initial bridge bank business occurs before the first onward transfer time, any liability of Bridge Bank in connection with that breach (whenever that liability may arise) remains that of Bridge Bank.

(8)   Sub-paragraph (7) does not apply to the extent that it would be incompatible with TUPE.

(9)   Bridge Bank and Nationwide may by agreement modify any provision of this Instrument to the extent permitted by section 36(7) of the Banking Act.

Provision of assistance

19. Bridge Bank must provide Nationwide with such information and assistance as is reasonably requested by Nationwide in writing—
   (1)   in relation to the initial bridge bank business; and
   (2)   for any other purpose relating to, in connection with or in consequence of this Instrument.

[2018]

PART 4
SECOND SUPPLEMENTAL TRANSFER

Second supplemental transfer

20. By virtue of this Instrument, all property, rights and liabilities of Dunfermline specified in paragraphs 23 and 24 (including relevant property, rights and liabilities specified in paragraphs 23 and 24 that fall within any of the descriptions specified in section 35(1) of the Banking Act) are transferred to Bridge Bank, other than the Nationwide additional loans excluded property, rights and liabilities.

21. The second supplemental transfer takes place at the second supplemental transfer time.

22. "Nationwide additional loans excluded property, rights and liabilities" means—
   (1)   any liability specified in paragraph 25(7);
   (2)   any liability in respect of (i) any award of damages or any fine imposed on or against Dunfermline by any court, tribunal or public body where the proceedings or investigations giving rise to that liability commenced before the second supplemental transfer time and (ii) any legal or other costs incurred by Dunfermline in connection with the defence of the proceedings or investigations that gave rise to that liability except that this sub-paragraph (2) does not apply to the extent that it would be incompatible with TUPE;

PART VI
OTHER MATERIALS

(3)   all rights and liabilities in respect of tax; and

(4)   any property, rights and liabilities the transfer of which would constitute a contravention of articles 3 to 7 of the Partial Property Transfers Order.

Nationwide additional loans property, rights and liabilities

23. All property, rights and liabilities in respect of the Nationwide additional loans.

24. All property, rights and liabilities in respect of any customer databases owned by Dunfermline relating exclusively to the property, rights and liabilities referred to in paragraph 23.

Nationwide additional loans continuity

25.—(1) As from the second supplemental transfer time, Bridge Bank is to be treated for all purposes necessary to give effect to the second supplemental transfer as the same person as Dunfermline except in relation to the Nationwide additional loans excluded property, rights and liabilities.

(2)   Agreements or other things done by or in relation to Dunfermline are, if they relate to the Nationwide additional loans immediately prior to the second supplemental transfer time, to be treated as made or done by or in relation to Bridge Bank.

(3)   Without limiting sub-paragraph (2), any payment received after the second supplemental transfer time by or in relation to Dunfermline that relates to the Nationwide additional loans immediately before the second supplemental transfer time other than a payment that relates to any Nationwide additional loans excluded property, rights and liabilities is to be treated as received by or in relation to Bridge Bank.

(4)   Subject to paragraph 22(2), anything (including legal proceedings)—
    (a)   that relates to some or all of the Nationwide additional loans immediately prior to the second supplemental transfer time; and
    (b)   which is in the process of being done by or in relation to Dunfermline immediately before the second supplemental transfer time,

shall be continued by or in relation to Bridge Bank.

(5)   Save in respect of the Nationwide additional loans excluded property, rights and liabilities, any reference (express or implied) to Dunfermline in a relevant Nationwide additional loans instrument or document is to have effect as if it were a reference to Bridge Bank.

(6)   For the purposes of sub-paragraph (5), "a relevant Nationwide additional loans instrument or document" is one which relates to some or all of the Nationwide additional loans.

(7)   Where any breach of contract or breach of duty in connection with some or all of the Nationwide additional loans occurs before the second supplemental transfer time, any liability of Dunfermline in connection with that breach (whenever that liability may arise) remains that of Dunfermline.

(8)   Sub-paragraph (7) does not apply to the extent that it would be incompatible with TUPE.

(9)   Dunfermline and Bridge Bank may by agreement modify any provision of this Instrument to the extent permitted by section 36(7) of the Banking Act.

Provision of assistance

26. Dunfermline must provide Bridge Bank with such information and assistance as is reasonably requested by Bridge Bank in writing—
    (1)   in relation to the Nationwide additional loans; and
    (2)   for any other purpose relating to, in connection with or in consequence of this Instrument.

[2019]

PART 5
SECOND ONWARD TRANSFER

Second onward transfer

27. By virtue of this Instrument, the property, rights and liabilities of Bridge Bank specified in paragraph 30 (including relevant property, rights and liabilities specified in paragraph 30 that fall within any of the descriptions specified in section 35(1) of the Banking Act) are transferred to Nationwide, other than the subsequent bridge bank excluded property, rights and liabilities.

28. The second onward transfer takes place at the second onward transfer time.

29. "subsequent bridge bank excluded property, rights and liabilities" means—
    (1)   any property, rights and liabilities the transfer of which would constitute a contravention of articles 3 to 7 of the Partial Property Transfers Order;
    (2)   all rights and liabilities in respect of tax;

(3)   any liability specified in paragraph 31(7); and

(4)   any liability in respect of (i) any award of damages or any fine imposed on or against Bridge Bank by any court, tribunal or public body where the proceedings or investigations giving rise to that liability commenced before the second onward transfer time and (ii) any legal or other costs incurred by Bridge Bank in connection with the defence of the proceedings or investigations that gave rise to that liability except that this sub-paragraph (4) does not apply to the extent that it would be incompatible with TUPE.

Subsequent bridge bank property, rights and liabilities

30. All property, rights and liabilities of Bridge Bank transferred to it by the second supplemental transfer by paragraph 20 of this Transfer Instrument.

Subsequent bridge bank continuity

31.—(1) As from the second onward transfer time, Nationwide is to be treated for all purposes necessary to give effect to the second onward transfer as the same person as Bridge Bank except in relation to the subsequent bridge bank excluded property, rights and liabilities.

(2)   Agreements or other things done by or in relation to Bridge Bank or treated as made or done by or in relation to Bridge Bank are, if they relate to the subsequent bridge bank business immediately prior to the second onward transfer time, to be treated as made or done by or in relation to Nationwide.

(3)   Without limiting sub-paragraph (2), any payment received, or treated as received, after the second onward transfer time by or in relation to Bridge Bank that relates to the subsequent bridge bank business immediately before the second onward transfer time other than a payment that relates to any subsequent bridge bank excluded property, rights and liabilities is to be treated as received by or in relation to Nationwide;

(4)   Subject to paragraph 29(4), anything (including legal proceedings)—

    (a)   that relates to some or all of the subsequent bridge bank business immediately prior to the second onward transfer time; and

    (b)   which is in the process of being done by or in relation to Bridge Bank or continued by or in relation to Bridge Bank immediately before the second onward transfer time,

shall be continued by or in relation to Nationwide.

(5)   Save in respect of the subsequent bridge bank excluded property, rights and liabilities, any reference (express or implied) to Bridge Bank in a relevant bridge bank instrument or document (including by virtue of paragraph 25(5)) is to have effect as if it were a reference to Nationwide.

(6)   For the purposes of sub-paragraph (5), "a relevant bridge bank instrument or document" is one which relates to some or all of the subsequent bridge bank business.

(7)   Where any breach of contract or breach of duty in connection with some or all of the subsequent bridge bank business occurs before the second onward transfer time, any liability of Bridge Bank in connection with that breach (whenever that liability may arise) remains that of Bridge Bank.

(8)   Sub-paragraph (7) does not apply to the extent that it would be incompatible with TUPE.

(9)   Bridge Bank and Nationwide may by agreement modify any provision of this Instrument to the extent permitted by section 36(7) of the Banking Act.

Provision of assistance

32. Bridge Bank must provide Nationwide with such information and assistance as is reasonably requested by Nationwide in writing—

    (1)   in relation to the subsequent bridge bank business; and

    (2)   for any other purpose relating to, in connection with or in consequence of this Instrument.

The Governor and Company of the Bank of England

[2020]

SCHEDULE 1
REFERENCE NUMBERS FOR DUNFERMLINE ADDITIONAL LOANS

Reference number
277142
277151
360805

PART VI
OTHER MATERIALS

Reference number
368709
487511

[2021]

SCHEDULE 2
REFERENCE NUMBERS FOR NATIONWIDE ADDITIONAL LOANS

Reference number
310689
829854
886378
944611

[2022]

SCHEDULE 3
REFERENCE NUMBERS FOR HOUSING ASSOCIATION DEPOSITS

Reference number
19791
20237
20636
20664
20718
20752
20836
21011
21139
21213
20916
680083
701018
858118
1609127
1702332
1816547
2130258
2428781
2506435
2691778
2745487
2839797
7310312
11904916

[2023]

SCHEDULE 4
REFERENCE NUMBERS FOR HOUSING ASSOCIATION LOANS

Reference number		
182788	381314	722812
184306	383082	722901
192791	391751	725790
200107	404608	729426
206202	405779	730939
214523	406635	737186
220388	406741	743135
222046	409774	743399
225592	418161	744298
226203	426199	745189
230171	429597	752959
233587	435431	753734
235440	439169	759007
238732	442887	762776
239534	443018	763781
240036	455296	776301
240559	455474	778117
240702	455687	782459
241571	467804	785571
245143	469815	785725
251330	482188	794635
251364	507415	801984
253359	521141	802948
255637	531804	805181
260274	538990	805599
260967	539082	816965
261211	564435	818852
262803	572322	824585
264016	588661	827983
264032	595047	830321
264695	595527	831069
267848	596213	841536
269859	596221	845833
269867	597970	850764
271586	605336	854352
274631	606669	880493
276766	606855	880752
279617	606952	881074
279625	607002	881538
280526	608751	883786
286516	608891	887064
291421	608904	887412
292184	610178	888958

PART VI
OTHER MATERIALS

Reference number		
295469	612448	896632
299871	621161	900168
303038	632473	900401
303500	641189	902233
304158	644129	904210
304743	656488	905739
312657	660256	907502
312673	663841	909831
312789	665827	913251
313912	666751	920371
314251	675580	920568
316431	679917	923656
318884	680117	927121
321061	685551	929565
323705	686361	932558
325961	686891	943002
327174	687103	943941
329606	687839	950718
332534	690708	954403
334341	690732	954691
335282	692573	956732
337978	693278	958492
347477	694487	960276
352683	694894	963291
352748	701653	964549
353001	703338	967173
355500	705390	970620
360937	718327	971090
362735	720003	971375
366099	720364	971839
372269	721263	

[2024]

SCHEDULE 5
REFERENCE NUMBERS FOR PIPELINE LOANS

Reference number
7
8
9
10
11
12
13
14

Reference number
15
16
17
18
19
20
21
22
23
24
25
26
27

[2025]

PART VI
OTHER MATERIALS

Index